2/07

The **Rough** Gu

D0459971

Malaysia, Singapore and Brunei

written and researched by

**Charles de Ledesma, Mark Lewis, Richard Lim,
Steven Martin and Pauline Savage**

ROUGH
GUIDES

NEW YORK · LONDON · DELHI

www.roughguides.com

915.95
MAL
2006

Contents

Malay life colour
section following p.312

Longhouse culture
colour section following
p.440

◄◄ Rhinoceros hornbill in flight ◄ Fishing village, Pulau Mabul, Sabah

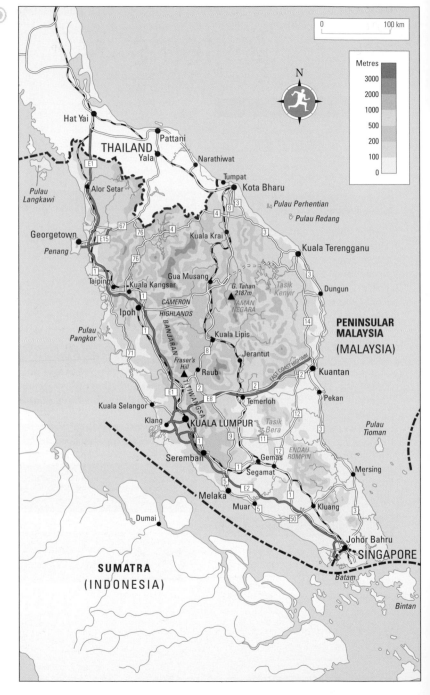

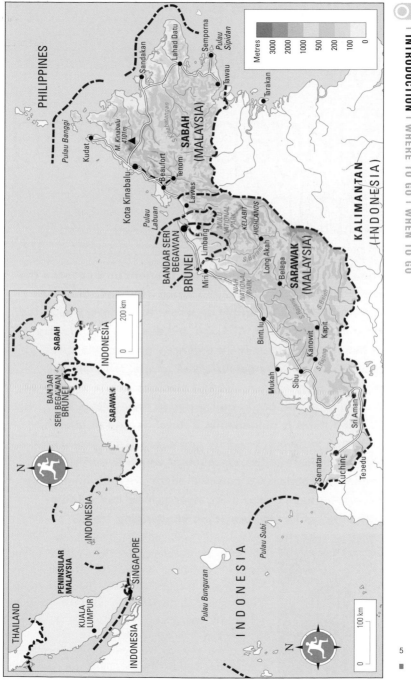

Introduction to

Malaysia, Singapore and Brunei

Though Malaysia, Singapore and Brunei don't possess the grand ancient ruins of neighbouring Thailand, their rich cultural heritage is readily apparent to visitors. Populated by a blend of Malays, Chinese, Indians and – in the case of Malaysia and Brunei – indigenous groups, the three countries boast a huge variety of annual festivals as well as a wonderful mixture of cuisines, while traditional architecture and crafts still thrive in rural areas. In addition there is astonishing natural beauty to take in, including gorgeous beaches and some of the world's oldest tropical rainforest, much of which is surprisingly accessible. Malaysia's national parks are a high spot, superb for cave exploration, river-rafting and wildlife-watching, while also providing challenging treks.

Malaysia, Singapore and Brunei have had a dramatic and at times turbulent past, born of a common **history** and ethnic composition that links the entire Malay archipelago, from Indonesia to the Philippines. Each became an important port of call on the trade route between India and China, the two great markets of the early world, and later formed the colonial lynchpins of the Portuguese, Dutch and British empires. Today the dominant

▲ Lanterns at Thian Hock Keng Temple, Singapore

cultural force in the region is undoubtedly **Islam**, adopted by the Malays in the fourteenth century, though in Chinese-dominated Singapore, **Buddhism** and **Taoism** together hold sway among half the population. But it's the commitment to religious plurality – there are also sizeable Christian and Hindu minorities – that is so attractive, often providing startling juxtapositions of mosques, temples and churches.

Malaysia has only existed in its present form since 1963, when the federation of the eleven Peninsula states, along with Singapore and the two Bornean territories of Sarawak and Sabah, became known as Malaysia. Singapore left the union in 1965, gaining independence in its own right; Brunei, always content to maintain its own enclave in Borneo, only lost its British colonial status in 1984. Since then, Malaysia, Singapore and Brunei have been united in their **economic predominance** amongst Southeast Asian nations. While Brunei is locked into a paternalistic regime, using its considerable oil wealth to guarantee its citizens an enviable standard of living, the city-state of Singapore has long been a model of free-market profiteering, transformed from a tiny port with no natural resources into a capitalist giant. Malaysia too has an ambitious manifesto – to achieve First World status by 2020, to which end the country is investing heavily in new infrastructure, from highways to ports and factories. Despite unforeseen problems, including the economic meltdown which plagued the region

> **It's Malaysia's commitment to religious plurality that is so attractive, often providing startling juxtapositions of mosques, temples and churches**

7
■

Fact file

- With 26 million inhabitants, Malaysia is divided into two distinct regions. **Peninsular Malaysia**, where the capital Kuala Lumpur is situated, is separated by more than 600km of the South China Sea from East Malaysia, comprising the states of **Sabah** and **Sarawak** on the island of Borneo.

- At just 700 square kilometres in size, **Singapore** is a crowded nation of around 4 million people, its main island linked to the southern tip of Peninsular Malaysia by two bridges.

- Made up of two enclaves in eastern Sarawak, **Brunei** is nearly ten times the size of Singapore, but has only one-tenth the population.

- Both Malaysia and Singapore are British-style **parliamentary democracies**, the former with a ceremonial head of state known as the Yang di-Pertuan Agung (the post rotates among the sultans from each state of the federation). Brunei is ruled by its **sultan**.

- Historically dominated by agriculture and mining, Malaysia's **economy** now features a healthy manufacturing sector, as does Singapore, where shipping and financial services are also key industries. Brunei profits handsomely from its reserves of oil and gas.

in the late 1990s, the rise in terrorism linked with September 11, 2001 and the cruel SARS virus of 2003, Malaysia and Singapore have bounced back with characteristic Southeast Asian tenacity, and remain two of the region's most dynamic, forward-looking countries.

Where to go

Malaysia's fast-growing capital, **Kuala Lumpur** (usually just referred to as KL) makes much the same initial impression as the city-state of Singapore, with high-rise hotels and air-conditioned shopping malls alongside characterful areas such as Chinatown and Little India. KL is also the social and economic driving force of a nation eager to better itself, a fact reflected in the growing number of designer bars and restaurants in the city, and in the booming manufacturing industries surrounding it. But this is a city firmly rooted in tradition, where the same Malay executives who wear suits to work dress in traditional clothes at festival times, and markets and food stalls are crowded in amongst new banks and businesses.

Less than three hours' drive south of the capital lies the birthplace of Malay civilization, **Melaka**, a must on anybody's itinerary for its proud architecture and mellow atmosphere. Much further up the **west coast** is the first British settlement, the island of **Penang**, with its beautifully restored old colonial buildings and a vibrant Chinatown district adorning its capital, **Georgetown**. For a taste of Old England, head for the hill stations of

Although development strategies and environmental and ecological changes have all made their mark in hindering wildlife-spotting opportunities, Peninsular Malaysia, Borneo and Singapore remain a paradise for lovers of the natural world, harbouring over 600 types of birds and more than 200 mammal species. The national parks of Peninsular Malaysia are home to Asian elephants, tigers, sun bears and clouded leopards, as well as tapirs, barking deer, macaques and gibbons. Hornbills and eagles can be spied in the skies, while back at ground level pythons and cobras can grow up to nine metres long. Travellers to certain of Borneo's forests and parks stand a good chance of seeing the elusive proboscis monkey, so-called because of its bulbous, drooping nose. The island is also one of only two habitats in the world (the other is Sumatra) for orang-utans in the wild – indeed, the name is Malay for "man of the forest".

The region's marine life is equally diverse: divers off the east coast of Sabah can swim with white-tip sharks, clown fish and barracuda, while along the east coast of the Peninsula, as well as northeast Sabah, green and hawksbill turtles drag themselves ashore to lay their eggs by night, in season. Even cosmopolitan Singapore maintains a pocket of primary rainforest that's home to anteaters, long-tailed macaques and snakes.

Fraser's Hill and the **Cameron Highlands**, where cooler temperatures and lush countryside provide ample opportunities for walks, bird-watching, rounds of golf and cream teas. North of Penang, Malay, rather than Chinese, traditions hold sway at **Alor Setar**, the last major town before the Thai border. This far north, the premier tourist destination is **Pulau Langkawi**, a popular duty-free island with world-class resorts and picture-postcard beaches.

Ethnic groups

While much of the Peninsula's population is a result of migration from other parts of Asia over the last two millennia, the Orang Asli ("original people") are believed to have arrived from the present day Philippines around 50,000 years ago. Few in number, they live mostly in the forested interior, where traditionally they practised shifting cultivation and held hard to animist beliefs in vital areas like weddings and burials, though these days the Orang Asli have increasingly become settled in new villages. Over in Sarawak the plethora of indigene groups is far more visible, ranging from the semi-nomadic Penan, who prefer to live deep in the forests, to modern communities like the Kelabit and Iban, many of whom welcome visitors into their splendid longhouses and work hard for high educational standards. Add to this the colour and chutzpah evident in Chinese temples and street fairs, Indian festival days and everyday life in Malay kampungs (villages), and the nations' pluralism draws the visitor into a vibrant celebration of ethnic diversity.

Travelling down the Peninsula's **east coast** is more relaxing, running past the sleepy villages of the mainland and the stunning islands of **Pulau Perhentian** and **Pulau Tioman**, busy with both backpackers and package tourists. The state capitals of **Kota Bharu**, near the northeastern Thai border, and **Kuala Terengganu**, further south, are showcases for the best of Malay traditions, craft production and performing arts.

Crossing the Peninsula's mountainous interior by road or rail allows you to venture into the unsullied tropical rainforests of **Taman Negara**. The national park's four thousand square kilometres have enough to keep you occupied for a week or two: trails, salt-lick hides for animal-watching, an aerial forest-canopy walkway, limestone caves and waterfalls. Here you may well also come across the **Orang Asli**, the Peninsula's indigenous peoples, a few of whom cling to a semi-nomadic lifestyle within the park.

Across the sea from the Peninsula are the East Malaysian states of Sarawak and Sabah. For most travellers, their first taste of **Sarawak** is **Kuching**, the old colonial capital, and then the Iban **longhouses** of the Batang Ai river system. **Sibu**, much further to the north on the Rajang River, is the starting point for trips to less touristed Iban, Kayan and Kenyah longhouses. In the north of the state, **Mulu National Park** is the principal destination, its extraordinary razor-sharp limestone needles

providing demanding climbing, while within the park's mountains lay vast chambers and deep, snaking caves. More remote still are the rarely explored **Kelabit Highlands**, further to the east, where the mountain air is refreshingly cool and flora and fauna abundant.

The main reason for a trip to **Sabah** is to conquer the 4101-metre granite peak of **Mount Kinabalu**, which is set in its own national park, though the lively modern capital **Kota Kinabalu** and its idyllic offshore islands, Gaya and Manukan, have their appeal, too. Beyond this, Sabah is worth a visit for its **wildlife**: turtles, orang-utans, proboscis monkeys and hornbills are just a few of the exotic residents of the jungle and plentiful islands. Marine attractions feature in the far east at **Pulau Sipadan**, pointing out towards the southern Philippines, which has a host of sharks, fishes and turtles, while its neighbour, **Pulau Mabul**, contains hip, but often pricey, diving resorts.

For many first-time travellers to Asia, **Singapore** is the ideal starting point, with Western standards of comfort and hygiene, as well as dazzling consumerism, alongside Chinese, Malay and Indian enclaves and the architectural remnants of the state's colonial past. Singapore also rightly holds a reputation as Asia's **gastronomic capital**, a place to savour snacks at simple hawker stalls or an exquisite Chinese banquet, all of the highest quality. Most people find a few days in the metropolis is long enough to see the sights, fill shopping bags and empty pockets, before moving on.

For those who venture into the tiny kingdom of **Brunei**, sandwiched between Sarawak's two most northerly divisions, there are few more stirring sights than the spectacle of the main mosque in the capital **Bandar Seri Begawan**, close to Kampung Ayer water village. In the sparsely populated Temburong district, you can visit unspoiled rainforest at the **Ulu Temburong National Park** where abundant wildlife roam and the rivers are clear. If these don't appeal, culturally a million miles away are the state's Disneyland-style **Jerudong Playground**, its futuristic, consumer-obsessive malls, and the jaw-droppingly opulent seven-star hotel, *The Empire*, built by the royal family.

▼ Orang Asli settlement, Cameron Highlands

When to go

Temperatures vary little in Malaysia, Singapore and Brunei, hovering across the vast bulk of the region constantly at or just above 30°C by day, while humidity is high all year round. The major distinction in the seasons is marked by the arrival of the northeast monsoon (during what is locally called the "rainy season"). This particularly affects the east coast of Peninsular Malaysia and the western end of Sarawak, with late November to mid-February seeing the heaviest rainfall. On the Peninsula's west coast and in Sabah, September and October are the wettest months. Monsoonal downpours can be heavy and prolonged, sometimes lasting two or three hours and prohibiting more or less all activity for the duration; boats to most of the islands in affected areas will not attempt the sea swell during the height of the rainy season. It's worth noting, too, that tropical climates are prone to showers all year round, often in the mid-afternoon, though these short, sheeting downpours clear up as quickly as they arrive. In mountainous areas like the Cameron Highlands, the Kelabit Highlands, and in the hill stations and upland national parks, you may experience more frequent rain as the high peaks gather clouds more or less permanently.

> **The ideal time to visit most of the region is between March and early October, when you will avoid the worst of the rains and there is less humidity**

▼ Pulau Lang Tengah, one of several idyllic east-coast islands

The **ideal time** to visit most of the region is between March and early October, when you will avoid the worst of the rains and there is less humidity, though note that both ends of this period can be characterized by a stifling lack of breezes. Arriving just after the rainy season can afford the best of all worlds, with an abundant water supply, verdant countryside and bountiful waterfalls, though there is still a clammy quality to the air. Arrive in Sabah a little later, in May, and you'll be able to take in the Sabah Fest, a week-long celebration of Sabahan culture, while in Sarawak, June's Gawai Festival is well worth attending, when longhouse doors are flung open for two days of rice-harvest merry-making, with dancing, eating, drinking and music. Despite the rains, the months of January and February can also be particularly rewarding, with a number of significant festivals, notably Chinese New Year and the Hindu celebration of Thaipusam, taking place over this period.

Average daily temperatures and rainfall

	Jan	Feb	Mar	Apr	May	Jun	July	Aug	Sep	Oct	Nov	Dec
Bandar Seri Begawan												
max °C	30	30	31	32	32.5	32	31.5	32	31.5	31.5	31	31
min °C	23	23	23	23.5	23.5	23.5	23.5	23.5	23	23	23	23
rainfall mm	133	63	71	124	218	311	277	256	314	334	296	241
Cameron Highlands												
max °C	21	22	23	23	23	23	22	22	22	22	22	21
min °C	14	14	14	15	15	15	14	15	15	15	15	15
rainfall mm	120	111	198	277	273	137	165	172	241	334	305	202
Kota Bharu												
max °C	29	30	31	32	33	32	32	32	32	31	29	29
min °C	22	23	23	24	24	24	23	23	23	23	23	23
rainfall mm	163	60	99	81	114	132	157	168	195	286	651	603
Kota Kinabalu												
max °C	30	30	31	32	32	31	31	31	31	31	31	31
min °C	23	23	23	24	24	24	24	24	23	23	23	23
rainfall mm	153	63	71	124	218	311	277	256	314	334	296	241
Kuala Lumpur												
max °C	32	33	33	33	33	32	32	32	32	32	31	31
min °C	22	22	23	23	23	23	23	23	23	23	23	23
rainfall mm	159	154	223	276	182	119	120	133	173	258	263	223
Kuching												
max °C	30	30	31	32	33	33	32	33	32	32	31	31
min °C	23	23	23	23	23	23	23	23	23	23	23	23
rainfall mm	683	522	339	286	253	199	199	211	271	326	343	465
Mersing												
max °C	28	29	30	31	32	31	31	31	31	31	29	28
min °C	23	23	23	23	23	23	22	22	22	23	23	23
rainfall mm	319	153	141	120	149	145	170	173	177	207	359	635
Penang												
max °C	32	32	32	32	31	31	31	31	31	31	31	31
min °C	23	23	24	24	24	24	23	23	23	23	23	23
rainfall mm	70	93	141	214	240	170	208	235	341	380	246	107
Singapore												
max °C	32	32	32	32	31	31	31	31	31	31	31	31
min °C	23	23	24	24	24	24	23	23	23	23	23	23
rainfall mm	70	93	141	214	240	170	208	235	341	380	246	107

things not to miss

It's not possible to see everything that Malaysia, Singapore and Brunei have to offer in one trip – and we don't suggest you try. What follows is a selective taste of the countries' highlights: natural wonders, stunning buildings and a colourful heritage. They're arranged in five colour-coded categories, which you can browse through to find the very best things to see and experience. All highlights have a page reference to take you straight into the guide, where you can find out more.

01 Longhouses in Sarawak See *Longhouse culture* **colour section** • These vast communal dwellings, home to members of indigenous tribes, are found on rivers and in remote mountain locations.

02 **Ulu Temburong Park** Page **611** • Brunei's only national park has a beautiful approach by longboat, while treks and a canopy walkway will keep you busy during your stay.

04 **Sungai Kinabatangan** Page **574** • Cruise through pristine jungle along this spectacular river, spotting proboscis monkeys and occasionally, the father of the forest, the orang-utan.

03 **Georgetown** Page **197** • Bustling Chinese-dominated haven with elaborate temples, the mansions of colonial Penang and beaches galore.

05 **Little India, Singapore** Page **671** • A walk down Serangoon Road, Singapore's equivalent of downtown Chennai, has all the sights, sounds and smells of the subcontinent.

06 **Street food** Page **59** • From Malay hawkers to elaborate Chinese restaurants, the region's food simply excels.

08 **Omar Ali Saifuddien Mosque** Page **601** • The centre of Brunei's capital is dominated by the magnificent Omar Ali Saifuddien Mosque.

07 **Diving at Pulau Sipadan** Page **583** • The spectacular islands off Borneo offer the thrill of swimming with sharks and turtles.

09 **Cameron Highlands** Page **162** • Misty tea plantations, afternoon tea and jungle trails in cool mountain air.

10 **The Perhentian Islands** Page **306** • With gorgeous, pale sandy beaches, some excellent snorkelling and a fine range of accommodation, these two east-coast islands appeal to backpackers and vacationing families alike.

11 **Langkawi** Page **225** • Sublime beaches and luxurious resorts characterize these west-coast islands, close to the border with Thailand.

13 **Shopping** Page **143** • KL has some of the best mall shopping in the world, complemented by miles of vibrant street markets.

12 **Rainforest Music Festival** Page **447** • Held annually on the edges of the Borneo jungle, this world-music festival is an opportunity to see indigenous performers alongside practitioners from across the globe.

14 **Proboscis monkeys, Bako** Page **448** • These odd-looking creatures roam *kerangas* forest and mangrove swamps in the national park, not far from Kuching.

15 **Bukit Timah Nature Reserve** Page **682** • Mature rainforest, macaques and walking trails – all just a short bus ride from downtown Singapore.

16 Singapore's arts scene

Page **718** • Once stultifyingly dull, Singapore is now channelling its wealth into a broad range of artistic activity, from experimental theatre to indie rock shows.

17 **Kampung Ayer** Page **602** • Bandar Seri Begawan's colourful water village is reached by "flying coffin" – an essential Bruneian experience.

18 **Mount Kinabalu** Page **556** • Watch dawn over Borneo from the summit of Southeast Asia's highest mountain.

20 **Traditional crafts** Page **83** • Malaysia boasts a wide range of crafts, from batik and *songket* (brocade) to rattan baskets and *labu*, gourd-shaped ceramic jugs.

19 **Dizzy heights** Page **121** • Enjoy the panoramic views from the Petronas Towers' Skybridge.

21 Traditional entertainment

See *Malay life* **colour section** ● Ranging from street performances of Chinese opera in Singapore to Malay shadow-puppet plays on the Peninsula's east coast, the traditional arts can be among the most enthralling events to witness.

22 Sunset at Kuching waterfront
Page **431** ● As the heat withers in Sarawak's capital city, the evening crowd come out to chat and enjoy the river.

23 Caving in Mulu
Page **505** ● Explore the park's subterranean limestone passages, which teem with wildlife.

24 Spectacular rainforests
Page **245** ● Malaysia's premier national park, Taman Negara, is one of the world's oldest rainforests, and there are numerous smaller, less discovered habitats throughout the region.

25 Melaka Page **360** • The city's complex historical heritage is evident in its Portuguese, Dutch and British buildings and Peranakan ancestral homes.

27 Adventure tourism Page **81** • Exhilarating white-water rafting, caving and paragliding, amongst other activities, are becoming more popular and widely available across the region.

26 Mulu National Park Page **501** • A sea of razor-sharp limestone pinnacles reward the challenging haul up Gunung Api.

Basics

Basics

Getting there

Located at the heart of Southeast Asia, and on the busy aviation corridor between Europe and Australasia, Malaysia and Singapore enjoy excellent international air links. Malaysia naturally has sited its chief international airport in the Kuala Lumpur (KL) area, but also has international airports in Kuching, Kota Kinabalu, Langkawi and Penang; note, however, that for the most part these four handle flights within East Asia only. If you're flying long-haul to East Malaysia or, for that matter, Brunei, you may well find yourself having to transit in Kuala Lumpur or Singapore.

Singapore and Bangkok are very much the **regional air hubs**, as a result of which fares to these two airports are especially competitive. If your focus is Malaysia, you could look for a good fare to Singapore or perhaps Bangkok, then continue to Malaysia overland or by taking advantage of one of the region's **budget flights** (thanks to which, incidentally, it's easier than ever to visit Malaysia, Singapore or Brunei as part of a wider trawl through Asia, with connections from as far afield as India and southeast China; see p.34 for more on Southeast Asian connections). That said, even if you pay slightly more to fly into **KL**, you often recoup this by not allotting additional time and expense to onward journeys or overnight stays elsewhere.

If you're arriving in the region on a long-haul flight with either **Malaysia Airlines** (often called **MAS** for short) or **Singapore Airlines (SIA)**, note that in general you'll be allowed to add free flights from their hub to and from one of several Peninsular Malaysia airports (and Singapore, on MAS). However, if it's Sarawak, Sabah or Brunei you want to fly on to, reckon on paying an extra £50/$85 to do so with either airline.

The **peak seasons** for fares to Southeast Asia are the Christmas/New Year period, typically from mid-December until the first few days of January, and, to a lesser extent, July and August. Fares to fly during these periods can be twenty percent higher than for other times of year, unless you book well in advance. Note that fares can also rise a few days either side of major local festivals, such as Islamic holidays and the Chinese New Year, and that weekend flights also tend to command a premium.

It can be worth looking out for **package** deals: some combine flights and accommodation, sometimes for little more than the airfare, while others offers short guided itineraries with accommodation but excluding flights. In both cases such packages can serve as starting points around which to plan a more ambitious trip.

If Malaysia, Singapore and Brunei are just one stage on a much longer journey, it's worth considering Round the World (**RTW**) tickets or **air passes** such as the Circle Pacific ticket; the latter is valid for travel in the Asia Pacific region, Australasia and the west coast of North America. Airline consortiums such as Star Alliance (ⓦwww .staralliance.com) and Oneworld Alliance (ⓦwww.oneworldalliance.com) are behind many of these deals, and their websites provide more details of the tickets. Specialist travel agents can help you choose the most suitable option for your route and budget.

Online booking agents

Ebookers ⓦwww.ebookers.com (UK), ⓦwww .ebookers.ie (Ireland).
Expedia ⓦwww.expedia.com (multiple locations).
Flightcentre ⓦwww.flightcentre.com (US, Canada, UK, Australia, New Zealand and South Africa).
lastminute.com ⓦwww.lastminute.com (multiple locations).
Opodo ⓦwww.opodo.co.uk (UK).
Travelocity ⓦwww.travelocity.co.uk (UK), ⓦwww.travelocity.com (US), ⓦwww.travelocity.ca (Canada), ⓦwww.zuji.com.au (Australia), ⓦwww .zuji.co.nz (New Zealand).

Fly less – stay longer! Travel and climate change

Climate change is a serious threat to the ecosystems that humans rely upon, and air travel is among the fastest-growing contributors to the problem. Rough Guides regard travel, overall, as a global benefit, and feel strongly that the advantages to developing economies are important, as is the opportunity of greater contact and awareness among peoples. But we all have a responsibility to limit our personal impact on global warming, and that means giving thought to how often we fly, and what we can do to redress the harm that our trips create.

Flying and climate change

Pretty much every form of motorized travel generates CO_2 – the main cause of human-induced climate change – but planes also generate climate-warming contrails and cirrus clouds and emit oxides of nitrogen, which create ozone (another greenhouse gas) at flight levels. Furthermore, flying simply allows us to travel much further than we otherwise would do. The figures are frightening: one person taking a return flight between Europe and California produces the equivalent impact of 2.5 tonnes of CO_2 – similar to the yearly output of the average UK car.

Fuel-cell and other less harmful types of plane may emerge eventually. But until then, there are really just two options for concerned travellers: to reduce the amount we travel by air (take fewer trips – stay for longer!), and to make the trips we do take "climate neutral" via a carbon offset scheme.

Carbon offset schemes

Offset schemes run by ⓦwww.climatecare.org, ⓦwww.carbonneutral.com and others allow you to make up for some or all of the greenhouse gases that you are responsible for releasing. To do this, they provide "carbon calculators" for working out the global-warming contribution of a specific flight (or even your entire existence), and then let you contribute an appropriate amount of money to fund offsetting measures. These include rainforest reforestation and initiatives to reduce future energy demand – often run in conjunction with sustainable development schemes.

Rough Guides, together with Lonely Planet and other concerned partners in the travel industry, are supporting a **carbon offset scheme** run by climatecare.org. Please take the time to view our website and see how you can help to make your trip climate neutral.

ⓦwww.roughguides.com/climatechange

From the US and Canada

Malaysia, Singapore and Brunei are roughly halfway around the world from North America, so whichever route you fly to Southeast Asia, you have a long journey ahead of you. In most cases the trip, including a stopover, will take at least 20 hours if you fly the **transatlantic** route from the eastern seaboard, or 19 hours minimum if you cross **the Pacific** from the west coast. These two options aren't necessarily the obvious choices however; for example, it can sometimes be cheaper to fly westwards from the east coast, stopping off in Northeast Asia en route.

If you must race across the globe to Southeast Asia, you could take advantage of either of two of the longest nonstop passenger flights in the world, with **Singapore Airlines**, which will have you touching down in Singapore after seventeen hours out of Los Angeles, or eighteen hours out of New York. The only other airline that won't have you changing planes en route is **Malaysia Airlines**, which operates direct to KL from the same two cities.

Otherwise, you're almost spoilt for choice – plenty of airlines operate to East Asia from major North American cities, and with most of the East Asian carriers offering onward flights to Malaysia and Singapore from their hub city, potential connections are legion. If your target is Borneo, it's worth investigating the possibility of connecting onto Malaysia Airlines, who fly Hong Kong–Kota Kinabalu, or one of Royal Brunei Airlines' flights from Hong Kong or Shanghai. **Fares** start at around US$800 or Can$1400 if you're flying from a major US or Canadian airport on either coast.

Malaysia **package** trips from North America tend to be quite predictable, concentrating on the usual historical cities or resorts of Peninsular Malaysia, or on the natural attractions of East Malaysia. Prices often exclude the cost of flights to Southeast Asia.

Airlines

Asiana Airlines ☏1-800/227-4262, ⓦwww .flyasiana.com. To Seoul from Boston, Los Angeles, New York, San Francisco and Seattle, with onward flights to Singapore operated by itself or Singapore Airlines.
British Airways ☏1-800/AIRWAYS, ⓦwww .ba.com. Daily nonstop services from many North American cities to London, with connections to Singapore.
Cathay Pacific US ☏1-800/233-2742, Canada ☏1-800/268-6868, ⓦwww.cathaypacific.com. Flights to Hong Kong from Los Angeles, New York, San Francisco Toronto and Vancouver, with connections to KL, Penang and Singapore.
China Airlines ☏1-800/227-5118, ⓦwww .china-airlines.com. From several North American cities to Taipei, with onward connections to KL, Penang and Singapore.
Emirates ☏1-800/777-3999, ⓦwww.emirates .com. From New York (JFK) to KL and Singapore, via Dubai.
EVA Airways ☏1-800/695-1188, ⓦwww .evaair.com. To Singapore and KL, via Taipei, from Honolulu, Los Angeles, New York, San Francisco, Seattle and Vancouver.
Japan Airlines ☏1-800/525-3663, ⓦwww .japanair.com. Daily flights to KL and Singapore, via Tokyo, from Chicago, Las Vegas, Los Angeles, New York, San Francisco and Vancouver.
Korean Airlines ☏1-800/438-5000 or 213/484 1900, ⓦwww.koreanair.com. From several major US cities, as well as from Vancouver and Toronto, to Seoul, with onward flights to KL, Penang and Singapore.
Malaysia Airlines (MAS) ☏1-800/552-9264, ⓦwww.mas.com.my. From LA and New York (Newark) direct to KL daily, via Taipei and Stockholm respectively.
Northwest/KLM ☏1-800/447-4747, ⓦwww .nwa.com. Flights to Singapore from its Asian hub in Tokyo, to which it has plenty of connections from North American cities. Also flights to KL and Singapore via Amsterdam or Paris with its partner airline KLM.

Singapore Airlines ☏1-800/742-3333 or 323/934 8171, ⓦwww.singaporeair.com. To Singapore from Los Angeles and New York (Newark), either with one stopover or nonstop (expect to pay a premium for the latter). Also flies from Vancouver and San Francisco to Singapore, via Seoul or Hong Kong.
Thai Airways US ☏1-800/426-5204, Canada ☏1-800/668-8103, ⓦwww.thaiair.com. From Los Angeles to KL, Singapore, Bandar Seri Begawan and Penang, via Bangkok.
United Airlines ☏1-800/538-2929, ⓦwww.ual .com. Daily flights from major North American cities to Hong Kong and Tokyo, with connections on to Singapore.

Flight agents

Air Brokers International ☏1-800/883-3273, ⓦwww.airbrokers.com. Specialist in RTW and Circle Pacific tickets.
Airtreks ☏1-877/AIRTREKS, ⓦwww.airtreks.com. RTW and Circle Pacific tickets.
Educational Travel Center ☏1-800/747-5551 or 608/256-5551, ⓦwww.edtrav.com. Student/youth discount agent.
Flightcentre US ☏1-866/967-5351, ⓦwww .flightcentre.us, Canada ☏1-877/967-5302, ⓦwww.flightcentre.ca. Rock-bottom fares worldwide.
STA Travel ☏1-800/781-4040, ⓦwww.sta-travel .com. Worldwide specialists in independent travel; also student IDs, travel insurance, etc.
Travel Cuts Canada ☏1-866/246-9762, US ☏1-800/592-2887, ⓦwww.travelcuts.com. Canadian student-travel organization.

Specialist tour operators

Adventure Center ☏1-800/228-8747, ⓦwww .adventurecenter.com. Offers a good range of Malaysia packages from various adventure-tour operators, mainly focused on East Malaysia, and including options such as wildlife-spotting, climbing and trekking.
The Adventure Travel Company Canada ☏1-888/238-2887, ⓦwww.atcadventure.com. A large range of East Asian tours geared towards independent travellers. Malaysia trips include two tours of Borneo plus one of the Peninsula.
Asian Affair Holidays ☏1-800/742-3133, ⓦwww.asianaffairholidays.com. Singapore Airlines' travel arm organizes packages from the US, including flights, hotels and sightseeing. Trips to Singapore, Langkawi and East Malaysia are among the offerings.
Asian Pacific Adventures ☏1-800/825-1680, ⓦwww.asianpacificadventures.com. Their

chief Malaysia tour is a Borneo trip aptly billed as "Headhunters, Hornbills and Orang-utans", with a few extensions possible in Sarawak or the Peninsula.

A Touch of Class Tours ☎1-800/203-0438, ⊛www.asianpacificadventures.com. A twelve-day "Multicultural Malaysia" package, dominated by Borneo but commencing in KL.

Bestway Tours ☎1-800/663-0844, ⊛www .bestway.com. Cultural tour specialist, though their two Borneo offerings are dominated by wildlife-spotting. They also offer a comprehensive two-week tour of Peninsular Malaysia and Singapore.

Borneo Lifestyles ☎310/674-9473, ⊛www .borneolifestyles.com. A limited range of East Malaysia tours, but with the possibility of adding on customized trips.

Deep Discoveries ☎1-800/667-5362, ⊛www .deepdiscoveries.com. Dive packages which discover not just the deeps off the coast of Sabah but can be customized to include wildlife sites.

eMalaysiaTravel.com ☎618/529-8033, ⊛www .emalaysiatravel.com. Various Malaysia offerings – KL city breaks, diving off Sabah, Taman Negara trips and so forth.

Explorient ☎1-800/785-1233, ⊛www.explorient .com. A range of short tours, focused on major cities and with a cultural emphasis, which can be combined with one another.

Gala Tours ☎562/692-5000, ⊛www.galatour .com. A range of short breaks, focused either on KL or Singapore, or taking in KL plus Penang, Kuching or Kota Kinabalu.

ITC Golf Tours ☎1-800/255-8735, ⊛www .itcgolf-africatours.com. Golf tours to both Malaysia and Singapore.

Intrepid Travel USA ☎1-866 847 8192, Canada ☎1-866/732 5885, ⊛www.intrepidtravel.com. Australia-based company with a long list of Malaysia packages, from loops around Peninsular Malaysia to Sabah trips taking in Mount Kinabalu, Turtle Island and the Sepilok Orang-utan Sanctuary.

Journeys International ☎1-800/255-8735, ⊛www.journeys-intl.com. Their two-week Borneo Adventure package is a thorough tour of Sabah, Sarawak and, unusually, Brunei.

Pacific Holidays ☎1-800/355-8025, ⊛www .pacificholidaysinc.com. A range of Malaysia packages, including a Malay Peninsula tour that unaccountably includes Bangkok, and a two-week East Malaysia itinerary.

Travel Masters ☎512/323-6961, ⊛www .travel-masters.net. Dive specialist; they can arrange not just Borneo dive packages but also also side trips in Sabah.

Worldwide Quest Adventures ☎1-800/387-1483, ⊛www.worldwidequest.com. Just one Malaysia offering, the two-week Borneo Panorama, including trekking in Sarawak plus an ascent of Mount Kinabalu.

From the UK and Ireland

London Heathrow has daily **nonstop** flights to KL (with Malaysia Airlines) and to Singapore (British Airways, Qantas and Singapore Airlines), taking around thirteen hours. It's also possible to fly nonstop to Penang or Langkawi with Malaysia Airlines, from London Heathrow, and to Singapore from **Manchester** with Singapore Airlines. Flying with any other airline will involve a change of plane in their hub city, and possibly an additional stopover elsewhere. From the **Republic of Ireland**, you'll have to change planes at London Heathrow or Manchester or at a hub elsewhere in Europe.

The very best **fares** to KL or Singapore are around the £400/€600 mark, midweek outside high season, including taxes, but these are usually for indirect flights, although Malaysia Airlines specials, on sale sporadically (particularly in December for travel the following year), can bring their KL fares down to this level. More typical are fares in the £450–550/€650–850 range.

Airlines

Air France UK ☎0845/359 1000, Republic of Ireland ☎01/605 0383, ⊛www.airfrance.com. Paris to Singapore, with connections from several UK and Irish airports.

Air India ☎020/8560 9996, ⊛www.airindia.com. Flights to KL and to Singapore via Bombay, Delhi or Madras.

Austrian Airlines UK ☎0870/124 2625, ⊛www .aua.com. London Heathrow to KL and to Singapore, via Vienna.

British Airways UK ☎0870/850 9850, Republic of Ireland ☎1890/626 747, ⊛www.britishairways .com. Daily nonstop flights from London Heathrow to Singapore. Connections available from UK regional airports and Dublin.

Cathay Pacific UK ☎020/8834 8888, ⊛www .cathaypacific.com. London Heathrow to Hong Kong, with onward connections to KL, Kota Kinabalu, Penang and Singapore.

Emirates UK ☎0870/243 2222, ⊛www.emirates .com. From London Heathrow, London Gatwick and Manchester to Dubai, with onward flights to KL and to Singapore.

Finnair UK ☏0870/241 4411, Republic of Ireland
☏01/844 6565, ⓦwww.finnair.com. London and
Dublin to Singapore via Helsinki.
Gulf Air UK ☏0870/777 1717, ⓦwww.gulfairco
.com. London Heathrow to KL and Singapore via
Bahrain.
KLM UK ☏0870/507 4074, ⓦwww.klm.com.
Daily flights via Amsterdam to both KL and Singapore;
connections from UK and Irish airports.
Lufthansa UK ☏0870/837 7747, ⓦwww
.lufthansa.com. Frankfurt to Singapore (nonstop) and
to KL, with connections from UK and Irish airports.
Malaysia Airlines (MAS) UK ☏0870/607 9090,
Republic of Ireland ☏01/676 1561, ⓦwww.mas
.com.my. Flies nonstop to KL, twice a day from London
Heathrow. Also nonstop flights from London Heathrow to
Penang and to Langkawi, a couple of times each week.
Qantas UK ☏0845/774 7767, ⓦwww.qantas.co
.uk. Nonstop London Heathrow to Singapore flights;
connections available from UK regional airports.
Qatar Airways UK ☏020/7896 3636, ⓦwww
.qatarairways.com. Flies from London Gatwick and
Heathrow and from Manchester to KL and Singapore;
all flights via Doha.
Royal Brunei Airlines UK ☏020/7584 6660,
ⓦwww.bruneiair.com. London Heathrow to Brunei
daily, with a stopover in Dubai.
Singapore Airlines (SIA) UK ☏0870/608 8886,
Republic of Ireland ☏01/671 0722, ⓦwww
.singaporeair.com. Nonstop flights to Singapore from
London Heathrow and Manchester, with connections
from other UK airports. Onward connections to
Malaysia (KL, Penang, Kota Kinabalu and Kuching)
and Brunei.
SriLankan Airlines UK ☏020/8538 2001,
ⓦwww.srilankan.aero. London Heathrow to Kuala
Lumpur and to Singapore, via Colombo.
Thai Airways ☏0870/606 0911, ⓦwww.thaiair
.com. Daily nonstop flights to Bangkok from London
Heathrow, with onward connections to Bandar Seri
Begawan, KL, Penang and Singapore.

Flight agents

Lee Travel Republic of Ireland ☏021/427 7111,
ⓦwww.leetravel.ie. Flights worldwide.
Lee's Travel UK ☏0870/027 33 88, ⓦwww
.leestravel.com. Far Eastern travel deals, including
off-loaded Malaysia and Singapore Airlines tickets.
North South Travel UK ☏ & ☏01245/608 291,
ⓦwww.northsouthtravel.co.uk. Discounted fares
worldwide; profits are used to support projects in the
developing world.
Rex Air ☏020/7437 4499. Specialist in flights to
the Far East with some good-value specials, always
worth a call.

STA Travel UK ☏0870/160 0599, ⓦwww
.statravel.co.uk. Worldwide specialists in low-cost
flights and tours for students and under-26s, though
other customers welcome.
Trailfinders UK ☏0845/058 5858, ⓦwww
.trailfinders.com; Republic of Ireland ☏01/677
7888, ⓦwww.trailfinders.ie. Efficient agent geared
up to independent travellers.
Travel Bag UK ☏0800/082 5000, ⓦwww
.travelbag.co.uk. Discount long-haul flights.
USIT Northern Ireland ☏028/9032 7111, ⓦwww
.usitnow.com, Republic of Ireland ☏01/602 1904,
ⓦwww.usit.ie. Student and youth travel.

Specialist tour operators

Bales Worldwide ☏0870/752 0780, ⓦwww
.balesworldwide.com. Upmarket package tours,
including a Borneo Discovery tour taking in both
Sabah and Sarawak.
Eastravel ☏01473/214305, ⓦwww.eastravel
.co.uk. A three-week East Malaysia tour, plus a
slightly shorter self-drive Peninsula trip.
Emerald Global ☏020/7312 1708, ⓦwww
.etours-online.com. Flight-plus-accommodation
Malaysia packages based in cities or resorts,
including a few based around activities such as
diving or golf.
Exodus ☏0870/240 5550, ⓦwww.exodus.co.uk.
Two-week East Malaysia tours, concentrating on
natural attractions and including some trekking.
Explore Worldwide ☏0870/333 4001 (Ireland
(o/o Maxwell's Travel ☏01/677 9479), ⓦwww
.exploreworldwide.com. Peninsular and East
Malaysia excursions of ten days to three weeks, taking
in the key cities as well as beaches and reserves.
Golden Days in Malaysia ☏020/8893 1781,
ⓦwww.goldendays.co.uk A range of itineraries,
each one of which covers a handful of major
attractions, with a choice of upmarket accommodation
at each stop.
Guerba ☏01373/826611, ⓦwww.guerba.com. A
couple of East Malaysia itineraries, taking in the usual
reserves and wildlife sites.
Intrepid Travel ☏0800/917 6456, ⓦwww
.intrepidtravel.com. An excellent range of tours from
this Australia-based company, from culinary itineraries
to Borneo packages involving wildlife-spotting and
Sarawak longhouses.
Kuoni ☏01306/740500, ⓦwww.kuoni
.co.uk. A handful of guided tours, including Borneo
Adventure, which sandwiches Sarawak and Sabah
between visits to Singapore and KL. Also resort deals
and customized itineraries.
Magic of the Orient ☏0117/311 6051, ⓦwww
.magic-of-the-orient.com. A variety of East Malaysia

tours, such as the weeklong "Wildlife of Borneo" tour, which whisks you around Sabah.

Malaysia Experience ☎020/8424 9548, ⊕www .malaysiaexperience.co.uk. Upmarket resort- and city-based packages.

Premier Holidays ☎0870/889 0854, ⊕www .premierholidays.co.uk. City- and resort-based packages in Peninsular Malaysia and Singapore.

Scott Dunn World ☎020/8682 5010, ⊕www .scottdunn.com. Top-end package holidays centred on Malaysia's island and beach resorts, plus a wildlife tour of East Malaysia and luxury breaks in KL and Singapore.

Silverbird ☎020/8875 9090, ⊕www.silverbird .co.uk. Far East travel specialist, all of whose tours are individually customized.

Skedaddle ☎0191/265 1110, ⊕www.skedaddle .co.uk. Cycling tours worldwide, including itineraries around both Peninsular and East Malaysia, using specialist knowledge of suitable routes.

Steppes East ☎01285/651010, ⊕www .steppeseast.co.uk. Specializing in Asia, Latin America and Africa, Steppes East can customize a variety of Malaysian tours.

Symbiosis ☎0845/123 2844, ⊕www.symbiosis -travel.com. Cycling, diving, trekking and other adventure activities in various Malaysian locations, plus a few resort-based holidays.

Transindus ☎020/8579 3739, ⊕www .transindus.co.uk. A variety of Malaysia itineraries

featuring flights, accommodation and local transport, but leaving the sightseeing up to you, and with no group travel involved.

Travelmood ☎0870/066 0044, ⊕www .travelmood.com. Malaysia offerings focus on beach and island packages.

Voyana ☎0871/271 5200, ⊕www.voyana.com. Resort-based holidays in Malaysia, plus Singapore city breaks.

From Australia and New Zealand

The relative proximity of Australia and New Zealand to Southeast Asia makes for a particularly good range of flights into Malaysia, Singapore and Brunei, including several direct connections into **Borneo** with Royal Brunei Airlines.

Fares depend not just on the season but also on exactly how far your starting point is from Southeast Asia. If you're flying from Darwin to Singapore (4hr 30min), you could pay as little as A$350 return with low-cost carrier Tiger Airways. At the other end of the scale, Sydney to Singapore (8hr) will set you back at least A$800, while Auckland to Singapore (10hr) generally starts at NZ$1200 return.

Airlines

Air New Zealand New Zealand ☎0800/737 000. Auckland nonstop to Singapore. Also through tickets from NZ airports to KL via Sydney or Melbourne, with the KL leg furnished by Malaysia Airlines.

Australian Airlines ☎13 13 13, ⊕www .australianairilnes.com.au. Cairns to Singapore, sometimes via Darwin; also Sydney to Singapore via Bali.

British Airways Australia ☎1300/767 177, New Zealand ☎09/966 9777, ⊕www.ba.com. Nonstop from Sydney and Melbourne to Singapore.

Emirates Australia ☎1300/303 777, New Zealand ☎09/968 2200, ⊕www.emirates.com. Auckland to Singapore via Brisbane, and Melbourne to Singapore.

Gulf Air Australia ☎1300/366 337, ⊕www .gulfairco.com. Sydney nonstop to Singapore.

Malaysia Airlines Australia ☎13 26 27, New Zealand ☎0800/777 747, ⊕www.mas.com.my. Nonstop to Kuala Lumpur from Auckland, Adelaide, Brisbane, Melbourne, Perth and Sydney; also Perth–Kuching nonstop.

Qantas Australia ☎13 13 13, New Zealand ☎0800/808 767, ⊕www.qantas.com.au. Brisbane,

Melbourne, Perth and Sydney nonstop to Singapore, plus Adelaide–Darwin–Singapore.

Royal Brunei Airlines Australia ☎1300/721 271, New Zealand ☎09/977 2209, ⓦwww .bruneiair.com. Auckland, Brisbane, Darwin, Perth and Sydney to Bandar Seri Begawan.

Singapore Airlines Australia ☎13 10 11, New Zealand ☎0800/80 89 09, ⓦwww.singaporeair .com. Nonstop flights to Singapore from Adelaide, Auckland, Brisbane, Christchurch, Melbourne, Perth, Sydney.

Tiger Airways ⓦwww.tigerairways.com. Budget airline with daily flights between Darwin and its home base, Singapore.

Flight agents

Destinations Unlimited New Zealand ☎9/414 1680, ⓦwww.travel-nz.com. Good deals on airfares and holidays.

STA Travel Australia ☎1300/733 035, ⓦwww .statravel.com.au, New Zealand ☎0508/782 872, ⓦwww.statravel.co.nz. Worldwide specialists in low-cost flights for students and under-26s; other customers also welcome. Over 200 branches overseas.

Trailfinders Australia ☎1300/780 212, ⓦwww .trailfinders.com.au. Australian branch of large UK-based independent travel specialists.

Specialist tour operators

Adventure World Australia ☎02/8913 0755, ⓦwww.adventureworld.com.au, New Zealand ☎09/524 5118, ⓦwww.adventureworld.co.nz. A range of East Malaysia and Brunei options, with mid-range or upmarket accommodation.

Allways Dive Expeditions ☎1800/338 239, ⓦwww.allwaysdive.com.au. Dive holidays to the prime dive sites of Sabah.

Borneo Holidays ☎08/941 1394. A range of trips to East Malaysia and Brunei; accommodation bookings also taken.

Intrepid Travel Australia ☎1300/360 667, New Zealand ☎0800/174 043, ⓦwww .intrepidtravel.com. Plenty of Malaysia offerings to suit different budgets and tastes – from a three-week East Malaysia package that takes you up Mount Kinabalu and includes a homestay, to a foodie-geared trawl up the west coast from Singapore to Penang.

Peregrine Adventures Australia ☎03/9663 8611, ⓦwww.peregrine.net.au. Experienced operator with a handful of East Malaysia packages, including a family-oriented Sabah trip that includes rafting and encounters with orang-utans.

San Michele Travel ☎1800/222 244, ⓦwww .asiatravel.com.au. Southeast Asia specialist with a small number of Malaysia trips.

Travel Clearance Australia ☎1300/900 800, ⓦwww.travelclearance.com.au. Discounted deals on Malaysia and Singapore holidays.

From South Africa

The quickest way to reach Malaysia or Singapore from South Africa is to fly with **Malaysia Airlines** or **Singapore Airlines**, both of which offer nonstop flights to their home countries from Johannesburg, with connections from Cape Town (Singapore Airlines also has some nonstop flights from Cape Town). Reckon on around eleven hours' flying time with either airline. Of the few indirect flights available, the most plausible connections involve a change of plane elsewhere in Africa or in the Middle East.

Fares from South Africa to Malaysia or Singapore aren't especially cheap, starting at around R6800 return, including taxes, though you may be lucky enough to turn up a few flight-and-accommodation packages for only a little more outlay.

Airlines

Air Mauritius ☎ 011/444 4600, ⓦ www
.airmauritius.com. Flights from Cape Town, Durban
and Jo'burg to Mauritius, where you change for one of
their flights on to KL or Singapore.

Cathay Pacific ☎ 011/700 8900, ⓦ www
.cathaypacific.com. Hong Kong to Singapore (and
to KL through a Malaysia Airlines code-share);
connections from Jo'burg.

Emirates ☎ 0861/3647 2837, ⓦ www.emirates
.com. Jo'burg to either KL or Singapore, via Dubai.

GulfAir ☎ 011/202 7626, ⓦ www.gulfairco.com.
Jo'burg to Kuala Lumpur via Bahrain.

Malaysia Airlines (MAS) ☎ 021/419 8010 or
011/880 9614, ⓦ www.mas.com.my. Cape Town to
Jo'burg, and thence nonstop to KL.

Qantas ☎ 011/441 8550, ⓦ www.qantas.com.au.
Johannesburg to Singapore via Perth.

Singapore Airlines (SIA) ☎ 021/674 0601 or
011/880 8560, ⓦ www.singaporeair.com. Several
flights a week to Singapore from Jo'burg (nonstop)
and from Cape Town (some nonstop, others via
Jo'burg).

Flight and travel agents

Flight Centre ☎ 0860/400 727, ⓦ www
.flightcentre.co.za. Budget travel specialist, with a
few Malaysia packages as well as flights.

Pentravel ⓦ www.pentravel.co.za. Travel agent
chain with offices in KwaZulu-Natal, Gauteng and
Western Cape, selling budget flights plus Qantas
Holidays packages to Malaysia.

Planet Travel ☎ 0860/100 739, ⓦ www
.planet-travel.co.za. Flights and packages, with some
Far Eastern offerings.

STA Travel ☎ 0861/781 781, ⓦ www.sta-travel
.co.za. Focused (though by no means exclusively) on
student travel, with good fares worldwide (including
RTW tickets). They're also agents for a selection of
Malaysian adventure tours.

Student Flights ☎ 0860/400 737, ⓦ www
.studentflights.co.za. The youth travel wing of Flight
Centre, offering discounted flights, including RTW fares.

Thompsons Tours ☎ 011/770 7677 or 021/408
9555, ⓦ www.thompsons.co.za. Flights and various
packages to Southeast Asia.

Travel.co.za ☎ 011/790 0010, ⓦ www.travel
.co.za. Online flight and tour agent with a few
Malaysian packages.

From elsewhere in Southeast Asia

It's both a cliché and a fact: **budget air
travel** has taken off in a big way in Asia. If

you plan it right, you can now easily take in
Malaysia, Singapore or Brunei as part of a
general meander through the region, taking
advantage of efficient, cheap air connections
with most other Southeast Asian countries
(barring, at the time of writing, Laos), and
with a minimum of backtracking.

The most useful no-frills carriers for the
three countries covered in this book are
the Malaysia-based **AirAsia** (ⓦ www.airasia
.com) and Singapore's **Jetstar Asia** (ⓦ www
.jetstarasia.com) and **Tiger Airways** (ⓦ www
.tigerairways.com). Though fuel surcharges
and taxes do take some of the shine off the
fares, prices can still be keen, especially if
you book well in advance of your journey: for
£35/$60 all-in, you can fly one-way from Bali
to KL, or from Ho Chi Minh City or Chiang
Mai to Singapore.

You can, of course, reach Malaysia or
Singapore from their immediate neighbours
by means other than flying. There are **road**
connections from Thailand and from Kalimantan (Indonesian Borneo), **ferries** from
the Indonesian island of Sumatra and from
the southern Philippines, and **trains** from
Thailand. The sections below explore in more
detail the travel options from these countries
to Malaysia and Singapore.

There's a round-up below of the most
popular border crossings, and details of the
routes are included in the text throughout.

From Thailand

There are two daily **rail** services between
Thailand and Malaysia, supplemented by the
luxurious Eastern and Oriental Express, which
runs all the way to Singapore (see box, opposite). The two ordinary rail services comprise
a stopping service between the southern
Thai city of **Hat Yai** and **KL**, run by the
Malaysian rail company KTM (ⓦ www.ktmb
.com.my), and an express service between
Bangkok and the Malaysian west-coast city
of **Butterworth** (close to Penang island), run
by State Railway of Thailand (ⓦ www.railway
.co.th). The KTM service departs Hat Yai at
2.50pm, taking seventeen hours to reach KL.
The express leaves Bangkok's Hualamphong
Station at 2.20pm stopping nine times en
route (notably at Hua Hin, Surat Thani, Hat
Yai and Alor Setar in Kedah), and arriving in
Butterworth almost exactly 24 hours later.

The Eastern & Oriental Express

Unlike some luxury trains in other parts of the world, the **Eastern & Oriental Express** isn't a re-creation of a classic rail journey from colonialism's heyday, but a sort of fantasy realization of how such a service might have looked had it existed in the Far East. Employing 1970s Japanese rolling stock, given an elegant old-world cladding with wooden inlay work and featuring Thai and Malay motifs, the train departs Bangkok on certain Sundays bound for Singapore, returning on Thursdays. En route there are extended stops at Kanchanaburi, for a visit to the infamous bridge over the **River Kwai**, and at Butterworth, where there's time for a half-day tour of **Georgetown**. An observation deck at the rear of the train makes the most of the passing scenery, while Thai dance performances help keep you entertained after dark.

Taking altogether four days and three nights (three days and two nights if done from Singapore), the trip costs around £1000/US$1750 per person in swish, en-suite Pullman accommodation, including meals from a menu of Eurasian fusion food, though alcohol costs extra. On the southbound leg, leaving the train at KL is perhaps better value, as this eliminates the third night of the journey and so brings the fare down to £700/$1225.

Bookings can be made through Venice Simplon-Orient-Express Limited in the UK (℡0845/077 2222, ⓦ www.orient-express.com) or in Singapore at E&O Services, #32-01/03 Shaw Towers, 100 Beach Rd (℡6392 3500). For booking contacts in other countries, see the company's website.

Also useful is the Thai rail service from Hat Yai, which is on the west coast of southern Thailand, across to **Sungai Golok** on the east coast, close to the Malaysian border crossing at Rantau Panjang, from where buses run to Kota Bharu, with a couple of services a day to Kuala Lumpur.

Hat Yai–KL **fares** start at RM44 in an ordinary seat, rising to RM57 in a lower-berth sleeper. Schedules and fare tables can be downloaded from the Malaysian Railways website ⓦ www.ktmb.com.my; for more on the Malaysian rail network, see p.49.

As regards **flights**, there are of course plenty of services connecting Bangkok and Chiang Mai with KL and Singapore. Some of the less obvious connections include a very useful Bangkok to Kota Kinabalu service (AirAsia), Bangkok to Penang (AirAsia), Ko Samui to KL (Berjaya Air) and Singapore (Bangkok Airways); Krabi to Singapore (Tiger Airways); Phuket to KL (AirAsia) and Singapore (Jetstar Asia & Tiger Airways). Note that Bangkok Airways (ⓦ www.bangkokair.com) and Berjaya Air (ⓦ www.berjaya-air.com) are not budget operators.

A few scheduled **ferry** services sail from the most southwesterly Thai town of Satun to the Malaysian west-coast town of Kuala Perlis (30min) and to Pulau Langkawi (1hr 30min). Boats leave from Thammalang pier, 10km south of Satun. Departing Thailand by sea for Malaysia, you should get your passport stamped at the immigration office at the pier to avoid problems with the Malaysian immigration officials when you arrive. Another option is the ferry from the southern Thai town of Ban Taba to the Malaysian town of Pengkalan Kubor, where frequent buses run to Kota Bharu, 20km away. There are buses to Ban Taba from the provincial capital, Narathiwat (1hr 30min).

The easiest road access from Thailand is via the rail junction town of Hat Yai, from where **buses** and shared taxis run regularly to Butterworth (4hr) and nearby Georgetown on Penang island. From the interior Thai town of Betong, there's a road across the border to the Malaysian town of **Keroh**, from where Route 67 leads west to meet Route 1 at Sungei Petani; shared taxis run along the route. You can also get a taxi from Ban Taba the few kilometres south to Kota Bharu.

From Indonesia

There are plenty of budget flights from Indonesia to Malaysia and Singapore, though on some routes you'll have to rely on full-cost airlines. **From Java**, AirAsia operates flights to KL from Bandung, Jakarta and Surabaya (Yogyakarta–KL is also served, by Malaysia Airlines) while there are flights to Singapore from Jakarta and Surabaya with Jetstar Asia. You can reach northern Borneo from Jakarta and Surabaya with Royal Brunei Airways into Bandar Seri Begawan. **From Sumatra**, AirAsia operates from Medan, Padang and Pekanbaru to KL, as well as from Medan to Penang; there are also flights to Singapore from Medan and Palembang (with Singapore Airlines subsidiary **SilkAir**, not a budget carrier; Ⓦwww.silkair.com), and from Padang (Tiger Airways). There are also flights **from Bali** to Bandar Seri Begawan (Royal Brunei), KL (AirAsia), Singapore (Jetstar Asia); and **from Lombok** to Singapore (SilkAir).

Surprisingly there aren't many flights **from Kalimantan** to Malaysia. AirAsia does operate from Balikpapan to KL, while Malaysia Airlines flies between Pontianak and Kuching.

It's possible to reach Sarawak from Kalimantan on just one road route, through the border town of Entikong and onwards to Kuching in the southwest of the state. The bus trip from the western city of Pontianak to Entikong takes seven hours, crossing to the Sarawak border town of Tebedu; you can stay on the same bus for another three hours to reach the Sarawak capital, Kuching.

As for **ferries**, a service operates from Medan in northern Sumatra to Penang (4hr) and, from Dumai further south, there's a daily service to Melaka (2hr). There are also a few services from Pulau Batam in the Riau archipelago (accessible by plane or boat from Sumatra or Jakarta) to Johor Bahru (30min) or Singapore (30min); and a minor ferry crossing from Tanjung Balai to Kukup (45min) just to the southwest of Johor Bahru. Over in Borneo, there are daily ferries to Tawau in **Sabah** from Nunakan (1hr).

From the Philippines

Despite the proximity of Sabah to the southern Philippines, there aren't many transport links between the two. A ferry service operates between Zamboanga and Sandakan. As for **flights**, there are low-cost options from Manila to KL (AirAsia), Kota Kinabalu (AirAsia) and Singapore (Jetstar Asia and Tiger Airways). Full-cost flights on Philippine Airlines (Ⓦwww .philippineairlines.com) include Cebu to KL and to Kota Kinabalu, and Manila to Bandar Seri Begawan.

Visas and red tape

Nationals of the UK, Ireland, the US, Canada, Australia, New Zealand and South Africa don't need visas to stay in Malaysia, Singapore or Brunei for up to fourteen days, longer in some cases. When you arrive you're automatically given right of entry, and it's straightforward to extend your permission to stay. That said, it's always a good idea to check with the relevant embassy or consulate, as the rules on visas are complex and subject to change. Ensure that your passport is valid for at least six months from the date of your trip, and has several blank pages for entry stamps.

Malaysia

Upon arrival in Malaysia, citizens of the **UK**, **Ireland**, **US**, **New Zealand** and **South Africa** are given a passport stamp entitling them to a **three-month stay** (two months for Canadians and Australians). Visitors who enter via Sarawak receive a one-month stamp (see below). It's a straightforward matter to **extend** this permit by applying at the Immigration Department, who have offices (listed in the Guide) in Kuala Lumpur and major towns. If you're in the south of the Peninsula, though, it's simpler just to cross into Singapore and back, whereupon you'll be granted a fresh Malaysia entry stamp. In theory, visitors can extend their stay for up to six months, but this is subject to the discretion of the official you encounter although in practice, there's rarely a problem.

Arriving by air, you'll be given a lengthy **landing card** to complete – note that you need to hang on to the small departure portion of the card for when you leave Malaysia.

Tourists travelling from the Peninsula to **East Malaysia** (Sarawak and Sabah) must carry a valid passport and be cleared again by immigration; visitors to Sabah can remain as long as their original entry stamp is valid.

If you would like to live part of the time in Malaysia without working there, you can get **long-stay multiple-entry visas** under the country's "Malaysia My Second Home" scheme (Ⓦmm2h.motour.gov.my), though note that a basic condition is that you deposit a sizeable amount of money in a local bank.

Malaysian embassies and consulates abroad

Australia 7 Perth Ave, Yarralumla, Canberra, ACT 6000 Ⓣ06/273 1543.
Brunei No. 61, Simpang 336, Kg Sungai Akar, Jalan Kebangsaan, P.O. Box 2826, Bandar Seri Begawan Ⓣ02/381095.
Canada 60 Boteler St, Ottawa, ON K1N 8Y7 Ⓣ613/237-5182.
Indonesia Jalan H.R. Rasuna Said, Kav. X/6, No. 1-3 Kuningan, Jakarta Selatan 12950 Ⓣ021/5224947.
Ireland Shelbourne House, Level 3A-5A, Ballsbridge, Dublin 4 Ⓣ01/667 7280.
New Zealand 10 Washington Ave, Brooklyn, Wellington Ⓣ04/801385 2439.
Singapore 301 Jervois Rd, Singapore 249007 Ⓣ6325 0111.
South Africa 1007 Schoeman Street, Arcadia, Pretoria 0083 Ⓣ3425990
Thailand 33-35 South Sathorn Rd, Bangkok 10120 Ⓣ02/679 2190.
UK 45 Belgrave Square, London SW1X 8QT Ⓣ020/7235 8033.
USA 3516 International Court, NW Washington, DC 20008 Ⓣ202/572-9700; 313 East, 43rd Street, New York Ⓣ212/490-2722; 550 South Hope St, Suite 400, Los Angeles 90071, Ⓣ213/892-9031.

Singapore

Upon arrival in **Singapore**, citizens of the UK, Ireland, the US, Canada, Australia, New Zealand and South Africa are normally stamped in for fourteen days, though they are given a month's stay if they request this. **Extending** your stay for up to three months is possible but extensions beyond this are rare. If you have any problems extending your stay, there's always the option of taking a bus up to Johor Bahru just inside Malaysia, then returning to Singapore, whereupon you're given a new entry stamp.

Sarawak

When you arrive in **Sarawak**, you receive an entry stamp permitting you to stay for **one month**, easily extendable for an additional month at the immigration offices in Kuching, Bintulu or Miri. If Sarawak is also the place where you entered the country, and you want to head to the Peninsula or Sabah subsequently, you need to go to the immigration office in Kuching (see p.443) and have your passport stamped with the usual pass. However, if you arrived in Sarawak after entering Malaysia through the Peninsula or Sabah, note that your original entry stamp must be valid in order for you to return to either. It's straightforward to have the stamp renewed at the immigration office in Kuching; note also that it doesn't matter if the stamp lapses while you're in Sarawak, as long as your presence is covered by a valid Sarawak entry stamp. Certain trips within Sarawak also require special **travel permits**; details are given in the text.

Singaporean embassies and consulates abroad

Australia 17 Forster Crescent, Yarralumla, Canberra, ACT 2600 Ⓣ06/273 3944.
Canada Suite 1820, 999 Hastings St, Vancouver, BC V6C 2W2 Ⓣ604/669 5115.
Indonesia Block X/4 Kav No. 2, Jalan H.R. Rasuna Said, Kuningan, Jakarta Ⓣ021/5201489.
Ireland No office; contact their UK representation.

Drugs: a warning

In Malaysia, Singapore and Brunei, the possession of **illegal drugs** – hard or soft – carries a hefty prison sentence. If you are caught smuggling drugs into or out of the country, at best you face a long stretch in a foreign prison; at worst, you could be hanged. This is no idle threat, as the authorities have, in the recent past, shown themselves to be prepared to pass the death sentence on Western travellers. The simple advice, therefore, is not to have anything to do with drugs in any of these countries, and never agree to carry anything through customs for a third party.

Malaysia 209 Jalan Tun Razak, Kuala Lumpur 50400 ☏ 03/2161 6404.
New Zealand Johnsonville PO Box 13-140, Wellington ☏ 04/479 2076.
South Africa 980 Schoeman Street, Arcadia, Pretoria 0083 ☏ 4306035
Thailand 129 South Sathorn Road, Yannawa, Bangkok 10120 ☏ 02/286-2111.
UK 9 Wilton Crescent, Belgravia, London SW1X 8SP ☏ 020/7235 8315.
USA 3501 International Place NW, Washington, DC 20008 ☏ 202/537-3100.

Brunei

US nationals can visit **Brunei** for up to ninety days without a visa, while British and New Zealand passport holders are granted thirty days, and Canadians, Australians and South Africans fourteen. Once you're in Brunei, **extending** your permission to stay is usually a formality; apply at the Immigration Department in Bandar Seri Begawan.

Bruneian embassies and consulates abroad

Australia 10 Beale Crescent, Deakin, ACT 2600 Canberra ☏ 06/285 4500.
Canada 395 Laurier Ave, Ottawa, ON, KIN 6R4 ☏ 613/234-5656.
Indonesia Jalan Tanjung Karang No. 7, Jakarta Pusat ☏ 021/3190 6080.
Ireland No office; contact their UK representation.
Malaysia No. 19-10 Tingkat 19, Menara Tan & Tan, Jalan Tun Razak, Kuala Lumpur 50400 ☏ 03/2161 2800.

New Zealand No office; contact their Australia representation.
The Philippines Eleventh Floor, BPI Building, Ayala Ave, Paseo De Roxas, Makati City, Metro Manila ☏ 02/816 2836.
Singapore 325 Tanglin Rd 247955 ☏ 7339055.
South Africa see the Singapore embassy.
Thailand No. 132 Sukhumvit Soi 23, Sukhumvit Road, Wattana District, Bangkok 10110 ☏ 02/204-1476.
UK 19/20 Belgrave Square, London SW1X 8PG ☏ 020/7581 0521.
USA 3520 International Court NW, Washington, DC 20008 ☏ 202/237-1838.

Customs allowances

Malaysia's duty-free allowances let you bring in 200 cigarettes, 50 cigars or 250g of tobacco, and wine, spirits or liquor not exceeding 1 litre. There's no customs clearance for passengers travelling from Singapore or Peninsular Malaysia to East Malaysia, nor for people passing between Sabah and Sarawak.

Entering **Singapore** from anywhere other than Malaysia (with which there are no duty-free restrictions), you can bring in 1 litre each of spirits, wine and beer duty-free; duty is payable on all tobacco.

Visitors to **Brunei** may bring in 200 cigarettes, 50 cigars or 250g of tobacco, and 60ml of perfume; non-Muslims over 17 can also import two quarts of liquor and twelve cans of beer for personal consumption (any alcohol brought into the country must be declared upon arrival).

Information

Malaysian tourist information can be frustratingly incoherent. There just isn't a tradition of collating and communicating useful details of buses, accommodation or other facilities. Even where brochures, maps or websites attempt to cover these subjects, you'll find that much-needed updates are few and far between. Also, organizations that should be cooperating with one another often seem keener to run their own little show; thus tourist offices may not be aware of new transport options or changes at local attractions. Phoning is often the best way to make enquiries as, for every resort or agency that deals promptly with an email or fax, you'll find another that doesn't get back to you for weeks.

Singapore is, of course, a much more sophisticated affair, with plenty of concrete information available – particularly online – right down to bus timetables and museum opening hours.

Tourist offices

There are two official sources of tourist information in Malaysia. The first is the country's tourism board, **Tourism Malaysia**, which has offices in most of the state capitals. They're complemented by tourist offices, sometimes called **Tourism Information Centres**, run by the state governments, which again are to be found in most of the state capitals. As a rule, all these offices are more than happy to furnish you with glossy brochures and leaflets, organized on a state-by-state basis, and though staff are not likely to have personal experience of off-the-beaten-track destinations, they can usually provide some nitty-gritty information on matters like bus travel or contact details for accommodation throughout their area of coverage.

In Singapore, tourist information is put out by the **Singapore Tourism Board**, which has several downtown **Visitors' Centres** (see p.631 for details), each with a huge range of handouts. **Brunei**'s fledgling tourist industry is mainly represented by the **Tourist Information Centre** in Bandar Seri Begawan (see p.600), who produce the useful *Explore Brunei* booklet.

National tourist office websites

ⓦ **www.tourismmalaysia.gov.my** Appropriately categorized according to the country's chief attractions – its nature and wildlife, islands and multicultural heritage. Includes lists of tour operators abroad with Malaysia offerings.

ⓦ **www.visitsingapore.com** Suggested itineraries; lists of attractions, upcoming events and festivals; an accommodation directory and plenty more.

ⓦ **www.tourismbrunei.com.** Unsurprisingly low-key site, best for its bread-and-butter details of travel formalities, tour operators and so forth.

Malaysian state tourism contacts

Johor ☏ 07/223 4935, ⓦ www.tourismjohor .gov.my.

Kedah ☏ 04/735 1030, ⓦ www.kedah.gov my/tourism.

Kelantan ☏ 09/748 5534.

Labuan ☏ 087/408600, ⓦ www.labuantourism .com.my.

Melaka ☏ 06/281 4803, ⓦ www.melaka.gov .my/eng/tourism.asp.

Negeri Sembilan ☏ 06/765 9870, ⓦ www .tourismnegerisembilan.com.

Pahang ☏ 09/516 1007, ⓦ www.pahangtourism .com.my.

Penang ☏ 04/262 0202, ⓦ www.tourismpenang .gov.my.

Sabah ☏ 088/212 121, ⓦ www.sabahtourism.com.

Sarawak ☏ 082/423 600, ⓦ www .sarawaktourism.com.

Terengganu ☏ 09/617 3553, ⓦ www.tourism .terengganu.gov.my.

Tourism Malaysia offices abroad

Australia Ground Floor, MAS Building, 56 William St, Perth ☎ 09/9481 0400, ✉ mptb.perth@tourism .gov.my; Level 2, 171 Clarence St, Sydney ☎ 02/9299 4441, ✉ mptb.sydney@tourism.gov.my.
Canada 1590-1111 West Georgia St, Vancouver ☎ 604/689-8899, ✉ mtpb.vancouver@tourism .gov.my.
Singapore #01-01B/C/D 80 Robinson Rd ☎ 6532 6321, ✉ mtpb.singapore@tourism.gov.my.
South Africa 1st Floor, Building 5, Commerce Square, 39 Rivonia Rd, Sandhurst, Johannesburg ☎ 011/268 0292, ✉ mtpb.johannesburg@tourism .gov.my.
UK 57 Trafalgar Square, London ☎ 020/7930 7932, ✉ mptb.london@tourism.gov.my.
US 120 East 56th St, Suite 810, New York, NY 10022 ☎ 212/745 1114, ✉ mptb.ny@tourism .gov.my; 818 West 7th St, Suite 970, Los Angeles ☎ 213/689 9702, ✉ mptb.la@tourism.gov.my.

Singapore tourism board offices abroad

Australia Level 11, AWA Building, 47 York St, Sydney ☎ 02/9290 2888, ✉ stb-syd@stb-syd .org.au.
Malaysia Ground Floor, Menara Keck Seng, 203 Jalan Bukit Bintang, KL ☎ 03/2142 7133, ✉ stb@stbmalaysia.com.my.
New Zealand c/o Vivaldi World Limited, Suite 10K, 18 Ronwood Avenue, Manukau City, Auckland ☎ 09/262 3933, ✉ stb.auckland@xtra.co.nz.
UK 1st floor, Carrington House, 126–130 Regent St, London ☎ 020/7437 0033, ✉ info@stb.org.uk.

US 1156 Avenue of the Americas, Suite 702, New York ☎ 212/302 4861, ✉ newyork@stb.gov .sg; 4929 Wiltshire Blvd, Suite 510, Los Angeles ☎ 323/677 0808, ⓦ www.singapore-usa.com.

Other tourist information sources

There are plenty of **websites** concerned with Malaysia tourism. Many of these are thinly disguised fronts for travel agencies intent on marketing their packages, but the best of these sites boast in-depth accounts of the more off-the-beaten-track towns and sights, sometimes reportage on tourism-related issues too, and are certainly worth a browse, though don't assume the information is up to date.

ⓦ **www.allmalaysia.info** Excellent tourism compendium put together by *The Star* newspaper, featuring travel-related news stories, state-by-state accounts of sights, and background articles on culture and events.

ⓦ **www.virtualmalaysia.com** Similar in scope to the All Malaysia site, with coverage of plenty of less visited sights, plus a message board which can throw up unusual pointers.

ⓦ **www.wildasia.net** Dedicated to promoting sustainable and responsible tourism, this Malaysia-based site features numerous articles on Southeast Asia, with plenty on Malaysia itself, of course, including descriptions of forest reserves and dive sites, plus a list of the more environmentally aware resorts.

Insurance

It's wise to take out an insurance policy before travelling to cover for medical emergencies, loss of personal belongings, injury and adventure sports.

You might want to contact a specialist travel insurance company, or consider the travel insurance deal we offer (see box opposite). A typical travel insurance policy usually provides cover for the loss of bags, tickets and – up to a certain limit – cash or cheques, as well as cancellation or curtailment of your

journey. Some policy premiums now include so-called **dangerous sports**; in Malaysia, for example, this can mean scuba diving, white-water rafting or trekking. Always ascertain whether medical coverage will be paid out as treatment proceeds or only after return home, and whether there is a 24-hour

Rough Guides travel insurance

Rough Guides has teamed up with Columbus Direct to offer you **travel insurance** that can be tailored to suit your needs. Products include a low-cost **backpacker** option for long stays; a **short break** option for city getaways; a typical **holiday package** option; and others. There are also annual **multi-trip** policies for those who travel regularly. Different sports and activities (trekking, skiing, etc) can be usually be covered if required.

See our website (ⓦwww.roughguidesinsurance.com) for eligibility and purchasing options. Alternatively, UK residents should call ☎0870/033 9988; US citizens should call ☎1-800/749-4922; Australians should call ☎1-300/669 999. All other nationalities should call ☎+44 870/890 2843.

medical emergency number. When securing baggage cover, make sure that the per-article limit – typically under £500 – will cover your most valuable possession. If you need to make a claim, you should keep receipts for medicines and medical treatment, and in the event you have anything stolen, you must obtain an official statement from the police.

Health

No inoculations are required for visiting Malaysia, Singapore or Brunei, although the immigration authorities may require a yellow-fever vaccination certificate if you have transited an endemic area, normally Africa or South America within the preceding six days.

It's a wise precaution to visit your doctor no loco than two months before you leave to check that you are up to date with your polio, typhoid, tetanus and hepatitis A inoculations, and to check the malarial status of the areas you are visiting. Only rural areas of Malaysia constitute a malaria risk and a small one at that; note that for some years Singapore has been completely malaria free. Brunei can lay claim to the same status too.

Medical resources for travellers

US and Canada

CDC ⓦwww.cdc.gov/travel. Official US government travel health site.
Canadian Society for International Health ⓦwww.csih.org. Extensive list of travel health centres.

International Society for Travel Medicine ⓦwww.istm.org. Has a full list of travel health clinics.

Australia, New Zealand and South Africa

Travellers' Medical and Vaccination Centre ⓦwww.tmvc.com.au, ☎1300/658 844. Lists travel clinics in Australia, New Zealand and South Africa.

UK and Ireland

Hospital for Tropical Diseases Travel Clinic ☎020/7387 5000 or 0845/155 5000, ⓦwww.thehtd.org.
MASTA (Medical Advisory Service for Travellers Abroad) ⓦwww.masta.org or ☎0113/238 7575 for the nearest clinic.
Travel Medicine Services ☎028/9031 5220.
Tropical Medical Bureau ☎1850/487 674, ⓦwww.tmb.ie.

Medical problems

The levels of **hygiene** and **medical care** in Malaysia, Singapore and Brunei are higher than in much of the rest of Southeast Asia; with any luck, the most serious thing you'll go down with is an upset stomach or insect or leech bites.

Heat problems

Travellers unused to tropical climates periodically suffer from **sunburn** and **dehydration**. The easiest way to avoid this is to restrict your exposure to the midday sun, use high-factor sun screens, wear sunglasses and a hat. You should also drink plenty of water and, if you do become dehydrated, keep up a regular intake of fluids. Rehydration preparations such as Dioralyte are handy; the DIY version is a handful of sugar with a good pinch of salt added to a litre of water, which creates roughly the right mineral balance. **Heat stroke** is more serious and can require hospitalization: its onset is indicated by a high body temperature, dry red skin and a fast pulse. To prevent **heat rashes**, prickly heat and fungal infections, use a mild antiseptic soap and dust yourself with prickly-heat talcum powder, which you can buy all over Malaysia and Singapore.

Stomach problems: food and water

The most common complaint is a **stomach problem**, which can range from a mild dose of diarrhoea to full-blown dysentery. The majority of stomach bugs may be unpleasant, but are unthreatening; however, if you notice blood or mucus in your stools, then you may have amoebic or bacillary dysentery, in which case you should seek medical help.

Since stomach bugs are usually transmitted by contaminated food and water, steer clear of raw vegetables and shellfish, always wash unpeeled fruit, and stick to freshly cooked foods, avoiding anything reheated. But however careful you are, food that's spicy or just different can sometimes upset your system, in which case, try to stick to relatively bland dishes and avoid fried food.

Tap water is drinkable throughout Malaysia, Singapore and Brunei but when in rural areas it's best to buy bottled water, which is widely available. If you're trekking in the back of beyond, or travelling upriver in deepest Sarawak, all drinking water should be regarded with caution and purified (see box below).

Malaria

Although the risk of catching **malaria** is extremely low, if you're planning to travel

Water purification

Apart from drinking bottled water, there are various ways to avoid disease by **treating your water source**, whether it be a tap, a river or stream. **Boiling**, the time-honoured method, is effective in sterilizing water, although it will not remove unpleasant tastes. A minimum boiling time of ten minutes (longer at higher altitudes) is sufficient to kill micro-organisms.

Chemical sterilization can be carried out using either chlorine or iodine tablets (it's essential to follow the manufacturer's dosage), or a tincture of iodine liquid – add a couple of drops to one litre of water and leave to stand for twenty minutes. Iodine tablets are preferable to chlorine as the latter leaves an unpleasant taste in the water and isn't effective in preventing such diseases as amoebic dysentery and giardiasis. A water filter is also useful, not least to improve the taste. However, note that a water filter alone will not remove viruses which, due to their microscopic size, will pass through into the filtered water.

Purification, a two-stage process involving both filtration and sterilization, gives the most complete treatment. Portable water purifiers range in size, from pocket-sized 60g models to bulky 800g versions.

for a long time or think you might be staying in remote areas such as the border region with Thailand, or are taking extended treks into East Malaysia's rainforests, then you should consider protection against it. The illness, which cannot be passed directly from one person to another, begins with flu-like symptoms, with a fluctuating high fever. The **prevention of mosquito bites** is the most reliable way to avoid the disease: apply insect repellent at regular intervals and sleep with a mosquito net where possible – some places provide these but it is safer to take your own. Mosquito coils, which you light to release smoke that deters the insects, are very cheap and widely available in shops throughout Malaysia and Singapore.

Most doctors will advise the additional use of malaria tablets. Although these aren't completely effective in protecting against malaria, they do at least help reduce the symptoms should you develop the disease. Bear in mind you have to start taking the tablets before you arrive in a malaria zone, and continue taking them for four weeks after you return – ask your doctor for the latest advice.

Dengue fever

Another mosquito-borne disease to be aware of is **dengue fever**, a virus which causes severe headaches, pain in the bones (especially of the back), fever and often a fine, red rash over the body. There's no specific treatment, just plenty of rest, an adequate fluid intake and painkillers when required. As with malaria, the best advice is to to try and prevent being bitten. A rare complication known as **dengue haemorrhagic fever** (DHF), is more serious and causes high fever, bleeding and in severe cases, circulatory failure. DHF requires urgent medical attention as blood transfusions may be needed.

There has been an upsurge in the number of cases of dengue fever across Southeast Asia. In Malaysia, particularly in Kuala Lumpur and the surrounding state of Selangor, there were over fifty deaths in 2002. Malaysia's opposition parties have accused the government of concealing the true scale of the problem.

Other diseases

Typhoid is a lethal disease that is spread by contact with infected water or food. It begins with a headache and a consistently high fever, followed by red spots on the chest and back, dehydration and occasional diarrhoea. If you think you have these symptoms you should seek immediate medical treatment.

Hepatitis is an inflammation of the liver, which may manifest itself as jaundice – a yellow discolouration of the skin and eyes – though extreme tiredness is a common characteristic. Viral hepatitis is most commonly hepatitis A or B. **Hepatitis A** is one of the most likely infections encountered in Asia, and is spread via contaminated food and water. Rest, lots of fluids and a total abstinence from alcohol are the major elements in the cure, as well as a simple, bland diet. One vaccine, Havrix, provides immunity against hepatitis A for up to ten years; one jab is required. The rarer **Hepatitis B** is transmitted through infected blood and blood products, so intravenous drug-users, together with those who have had unprotected sex, are most at risk. The Hepatitis B vaccine (three jabs over six months, plus a booster after five years) is recommended to anyone falling into one of these high-risk categories.

Cholera, outbreaks of which are reported in Malaysia from time to time, is caught by contact with infected water and food. The disease begins with fever, severe vomiting and diarrhoea, followed by weakness and muscle cramps – seek medical help immediately and watch out for dehydration. There is a vaccine, though it's considered so ineffectual nowadays that there's little point in having it.

Altitude sickness

Altitude sickness (or acute mountain sickness) is a potentially life-threatening illness affecting people who ascend above around 3500m. Symptoms include dizziness, headache, shortness of breath, nausea; in severe cases it can lead to a swelling of the brain and lungs which can prove fatal. In Malaysia it's only likely to be relevant to those climbing Mount Kinabalu (4101m), and most people report only mild symptoms at this altitude. If affected, there's little you can do apart from descending to lower altitude although there are prescription drugs which may temporarily control the symptoms. Your best bet is to acclimatize at lower altitude and ascend slowly.

Cuts, bites and stings

Wearing protective clothing when swimming, snorkelling or diving can help avoid sunburn and protect against any sea stings. **Sea lice**, minute creatures which cause painful though harmless bites are the most common hazard; more dangerous are **jellyfish**, whose stings must be doused with vinegar to deactivate the poison before you seek medical help.

Coral can also cause nasty cuts and grazes; any wounds should be cleaned and kept as dry as possible until properly healed. The only way to avoid well-camouflaged **sea urchins** and **stone fish** is by not stepping on the seabed: even thick-soled shoes don't provide total protection against their long, sharp spines, which can be removed by softening the skin by holding it over a steaming pan of water.

For many people, the ubiquitous **leech** – whose bite is not actually harmful or painful – is the most irritating aspect to jungle trekking. Whenever there's been a heavy rainfall, you can rely upon the leeches to come out. Always tuck your trousers into your socks and tie your bootlaces tight. The best anti-leech socks are made from calico; you can buy these for around RM10 a pair from the Malaysian Nature Society, JKR 641, Jalan Kelantan, 50480 KL (☏03/22879422, ⓦwww.mns.org.my). If you find the leeches are getting through, the best remedy is to soak the outside of your socks and your boots in insect repellent, or dampen tobacco and apply it in between your socks and shoes. It's best to get into the habit of checking your feet and legs every twenty minutes or so for leeches.

Poisonous **snakes** are rare, but if you are bitten you must remain absolutely still and calm until help arrives. Meanwhile, get someone to clean and disinfect the wound thoroughly (alcohol will do if nothing else can be found), and apply a bandage with gentle pressure to the affected area. It helps if you can kill the snake and take it to be identified. Poisonous **spiders** are relatively rare; as with snake bites, keep calm and seek medical help as soon as possible.

Treatment: pharmacies, doctors and hospitals

Medical services in Malaysia, Singapore and Brunei are excellent, with staff almost everywhere speaking good English and using up-to-date treatments. In the Guide, we've included details of local pharmacists and hospitals in the "Listings" sections for cities and major towns.

Pharmacies stock a wide range of medicines and health-related items, from contraceptives to contact lens solution; opening hours are usually Monday to Saturday 9am to 6pm (except in Kelantan, Terengganu, Kedah and Perlis states, where Friday and not Sunday is the day of closing). Pharmacists can recommend products for skin complaints or simple stomach problems, though it always pays to get a proper diagnosis.

Private **clinics** are found even in the smallest towns – your hotel or the local tourist office will be able to recommend a good English-speaking doctor. A visit costs around RM30, not including the cost of any prescribed medication. Don't forget to keep the receipts for insurance-claim purposes. Finally, the emergency department of each town's **General Hospital** will see foreigners (usually allowing you to jump the queue) for a small fee, though obviously costs rise rapidly if continued treatment or overnight stays are necessary.

Services in **Singapore** are broadly similar to those in Malaysia; for the location of Singapore pharmacies and hospitals, turn to p.723. Note that one location in Singapore, the Mustafa Centre plaza, in Little India, is open 24 hours a day, seven days a week. **Brunei** actually offers free medical treatment, although it is highly unlikely that you will need it given that most visitors stay a very limited amount of time in the sultanate.

Costs, money and banks

Those entering Malaysia from Thailand will find that costs will take a step up – both food and accommodation are noticeably more expensive – whereas travellers arriving from Indonesia will find overall prices are decidedly lower. Once in the region, daily necessities like food, drink and travel are marginally more expensive in Singapore than in Malaysia; over in East Malaysia, room rates tend to be somewhat higher than on the Peninsula, and you'll also find yourself forking out for river trips and nature tours.

Bargaining is de rigueur throughout Malaysia and Singapore, especially when shopping or renting a room for the night, though note that you don't haggle for meals.

Travelling in a group helps keep accommodation and eating costs down. The region affords some savings for senior citizens, and an **ISIC student card** might occasionally pay dividends. Most tourist attractions offer discounted entrance fees for children, while Malaysia's public transport network has a variety of special deals on tickets that help keep costs down (see "Getting Around" for more).

Accessing your funds

The quickest way to access your funds is to withdraw money from local **automatic teller machines** (ATMs). ATMs in Singapore and Malaysia can be found everywhere in urban areas, including shopping malls and transportation hubs, as well as outside banks. Before using an ATM, make sure its network (Plus, Maestro, etc) matches the one on your card. If you are worried that an ATM will eat your card – as sometimes happens – it is a good idea to use only those that are attached to banks and then only during banking hours; that way if your card is swallowed by the machine, you can usually get it right back. To check your card will work abroad, contact your credit card company or bank before you leave home; you should also ask about withdrawl charges.

Major **credit cards** are widely accepted in the more upmarket hotels, shops and restaurants throughout the region, though beware of the illegal surcharges levied by some establishments – check before you pay that there's no surcharge; if there is, contact your card company and tell them about it. Banks will often advance cash against major credit cards.

As well as debit and credit cards it's wise to carry some of your cash in the form of **traveller's cheques** – either sterling or US dollar cheques are acceptable. Cheques can be cashed at Malaysian, Singaporean and Bruneian banks, licensed moneychangers and some hotels, upon presentation of a passport. Some shops will even accept traveller's cheques as cash.

To report lost or stolen traveller's cheques or credit cards, call: Visa in Malaysia (①1-000 80 2997), in Singapore (☎800-110-0344); MasterCard in Malaysia (☎1-800 80 4594), in Singapore (☎800-1100-113); American Express in Malaysia (☎03/2050 0000), in Singapore (☎1-800-737-8188).

Malaysia

Malaysia's unit of currency is the Malaysian **ringgit** (denoted "RM" before the price, and often informally called a "dollar"), divided into 100 sen. Notes come in RM1, RM2, RM5, RM10, RM20, RM50 and RM100 denominations; coins are minted in 1 sen, 5 sen, 10 sen, 20 sen and 50 sen denominations.

At the time of writing, the **exchange rate** was RM3.7 to US$1. and around RM6.5 to £1. Rates are posted daily in banks and exchange kiosks, and published in the *New Straits Times*. Online, ⓦwww.xe.com gives live conversion rates between any two currencies. There is no currency black market in Malaysia, and no limit on the amount of foreign currency you can carry in or out of the country, although it must be declared at customs. There is however a limit of RM1000 on the amount of ringgit allowed into or out of Malaysia.

Major banks represented in Malaysia include Maybank, HSBC, Citibank, Standard Chartered, RHB Bank and Bank Bumiputra Commerce. **Banking hours** are generally Monday to Friday 9.30am to 4pm and Saturday 9.30 to 11.30am (closed on every first and third Saturday of the month), though in the largely Muslim states of Kedah, Perlis, Kelantan and Terengganu, Friday is a holiday and Sunday a working day. Licensed **moneychangers'** kiosks, found in bigger towns all over the country, tend to open later, until around 6pm, with some opening at weekends and until 9pm, too; some hotels will exchange money at all hours. Exchange rates tend to be more generous at moneychangers. It's not generally difficult to change money in Sabah or Sarawak, though if you are travelling along a river in the interior for any length of time, it's a wise idea to carry a fair amount of cash, in smallish denominations.

Malaysia is one of those countries where you can live fairly cheaply or spend a fortune. In **Peninsular Malaysia** you get by on £12/US$20 per day staying in dorms, eating at hawker stalls and getting around by bus. Double that and you'll be able to exist in relative comfort and not have to think too hard about occasionally treating yourself. Stay a night or two at the country's world-class hotels, however, or hang out in some of KL's smartest nightclubs and restaurants and the sky's your limit. Over in **East Malaysia** the average cost of living is higher, hotel rates can be half as much again as on the Peninsula and having to organize your own transport can make a significant difference to the budget; there are more details at the beginning of the relevant chapters.

Singapore

The currency is the **Singapore dollar**, written simply as $ (or – occasionally in this book – S$ to distinguish it from other dollars) and divided into 100 cents. Notes are issued in denominations of $1, $2, $5, $10, $20,

$50, $100, $500, $1000 and $10,000; coins come in denominations of 1, 5, 10, 20 and 50 cents, and $1. At the time of writing, the **exchange rate** was around S$2.80 to £1, S$1.60 to US$1. Singapore dollars are not accepted in Malaysia, but are legal tender in Brunei (see below).

Singapore **banking hours** are generally Monday to Friday 9.30am to 3pm and Saturday 9.30 to 11.30am. Major banks represented include Overseas Union Bank, United Overseas Bank, OCBC, Standard Chartered Bank, HSBC and Citibank. Rates at **moneychangers** are as good as you'll find in the banks. No currency black market operates in Singapore, nor are there any restrictions on carrying currency into or out of the state.

Singapore is generally a little more expensive than Malaysia – some reckon that whatever the cost in Malaysia in ringgit you'll pay the same number of Singapore dollars for it over the causeway. Again, if money is no object, you'll be able to take advantage of hotels, restaurants and shops as sumptuous as any in the world, but, equally, with budget dormitory accommodation in plentiful supply, and both food and internal travel cheap in the extreme, you'll find it possible to live on a budget of less than £15/US$30 a day. Upgrading your lodgings to a private room in a guesthouse, eating in a restaurant and having a beer or two could require £30/US$55 a day.

Brunei

Brunei's currency is the **Brunei dollar**, which is divided into 100 cents; you'll see it written as B$, or simply as $. The Bruneian dollar has parity with the Singapore dollar and both are legal tender in either country. Notes come in $1, $5, $10, $50, $100, $500, $1000 and $10,000 denominations; coins come in denominations of 1, 5, 10, 20 and 50 cents.

Brunei **banking hours** are Monday to Friday 9am to 3pm and Saturday 9 to 11am. Banks represented in Bandar Seri Begawan include the International Bank of Brunei, Citibank, Standard Chartered Bank and the Overseas Union Bank – all have ATMs and cash traveller's cheques for a small transaction fee.

Costs in Brunei are broadly similar to Singapore. However, as there is very little in the way of budget accommodation, an average daily budget is likely to start at around £40–50/US$70–90. In addition, if you want to see anything outside the capital, you are largely dependent on expensive taxis since the public transport network, though slowly being developed, is still minimal.

Getting around

Public transport in Malaysia, Singapore and Brunei is reliable, though not as cheap as in other Southeast Asian countries. Much of your travelling, particularly in Peninsular Malaysia, will be by bus, minivan or, less often, long-distance taxi. Budget flights are a great option for making large hops within the Peninsula or around the region, especially in view of the fact that there are no ferries between Peninsular and East Malaysia. The Malaysian train system, limited to the Peninsula (apart from a small stretch of railway in Sabah), has to a degree been superseded by fast highways which ensure buses actually outpace the trains, though it still has its uses, particularly in the interior and on the express run north from Butterworth to Bangkok.

Sabah and **Sarawak** have their own travel peculiarities – in Sarawak, for instance, you're reliant on boats, and occasionally planes, for some long-distance travel. **Brunei's** bus service, covering routes through the main towns, is supplemented by boats in remote areas such as the Temburong district. The chapters on Sarawak, Sabah, Brunei and Singapore contain detailed information on their respective transport systems; the emphasis in the rest of this section is largely on Peninsular Malaysia.

Note that the transport system is subject to heavy pressure whenever there's a nationwide **public holiday** – particularly during Muslim festivals, the Chinese New Year, Deepavali, and Christmas and New Year. A day or two before each festival, whole communities embark upon what's called **balik kampung**, which literally means returning to their home villages and towns to be with family, and making the exodus in reverse a day or two afterwards. You should make bus, train or flight reservations at least a week in advance to travel at these times; if you're driving, steel yourself for more than the usual number of jams.

For a rundown of public transport routes in each region covered by this book, see the "Travel details" sections at the end of each guide chapter.

Buses

The national **bus network** is generally the easiest, quickest and cheapest way of getting around Malaysia, with regular services between all major Peninsula cities and towns. Besides intercity services, which operate largely on an **express** basis, there are also **local buses** which run to destinations up to 100km away, though being stopping services they may well take up to three hours to cover this relatively short distance. For more on local buses, see p.56.

The chief difficulty you might experience in using buses is simply the sheer profusion of options, for the network is about as far from being integrated as it's possible to get. Any major bus station in Malaysia feels not unlike a traditional street market; turn up and you'll find a zillion and one vendors with broadly similar offerings at similar prices. While all this might seem like a recipe for chaos, in practice things do work reasonably well.

Finding out about available bus connections is usually straightforward but if not, local tourist offices should be able to help. In any case, on the main routes (in practice, along the major highways), the plethora of bus companies means departures are pretty **frequent** (in practice, hourly or every other hour during daylight hours). Much of the time you can just turn up and get a ticket for the next available bus.

For intercity journeys, you'll often find yourself relying on a handful of well-established bus companies. The largest of these is **Transnasional** (Ⓦ www.transnasional .com.my), whose services have the entire Peninsula pretty well covered. Their website has a useful timetable search facility which allows you to establish likely departure and journey times, with fares, for a large number of routes. Other major bus companies include **Plusliner** (Ⓦ www.plusliner.com) and **Konsortium Bas Ekspres** (Ⓣ 05/891 8888, Ⓦ www.kbes.com.my). Complementing these outfits are numerous small-scale intercity operators which generally focus on services between their home state and one or two adjacent states.

Whichever bus company you travel with, you'll find that practically all intercity buses are reasonably comfortable, with **air conditioning** and curtains to help screen out the blazing tropical sun, though on the down side, the way seats are packed together can make things awkward for taller travellers. The buses generally don't have toilets, but on the longer journeys there'll be an extended rest stop every couple of hours or so, and there's

often a half-hour meal stopover at lunchtime or dinnertime as well. On a few plum routes, notably KL–Singapore and KL–Penang, there are additional **luxury** or "executive" coaches to choose from, charging premium prices and featuring greater legroom and on-board TVs and toilets.

All intercity **fares** are eminently reasonable (see the box, below), but note that if you want to leave the bus at a small town en route, you may be charged the full fare or the fare until the next major town. Local buses, where available, are more cost-effective for such journeys, though they take much longer.

Finally, note that express and local buses usually operate from separate stations; the local bus station is often fairly central, the express-bus station a little further out. In some towns, buses may call at both stations before terminating.

Various buses ply the long-distance routes across **Sabah**, but they are heavily outnumbered by the minivans that buzz around the state, which generally leave from the same terminals. Faster and slightly more expensive than the scheduled bus services, minivans only leave when jam-packed and are often very uncomfortable as a result. Also prevalent in Sabah are four-wheel-drives (4WDs), usually Toyota Land Cruisers, which take only eight passengers and whose fares are at least twenty percent higher than going by minivan.

In **Sarawak**, modern air-con buses ply the trans-state coastal road between Kuching and the Brunei border, serving Sibu, Bintulu and Miri en route. Again, fares are

Sample intercity bus fares

Kuala Lumpur to:

Alor Setar (Kedah)	5hr 30min	RM30
Butterworth	5hr	RM25
Ipoh	2hr 30min	RM13
Johor Bahru	4hr 30min	RM24/50*
Kota Bharu	9hr	RM33
Kuala Lipis	4hr	RM12
Kuala Terengganu	8hr	RM30
Kuantan	4hr	RM18
Melaka	2hr	RM10
Penang	5hr 30min	RM27/53*
Singapore	5–6hr	RM30/55*
(* = luxury coach)		

very reasonable: the fifteen-hour trip from Kuching to Miri costs RM70, for example. In addition, local buses serve the satellite towns and villages around the state's main settlements. These buses are particularly useful when exploring southwestern Sarawak and for the cross-border trip to Pontianak in Indonesian Kalimantan. Four-wheel-drives are increasingly coming into use for navigating the logging tracks which have opened up remote inland areas; details of routes are given in the Guide.

Trains

The Peninsula's intercity train service, operated by **KTM** (short for "Keretapi Tanah Melayu" or Malay Land Trains; ☎03/2267 1200, ⓦwww.ktmb.com.my), is limited to a network shaped roughly like a Y, the arms of which, for historical reasons, don't intersect at KL, but an annoying 170km further south at Gemas, close to the Negeri Sembilan/Johor boundary. One arm from Gemas up to Thailand, another down to Singapore; the remaining branch cuts its way through the jungled interior up to Tumpat, on the east coast near the Thai border. KTM also runs the Komuter rail service in KL and its environs, for details of which, see p.103.

There are two main classes of train: **express** services, which call mostly at major stations and are generally modern, fully air-conditioned and well maintained; and **local** ("Mel" on timetables) trains, not air-conditioned and of variable quality, which operate on various segments between Singapore and Tumpat and call at every town, village and hamlet en route. Somewhere in between are the KL–Hat Yai service and the Ekonomi Siang train between Singapore and Gemas, both of which call at minor stations but are faster than the Mel trains; the Hat Yai service is actually called an express.

Unfortunately, not even the express trains can keep up with buses where modern highways exist alongside. The 370-kilometre journey from KL to Johor Bahru, for example, takes the train five and a half hours at best; on a good day on the roads, buses are roughly an hour quicker. Until the railway tracks themselves and the infrastructure attending them are

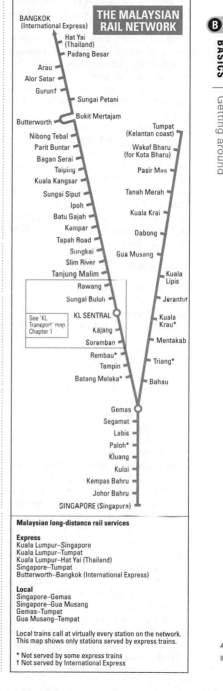

THE MALAYSIAN RAIL NETWORK

BANGKOK (International Express)
Hat Yai (Thailand)
Padang Besar
Arau
Alor Setar
Gurun†
Sungai Petani
Bukit Mertajam
Butterworth
Nibong Tebal
Parit Buntar
Bagan Serai
Taiping
Kuala Kangsar
Sungai Siput
Ipoh
Batu Gajah
Kampar
Tapah Road
Sungkai
Slim River
Tanjung Malim
Rawang
Sungai Buloh

Tumpat (Kelantan coast)
Wakaf Bharu (for Kota Bharu)
Pasir Mas
Tanah Merah
Kuala Krai
Dabong
Gua Musang
Kuala Lipis
Jerantut
Kuala Krau*
Mentakab
Triang*
Bahau

KL SENTRAL
See 'KL Transport' map Chapter 1
Kajang
Seremban
Rembau*
Tampin
Batang Melaka*

Gemas
Segamat
Labis
Paloh*
Kluang
Kulai
Kempas Bahru
Johor Bahru
SINGAPORE (Singapura)

Malaysian long-distance rail services

Express
Kuala Lumpur–Singapore
Kuala Lumpur–Tumpat
Kuala Lumpur–Hat Yai (Thailand)
Singapore–Tumpat
Butterworth–Bangkok (International Express)

Local
Singapore–Gemas
Singapore–Gua Musang
Gemas–Tumpat
Gua Musang–Tempat

Local trains call at virtually every station on the network. This map shows only stations served by express trains.

* Not served by some express trains
† Not served by International Express

modernized, you're unlikely to be heavily reliant on the trains for journeys along the west coast and in the south.

The rail system does, however, retain a couple of advantages. **Sleeper services** – between KL and Singapore, between KL and Hat Yai, and between Singapore and Tumpat, not to mention the international service from Butterworth to Bangkok – can save on a night's accommodation. Express trains also remain the quickest way to reach some parts of the forested **interior**, and local trains through the interior can also be handy for reaching certain small settlements; for more on the interior's rail service, see the box on the "Jungle Railway", p.243. Moreover, there's still a certain thrill in arriving at some of the splendidly solid colonial stations, built when the train was the prime means of transport.

Ticket types and bookings

Most **express** trains run by night, and so offer the option of **sleeper berths**, which come in **standard** and **premier** class, while the seats divide into **standard** and **economy** versions. The chief distinction between these labels boils down to nothing more complex than how many berths or seats there are per carriage. Standard sleepers comprise twenty pairs of berths (upper and lower), premier eight cabins with two berths. Standard seats are less packed together than their economy counterparts and come with minor extras like aircraft-style trays on seat backs and the odd TV screen.

There are exceptions to this picture, notably on the Senandung Malam KL–Singapore service, which has an additional tier of comfort in the form of a **premier deluxe** carriage, featuring six en-suite cabins each containing two berths; lone travellers can pay a supplement to have the whole cabin to themselves. As for the two **daytime express** services, which run between KL and Singapore, they're something of a hybrid, with **standard** and **premier seats**. The latter have fewer, posher seats to each carriage. The table of sample fares opposite makes clear which seat and berth classes you can expect on the various services.

Local trains, plus the Ekonomi Siang Singapore–Gemas service, feature economy-class seats only. Note, however, that these trains are older and scruffier than their express counterparts (the Gua Musang–Tumpat service, in particular, is positively dilapidated). Tickets on local trains are very cheap; the longest possible local train journey, Gemas–Tumpat (a numbing 15hr, compared to 10hr by express train), costs RM20.

Buying tickets

While tickets can be **bought in advance** for any train, it's only on express trains that seat and berth reservations can be made. Reserving a day or two in advance is certainly recommended, particularly if you want a berth. Bookings can be made at major stations and online at KTM's website.

Timetables are usually available at major train stations and can sometimes be downloaded from KTM's website, which may also have **fare tables**. Some of these are displayed in a cumulative format, showing how fares build with distance from the starting point; to work out the fare between adjacent stations, simply take the difference between fares from the train's starting point.

Given the various limitations of the trains, you'd have to be a hardcore rail buff to want to make use of KTM's **tourist rail-pass**, which offers foreigners (excluding Singaporeans) unlimited travel on intercity trains for a defined period. It looks reasonable value at US$35 (RM130) for five days (ten- and fifteen-day versions are available), but there is a catch: it doesn't cover berths. The passes are sold at the stations in KL, Singapore, Butterworth, Johor Bahru, Padang Besar (at the Thai border), Port Klang, Wakaf Bharu, and at the KTM ticket office in Georgetown.

Long-distance taxis

Most towns in Malaysia have a **long-distance taxi** rank, usually close to or sited in the express bus station. The taxis serve long-distance routes throughout the country, and can be a lot quicker than the buses. The snag is that they operate on a **shared** basis, meaning you have to wait for enough people show up to fill the four passenger

Sample express-train fares

Prices for berths in this table refer to upper berths; lower berths command a premium of around RM5, RM8 and RM20 in standard, premier and premier deluxe classes respectively.

Journey	Premier deluxe berth	Premier berth	Standard berth	Premier seat	Standard seat	Economy seat
KL–Singapore (sleeper; 9hr)	RM110	RM78	RM38	–	RM30	RM19
KL–Singapore (daytime; 6hr 30min)	–	–	–	RM68	RM34	–
Wakaf Bharu– Jerantut (for Taman Negara; 6hr 30min)	–	–	RM25	–	RM17	RM13
KL–Butterworth (9hr 15min)	–	RM77*	RM38	–	RM30*	RM17

* not available southbound

seats in the vehicle, but in most major towns this shouldn't take more than thirty minutes, especially to set off before 10am; afternoon journeys can involve a bit of thumb-twiddling. **Fares** usually work out to be two to three times the corresponding fare in an express bus; see the table on p.52 for sample prices. Note that long-distance taxi fares, in particular, may be subject to jumps when fuel prices are rising rapidly.

For many visitors travelling in small groups, the real advantage of these taxis is that you can **charter** one for your journey, the price for which is the same as paying for all four passenger places. Not only does this mean you'll set off immediately, but it also allows you to access destinations that may not be served directly by buses or, indeed, by shared taxis. There's no danger of being ripped off: charter prices to a large number of destinations, both the popular and the obscure, are set by the authorities and are usually chalked up on a board in the taxi office or listed on a laminated tariff card (*senarai tambang*), which you can ask to see. If you want to charter a vehicle for a **specific itinerary** (if not a taxi, your accommodation can usually find you a car with a driver), spending several hours meandering around town and out to the surrounding countryside, reckon on paying RM30 per hour.

Some taxi operators assume any tourist who shows up will want to charter a taxi; if you want to use the taxi on a shared basis, say "*nak kongsi dengan orang lain*".

Ferries and boats

Ferries sail to all the major islands off Peninsular Malaysia's east and west coasts. The traditional *penambang* (sometimes called "bumboats"), compact motorized craft originally used for fishing, are rapidly being replaced by larger, sleeker express models. On most ferries, you buy your ticket in advance from booths at the jetty (on some you can pay on the boat as well); details are given in the text. Barring rainy-season storms, there are daily services from the mainland to Tioman and the Perhentian islands (other east-coast islands are hard to reach off-season), and a regular catamaran service from Singapore to Tioman.

Within **Sarawak**, the most common form of public transport, buses aside, are the long and narrow express boats which ply the state's river systems. A lifeline for the inhabitants of the interior, these low-lying craft run to a regular timetable; buy your ticket on board. On the smaller tributaries, travel is by longboat, which can turn out to be more expensive if you have to charter the whole vessel, although you rarely need to do so.

Sabah has no express-boat river services, though regular ferries connect Pulau

Labuan with Kota Kinabalu, Sipitang and Menumbok, all on the west coast; details are given in the text. In **Brunei**, there are some useful boat services, including the speedboat service from Bandar Seri Begawan to Bangar for Temburong Park, and the regular boats from Bandar to Lawas or Limbang in Sarawak and Pulau Labuan in Sabah.

Planes

With the advent of Far Eastern low-cost airlines, **flying** around the region is now within the reach of all but the most thrifty of backpackers. Malaysian domestic flights are operated by Malaysia Airlines (**MAS**) and the budget carrier **AirAsia**, while **Singapore Airlines** and **Royal Brunei Airlines** offer a range of connections to the major Peninsular and East Malaysian cities from Singapore and Bandar Seri Begawan.

If you're flying within Malaysia, note that although there are airports throughout the country, with daily flights, many connections between regional airports require a change of plane in KL, making flying much less of a time-saver than it might appear at first sight. The chief exceptions to this rule are AirAsia's flights **from Johor Bahru** to East Malaysia

and to the north of Peninsular Malaysia, and flights **within East Malaysia**.

Note also that flights between Malaysia and **Singapore** or **Brunei** are substantially more expensive than the distances involved would suggest, as these count as international services; there are, as of the time of writing, no budget operators offering such connections.

Airfares throughout this section are for one-way tickets (return fares are usually double the cost) and include taxes and any fuel surcharges.

MAS

MAS (W www.mas.com.my) used to offer comprehensive domestic connections but, dogged by losses and with the upstart AirAsia nipping at its heels, has had to rationalize its domestic coverage. The airline now flies mainly between KL and state capitals, though it also operates a few flights between East Malaysian cities and from Johor Bahru.

Fares are generally twenty to fifty percent higher on MAS than on AirAsia, so if you're being cost-conscious, you'll want to use MAS only on routes where AirAsia isn't an alternative, such as Kuching–Kota Kinabalu (RM135) or Penang–Singapore (RM350).

Fare comparisons

Journey	By bus	By shared taxi	By rail (standard class, upper berth/seat)	By air (including any taxes and fuel surcharges)
KL–Johor Bahru	RM24; 4hr 30min	RM100; 4hr	RM33 (seat only, daytime express); 5hr 30min	RM90 (MAS); RM55 (AirAsia); 40min
KL–Penang	RM27 (RM55 executive coach); 5hr 30min	RM90; 4hr 30min	RM38/30; 9hr 30min	RM100 (MAS); RM65 (AirAsia); 45min
KL–Kota Bharu	RM33; 9hr	RM100; 8hr	RM46/38, 12hr to Wakaf Bharu, then a short bus/taxi ride	RM100 (MAS); RM85 (AirAsia); 50min
Kuantan–Kuala Terengganu	RM13; 4hr	RM35; 3hr 30min	–	–
Johor Bahru–Kota Bharu	RM45; 12hr	–	RM48/RM40, 11hr 30min	RM65 (AirAsia); 1hr

AirAsia

The efficient no-frills carrier **AirAsia** (T03/8775 4000 or 1300 88 99 33, Wwww .airasia.com) has rewritten the book on Malaysian internal flights since it arrived on the scene a few years ago. It not only charges considerably less than MAS on some routes, but has a two-hub approach to its network, with flights radiating not just **from KL** but increasingly also **from Johor Bahru** (something of a surrogate for Singapore, which has largely cold-shouldered the airline up to the time of writing). From Johor Bahru, they offer convenient nonstop connections with the north of the Peninsula (Penang, Kota Bharu and Ipoh), and also with East Malaysia, including Kuching, Labuan, Miri, Kota Kinabalu and Sandakan.

If you're among the more intrepid visitors, you may even end up making use of their turboprop **rural air services** which represent something of a lifeline for back-of-beyond Borneo communities. Once operated by MAS, these flights are now run by AirAsia subsidiary **Fly Asian Xpress** (T03/8660 4343, Wwww .flyasianexpress.com). For more details, see the Sarawak and Sabah chapters.

Despite the inevitable fuel surcharges and taxes, AirAsia's prices really are attractive – fares for short hops within the Peninsula are as low as RM50, while the very longest domestic route offered, from KL to Sandakan in eastern Sabah (2hr 30min), weighs in at RM150. The best fares are usually to be had not just by booking early, but also by doing it online rather than on the phone or through their offices (which, for convenience, they maintain in major cities and airports). Note that the lowest fares may be unavailable for travel on or close to public holidays, and during the school holidays.

Other airlines

Singapore Airlines (Singapore T6223 8888, Malaysia T03/2692 3122, Wwww .singaporeair.com) and its subsidiary **SilkAir** (Singapore T6223 8888, Wwww.silkair .com) between them fly from Singapore to several key Malaysian destinations, including KL, Kota Kinabalu, Kuching, Langkawi and Penang, plus Brunei. Fares are a little higher than on MAS; expect to pay around S\$230 to Penang, S\$250 to Kuching, S\$450 to Kota Kinabalu. Similar prices are charged by **Royal Brunei Airways** (Brunei T221 2222, Malaysia T03/2070 7166, Singapore T6235 4672, Wwww.bruneiair.com), who fly to KL, Singapore and Kota Kinabalu from Brunei.

It's no accident that three Malaysian resort islands, **Pangkor**, **Redang** and **Tioman**, have airstrips served by **Berjaya Air** (Malaysia T03/2145 2828, Singapore T6227 3688, Wwww.berjaya-air.com), for all play host to resorts owned by the airline's parent company, the giant Malaysian conglomerate Berjaya Corporation. Berjaya Air flies to all three from KL, and to Redang and Tioman from Singapore. Unsurprisingly, prices are distinctly elevated – for example, RM235 to Pangkor from KL, S\$170 to Redang from Singapore.

Driving and vehicle rental

The **roads** in **Peninsular Malaysia** are generally excellent, making driving there a viable prospect for tourists. It's mostly the same story in **Sarawak** and **Brunei**, though **Sabah** is the odd one out; a sizeable minority of roads there are rough, unpaved and highly susceptible to flash flooding. **Singapore** is another tale altogether, boasting a hi-tech road-use charging system that requires all cars to have a black-box gizmo which talks electronically to gantries on some highways.

Despite these disparities, the three countries do share certain practices on the roads. All use the UK system of **driving on the left**. It's compulsory to wear seat belts in the front of the vehicle (and in the back too, in Singapore). To **rent a vehicle**, you must be 23 or over and have held a clean driving licence for at least a year; a national driving licence, particularly if written in English, is sufficient, though there's no harm in acquiring an International Driving Licence.

Because of Singapore's unique road pricing technology, and the fact that some car rental outlets don't allow their cars to be driven between Malaysia and Singapore, the rest of this section concentrates on Malaysia. For information on driving in Singapore and Brunei, see the respective chapters.

Highways in Peninsular Malaysia

Listed below are the main **expressways** ("E" roads, plus the East Coast Highway) and the most important of the older **trunk roads**, the latter generally nothing more than two-lane affairs threaded through the main towns. We've prefixed the trunk roads with "Route", though on roads signs these are usually referred to by their number alone. Note that the E1 and E2 together make up what's sometimes called the **North–South Expressway (NSE)**.

Road name	Route
E1	Main west-coast highway from Sungai Buloh, north of KL, up to the Thai border, via Ipoh and Butterworth
E2	Main southern highway from Sungai Besi, south of KL, to Johor Bahru, via Seremban
E3	From the E2 at Senai, near Johor Bahru airport, to Singapore via the Second Crossing
E6	Curling round to the west of KL, this links the E1 and E2
E8 (Karak Highway)	KL northeast to Karak, passing close to Genting Highlands; the first stage of the journey from KL to Kuantan or the interior
Lebuhraya Pantai Timur (Phase I)	East Coast Highway, from Karak (at the end of the E8) to Kuantan port, just north of Kuantan
Lebuhraya Pantai Timur (Phase II)	From Kuantan port to Kuala Terengganu (to be completed in 2008)
Lebuhraya Persekutuan	KL–Port Klang; the main thoroughfare of the Federal Territory along the Klang Valley
Route 1	Old north–south trunk road traversing KL and most of the main towns on the west of the Peninsula, right down to the Causeway to Singapore; now shadows the E1 and E2 for much of its length
Route 2	Old road from KL to the east coast, ending at Kuantan
Route 3	The main east-coast road, from Kota Bharu to Johor Bahru
Route 4	West–east road in the very north of the Peninsula, between Gerik in Perak and Machang in Kelantan
Route 5	The main west-coast road, from Lumut near Ipoh to Johor Bahru, via Melaka
Route 8	The main interior road, from Bentong near KL to Kota Bharu
Route 14	Kuantan–Kuala Terengganu, inland; will be superseded by Phase II of the East Coast Highway

Malaysian roads

Where you've a choice between using an expressway and a trunk road (see the box above for the most useful in the Peninsula), it's almost always quicker to head out of town for the expressway even if the trunk road passes through the town itself, unless your destination isn't particularly far away.

The **speed limit** is 110kph on expressways, 90kph on trunk roads, and 50kph in built-up areas. You'd be wise to stick religiously to these limits, since speed traps are commonplace and fines hefty. In the event you are pulled up for a traffic offence, note that it's not unknown for Malaysian police to ask for a bribe, which will set you back less than the fine. Never offer to bribe a police officer and think carefully before you give in to an invitation to do so.

Tolls are payable on all expressways, generally at a rate of around RM12.50 per

100km, though on some roads a flat fee is levied. At toll points (signed "Tol Plaza"), you can pay in cash (there are cashiers on hand to dispense change) or by waving a stored-value **Touch 'n Go** card in front of a sensor. For most visitors, the convenience of using these cards – which also work on KL's transport system – is unfortunately negated by the fact that outlets where you can buy them or add credit are far from ubiquitous; see Ⓦwww.touchngo.com.my for a list of vendors, or p.101 for agents in KL. Get in the appropriate lane as you approach the toll points; some lanes are for certain types of vehicle only, some (signed "Touch 'n Go sahaja") require card payments.

While Malaysian highways can be a pleasure to drive, wide and efficient, and featuring convenient **rest stops** with toilets, shops and small food courts, the streets of major cities can be a pain. They're regularly traffic-snarled, with patchy sign-posting and confusing one-way systems to boot. At least most cities and towns do boast a liberal sprinkling of **car parks**, and even where you can't find one, there's usually no problem with parking in a lane or side street.

Once out on the roads, you'll rapidly become aware of the behaviour of some Malaysian motorists, which could very generously be termed "enterprising", though a plausible alternative description would be *gila* (Malay for "insane"). Swerving from lane to lane in the thick of the traffic, overtaking close to blind corners and careering down hill roads are not uncommon, as are tragic stories in the press of pile-ups and road fatalities. Not for nothing do exhortations reading "*pandu cermat*" (drive safely) appear on numerous highway signboards, though the message still isn't getting through.

If you're new to driving in Malaysia, the best approach is to take all of this with equanimity and drive conservatively. Concede the right of way if you're not quite sure of the intentions of others; one confusing habit that some local drivers have adopted is that they flash their headlights when they are claiming the right of way, not the other way around.

Car and bike rental

Car rental rates begin at around RM160 per day for a week's rental of a basic 1.5-litre Proton, including unlimited mileage and collision damage waiver insurance. The excess can be RM1000 or more but this can be reduced or set to zero by paying a surcharge of up to ten percent on the daily rental rate. **Fuel** costs around RM2 per litre.

Malay vocabulary for drivers

The list which follows should help decipher road signage in Peninsular Malaysia and parts of Brunei, much of which is in Malay.

Utara	North	**Ikut kiri/kanan**	Keep left/right
Selatan	South	**Jalan sehala**	One-way street
Barat	West	**Kawasan rehat**	Highway rest stop
Timur	East	**Kurangkan laju**	Reduce speed
Di belakang	Behind	**Lebuhraya**	Expressway/
Di hadapan	Ahead		highway
Awas	Caution	**Lencongan**	Detour
Berhenti	Stop	**Pembinaan di**	Road works
Beri laluan	Give way	**hadapan**	ahead
Dilarang meletak	No parking	**Pusat bandar/**	Town/city centre
kereta		**bandaraya**	
Dilarang memancing	No fishing	**Simpang ke …**	Junction/turning
	(common at		for …
	bridges)	**Zon had laju**	Zone where
Dilarang memotong	No overtaking		speed limit
Had laju/jam	Speed limit/		applies
	per hour		

Motorbike rental is much more informal, usually offered by Malaysian guesthouses and shops in more touristy areas. Officially, you must be over 21 and have an appropriate driving licence, though it's unlikely you'll have to show the latter; you'll probably need to leave your passport as a deposit, however. Wearing helmets is compulsory. The cost of rental is around RM25 per day, while **bicycles**, which can be useful in rural areas, can be rented for around RM5 a day.

Car rental agencies

Avis ☎ 1800/881 054, ⊛ www.avis.com.my. Locations include KL airport, Johor Bahru, Kota Bharu and Penang.
Hawk ☎ 03/5631 6488, ⊛ www.hawkrentacar .com.my. KL airport, Johor Bahru, Melaka, Kota Bharu, Kuantan and Penang.
Hertz ☎ 1800/883 086 or 03/2148 6433, ⊛ www .hertz.com. KL, Alor Setar, Johor Bahru, Kuantan, Kuching, Kota Kinabalu and Penang.
Mayflower ☎ 1800/881 688, ⊛ www .mayflowercarrental.com.my. KL, Johor Bahru, Kota Kinabalu, Kuantan, Kuching and Langkawi.
National ☎ 03/2148 2823, ⊛ www.nationalcar .com. KL, Alor Setar (Kedah) and Penang.
Orix ☎ 03/9284 7799, ⊛ www.orixrentacar .my. KL, Johor Bahru, Kuantan and Penang.

City and local transport

Most Malaysian cities and towns have some kind of **bus service** serving both urban areas and hinterland; details are given in the text wherever appropriate. Fares are always very cheap even if some of the bus networks – in places like KL and Georgetown – appear absolutely unfathomable to visitors (and to some locals); journeys of an up to hour often cost no more than RM3. As a result, in this book, fares for local buses are given only where they exceed RM3. In KL, there are also the Komuter train and metro-style light rail and monorail systems, which are fairly efficient. **Taxis** are always metered, but you may find that taxi drivers would prefer to turn off the meter and negotiate a fare, which isn't legal.

Trishaws (bicycle rickshaws), seating two people, are seen less and less these days, but they're still very much part of the tourist scene in places like Melaka, Penang, Kota Bharu and Singapore. Taking a trishaw tour can be a useful, atmospheric introduction to the town and the drivers often provide interesting, anecdotal information. In most cases, they aren't much cheaper than taking a taxi – bargain hard to fix the price in advance. You can expect to pay a minimum of RM3 for a short journey, while chartering by the hour can cost as much as RM25.

Accommodation

While accommodation in Malaysia and Singapore is not the cheapest in Southeast Asia, in most places you can still get pretty good deals on simple rooms: in Malaysia it is possible to find double rooms for under RM30 (£6/US$9); under S$25 (£10/US$15) in Singapore. East Malaysia is a little more expensive; expect to pay RM40–50 (£7–9/US$11–13.50) for a room that's often just basic. While in Brunei, prices are significantly higher, starting at around B$55 (£27/$42).

This section focuses on accommodation across Malaysia; for more on Singapore and Brunei see p.636 & p.594 respectively.

The very cheapest form of accommodation is in a **dormitory bed** at a guesthouse, backpacker hostel or lodge, but these generally only exist in the more obvious tourist spots – Kuala Lumpur, Georgetown, Kota Bharu, Cherating, Kuching and Kota Kinabalu. At the other end of the scale, the region's luxury **hotels** offer a level of comfort and style to rank with any in the world. Prices in some of these, relatively speaking, have gone down in recent years with many hotels offering promotional discounts which can slash twenty percent or more off the rack rate; for example, an en-suite room with balcony plus breakfast, can go for as little as RM120 (£25/US$35) or you can secure a room in a luxurious five-star hotel in Kuala Lumpur or Kota Kinabalu for RM200–250 (£40–50/US$60–75) with a little shopping around.

At the budget end of the market you'll have to share a **bathroom**, which in most cases will feature a shower and Western-style toilet. Instead of showers, a few older places, usually in rural areas, sometimes have a *mandi* – a large basin of cold water which you throw over yourself with a bucket or ladle. **Air-conditioning** is standard in most hotels, while at the budget end you're more likely to find fan-only rooms, although increasingly even these places have transferred to air-con.

Room rates remain relatively stable throughout the year, rising slightly during the major holiday periods – Christmas, Easter, Chinese New Year and *Hari Raya*. It's always worth bargaining during the monsoon lull on the east coast of the Peninsula (Nov–Feb) when prices drop sharply and hotels are almost empty, or if you're staying for a couple of weeks in one place. When asking for a room, note that a single room usually means it will contain one double bed, while

a double can have a double bed, two single beds or even two double beds; a triple will usually have three doubles or a combination or doubles and singles. Baby cots are usually available only in more expensive places.

In popular resorts, you'll often be accosted by people at bus or train stations advertising rooms: it's rarely worth going with them, although they might be useful in securing you a room in the peak holiday season, saving you a lot of fruitless trudging around.

Guesthouses, chalets, homestays and hostels

The mainstay of the travellers' scene in Malaysia and Singapore are the **guesthouses** or as they are sometimes called, **B&Bs** or **backpackers**, located in popular tourist areas and often excellent places to meet other people and pick up information. They can range from simple beachside huts to modern multi-storey apartment buildings complete with satellite TV, DVD players and Internet. Their advantage for the single traveller on a tight budget is that almost all offer dorm beds costing RM10–20. There are usually basic double rooms available, too, usually with a fan and possibly a mosquito net, from RM20 (S$20) upwards. Fierce competition on the Malaysian east coast means that prices there occasionally drop as low as RM15 for a double room, though this is somewhat offset by the pricier options on the islands in the south, where you'll be hard pushed to find anything for under RM25.

Accommodation price codes

Accommodation in the Malaysia chapters of this book has been categorized according to the following price codes, reflecting the price of the **cheapest double room** (for Singapore and Brunei price codes see p.637 and p.594 respectively). In view of the fact that many Malaysian hotels offer frequent promotional discounts, the price codes represent **discounted rates** if these are likely to be available most of the year; otherwise the published rates are used. Promotional rates become much harder to come by during major festivals or during the school holidays (see p.76). As a rule, always ask about discounts when you email, telephone or turn up somewhere.

In the case of luxury hotels, the price codes have been calculated to include taxes. Breakfast isn't usually included in the price, unless otherwise stated.

❶ RM20 and under
❷ RM21–40
❸ RM41–60
❹ RM61–80
❺ RM81–110
❻ RM111–160
❼ RM161–220
❽ RM221–360
❾ RM361 and above

In national parks, islands and in resort-style compounds you'll often come across **chalet** accommodation. Usually sleeping two with an en-suite bathroom, these range from simple A-frame huts to luxury affairs with a sitting area, TV, mini bar, etc. Prices vary accordingly from RM20–40 per night for the most basic to upwards RM1000 for a two-night package at the resorts on Mabul and Kapalai islands in Sabah.

In certain places **homestay programmes** are available, whereby you stay with a Malaysian family, paying for your bed and board. The facilities are modest, and although some people find staying with a family too restrictive, it can be a good way of sampling Malay home cooking and culture. It may be hard to find details on homestays in the region you're visiting; a good bet is contacting the local tourist office for a list.

Official **youth hostels** in Malaysia are often hopelessly far-flung and no cheaper than guesthouses – the rare exceptions are noted in the text. As a rule, it's not worth becoming an HI member just for the trip to Malaysia, though if you're travelling further afield it might pay for itself eventually. Each major town generally has both a YMCA and a YWCA. Like the youth hostels, these are rarely conveniently located, though their facilities are better than those at the youth hostels. However, at RM50 a night (double with shared bathroom) the YMCA and YWCA are poor value compared to the budget hotels.

Hotels

The cheapest **hotels** in Malaysia tend to cater for a predominantly local clientele. These places are generally clean and well kept and there's never any need to book in advance: just go to the next place around the corner if your first choice is full. Ordinary rooms, starting at RM25 a night, are usually divided from one another by thin partitions and contain a washbasin, table and ceiling fan, though never a mosquito net. In the better places – often old converted mansions – you may also be treated to polished wooden floors and antique furniture. Showers and toilets (squat-style almost everywhere) are shared and can be pretty basic. Another consideration is the noise

level, which can be very considerable since most places are on main streets. A word of **warning**: some of the hotels at the cheaper end of the scale also function as brothels, especially those described using the Malay term *Rumah persinggahan* or *Rumah Tumpangan*.

Further up the scale are the **mid-range hotels**, often the only alternative in most towns, though they're rarely better value than a well-kept budget place. The big difference is in the comfort of the mattress – nearly always sprung – and getting your own Western-style, but cramped, bathroom. Prices range from RM40–100 (S$50–150 in Singapore), for which expense you can expect a carpeted room with air-con and TV, and, towards the upper end of the range, a telephone and refrigerator. In these places, too, a genuine distinction is made between single rooms and doubles.

One category of accommodation hard to find these days are **government resthouses** (*rumah rehat*), which once provided accommodation for visiting colonial officials. Their facilities, which range from antiquated to semi-modern, are generally good value: the best retain something of their old character and can be atmospheric places to stay; rooms tend to be large and well equipped, with private bathrooms, and even a separate lounge area.

Moving to the top of the scale, the **high-class hotels** are as comfortable as you might expect, many with state-of-the-art facilities. Recently, the trend has been to reflect local traditions with the incorporation of quasi kampung-style architecture – low-level timber structures with saddle-shaped roofs and open-sided public areas; hotels with such features still have all the usual trappings though, such as swimming pools, air-conditioning and business facilities. While prices can be as reasonable as RM120 per room, rates in popular destinations such as Penang and Kota Kinabalu can rocket to RM300 and above – though this is still relatively good value compared to hotels of an equivalent standard in London or New York. Don't forget that the price quoted by the hotel rarely includes the compulsory ten percent **service charge** and five percent **government tax** (four percent in Singapore), often signified by "++" after the price. It is always cheaper to stay at top hotels if you can do so as part of a **pre-booked package** – ask your travel agent if you want to stay at a specific hotel.

Longhouses

Staying in a wood-and-bamboo stilted **longhouse** is a de rigueur experience for many travellers visiting **Sarawak**. Increasingly, the most practical way to do this is as part of an organized **tour**, inevitably more a commercialized experience than visiting independently. However, it's still possible to travel along the rivers and, with only a minimal command of Malay at your disposal, be directed to communities off the beaten track which seldom see visitors. Visiting groups usually get a room to themselves in the longhouse, though during a festival the place may be so crowded that you end up sleeping sardine-fashion in the communal areas.

Traditionally, there's no charge to stay in a longhouse, though it is good manners to bring **gifts** such as exercise books and pens and pencils for children, or to give a donation of, say, RM20 per visitor. Once

there, you can participate in many activities including weaving, cooking, using a blowpipe, fishing, helping in the agricultural plots, and perhaps going out on a wild-boar hunt. For more details, including etiquette during your stay, see the *Longhouse culture* colour section.

Camping

Despite the rural nature of most of Malaysia, there are few official opportunities for **camping**, perhaps because guesthouses and hotels are so reasonable, and because the heat and humidity, not to mention the generous supply of insects, make camping something that only strange foreigners willingly do. Where there are campsites, they charge around RM10 per person per night, and facilities are very basic. A few lodges and camps have sturdy A-frame tents for hire, the *Pulau Tiga Survivor Resort* in Sabah is one such example.

If you go trekking in more remote regions, for example in Endau-Rompin National Park in Peninsular Malaysia, camping is about your only option; note that equipment is rarely included in the advertised price of an organized trip.

Eating and drinking

One of the best reasons to come to Malaysia and Singapore (even Brunei, to a lesser extent) is the food, comprising two of the world's most sophisticated and venerated cuisines – Chinese and Indian – and one of the world's most underrated – Malay. Even if you think you know two out of the three pretty well, be prepared to be surprised: Chinese food here boasts a lot of the provincial diversity that you just don't find in the West's Cantonese-dominated Chinese restaurants, while Indian fare is predominantly southern Indian, lighter and spicier than better-known northern food.

Furthermore, each of the three cuisines has learnt more than a few tricks off the other two, giving rise to some great, distinctive fusion food. For example, the Chinese do curries, the Indians and Malays cook tofu – and everyone does noodle dishes, with rice the universal staple. Add to this cross-fertilization the existence of a range of regional variations and specialities, plus excellent seafood and unusual tropical produce, and the result is – if you dare to order enterprisingly – a dazzling gastronomic experience.

None of this need come at great expense. From the ubiquitous food stalls and cheap roadside diners called **kedai kopis**, to restaurants in world-class hotels, the standard of cooking is high and food everywhere is remarkably good value. Basic noodle- or rice-based one-plate meals at a stall or *kedai kopi* rarely come to more than a few ringgit or Singapore dollars, and even a full meal with drinks in a fancy restaurant seldom runs to more than RM40 or S$30 a head. The most renowned culinary centres are Singapore, Georgetown, KL, Melaka and Kota Bharu, although other towns, like Johor Bahru, Ipoh, Kuching and Sibu all have their own distinctive dishes too.

Places to eat

One myth to bust immediately is the notion that you will get **food poisoning** eating at street stalls and cheap diners. Standards of hygiene are usually good, and as most food is cooked to order (or, in the case of rice-with-toppings spreads, only on display for a few hours), it's generally pretty safe.

Food stalls and food courts

Some of the cheapest and most delicious food available in Malaysia and Singapore comes from **food stalls**, traditionally wooden pushcarts on the roadside, surrounded by a few wobbly tables with stools to sit at. Most stalls serve one or a few standard **noodle** and **rice dishes** or specialize in certain delicacies, from oyster omelettes to cuttlefish curry. Particularly in Singapore and KL, you'll

even come across stalls with Western food like burgers and steak, or even Japanese and Korean food. There's usually a hot and cold drinks stall on hand; in Singapore and most Malaysian cities, you'll be able to get a **beer** or **stout**, too.

For many visitors, however, there is a psychological barrier to having a meal by the roadside. To ease yourself into the *modus operandi* of stalls, take advantage of the fact that many are nowadays assembled into user-friendly **food courts** or **medan selera** (literally "appetite squares"), also known as **hawker centres** in Singapore. Usually taking up a floor of an office building or shopping mall, or housed beneath pavilions, food courts conveniently feature stall lots with menus displayed and fixed tables, plus toilets. You don't have to sit close to the stall you're patronizing: find a free table, and the vendor will track you down when your food is ready (some Singapore food centres have tables with numbers that must be quoted when ordering). You generally pay when your order is delivered, though payment is sometimes asked for when you order.

Most stalls open at around 10am, though some open at breakfast time, and close well before midnight except in the big cities. During the Muslim fasting month of **Ramadan**, however, Muslim-run stalls don't open until mid-afternoon, though this is also when you can take advantage of the **pasar Ramadan**, afternoon food markets at which stalls sell masses of savouries and sweet treats to take away; tourist offices can tell you where one is taking place. Ramadan is also the time to stuff yourself at the massive

Eating etiquette

Malays and Indians often eat with the **right hand**, using the palm as a scoop and the thumb to help push food into the mouth. **Chopsticks** are, of course, used for Chinese food, though note that a spoon is always used to help with rice, gravies and slippery fare such as mushrooms or tofu, and that you don't attempt to pick up rice with chopsticks (unless you've a rice bowl, in which case you lift the bowl to your mouth and use the chopsticks as a sort of shovel). If you can't face either local style of eating, note that **cutlery** is universally available – for local fare, always a fork and spoon, the fork serving to push food on to the spoon, which does the transferring to the mouth.

fast-breaking buffets which most major hotels lay on throughout the month.

The kedai kopi

Few streets exist without a **kedai kopi**, sometimes known as a *kopitiam* in Hokkien Chinese. Both terms literally mean "coffee shop", but despite the name, a *kedai kopi* is actually an inexpensive diner rather than a café – though beverages are always available. Most serve noodle and rice dishes all day, often with a *campur*-style spread (see below) at lunchtime, sometimes in the evening too. Some *kedai kopis* function as miniature food markets, housing a handful of vendors – perhaps one offering curries and griddle breads, another doing a particular Chinese noodle dish, and so on. Menus, where available, are often written up on a board, though a few of the slicker *kedai kopis* have printed à la carte menus of meat and seafood dishes.

Most *kedai kopis* open at 8am to serve breakfast, and don't shut until the early evening, a few staying open as late as 10pm. Culinary standards are seldom spectacular but are satisfying all the same, and you're unlikely to spend more than small change for a filling one-plate meal. It's worth noting that in some Malaysian towns, particularly on the east coast, the Chinese-run *kedai kopis* are often the only places where you'll be able to get **alcohol**.

Restaurants, cafés and bakeries

More sophisticated restaurants only exist in the big cities. Some are simply upmarket versions of *kedai kopis*, serving a more diverse list of local favourites in slick surroundings. Don't expect a stiffly formal ambience in these places, however – while some places can be sedate, the Chinese community, in particular, prefer restaurants to be noisy, sociable affairs.

Where the pricier restaurants come into their own is for **international fare** – anything from Vietnamese to Mediterranean to Tex-Mex. KL, Singapore and Georgetown all have dynamic restaurant scenes, and the five-star hotels, whether in the cities or on resort islands, usually boast a top-flight restaurant of their own.

Elaborate **buffet** breakfasts and lunches are a feature of some hotel restaurants and can be good value and worth looking out for. The chief letdown is that the service can be a little amateurish, reflecting how novel this sort of dining experience is for many of the staff.

Most large Malaysian towns feature a few attempts at Western **cafés**, serving passable fries, sandwiches, burgers, shakes and so forth. It's also easy to find **bakeries**, which can represent a welcome change from the local rice-based diet – though don't be surprised to find chilli sardine buns and other Asian/Western hybrids, or cakes with decidedly artificial fillings and colourings. For anything really decent in the café or bakery line, you'll need to be in one of the big cities.

Phone numbers are included in our restaurant reviews where it's advisable to make reservations. Note that **tipping** is not expected in restaurants; bills arrive complete with service charge and, in Malaysia and Singapore, government tax.

The cuisines

A convenient and inexpensive way to get acquainted with a variety of local dishes is to sample the food spreads available at many of the *kedai kopis*. The concept is pretty much summed up by the Malay phrase **nasi campur** ("mixed rice"), though Chinese and Indian *kedai kopis*, too, offer these arrays of stir-fries, curries and other savouries, set out in metal trays or platted, particularly at lunchtime. As in a cafeteria, you simply tell the person behind the counter which items appeal to you, and a helping of each will be piled atop a largish serving of rice. If the plainness of the rice soon palls, you should ask for it to be doused with a scoopful of gravy (*kuah* in Malay) from any stew or stir-fry on display, for which you'll be charged very little extra (if anything).

Campur food is not haute cuisine – and that's precisely the attraction. Whether you have, say, *ikan kembong* (mackerel) deep fried and served whole, or chicken pieces braised in soy sauce, or bean sprouts stir-fried with salted fish or shrimp, any *campur* spread is much closer to **home cooking** than anything served in formal restaurants.

Nasi campur and noodle dishes are meals in themselves, but otherwise eating is generally a **shared** experience – stir-fries and other dishes arrive in quick succession and everyone present helps themselves to several servings of each, eaten with rice, as the meal progresses.

Breakfast can present a conundrum in small towns, where the rice and noodle dishes that locals enjoy at all times of day may be all that's easily available. If you can't get used to the likes of rice porridge at dawn, try to find a stall or *kedai kopi* offering *roti bakar*, toast served with butter and **kaya**. The latter is a scrumptious sweet spread not unlike English lemon curd in that it's made with eggs, though creamed coconut is the magic ingredient that accounts for most of the flavour. *Kaya* is often an orangey colour, but don't fret if you're served some that's a murky green – this is down to the aromatic pandan leaf having been added to the mixture during cooking.

Malay food

In its influences, Malay cuisine looks to the north and east, most obviously to China in the use of noodles and soy sauce, but also to neighbouring Thailand, with which it shares an affinity for ingredients such as lemon grass, the ginger-like galingale and fermented fish sauce (the Malay version, *budu*, is made from anchovies). But the cuisine also draws on Indian and Middle East flavours, in the use of spices, and in dishes such as biryani rice. The resulting cuisine is characterized by being both spicy and a little sweet. Naturally there's a particular emphasis on **local ingredients**. *Santan* (coconut milk) lends a sweet, creamy undertone to many stews and curries, while *belacan*, a pungent fermented prawn paste (something of an acquired taste), is found in chilli condiments and sauces. A range of unusual **herbs**, including curry, kaffir lime and turmeric leaves, also play a prominent role.

The cuisine of the southern part of the Peninsula tends to be more *lemak* (rich) than further north, where the Thai influence is strongest and where you'll thus find many a *tom yam* stew – spicy and sour (the latter by dint of lemon grass) – on offer. The most famous Malay dish is arguably **satay** (see box opposite), but this can be hard to find outside the big cities; another classic, and this time ubiquitous, is *nasi lemak* (see the same box), standard breakfast fare. Also quintessentially Malay is **rendang**, a dryish curry made by slow-cooking meat (usually beef) in coconut milk flavoured with galingale and a variety of herbs and spices.

For many visitors, one of the most striking things about Malay food is the bewildering array of **kuih-muih** (or just *kuih*), or sweetmeats, on display at markets at street stalls. Often featuring coconut and sometimes sweetened with *gula melaka* (palm-sugar molasses, with the bouquet of caramel), they come in all shapes and sizes, and in as many colours as you find in a paints catalogue – rainbow-hued layer cakes of rice flour are about the most extreme example. Sweet-toothed Malays must tolerate a very high intake of food additives, for these days artificial colours are used in place of natural extracts.

Malay cuisine at its best is as sophisticated as any of the world's great culinary styles, but unfortunately the best cooking is often confined to the home (make the most of it if you're doing a village homestay). The few Malay restaurants that do exist are of a good standard, presenting dishes with a loving attention to detail.

Chinese food

The range of Chinese cooking available in Malaysia and Singapore represents a mouth-watering sweep through China's southeastern seaboard, reflecting the historical pattern of emigration from **Fujian**, **Guangzhou** and **Hainan Island** provinces. This diversity is evident in popular dishes served at any collection of stalls or *kopitiams* (*kopitiam* being *kedai kopi* rendered in Hokkien/Fujianese). Cantonese *char siew* (roast pork, given a reddish honey-based marinade) is frequently served over plain rice as a meal in itself, or as a garnish in noodle dishes such as *wonton mee* (noodles with Cantonese pork dumplings); also very common is chicken rice, comprising Hainanese-style steamed chicken, accompanied by savoury rice cooked in chicken stock. Fujian province contributes dishes such as *hae mee*, yellow noodles in a rich prawn broth; *yong tau foo*, from the Hakka ethnic group on the border with Guangzhou, and comprising bean curd, fishball dumplings and assorted vegetables, poached and served with broth and sweet dipping sauces; *char kuay teow*, tagliatelle-like rice noodles fried with a dark, sweetish soy sauce; and *mee pok*, a Teochew (Chaozhou) dish featuring ribbon-like noodles with fishball dumplings and a spicy dressing.

Restaurant dining, on the other hand, is dominated by **Cantonese** food, in line with the importance of Guangzhou (Canton) cuisine in Chinese cooking generally. Menus are sometimes predictable – including standbys such as lemon chicken, mapo tofu, steamed sea bass, sweetcorn soup, Yangzhou fried rice, claypot rice (rice cooked in an earthenware pot with sweet *lap cheong* pork sausage) and so forth – but the quality of cooking is usually very high.

Many Cantonese places offer great **dim sum** lunches, at which small servings of numerous savouries such as *siu mai* dumplings (of pork and prawn), crispy yam puffs and *chee cheong fun* (rice-flour rolls stuffed with pork and dredged in sweet sauce) are consumed. Traditionally, they're all served in bamboo steamers and ordered off trolleys wheeled around by waitresses, though these days you might well make your selection from a menu, with the food arriving directly from the kitchen.

Where available, take the opportunity to try **specialities** such as steamboat, a sort of Chinese fondue involving the dunking of raw vegetables, meat and seafood into boiling stock to cook (the stock itself is drunk as part of the meal), or chilli crab (served at some seafood places), in which crab pieces are served up in a spicy tomato sauce. It's also worth sampling humdrum but very commonplace stomach-fillers such as **rice**

Six of the best

The culinary highlights listed below are mostly fairly easy to find, and many of these foods cut across racial boundaries as well, with each ethnic group modifying the dish slightly to suit its own cooking style. For a much more comprehensive run-down of local dishes, snacks and desserts, see the section on pp.793–799.

Nasi lemak Rice fragrantly cooked in coconut milk and served with fried peanuts, tiny fried anchovies, cucumber, boiled egg and spicy *sambal*.

Roti canai Called *roti prata* in Singapore, this Indian-inspired griddle-cooked flat bread comes with a thin, slightly sweet curry sauce made with dhal or fish. The most ubiquitous of a long list of *rotis*, it's served by Malay and Indian *kedai kopis* and stalls.

Nasi goreng Literally, fried rice, though not as in Chinese restaurants; Malay and Indian versions feature a little spice and chilli, along with the usual mix of vegetables plus shrimp, chicken and/or egg bits.

Mee goreng Literally, fried noodles, though again not as in Chinese restaurants; as with *nasi goreng*, the Malay and Indian versions are seasoned with spice and chilli, possibly tomato ketchup too. Versions using noodles other than *mee* (eg *bihun goreng*, made with vermicelli) are also available.

Satay A Malay dish of chicken, mutton or beef, kebabed on twig-like skewers made of bamboo, given a sweet marinade and barbecued. Sold by the stick, the meat is accompanied by sliced onion and cucumber, and *ketupat*, which is sticky-rice cubes steamed in a wrap of woven leaves; all these are meant to be dipped in a spicy peanut sauce, which at its best boasts a depth of flavour that blows peanut butter out of the water. Chinese versions of satay featuring pork also exist.

Laksa A spicy seafood noodle soup, Nonya in origin. Singapore *laksa*, served with fishcake dumplings and beansprouts, is rich and a little sweet thanks to copious use of coconut milk, while Penang's *asam laksa* features flaked fish and a hot and sour flavour thanks to tamarind.

porridge – either plain, with salted fish and omelette strips added for flavour, or already flavoured by being cooked with chicken or fish – and **pow**, steamed buns containing a savoury filling of *char siew* or chicken, or sometimes a sweet filling of red bean paste. Both porridge and *pow* are widely available as breakfast fare, while *pow* is sold throughout the day as a snack.

Of late, there's also been something of a fad for foods from Beijing and Shanghai, including *xiaolongbao* and *guotie* dumplings – though these are as yet found only in a few restaurants.

Nonya food

Named after the word used to describe womenfolk of the Peranakan communities (see p.753), Nonya food is to Penang, Melaka and Singapore as Creole food is to Louisiana, a product of the melding of cultures. In the case of Nonya food, the blend is of Chinese and Malay (and also Indonesian) cuisines. Employing a far wider range of spices than in Chinese cooking, the cuisine can seem more Malay than Chinese, apart from the fact that pork is widely used.

Nonya **popiah** (spring rolls) is one of the trademark dishes: rather than being fried, the rolls are assembled by coating a steamed wrap with a sweet sauce made of palm sugar, then stuffed mainly with stir-fried *bangkwang*, a crunchy turnip-like vegetable. Another classic is **laksa**, noodles in a spicy soup flavoured in part by *daun kesom* – a herb fittingly referred to in English as laksa leaf (see the box on p.63 for more). Other well-known Nonya dishes include **kuih pai tee**, not unlike fried spring rolls in texture but shaped like cup cakes, with the filling spooned in; and **asam fish**, a spicy, tangy fish stew featuring tamarind (the *asam* of the name); and **otak-otak**, fish mashed with coconut milk and chilli paste, then put in a narrow banana-leaf envelope and steamed or barbecued.

As with Malay food, the very best Nonya cooking is prepared in the home, these days often by elderly matriarchs, though a younger generation of cooks is perpetuating the tradition. There are Nonya restaurants in KL, Penang, Melaka and Singapore, but otherwise your main chance of encountering it is through being invited into the home of a family with Peranakan roots.

Indian food

The classic **southern Indian** dish is the *dosai* or *thosai*, a thin rice-flour pancake, often stuffed with a vegetable mixture. It's usually served accompanied by *sambar*, a coconut chutney; *rasam*, a tamarind broth; and perhaps a few small helpings of vegetable or dhal curries. Also very common are a range of *roti* griddle breads, plus the similar but more substantial *murtabak*, thicker than a *roti* and stuffed with egg, onion and minced meat, with sweet banana versions sometimes available. At lunchtime many South Indian cafés turn to serving *daun pisang* (literally, banana leaf), a meal comprising rice heaped on a banana-leaf platter and small, replenishable heaps of various curries placed alongside. in some restaurants, more substantial dishes, such as the popular fish-head curry (don't be put off by the idea – the "cheeks" between the mouth and gills are packed with tasty flesh) are also available.

A notable aspect of the Indian eating scene in Malaysia is the "**mamak**" *kedai kopi*, run by Muslims of Indian descent. With Malay restaurants not that common, *mamak* establishments have become the de facto meeting places for all creeds, being halal and open late. Foodwise, they're very similar to other South Indian places, though there's perhaps more of an emphasis on meat in *mamak* joints. Tamil and *mamak* eating places aren't hard to tell apart, as the former display pictures of Hindu gods, while the latter have framed Arabic inscriptions on the walls. There are also a few Indian Muslim coffee shops in Singapore, particularly in Little India and the Arab quarter, but the term *mamak* isn't really used there.

The food served in **northern Indian** restaurants (really only found in big cities), is richer, less fiery and more reliant on mutton and chicken. The most famous style of **north Indian** cooking is *tandoori* – named after the clay oven in which the food is cooked; you'll commonly come across tandoori chicken marinated in yoghurt and

Special diets

Malay food is, unfortunately, a tough nut to crack for **vegetarians**, as meat and seafood are well integrated into the cuisine. Among the standard savoury dishes, it's really only *sayur lodeh* (a rich mixed-vegetable curry made with coconut milk), *tauhu goreng* (deep-fried tofu with a peanut dressing similar to satay sauce) and *acar* (pickles) that veggies can handle. Eating places run by the **Chinese** and **Indian** communities are the best bets, as these groups have some familarity with vegetarianism thanks to the cultural influence of Buddhism and Hinduism. Chinese restaurants can always whip up veg stir-fries to order and many places now feature **Chinese vegetarian** cuisine, featuring the use of textured veg protein and gluten mock meats, often uncannily like the real thing, and delicious when done right.

If you're a strict vegetarian, you'll want to avoid **seafood derivatives** commonly used in cooking. This means eschewing dishes like *rojak* (containing fermented prawn paste) and the chilli dip called *sambal belacan* (containing *belacan*, the Malay answer to prawn paste) – though for some visitors, vegetarian or not, the pungency of prawn paste is enough of a deterrent. Oyster sauce, used in Chinese stir-fries, is omitted for vegetarian purposes in favour of soy sauce or just salt. Note also that the delicious gravy that accompanies **roti canai** is only likely to be suitable for veggies if you spot telltale lentils.

If you need to **explain in Malay** that you're vegetarian, try *saya hanya makan sayuran* ("I only eat vegetables"). Even if the person taking your order speaks English, it can be useful to list the things you don't eat (in Malay you'd say, for example, *saya tak mahu ayam dan ikan dan udang* for "I don't want chicken or fish or prawn" – see "Language", p.793, for more terms). Expect a few misunderstandings. The cook may leave out one thing on your proscribed list, only to substitute another; certain ingredients, such as dried shrimp, are so commonplace that the cook will mechanically add them without realizing it.

Halal food

Halal fare doesn't just feature at Malay and *mamak* restaurants and stalls. The catering at mid-range and top-tier Malaysian hotels is in fact mostly halal, or at least "pork free" and even the Chinese dishes served at top hotel restaurants have their pork content replaced with something else. Of course, the pork-free billing doesn't equate to being halal, but many local Muslims are prepared to overlook this grey area or get round it by ordering seafood.

In **Singapore**, most hawker centres have a row or two of Muslim stalls, and in areas where the great majority of the population is Muslim, such as **Kelantan** and **Terengganu**, halal or pork-free food is the norm, even at Chinese and Indian restaurants.

spices and then baked. Breads such as nan also tend to feature, more so than rice, though just about every Indian restaurant has a version of biryani.

Borneo cuisine

Much of the diet of the indigenous groups living in settled communities in **East Malaysia** tends to revolve around standard Malay and Chinese dishes. But in the remoter regions, or at festival times, you may have an opportunity to sample indigenous cuisine. In **Sabah**'s Klias Peninsula and in **Brunei**, villagers still produce *ambuyat*, a glue-like, sago-starch porridge that's dipped in sauce; or there's the Murut speciality of *jaruk* – raw wild boar, fermented in a bamboo tube, and definitely an acquired taste. Most famous of Sabah's dishes is *hinava*, or raw fish pickled in lime juice. In **Sarawak**, you're most likely to eat with the Iban or Kelabit, sampling wild boar with jungle ferns and sticky rice.

Tropical fruit

Markets feature a delightful range of locally grown **fruit**, though modern agricultural practices are leading to a decline in some varieties. Below are some of the more unusual fruits to watch out for.

Bananas (pisang) Look out for the delicious *pisang mas*, small, straight, thin-skinned and aromatically sweet; *pisang rastali*, slightly bigger, with dark blotches on the skin and not quite so sweet; plus green- and even red-skinned varieties.

Chempedak This smaller version of the *nangka* (see jackfruit below) is normally deep-fried, enabling the seed, not unlike new potato, to be eaten too.

Ciku Looks like an apple; varies from yellow to pinkish brown when ripe, with a soft, pulpy flesh.

Durian One of the most popular fruits in Southeast Asia, durians are also, for many visitors, the most repugnant, thanks to their unpleasant smell. In season from March to May, June to August and November to February, they're the size of soccer balls and have a thick green skin covered with sharp spikes. Inside, rows of large seeds are coated with squidgy yellow-white flesh, whose flavour has been likened to vomit-flavoured custard.

Guava Has a green, textured skin and flesh with five times the vitamin C content of oranges.

Jackfruit Like some kind of giant green grenade, the jackfruit (*nangka*) grows up to 40cm long and has a coarse greenish-yellow exterior, enclosing large seeds whose sweet flesh has a powerful odour, vaguely like overripe pineapple.

Langsat Together with its sister fruit, the *duku*, this looks like a small, round potato, with juicy, segmented white flesh containing small, bitter seeds.

Longan Not unlike the lychee, this stone fruit has sweet, juicy translucent flesh inside a thin brown skin.

Mangosteen Available from June to August and November to January, mangosteens have a segmented white flesh with a sweet, slightly tart flavour. Be warned: the thick purple rind contains juice that stains clothes indelibly.

Papaya Among the easiest fruits to grow, frequently getting to 30cm in length. The sweet orange flesh has a slight unpleasant odour to it, but is a rich source of vitamins A and C.

Pomelo Pale green on the outside, this is the largest of all the citrus fruits, slightly smaller than a soccer ball. At its best, it's a fantastic thirst quencher, juicy and sweeter than grapefruit. Slice away the rind with a knife, then separate and peel the giant segments with your hands.

Rambutan Rambutans are the shape and size of small hen's eggs, with a soft, spiny exterior (the redder, the riper) that gives them their name – *rambut* means "hair" in Malay. To get beneath the skin, simply make a small tear with your nails and twist open. The translucent white flesh coating the stone inside has a sweet, delicate flavour.

Salak Teardrop-shaped, the *salak* has a skin like a snake's and a bitter taste.

Soursop Inside the bumpy, muddy-green skin of this fruit is smooth white flesh like blancmange. Margaret Brooke, wife of Sarawak's second rajah, Charles, described it as "tasting like cotton wool dipped in vinegar and sugar".

Star fruit This waxy, pale green fruit, star-shaped in cross-section, is said to be good for high blood pressure. The yellower the fruit, the sweeter its flesh – though in general it can be rather insipid.

Drinks and desserts

Stalls at every food centre sell a variety of fresh fruit drinks as well exotic desserts. You need a pretty sweet tooth to cope with any of these, though, as they're usually laced with syrup; alternatively, concentrate on **bottled water**, which is widely available at around RM2 a litre.

Among the freshly squeezed **juices**, watermelon, orange and carrot are pretty common, as is the faintly sappy but invigorating sugar cane, extracted by pressing the canes through large mangles. Some street stalls also do a range of cordial-based drinks, nowhere near as good. Rather better are lychee and longan drinks, made with diluted tinned juices and served with some of the fruit at the bottom. The usual range of **soft drinks** is available everywhere for around RM1.50 a can/carton, with the F&N and Yeo companies providing more unusual flavours. Sweetened soya milk in cartons or – much tastier – freshly made at stalls is another popular local choice, as is the refreshing *chin chow*, which is sweet and dark like cola but is in fact made with a carrageenan-type seaweed, and comes with strands of seaweed jelly.

Tea (*teh*) and **coffee** (*kopi*) are as much national drinks as they are in the West. If ordered with milk, they'll come with a generous amount of the sweetened condensed variety (only large hotels and smarter Western-style cafés have ordinary milk). If you don't have a sweet tooth, either ask for your drink *kurang manis* (literally "lacking in sweetness"), in which case less condensed milk will be added, or have it black (use the suffix "o", eg *kopi o* for black coffee) or neat, with neither milk nor sugar (*kosong*).

Locals adore their tea or coffee **tarik**, literally "pulled", which in practice means frothing the drink by repeatedly pouring it out of a container in one hand to another container in the other hand, and back. Occasionally this is quite an entertaining performance, the drink being poured from head height with scarcely a drop being spilt.

Alcohol

In **Malaysia** and **Singapore**, alcohol is generally not hard to find. Most of the big cities have fairly sophisticated bar scenes, though in the towns drinking is limited to a few non-Muslim restaurants, Chinese *kedai kopi*s and Chinese-style bars – often no better than tarted-up *kedai kopi*s, the walls sometimes plastered with posters of Hong Kong showbiz poppets. However, in the strongly Muslim areas, particularly Kelantan and Terengganu, only a small number of establishments, often Chinese *kedai kopi*s and stalls, are licensed. **Brunei** is officially a dry state, though non-Muslim visitors may bring a small quantity into the country for their own consumption (see p.38).

Anchor and Tiger **beer** (lager) are locally produced and are probably the best choice, though you can also get Western and Thai brands, as well as the Chinese Tsingtao and a variety of **stouts**, including Guinness and the Singaporean ABC. Locally produced **whisky** and **rum** are cheap enough, too, though they're pretty rough stuff and can well do with mixing with Coke. **Brandy**, which is what the local Chinese drink, tends

to be better. The more upmarket restaurants serve cocktails and imported wine, though the latter is pretty expensive. In the longhouses of Sabah and Sarawak, you might be invited to sample *tuak*, a rice wine made by most families, that's about the same strength as beer.

Where bars exist in numbers, fierce competition ensures **happy hours** are a regular feature (usually daily 5–7pm), bringing the price down to around RM6 a glass, though spirits still remain pricey. While there are some bars which open from lunchtime till late, most tend to double as clubs, opening in the evenings until 3 or 4am.

Desserts

Appropriately, given the steamy climate, stalls offer a range of desserts which often revolve around ice milled down to something resembling snow or slush. One ingredient you might be surprised to find in desserts is **pulses** such as red beans and lentils. You'll even find delicious red bean ice cream on sale, its flavour dominated by coconut milk rather than the beans.

At their best, these icy concoctions are certainly a lot more interesting than most ice-cream sundaes ever get. Worth trying is **els kacang** (also known as *air batu campur* – "mixed ice" – or ABC), comprising a small helping of aduki beans, sweetcorn and bits of jelly, covered with a snowy mound which is doused in colourful syrups. Even better, though high in cholesterol, is **cendol**, luscious coconut milk sweetened with *gula melaka* and mixed with green fragments of mung-bean-flour jelly.

Communications

It's not just ultra-hi-tech Singapore that boasts an efficient, modern communications network. Mobile coverage is fairly widespread in Malaysia and Brunei, as is Internet access, though connections may not be as quick as you might like.

Mail

Malaysia has a well-organized postal service operated by Pos Malaysia (☎1300/300 300, ⓦwww.pos.com.my), whose website gives thorough details of postage rates, express mail and courier ("PosLaju") options and so forth. **Aerogrammes** are the most cost-effective way to send airmail letters, at RM0.50 apiece, as compared to RM1.50 to airmail the lightest letters to Australasia. **Surface mail** – which can be useful as a relatively cheap way to send parcels – takes at least six weeks. Usual post office opening hours are Monday to Saturday 8am–6pm.

Each Malaysian town has a **General Post Office** (GPO) with a **poste restante** section, where mail will be held for two months. If you're having mail sent this way, tell the sender to underline your surname or put it in capitals, and to address the letter as follows: name, Poste Restante, GPO, town or city, state. When picking up mail, be sure to have staff check under first names as well as family names – misfiling of letters is common.

In **Brunei**, post offices are open Monday to Thursday between 8am and 4.30pm, and on Friday and Saturday from 8am till noon. Some hotels can also provide basic postal facilities. For details of postal services in **Singapore**, see p.723.

Telephones

Coin- and card-operated phones aren't hard to find in towns and cities and for many travellers these suffice for the occasional call. Domestic calls are fairly cheap, and with VoIP (calls which are Internet-routed, and thus discounted) becoming available via certain phone cards and to mobile users, even international calls won't cost a fortune.

For the greatest convenience, it's a good idea to bring your **mobile/cell phone** and enable **roaming**. Bear in mind that for roaming to work, your phone must be **GSM/triband** (older North American phones may not satisfy this). The same condition applies if you want to use a prepaid **local SIM card**, which is a much cheaper option than roaming, though do also ensure your phone isn't

---

International calls

To make international calls to any of the countries below, dial your international access code (☎00 in Malaysia and Brunei, ☎001 in Singapore) then the relevant country code from the list, then the number (including any area code, but excluding any initial zero). However, note that it is still possible to dial a Singapore number from Malaysia using ☎02 (the area code for Singapore from the days it was part of Malaysia), then the number. From Singapore, you can call Malaysia by dialling ☎020, then the area code (omitting the initial zero), then the number.

IDD country codes

Australia ☎61	New Zealand ☎64
Brunei ☎673	Singapore ☎65
Canada ☎1	South Africa ☎27
Ireland ☎353	UK ☎44
Malaysia ☎60	USA ☎1

Operator and directory services

Malaysia
Local directory enquiries: ☎103
Operator-assisted calls (including international collect/reverse charge) : ☎101
Business number online searches: ⊛www.yellowpages.com.my – you may need to search using Malay category words, especially if you don't know the exact name of the organization

Singapore
Local directory enquiries: ☎100
Operator-assisted international calls: ☎104
Business number online searches: ⊛www.yellowpages.com.sg

Brunei
Local directory enquiries: ☎113

---

locked to your current network. Outlets specializing in "hand phones" (as mobile phones are referred to locally) where you can buy or add credit to a local SIM card are easily found, even in small towns. When you buy additional air time, you usually receive a scratch card or receipt bearing a numerical code, which you transmit to the phone company (for example, via SMS). It doesn't hurt to call the service provider early on, to ask about budget international calls and other discount deals they may offer.

Malaysia

There are public phones in most Malaysian towns. Local calls are very cheap at just 10 sen for three minutes, but for long-distance calls, it can be more convenient to buy a **phonecard**. Your best bet is to use a card such as iTalk or Ring Ring, both from Telekom Malaysia, which enable you to make discounted calls (iTalk uses VoIP) from the line in your hotel room as well as from payphones. Several companies issue conventional phonecards that only work in card-operated phones run by the issuing firm; the most widely available are those of Telekom Malaysia, whose phonecards (Kadfon) come in denominations from RM5 right up to RM100. Whichever phonecard you want, Shell and Petronas service stations, 7-Eleven outlets and newsagents are the best outlets to try.

All cities and most towns have a **TM Point office** (locations are given in the text and on ⊛www.telekom.com.my) where it used to be possible to make collect calls. These days, however, TM Point offices merely have the same card-operated phones as you'll find elsewhere.

There are two big players in the **mobile phone** market, namely Hotlink/Maxis and Celcom, with the smaller DiGi bringing up the rear. On the Peninsula you'll usually get a signal on both coasts, along highways and major roads, and on touristed islands. In the forested interior, as a rule your phone will work in any town large enough to be served by express trains (as well as at the Taman Negara headquarters). Sabah and Sarawak coverage is much patchier, focusing on cities and the populated river valleys, though even in the Kelabit Highlands mobile calls are possible.

In general, a **prepaid SIM card** will cost up to RM20, including a certain amount of call time. Note that in Malaysia you're required to bring **ID**, such as your passport, when buying a SIM card. Mobile **tariffs** are complex, with charges affected by the relative locations of the caller's mobile and the receiver's phone, but in the evening off-peak period, RM0.50 per minute is typical for a call to a mobile or fixed phone in the same billing region.

Singapore

You couldn't have more options for keeping in touch with the outside world than in tech-savvy Singapore, endowed with ubiquitous payphones, mobile coverage and fast Net access. All cardphones allow international calls, and some even accept credit cards for payment; otherwise you can pay using a variety of **phonecards**, available in denominations starting from $5; they're on sale at the Comcentre (see p.723) and post offices, as well as in 7-Elevens, stationers and bookshops. Domestic calls from payphones cost just 10¢ for three minutes. Major **mobile** providers include Singtel (Ⓦ www.singtel .com) and Starhub (Ⓦ www.starhub.com).

Brunei

International calls can be made in booths at the Telekom office in the capital, or from cardphones; if you want to call collect, substitute ☎01 for the usual ☎00 international code, then dial the number as though making an ordinary international call; this brings the number up on the operator's system. Phonecards start at $10, and can be bought from the Telekom office and post offices.

Internet access

Internet cafés and shops can be found in all Malaysian cities and large towns, often in malls or in upstairs premises along central streets. While many may serve the odd coffee or Coke, the emphasis often isn't on beverages or even getting online, but on networked gaming, the computers swamped by kids playing noisy shoot-em-ups late into the night. Periodic crackdowns temporarily compel the Internet cafés to keep sensible hours and, it's hoped, the youths in their beds. At least the cafés do provide reliable, if not always superfast, Internet access, costing RM3–6 per hour in practically all cases. In small towns, Net access may be available in guesthouses that see foreign travellers, or mobile-phone shops, both charging standard rates.

Likewise, it's not hard to get online in **Brunei** or **Singapore**, though expect prices to be around fifty percent higher than in Malaysia. For more details, see the respective chapters.

The media

In Malaysia some aspects of media control have loosened in recent years with a plethora of websites offering a wide range of news, satire, environmental awareness and cultural information. However, traditional media still operate under significant restrictions. Singapore and Brunei are less progressive still – the former has even banned the use of blogs by opposition party members or indeed by anyone writing about political matters. But the proliferation of websites goes on, reflecting a change in the way young people especially view and absorb information.

Not surprisingly perhaps, the foreign media is often attacked across the three nations for putting forward an interpretation of events that differs from the "official" one, notably regarding any perceived criticism of Islam (Malaysia and Brunei), or the government (Singapore). However, **Western newspapers** and magazines are widely available in the main cities (usually the day after publication) but you'll have to wait a few days to get them in small towns.

There is also a well-established local English-language press and various domestic **television** and **radio** channels to choose from which now compete with regional satellite broadcasters.

Newspapers, magazines and online news

Daily **English-language newspapers** are published across the three territories (see below). **Malaysia** boasts four which have Sunday editions as well; particularly impressive, though, are their polished **online editions** which appear more reactive to news developments. Although these papers are available in urban centres in East Malaysia, the local English-language dailies such as *Borneo Post* in Sarawak and the *Daily Express* in Sabah are more popular.

Malaysia and Singapore also have Chinese-, Tamil- and Malay-language newspapers and a variety of weekly and monthly English-language **magazines**.

News websites across the region tends to be less subject to censorship compared with print and broadcast outlets and are well worth checking out.

Malaysia

Aliran Monthly Ⓦ www.aliran.com. Magazine which reports on economic and political issues from a less centralized, more independent perspective.
Malay Mail Ⓦ www.mmail.com.my. Populist paper focusing on the domestic front with tabloid-style scoops and an extensive "What's on" section.
Malaysiakini (Malaysia Now) Ⓦ www .malaysiakini.com. Website offering balanced and invigorating reporting, columns and reader exchange. It's sometimes accused of being pro-opposition, though opposition parties also may expect to receive rough treatment.
New Straits Times Ⓦ www.nst.com.my. Sister paper to Singapore's *Straits Times* but to all intents a separate entity, this tabloid offers government-slanted political news, some thought-provoking columns and wide arts coverage.
Rengah Sarawak Ⓦ www.rengah.c2o.org. Website with stories and information relating to Sarawak including articles, updates on campaigns, forums and links.
Sarawak Alive Ⓦ www.sarawak.com.my. Well-presented Sarawak website, full of articles on indigenous lifestyle, food and arts.
The Star Ⓦ www.thestar.com.my. News-heavy tabloid with an exceptional website presenting a wide picture of Malaysian news, culture and environment (its articles are available free online one month after publication).
The Sun Ⓦ www.sun2surf.com. Strong on populist columns about all things Malaysian and has an excellent weekly listings magazine – *Time Out* – on Thursdays and is the most independent of the four.

Singapore

New Paper Ⓦ www.newpaper.asia1.com.sg. An amusingly tame tabloid which hits the streets every afternoon.
Straits Times Ⓦ www.straitstimes.asia1.com .sg. Quality daily broadsheet with good coverage of international events.
Talking Cock Ⓦ www.talkingcock.com. Satirical Singapore-based website which takes amusing swipes at the establishment and the local *Ah Bengs* (Chinese gang members).

Brunei

Borneo Bulletin Ⓦ www.brunet.bn/news/bb. The main paper in Brunei, the *Bulletin* has limited news content but a fascinating letters page where topics seldom discussed in this strict state can get an airing. The online version is worth a look particularly if you are after the latest news on the royal family.

Television

Malaysia

RTM1 & RTM2 Ⓦ www.rtm.net.my. Malaysia's staple, government-owned channels, broadcasting in Malay, with some material in Chinese, Tamil and English. News in English is broadcast on RTM2 at 8pm daily.
TV3 Ⓦ www.tv3.com.my. Commercially owned showing English-language news and documentaries, Chinese kung fu, and Tamil, British and American films and soaps.
TV 7 Ⓦ www.ntv7.com.my. Part of the TV3 stable, featuring youth-orientated programming and some news slots.
8TV Ⓦ www.8tv.com.my. Again, caters for the youth market, in various languages.
Astro Ⓦ www.astro.com.my/v5. Satellite service with around forty channels carrying news (including the BBC's World channel and CNN), movies, documentaries as well as Cantonese and Tamil/Bollywood channels.

Singapore

As well as the main station listed below, Singaporean TV sets are able to receive Malaysia's RTM1, RTM2 and TV3 channels; similarly, in southern Malaysia it's possible to pick up Singaporean TV and radio.
Mediacorp TV Ⓦ www.mediacorptv.com. Previously the Television Corporation of Singapore (TCS), it screens various channels in English, Chinese, Malay and Tamil. Channel 5 and Channel News Asia feature largely English-language programmes and Channel 8 specialises in Chinese soap operas.

Brunei

Radio and Television Brunei (RTB) ⓦ www.rtb .gov.bn. Brunei's national network imports most of its programming from Malaysia; short English-language news broadcast in the evening.

Radio

Radio in Malaysia has expanded in recent years responding to the needs of a very diverse market. The Malaysian government owns 32 stations across the sector, under Radio Malaysia, part of RTM. Some of the RTM stable broadcast in Malay, Chinese and Tamil while the ones below broadcast all or partly in English. Sabah and Sarawak have a few FM stations of their own; the latter's English language CATS Radio offers news from a local perspective, plus music.

Malaysia

Muzik FM ⓦ www.u2muzikfm.com. Online music station.

Nasional FM (formerly Radio 1) ⓦ www.radio1 .com.my. Popular mix of news and music available online and on FM regionally: 98.3 Klang Valley, 94.9 Penang, 106.7 Johor and 88.3 Ipoh.

Red FM ⓦ www.red1049.com. On 104.9 FM, this English-language station owned by the *Star* newspaper group has a populist diet of music and general chat.

Trax FM ⓦ www.traxxfm.net. Broadcasts in English with a mix of news and music. Frequencies 90.3 Klang, 98.7 Penang, 102.9 Johor South and 90.1 Ipoh.

BBC World Service ⓦ www.bbc.co.uk /worldservice. Can be received on shortwave; in Johor, you might be able to pick it up on 88.9 FM.

Singapore

As well as the listings below there are daily broadcasts in Chinese (95.8FM), Malay (94.2FM) and Tamil (96.8FM). For programme listings check the daily newspapers, or *8 Days* magazine.

Mediacorp Radio ⓦ www.mediacorpradio.sg. Broadcasts several English-language radio shows daily including Gold (90.5FM), an information and music channel; Heart (91.3FM), offering music and "infotainment"; Symphony FM (92.4FM), featuring classical music; Perfect 10 (98.7FM), playing pop music; and Class (95FM), playing middle-of-the-road hits.

BBC World Service Can be picked up 24 hours a day on 88.9FM.

Brunei

RTB broadcasts two channels a day on the medium-wave and FM bands – one in Malay, the other in English and Chinese.

Festivals

With so many ethnic groups and religions represented in Malaysia, Singapore and Brunei, you'll be unlucky if your trip doesn't coincide with some sort of festival, either secular or religious. Religious celebrations range from exuberant, family-oriented pageants to blood-curdlingly gory displays of devotion. Secular events might comprise a carnival with a cast of thousands, or just a local market with a few cultural demonstrations laid on. If you're keen to see a major religious festival, it's best to make for a town or city where there is a large population of the particular ethnic group involved – all the relevant details are given in the list of festivals and events below, and are backed up by special accounts throughout the text.

If you're particularly interested in specifically **Malay festivities**, it's worth noting that in Kota Bharu, a cultural centre has been established as a platform for traditional Malay pastimes and sports – see also *Malay life* colour section. Chinese religious festivals – in particular, the Festival of Hungry Ghosts – are the best times to catch a free performance of a Chinese opera, or *wayang*, in which characters act out classic Chinese legends, accompanied by crashing cymbals, clanging gongs and stylized singing.

Bear in mind that the major festival periods may play havoc with even the best-planned travel itineraries. Over Ramadan in particular, transport networks and hotel capacity are stretched to their limits, as countless Muslims engage in *balik kampung* – the return to one's home village; Chinese New Year wreaks similar havoc. Some, but by no means all, festivals are also public holidays (when everything closes); check the lists on p.76 for those.

Most of the festivals have no fixed dates, but change annually according to the lunar calendar; the **Islamic calendar** shifts forward relative to the Gregorian calendar by about ten days each year, so that, for example, a Muslim festival which happens in mid-April one year will be nearer the beginning of April the following year. We've listed rough timings, but for specific dates each year it's a good idea to check with the local tourist office.

A festival and events calendar

January–February

Ponggal A Tamil harvest and new year festival held at the start of the Tamil month of Thai. *Ponggal* translates as "overflow" and the festival is celebrated by boiling sugar, rice and milk together in a new claypot over a wood fire. The milk boils and overflows, forcing out the rice symbolising prosperity and plenty; offerings of food are made at Hindu temples such as Singapore's Sri Srinivasa Perumal Temple on Serangoon Road (mid-Jan).

Thaipusam Entranced Hindu penitents carry elaborate steel arches (*kavadi*), attached to their skin by hooks and skewers, to honour Lord Subramaniam. The biggest processions are at Kuala Lumpur's Batu Caves and from the Sri Srinivasa Perumal Temple to the Chettiar Hindu Temple in Singapore (late Jan).

Chinese New Year Chinese communities spring spectacularly to life, to welcome in the new year. Old debts are settled, friends and relatives visited, and red envelopes (*hong bao/ang pao*) containing money are given to children; Chinese operas and lion-and-dragon-dance troupes perform in the streets, while ad hoc markets sell sausages and waxed ducks, pussy willow, chrysanthemums and mandarin oranges. Colourful parades of stilt-walkers, lion dancers and floats along Singapore's Orchard Road and through the major towns and cities of west-coast Malaysia celebrate the Chingay holiday, part of the new year festivities (Feb).

Chap Goh Mei The fifteenth and climactic day of the Chinese New Year period, and a time for more feasting and firecrackers; women who throw an orange into the sea at this time are supposed to be granted a good husband; the day is known as *Guan Hsiao Chieh* in Sarawak (generally Feb).

Brunei National Day The sultan and 35,000 other Bruneians watch parades and fireworks at the Sultan Hassanal Bolkiah National Stadium, just outside Bandar Seri Begawan; the rest watch on TV (Feb 23).

Birthday of the Monkey God To celebrate the birthday of one of the most popular deities in the Chinese pantheon, mediums possessed by the Monkey God's spirit pierce themselves with skewers; elsewhere street operas and puppet shows are performed. Make for Singapore's Monkey God Temple on Seng Poh Road, or look out for ad hoc canopies erected near Chinese temples (Feb & Sept).

March–May

Easter Candlelit processions held on Good Friday at Christian churches like St Peter's in Melaka and St Joseph's in Singapore (March/April).

Qing Ming Ancestral graves are cleaned and restored, and offerings made by Chinese families at the beginning of the third lunar month – signals the beginning of spring and a new farming year (April).

Vesak Day Saffron-robed monks chant prayers at packed Buddhist temples, and devotees release caged birds to commemorate the Buddha's birth, enlightenment and the attainment of Nirvana (May).

Pesta Kaamatan Celebrated in the villages of Sabah's west coast and interior, the harvest festival of the Kadazan/Dusun people features a ceremony of thanksgiving by a *bobohizan* (high priestess), followed by lavish festivities; the festival culminates in a major celebration in Kota Kinabalu (May).

Sabah Fest A week of events in Kota Kinabalu, offering a chance to experience Sabah's food, handicrafts, dance and music (late May). *Rumah Terbuka Malaysia Tadau Kaamatan* (Harvest Festival), Kota Kinabalu, Sabah (May 31).

Brunei Armed Forces Day The formation of Brunei's armed forces is celebrated with parades and displays on the padang (May 31).

June–August

Yang di-Pertuan Agong's Birthday Festivities are held in KL to celebrate the birthday of Malaysia's king, elected every five years by the country's nine sultans or rajahs from among their number (June).

Gawai Dayak Sarawak's Iban and Bidayuh peoples celebrate the end of harvesting with extravagant longhouse feasts. Aim to be in an Iban longhouse on the Sunjei Rajang or along the Batang Ai River, or on dry land around Serian or Bau (June).

Feast of Saint Peter Melaka's Eurasian community decorate their boats to honour the patron saint of fishermen (June 24).

Dragon Boat Festival Rowing boats, bearing a dragon's head and tail, race in Penang, Melaka, Singapore and Kota Kinabalu, to commemorate a Chinese scholar who drowned himself in protest against political corruption (June/July).

Sultan of Brunei's Birthday Celebrations Starting with a speech by the sultan on the padang, celebrations continue for two weeks with parades, lantern processions, traditional sports competitions and fireworks – see local press for details (July 15).

Flower Festival Based in the Cameron Highlands, with a display of floral arrangements and a competition for the best flower-covered float (Aug).

Sarawak Extravaganza Kuching hosts a month of arts and crafts shows, street parades, food fairs and traditional games, all celebrating the culture of Sarawak (Aug).

Singapore National Day Singapore's independence is celebrated with a huge show at the National Stadium, featuring military parades and fireworks (Aug 9).

Festival of the Hungry Ghosts *Yue Lan*; held to appease the souls of the dead released from purgatory during the seventh lunar month, when Chinese street operas are held, and joss sticks, red candles and paper money burnt outside Chinese homes (late Aug).

Malaysia National Day Parades in Dataran Merdeka, KL, Kuching and Kota Kinabalu to mark the formation of the state of Malaysia. Often preceded by weeks of flag waving (Aug 31).

September–December

Moon Cake Festival Also known as the Mid-Autumn Festival (held during the eighth lunar month), when Chinese people eat and exchange moon cakes (made from sesame and lotus seeds and sometimes stuffed with a duck egg) to honour the fall of the Mongol Empire, plotted, so legend has it, by means of messages secreted in cakes. After dark, children parade with gaily coloured lanterns. Chinatowns are the obvious places to view the parades, but Singapore's Chinese Gardens and Kuching's Reservoir Park also have particularly good displays (Sept).

Navarathiri Hindu temples devote nine nights to classical dance and music in honour of the consorts of the Hindu gods, Shiva, Vishnu and Brahman; one reliable venue is Singapore's Chettiar Temple (Sept–Oct).

Thimithi Hindu firewalking ceremony in which devotees prove the strength of their faith by running across a pit of hot coals; best seen at the Sri Mariamman Temple in Singapore (Sept–Nov).

Festival of the Nine Emperor Gods The nine-day sojourn on earth of the Nine Emperor Gods – thought to bring good health and longevity – is celebrated in Singapore at the Kiu Ong Yah Temple (Upper Serangoon Road) by Chinese operas and mediums cavorting in the streets (Oct).

Pilgrimage to Kusu Island Locals visit Singapore's Kusu Island in their thousands to pray for good luck and fertility at the Tua Pekong Temple and the island's Muslim shrine (Oct/Nov).

Kota Belud Tamu Besar Sabah's biggest annual market, attended by Bajau tribesmen on horseback, features cultural performances and handicraft demonstrations (Oct/Nov).

Deepavali Hindu festival celebrating the victory of Light over Dark: oil lamps are lit outside homes to attract Lakshmi, the Goddess of Prosperity, and prayers are offered at all temples (Oct).

Ramadan Muslims spend the ninth month of the Islamic calendar fasting in the daytime, and breaking their fasts nightly with delicious Malay sweetmeats served at stalls outside mosques (mid-Sept to mid-Oct 2007).

Hari Raya Haji An auspicious day for Muslims, who gather at mosques to honour those who have completed the *hajj*, or pilgrimage to Mecca; goats are sacrificed, and their meat given to the needy. Known as *Hari Raya Aidiladha* in Brunei and sometimes in Malaysia and Singapore too.

Hari Raya Puasa The end of Ramadan which Muslims celebrate by feasting, and by visiting family and friends; this is the only time the region's royal palaces are open to the public, including Brunei's, where the holiday is known as *Hari Raya Aidilfitri* (mid October in 2007).

Christmas Shopping centres in major cities compete to create the most spectacular Christmas decorations (Dec 25).

Opening hours and public holidays

Specific opening hours are given throughout the text, but check below for the general opening hours of businesses and offices in Malaysia, Singapore and Brunei. It's worth noting that in Malaysia's more devout Muslim states, Friday – not Sunday – is the day of rest. Businesses and offices close after lunch on Thursday to accommodate this, while government offices in Brunei close on Fridays and Sundays.

Singapore and Malaysia share several common public holidays, as well as each having their own. Transport becomes a headache on these days, though you're only likely to be really inconvenienced around Chinese New Year (Jan–Feb) and at the end of the Muslim month of **Ramadan** (Sept/Oct). Local tourist offices can tell you exactly which dates these holidays fall upon annually. In Malaysia, a further complication is that some public holidays vary from state to state, depending on each state's religious make-up. In addition, countless localized state holidays mark the birthdays of sultans and governors. Don't be surprised to turn up somewhere and find everything closed for the day.

Opening hours

In **Malaysia**, shops are open daily 9.30am–7pm and shopping centres typically open daily 10am–10pm. Government offices tend to work Monday to Thursday 8am–12.45pm and 2–4.15pm, Friday 8am–12.15pm and 2.45–4.15pm, Saturday 8am–12.45pm; however, in the states of Kedah, Kelantan and Terengannu, on Thursday the hours are 8am–12.45pm, with offices closing on Friday and opening on Sunday. Banks open Monday to Friday 9.30am–4pm and alternate Saturdays 9.30–11.30am; as with government offices, Thursday is a half-day and Friday a holiday in the states of Kedah, Kelantan and Terengganu. It's impossible to give general opening hours for temples, mosques and museums – check the text for specific hours, given where appropriate.

In **Singapore**, shopping centres open daily 10am–10pm; banks are sure to open at least Monday to Friday 10am–3pm, Saturday 9.30am–1pm and sometimes longer; while offices generally work Monday to Friday 8.30am–5pm and sometimes on Saturday mornings. In general, Chinese temples open daily from 7am to around 6pm, Hindu temples from 6am to noon and 5 to 9pm and mosques from 8am to 1pm; specific opening hours for all temples and museums are given in the text.

Government offices in **Brunei** open 7.45am–12.15pm and 1.30–4.30pm, except Friday and Sunday; shopping centres daily 10am–10pm; and banks Monday to Friday 9am–3pm and Saturday 9–11am.

Public and school holidays

Below are listed the public holiday dates for **2007** (note that Muslim holidays move forward ten or eleven days each year). In addition there are local state holidays in Malaysia, for example *Pesta Keamatan* celebrated in May in Sabah and *Gawai* Festival is celebrated in June in Sarawak. For an explanation of the festivities associated with some of the holidays below, see pp.73–75.

It pays to be aware of not just public holidays but also the local **school holidays**, as Malaysian accommodation is often harder to come by during these periods. In Malaysia, schools get a week off in mid-March and late August, and two weeks off at the start of June, with a long break from mid-November to the end of the year. Singapore school breaks are almost identical, except that the June holiday lasts the whole month, and kids get a week off in early September rather than late August.

Malaysia

January 1 New Year's Day
January 22 *Maal Hijrah* (the Muslim New Year)
February 18 & 19 Chinese New Year
March 31 Birthday of the Prophet Mohammed
April 6 Good Friday
May 1 Labour Day
May 31 Vesak Day
June 3 Yang Dipertuan Agong's Birthday
August 31 National Day
October 13 & 14 *Hari Raya Puasa*
November 8 *Deepavali*
December 20 *Hari Raya Haji* (Korban)
December 25 Christmas Day

Singapore

January 1 New Year's Day
February 18 & 19 Chinese New Year
April 6 Good Friday
May 1 Labour Day
May 31 Vesak Day
August 9 National Day
October 13 *Hari Raya Puasa*
November 8 *Deepavali*
December 20 *Hari Raya Haji*
December 25 Christmas Day

Brunei

January 1 New Year's Day
January 22 *Maal Hijrah* (the Muslim New Year)
February 18 & 19 Chinese New Year
February 23 National Day
March 31 Birthday of the Prophet Mohammed
May 31 Armed Forces' Day
July 15 Sultan's Birthday
September 2 *Israk Mikraj* (the night when the Koran was revealed to the Prophet)
September 13 First day of Ramadan
October 13 *Hari Raya Aidilfitri*
November 12 Anniversary of Revelation of the Koran
December 20 *Hari Raya Aidiladha*
December 25 Christmas Day

Crime and personal safety

If you lose something in Malaysia, Singapore or Brunei, you're more likely to have someone running after you with it than running away. Nevertheless, you shouldn't become complacent: pickpockets and snatch thieves are still on the prowl in Malaysia's more touristed cities, and don't forget that theft from dormitories by other tourists is a common complaint.

Crime

Most people carry their passport, traveller's cheques and other valuables in a concealed money belt, and guesthouses and hotels will often have a safety deposit box. Always keep a separate record of the numbers of your traveller's cheques, together with a note of which ones you've cashed. It's probably worth taking a photocopy of the relevant pages of your passport, too, in case it's lost or stolen. In the more remote parts of Sarawak or Sabah there is little crime, and you needn't worry unduly about carrying cash – in fact, the lack of banks means that you'll probably have to carry more than you might otherwise.

It's worth repeating here that it is very unwise to have anything to do with **illegal drugs** of any description in Malaysia and Singapore. If you are arrested for drugs offences you can expect no mercy from the authorities (see box, p.38) and little help from your consular representatives.

A plus for **women travellers** is that sexual harassment in Malaysia and Singapore is minimal, and certainly no more than you might encounter at home – the level of contact rarely goes beyond the odd whistle or shy giggles. Irritating though it can be, you have to expect some attention both as a foreigner and as a woman, but it's often down to no more than pure curiosity and your novelty value. See p.80 for further advice for women travellers alone.

Malaysia

If you do need to **report a crime** in Malaysia, head for the nearest police station (marked on the maps and included in the text), where there'll invariably be someone who speaks English; you'll need a copy of a police report for insurance purposes. In many major tourist spots, there are specific **tourist police stations** which are geared up to problems faced by foreign travellers. The police are generally more aloof than in the West, dressed in blue trousers and white short-sleeved shirts, and armed with small handguns. While you're likely to be excused any minor misdemeanour as a foreigner, it pays to be deferential if caught on the wrong side of the law.

Restrictions on contact between people of the opposite sex (such as the offence of *khalwat,* or "close proximity") and eating in public during daylight hours in the Ramadan month apply to Muslims only.

Singapore

Singapore is known locally as a "fine city". There's a fine of S$500 for smoking in public places such as cinemas, trains, lifts, air-conditioned restaurants and shopping malls, and one of $50 for "jaywalking" – crossing a main road within 50m of a designated pedestrian crossing or bridge.

Emergencies

In an emergency, dial the following numbers:
Malaysia
Police ☎999
Fire Brigade/Ambulance ☎994
Singapore
Police ☎999
Fire Brigade/Ambulance ☎995
Brunei
Police ☎993
Ambulance ☎991
Fire Brigade ☎995

Littering carries a $1000 fine, with offenders now issued Corrective Work Orders and forced to do litter-picking duty, while eating or drinking on the MRT could cost you $500. Other **fines** include those for urinating in lifts (legend has it that some lifts are fitted with urine detectors, while in Malaysia the government proposed see-through lifts as a deterrent), not flushing a public toilet and chewing gum (which is outlawed in Singapore). It's worth bearing all these offences in mind, since foreigners are not exempt from the various Singaporean punishments – as the American Michael Fay discovered in 1994, when he was given four strokes of the cane for vandalism.

Singapore's **police**, who wear dark-blue uniforms, keep a fairly low profile, but are polite and helpful when approached. For details of the main police station, and other emergency information, check the relevant sections of "Listings".

Terrorism

In the wake of the terrorist bombings in Bali as well as religious violence in southern Thailand and the southern Philippines, personal security has become a prime concern for travellers throughout Southeast Asia. Although there is undoubtedly a connection between Malaysia and fundamentalist Islamic groups, security forces have been working hard recently and believe that after numerous arrests many of the networks have now been broken. This has led local politicians to claim that there is no more likelihood of terrorist activity in Malaysia, Singapore or Brunei than there is in Europe, the US, Australia or New Zealand, although this advice often conflicts with the more cautious line taken by Western governments, particulary the US and Australia.

Muslims in Malaysia have a fairly sophisticated view of Westerners. They know that many have been opposed to recent military action undertaken by their governments. Pictures showing Westerners volunteering to act as human shields in the occupied West Bank and in Iraq were widely shown on the region's television. Most Muslims in Malaysia would respond to any attack on Westerners in Malaysia with complete outrage.

Culture and etiquette

Despite the obvious openness to influences from around the globe, and the urbanity of Kuala Lumpur, Singapore, Penang and Kuching, society in Malaysia, Singapore and Brunei remains fairly conservative and conformist. Behaviour that departs from established cultural and behavioural norms – basically, anything that draws attention to the individuals concerned – can create a bit of a scene and become problematic. These norms are well worth noting, being both tricky for outsiders to discern and widely applicable elsewhere in Asia.

Though allowances are made for foreigners, until you acquire some familiarity with where the limits lie, it's best to err on the side of caution. Get the balance right and you'll find locals helpful and welcoming, while respectful of your need for some privacy – the cliché about there being no concept of personal space in Southeast Asia seldom applies here.

Incidentally, one area where you'll probably not want to conform to local norms is that of **punctuality**: locals often seem not so much fashionably as congenitally late.

It's always best to keep to the agreed time of any social rendezvous – just don't be surprised if you then wait for half an hour for local friends to show.

Dress

For both men and women, exposing lots of **bare flesh** is generally a no-no in Asia, and the minimum degree to which you should cover up can seem surprisingly prim. Islamic tradition suffuses the **dress code** for locals, Muslim or otherwise, and dictates that both men and women should keep torsos covered; shirt sleeves, if short, should come down to the elbow (vests are thus not okay, and for women, long-sleeved tops are preferable), while shorts (or skirts) should extend down to the knee (long trousers are ideal). Figure-hugging clothes are often frowned upon, particularly for women.

Of course dress codes are more liberal in most cities (Singapore in particular), on the beach and when pursuing sporting activities, but it's surprising how often the minimum standards mentioned above are complied with. Conversely, in conservative Muslim cities such as Kota Bharu and Kuala Terengganu, local men of any creed just aren't seen in shorts. Likewise, on public beaches in rural Muslim areas, stripping off for a swim may cause offence or attract unwanted attention.

Given that dress matters, locals always make an effort to be smartly turned out, and you'd gain a modicum of respect in the eyes of others if you do the same. Also, remember that in Muslim tradition, the soles of shoes are considered unclean, having been in contact with the dirt of the street, and before entering any home (Muslim or otherwise), it's almost universal practice to **remove your footwear** at the threshold or before stepping onto any carpeted or matted area. Your hosts will politely remind you if you forget.

Discretion and body language

Given the fairly conformist nature of society, **discretion** should be your watchword. **Canoodling** in public will not win you any friends and could make you the subject of unwanted attention; also, arguing or raising your voice in public is not the done thing. In a situation where you need to make a complaint, the most effective approach is to swallow your frustration and go out of your way to be reasonable while stating your case. **Drinking in public** is not acceptable away from restaurants, bars and street dining areas.

In relation to **body language**, note that touching someone's head, be they Muslim or otherwise, is to be avoided, as the head is considered sacred in Eastern culture. **Handshakes** are fairly commonplace when meeting someone; Muslims often follow this by touching the palm of the right hand to their own chest. Some Muslims may be reluctant to shake hands with the opposite sex, however, in which case a smile, nod and the right-hand-palm gesture mentioned above will suffice.

Finally, if using your hands while **eating**, note that the left hand is not used to bring food to your mouth, as in Islamic culture the left hand is used for cleaning yourself when going to the toilet. Likewise, it's best not to hand over cash or a gift or point with your left hand, as this could be considered impolite.

Visiting places of worship

It's not uncommon to see various temples and mosques happily existing side by side, each providing a social as well as a religious focal point for the corresponding community. Architectural traditions mean that the Chinese and Indian temples, built out of brick, have long outlasted the timber Malay mosque, and some are among the oldest structures you're likely to see in the region. Many of these building are worth a look around, and the good news is that they usually can be visited, though only at the largest temples might you get a little tour, courtesy of the caretaker.

Most **mosques** can be visited by non-Muslims at certain times, usually in the morning (it's always worth checking first with the local tourist office). Visitors should be appropriately dressed. For men and women this means long trousers and a shirt or top with sleeves coming down to the elbows (long sleeves are even better); women will also have to don a long cloak and headdress, which is provided by most mosques. You'll be required to **remove your shoes** before entering the mosque. No non-Muslim is allowed to enter a mosque during prayer time or go into the prayer hall at any time, although it's possible to stand just outside and look in.

Most Chinese and Hindu **temples** are open from early morning to early evening; devotees go in when they like, to make offerings or to pray – there are no set prayer times. At Hindu temples, as with mosques, you're expected to remove your shoes before entering. Some Chinese temples offer the bonus of weekly musical and theatrical **performances**, which can be enjoyed by visitors as well as locals.

Women travellers

Women who respect local customs and exercise common sense should have few problems travelling alone or with other women. A basic rule is not to do things you wouldn't do at home, so hitch-hiking, for example, is best avoided.

Some Western women have been known to find the atmosphere in largely Muslim areas, such as Kelantan or Terengganu, offputting. Arriving there from Thailand or from a more cosmopolitan part of Malaysia, some women travellers go out of their way to observe the dress code mentioned earlier, yet an unlucky few still find themselves being stared at or, worse, subjected to wolf-whistles or lewd gestures. This is all the more annoying if you spot local Chinese women wandering around in skimpy tops without anyone batting an eyelid. Though it's no consolation, it's worthwhile to note that the ground rules are different for locals; the Malay, Chinese and Indian communities, having lived together for generations, have an unspoken understanding as to how the respective communities can behave in public. Besides, Western movies and TV shows have led some locals to think that Western women are somehow "loose". Conversely, if you're a tourist of, say, Japanese or Indian extraction, you may find that the concessions local women enjoy automatically apply to you.

Attitudes to homosexuality

Though Malaysia's largest cities, plus Singapore, have long had a discreet gay scene, the public profile of gays and lesbians was until recently still summed up by the old "don't ask, don't tell" maxim. However, the advent of cyberspace has helped galvanize gay people in both countries, providing a virtual refuge within which to socialize. Hitherto strait-laced **Singapore** is now the home of an excellent gay news and lifestyle website (@www.fridae.com), permits exploration of gay themes in the arts and has even played host to gay rave parties which drew significant international participation. While things have relaxed slightly in **Malaysia** too, the environment there is always going to

---

The status of Malay women

Malay women are among the most emancipated in the Islamic world. They often attain prominent roles in business, academia and all other aspects of public life, and are not lacking in confidence or social skills, as a visit to any Malay-run shop, hotel or market stall will attest. Malay women are also very much the linchpin of the family, and husbands often give way to their wives in domestic matters.

The more conservative tide running through the Islamic world has had hardly any impact on this situation although many Malay women now wear **headscarfs** whereas, a generation or two ago, they were often content not to wear one. Sometimes, this indicates an acceptance of the trappings of religion, or possibly a desire to please parents, but nothing more – it's not unusual to see young Malay women at clubs partying away dressed in the unlikely combination of headscarf, skimpy T-shirt and tight jeans.

All of this is not to say that the outlook for Malay women is entirely rosy. Women's rights groups are concerned over amendments to Malaysia's Islamic family law, changes which they argue weaken the hand of Muslim women, and which were only passed in the face of considerable disquiet among the government's own women senators. At least the government has agreed to delay implementation of these new laws for further consultation.

be more conservative – amply illustrated by the fact that *Brokeback Mountain* failed to be screened north of the Causeway. That said, the Malaysian government does not, despite occasional gay-hostile reporting in the Malay-language press, have any obvious Islamically inspired appetite to clamp down on the limited gay nightlife that exists.

For all the general loosening up of the last ten or fifteen years, it's very much a case of two steps forward and one step back. Singapore's gay raves were, at the time of writing, increasingly being blocked by the authorities, who have also consistently declined to give official recognition to its gay lobby group, People Like Us (ⓦwww.plu.sg). In Malaysia, while a few gay-friendly bars continue to thrive, any gay campaigning that

exists tends to be channelled into the relatively uncontentious issue of HIV/AIDS.

Given the prevailing social and political climate, the best that Malaysia's and Singapore's gays and lesbians can presently hope for is to be accepted on sufferance. Archaic colonial-era laws prohibiting sex between men are unlikely to be repealed, let alone be debated in parliament; legal recognition of gay partnerships is a very distant prospect.

This mixed picture shouldn't deter gay visitors from getting to know and enjoy the local scene, such as it is. A small number of gay establishments are reviewed in this guide, but for listings of the latest venues in both Singapore and Malaysia, check out ⓦwww.fridae.com and the Bangkok-based ⓦwww.utopia-asia.com.

Outdoor pursuits

With some of the oldest tropical rainforest in the world and countless beaches and islands, trekking, snorkelling and scuba diving are common pursuits in Malaysia, while Singapore is only a short step away from these diversions. The more established resorts on the islands of Penang, Langkawi and Tioman offer more elaborate sports such as jet skiing and paragliding, while Cherating (the budget-travellers' centre on the east coast), with its exposed, windy bay, is a hot spot for windsurfers. Although all these places and activities are covered in more detail in the relevant chapters, below are some pointers to consider.

If you intend to take up any of these pursuits, check that your **insurance** policy covers you. For details of any problems you might encounter out in the Malaysian wilds, see "Health" (p.41).

Snorkelling, diving and windsurfing

The crystal-clear waters of Malaysia and its abundance of tropical fish and coral make **snorkelling** and **diving** a must for any underwater enthusiast. This is particularly true of Sabah's Pulau Sipadan and the Peninsula's east coast, where islands like Perhentian, Redang, Kapas and Tioman are turning their natural resources into a

lucrative business. Pulau Tioman offers the most choice for schools and dive sites – though some damage has already been caused to the coral reefs by over-eager visitors. However tempting the coral looks, you should never touch it as this can cause irreparable damage to the reefs and upset the delicate underwater ecosystem.

Most beachside guesthouses have snorkelling equipment for rent and rates are very reasonable at RM15–20 per day – check before you set out that the mask makes a secure seal against your face. Dive shops offer courses ranging from a five-day beginner's open-water course, typically around RM700, right through to the dive-master certificate, a fourteen-day course costing about RM1200. Make sure that the shop is registered with PADI (Professional Association of Diving Instructors) or SSI (Scuba Schools International); it's also a good idea to ascertain the size of the group, and that the instructor speaks good English. All equipment and tuition should be included in the price: it's worth checking the condition of the gear before signing on the dotted line.

In some popular snorkelling areas there are lanes for **motorboats** clearly marked with buoy lines – always stay on the correct side of the line or you risk a nasty accident. If you're not sure in which areas it is safe to swim or snorkel, always seek local advice.

Windsurfing has yet to take off in all but the most expensive resorts in Malaysia, with the notable exception of Cherating. Its large, open bay and shallow waters provide near-perfect conditions for the sport, and a few local entrepreneurs are catching on by renting out equipment – usually for around RM15 per hour – but don't expect expert coaching.

White-water rafting

White-water rafting has become a highly popular activity near the Sabah capital Kota Kinabalu. Two hours drive south lies Sungai Padas, a fast moving river which, at its northern end, runs through the spectacular Padas Gorge. Most tour operators provided a day's rafting for less than RM200; there's no need to bring specialist equipment as life jackets are provided. Expect, however, to get drenched and have an exhilarating time.

Trekking

The majority of **treks**, either on the Malay Peninsula or in Sarawak and Sabah, require some forethought and preparation. As well as the fierce sun, the tropical climate can unleash torrential rain without any warning, which rapidly affects the condition of trails or the height of a river – what started out as a ten-hour trip can end up taking twice as long. That said, the time of year is not a hugely significant factor when planning a trek. Although the **rainy season** (Nov–Feb) undoubtedly slows your progress on some of the trails, conditions are less humid then, and the parks and adventure tours not oversubscribed.

Most visitors trek in the large **national parks** to experience the remaining primary jungle and rainforest at first hand. Treks in the parks often require that you go in a group with a guide, although it's quite possible to

---

Check list of trekking equipment

The list below assumes you'll be staying in hostels and lodges. This may not always be possible and if you plan to camp, you'll need more equipment, not least your own tent (since most tours don't include camping equipment).

Essentials
Backpack
Sleeping bag
Mosquito net
Water bottle
Toiletries and toilet paper
Torch (and/or head torch)
Sewing kit
Pocket knife
Sunglasses (UV protective)
Sun block and lip balm
Insect repellent
Compass

Clothing and footwear
Breathable shirts/T-shirts
Lightweight, quick-drying trousers
Rainproof coat or poncho
Cotton hat with brim
Fleece jacket
Trekking boots
Cotton and woollen socks
Anti-leech socks (see p.44)

Other useful items
Plastic bag (to rainproof your pack)
Emergency snack food
Candles
Spare bootlaces
Small towel
Soap powder
Insulation mat
Large mug and spoon
Basic first-aid kit

go to most parks on your own and then join a group once there. Costs and conditions vary among the parks; each park account in the Guide contains full practical details. For inexperienced trekkers, Taman Negara is probably the best place to start, boasting the greatest variety of walks, while Bako National Park in southwest Sarawak offers fairly easy, day-long hikes amidst spectacular scenery. For the more experienced, other parks in Sarawak, especially Gunung Mulu, should offer sufficient challenges for most tastes; the largely inaccessible Endau-Rompin park in the south of Peninsular Malaysia is for serious expedition fiends only. Mount Kinabalu Park in Sabah is in a class of its own, the hike to the top of the mountain a demanding but highly rewarding combination of trekking and climbing. Tour operators in your home country (see the various "Getting there" sections), and those based in Kuala Lumpur, Kuching, Miri and Kota Kinabalu (listed throughout the Guide), are the best places for more information on conditions and options in the parks.

Shopping and souvenirs

Southeast Asia offers real shopping bargains, with electrical equipment, cameras, clothes, fabrics, tapes and CDs all selling at competitive prices. What's more, the region's ethnic diversity means you'll be spoilt for choice when it comes to souvenirs and handicrafts.

Unless you're in a department store, prices are negotiable, so be prepared to **haggle**. If you're planning to buy something pricey – a camera, say, or a stereo – it's a good idea to pay a visit to a fixed-price store to check the correct retail price; this way, you'll know if you're being ripped off. Asking for the "best price" is always a good start to negotiations; from there, it's a question of technique, but be realistic – shopkeepers will soon lose interest if you offer an unreasonably low price. Moving towards the door of the shop often pays dividends – it's surprising how often you'll be called back. If you do buy any electrical goods, make sure you get an international guarantee, and that it is endorsed by the shop.

Throughout the Guide, good buys and bargains are picked out and there are features on the best things to buy in specific regions. Malaysian pastimes throw up some interesting purchases: *wayang kulit* (shadow play) puppets, portraying characters from Hindu legend, are attractive and light to carry; equally colourful but completely impractical if you have to carry them around are the Malaysian kites, which can be several metres long. There's a round-up below of the other main souvenir items you might want to bring back.

In East Malaysia, the craft shops of Kota Kinabalu in Sabah have a wide variety of ethnic handicrafts native to the state. Most colourful of these are the *tudong duang*, a multicoloured food cover that looks more like a conical hat, and the painstakingly elaborate, beaded necklaces of the Runggus tribe. Also available are the bamboo, rattan and bark haversacks that locals use in the fields. For more unusual mementoes, look out for the *sumpitan*, a type of blowpipe, or the *sompoton*, a musical instrument consisting of eight bamboo pipes inserted into a gourd, which sounds like a harmonica. Kota Kinabalu's stalls and markets also sell Indonesian and Filipino products, some of which are worth a look, such as mats and wooden sculptures of animals and birds.

Sarawak's peoples also produce a wide range of handicrafts using raw materials from the forest, with designs that are inspired by animist beliefs. In longhouses, you may see blowpipes and tools being made. If you travel deep into the forested interior you might get a chance to meet the semi-nomadic Penan peoples, who are experts at firing metal and making *parangs* (long knives). Kuching is also renowned for its pottery, ceramic vases and bowls designed with Iban and Bidayuh native designs. If you travel a few miles out of town you can visit the pottery factories where craftsmen use traditional methods (see p.441).

Fabrics

The art of producing **batik** cloth originated in Indonesia, but today batik is available across Southeast Asia and supports a thriving industry in Malaysia. To make batik, hot wax is applied to a piece of cloth with either a pen or a copper stamp; when the cloth is dyed, the wax resists the dye and a pattern appears, a process that can be repeated many times to build up colours. Batik is used to create shirts, skirts, bags and hats, as well as traditional sarongs – rectangular lengths of cloth wrapped around the waist and legs to form a sort of skirt worn by both males and females. These start at around RM15 and are more expensive, depending on how complex and colourful the design is. Note that some vendors try to pass off printed cloth as batik. Make sure the brightness of the pattern is equal on both sides – if it's obviously lighter on one side, it is likely the cloth is just printed and not a true batik. In some of the Malaysian east-coast towns, little cottage industries have sprung up enabling tourists to make their own batik clothes; we've given details where relevant.

The exquisite style of fabric known as **songket** is a big step up in price from batik; made by hand-weaving gold and silver thread into plain cloth, *songket* is used to make sarongs, headscarves and the like. Expect to pay at least RM100 for a sarong-length of cloth, and RM300–400 for the most decorative pieces. The other thing you'll be able to buy in Indian enclaves everywhere is primary-coloured silk **sarees** – look in Little India in Singapore and the Chow Kit and Lebuh India enclaves in Kuala Lumpur for the best bargains. Prices start at around RM50.

Unique to Sarawak is *pua kumbu* (in Iban, "blanket"), a textile whose complex designs are created using the *ikat* method of weaving (see p.459 for more details). The cloth is best picked up in the bazaar towns or longhouses along the state's many rivers.

Metalwork and woodcarving

Of the wealth of metalwork on offer, **silverware** from Kelantan is among the finest and most intricately designed; it's commonly used to make earrings, brooches and pendants, as well as more substantial pieces. Selangor state is renowned for its **pewter** – a refined blend of tin, antimony and copper, which makes elegant vases, tankards and ornaments. Prices for pewter are fixed throughout Malaysia.

Over in Brunei, the speciality is **brassware** – cannons, kettles (called *kiri*) and gongs – decorated with elaborate Islamic motifs. Brunei brassware, however, is substantially more expensive than similarly sized Malaysian pewter articles.

Natural resources from the forest have traditionally been put to good use, with rattan, cane, wicker and bamboo used to

---

Duty-free goods

Duty-free products in Singapore include electronic and electrical goods, cosmetics, cameras, clocks, watches, jewellery, precious stones and metals. Malaysia has no duty on cameras, watches, cosmetics, perfumes or cigarettes. Pulau Labuan, Pulau Langkawi and Pulau Tioman are duty-free islands, which in practice means that goods there (including alcohol) can be twenty percent cheaper than on the Malaysian mainland, though it's not as though a particularly impressive range of products is on sale.

make baskets, bird cages, mats, hats and shoulder bags. **Woodcarving** skills, once employed to decorate the palaces and public buildings of the early sultans, are today used to make less exotic articles such as mirror frames. However, it's still possible to see one of the dynamic **statues** created by the Orang Asli, at cultural shows and festivals in Kuala Lumpur and Kuantan. As animists, Orang Asli artists draw upon the natural world – animals, trees, fish, as well as more abstract elements like fire and water – for their imagery. Of particular interest are the **carvings** of the Mah Meri of Selangor, which are improvisations on the theme of *moyang*, literally "ancestor", which is the generic name for all spirit images. Dozens of *moyang*, each representing a different spirit, are incorporated into the Meri's beliefs and inspire the wooden-face sculptures which they carve. Also popular are *topeng*, or face masks. Look out too, for the exquisite woodcarving made by Sarawak's indigenous tribespeoples, much of it representing slender rice-gods; you'll find this work sold along Kuching's waterfront.

Travellers with disabilities

Of the three countries, Singapore is the most accessible to travellers with disabilities; hefty tax incentives are provided for developers who include access features for the disabled in new buildings. In contrast, Malaysia and Brunei make few provisions if any.

Across the region, life is made a lot easier if you can afford the more upmarket hotels (which usually have specially adapted elevators) and to shell out for taxis and the odd domestic flight. Similarly, the more expensive international airlines tend to be better equipped to get you there in the first place: MAS, British Airways, KLM and Qantas all carry aisle wheelchairs and have at least one toilet adapted for disabled passengers. However, few, if any, tour operators offering holidays in the region accommodate the needs of those with disabilities.

Access is slowly improving in **Singapore** and most hotels now make some provision for disabled guests, though often there will only be one specially designed bedroom in an establishment – always call first for information, and book in plenty of time. Getting around the city is less straightforward: buses are not accessible to wheelchairs and there are no elevators in the MRT system. However, wheelchair-accessible Maxicab taxis can be booked through firms such as Citycab (ⓦwww.citycab.com.sg), and there are acoustic signals at street crossings.

In **Malaysia**, wheelchair-users will have a hard time negotiating the uneven pavements in most towns and cities, and will find it difficult to board buses, trains, ferries and the LRT metro system in Kuala Lumpur, none of which has been adapted for wheelchairs. Although most modern hotels in KL and Georgetown have good access, much budget accommodation is located up narrow stairways and presents difficulties for the disabled. One taxi operator in the KL area, E-Smartcab (see p.103), has vehicles fitted with **wheelchair** ramps; if requested, they can arrange airport pick-up.

Contacts for travellers with disabilities

Malaysian Confederation of the Disabled 931 Jalan 17/38 Petaling Jaya, ☏3/79562300 ⓔmymcd@tm.net.my. A member of Disabled Peoples International, working for equal opportunities for disabled people in Malaysia.
Malaysia Federation of the Deaf 9 Kompleks Perniagaan Sri Selangor Jalan San Peng, Kuala Lumpur, ☏3/2230690, ⓦwww.mfd.org.my. Member of the World Federation of the Deaf (WFD), an organization that works towards improving sign

language, access to education, information and services for deaf people.

Disabled People's Association Singapore
150A Pandan Gardens, #02-00, Day Care Centre, Ayer Rajah Community Center Singapore 609342 ☎68991220, 🌐www.dpa.org.sg. Non-profit

organization representing people with all types of disabilities. Produces *Access Singapore*, a thorough and informative brochure detailing amenities for the disabled across the city state (available via their website).

Directory

Barbers Barber shops (*kedai gunting rambut*) can be found in most towns of any size, and function like barbers anywhere else, though you may find Tamil-run places scarily attempting to snip nasal and ear hair, and many barbers throw in a post-haircut neck-and-shoulders massage (practically a pounding in some cases). In Malaysia, a haircut in an ordinary barber's costs around RM10; a small tip is appreciated.

Children Malaysia, Singapore and Brunei are very child-friendly countries in which to travel. Disposable nappies and powdered milk are easy to find (fresh milk is sold in supermarkets), and bland Chinese soups and rice dishes, or bakery fare, are ideal for systems unaccustomed to spicy food. Many restaurants and the slicker *kedai kopi*s have high chairs, though only upmarket hotels provide baby cots or a baby-sitting service. However, rooms in the cheaper hotels can usually be booked with an extra bed for little extra cost. Children under 12 get into many attractions for half-price, and enjoy discounts on buses and trains.

Electricity Mains voltage in Malaysia, Singapore and Brunei is 230 volts, so any equipment which uses 110 volts will need a converter. In all three countries, the plugs have three square prongs like British ones.

Laundry Most Malaysian towns have laundries (*dobi*), where you can have clothes washed cheaply and quickly, according to weight, picking them up later in the day or early the next day. In addition, an increasing number of budget hostels have washing machines available for guests for a small

charge. Small sachets of soap powder are readily available from general stores if you prefer to hand-wash. Dry-cleaning services are less common, though any hotel of a decent standard will be able to oblige.

Time zone For administrative convenience, Malaysia, Singapore and Brunei are all eight hours ahead of Universal Time (GMT in UK), all year, which means that Peninsular Malaysia and Singapore in effect have permanent Daylight Saving Time, as geographically speaking they ought to be seven hours ahead (as is Thailand). This close to the equator, you can rely on dawn being around 6.30am in the Peninsula and Singapore, dusk at around 7.30pm; in Borneo both happen roughly an hour earlier. Not taking into account daylight saving time elsewhere, the three countries are two hours behind Sydney, eight hours ahead of the UK and Ireland, 13 hours ahead of US Eastern Standard Time and 16 hours ahead of US Pacific Standard Time.

Work Opportunities for non-residents to find short-term employment in Malaysia and Singapore are few and far between. On an unofficial basis, helpers are often required in guesthouses; the wages you'll get for these tasks are low, but board and lodging are often included. On a more formal level, both Singapore and KL in particular have large expat communities who've secured work permits with the help of local employers. In Malaysia you can still expect an elevated expat salary, but this perk is increasingly rare in Singapore, where living standards are high enough as it is.

Guide

Guide

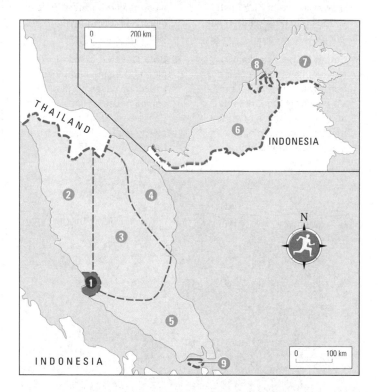

1

Kuala Lumpur
and around

CHAPTER 1 # Highlights

✳ **Islamic Arts Museum** One of the most sophisticated museums in the capital, documenting Muslim cultures through arts and crafts. See p.118

✳ **Petronas Towers** Come to gawp at these surprisingly serene twin structures, then browse in one of KL's best shopping malls, right beneath. See p.121

✳ **Eating** KL has excellent restaurants offering cuisine from around the world, but it's the street food, notably at Jalan Alor, that's often the most memorable dining experience. See p.129

✳ **Clubbing** KL is definitely Malaysia's party capital, home to some exceptional clubs that regularly draw big-name DJs. See p.138

✳ **Shopping** Whether you prefer the bright lights of the state-of-the-art malls or the bustle of the city's endless street markets and bazaars, KL is a city made for shopping. See p.143

✳ **Batu Caves** A blend of religion and theme park, these limestone caves north of the capital house a Hindu temple complex, and offer adventure caving explorations in a side cavern. See p.148

△ KL's skyline, dominated by the Menara KL and Petronas Towers

Kuala Lumpur and around

Founded in the mid-nineteenth century, **KUALA LUMPUR** – or **KL** as it's known to residents and visitors alike – has never had a coherent style, a situation only aggravated by the fact that the city has changed almost beyond recognition over the last thirty years. The first grand buildings around Merdeka Square, dating from the 1890s, were eccentric mishmashes themselves, the result of British engineers and architects fusing, or perhaps confusing, influences from around the empire and the world – Moghul, Malay, Moorish and Victorian elements jumbled together. Today, those colonial buildings that remain are overshadowed by stowering modern buildings – most notably the Petronas Towers – that wouldn't be out of place in Hong Kong or New York, reflecting the fact that this, the youngest of Southeast Asia's capitals, is also the most economically successful after Singapore. A sociable and safe place, KL has a real buzz to it, with good nightlife and enough interesting monuments to keep visitors busy for a few days at least. The ethnic and cultural mix of Malays, Chinese and Indians makes itself felt throughout: in conversations on the street, in the sheer variety of food for sale, and in the profusion of mosques, Buddhist temples and Hindu shrines.

Yet many visitors, as well as some Malaysians, have mixed feelings about KL. Malaysia's Prime Minister, Abdullah Badawi, has spoken of the country being able to afford first-class infrastructure while retaining a third-world mentality, lagging behind when it comes to understanding planning, maintenance and service. You'll see ample evidence of this in KL, where it's also clear that untrammelled development has given the city more than its share of featureless buildings and follies, terrible traffic snarl-ups and some urban poverty. For some locals, the capital is only worth tolerating as a place to acquire good money and experience before returning to a cherished provincial village; others say that KL has been their salvation, the only city in the country big and broad-minded enough to allow them to explore their true artistic or spiritual identity.

For the many travellers who visit both KL and Singapore, it's hard not to conclude that if only KL took some of Singapore's ability to organize systematically and transparently, while Singapore had some of KL's pleasingly organic qualities, and didn't take itself quite so seriously, then both cities would genuinely be enriched. As things stand, they remain rivals, competing in their own way for investment and recognition while grudgingly admiring each other,

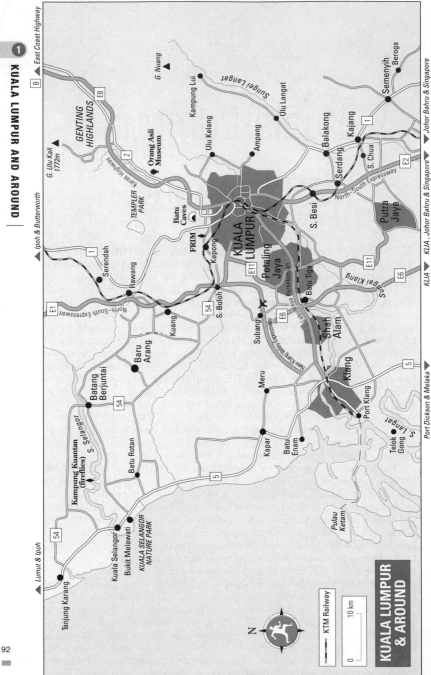

KUALA LUMPUR & AROUND

KTM Railway

0   10 km

N

East Coast Highway ▲

8 ▲

Ipoh & Butterworth ▲

Lumut & Ipoh ▲

Port Dickson & Melaka ▲

KLIA ▲   KLIA, Johor Bahru & Singapore ▲

Johor Bahru & Singapore ▲

tacitly recognizing that, as metropolises dedicated both to multiculturalism and conspicuous consumption, they are probably more like each other than anywhere else in the world.

A stay of a few days is enough to appreciate the best of KL's **attractions**, including the colonial core around **Merdeka Square** and the adjacent enclaves of **Chinatown** and **Little India**, plus, to the east, the restaurants, shops and nightlife of the so-called **Golden Triangle**, the modern sector of downtown KL. It can be equally rewarding just strolling and taking in KL's street life, in particular its boisterous **markets**, ranging from fish and produce markets stuffed into alleyways, to stalls selling cooked food of every shape and description, or inexpensive clothes and accessories. KL's hinterland isn't devoid of genuinely worthwhile sights either, among them the rugged limestone **Batu Caves**, which contain the country's most sacred Hindu shrine; showcasing the lifestyle and culture of the Peninsula's indigenous peoples; the **Forest Research Institute of Malaysia**, with a treetop canopy walkway for a quick taste of the rainforest; and **Kuala Selangor**, home to numerous fireflies that magically flash in unison.

Some history

KL was founded in 1857 when the ruler of Selangor State, Raja Abdullah, sent a party of Chinese prospectors to explore the area at the union of Gombak and Klang rivers. The aim was to find extractable deposits of **tin** – a metal that had already brought great wealth to the northern town of Ipoh. Though four-fifths of the party died from malaria within a month as they hacked through the dense jungle, the pioneers had their reward in the discovery of rich deposits 6km from the confluence, near **Ampang**, which grew into a staging post for Chinese labourers who arrived to work in the mines. Settlements at confluences were commonplace in the Peninsula, but uncommonly this particular village acquired the name Kuala Lumpur ("muddy confluence" in Malay) rather than, as convention dictated, being named after the lesser of the two fusing rivers (KL should, by rights, have been called Kuala Gombak)

The first Chinese *towkays* (merchants) set up two secret societies in Ampang, and fierce competition between them for the economic spoils soon developed. Until the 1870s, this rivalry effectively restrained the growth of Ampang (which, though it was the initial nucleus of KL, lies to the east of the present-day city). The arrival of an influential Chinese merchant, **Yap Ah Loy**, helped unify the divergent groups. Ah Loy's career symbolized the Eldorado lifestyle of KL's early years. Having left China with hardly a penny to his name, he had become KL's Kapitan Cina, or Chinese headman, by the time he was 30. He is reputed to have brought law and order to the frontier town by ruthlessly making an example of criminals, parading them through the streets on a first offence and, if they reoffended twice, executing them. He led the rebuilding of KL after it was razed during the Selangor Civil War (1867–73) and personally bore much of the cost for another rebuilding after the fire of 1881.

Until the 1880s, KL was little more than a shantytown of wooden huts precariously positioned on the edge of the river bank. Reaching the settlement was a tough job in itself. Small steamers could get within 30km of the town along Sungai Klang, but the rest of the trip was either by shallow boat or through the jungle. Getting to the tin mines was even worse. In his memoirs, *Footprints in Malaya*, the British Resident of Selangor State, **Frank Swettenham**, remembered it being "... a twelve-hour effort ... there was no discernible path and much of the distance we travelled up to our waist in water. Torn by thorns, poisoned by leech bites and stung by scores of blood-sucking insects, the struggle was one long misery." And yet people were drawn to the town like bees to honey. Early British investors, Malay farmers, Chinese *towkays* and workers – and, in the first years of the twentieth century, Indians from Tamil Nadu – all arrived looking for work, whether it was in the tin mines, on surrounding rubber estates or, later, on roads and railway construction.

Swettenham demolished most of KL's wooden huts and imported **British architects** from India to design solid, grand edifices, suitable for a new capital. He faced an initial setback in the devastating fire of 1881; nevertheless, by 1887 the city had five hundred brick buildings, and eight times that number by the early 1900s, by which time KL had also become capital of the Federated Malay States. He encouraged local businessmen to set up brickworks to the south of the city which later gave their name to the Brickfields district. The population, which grew from four thousand to forty thousand in the 1880s, was predominantly Chinese, and was further swollen by the arrival of the Tamils. The seeds of KL's staggering modern growth had been sown.

Development continued steadily in the first quarter of the twentieth century. Catastrophic floods in 1926 inspired a major engineering project which straightened the course of Sungai Klang, confining it within reinforced, raised banks. By the time the **Japanese invaded** the Peninsula in December 1941, overrunning the British army's positions with devastating speed, the commercial zone around Chinatown had grown to eclipse the original colonial area, and the *towkays*, enriched by the rubber boom, were already installed in opulent townhouses along today's Jalan Tuanku Abdul Rahman and Jalan Ampang. The city suffered little physical damage during World War II, but the Japanese inflicted terrible repression on their historic enemies, the Chinese (at least five thousand were killed in the first few weeks of the invasion alone), and sent thousands of Indians to Burma to build the infamous railway; very few of them survived. At the same time, the Japanese ingratiated themselves with some Malays, by suggesting that loyalty to the occupiers would be rewarded with independence after the war.

Following the **Japanese surrender** in September 1945, the British found they couldn't pick up where they had left off. Nationalist demands had replaced the Malays' former acceptance of the colonizers, while for some of the Chinese population, identification with Mao's revolution in 1949 led to a desire to see Malaya become a communist state. The alienation of many Chinese was heightened by Malay reluctance to allow the Chinese full rights of citizenship. The following period of unrest (1948–60), which stopped just short of civil war, became known as the **Emergency**. Although very few incidents occurred in KL itself during the period – the guerrillas were aware that they couldn't actually take the capital – the atmosphere in the city remained tense. The look of the city changed, too, during this postwar period, with the nineteenth-century buildings which had dominated KL – the Sultan Abdul Samad Building, the railway station and other government offices – gradually being overshadowed by a plethora of modern developments.

Malaysia was twelve years into its independence when simmering rivalries between the Malays and the Chinese spilled over into the May 1969 **race riots** in the city, in which at least two hundred people lost their lives. Thanks partly to pragmatism on both sides (and also to the imposition of a state of emergency), the city quickly managed to return to normal. In 1974, KL was plucked from the bosom of Selangor and designated **Wilayah Persekutuan** (Federal Territory), an administrative zone in its own right; **Shah Alam**, west along the Klang Valley, replaced KL as Selangor's capital.

After a period of consolidation, in the 1990s KL and the rest of the Klang Valley, including KL's satellite new town of **Petaling Jaya**, became a thriving conurbation. The decade, and the early part of the new millennium, saw the realization of several huge infrastructural ventures that are part and parcel of local life today – KL's international **airport** and the **Formula One race-track**, both at Sepang in the far south of Selangor; the downtown **Menara KL** communications tower; the **Petronas Towers** and the attendant **KLCC** shopping development, also downtown; **KL Sentral**, the new rail hub; and **Putrajaya**, the government's administrative hub (though KL remains the legislative centre and seat of parliament). Ironically, many of these prestige projects came onstream with the economy being buffeted by the Asian financial crisis of the late 1990s, and with the country in some turmoil over the **Anwar affair**, which several times saw security forces and pro-reform demonstrators out on the streets of KL, a city largely unused to public displays of dissent. The economy has been back on an even keel in recent years, however, and the transformation of swaths of KL and much of Selangor is once again burgeoning – so much so that concerns are now being voiced over the potential strain on water resources and other environmental repercussions.

Orientation and arrival

Many visitors find it hard to discern a distinct centre within Kuala Lumpur. Indeed, there are two hubs of activity: the **historical heart** of the city, centred on the now no-longer-muddy confluence, with Chinatown, the Jamek mosque, the old train station and Little India close by; and an altogether different modern core, the **Golden Triangle**, its focus being the upmarket hotels, restaurants and malls of **Bukit Bintang**, just 2km east of the old centre. Most points of interest lie within the loop technically known as Middle Ring Road I, comprising Jalan Tun Razak, Lebuhraya Mahameru, Jalan Damansara and so forth along its length. Inside this circuit are the **Lake Gardens** and their attendant museums and specialist parks, which lie just to the west of the historical zone, while on the northeastern fringe of the Golden Triangle lies the stretch of prime real estate known as **KLCC** (confusingly, standing for Kuala Lumpur City Centre), boasting the **Petronas Towers**.

Arrival

The only arrival points that aren't fairly central are KL's airports, in particular the massive Kuala Lumpur International Airport at Sepang, near the coast on the southern edge of Selangor. For more on using the various KL transport options mentioned below, see the section on p.101.

By air

KLIA, as KL's main airport is usually referred to (ⓦwww.klia.com.my), is divided into two separate terminal complexes, both reachable off the E6 highway. The **main terminal**, used by most airlines except budget carriers, is some 50km south of KL as the crow flies, and actually closer to Seremban than KL. The arrivals hall is broadly divided into international and domestic sections, the former containing a **tourist office** (daily 6am–midnight; ☎03/8776 5651) and 24-hour bureau de change operated by the RHB bank, with various ATMs and other exchange facilities dotted around both sections. There are also plenty of desks representing the main car rental outlets and KL's pricier hotels; the airport also has a five-star hotel of its own, the *Pan Pacific* (☎03/8787 3333, ⓦklairport .panpacific.com). Malaysia Airlines has a sales counter in arrivals.

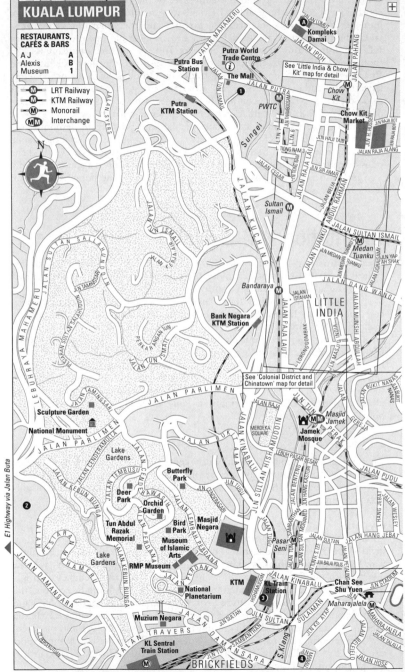

KUALA LUMPUR

RESTAURANTS, CAFÉS & BARS

A J	**A**
Alexis	**B**
Museum	**1**

Ⓜ	LRT Railway
Ⓜ	KTM Railway
Ⓜ	Monorail
ⓂⓂ	Interchange

N

See 'Little India & Chow Kit' map for detail

See 'Colonial District and Chinatown' map for detail

Sentul & E8 Highway ▲   ▲ Pekeliling Bus Station & Titiwangsa Stations

Kompleks Damai

Putra World Trade Centre
ⓘ
The Mall
Putra Bus Station

Putra KTM Station

Chow Kit

PWTC

Chow Kit Market

Sungei

JALAN IPOH

JALAN PAHANG

JALAN PUTRA

JALAN TUN ISMAIL

JALAN SYERS

JALAN SULTAN SALAHUDDIN

LEBUHRAYA MAHAMERU

PERSIARAN SULTAN SALAHUDDIN

JALAN TUN ISMAIL

JALAN KUCHING

Sultan Ismail
Ⓜ

Medan Tuanku
Ⓜ

JALAN SULTAN ISMAIL

JALAN TUANKU

Bandaraya
Ⓜ

LITTLE INDIA

JALAN DANG WANGI

JALAN RAJA LAUT

JALAN TUANKU ABDUL RAHMAN

Bank Negara KTM Station

JALAN PARLIMEN

JALAN PARLIMEN

Sculpture Garden
National Monument

Lake Gardens

Butterfly Park

Deer Park
Orchid Garden
Tun Abdul Razak Memorial

Bird Park

Masjid Negara

Museum of Islamic Arts

Lake Gardens

RMP Museum

National Planetarium

Muzium Negara

KTM

KL Sentral Train Station

JALAN DAMANSARA

JALAN TEMBUSU

JALAN CENDERAMULIA

JALAN KEBUN BUNGA

JALAN KEBUN BUNGA

JALAN PERDANA

JALAN PERDANA

PESIARAN MAHAMERU

JALAN TRAVERS

JALAN DAMANSARA

S. Klang

JALAN BUKIT AMAN

JALAN KINABALU

JALAN SULTAN HISHAMUDDIN

JALAN RAJA

MERDEKA SQUARE

Jamek Mosque
ⓂⓂ
Masjid Jamek

LEBUH PASAR BESAR

JALAN TUN PERAK

BUKIT NANAS

Pasar Seni
Ⓜ

JALAN PUDU

JALAN SULTAN

JALAN HANG JEBAT

Chan See Shu Yuen

Maharajalela
Ⓜ

KTM

KL Train Station

JLN SULTAN

BRICKFIELDS

◄ E1 Highway via Jalan Buta

▼ Bangsar, Midvalley Megamall & E1 Highway via E23

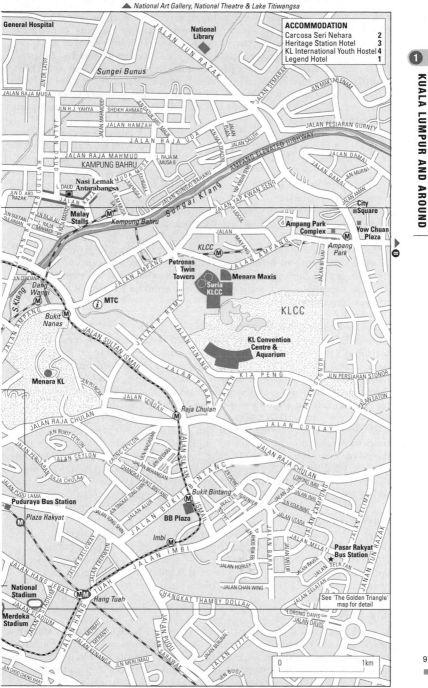

▲ National Art Gallery, National Theatre & Lake Titiwangsa

ACCOMMODATION

Carcosa Seri Nehara	2
Heritage Station Hotel	3
KL International Youth Hostel	4
Legend Hotel	1

General Hospital

National Library

JALAN TUN RAZAK

Sungei Bunus

JALAN RAJA MUDA

JLN H.J. YAHYA

JALAN MAHMOOD

SHEIKH AHMAD

JALAN DATUK ABD

JALAN TUAN

JLN MAKTAB ENAM

JALAN SEMARA

JALAN PESIARAN GURNEY

JALAN HAMZAH

JALAN DAMAI

JLN MURNI

JALAN RAJA UDA

JALAN SALEH

JALAN DAMAI

JALAN RAJA MAHMUD

RAJA M. MUDA MUSA 6

KAMPUNG BAHRU

JLN D. ABD RAZAK

Nasi Lemak Antarabangsa

L. DAUD

JALAN RAJA ALANG

JALAN SUNGAI BAHARU

AMPANG ELEVATED HIGHWAY

JLN YAP KWAN SENG

JALAN AMAN

City Square

JLN SULTAN SULAIMAN

JLN RAJA ALI

EL RAJA MAHADI

Malay Stalls

Ⓜ

Kampung Bahru

Sungai Klang

JALAN PUDU OL

Ampang Park Complex

Yow Chuan Plaza

JALAN

MAYANG

KLCC

Ⓜ

JALAN AMPANG

Ampang Park

Ⓜ

S. KLANG

JLN CENDANA

Dang Wangi

Ⓜ

JALAN AMPANG

Petronas Twin Towers

Suria KLCC

Menara Maxis

JALAN BINJAI

JLN PINANG

Bukit Nanas

Ⓜ

JALAN SULTAN ISMAIL

JALAN P RAMLEE

KLCC

JLN STONOR

JALAN PINANG

Menara KL

JALAN PUNCAK

JALAN PERAK

KL Convention Centre & Aquarium

KIA PENG

JLN PERSIARAN STONOR

JLN EATON

JALAN CONGAH

Raja Chulan

Ⓜ

JALAN PERAK

JALAN CONLAY

JALAN RAJA CHULAN

JLN BUKIT CEYLON

JALAN CEYLON

LORONG CEYLON

JLN NAGASARI

JALAN BEDARA

JALAN SULTAN

JALAN RAJA CHULAN

LORONG IMBI

JALAN JATI

JALAN INAI

JLN KEMUNING

JALAN KAMPUNG

JLN CELTAA

JALAN PERMAISURI RAJA CHULAN

CHANGKAT BUKIT BINTANG

JALAN BUKIT BINTANG

Bukit Bintang

Ⓜ

WALTER GRENIER

JALAN UTARA

JALAN MELATI

Pasar Rakyat Bus Station

Puduraya Bus Station

Ⓜ

Plaza Rakyat

JLN TINGKAT TONG SHIN

JALAN ALOR

BB Plaza

JALAN SULTAN ISMAIL

JLN KHOO TEK KTK

JALAN BARAT

JALAN MELUR

JALAN RANA

JALAN TUN RAZAK

JALAN YONG SHIN

JALAN BERIVEEN

Imbi

Ⓜ

JALAN IMBI

JALAN HORLEY

JALAN SELATAN

JALAN PUDU LAMA

JALAN GALLOWAY

JALAN HANG JEBAT

JALAN CHAN WING

See 'The Golden Triangle' map for detail

National Stadium

ⓂⓂ

Hang Tuah

CHANGKAT THAMBY DOLLAH

LORONG DAVIS

JALAN DAVIS

Merdeka Stadium

JLN STADIUM

JALAN HANG TUAH

JALAN MERBAU

JALAN MERANTI

JALAN PUDU

JALAN PUDU SARAWAK

JALAN BERUNAI

JALAN 1777C

JLN CHOO CHENG KHAY

JLN BUGIS

0   1km

MTC ⓘ

Ⓑ

▼ E2 Highway via E7 & E9

Various trains and buses connect the main terminal with other parts of the country. For many visitors heading to downtown KL, the most convenient option is to use one of the two light rail links (sometimes labelled ERL on route maps; @ www.kliaekspres.com) from level 1: either the **KLIA Ekspres** (daily 5am–midnight; every 15–20 min; 28min) or the fractionally slower **KLIA Transit** (every 30min 5.30am–midnight), which calls at three stops outside KL en route. Fares to KL on each service are RM35 one-way. Both services terminate at KL Sentral, the downtown rail hub; see below for onward transport details from KL Sentral.

Airport **coaches**, leaving from the main terminal's bus station (signed from level 2), are also convenient, if much slower than the trains. Among the KL services are one to the downtown hotels (hourly 7am–12.30am; 1hr 30min; one-way/return RM25/45) and another to Chan Sow Lin station (hourly 6.30am–9.30pm; 1hr; RM10/18) on the light rail transit network, with connections to Bukit Bintang, Chinatown and Little India. There are also Triton Express buses (☎03/8787 4258) to **Ipoh** (every 3hr 9am–midnight; 3hr 30min; RM42) and **Kuantan** (at 9am and 4pm; 6hr; RM35). For details of transport to Seremban, see p.357.

Taxis are a good option for leaving the airport, but to avoid getting ensnared in tricky bargaining with touts, buy a fixed-fare ticket for your journey from the counter near the arrivals exit. Fares vary according to your destination, and are quite reasonable; the hour-long drive to downtown KL costs RM70 for up to three passengers.

The low-cost-carrier terminal

Though KLIA's main terminal is far from close to capacity, a **low-cost-carrier terminal** (@ www.klia.com.my/LCCTerminal), used mainly by AirAsia, has been created 20km south of the main terminal. Facilities here are much more limited than at the main terminal, but include a couple of ATMs and a bureau de change. As at the main terminal, there are a multitude of options for onward travel, including the **Skybus** service to KL Sentral (every 15–30min 7.15am–12.30am; 1hr 15min; RM9; @ www.skybus.com.my) and **airport coaches** to Chan Sow Lin station (every 45min 5am–12.30am; RM10; 1hr). There are also buses to Nilai station (for Komuter trains; RM1.50) and to Salak Tinggi (for the KLIA Transit service; RM2 to the station, then RM12.50 to KL Sentral). **Taxis** to KL start at RM60 depending on the type of vehicle (buy a ticket from the taxi counter). Shuttle buses connect the two airport terminals (every 20min 6am–12.30am; RM1.50); if you want to reach Seremban, see p.357.

Subang airport

Once KL's main air terminal, **Subang airport** is now used only by a few flights to and from resort locations, operated by Berjaya Air. The airport is some 20km due west of downtown KL; bus #47 heads to Chinatown from here, or you could get a taxi into the city (around RM40) or to the Kelana Jaya LRT terminus, which is only a couple of kilometres away.

By train

Located just to the southwest of downtown KL, **KL Sentral station** (☎03/2279 8699) is the hub for the Peninsula's rail services – not just intercity trains to Singapore, Kelantan and Thailand, but also the two local Komuter lines (see p.103) and the two KLIA light rail links. It's also a stop on the Kelana Jaya–Gombak **LRT** service (see p.103), making it easy to get to Chinatown

Destinations in the Peninsula are easily reached by bus or train, but low-cost flights do speed up the journey to Kota Bharu or Kuala Terengganu. **Driving** around the Peninsula is quite feasible (see p.56 for car-rental agencies); the main hurdle is how to reach the highways from downtown KL, with its confusing road signage, one-way systems and countless express bypasses. The **E1** (North–South Expressway northbound) is signed from Jalan Duta, which branches off Middle Ring Road I west of the Lake Gardens; the **E2** (North–South Expressway southbound) starts at Sungei Besi 2km south of Chinatown, and can be reached by following signs along Jalan Tun Razak and the southern stretch of Middle Ring Road I. For the **E8** (linked to the **East Coast Highway** to Kuantan, and **Route 8** into the interior), get onto Jalan Tun Razak (or use Jalan Raja Laut if starting from Chinatown) and head northwest to Jalan Ipoh; proceed up this for a short distance, then turn right onto Jalan Sentul and follow signs for the highway.

By bus or long-distance taxi

Most long-distance buses and taxis leave from the **Puduraya bus station**. From street level, various staircases lead up to the main concourse where at least seventy bus companies are represented. Most routes are served by more than one operator, meaning there are several departures a day for most destinations. Also split into two groups are the 23 flights of steps leading down to the bus bays on the ground floor; make sure to ask which bay your bus leaves from. **Long-distance taxis** leave from the car parks on the upper floors; fares per vehicle are around RM200 to Cameron Highlands, RM300 to Kuala Tahan (the main Taman Negara entrance) and RM320 to Kota Bharu or Kuala Terengganu.

Some buses to **Kuantan** leave from Puduraya, but others, along with buses to the **interior**, use the small **Pekeliling bus station**, very close to Titiwangsa station on the Monorail and LRT. For buses to coastal **Kelantan** and **Terengganu** (including Kota Bharu and Kuala Terengganu), as well as yet more services to Kuantan, go to the **Putra bus station**, by the Putra World Trade Centre (and a short walk from the PWTC LRT or the KTM Putra station). For buses west to Port Klang, Klang and Shah Alam, use the **Klang bus station** in Chinatown. While there are plenty of buses from Puduraya to Singapore, some luxury services leave from the **Pasar Rakyat bus station** and from the **old railway station**.

As usual, there are no central enquiry numbers for the bus stations; to buy tickets, it's best to turn up and speak to the various bus companies directly. Numbers for a few of the larger companies are listed on p.145.

By air

Malaysia Airlines (MAS; ☎1300/883000, ⊛www.mas.com.my) has a ticket office, keeping extended hours, at KL Sentral (near the KLIA Express departure area; ☎03/2272 4248; daily 4.30am–midnight). You can also buy tickets at the MAS Building, Jalan Sultan Ismail (☎03/2165 5319). **AirAsia** (☎1300/889933, ⊛www.airasia.com.my) also has an office at KL Sentral (near *McDonalds*; ☎03/2274 2714; daily 8am–10pm). **Berjaya Air** is on level 6 of KL Plaza, Bukit Bintang (☎03/2145 2828, ⊛www.berjaya-air.com). International airlines are listed on p.145. For **flight information**, check ⊛www.klia.com.my, or call ☎03/8776 2000 (KLIA main terminal), ☎03/8777 6777 (KLIA low-cost-carrier terminal, for AirAsia) or ☎03/7846 1833 (Subang).

By train and ferry

For timetables and ticket reservations for **express trains** to Singapore, Tumpat (via the interior) and Hat Yai in Thailand (via Butterworth and the west coast), call KTM on ☎03/2267 1200, or check ⊛www.ktmb.com.my. The only **ferries** from the vicinity of KL are those to Tanjung Balai in Sumatra, which sail from Port Klang (see p.154), reachable by Komuter train.

(use the Pasar Seni stop), Little India (Masjid Jamek or Bandaraya stations) and KLCC (KLCC station). KL's **Monorail** service begins at KL Sentral but, in just one of many little planning lapses that you'll encounter in the city, the station is a poorly signposted 200m away in Brickfields (see map, p.128) – to reach it, descend to street level on the southeast side of KL Sentral (where a handful of buses leave, none of much use for downtown), then wander through the informal market here across to Jalan Tun Sambanthan.

Taxis queue up at the rank on the southern side of the station (follow the signs for feeder buses) and can also be flagged down on Jalan Tun Sambanthan. You can also use the taxi rank on the northern side of KL Sentral, where the *Hilton* and *Meridien* hotels are located, but fares from here are fixed according to your destination (buy a ticket from the counter just inside the exit) and are several ringgit higher than the metered fare would be. Note that there's no pedestrian access to Jalan Travers on the north side of the station, which rules out walking the 2km to Chinatown – even if you manage to descend to Jalan Travers, you'll find the trek northeast is along frenetic highways with few pedestrian crossings.

By bus or taxi

KL's main **bus station** is **Puduraya**, at the base of an undistinguished concrete lump on Jalan Pudu, just to the east of Chinatown. On the main passenger level of the station (where the ticket booths are located), you'll find a moneychanger (hidden amid the kiosks at the opposite end from the food stalls) and a couple of ATMs, with a bank upstairs. Close to the back of the station is the Plaza Rakyat LRT station (an unsigned exit at the back of the Puduraya's passenger concourse gives onto a lane leading to the LRT). There are several backpacker hostels opposite and around the station, while Chinatown is within easy walking distance, and the guesthouses of Tengkat Tong Shin are also not hard to reach on foot. Alternatively, for Bukit Bintang, take bus #29, which heads east along Jalan Pudu and Jalan Imbi, then north up Jalan Sultan Ismail to the Lot 10 Shopping Centre.

Buses from the east coast (Kelantan and Terengganu, especially) end up at **Putra bus station**, a smaller, more modern terminus to the northwest of the city centre, close to the Putra World Trade Centre. Around 500m east is the PWTC LRT station. Fractionally closer to the south is Putra station, served by Komuter trains to the old Kuala Lumpur station (on the edge of Chinatown) and KL Sentral. About 1km northeast of the Putra bus station is **Pekeliling bus station** on Jalan Tun Razak, used by buses from the interior and some services from Kuantan. Conveniently, the separate Titiwangsa stations on the Monorail and the LRT are very close at hand, just to the north.

Some buses from Singapore use the **Pasar Rakyat bus station**, in a nondescript area close to the eastern section of Jalan Tun Razak. Head 500m north up any of the quiet lanes here and you're on the eastern section of Jalan Bukit Bintang, with the bright lights of Bukit Bintang 1km uphill to the west; taxis aren't hard to find at the bus station itself, while bus #4B is also available, travelling up Jalan Tun Razak to KLCC. Back in Chinatown, the **Klang bus station**, at the south end of Jalan Sultan Mohammed is used by Klang Valley buses to and from Port Klang, Klang and Shah Alam; virtually next door is an LRT stop, Pasar Seni.

Finally, most **long-distance taxis** arrive at the bus stations: most end up on the upper floors of Puduraya bus station, though a few use Putra or Pekeliling stations depending on where they started out.

Information and city transport

Of KL's three tourist offices, the biggest is the **Malaysia Tourism Centre** at 109 Jalan Ampang (MTC; daily 7am–10pm; ☎03/2164 3929, ⓦwww.mtc .gov.my), not far from the Bukit Nanas Monorail stop; you can also get here on bus #23, #24a, #176 or #182 from Jalan Hang Lekir in Chinatown. Like its two smaller counterparts, which are located at **KL Sentral** (hidden away amid the shops on level 1; daily 9am–6pm; ☎03/2272 5823) and at the **Putra World Trade Centre** (level 2; Mon–Fri 9am–6pm; ☎03/2615 8450), the MTC is mainly of use for leaflets and free city **maps**, though staff at all three offices can offer good general advice. The MTC also houses exchange facilities and payphones, plus a **travel agent** (☎2163 0162) which can arrange trips to Taman Negara and other attractions.

If you want to keep an ear to the ground on happenings around town then, besides scanning the newspapers, you should seek out the **listings** magazine *Klue* (ⓦwww.klue.com.my). Also worth a look is ⓦwww.visionkl.com, a handy repository of sights, restaurants, clubs and events, including a slew of useful phone numbers. The most detailed **map** of the city and the surrounding conurbation, handy for drivers, is the one-hundred-page *Kuala Lumpur & Klang Valley Street Atlas*, published by World Express Mapping and available at many bookshops (RM24).

One thing to bear in mind is that most literature about KL tends to go out-of-date fairly quickly, so don't be surprised if places have moved, or if roads and buildings have sprung into existence or ceased to be. Sometimes the material simply isn't quite right to start with, as is the case with a lot of the transport maps in circulation.

City transport

Downtown KL isn't that large, so it's tempting to do a lot of exploration **on foot**, but many pedestrians soon find themselves wilting thanks to the combined effects of humidity and traffic fumes. Furthermore, the narrow roads in the old centre are relentlessly jammed with slow-moving cars, while in the newer parts of town, and where roads have been upgraded to highways, it's the

---

Touch 'n Go cards

With KL only toddling towards having a properly integrated transport system, you'll find you need to line up to buy a ticket every time you change from one service to another – if you transfer from the LRT to the Monorail, for example. It soon becomes a drag, one which can only be avoided by having a stored-value **Touch 'n Go card** (ⓦwww.touchngo.com.my), worthwhile if you're spending a lot of time in KL or driving around the Peninsula. Originally introduced to ease toll payments on the Peninsula's privatized highways, the cards are accepted at LRT, Monorail and KTM stations (look for ticket gates bearing the card's logo) and by machines on some buses; simply press the card against the sensor to have the fare deducted. The card itself costs RM10 and is available in several denominations starting from a stored value of RM20. The snag is that only a few stations sell the cards – at the time of writing, KL Sentral, KLCC, Masjid Jamek and KTM's Mid Valley – and these are also the only stations where you can load the cards with new credit. It's also possible to add credit at a handful of small outlets (the odd convenience store, pharmacy, etc – see the website for details), at ATMs (but you'll need a Malaysian bank card) and at highway toll points.

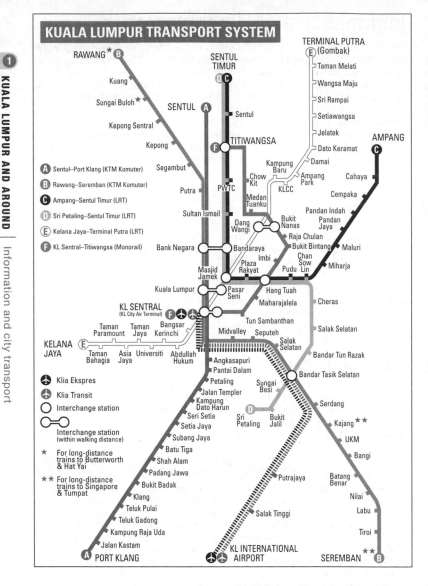

KUALA LUMPUR TRANSPORT SYSTEM

- **A** Sentul–Port Klang (KTM Komuter)
- **B** Rawang–Seremban (KTM Komuter)
- **C** Ampang–Sentul Timur (LRT)
- **D** Sri Petaling–Sentul Timur (LRT)
- **E** Kelana Jaya–Terminal Putra (LRT)
- **F** KL Sentral–Titiwangsa (Monorail)

- Klia Ekspres
- Klia Transit
- ○ Interchange station
- Interchange station (within walking distance)
- ★ For long-distance trains to Butterworth & Hat Yai
- ★★ For long-distance trains to Singapore & Tumpat

sheer volume and pace of the traffic that can wear you down, as you wander around in search of a pedestrian crossing or an opportunity to race across.

Thankfully, the two light rail transit (LRT) lines and the Monorail, together with the Komuter train services and taxis, are reasonably efficient and inexpensive. However, the various transport lines, having been created piecemeal, don't coordinate well with one another – interchanges sometimes involve inconvenient walks, and network-wide tickets don't exist. These issues are slowly being addressed by a new management body, **RapidKL** (☏1800/388 228,

@ www.rapidkl.com.my), whose website includes network maps, details of monthly LRT/bus passes and service announcements, though it doesn't have detailed information on the Monorail or KTM trains.

The LRT and the Monorail

The **Light Rail Transit** (**LRT**; every 5–10min 6am–midnight, or until 11.30pm on Sun) is a metro network comprising two, mostly elevated, lines, with a convenient central **interchange** at Masjid Jamek near Little India. The **Kelana Jaya** line (often known by its old name, **Putra**), is the more useful of the two, passing through KL Sentral, Chinatown and the old colonial district (Pasar Seni/Masjid Jamek stations) and KLCC. The other line, officially **Ampang and Sri Petaling** (its old name, **Star**, is still used), has two branches which join at Chan Sow Lin station and continue up to Sentul Timur in the north of the city. For visitors, it's mainly of use for travel between Chinatown (Plaza Rakyat station) and Little India (Masjid Jamek or Bandaraya stations) and Chow Kit Market (Sultan Ismail station). **Fares** start at around RM1 and climb in small steps up to RM2.50.

The LRT is complemented by the **Monorail** (every 5–10min 6am–midnight; @ www.monorail.com.my), an elevated rail system with a noticable tilt as it cambers around bends, and each station is shamelessly associated with a different commercial sponsor. From its KL Sentral terminus (200m from the KL Sentral rail hub), the line at first heads east, through Brickfields and the southern edge of Chinatown, then swings north and west through Bukit Bintang and along Jalan Sultan Ismail, nearly reaching Jalan TAR before heading north through Chow Kit to terminate at Titiwangsa station on Jalan Tun Razak. There are interchanges with the LRT at Bukit Nanas (requiring a five-minute walk to Dang Wangi station) and at Hang Tuah. **Fares** range from RM1.20 for a trip of a couple of stops, up to RM2.50 to ride the line end-to-end.

The LRT and Monorail together take care of most journeys visitors need to make within downtown KL, with one very notable exception, namely Chinatown/Masjid Jamek to Bukit Bintang The Monorail just about covers this, if you're prepared to trudge south to Maharajalela station; otherwise, you could brave KL's bus system (see p.104 for details of this journey) or steel your lungs for the hike east along busy Jalan Pudu and Jalan Bukit Bintang.

Komuter trains

Modern **Komuter** trains, run by national rail operator KTM (☎ 03/2267 1200, @ www.ktmb.com.my) travel on two lines – one from Rawang, northwest of KL, southeast to Seremban, the capital of Negeri Sembilan, and the other from the northern suburb of Sentul west to Port Klang. Both connect at four downtown stations, namely Putra, near the Putra World Trade Centre; Bank Negara, near Little India; the old Kuala Lumpur train station, in the colonial district; and KL Sentral. The trains run at every fifteen to twenty minutes during the day, but only every half hour after 8pm. **Tickets** (RM1–8), can be purchased from the stations and automatic machines at the stops; return tickets cost double the one-way fare. Weekly and monthly passes for designated journeys are also available.

Buses

Though KL's **bus** services are pretty comprehensive, most visitors avoid them as they seem impossible to fathom. The small grid of streets around Puduraya and Central Market is very much the **hub** of the network, but there are no proper terminuses – you just have to check out the numerous bus stops, which don't always display the numbers of buses which pass by. Buildings with key stops close by, including the Sinarkota Building, the Kotaraya Building and the Bangkok Bank, appear on the Chinatown map on p.111.

A handful of companies operate city buses, notably RapidKL and Metrobus (☎03/5635 7897). Note that the bus network is gradually being revamped, so you may want to double-check routes and numbers with one of the bus companies or a tourist office before travelling. Two routes within downtown KL are useful as they cover the **Chinatown–Bukit Bintang** journey, namely #29 (from Pasar Seni east along Jalan Pudu and Jalan Imbi, then north up Jalan Sultan Ismail) and the City Shuttle #113 (Pasir Seni northeast up Jalan Raja Chulan, then south along Jalan Sultan Ismail). Also useful are a couple of other City Shuttles: #110 from KL Sentral to the Central Market; and #115 from KL Sentral to the Lake Gardens, via the National Museum and Masjid Negara.

Fares are very low; on most RapidKL buses, they start at RM1 and climb in three steps to RM2.50, which would cover a journey of nearly 20km from downtown. On City Shuttles, however, you buy a day ticket (RM2) which allows unlimited travel on any shuttle. On some buses you pay the conductor; on others you pay the driver or drop the money into a machine close to the driver (in which case change isn't given). Services start up around 6am and begin winding down from 10pm onwards. Given KL's frequent traffic snarl-ups, do allow plenty of time for your journey, particularly if you're starting out in Chinatown.

Finally, at the time of writing, plans were being finalized to operate open-top double-decker tourist buses, making a circuit of certain hotels and sights; check with any of the tourist offices for details.

Taxis

KL taxis come in several **classes**. Ordinary taxis are painted in various colours, but always display the words "Teksi Bermeter" on a sign on the roof; slightly smarter vehicles, usually in yellow, display "Teksi Premier" instead. At night, these roof signs are lit to indicate the taxi is available (though some drivers have a habit of leaving the light on even when they already have a passenger). A third class of taxis comprises the smart, high-side Enviro 2000 vehicles, powered by natural gas.

Fares are low: in ordinary taxis the flagfall is RM2, and the tariff is 10 sen for every 150m travelled. This translates into just RM4 for a typical journey between Bukit Bintang and Chinatown, or RM6 for Bukit Bintang to KL Sentral, or Chinatown to KLCC. Teksi Premier and Enviro 2000 vehicles have somewhat higher charges: a flagfall of RM3 or RM4, and 20 sen for every 150m travelled. While it's compulsory for fare **meters** to be used, some drivers try to flout the rule by asking a flat fee, so it's worth knowing how much your trip should cost (ask beforehand at your accommodation). If you don't want to get into bargaining with the driver, either insist the meter be used or wait for another taxi.

Both ordinary taxis and the premier-class cars are easily flagged down in the street, other than during heavy rain when, understandably, demand for taxis soars. Enviro 2000 vehicles tend to cluster around upmarket hotels. There are numerous taxi **ranks** around the city, usually situated beside bus stops and outside shopping malls. It's a good idea to wait on the correct side of the road for the direction you want to head in, since some drivers refuse to turn their cab round. Some drivers don't speak much English, so it's a good idea to have the address you want written down in Malay, or to have a map handy, or to mention a well-known landmark near where you want to head.

There are plenty of companies you can call to book a taxi, among them Comfort Taxi (☎03/2692 2525), Radio Teksi (☎03/9221 7600), Supercab

(☎03/2095 3399) and SW Taxis (☎03/2693 6211); you'll be charged an extra couple of ringgit for the booking. E-Smartcab has premier taxis fitted with **wheelchair** ramps (☎5192 2773 or 5192 1775, Ⓦwww.cabcharge.com.my).

Accommodation

There's a wide range of accommodation available in KL, and though rates are higher here than anywhere else in the country, they remain very reasonable, thanks to an oversupply of rooms at most times of year. As elsewhere in Malaysia, many hotels offer **promotional rates** – which may in fact apply more often than their official rates, and which are well worth asking about (or checking on their websites). Additionally, a few places have discounts outside weekends (price codes below correspond to weekend rates). It's only during peak periods – the tourism high season (see below), key festivals and events, and the school holidays that special deals can be tricky to come by; during the Formula One weekend, many hotels actually push up their rates. Even without a discount, it's usually not hard to find a good double in a guesthouse with shared facilities for RM60 a night, while a decent mid-range hotel room can be had for around RM150; anything costing above RM250 a night will certainly be pretty luxurious.

Historically, it's been **Chinatown**, very close to Puduraya bus station, that's been the mecca for KL's budget travellers. The area still boasts the old-fashioned colour – sometimes verging on chaos – that epitomizes many Southeast Asian cities, as well as plenty of hostels, plus several inexpensive and mid-range hotels and lodgings. These days, however, it's in danger of being usurped as a travellers' haunt by the more sedate, and much more modern, **Bukit Bintang**, fifteen minutes' walk to the east. Here, just a few streets from the fancy hotels and malls which dominate the area, and close to the celebrated Chinese food stalls of Jalan Alor, you'll find plenty of excellent guesthouses on and around Tengkat Tong Shin. Though slightly more expensive than the hostels of Chinatown, these guesthouses are better value generally – much less cramped and noisy, with modern facilities, pleasant lounges and a relaxed feel.

Slightly further afield, there are more upscale hotels to be found along **Jalan Sultan Ismail** and the northern end of **Jalan Ampang**, which, together with Bukit Bintang, form part of KL's so-called **Golden Triangle**. All other parts of KL pale as regards accommodation, though **Little India** and nearby **Chow Kit**, linked by the fiendishly busy **Jalan Tuanku Abdul Rahman**, feature a number of mid-range hotels, while **Brickfields**, convenient for KL Sentral, has a couple of places worth considering, though some hotels here verge on seedy.

During busy periods – July, August, November and December – it's advisable to **book** your accommodation in advance. If you prefer to book **online**, try Ⓦwww.hostelworld.com or Ⓦwww.hostelz.com for up-to-date lists of hostels and guesthouses, or the many KL hotel-booking websites which can be found on the Net – though note that it's always worth comparing these websites' deals with any promotional rate the hotel may be offering.

Chinatown and around

Old-style Chinese flophouses are now rather scarce in Chinatown, having been edged out by backpacker-oriented places, not to mention hotels. The most mundane places tend to be clustered around the bus station; if it's inexpensive accommodation you're after, you'd do better to pay a little bit more to stay in one of the establishments close to the popular Petaling Street Market. The places reviewed below appear on the map on p.111, except for the *International Youth Hostel* and the *Heritage Station Hotel*, for which see the map on pp.96–97.

Hostels and guesthouses

Anuja Backpackers Inn First to third floors, 28 Jalan Pudu ☎03/2026 6479, ✉anujainn@sgsmc .com. Boxy and rather bare rooms, though reasonably kept. Some rooms, including the dorms, have a/c, but all share facilities. Internet access is available, as are banana-leaf-style meals from their own restaurant. Dorms RM10, ❷

Backpackers Travellers Inn Second floor, 60b Jalan Sultan ☎03/2078 2473, ⓦwww .backpackerskl.com. Narrow corridors lined with plain rooms with louvred windows. Some rooms and the three eight-bed dorms have a/c; attached bathrooms also available with some rooms. The chief attractions are the cool rooftop bar with affordable beers, and the fact that the management can organize a variety of trips – Taman Negara, the Kuala Selangor fireflies and the Kuala Gandah elephant sanctuary being the most obvious prospects. Established and popular. Dorm beds RM10, ❷

Backpackers Travellers Lodge First floor, 158 Jalan Tun H.S. Lee ☎03/2031 0889, ☏2078 1128. Unadorned, somewhat cell-like rooms and dorms with tiled floors and small shared bathrooms. A few rooms have a/c and en-suite facilities. Simple breakfasts of coffee or tea and toast or sandwiches can be ordered. Internet access. Dorm beds RM10, ❷

Kameleon Travellers Lodge 35–37 Jalan Pudu Lama ☎03/2070 7770, ✉kameleontravellerslodge .hotmail.com. Pleasant Indian-run guesthouse with simple rooms, sharing facilities and the option of a/c in a few doubles. Internet access is available and there's a small terrace with cane furniture to sit out on. A better choice than many of the places on Jalan Pudu itself. Dorms RM10, ❷

KL City Lodge 16 Jalan Pudu ☎03/2070 5275, ☏2031 3725. Another fairly basic affair, with the usual mix of fan and a/c rooms, some en suite, plus a laundry service and Internet access, but no dorms. ❷

KL International Youth Hostel Jalan Manau, off Jalan Kampung Atap ☎03/2273 6870, ☏2274 1115. Dorms with four, six or ten beds, plus a café, TV lounge and a laundry service. The chief drawback is the location: visiting Jalan Petaling from here means braving the multi-lane traffic of Jalan Maharajalela, though at least the monorail station is within easy reach. ❶

Pudu Hostel Third floor, Wisma Lai Choon, 10 Jalan Pudu ☎03/2078 9600, ⓦwww.puduhostel.com.

It's prominently signed at the start of Jalan Pudu, but this place is a bit of a let-down, as institutional as hostels get, and just a little tatty throughout. Still, they do have Net access, and pool and snooker tables. Dorms RM12, ❷

Red Dragon Hostel 80 Jalan Sultan ☎03/2078 9366, ⓦwww.hostelreddragon.com. A substantial affair, and thus inevitably institutional though well run, with over thirty rooms and three dorms (all with a/c), an enormous lounge and a restaurant and café open to the hubbub of Jalan Sultan. A few en-suite rooms are available for a premium of RM20. Internet access and bigscreen TV available. Dorms RM15, ❷

Le Village Guesthouse 99a Jalan Tun H.S. Lee ☎013/355 0235. The funky abstract paintings in the entrance stairway set the tone at this homely place, housed in an attractive early twentieth-century shophouse dominated by the *Kamal Curry House*. Inside there's more artwork on multicoloured walls, and simple rooms and three-bed dorms with sliding doors, all set around a sitting area with rattan furniture and satellite TV. All rooms have fan (the windowless ones can be still be stuffy, though) and share facilities; there's also a simple kitchen with fridge and stove. Dorms RM12, ❷

YWCA 12 Jalan Hang Jebat ☎03/2070 1623, ☏2031 7753. Safely removed from the noise of Chinatown, the well-kept *YWCA* lets its rooms only to women, couples and families. All rooms have fan and share facilities. ❸

Hotels

Ancasa Jalan Tun Tan Cheng Lock ☎03/2026 6060, ⓦwww.udaancasa.com. Slick, well-run hotel with decent-sized and comfortably furnished rooms, boasting satellite TV. There's also a pricey spa for massages, aromatherapy and other treatments, plus a decent restaurant and a bar, though breakfast isn't included in the basic rate (it can be added for around RM15 extra per day). Rates rise by ten percent at weekends. ❻

Chinatown Inn 52–54 Jalan Petaling ☎03/2070 4008, ⓦwww.chinatowninn.com. Reached by an unobtrusive doorway behind the market stalls, this is a little haven in the heart of Chinatown. The rooms are bland, but spacious enough; all have TV and attached bathroom, and most have a/c – which is just as well, as many are windowless. Internet access available. RM20 discounts on fan rooms outside weekends. ❹

China Town 2 70–72 Jalan Petaling ☏03/2072 9933, ⓦwww.hotelchinatown2.com. Sister hotel to the *Chinatown Inn*, and pretty much identical in concept and feel, with rooms (including singles and some dorms) crammed deep into the building, which runs all the way to Jalan Sultan. Internet access. Dorms from RM20, ❹

Heritage Station Kuala Lumpur Station, Jalan Sultan Hishamuddin ☏03/2272 1688, ⓦwww .heritagehotelmalaysia.com. The city's finest hotel during the colonial era, now trading on past glories and beset by a sleepy ennui. The big attraction is, of course, the building itself, though it's not nearly as atmospheric as you might hope; the rooms are very spacious but blandly furnished. Amenities are limited to a simple restaurant and a humdrum lounge. Rate includes breakfast. ❺

Katari 38 Jalan Pudu ☏03/2031 7777, ⓦwww .katari.com.my. A compact, modern hotel with a/c, en-suite rooms with TV. Though on the small side, the rooms are well kept, and the rate includes breakfast. ❺

Lok Ann 113a Jalan Petaling ☏03/2078 9544. Aging Chinese hotel with simple a/c, en-suite rooms, though no TV. ❷

🏃 Malaya Jalan Hang Lekir ☏03/2072 7722, ⓦwww.hotelmalaya.com.my. An old faithful of a hotel, with a dreary 1970s façade to prove it.

Rooms – all a/c and en suite – are comfortable if unremarkable, and the place isn't as slick as some other mid-range hotels, but it's also slightly cheaper, and has a great location bordering on the thick of the Jalan Petaling action. Rate includes breakfast. Promotional rates, available much of the time, make it a good deal. ❻

Mandarin Pacific 2–8 Jalan Sultan ☏03/2070 3000, ⓕ2070 4363. Not unlike the *Malaya*, with an unappealing exterior and decent en-suite rooms, but a bit staid, for which it compensates by being slightly cheaper. Breakfast included. ❺

Petaling 121–123 Jalan Petaling ☏03/2078 9870. No-frills hotel, featuring slightly tatty, en-suite rooms with a/c and TV. They knock fifteen percent off the rate outside weekends. ❹

Puduraya Above Puduraya bus station ☏03/2072 1000, ⓕ2070 5567. Several floors up from the bus station is this functional Chinese-run hotel which, despite a rather uninviting lobby, is pretty efficient. Rooms have a/c and bathroom, and some have good views over the city. Ten-percent discounts outside weekends. ❺

Swiss Inn 62 Jalan Sultan ☏03/2072 3333, ⓦwww.swissinnkualalumpur.com. Pleasant, well-regarded hotel, with satellite TV in the rooms and a coffee house that affords a bird's-eye view of the Jalan Petaling Market. ❺

The Golden Triangle, including Bukit Bintang

Many of Bukit Bintang's guesthouses occupy nicely restored old **shophouses** (or sometimes pairs of shophouses with their separating walls knocked through), and may feature small, comfortable rooms partitioned using plywood, often with a chunk cut out at the top to allow pairs of rooms to share an air-conditioning unit. It's hard to go wrong with any of these, just as it's difficult to be disappointed with any of the Golden Triangle's many upmarket hotels. For the locations of the places reviewed below, see the map on pp.122–123.

Guesthouses

Bintang Guesthouse 27 Jalan Tong Shin ☏03/2144 3398, ⓦwww.bintangguesthouse.com .my. With local and foreign businessmen among the clientele this doesn't feel like a backpacker place. It's also surprisingly large, with 42 rooms, a well-equipped kitchen and a laundry area lurking in the depths of the two renovated shophouses that it occupies. The rooms, which include good-value singles and family rooms, can be a bit small but do include a few original features like the colourful floor tiles. En-suite facilities and a/c available in some rooms. Dorms RM15, ❷

🏃 Green Hut 48 Tengkat Tong Shin ☏03/2142 3339, ⓦwww.thegreenhut.com. Easily spotted thanks to its lime green exterior, with more bright multicoloured walls and a suitably

romantic jungle mural within, *Green Hut* is a relaxed place with spotless facilities. A few rooms are en suite. The cosy lounge has Internet terminals and satellite TV. Dorms RM20, ❸

🏃 Number 8 Guesthouse 8–10 Tengkat Tong Shin ☏03/2144 2050, ⓦwww.numbereight .com.my. A sleek setup with a unique minimalist designer feel throughout – the dorm bunk beds even have adjoining lockers with built-in reading lights. All rooms have a/c and marble-topped sinks, though bathrooms and showers are shared. There's also a very smart kitchen with microwave oven, and a lounge with Net access. Dorms RM30, ❺

Pondok Lodge 20-2c Changkat Bukit Bintang ☏03/2142 8449, ⓦwww.pondoklodge.com. One of the better-established guesthouses, with simply furnished, somewhat boxy rooms, plus a four-bed dorm. All have a/c but share bathrooms. Satellite TV and Internet access are available in the lounge, and a simple breakfast is included in the rate, but note that you pay a small premium for the use of their blankets or towels. Dorms RM23, ❸

Pujangga Homestay 21 Jalan Berangan ☎03/2141 4243, ⓦwww.pujangga-homestay.com. Just four rooms – one single, two doubles and a six-bed dorm, all with a/c – in a 1970s terraced house. Facilities include a little lounge with TV, a kitchen and Internet access. The rates include breakfast; help yourself to coffee or tea, toast and cornflakes. As homely as you could wish for – a good choice. Dorms RM25, ❸

🏃 **Rainforest B&B** 27 Jalan Mesui ☎03/2145 1466, ⒺRainforest_kl@hotmail.com. Characterful Malay-run place that towers over the neighbouring houses in the terrace, each of its upper floors overflowing with potted palms, ferns and bougainvillea. All the rooms have cool wooden floors, a/c, attached bathroom and TV; there's also an enormous dorm taking up most of the first floor, with six single beds and its own sofa. Rate includes breakfast. Dorms RM36, ❹

🏃 **Red Palm** 5 Tengkat Tong Shin ☎03/2143 1279, ⓦwww.redpalm-kl.com. Well-regarded, friendly and informal establishment with just three rooms and a dorm upstairs, all sharing facilities. Downstairs is a spacious lounge with a number of Internet terminals. Rates include a simple breakfast. Reservations advised. Look for them opposite the *Number Eight Guesthouse*. Dorm beds RM25, ❹

Hotels

Allson Genesis 45 Tengkat Tong Shin ☎03/2141 2000, ⓦwww.allson-genesis.com. Modern hotel that has the distinction of being a little cosier than many others in the same price bracket. Rate includes breakfast. ❼

Comfort Inn 65 Changkat Bukit Bintang ☎03/2141 3636, ⓦwww.hotelcomfort.biz. Behind the ghastly concrete exterior is a tiny hotel with tiny, plain a/c rooms and even tinier attached bathrooms. Still, this ranks among the cheapest hotels in the area and staff are friendly. ❹

🏃 **Corus** Jalan Ampang ☎03/2161 8888, ⓦwww.corushotelkl.com. A tried-and-tested mid-1980s hotel that's maturing well. Besides plush rooms, it boasts Chinese and Japanese restaurants and a swimming pool. Recommended, especially as frequent promotions make it a bargain. ❼

Equatorial Jalan Sultan Ismail ☎03/2161 7777, ⓦwww.equatorial.com. Vast five-star hotel with a swimming pool, wireless Internet access and some good restaurants and cafés. Published rates are

sky-high, but good discounts are available most of the year. ❽

🏃 **Federal** 35 Jalan Bukit Bintang ☎03/2148 9166, ⓦwww.fhihotels.com. Venerable hotel dating from the year of Malaysia's independence, and nicely updated through the years, the current incarnation sporting a beautiful marbled lobby. Facilities include a pool, bowling alley and the revolving *Bintang* restaurant which, like some of the rooms, offers views over the concrete jungle of malls that dominate Bukit Bintang. ❼

Istana 73 Jalan Raja Chulan ☎03/2141 9988, ⓦwww.hotelistana.com.my. Five-star, five-hundred-room hotel, one of the best in town, with a strong Islamic feel to the decor, including a gorgeous black marble water feature and plenty of geometrical motifs. Despite the rather bare corridors and muted colour schemes throughout, the rooms themselves are slick and spacious, and some have good views of the Petronas Towers. There's the obligatory range of restaurants, plus a pool and gym. ❽

Mandarin Oriental KLCC ☎03/2380 8888, ⓦwww.mandarinoriental.com. Enormous hotel (it only looks small by virtue of being conveniently next to Suria KLCC) and as sumptuous as they come. Pointedly bills itself as "for affluent travellers" – which is spot-on, given that the lowest regularly available rate is around RM640 a night, though limited specials are available online. ❾

Marriott 183 Jalan Bukit Bintang ☎03/2715 9000, ⓦwww.marriott.com. Among the crème de la crème of KL hotels, with top-notch rooms and facilities, including a restaurant featuring one of the rarer strands of Chinese cuisine in KL, Shanghainese. ❾

🏃 **Maya** 138 Jalan Ampang ☎03/2711 8866, ⓦwww.hotelmaya.com.my. This stunning boutique hotel has two hundred rooms arranged around a vast, futuristic central atrium and is distinguished by chic designer furnishings throughout. In the cheapest studio rooms (a range of suites are also available) there are even glass-walled bathrooms (with privacy curtains) so you can watch the bigscreen TV from the bathtub. Room safes have power points so you can store and recharge your gadgets, and every room has Net access. The hotel also boasts a range of spa treatments and restaurants, plus free transfers to and from KL airport or KL Sentral. Rates typically start at around RM570, though tempting discounts are sometimes available online. ❾

Nikko 165 Jalan Ampang ☎03/2161 1111, ⓦwww.hotelnikko.com.my. Swanky and sleek five-star affair with a great range of restaurants, satellite TV and a pool. As it caters mainly to business travellers, rates fall at weekends – though in general the hotel is only worthwhile if you get a promotional deal (typically around RM440 for a double), as the rack rate is extortionate. ❾

Radius 51a Changkat Bukit Bintang ☎03/2715 3888, ⓦwww.radius-international.com. Substantial hotel with a variety of comfy rooms, a restaurant and café, a terrace swimming pool and WiFi Internet access (RM8/hr) in the lobby. Promotional rates apply much of the time, which is just as well as the rack rate is steep. ❼

Renaissance/New World Junction of Jalan Sultan Ismail and Jalan Ampang ☎03/2162 2233, ⓦwww.renaissance-kul.com. Part of the Marriott group, this is actually two hotels in one, sharing facilities – including an excellent outdoor swimming pool, gym and restaurants. The New World wing is around twenty percent cheaper. Rates exclude breakfast. New World ❽, Renaissance ❾

🏃 **Seasons View** 61 Jalan Alor ☎03/2145 7577, ⓦwww.seasonsview.com. On one level, a mundane, smallish, lower-mid-range hotel – but it's competently run, has modern en-suite rooms, a good location amid the culinary splendour of Jalan Alor, and great rates (which include breakfast). ❺

Westin 199 Jalan Bukit Bintang ☎03/2731 8333, ⓦwww.westin.com/kualalumpur. A bunch of great restaurants and amenities such as a gym with skyline views add up to a pretty strong hand for the five-star Westin, sometimes unfairly overshadowed by the rival Marriott next door. ❾

Serviced apartments

🏃 **KL Plaza Suites** ☎03/2145 6988, ⓦwww .berjayaresorts.com.my. Great-value serviced apartments affording a lot more space than you'd get in a similarly priced hotel room, including a lounge area and, for only a small premium, a kitchenette. Facilities include a swimming pool and squash courts. A simple breakfast can be ordered, but with the numerous cafés of Bintang Walk close at hand, it's hardly worth bothering with. ❼

Pacific Regency Menara Panglobal, Jalan Puncak, off Jalan P. Ramlee ☎03/2332 7777, ⓦwww .pacific-regency.com. Luxury apartments complete with kitchenette, satellite TV, wireless Internet access and, on the roof, a swimming pool and the brilliant Luna bar (see p.138). The location, partway up Bukit Nanas near Menara KL, isn't near any stations – though if you can afford the rates, taxi fares won't trouble you in the least. ⓿

Little India, Chow Kit and the Putra World Trade Centre

The places reviewed below appear on the map on p.119, except for the *Legend* which appears on the map on pp.96–97.

Champagne 141 Jalan Bunus, off Jalan Masjid India ☎03/2698 6333. Reasonably spacious rooms with a/c and en-suite facilities, though slightly fraying at the edges. ❺

Coliseum 98–100 Jalan TAR ☎03/2692 6270. One of KL's most famous old-style hotels – a few mod cons apart, little about this place seems to have changed since it was built in the 1920s. The rooms are large, with ceiling fans (a/c available in some rooms), cast-iron bedsteads and Bakelite light fittings. Bathrooms are shared. It can be a bit noisy, but is kept fairly clean and oozes atmosphere. ❸

Garden City Hotel 214 Jalan Bunus, off Jalan Masjid India ☎03/2711 7777, ⓦwww .gardencityhotel.net. One of the tidier hotels in the Masjid India area, with slightly aging compact a/c rooms; there's also a decent café serving North and South Indian fare. Rate includes breakfast. ❻

Kowloon 142–146 Jalan TAR ☎03/2693 4246, ⓦwww.kowloonhotelkl.com. The rooms are showing their age and can be a little musty, though they're decent enough, with TV, a/c and tidy bathrooms. ❺

Legend Putra Place, 100 Jalan Putra ☎03/4042 9888, ⓦwww.legendsgroup.com. Above the Mall shopping development, this luxury hotel boasts a rooftop pool and good restaurants and bars. ❽

Noble Fourth floor, 165 Jalan Tunku Abdul Rahman ☎03/27117111, ⓦwww.hotelnoble.com. Slightly scruffy but otherwise predictable a/c rooms, some with good views over the pasar malam. Rate includes breakfast. ❻

Palace 40–46 Jalan Masjid India ☎03/2698 6122, ⓔpalacehotel@myjaring.net. Well-run hotel with modern a/c, en-suite rooms in the thick of the night market. Rate includes breakfast. ❻

Plaza Jalan Raja Laut ☎03/2698 2255, ⓦwww .hotelplazakl.com.my. A modern mid-range affair with comfy rooms, all with bathroom, TV and a/c. Convenient for both the LRT and the monorail. Rate includes breakfast. ❻

Stanford 449 Jalan TAR ☎03/2691 9833, ⓦwww .stanfordhotel.com.my. A refuge amid the clamour of Chow Kit Market, featuring bland but serviceable en-suite rooms (with bathtubs). Rooms on the east side having great views of the Petronas Towers against the backdrop of the Genting Highlands. ❻

Brickfields and KL Sentral

The places reviewed below appear on the map on p.128.

Florida 71–73 Jalan Thambypillai ☎03/2260 1333, ℻2274 9107. A functional hotel lacking the seediness that taints many lodgings in the area. En-suite rooms with a/c and TV. ❹

Hilton 3 Jalan Stesen Sentral ☎03/2264 2264, ⓦwww.kuala-lumpur.hilton.com. Lavish hotel whose lobby wouldn't look out of place fronting a modern art museum and rooms straight out of the style magazines. Rates are extremely variable, but reckon on at least RM420 a night. ❾

Le Meridien 2 Jalan Stesen Sentral ☎03/2263 7888, ⓦkualalumpur.lemeridien.com. Not quite as opulent as the *Hilton* next door, but grand by

anyone else's standards, with a pool and spa, and a fancy Lebanese restaurant. As at the *Hilton*, rates wander all over the place although rooms don't come cheaper than RM360 a night. ❾

YMCA 95 Jalan Padang Belia ☎03/2274 1439, ⓦwww.ymcakl.com. A well-maintained place reminiscent of campus accommodation, and open to male and female guests. Rooms, all with a/c and TV, range from singles to quads, with the option of attached bathrooms with the singles and doubles. Facilities include a café, laundry, barber's and tennis courts (you'll need your own gear, though). Good value, particularly as breakfast is included. ❹

Further out

Carcosa Seri Negara Taman Tasik Perdana ☎03/2282 1888, ⓦwww.carcosa.com.my. See map, pp.96–97. Set in its own grounds, just west of the Lake Gardens, these two colonial mansions

are without doubt the most exclusive places to stay in KL – the management can truthfully boast "Queen Elizabeth slept here". For more, see p.127. Suites from RM1250, ❾

The City

Most visitors divide their time about equally between old and new KL, which is probably the best strategy for seeing the city. Very close to the historic "muddy confluence", **Merdeka Square**, with its colonial-era courthouses and administrative buildings, is pretty much on everyone's list, as is **Chinatown** to the southeast; in between lie the city's old **Jamek Mosque** and **Pasar Seni**, one of KL's main crafts markets. Worthwhile forays can be made north to **Little India** (and, if you're so inclined, on up to **Chow Kit Market**); south to the **old railway station**, **Masjid Negara** (the National Mosque) and the adjacent **Islamic Arts Museum**; further south to the **National Museum** and the **Brickfields** district, both close to KL Sentral; and west to the **Lake Gardens**, one of surprisingly few green lungs in this tropical city.

All the while, you'll probably be shuttling across to the **Golden Triangle**. Not actually a triangle, it takes in the **Menara KL** communications tower, just northeast of Chinatown; as well as the numerous hotels, malls, restaurants and clubs of **Bukit Bintang**, focused on Jalan Bukit Bintang, Jalan Imbi and Jalan Sultan Ismail. The Golden Triangle is bounded on its northern edge by **Jalan Ampang**, one of the first streets to be developed as a residential area for rich tin *towkays* and colonial administrators at the start of the twentieth century, and which still retains a few mansions, some now housing embassies. Close to the junction of Jalan Ampang and Jalan Tun Razak are the **Petronas Towers**.

If you've a particular interest in KL's architectural heritage, it's worth arranging a **walking tour** with the Malaysian Tourist Guides Council (Ⓔmtgc@po .jaring.my). Their three-hour guided walks typically start from Merdeka Square and cost RM200 for up to twelve people.

Around Merdeka Square – the colonial quarter

The small **colonial quarter**, which developed around the confluence of the Gombak and Klang rivers in the 1880s, is the area of KL that arguably best retains its historic character, with an eccentric fusion of building styles, including practically all of the city's Moorish-style buildings. At its heart on the west bank of the Klang is a beautifully tended English cricket ground and *padang* (field), revered for its place in Malaysian history, for it was here that on August 31, 1957, Malaysia's first prime minister, Tunku Abdul Rahman, declared *merdeka*, or independence. Subsequently, the space was renamed Dataran Merdeka, or **Merdeka Square**.

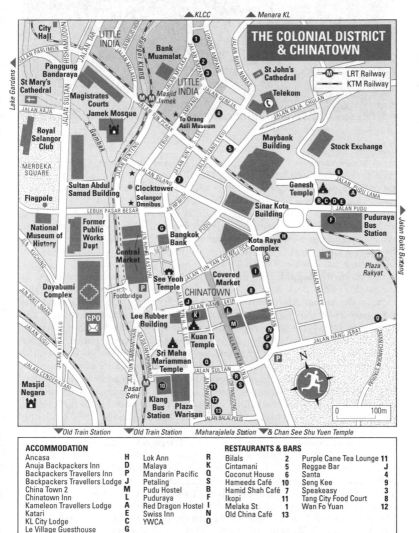

THE COLONIAL DISTRICT & CHINATOWN

ACCOMMODATION				RESTAURANTS & BARS			
Ancasa	H	Lok Ann	R	Bilals	2	Purple Cane Tea Lounge	11
Anuja Backpackers Inn	D	Malaya	K	Cintamani	5	Reggae Bar	J
Backpackers Travellers Inn	P	Mandarin Pacific	Q	Coconut House	6	Santa	4
Backpackers Travellers Lodge	J	Petaling	S	Hameeds Café	10	Seng Kee	9
China Town 2	M	Pudu Hostel	B	Hamid Shah Café	7	Speakeasy	3
Chinatown Inn	L	Puduraya	F	Ikopi	11	Tang City Food Court	8
Kameleon Travellers Lodge	A	Red Dragon Hostel	I	Melaka St	1	Wan Fo Yuan	12
Katari	E	Swiss Inn	N	Old China Café	13		
KL City Lodge	C	YWCA	O				
Le Village Guesthouse	G						

△ The Sultan Abdul Samad Building

On the western side of the square, the **Royal Selangor Club** was the British elite's favourite watering hole. The club itself was founded in the 1880s, though the present clubhouse, a low, black-and-white mock Tudor structure, is a 1970s rebuilding of a structure built by A.B. Hubbock in 1910, after the original was badly damaged by fire. Colonial wags used to refer to the building as "the Spotted Dog", supposedly in memory of the club mascot, a Dalmatian, which a former member used to tie up at the steps. To the north, the Anglican **St Mary's Cathedral** (1894), usually open in the daytime, welcomed the city's European inhabitants every Sunday before they repaired to the club.

The 95-metre **flagpole** just south of the square is supposedly the tallest in the world. Locals flock here on weekend evenings to parade beside the fairy lights of the **Sultan Abdul Samad Building**, across Jalan Sultan Hishamuddin from here. Now the High Court, it has a two-storey grey-and-red brick facade dominated by a forty-metre-high clock tower, and curved colonnades topped with impressive copper cupolas; the building isn't open to the public. Designed by Anthony Norman (also responsible for St Mary's) and finished in 1897, the building was constructed to house the colonial administration's offices, and was among the earliest of the capital's **Moorish-style buildings**. Picturesque fantasies predominate, featuring onion domes, cupolas, colonnades, arched windows and wedding-cake plasterwork. One man was largely responsible for this original urban fabric – Charles Edwin Spooner, the state engineer in the 1890s. Under his guidance, architect A.C.A. Norman came up with an initial design for the Sultan Abdul Samad Building – in the Neoclassical Renaissance style, which was then the general standard for government buildings throughout the British Empire. But Spooner argued that the symbols of the Federated Malay States, a protectorate rather than a colony, should reflect the Islamic sensibilities of the Malay rulers. So a more "Eastern" design was eventually used, though not one based on traditional Malay timber buildings but imported from colonial India. Other buildings by Norman which followed in this mould include the Post Office (now the Federal Courts), the Public Works Department and the High Court.

The Hash House Harriers

Dotty Englishmen took their dottiness with them all around the empire. Among them was one A.S. Gispert who joined a club in Melaka, the Springgit Harriers, that indulged in a version of the English running game Hare and Hounds. The game is simple; a runner or "hare" sets a paper trail for a group – the "hounds" – that later sets off in pursuit. The paper trail, often laid through stretches of woodland, might periodically break or veer off in a different direction; the "hounds" would fan out and try and pick it up. In 1938 Gispert managed to enthuse some of his fellow drinkers who peopled the Hash House, as the dining room of the Royal Selangor Club was affectionately known, into taking part in the game. The dozen or so founding members of the **Hash House Harriers**, as the group became known, would run on Mondays after their weekly training session for the Malay States Volunteer Reserves. Gispert was killed helping to defend Singapore in early 1942, but after the war the other founders revived the tradition, and the Hash House Harriers went on to become an international running club. The original KL group, respectfully regarded as the mother of all hashing groups, is still in existence (Ⓦ www.motherhash.org).

To the north stands the black domed old **City Hall**, and to the south the **National Museum of History** (daily 9am–6pm; free; Ⓦ www .nationalhistorymuseum.gov.my). Once the workplace of former British prime minister John Major in his days as a banker, this cream-coloured building, also in a Moorish style, on the corner of Jalan Raja was converted in 1996 from government offices into a museum. It provides an informative romp, which can be covered in half an hour, through the main points of the nation's history, spanning everything from the geological formation of the Malay Peninsula to the Vision 2020 programme, which aims for Malaysia to achieve full industrialized status by that year. On the opposite corner is the original Public Works Department (now housing courts of law), with striped brickwork and keyhole archways.

Jamek Mosque and Central Market

East of Merdeka Square, Lebuh Pasar Besar includes KL's busiest bridge, connecting the colonial quarter with the more frenetic life of the old commercial district on the east side of the Klang River. Just north of the bridge is the **Jamek Mosque** (Masjid Jamek; open to visitors in between prayer times; free), on a promontory at the confluence of the Klang and Gombak rivers. It was here – on a section of dry land carved out from the enveloping forest – that tin prospectors from Klang established a base in the 1850s, which soon turned into a boom town. The mosque, part of the second great period of expansion in KL, was completed in 1909 by the British architect A.B. Hubbock, who took over from Anthony Norman after the latter was compulsorily retired in 1903 on grounds of inefficiency. Hubbock had previously lived in India, and thus the Jamek Mosque incorporates features copied from Mogul mosques – pink brick walls and arched colonnades, topped by oval cupolas and squat minarets. There's an intimacy here that isn't obvious at the modern, much larger national mosque to the south, and the grounds, bordered by palms, are a pleasant place to sit and rest. The main entrance is on Jalan Tun Perak.

Head south off Lebuh Pasar Besar and you reach the Art Deco **Central Market** (daily 9am–10pm). Backing onto Sungei Klang, this large pastel-coloured brick hangar was built in the 1920s as the capital's wet market, though the butchers and fishmongers have long since left for places like Chow Kit

Market and the back alleys of nearby Chinatown. In the mid-1980s the market was converted into what's known as **Pasar Seni**, meaning "art market", though most of the shops within actually sell **crafts** and souvenirs – anything from porcelain statues of Hindu and Chinese deities to woodcarvings and T-shirts. It was originally hoped that Pasar Seni would follow in the footsteps of London's famous Covent Garden Market and become a major tourist draw, but instead there's a distinctly dowdy feel to the place, and for every worthwhile outlet showcasing *songket* or silverware, there's a mundane shop selling watches or magazines. Still, the market is definitely worth a browse, and is a lively meeting point at weekends and most evenings, when a few buskers entertain the kids with Malay pop covers. Plans have been mooted to raise rents and take the whole complex upmarket; it's to be hoped this doesn't result in yet another designer-goods arcade that only the city's elite will appreciate.

Chinatown

Spreading out east from Central Market is **Chinatown**, once KL's commercial kernel, dating from the arrival of the first traders in the 1860s. Bordered by Jalan Sultan to the east, Jalan Tun Perak to the north and Jalan Maharajalela to the south, the area had adopted its current extent by the late nineteenth century, with southern-Chinese shophouses, coffee shops and temples springing up along narrow streets such as Jalan Tun H.S. Lee (formerly Main Street) and Jalan Petaling. Although rather dwarfed by surrounding skyscrapers, KL's Chinatown is still a warren of old Chinese shophouses, though unlike those in Melaka's Jonkers Walk area or around Penang's Lebuh Chulia, these are fairly workaday. While the threat of redevelopment constantly hangs over the area, it's encouraging that a few of the period buildings are being refurbished.

For locals and visitors alike, **Jalan Petaling** is very much the main draw. Home to brothels and gambling dens in KL's early years, these days it's the haunt of market traders who, under a modern blue glass roof, do a roaring trade in fake watches and handbags, and pirated DVDs, from late morning until well into the evening. The buzz spills over into neighbouring streets, which feature shops and hawkers selling all manner of foodstuffs, from *ba kwa* (slices of pork, given a sweet marinade and grilled) to local fruits and molasses-like herbal brews in tureens. The Chinese restaurants and stalls in the vicinity are among the most popular eating places in KL, some staying open into the small hours.

See Yeoh and Chan See Shu Yuen temples

Just past the junction of Jalan Tun H.S. Lee and Jalan Cheng Lock is the **See Yeoh Temple**, founded in 1883 by Yap Ah Loy, KL's early Chinese headman, who funded its construction; a photograph of him is often prominently displayed on one of the altars. The temple is atmospheric but not particularly interesting, though it comes to life on festival days. You're better off visiting the area's largest temple, **Chan See Shu Yuen**, at the very southern end of Jalan Petaling. The main deity here is Chong Wah, a Sung-dynasty emperor. The inner shrine is covered in scenes of lions, dragons and mythical creatures battling with warriors. Statues representing the temples' three deities stand behind a glass wall, with a mural of a brilliant-yellow sun above them. From outside, you can see the intricately carved roof, its images depicting more monumental events in Chinese history and mythology, while decorating the edge of the pavilion are blue ceramic vases and small statues of peasants – the guardians of the temple – armed with poles crowned with lanterns.

Sri Maha Mariamman Temple

Oddly perhaps, one of KL's main Hindu shrines, the **Sri Maha Mariamman Temple**, is also located in the heart of Chinatown, on Jalan Tun H.S. Lee (where you can also pause to take a look at the nearby **Kuan Ti Temple**, an attractively restored Taoist affair dating back to the late nineteenth century). The earliest shrine on the Sri Maha Mariamman site was built in 1873 by Tamil immigrants and named after the Hindu deity, Mariamman, whose

△ Striking a deal, Jalan Petaling

intercession was sought to provide protection against sickness and "unholy incidents". In the case of the Tamils, who had arrived to build the railways or work on the plantations, they needed all the solace they could find from the appalling rigours of their working life.

Significant rebuilding of the temple took place in the 1960s, when sculptors from India were commissioned to design idols to adorn the five tiers of the gate tower – these now shine with gold embellishments, precious stones and exquisite Spanish and Italian tiles. Above the gate is a hectic profusion of Hindu gods, frozen in dozens of scenes from the *Ramayana*. Outside the pyramid-shaped entrance, you may come across garland-makers selling their wares.

During the Hindu **Thaipusam** festival, the temple's golden chariot is paraded through the streets on its route to the Batu Caves, on the northern edge of the city (see p.149). The rest of the year, the chariot is kept in a large room in the temple; you can ask an attendant to unlock the door and let you have a peek.

The temple is always open to the public and is free to visit, although you may want to contribute a ringgit or two towards its upkeep. Visitors must leave their shoes at a rack situated to the left of the entrance.

Chinatown's eastern edge

Chinatown's main west–east thoroughfares, Jalan Tun Perak and Jalan Tun Tan Cheng Lock (the latter the route of the original rail line through KL) converge at the Puduraya intersection, just off which stands the **Maybank Building**. Built in the late 1980s by Hijjas Kasturi, it's a structure typical of the new KL, designed with Islamic principles of purity in mind. Unlike many of the other modern skyscrapers here, there's actually a reason to venture inside – to visit either the small art gallery or the **Numismatic Museum** (Mon–Sat 10am 6pm; free), both on the main lobby floor. The latter is an unusually interesting collection, arranged in chronological fashion, starting with pre-coinage artefacts once used for transactions in Southeast Asia – tin ingots, gold dust and bars of silver or, for what the caption describes as "ordinary people", cowrie shells, rice and beads. Coins were gradually introduced into the region along with the arrival of the various colonizing powers; early sixteenth-century Portuguese coins on display are delicately engraved with miniatures of the Malay Peninsula and tiny kites billowing in the air. The first mass-produced coins, issued by the British East India Company, bore the company's coat of arms – a practice echoed later by timber and rubber companies, who until the late eighteenth century minted tokens to pay their expanding labour pool. The very first notes were produced by a private bank in 1694, although the first official notes were only issued at the end of the nineteenth century, by the British. During the Japanese invasion, the occupying administration produced its own notes which, after the Japanese surrender, the British diligently collected and stamped "not legal tender".

East of here, a little street, Jalan Pudu Lama, is the location of KL's second most important Hindu shrine, the **Court Hill Ganesh Temple** (daily 9am–6pm; free), a small and often crowded place, with stalls outside selling garlands, incense, sweetmeats and charms. This was a favoured stop for visitors on their way to KL's original law courts, once sited nearby. Suppliants prayed to the chief deity, Lord Ganesh, who specializes in the removal of all obstacles to prosperity, peace and success.

The old train station and around

One the city's best-known colonial buildings, the old **Kuala Lumpur train station** now feels distinctly unloved and cut off from its colonial cousins.

KL's new architecture

The explosion of giant-scale **architecture** projects in and around KL began in the 1970s, when KL's first construction boom gave room for inventive architects to expand on themes suited to its tropical climate. The resulting buildings saw traditional elements interacting with innovative architectural expressions, often to striking effect. One of the earliest examples of this is the **Dayabumi Complex** just south of Merdeka Square. Malay architect Nik Mohammed took modern mosque architecture as his model and produced this tower, whose high-vaulted entrance arches and glistening white open fretwork has become characteristic of progressive Malaysian city architecture.

The architect who best demonstrates the fusing of essentially religious motifs with new design is **Hijjas Kasturi**. His most impressive work is perhaps the **Maybank Building**, where the predominance of white denotes purity, while its great height, sleekness and grandeur are reminiscent of a minaret. In his **Tabung Haji Building**, close to the intersection of Jalan Ampang and Jalan Tun Abdul Razak (and very near the *Hotel Nikko*, which he also designed), the five columns supporting the bottle-like structure represent the five pillars of Islam, the single tower unity with God; appropriately, the building is the headquarters of the Pilgrims Fund, which provides Islamic banking services and coordinates matters to do with the Hajj. A more recent and equally striking design of his is the Telekom Malaysia headquarters, close to Jalan Klang Lama south of Brickfields, which, from certain angles, resembles a shark's fin slicing through the sky.

These themes were developed throughout the 1990s, during which a trio of buildings, the **National Library**, **Art Gallery** and **Theatre**, on Jalan Tun Razak, have reinterpreted traditional Malay forms. Although the library, designed by Shamsuddin Mohammed, is dominated by a gleaming roof covered in large blue ceramic tiles, the grandeur of the exterior contrasts with the interior's incorporation of everyday cultural symbols, with sculpture that utilizes the shapes of traditional earthenware pots, and walls bearing the patterns of the traditional woven *songket* cloth. Another modern take on traditional Malay building styles, the **Bank Muamalat Building**, can be seen on Jalan Melaka, near Masjid Jamek LRT station. Of course, the manic expansion of KL in the 1990s also gave rise to Malaysia's one world-famous icon, with its own Islamic touches, in the **Petronas Twin Towers** (see p.121).

The next phase is in the hands of architects like Zaini Zainul who continues in the tradition of East-meets-West design. He designed parts of the new seat of government at Putrajaya, set around a lake south of KL. However, while Putrajaya exhibits excellent attention to detail in its design, many of the buildings so far completed could better be described as ostentatious and imperial rather than distinctively Southeast Asian.

It ought to be easy enough to reach from Merdeka Square, but Jalan Sultan Hishamuddin here becomes a broad, feverishly busy highway, with hardly any designated crossings. It's easier to get to the station by simply taking a Komuter train, in which case, if you happen to arrive on one of the atmospheric older platforms, you immediately get to take in the arched ceilings, so evocative of those at the larger train stations in London. Otherwise, the station is a five-hundred-metre walk southwest from Central Market, across the bridge and down along the western side of the river, past the Dayabumi Complex and the modern General Post Office; eventually you'll come to a small gate opening onto newer platforms at the far northern end of the station.

The station was completed in 1911 by A.B. Hubbock and, as with his Jamek Mosque, reflects his inspiration from North Indian Islamic architecture in its meshing spires, minarets and arches. For the best view of the facade, you'll need to get across to the western side of Jalan Sultan Hishamuddin – thankfully, you can avoid the traffic by scooting through the pedestrian subway linking the station with KTM's headquarters opposite – itself an attractive Moorish structure designed by Hubbock, completed around the same time as the station and actually more imposing than its counterpart.

Masjid Negara

Once at the KTM building, you can easily take the opportunity to walk to a few attractions on the fringes of the Lake Gardens, beginning with the **Masjid Negara** (National Mosque; daily 9am–6pm except Fri 2.45–6pm). Opened in 1965, it's starting to look rather dated, but does feature impressive rectangles of white marble bisected by pools of water, and a hall that can hold up to ten thousand worshippers. In the prayer hall, size gives way to decorative prowess, the dome adorned with eighteen points signifying the five pillars of Islam and the thirteen states of Malaysia. To enter as a visitor (between prayers only), you need to be properly dressed: robes can be borrowed (free) from the desk at the mosque entrance.

The Islamic Arts Museum

Just up Jalan Lembah Perdana from the mosque is the ultramodern **Islamic Arts Museum** (Tues–Sun 10am–6pm; RM10, or RM12 if there are temporary exhibitions; Ⓦ www.iamm.org.my). In a city that's, frankly, lacking in good museums, this well-documented collection is a real standout, housed in an open-plan building with gleaming marble floors; allow around ninety minutes to do it justice. Note that if you're arriving by taxi, you may find that the driver will know only its Malay name, Muzium Kesenian Islam (and if that doesn't work, just ask for the Masjid Negara).

Things begin rather unpromisingly on **level 1** with a mundane collection of dioramas of Muslim holy places. Most interesting of these is the Great Mosque of Xi'an in central China, looking for all the world like a Chinese temple; it's the first of a number of exhibits that give deserved attention to the often neglected subject of Islam in the Far East, a theme continued elsewhere on this level in the India, China and Malay galleries. In the India gallery, devoted to the Moguls, look out in particular for an intricately carved wooden locking mechanism, designed to cloister the harem away from the rest of the world; the China gallery boasts some good examples of porcelain bearing Arabic calligraphy, and yet more Arabic script in scroll paintings on the far wall. Best of all here is the Malay gallery, featuring, among other items, an impressive three-metre-high archway, once part of a house belonging to an Indonesian notable, with black, red and gold lacquering and a trelliswork of leaves as its main motif. Below it is displayed an equally fine trunk that was used as a travelling box by Terengganu royalty. Built of the much-prized *cengal* hardwood, it's decorated in red and gold and bears the names of Islam's revered first four caliphs.

On **level 2**, there are some good displays of richly embroided textiles and marquetry, as well as some unusual examples of Western European ceramic crockery, mostly from the eighteenth and nineteenth centuries, influenced by the Islamic world in their design and in some cases actually produced for that market. But what's likely to excite your interest most here is the terrace containing the museum's main **dome**, a blue-and-white affair with floral ornamentation. Built by Iranian craftsmen, it's just one of several gorgeous domes in the building, but the only one that's meant to illustrate the exterior of a grand mosque. Finally, look out for the bizarre reversed dome ceiling, bulging downwards from above – it's the last thing you see as you make your way back to the foyer from the area containing the **gift shop** and Arabic **restaurant**, both excellent.

The RMP Museum

Behind the Islamic Arts Museum, the **RMP Museum** (Tues–Sun 10am–6pm; free), on Jalan Perdana, covers the vivid history of the Malaysian police force. Among the photographs are some fascinating images (*c.* 1900), including a shot of British officers and their local charges on patrol on buffaloes. The museum also has a variety of weapons confiscated from the communists during the Emergency, including a vicious assortment of *parangs* and a curved, bladed implement known as a Sarawak or Iban axe. Once you've had a look around, you can, if you're feeling energetic, continue up Jalan Perdana into the Lake Gardens (see p.125).

Little India to Chow Kit Market

Just to the north of Chinatown, **Little India** – the commercial centre for KL's Indian community – lies on the site of a Malay kampung dating from the very earliest days of the settlement. Much smaller than Chinatown, though equally fascinating, Little India is traditionally the main area in the city for buying garments, especially saris and *songket*s, as well as jewellery.

If you approach from Chinatown, you'll notice Indian restaurants and shops beginning to figure on the streets as soon as you head north from Jalan Tun Perak. Only a few steps north from the Masjid Jamek LRT station is **Jalan Melayu**, its name indicative of the former Malay community here; these days it's home to quite a few Indian stores, some selling excellent *burfi* and other sweet confections. Approaching **Jalan**

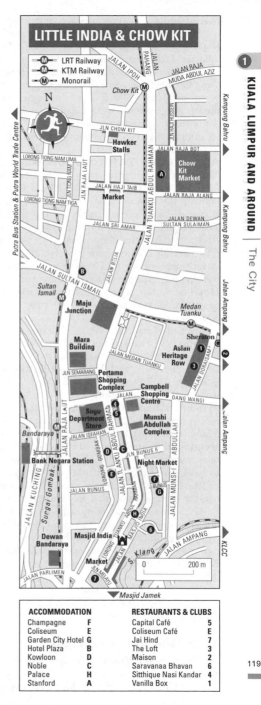

ACCOMMODATION		RESTAURANTS & CLUBS	
Champagne	**F**	Capital Café	**5**
Coliseum	**E**	Coliseum Café	**E**
Garden City Hotel	**G**	Jai Hind	**7**
Hotel Plaza	**B**	The Loft	**3**
Kowloon	**D**	Maison	**2**
Noble	**C**	Saravanaa Bhavan	**6**
Palace	**H**	Sitthique Nasi Kandar	**4**
Stanford	**A**	Vanilla Box	**1**

Masjid India, you encounter a popular covered market much smaller than the one in Chinatown's Petaling Street, but otherwise not that dissimilar, and selling a few fake accessories too. Further up is **Masjid India** itself, a reddish-brown Indian-influenced affair dating from the 1960s; the first mosque on the site, a mere hut, had been built one hundred years earlier. If you continue a few minutes further along the street you come to a little square, to the right (east) of which you'll find plenty of *kedai kopis* and, come evening, street vendors selling food; turn off to the left and you come to Lorong Tuanku Abdul Rahman, whose northern end is dominated by a **night market**, busiest at weekends. Mainly Malay-run, the stalls sell both food and an eclectic range of bits and pieces, from T-shirts to trinkets.

Along Jalan TAR to Chow Kit

Chow Kit Market, most easily reached by Monorail, is some 1500m north of Little India, along **Jalan Tuanku Abdul Rahman** (or **Jalan TAR** as it's always known). If you want to save yourself the walk from Little India, head west to Jalan Raja Laut, where virtually any bus will take you north to Chow Kit (Jalan TAR carries southbound traffic only – an unsuccessful attempt at easing the city's chronic traffic congestion). The walk along Jalan TAR does, however, offer occasional glimpses of Neoclassical and Art Deco buildings and shops, in various states of repair, as some compensation for the furious traffic. The most well-known example of one of these period pieces is the modest **Coliseum Hotel** (at no. 98), where the British owners of the rubber plantations once met to sink tumblers of whisky and water and eat steak. Dating from the 1920s (the adjacent Coliseum Cinema is of the same vintage), it has a rather bare facade for a Neoclassical structure, but the interior is genuinely atmospheric – it scarcely seems to have changed for decades. Come here for a cold beer rather than the food, which can be very ordinary.

At the northern end of Jalan TAR, **Chow Kit** has a noticable Indonesian presence; you'll come across Indonesian music and snacks on sale among the stalls in the sprawling produce and goods **market** that permeates the back alleys east of Jalan TAR, though more prominent are numerous vendors offering more usual items such as sandals, satay or *songkoks* (black caps resembling flattish fezzes, worn by Malay men). Chow Kit has a reputation as a good place to buy **secondhand clothes** (sometimes called "*baju* bundle"), but most clothes outlets offer mundane new items. To track down secondhand garments, you may need to head out of the main market and across to Jalan Haji Taib on the west side of Jalan TAR; here you may chance upon items like Levi's 501s in reasonable condition and at prices that are almost too reasonable to be true – starting from RM20 a pair. The market operates much of the day and into the evening, but note that some locals prefer to give Chow Kit a wide berth after dark.

If you've time on your hands and enjoy a wander, you could head 1km east from Chow Kit (along either Jalan Raja Bot or Jalan Raja Alang) into **Kampung Bahru**, once a Malay enclave with a distinct village feel. These days the area is rapidly modernizing, however, and people are leaving for other neighbourhoods, though Jalan Raja Muda Musa here still features some of the best Malay **food stalls** in the city. Hidden away off a side road to the south is Kumpung Bahru LRT station.

The Golden Triangle

The heart of modern KL, the **Golden Triangle** has two main focal points. Many visitors make a bee-line for the huge development that is **KLCC** (Kuala Lumpur City Centre; Ⓦ www.klcc.com.my), which occupies a site once home to the Selangor Turf Club. The chief attraction here is the **Petronas Towers**, soaring above one of KL's best malls, **Suria KLCC**; also here is the city's glossy **aquarium**. But often it's **Bukit Bintang** ("Star Hill"), home to many of KL's best hotels and restaurants, that makes a deeper impression.

The Petronas Towers and the aquarium aside, there are few specific sights in the Golden Triangle, though you may want to head east from Bukit Bintang to **Kompleks Budaya Kraf**, the city's largest handicrafts gallery, or – if you've a head for heights – northwest to Bukit Nanas, which affords great views of the city from the communications tower, **Menara KL**. Just to the south of Bukit Bintang, the disused **Pudu Jail** is a perverse sight of sorts, looking like a nightmarish concentration camp, its yellowing walls overlooked by grim watchtowers; you get a bird's-view from the Monorail as its swings past. Sections of the exterior wall are still covered with what's claimed to be the longest mural in the world, depicting lush jungles and lazy beaches – the work of the prisoners, who used their hands to apply the paint. Somehow this piece of prime real estate has escaped redevelopment for several years, though it's likely it will be turned into an area of luxury apartments and shops.

The Petronas Towers

Much of KLCC is taken up by a mundane park, but there's no mistaking the grandiosity of the **Petronas Towers**, in the northwest of the site, at the junction of Jalan Ampang and Jalan P. Ramlee. The towers are the home of Petronas – the state-owned oil company – as well as several other multinational companies. Though many questions were raised over whether the construction costs (US$2 billion) were an unwarranted drain on the Malaysian economy, the tapering steel-clad structures have undoubtedly become a symbol of modern Malaysia and a striking, even beautiful piece of architecture in their own right. Their unusual cross-sectional profile, an eight-pointed star, obviously draws on Islamic art, while the designs on the interior walls are a profusion of squares and circles symbolizing harmony and strength. The project is also subtly permeated by Chinese numerological beliefs, in that the towers have 88 floors and the postcode 59088 – eight being a very auspicious number to the Chinese.

Standing 452m high (and still ranking among the world's very tallest buildings), the towers were designed by the Argentinian architect Cesar Pelli, who was also responsible for the Canary Wharf Tower in London. One tower was built by a Japanese team, the other by rivals from Korea; the Japanese topped out first, but the Koreans engineered the **skybridge** (Tues–Sun 9.30am–5pm), which joins the towers at both the forty-first and forty-second floors. The skybridge's views aren't quite as fine those as from Menara KL, but if you do want to visit, you can take advantage of free skybridge passes, issued on level 4 at the **Petrosains Museum** (devoted to the technology of the oil industry; Tues–Thurs 9.30–5.30pm, Fri 1.30–5.30pm, Sat & Sun 9.30–6.30pm; Ⓦwww .petrosains.com.my; RM12). Skybridge visitors are limited to eight hundred per day (children under 12 not allowed), so it may be best to turn up early. The **Podium** at the base of the towers also contains a concert hall (home to the Malaysian Philharmonic; see p.140) and the Petronas **art gallery** (see p.142).

The aquarium

KL's newest big attraction at the time of writing, its **aquarium** (daily 11am–8pm, last tickets sold at 7pm; RM38; Ⓣ03/2333 1888, Ⓦwww.klaquaria.com), is housed within its newest prestige project, the **KL Convention Centre**, which takes up a sizeable chunk of the southern section of KLCC. It's most easily reached via Jalan Pinang, though you can get here using a long pedestrian

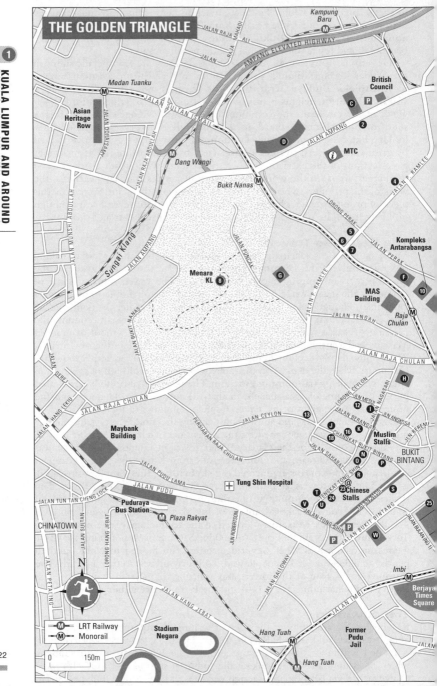

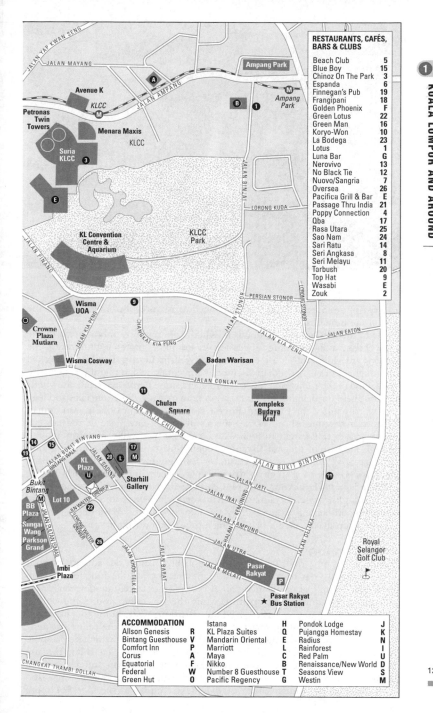

RESTAURANTS, CAFÉS, BARS & CLUBS

Beach Club	5
Blue Boy	15
Chinoz On The Park	3
Espanda	6
Finnegan's Pub	19
Frangipani	18
Golden Phoenix	F
Green Lotus	22
Green Man	16
Koryo-Won	10
La Bodega	23
Lotus	1
Luna Bar	G
Nerovivo	13
No Black Tie	12
Nuovo/Sangria	7
Oversea	26
Pacifica Grill & Bar	E
Passage Thru India	21
Poppy Connection	4
Qba	17
Rasa Utara	25
Sao Nam	24
Sari Ratu	14
Seri Angkasa	8
Seri Melayu	11
Tarbush	20
Top Hat	9
Wasabi	E
Zouk	2

Avenue K

KLCC

Ampang Park

Ampang Park

Petronas Twin Towers

Menara Maxis

KLCC

Suria KLCC

KLCC Park

KL Convention Centre & Aquarium

Wisma UOA

Crowne Plaza Mutiara

Wisma Cosway

Badan Warisan

Chulan Square

Kompleks Budaya Kraf

KL Plaza

Starhill Gallery

Bukit Bintang

Lot 10

BB Plaza

Sungai Wang Parkson Grand

Imbi Plaza

Royal Selangor Golf Club

Pasar Rakyat

Pasar Rakyat Bus Station

ACCOMMODATION					
Allson Genesis	R	Istana	H	Pondok Lodge	J
Bintang Guesthouse	V	KL Plaza Suites	Q	Pujangga Homestay	K
Comfort Inn	P	Mandarin Oriental	E	Radius	N
Corus	A	Marriott	L	Rainforest	I
Equatorial	F	Maya	C	Red Palm	U
Federal	W	Nikko	B	Renaissance/New World	D
Green Hut	O	Number 8 Guesthouse	T	Seasons View	S
		Pacific Regency	G	Westin	M

123

△ Under the Living Ocean tank

underpass from Suria KLCC (you may need to ask directions in the mall, as the start of the tunnel isn't obvious).

One of the costliest tourist draws in KL, the aquarium is only just worth the price of admission. Labelling is occasionally lost in the muted lighting, but some sections are wonderful – for example the well-lit **Living Reef** tank, packed with multicoloured, multiform anemones and corals, which might just help you make sense of the riches on view to snorkellers at the Perhentians and elsewhere; look out here for delightful little crimson prawns with white tentacles and legs. Also worthwhile is the **Flooded Forest** tank, with its pair of hefty Amazonian arapaima freshwater fish, all of two metres in length. The pièce de résistance is the obligatory transparent tunnel, whose moving belt walkway transports you through the base of the vast **Living Ocean** tank, replete with menacing sand tiger sharks, all with parasitic sharksucker fish clinging to their front and back edges. It's possible to arrange to **dive** with the sharks, for around RM400 (the fee includes a DVD of your dive, plus equipment rental); contact the aquarium for details. Otherwise, the aquarium has worthwhile diversions on coastal and other wetland habitats, populated by the likes of gigantic grasshoppers and by oriental whip snakes, such a bright green they're almost fluorescent.

Bukit Bintang

Even if you're on a tight budget, you'll probably spend a fair amount of your time wandering – as many locals do – the area around the junction of Jalan Bukit Bintang and Jalan Sultan Ismail. A profusion of largely modest malls here offer plenty of affordable **shopping**, while the pavement around the Lot 10 Mall, east of the junction, has evolved into **Bintang Walk**, home to a parade of smart cafés, not to mention smart, debonair locals. By night the centre of attention, at least as regards dining, switches to nearby **Jalan Alor**, which boasts some of the best Chinese eating in the city; close by on Changkat Bukit Bintang and Tengkat Tong Shin are more excellent restaurants, serving up a variety of cuisines. A little further to the north, the junction of Jalan Sultan Ismail and **Jalan P. Ramlee** features some of the slickest **clubs** in the city. For more on Bukit Bintang, see the "Eating", "Drinking", "Nightlife" and "Shopping" sections later in the chapter.

Menara KL

The area north of the western stretch of Jalan Raja Chulan is dominated by **Bukit Nanas**, on which stands the **Menara KL** communications tower (daily 9am–10pm; RM20; Ⓦ www.menarakl.com.my). At 421m, the tower is a striking addition to the KL skyline, and the best lookout from which to piece together the disparate parts of the city and its surroundings. The usual approach to the tower is via Jalan Puncak, to the south (shuttle buses are on hand for the drive up); bus #61 from Jalan Yap Ah Loy in Chinatown or from Jalan Sultan Ismail in Bukit Bintang can drop you close by at the junction of Jalan Raja Chulan and Jalan P. Ramlee, or you could walk from the Raja Chulan monorail station.

Before heading up to the top of the tower, you can catch an informative short film about its construction and take in the beautiful geometrical patterns – courtesy of Iranian craftsmen – decorating the entrance to the high-speed lifts. The **observation deck** is at the base of the bulbous portion of the tower, which was designed in the shape of the *gasing*, the Malay spinning top. Immediately above it is the *Seri Angkasa*, a revolving restaurant which has to qualify as one of the city's most striking locations for a meal (see p.133). The lights around the tower's crown change colour for special occasions – green for Muslim festivals, purple for Deepavali and red for the Chinese New Year.

To the west of the tower's base, on Jalan Bukit Nanas, are a fine collection of **colonial school buildings**, including the St John's Institution (1904) and Bukit Nanas Convent School, which remain among KL's top schools.

Kompleks Budaya Kraf and Badan Warisan

Just south of KLCC, Jalan Conlay has two places worth making time for. Most people who come this way are bound for **Kompleks Budaya Kraf** (daily 9am–6pm; free), devoted to the country's wide range of arts and crafts, including silver-, pewter- and brassware, batik, woodcarvings and ceramics. This is a good opportunity to see excellent examples of Malaysia's crafts in one place, and to do some serious souvenir shopping. There's also a small **crafts museum** within the complex (RM3).

If you're heading this way, it would be a shame not to pop in to **Badan Warisan** at 2 Jalan Stonor (Mon–Sat 10am–5.30pm; free; Ⓦ www .badanwarisan.org.my). This is Malaysia's architecture conservation trust, campaigning to preserve the rich heritage of shophouses, temples and colonial buildings that developers and many municipal authorities seem intent on destroying. It's housed in a 1925 colonial mansion which contains a gift shop, good for books on local architecture, and hosts occasional temporary exhibitions, focusing on anything from colonial furniture to restoration work. Also in the grounds is the beautifully restored **Rumah Penghulu Abu Seman**, a traditional timber house that once belonged to a Malay chieftain. Moved here from Kedah, it can only be visited on a guided tour (11am & 3pm; RM5).

The Lake Gardens

West of the colonial quarter, the **Lake Gardens** (aka Taman Tasik Perdana), are an expanse of close-cropped lawns, gardens and hills, originally laid out in the 1890s by the British state treasurer to Malaya, Alfred Venning, though much of the landscaping has been carried out in the last 25 years. The park, spread around a lake, incorporates a number of sights – including the National Monument, the

Butterfly Park and Bird Park, and the National Planetarium – while just 1km west of the National Monument is Malaysia's Parliament House.

Most people enter the gardens either from the north, along **Jalan Parlimen**, or from the south using **Jalan Lembah Perdana** (where Masjid Negara and the Islamic Arts Museum are located) or **Jalan Damansara** (where the National Museum lies; a footbridge connects the museum with the planetarium). Note that both Jalan Parlimen and Jalan Damansara are busy highways, and that many of the gardens' attractions are a little way from the main road; it's much easier to get here by taxi or bus (Jalan Parlimen is served by City Shuttle #115 from Merdeka Square and KL Sentral, and by bus #32 from Jalan Tun Perak in Chinatown).

In the gardens

Opposite the main entrance, off Jalan Parlimen, is the **National Monument**, a great bronze sculpture designed by Felix de Weldon, better known for his work on the Iwo Jima Memorial in Washington DC. The monument was constructed in 1966 to commemorate the nation's heroes, yet strangely the seven military figures protruding from it appear European rather than from any of the various Malaysian ethnic groups who fought in World War II and during the Emergency. Reached by a path leading up from the car park, the monument stands in a tranquil spot surrounded by a moat with fountains and ornamental pewter water lilies. Back at the car park is the **Taman ASEAN Sculpture Garden**, to which neighbouring countries have contributed abstract works in marble, iron, wood and bamboo.

Five minutes' walk south of the National Monument is the **Butterfly Park** (daily 9am–6pm; RM15), an unexpected delight featuring a large collection of amazingly colourful butterflies – some with fifteen-centimetre wing spans – flitting around a pretty garden under netting; just as impressive are the giant koi carp in the garden's ponds. Also worth seeing is the **Bird Park**, which bills itself as the world's largest covered bird park (daily 9am–7.30pm; RM28; Ⓦ www.birdpark.com.my); retrace your steps from the Butterfly Park to Jalan Cenderawasih and turn left uphill, following the road for 200m to the Bird Park entrance. Within, walkways loop around streams and pools taking in the enclosures of indigenous species such as East Malaysia's distinctive hornbills, the brahminy kite and the hawk eagle, and specimens of the largest pheasant in the world, the argus pheasant, not to mention parrots, toucans, flamingoes and birds of prey. If you're into tropical plants, you'll love the **Orchid** and **Hibiscus** (*bunga raya*) **Gardens** (daily 9am–6pm; Sat & Sun RM1, otherwise free), just north of the Bird Park, where hundreds of plants are grown and sold.

The main road through the gardens then weaves down past a field of deer, to the **Tun Abdul Razak Memorial**, a house built for the second Malaysian prime minister, who is commemorated by a collection of memorabilia inside, while his motorboat and golf trolley are ceremonially positioned outside. From here, you're only twenty minutes from the southern entrance. Beyond is the **lake** itself, which takes nearly an hour to walk around.

The planetarium

On a hill to the east of the lake is yet another public edifice with obligatory Islamic-influenced architecture, the **National Planetarium** (daily 9.30am–4.30pm; RM3). Aside from the usual shows, some in English, detailing the constellations, there are static displays illuminating the Islamic origins of astronomy as well as Malaysia's own space-age ambitions. In a country obsessed with record-setting and prestige projects, one of the latest crazes is to put a Malaysian in space, which may well happen as part of a Russian mission in 2007, though the focus often seems to be not on scientific work but on whether Malaysian snacks can be adapted for space consumption and how Islamic rites should be observed from the cosmos. For an extra RM6, you can enter the Space Theatre and watch a film from a changing programme of wide-screen IMAX movies (10am, noon, 2pm, 4pm). Those with cast-iron stomachs may also care to taste weightlessness in the Shuttle Spaceball, where the would-be astronaut is spun within a man-sized gyroscope – to the amusement of onlookers. The viewing gallery on the fourth floor provides a panoramic view of Kuala Lumpur's skyline and the surrounding Lake Gardens.

Having taken your fill of the planetarium, you could take the pedestrian bridge south to National Museum (see below).

The Carcosa Seri Negara

The **Carcosa Seri Negara** is KL's most exclusive hotel, secluded up a winding hill road to the west of the lake. This former colonial residence of the British governor of the Malay States comprises two elegant whitewashed mansions with Neoclassical touches – the "Carcosa", built in 1904 for Sir Frank Swettenham; and the "Seri Negara", formerly called the "King's House", which was used for guests. At independence, Malaysia's first prime minister, Tuanku Abdul Rahman, gifted the buildings to Britain who used them as the official residence of the British high commissioner. Abdul Rahman's successor, Dr Mahathir, secured the return of the buildings, and in 1989, after an inaugural visit by Queen Elizabeth II, the mansion and guesthouse became a hotel.

The hotel's oh-so-English **cream tea** is a fitting reward for a hot day's wandering around the Lake Gardens – as long as you don't mind paying RM70 a head for the privilege. Just don't turn up looking sweaty and dishevelled, as you will be if you attempt to tramp up here along Persiaran Mahameru, which starts on Jalan Damansara south of the Lake Gardens; much better is to take a taxi.

The National Museum

Built in 1963, the **National Museum** (Muzium Negara; daily 9am–6pm; RM2; ⓦ www.museum.gov.my) makes a positive first impression, with its sweeping roof characteristic of Sumatran Minangkabau architecture. Much of the museum's original collection was destroyed by World War II bombing, but the extensive ethnographic and archeological exhibits on display are worthy of an hour's wander. The only public transport here is bus #35 from Jalan TAR and Jalan Sultan Hishamuddin; ironically, the museum can't be reached from KL Sentral (diagonally across on Jalan Damansara) because of the lack of a northern exit from the station. In practice, the museum is best reached by taxi, perhaps combined with a trip to the planetarium (see opposite), to which it's linked by a footbridge.

The **first floor**, on which you enter the building, is mostly taken up with rather artless life-size dioramas depicting various aspects of traditional Malaysian life, from the prosaic activities of the Malay kampung (village) – fishing, farming and weaving – to the pomp and ritual of a wedding and a Malay circumcision ceremony. At the end of the room, a cross-section of a Melaka Baba house is revealed, loaded with mahogany furniture, intricate carpets and ornaments made from silver, brass and gold. Also on this floor are *wayang kulit* (shadow puppetry) displays, showing a variety of the hide puppets used in this ancient artistic tradition.

On the **second floor**, a large but uninspiring section of stuffed birds and animals needn't detain you long, certainly not if you're waylaid by the much more impressive collection of weapons, including a large number of *kris* daggers, *parang*s (machetes), swords and miniature cannons. Finally, there's a worthwhile section on traditional musical instruments: the *serunai*, a reed flute with a multicoloured end; the *rebab*, a kind of fiddle played with the instrument held upright, its base in the musician's lap; numerous two-metre-long Kelantanese drums and smaller *rebana* drums; and Chinese lutes, gongs and flutes.

Brickfields and KL Sentral

Located 2km south of the city centre, the **Brickfields** district was first settled by Tamils employed to build the railways, and named after the brickyards which lined the railway tracks. The area retains a strong South Indian presence, as well as some buildings and shophouses dating from the turn of the last century. However, with the completion of **KL Sentral** station in 2001, and the subsequent opening of two five-star hotels on the station's doorstep, the area has undoubtedly lost something of its original flavour. Still, if you arrive at KL Sentral and have a little time to spare, Brickfields does make for a pleasant wander, has a few worthwhile places to eat (see p.135) and, for the time being, retains a laid-back feel, in contrast with bustling Little India.

Arriving by Monorail puts you right on Jalan Tun Sambanthan, the main thoroughfare, which once ran along the back of the original railway line. The space between the road and KL Sentral is now taken up by a thriving **market** selling trinkets and Indian snacks, among other items. Specific attractions are few, but a wander through the streets south of, and parallel to, Jalan Tun Sambanthan reveals a profusion of old mission schools, churches and temples, notably the **Maha Vihara Buddhist Temple** on Jalan Berhala. A serene affair with a

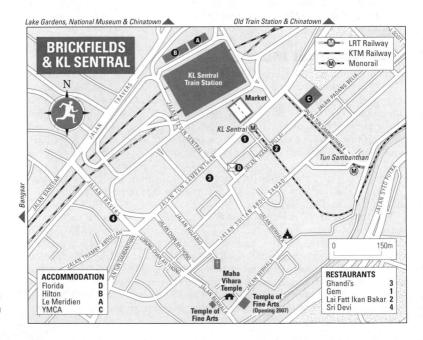

prominent white stupa, it's the centre of Sinhalese Buddhism in Malaysia. Also here is the **Temple of Fine Arts**, an Indian cultural centre featuring a crafts shop, an excellent café (run by the same people behind the superb *Annalakshmi* restaurant, p.135) and concerts of Indian music and dance. At the time of writing, they were housed in a small building at no. 128, but will shift into a grand purpose-built complex at no. 116 some time in 2007. In the northeast of the area, on Jalan Scott, you'll find one of many worthwhile independent art galleries in KL, the Wei-ling Gallery (see p.143).

Out from the centre

Outer KL offers fairly slim pickings for visitors, which is just as well given the chaotic traffic. The one attraction that you may want to make time for is the terrific **Thean Hou Temple** in Seputeh, just to the south of the city. If you've an interest in local art, you could head to the **National Art Gallery** (see the "Visual arts" section on p.142) on Jalan Tun Razak, just south of the mundane, man-made Lake Titiwangsa and its gardens. You may find the National Art Gallery a bit of a mixed bag, however; more consistent art galleries can be found southwest of the centre in trendy **Bangsar**, which also has some of the best restaurants and bars in the city (see p.135 and p.138). For attractions which are some way outside KL proper, see the "Around KL" section (p.147).

Thean Hou Temple

KL's huge and colourful Buddhist **Thean Hou Temple** (daily 8am–6pm; free), completed in 1987, is located on a hilltop in Seputeh, on the south side of the Sungai Klang 1km south of Brickfields. The temple is always busy, with busloads of tourists descending for the marvellous views north over the city. It's also the most popular place in KL for Chinese marriages, and has its own registry office on the first floor of the temple complex.

The main focus of excitement is the pagoda, in whose inner temple stands the shrine to Thean Hou's main deity, Kuan Yin, the goddess of mercy, who – legend has it – appears on earth in a variety of forms and can be identified by the precious dew flask which she always holds. The decor is as ornate as you'd expect, with a ceiling whose intricate patterns contain hundreds of green lanterns. In the centre of the line of sculpted deities sits Thean Hou, with Kuan Yin to her right, in front of whom visitors gather to burn offerings of joss sticks and paper money. During major Chinese festivals, particularly the Lunar New Year, the temple becomes extremely crowded.

The easiest way to get here is by bus #51 from Klang bus station, getting off at Wisma Belia on Jalan Syed Putra (tell the driver you want to be let off at the temple). From here, the temple is five minutes' walk southeast up a steep hill on the right. Walking here from Brickfields isn't practical, as you need to head some way south along Jalan Tun Sambanthan to where it crosses the river, then double back along Jalan Syed Putra.

Eating

Food is without doubt one of the highlights of any visit to KL. There are simply many more opportunities to enjoy high-calibre cooking here, in a variety of local and international styles, than anywhere else in the country, and whether you dine in a chic bistro-style restaurant or at a humble roadside stall, prices are almost always very reasonable.

Despite plenty of scope for cosmopolitan, upmarket dining, for many locals eating is still fundamentally about Malay, Chinese and Indian **street food**. The best-known food stalls are held in the same kind of reverence as a top-flight restaurant might be in a Western city, and people will travel across KL just to seek out a stall whose take on a particular dish is said to be better than anyone else's. If you find customers lining up to partake of some stall's spring rolls or *laksa*, it's a surefire indicator of quality. Stalls, whether on the street or collected into **food courts** (to be found in or close to major office blocks and shopping malls), are your best bets for inexpensive, satisfying meals, as are **kedai kopis**, also very common though a little thin on the ground in the Golden Triangle.

KL's **restaurants**, ranging from characterful little affairs in beautifully refurbished shophouses to banqueting halls in five-star hotels, are an equally vital part of the food experience. Be aware, however, that price and decor are not a watertight indicator of consistency or quality, and that service can be hesitant even in big hotels. At least the food in the better hotels is usually reliable if not necessarily top-drawer, whereas independent restaurants can range from inspired to downright amateurish.

Chinatown and around

There are some superb food **stalls** in Chinatown, serving up everything from rich yet subtle *bak kut teh* (pork-rib consommé, flavoured with herbs) to cooling sweet treats like *cendol*. The stalls here aren't always that easy for foreign visitors to get to grips with, however, particularly when some of the best lurk in the market alleys between Jalan Tun H.S. Lee and Jalan Petaling, and may be signed only in Chinese or not at all. Still, you can get an excellent taster of how stalls operate, and of street food, in the *Tang City Food Court* (see opposite).

Otherwise, the area has plenty of *kedai kopis* and a few cheap or mid-priced **restaurants**, with a few particularly touristy places at the eastern end of Jalan

△ Outdoor food stalls, Chinatown

Hang Lekir. You're not limited to Chinese food either, since the fringes of Chinatown, especially the zone north of Jalan Hang Lekir and around the Central Market, feature plenty of **Indian** and **mamak** places, and there's an excellent, mainly **Malay** food court in Central Market itself, with stalls offering regional fare from around the Peninsula. If you really are unadventurous, try the coffee house at the *Swiss Inn*, which offers predictable Western and local food, though the main reason to come here is the view of proceedings in the Petaling Street Market.

Bilals 33 Jalan Ampang. Better than average *mamak* joint, with chicken, mutton and squid curries, among others.

Cintamani 37 & 39 Jalan Hang Lekir; entrance also on Jalan Raja Chulan. Terrific Tamil-run vegetarian restaurant taking up two refurbished shophouses. They major on great meat-free versions of street-food favourites like *nasi lemak*, as well as a few Western-style offerings such as spicy potato skins. Best of all, though, is the great lunchtime buffet spread of soups, stews, stir-fries and rice and noodles, all for RM11. Good yoghurt shakes and local desserts too. Daily except Sat 7am–10pm.

Coconut House 28 & 30 Jalan Pudu Lama ☏03/2031 2830. Chinese-run Italian which, happily, turns out not to be a culinary oxymoron, serving up over a dozen very decent thin-crust pizzas (costing around RM15) from their own wood-fired oven. Also a range of mains (RM25 and up) such as *osso bucco*, and pasta dishes (RM15), plus a cool soundtrack of world music and left-field pop. Daily 10am till late.

Hameeds Café Klang bus station. Busy *kedai kopi* serving tandoori chicken, curries and rice dishes; fish-head curry is the house speciality.

Hamid Shah Café Jalan Silang. Excellent, busy *kedai kopi* for Malay and North Indian curries and *roti*. Daily 8am–6pm.

Ikopi First floor, 6 Jalan Panggong. Smart café with modern decor and parquet flooring, serving up a range of pricey speciality coffees (from RM14) plus more affordable lattes, macchiatos and so forth (around RM5). A few local and Western snacks available. If they're not busy, staff can tell you about their brewing techniques and the gadgets involved. Daily except Tues 11am–late.

Melaka St 37 Jalan Ampang. Hole-in-the-wall Indian-run place with *thosais*, *rotis* plus several noodle offerings. Inexpensive.

Old China Café 11 Jalan Balai Polis ☏03/2072 5915. Nonya restaurant atmospherically housed in a 1920s shophouse which was once home to KL's laundry guild; much of the decor, including the saloon-style swing doors at the entrance, is original and lovingly preserved. Among must-trys are classic dishes such as *itek tim*, duck

soup; *asam* fish, (spicy and sweet-yet-sour with tamarind); *chap chye*, the classic Nonya veg stir-fry; and desserts such as *bubur cha cha* or sago with *gula melaka*. Not expensive either – RM50 is ample to feed two. Daily 11am–11pm.

Purple Cane Tea House Third floor, 6 Jalan Panggong. Chinese tea shop where you can appreciate a variety of speciality teas, from relatively mundane green tea to varieties such as *pu'er*, reddish-brown like some of Malaysia's jungle rivers and imbued with a strong smoky flavour. They also do bizarre concoctions of tea, egg and various fruit flavours – actually pretty palatable – plus some rice and noodle snacks. Their teas are available to buy in leaf form, along with a range of tea-related paraphernalia, from their shop around the corner at 11 Jalan Sultan. Daily 11am–8pm.

Santa 7 Jalan Tun H.S. Lee, at the street's northern end. A lively *kedai kopi*, where chapati, rice and a choice of curries are unlikely to set you back more than RM5.

Seng Kee 50 Jalan Sultan. Frenetically busy, quintessentially Chinese restaurant serving up great Cantonese fare – everything from standards like beef with *kai lan* to occasional riverfish dishes, depending on supply. The house speciality, however, is *loh shee fun*, which unappetizingly translates as mouse-tail noodles, but is actually fantastic: stubby lengths of noodle fried with soy sauce, served in a clay pot and topped with pork crackling and a raw egg. Daily 10.30am till late.

Tang City Food Court Jalan Hang Lekir. A fine collection of fairly priced, tourist-friendly stalls, all recommended, from the Economy Mixed Rice *campur*-type spread at the front onwards. This is a great place to try *popiah*, spring rolls in the local, unfried fashion (RM3 buys a large portion at the Lim Kee stall), or prawn *mee* (also available from Lim Kee) or *yong tau foo* (available at a couple of other stalls – scan the signs). For afters, try the whimsically named Summer Shala'la stall at the front on the left, which does souped-up versions of local desserts, such *air batu campur* augmented with various fruit toppings.

Wan Fo Yuan Vegetarian Restaurant Jalan Panggong. Tiptop though unprepossessing a/c place, lurking behind dark glass doors.

The extensive picture menu features teppenyaki ribs, fried goose rice and other "meaty" treats – all made with soya- or gluten-based substitutes or occasionally yam, and often boasting depths of smoky flavour that seem miraculous considering the vegetarian ingredients. Most dishes cost around RM10 (rice or noodle one-plate meals RM6) and servings are generous. Daily 10am–10pm.

The Golden Triangle and Kampung Bahru

Besides numerous upmarket restaurants, the Golden Triangle also boasts some of the best Chinese food stalls in KL, along **Jalan Alor**. The street actually has a double layer of food outlets, being lined with mid-priced, open-air Chinese restaurants, which have stalls lined up in front of them. It's all pretty informal: if you choose a table on the street, you can order from nearby stalls or restaurants, and if you sit in one of the restaurants you can order from stalls outside or even across the road, as long as you can explain where your table is; English signage at the stalls is limited to their name and a terse description of what they serve, but many restaurateurs speak some English and have English-language menus. A few of the restaurants open around lunchtime, but things really gets going from late afternoon onwards, and the stalls stay open right into the small hours. As for the food, KL Chinese absolutely swear by the Hokkien noodles (*fu-kien meen* in Cantonese), comprising egg noodles fried in lard, seasoned with dark soy sauce and garnished with prawn, pork and fish-cake slices, and greens; look for a popular stall serving it near the Changkat Bukit Bintang end of the road. For the really daring, there are at least two stalls serving up frog porridge: rice gruel containing, well, bits of frog, actually hard to distinguish from chicken.

As for inexpensive eats elsewhere in the Golden Triangle, there are convenient stalls on the fourth floor of the Sungai Wang Plaza, close to the junction of Jalan Sultan Ismail and Jalan Imbi, and also plenty of Malay stalls at Suria KLCC. Close to Jalan Alor, there are a number of Malay and *mamak* places on Jalan Nagasari.

On the northern fringes of the Golden Triangle, **Kampung Bahru** is noteworthy for hosting one of KL's most extensive collections of Malay stalls, on and around Jalan Raja Muda Musa; they're easily reached using the Kampung Baru LRT stop. Among these is the *Nasi Lemak Antarabangsa* outlet, which devotees say does the best *nasi lemak* breakfast in the city. The stall shuts by 11am, but many of the other stalls are open late into the evening.

La Bodega 31 Tengkat Tong Shin ☎03/2142 6368, ⓦwww.bodega.com.my. Offshoot of the Bangsar-based outfit (see p.136), with the usual tapas plus more formal fare, and occasional live music. Daily noon till late (Sat & Sun from 10am).

Chinoz On The Park G47, Suria KLCC ☎03/2166 8277. Smart, convivial café-restaurant with generally Mediterranean-slanted food, from Lebanese lamb wraps to various pizzas (some of the best in town, from RM25), plus a good range of cocktails. The icing on the cake is the great location facing KLCC's kitsch musical fountains and with the Petronas Towers, though screened by the mall's bulk, looming right behind. Daily 8am–midnight.

Golden Phoenix *Hotel Equatorial*, Jalan Sultan Ismail ☎03/2161 7777. Top-flight, non-halal Cantonese restaurant (with a touch of Sichuan) with good seafood dishes. The *belacan* fish (decidedly not mainland Chinese fare) is worth tackling – if you've never had pungent *belacan* before, you'll either adore it or decide you'll never touch the stuff again. Daily noon–2.30pm & 6.30pm till 11pm.

Green Lotus Café Jalan Walter Grenier ☎03/2141 3007. Nestling anonymously behind a tiny oriental garden, this is something of a gay Chinese hangout. The menu features a good pan-East Asian mix, while the decor is amusingly chichi – red drapes, a wall-mounted moose's head and faux baroque mirror. Dishes from RM10; portions are generous. Mon–Sat noon till late, Sun 3pm till late.

Koryo-Won Antarabangsa Complex, 37 Jalan Sultan Ismail ☎03/2142 7655. Halal Korean restaurant specializing in good old Korean barbecue, done to a turn at your table. Not cheap at RM50 per person, excluding rice.

Lotus 2 Jalan Binjai. Phenomenal 24hr Tamil joint, the size of a small supermarket, that's a major social hub by evening and into the post-clubbing hours. They do all the usual South Indian favourites, plus *nasi kandar*, with some of the food laid out in self-service spreads.

Nerovivo 3a Jalan Ceylon ☎03/2070 3120. This upmarket restaurant is among the best Italian places in KL, with chic modern decor and an extensive menu majoring on seafood. Though they can be a little inconsistent at times, they do have fantastic pizzas and pasta dishes (including excellent *linguine vongole*). Not cheap – pizzas start at RM25, while main courses start around the RM40 mark – and not great for an intimate meal either, as both the background music and conversation can be pretty loud. Daily noon till late, except Sat closed lunchtime.

Oversea 84–88 Jalan Imbi ☎03/2148 7567. Established and much loved Cantonese restaurant, well known for excellent roast meats such as *char siew*, plus *dim sum* at lunchtime and great seafood, including its trademark (non-Cantonese) *asam* fish head. Daily 11am–2.30pm & 6–11pm.

Pacifica Grill & Bar *Mandarin Oriental*, KLCC ☎03/2179 8882. Specializing in international cuisine mixing influences from the Pacific and the Mediterranean, this place is particularly strong on fish and steaks. Expensive – even the set meals start at RM70 for two courses.

Passage Thru India 4 Jalan Delima, close to the junction of Jalan Bukit Bintang and Jalan Tun Razak ☎03/2145 0366. Well-regarded place drawing its menu from every part of the subcontinent. Prices are reasonable – tandoori chicken will set you back around RM14, lassis RM6.

Qba *Westin Hotel*, 199 Jalan Bukit Bintang. Latin American-themed restaurant, on the pricey side – plenty on the menu is around the RM50 mark – but with generous portions and a cosy ambience. Put together your own grill platters featuring steak, chicken or seafood (charged by weight) or go for lighter tapas or other options. Daily from 5pm till late.

Rasa Utara Basement of BB Plaza, Jalan Bukit Bintang ☎03/2141 9246. Specializing in northern Malay food, specifically that of Kedah. Try the *laksa*, featuring mackerel pieces, or *passambur*, an appetizer not unlike the Indonesian *gado-gado*, comprising various vegetables dressed in a satay-style peanut sauce. Moderately priced. Daily 11am–9.30pm.

Sao Nam 21 Tengkat Tong Shin ☎03/2144 1225. You don't have to be mad about Vietnamese food to warm to this unpretentious restaurant. Beneath wall posters extolling the collectivist life, definitive beef *pho* noodles are served up, alongside delightful mangosteen salad – a house speciality – and, to wash it down afterwards, Vietnamese drip-style coffee, brewed in a filter placed over your cup. Good-value set lunches too (RM20), typically featuring a main course, salad plus a drink. Tues–Sun noon–2.30pm & 6–10.30pm.

Sari Ratu 42–4 Jalan Sultan Ismail ☎03/2141 1811. Indonesian restaurant serving good-value food from around the archipelago. Daily 11am–11pm.

Seri Angkasa Revolving atop Menara KL ☎03/2020 5055. The buffets, which are what most customers end up going for (lunch RM67, tea RM25, dinner RM115), aren't that spectacular – but the views are. Smart casual dress required (no shorts, sleeveless tops or sandals). Daily: lunch noon–3pm, tea 3.30–5.30pm, dinner 6.30–11.30pm; Sat & Sun additional brunch (11.30am–5.30pm) and high tea (3.30–5.30pm) options.

Tarbush LG16, Starhill Gallery ☎03/2144 6393. Part of the maze of elegant restaurants at Starhill, *Tarbush* is a classy Lebanese par excellence. There's plenty for carnivores, including classic *shish tawook* (grilled chicken breast) plus a best-of-everything mixed grill at RM35, as well as loads for veggies if you order up meze (selections, all at around RM10, include hummus, stuffed vine leaves and tabbouleh). The fruity milk shakes are as luscious as anything sold on the streets of Beirut. Daily 11am till late.

Top Hat 7 Jalan Kia Peng, close to KL Convention Centre ☎03/2142 8611. Classy restaurant based in a renovated 1930s mansion. Nonya food dominates proceedings, from the *kuih pai tee* appetizers (their signature dish, thanks to the resemblance to top hats) to mainstays like *laksa*, but there's a fair amount of Western and fusion fare as well. Desserts, mainly gateaux, are particularly sinful. A wide range of three-course set meals (RM35–100) can be good value.

Wasabi *Mandarin Oriental*, KLCC ☎03/2163 0968. Japanese food of a very high order in a stylish setting in the hotel's basement. Sushi and sashimi sets from around RM50. Mon–Fri noon–2.30pm & 7–11pm, Sat 7–11pm, Sun 11.30–3.30pm.

Little India to Chow Kit and beyond

Little India is a good area for both Indian and Malay food – there are a number of inexpensive Indian restaurants and sweetmeat shops along Jalan Melayu, while in and around Lorong TAR's *pasar malam* are quite a few Malay food stalls and Indian *kedai kopis*. There's also a useful food court opposite the *Palace Hotel* that stays open late. A few truly venerable *kedai kopis*, some housed in equally venerable shophouses, can be found along hectic Jalan TAR, while there are more stalls, Malay and even Indonesian, around Chow Kit Market.

For upmarket eating, you'll have to head to the eastern fringe of the area. Here, close to Medan Tuanku monorail station and the *Sheraton* hotel, the newish **Asian Heritage Row** on Jalan Doraisamy is a terrace of refurbished shophouses, home to a string of smart restaurants, bars and clubs, with more springing up nearby. For the locations of most places reviewed below, see the map on p.119, otherwise check the main KL map, pp.96–97.

A J Kompleks Damai, 50 Jalan Lumut, off Jalan Ipoh ☏03/4044 8888. A Malay diner like no other, with funky modern decor on the walls and a world-music soundtrack. They do amazing, good-value buffet spreads, typically costing RM10–15 depending on what you have, and featuring several fish curries and the likes of *ayam kicap* (chicken and potatoes cooked in soy sauce), *tempeh goreng* (fried fermented bean cakes) and *ulam* (Malay salad). The proprietor hails from Johor, hence the presence of southern fare like *laksa Johor* on the menu. The place is a few minutes' walk south along Jalan Pahang Barat from Titiwangsa station.

Capital Café 213 Jalan TAR. Housed in a Neoclassical block, this endearing *kedai kopi* is something of a period piece itself, looking as though little has been altered since it first opened in the 1950s. The halal food caters to all tastes: there's *nasi lemak* in the morning, *rojak* and *nasi padang* during the day, and excellent satay in the evenings, plus Chinese rice and noodle dishes cooked to order throughout. Daily 7am–8pm.

Coliseum Café 98 Jalan TAR. Colonial-era hotel restaurant known for bland meat-and-two-veg meals, once served up by Hainanese chefs who emulated English cooking to please their colonial masters. The restaurant still serves up steaks and fish-and-chips today, of variable quality; you may be better off sticking to the rice and noodle repertoire. Despite the waiters' crisp uniforms, the service can be a bit shambolic, but the atmosphere partly makes amends. Daily 8am–10pm.

Jai Hind 11–15 Jalan Melayu. Friendly Sikh-run *kedai kopi* which, besides an impressively wide-ranging *campur*-type spread of curries and stir-fries, also has an extensive menu of North Indian savouries and sweets, as good as you'll get in much posher restaurants but at half the price. Mon–Sat 8am–9pm, Sun 10am–7pm.

Museum Restaurant *Legend Hotel*, Putra Place ☏03/4042 9888. Cantonese and spicy Sichuan cuisine served amid beautifully displayed antiques and paintings.

Saravanaa Bhavan Jalan Masjid India. Member of a slightly eccentric Madras-based chain of vegetarian restaurants that's spread its tentacles as far afield as London and New York. The menu features all the usual South Indian delights – *thosai*, *idli*, *uthapam* and so forth – plus a few allegedly Chinese aberrations, including *paneer* fried rice and various "Manchurian" affairs. The cooking's generally good, but be warned that spicing can be incendiary, even by South Indian standards. Inexpensive, with main courses under RM10. Daily 8am–10pm.

Sithique Nasi Kandar 233 Jalan TAR. One of a handful of popular *kedai kopis* on Jalan TAR serving Penang-style variations on *mamak* fare, with an impressive range of fiery curries, including fish head as well as cuttlefish. Daily 7.30am–7.30pm.

Vanilla Box Asian Heritage Row, 58 Jalan Doraisamy. Delightful, intimate café-deli with magazines and papers to read, and a range of soups, salads, snacks and light meals (including quiche and beef or vegetable lasagnes). For dessert, tuck into their mouthwatering range of gateaux – the cheesecake hits the spot. Heineken, Guinness and Tiger available. Very reasonably priced, with appealing set breakfasts (RM10), main courses RM25. Mon–Fri 8am–9pm, Sat 10am–9pm.

Brickfields and Mid Valley

Naturally enough, **Indian food** dominates the Brickfields eating scene, such as it is, though one of the best Indian places in KL isn't in Brickfields but 1km to the southwest at the Mid Valley Megamall, served by Mid Valley station on the Seremban Komuter line. The Brickfields restaurants reviewed are shown on the map on p.128.

Annalakshmi Ground Floor Boulevard, Mid Valley Megamall ☎03/2284 3799. Community-run South Indian vegetarian restaurant with a stupendous eat-all-you-want buffet, featuring terrific home cooking. You actually pay what you feel the meal is worth to you, and the profits go to support the work of the Temple of Fine Arts (see p.142), among other projects. Daily 11.30am–3pm & 6.30–10pm.

Gem 124 Jalan Tun Sambanthan, Brickfields ☎03/2260 1373. Reliable a/c restaurant serving up South Indian chicken, mutton and seafood curries from RM10 and up. As ever, the *thali* platters make for a good deal, costing around RM10. Conveniently close to the monorail station. Daily 11.30am till late.

Ghandhi's Jalan Thambypillai, close to the Brickfields post office. Nothing more than a shack hidden off the main road, shaded by trees and with a few tables placed around. Humble it may be, but they cook to order a range of delicious if oddly named Indian vegetarian dishes (Y2K Chicken, and so forth), making use of soya chunks and other meat substitutes. Friendly and inexpensive. Daily 6pm till late.

Lai Fatt Ikan Bakar Jalan Thambypillai. *Kedai kopi* doing delicious *ikan bakar* and barbecued stingray, covered in spices and served on banana leaves.

Sri Devi Jalan Travers. Widely reckoned to sell some of Brickfields' best Indian food, this little place does excellent banana-leaf curries from midday onwards and wonderful *dosais* all day. The *masala dosai* is particularly fine. Inexpensive.

Bangsar

Of the handful of suburbs to have enjoyed a mushrooming of upmarket restaurants and bars, **Bangsar** is the closest to downtown KL. Just four kilometres' southwest from Chinatown is the epicentre of the area's thriving eating and drinking scene, the small grid of streets known as **Bangsar Baru**, beginning pretty much at the junction of Jalan Maarof and the southern part of Jalan Ara. Along Jalan Ara itself, just west of the main action, is a newish, extremely smart terraced development known as **One Bangsar**, housing yet more restaurants. Altogether the area is very much an expat ghetto, as well as catering to well-heeled local professionals. This is not to say that more typically Malaysian eating doesn't get a look in: Bangsar Baru also boasts a great *mamak*, Devi's Corner, that's crammed most nights, and a heaving Sunday **pasar malam** that's one of the city's best markets for takeaway cooked food, with some fresh produce also available. A little incongruous here are a smattering of Tamil clubs, a spillover from Brickfields just to the east.

Bus #5 travels to Bangsar Baru from the Sultan Mohamed terminal in Chinatown, via Brickfields. The LRT isn't convenient for Bangsar Baru, however: from Bangsar station, you face a short walk southwest along Jalan Bangsar, then a slightly uphill ten-minute walk northwest along Jalan Maarof; both are frenetically busy highways that really weren't meant for pedestrians to tramp alongside or get across. A **taxi** to Bangsar Baru from Chinatown shouldn't cost more than RM6.

Alexis Bistro 29 Jalan Telawi 3 ☎03/2284 2880. The de facto clubhouse of Kuala Lumpur's movers and shakers – you'll see newspaper editors, academics, film-makers and politicos chewing the fat and putting Malaysia to rights here. Both local and Western fare is served, so don't be surprised

that slick noodle and pasta dishes feature on the menu. There's also a formidable gateaux counter. Main courses from around RM15.

Assam and Garam One Bangsar, Jalan Ara ☎03/2282 6286. A most unusual entity, an upmarket Malay restaurant run by a Chinese cook who's

BANGSAR BARU

JALAN TELAWI 6

JALAN TELAWI 5

JALAN TELAWI 3

JALAN TELAWI

JALAN TELAWI 4

JALAN TERASEK 4

N

JALAN TERASEK

Sunday Market

JALAN TELAWI 2

JALAN TELAWI 1

Food Centre

MPH Bookstore

JALAN MAAROF

LORONG MAAROF

Bangsar Seafood Village

Bangsar Village

JALAN MAAROF

JALAN ARA

0   100m

▼ No. 5 Bus stop

Brickfields ▼

◀ T & 9ne Bangsar

RESTAURANTS, CAFÉS & BARS	
Alexis Bistro	11
Assam and Garam	17
Bon Bon Brasserie	9
Delicious by Ms Read	16
Devi's Corner	15
Finnegan's	1
Fu Yu	12
Grappa Trattoria	4
House Frankfurt	2
La Bodega	6
Madam Kwan's	14
Modesto's	7
Planet Jim's	5
Ronnie Q's	10
Saravanaa Bhavan	8
The Social	13
Telawi Street Bistro	3

passionate about the cuisine. Their *tok* beef really sets the standard: basically a *rendang*, it melts in the mouth, with no hint of the stringiness that plagues inferior attempts. Also try the great *asam pedas* fish, flavoured with lemon grass, ginger flower and *daun kesom*. Great *kuih* for dessert too, such as *talam ubi*, a steamed coconut and tapioca pudding. The food is halal, but alcohol is available. Daily noon–3pm & 6.30–11pm; separate deli section 9.30am till late.

La Bodega 16 Jalan Telawi 2 ☎03/2287 8318, ⓦwww.bodega.com.my. Basically a tapas bar, augmented by a bistro and deli. The tapas part has the most authentically Spanish menu, while the bistro features plenty of appealing modern European fare, and the deli majors on all-day breakfasts and great sandwiches and cakes. There's also a lounge with cosy armchairs, cocktails and yet more tapas.

Bon Bon Brasserie 20 Jalan Telawi 2 ☎03/2283 1100. Sister restaurant to the *Alexis*,

this is a good spot from which to watch fashionable Bangsar sashay by. Lots of modern European-style dishes from around RM25. Daily noon–3pm and 6pm till late.

🏃 **Delicious By Ms Read** In the Bangsar Village mall ☎03/2288 1770. Once upon a time, a store selling clothes for the large woman decided to branch out into health-conscious catering – and this superb café-restaurant was the result. The food's not actually starved of fat, sugar and salt, but is expertly prepared, features fresh ingredients and is very reasonably priced – sandwiches, quiches, pastas and salads start at RM15. The deep-dish pies, if available (the menu changes regularly; RM20), are recommended, as are the luscious cakes, which probably boost their clothing sales. Breakfasts (cooked or featuring French toast or waffles) available at weekends. Mon–Thurs 11am–10pm, Fri–Sun 8am–10pm.

Fu Yu 14 Jalan Telawi 4 ⊕03/2282 0009. Popular Cantonese restaurant, strong on seafood, not just fish and prawn but also featuring rubbery sea cucumber – definitely an acquired taste. Separate veggie menu. Dishes from RM10. Daily noon–3pm & 6pm–midnight.

Grappa Trattoria 1 Jalan Telawi 5 ⊕03/2287 0080. Very classy affair, with modern, uncluttered decor and food with Italian influences. Pasta starts at around RM20, main fish courses from RM40.

House Frankfurt 12 Jalan Telawi 5 ⊕03/2284 1624. If the pork-free nature of a lot of KL dining is getting you down, come to this agreeable bar-restaurant to enjoy *schweinfleisch* – as grilled pork knuckle, *wurst* or schnitzel. They also do classic southern German *spätzle*, little pasta bits with cheese and bacon. Mon–Sat 4pm–midnight, Sun noon–midnight.

Madam Kwan's 65 Jalan Telawi 3 ⊕03/2284 2297. If stalls and *kedai kopis* don't appeal, come here to try Madam Kwan's elaborate takes on classic local fare, from *nasi lemak* to chicken rice. Often busy. Main courses from RM10. Daily 11.30am till late.

Planter Jim's 6–8 Jalan Telawi 2 ⊕03/2282 4084. Consistently good Thai food with an eclectic twist – it's doubtful that their grilled ostrich with black pepper is much seen on the streets of Chiang Mai. Good desserts too, including a Thai-style *air batu campur* with jackfruit and water chestnut. Dishes from RM10. Daily noon till late.

Saravanaa Bhavan 52 Jalan Maarof. See review on p.134. Daily 8am–10pm.

The Social 57–59 Jalan Telawi 3. Convivial bar-restaurant with a mix of Asian and Western fare, plus football matches on satellite TV. Set lunches at RM25 are good value. Best of all, the terrace tables offer a superb view of the hectic Sunday *pasar malam*. Daily noon–2am.

Telawi Street Bistro 1 Jalan Telawi 3 ⊕03/2284 3168, ⓦwww.telawi.com.my. The decor is modern, the food influenced by Western bistros – so modern continental European and Mediterranean flavours predominate. Very strong on pizza, not just in its traditional form but also in pocket (stuffed, à la calzone) and plank (long rectangular crusts with up to four toppings) varieties. Open till late; Mon–Fri from noon, Sat & Sun from 10am.

Drinking, nightlife and entertainment

The most fashionable of KL's **bars** and **clubs** are concentrated in the Golden Triangle, with Bangsar also playing host to a few slick bars. If the drinking scene seems to tick over healthily enough, KL's **clubbing** appears surprisingly buoyant for the size of the city. A few years ago, the city was one of the party capitals of Southeast Asia, with frequent large-scale raves and locals muttering darkly about so-called sarong party girls, local women prowling the clubs hoping to land a white boyfriend. Things have come off the boil somewhat recently but there remain a number of stalwart venues where you're guaranteed a range of good sounds through the week. It's only during Ramadan that both the bars and clubs are distinctly quiet.

The local **performing arts** scene is distinctly modest, and furthermore is split between KL and its satellite Petaling Jaya, which, with its incredibly complex system of numbered roads which even local residents don't understand, is best accessed by taxi. **Theatre** is probably the strongest suit, and throughout the year there are concerts, musicals and so forth, by local as well as visiting international performers and troupes. There's also a dedicated community of people working in the **visual arts**. For event **listings**, check the national press, such as Thursday's *Star* newspaper, and also KL's excellent culture and lifestyle magazine, **Klue** (ⓦwww.klue.com.my), which features intelligent interviews with local writers, musicians, actors and directors. In a similar spirit, ⓦwww.kakiseni.com is worth consulting not only for listings but also for an intelligent look at how the performing arts can reach a *modus vivendi* with the multicultural Asian and Muslim values that hold sway in Malaysia.

Bars and pubs

Bar **hours** vary from one venue to the next, but most places are open from mid-afternoon till midnight, at least. Beer in KL costs around RM12 a pint (when available on draught; bottles and cans are more common), a couple of ringgit less during the happy hours which most places offer.

Coliseum Hotel 98 Jalan TAR. Endearingly antiquated, the bar here has a rich history and relaxed atmosphere, though some of the cocktails are a bit iffy. Sip a chilled beer and imagine the planters and colonial administrators of yesteryear gathering to quench their thirst. Daily 10am–10pm.

Finnegan's Pub 51 Jalan Sultan Ismail, Bukit Bintang; 6 Jalan Telawi 5, Bangsar. This chain bills itself as "Malaysia's leading Irish pubs", which isn't saying much, though the venues are pleasant enough. Guinness, Kilkenny and Strongbow cider on tap, plus a menu of generic pub food – ploughman's lunches, pies – as well as pricier steaks and the obligatory Irish stew. Also good for football on satellite TV.

Frangipani 25 Changkat Bukit Bintang. Behind the impressive Art Deco-style facade is a bar with sleek minimalist decor, excellent cocktails, pumping house sounds and a beautiful straight and gay clientele, almost as pretty as the downstairs restaurant's pricey nouvelle cuisine. Tues–Sun: bar from 6pm till late, restaurant Tues–Sun 7.30–10.30pm.

The Green Man 40 Changkat Bukit Bintang. Small, likeable pub serving reasonably priced local and imported beer and bacon and cheese toasties. Particularly busy when there's football or rugby on TV (there's also a pool table). Mon–Thurs 4pm till late, Fri–Sun noon till late.

House Frankfurt 12 Jalan Telawi 5, Bangsar. Relaxed venue with amicable management and walls lined with vintage photos of German movie stars. They offer a terrific range of Pilseners and German dark beers and *weissbier* (a 330ml bottle costs RM8), plus *schnapps* (RM15). Mon–Sat 4pm–midnight, Sun noon–midnight.

Luna Bar Level 34, *Pacific Regency Hotel Apartments*, Menara Panglobal, Jalan Puncak, off Jalan P. Ramlee. If you've only time to take in a couple of bars while in KL, you could do far worse than drop by at this gorgeous rooftop poolside venue, with loungey sounds and breathtaking views of KL's skyline.

Reggae Bar 158 Jalan Tun H.S. Lee, Chinatown. No-frills bar below a hostel and thus very popular with backpackers, though a few locals drop by too. The wall is plastered with Bob Marley memorabilia, though the DJs do recognize that other reggae artistes are available. Daily 6pm till late.

Ronnie Q's 32 Jalan Telawi 2, Bangsar. Plenty of bars feature football matches on satellite TV, but at *Ronnie Q's* the focus is very much on sport – not just soccer but also cricket and rugby. The closest thing KL has to a Western sports bar.

Speakeasy 9 Jalan Ampang. A rare example of its species in the Chinatown area, this bar-restaurant does a good range of wines and spirits, as well as a menu of light meals, with more interesting fusion fare at lunchtime. Pool tables available. Mon–Fri noon–midnight.

Clubs and live music

KL's clubland is largely focused around the junction of **Jalan Sultan Ismail** and **Jalan P. Ramlee** in the Golden Triangle, and there are also a number of venues springing up around **Asian Heritage Row** on Jalan Doraisamy, close to Medan Tuanku station on the monorail. The music policy at any venue can change as often as KL experiences a thunderstorm, but as a general rule weekends tend to feature more hardcore dance sounds, while during the week retro hits and fairly accessible R&B take over. To keep up with happenings, including which big-name DJs might be in town, check out the Friday club listings in the *Star* newspaper, the free *Juice* magazine (available at bars and clubs, or at ⓦwww.juiceonline.com) or the clubs' own websites, though don't be surprised if some haven't been updated in a while. Most clubs get going late and don't wind down until 3am or so; a **cover charge** of RM20–40 often applies (more if well-known DJs are playing), though women get in free at some venues during mid-week. Post-clubbing, you could do worse than join locals for food or a *teh tarik* nightcap down Jalan Alor (see p.132) or at one of several 24-hour restaurants (such as the *Lotus*, p.133, or one of a couple of *mamak* places on Jalan Nagasari, downhill from Jalan Alor).

Unfortunately, **live music** in KL isn't much to write home about. With Malaysia a recognized centre for music piracy, and standards of living not quite up to those of the other Asian "tiger" economies, it's simply uneconomic for most international bands to play here, though there are occasional concerts by very safe big-name pop, soul or country artists. If you want to enjoy cutting-edge gigs by foreign acts, you'll have to join the Malaysian music fans shuttling down to Singapore. That said, the Malaysian music scene is worth investigating: KL has a few small venues where local singer-songwriters and bands performing in English get to strut their stuff, and there are a few live shows by Malay pop-stars and old-school rockers, which are publicized in the press.

Clubs

Beach Club 97 Jalan P. Ramlee, Golden Triangle. Established venue, with a somewhat clichéd thatched tropical hut theme and definitely something of a meat market. Still, the mix of commercial chart and house sounds does pull in the punters.

Espanda 97 Jalan Sultan Ismail, Golden Triangle ⓦ www.espandaclub.com. A sizeable modern venue spinning house at weekends, with more generic sounds during the rest of the week. Look out for occasional independently promoted nights with big-name DJs.

The Loft/Cynna Asian Heritage Row, Jalan Doraisamy ⓣ 03/2691 5668. A mixture of house (more hardcore at *Cynna*), R&B and retro sounds at this sleek and surprisingly spacious venue.

Maison Jalan Yap Ah Shak, behind the *Sheraton* and very close to Asian Heritage Row ⓦ www .maison.com.my. An impressive conversion of colonial-era property, retaining the period facade but all minimalist decor within. Nightly except Mon, Wed tends to be R&B, Fri & Sat house.

Nouvo/Sangria 16 Jalan Sultan Ismail, Golden Triangle (at the junction with Jalan P. Ramlee) ⓦ www.nouvoclub.com. Two venues in one: upstairs is the rather owish club *Nouvo*, while *Sangria* downstairs is a bar with alfresco seating. The music is mainly fairly commercial R&B and hip-hop; much hipper are the drum-and-bass parties twice a month. As at *Espanda*, there are more interesting big-name DJ nights from time to time.

Poppy Collection 18-1 Jalan P. Ramlee ⓦ www .poppy-collection.com. Swanky designer venue, spinning soul and R&B downstairs in the *Poppy Garden*, with largely unadulterated house sounds above in the *Passion* lounge. No cover charge except during special events.

Zouk 113 Jalan Ampang, Golden Triangle ⓦ www .zoukclub.com.my. Operating out of its own hyper-modern building, this offshoot of one of Singapore's top clubs has rapidly become a mainstay of the KL scene too. There are several venues within, spinning an eclectic range of music, including trance (Sat) and a smidgen of indie. There's also a relaxed terrace bar.

Live venues

Alexis Bistro & Wine Bar Ground floor, Great Eastern Mall, 303 Jalan Ampang ⓣ 03/4260 2288, ⓦ www.alexis.com.my. Smart venue with occasional live jazz or blues sets by local or low-key international groups. Worth the trek – it's 2km east of the Ampang Park LRT stop.

La Bodega 16 Jalan Telawi 2, Bangsar; 31 Tengkat Tong Shin, Bukit Bintang ⓦ www.labodega.com .my. Regular open-mike music nights at this popular tapas bar and lounge.

No Black Tie 17 Jalan Mesui, Bukit Bintang ⓣ 03/2142 3737. Occasional music venue, gorgeously done out in tropical timbers. They major on jazz but take pride in putting on left-field performers from various musical genres – here you just might stumble upon the likes of satirical songwriter Rafique Rashid. Sadly, they tend to keep their events hush-hush, so either call to find out what's on or turn up on spec.

Top Hat 7 Jalan Kia Peng, close to KLCC ⓣ 03/2142 8611. At weekends this swish restaurant has its upstairs section turned over to jazz sessions involving local enthusiasts of the genre – always decidedly non-loungey, though it varies from week to week. Pricey, though, at RM58 including two drinks.

Gay KL

KL's gay community, while fairly discreet, is not closeted, as a stroll down fashionable **Bintang Walk** – the stretch of Jalan Bukit Bintang just east of Jalan Sultan Ismail – will confirm, the smart café terraces here attracting a noticably gay clientele. Plenty of the mainstream clubs have euphemistically named boys' nights (at the time of writing, *Espanda* or *Maison* of a Sunday·evening were good bets), and there are also a few discreet saunas.

The chief gay venue proper is *Blue Boy*, 50 Jalan Sultan Ismail, actually in a dingy lane off the main drag. It attracts a local and foreign crowd, though beware the odd hustler. Much more agreeable is *Liquid* (Wed–Sun 5pm–3am; RM25 cover), something of a veteran survivor on KL's clubbing scene. With a mixed clientele (particularly gay at weekends), it's housed in a perfect little venue in the Central Market Annexe, with a quieter terrace overlooking Sungai Klang that's good for a chat. Wednesday nights tend to be for retro sounds, Fridays and Saturdays house, which is also when its upstairs *Disco* offshoot opens up for the crowd to get down to handbag and yet more house. Both *Frangipani* (see p.138) and the *Green Lotus Café* (see p.132) are also gay hangouts. For more on gay venues and social events in the city, try the excellent website Ⓦ www.mylpg.net.

Theatre and classical music

Most prominent among KL's **theatre** companies is the Actors Studio. Based in Bangsar, it mounts several productions each year, ranging from Malaysianized versions of foreign classics to work by local playwrights, and has been instrumental in the creation and running of one of the city's more impressive independent arts centres, KLPac (see below). Other drama companies worth making time for include the Five Arts Centre (Ⓦ www.fiveartscentre.org), the Straits Theatre Company and the satirical Instant Café.

If you're interested in classical music, there are two home-grown **orchestras** to choose from, namely the Malaysian Philharmonic Orchestra (Ⓦ www .malaysianphilharmonic.com) and the Dama Orchestra (Ⓦ www.damaorchestra .com), the latter specializing in Chinese classical music and musicals. Watch the press for news of international recitals.

Theatres, performance spaces and concert halls

Besides the **venues** listed here, you'll find that there are occasional concerts at the KL Convention Centre and also at out-of-town resorts such as Genting Highlands; check the press for details.

Actors Studio Bangsar Bangsar Shopping Centre, 285 Jalan Maarof ☎ 03/2094 0400, Ⓦ www .theactorsstudio.com.my. About 1500m uphill from Bangsar Baru, this hosts drama by the Actors Studio and other companies, plus a variety of concerts.

Dewan Philharmonik Petronas Twin Towers, KLCC ☎ 03/2051 7007. The home of the Malaysian Philharmonic, and also hosts concerts by other performers, not just in the classical domain. Box office is on the ground floor, Tower 2 (Mon–Sat 10am–6pm).

Istana Budaya (National Theatre) Jalan Tun Razak, east of the junction with Jalan Pahang and south of Titiwangsa Gardens ☎ 03/4025 5932, Ⓦ www.istanabudaya.com.my. Besides providing a spacious modern home for the National Theatre Company and the National Symphony Orchestra, this venue sees performances by visiting international orchestras as well as staging pop concerts, plays and ballets. Just over 1km from Titiwangsa (LRT/monorail) or Chow Kit (monorail) stations.

KLPac Jalan Strachan, off Jalan Ipoh ☎ 03/4047 9000 or 4042 7500, Ⓦ www.klpac.com. A joint project of the Actors Studio and the construction conglomerate which is redeveloping the area, the KL Performing Arts Centre is housed in a former rail depot revamped to look like something Frank Lloyd Wright could have doodled. It hosts a few jazz, indie and dance events, plus, of course, plays by various companies. The location couldn't be more awkward, however, in the depths of a disused golf course and cut off from the nearby Sentul Komuter station by the rail line, which you can't cross safely without a big detour. Get here by taxi; just pray that the driver is a culture vulture or remembers the Sentul Raya Golf Club. As for heading back, be prepared for a trudge out to Jalan Ipoh, where you can pick up a taxi.

Panggung Bandaraya Corner of Jalan Sultan Hishamuddin and Jalan Tun Perak ⓦ www.dbkl .gov.my/panggung. Occasional performances of Malay drama (*bangsawan*) take place in this historic theatre, with a Moorish facade.

Film

Cinema in KL is something of a let-down. Hollywood blockbusters are easy enough to find, though expect the censor's scissors to have excised any unusually torrid bits. However, more adventurous international films are thin on the ground, and local independent productions, which often hold a mirror up to taboo or sensitive social issues, don't get the popular acclaim they deserve despite going through something of a purple patch. Still, it's worth looking out for screenings or VCDs of films by the likes of Yasmin Ahmad, whose *Sepet* (2004) dealt amusingly yet touchingly with a Chinese–Malay love affair; its sequel *Gubra* (2006) sees the Malay woman of the romance plunged into a complex tale whose main theme is betrayal. Also worth keeping an eye out for is the work of opinionated writer and director Amir Muhammad. His latest film at the time of writing, *Lelaki Komunis Terakhir* (*The Last Communist*; 2006), was banned by the government just as it was about to open, apparently because it dealt with the awkward subject of Chin Peng, the ringleader behind the violent Emergency of the 1950s. While it's to be hoped the ban will prove temporary, the episode is a timely reminder that despite rising living standards and levels of educational attainment, freedom of expression remains very much a live issue in Malaysia.

The two main **cinema chains**, both with online booking facilities, are Golden Screen Cinemas (ⓦ www.gsc.com.my) and TGV (ⓦ www.tgv.com .my). GSC's screens at Mid Valley Megamall (ⓣ 03/8312 3456) are your best bet for occasional art-house films from abroad; TGV has a conveniently located multiplex at Suria KLCC (ⓣ 03/7492 2929). Also worth a look-in for its local cachet – even if the Indian and Cantonese action flicks it's specialized in for generations aren't your thing – is the Coliseum Cinema on Jalan TAR. An institution dating back to the 1920s, it is, however, threatened with conversion into a newfangled arts centre. Finally, there's also the DiGi IMAX cinema on level 10 of the Berjaya Times Square mall, Jalan Imbi (ⓣ 03/2117 3046).

Cultural shows

Traditional dance can be seen at the **cultural shows** put on by the MTC and by a couple of restaurants for diners, though what's on offer is a little touristy. Indian dance is better catered for, thanks to the Temple of Fine Arts (see below). Traditional festivals may see more authentic performances being staged; check the press or ask at MTC for details.

Malaysia Tourism Centre (MTC) 109 Jalan Ampang ⓣ 03/2164 3929, ⓦ www.mtc.gov.my. Half-hour dance shows, featuring performers from Borneo as well as the Peninsula, are held Tues, Thurs, Sat & Sun from 2pm (RM5). More interesting are the weightier music sessions, featuring *dikir barat*, improvised Malay folk music from the east coast; call for details.
Nelayan Titiwangsa Titiwangsa Gardens ⓣ 03/4022 8400. On a platform out over the lake, this restaurant serves a variety of local

fare, including steamboats. They also offer good-value buffet spreads (lunchtime RM20, eves RM25–28). The main reason to make the trek out here (best done by taxi), however, is the show of traditional Malay song and dance (eves at 8.30pm, except Mon). Daily noon–2.30pm and 6.30–11pm.
Seri Melayu Jalan Conlay ⓣ 03/2145 1833. In a traditional Malay-style house, this restaurant serves up Malay buffets (eves RM68) and does nightly traditional dance shows (8.30pm). Smartish dress

required (avoid shorts and sleeveless tops). Daily noon–3pm & 6.30pm till late.

Temple of Fine Arts Jalan Berhala, Brickfields ☎03/2274 3709. Community-run cultural centre set up to preserve Tamil culture by promoting dance, theatre, folk, classical music and

craft-making. Probably the best place in KL to see traditional Indian dance – call to check their programme. By the time you read this, their brand new complex at no. 116 should be up and running; otherwise look for their temporary premises around the corner at no. 128.

Visual arts

KL has been developing a strong visual arts scene over the years. At first artists were mainly reliant on the support of state- or corporate-funded galleries, but with standards of living rising all the time, artists are increasingly autonomous and audacious, sustained by interest from private buyers and by showings at a number of excellent independent galleries. Painting is the dominant medium and, despite an extended flirtation with expressionism, these days it's **figurative art** that's making the strongest impression.

As for names to look out for, the older generation of Malaysian **artists** includes the likes of Latif Mohidin and Jolly Koh, both colourful abstract painters; Ibrahim Hussein, specializing in design-based pop art; and Redza Piyadasa, whose work ranges from conceptual art to mixed-media studies with more of an obvious social conscience. Also worth checking out are Sylvia Lee Goh from Penang, whose oils often reflect her Baba-Nonya background; and Loh Ek Sem and Anuar Dan, both of whom focus on Malaysia's vanishing rural life. Among the new wave of artists, keep an eye out for the **Matahati** group, young Malay artists led by Sabah-born Bayu Utomo Radjikin, whose works, exploring issues of identity in modern Malaysia, have a distinctively Malay sensibility; you're also likely to come across work by Wong Hoy Cheong and Jalaini Abu Hassan, both making big waves at the moment. **Sculpture** and installations are a worthwhile minority interest, and one of the more challenging practitioners is Abdul Multhalib Musa, whose creations resemble giant abstract combs or slinky springs.

Art Folio Second floor, City Square, 182 Jalan Tun Razak ☎03/2162 3339. Stacks of watercolours, oil paintings and ceramics, at high prices; gives a reasonable picture of current trends. Mon–Sat 10am–7pm.

Art House Second floor, Wisma Cosway, Jalan Raja Chulan (close to the junction with Jalan Perak), Golden Triangle ☎03/2148 2283. Specializes in high-quality brush paintings and ceramics from China, and represents a few local Chinese artists. Mon–Sat 10am–7.30pm.

Artists' Colony Kompleks Budaya Kraf, Jalan Conlay, Golden Triangle. Around the edges of the crafts complex are a bunch of cottages rented out as inexpensive studios to up-and-coming artists, mainly Malay, whom you can watch at work. It's all very down to earth and they charge reasonable prices if you're buying. Sunday is the best day to turn up, as most of the artists are around then.

Galeri Petronas Petronas Twin Towers, KLCC ☎03/2051 7090, ⊛www.galeripetronas.com.my. Large space with interesting temporary exhibitions,

though perhaps not quite as cutting-edge as it once was. Tues–Sun 10am–8pm.

Maya Gallery First floor, 12 Jalan Telawi 3, Bangsar Baru ☎03/2282 2069, ⊛www .mayagallery.com.my. Enterprising gallery, not afraid to show young artists. Tues–Fri 11am–7pm, Sat & Sun noon–6pm.

National Art Gallery (Balai Seni Lukis Negara) Jalan Tun Razak ☎03/4025 4990, ⊛www .artgallery.gov.my. A striking, vaguely pyramidal building whose interior has shades of New York's Guggenheim about it, but the quality of the exhibitions varies. On the first Saturday of the month the gallery plays host to Laman Seni, an informal arts-and-crafts bazaar. Best reached by taxi; Jalan Tun Razak is too busy to make the 1km walk from Titiwangsa station worthwhile. Daily 10am–6pm.

Rimbun Dahan Kilometer 27, Jalan Kuang, Kuang ☎03/6038 3690, ⊛www.rimbundahan.org. The estate of renowned Malaysian architect Hijjas Kasturi is also a key centre for artistic endeavour, supporting several artist residencies every year.

Exhibitions are held twice a year (usually March & Sept; call for details), at which you can not only get acquainted with the artists and their work but also take in the splendid architecture of the estate. To get here, take the Komuter train to Sungei Buloh, then a taxi (you may need to ask for "*rumah* Hijjas Kasturi"; RM8).

Starhill Gallery Next to the *Marriott*, Bintang Walk ⓦ www.starhillgallery.com. Amid all the designer outlets here are a few actual galleries, slightly too fashionable for their own good, though a few gems pop up for sale occasionally.

Valentine Willie Fine Art First floor, 17 Jalan Telawi 3, Bangsar Baru ⓦ www.artsasia.com.my. Specializing in modern Southeast Asian artists, particularly from Thailand and Indonesia, and of course home-grown talent. Mon–Fri noon–8pm, Sat noon–6pm.

Wei-ling Gallery 8 Jalan Scott, Brickfields (just a little northeast of the *YMCA*) ☏ 03/2260 1106, ⓦ www.weiling-gallery.com. A great venue in an old shophouse, showcasing the most interesting of the new wave of artists plus established names. Mon–Fri noon–7pm.

Shopping

There's no city in Malaysia where consumerism is as widespread and in-your-face as KL. The malls of the Golden Triangle are big haunts for youths and yuppies alike, while **street markets** remain a draw for everyone, offering a gregarious atmosphere and goods of all sorts. Jalan Petaling in Chinatown (see p.114) is, of course a big draw day and night, particularly for fake watches and leather goods; some of these have started to creep into the covered market on Jalan Masjid India and the nearby Lorong Tuanku Abdul Rahman *pasar malam* (see p.120), but their mainstays remain Malay- and Indian-style clothes and fabrics, plus a few eccentricities such as herbal tonics and various charms alleged to improve male vigour. Chow Kit Market (see p.120) has some clothing bargains but little else of interest. A great just-out-of-town market for knick-knacks and general bric-a-brac happens every weekend inside the **Amcorp Mall** in Petaling Jaya, close to Taman Jaya station on the LRT.

If no specific **business hours** are given in the shop listings that follow, then the establishment keeps the usual Malaysian shopping hours, opening by mid-morning and shutting at 8pm (an hour or two later in the case of outlets within malls), six or seven days a week.

Handicrafts

Malaysian crafts tend to be available a little more cheaply in the provincial areas where they originate. Nevertheless, KL is a good place to bone up on handicrafts – there's an excellent range on sale, though some of the items are made in other Southeast Asian countries – and if the capital is your final stop before you leave the country, it can be better to buy here than to lug around items acquired elsewhere.

Central Market (Pasar Seni) Jalan Hang Kasturi, Chinatown. The selection of wares here is all a bit *rojak*, as locals would say – like the Malaysian salad, a bit of a jumble. Despite its Malay name translating as "art market", the complex is largely given over to batik clothing, *songket* and handi-crafts such as Malay kites and African-style masks. If plans to smarten up the place come to fruition, expect even this mixed bag to be diluted by the designer accessories.

Karyaneka Kompleks Budaya Kraf, Jalan Conlay ☏ 03/2164 4344. There's a bit of everything at this crafts emporium – Kelantan kites in silver filigree (RM60 buys a small ornamental example, while for one 30cm across you could pay RM2000); baskets and bags of woven *mengkuang* (pandanus) leaves, sometimes with attractive designs; and so forth. For a taster, visit their much smaller shop on the lower ground level of BB Plaza, Jalan Bukit Bintang. Daily 10am–8pm.

Lavanya Arts Temple of Fine Arts, 128 Jalan Berhala, Brickfields. If you've an interest in Indian handicrafts, this small outlet is the place to come. Some time in 2007 they will, along with the Temple

143

of Fine Arts, move to a new complex at no. 116. Tues–Sat 10am–8pm, Sun 10am–2pm.

Peter Hoe Second floor, Lee Rubber Building, corner of Jalan Tun H.S. Lee and Jalan Hang Lekir, and also at 2 Jalan Hang Lekir. The latter outlet specializes in batik, made in Indonesia to their own designs and in less garish colours than usual. Their main shop (reached by the side entrance of the Lee Rubber Building) is much larger and sells a variety of soft furnishings, knick-knacks, textile bags and so forth, mostly imported from around the region. Daily 10am–7pm.

Pucuk Rebung Level 3, Suria KLCC ☎03/2162 0069. There are several crafts places in Suria KLCC, but this is one of the better places for items that reflect Malay culture, including batik, *songkets* and silverware, although prices are on the high side. Daily 10am–10pm.

Royal Selangor Pewter Factory 4 Jalan Usahawan Lima, Setapak Industrial Area ⓦ visitorcentre.royalselangor.com. For years pewter was something of a souvenir cliché in Malaysia. Still, pewter platters, mugs and other objects can be elegant, and the Royal Selangor factory has been turning them out longer than most. Their visitor centre (daily 9am–5pm) offers guided tours (free; just turn up), workshops at which you can make your own plates (by arrangement; RM50 per person for at least five people) and, of course, the opportunity to buy their products. The factory is at least 5km north-east of Chow Kit, and 2km west of the Wangsa Maju LRT stop; best to take a taxi from the latter. They also have stores at Suria KLCC and at the Lot 10 Shopping Centre, Bukit Bintang.

Malls and supermarkets

Locals and visitors alike come to KL's **shopping malls** to seek refuge from the heat as much as to shop; for local young people, the malls are also important places to socialize. Mostly located outside the old centre, particularly in the Golden Triangle, the malls divide into two categories – gargantuan affairs in the manner of Western malls and featuring international chains and designer names, and smaller, denser Southeast Asian-style complexes, basically indoor bazaars with row upon row of tiny independent retailers. Ironically, the simpler malls tend to be much more popular than their more sophisticated, pricier counterparts, and can be atmospheric places to wander. Many malls, of whatever type, house a **supermarket** or department store of one sort or another.

Bukit Bintang

BB Plaza Jalan Bukit Bintang, just west of Jalan Sultan Ismail. Teeming local-style mall with good deals on cameras and electronic equipment.

Berjaya Times Square Jalan Imbi, the monorail's Imbi stop is right opposite ⓦ www.timessquarekl .com. Ginormous mall with indoor theme park rides and an IMAX cinema. It also houses the UK chain store Debenhams, a large Borders and the Shasta supermarket. Not as buzzing as it should be, however.

Lot 10 Shopping Centre Bintang Walk. Specializes in designer clothes and accessories, as well as playing host to the Japanese department store, Isetan.

Starhill Gallery Next to the *Marriott*, Bintang Walk ⓦ www.starhillgallery.com. More designer names than is healthy, orbiting a suitably grand atrium. Just as noteworthy is the maze of top-notch restaurants at the base of the building.

Sungei Wang Plaza Jalan Sultan Ismail ⓦ www .sungeiwang.com. Joined onto BB Plaza and just as popular as its neighbour, KL's first mall offers everything from clothes to consumer electronics. Generally keenly priced.

KLCC

Avenue K 156 Jalan Ampang, just across from the Petronas Twin Towers and over KLCC LRT station. Worth a look if you're into designer outlets, but a bit staid.

Suria KLCC At the base of the Petronas Twin Towers ⓦ www.suriaklcc.com.my. A mall so large it's subdivided into sub-malls for ease of reference, Suria KLCC's oval atriums are home to UK department store Marks & Spencer, Isetan and Cold Storage supermarkets, plus numerous restaurants and a TGV multiplex cinema. Arguably the best of the Western-style malls.

Bangsar and Mid Valley

Bangsar Shopping Centre 285 Jalan Maarof, Bangsar. Upmarket affair, a good place to have a suit made, buy gifts or just find some food from home that you miss. Plenty of restaurants and coffee shops to boot, with more restaurants in Bangsar Baru 1500m downhill to the south.

Mid Valley Megamall Off Jalan Syed Putra, 2km south of Brickfields Ⓦ www.midvalley.com.my. This sprawling affair certainly gives Suria KLCC a run for its money, and is easy to get to as well, with KTM's Mid Valley station next door. Come here for the Carrefour hypermarket, the Jusco and Metrojaya department stores, the MPH bookstore and the usual plethora of outlets selling everything from cosmetics to computers. Also houses a GSC multiplex cinema.

Books and CDs

The larger KL **bookshops** are pretty impressive, carrying a range of English publications similar in scope to what you'll find at a good bookshop in the West, though in less depth. You'll also find a very good range of literature on Malaysia and the rest of Southeast Asia – everything from historical monographs to coffee-table books about local architecture. Unfortunately, in this country of rampant piracy, **music** shops are nothing to write home about.

Borders Berjaya Times Square, Bukit Bintang. One of the world's largest examples of the chain, on two expansive floors. Fantastic for books, not so great for CDs. Daily 9am–11pm.

Kinokuniya Level 4, Suria KLCC. Efficient Japanese chain with plenty of English publications, including a decent travel section.

MPH Unit JA1, ground floor, Mid Valley Megamall; smaller outlets on the ground floor at BB Plaza, Bukit Bintang; level 1, KL Sentral; and in Bangsar Baru at the Bangsar Village Shopping Centre and at 2, Jalan Telawi 2; Ⓦ www.mph.com.my. The veteran survivor of the local book trade still carries a good mix of novels and nonfiction titles.

Music Magic M26 Central Market ☎03/2274 6649. Small independent CD retailer, good for foreign rock and indie; special orders taken for imports, too. Daily 11am–5.30pm.

Silverfish Books 67-1 Jalan Telawi 3, Bangsar, next to *Madam Kwan's* ☎03/2284 4837. Not just a bookshop but an independent publisher to boot. They're not bad for material on Malaysia, but sometimes stock obscure items at the expense of worthwhile mainstream titles.

Tower Records Third floor, Suria KLCC; first floor, Mid Valley Megamall. The main outlet for chart music of all sorts, including a small selection of local music.

Listings

Airlines For details of MAS, AirAsia and Berjaya Air offices, see p.99. Air France, c/o KLM; Air Mauritius, Central Plaza, Jalan Sultan Ismail ☎03/2142 9161; Austrian Airlines, Central Plaza, Jalan Sultan Ismail ☎03/2148 8033; British Airways, c/o Qantas; Cathay Pacific, Menara IMC, Jalan Sultan Ismail ☎03/2078 3377; China Airlines, Amoda Building, 22 Jalan Imbi ☎03/2142 7344; Delta Airlines, Wisma SIA, Jalan Dang Wangi ☎2691 5490; Emirates, UBN Tower, Jalan P. Ramlee ☎03/2058 5888; Garuda, Menara Citibank, Jalan Ampang ☎03/2162 2811; Gulf Air, Central Plaza, Jalan Sultan Ismail, ☎03/2141 2676; Japan Airlines, Menara Citibank, Jalan Ampang, ☎03/2178 5931; KLM, *Parkroyal Hotel*, Bukit Bintang ☎03/2711 9811; Korean Air, Mui Plaza, Jalan P. Ramlee ☎03/2144 0200; Qantas, Menara IMC, Jalan Sultan Ismail ☎1800/881 260; Royal Brunei, UBN Tower, Jalan P. Ramlee ☎03/2070 7166; Singapore Airlines, Wisma SIA, Jalan Dang Wangi ☎03/2692 3122; SriLankan Airlines, Mui Plaza, Jalan P.

Ramlee ☎03/2072 3633; Thai Airways, Wisma Goldhill, Jalan Raja Chulan ☎03/2031 2900.

Banks and exchange There are banks with ATMs throughout KL. Maybank is usually your best bet for foreign exchange. You may get better rates from official moneychangers, which can be found in shopping malls and in and around transport hubs.

Buses For intercity bus enquries, the following numbers may come in handy. KL Sentral: Transnasional ☎03/2273 6473. Pasar Rakyat bus station: Transtar ☎03/2141 1771 (luxury buses to Singapore). Pekeliling: Plusliner ☎03/4042 1256. Puduraya: Konsortium Bas Ekspress ☎03/2070 9410 (Penang/Kedah), ☎03/2070 1321 (JB/Singapore); Plusliner ☎03/2070 2617; Transnasional ☎03/2070 3300; Utama Ekspres ☎03/2070 3940. Putra: Ekspres Mutiara ☎03/4045 2122; Ekspres Sutera ☎4042 5699; Transnasional ☎03/4043 8984; Triton ☎03/4044 6591; Utama Ekspres ☎03/4045 2122. Old Railway Station: Plusliner/Nice ☎03/2272 1586 (luxury buses to Penang, Singapore).

Casino KL has long had a casino at Genting Highlands (ⓦ www.genting.com.my), which also features several fairly pricey hotels, a theme park, shopping malls and so forth. It's 30km out of town, best reached via the Karak Highway (E8); express buses head there from Puduraya or Pasar Rakyat bus stations (RM8 one-way), and there are also shared taxis from Puduraya.

Cultural centres Alliance Française, 15 Lorong Gurney ⓣ 03/26 94 7880; British Council, West Block, Wisma Selangor Dredging, Jalan Ampang (next to the *Maya* hotel) ⓣ 03/2723 7900; Goethe-Institut, 1 Jalan Langgak Golf ⓣ 03/21422011.

Embassies and consulates Australia, 6 Jalan Yap Kwan Seng ⓣ 03/2146 5555; Brunei, 19th floor, Menara Tan & Tan, 207 Jalan Tun Razak ⓣ 03/2161 2800; Cambodia, 46 Jalan U Thant ⓣ 03/4257 3711; Canada, 17th floor, Menara Tan & Tan, 207 Jalan Tun Razak ⓣ 03/2718 3333; China, 229 Jalan Ampang ⓣ 03/2163 6815 or 2142 8585; India, 2 Jalan Taman Duta ⓣ 03/2093 3504; Indonesia, 233 Jalan Tun Razak ⓣ 03/2145 2011; Ireland, The Amp Walk, 218 Jalan Ampang ⓣ 03/2161 2963; Japan, 11 Persiaran Stonor ⓣ 03/2143 1739; Laos, 25 Jalan Damai ⓣ 03/2148 7059; Netherlands, seventh floor, The Amp Walk, 218 Jalan Ampang ⓣ 03/2168 6200; New Zealand: level 21, Menara IMC, Jalan Sultan Ismail ⓣ 03/2078 2533; Philippines, 1 Changkat Kia Peng ⓣ 03/2148 9989; Singapore, 209 Jalan Tun Razak ⓣ 03/2161 6277; South Africa, 12 Lorong Titiwangsa 12 ⓣ 03/4026 5700; Thailand, 206 Jalan Ampang ⓣ 03/2148 8222; UK, 185 Jalan Ampang ⓣ 03/2170 2345; USA, 376 Jalan Tun Razak ⓣ 03/2168 5000; Vietnam, 4 Persiaran Stonor ⓣ 03/2148 4036.

Formula 1 Check ⓦ www.malaysiangp.com.my for details of the Sepang circuit, ticketing and special buses that run from Nilai station during the event. There are a few hotels in the vicinity, such as the *Concorde* (ⓦ www.concorde.net/sepang) and *Empress* (ⓦ www.empresshotelsepang.com), but trains make commuting from downtown KL fairly quick.

Hospitals and clinics General Hospital, Jalan Pahang ⓣ 03/2692 1044; Gleneagles Hospital, Jalan Ampang ⓣ 03/4257 1300; Pantai Medical Centre, Jalan Bukit Pantai, not far from Kerinchi LRT station ⓣ 03/2296 0888; Tung Shin Hospital, Jalan Pudu ⓣ 03/2072 1655.

Internet access Chinatown has a couple of Internet places along Jalan Sultan, close to Jalan Tun Tan Cheng Lock. In Bukit Bintang, there's a 24hr cybercafé on Tengkat Tong Shin, more or less next to *La Bodega* restaurant, and there are several

places on the stretch of Jalan Bukit Bintang just west of the junction with Jalan Sultan Ismail. Some malls have Internet cafés too. The usual charges apply (RM3–6/hr), with Bukit Bintang rates tending to be more expensive.

Left luggage Luggage can be stored for a few ringgit per day at KL Sentral station and Puduraya bus station (look out for a couple of counters at the back of the passenger level). At KLIA, the service costs RM10–30 per day depending on the size of the bags; see the "Facilities" section of ⓦ www.klia.com.my for more.

Police KL has its own Tourist Police station, where you can report stolen property for insurance claims. Useful locations include at MTC, 109 Jalan Ampang (ⓣ 03/2163 3657), and at Puduraya bus station.

Post office The General Post Office is just south of the Dayabumi Complex (Mon–Fri 8am–4pm, Sat 8am–2pm); poste restante/general delivery mail comes here. In Chinatown, there's a post office upstairs at the Puduraya bus station; a post office with extended hours can be found at Suria KLCC (daily 10am–6pm).

Sports facilities and health clubs Publicly run sports facilities in KL are surprisingly limited. Bangsar has a sports complex at Jalan Terasek 3 (just west of Bangsar Baru; ⓣ 03/2284 6065) with badminton and tennis courts, and a pool. Some way south of the centre, but close to the Bukit Jalil LRT station, is the National Sports Complex (ⓣ 03/2094 8211, ⓦ www.ksn.com.my), which has a swimming pool (daily 2.30–4.30pm & 6–8.30pm, Sat & Sun also 10am–12.30pm) and squash courts (Mon–Fri 2–4pm & 6–8pm, Sat & Sun 10am–noon). More centrally, there are a number of private health clubs, which feature gyms and aerobics programmes; some may also have a sauna and a swimming pool. Fitness First (ⓦ www.fitness.com.my) and California Fitness (ⓦ www.californiafitness.com) both have convenient locations on Jalan Sultan Ismail, at no. 22 and no. 30 respectively; Fitness First is also in the Menara Maxis, next to Suria KLCC. There's also the Clark Hatch Fitness Centre at City Square Plaza, Jalan Tun Razak, close to the Ampang Park LRT station. For a round of golf, try the KL Golf and Country Club at Bukit Kiara, just west of Bangsar (take a taxi); non-members can usually get in on weekdays (book in advance on ⓣ 03/2093 1111), but be prepared to show proof of your handicap.

Travel agents and tour operators International flights and tours can be booked through, among others, Holiday Tours & Travel, fifth floor, Wisma UOA II, Jalan Pinang (ⓣ 03/2163 3006, ⓦ www.holidaytours.com.my), and at level 1, KL Sentral

(☎03/2273 2200); Reliance Tours, third floor, Sungei Wang Plaza, Bukit Bintang (☎03/2148 6022, ⓦwww.reliancetravel.com); or STA, fifth floor, Magnum Plaza, 128 Jalan Pudu (☎03/2148 9800, ⓦwww.statravel.com.my). For packages within Malaysia, you could try Angel Tours, 148A Jalan Bukit Bintang (☎03/2148 8288); Discovery Overland, Block B, Megan Avenue II, 12 Jalan Yap Kwan Seng (☎03/2164 8113, ⓦwww.discovery overland.com); Holiday Tours, listed above; Jet Asia, Pudu Plaza, Jalan Landak (near the Pudu LRT station; ☎03/2142 1911, ⓦwww.jetasiatravel .com); or Malaysian Travel Business, at the MTC tourist office (☎03/2163 0162).

Visa extensions The Immigration Office is at Block 1, Pusat Bandar Damansara (☎03/2095 5077); buses #21C or #48C from the Kota Raya Building in Chinatown or #309 from KL Sentral will get you there.

Around Kuala Lumpur

The most obvious attractions around KL proper are to the **north**, where limestone peaks rise up out of the forest and the roads narrow as you pass through small kampungs. There is dramatic scenery as close as 13km from the city, where the Hindu shrine at the **Batu Caves** attracts enough visitors to make it one of Malaysia's main tourist attractions. Nearby, the **Forest Institute of Malaysia** and **Templer Park** encompass the nearest portion of primary rainforest to the capital. Northwest of KL is the quiet town of **Kuala Selangor** which offers the chance to observe the nightly dance of **fireflies**.

West of KL is Selangor's former capital, **Klang**, where there's a fascinating tin museum, and one of the country's most atmospheric mosques. Another appealing day-trip is to the quaint Chinese fishing village of **Pulau Ketam**, an hour's ferry ride from the coastal town of Port Klang.

As some of the sights mentioned in this section can be a bit of a slog to get to by public transport, you may want to take advantage of excursions offered by some travel agents, for example at the *Backpacker's Travellers Inn* (see p.106) or MTC (see above).

FRIM, Batu Caves and the Orang Asli Museum

Malaysia's **Forest Research Institute** (FRIM), the **Orang Asli Museum** and – one of the most popular attractions around KL – the **Batu Caves** lie to the north of the capital, along or off the so-called Middle Ring Road II, which is called Jalan Batu Caves in the vicinity of the caves themselves. Their proximity to this road makes it feasible to visit all three in a circuit, if you're driving. There are two routes out here: either take the **E8** highway, which intersects Jalan Batu Caves, or use **Jalan Ipoh**, which starts at Chow Kit and meets Jalan Batu Caves 4km west of the E8. FRIM is west of Jalan Ipoh, the Orang Asli Museum close to the E8, and the caves are in between the two. With a car, it's also feasible to continue up Jalan Ipoh to Templer Park, a stretch of forest northwest of the caves (see p.151). Inconveniently, it's largely impossible to go from one sight to the next by bus.

FRIM

If you can't make it out to Taman Negara and its forest-canopy walkway, you can instead stroll through the treetops at the **Forest Research Institute of Malaysia (FRIM)** (daily 8am–6.30pm; RM3; ☎03/6279 7000, ⓦwww.frim .gov.my). The canopy walkway here (Tues–Sat 10am–1.30pm; RM5) provides a unique view of KL's skyscrapers through the trees. The fifteen-square-kilometre park also has several worthwhile trails, for which you should bring along drinking water and insect repellent, and wear shoes rather than sandals. For those who wish to learn more about Malaysia's ecological heritage, there's also a museum containing details of the institute's research, an arboretum and an eclectic range of wood-based antiques and implements, including an intricately carved boat, treasure chests and a four-poster bed.

FRIM is signposted 4km west of the junction of Jalan Ipoh and Middle Ring Road II. **Bus** #94a from Jalan Hang Kasturi in Chinatown heads all the way to FRIM, taking around an hour to get there; alternatively, catch a Komuter **train** to the Kepong station, 2km from the site, to which you can continue by taxi.

Batu Caves

Long before you reach the entrance to the **Batu Caves**, you'll see them ahead: small, black holes in the vast limestone thumbs which comprise a ridge of hills in Gombak, on the very fringes of greater KL. In 1891, ten years after the caves were noticed by the American explorer William Hornaby, local Indian dignitaries convinced the British colonial authorities that the caves were ideal places in which to worship (probably because their spectacular geography was thought reminiscent of the sacred Himalayas). Soon ever-increasing numbers of devotees were visiting the caves to pray at the shrine established here to Lord Muruga, also known as **Lord Subramaniam**; later the temple complex was expanded to include a shrine to the elephant-headed deity **Ganesh**. Today the caves and shrines are surrounded by the full panoply of religious commercialism, with shops selling Hindu idols, pamphlets, bracelets, postcards and cassettes. The caves are incredibly popular, and always packed with visitors, but the numbers most days are nothing compared to the thousands upon thousands of devotees who descend here during the annual three-day **Thaipusam festival** (see box opposite).

The caves

To the left of the brick staircase leading up to the main Temple Cave, a small path leads off to the so-called **Art Gallery Cave** (daily 8.30am–7pm; RM1), which contains dozens of striking multicoloured statues of deities, portraying scenes from the Hindu scriptures. As well as these psychedelic dioramas – including a naked goddess astride a five-headed snake, flanked by figures with goats' heads carrying farming implements – flamboyant murals line the damp walls of the cave depicting jungle settings, mythic battles and abstract designs.

At the top of the main staircase, there's a clear view through to the **Subramaniam Swamy Temple** (daily 8am–7pm), set deep in a cave around 100m high and 80m long, the cave walls lined with idols representing the six lives of Lord Subramaniam. The temple, illuminated by shafts of light from gaps in the cave ceiling high above, has an entrance guarded by two statues, their index fingers pointing upwards towards the light. Within the temple, devoted to Lord Subramaniam and another deity, Rama, a dome is densely sculpted with more scenes from the scriptures. In a chamber at the back of the temple is a statue of Rama, who watches over the well-being of all immigrants, adorned with silver jewellery and a silk sarong. If you want to look closely at this inner sanctum, the temple staff will mark a small red dot on your forehead, giving you a spiritual right to enter.

About three-quarters of the way up to the Temple Cave, a turning on the left leads to a vast side cavern known, somewhat unimaginatively, as the **Dark Caves**. Here a two-kilometre passageway gives onto five chambers populated by a large variety of insects and at least three types of **bats**, which can be

Thaipusam at the Batu Caves

The most important festival in the Malaysian Hindu calendar (along with Deepavali), **Thaipusam** honours the Hindu deity Lord Subramaniam. Originally a Tamil festival from Southern India, it's a day of penance and celebration, held during full moon in the month of "Thai" (relative to the Gregorian calendar, it always falls between mid-Jan and mid-Feb), when huge crowds arrive at the Batu Caves. What was originally intended to be a day of penance for past sins has now become a major tourist attraction, with both Malaysians and foreigners flocking to the festival every year.

The start of Thaipusam is marked by the departure at dawn, from KL's Sri Maha Mariamman Temple, of a golden chariot bearing a statue of Subramaniam. Thousands of devotees follow on foot as it makes its seven-hour procession to the caves. Once there, the statue is placed in a tent before being carried up to the temple cave. As part of their penance – and in a trance-like state – the devotees carry numerous types of *kavadi* ("burdens" in Tamil), the most popular being milk jugs decorated with peacock feathers placed on top of the head, which are connected to the penitents' flesh by hooks. Others wear wooden frames with sharp spikes protruding from them which are carried on the back and hooked into the skin; trident-shaped skewers are placed through some devotees' tongues and cheeks. This rather grisly procession – which now only occurs in Malaysia, Singapore and Thailand – has its origins in India, where most of Lord Subramaniam's temples were sited on high ridges which pilgrims would walk up, carrying heavy pitchers or pots to honour the deity. At Batu Caves, the 272-step climb up to the main chamber expresses the idea that you cannot reach God without expending effort.

Once in the temple cave, the devotees participate in ceremonies and rituals to Subramaniam and Ganesh, finishing with a celebration for Rama, when milk from the *kavadi* vessel can be spilt as an offering; incense and camphor are burned as the bearers unload their devotional burdens. The festival takes many hours to complete, in an atmosphere so highly charged that police are needed to line the stairs and protect onlookers from the entranced *kavadi*-bearers and their instruments of self-flagellation.

Extra buses run to the caves during Thaipusam. It's advisable to get there early (say 7am) for a good view of the proceedings. Although there are numerous vendors selling food and drink at the caves, it's a good idea to take water and snacks with you, as the size of the crowd is horrendous.

distinguished by their faces and calls. The caves also house a variety of interesting limestone formations, including several towering **flow stones**, so called because they have a continuous sheet of water running down them. The Dark Caves can only be visited on a guided tour (see "Practicalities" below).

Practicalities

The caves are on Jalan Batu Caves, roughly midway between the junctions with Jalan Ipoh and the E8. You can get here on **bus** #14D from Lebuh Ampang, close to Central Market (hourly; 1hr) or from Jalan Raja Laut in Chow Kit; it's also possible to hop on the LRT to the Gombak terminus, then get a taxi the rest of the way (RM10).

There are two tours to the **Dark Caves**, both of which need to be booked two days in advance (℡012/430 7011, ✉enquiry@darkcaves.com.my). The education tour is simply a guided walk around the caves (1hr; RM35), on which various creatures and rock formations are pointed out. Much more memorable is the adventure tour (3–4hr; RM50), on which you get to clamber up, down and through some of the more interesting nooks and crannies of the system.

△ Devotees drag *kavadi* (burdens) at the Thaipusam Festival, Batu Caves

Boots (in a limited range of sizes), helmets and torches are provided, but it's best to bring a change of clothes and a towel for freshening up later in the temple's facilities.

The Orang Asli Museum

Run by the government's Department for Orang Asli Affairs, the **Orang Asli Museum** (daily except Fri 9am–5pm; free), holds a certain interest if this is as far into rural Malaysia as you're going to get. Located about 20km northeast of KL as the crow flies, the museum aims to present a portrait of the various groups of Orang Asli, once nomadic hunter-gatherers in the jungle, though now largely resident in rural settlements.

The foyer contains a large map of the Peninsula making clear that the Orang Asli are found, in varying numbers, in just about every state, a fact which surprises some visitors, who see little sign of them during their travels. Besides collections of the fishing nets, guns and blowpipes the Orang Asli use to eke out their traditional existence, the museum also has photographs of Orang Asli press-ganged by the Malay and British military to fight the communist guerrillas in the 1950s (see p.739). Other displays describe the changes forced on the Orang Asli over the past thirty years – some positive, like the development of health and school networks, others less encouraging, like the erosion of the family system as young men drift off to look for seasonal work.

Particularly interesting, hidden in an annexe to the rear of the building, are examples of traditional handicrafts, including the **head carvings** made by the Mah Meri tribe from the swampy region on the borders of Selangor and Negeri Sembilan, and the Jah Hut from the slopes of Gunung Benom in central Pehang. The carvings, around 50cm high, show stylized, fierce facial expressions, and are fashioned from a particularly strong, heavy hardwood.

They still have religious significance – the most common image used, the animist deity Moyang, represents the spirit of the ancestors – and are prevalent in current religious ceremonies, when similar masks are worn during dances honouring a pantheon of gods. The Orang Asli's **animist religion** is influenced by early Hindu beliefs, and the carvings here show similarities with those of some Hindu deities.

Practicalities

The Orang Asli Museum is off Jalan Gombak, some 5km east of Batu Caves. Two **buses** head here from Lebuh Ampang in Chinatown (around RM3), one operated by Len Seng, signed "Gombak Batu 12", the other by Permata Kiara (#174). Ask the driver to tell you when you've arrived, as it's not obvious; leaving the bus, cross to the east side of the road and head 50m further up, where a steep side road leads to the museum. Arriving by **car**, turn east off the E8 onto Jalan Batu Caves and you'll come to Jalan Gombak after 1km; turn left (north) up this and continue another 2km or so to reach the site.

Templer Park

Named after Sir Gerald Templer (the last of Malaya's British high commissioners), **Templer Park** (unrestricted access) is the closest you'll get to primary **rainforest** if you haven't got time to visit the state parks in the interior, though development all around means you're unlikely to see much wildlife.

The park covers over a square kilometre of forest, dominated by a belt of limestone outcrops set in a valley, cutting through the hills for 5km. A narrow road winds from the entrance to an artificial lake, 300m to the east, before shrinking to a narrow path, which snakes up into the forest. This trail leads back and forth across the shallow, five-metre-wide Sungai Templer, reaching a dramatic waterfall after an hour's walk. From here you can follow the riverside path through primary jungle for another hour or so, but you'll have to return by the same route. An alternative is to leave the main path on a trail to the left of the waterfall, from where a one-hour trek hugs the edge of the hillside and later meets the road near the park entrance. Other paths snake up into the forested hills and pass natural swimming lagoons and waterfalls. The park's highest point is the hump-like **Bukit Takun** (350m), in its northern corner, rising on the western side of the river; the trail peters out at the base of the hill, though.

Practicalities

Rawang-bound **buses** operated by Metrobus (#43) come here from outside the Bangkok Bank in the Chinatown area. You could combine a visit to the park with one to the Batu Caves, from where you catch the bus back out to Jalan Ipoh and then wait for a bus to the park. By **car**, continue north up Jalan Ipoh beyond the Batu Caves exit for about 7km; the park is clearly signposted on the right. Bring your own food and drink, as there's nowhere at the park to buy refreshments.

Kuala Selangor and around

KUALA SELANGOR lies close to the coast on Route 5, some 70km northwest of KL, on the banks of Sungei Selangor. A former royal town, today it's a small, sleepy affair; the chief reason a stream of visitors continue to come here is to see the **fireflies** of the surrounding area. It's possible to visit on a long daytrip from KL, taking in the town's fort and nature park by day and the fireflies after dark, then catch a bus back to the capital, though there are a couple of places to stay in the vicinity. Just pray there's no outbreak of **rain**, as the fireflies don't perform in wet conditions.

All that remains of Kuala Selangor's more glorious past are the remnants of two forts overlooking the town, the largest of which, **Fort Altingberg** (daily 9am–4.30pm; free), recalls a period in Malaysian history when this part of the country changed hands, bloodily, on several occasions. Originally called Fort Melawati, Altingberg was built by local people during the reign of Sultan Ibrahim of Selangor in the eighteenth century, and was later captured by the Dutch (who renamed it) as part of an attempt to wrestle the tin trade from the sultans. The fortress was partly destroyed during local skirmishes in the Selangor Civil War (1867–73). Within its grounds is a cannon, reputed to be from the Dutch era, and a rock used for executions. **Bukit Melawati**, the hill on which the fort is based, also has a lighthouse and a resthouse built during the British colonial period. On Saturdays the road from the town up to the fort is closed to traffic and all visitors ascend by way of a trolley car (RM5).

Kuala Selangor Nature Park

Its edges lying directly below the fort, the **Kuala Selangor Nature Park** (daily 9am–5.30pm) encompasses mud flats, mangroves and a small patch of forest; together, they're host to around 150 species of birds, with thirty more passing along the coastline annually. The park is also home to silverleaf monkeys, which live in the forest, and a variety of crabs and fish in the mangroves. There are several clearly marked **trails** in the park, the longest 1500m in length.

The park is a five-hundred-metre walk from Bukit Melawati (follow signs for "Taman Alam"). You can also get here on the **buses** which run up Route 5 from Klang; ask to be let off at the park, and you'll be dropped at a petrol station, from where the park is 200m up Jalan Klinik.

Most people who make the trip to Kuala Selangor come to see the **fireflies**, which glow spectacularly in the early evening along the banks of the narrow Sungei Selangor. For a time, however, this natural spectacle looked to be in terminal decline, thanks to uncontrolled development: the fireflies' mangrove habitat was rapidly being cleared, and the river was becoming increasingly polluted with refuse. Belatedly, the authorities have stepped in with public education programmes to ensure better waste management, and there's talk of

Fireflies

There are more than a hundred species of firefly, among which those found in Southeast Asia give some of the most striking displays. Known as *kelip-kelip* in Malay, the **fireflies** are actually six-millimetre-long **beetles** which belong to the *Lampyridae* family, and are found in a region stretching from India to the Philippines and Papua New Guinea.

During the day, the fireflies rest on blades of grass or in palm trees behind the river's **mangrove swamps**. After sunset they move to the mangroves themselves, attracting mates with **synchronized flashes** of light at a rate of three per second. All the male fireflies flash within one-thirtieth of a second of one another (scientists are still trying to work out exactly why); the females also produce a bright light, but don't flash in the same flamboyant way as the males. The most successful males are apparently those that flash most brightly and which fly fastest. Mating is initiated by the female who flashes the male to indicate her interest. It's important for visitors to remain quiet when watching the firefly display and not to take flash photographs, as such behaviour scares the insects away.

setting aside part of the river as a reserve, though the fact that some land alongside is privately owned will complicate matters. For the moment, things appear to have stabilized, and you stand a reasonable chance of enjoying a decent light show, weather permitting.

Boats leave on firefly-spotting trips from two locations several kilometres from town: **Bukit Belimbing**, on the north bank across the river bridge; and at **Kampung Kuantan**, on the south bank. At Bukit Belimbing, trips are run by the **Firefly Park Resort**, from whose jetty motorized boats set out on half-hour trips (daily 7.45–10.30pm; RM10 per person); boats from Kampung Kuantan's jetty operate to a similar schedule and at similar prices. There are no buses to either of the jetties, so taxis from Kuala Selangor get away with pretty steep prices – expect a ride to the resort to cost at least RM15.

Practicalities

Kuala Selangor is very close to the junction of Route 5 and Route 54, which leads here from KL via Sungei Buloh. Red-and-white Selangor Omnibus **buses** (#141; RM5.50; 2hr) head to Kuala Selangor roughly hourly, either from bay 23 in Puduraya station or from just outside the station; you can also pick up the service in the Chow Kit area, though you'll need to ask around to find the correct stop. The last bus back to KL leaves around 10pm. Kuala Selangor has a newish **bus station** along Route 5, about 2km south of the centre. Local buses leave here bound for the centre, which is a nondescript square, but you'll probably find that buses pass through the station and terminate at the square itself, very close to Bukit Melawati. The **drive** from KL takes at least an hour depending on traffic and your starting point; take the E1 northbound from KL (as described on p.99) and turn off onto Route 54 at the Sungei Buloh exit. If you're heading for Kampung Kuantan, look out for a signed turning on the right as you near Kuala Selangor.

The only **hotel** in town itself is the *Kuala Selangor*, on the central square (☎03/3289 2709; RM30). A simple, surprisingly homely place, it has a variety of rooms, including some with a/c and en-suite facilities. Basic chalets with fan and bathroom are available in the Nature Park (☎03/3289 2294, @ksnaturepark@yahoo.com; RM45), for which you'll generally need to reserve at weekends. As there's nowhere to get food here, you may want to bring your own provisions. The slickest accommodation in the area is at the *Firefly Park Resort* (☎03/3289 1208, @www.fireflypark.com; RM120), where chalets have all mod cons. The resort has its own café (rates include breakfast), but for food, it's a better idea to try one of the **seafood restaurants** at Pasir Penambang, on the north bank of the Selangor River 5km from Kuala Selangor; make your way across the river bridge, turn left and it's signed down a turning on the left.

Klang

From the early sixteenth century onwards **KLANG**, 30km southwest of KL, was at the centre of one of the most important tin-producing areas in Malaysia. However, in this was sown the seeds of its own decline – it was from Klang that the expedition up Sungei Klang to seek new tin deposits was organized, the success of which led to the founding of Kuala Lumpur in the 1850s. In 1880, KL superseded Klang as state capital, and the old river port ceased to have any political or ceremonial importance, though the Klang Valley remained ripe for development as KL expanded rapidly. The first road linking Klang to KL wasn't built until the 1920s – previously all goods were carried along a narrow horse track or went by river – but a decade later the rail line between the two towns came into existence. So important is the Klang Valley conurbation today that there are two highways down to Klang, the Federal Highway (signed Lebuhraya Persekutuan) and the New Klang Valley Expressway (NKVE), linking up with the E1 at Sungai Buloh.

The Town

Although Klang remains a bustling, commercial centre, its historic buildings – the tin museum, the mosque, the government offices and the old *istana* (palace) – reflect a more dignified, graceful past, where the call to prayer dictated the pace of life. Most of these buildings, as well as the train station (trains are the easiest way to get here from KL), are found in the compact **old quarter** of town on the south side of the river. Leaving the station, head west past the foot of the river bridge and you'll find the **Gedung Raja Abdullah Museum**, devoted to the town's tin mining heritage. Housed in an old tin warehouse built in 1856 by Raja Abdullah, the Sultan of Selangor's son (it was at Abdullah's prompting that the pioneers rafted up the Sungei Klang in 1857 to look for new sources of tin), the museum was undergoing renovations at the time of writing, but is scheduled to reopen in late 2006.

You can only visit the magnificent nineteenth-century **istana** during the two-day Hari Raya Puasa festival (at the end of Ramadan), but the walk up the road there, past well-tended plants, trees and flowerbeds offers a ravishing prospect, with the main golden spire of the palace gleaming in the background. It's a ten-minute walk south from the train station along Jalan Stesen, which becomes Jalan Istana. If you return the way you came and take the first right onto Jalan Dato Hamzah Raja past the padang, then another right onto Jalan Raya Timur, you'll reach Klang's mosque, the intimate and atmospheric **Masjid Sultan Suleiman**, ten minutes' walk further on, with seven yellow domes and grey-stone outer walls. Here, low, arched entrances set into the walls lead into narrow passages where the worshippers sit and read the Koran; the inner prayer room has stained-glass windows. The mosque is open to visitors in between prayers.

Practicalities

Komuter **trains** from KL arrive in Klang every fifteen to thirty minutes (RM3.60 one-way; 45min). There are also frequent **buses** from KL's Klang bus station, but these can take up to twice as long as the train. Buses arrive on the north side of the river, from where it's best to use the more easterly of the two bridges (ask for Jambatan Tengku Musaeddin) to reach the old part of town; once on the south side of the river, a ten-minute walk away, you'll find the train station to the left and the Gedung Raja Abdullah Museum to the right. It's possible, incidentally, to combine a trip to Klang with Kuala Selangor, served by hourly buses up Route 5 from Klang (RM4; 1hr 15min).

Port Klang and Pulau Ketam

Eight kilometres west of Klang is **PORT KLANG**, from where ferries run to Sumatra and to Pulau Ketam, a quaint Chinese fishing village on the most westerly of the Malaysian islands opposite the port. Port Klang itself has little of interest, but if you are there in the third week of November, around the beginning of the rainy season, watch out for the **Raja Muda Regatta**, a competition pitting top yachts against the elements. There are also some good Chinese **seafood restaurants** by the riverside; the most popular places are usually a good bet.

The Komuter train from Klang stops directly opposite the main jetty; bus passengers disembark 100m further along the road from here. The jetty is where comfortable air-conditioned boats leave for **Tanjung Balai** (Asahan) in Sumatra (daily at 1pm; 3hr 30min; RM100). To travel on these boats, you need a prearranged visa, which you can get from the Indonesian Embassy in KL (see p.146). Arriving from Sumatra, you can get to KL on the Komuter train (every 30 min; 7am–10pm); the Customs building near the Pulau Ketam jetty has facilities for changing money. Conveniently opposite the bus stop is a **café**, the *Sri Thankashmi Villas*, that serves tasty *masala dosai*.

Pulau Ketam

An hour's ferry ride from Port Klang through the mangrove swamps is the fishing village of **PULAU KETAM** (the name means "Crab Island"), a Chinese stronghold since three fishermen established a community here at the beginning of the twentieth century. Today, it is most appealing for its clapboard houses built on stilts, its lack of cars, and its seafood restaurants. **Ferries** (daily 7am–8pm) from Port Klang leave every thirty minutes from the pier 50m west of Tanjung Balai jetty.

Bicycles can be rented at the *Sea Lion Villa Lodge*, next to the jetty, for RM5 an hour, but everything on the island is within easy walking distance. The **Hock Leng Keng Temple** at the end of Jalan Merdeka – the main shopping street with old painted movie banners strung across it to provide shade – is worth checking out, as is the local Chinese Association hall, the balcony of which provides a pleasant view across the village. Rather less pleasant is the pollution in the water around the houses, all too apparent at low tide.

While most visitors do the island as a day-trip, it's possible to **stay** there at the *Sea Lion Villa Lodge* (☏03/3110 4121; ❷) and the *Pulau Ketam Lodge* (☏03/3110 4200; ❷) on Jalan Merdeka, although there is little to do in the evening with the exception of one or two karaoke joints. The best option is to sample the reasonably priced seafood on offer; the local speciality is crab and it's best eaten at the *Kuai Lok Hian* restaurant by the jetty (around RM15), where the sea breeze will keep you cool as you watch the fishing boats plough up and down the estuaries between the islands.

Travel details

Trains

KL to: Alor Setar (daily; 11hr 45min); Butterworth (daily; 9hr); Dabong (daily; 11hr); Gemas (5 daily; 3hr 30min); Gua Musang (daily; 10hr); Jerantut (daily; 6hr 30min); Hat Yai (Thailand; 14hr 30min); Ipoh (daily; 3hr 15min); Johor Bahru (4 daily; 6hr); Klang (frequent; 45min); Kuala Kangsar (daily; 5hr 45min); Kuala Lipis (daily; 8hr 15min); Port Klang (frequent; 1hr); Seremban (frequent; 1hr–1hr 30min); Singapore (4 daily; 7hr 30min); Sungai Petani (daily; 10hr 45min); Wakaf Bharu (for Kota Bharu; daily; 13hr 15min).

Buses

Buses depart from KL for major destinations around the Peninsula frequently, typically hourly or every two hours throughout the day, with additional night-time departures on the longest routes. Frequencies are given below only where there are significant departures from this pattern.

Pasar Rakyat station to: Singapore (several daily; 6hr).

Pekeliling station to: Jerantut (3hr); Kuala Lipis (6 daily; 4hr 30min); Kuala Terengganu (several daily; 7hr); Kuantan (3hr 30min); Temerloh (2hr 30min); Triang (several daily; 4hr).

Pudu Raya station to: Alor Setar (9hr); Butterworth (5hr 30min); Cameron Highlands (4hr 30min); Genting Highlands (1hr); Georgetown (6hr); Hat Yai (Thailand; several daily; 9hr); Ipoh (4hr); Johor Bahru (5hr); Kuantan (4hr); Lumut (4hr); Melaka (2hr); Mersing (at least 5 daily; 6hr); Seremban (1hr); Singapore (6hr); Taiping (4hr 30min).

Putra station to: Gua Musang (several daily; 5hr); Kota Bharu (9hr); Kuala Terengganu (several daily; 7hr); Kuantan (3 daily; 3hr 30min); Tasik Kenyir (2 daily; 8hr).

Ferries

Port Klang to: Pulau Ketam (every 30min; 1hr).

Flights

Besides the flights listed below, there are also several flights a day with Singapore Airlines and Royal Brunei Airways to Singapore and Bandar Seri Begawan respectively.

MAS

KLIA to: Alor Setar (3 daily; 50min); Bandar Seri Begawan (2 daily; 2hr 20min); Bintulu (1–2 daily; 2hr 15min); Johor Bahru (4 daily; 45min); Kota Bharu (5 daily; 55min); Kota Kinabalu (at least 12 daily; 2hr 30min); Kuala Terengganu (4 daily; 45min); Kuantan (5 daily; 40min); Kuching (10 daily; 1hr 45min); Labuan (3 daily; 2hr 25min); Langkawi (5 daily; 55min); Miri (4 daily; 2hr 15min); Penang (14 daily; 45min); Sandakan (daily; 2hr 45min); Sibu (1–2 daily; 2hr); Singapore (7 daily; 55min); Tawau (daily; 2hr 45min).

AirAsia

KLIA Low-Cost-Carrier Terminal to: Alor Setar (daily; 55min); Bintulu (2 daily; 2hr); Johor Bahru (4 daily; 50min); Kota Bharu (3 daily; 55min); Kota Kinabalu (7 daily; 2hr 30min); Kuala Terengganu (2 daily; 55min); Kuching (7 daily; 1hr 40min); Labuan (daily; 2hr 25min); Langkawi (3 daily; 1hr); Miri (3 daily; 2hr 15min); Penang (3 daily; 40min); Sandakan (2 daily; 2hr 45min); Sibu (3 daily; 1hr 45min); Tawau (2 daily; 2hr 45min).

Berjaya Air

Subang Airport to: Pulau Pangkor (5 weekly; 40min); Pulau Redang (March–Oct, 9 weekly; 50min); Pulau Tioman (2 daily; 1hr).

The west coast

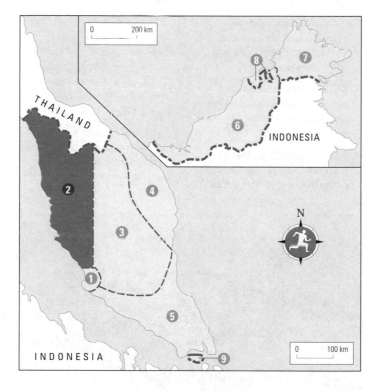

CHAPTER 2 # Highlights

* **Cameron Highlands** Cool down amidst the tea plantations and jungle trails of this colonial hill station. See p.162

* **Kellie's Castle** Picturesquely crumbling 1920s Scottish mansion set in the hills near Ipoh. See p.179

* **Pulau Pangkor** Laid-back tropical island with some of the best beaches on the west coast. See p.180

* **Kuala Kangsar** Sleepy but picturesque royal capital with a splendid mosque and Sultan's palace. See p.186

* **Taiping** Bustling traditional town with tranquil gardens and a mini hill station. See p.189

* **Georgetown** Bustling Chinese-dominated haven with elaborate temples, colonial mansions and beaches galore. See p.197

* **Lembah Bujang** There's much to learn from recent excavations at this 1000-year-old architectural site. See p.220

* **Alor Setar** An appealing city that successfully blends modern with Malay/Muslim architecture; there's also an impressive Thai temple. See p.222

* **Langkawi** Perfect beaches and exotic resorts characterize these islands close to Thailand. See p.225

△ Khoo Kongsi, Georgetown

2

The west coast

The **west coast** of Peninsular Malaysia, from Kuala Lumpur north to the Thai border, is the most industrialized and densely populated – not to mention cosmopolitan – part of the whole country. Its considerable natural resources have long brought eager traders and entrepreneurs here, but it was the demand for the region's tin in the late nineteenth century that spearheaded Malaysia's phenomenal economic rise. Immigrant workers, most of whom settled in the region for good, bestowed a permanent legacy here – the predominantly Chinese towns that punctuate the route north. **Perak State** (*perak* meaning "silver") once boasted the richest single tin field in the world. When the light industry surrounding Malaysia's other major commodity, rubber, took over from the dying tin trade in the 1950s, the essentially agricultural nature of much of the region wasn't quite obliterated. The states of **Kedah** and **Perlis**, the latter tucked into the northern border, share the distinction of being the historical *jelapang padi*, or "rice bowl", of Malaysia, where rich, emerald-green paddy fields and jutting limestone outcrops form the Peninsula's most dramatic scenery.

This is the area in which the **British** held most sway, attracted by the political prestige of controlling such a strategic trading region. Although the British had claimed administrative authority since 1826 through the Straits Settlements (which included Singapore and Melaka as well as Penang), it was the establishment of the Federated Malay States of Perak, Pahang, Selangor and Negeri Sembilan fifty years later, that extended colonial rule to the whole Peninsula.

Most visitors are too intent on the beckoning delights of Thailand to bother stopping at anything other than the major destinations. But nowhere are the rural delights of the country more apparent than at the **hill stations** north of the capital, once cool refuges for colonial administrators. The largest of these, the **Cameron Highlands**, some 150km north of KL, is one of the country's most significant tourist spots, a locally popular mountain retreat with opportunities for forest treks and indulgence in the traditional British comforts of crackling log fires and cream teas.

Due west of here, tiny **Pulau Pangkor**, though not as idyllic as the islands of the Peninsula's east coast, is an increasingly visited resort, with the best beaches in the area. However, the fastest development is on its far northern rival, **Pulau Langkawi**, the largest island in the glittering and largely unpopulated Langkawi archipelago. Most travellers wisely have little time for the mainland port of **Butterworth**, just using it for access to the holiday island of **Penang**, whose vibrant capital, **Georgetown**, combines modern shopping malls with ancient Chinese shophouses.

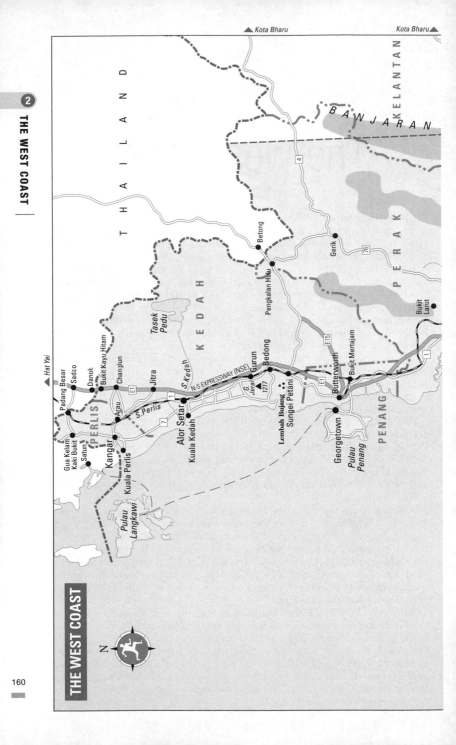

THE WEST COAST

N

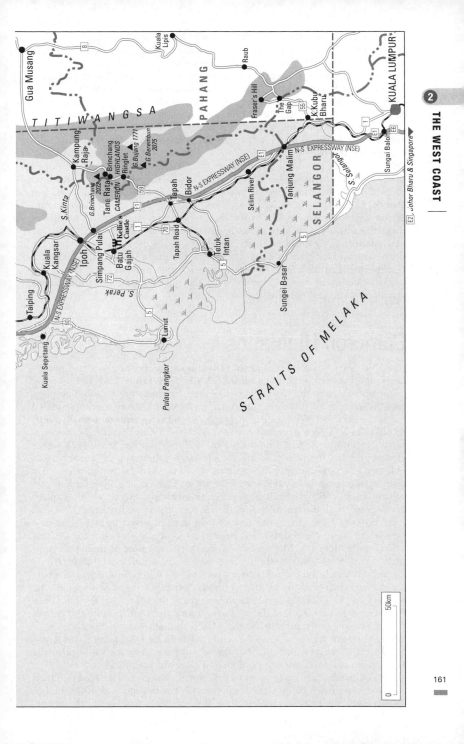

These main destinations aside, there's a whole host of intriguing and under-visited places off the beaten track, such as the old tin-boom city of **Ipoh**, 200km northwest of Kuala Lumpur, which has elegant colonial buildings and mansions at every turn, and its northern neighbour the royal town of **Kuala Kangsar**, a quiet place of architectural interest. The route north also passes through the scenic old mining town of **Taiping**. The state capital of Kedah is **Alor Setar**, the last major town before the border. Long a stamping ground for successions of invaders, the region still reveals a Thai influence in its cuisine, although Alor Setar itself is a staunch Muslim stronghold. From here it's a short hop via any of the **border towns** – Kuala Perlis, Kangar and Arau – into Thailand itself.

Because of its economic importance, the west coast has a well-developed transport infrastructure. The wide **North–South Expressway** (also referred to as "NSE"), pleasantly free of heavy traffic north of KL, virtually shadows **Route 1**, and runs from Malaysia's northern border at Bukit Kayu Hitam all the way to Singapore. The **train line**, which runs more or less parallel to these roads, is used less, though its border crossing at Padang Besar facilitates easy connections with Hat Yai, the transport crossroads of southern Thailand. Both roads and the train line pass through all the major towns – Ipoh, Taiping, Butterworth and Alor Setar – with **express buses** providing the fastest and most frequent way of travelling between the major towns, and **local buses** serving the hills and the coast.

Cameron Highlands

Amid the lofty peaks of **Banjaran Titiwangsa**, the Peninsula's main mountain range, the various outposts of the **CAMERON HIGHLANDS** (Ⓦwww .cameronhighlands.com) form Malaysia's most extensive hill station. The place took its name from William Cameron, a government surveyor who stumbled across the area in 1885 during a mapping expedition. Cameron actually failed to mark his find on a map, and it wasn't until the 1920s that the location was officially confirmed. When he visited in 1925, Sir George Maxwell, a senior civil servant, saw the same potential for a hill station here as he'd seen at Fraser's Hill (see p.265). Others, too, were quick to see the benefits of the region. Tea planters migrating from India were followed by Chinese vegetable farmers and wealthy landowners in search of a weekend retreat; the Highlands' subsequent development culminated in today's hotels and luxury apartments. Malaysia's rapid economic growth of the past decade has also given birth to a middle class who have discovered the Highlands as an ideal place for enjoying cool air amidst exotic flora. For Malaysians who don't have the time or money to vacation in temperate climates, the resort towns of the Cameron Highlands have the answer: watch the fog roll in from your mock-Tudor condo, don a tweedy flat cap, and then pose for a souvenir photo next to a red London-style phone booth. The "Ye Olde English" atmosphere really does feel contrived at times, but there is no denying that the locals get a kick out of it. Despite the crowds and crassness – especially during the March through May hot season school holidays – there are some leisurely nature walks to be had up here, and if you have been in the lowlands of Malaysia or Southeast Asia for some time, the Highlands are a good place to cool off and clear out your lungs.

The highlands encompass three small towns: **Ringlet**, a rich agricultural area and site of the famous tea plantations; 13km beyond and 300m higher, **Tanah Rata**, the principal settlement of the highlands; and 5km further north,

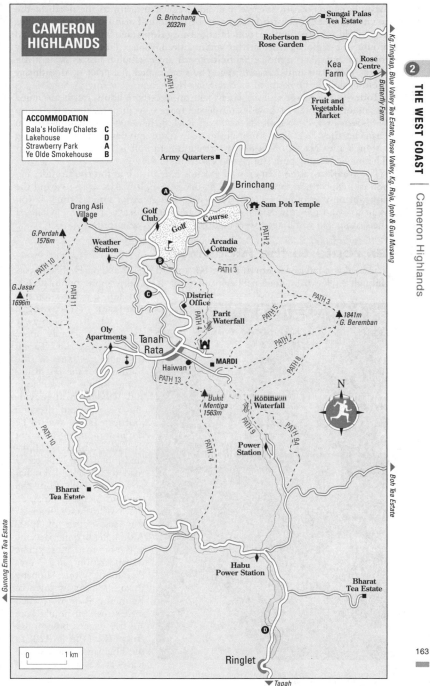

CAMERON
HIGHLANDS

ACCOMMODATION
Bala's Holiday Chalets   C
Lakehouse   D
Strawberry Park   A
Ye Olde Smokehouse   B

G. Brinchang
2032m

Sungai Palas
Tea Estate

Robertson
Rose Garden

Kea
Farm

Rose
Centre

Fruit and
Vegetable
Market

Kg. Tringkap, Blue Valley Tea Estate, Rose Valley, Kg. Raja, Ipoh & Gua Musang

Butterfly Farm

PATH 1

Army Quarters

Brinchang

Sam Poh Temple

Orang Asli
Village

Golf
Club

Golf Course

Arcadia
Cottage

PATH 2

G.Perdah
1576m

Weather
Station

Golf

PATH 10

PATH 3

PATH 11

G.Jasar
1696m

District
Office

Parit
Waterfall

PATH 5

PATH 3

1841m
G. Beremban

PATH 4

Oly
Apartments

Tanah
Rata

PATH 7

PATH 8

MARDI

Haiwan

PATH 13

Robinson
Waterfall

N

Bukit
Mentiga
1563m

PATH 4

PATH 9

PATH 9A

PATH 10

Power
Station

Bharat
Tea Estate

Gunong Emas Tea Estate

Boh Tea Estate

Habu
Power Station

Bharat
Tea Estate

D

0   1 km

Ringlet

Tapah

Brinchang, renowned for the fruit and vegetable farms to the north of the town. The best **accommodation** is to be found in Tanah Rata and Brinchang; you could also try renting one of the **bungalows** and **apartments** dotted around the region, particularly if you're travelling in a group or plan to stay for some time. Accommodation **prices** soar at peak holiday times (Christmas, Easter, *Hari Raya* and *Deepavali*) when you can expect the price of an ordinary room to double; book ahead to ensure a place.

Tours of the whole region, which take around three hours, can be arranged by any of the hotels or hostels and depart from your place of accommodation at 8.45am or 1.45pm daily (typical cost RM25). Though a bit whistle-stop in character, they do at least cover all the main sights and destinations – including a stop at a tea plantation, butterfly farm and Sam Poh Temple – in one swoop. The inevitable shopping stop at the end is mercifully low-key.

The **weather** in the Cameron Highlands is as British as the countryside, and you can expect rainstorms even in the dry season. It makes sense to avoid the area during the monsoon itself (Nov–Jan), and at major holiday times if you want to avoid the crowds. Temperatures drop dramatically at night – whatever the season – so you'll need warm clothes, as well as waterproofs.

En route to the Highlands

The road and rail routes **north from KL** towards the Cameron Highlands pass through endless pale-green rubber plantations. It's a fairly monotonous stretch, but for the 350-kilometre **Banjaran Titiwangsa** range, which rises up away to the east. Hardly more than a crossroads, **Tapah** lies about 40km to the southwest of the Highlands along Route 59 (a long and winding road providing a scenic, but dizzying journey). Tapah used to be the main jumping-off point for the Cameron Highlands, but a much easier road to the Highlands has now been built from the town of Simpang Pulai, on the North-South Expressway just south of Ipoh. Although not quite as scenic as the old road, most public transportation now uses this route. From Simpang Pulai, the gateway town of Kampung Raja is reached in less than an hour. There are five express buses a day **from KL** (4hr; RM22) to the Highlands (the last one leaves at 3.30pm).

△ British phone booth in the Cameron Highlands

Some people coming from the south still travel via Tapah, which you can reach by **express bus** from many major towns on the peninsula. If you're **driving from KL**, you may still want to go via Tapah, but continue your journey north via the new road through Kampung Raja rather than doubling back on Route 59. If you have time to spare and want to get off the main highways, a less direct but more interesting route is the coastal Route 5, running through low-lying marshland almost all the way to **Teluk Intan**, 157km northwest of the capital. Here you can stop off at the leaning pagoda-like clock tower and grab a bowl of noodles, before taking the minor back roads to **Bidor**, 14km south of Tapah, to connect with the North–South Expressway and Route 1.

If you're coming from the **east coast** via motorbike or four-wheel drive, you can take the rather rough road from Gua Musang to Brinchang (90km).

Tapah

The north–south Jalan Besar is Tapah's main street, west off which run Jalan Raja and Jalan Stesen. Local bus services use the **bus station** on Jalan Raja; there are hourly departures from here to Tanah Rata (8am–5.30pm; 2hr; RM5). **Ticket agencies** for these services can either tell you where to catch your bus, or more than likely flag it down for you. Try Kah Mee (℡05/412 973), 10 Jalan Raja, opposite the bus station, or *Caspian* – which is also a restaurant – nearby on the main road. The **train station**, called "Tapah Road", where trains from destinations up and down the west coast arrive, is a few kilometres west of town; it's easy enough to get from the station into town by taxi (RM7) or the hourly local bus (90 sen).

You're unlikely to need to stay in Tapah, though it has some very reasonable **hotels**, including the *Hotel Bunga Raya*, 6 Jalan Besar (℡05/401 1436; ❷), on the corner with Jalan Raja; it's basic and clean, and all its rooms are en suite. Two other options are two minutes' walk away on Jalan Stesen. The good-value *Timuran*, 23 Jalan Stesen (℡05/401 1092, ℻401 2570; ❷), has spotless rooms, some with air-con, and there's also a busy restaurant downstairs. A slightly more comfortable place is just opposite, the *NH Hotel*, 24 Jalan Stesen (℡&℻05/401 7188; ❸), which has en-suite rooms with air-con and TVs. There are a number of nondescript cheap Indian and Chinese **restaurants** dotted around town.

Ringlet and the Boh Tea Estate

There's not much to **RINGLET**, the first settlement you reach in the Cameron Highlands, 47km from Tapah. There are several **tea plantations** in the area; one of the most worthwhile to visit is the **Boh Tea Estate** (Tues–Sun 11am–3pm), 8km northeast of town. There's a free tour on which you'll see the whole production process – from the picking to the packing of the tea, which you cannot do at the estate's more frequented **Palas** division, north of Brinchang (see p.173). There are buses from Ringlet to Habu daily at approximately hourly intervals from 8am til 5.30pm. From here, it's approximately another 10km on a hilly and winding road to the estate. The quickest way to get to the tea estate is to take a taxi (RM30 one-way) from Tanah Rata. **Buses** from Tapah stop on the main road in Ringlet before moving on to Tanah Ratah, from where there are buses eight times a day back to Ringlet starting at 8am, with the last service at 5.30pm. Although this is a rather isolated place to base yourself, there is one deluxe **place to stay**, the *Lakehouse* (℡05/495 6152, ⓦwww.lakehouse -cameron.com; ❾), an elegant Tudor-style mansion with a lounge, games room, and restaurant serving traditional English fare, including cream teas.

Walking in the Cameron Highlands

The Cameron Highlands offer a number of **walks** of varying difficulty. Although the forest sometimes obscures the view, the trails here take in some of the most spectacular scenery in Malaysia, encompassing textured greenery and misty mountain peaks. Some of the walks are no more than casual strolls, while others are romps through what seems like the wild unknown, giving a sense of isolation rarely encountered in lowland Malaysia. Despite the presence of large mammals in the deep forest, such as honey bears and monkeys, you're unlikely to come across many animals on the trails, perhaps only the odd wild pig or squirrel. At all times of year the **flora** is prolific, with ferns, pitcher plants and orchids amongst the tremendous canopy of trees.

Unfortunately, the trails are often badly signposted and maintained, though there are various sketch **maps** on sale in Tanah Rata (RM1) and at many of the hotels. Despite their apparent vagueness, they do make some sort of sense on the ground, although some of the trails marked no longer exist. The *Cameronian Inn* and *Father's Guest House* (see p.169) are good contacts for trail information and hiring guides. There used to be more official trails but many were closed during the 1970s due to the supposed threat of Communist guerrillas. Although they are no longer perceived as a threat today, the trails have not been reopened. If you want to attempt any **unofficial routes**, a guide is essential and you must also obtain a permit from the District Office (see "Listings", p.170), which is tricky and expensive.

However, the **official trails**, detailed below (and marked on the map on p.163) are varied enough for most tastes and energies. The timings given are for one-way walks for people with an average level of fitness. You should always inform someone, preferably at your hotel, where you are going and what time you expect to be back. On longer hikes, take warm clothing, water, a torch and a cigarette lighter or matches for basic survival should you get lost. If someone doesn't return from a hike and you suspect they may be in **trouble**, inform the District Office immediately. It's not a fanciful notion that the hills and forests are dangerous – mudslides, for example, are not uncommon in some spots. The most notorious incident to date concerns the American silk entrepreneur **Jim Thompson**, who came on holiday here in Easter 1967 and disappeared in the forest. The services of Orang Asli trackers, dogs and even mystics failed to provide any clue to his fate – a warning to present-day trekkers of the hazards of jungle life.

The following paths are numbered according to the local area map. Check before departing as several paths may be closed or out of use.

Path 1 (2hr) This is a steep climb, but you can do the walk downhill only by taking a taxi (from Brinchang for RM10) to the top of Gunung Brinchang. At 2000m, this is the highest road in Peninsular Malaysia and there's a terrific view of the highlands from the summit. If going uphill, start just north of Brinchang, on a rarely used and unmaintained track near the army quarters. Look for the white stone marker 1/48 which

Tanah Rata

The tidy town of **TANAH RATA** is the Highlands' most developed settlement, a bustling place festooned with hotels, white-balustraded buildings, flowers and parks. It comprises little more than one street (officially called Jalan Besar, but usually just known as "Main Road"), which is where you'll find most of the hotels, banks and other services, as well as some of the best restaurants in the Cameron Highlands, all lined up in a half-kilometre stretch. Since the street also serves as the main thoroughfare to the rest of the region, it suffers from the constant honking of departing buses during the day, but at night becomes the centre of the Cameron Highlands' social life, with restaurant tables spilling out onto the pavement.

marks the beginning of the trail. Once you reach the summit, you can either return the way you came or by walking east along the sealed access road back to the main road, passing an access road to the Sungai Palas Tea Estate en route (see p.173).

Path 2 (1hr 30min) Begins just before the Sam Poh Temple below Brinchang – not clearly marked, and often a bit of a scramble, you'll need to be reasonably fit and well prepared for this option. The route undulates severely and eventually merges with Path 3.

Path 3 (2hr 30min) Starts at *Arcadia Cottage* to the southeast of the golf course, crossing streams and climbing quite steeply to reach the peak of Gunung Beremban (1841m). Once at the top, you can retrace your steps, or head down Path 5, 7, or 8.

Path 4 (20min) Paved in stretches, this walk starts south of the golf course and goes past Parit Waterfall, leading on to a watchtower with good views over Brinchang. The last stop is the Forest Department HQ from where a sealed path leads back to the main road.

Path 5 (1hr) Branches off from Path 3 and ends up at the Malaysian Agriculture Research and Development Institute (MARDI). It's an easy walk through peaceful woodland, after which you can cut back up the road to Tanah Rata.

Path 7 (2hr) Starts near MARDI and climbs steeply to Gunung Beremban; an arduous and very overgrown hike best recommended as a descent route from Path 3.

Path 8 (3hr) Another route to Gunung Beremban, a tough approach from Robinson Waterfall; more taxing than Path 7.

Path 9 and **9A** (1hr) The descent from Robinson Waterfall to the power station is steep and strenuous; the station caretaker will let you through to the road to Boh. Path 9A, an easier downhill grade than Path 9, branches off from the main route and emerges in a vegetable farm on the Boh road.

Path 10 (2hr 30min) Starts just behind the *Oly Apartments* and involves a fairly strenuous climb to Gunung Jasar (1696m). It then drops down to the Orang Asli village, where you join a small road leading back to the main road.

Path 11 (2hr) Takes you up to Gunung Perdah (1576m), a slightly shorter and less challenging route than Path 10. Again, you come out at the Orang Asli village and take the small road back into town.

Path 13 (1hr) An alternate access to Path 14, its starting point is a half-hour's walk southwest of the *Cameronian Holiday Inn* in Tanah Rata.

Path 14 (3hr) This is a tricky and initially steep route via Bukit Mentiga (1563m), with great views. It begins at Haiwan (a veterinary centre) and continues south, becoming very hard to make out until it joins the road 8km from Tanah Rata. Best not to do this one alone.

All the local and long-distance **buses** go only as far as Tanah Rata; to move further on to Brinchang and other destinations you'll have to change here. The **bus station** is about halfway along the main road, and Tanah Rata's **taxi rank** is just a little further north. At the far end of town, past the hospital and the police station, the road bends round to the west to continue on to Brinchang. There is no official tourist office in the Cameron Highlands, but you can purchase **maps** at many of the local shops or hostels.

Tanah Rata is an ideal base to explore the Cameron Highlands, with many **walks** starting nearby, a couple of waterfalls, a mosque and three reasonably high mountain peaks all within hiking distance. Several of the walks pass through, or close to, the **Malaysian Agriculture Research and Development**

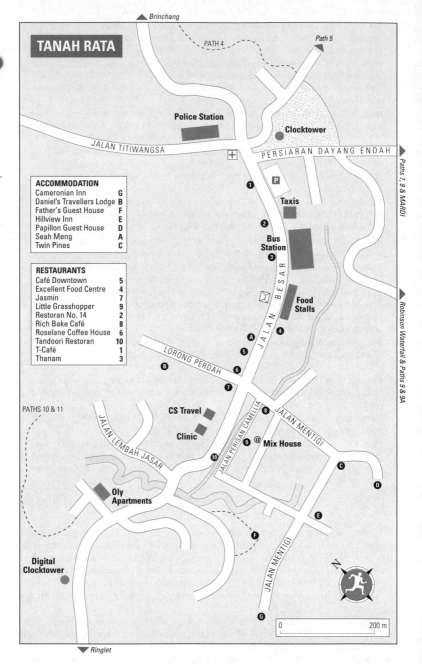

TANAH RATA

▲ Brinchang

PATH 4

Path 5 ▶

Police Station

Clocktower

JALAN TITIWANGSA

PERSIARAN DAYANG ENDAH

▶ Paths 7, 8 & MARDI

P

Taxis

Bus Station

Food Stalls

▶ Robinson Waterfall & Paths 9 & 9A

JALAN BESAR

LORONG PERDAH

CS Travel

Clinic

JALAN PERISAN CAMELLIA

@ Mix House

JALAN MENTIGI

PATHS 10 & 11

JALAN LEMBAH JASAR

Oly Apartments

JALAN MENTIGI

Digital Clocktower

N

0   200 m

▼ Ringlet

ACCOMMODATION
Cameronian Inn	G
Daniel's Travellers Lodge	B
Father's Guest House	F
Hillview Inn	E
Papillon Guest House	D
Seah Meng	A
Twin Pines	C

RESTAURANTS
Café Downtown	5
Excellent Food Centre	4
Jasmin	7
Little Grasshopper	9
Restoran No. 14	2
Rich Bake Café	8
Roselane Coffee House	6
Tandoori Restoran	10
T-Café	1
Thanam	3

Institute (MARDI; ☎05/491 1255) a couple of kilometres east of town, which is open for tours by appointment, though it's rather dry for anyone other than a specialist. This is the location for the annual **Flower Festival** held most years in August, when colourful floats compete for prizes.

Accommodation

Budget lodging is of a good standard in Tanah Rata, with even the simplest **hostels** offering hot showers and higher levels of service and cleanliness for the price than in many other parts of the Peninsula. Many of the budget places have touts at the bus station. The places strung along the main road can be a bit noisy; for a quieter stay you'll have to pay the higher prices charged at the comfortable hotels out on the road to Brinchang, or rent one of the **apartments** or cottages in the locality. These are advertised in shop windows in Tanah Rata – rates quoted are usually per day, and a residential cook or caretaker can often be hired at an additional cost. Try the *Golf View Villa*, a six-room bungalow for RM360 (☎05/491 1624); the *Star Regency Apartments*, with a wide range of rooms for all budgets (☎05/491 5133); *Rose Cottage*, which has two rooms and costs RM250 (☎05/491 1173); or *Country Lodge*, which sleeps six people for RM270 (☎05/491 1811).

In Tanah Rata

See Tanah Rata map opposite.

Cameronian Inn 16 Jalan Mentigi ☎05/491 1327, ℱ491 4966. This friendly, clean converted house with Internet access, a washing machine and a library is set in a quiet garden. Double rooms with shared facilities are rather dank, while the brighter en suites are better value. There's also a small dorm (RM8). Organized treks set off from here at 9.30am most mornings, with non-guests welcome at no charge. ❶–❷

Daniel's Travellers Lodge 9 Lorong Perdah ☎05/491 5823, ⓦdaniels.cameronhighlands.com. This place is very popular with travellers and has one huge attic dorm (RM7–8) and doubles with fans and shared or private toilets. There's a good communal sitting area and café with comfy chairs and pumping music – less pleasant at night when you're trying to sleep. ❶

Father's Guest House A4 Jalan Gereja ☎05/491 2484, ℰfathersonline@hotmail .com. The best of the budget places, set on a quiet hill in the outskirts. There are doubles in a stone house with French doors opening onto a secluded garden, and dorm beds in aluminium huts (RM9). They also have a large collection of books, a few Internet terminals and very friendly, well-travelled staff. There's also a nice little restaurant with home-made cakes. ❶

Hillview Inn 17 Jalan Mentigi ☎05/491 2915, ℰhillviewinn@hotmail.com. New and clean, this hotel has spacious rooms, all with balconies and hot showers. Amenities include a laundry, restaurant and Internet access. Good value. ❸

Papillon Guest House 8 Jalan Mentigi ☎05/491 5942. Head out to the *Twin Pines*, then follow the road left for another 100m to reach this friendly family house with clean dorms (RM10), singles (RM25) and en-suite doubles. There's a kitchen, laundry, and pleasant lounge. Rates include a light breakfast. ❷

Seah Meng 39 Jalan Besar ☎05/491 1373. Located in a rather ugly shophouse, the basic but clean and well-kept rooms are one of the best deals in town. ❷

Twin Pines 2 Jalan Mentigi ☎05/491 2169, ⓦtwinpines.cameronhighlands.com. Set back from the road with a blue roof, this laid-back place is popular with travellers, though it can be noisy due to the thin-walled rooms. There's an attractive patio garden, a café and online facilities. Dorms are RM6–7 and there are small doubles with shared bath. ❶

On the road to Brinchang

See Cameron Highlands map on p.163.

Bala's Holiday Chalets ☎05/491 1660, ⓦwww.balaschalet.com. A kilometre or so towards Brinchang, this lovingly refurbished colonial-era boarding school has a variety of tastefully furnished rooms. There's a lounge, dining rooms and a log fire plus beautiful gardens, which are a great spot for afternoon tea. Internet service and free shuttle pick-up from Tanah Rata. ❹

Strawberry Park ☎05/491 1166, ℱ491 1949. A modern apartment-syle hotel in a superb location at the top of a hill, which makes it rather inaccessible, though a hotel minibus leaves on request.

There's an indoor swimming pool and sauna, which are also available to non-guests for day-use. Check for special promotions. ⑧

Ye Olde Smokehouse Hotel ☎05/491 1215, ⓦwww.thesmokehouse.com.my. Midway along the Tanah Rata–Brinchang road. Twelve suites, most with four-poster beds, are rather overpriced when compared to others in this category. The hotel was built in 1937 and its colonial-era pedigree is what you pay for. Leaded windows and wooden beams give a country pub feel. Rates include English breakfast. ⑨

Eating and drinking

The local Highlands speciality is Chinese **steamboat**. It's similar to a meat fondue, and involves cooking your food at the table on a burner. You get vegetables, meat and prawns, which you dip in a boiling pot filled with stock. The Malay **food stalls** along the main road are open in the evening and serve satay, *tom yam* (spicy Thai soup) and the usual rice and noodle combinations, for about RM2 per dish.

Café Downtown 41 Jalan Besar. Downstairs from the *Hotel Downtown*, this is a good spot for breakfast and lunch. Does tasty pastries and cakes as well as set meals of noodles and rice.
Excellent Food Centre Jalan Besar, opposite the post office. Lives up to its name with a large, inexpensive menu of Western and Asian dishes – it's great for breakfast. Open during the day only. In the adjacent Fresh *Milk* Corner, you can get wonderful shakes and lassis.
Jasmin 45 Jalan Besar. The *rijsttafel* (a Dutch Indonesian dish of rice and various curries) served here is popular with German and Dutch travellers. There's karaoke in the evening.
Little Grasshopper 57b Perisan Camellia 3. On the second floor above the new shophouses. Excellent-value steamboats – starting at just RM9 – served by friendly staff in a tasteful setting. Also has traditional Chinese tea.
Restoran No. 14 Jalan Besar, across from the petrol station. This popular banana-leaf restaurant serves cheap and tasty *masala dosas*.
Rich Bake Café Jalan Besar. Bright, jazzy spot which sometimes has live music; serves good pancakes.
Roselane Coffee House 44 Jalan Besar. The various set menus and low-price meat grills here make up for the twee decor.
Tandoori Restoran Jalan Besar. Tasty, good-value Indian food, including naan breads and tandoori dishes.
T-Café Jalan Besar. This newish eatery has the Highland's best baked goodies, as well as an excellent selection of vegetarian dishes. The apple pie is a house specialty.
Thanam Jalan Besar. This little eatery has it all: they serve good Hainanese chicken rice as well as Indian Muslim food and Western breakfast, lassi and juices.
Ye Olde Smokehouse On the Tanah Rata–Brinchang road ☎05/491 1215. The hotel opens its restaurant to non-guests, but enforces an absurdly formal (given the décor) dress code. Unless you're absolutely dying for a traditional English roast – and are ready to pay dearly for it – it's probably better to wait until you get home.

Listings

Banks There is a branch of HSBC on Jalan Besar, north of the post office, and a Maybank with an ATM on the northern branch of Jalan Mentigi.
District office 39007 Tanah Rata ☎05/491 1066, ⓕ491 1843 (Mon–Thurs 8am–1pm & 2–4.30pm, Fri 8am–12.15pm & 2.45–4.30pm, Sat 8am–12.15pm). Contact them immediately if you suspect someone has got lost on a walk. Also call here to obtain permits for unofficial trails.
Hospital Jalan Besar, opposite the park ☎05/491 1966. There's also a clinic at 48 Main Rd (8.30am–12.30pm, 2–5.30pm & 8–10pm). Ring doorbell after clinic hours in emergencies.
Internet access Mix House Net, 76b Jalan Perisan Camellia.
Laundry Highlands Laundry on Jalan Besar (☎05/491 1820) is reasonably priced, plus most hostels also have laundry services.
Police station Jalan Besar, opposite the *New Garden Inn* ☎05/491 1222.
Post office Jalan Besar ☎05/491 1051.
Service station There are service stations in both Tanah Rata and Brinchang.
Sport Cameron Highlands Golf Club has an eighteen-hole course (RM40 on weekdays, RM60 on weekends and holidays), caddy fees and equipment rental extra; ☎05/491 1126; there's a strict

dress code (no collarless shirts, shorts or flip-flops). Tennis courts at the golf club (RM4/hr for court, RM5 for racket). **Taxi rank** Jalan Besar ☏ 05/491 1234.

Travel agent CS Travel, 47 Jalan Besar ☏ 05/491 1200, ⊛ www.cstravel.com. They can help with express bus tickets from Tapah to all major destinations and will also book Highlands' tours.

Brinchang and around

After Tanah Rata, **BRINCHANG**, 5km or so further north, seems rather scruffy. Sprawling around a central square and the main road – Jalan Besar – through town, some say it lacks the charm of its neighbour. Most visitors however will find there is little difference between the two settlements. If anything, Brinchang has more of a traffic problem. On the bright side, Brinchang also has a lively **night market** from 4pm on Saturdays and holidays. In peak periods, you may have to resort to Brinchang as an alternative to Tanah Rata in order to find a room – not a disaster, since Walks 1 to 3 are easily approached from here, and reaching the **farms** and **tea estates** to the north is quicker from here too. A more challenging alternative to the local trails is to hike to the summit of **Gunung Brinchang** (2032m), the highest peak in Malaysia accessible by road. This takes two to three hours from Brinchang and although the road there is sealed, it's an extremely steep and exhausting climb. On a clear day though, the views back down the broad valley are wonderful. You can also walk to the **Sam Poh Temple**, 1km southeast of Brinchang, a gaudy modern place with a monastery that was built in 1965.

Practicalities

Buses leave Tanah Rata for Brinchang and Kampung Raja (the furthest point north of here that's served by public transport) every hour or so between 6.30am and 6.30pm, from the **bus stop** just south of the square. A **taxi** from Tanah Rata to Brinchang costs around RM5.

Accommodation

Most of the **hotels** in Brinchang line the east and west sides of the central square, and although the numbering system leaves much to be desired, you shouldn't have too much difficulty locating them. When you do, you'll find them uniformly overpriced. Brinchang has only a few budget options and sees very little of the backpacker scene. The standard high-season price hikes apply.

Equatorial Resort Kea Farm ☏ 05/496 1777, ⓔ info@cam.equatorial.com. Luxury resort, about 2km north of Brinchang, near the Rose Centre. Has modern rooms in high-rise towers; facilities include cinema complex and gym. ❽
Golden Star Hotel 26 Jalan Besar ☏ 05/491 2233. The next best choice after the *Silverstar* for an inexpensive night's sleep; the rooms are nothing special but they're clean and well looked-after. ❸

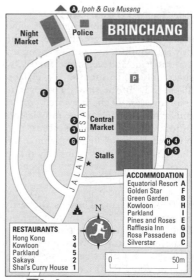

RESTAURANTS	
Hong Kong	3
Kowloon	4
Parkland	5
Sakaya	2
Shal's Curry House	1

ACCOMMODATION	
Equatorial Resort	A
Golden Star	F
Green Garden	B
Kowloon	H
Parkland	I
Pines and Roses	E
Rafflesia Inn	G
Rosa Passadena	D
Silverstar	C

Green Garden Lot 13, Jalan Besar ☏ 05/491 5824, Ⓕ 05/491 5824. In a gardenless shophouse on the northwest corner of the square, this hotel has clean rooms with well-equipped bathrooms. They're overpriced for what you get, though. ❺

Kowloon 34–35 Jalan Besar ☏ 05/491 1366, Ⓕ 491 1803. Above the Chinese restaurant of the same name, this place has small, comfortable rooms with TVs and bathrooms – good value by Brinchang standards. ❹

Parkland 45 Jalan Besar ☏ 05/491 1299, Ⓕ 491 1803. In a five-storey shophouse with the obligatory mock-Tudor gables, the *Parkland* is run by the same management as the *Kowloon* with similar standards but larger rooms. ❺

Pines and Roses ☏ 05/491 2203. Located in a nondescript shophouse, this place has friendly service and simple, clean doubles. Good value. ❸

Rafflesia Inn Lot 30, Jalan Besar ☏ & Ⓕ 05/491 2859. This new backpacker operation is the only real budget accommodation in town. It has a comfy TV lounge and dorm beds (RM10). The owner, Mr Rama, is a wellspring of information. ❷

Rosa Passadena 1 Bandar Baru Brinchang ☏ 05/491 2288. Large, modern, professionally run hotel offering small but cosy rooms with mini bars and hot tubs. ❻

Silverstar 10 Jalan Besar ☏ 05/491 1387. Fifteen basic, fair-sized rooms with *mandi*-style bath. One of the few places in Brinchang where you won't pay over the odds for clean sheets and a place to sleep. The Chinese restaurant on the ground floor is very popular. ❷

Eating and drinking

As well as the Malay **food stalls** in the central square, the following cafés and restaurants are worth a try.

Hong Kong Jalan Besar, west side of square. This posh-looking place serves the usual Chinese dishes and steamboats.

Kowloon 34–35 Jalan Besar. Downstairs from the *Kowloon Hotel*, this smart, efficient restaurant has prices to match. The dishes from the very large Chinese menu are worth the extra cost.

Parkland 45 Jalan Besar. Part of the hotel, this pleasant, airy restaurant has good views over town

but is fairly pricey considering the bland, international cuisine it serves.

Sakaya Jalan Besar. Near the *Hong Kong*, this inexpensive Chinese eating house does buffet lunches, costing from RM3 for three dishes, including rice.

Shal's Curry House 25 Jalan Besar. Good South Indian cuisine, spiced teas, and apple strudel. Recommended.

North of Brinchang

All over the Cameron Highlands – but especially north of Brinchang – you'll pass small sheds or greenhouses by the roadside, selling cabbages, leeks, cauliflowers, mushrooms and strawberries. These are the produce of the area's various fruit and vegetable **farms**, where narrow plots are cut out of the sheer hillsides to increase the surface area for planting, forming giant steps all the way up the slopes. However, terrace farming poses a problem for the transportation of the harvested crop, since the paths between the terraces are only wide enough for one nimble-footed person. This has been solved by the introduction of a **cable system**, initially operated by brute force but now powered by diesel engines, which hoist the large baskets of vegetables from the terraces to trucks waiting by the roadside high above, from where they are taken to market – over forty percent of the produce is for export to Singapore, Brunei and Hong Kong.

A couple of more specific targets might entice you out into the countryside north of Brinchang. There's a **Butterfly Farm** and a **Butterfly Garden** (daily 8am–5pm; RM3), 5km to the north at Kea Farm. Both establishments are very similar and just a hundred metres away from each other. Both have hundreds of butterflies of various species flittering among the flowers and ponds; the Kampung Raja bus from Brinchang passes both places, or you can get a taxi from Tanah Rata for about RM15. Flower lovers are well served by the **Rose Centre** at Kea

Farm (daily 8am–5pm; RM3), which has a spectacular view of the surrounding valleys from its summit, crowned in surreal fashion by a colourful Mother-Hubbard-like boot. The sculptures here, of which the boot is one, were created by Burmese craftsmen and do a lot to liven up a potentially dull attraction. Besides roses, there are also other temperate-climate flowers – rare and expensive in tropical Southeast Asia – being cultivated here.

The Sungai Palas Tea Estate

Set high in the hills north of Brinchang, the **Sungai Palas Tea Estate** (Tues–Sun 8.30am–3pm, tours roughly every 10min; free) doesn't attract crowds of people. Despite the romantic imagery used on tea packaging, handpicking – though the best method for producing the highest quality tea – is now far too labour-intensive to be economical. Instead, the Tamil, Bangladeshi and Malay workers who live on the estates pick the small, green leaves with shears. Once in the factory, the full baskets are emptied into large wire vats where the leaves are withered by alternate blasts of hot and cold air for sixteen to eighteen hours; this removes around fifty percent of their moisture. They are then sifted of dust and impurities and rolled by ancient, bulky machines. This breaks up the leaves and releases the moisture for the all-important process of **fermentation**. Following ninety minutes' grinding, the soggy mass is fired at 90°C to halt the fermentation process, and the leaves turn black. After being sorted into grades, the tea matures for three to six months before being packaged and transported to market.

How much you glean of this process from your guide is variable, as the noise in parts of the factory is so deafening that all sound save the roar of the dryers is obliterated. Some areas of the building are also made extremely dusty by the tea impurities, so take a handkerchief to cover your mouth and nose. There's a pleasant **café** and garden on the premises where you can enjoy a cup of tea before or after the tour.

Six **buses** run back and forth from Tanah Rata to the estate from Brinchang's bus station between 6.30am and 6.30pm. To return, it is also possible to walk the 6km or so along the road back to Brinchang, though the hilliness of the route may put you off. From Tanah Rata a taxi should cost around RM20–25.

Ipoh and around

Eighty kilometres north of Tapah in the Kinta Valley is **IPOH**, the state capital of Perak and third-biggest city in Malaysia. It grew rich on the tin trade, which transformed it within the space of forty years at the end of the nineteenth century from a tiny kampung in a landscape dominated by dramatic limestone outcrops to a sprawling boom town. Now a metropolis of over half a million people, Ipoh (the name comes from that of the *upas* tree which thrived in the area, and whose sap was used by the Orang Asli for blowpipe dart poison) is a far cry from the original village on this site. Perak had been renowned for its rich tin deposits since the sixteenth century, which made it vulnerable to attempts from rival chiefs to seize the throne and thus gain control of the lucrative tin trade. However, it wasn't until the discovery of a major field in 1880 that Ipoh's fortunes turned; before long it became a prime destination for pioneers, merchants and fortune-seekers from all over the world, and a cosmopolitan city, something reflected in the broad mix of cultures today. To accommodate the

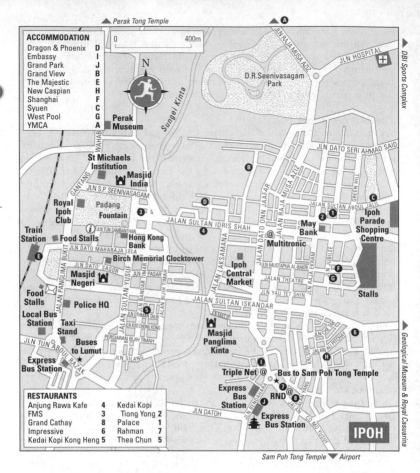

▲ Perak Tong Temple

ACCOMMODATION
Dragon & Phoenix	D
Embassy	I
Grand Park	J
Grand View	B
The Majestic	E
New Caspian	H
Shanghai	F
Syuen	C
West Pool	G
YMCA	A

RESTAURANTS
Anjung Rawa Kafe	4	Kedai Kopi	
FMS	3	Tiong Yong	2
Grand Cathay	8	Palace	1
Impressive	6	Rahman	7
Kedai Kopi Kong Heng	5	Thea Chun	5

Sam Poh Tong Temple ▼ Airport

rapidly increasing population, between 1905 and 1914 the city expanded across
Sungai Kinta into a "new town" area, its economic good fortune reflected in a
multitude of **colonial buildings** and Chinese mansions. The demand for the
metal later declined, although the export of tin is still the fifth largest earner of
foreign currency in the country, and Ipoh is still a major player.

Yet despite its historical significance and present-day administrative
importance, Ipoh's new town doesn't have much to offer the visitor.
Although the colonial architecture around the padang is certainly worth a
look, the main reason people stop here is to visit Ipoh's outlying attractions
– the Chinese cave temples of **Sam Poh Tong** and **Perak Tong**, the anach-
ronistic ruin of **Kellie's Castle** and the unique development at the **Tambun
Hot Springs**. To do these sights justice, you're likely to have to spend at least
one night in the city.

Arrival and information

The **layout** of central Ipoh is reasonably straightforward, since the roads
more or less form a grid system. What *is* confusing is that some of the old

△ Kellie's Castle

colonial **street names** have been changed in favour of something more Islamic, though the street signs haven't always caught up; hence, Jalan C.M. Yusuf instead of Jalan Chamberlain, Jalan Mustapha Al-Bakri for Jalan Clare and Jalan Bandar Timar for Jalan Leech. In practice, people recognize either name. The muddy and lethargic **Sungai Kinta** cuts the centre of Ipoh neatly in two; most of the hotels are situated east of the river, while the **old town** is on the opposite side between the two major thoroughfares, Jalan Sultan Idris Shah and Jalan Sultan Iskander.

Both the North–South Expressway and Route 1 pass through Ipoh, which is also a major stop for express buses and trains between Butterworth and KL. The **train station** is on Jalan Panglima Bukit Gantang Wahab (more simply Jalan Panglima), west of the old town, but there are only a few trains passing through Ipoh, and given that they stop here in the middle of the night, it is unlikely that you will be arriving or departing by train. Just south of the train station, at the junction of Jalan Tun Abdul Razak and Jalan Panglima, is the **local bus station** (buses to Taiping and Kuala Kangsar every 15min), opposite which is a **taxi stand**. Local buses to **Lumut** (hourly 6am–6pm; 1hr 30min), the departure point for Pulau Pangkor (see p.180), use a separate forecourt, beside a row of shops, a little further along Jalan Tun Abdul Razak. There are two **express bus** stations: one behind a bank of ticket booths across the road from the local bus station, and another one near the roundabout on Jalan Bendahara (near the Chinese Temple). The Sultan Azlan Shah **airport** is 15km from the city; a taxi into the centre costs RM25.

The **tourist office** is in the State Economic Planning Unit, close to the train station on Jalan Tun Sambanthan (Mon–Thurs 8am–1pm & 2–4.30pm, Fri & Sat 8am–12.15pm & 2.45–4.30pm, closed first and third Sat of every month; ℡05/241 2959, ℻241 2958); besides assistance on Ipoh, it can provide information on travel throughout Perak State.

Accommodation

Most of the **places to stay** in Ipoh are found east of the river, around Jalan C.M. Yusuf and Jalan Mustapha Al-Bakri; the latter has a more seedy feel, though it's generally much quieter. At the time of publication, most hotels in town were offering promotional rates of approximately thirty percent off their published rates; these lower rates are expected to prevail indefinitely and are quoted below.

Dragon & Phoenix 23–25 Jalan Toh Puan Chah ☎ 05/253 4661, ℱ 253 5096. A relatively quiet hotel set back from the main road with clean, bright rooms. Good value. ❹

Embassy Jalan C.M. Yusuf ☎ 05/254 9496. The best budget place if you want your own bathroom. All rooms are clean and have hot water and a/c. ❷

Grand Park Hotel 19 Jalan Bendahara ☎ 05/241 1333. Conveniently close to one of the express bus stations, this old colonial building with wood and tile floors has reasonable rooms with a/c. ❸

Grand View Hotel 36 Jalan Horley ☎ 05/243 1488, ℱ 243 1811. Although a bit out of the way, this well-run hotel has clean bright rooms and a good view from the side and back (the front rooms look onto a parking garage). All rooms are en suite, with a/c, TV and kettle. ❹

The Majestic Above the train station, set back a little from Jalan Panglima ☎ 05/255 5605, ℱ 255 3393. Although the basic rooms in this colonial-era hotel are nothing special, an extra RM25 will get you a spacious en-suite room off of the huge tiled veranda complete with wicker chairs. Its location in the old town and proximity to the bus station are a plus. Breakfast is included. ❹

New Caspian Hotel (formerly Central Hotel) 20–26 Jalan Ali Pitchay ☎ 05/243 9254, ℱ 243 9258. Well-kept and friendly place where the en-suite rooms come with a/c, TVs and fridges. Excellent value, and first choice in the mid-range category. ❸

Shanghai 85 Jalan Mustapha Al-Bakri ☎ 05/241 2070. Standard Chinese-run hotel that's clean and functional enough for the money. Also has some a/c rooms. ❷

Syuen 88 Jalan Sultan Jalil ☎ 05/253 8889, ℱ 253 3335, ℮ syuenht@tm.net.my. The top hotel in Ipoh. Of international standard with all the trimmings, including a stately lobby and a swimming pool. ❼

West Pool 74 Clare St ☎ 05/254 5042. The least expensive place in town, above a furiously busy Chinese restaurant. Manages a high degree of cleanliness. The communal showers are of the *mandi* type. There are a few signs up warning you to leave your firearms at reception, and not to drill peepholes in the walls, but otherwise it's okay. ❶

YMCA 311 Jalan Raja Musa Aziz ☎ 05/254 0809. Located about a kilometre north of the town centre in a leafy suburb, the local Y has clean rooms and excellent security, although not the cheapest rates in town. ❸

The City

Although most of Ipoh's attractions are on the outskirts, there are a few buildings in the centre that make a leisurely stroll through the old town worthwhile. The most prominent reminder of Ipoh's economic heyday is the **train station**, built in 1917 at the height of the tin boom. With its Moorish turrets and domes, and a veranda that runs the entire two-hundred-metre length of the building, it's a typical example of the British conception of "East meets West". Like other colonial train stations in KL and Hong Kong, it boasted a plush hotel (the *Majestic*) in which the planters, traders and administrators sank cocktails.

From the train station, it's a short walk northeast past the tourist office, to the **padang**, around which there are several interesting colonial-era buildings including, on the north side, St Michael's School (opened in 1912 and still running today) built in Neo-Gothic style, which was used as the Japanese army administration and medical centre during World War II. Next door is the **Masjid India** (1908), which was built in the Chettia style by a sheikh who migrated from South India; today, it serves the Indian Muslim community. Walking south away from the padang, you'll come to the modern

Masjid Negeri on Jalan Sultan Iskandar. This is one of the more conspicuous landmarks in the centre of town, all tacky 1960s cladding, with a minaret that rises over 40m above its mosaic-tiled domes. Directly opposite the mosque, on the parallel Jalan Dato' Sagor, stands the **Birch Memorial Clock Tower**, a square, white tower incorporating a portrait bust of J.W.W. Birch, the first British Resident of Perak, who was murdered in 1874. When Birch was installed as Resident (see p.188), his abrupt manner and lack of understanding of Malay customs quickly offended Sultan Abdullah, who resented his attempts to control rather than advise. Birch's manner proved to be an insult to the sensibilities of the Perak royalty for which he paid with his life – on November 2 he was shot while bathing in the river at Kuala Kangsar, on a trip to post notices of his own reforms. Another interesting mosque is the **Masjid Panglima Kinta**, on Jalan Masjid just off Jalan Sultan Iskandar. It was the first mosque in Ipoh as well as the site of the first madrasah (Islamic school) and has unusual Moorish-style arches.

The **Perak Museum** (daily 9.30am–5pm; free) is housed in an elegant, former tin miner's mansion, only a short walk north from the station. Covering two floors, the museum has evocative photos of Ipoh's glory days during the tin boom, but otherwise the displays lack imagination.

Ipoh's **Geological Museum** (Mon–Thurs 8am–1pm & 2–4.30pm, Sat 8am–12.45pm, closed first and third Sat of every month; free), on Jalan Sultan Azlan Shah on the far eastern outskirts of the city (RM5 by taxi from the centre), does its best to make tin seem interesting, but other than granting a perfunctory insight into what made the city rich, the only achievement here is comprehensiveness – over six hundred samples of minerals and an array of fossils and precious stones are displayed.

Eating and drinking

Ipoh is an excellent place to sample both local Chinese and Malay dishes. At lunchtime, regional specialities are available at most Chinese **restaurants** and **cafés**, including *sar hor fun*. On Jalan Pitchay, near the *New Caspian Hotel*, is the clean and bright *Impressive* hawker centre, a good choice for cheap Chinese stir-fry and Indian sweets. Many of Ipoh's restaurants close in the evenings, so you may have to turn to the **food stalls**, some of which lie near the train station and at the top of Jalan C.M. Yusuf. The best stalls, however, are at the southern end of Jalan Greenhill, east of the *Shanghai Hotel*, where nearly a hundred stay open well into the night, serving just about anything you care to name. On Jalan Sultan Abdul Jalil you'll also find some very good-quality Indian stalls, and the *No.1* banana-leaf curry house.

Anjung Rawa Café Across the street from the *D&P Hotel* on Jalan Sultan Idris Shah, this relaxing, friendly and family-run café serves good Malay food and fresh juices.

FMS Bar and Restaurant Overlooking the padang, this is said to be Malaysia's oldest bar, opened here in the Federated Malay States building in 1906. The colonial-era setting with marble-topped Peranakan tables is a venue for Chinese and Western food.

Grand Cathay On Jalan C.M. Yusuf, this place is very popular with Chinese locals.

Kedai Kopi Kong Heng On Jalan Othman Talib. The oldest and best of the lunchtime only Chinese cafés. Satay is their specialty.

Kedai Kopi Tiong Yong On Jalan Raja Ekram. A hole-in-the-wall café offering cheap Chinese stir fry.

Noor Jahan Bakery On Jalan Raja Ekram. A good breakfast option with fresh bread and pastries.

Palace Restaurant Situated in the *Excelsior Hotel*, this Chinese restaurant is worth the modest splurge.

Rahman On Jalan C.M. Yusuf, this is a cheap and extremely friendly Indian restaurant.

Thean Chun Next to the *Kedai Kopi Kong Heng*, this Chinese hole-in-the-wall has the town's signature *ipoh kuey tiow* noodles on offer.

Listings

Airlines MAS, Lot 108, Bangunan Seri Kinta, Jalan Sultan Idris Shah ☎05/241 4155.

Airport ☎05/312 2459 for flight information.

Banks Maybank and Bank Bumiputra are on Jalan Sultan Idris Shah; there's an Oriental Bank on Jalan Yang Kalsom.

Buses Tickets for Lumut buses can be bought from Perak Roadways, under the advertising hoardings on Jalan Tun Abdul Razak, opposite the express bus station.

Car rental Hertz (☎05/312 7109) and Pacific (☎05/313 7949) both have offices at the airport.

Cinemas Fourth floor of the Ipoh Parade shopping complex, Jalan Sultan Abdul Jalil, just east of the *Syuen Hotel*.

Hospital Jalan Hospital ☎05/254 1835.

Internet access MultiTronic, 133 Jalan Sultan Idris Shah, ☎05/254 4893; RND Internet Café, 92 Jalan C.M. Yusuf ☎05/243 7578; Triple Net, 41 Jalan C.M. Yusuf ☎05/254 4725.

Police On Jalan Panglima between the bus and train stations ☎05/253 5522.

Post office The GPO is practically next door to the train station, on Jalan Panglima.

Taxis There's a taxi stand at the bus station. To phone for a cab, call Nam Taxi (☎05/241 2189) or Ipoh Radio Cab (☎05/241 1753).

Trains ☎05/254 0481 for information.

Travel agents HWA Y/K Tours and Travel, 23 Jalan Che Tak (☎05/250 4060), and K&C Travel & Tours, 250 Jalan Sultan Iskandar (☎05/250 6999), both sell airline tickets.

Visa extensions The Immigration Office is at Level 2, Bangunan Serikinta, Jalan Sultan Idris Shah (Mon–Thurs 8am–1pm & 2–4.30pm, Fri 8am–12.15pm & 2.45–4.30pm; ☎05/254 9316). Note that they stop accepting applications an hour before they close for the day.

Around Ipoh

Much of Ipoh's striking surroundings have been marred by unsightly manufacturing industries. Nevertheless, it's not long before you escape the industrialization and find yourself in the heart of extensive rubber plantations, typical of so much of this part of the country. To the north and south of Ipoh are craggy **limestone peaks**; those nearest to the city are riddled with caves where Ipoh's immigrant workers established **Buddhist temples**, now popular pilgrimage centres, particularly during the Chinese New Year celebrations. **Kellie's Castle** and the **Tambun Hot Springs** make interesting excursions.

The Perak Tong and Sam Poh Tong temples

The **Perak Tong Temple** (daily 8am–5pm; free), 6km north of Ipoh, is the more impressive of the two Chinese cave temples just outside the city, situated in dramatic surroundings and doubling as a centre for Chinese art; to get here, take the #141 Kuala Kangsar bus from the local bus station (20min). The gaudiness of the temple's exterior – bright red-and-yellow pavilions flanked by feathery willows and lotus ponds – gives no hint of the eerie atmosphere inside, where darkened cavern upon cavern honeycombs up into the rock formation. The huge first chamber is dominated by a fifteen-metre-high golden statue of the Buddha flanked by two startled-looking companions dancing and playing instruments. A massive bell, believed to be more than a century old, fills the chamber with booming echoes from time to time – it's rung by visiting devotees to draw attention to the donation they've just offered. Walking past the bell into the next chamber, as your eyes become more accustomed to the gloom, you'll notice the decorated walls, covered with complex calligraphy and delicate flower paintings. Towards the back of this musty hollow, a steep flight of 385 crudely fashioned steps climbs up and out of the cave to a sort of balcony, with views of great limestone outcrops and ugly factory buildings.

The **Sam Poh Tong Temple** (daily 8am–4.30pm; free), just south of the city, is also a popular place of pilgrimage for Chinese Buddhists. Built into a rock face, the huge limestone caverns open towards the rear to give more impressive views over the surrounding suburbs and hills. Unfortunately, the upkeep of the temple leaves a lot to be desired; the place is covered with litter and graffiti. There's an expensive bar nearby and a good Chinese vegetarian restaurant. A visit to the temple makes an easy half-day trip: catch the green "Kinta" bus #66 or #73 (to Kangar) from the local **bus** station, or from the roundabout near the *Ritz Garden Hotel*; it's a ten-minute journey.

Kellie's Castle

If you only have time for one trip from Ipoh, make it **Kellie's Castle**, a mansion situated in the Kinta Kelas Rubber Estate, 12km south of Ipoh. It stands as a symbol of the prosperity achieved by many enterprising foreigners who capitalized on the potential of the rubber market in the early 1900s. The mansion, with a weighty rectangular tower and apricot-coloured bricks, was to have been the second home of William Kellie Smith, a Scottish entrepreneur, who settled here in order to make his fortune. Designed with splendour in mind, there were even plans for a lift to be installed, the first in Malaysia. However, during the mansion's construction in the 1920s, an epidemic of Spanish influenza broke out, killing many of the Tamil workers. In an act of appeasement, Smith had a Hindu temple built near the house; among the deities represented on the temple roof is a figure dressed in a white suit and pith helmet, presumably Smith himself. While work resumed on the "castle", Smith left on a trip to England in 1925; however, he fell ill and died in Portugal. The crumbling, warren-like remains, set in lush, hilly countryside, are now covered in graffiti dating back to 1941.

   Getting to the castle from Ipoh is best done by taxi (about RM30 one-way, or RM50 return including a wait while you look around). For a cheaper but more complicated transportation option you can take bus #36 or #37 from the local bus station to Batu Gajah (departures every 1hr 20min or so; 30min), from where you can walk the remaining 4km on the A8 road (clearly signposted), or catch bus #67, which passes the castle fairly frequently, or take a taxi from the main road (around RM5).

Tambun Hot Springs and Gua Tambun

Eight kilometres northeast of Ipoh, at the **Tambun Hot Springs** (Tues–Sun 8am–9pm; RM5) you can indulge in mineral-rich soaks in the two thermal swimming pools, one cooler than the other, which are fed by hot springs. All around you, steaming slimy water breaks through the surface of the earth; you can even crawl into the corner of a nearby limestone cave for a natural sauna (not for the claustrophobic). Another of the surrounding caves, once inhabited by Japanese monks, was later home to Japanese soldiers hiding out during World War II; they left painted characters on some of the cave walls.

   In the 1930s, evidence of a prehistoric civilization dating back 10,000 years was discovered at the nearby **Gua Tambun** (Tambun Cave). Drawings on the cave walls and limestone cliffs include that of a large meat-eating fish, the *degong*.

   To get there, take the Tambun **bus** from Ipoh's local bus station for about thirty minutes until you see the signpost for "Resort Air Panas", off to the right of the main road; the springs are a further kilometre down a dirt track.

Pulau Pangkor

With some of the best beaches to be found on this side of the Malay Peninsula, **PULAU PANGKOR** is one of the west coast's more appealing islands. It's also one of the most accessible, lying just a forty-minute ferry ride from the port of **Lumut**. This fact has turned Pangkor into an increasingly popular weekend resort, with an airport and three international-standard hotels, while the adjacent, privately owned island of Pangkor Laut, just off the southwest coast of Pulau Pangkor, is home to one of Malaysia's most exclusive resorts. These facilities are disproportionate to Pangkor's small size and at odds with its quiet, almost genteel, atmosphere. The inhabitants still live largely by fishing and boat-building rather than tourism – although development around Teluk Nipah looks set to tip the balance. For all its tranquillity, Pulau Pangkor played an important part in the development of modern Malaysia, witnessing the signing of the ground-breaking **Pangkor Treaty** of 1874, which led to the creation of the Residential System (see p.188).

Most of the thriving local villages lie in a string along the island's east coast, while tourist accommodation and the best **beaches** are on the west side. The interior is mountainous and densely forested, inaccessible but for a few tiny trails and one main road that connects the two coasts, but there's plenty to occupy you around the rim, from superb stretches of sand to historical sites, including **Kota Belanda**, a seventeenth-century Dutch fort and several **temples**.

It's worth remembering that **Thaipusam** is celebrated roughly a month late here, falling on the full moon in mid-February or early March. The unmissably gruesome spectacle of Hindu religious fervour goes on for two days, with the processions starting out on the beach at Pasir Bogak, and ending up at the Sri Pathirakaliaman Temple (see p.185) on the island's east coast.

Travel practicalities

Berjaya Air (℡05/685 5828) flies from KL's Subang airport (RM225 one-way) to the north of the island. The passenger-only **ferries** from Lumut (see p.182) to Pulau Pangkor run approximately every half-hour (Mon–Fri 7am–7pm, Sat & Sun 7am–8pm; RM3 one-way; 40min), calling at Kampung Sungai Pinang Kecil before reaching the main jetty at Pangkor Town. Alternatively, catamarans depart hourly from the same jetty (Mon–Fri 7am–7pm, Sat & Sun 7am–8pm; RM5), which will get you to the island in twenty minutes. In addition, seven boats a day, run by Pan Silver (℡05/683 5541; RM8 return), go from Lumut jetty to a jetty 1km east of the *Pan Pacific Resort* (from where a shuttle bus takes you to the resort).

Pulau Pangkor has a sealed **road** of varying quality forming a loop that takes in much of the island's circumference, avoiding the mountainous interior and cutting inland only between Pangkor Town, where the ferry docks, and the tourist developments at Pasir Bogak, 2km away on the west coast. **Renting a motorbike** or **pushbike** in Pangkor Town or from a hotel or guesthouse on the west coast costs around RM30 or RM10 per day respectively; the *Pangkor Standard Camp* has a good selection. As Pulau Pangkor is only 3km by 9km, a trip around the island is easily accomplished in a day. You could see all the sights by motorbike in about five hours, stopping en route for lunch – add another few hours if you're on a bicycle. Otherwise the only other means of transport are the bright pink, shared **minibus taxis** (RM4 from Pangkor Town to Pasir Bogak, RM10 to Teluk Nipah and RM24.30 for a round-island trip), and the **local buses**, which run hourly between 8am and 6pm from Pangkor Town to Pasir Bogak.

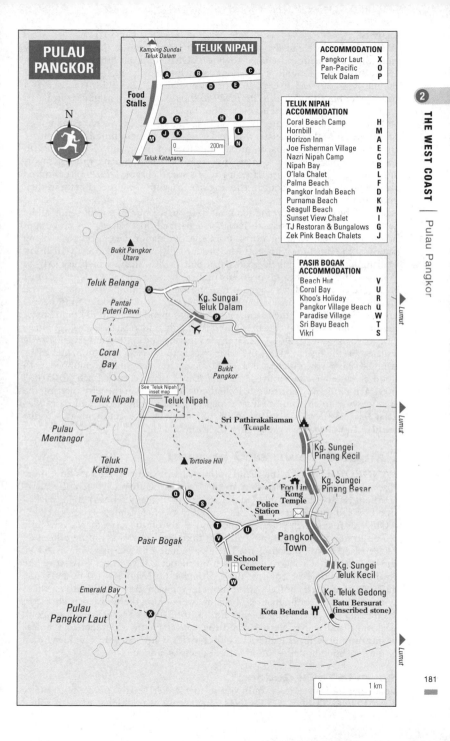

PULAU PANGKOR

TELUK NIPAH

Kamping Sundai
Teluk Dalam

Food Stalls

0   200m

Teluk Ketapang

N

ACCOMMODATION

Pangkor Laut	X
Pan-Pacific	O
Teluk Dalam	P

TELUK NIPAH ACCOMMODATION

Coral Beach Camp	H
Hornbill	M
Horizon Inn	A
Joe Fisherman Village	E
Nazri Nipah Camp	C
Nipah Bay	B
O'lala Chalet	L
Palma Beach	F
Pangkor Indah Beach	D
Purnama Beach	K
Seagull Beach	N
Sunset View Chalet	I
TJ Restoran & Bungalows	G
Zek Pink Beach Chalets	J

PASIR BOGAK ACCOMMODATION

Beach Hut	V
Coral Bay	U
Khoo's Holiday	R
Pangkor Village Beach	u
Paradise Village	W
Sri Bayu Beach	T
Vikri	S

Bukit Pangkor Utara

Teluk Belanga

Pantai Puteri Dewi

Kg. Sungai Teluk Dalam

Coral Bay

Bukit Pangkor

See Teluk Nipah inset map

Teluk Nipah

Pulau Mentangor

Sri Pathirakaliaman Temple

Teluk Ketapang

Tortoise Hill

Kg. Sungei Pinang Kecil

Kg. Sungei Pinang Besar

Foo Lin Kong Temple

Police Station

Pasir Bogak

Pangkor Town

School
Cemetery

Kg. Sungei Teluk Kecil

Kg. Teluk Gedong

Emerald Bay

Batu Bersurat (inscribed stone)

Pulau Pangkor Laut

Kota Belanda

0   1 km

Lumut

Although it's possible to fly to Pangkor, most people cross to the island by ferry from the quiet mainland coastal town of **LUMUT**, about 80km southwest of Ipoh. **Buses** run roughly every hour from Ipoh (daily; 9.30am–7.50pm; 1hr 30min; RM4.30) and five times a day from Taiping (2hr; RM6), as well as a daily direct bus from Tapah (2hr; RM9), although the latter originates in Kuala Lumpur and is often full when it reaches Tapah.

Once a relatively obscure fishing village, Lumut has become the main base of the Royal Malaysian Navy, whose towering apartment buildings dominate the coastline from the sea. In an attempt to cash in on the success of Pulau Pangkor, Lumut too has seen its own spate of development, though this is still low-key. The town manages to retain some charm, with multicoloured fishing boats bobbing about in the tiny marina, and stores specializing in shell and coral handicrafts.

Lumut's **bus station**, on the road out to Ipoh, is a minute's walk south of the **jetty** from where the boats to Pangkor depart; all boat tickets can be bought at the jetty itself. Walking north from the bus station takes you to a filling station at the junction with both the shore road (Jalan Iskandar Shah/Jalan Titi Panjang) and another inland road (Jalan Sultan Idris Shah), which leads off to your left. If you need to **change money**, it's better to do so here, as it can be hard to change traveller's cheques in Pangkor Town; most of Lumut's several moneychangers and banks are on Jalan Sultan Idris Shah. Although most people continue straight on to the island, if you need to spend the night in Lumut, there are a few **places to stay**. Further down Jalan Sultan Idris Shah there's the *Orient Star* (☎05/683 4199, ⓕ683 4223; ➒). It's the top spot in town, very pleasantly situated on the beach. Along the same road is the *Galaxy Inn* (☎05/683 8731, ⓕ683 8723; ➌), the quietest of the mid-range choices. Similarly equipped, with good en-suite air-con rooms, is the *Indah*, 208 Jalan Iskandar Shah (☎05/683 5064; ➌), a little way northwest along the waterfront from the jetty, offering the best views in town. Lumut's least expensive option is the clean and basic *Phin Lum Hooi*, 93 Jalan Titi Panjang (☎05/683 5641; ➋) – to get there, walk to the service station, and turn right onto the shore road.

Pangkor Town and around

PANGKOR TOWN is the island's principal settlement, though it's little more than a few dusty streets. The best area by far is the lively port, where the early-morning catch – the *ikan bilis* (anchovies) are particularly renowned – is packed into boxes of crushed ice to be despatched to the mainland.

Other than to stretch your legs once you've got off the ferry, there's very little reason to stop long; bright pink minibus **taxis** to the beaches on the other side of the island leave from the jetty. There's a branch of Maybank with an **ATM**, just to your left as you come ashore from the jetty. If you decide **to stay**, the town has a couple of options: the *Chuan Fu*, 60 Main Rd (☎ & ⓕ05/685 1123; ➊), is the best choice, with rooms ranging from basic doubles to en suites with air-con; the communal rear balcony overlooking the water adds character. Nearer the jetty, *Hotel Min Lian* at no. 1a (☎05/685 1294; ➌) charges a good deal more and delivers less. Around the *Chuan Fu* are a number of Chinese **restaurants** as well as a handful of **cyber-cafés** whose rates are a bit lower than at the beachside hostels – and there's also less of a queue.

South to Teluk Gedong

Following the coastal road south out of town, after 1.5km you come to pretty **KAMPUNG TELUK GEDONG**, a gathering of traditional wooden stilted houses named after the bay in which they are cradled. Here, set back from the road on the right, is the **Kota Belanda**, or Dutch Fort, originally built in 1670 to store tin supplies from Perak and keep a check on piracy in the Straits, but destroyed in 1690 by the Malays, who were discontent with Dutch rule. The fort was rebuilt in 1743 but only remained in use for a further five years, when the Dutch finally withdrew after being subjected to several more attacks. The abandoned site was left to decay, and the disappointing half-built structure that you see today is, unbelievably, a recent reconstruction.

A few metres further along the road, on the left, lies the **Batu Bersurat**, a huge boulder under a canopy. On the rock, the year 1743 is inscribed beside a drawing which – with the use of some imagination – depicts a tiger mauling a child, a grisly memorial to a Dutch child who disappeared while playing nearby. A more plausible account of the incident is that the infant was kidnapped by the Malays, in retribution for the continuing Dutch presence.

West to Pasir Bogak and Teluk Ketapang

A two-kilometre road connects the east and west coasts of Pulau Pangkor, terminating in the west at the holiday village of **PASIR BOGAK**, the biggest and most upmarket development on the island. Only a few of the **chalets** front the beach itself; most line the nearby road that continues north along the west coast.

Better beaches are to be found about 2km further north at **TELUK KETAPANG** ("Turtle Bay"), named for the sometime resident – the increasingly rare giant **leatherback turtle**. The creatures swim thousands of miles to lay their eggs on Malaysia's beaches, normally favouring the Peninsula's eastern coast assuming they show up at all – they're practically extinct in the Pacific. If not, take the opportunity to stretch out on white-sand beaches – edged by palm trees – which are slightly less crowded than Pasir Bogak's, and much wider and cleaner. There's no accommodation at Teluk Ketapang; you'll have to make do with either staying in Pasir Bogak or a few kilometres further north in Teluk Nipah. Whereas Teluk Nipah boasts nicer beaches, Pasir Bogak is a quieter place to stay. Most of the hotels in Pasir Bogak have **restaurants** attached and there are some food stalls (evenings only) on the seafront just south of *Vikri Huts*. Otherwise, the food in town is generally overpriced.

Accommodation

Hotels in Pasir Bogak arrange their prices into three categories: low (weekdays), high (weekends) and peak (holidays), with peak prices being around fifty percent higher than low season. Prices listed below are for double rooms during low season.

Beach Hut Hotel ☎ & ⓕ 05/685 1159. Friendly, mid-range collection of pleasant beachfront chalets and simple double rooms. **❹**

Coral Bay ☎ 05/685 5111. This high-rise hotel has high-quality though rather bland rooms at a reasonable rate. Breakfast included. **❻**

Khoo's Holiday Resort ☎ 05/685 2190. Large complex of tasteful doubles perched on the hillside. Great views and friendly staff; the owner will take guests on fishing trips. Breakfast included. **❸**

Pangkor Village Beach ☎ 05/685 2227, ⓕ 685 3787. Has a wide choice of accommodation from A-frames (**❷**) to overpriced chalets (**❻**) set in a pleasant garden just off the beach. There's a restaurant and breakfast is included. Great location with watersports facilities right next door.

Paradise Village (no phone). The secluded chalets are nothing special, but because it's a short hike from the main road, this is the best option for those who really want to get away from it all; you practically have your own private beach. **❹**

Sri Bayu Beach ☎ 05/685 1929. The spacious lobby leads onto a well-landscaped garden and deluxe chalets. The rooms themselves though,

while comfortable enough, aren't quite up to the whopping price tag. **❼**
Vikri ☎05/685 4258. A-frame huts (**❷**), as well as new chalets (**❹**) shaded by tall trees, across the road from the beach. Restaurant serving banana-leaf curries for lunch and dinner.

Teluk Nipah

TELUK NIPAH has become something of a travellers' hangout mainly because of its good beaches. Of these, **Coral Bay** is the best – a perfect cove with crystal-clear sea and smooth, white sand, backed by dense jungle climbing steeply to Bukit Pangkor, one of the island's three peaks. The bay is inaccessible by road; to reach it, you have to climb over the rocks at the northern end of Teluk Nipah – watch the tide or you might have to swim back. This is the best spot on the island for **snorkelling**, and most of the hostels here rent out masks, snorkels and fins for about RM20 a day.

There are **food stalls** lined up along the beach in between the two roads into the kampung, and a few **restaurants** further up. Most popular for dinner is *TJ Restoran,* a little way up the first (southernmost) road leading inland. Arrive early unless you don't mind a bit of a wait. They serve excellent freshly caught grilled fish as well as less expensive Western and Indonesian dishes. **Internet** access is available at *Nipah Bay Villa, Purnama Beach Resort*, and *Seagull Beach Resort*.

Accommodation

Much of the recent development on the island has focused on Teluk Nipah because of its beaches. There are new places opening all the time, but the atmosphere is still quiet and informal. Standards within each price category tend to be pretty much uniform, so you're best off choosing a place by atmosphere and location. Most accommodation here is in the form of private chalets. Seasonal price categories are the same as at Pasir Bogak. All the accommodation listed below is marked on the map on p.181.

Inexpensive

Coral Beach Camp ☎05/685 2711, ℻685 2796. Simple, double chalets with showers in a small, well-kept garden. There are some A-frames at half the cost. **❸**

Joe Fisherman Village ☎05/685 2389. One of the first establishments here. The A-frames (**❷**) and chalets (**❸**) are a bit on the rustic side (although they come equipped with mosquito nets). There's a small very friendly café. Bicycles for rent (RM15).

O'lala ☎05/685 5112. These chalets have air-con and TVs in every room. Friendly atmosphere and good value. **❸**

Nazri Nipah Camp ☎05/685 2014. Laid-back traveller place with good value A-frames (**❶**) and chalets (**❷**). There's a cosy café as well as kitchen facilities. Can provide lots of advice on watersports and treks.

Purnama Beach ☎05/685 3530, ℮pbr2000@tm.net.my. Large development with a good range of options, from comfortable doubles with shared bath to plush chalets. There's a pool and a restaurant, plus laundry and Internet services. **❷**

Seagull Beach ☎05/685 2878, ℻685 2857. Another large complex with a variety of room styles. This well-run place has a restaurant, launderette, and Internet access as well as billiards, ping-pong and volleyball facilities. **❸**

🏃 **TJ Restoran & Bungalows** ☎05/685 3477. The best-value accommodation in Teluk Nipah, boasting chalets at half the price of elsewhere. The management is very friendly and doesn't hike the price up too much at peak times. The restaurant serves great food. **❷**

Moderate and Expensive

Horizon Inn ☎05/685 3398, ℻05/685 3339. This two-storey building sits at the north end of the coast road and has nice sea-view rooms and a restaurant. **❺**

Hornbill ☎05/685 2005, ℻685 2006. The first place reached on the coast road from Teluk Ketapang. All the rooms in this two-storey building boast wooden floors, balconies and a view of the beach. You can, however, get a similarly equipped chalet at one of the inland places for less. Breakfast included. **❻**

Nipah Bay Villa ☎ 05/685 2198. There are many types of chalets available, from doubles to family rooms housing eight people. All rooms have air-con, satellite TV and hot water. There's a restaurant plus Internet access. ❺

Palma Beach ☎ 05/685 3693, ⓕ 685 4431. Well-designed, sturdy chalets with air-con, TVs and an efficient management. ❺

Pangkor Indah Beach ☎ 05/685 2107. These pleasant, wooden chalets have a/c and TVs. ❹

Sunset View ☎ 05/685 6855, ⓔ sunsetvu@hotmail.com. The chalets here are well maintained by the friendly owner. Cooking facilities available. ❹

Zek Pink Beach Chalets ☎ & ⓕ 05/685 3529. These pink-painted chalets live up to their name; even the furniture is in rosy shades. ❹

The north coast

The road cuts inland from Teluk Nipah and crosses to the northeastern tip of the island, where it branches off west to the high-class *Pan Pacific Resort* (☎ 05/685 1091, ⓕ 685 2390; ❾), situated in secluded **TELUK BELANGA**. A direct ferry also runs here from Lumut, though unless you're staying at the resort you'll be charged RM40 to use the beach – Pantai Puteri Dewi ("Beach of the Beautiful Princess"), a fine stretch of crunchy white sand. The fee covers use of the sports facilities – except for the golf course – and a snack.

Doubling back to the junction with the main road, you'll pass the airport and come to the pleasant *Teluk Dalam Resort* (☎ 05/685 5000, ⓕ 685 4000; ❾), large chalets set around a quiet bay, with a couple of restaurants. After continuing up the steep hill and craggy headland, the road descends into the first bay on the east coast. There's not much to see on this side of the island for the next 3km until you reach the **Sri Pathirakaliaman** Hindu temple, overlooking the sea. Only worth a cursory glance, it lies just north of **Kampung Sungai Pinang Kecil**, little more than a few straggling dwellings by the roadside, and the first stop for the ferry from Lumut. One kilometre further north of the more substantial Kampung Sungai Pinang Besar is the **Foo Lin Kong** Temple, a cross between a place of worship and a theme park. Inside the dim, rather spooky room that houses the shrine are some authentic-looking shrunken heads designed to ward off evil spirits, and a few incongruous Guinness bottles acting as offerings. Surrounding the temple itself is a miniature Great Wall of China spreading up the hillside, a small children's playground and a dismal zoo. Pangkor Town is just 1km or so south from here along the main road.

Other islands: Pulau Pangkor Laut and Pulau Sembilan

Some of the Pulau Pangkor hotels arrange **fishing and snorkelling day-trips** to the small islands around (about RM25 per person). No accommodation is available except on **PULAU PANGKOR LAUT** to the southwest, a privately owned island which is the exclusive domain of the **Pangkor Laut Resort** (☎ 05/699 1100, ⓦ www.pangkorlautresort.com; ❾). With its sympathetically designed accommodation and top-class restaurants, this luxurious resort is well worth visiting for Emerald Bay alone, whose superb sand and waters make it one of the most beautiful beaches in Malaysia. There are eight daily ferries to the island, run by the resort itself; you can use them for a day-trip.

PULAU SEMBILAN, an archipelago of nine islands two hours south by boat from Pulau Pangkor, is the setting for an annual **fishing safari**, a competitive event held in conjunction with the lavishly celebrated **Lumut Pesta Laut**, a popular festival that takes place in Lumut every August. Only one island in the clump, Pulau Lalang, has fresh water and accessible beaches, and at present there is nowhere to stay. You can charter a boat there from Lumut jetty or Pasir Bogak for around RM300.

Kuala Kangsar

While Ipoh is the state administrative capital of Perak, **KUALA KANGSAR** – 50km to the northwest – is its royal town, home to the Sultans of Perak since the fifteenth century, with monuments to match. Built at a grandiose sweep of Sungai Perak, it's a neat, attractive town of green parks and flowers, little-visited by tourists – another reason to make time for at least a couple of hours' stopover between Ipoh and Taiping. Nineteenth-century accounts of Kuala Kangsar rhapsodized about its situation: Ambrose B. Rathborne wrote in his *Camping and Tramping in Malaya* (1883) that it had "one of the prettiest views in the Straits …overlooking Sungai Perak, up whose beautiful valley an uninterrupted view is obtained". Rathborne camped and tramped his way through the jungle on an elephant, which was the only way to reach Kuala Kangsar at the time.

With the planting of nine **rubber-tree** seedlings here at the beginning of Hugh Low's Residency in 1877 (see box, p.188), Kuala Kangsar was in at the start of colonial Malaya's most important industry (one of the original trees survives in a compound next to the district office). Despite the town's erstwhile importance as an administrative centre, not much has survived from that period, but a clutch of monuments on the outskirts of town provides a snapshot of Kuala Kangsar's royal and religious importance for the Malays.

Several places of interest are within easy walking distance of the town centre. Heading east from the clock tower in the centre of town, follow Jalan Istana as it curves around the fast-moving river, passing through the ornamental gateway that straddles the street. After about 2km, as the gentle gradient of Bukit Chandan begins, you'll reach the **Masjid Ubudiah**, whose large, gold, onion domes soar skywards; non-Muslims should ask permission before entering.

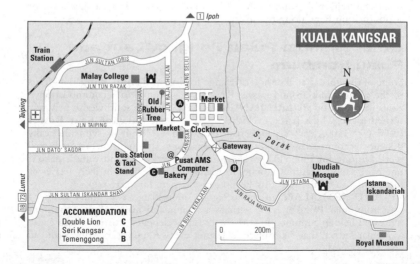

A king without his crown

There is **no crown** in the sultan's regalia, a fact explained by an early legend associated with Sungai Perak: a former prince was caught in a severe storm while sailing on the river. Throwing his crown overboard to calm the waves, he saved the sinking ship – but not his headgear. Since that day, new sultans have been enthroned to the sound of drumming rather than by being crowned.

Disproportionately tall, it looks like Islam's answer to Cinderella's castle. Its construction, in 1917, was interrupted several times, most dramatically when two elephants belonging to Sultan Idris rampaged all over the imported Italian marble floor.

A five-minute walk onward up the same road brings you to the imposing white marble **Istana Iskandariah**, the sultan's ultramodern official palace. It's closed to the public, though a stroll round to the left of the huge gates gives a good view down the river.

Close by, off to the left as you circle the palace to rejoin the road, the **Royal Museum** (Mon–Thurs, Sat & Sun 9.30am–5pm, Fri 9.30am–12.15pm & 3–5pm; free) is of greater architectural significance. This former royal residence, the erstwhile Istana Kenangan, is a traditional stilted wooden structure built without the use of nails and decorated with intricate friezes and geometric-patterned wall panels. Inside, the museum displays a collection of royal artefacts (medals, costumes and so on), although its photographs of past and present royalty in Perak are of more interest.

Back in town, the most evocative memory of colonial days is provided by the **Malay College** on Jalan Tun Razak, its elegant columns and porticoes visible as you approach the centre from the train station. Founded in January 1905, it was conceived by British administrators as a training ground for the sons of Malay nobility, an "Eton of the East", where discipline and tradition was more English

△ Royal Museum, Kuala Kangsar

than in England – although the schoolboys were required to wear formal Malay dress, as they still do today. The success of many of the college's pupils in finding good jobs in the newly created Malay Administrative Service left parents clamouring for places for their offspring, and started a craze for English education elsewhere in the country. The school is still an elite training ground today, one of its most famous alumni being former deputy prime minister Anwar Ibrahim.

Practicalities

Kuala Kangsar lies on Route 1 and on the main west-coast train line. The **train station** is on the northwestern outskirts of town, a twenty-minute walk from

The Resident system

Late in 1873, Raja Abdullah of Perak invited the new Governor of the Straits Settlements, Andrew Clarke, to appoint a **Resident** (colonial officer) to Perak, in exchange for Abdullah being recognized as the Sultan of Perak instead of his rival, the intractable Sultan Ismail. This held some appeal for the British, whose involvement in Malay affairs had hitherto been unofficial, and who were eager to foster stability and facilitate economic progress in the region. So on January 20, 1874, the **Pangkor Treaty** was signed by Clarke and Abdullah; the idea was that the Resident – each state would have its own – would play an advisory role in Malay affairs of state in return for taking a sympathetic attitude to Malay customs and rituals.

It is doubtful that the Malays had any idea of the long-term consequences of the treaty, whose original version indicated that the decision-making process would be collective, much like the Malays' own courts; more significantly, the distinction between the political and the religious was from the start a nonsensical concept for the Malays, for whom all action was dictated by the laws of Islam. The interpretation of the newly created post was in the hands of **Hugh Low** (1824–1905), one of the early Residents, whose jurisdiction of Perak (1877–89) was based in Kuala Kangsar. The personable Low lived modestly by British standards and, with two pet chimpanzees for company, kept open house during his ten-hour working day. Low's linguistic skills won him favour with the local chiefs, with whom he could soon converse fluently, and whose practices he quickly understood. Having spent nearly thirty years in Borneo, Low had become great friends with Charles and James Brooke (see pp.423–424), and sought to emulate their relatively benign system of government.

The approval of the Malay nobility – by no means guaranteed, as the Birch incident shows (see p.177) – was vital to the success of the Residency scheme, and was secured principally by compensating them for the income they had lost from taxes and property. This suited the sultans well, who not only obtained financial security for themselves by virtue of their healthy stipends, but also got protection from other rivals. As time went on, lesser figures were given positions within the bureaucracy, thus weaving the Malays into the fabric of the administration, of which the cornerstone was the **State Council**. Although the sultan was its ceremonial head, the Resident chose the constituent members and set the political agenda, in consultation with his deputies – the district officers – and the governor.

The increasing power of central government soon began to diminish the consultative side of the Resident's role, and by the 1890s fewer and fewer meetings of the council were being held. Even in religious matters, the goal posts were often moved to suit British purposes. Furthermore, there were few Residents as talented and sympathetic as Hugh Low and so, predictably, the involvement of the British in Malay affairs became less to instruct their subjects in new forms of government and more to affirm British status. Sultan Abdullah, bent on acquiring local power and status, thereby inadvertently provided a foot in the door for the British, an act which ultimately led to their full political intervention in the Peninsula.

the clock tower in the centre of town. Buses from Ipoh, Butterworth and Taiping pull up at the **bus station** at the bottom of Jalan Raja Bendahara, close to the river. There are a couple of **places to stay** including the simple but friendly *Double Lion* at 74 Jalan Kangsar (T05/776 1010; ❷), just south of the bus station, with clean rooms, ranging from fan singles with shared bath (❷) to en-suite air-con rooms with TVs (❹). In the middle of town near the clock tower, the *Seri Kangsar*, at 33 Jalan Daeng Selili T05/777 7301, F777 7101; ❹), has simple en-suite rooms also with air-con and TVs. A quieter option is the *Temenggong* (T05/776 3872; ❹), along Jalan Istana, half a kilometre southeast of the clock tower. Although it's a bit run down, this is a friendly place with a stately riverside location. There's **Internet** access at Pusat AMS Computer, second floor, 86 Jalan Kangsar (T05/777 6320), which is close to most of the town's **restaurants** serving the usual fare.

Taiping and Bukit Larut

Set against the backdrop of the mist-laden Bintang Hills, **TAIPING** – like so many places in Perak – has its origins in the discovery of tin here in the first decades of the nineteenth century. As a mining centre, overrun by enthusiastic prospectors, it had an unsurprisingly turbulent early history. Originally known as Larut, the town was torn apart in 1871 by violent wars between various Chinese secret societies, whose members had come to work in the mines. A truce was finally declared in 1874, after British intervention as a result of the Pangkor Treaty, and the town was – somewhat hopefully – renamed Taiping, meaning "everlasting peace" – which, incidentally, makes it the only sizeable town in Malaysia today with a Chinese name.

Despite these shaky beginnings, Taiping began to thrive. Its growing prosperity helped fund many firsts at a time when Kuala Lumpur was barely on the map: the first railway in the country (built to facilitate the export of the tin, connecting Taiping with the coastal port of Port Weld, now called Kuala Sepetang); the first English-language school in 1878; the first museum in 1883; and the first English-language newspaper (the *Perak Pioneer*) in 1894. With the establishment of the nearby hill station of **Bukit Larut** (formerly Maxwell Hill) as a retreat for its administrators, Taiping was firmly at the forefront of the colonial development of the Federated Malay States. For years, tin was its life force, mined and traded by a population that was largely Chinese, and superstitious: the mere presence of a European close to a tin mine was disliked and resented. Ambrose B. Rathborne noted that "No greater offence can be given to a gang of miners than by descending their mine with boots on and an umbrella opened overhead, as it is popularly supposed that such a proceeding is an insult to the presiding spirits, who, out of revenge will make the tin ore disappear." Geology was the actual reason for the eventual depletion of the tin deposits, with the declining market for tin in later years taking an additional toll on the wealth of the town. Taiping became the headquarters of the Japanese military administration of Malaya and Sumatra during World War II.

Nowadays, bypassed by the North–South Expressway and replaced in administrative importance by Ipoh, Taiping is declining gracefully, its tattered two-storey shop fronts indicative of the run-down atmosphere that pervades the town. Although the main reason people visit is to relax at Bukit Larut, allow yourself at least a day to explore the sights of Taiping – the **gardens**, **Perak Museum** and the fine buildings which line the wide roads.

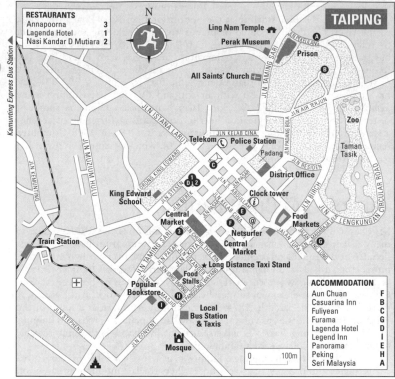

RESTAURANTS
Annapoorna — 3
Lagenda Hotel — 1
Nasi Kandar D Mutiara — 2

ACCOMMODATION
Aun Chuan — F
Casuarina Inn — B
Fuliyean — C
Furama — G
Lagenda Hotel — D
Legend Inn — I
Panorama — E
Peking — H
Seri Malaysia — A

▼ Penang & Ipoh

Arrival and information

The **train station** is on Jalan Stesen behind the hospital, just over a kilometre west of the centre of Taiping. An inconvenient 7km taxi ride (RM5) north of the centre is the Kamunting **express bus station**. The **local bus station** is on Jalan Panggung Wayang. The friendly **visitor's information centre** (Mon–Fri 8.30am–5.30pm, Sat 8.30am–3:00pm; often closed for an hour at noon), where you can get a good heritage tour **map** of Taiping, is located in the clock tower building, which also houses the old, historic **police station**, on the corner of Jalan Kota and Lanal S. Abdullah. There are several places with **Internet** access including Helmi Computer Technology Centre at 200 & 200A Jalan Kota, DiscoverdeInternet at 3 Jalan Panggong Wayang, and Net Surfer, 36–38 Jalan Tupai (☎05/805 9596).

Accommodation

For a town of its size, Taiping has a remarkable number of **hotels**, which is just as well because in high season it often has to cater for the overspill from Bukit Larut. For those on a tight budget, or who prefer a bit more action, the town rather than the hill station is definitely the place to stay. It's worth noting that the striking Peranakan-style *Peace Hotel* on Jalan Panggung Wayang is not a regular hotel at all, but a brothel.

Aun Chuan 25 Jalan Kota ☎ 05/807 5322, on the junction with Jalan Halaman Pasar, above KFC. The least expensive option in town, it's clean and spacious, with wooden floors and en-suite rooms. ❶

Casuarina Inn Taman Tasik ☎ 05/804 1339, ⓕ 804 1337. Standing on the site of the former official quarters of the British Resident in Perak State, overlooking the lake gardens, this hotel offers huge but rather musty en-suite rooms. ❹

Fuliyean 14 Jalan Barrack ☎ 05/806 8648, ⓕ 807 0648. Good-value spotless rooms with TVs and en-suite bathrooms. ❸

Furama 30 Jalan Peng Loong ☎ 05/807 1077, ⓦ www.cyberoffice.com.my/furama. This clean, bright hotel is located between the Lake Garden and one of the large hawker centres. The well-maintained en-suite rooms come with air-con, TVs and kettles. Laundry service is available. Good value. ❹

🏃 Lagenda Hotel 101 Jalan Stesen ☎ 05/805 3333, ⓕ 805 3355. Formerly the governor's residence, this colonial building has been successfully transformed into a small hotel and café. It's pleasantly situated in green and quiet surroundings; rooms are set around a courtyard with a tiny wading pool. ❹

Legend Inn Corner of Jalan Convent and Jalan Masjid ☎ 05/806 0000, ⓦ www.legendinn.com. Conveniently located near the bus station, this is the best hotel in town, a little smarter and less expensive than the *Seri Malaysia*, but without the view. ❺

Panorama 61–79 Jalan Kota ☎ 05/808 4111, ⓔ panoramatpg@hotmail.com. A reasonably priced and centrally located (although rather run-of-the-mill) hotel. ❹

🏃 Peking 2 Jalan Idris Taiping ☎ 05/807 2975, ⓕ 808 5698. A real gem of a traditional Chinese wooden house (built in 1929) with original carvings and coloured glass. The rooms are simple but clean, apart from the rather grotty carpet. Good value. ❷

Seri Malaysia Taman Tasik ☎ 05/806 9502, ⓦ www.serimalaysia.com.my. Part of the Seri Malaysia chain, the hotel itself is nothing special but it has a quiet lakeside location with lovely garden views. Breakfast included. ❻

The Town and around

Taiping is easily walkable, and since the central streets are laid out on a grid system, there's no problem finding your way around. The four main streets, which run parallel to each other, are Jalan Taming Sari, Jalan Pasar, Jalan Kota and Jalan Panggung Wayang. Up Jalan Pasar are the **padang** and the sparkling-white **District Office**, which marks the northern limit of the Chinese district. The gardens – Taman Tasik – spread to the northeast of here, close to the foot of Bukit Larut, with the museum a little to the northwest; on the opposite side of town, on its southwestern outskirts, are three **temples** for the Hindu, Chinese and Muslim communities respectively.

A wander around the shop-lined streets surrounding Taiping's **central market** – you see wizened *towkays* lurking at the rear of musty shophouses and dingy *kedai kopis* – does little to detract from its reputation as a murky old mining town, though Taiping's numerous, lively **night markets** (see p.192) bring welcome splashes of colour and life. North of here up Jalan Taming Sari is **All Saints' Church**, founded in 1887. The oldest church in Malaysia cuts a forlorn figure these days: termites are slowly destroying the wooden structure, and there's talk of completely demolishing and rebuilding the church. In some ways, the tiny churchyard is more interesting, containing the graves of the earliest British and Australian settlers, many of whom died at an early age; others, after many years of service to the Malay states, failed to obtain a pension to allow them to return home.

Another hundred metres further on, the **Perak Museum** (daily 9.30am–5pm; closed Fri noon–2.45pm; free), housed in a cool and spacious colonial building, boasted as many as thirteen thousand exhibits when it opened in 1883. There are displays of stuffed local fauna as well as an extensive collection of ancient weapons and Orang Asli implements and ornaments. Next door to the museum, the **Ling Nam Temple** is one of Taiping's main Chinese centres of worship, while opposite the museum is a **prison**, built in 1885 and subsequently used by the Japanese during World War II – today it's where many of the executions of Malaysia's drug offenders are carried out.

Backtracking down Jalan Taming Sari takes you to the padang, from where it's a ten-minute stroll east to **Taman Tasik**, the extensive lake gardens which are landscaped around two former tin-mining pools. At the height of the industry's success, large areas of countryside were being laid waste, creating unsightly muddy heaps and stagnant pools. In Taiping, at least, the Resident retained a colonial sense of propriety and turned this area into a park in 1880. It's still immaculately kept, with a gazebo, freshwater fish in the lakes, and a profusion of flowers. There's also a nine-hole golf course and even a small zoo (daily 8:30am–6:30pm; RM4; ⓦwww.zootaiping.gov.my).

A few minutes' walk to the northeast of the park, past the lotus pond, is the **Commonwealth War Cemetery**, a serene memorial to the casualties of World War II, containing the graves of 866 men, many of whom could not be identified. Split in two by the road to Bukit Larut, the cemetery is divided between Hindu and Muslim Indians on one side and Christian British and Australians on the other. Close by are the **Burmese Pools**, a series of natural rock pools that are not nearly as inviting as they sound. A much better bet for a cool dip are the more traditional **Coronation Pools** (RM1), just at the base of Bukit Larut, where the chlorine-free water comes straight from the hills.

Eating and drinking

The most atmospheric meals to be had in town are those at Taiping's numerous **food markets**, which are located on almost every street. The largest is along Jalan Chung Thye Phin (Cross Street), while the eastern side of the food market on Jalan Tupai is great for ice-cream sundaes and fruit salads, as well as all manner of main courses. Opposite the *Peking* hotel on Jalan Idris Taiping is another large row of stalls, where you can get a burger or seafood. *Restoran Annapoorna* on the corner at 164 Jalan Taming Sari is recommended for its good-value and tasty Indian food. There's a pleasant café at the *Lagenda Hotel* as well as a restaurant next door, *Nasi Kandar D Mutiara*, which serves a wide variety of good Indian food.

Bukit Larut (Maxwell Hill)

BUKIT LARUT (formerly Maxwell Hill) – 12km northeast of Taiping – is Malaysia's smallest (and oldest) hill station. Named after the first Assistant Resident of Perak, George Maxwell, the name changed back to Bukit Larut in 1979 as part of a general trend to return to local rather than English place names. At approximately 1035m above sea level, the climate is wonderfully cool, and on a clear day there are spectacular views down to the west coast. Unfortunately its status as reputedly the wettest place in Malaysia, with 5m of rainfall annually, also means that it's frequently too cloudy at the top to see much at all. That said, the cloud cover can be very atmospheric and the air of colonial nostalgia makes Bukit Larut well worth visiting. There are a few tame forest **walks** here too; most walkers stick to the main road winding up the mountain. There are a few forest paths leading off the main road, but these are unmarked. The climb to The Cottage – a stone bungalow built in the 1880s for British officialdom – leads through groves of evergreens and the largest variety of flowers in the country, to the only accessible **summit**. Protect yourself against leeches, which can be a problem in the forest, by wearing long trousers, and socks and shoes, rather than sandals.

The narrow road up to the hill station twists and turns round some terrifying bends and is only accessible by government Land Rover or on foot; private vehicles are not allowed up. The service (hourly 8am–5:30pm; 35min; RM4 round trip) begins at the foot of the hill, twenty minutes' walk from the lake gardens in Taiping. If you're only making a day-trip, it's especially advisable to **book your seat** in advance (either in person at the booking office where the service begins, or by calling ☏05/807 7241 or 807 7243), otherwise at busy times you could find yourself hanging around waiting for a space. Book the return journey up at the hill station itself, in the booth by the *Rumah Beringin* resthouse (if you're in the last jeep down, beware that they sometimes leave ahead of schedule).

Many people prefer to **walk** up from Taiping instead, which takes from two and a half to three hours; the marked path starts at the Land Rover pick-up point. You'll need to be quite fit, but this way you get more time to take in the views and can still make it down again by early evening. About midway to the summit is the Tea Garden House, little more than a shelter now, though once part of an extensive tea estate. It's an ideal place to stop for a rest, as the view at this point is superb, with the town of Taiping and the mirror-like waters of the gardens visible below.

Practicalities

The choice for **accommodation** on Bukit Larut is between resthouses and bungalows. Standards are pretty uniform, with most places offering hot water, kitchen facilities and spacious rooms. As there's only room for a total of 53 people, you'll need to **book in advance** at the office at the foot of the hill, where you book the Land Rovers (☏05/807 7241 or 807 7243). Bungalow prices are for the whole building (sleeping six), while the resthouses rent out individual rooms. **Food** is available at each of the resthouses, while at the bungalows, the caretaker can arrange for food to be prepared for you, or you can do your own cooking – buy your provisions in Taiping.

The Land Rover stops right next to the *Rumah Beringin* (RM150) bungalow, not quite as quiet as the other places as day-trippers often come here for a couple of hours before heading back down. All the other places to stay are of an equally basic standard and dotted around the hills within a mile of the drop-off point; the driver will take you to your door if you ask. A one-hundred-metre walk downhill from the stop is the *Rehat Bukit Larut* resthouse (❷); a minute's walk up from here brings you to the *Rumah Angkasa* (❻). A quarter of a mile uphill from the Land Rover stop, there's a junction to the left where there are the *Rumah Cendana* (❻), *Rumah Tempinis* (❻), and the VIP-class *Sri Kayangan* (❼) bungalows, all spaced well away from each other; taking a right leads, after about 400m, to the *Rumah Rehat Gunung Hijau* resthouse, which is the most secluded accommodation option up here (❷).

Penang

North of Taiping, towards the coast, the landscape becomes increasingly flat and arid as the road eases away from the backbone of mountains that dominate the western seaboard. Sitting 94km north of Taiping is the dusty, industrial port town of **Butterworth**, part of **PENANG**, a confusing amalgam of state and island. Everything of interest in Penang State is on **Pulau Pinang** ("Betel Nut Island" in Malay) – a large island, 285 square kilometres in area, upon which

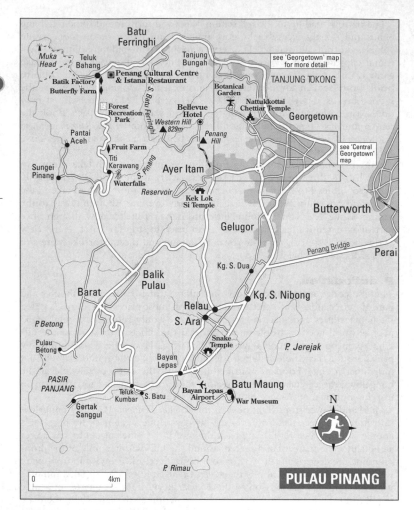

the first British settlement on the Malay Peninsula was sited. The confusion gets worse, as the island's city (Malaysia's second largest), the likeable **Georgetown**, is also often referred to as "Penang". A fast-moving, go-ahead place, Georgetown has a reputation as a duty-free shopping mecca that accords with its history as a trading port. Despite the gigantic high-rise **KOMTAR building** – visible even from the mainland – epitomizing its commercial development, Georgetown has sacrificed a relatively small number (when compared to KL or Singapore) of its traditional buildings and customs to modernity. In its Chinatown – one of Malaysia's most vibrant – faded two-storey shophouses and ornate temples predominate, legacies of the massive influx of immigrants attracted here by the early establishment of a colonial port. Hot on their heels were the Indian merchants, bringing with them spices, textiles and religious customs, nowhere more evident in the city than during the festival of *Thaipusam* in February (see p.73). To the northwest of the town centre, a few remaining huge mansions and elegant gardens bear witness to the rewards reaped by early entrepreneurs. Georgetown also has some of the country's best British colonial architecture in the area surrounding crumbling Fort Cornwallis, the island's oldest building. Visiting the many sites of architectural and historical interest could take you several days so if you want to spend some time hanging out on Penang's beaches, you may want to extend your stay. It's an easy place to get stuck for a while.

Georgetown is likely to be your base during a stay on Pulau Pinang, but some visitors also make trips out to the beaches at **Batu Ferringhi** or the much quieter **Teluk Bahang** along the north coast, which can be done in a day-trip, although you may want to stay longer. Its hippie hangout days of the 1970s long gone, this stretch is now mostly five-star resort territory, though some budget places nestle between the plush high-rises. Although pollution and over-development have taken their inevitable toll, the beaches themselves aren't bad (though not recommended for swimming as the water is rather polluted) and the nightlife keeps most people happy. The beaches, however, are not the only reason to come to Penang: to add to the diversions of Georgetown, journeys to the south and west of the island reveal a startlingly rural and mountainous interior, with a population that retains many of its traditions and industries. There are also about thirty **hiking trails** around the island, well described in *Nature Trails of Penang Island*, which is published by the Malaysian Nature Society and available at the tourist office (see p.199).

The island is the focus of several important **festivals** and events throughout the year, starting with *Thaipusam*. Perhaps the best known of the rest is the Penang Bridge Run held in May, when thousands of competitors hurtle across the bridge to Butterworth at dawn as part of a half-marathon. June is also a busy month, witnessing the International Dragonboat Race, the Equestrian Carnival and, on the northern coast, a beach volleyball tournament. In July, Georgetown's flower festival and Grand Parade provide colour, while the Cultural Festival provides a showcase for Penang's Malays, Chinese and Indians.

Some history

Pulau Pinang was ruled by the **sultans of Kedah** until the late eighteenth century. In the wake of years of harassment by Kedah's enemies, the sultan, Mohammed J'wa Mu'Azzam Shah II, was prepared to afford trade facilities to any nation that would provide him with military protection. Enter **Francis Light** in 1771, a ship's captain of the European trading company of Jourdain, Sullivan and de Souza, who was in search of a regional trading base for both his company and the **East India Company**. According to contemporary accounts, Captain Light was a charming man, well trained in the art of diplomacy, and it was not long before the sultan had housed the captain in his fort at Kuala Kedah, conferring upon him the honorary title of "Deva Raja" (God-king) and taking him into his confidence.

Light knew that the East India Company wanted to obtain a strategic port in the region to facilitate its trade with China, and as a refuge from its enemies in the Bay of Bengal. In forwarding the sultan's offer of the island of Penang to the company, Light drew particular attention to its safe harbour, and to the opportunities for local commerce. In 1772 the company sent its own agent, Edward Moncton, to negotiate with the sultan, but the talks soon broke down. It was another twelve years before agreement was reached, spurred on by the accession of a new sultan, Abdullah, and the East India Company's mounting concern that other countries were gaining a regional foothold – the French, at war with Britain, had acquired port facilities in northern Sumatra, having already made a pact with Burma, and the Dutch were consolidating their position in the Straits of Melaka.

In accordance with an agreement arranged by Light, the company was to pay Sultan Abdullah RM30,000 a year. Unfortunately for the sultan, the company's new governor-general, Charles Cornwallis, firmly stated that he could not be party to the sultan's disputes with the other Malay princes, or promise to protect him from the Burmese or Siamese. This rather pulled the rug from under Light's feet because it was on the basis of these promises that the sultan had ceded the island of Penang in the first place. Undeterred, Light decided to conceal the facts from both parties, and on his own initiative formally **established a port** at Penang on August 11, 1786. For the next five years, Light adopted stalling tactics with the sultan, assuring him that the matter of protection was being referred to authorities in London. The sultan eventually began to suspect that the company had reneged on the agreement, and attempted to drive the British out of Penang by force, but the effort failed; the subsequent settlement imposed by the British allowed the sultan an annual payment of only RM6000, and no role in the future government of the island.

So it was that Penang, then inhabited by less than a hundred indigenous fishermen, became the **first British settlement** in the Malay Peninsula. Densely forested, the island was open to settlers to claim as much land as they could clear – in somewhat debonair mood, Light encouraged the razing of the jungle by firing coins from a cannon into the undergrowth. After an initial, late-eighteenth-century influx of mainly Chinese immigrants, attracted by the possibilities of new commerce, Penang quickly became a major colonial administrative centre – within two years, four hundred acres were under cultivation and the population had reached ten thousand. Francis Light was made superintendent and declared the island a free port, renaming it "Prince of Wales Island" after the British heir apparent, whose birthday fell the day after the founding of the island. Georgetown, named – unsurprisingly – after the British king at that time, George III, has retained its colonial name even though the island's name has reverted to Penang.

For a time, all looked rosy for Penang, with Georgetown proclaimed as capital of the newly established **Straits Settlements** (incorporating Melaka and Singapore) in 1826. But the founding of Singapore in 1819 was the beginning of the end for Georgetown, and as the new colony overtook its predecessor in every respect (replacing it as capital of the Straits Settlements in 1832), Penang's fortunes rapidly began to wane. In retrospect, this had one beneficial effect: with Georgetown stuck in the economic doldrums for a century or more, there was no significant development within the city, and consequently many of its colonial and early Chinese buildings survive to this day. Although Penang was occupied by the Japanese during World War II, the strategic significance of Singapore once more proved to be Penang's saving grace, and there was little or no bomb damage to Penang island.

Butterworth

Realistically, the only reason to spend any time at all in **BUTTERWORTH**, 370km from KL, is to sort out your transport to Penang island – which can usually be done within half an hour of arrival. The **bus station**, **ferry pier**, long-distance-**taxi stand** and **train station** are all next door to each other, lying right on the quayside, so you shouldn't have to venture any further.

There are plenty of **places to stay**, although the decent hotels are a fair way from the port; none of the nearby options are particularly appealing, so unless you're really pressed for time, spending the night in Georgetown is the better option. The closest place to the front is the *Beach Garden Hotel* (☎04/332 2845; ❸) at 4835 Jalan Pantai, which, although there's neither a beach nor garden is serviceable and friendly. There are many other nondescript options along Jalan Bagan Luar, the main road running out of Butterworth. The stalls on the top floor of the bus terminal offer the best **eating** in town, staying open well into the night.

The passenger and car **ferry service to Georgetown** takes fifteen minutes (passengers 60 sen return, cars RM1 return); from the top floor of the bus station, you can walk over the signposted causeway to the ferry ticketing booths. The ferry runs from 5am until 11pm. When you have disembarked from the train you will soon be approached by taxi drivers who will offer to take you to Penang. The ferry is faster and cheaper, so keep on walking and follow the signs to the ferry landing.

The **Penang Bridge**, the longest in Asia at 13km, crosses from just south of Butterworth – turn west off Route 1, 5km south of Butterworth, for the bridge – to the east coast of the island, 8km south of Georgetown (a **toll** of RM7 is payable only on the journey out from the mainland); if you are coming over by **long-distance taxi** from any point on the Peninsula, check whether the toll is included in the fare.

Georgetown

Visiting **GEORGETOWN** in 1879, stalwart Victorian traveller Isabella Bird called it "a brilliant place under a brilliant sky", a simple statement on which it's hard to improve – Malaysia's most fascinating city retains more of its cultural history than virtually anywhere else in the country. Fort Cornwallis, St George's Church and the many buildings on and around Lebuh Pantai all survive from the earliest colonial days, and the communities of Chinatown and Little India have contributed some fine temples. Later Thai and Burmese arrivals left their mark on the city, but its predominant feature are the rows of peeling two-storey **Chinese shophouses**, their shutters painted in pastel colours, with bright-red Chinese lettering covering their colonnades and cheerfully designed awnings to shield the goods from the glaring sun. While the confusion of rickshaws, buses, lorries and scooters make parts of Georgetown as frenetic and polluted as most other places in the region, life in the slow lane has changed very little over the years. The rituals of worship, eating out at a roadside stall and the running of the family business, have all continued with little concern for Georgetown's contemporary technological development. It may no longer be a sleepy backwater – most of the island's one-million strong population now lives here – but the city's soul is firmly rooted in the past.

Strategically sited Georgetown is no stranger to visitors, since ships from all over the world have been docking at present-day Swettenham Pier since Francis Light first established his port here in 1786. Where once ships' chandlers and supply merchants ran thriving businesses, modern-day maritime trade is of an entirely different nature: neon-lit bars and dingy brothels help to boost the spirits of foreign navy crews who make regular forays around the city's streets. There's been a gradual change though, especially since the late 1970s, when foreign tourists first descended upon Penang in significant numbers. Nowadays, parts of downtown Georgetown sparkle with the state-of-the-art hotels and air-con shopping malls familiar to much of modern

Malaysia. But perhaps more than any other place in the country Georgetown is a magnet for budget travellers – the city is something of a hangout, a place not only to renew Thai visas, but to relax and observe street life from a pavement café, in between trips to the beach.

Arrival and information

Passenger and car **ferries from Butterworth** (15mins) dock at the centrally located terminal on **Pengkalan Weld** in Georgetown; those **from Medan** (Indonesia) and **Langkawi** dock at **Swettenham Pier**, a few hundred metres north along the dockside. The **express-bus station** and taxi stand at the KOMTAR building are just a short walk from the hotels and major amenities. The Penang Bridge brings **drivers** into the island on Jalan Udini, 8km south of Georgetown on the east coast. Driving into the city is not for the traffic-shy, though the major routes are well signposted. It's easiest to park in the KOMTAR building on Jalan Penang, which is within easy walking distance of the hotel area (mid-range and above hotels usually have private car parks). The **airport** is at Bayan Lepas on the southeastern tip of the island. Yellow bus #83 (roughly hourly, 6am–9pm; RM1.45) takes about 45 minutes to run into Georgetown, stopping at the KOMTAR building and subsequently at the Pengkalan Weld ferry terminal; a taxi into the city costs RM29 – buy a coupon beforehand from inside the terminal building.

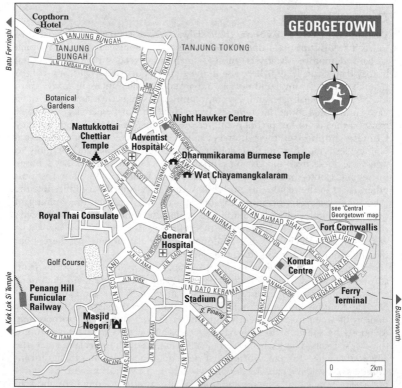

If you arrive by ferry, the most convenient tourist office is the **Penang Tourist Centre** (Mon–Thurs 8.30am–1pm & 2–4.30pm, Fri 8.30am–12.30pm & 2.30–4.30pm, Sat 8.30am–1pm; ☎04/261 6663, ⓦwww.penang.net.my), on the ground floor of the Penang Port Commission building on Jalan Tun Syed Sheh Barakbah. A couple of doors down at no. 10 is **Tourism Malaysia** (Mon–Thurs 8am–12.45pm & 2–5pm, Fri 8am–12.15pm & 2.45–4.15pm, Sat 8am–1pm, closed first and third Sat of every month; ☎04/262 0066), which is more helpful. Better still is the **Tourist Information Centre** (daily 10am–6pm; ☎04/261 4461) on the third floor of the KOMTAR building, where

Moving on from Penang island

Most journeys from Penang island involve changing in Butterworth, where you can pick up long-distance buses and trains to destinations in the Peninsula and on to Hat Yai, Surat Thani and Bangkok in Thailand (although you can also catch many buses directly from Penang).

By air

Among the direct international **flights** from Georgetown are services to **Medan** in Sumatra, **Bangkok** and **Phuket** in Thailand, and **Singapore**. To get to Bayan Lepas International Airport, take yellow bus #83 (hourly on the hour 6am–9pm; 45min; RM1.45) from Pengkalan Weld or the KOMTAR building.

By ferry

The passenger and car **ferry** from the Pengkalan Weld terminal is free on the leg to **Butterworth**, a fifteen-minute journey (daily 5am–11pm, every 20min). Express ferries to **Medan** (Sumatra, Indonesia; 4hr) and **Langkawi** (2hr 30min) depart daily from Swettenham Pier. The ferry to Langkawi departs Penang at 8am and 8.45am (RM35 one-way); the return trip departs Langkawi at 5.30pm. Tickets for both Langkawi and Sumatra can be purchased in advance from the office next to the Penang Tourist Association and from the tourist office at the KOMTAR building. Tickets for Langkawi are also sold by the Kuala Perlis Langkawi Ferry Service (☎04/262 5630) and Langkawi Ferry Service (☎04/264 2088), both at the Penang Port Commission building; the travel agencies on Lebuh Chulia will also book tickets for you.

By bus

Buses depart from the KOMTAR building for many destinations on the Peninsula (including KL, Kota Bharu, Kuala Terengganu and the Cameron Highlands), as well as Singapore and Thailand, but they can get busy, so book ahead at SIA Tours & Travel, 35 Pengkalan Weld (☎04/262 2951), or simply purchase your tickets from one of the many agents in town. There are more services from the terminal at Butterworth, which are so numerous that you can just turn up without booking beforehand.

By train

The nearest **train station** is in Butterworth (☎04/323 7962); there is a booking office in the Pengkalan Weld ferry terminal where you can reserve tickets to anywhere on the Peninsula as well as for the International Express to Bangkok.

By taxi

Taxis from the Pengkalan Weld ferry terminal charge about RM80 per vehicle to **Butterworth** station, so you're much better off taking the ferry, which is faster and free in this direction. Long-distance taxis to **Hat Yai** in Thailand (RM250 for up to four passengers) depart from several hostels on Lebuh Chulia.

knowledgeable staff can provide any information you might need. They also arrange half-day **tours** of the city and the island (from around RM30), which are not a bad way to see Penang if your time is limited. They sell a **tourist newspaper** (RM2; it's also available for free at some hotels), which provides a map of the free city-centre shuttle bus service.

Also worth checking out is the **Penang Heritage Trust** (Mon–Fri 9.30am–noon & 2pm–4.30pm; ☏04/264 2631, ⓦwww.pht.org.my) at 26A Lorong Stewart. It's staffed by knowledgeable volunteers who can provide you with free heritage trail maps.

City transport

The city is fairly small – you can walk from Pengkalan Weld to the top of the main street, Lebuh Chulia, in about twenty minutes – and so it's best to get around **on foot**; you'll miss most of the interesting alleyways otherwise. For longer journeys in town, and for travelling around the island, you'll need to master the excellent **bus service**. Red-and-white **Transit Link** buses – the most common of the lot – run on most routes through the island and around the city from a station on Lebuh Victoria, a block north of Pengkalan Weld. Leaving from the station next to the ferry terminal on Pengkalan Weld, blue buses service the north of the island, and yellow buses the south and west. There are also a number of minibuses operating; we've given details of useful services in the text. All buses stop on Jalan Ria, by the KOMTAR building. **Fares** are rarely more than a ringgit and services are frequent, though by 8pm in the evening they become more sporadic and stop completely at 10pm. There's also a **free shuttle bus service** around the city centre (Mon–Fri 7am–7pm, Sat 7am–2pm); the tourist newspaper available at the Tourist Information Centre provides a routemap.

The traditional way of seeing the city is by **tricycle-rickshaw**. If you can afford it, a ride in one of these is a fun way to see some of the city. Unfortunately, drivers act as though being hailed by a foreign visitor is tantamount to winning the lottery. Expect to pay about ten times the local rate, and don't be surprised if you have little luck haggling the price down. Business is so good apparently that most pedicab drivers would rather drive away without a fare than lower their expectations. Most of the city's tricycle-rickshaw drivers tout for customers outside the major hotels and all along Lebuh Chulia. Negotiate the price in advance; a ride from the ferry terminal at Pengkalan Weld to the

Street names in Georgetown

The most confusing thing about finding your way around Georgetown is understanding the **street names**, which all used to reflect the city's colonial past; however, the current political climate encourages either a Malay translation of an existing name (Penang Road has become Jalan Penang, Penang Street is Lebuh Penang, Weld Quay has become Pengkalan Weld, and Beach Street is now Lebuh Pantai) or complete renaming. This would be relatively straightforward were it not for the fact that the new names have not always been popularly accepted – Lorong Cinta, for example, is almost universally known as Love Lane – and even on official maps you'll sometimes see either name used. The most awkward of the new names is Jalan Masjid Kapitan Kling for the erstwhile Pitt Street, which more often than not is referred to simply as Lebuh Pitt. Several street names are also used repeatedly, such as Lorong Chulia and Lebuh Chulia, Lorong Penang and Lebuh Penang; also, don't confuse Lorong Cinta with Lebuh Cintra.

northern end of Lebuh Chulia costs around RM20. It's good to be aware too, that drivers will try to exact a commission from your place of accommodation if you are foolish enough to take a pedicab to look for a room. There are **taxi** stands by the ferry terminal and on Jalan Dr. Lim Chwee Long, off Jalan Penang. Drivers don't use their meters, so agree the fare in advance – a trip to the Thai Embassy costs about RM15, while a ride out to the airport or Batu Ferringhi costs RM30–40. To book a taxi in advance, call Jade Auto (℡04/226 3015), C.T. Taxis (℡04/229 9467) or J.R.I. Taxis (℡04/229 0501). For **bike or car rental** – particularly useful if you plan to see the rest of the island – see p.214.

Accommodation

Georgetown has a profusion of hotels and guesthouses, with plenty of choice at the budget end of the scale. The budget places, mostly on and around **Lebuh Chulia**, are usually within ramshackle wooden-shuttered mansions, often with courtyards and elegant internal staircases. Most have dorm beds as well as private rooms, and offer other useful services, such as selling bus tickets to Thailand and obtaining Thai visas. The two official **youth hostels** are a long way from the city centre: the *YMCA* is at 211 Jalan Macalister, 4km west from the KOMTAR building (℡04/229 2349; ❷), and the *YWCA* is 7km southwest of the centre at 8 Jalan Masjid Negeri (℡04/828 1855; ❷).

Budget on Lebuh Chulia & Jalan Penang

Ai Goh 465 Jalan Penang ℡04/262 9922, ℻263 2922. On the corner of Jalan Penang and Lebuh Kimberly, this very basic hotel has fan cubicle rooms with shared facilities for RM20. An extra RM5 will get you a private shower. Although the place could use some paint, it's relatively quiet, as it's set back from the street. ❷

Hang Chow 511 Lebuh Chulia ℡04/261 0810. Clean and tidy fan rooms. A few ringgit more will get you your own shower; some of the rooms have air-con. There's a nice *kopitiam* restaurant downstairs. ❷

New Eng Aun 380 Lebuh Chulia ①04/262 3080. Basic but very clean Chinese-run place. Fan and air-con rooms with shared facilities. The ornate Chinese gate in front makes it hard to miss. Between the gate and the hotel is a small beer garden. ❷

Olive Spring 300–302 Lebuh Chulia ℡04/261 4641. Friendly hotel with clean fan singles (❶) and doubles (with sink ❷). The upstairs rooms at the back near the balcony are the most popular as it's quieter there. There's also a dorm (RM8). All rooms have shared facilities.

Swiss Hotel 431F Lebuh Chulia ℡04/262 0133. A bland but clean and functional hostel – as the name suggests – and with sturdier walls than most. It's set back from the road, with parking and an airy café. ❷

White House 72 Jalan Penang ℡04/263 2385, ℻263 2386. Very clean, large rooms, with hot showers and optional a/c, for half what you'd pay elsewhere. This friendly, family-run place offers some of the best-value rooms in town. ❷

Budget elsewhere

These places are off the main drags of Chulia and Penang and so tend to be quieter.

Broadway Hostel 35F Jalan Masjid Kapitan Kling ℡04/262 8550, ℻262 8560. In a modern building, this friendly place has small and very basic but tidy fan rooms with thin walls as well as a dorm (RM7) and a/c rooms with two double beds. All rooms have shared facilities. ❷

Coral Hostel 99–101 Lebuh King ℡04/264 4909 ℻262 4775. Located in Little India, this clean, friendly and well-run place has a spacious dorm (RM8), but some of the other rooms have very thin walls. There's a lounge as well as breakfast-making facilities. A/c rooms also available. ❷

D'Budget Hostel 9 Lebuh Gereja ℡04/263 4794. Conveniently close to the ferry terminals, this friendly Indian-run place has spartan but clean, well-kept and secure rooms. There's a large roof patio plus Internet access, laundry facilities and a TV room. Dorm beds RM8; quad RM10. ❷

Love Lane Inn 54 Lorong Cinta ℡019/471 8409. The rooms are spartan and clean, but rather sterile, although there's lots of information for travellers, both from the notice-board and the knowledgeable staff. Dorms (RM8) and very simple singles (❶) as well as doubles (❷).

Modern 179C Lebuh Muntri ℡04/263 5424. On the corner of Lebuh Leith, this basic hotel is friendly, but far from modern. There are a variety of rooms: fan or a/c, en-suite or shared showers. The nicest rooms are the large doubles with private balconies and 1930s dark wood furniture. ❶

Noble 36 Lorong Pasar ☎04/261 2372, ℱ263 2372. Tucked away on a quiet side street, this friendly place has fan rooms with wood floors. The en-suite rooms are especially good value. Spacious common area with drinks and a kettle. ❶

Oasis Hotel 23 Lorong Cinta ☎019/261 6778. A good budget option in an old house set back in a gated compound shaded by a banyan tree. The rooms are spartan but clean and bathrooms are shared. The pleasant sitting area on the porch is a plus. ❶

Oriental Guest House 81 Lebuh Muntri ☎04/261 3378, ℱ263 3378. A little more traditional than most, the rooms have high ceilings and the ones downstairs have original tile floors. All fan rooms with shared facilities. ❷

Pin Seng 82 Lorong Cinta ☎04/261 9004. Relatively quiet because it's set back from the road, this simple place has a pleasant small lobby with an original tiled floor and wooden tables. ❶

75 Travellers Lodge 75 Lebuh Muntri ☎04/262 3378, ℱ263 3378. Small but clean thin-walled rooms with sinks, on a quiet street. Hot showers and laundry service plus a nice balcony at the back. Dorm RM8, fan rooms (❶); en-suite and a/c rooms (❷).

🏃 **Wan Hai** 35 Lorong Cinta ☎04/261 6853. Friendly hotel that's got lots of old embellishments, including carved wooden partitions above the cubicles. There's a spacious patio on the roof and the rooms are large and include more furniture than most. The *Wan Hai* boasts two dorms but the airy one at the front of the building affords a real taste of the sound effects of Penang's streetlife, from hawker's calls to the shuffling of mahjongg tiles. Dorms cost RM8. ❶

Moderate

🏃 **Cathay** 15 Lebuh Leith ☎04/262 6271, ℱ263 9300. Stylish colonial mansion dating from 1910. The cool greys of the decor, spacious rooms and courtyard fountain make for a tranquil environment. Fan rooms on the second floor are airy and bright but lack bathrooms. Rooms with en-suite bath and a/c are small and dark. The hotel was used as a set for the film *Beyond Rangoon*. ❹

Hong Ping 273B Lebuh Chulia ☎04/262 5243, ℱ262 3270. This hotel above the *Co Co Island* restaurant is the only mid-range option on Lebuh Chulia; it's clean and well run and all rooms have a/c, TVs and hot showers. Good value. ❹

Malaysia 7 Jalan Penang ☎04/263 3311, 🌐www.hotelmalaysia.com.my. Best of the hotels along this strip. Back rooms face the Cheong Fatt Tze Museum. The smartly decorated rooms have kettles and breakfast is included in the price. ❺

Merchant 55 Jalan Penang ☎04/263 2828, ℱ262 5511. Slightly smarter than the *Oriental* at the same price, all rooms have bathtubs and fridges. Continental breakfast included. ❺

Oriental 105 Jalan Penang ☎04/263 4211, ✉hostpg@pd.jaring.my. Reasonable rooms with helpful, professional staff. There's a North Indian restaurant in the basement as well as a karaoke lounge and a café with Internet access. ❺

Peking 50A Jalan Penang ☎04/263 6191. Large, clean rooms with nice tile floors, but the walls could use a lick of paint. All rooms are en suite, with a/c and TV. ❹

Expensive

🏃 **Cheong Fatt Tze Mansion** 14 Lebuh Leith ☎04/262 0006, 🌐www .cheongfatttzemansion.com. Hyperbole aside, this is the best place of accommodation in all of Malaysia. This huge, century-old Chinese mansion with fifteen stylish en-suite rooms was used as a set for the movie Indochine. Guests have the run of the place – there are no roped off areas or "staff only" signs here. Besides the reading & TV room, there is a games room with ping-pong table and free Internet access, as well as a stunning courtyard open to the sky, where you can while away the day sipping beer and admiring the intricately carved Chinese scrollwork. If you're really lucky you'll be in the courtyard during a cloudburst and experience the house being naturally cooled by the rain as the architects intended. Rate includes breakfast. Book ahead. ❽

Cititel 66 Jalan Penang ☎04/370 1188, 🌐www.cititelhotel.com. Large new business hotel with well-appointed but smallish rooms. There's a large Jacuzzi and three restaurants: Japanese, Chinese, and a 24-hour café. Rate includes breakfast. ❻

City Bayview 25A Lebuh Farquhar ☎04/263 3161, ✉cbvpg@tm.net.my. Modern luxury high-rise close to the sea, with its own pool and fantastic views over the bay from the revolving rooftop restaurant. Good value. ❻

Eastern & Oriental (E&O) Hotel 10 Lebuh Farquhar ☎04/222 2000, 🌐www.e-o-hotel.com. This atmospheric colonial hotel recently underwent an extensive facelift – all rooms were converted into beautifully appointed suites and there are several upscale restaurants to choose from. If you can't afford to stay here have a beer in the bar. This will give you an excuse to stand under the huge domed ceiling in the lobby and listen to a most remarkable echo. ❾

Traders Hotel Jalan Magazine ☎04/262 2622, ℻262 6526. Formerly the *Shangri-La*, this modern deluxe hotel is conveniently located next to the KOMTAR building; all the facilities you would expect for a place of its price. ❾

The city centre

The main area of interest in Georgetown is the central square-kilometre or so bordered by Jalan Penang, Jalan Magazine and the sharply curving coast. The most prominent, if not most aesthetically pleasing, landmark is the Komplex Tun Abdul Razak (or KOMTAR), a huge high-rise of shops and offices towering over the western corner of the city centre. You can visit the **viewing deck**, on the fifty-eighth floor of the KOMTAR building, which affords fantastic views of the harbour, Penang Hill, temples and other sites within the city. The entry fee is RM5, but if you take the elevator to the fifty-ninth floor and eat in the restaurant, admission is free.

The entire centre of Georgetown could effectively be termed **Chinatown**, since it is dominated by shuttered two-storey shophouses and a liberal scattering of *kongsis* (clan associations) that have stood here in various forms since the late eighteenth century. In the thick of it is tiny **Little India**, between Lebuh King and Lebuh Queen, while the remnants of the city's **colonial** past – Fort Cornwallis, St George's Church and the building housing the Penang Museum – are all clustered relatively close together at the northeastern end of town, not far from Swettenham Docks. For a reminder of Penang's past economic success, the area around **Lebuh Leith**, west of the central area, is worth exploring. It's typified by the mansions of "millionaires' row" and the *Eastern and Oriental (E&O) Hotel*. Built in 1885 by the Armenian Sarkies brothers (who also ran Singapore's *Raffles Hotel*), former guests included Somerset Maugham and Noel Coward. Even if you can't afford to stay here, stroll through the grand lobby with its cool marble floors and high dome.

△ Rickshaws outside Cheong Fatt Tze Mansion, Georgetown

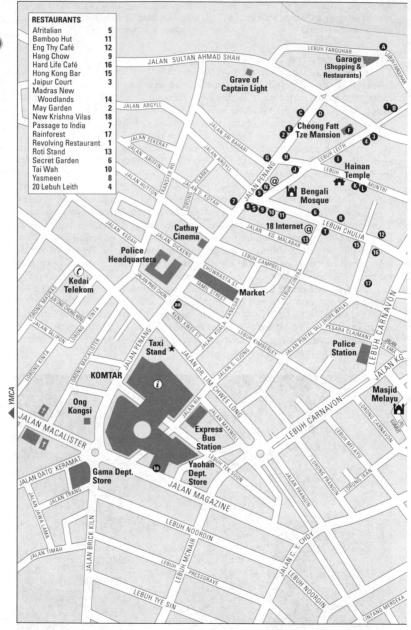

RESTAURANTS

Afritalian	5
Bamboo Hut	11
Eng Thy Café	12
Hang Chow	9
Hard Life Café	16
Hong Kong Bar	15
Jaipur Court	3
Madras New Woodlands	14
May Garden	2
New Krishna Vilas	18
Passage to India	7
Rainforest	17
Revolving Restaurant	1
Roti Stand	13
Secret Garden	6
Tai Wah	10
Yasmeen	8
20 Lebuh Leith	4

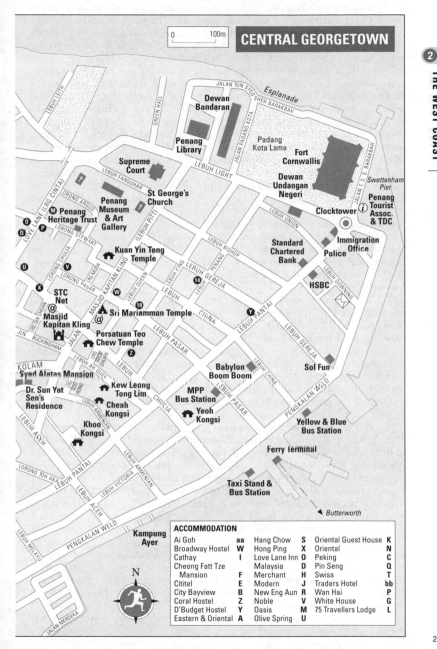

CENTRAL GEORGETOWN

0 — 100m

Esplanade

Dewan Bandaran

JALAN TUN SYED SHEH BARAKBAH

Penang Library

Padang Kota Lama

Fort Cornwallis

JALAN T S S BARAKBAH

Swettenham Pier

Supreme Court

LEBUH FARQUHAR

Dewan Undangan Negeri

LEBUH LIGHT

JALAN PADANG KOTA

GREEN HALL

LEBUH LEITH

LORONG ARGUS

LORONG CINTAI (LRG ANE)

Penang Heritage Trust

Penang Museum & Art Gallery

St George's Church

Clocktower

Penang Tourist Assoc. & TDC

LORONG STEWART

Immigration Office

LEBUH UNION

Police

Kuan Yin Teng Temple

LEBUH PITT

LEBUH BISHOP

LEBUH PENANG

Standard Chartered Bank

LOVE LANE

LORONG CHULIA

LORONG PASAR

MASJID KAPITAN KLING

LRG MUDA

LEBUH QUEEN

LEBUH KING

LEBUH PENANG

LEBUH GEREJA

HSBC

STC Net

Sri Mariamman Temple

LEBUH CHINA

LEBUH PANTAI

Masjid Kapitan Kling

JALAN

JLN BUCKINGHAM

DESAK CHIAN

Persatuan Teo Chew Temple

LEBUH PASAR

LEBUH GEREJA

KOLAM

LRG SOO HONG

Syed Alatas Mansion

LEBUH AH QUEE

Babylon Boom Boom

LEBUH CHINA

Sol Fun

PENGKALAN WELD

Dr. Sun Yat Sen's Residence

Kew Leong Tong Lim

Cheah Kongsi

LEBUH ARMENIAN

MPP Bus Station

LEBUH PASAR

Yeoh Kongsi

Yellow & Blue Bus Station

Khoo Kongsi

LEBUH ACHEH

LORONG TOH AKA

LEBUH PANTAI

LEBUH VICTORIA

LEBUH ARMENIAN

LEBUH ACEH

Ferry Terminal

Taxi Stand & Bus Station

Butterworth

LEBUH MELAYU

PENGKALAN WELD

Kampung Ayer

N

JALAN MERDEKA

ACCOMMODATION

Ai Goh	aa	Hang Chow	S	Oriental Guest House	K
Broadway Hostel	W	Hong Ping	X	Oriental	N
Cathay	I	Love Lane Inn	O	Peking	C
Cheong Fatt Tze		Malaysia	D	Pin Seng	Q
Mansion	F	Merchant	H	Swiss	T
Cititel	E	Modern	J	Traders Hotel	bb
City Bayview	B	New Eng Aun	R	Wan Hai	P
Coral Hostel	Z	Noble	V	White House	G
D'Budget Hostel	Y	Oasis	M	75 Travellers Lodge	L
Eastern & Oriental	A	Olive Spring	U		

Fort Cornwallis and the waterfront

The site of **Fort Cornwallis** (daily 8.30am–7pm; RM1) on the northeastern tip of Pulau Pinang marks the spot where the British fleet, under Captain Francis Light, disembarked on July 16, 1786. A fort fronting the blustery north channel was hastily thrown up to provide barracks for Light and his men, and was named after Lord Charles Cornwallis, Governor-General of India, as well as the man whose surrender to George Washington in 1781 cost Britain its American colonies. The present structure dates from around twenty years after, but for all its significance little remains to excite the senses, just peeling walls and the seventeenth-century **Sri Rambai cannon**, sited in the northwest corner of the citadel. Presented to the Sultan of Johor by the Dutch, this was confiscated by the British in 1871 during their attack on Selangor – they loaded 29 guns, including the cannon, onto the steamer *Sri Rambai* and upon reaching Penang, threw it overboard; it remained submerged for almost a decade. According to local legend, the cannon refused to leave the seabed during the subsequent salvage operation and only floated to the surface when Tunku Qudin, the former Viceroy of Selangor, tied a rope to it and ordered it to rise. Since then it's been considered a living entity with mystical powers; the local belief is that barren women can conceive by laying flowers on its barrel.

Inside the fort, there's a replica of a traditional Malay house, a craft shop and, close to the cannon, a claustrophobic underground bunker detailing the history of Penang – unimaginatively presented, but informative. An open-air auditorium hosts music and dance festivals – keep an eye on the local press for details of shows.

The large expanse of green that borders the fort, the **Padang Kota Lama**, was once the favourite promenade of the island's colonial administrators and thronged with rickshaws and carriages. On the south side, opposite the grand sweep of the **Esplanade**, was a bandstand where Filipino musicians played to strolling passers-by. Now used for sports and other public events, the padang is bordered by some superb examples of Anglo-Victorian architecture: the **Dewan Undangan Negeri** (State Legislative Building) with its weighty portico and ornate gables, and the **Dewan Bandaran** (town hall), of equal aesthetic if not political merit, the city's affairs now being conducted from the KOMTAR building.

There's a Moorish-style **clock tower** on the southeast corner of the padang, at the junction of Lebuh Light and Lebuh Pantai. Presented to the town in 1897 to mark Queen Victoria's Diamond Jubilee, it is sixty feet (20m) high, each foot representing a year of her reign. A bomb dropped during World War II caused the tower to tilt slightly. Turn to the right here and you're at the top of one of Georgetown's oldest streets, **Lebuh Pantai**, the heart of the business district. This narrow and congested road once fronted the beach – its swaying palms were the first sight of the island for anyone approaching from the mainland. The street is a far cry from this today, with scores of moneylenders squeezed cheek-by-jowl between the imposing bank and government buildings, not to mention the constant buzz of motor scooters. Gracefully lining an otherwise ill-proportioned street are some of Georgetown's best colonial buildings, including the Standard Chartered Bank and HSBC, the heavy pillars of the former creating an elegant archway. Across the street is a pretty pale blue confection, the Majlis Jabatan Agama.

A left turn down any of the adjoining streets leads to the **waterfront**, but there's little of interest here except the passage of the lumbering yellow ferries to and from Butterworth. The ferry terminal is also known as "Clan Piers", since each of the jetties is named after a different Chinese clan.

On the western side of Lebuh Pantai you're in Chinatown. A leisurely five-minute stroll from here, along Lebuh Chulia or down any of the parallel side streets running northwest, brings you to Jalan Masjid Kapitan Kling (or Lebuh Pitt), one of the city's main thoroughfares. Around its intersection with Lebuh Chulia you'll find a mosque, a Chinese temple, and a Hindu temple, testament to Penang's multi-ethnicity. The area east of here, enclosed by the parallel roads of Lebuh King and Lebuh Queen, forms Georgetown's compact **Little India** district. Surrounded on all sides by Chinatown, it's a vibrant, self-contained community comprising sari and incense shops, banana-leaf-curry houses, and the towering **Sri Mariamman Temple** (open daily from early morning to late evening) on the corner of Lebuh Queen and Lebuh Chulia. A typical example of Hindu architecture, the lofty entrance tower teems with brightly coloured sculptures of gods and swans devoted to the main deity, Mariamman; the inner sanctum has a nine-metre-high dome, with statues of forty other deities and lions. On the other side of Lebuh Chulia is the Chinese **Persatuan Teochew Temple**, which features fearsome guardians painted on the insides of the temple doors.

Lebuh Chulia itself – the central artery of Chinatown – was where the southern Indian immigrants chose to establish their earliest businesses (*chulia* being the Tamil word for "merchant"), and the Indian shops here still deal in textiles. But the area (like much of central Georgetown) looks predominantly Chinese with its shophouses and arcades selling everything from antiques and bamboo furniture to books and photographic services.

Back on Jalan Masjid Kapitan Kling (Lebuh Pitt), at the corner of Jalan Buckingham, stands the **Masjid Kapitan Kling**. Built in the early nineteenth century by Indian Muslim settlers (originally East India Company troops), the yellow mosque is built in Indian-influenced Islamic style and has a single minaret. A few minutes' walk north you reach the **Kuan Yin Teng Temple**, which is dedicated to Bodhisattva, the goddess of mercy, probably the most worshipped of all the Chinese deities, much-revered by Buddhists, Taoists and Confucians alike. While not the finest example of a *kongsi* (that honour goes to the Khoo Kongsi below), this Chinese temple can claim the title of the oldest in Penang. Originally constructed around 1800, it was completely ravaged during World War II; what you see today, including the massive roof dominated by two guardian dragons, is a restoration.

Lebuh Aceh, Lebuh Armenian and the Khoo Kongsi

Going south on Jalan Masjid Kapitan Kling and turning right into Lebuh Armenian, you'll find a blue house at no. 120, which dates from the 1870s. It served as the base of **Dr Sun Yat Sen** (Mon–Fri 9am–5pm, Sat 9am–1pm; free admission), president of the first Chinese Republic, from 1910 to 1911. The interior has been handsomely preserved with carved timber screens and air wells. Next door is the elegantly restored **Syed Alatas Mansion** (same opening hours; free), a lovely double-storey colonial building which originally belonged to a wealthy Achenese merchant of Arab descent. As you reach Lebuh Aceh, you'll see the oldest mosque in Penang, **Masjid Melayu**, built in 1808, unusual for its Egyptian-style minaret – most in Malaysia are Moorish. The hole halfway up was supposedly made by a cannonball fired from Khoo Kongsi during the clan riots in 1867 (see box p.208).

Across Lebuh Aceh, in a secluded square on an alleyway connecting Jalan Masjid Kapitan Kling and Lebuh Pantai, stands the **Khoo Kongsi** (Mon–Fri 9am–5pm, Sat 9am–1pm; RM5 admission), *kongsi* being the Hokkien term for (clan) association (and by extension applied to the clan house), a building in which Chinese families gather to worship their ancestors. In Penang, the *kongsi*s were originally formed to provide mutual help and protection for nineteenth-century immigrants, who naturally tended to band together in clans according to the district from which they came. At one time this led to rivalry and often violence between the different Chinese communities, though these days the *kongsi*s have reverted to their supportive role, helping with the education of members' children, settling disputes between clan members or advancing loans. Consequently, they are an important means of preserving solidarity, although traditionally women have been excluded from many of the functions and are rarely represented in the hierarchy.

Many of the *kongsi*s in Penang are excellent examples of traditional Chinese architecture, well over a hundred years old. There is generally a spacious court-yard in front of the clan house, opposite which is a stage for theatrical perform-ances, and two halls in the main building itself, one for the shrine of the clan deity, the other for the display of the ancestral tablets (the equivalent of grave-stones). Completed in 1894, the Khoo Kongsi was an ambitious and extensive project with a roof styled in the manner of a grand palace; it took eight years to complete but was immediately gutted in a mysterious fire. Suspecting sabotage, the clan members rebuilt the house on a lesser scale, making the excuse that the previous design had been too noble to house the ancestral tablets of ordinary mortals. The resulting structure, meticulously crafted by experts from China,

The Penang Riots

Chinese immigrants in Penang brought their traditions with them, including the establishment of **triads** (secret societies), branches of organizations that had evolved in China during the eighteenth century as a means of overthrowing Manchu rule. Once in Penang, the societies provided mutual aid and protection for the Chinese community, their position later bolstered by alliances with Malay religious groups originally established to assist members with funerals and marriages.

As the societies grew in wealth and power, gang warfare and extortion rackets became commonplace. The newly appointed governor-general, Sir Harry Ord, and his inefficient police force (largely composed of non-Chinese) proved ineffective in preventing the increasing turmoil. In 1867, matters came to a head in the series of events known subsequently as the **Penang Riots**. For nine days Georgetown was shaken by fighting between the Tua Peh Kong society, supported by the Malay Red Flag, and the Ghee Hin, allied with the Malay White Flag. Police intervention resulted in a temporary truce, but a major clash seemed inevitable when, on August 1, 1867, the headman of the Tua Peh Kong falsely charged the Ghee Hin and the White Flag societies with stealing cloth belonging to Tua Peh Kong dyers. All hell broke loose and fighting raged around Lebuhs Armenian, Church and Chulia. Barricades were erected around the Khoo Kongsi, where much of the fiercest fighting took place, and you can still find bullet holes in the surrounding shops and houses. The authorities were powerless to act, since the battery of artillery normally stationed at Fort Corn-wallis had just left for Rangoon and relief forces had not yet arrived. Countless arrests were made, but the police soon had to release many from custody as there was not enough room in the overflowing jails.

The fighting was eventually quelled by **sepoys** (Indian troops) brought in from Sin-gapore by the governor-general, but by then hundreds had been killed and scores of houses burned. As compensation for the devastation suffered by the city, a penalty of RM5000 was levied on each of the secret societies, some of which was later used to finance the building of four police stations to deal with any future trouble.

has a saddle-shaped roof that reputedly weighs 25 tonnes. Its central hall is dark with heavy, intricately carved beams and pillars and bulky mother-of-pearl inlaid furniture; an Art Deco grandfather clock stands somewhat incongruously in the corner. Behind this is a separate chamber, with delicate black-and-white line drawings depicting scenes of courtly life. The hall on the left is a richly decorated shrine to Tua Peh Kong, the god of prosperity; the right-hand hall contains the gilded ancestral tablets. Connecting all three halls is a balcony minutely decorated in bas-relief, whose carvings depict episodes from folk tales – even the bars on the windows have been carved into bamboo sticks.

Exiting the compound and turning back into Lebuh Armenian you'll come across **Cheah Kongsi** (free admission). Like its more illustrious cousin, this clan house stands in a large compound, only accessible through a narrow entrance from the street. Not as grand as the nearby Khoo Kongsi, Cheah Kongsi gets fewer tourists, making it more serene, with a pleasant shaded balcony where old Chinese men play chess in the long hot afternoons.

Lebuh Farquhar and Lebuh Leith

Near the northern end of Jalan Masjid Kapitan Kling, opposite the junction with Lebuh Bishop, is the Anglican **St George's Church** (Tues–Sat 8.30am–12.30pm & 1.30–4.30pm, Sun 8.30am–4.30pm). One of the oldest buildings in Penang, and as simple and unpretentious as anything built in the Greek style in Asia can be, it was constructed in 1817–19 by the East India Company using convict labour; its cool, pastel-blue interior must have been a welcome retreat from the heat for the new congregation. In 1886, on the centenary of the founding of Penang, a memorial to Francis Light was built in front of the church in the form of a Greek temple. Next to the church, on **Lebuh Farquhar** (which takes its name from a former lieutenant-governor of the settlement), is the **Penang Museum and Art Gallery** (daily except Fri 9am–5pm; RM1), housed in a building dating from 1821 that was originally the first English-medium public school in the east. It has an excellent collection of memorabilia: rickshaws, Peranakan furniture, clothing and ceramics, faded black-and-white photographs of early Penang's Chinese millionaires and a panoramic photograph of Georgetown taken in the 1870s – note just how many buildings still survive. The art gallery upstairs displays original watercolours, oil paintings and heritage photos of colonial Georgetown. In front of the museum stands a statue of Francis Light, cast in 1936 for the 150th anniversary of the founding of Penang. As there was no image available, Sir Francis' features were copied from a portrait of his son, Colonel William Light, founder of Adelaide in Australia. During World War II, the Japanese removed the statue and later returned it (minus the sword).

Continuing west underneath a footbridge and turning left on **Lebuh Leith**, you'll soon reach the stunning **Cheong Fatt Tze Mansion** at no. 14 (T04/262 0006, Wwww.cheongfatttzemansion.com), whose outer walls are painted a striking indigo blue. Built by Thio Thiaw Siat, a Cantonese businessman, it's the best example of eclectic nineteenth-century Peranakan architecture in Penang. The mansion, with its elaborate ceremonial halls, bedrooms and libraries, separated by cobbled courtyards, small gardens and heavy wooden doors, has been magnificently restored. The interior can only be seen by joining an hour-long guided tour (Mon–Fri at 11am & 3pm; Sat, Sun & public holidays at 11am), which is well worth the RM10 entrance fee. The mansion also runs a bed and breakfast (see "Accommodation").

Turning back north on Lebuh Leith and then left on Lebuh Farquhar, you'll find the legendary **Eastern & Oriental Hotel**, once part of the Sarkies brothers' select chain of colonial retreats (as was the *Raffles* in Singapore; see p.650). Rudyard Kipling and Somerset Maugham both stayed here, taking tiffin on the terrace and enjoying the cooling sea breeze. About five minutes' walk west along Lebuh Farquhar, the road merges with sea-facing Jalan Sultan Ahmad Shah, across which you'll find the overgrown churchyard where Francis Light is buried. Further along, the huge crumbling mansions set back from the road in acres of seedy lawn give the road its nickname – "millionaires' row" – and though the costs of upkeep have seen several of the houses fall into disrepair, the road remains a reminder of the ostentatious wealth of colonial Penang.

Eating

Georgetown's status as Malaysia's second city means there is no shortage of cafés and restaurants. There's a wide choice of Malay, Chinese and South Indian food as well as North Indian and Nonya specialities. **Hawker stalls** dish out the cheapest meals and are located either in permanent sites, in which case they're open all day and evening, or by the roadsides and down alleyways, when they spring up at meal times only. In addition, a roving **pasar malam** (night market), with stalls selling all manner of food, is held every two weeks at various venues around town – any of the tourist offices will have the details.

Of the **cafés** (usually open 8am–11pm), the ubiquitous **Chinese** *kedai kopi*s serve reliable rice and noodle standards, with many also specializing in fine Hainan chicken rice. The other local favourite is Penang *laksa*, noodles in thick fish soup, garnished with vegetables, pineapple and *belacan* (shrimp paste). The **South Indian** *kedai kopi*s on Lebuh Penang (the eastern edge of Little India) offer *murtabak, roti* and biriyani as well as a bewildering array of vegetarian banana-leaf curries; none serve alcohol. The main travellers' hangouts are dotted on or around Lebuh Chulia, often little more than hole-in-the-wall joints serving **Western breakfasts**, banana pancakes and milk shakes at reasonable prices. These tend to open from around 9am to 5pm (the exceptions are noted below). For more **upmarket restaurants**, head to Gurney Drive, where some good seafood places housed in old villas with outdoor tables facing the sea make for an atmospheric treat.

Hawker stalls

Chinatown Lebuh Kimberley and Lebuh Cintra. Open late into the night, this place does every sort of noodle and rice dish, each for just a few ringgit.

Food Court KOMTAR building. On the ground floor and on the roof. The atmosphere's a little sterile, but there's a good range of Chinese, Malay and Indian food.

Jalan Tun Syed Shah Barakah Near Fort Cornwallis, at the west end of the esplanade. Most of the stalls serve Chinese food, though a few do Malay fare too. The fruit juices here are particularly fine.

Pesiaran Gurney (Gurney Drive) 3km northwest along the coast before Tanjung Tokong (take any bus going to Batu Ferringhi). This area with many hawker-style restaurants specializing in seafood becomes very lively at night, when the locals come out to stroll along the promenade.

Cafés

Bamboo Hut 481 Lebuh Chulia. Good for all-day breakfasts and Indian dishes. Also has great milk shakes served in bamboo cups.

Eng Thy Café 340 Lebuh Chulia. Popular with travellers, this place serves good fruit shakes and Western breakfasts as well as a large variety of inexpensive snacks. Movie screenings in the evenings make for a noisy dinner. Daily 8am–midnight.

Hang Chow Café 511 Lebuh Chulia. On the ground floor of the *Hang Chow Hotel*, this place serves good Western food including home-made yoghurt as well as pizza and shakes in a traditional *kopitiam* setting.

Hard Life Café 363 Lebuh Chulia. Bob Marley and the like plastered across the walls plus mellow tunes make this a laid-back spot for drinks, snacks and beers.

Madras New Woodlands 60 Lebuh Penang. Excellent South Indian cuisine at bargain prices.

Lunchtime *thalis* – an array of spicy dishes with crispy pancakes – cost RM4.

New Krishna Vilas 75 Lebuh Pasar. Excellent banana-leaf-curry house with rock-bottom prices. Try their *dhosas* (crispy crêpes). Daily 7am–9.30pm (closed one Wed each month).

Rainforest 294A Lebuh Chulia. Roomy and comfortable, with tasteful rattan and bamboo decor, this café serves international veggie food and wonderful wholemeal bread.

Secret Garden 414 Lebuh Chulia. A spacious and airy place that's popular with travellers. It serves good breakfasts until 2pm and has an extensive international menu.

Yasmeen Jalan Penang. Delicious and cheap halal Indian food, including lots of spicy, cumin-coloured vegatables and curries to dip your *roti* into. The tandoori chicken is good too.

Restaurants

Afritalian Restoran & Kafe On the corner of Jalan Penang and Lebuh Chulia (in the same building as the *Oriental Hotel*). Set Western breakfast for RM10 and African as well as Italian dishes starting at RM9.

Jaipur Court 11 Lebuh Leith. Expensive but tasty North Indian cuisine in an attractive old colonial building with some outdoor seating.

May Garden 70 Jalan Penang. Plush but affordable Cantonese restaurant with excellent food. Very popular with tourists from the nearby high-rise hotels.

Passage to India 132–134 Jalan Penang. Serves good North and South Indian cuisine in a colourful setting. Dinner only.

Revolving Restaurant Fourteenth floor, *City Bayview Hotel*, Lebuh Farquhar. Serves Western and Asian dishes, with a colourful all-you-can-eat dinner buffet (RM44) featuring live music.

Roti Stand Lebuh Cintra. Tables are set up in a lot at dusk and a menu of nearly one hundred types of *roti* is displayed on a wall. There are both sweet and savoury *roti* to choose from, as well as coffee, tea and soft drinks. Try the *roti tisu*, so called because it's deep fried until it resembles a crumpled piece of tissue paper, and then glazed with butter and honey. Wash it down with a piping hot glass of ginger tea.

Drinking, nightlife and entertainment

Most of Georgetown's **bars** are comfortable places in which to hang out – some of the best are detailed below. With the periodic arrival of the Malaysian navy, though, a good many turn into rowdy meat markets, and a place that may have been fine the night before can become unpleasant for women visitors. Usual opening hours are 6pm to 2am with happy hours often running from 6pm to 8pm. If there's live music, it usually starts at 10.30pm. In Georgetown's **discos**, which stay open until the early hours (a cover charge of around RM50 usually applies), you're more likely to hear local pop music than the latest Western club sounds.

Other entertainment is thin on the ground: the Cathay (Jalan Penang) and Rex (Jalan Burma) **cinemas** show recent releases of English-language movies; check the *New Straits Times* and other Penang listings.

Bars

Cheers Jalan Penang. Standout sports bar that emphasizes pitchers of beer and a generous happy hour (5–9pm). There's an adjacent wine bar if you prefer something more intimate.

Hong Kong Bar Lebuh Chulia. A classic liberty-port dive with command plaques and photos of warships adorning the walls – although if you happen to be here when the Australian fleet is in port, give this place a wide berth. Open daily 5pm til late.

Old China Café Lebuh Pantai. Authentic colonial style of the 1930s, packed with so much atmosphere you'll feel like you've landed a part in a remake of *Casablanca*.

Tai Wah Lebuh Chulia. This daytime café turns into a lively bar full of Indonesian guest workers in the evening; serves some of the cheapest beer in town.

20 Lebuh Leith This renovated 1930s Straits-style mansion, festooned with film memorabilia, has a large video screen, plenty of tables in the beer garden and a good but rather pricey teriyaki grill out front.

Clubs

The Bungalow 4 Jalan Penang. Classy decor in a renovated colonial building. Something for everyone with live pop music nightly (except Sun), sports on TV, a well-stocked bar, and a small menu.

California Pub & Beer Garden 20 Lebuh Leith. This colonial building has live music – English and Chinese pop – nightly (except Sun). There's a snack menu and the prices are more reasonable than at similar places.

Carmen Inn Basement, City Bayview, 25a Lebuh Farquhar. One of the better hotel clubs in George-town, which concentrates on Sixties and Seventies sounds.

Slippery Señoritas Garage, 2 Jalan Penang. A Latin-themed disco of the kind that has popped up all over Asia in the last half decade. Except for half the name, there's really nothing Latin about it, but this is the island's most lively pick-up joint.

Uptown Bistro 20 Jalan Sultan Ahmad Shah. This bright purple building is hard to miss. There's a nightly live band (Chinese pop) indoors as well as a beer garden in the courtyard.

Out from the city centre

There are several sights on the western and northern **outskirts** of Georgetown that are worth exploring, most of which provide a welcome break from the frenetic city. In particular, trips to **Penang Hill**, the **botanical gardens**, and **Ayer Itam** with its sprawling **Kek Lok Si temple** are a cool alternative to heading for the northern beaches for the day. For true temple buffs, there are three more worth visiting: the Thai **Wat Chayamangkalarm**, the Burmese **Dharmmikarama Temple**, and the **Nattukottai Chettiar Temple**. **Buses** run to all the destinations below from the station at the KOMTAR building on Jalan Ria.

Three temples and the Botanical Gardens

A fifteen-minute bus ride (Transitlink #202, #212, minibus #31, #31a, #88, #88a or blue bus #93) towards Batu Ferringhi brings you to **Wat Chayamangkalaram** on Lorong Burma, a Thai temple painted in yellow and blue and flanked by two statues, whose fierce grimaces and weighty swords are designed to ward off unwanted visitors. Inside, a 33-metre-long statue of the Reclining Buddha is surrounded by other, elaborately decorated Buddha images covered with gold leaf. The Burmese **Dharmmikarama Temple** across the road is less spectacular, although the white-stone elephants at the entrance are attractive and the temple's two *stupas* are lit to good effect at night. Both temples are open between sunrise and sunset (free).

Further west on Jalan Kebun Bunga is the **Nattukottai Chettiar Temple**, a seven-kilometre bus ride from the city centre on the hourly Transitlink #7; ask to be dropped off at *The Waterfall Hotel*, from where the temple is a five-minute walk north. This is the focus of the Hindu **Thaipusam** festival in February, in honour of Lord Subramanian, when thousands of devotees walk through the streets bearing *kavadis* (sacred yokes) fixed to their bodies by hooks and spikes spearing their flesh. The biggest such event in Malaysia is at Kuala Lumpur's Batu Caves (see p.149); the festivities in Georgetown are a similar blend of hypnotic frenzy and celebration. At other times of the year, you're free to concentrate on the temple itself, in which an unusual wooden colonnaded walkway with exquisite pictorial tiles leads up to the inner sanctum, where a life-sized solid-silver peacock – the birds crop up throughout the temple – bows its head to the deity, Lord Subramanian.

Just five more minutes further up Jalan Kebun Bunga (formerly Waterfall Road) from the temple lie the **Botanical Gardens** (daily 7am–7pm; free) in a lush valley. They are a good place to escape the city and enjoy some fresh air. Unfortunately, the waterfall that gave the road its name has been cordoned off, and can't be easily seen from a distance either.

Ayer Itam and the Kek Lok Si Temple

A thirty-minute bus ride west (take Transitlink #1, #101, #130, #351, #361, yellow bus #85 or minibus #21), **Ayer Itam** is an appealing wooded hilly area, spread around the Ayer Itam Dam, built in the early 1960s. As you approach Ayer Itam, the sprawling, fairytale complex of **Kek Lok Si Temple** (open morning to late evening; free) makes an intriguing sight, the tips of its colourful towers peeking cheekily through the treetops. Supposedly the largest Buddhist temple in Malaysia, it's a serious place of worship as well as being a major tourist spot, with fantastic shrines and pagodas, linked by hundreds of steps, and bedecked with flags, lanterns and statues. The abbot of the Kuan Yin Temple on Lebuh Pitt arrived from China in 1885 and chose this site because the landscape around Ayer Itam reminded him of his homeland. He raised money from rich Chinese merchants to fund the construction of the huge temple, set across twelve hectares, modelled on Fok San Monastery in Fuchow, China. The entrance to the complex is approached through a line of trinket stalls, their awnings forming a tunnel stretching a few hundred metres uphill. On the way up is a pond for turtles, which represent eternity. The seven-tier Ban Po, or "Million Buddhas Precious Pagoda" is the most prominent feature of the compound and is built in three different styles. The lower section of simple Chinese saddle-shaped eaves represents the goddess of mercy; the central levels represent the laughing Buddha and have elaborate Thai arched windows; at the top is a golden Burmese *stupa*, representing the historical Buddha. It costs RM2 to climb the 193 steps to the top, where there is a great **view** of Georgetown and the bay.

Penang Hill

Just on the outskirts of Georgetown is the small hill station of **Penang Hill** (Bukit Bendera), an 821-metre-high dome of tropical forest due west of the city. It was the first colonial hill station in Peninsular Malaysia and once the retreat for the colony's wealthiest administrators. Nowadays it's a popular excursion for the locals and can get quite crowded at weekends. The cooler climate (the average temperature is 5 degrees lower than Georgetown) benefits flowering trees and shrubs, and there are several gentle, well-marked walks through areas whose names (Tiger Hill, Strawberry Hill) hark back to colonial days. You can also walk down to the Botanical Gardens, a steep descent that takes about an hour.

To get to the hill, take Transitlink #1, #101, #130, #351, #361, yellow bus #85 or minibus #21 to the terminus and then either walk the remaining fifteen minutes or take the Transitlink #8 which terminates at the base of Penang Hill. The last part of the journey is made by **funicular railway** (daily 6.30am–11.30pm; every 30min; 30min journey; RM4 return), which deposits you at the top of the hill. It was then re-built by the Swiss in 1922. At the top there's a temple, a mosque, a post office, a police station, a few restaurants and food stalls and a **hotel**, the *Bellevue* (☎04/829 9500, ℱ829 2052; ❺), with large comfortable rooms and a terrace affording superb views over Georgetown; a drink or a meal here is perfect at sunset when the city's lights flicker on in the distance.

Listings

Airlines Cathay Pacific, Menara PSCI, Jalan Sultan Ahmed Shah ☎04/226 0411; Malaysia Airlines, ground floor, KOMTAR building, Jalan Penang ☎04/262 0011; Singapore Airlines, Wisma Penang Gardens, Jalan Sultan Ahmed Shah ☎04/226 3201; Thai International, Wisma Central, Jalan Macalister ☎04/226 6000.

Airport ☎04/643 0373 for flight information.
American Express c/o Mayflower Acme Tours, MWE Plaza Lebuh Farquhar (Mon–Fri 8.30am–5.30pm, Sat 8.30am–1pm; ☎04/262 8196, ℱ261 9024). Credit card and traveller's cheque holders can use the office as a poste restante/general delivery address.

Bakeries Both Diner's Bakery at 153 Lebuh Campbell and Ng Kee Cakeshop at 61 Lebuh Cintra offer good variety. There's also a small outlet of Eden Bakery across from the *Modern Hotel* on Lebuh Muntri.

Banks and exchange Major banks (Mon–Fri 10am–3pm, Sat 9.30–11.30am) are along Lebuh Pantai, including Standard Chartered and HSBC Bank, but since they charge a hefty commission, the licensed moneychangers on Lebuh Pantai, Lebuh Chulia and Jalan Masjid Kapitan Kling (daily 8.30am–6pm) are preferable – they charge no commission and their rates are often better.

Bike rental Outlets on Lebuh Chulia rent out motorbikes (RM20 a day) and bicycles (RM8 a day). Try Tanjung Mutiara Mini Market at no. 417B or Sam Bookstore at no. 473.

Bookshops United Books Ltd, Jalan Penang, has a large selection of English-language books. There are several bookshops in the KOMTAR building, including Popular Books on the second floor. Times Books in the nearby Lifestyle department store also has a good selection. In addition, there are a few secondhand bookshops on Lebuh Chulia, the best of which is Sam Bookstore at no. 473 (the friendly and enterprising owner also rents bikes, books tickets, handles Thai visas, and stores luggage).

Car rental Avis, at the airport ☎04/643 9633; Hertz, 38 Lebuh Farquhar ☎04/263 5914 and at the airport ☎04/643 0208; Orix, at the airport ☎04/644 4772. See also p.56.

Consulates Australia: c/o Denis Mark Lee, 1C Lorong Hutton ☎04/263 3320; Indonesia: 467 Jalan Burma ☎04/227 4686; Thailand: 1 Jalan Tunku Abdul Rahman ☎04/262 8029; UK: Standard Chartered Bank Chambers, Lebuh Pantai ☎04/262 5333. There is no representation here for citizens of the USA, Canada, Ireland or New Zealand – KL has the nearest offices (see p.146).

Hospitals Adventist Hospital, Jalan Burma (☎04/226 1133; to get there, take blue bus #93 or minibus #26, #31 or #88 or Transitlink #202 or #212); General Hospital, Jalan Utama (☎04/229 3333).

Internet access As well as a few places in the KOMTAR building, you'll find no shortage of Internet terminals on and around Lebuh Chulia (see map of Central Georgetown for locations). The going rate is around RM2 for half an hour, although The Big Apple at 94 Love Lane charges only RM1.

Pharmacy There are several along Jalan Penang (10am–6pm).

Police The police headquarters is on Jalan Penang; in emergencies call ☎999.

Post office The General Post Office is on Lebuh Downing (Mon–Fri 8.30am–5pm, Sat 8.30am–4pm). The efficient poste restante/general delivery office is here; a parcel-wrapping service is available at book and stationery shops on Lebuh Chulia.

Sport You can play golf at Bukit Jambul Country Club, 2 Jalan Bukit Jambul (☎04/644 2255; green fee RM74), or the Penang Turf Club Golf (☎04/226 6701; green fees RM84). There's racing at the Penang Turf Club, Jalan Batu Gantung (☎04/226 6701) – see the local paper for fixtures. You can swim at the Pertama Sports Complex, Paya Terubong, near Ayer Itam (daily 9–11am & 4–9pm; RM4).

Telephone offices Calls within Penang made from public telephone booths cost a flat rate of 10 sen. For international calls you can buy a phonecard or use the Telekom office at the GPO on Lebuh Downing, open 24 hours.

Travel agents Try MSL Travel in the *Angora Hotel*, 202 Jalan Macalister, for student and youth travel. There are a large number of other agencies along Lebuh Chulia.

Visa extensions Pejabat Imigresen, Lebuh Pantai, on the corner of Lebuh Light (☎04/261 5122). For on-the-spot visa renewals.

The northern coast

The narrow strip, about 15km in length, along Pulau Pinang's **north coast** has been aggressively marketed since the early days of package tourism in the 1970s. The area already feels overdeveloped, but there are huge apartment buildings still springing up.

Hemmed in by the densely forested interior, this stretch of coast is punctuated by a series of bays and beaches, linked by a twisting road lined with resort hotels which advertise themselves as being part of the "Pearl of the Orient". However, the filthy ocean rather detracts from this image, and there's nothing here to touch the east coast waters of the Peninsula. There are three main developments strung out along the northern coast: Tanjung Bungah, Batu Ferringhi and Teluk Bahang. The first two have arisen purely to serve the needs of tourism; this is particularly obvious at Tanjung Bungah, where you wonder if there are any locals at all. Occupied for the most part by a string of deluxe resorts, **Batu Ferringhi** is the biggest of the three, and has gone a fair way towards establishing a community and spirit of its own, while **Teluk Bahang**, with just one modern hotel, is the only place to maintain its fishing-village roots. If you want to stay at any of the beaches, it's wise to ring the hotels and guesthouses first to check on space, especially during Christmas, Easter and *Hari Raya*.

Batu Ferringhi

BATU FERRINGHI ("White Man's Rock"), a twenty-minute bus ride from Georgetown on Transitlink #202 or Transitlink air-con #93 (but not the standard #93), was a popular hippie hangout in the 1970s. Things have changed dramatically since then. Now there are high-rises towering all along the far from pristine beach, as well as expensive restaurants and shops. A fair number of Batu Ferringhi's visitors are moneyed and from the Middle East. For them it seems the existence of a beach is inconsequential – they have come for shopping and eating during the day, and drinking at night in the bars and discos. If your main interest is swimming or snorkelling, or if you've spent some time at one of the beaches on the east coast and are looking for more of the same, you'll be sorely disappointed. The sand and sea, simply put, are dirty.

Orientation is very simple: the road – along which all the hotels and restaurants are lined up – runs more or less straight along the coast for 3km. The centre, such as it is, lies between two bridges a couple of kilometres apart and has a Telekom office, post office and police station, almost opposite which are a mosque and a clinic; the bus from Georgetown stops here, and will take you wherever you want along the main road if you ask. There are several **Internet** cafés and **moneychangers** along the main road. Happily for visitors with money, every major hotel has a pool. During the day the trinket stalls, tailors' shops and street hawkers remain fairly unobtrusive, but when the sun goes down the road comes alive with brightly lit stalls selling batik, T-shirts and fake designer watches.

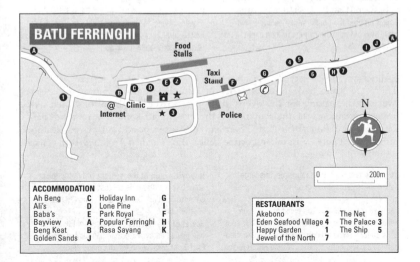

Accommodation

Towards the western end of Batu Ferringhi there's a small enclave of **budget guesthouses** facing the beach, reached by the road next to the *Guan Guan Café*. The standards tend to be lower than in Georgetown and the prices higher. If you come here by taxi, just have the taxi drop you on the main road (near the post office), as they will charge you a RM10 commission if they take you directly to a guesthouse. Independent travellers don't get particularly good deals in the expensive **hotels**, most of whose business is with tour groups, but it's definitely worth enquiring about discounts, as there are often special offers of up to fifty percent off the advertised rate during non-peak times.

Budget

Ah Beng ℡04/881 1036. This is a serene, family-run place with polished wood floors, a communal balcony overlooking the sea, and a washing machine. Fan rooms ❷; en suite with air-con ❸.

Ali's ℡04/881 1316, ✉alisgues@tm.net.my. This very popular place fills up early, and for good reason. It's the best budget place on the beach, with a relaxing open-air café and garden, and a pleasant wooden veranda. A five-bed dorm is the cheapest place to stay in town. Dorm ❶; fan rooms ❷.

Baba's ℡04/881 1686. A spotless and friendly guesthouse with a sea-view communal balcony. Fan rooms ❷; en suite with air-con ❸.

Beng Keat ℡ & ℡04/881 1907. Set away from the beach, this friendly place has clean, comfortable en-suite rooms with hot shower, plus a garden and a small kitchen for self-catering as well as a laundry and book exchange. Each room has a tiny veranda with table and chairs. Good value. ❷

Moderate and expensive

Bayview ℡04/881 2123, ✉bbr@po.jaring.my. This is grander than most, with a ballroom and glass lifts, but no more expensive than some of its neighbours. ❼

Golden Sands ℡04/881 1911, ⊛www.shangri-la.com. This plush mid-size resort hotel has a comfortable open-air lobby and many sports activities available. ❾

Holiday Inn ℡04/881 1601, ⊛www.penang.holiday-inn.com. Well-appointed rooms, some with parquet flooring. Their kids' club makes this a good option for families. ❽

Lone Pine ℡04/881 1511, ⊛www.lonepinehotel.com. Established in 1948, this boutique hotel situated around a colonial-era bungalow was the first in Batu Ferringhi. It's now been refurbished along clean modern lines. Its seaside *Bungalow Restaurant* serves Hainanese and Western cuisine. ❽

Park Royal ℡04/881 1133, ℻881 2233. Recently renovated, this medium-rise hotel boasts an elegant colonial-style Indonesian restaurant, *Tiffins*. There's also a Japanese restaurant. ❼

Popular Ferringhi Motel and Restaurant ℡04/881 3333, ℻881 3494. Set back from the beach behind a row of restaurants, this place has better air-con rooms than the beachfront backpackers' places. ❸

Rasa Sayang Resort & Spa ℡04/881 1811, ⊛www.shangri-la.com. This classy low-rise hotel boasts traditional Malay architecture with its Minangkabau-style roofs. ❾

Eating and drinking

There are some budget **restaurants** in Batu Ferringhi, but most places are overpriced, catering for the overspill from the large hotels, all of which have several restaurants of their own. By the beach are some cheap food stalls, including the *Rastafarian Café*. There are also some good (but pricey) seafood restaurants. There's a **hawker centre** called the *Matahari Food and Beer Garden* near the first bridge.

Akebono Just north of the mosque, this large Japanese restaurant has good-value set lunches at RM12.

Eden Seafood Village The boast at this huge beachfront place is "Anything that swims, we cook it". A cultural show accompanies the evening meal, but you'll pay a hefty price, at around RM20 a dish.

Happy Garden At the western end of the main strip, this restaurant is set just off the road in a colourful garden. Serves good-value Chinese and Western food.

Jewel of the North Located east of the stream, this place has tasty North Indian food at around RM15 per dish. Open for lunch and dinner.

The Net Inexpensive banana-leaf curries served from 10.30am to 2.30pm, as well as other South Indian meals at lunchtime and evenings.

The Palace Across from the mosque, this colourfully decorated restaurant serves Western as well as Indian food at RM5–12 per dish. Open for lunch and dinner.

Teluk Bahang

Five kilometres west of Batu Ferringhi, the small fishing kampung of **TELUK BAHANG** is the place to come to escape the development. Towards the western end of the village, the long spindly pier, with its multitude of fishing boats, is the focus of daily life. The small path which disappears into the forest beyond the pier is the start of a two-hour trek west to the lighthouse at **Muka Head**, a rocky headland where the beaches are better than the ones at Teluk Bahang itself; however, since the big hotels run boat trips out there, it's unlikely that you'll have the sands to yourself. Just to the south is a Butterfly Farm and Forest Recreation Park and the Penang Cultural Centre (see p.219).

Practicalities

Accommodation in Teluk Bahang is limited. The very friendly *Rama's Guest House* (☎04/885 1179; ❶) is a hippie homestay that survived the 1970s, with some dorm beds (RM8) as well as two fan rooms (RM15) with use of kitchen facilities; take the north (beachward) turn at the Teluk Bahang roundabout and it's about 25m down the road on the right. Further along the beach past the bridge is the *Fisherman's Village* (❶), with simple rooms in a Malay family home. At the other end of the scale, the beautifully decorated *Penang Mutiara* (☎04/885 2828, ℱ885 2829; ❾), on the eastern end of the shore road, has a good range of restaurants, watersports and a better beach than its rivals in Batu Ferringhi, though it's considerably more expensive. There's also one mid-range option, the *Hotbay* (❸), between the *Mutiara* and the roundabout, with simple fan or air-con en-suite rooms.

Teluk Bahang's real attraction is its plethora of inexpensive **places to eat** on the little stretch of main road, including an excellent seafood restaurant (open daily 6–10pm) called *The End of the World*, just by the pier. Off the northeast corner of the roundabout is *Restoran Khaleel*, which serves tasty and inexpensive *nasi campur*, banana *roti*s and ice cream. Set in a park incorporating traditional buildings from the nation's states, the *Istana Malay Theatre Restaurant* (☎04/885 1175) features a nightly traditional dinner and dance show from 6pm to 10.30pm, which will put you back around RM130.

The rest of the island

Given that all the accommodation on Penang island is either in Georgetown, near the airport or on the north coast, seeing the **rest of the island** generally means making day-trips. Public transport takes in most of the points of interest picked out below; indeed, it's possible to do a circuitous day-trip by bus: yellow buses #66 and #352 head southwest from Georgetown via Jelutong to Balik Pulau, from where yellow bus #76 (4 daily) continues to Teluk Bahang; here you can change to blue bus #93, which heads east through Batu Ferringhi and back to Georgetown. You'll need to leave Georgetown by 8 or 9am in order to complete your trip the same day. However, getting around by bus rather misses the point, which is to get away from the main road and explore the jungle, beaches and kampungs at leisure. It's much better to **rent a motorbike**, or even a **bicycle**, from one of the outlets on Lebuh Chulia – the bus circuit already mentioned is a seventy-kilometre round trip, so you have to be fairly fit to accomplish it using pedal-power, especially since some parts of the road are very steep. Once clear of the outskirts of Georgetown the traffic eases up; the interior is blissfully free of traffic, though it can get busy along the northern and eastern shore roads.

South from Georgetown to Gertak Sanggul

The road south from Pengkalan Weld in Georgetown heads past the university to the **Snake Temple**, 12km from the city (reachable on yellow bus #66). This is a major attraction for Asian bus-tour groups and the usual souvenir and food stalls clutter the otherwise impressive entrance which is guarded by two stone lions. The temple was founded in memory of Chor Soo King, a monk who arrived from China over a hundred years ago and gained local fame as a healer. His statue sits in the main square in front of the temple, clothed in red and yellow. Inside, draped lazily over parts of the altar, are a handful of poisonous green snakes (mostly Wagler's pit vipers) which, legend has it, mysteriously appeared upon completion of the temple in 1850 and have made the temple their refuge ever since. The snakes seem rather lethargic and the temple caretaker says that their fangs have been pulled out. He also claims that it's safe to have your photograph taken with the snakes curled around your neck and shoulders, and he'll charge you RM10 if you choose to do so. He'll even snap the photo for you if you've come alone. Don't, however, come crying to us if you try this and get bitten.

Continuing south, the road leads past the airport at Bayan Lepas to **Batu Maung**, 7km from the Snake Temple, which can also be reached directly on yellow bus #68 or #96, or minibus #27 or Transitlink #303, all of which leave from Georgetown's KOMTAR building. Apart from the pretty coastal scenery, the only other reason to come here is to visit the **Penang War Museum** (daily 9am–7pm), located on the site of a British military fortress built in the 1930s. Situated on twenty acres of land, the fort was blasted and dug into the hill by local labourers. It includes underground tunnels, an observation tower, a cook house and an infirmary. Backtrack a couple of kilometres to Bayan Lepas and carry on west for 3km along the main road to reach **Teluk Kumbar**, where the sea looks particularly uninviting and the beach, though reasonable, gets very crowded at weekends. West of here, the four-kilometre stretch of road along the south coast towards **Gertak Sanggul** is one of the most attractive parts of the island, gently winding and tree-lined, with the odd tantalizing glimpse of glittering ocean. The road ends at a scenic bay where you can watch the local fishing boats at work. It's possible to reach Gertak Sanggul directly from Georgetown on yellow **bus** #67 or #80 from the KOMTAR building.

North to Teluk Bahang

Just to the east of Teluk Kumbar, the road north winds steeply up to the village of **Barat**, where you have the choice of heading northeast to **Balik Pulau** or southwest to **Pulau Betong**. Neither are particularly enthralling, though there's something attractive in the quiet pace of life and the friendliness of the local people. Balik Pulau is probably the better choice, simply because of the string of good cafés along the main road.

Back on the main road, the route climbs very steeply as it winds round the jungle-clad hillside, offering the occasional view over the flat, forested plain which stretches toward the sea. A couple of kilometres from the turning for Sungai Pinang are the disappointing **Titi Kerawang Waterfalls**, outside the rainy season little more than a dismal, rubbish-strewn trickle; however, they're worth a stop to buy fresh fruit from the roadside stalls. Continue 1km further to the **Tropical Fruit Farm** (daily 9am–6pm; ☎04/866 5168), where over two hundred varieties of tropical and sub-tropical fruits are grown on 25 hectares. A tour of the farm, which includes a fresh fruit platter, costs RM20. They also run their own buses to several hotels in town, but this will almost double the fee. The road then levels and straightens out for the next 4km before reaching the **Forest Recreation Park** (Tues–Sun 9am–5pm; free) on the east side of the road. The museum here (RM1) introduces visitors to the different types of forest on Penang, and there are several well-marked forest trails and a children's playground nearby. They also run guided jungle discovery tours (2–5 hrs; RM13–33). If you're joining a tour, you can be picked up from various hotels in town (transportation RM5–10 extra). Another kilometre further along the road to Teluk Bahang is the **Butterfly Farm** (Mon–Fri 9am–5pm, Sat & Sun 9am–6pm; RM4). This is home to all manner of creepy-crawlies, including frogs, snakes, stick insects and scorpions, as well as four thousand butterflies of around 120 different species. Also nearby is a **Batik Factory** (9am–6pm; free) where you can watch Malaysian-style batik being made and buy the finished product. Less than 1km further north is the roundabout at Teluk Bahang (see p.217). Nearby is the newly built **Penang Cultural Centre,** which has daily "cultural tours" that include guided tours of examples of Malay architecture, as well as demonstrations of Malay dance and even a mock Muslim wedding ceremony. Each tour lasts a couple of hours, and there's a nightly dinner show at 6pm. Reservations can be booked through major hotels, or travel agencies along Lebuh Chulia in Georgetown. A right turn here brings you onto the northern coastal road, 20km or so from Georgetown.

Sungai Petani and around

From Butterworth, the train line and highways run north, into the state of **Kedah** and through the small town of **Sungai Petani**, 35km away. Few people stop here, but those who do are drawn by two fairly specialist attractions: the **archeological remains** at Lembah Bujang (Bujang Valley) 10km further northwest; and **Gunung Jerai** (Kedah Peak), 9km north of the valley.

The Town

SUNGAI PETANI is the nearest point from which to reach both the Bujang Valley and Kedah Peak. If you plan to visit both Lembah Bujang and Gunung Jerai in one day, you'll need to stay overnight at one of Sungai Petani's few **hotels**, which are close to the centre; otherwise, you can just make a short detour from Sungai Petani and continue on from there to your next destination, as there's no particular reason to stay in Sungai Petani itself.

A clock tower dominates Jalan Ibrahim, the main north–south road through town; from here, a side road directly to the east leads to the **train station**. One block south of the clock tower, another side road branching east, Jalan Kuala Ketil, crosses over the tracks and leads to the **express bus stop** – little more than a yard and some food stalls. A further block south and to the west is Jalan Petri, which continues west past the local bus station, taxi stand and budget **hotels**.

West along Jalan Petri from the local bus station, at no. 7 is the *Duta* (☎04/421 2040; ❸), which is the best-value option in town, with large, colourful and comfortable en-suite rooms and friendly, well-informed staff. Satellite TV, air-con and hot showers await at the *Seri Malaysia* (☎04/423 6524, ⓕ423 4106; ❺),

A short history of Kedah

Kedah's history is a sad catalogue of invasion and subjugation, mainly by the Thais, lasting more or less up until the beginning of the twentieth century. The state has long been noted for its **independent spirit**: an eleventh-century Chola-dynasty tablet inscription mentions "Kadaram [Kedah] of fierce strength". By the thirteenth century, Kedah was already asserting its own economic superiority over the Srivijaya Empire (see p.728) by sending ships to India to trade jungle products for such exotic goods as Arabian glass and Chinese porcelain. Despite becoming a vassal state of **Ayuthaya** – the mighty Thai kingdom – during the mid-seventeenth century, Kedah still managed to express its defiance. For decades, the Malay states had been left to get on with their own affairs, provided they sent monetary tributes to Thailand from time to time. But when, in 1645, the Kedah ruler was summoned to appear at the Thai court in person – an unprecedented request – he refused point-blank, claiming that it was beneath the dignity of a sultan to prostrate himself before another ruler. In a climb-down, the king of Ayuthaya sent a statue of himself to Kedah, instructing the court, rather hopefully, to pay homage to it twice a day. At the beginning of the nineteenth century, Kedah's relationship with its Thai conquerors degenerated into a **jihad**, or holy war, led by Sultan Ahmad. The strength of religious feeling frightened the Bangkok government, who deposed Ahmad, but in 1842 the British, anxious to see peace in the region and realizing the strength of Ahmad's hold over his people, forced the sultan's reinstatement. Even this gesture had little effect on stubborn Kedah: as recently as the beginning of the twentieth century, when Kedah was transferred by the Thais to British control, it adamantly refused to become part of the Federated Malay States.

at 21 Jalan Pasar, just two minutes' walk north of the express bus stand, but it's rather grubby for the price. For good cheap Malay and Indian **food**, try *Restauran Lih Pin*, across from the *Duta* hotel. Further west along Jalan Petri, the *Restauran Bee Ah Ton*, is a more stylish *kopitiam*. For Chinese food, there's a restaurant at the *Lucky Hotel* on the other side of Jalan Petri, and a small but lively **night market** one block north on Jalan Dewa – the street leading north from the local bus station.

Lembah Bujang

Ten kilometres northwest of Sungai Petani, on the banks of the Sungai Bujang and in the shadow of Gunung Jerai, lies Malaysia's most important archeological site, **Lembah Bujang** proving the existence of a significant Hindu–Buddhist kingdom here as far back as the fourth century. By the seventh century the Lembah Bujang kingdom was part of the large Srivijaya Empire of Sumatra, reaching its architectural peak in the ninth and tenth centuries (contemporaneous with Borobudur in Java). The kingdom had trading ties with the Khmers of Cambodia and was visited by the Chinese monk I-Tsing in 671. In 1025, Lembuh Bujang was attacked by the Chola Kingdom of India, but later formed an alliance with the Cholas against the waning Srivijaya Empire. Trading continued, but by the fourteenth century Lembah Bujang's significance had faded, and with the rise of Islam the temples were left to the jungle.

Much of the country's history before 1400 had been somewhat sketchily pieced together from unreliable or contradictory contemporaneous accounts. In the early nineteenth century, James Low, a member of the Madras Army stationed at Penang and a keen amateur archeologist, discovered "the relics of a Hindoo colony" in the Bujang Valley. This gave credence to the prevailing theory that Hinduism was the dominant ideology in early Malaya. However, early-twentieth-century excavations have revealed fifty or so **Buddhist temples** (known as *candi*s) in the Bujang basin, creating a controversy in academic circles.

Candi Bukit Batu Pahat, one of the tenth-century temples now reconstructed on the Lembah Bujang site, incorporates the styles of not only Mahayana Buddhism but also the cults of Shiva and Vishnu. The fact that India – the birthplace of Hinduism and Buddhism – has no direct equivalent of this architecture signifies that the religions must have been adapted to the local culture, creating a modified theology. Like the Hindu-Buddhist temples at Angkor in Cambodia, these ruins are remnants of a local interpretation of the ancient South Asian religions – at least that is the official word. Not surprisingly, to Malaysian archeologists, who are almost exclusively ethnic-Malay, the idea that there could be Indian ruins in Malaysia that predated anything Malay is highly controversial.

Since excavations are still taking place, most of the site is off-limits to the public, but you can visit the **archeological museum** (daily 9am–4pm, Fri 9am–12.15pm & 2.45–4pm; free), which displays photographs of some of the finds *in situ*, as well as a number of relocated carved stone pillars, pots and jewels. The historical information is fairly turgidly written and there are precious few contextual comments on the artefacts. Behind the museum, eight *candi*s (including Candi Bukit Batu Pahat) have been reconstructed using original materials. The entire complex is in a pleasant park setting alongside the Sungai Bujang – a good place for watching **butterflies**. It's easy to see why this area was attractive as a temple site: with Gunung Jerai as a backdrop and granite easily available from the outcrops in the river (the boreholes are still visible), it's both a practical and aesthetic location. There's a snackshop on the premises.

Getting there from Sungai Petani's local bus station is quite straightforward with a local (blue) bus (hourly; 30min journey) signposted for Merbok or Tanjung Dawai. Ask the bus driver to let you off in Merbok, a small village with one main road; follow the signpost for the museum for 2km through fruit orchards. To catch the bus back to Sungai Petani, you need to flag it down – locals can show you where. **Accommodation** is available at the nearby *Damai Park Resort* (signposted off the road from Merbok; ☏04/457 3340; fan ❹, a/c ❺), which has several clean en-suite chalets dotted around a shady park planted with fruit trees. There's a large clean dorm up a hill where RM15 gets you a mattress on the floor; kitchen facilities are available. It's a lovely quiet retreat during the week – all you hear are the sounds of the nearby stream; that said, it can get busy at weekends, when advance **reservations** are often necessary.

Gunung Jerai

Dominating the landscape, **Gunung Jerai** (1200m) is a massive limestone outcrop 9km north of Lembah Bujang as the crow flies. It's the highest peak in Kedah, and on clear days offers panoramic views over the rolling rice fields stretching up to Perlis in the north, and along the coastline from Penang to Langkawi. Gunung Jerai is replete with history and legend; tales abound of the infamous **Raja Bersiong** ("the king with fangs") who once held court over the ancient kingdom of Langkasuka, and archeological digs here have revealed the existence of a water temple (Candi Telaga Sembilan) which many believe was the private pool of Raja Bersiong. A few hours is enough to stroll around the **Sungai Teroi Forest Recreation Park** halfway up the mountain, with its rare orchids and wildlife including the lesser mouse deer and the long-tailed macaque, for which the conservation area is renowned. At the top of the path leading to the recreation park is a **Museum of Forestry** (daily 9am–3pm; free), which is of limited interest.

The jumping-off point for Gunung Jerai is just north of the town of **Gurun**, on Route 1. Local bus #2 from Sungai Petani (every 30min; 30min) drops you at the bottom of the mountain, from where you can walk up to the summit (a gentle two-hour climb) or get one of the **jeeps** that make the journey up every 45 minutes (daily 8.30am–5pm; RM5 return). On the peak a small settlement offers a pleasant overnight stay at the one **hotel**, the *Peranginan Gunung Jerai* (☎04/423 4345; ❹), which has a restaurant as well as tents for those who prefer sleeping alfresco (RM30).

Alor Setar and around

The last major stop before the Thai border, **ALOR SETAR**, the tidy state capital of Kedah, is a city keen to preserve its heritage, a fact attested to by its many royal buildings and museums. Though little-visited by tourists, it's a clean and compact city with a pleasant sea-breeze and enough architectural interest to make it a good place to stop and relax on your way to or from Thailand. Something of Kedah's past (see box, p.220) is evidenced by the many Thais still living in Alor Setar today, worshipping in the splendidly restored Thai temple and running businesses and restaurants. For all that, Alor Setar is one of the most Malay towns you'll find on the west coast, sustained in part by the predominance of Islam which, throughout the years of external domination, played an important part in the maintenance of traditional Malay values. It's a fact worth

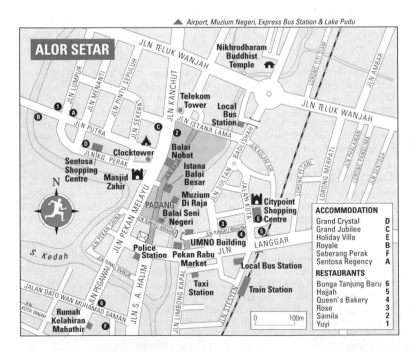

keeping in mind for women just returning from Thailand or Langkawi: shorts and sleeveless tops are better left on the beach. Alor Setar has also been the hometown of two of Malaysia's prime ministers: Tunku Abdul Rahman and Mahathir Mohamad.

Arrival and information

Located on Route 1 and the main west-coast train line, Alor Setar is something of a **transport hub**, with connections to Thailand and Singapore, as well as most cities on the Peninsula. Alor Setar's huge Shahab Perdana **express bus station** is located 5km north of the centre. Shahab Perdana is well connected to the city by municipal buses (60 sen) and taxis (RM7). Buses coming from the south usually stop in town first, so if you're staying in Alor Setar, get off in front of the large UMNO Building on Jalan Tungku Ibrahim. If you miss the stop, you can easily catch a local bus back into town from Shahab Perdana. Buses leave Shahab Perdana every fifteen minutes for the twelve-kilometre journey to the jetty at **Kuala Kedah**, from where ferries set sail for **Pulau Langkawi**. Shahab Perdana is also a departure point for the bus service to Kangar, from where there's a connecting service to the Langkawi ferry jetty at Kuala Perlis (however, from Alor Setar it's more convenient to take the ferry via Kuala Kedah). Buses to **Thailand** only go as far as the border, where you'll have to change to a Thai bus bound for Hat Yai or Bangkok. Confusingly, there are also several **local bus stations** in town; these all connect with Shahab Perdana as well as some local destinations. These buses also stop opposite the Pekan Rabu market on Jalan Tunku Ibrahim.

The **train** station, unsurprisingly on Jalan Stesyen, is just a minute's walk south of the local bus station. Alor Setar is a principal station on the west-coast route and a place to pick up the express train to Hat Yai and Bangkok. You can also take a **taxi** from the taxi station south of the Pekan Rabu market to the Thai border (RM33; 2hr), then transfer to a Thai taxi for the onward journey to Hat Yai (60km). The domestic **airport** (MAS office ☎04/721 1186), 11km north of town, is accessible by the hourly Kepala Batas bus from Shahab Perdana, or by taxi (around RM10); AirAsia has an office here too.

Most of the major **banks** are on Jalan Raja. There are many **cyber-cafés** in the Citypoint shopping centre.

Accommodation

Most of Alor Setar's hotels are in the mid-range category and they are generally well run with friendly staff.

Grand Crystal 40 Jalan Kampung Perak ☎04/731 3333, ⓕ731 6368. Reasonable business-class hotel with a pool. Rates include breakfast. ❺
Grand Jubilee 429 Jalan Kanchut ☎ & ⓕ04/733 0055. Friendly place with simple en-suite fan and air-con rooms. ❸
Holiday Villa Southeast corner of the Citypoint shopping centre, Jalan Tunku Ibrahim ☎04/734 9999, ⓦwww.holidayvilla.com.my. By far the most luxurious hotel in town, with tastefully appointed rooms, a classy lobby and nice views from the upper floors. Amenities include a pool and fitness centre. ❼
Royale 97 Jalan Putra ☎04/733 0921, ⓕ733 0925. This clean and bright hotel with

well-equipped rooms has a quiet riverside location and friendly staff. Good value. Recommended. ❹
Hotel Seberang Perak Lorong Kilang Ais, Jalan Dato' Wan Muhamad Saman ☎04/772 4329, ⓔibsoew@pd.jaring.my. Right behind the Ruhmah Kelahiran Mahathir, this friendly family-run hotel has small, pink-painted, basic but clean rooms with air-con and attached (Asian) toilets and shower. ❸
Sentosa Regency Hotel 250A-F Jalan Putra ☎04/730 3999, ⓦwww.sentosaregencyhotel .com. Business hotel with plush lobby and comfortable rooms. There's a gym and restaurant. Rate includes buffet breakfast ❻

The Town

The River Sungai Kedah runs along the western and southern outskirts of Alor Setar. The main sights are located in the west of the town around the padang, which has a large modern fountain at its centre. The area just to the west is dominated by impressive **Masjid Zahir**, claimed to be the oldest in Malaysia. Facing the mosque, the elegant **Istana Balai Besar** (Royal Audience Hall) – the principal official building during the eighteenth century – stands serene on the grounds of the padang. The present two-storey, open-colonnaded structure dates back only to 1904, when the original hall was rebuilt to host the marriages of Sultan Abdul Hamid's five eldest children. So grand was the refurbishment and so lavish the ceremony that the state was nearly bankrupted.

Just behind the Balai Besar, the old royal palace now serves as the **Muzium Di Raja** (daily 10am–6pm, closed Fri noon–2pm; free), an excellent way of preserving this dainty little 1930s building. The museum has its fair share of eulogistic memorabilia – medals and fond recollections of the current sultan's salad days – and some of the rooms have been kept exactly as they were used by the sultan and his family.

Across the way stands a curious octagonal tower, the **Balai Nobat**, housing the sacred instruments of the royal orchestra; unfortunately, the tower and its contents are not open for public view. Played only during royal ceremonies, the collection consists of three ornate silver drums, a gong, a long trumpet and a double-reeded instrument similar to the oboe, which combine to produce the haunting strains of *nobat* music (the name derives from a Persian word for a very large kettle drum, played in Malay royal palaces). Since the instruments are regarded as the most treasured part of the sultan's regalia, so the musicians themselves are given a special title, *Orang Kalur*, relating to the time when they were also keepers of the royal records. The Kedah Nobat, the oldest and most famous of these ensembles, played at the installation of independent Malaya's first constitutional monarch in 1947.

Just north of the padang on Jalan Kanchut is the **Telekom Tower** (daily 10am–10pm), the most modern sight in Alor Setar. A mini-version of the one in KL, it has a fast-food restaurant and viewing gallery. Continue north from here and then east along Jalan Telok Wanjah and you'll come to the **Nikhrodharam Buddhist Temple**, just beside the roundabout. The building of this glittering temple complex, decorated with many colourful statues, mosaics and paintings, began in the 1950s and was only finished in 1995. A match for many in Thailand, it is a testimony to the continuing influence of Thai culture in the city.

On the padang's south side, the grandiose, white-stucco **Balai Seni Negeri** (daily 10am–6pm, Fri closed noon–2pm; free) is an art gallery that was closed for renovation at time of writing. South of the padang, across the Sungai Kedah, is **Rumah Kelahiran Mahathir** (Tues–Sun 10am–5pm, closed fri noon–3pm; free), at 18 Lorong Kilang Ais, the birthplace and family home of Dr Mahathir Mohamad. It's now a museum, documenting the life of the local doctor who became the most powerful Malaysian prime minister of modern times. Even if you're not interested in Mahathir himself, it's worth taking a glimpse inside his former house to get an idea of what traditional middle-class Malay houses looked like in the Fifties.

For a glimpse of contemporary culture, head for the **Pekan Rabu**, a daily market running from morning to midnight. Situated in a large building on Jalan Tunku Ibrahim, it comprises a large collection of stalls selling everything from handicrafts to local farm produce, a good place to sample traditional Kedah food like *dodol durian*, a sweet cake made from the notoriously pungent durian fruit. South of here, past the police station on Jalan S. A. Halim, you can book evening **river cruises** (RM30 per hour) from the *Flora Inn*. The boat will stop at a village along the way, where you can observe the preparation of the local sweet *dodol*.

Hop on any bus heading north from Jalan Penak Melayu, adjacent to the padang, and after about 1500m you'll pass the **Muzium Negeri** (Tues–Sun 10am–6pm, closed Fri noon–3pm; free). On Jalan Lebuhraya Darulaman, it contains some background information on the archeological finds at Lembah Bujang (see p.220). Close to the entrance, there's a delicate silver tree, known as the *bunga mas dan perak* ("the gold and silver flowers"). The name refers to a practice, established in the seventeenth century, of honouring the ruling government of Thailand by a triennial presentation of two small trees of gold and silver, about 1m in height, meticulously detailed even down to the birds nesting in their branches. The cost of these ornaments was estimated at over a thousand Spanish dollars, no mean sum for those times. While the tradition was seen by Ayuthaya as a recognition of its suzerainty, Kedah rulers considered the gift a show of goodwill and friendship – characteristically refusing to acknowledge their vassal status.

Eating

Despite Alor Setar's Malay overtones, its restaurant sector seems to be predominantly Chinese. Chinatown is around the veritable restaurant row of Jalan Putera to the east of the padang, where there are also lots of hawkers to choose from. You'd also do well to sample some Thai cuisine while in town.

Hajjah Opposite Citypoint on Jalan Tungku Ibrahim. This is a good place to try Thai seafood dishes.
Queen's Bakery At 33 Jalan Tunku Ibrahim, this diner-style restaurant has a good variety of breads and cakes as well as ice-cream sundaes.
Restoran Bunga Tanjung Baru On the corner of Jalan Pegawai and Jalan Dato Wan Muhamad Saman, near the Rumah Kelahiran Mahatir, you'll find this eatery offering South Indian fare.

Restoran Yuyi Located underneath the shade of a banyan tree on the corner of Jalan Putra and Jalan Lumpur, this is the place to come for cheap Chinese vegetarian food.
Rose Restaurant On Jalan Sultan Badlishah, this place has dooont South Indian food
Samila Hotel Restaurant On the northwest corner of the padang. Head here if you're in the mood for Western food.

Pulau Langkawi

Situated 30km off the coast, at the very northwestern tip of the Peninsula, is a cluster of 104 tropical islands known collectively as **LANGKAWI**. The archipelago's beauty has fostered many traditional stories, so much so that Langkawi has become known as the "Islands of Legends". In true Malay fashion, almost every major landmark here has a myth associated with it, each story hijacked by the tourist authorities to promote the islands. Most are little more than tiny, deserted, scrub-clad rocks jutting out of the sea; only three are inhabited, including the largest of the group, **Pulau Langkawi** (around 500 square kilometres), once a haven for pirates, now a sought-after refuge for wealthy tourists. With the encouragement of its biggest fan, Dr Mahathir, who once worked here as a doctor, Pulau Langkawi has in recent years seen unparalleled development, enhanced by its duty-free status, making it Malaysia's premier island retreat. Some of the country's most luxurious hotels are here, and a new airport has been built to cope with the increasing number of visitors. Langkawi is not a

△ Pulau Langkawi beach

budget destination: to appreciate all the islands have to offer, you need to spend quite a bit of money, though you could scrape by on RM100 a day if all you do is sit on the beach.

Most of Pulau Langkawi's inhabitants still live simply, in a traditional fashion. Consequently, its natural attractions – a mountainous interior, white sands, limestone outcrops and lush vegetation – have remained relatively unspoiled despite development along the shores. The island's charms consist largely of lazing around on beaches and enjoying the sunshine, although you can also visit various splendid waterfalls and the **Telaga Air Panas** hot springs, or take a gondola to the top of **Gunung Mat Cincang**. Parts of Langkawi were affected by the tsunami of 2004, but you'd never know it today.

The principal town on the island is **Kuah**, a boom town of hotels and shops in the southeast of the island, where you'll find most of the duty-free bargains. The main tourist development has taken place around two bays on the western side of the island, at **Pantai Tengah** and **Pantai Cenang**. The former is the more commercialized, although there is some budget accommodation available on both beaches. More recent building work has taken place at two beaches on the north coast, **Pantai Datai** and **Tanjung Rhu**, where accommodation is limited to top-class resorts.

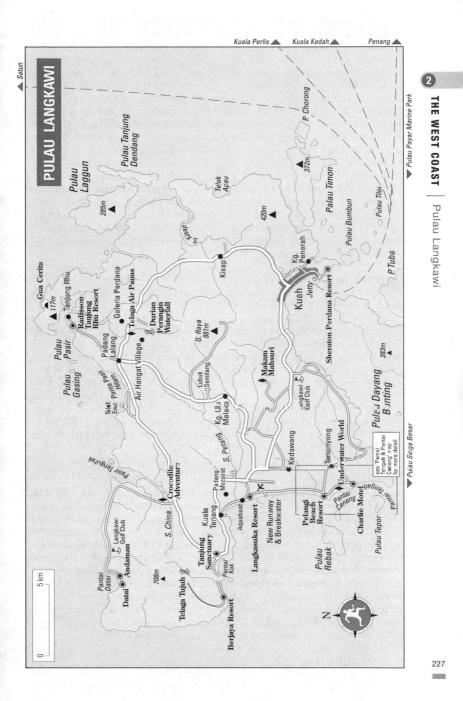

PULAU LANGKAWI

Satun ▲

Kuala Perlis ▲   Kuala Kedah ▲   Penang ▲

▼ Pulau Payar Marine Park

Pulau Laggun

Pulau Tanjung Dendang

P. Chorong

285m ▲

372m ▲

Teluk Apau

▶ Pulau Tiloi

Pulau Timon

420m ▲

Kisap

Kg. Penerah

Pulau Bumbun

P.Tuba

Kuah

Jetty

Sheraton Perdana Resort

Pulau Dayang Bunting

283m ▲

Gua Cerita

117m ▲

Tanjung Rhu

Radisson Tanjung Rhu Resort

Pulau Pasir

Galeria Perdana

Telaga Air Panas

Durian Perangin Waterfall

G. Raya 881m ▲

Makam Mahsuri

Langkawi Golf Club

Pulau Gasing

Padang Lalang

Air Hangat Village

Lubuk Semilang

Kg. Ulu Melaka

Kedawang

Temonyong

Pantai Pasir Hitam

S. Kisap

S. Petang

Underwater World

Pulau Singa Besar ▼

Toilet ▲ Ewa

Pasir Tengkorak

S. China

Crocodile Adventure

Padang Matsirat

S. Petang

Kg. Ulu

New Runway & Breakwater

Pelangi Beach Resort

Pantai Cenang

Charlie Motel

Pantai Tengah

see "Pantai Tengah & Pantai Cenang" map for more detail

Pulau Tepor

Pantai Datai

Datai Andaman

Langkawi Golf Club

708m ▲

Tanjung Sanctuary

Kuala Teriang

Aquabaat

Langkasuka Resort

Pulau Rebak

Telaga Tujuh

Pantai Kok

Berjaya Resort

5 km

0

N

227

There is basically one circular route around the island, with the other main road cutting the island in two, connecting north and south; even the minor roads are well surfaced and signposted. **Public transport** around the island is limited to **taxis**, the bus companies having gone out of business due to the increasingly upmarket island clientele relying on their resorts' private coaches. Taxis on Langkawi are very expensive. A trip from the Kuah jetty to Pantai Cenang costs RM30, while a three-hour taxi tour of the island runs to around RM250 per vehicle. If you think you can handle the local driving habits, it's definitely worthwhile to **rent a car** (from RM80) or **motorbike** (RM50) for the day, and see the island at your own pace; there are plenty of rental opportunities at the Kuah jetty, in Kuah town or Pantai Cenang. Some places also rent **bicycles** for RM25 per day.

On the neighbouring islands of Pulau Singa Besar and Pulau Payar, designated **wildlife and marine parks** provide a little extra interest. You can also dive and snorkel off some of the archipelago's other, uninhabited islands, though the only way to do this is by taking an expensive day-trip, organized either by the Pulau Langkawi tourist office or one of the hotels. There's a **website** (⊛www.langkawi-online.com) which offers general information on the island as well as bookings.

Getting to Langkawi

There are ferries every day from two points on the mainland, one from **Kuala Perlis** (see p.236; 1hr; RM12 one-way), close to the Thai border, and the other from **Kuala Kedah** (see p.223; 1hr 15min; RM15 one-way), 51km to the south, just 8km from Alor Setar. Fast ferries depart at least hourly (8am–7pm) from both jetties; there's no need to book tickets in advance. All ferry services run to the **Kuah jetty** on the southeastern tip of the island, about five minutes' drive from Kuah itself. One daily passenger boat sails here from **Penang** (departing at 8.30am; 2hr 30min; RM35 one-way; the return trip departs at 5.30pm). There are also ferry services from **Thailand**: four times daily from Satun, on the border (1hr 30min; RM19). You can leave **luggage** at the ferry terminal for RM1.50. There are domestic **flights** to Pulau Langkawi from KL, Georgetown and Ipoh, and international services from Singapore and Kansai airport in Japan.

Kuah

Lining a large sweep of bay in the southeastern corner of the island, **KUAH**, with a population of thirteen thousand, is easily the largest town on Langkawi. The centre has been greatly developed in recent years, with a new ferry terminal, hotels and shopping complexes popping up all along the bay. Beside the ferry terminal is **Dataran Lang** (Eagle Square), graced by an enormous sculpture of an eagle (Langkawi means "red eagle" and you're likely to spot several brahminy kites and white-bellied fishing eagles during your stay here). Next to the square is **Lagenda Langkawi Dalan Taman** (daily 9am–9pm; RM5), a theme park based around the legends of the islands, its twenty hectares of landscaped gardens punctuated by more giant sculptures. There are vantage points over the bay and surroundings, but no shade or place to buy refreshments. Most of the hotels and shopping complexes are further around the bay.

Practicalities

Ferries run to the jetty on the southeastern tip of the island, about five minutes' drive from Kuah itself. A taxi from the jetty into Kuah costs around RM10.

The **airport** (☎04/955 1311) is 20km west of Kuah, near Pantai Cenang; a taxi from here to any of the western beaches or Kuah costs less than RM60–80.

The Langkawi **tourist office** (daily except Fri 9am–5pm; ☎04/966 7789, Ⓕ966 7889) located on Jalan Persiaran Putera (the route into Kuah from the jetty) next to the mosque, has very helpful staff; there's also an information booth at the airport (same times as main tourist office). Kuah is not an unattractive place, but despite the multitude of hotels it's not somewhere you're likely to want to stay. As well as the numerous duty-free shops along the main road, selling everything from hooch to handbags, you'll find the **post office** (daily except Fri 9am–5pm), **police station** (☎04/966 6222) and **hospital** (☎04/966 3333) close to each other. Behind the MAYA shopping complex, also on the main road, are three parallel streets where all the **banks** (virtually the only places to change money on the island) and the **Telekom centre** are located. There are **Internet cafés** at Jalan Pandak Maya 1 and Jalan Pandak Maya 3. There's an MAS office (☎04/966 6622) in the Tabung Haji building.

Accommodation

As with the rest of Langkawi, there's little in the way of budget **accommodation** in Kuah. Most people head directly to one of Langkawi's beaches rather than spending the night in town. It's possible to walk to the places listed here, which are all between one and two kilometres from the jetty on the right side of the road. It's best to just head off on your own, rather than going through the agents at the ferry terminal, who'll take twenty percent commission. If you're foolish enough to take a taxi into town to look for accommodation, prepare yourself for a thorough fleecing.

Just about a kilometre from the jetty, on Jalan Persiaran Putera, past the giant Lada Complex on the right, there's the *Hotel Central* (☎04/966 8585, Ⓕ966 7385; ❺) with good-value clean and comfortable rooms. Further along the road there's the *Asia Hotel,* (☎04/966 6216; ❹), with good-sized en-suite doubles. After crossing a bridge, you'll see the high-rise *City Bayview* up a small hill (☎04/966 1818, ⓦwww.bayviewintl.com; ❻). It's the top hotel along this strip, though not really worth paying more for, unless you want a pool. Two kilometres southeast down the main road from the ferry terminal is the *Sheraton Perdana Resort,* Jalan Pantai Dato' Syed Omar (☎04/966 2020, Ⓕ966 6414; ❽) Set in landscaped grounds, with a private beach, sports facilities and several swimming pools, this hotel commands a spectacular view of island-dotted Langkawi Bay.

Eating

Kuah has numerous eating places of various standards, from the **hawker stalls** – past the post office heading towards the jetty – to the pricier seafood **restaurants** on the seafront, like *Prawn Village,* next to the *Asia* hotel. Despite the ready availability of fresh fish, these places are fairly expensive, each dish setting you back at least RM8 – there are better places elsewhere on the island.

To the west coast: Makam Mahsuri

Taking the main road west out of Kuah, just past the Langkawi Golf Club, about 10km from town, you see a signpost for **Makam Mahsuri** (the tomb of Mahsuri; daily 10am–6pm; RM2). In **Kampung Mawat**, a couple of kilometres off the main road west of Kuah, the tomb is enshrined in Langkawi's most famous legend, which tells of a young woman named Mahsuri, born over two hundred years ago. Her beauty was such that it inspired a vengeful

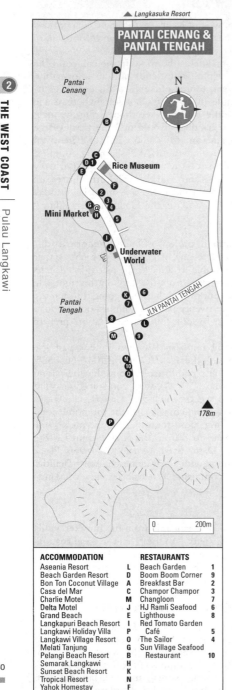

▲ Langkasuka Resort

PANTAI CENANG & PANTAI TENGAH

Pantai Cenang

N

Rice Museum

Mini Market

Underwater World

Pantai Tengah

JLN PANTAI TENGAH

▲ 178m

0   200m

ACCOMMODATION		RESTAURANTS	
Aseania Resort	L	Beach Garden	1
Beach Garden Resort	D	Boom Boom Corner	9
Bon Ton Coconut Village	A	Breakfast Bar	2
Casa del Mar	C	Champor Champor	3
Charlie Motel	M	Changloon	7
Delta Motel	J	HJ Ramli Seafood	6
Grand Beach	E	Lighthouse	8
Langkapuri Beach Resort	I	Red Tomato Garden	
Langkawi Holiday Villa	P	Café	5
Langkawi Village Resort	O	The Sailor	4
Melati Tanjung	G	Sun Village Seafood	
Pelangi Beach Resort	B	Restaurant	10
Semarak Langkawi	H		
Sunset Beach Resort	K		
Tropical Resort	N		
Yahok Homestay	F		

accusation of adultery from a spurned suitor – or, as some versions have it, a jealous mother-in-law – while her husband was away fighting the invading Siamese. Mahsuri protested her innocence but was found guilty by the village elders, who sentenced her to death. She was tied to a stake, and as the ceremonial dagger was plunged into her, began to bleed white blood, a sign that proved her innocence. With her dying breath, Mahsuri muttered a curse on Langkawi's prosperity, to last seven generations – judging by the island's increasing income in recent years, this must be starting to wear off.

Pantai Tengah and Pantai Cenang

Back on the main road, heading west, you travel a further 8km to a junction from where the first of the island's western beaches, **PANTAI TENGAH**, 6km away, is clearly signposted. It's a sleepy beach town, less crowded and catering more to locals than **PANTAI CENANG**, the next beach development along the coast. Although Pantai Cenang is more developed, the buildings at both beaches are unobtrusive, mainly because of the government's requirement that beach-front accommodation doesn't exceed the height of a coconut tree. The beach at Tengah is a quiet stretch of clean, crunchy sand, but there are sometimes jellyfish in the water, so take local advice before you swim.

To the north, at Underwater World, there's a rocky outcrop which separates the bays of Pantai Tengah and Pantai Cenang. The bay at Pantai Cenang forms a large sweep of wide beach with sugary sand. Plenty of places on the beach offer **watersports** and

boat rental, one of the more organized centres being the Langkawi Marine Sports (℡04/955 1389). Its prices are negotiable and vary with the time of year – during low season (weekdays, non-holidays) expect to pay around RM200 per boat (for up to eight people) for a round-the-island boat tour, RM200 for half a day's fishing or RM50 for fifteen minutes' waterskiing, or thirty minutes on a jet ski.

Along the coast road, you'll find no shortage of **mini-markets** selling general provisions; most also provide **Internet** terminals, as does *AB Motel*. There are also plenty of outfits **renting cars, motorbikes and bicycles**.

The main attraction on the west coast, besides the beach, is **Underwater World** (daily 10am–6pm; RM18), boasting the largest aquarium in Asia; it houses over five thousand marine and freshwater fish. Although the attached duty-free shopping complex seems like the main reason for the operation, the fish are well presented, the highlight being a walk-through aquarium where sharks, turtles and hundreds of other sea creatures swim around and above boggle-eyed visitors in a transparent tunnel. There's also a touch pool where you can get feely with starfish, sea slugs and sea cucumbers.

At the northern end of Pantai Cenang is a rather deserted **rice museum** (10am–6pm; free), although you may be able to get a personal tour which provides a hands-on experience with traditional planting equipment and even gives you the opportunity to get your feet wet in a paddy field.

Accommodation

There are dozens of places to stay, but even the budget options start at RM40. However, discounts are usually given for stays of three nights or more. You'll get better rates at the luxury resorts by booking a package deal through a travel agent. Accommodation is a little sparser on Pantai Tengah than on Pantai Cenang.

Inexpensive

Grand Beach ℡04/955 1457, ℻955 3846. On the northern end of the beach, these clean bungalows with fans ❷ or air-con ❹ are priced more reasonably than others of equal standard.

Melati Tanjung Motel ℡04/955 1099. Individual wooden chalets with small patios right on the beach or set back in a grassy garden. The rooms are clean and come with refrigerators. Good value; fan ❷, air-con ❸.

Yahok Homestay ℡04/955 8120. Set back in a kampung, this spartan but friendly place with all fan rooms and shared facilities is popular with travellers. There's a common balcony overlooking a coconut grove. ❷

Moderate

Charlie Motel ℡04/955 1200, ℻955 1316. This beachfront place in a garden setting was recently renovated and has wooden A-Frame chalets sleeping up to four. There's also a decent restaurant on the premises. ❹

Delta Motel ℡04/955 2253, ℻953 1307. Closely spaced, large wooden chalets in a shady garden right by the beach. The restaurant serves local food (no alcohol allowed). ❹

Langkapuri Beach Resort ℡04/955 1202, ℻955 1959. A range of concrete chalets on a leafy patch of beach. All the rooms have air-con and hot showers. ❺

Semarak Langkawi Beach Resort ℡04/955 1377, ℻955 1159. A step up from most others in this price range, these spacious and well-maintained chalets are dotted around a garden shaded with coconut palms. There's a pleasant terrace restaurant. Fan rooms ❹, air-con ❺.

Tropical Resort ℡04/955 4075. It's only a few metres to the beach through some scrub from these two rows of very clean chalets, all with air-con and TV. Good value. ❹

Expensive

Aseania Resort ℡04/955 2020, ⓦwww.langkawi-resorts.com/aseaniaresort. Although the pink-palace exterior may be off-putting, the rooms themselves are nicely appointed. There's a 150m-long pool complete with waterfall and slides. ❻

Beach Garden Resort ℡04/955 1363, ⓦwww.beachgardenresort.com. More intimate than the large resorts, this German-owned place has tastefully decorated rooms surrounding a leafy courtyard. There's a small swimming pool and a restaurant on the beach. **⑥**

Casa del Mar ⏀04/955 2388, ⓦwww .casadelmar-langkawi.com. This German-managed boutique hotel's exterior and lobby have a colonial Mexican flavour. The rooms are tastefully decorated and there's a spa and small pool. **⑨**

Langkawi Holiday Villa ⏀04/955 1701, ⓦwww .holidayvillahotels.com. Large luxury resort with a spa and choice of restaurants, including Italian and Japanese. Extensive lawn and a large pool, but the rooms are slightly worn. Has a good range of watersports open to non-guests. **⑧**

Langkawi Village Resort ⏀04/955 1511, ⓦwww.langkawi-villageresort.com. Very pleasant, unpretentious kampung-style resort in a garden

setting. The accommodation is in well-designed, two-storey chalets with all the trimmings. There's a pool and a seaside restaurant. Rate includes buffet breakfast. Good value. **⑦**

Pelangi Beach Resort ⏀04/952 8888, ⓦwww .pelangibeachresort.com. Pantai Cenang's finest accommodation, an impressive five-star development of two-storey timber chalets, which echo traditional Malay architecture. All the luxuries you'd expect for the price. **⑨**

Sunset Beach Resort ⏀04/955 1751, ⓦwww .sunsetbeachresort.com. An intimate alternative to the big resorts, the tastefully decorated rooms surround a central courtyard with a lush garden. Friendly service. **⑥**

Eating and drinking

The large resorts all have attached **restaurants**, where the emphasis is on West-ernized Asian dishes. The smaller establishments tend to have restaurants right on the beach serving simpler local fare. Although there's more choice at Pantai Cenang, Pantai Tengah has a few good eateries and is usually less crowded.

Beach Garden A pretty beachside operation serving Western food including pizza and pasta with beer to wash it down.

Boom Boom Corner Serves tasty and inexpensive Pakistani food.

Breakfast Bar Friendly place serving sandwiches and good Western breakfasts from 7am to 10pm. This is by far the best breakfast place in town.

Champor Champor Meaning "mix mix", this small bar and restaurant, in a leafy, secluded spot, serves tasty if slightly pricey fusion cuisine.

Changloon This Thai/Chinese seafood place offers fresh fish as well as the usual noodle and rice dishes.

Delta Motel Has a terrace restaurant with good-value local dishes, but doesn't serve alcohol.

HJ Ramli Seafood One of the better seafood establishments on this beach, *HJ Ramli*

specializes in grilled fish; it doesn't get much fresher than this.

Lighthouse At the end of Jalan Pantai Tengah, this stylish restaurant has an extensive drinks list and is a good place to enjoy a cocktail at sunset. Their menu consists of Mediterranean and Malaysian cuisine served in an elegantly modern setting (open daily 11am–2am).

Red Tomato Garden Café Popular with travellers, this place serves Western breakfasts and home-made bread as well as some pricier pasta and main dishes for lunch and dinner. Try their pizzas from a wood-fired oven.

The Sailor Here you'll find German food as well as steaks and pizza for lunch and dinner.

Sun Village Seafood Restaurant In a wooden Malay-style building, this place has an extensive wine list and serves a variety of grilled seafood as well as less expensive curries.

North to Pantai Kok

Heading north 5km, a right turn after the airport brings you to the **Padang Matsirat** (literally, "Field of Burnt Rice"). Shortly after Mahsuri's death, the Siamese conquered Kedah and prepared to attack Langkawi. In order to halt the advance of the invaders, the island's inhabitants set fire to their staple crop and poisoned their wells. To this day, so the legend goes, traces of burnt rice resurface in the area after a heavy downfall of rain.

Just past the *Sheraton* complex is the beach of **PANTAI KOK**, which lies on the far western stretch of Langkawi. Previously considered Langkawi's most beautiful beach, it has now unfortunately been ruined by the construction of a marina. From here, you're only 2km from the splendid falls at Telaga Tujuh, just to the north (see below). Also nearby is the summer palace built for the film *Anna and the King* (1999), which is now open to visitors, but already crumbling back into the jungle.

Accommodation and eating

Unfortunately, the budget **accommodation** on the beach has been bulldozed to make way for a golf course, so pricier complexes are the only option. On the shore road north of Pantai Cenang, the mini-resort *Bon Ton Coconut Village* (℡04/955 1679, ✉bonton_coconutvillage@hotmail.com) has survived the development of the area; it consists of a few large but basic chalets (RM189) which are set in the middle of rice fields. The **restaurant** is worth visiting for its well-presented local food and home-made cakes. There's also a trendy **crafts shop**, which is surrounded by seven traditional kampung houses. Further up the coast is the *Langkasuka Resort* (℡04/955 6888 ❼), a luxurious place on a lovely beach, with promotional discounts of up to fifty percent. A couple of kilometres uphill along the coast road, near the junction with the road leading inland is the stylish *Tanjung Sanctuary Langkawi* (℡04/955 2977, ⓦwww .tanjung-sanctuary-langkawi.com; ❼), with luxurious accommodation in natural surroundings. It's on a forested rocky headland and has its own private beach, plus a swimming pool and a restaurant built on stilts over the water. Another 4km west at the end of the road, is the luxurious *Berjaya Resort* (℡04/959 1888, ⓦwww.berjayaresorts.com.my; ❽); the decor is somewhat kitsch, but the Japanese massages, facials and forest spa are its real attraction.

Telaga Tujuh

The road beyond the turn-off to the *Berjaya Resort*, leads to a car park, from where a dirt track heads up to the island's most wonderful natural attraction, **Telaga Tujuh** (literally, "Seven Pools"), a cascading freshwater stream that has pounded large recesses into the rock, forming several pools down a slope. During the rainy season, the slipperiness of the moss covering the rock in between the pools enables you to slide rapidly from one pool to another, before the fast-flowing water disappears over the cliff to form the ninety-metre **waterfall** you can see from below – it's only the depth of the water in the last pool that prevents you from shooting off the end too. This being Langkawi, there's an associated legend, suggesting the spot is the playground of mountain fairies. They're believed to have left behind a special kind of lime and the *sintuk* (a climbing plant with enormous pods), which grow around these pools; the locals use them as a hair wash, which is thought to rinse away bad luck.

The walk to the pools from the turning near the *Berjaya Resort* takes about 45 minutes, the last stage of which involves a steep two-hundred-metre climb up from the inevitable cluster of souvenir stalls at the base of the hill. Look out for the long-tailed macaques that bound around the trail; they are playful, but can be vicious if provoked. If you're lucky, you may spot a cream-coloured giant squirrel (famed in these parts) scampering up the tree trunks, or great hornbills hanging out in the treetops; the latter, with their huge, hooked orange beak and cackle-like call, are the most distinctive of all Malaysian birds.

Datai

From Pantai Kok, the main road north heads to Pulau Langkawi's **north coast**. On the way, after about 7km, you'll pass **Crocodile Adventure** (daily 9am–6pm; RM8), Malaysia's largest crocodile farm where you can view some 1500 saltwater crocodiles (*Crocodilus porosus*) at various stages of their development.

There are also the usual shows that feature "crocodile wrestling" and the like. More interesting perhaps are the feedings that take place before each show. Ten kilometres further on, there's a road off to the left which leads a further 12km to **DATAI**, the site of Langkawi's premier resort development. En route, the road curves and climbs to reveal a couple of secluded coves from where you can see several Thai islands in the distance; the sea at this point is a clear jewel-like blue. Just before you reach the resort area there's more development close to the top-notch Datai Bay Golf Club.

The *Datai* (T04/959 2500, W www.thedatai.com; 9) is the quintessential rainforest resort. Volcanic rock and wood have been used to stunning effect, creating architecture that's in harmony with the surrounding forest. The views across the bay to Thailand are stunning, as is the price. Under the same management is the *Andaman* (T04/959 1088, W www.theandaman.com; 9), which shares the beach at Datai Bay.

Tanjung Rhu and Durian Perangin Falls

Returning to the main north coast road and continuing 10km east, you reach **Pantai Pasir Hitam** ("Black Sand Beach"), where the cliff drops down away from the road to the streaks of black sand caused by mineral deposits from a spring, though there's no access to the narrow beach.

Five kilometres further east, the road intersects with the main north–south route across the island at the village of **Padang Lalang**. Turn left, and a couple of kilometres through some swampy land brings you to **TANJUNG RHU**, also known as "Casuarina Beach" because of the profusion of these pine-like trees here. The only development here is the *Radisson Tanjung Rhu Resort* (T04/959 1033, W www.tanjungrhu.com.my; 9), which is almost as luxurious as the *Andaman* and *Datai*. Not as isolated, it's within walking distance of a public beach and boat hire for day-trips. Outside on the approach road, past the sign that warns "Alcohol is the root of all evil", are some food and drink stalls – which don't sell beer. There's a beautiful beach and the sea here, sheltered by the curve of the bay, is unusually tranquil. The tide goes out far enough for you to walk out to the nearby islands of **PULAU PASIR** and **PULAU GASING**, perfect for a bit of secluded sunbathing. On a promontory accessible only by boat from Tanjung Rhu (RM80), you'll find the isolated **Gua Cerita** or "Cave of Tales", facing the Thai coastline. Despite the profusion of bat droppings, it's worth having a close look inside the cave, as you can make out ancient lettering on the walls – verses of the Koran.

Back at the crossroads, you can either head for the interior **Gunung Raya** or continue east to the site of **Telaga Air Panas**. To reach the top of Gunung Raya (881m), the tallest mountain on the island, take the curvy paved road which branches east after about 7km. As you climb higher through the jungle, the view on a clear day becomes ever more spectacular. The other option is to continue past the crossroads another 2km east to the site of Telaga Air Panas ("Hot Springs"), the result of another Langkawi legend: the area was reputedly formed during a quarrel between the island's two leading families over a rejected offer of marriage. Household items were flung about in the fight: the spot where gravy splashed from the pots became known as Kuah ("gravy"), and here, where the jugs of boiling water landed, hot springs spouted. There's not much to see and what there is has been subsumed within the **Air Hangat Village** (daily 10am–6pm; RM4; T04/959 1357), which encompasses the hot springs and an arts pavilion, designed in traditional Malay kampung style; demonstrations of folk and classical dance, kick boxing and *silat* are put on here at various times of the day. There's also an expensive **restaurant** that puts on a cultural show every evening, inevitably catering to tour groups.

Next along the road is the **Galeria Perdana** (daily 10am–5pm; RM5), which contains over ten thousand state gifts and awards presented to Prime Minister Dr Mahathir – an eclectic collection ranging from African wood carvings to Japanese ceramics. Further on is the turn-off for **Durian Perangin**, a waterfall reached along a difficult and rocky path, and fairly disappointing unless you happen to catch it during the wet season when the water level is high. Shortly after this, the road curves to the south for the remaining 10km to Kuah.

Other Langkawi islands

Expensive **day-trips** to some of the nearer islands to Pulau Langkawi are organized by various hotels at Pantai Tengah or Pantai Cenang and by a couple of local firms. These excursions are fine if you're into diving, snorkelling and fishing, but otherwise provide little incentive to leave the main island. It's also possible to get to some islands independently, taking the island-hopping boat which visits – among others – Pulau Singa Besar and Pulau Dayang Bunting; it leaves from the Marble Beach jetty, two minutes' walk southeast of the Kuah jetty (daily 9am & 2.30pm; RM45); the tourist office in Kuah has details of the current route.

Mountainous **Pulau Tuba**, 5km south of Langkawi, is the only other island with accommodation – just the one option, the *Sunrise Beach Resort* (☎04/966 9752, ✉putri51@hotmail.com; ④), with its own swimming pool. There's barely enough space around the rim of the island for the dirt track which encircles it, though it does take in some deserted beaches. It's awkward to get to Tuba – a matter of hanging round the Marble Beach jetty until someone offers to take you across in one of the small speedboats.

Pulau Dayang Bunting (literally, "Island of the Pregnant Maiden") is the second largest island in the archipelago, about fifteen minutes' boat ride from Marble Beach jetty. It's the exception to the rule in having at least a couple of specific points of interest, but you'll have to visit on a day-trip as there's nowhere to stay. A large and tranquil freshwater lake, **Tasik Dayang Bunting**, is believed to have magical properties making barren women fertile. According to legend, after drinking from the lake, a childless couple had a baby girl after nineteen years of unsuccessful attempts to conceive. Legend also has it that the lake is inhabited by a large white crocodile, but don't let that stop you from going for a swim in this lovely green lake surrounded by massive, densely forested limestone outcrops. The entire island is dotted with these, which are at their most dramatic around the **Gua Langsir** ("Cave of the Banshee"), a towering 91-metre-high cave on the island's west coast, which is said to be haunted – probably because of the sounds of the thousands of bats which live inside. The island-hopping boat drops you at a jetty near the lake before continuing to the cave, 8km to the north.

Langkawi's most recent attempt at green tourism is realized on **Pulau Singa Besar**, a wildlife sanctuary 3km off the southern tip of Pantai Tengah and also a stop for the island-hopping boat. The organized day-trip includes the services of a guide, since you're not allowed to roam around at will. Monkeys, mouse deer, iguanas and peacocks are among the wildlife to have been freed on the island, although how many animals you actually see is inevitably a matter of luck.

Pulau Payar Marine Park has great schools of tropical fish, including black-finned sharks. South of the island, 13km west of the Peninsula, lies a coral garden supporting the largest number of coral species in the country. A few companies organize day-trips to the marine park, including Langkawi Coral, which has an office at Kuah ferry terminal (℡04/966 7318, ⓦwww.langkawicoral.com) and Island and Sun at Simpang 3, Pantai Tengah (℡ & ℻04/955 7166). Prices range around RM130 and usually include hotel pick-ups, lunch, and all snorkelling equipment, although it's worth shopping around (there are also operators in Pantai Cenang) as some smaller outfits charge less for the same trip. No accommodation is available; to **camp** you must first obtain permission from the Fisheries Department at Alor Setar (℡04/732 5573).

North to the Thai border

The tiny state of **Perlis** – at 800 square kilometres, the smallest in Malaysia – lies at the northwestern tip of the Peninsula, bordering Thailand. Together with neighbouring Kedah, it's traditionally been viewed as the country's agricultural heartland, something reflected in the landscape which is dominated by lustrous, bright-green paddy fields. There's no special reason to stop here; most people pass quickly through the state's small towns on their way to Thailand.

Kangar, Arau and Kaki Bukit

KANGAR, the state capital of Perlis, is an unremarkable modern town. The centrally located **bus station** is where you change buses for the **Thai border** (see box opposite) or to **Kuala Perlis** in order to take the ferry to Langkawi. The nearest **train station** is 10km to the east at **ARAU**, the least interesting of all Malaysia's royal towns – its Royal Palace (closed to the public) on the main road looks like little more than a comfortable mansion. The town is only really handy for the daily morning train making the two-hour journey to Hat Yai, Thailand or the International Express from Butterworth to Bangkok, a journey of nineteen hours (check the latest train schedule: ⓦwww.ktmb.com .my). A morning southbound train departs Arau for the two-and-a-half hour journey to Butterworth; another southbound train departs Arau in the evening and terminates in Kuala Lumpur the following morning (again, make sure to check the latest timetable).

If you have some time to kill before crossing the border, you could visit **Gua Kelam Kaki Bukit** (literally, "a cave of darkness at the foot of a hill"), a 370-metre-long limestone cave once part of a working tin mine; it lies in a valley about 25km north of Kangar up Route 1. The town of **KAKI BUKIT**, 1km south of the cave, is easily reached by bus from Kangar. The stream that runs through the cavern was once used to carry away excavated tin ore to the processing plant near the cave's entrance. Access through the cave is by way of a suspended wooden walkway, also used by locals – and their motorbikes – as a means of getting to the other side of the valley, though for visitors the walkway's attraction is that it allows them to look down into the former mine.

Kuala Perlis

Though it's the second largest settlement in the state, the little town of **KUALA PERLIS**, 45km north of Alor Setar, has only two streets. There's no real reason to come here other than taking the ferry to Langkawi or Satun in Thailand; buses drop you at an unmarked stand adjacent to the jetty, from where a wooden footbridge connects with the older, more interesting part of town, a ramshackle collection of buildings on stilts. Though you can reserve tickets at

Crossing the Malaysia/Thailand border

There are two border crossings, both open from 6am to 10pm, one on the railway line at the village of **Padang Besar** and another, 20km southeast on Route 1, at **Bukit Kayu Hitam**. Make sure that your passport is stamped by the border police upon entry in either direction, or you can be fined for entering illegally when you leave the country.

There are regular **bus** connections from both border crossings to **Hat Yai**, southern Thailand's transportation hub, 60km away. If travelling by bus or taxi via Padang Besar, you'll have to get off before the border and cross the 2km of no-man's land on foot or catch a ride with the motorcyclists who ferry people back and forth for RM30 (350 Baht) each way.

The **train** comes to a halt at the border crossing of **Padang Besar**, where a very long platform connects the Malaysian service with its Thai counterpart. You don't change trains here, although you must get off and go through customs at the station. There are only two northbound trains a day, one terminating in Hat Yai and the other via Hat Yai to Bangkok. Due to heightened security on this line, the railway timetable is often at odds with actual arrival and departure times. If you plan on getting on a north- or south-bound train at Padang Besar, it's best to check the timetable posted at the station for the latest estimated arrival and departure times.

the Kuala Perlis–Langkawi Ferry Service's jetty office (☏04/985 4494), it's just as easy to turn up and board, with departures on the hour (7am–7pm), plus 9.30am, 3.30pm and 5.30pm (RM12; 1hr).

There are two **banks** in the main part of town, near the jetty. The town also has a couple of **hotels** in case you decide to stay. Close to the jetty is the *Kuala Perlis Seaview Hotel* (☏04/985 2171: ❺), with spacious and clean rooms (but no sea view). In the budget category, it's best to avoid the grimy options across from the ferry terminal and walk about a kilometre down the main road to the outskirts of town; opposite the mosque is a right turn from where the *Asia Hotel*, 18 Taman Sentosa (☏04/985 5392; ❷), is signposted. It has a better-than-average Chinese **restaurant** downstairs.

You can reach Satun in **Thailand** directly from Kuala Perlis: small boats from Langkawi stop here en route, leaving from the jetty when they are full (30min; RM4); at weekends you'll be charged an additional RM1 for the immigration officers' overtime payment.

Travel details

Trains

Alor Setar to: Arau (daily; 45min); Bangkok (Thailand; daily; 20hr) Butterworth (daily; 2hr 45min); Hat Yai (Thailand; 2 daily; 2hr 20min); Ipoh (daily; 8hr); Kuala Kangsar (daily; 6hr); Kuala Lumpur (daily; 13hr); Sungai Petani (daily; 1hr); Taiping (daily; 5hr 20min); Tapah Road (daily; 9hr).
Butterworth to: Alor Setar (1 daily; 2hr 45min); Bangkok (Thailand; daily; 22hr); Hat Yai (Thailand; 2 daily; 4hr 45min); Ipoh (daily; 5hr); Kuala Kangsar (daily; 4hr); Kuala Lumpur (daily; 13hr 30min);

Sungai Petani (daily; 1hr); Taiping (daily; 3hr 15min); Tapah Road (daily; 6hr 45min).
Ipoh to: Alor Setar (daily; 7hr 20min); Butterworth (daily; 5hr); Kuala Kangsar (daily; 2hr); Kuala Lumpur (daily; 5hr 15min); Sungai Petani (daily; 6hr 15min); Taiping (daily; 2hr); Tapah Road (daily; 1hr 30min).
Kuala Kangsar to: Alor Setar (daily; 6hr); Butterworth (daily; 4hr); Ipoh (daily; 2hr); Kuala Lumpur (daily; 7hr); Sungai Petani (daily; 5hr); Taiping (daily; 1hr); Tapah Road (daily; 3hr).
Taiping to: Alor Setar (daily; 5hr 20min); Butterworth (daily; 3hr 15min); Ipoh (daily; 2hr); Kuala

Kangsar (daily; 1hr); Kuala Lumpur (daily; 8hr); Sungai Petani (daily; 4hr 20min); Tapah Road (daily; 4hr).

Tapah Road to: Alor Setar (daily; 9hr); Butterworth (daily; 6hr 45min); Ipoh (3 daily; 1hr 30min); Kuala Kangsar (daily; 3hr); Kuala Lumpur (daily; 4hr); Sungai Petani (daily; 8hr); Taiping (daily; 4hr).

Buses

Alor Setar to: Butterworth (every 20min; 1hr 30min); Ipoh (7 daily; 4hr); Johor Bahru (6 daily; 12hr); Kangar (every 40 min; 1hr 15min); Kota Bharu (2 daily; 8hr); Kuala Kedah (every 15min; 15min); Kuala Lumpur (6 daily; 6hr); Kuala Terengganu (2 daily; 9hr); Kuantan (3 daily; 9hr); Melaka (4 daily; 8hr) Seremban (2 daily; 7hr); Singapore (4 daily; 13hr) Sungai Petani (every 30min; 1hr 15min).

Butterworth to: Alor Setar (every 30min; 1hr 30min); Ipoh (hourly; 3hr); Kota Bharu (2 daily; 6hr); Kuala Lumpur (at least 10 daily; 4hr 30min); Kuala Terengganu (1 daily; 8hr); Kuantan (2 daily; 9hr); Lumut (5 daily; 3hr); Melaka (1 daily; 7hr); Seremban (1 daily; 6hr); Singapore (at least 1 daily; 11hr); Sungai Petani (every 20min; 40min); Taiping (1 hourly; 2hr 15min).

Ipoh to: Alor Setar (7 daily; 4hr); Butterworth (hourly; 3hr); Hat Yai, (Thailand; 2 daily; 7hr); Johor Bahru (3 daily; 7hr 30min); Kangar (2 daily; 4hr); Kota Bahru (2 daily; 8hr); Kuala Kangsar (every 45min; 1hr); Kuala Lumpur (every 30min–1hr 30min); Kuala Terengganu (2 daily; 11hr); Kuantan (2 daily; 8hr); Lumut (hourly; 1hr 30min); Melaka (1 daily; 5hr); Penang (hourly; 2hr 30min); Singapore (2 daily; 9hr); Tapah (hourly; 1hr).

Kangar to: Alor Setar (every 40min; 1hr 15min); Butterworth (7 daily; 1hr 45min); Kuala Perlis (every 45min; 30min).

Lumut to: Butterworth (4 daily; 4hr); Ipoh (every 30min–1hr; 1hr 30min); Kuala Lumpur (8 daily; 5hr 30min); Kuantan (5 daily; 9hr 30min); Taiping (every 30min; 1hr 10min); Tapah (1 daily; 2hr).

Tapah to: Butterworth (2 daily; 4hr 30min); Hat Yai (Thailand; daily; 10hr); Ipoh (hourly; 1hr); Kuala Lumpur (at least 10 daily; 2hr); Kuala Terengganu (daily; 6hr); Kuantan (2 daily; 6hr); Lumut (1 daily; 2hr); Melaka (1 daily; 3hr 30min); Singapore (2 daily; 10hr).

Ferries

Butterworth to: Georgetown (every 20min–1hr, 5am–11pm service; 20min).

Georgetown to: Butterworth (every 20min–1hr, 5am–11pm service; 20min); Langkawi (daily; 2hr 30min); Medan (Indonesia; daily; 4hr).

Kuala Kedah to: Langkawi (20 daily; 1hr 15min).

Kuala Perlis to: Langkawi (16 daily; 1hr); Satun (Thailand; 3 daily; 30min).

Langkawi to: Kuala Kedah (20 daily; 1hr 15min); Kuala Perlis (16 daily; 1hr); Penang (2 daily; 2hr 30min); Satun (Thailand; 3 daily; 1hr 30min).

Lumut to: Pangkor (every 30min; 7am–7pm daily; 40min).

Flights

Georgetown to: Johor Bahru (10 weekly; 1hr); Kuala Lumpur (at least 15 daily; 45min); Langkawi (daily; 30min); Singapore (at least 4 daily; 1hr 20min).

Ipoh to: Johor Bahru (8 weekly; 1hr); Kuala Lumpur (daily; 45min).

Langkawi to: Kuala Lumpur (at least 10 daily; 55min); Penang (daily; 30min); Singapore (1–2 daily; 1hr 30min).

The interior

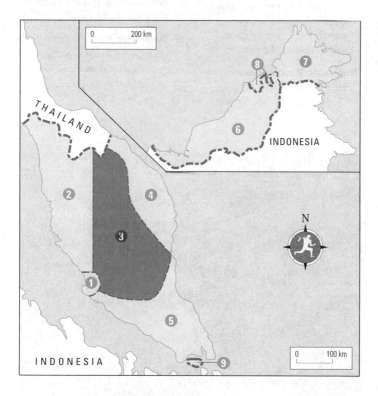

CHAPTER 3 # Highlights

✳ **Taman Negara** The Peninsula's largest and oldest nature reserve offers river trips, hikes and wildlife-spotting amid a vast tract of ancient rainforest. See p.245

✳ **Fraser's Hill** This relaxing hill station makes for a great overnight break, with short nature trails to tackle and varied birdlife. See p.265

✳ **Kenong Rimba** A little-developed reserve adjoining Taman Negara, offering its own trekking and wildlife-spotting opportunities. See p.275

✳ **Stong State Park** In the interior of Kelantan State, Stong boasts a picturesque waterfall and good trekking up a mountainside, though facilities are minimal. See p.279

✳ **Tasik Bera** Encounters with local Orang Asli are possible at this tranquil, isolated lake, as are boat rides and jungle hikes. See p.283

△ Orang Asli, Taman Negara

The interior

The peaks of the **Banjaran Titiwangsa**, the Peninsula's spine, form the western boundary of the **interior**; to their east is an H-shaped range of steep, sandstone peaks with knife-edge ridges and luxuriant valleys where small towns and kampungs nestle. The rivers which flow from these mountains – the Pahang, Tembeling, Lebir and Nenggiri, among many others – provide the northern interior's indigenous peoples, the Negritos and Senoi, with their main means of transport. Visitors, too, can travel by river, to reach **Taman Negara,** the country's first national park, straddling the borders of Pahang, Kelantan and Terengganu states. Further south, two lake systems, **Tasik Chini** and **Tasik Bera,** offer their share of boat trips and the chance to meet local Orang Asli communities. Other worthwhile stops include **Kuala Lipis,** the former capital of Pahang, **Kenong Rimba** and **Stong** state parks; and the hill station of **Fraser's Hill,** 75km north of Kuala Lumpur, which affords good **birdwatching** and relaxing walks in temperatures a pleasant 5°C or so cooler than in the lowlands.

Route 8 is the interior's main artery, running from Bentong near KL northeast to Kota Bharu. Taking around eight hours to drive in its entirety, it's not the wide conduit that more recently built highways are, so expect to be periodically slowed behind ponderous lorries. The quickest way to reach Route 8 from KL is the **E8** (the **Karak Highway**), a multilane rollercoaster of a road that careers through the foothills of the Genting Highlands to link with Route 8 just south of Bentong. Expect a few thrilling, cambered descents on this road – and be warned that there are often nasty accidents on it, too. The E8 also connects onto the **East Coast Highway** running east across the interior to Kuantan. Another new road slices across the northern part of the interior, from Gua Musang west to the Cameron Highlands and Ipoh, and, it's intended, east to Kuala Berang near Tasik Kenyir. Bus services along these routes are reasonably efficient, but unless you're in a real hurry to get from one coast to the other, consider a trip on the **jungle railway** (see box on p.243), serving most of the interior's attractions except Fraser's Hill and Tasik Chini.

Some history

The interior comprises much of Pahang and Kelantan, which were the last regions of Peninsular Malaysia to excite the interest of the British colonial authorities. Until the 1880s the Bendahara (Prince) of Pahang, Wan Ahmed, ran his state as a private fiefdom, unvisited by outsiders except for a hundred or so Chinese and European gold prospectors who had established contacts with some remote Malay villages and Orang Asli settlements. When explorer and colonial administrator **Sir Hugh Clifford** visited, he noted that the region "did

THE INTERIOR

THAILAND

Tumpat
Wakaf Bharu
Pasir Mas
disused
Kota Bharu

Pasir Putih
Kg. Raja

Tanah
Merah
Machang
Jeli

Kuala Krai

STONG
STATE PARK
Dabong

Kampong
Tembeling

Kuala Terengganu

K E L A N T A N

S. Nenggiri
S. Galas
S. Lebir
S. Terengganu

UNDER CONSTRUCTION

Gua Musang

Merapoh

TAMAN
NEGARA
G. Tahan
S. Tahan

TERENGGANU

Cameron
Highlands

KENONG RIMBA
STATE PARK

Kuala Tahan

S. Tembeling

S. Jelai

Batu
Sembilan

Kuala Lipis

Benta
Kerambit
Kuala Tembeling (Tembeling jetty)

P A H A N G

Jerantut

Fraser's
Hill
Raub

S. Pahang

Tanjung
Malim
The Gap

Kuantan

Kuala Kubu Bharu

Bentong

Genting
Highlands

Mentakab

Maran

EAST COAST HIGHWAY

Rawang

Temerloh

Tasik Chini

Kg. Belimbing
Kg. Chini

Pekan

Chini
Resort
Kg. Gumum
Felda
Chini

KUALA LUMPUR

Triang
Kerayong/Bandar Bera

SELANGOR

Ayer
Hitam

Tasik Bera
Pos Iskandar

Bahau

NEGERI
SEMBILAN

Seremban
Gemas
Segamat

Tampin

0   50 km

N

▼ Johor Bahru

not boast a mile of road and ... was smothered in deep, damp forest, threaded across a network of streams and rivers ... flecked here and there by little splashes of sunlight." What Clifford also noted – and indeed the reason for his visit – was that Pahang was "wonderfully rich in minerals". Wan Ahmed gave the British mining and planting rights, in exchange for military protection against the incursions of the Siamese and Kelantanese.

The jungle railway

It took indentured Tamil labourers eight years to achieve the remarkable feat of building the five-hundred-kilometre jungle railway from **Gemas**, southeast of KL, to **Tumpat** on the northeast coast. The first section from Gemas to Kuala Lipis opened in 1920, with the full extent of the line following in 1931. Initially it was used exclusively for freight – for tin and rubber, and later oil palm – before a passenger service, originally known as the "Golden Blowpipe", opened in 1938. Today the route is served by trains from both **KL** and **Singapore**.

By dint of its very existence, the line doesn't pass through virgin jungle; instead much of the route is flanked by *belukar*-type woodland, and the line often dips through cuttings below ferny embankments, or skirts the backs of kampung gardens, within eyeshot of bougainvillea and fruiting rambutan and mango trees. None of this is to detract from the fact that as a way of encountering **rural life**, a ride on the jungle train can't be beaten, giving you the chance to take in backwater scenery in the company of cheroot-smoking old men in sarongs, and fast-talking women hauling kids, poultry and vegetables to and from the nearest market.

For the unadulterated jungle railway experience, you need to be on one of the slow **local trains** ("Mel" services in the timetables), which call at just about every obscure hamlet on the route, some of which have Orang Asli names. Their express counterparts are much more efficient, but the rolling stock is relatively modern and charmless, and the air-conditioning insulates you from the onrushing countryside; moreover the schedules mean that they tend to do their run through the interior by night. The most atmospheric of the local services are those running in **Kelantan**, between Gua Musang and Tumpat on the coast. So dilapidated are these trains, with broken seats, non-functioning fans and fused lights (you may be plunged into pitch darkness on the several occasions when the train enters a tunnel), that it feels as though they must date from the colonial era. In fact, they were acquired in the 1980s, and should finally be replaced in the next few years, so ride them while they're still around; you'll be too absorbed in the whole experience to notice minor discomforts. The local service between Gemas and Gua Musang or Tumpat uses rather better-maintained rolling stock of about the same vintage, and takes you through the best stretch for actual **jungle vistas**, in Pahang south of Gua Musang, where hill after hill is blanketed in rainforest. Wherever you are, don't be tempted to rest your elbow on the window rim or, worse, stick your head out for a better look – lineside shrubbery packs a sharp punch when brushed past at speed. The open windows on some trains act in effect as mobile hedge trimmers, slicing away twigs and leaves which end up all over the carriages.

Timetables are to be taken with a pinch of salt, as delays on the line aren't uncommon, and it's not unknown for trains to show up early either; even if you've bought tickets in advance (not usually necessary except for express services), be at the station fifteen minutes ahead of the scheduled departure. Occasionally you may find that the time on the ticket doesn't match the timetable, in which case ask station staff for clarification. Even if everything appears to be going to schedule, note that there's only one set of tracks on long stretches of the route: delays elsewhere may mean your train being held at a siding (or even having to reverse) for an extended period to let an oncoming train pass.

△ The jungle railway

First to arrive were British officials, followed by tin and gold prospectors, then by investors in rubber and other plantation enterprises. The new arrivals initially used the rivers to get around, though the larger companies soon began to clear tracks – the forerunners of the area's roads – into the valleys and along the mountain ridges, and development was made easier again when the railway opened in the 1920s. Slowly, small towns like **Temerloh**, **Raub** and **Kuala Lipis** grew in size and importance, while new settlements like Gua Musang were established to cater for the influx of Chinese merchants and workers.

Since the 1980s, when the Route 8 **highway** into the interior was completed, much of the region has been transformed, and the primeval landscape tamed to a large extent, providing economic incentives for people from both coasts to move into these areas. The spread of the timber, rubber and palm-oil industries has had a huge impact, in particular upon the **Orang Asli**. Since the Emergency, when many Orang Asli were forcibly resettled into villages (see p.739), their lifestyle has been gradually diluting. Back in the 1970s an expert on the Orang Asli, Iskandar Carey, wrote: "there are groups of Senoi [one of the three main Orang Asli peoples] in the deep jungle who have never seen a road, although they are familiar with helicopters, a word for which has been incorporated into their language." These days many indigenous people have made their way into the cash economy and the fringes, at least, of mainstream society, a transition steered in large part by the government's Department of Orang Asli Affairs. However, three-quarters of the Orang Asli remain below the poverty line (compared to less than a tenth of the population as a whole), a fact which makes it all the harder for them to confront the many forces – from planning agencies to Christian and Muslim groups – seeking to influence their destiny. The issue of **land rights** is among the gravest of their problems, for while the country's Aboriginal People's Act has led to the creation of Orang Asli reserves, at the same time many Asli traditional areas have been gazetted as state land, rendering the inhabitants there, at best, tolerated guests of the government.

Taman Negara

Two hundred and fifty kilometres northeast of KL is Peninsular Malaysia's largest and most important protected area, **TAMAN NEGARA** (literally "national park"; ☎09/266 1122, ⓦwww.wildlife.gov.my). Spread over 4343 square kilometres, the park comprises dense lowland forest, higher altitude cloudforest (enveloping the Peninsula's highest peak, **Gunung Tahan**), numerous hills, Orang Asli settlements, hides, campsites and an upmarket jungle retreat. From the streams which snake down from the mountains and feed fierce waterfalls, to the lush flora and fauna, the park experience (as the tourist brochures never tire of telling you) is second to none.

The area was first protected by state legislation in 1925, when 1300 square kilometres was designated as the Gunung Tahan Game Reserve; thirteen years later it became the King George V National Park. At independence, the park was renamed Taman Negara and extended to its current boundaries. In 1991, the government's Department of Wildlife and National Parks (more simply known as the Wildlife Department) decided it would be best to split the running of the park, with the department continuing to oversee its ecological management, but accommodation and eating facilities privatized at the park's headquarters at **Kuala Tahan**. Since then there has been substantial investment here, resulting in over one hundred slick chalets at the park headquarters, and even more budget and mid-range accommodation in the nearby Malay village of the same name.

The park itself forms by far the largest undivided tract of rainforest in Peninsular Malaysia; indeed it contains some of the **oldest rainforest** in the world – older than the Congo or Amazon – which has evolved over 130 million years. Every trek into the forest has its fascinations. If you've never been inside tropical rainforest before, just listening to the bird, insect and animal sounds, marvelling at the sheer size of dipterocarp trees and peering into the forest canopy is a memorable experience. There are a myriad of entrancing sights: flowering lianas, giant bamboo stands with fungi which glow in the dark and chattering macaque monkeys rattling across the treetops. Some of the Peninsula's one thousand **Batek** Orang Asli, a subgroup of the Negritos, remain in the area; most are hunter-gatherers (the park authorities generally turn a blind eye to their hunting game here). You may pass their vine-and-forest-brush shelters, built to stand only for a few days before their inhabitants move on again, and you can even take a discreet look at a couple of semi-permanent settlements in the vicinity of Kuala Tahan.

Although for many visitors the chance of seeing sizeable mammals, especially **elephants**, is one of the park's big draws, bear in mind that success generally means making a three- or four-day trek into the forest, requiring the services of a guide. But stay overnight in the **hides** – tree houses positioned beside salt licks – and you might spot mousedeer, tapir and *seladang* (wild ox), especially during the rainy season, whilst wild pigs have been known to forage right in the midst of the park headquarters itself. **Birdlife** is ever present and a good prospect; the park has over three hundred species, many quite easy to spot with good binoculars and some patience. For a rundown of the park habitats and denizens, see the wildlife account in "Contexts" (p.765). If you're not a hardcore wildlife spotter, take advantages of opportunities for a river swim or even angling. On the other hand, if you're simply keen to glimpse something of primary rainforest, it's much easier to give Taman Negara a miss and instead make for FRIM on the outskirts of KL (see p.147), or the Bukit Timah Nature Reserve in Singapore (see p.682).

The **best time** to visit the park is between February and mid-October when the weather is less likely to be wet, though note that from May to August is the park's busiest period, when, for budget accommodation in particular, it makes sense to book ahead; at other times, discounted rates are often available. Between mid-November and mid-January in particular, a visit may well turn into a rather sodden experience – not just on the trails either, as the cheaper chalet accommodation can be leak-prone – and for your pains you may discover that movement within the park is restricted by the conditions.

Most of the park's trails don't require anything beyond an average level of fitness. Unless you're undertaking extended treks, you won't need special **gear**: T-shirts, long trousers and strong sports shoes (though hiking boots are better) are adequate. Though you'll be screened by the forest canopy much of the time, do have a sun hat and water to hand. It's a good idea to take **binoculars** to get the best possible look at birds from the jungle floor, while a **magnifying glass** can open up a whole new world of insects and leaf and bark formations. More mundanely, you'll need mosquito **repellent** and a good **torch**.

To **budget** for your trip, a useful rule of thumb is that for any trek involving overnighting in the forest (other than in a hide close to a park office or accessible by boat), you're likely to want to hire a guide. The charge for this may seem steep, and the cost of boat excursions can also mount up (see the box on p.256), but these are the only substantial outlays that you'll face, as inexpensive accommodation, eating and transport options are generally easy to find. Many visitors never do any serious trekking and stay for just two or three nights, enough to get a reasonable flavour of the park.

Unfortunately, the undoubted success of Taman Negara, with over sixty thousand visitors a year, brings its own problems. According to some local environmentalists, the increasing number of visitors is having an impact on the park's ecosystem: the popular trail to Gunung Tahan is suffering accelerated **erosion** and some littering due to the large number of hikers. Also of concern is the effect on the food chain of the drift of large mammals away from the much touristed Kuala Tahan area.

Access to the park

Officially there are four entry points to Taman Negara, but only one figures in the schemes of the vast majority of visitors, namely **Kuala Tahan** itself, location of not only the park headquarters but also the elevated canopy walkway and the only upmarket accommodation within the park, the *Mutiara Taman Negara Resort*. Tourist facilities spill across from here to the opposite bank of the Tembeling River, where the once-sleepy Kuala Tahan village positively brims with chalet developments. If you want a relatively solitary, at-one-with-nature experience, you may well not take to Kuala Tahan, but it does have sheer convenience as its trump card – besides an abundance of beds, it boasts reasonable transport connections, simple shops and restaurants, and even cell phone coverage, though **no banks** or ATMs. Of the other three park entrances, two are awkward to get to, and all three are isolated, with simple chalets their only amenities.

In view of the overwhelming popularity of Kuala Tahan, the coverage below focuses on entering the park here. But given the pressures building up at the site, it's in everyone's interest that more visitors get off the beaten track and use the other park entrances, for more on which, see the box opposite.

Taman Negara: alternative approaches

If you visit Taman Negara via any of these entry points, it's best to call in advance to book **accommodation** (through the park office, except in the case of Tanjung Mentong) and, for Kuala Koh and Tanjung Mentong, to check on the availability of **guides**. Park staff can give details of various hiking and wildlife-spotting options. Except where stated, the park and guide fees in the box on p.256 apply.

Entry point and features	Practicalities
Merapoh, Pahang (ⓣ & ⓕ 09/912 4894)	This entrance (aka Sungai Relau) offers the shortest route to Gunung Tahan; allow four days to get there and return. Guided night hikes are available, and there are caves to explore. This is also one of the more promising locations for wildlife-spotting; night "safaris" using jeep tracks can be arranged. Merapoh is on Route 8 and is served by local trains. The station is 7km from the park gates (locals can give you a lift there for RM5). Three-bed chalets, some with air-conditioning, are available (RM40), and there's a dorm (RM10); catering can be arranged. If climbing Tahan, book at least a month in advance; guide fees for Gunung Tahan are RM300 (for up to twelve people), or RM500 if ending up at Kuala Tahan.
Kuala Koh, Kelantan (ⓣ 09/928 2952)	In addition to trekking opportunities, this northern section of the park has reasonable wildlife-spotting (you might see elephants and mousedeer, among others) and fishing. Turn off Route 8 around 45km east of Gua Musang, at the junction for Felda Aring, and continue east for another 45km (the park is signed from Felda Aring). Taxi charter from Gua Musang costs around RM100. Six chalets (❷) and dorm beds (RM5) are available, as is a simple restaurant.
Tanjung Mentong, Terengganu (ⓣ 09/622 7751)	Fishing in Tasik Kenyir is one of the chief draws, plus there's a straightforward two-day hike to Gunung Gagau, and you can explore Gua Bewah, the caves just outside the park perimeter. Access is by boat from the Gawi jetty at Tasik Kenyir (see p.328). Accommodation with private facilities is available at the *Tanjung Mentong Resort* (ⓣ 09/623 6684), which has dorms and chalets (the latter have a/c). Package trips are the best way to visit: the resort offers a three-day, two-night stay in one of the chalets, with meals, boat transfers and some activities (including trekking and a cave trip), for around RM400 per person. Packages are also available from travel agents in Kuala Terengganu.

Whichever entrance you use, upon arrival you pay the nominal park **fees** at the local office of the Wildlife Department, whose staff can be hired as **guides** for jungle treks.

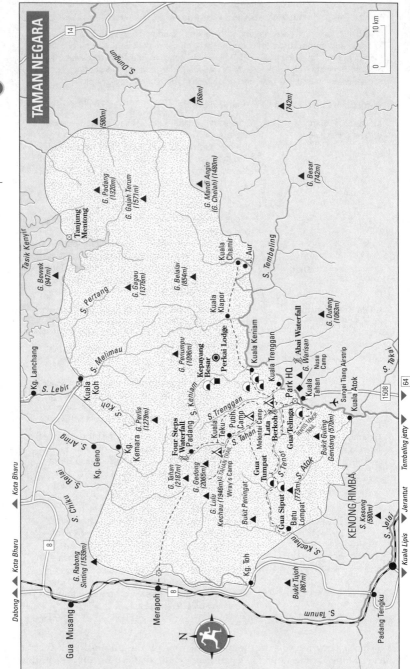

Tourist transfers and packages

Though the bus from Jerantut to Kuala Tahan makes reaching Taman Negara straightforward, many visitors prefer to book themselves a tourist transfer or package trip, with KL the most popular starting point. From the **Bukit Bintang** area, **SPKG** in Jerantut (see p.251) operates a bus to the Tembeling jetty leaving from the *Crowne Plaza Mutiara Hotel* on Jalan Sultan Ismail (departures every morning at around 8.30am; RM40 one-way). The same fare and departure time and place apply to Tembeling buses operated by the travel agent based at the MTC tourist office in KL (☎03/2163 0162), though unlike SPKG they don't sell boat tickets. From **Chinatown**, the very slick **NKS Travel** (☎03/2072 0336, ⓦwww.taman-negara.com) operates its own jetty buses from the *Mandarin Pacific Hotel* (daily 8am; RM35; see p.107), where tickets can be bought. Having cornered a large chunk of the backpacker market, NKS is introducing transfers to the park from further afield in the north of the Peninsula; contact them for their current offerings. Taman Negara **package trips** – available from NKS, SPKG and travel agents and hostels in various cities – usually offer two or three nights at Kuala Tahan, with a range of accommodation and meal options, and may include activities such as walks and boat excursions as well. While they're undoubtedly convenient and give you enough time to get a reasonable flavour of the park, you may well prefer the flexibility of an independent visit, eating where you please and organizing activities of your own choosing – which almost always works out cheaper. For details of the packages at the *Taman Negara Resort*, see p.255.

If you do want to make your own arrangements at the park, note that despite what you may hear in Kuala Tahan or elsewhere, there's no need to book your accommodation through, for example, the agent who arranges your transport to the park; simply shop around once you've arrived (the task is no trickier than anywhere else) or call or email ahead.

Travel to Kuala Tahan

There's only one road to Kuala Tahan, the recently completed **Route 1508**, branching north off Route 64 ten minutes east of Jerantut. **Driving** from KL, leave the East Coast Highway at Temerloh, heading up Route 98 for Jerantut, then pick up Route 64 eastwards for the Kuala Tahan road. Starting from Kuantan, pick up Route 64 at Maran.

Tourist transfers to the park headquarters are available from KL and elsewhere (see below), but if you want to reach Kuala Tahan by **public transport**, you'll almost certainly pass through **Jerantut** (see p.250), just over 50km from Kuala Tahan as the crow flies, and served by **express trains** from KL, Singapore and Kota Bharu (unfortunately, most of these arrive in the small hours). A humdrum little place, Jerantut is the only town with direct links to Kuala Tahan – a very convenient local **bus** departs for the village at 5.30am, 8am, 1.30pm and 5.15pm (RM6; 1hr 30min), as well as **shared taxis** (RM60). If you're starting out in KL or Kuantan, there's no problem finding buses for Jerantut, though you may need to change in Temerloh. **Kuala Lipis** (see p.270) is also a potential jumping-off point for the park – it's only slightly further from Kuala Tahan than Jerantut, it's also served by express trains, and it has some surviving colonial architecture to help while away any spare time you may have.

Much more alluring than reaching the park by road is **boating** up to Kuala Tahan on the muddy **Tembeling River**, taking in the age-old rainforest swathing both banks. For most visitors the ride, in motorized sampans seating ten or so, is an essential part of the Taman Negara experience, though not necessarily worth doing in both directions (you may prefer to save the trip for the finale: the ride back from Kuala Tahan is downriver and thus quicker by about half an hour). The **jetty** for the boat trips (daily 9am & 2pm except Fri 9am & 2.30pm; RM25 one-way, RM50 return; 3hr upriver) is at **Kuala Tembeling**, the access road for which leaves Route 64 just east of Jerantut. For the afternoon boats, you can reach the jetty from Jerantut on the 11.15am local bus to Kerambit, or chance getting a local train, the 8.15am Gemas–Tumpat, which calls at Jerantut at 12.47pm, then Tembeling (one stop along) at 1.04pm; keep your fingers crossed and hope that there are no delays. Note also that the jetty is a half-hour walk from Tembeling "station" (literally just a signboard next to the track); follow the nearby road to the junction where you need to take the fork for the new town (it's best to ask directions). For the morning boats, it's best to arrange a shared taxi in Jerantut (RM16 to the jetty) or book a transfer with the boat operator or a hostel there. Boat **tickets** can be bought at the jetty (which has *kedai kopi*s for a bite while you await your sailing) or in advance from any of three boat operators: the Taman Negara package specialist NKS Travel (with offices in KL and Jerantut; see p.249), Mutiara Hotels (who run the *Taman Negara Resort*; see p.255) and SPKG in Jerantut.

Jerantut

Small, busy **JERANTUT** used to be a tad busier not so long ago, when the town centre sat right on the Raub–Maran road. These days the bulk of the town lies just north of a modern bypass taking most of the through traffic. Yet another road has contributed to the dip in the town's activity, for with the completion of Route 1508 to Kuala Tahan, Jerantut's status as gateway to Taman Negara is somewhat diminished. An accommodation shakeout has ensued, though the town remains a very reasonable place to overnight.

The part of the centre of interest to visitors is shaped like an inverted L, which has the **train station** and **bus station** at its northern end, and which is lined

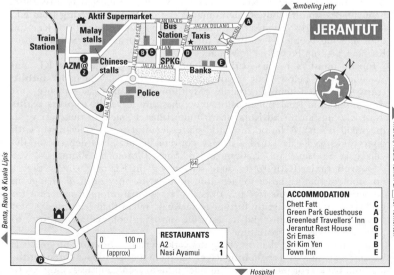

by most of the town's amenities, including a couple of **banks** at the eastern end of Jalan Tahan. An unofficial though very helpful **information** kiosk, really an agency offering tours, accommodation booking and so forth (daily 10am–6pm & 8–10pm except in Ramadan; ℡09/266 1472), is just a little way west of the bus station and the Aktif **supermarket**, one of the best places to stock up on supplies for the park. Not far from the train station is the best of a couple of **Internet** places in town, AZM.

The bus station has a little kiosk advertising bus tickets for Kuala Tahan, but in fact you pay the driver on board. Next door, shared taxis run not only to surrounding towns but also quite a few east-coast destinations – you could reach even Kota Bharu or Kuala Besut (for the Perhentian islands) this way (around RM300). Tickets for boats run by **SPKG** from Tembeling jetty to Kuala Tahan (and on to their *Nusa Holiday Village* accommodation further upriver) can be bought from their office at 16 Jalan Diwangsa (℡09/266 2639, Ⓔspkg@tm.net.my), next to the *KFC*.

Accommodation

Chett Fatt Jalan Diwangsa ℡09/266 5805. In need of a lick of paint, but decent value nonetheless. There's a choice of double rooms, some with a/c but no en suite, or larger rooms (sleeping up to four), some with attached bathroom. ❶

Green Park Guesthouse Jalan Bomba ℡09/266 3884, Ⓦwww.my-greenpark.com. Compact backpackers' place with a/c dorms and rooms, and sharing bathrooms. Apart from the usual Taman Negara transfers, they offer – uniquely – 4WD and boat transfers to Kenong Rimba State Park, where they manage the chalet facilities. Dorm beds RM10, rooms ❷

Greenleaf Travellers' Inn Jalan Diwangsa ℡ & Ⓕ09/266 2745. A homely if unexciting backpackers' place with dorm beds and a variety of rooms, including cheap singles. Some rooms have a/c and TV, though none have an attached bathroom. Unlike the *Sri Emas*, it's pretty laid-back. Dorm beds RM10, rooms ❶

Jerantut Rest House A few minutes' walk from the centre, just south of the end of Jalan Besar ℡09/266 3619. Once serenely removed from the centre, this complex of colonial-era bungalows now abuts the new bypass, and renovations have diluted whatever character it had left. Despite all this, it remains a pleasant place to stay, and is comfy enough, with en-suite a/c rooms with TV, and a large central lounge. It's popular with Malay groups, and when busy can feel appealingly like an extended Malay household. ❸

Sri Emas Jalan Besar ℡09/266 4499, Ⓦwww.taman-negara.com. Part of the NKS Travel juggernaut, with backpackers being shipped in and out every day as though on a conveyor belt. At the time of writing they had two premises on the west side of Jalan Besar, though one of these may shut when their new building on the east side is completed. Besides dorms, there's a wide variety of rooms, for two to four people, with fan or a/c, and with or without en-suite facilities and TV. Everything's well run, almost to a fault; there's also a laundry service, satellite TV in the lounge, and fast Internet access available downstairs. The full range of NKS packages are sold on site. Dorm beds RM8, rooms ❶

Sri Kim Yen Jalan Diwangsa ℡09/266 2168. Excellent value: reasonably well kept, simply furnished rooms, with a/c and en suite. The traffic noise can be irritating though, and mysteriously, the corridors are infernally hot. ❷

Town Inn Jalan Tahan ℡09/266 6811, Ⓦwww.towninn-hotel.com. A newish, friendly mid-range hotel, the rooms a little boxy but more than presentable, with a/c, bathroom and TV. Uniquely, just in case you packed your laptop in with your jungle gear, they also offer wireless Internet access for free. ❸

Eating

The most obvious – and justifiably popular – place to eat in Jerantut is the large open-air **food court** east of the train station. The stalls are largely Malay-run, and do an unusually good range of rice and noodle dishes. A smattering of Chinese stalls and restaurants can be found close to the station – among these is a decent *kedai kopi* that does tasty *dim sum* for breakfast; the *Nasi Ayamui* which, as the name suggests, specializes in chicken rice; and – a cut above the rest – the *A2 Restaurant*, for *char siew* or roast duck rice (RM4) plus seafood and vegetable dishes, cooked to order.

Kuala Tahan village

Travelling to Kuala Tahan by bus from Jerantut, you'll find the road undulates its way through the usual rural Malaysian mix of vast oil-palm estates, rubber plantations and *belukar*, with perhaps a detour through a kampung or two; there's a possibility the bus will pick up a few Batek passengers en route. As for the sixty-kilometre boat trip upriver to the village, that actually begins on the wide Sungai Pahang, but after a short distance the sampans branch off into the narrower **Sungai Tembeling**. At first, small pepper orchards and oil-palm plantations can be seen, but soon the moss-draped trees reach down to the water, the forest canopy thickens, with only the occasional dab of blossom or brown leaves to interrupt the various shades of green.

The confluence for which **KUALA TAHAN** is named is that of the Tembeling and Tahan rivers. Steps on the park side of the Tembeling lead up to the park entrance and the *Taman Negara Resort*; boats deposit new arrivals either here or on the opposite (village) bank, above which the road into Kuala Tahan ends in a small car park.

Practicalities

Little **"umbrella boats"** shuttle on demand between the tiny park jetty and the floating restaurants on the village side (daily roughly 7am–11pm; the fare is 50 sen per person, to be deposited in the boatman's tin). It's in the village that you'll find practically all the budget and mid-range places to stay in the vicinity (except for the campsite and hostel at the *Taman Negara Resort*, and a couple of places upriver on the village side), and all the cheap **eating**. A few accommodation options have their own restaurants, but most visitors eat in the row of floating, glorified *kedai kopi*s moored beside the shingle beach. Opening up daily for breakfast and staying open until 11pm, they offer the usual rice and noodle dishes, sometimes *roti canai*, plus Western travellers' fare such as pancakes, sandwiches and milk shakes. The *Family* restaurant (the names are generally signed on the village side only) has a slight edge over the rest in terms of ambience, with fancy lighting and bamboo roll-up blinds. Note that environmental compliance at some restaurants leaves something to be desired: if you witness scraps going straight in the river, you may want to raise the matter with the park

---

Leaving Kuala Tahan

The **Jerantut bus** leaves from Kuala Tahan's main road daily at 7.30am, 10am, 3.30pm and 7pm; pay the driver the RM6 fare. **Boats** downriver to the Tembeling jetty leave daily at 9am and 2pm, or 9am and 2.30pm on Fridays (RM25). If you didn't buy a return ticket when you came, reserve your ticket the day before your journey, at the SPKG or NKS booths among the floating restaurants. You can arrange the onward trip to Jerantut with them, or try to find a shared taxi once at Tembeling jetty (around RM20 per person). If you intend to use one of the afternoon boats, note that in low season some of these departures may be curtailed; to avoid any nasty surprises, double-check with the boat operator the day before your journey.

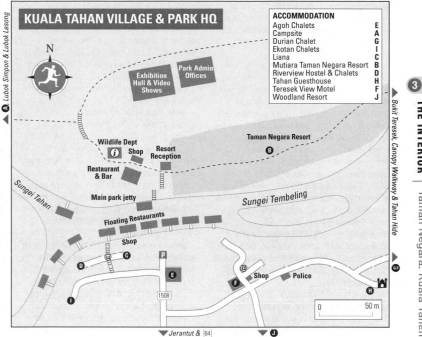

KUALA TAHAN VILLAGE & PARK HQ

N

Lubok Simpon & Lubok Lesong

Exhibition Hall & Video Shows

Park Admin Offices

Wildlife Dept

i Shop

Resort Reception

Taman Negara Resort
B

Restaurant & Bar

Sungei Tahan

Main park jetty

Sungei Tembeling

Floating Restaurants

Shop

@ C

D

P

E

1508

@

F Shop Police

I

H

0   50 m

Jerantut & 64

J

Bukit Teresek, Canopy Walkway & Tahan Hide

ACCOMMODATION

Agoh Chalets	E
Campsite	A
Durian Chalet	G
Ekotan Chalets	I
Liana	C
Mutiara Taman Negara Resort	B
Riverview Hostel & Chalets	D
Tahan Guesthouse	H
Teresek View Motel	F
Woodland Resort	J

authorities. You should take a torch with you in the evening, as **electricity** in the village can be flaky.

The tour operators SPKG and NKS each have an office in and among the restaurants; look out for their logos on the restaurant signs. The village has a few basic shops and stalls scattered about: there's a reasonably priced **convenience store** opposite the *Teresek View Motel*, and near this is one of a couple of places offering **Internet** access at a premium rate (RM6/hr).

Best established of the **upriver** places to stay is *Nusa Holiday Village*, run by SPKG (☎09/266 2639 or 03/40428369, ⓦ www.tamannegara-nusaholiday .com.my; dorm beds RM15, rooms ❸). Around fifteen minutes' boat ride away, it's not a vast complex, but does have quite a collection of accommodation, so the setting isn't as tranquil as it could be. Cheapest are the six- or eight-bed dorms, decent enough, with facilities in a separate block; and the en-suite A-frame chalets, which are slightly threadbare. Best of the lot, at around double the rate for the A-frames, are the so-called "Malay houses", with cane furniture, mosquito nets, a tiled bathroom, fan and air-conditioning; not dissimilar are the fractionally cheaper "Malay cottages", lacking air-conditioning but probably the best value here. The simple restaurant serves up fare very like what you get in Kuala Tahan itself. Budget a little extra for shuttling around on SPKG's boats (see p.258; the ride to Kuala Tahan is RM3 for residents, otherwise RM7). If you want to hike outside the park from here, you could walk to the **Abai Waterfall** in about an hour, or up the nearby peak of **Gunung Warisan**, two hours' away.

Village accommodation

Agoh Chalets ☎ & ℱ 09/266 9570. A range of two- and four-person en-suite chalets, all a/c and with bathroom, though otherwise fairly spartan. Decent if uninspired. ❸

Durian Chalet ☎ 09/266 8940. Delightful, rustic chalets of woven bamboo, clustered around a pretty garden with a teeming fish pond. They're all reasonably maintained and have shack-like bathrooms attached. There's also a separate brick "family house" (RM50), which can be rented out as an eight-person dorm. A great place to get away from it all. It's a 5min walk from the *Teresek View*, down a steep hill and through a small stand of rubber trees. Dorm beds RM10, chalets ❷

Ekotan Chalets ☎ 09/266 9897. Serviceable a/c, en-suite chalets in a small compound, plus dorms, some with a/c, for five to eight people. A tad over-priced. Dorm beds RM13, chalets ❺

Liana ☎ 09/266 9322. A barracks of a building, with four-bed dorms but thankfully not the rigours of boot camp. The management, when you can find them, are friendly, but it's best kept as a fallback. Dorm beds RM10.

Riverview Hostel & Chalets ☎ & ℱ 09/266 6766. Simple, slightly shabby en-suite timber chalets with thatched roofs, plus some four- and six-bed dorms. Resident here is Sulaiman, who speaks good English and can be hired as a guide for treks – not just here but as far afield as Jelawang, if you're so minded. Dorm beds RM10, chalets ❷

Tahan Guesthouse ☎ 09/266 7752, ℮ jungletreker@yahoo.com. A bizarre sight given its setting, this two-storey house is like a kindergarten gone native, painted in bright colours and decorated with wildlife-related murals. Accommodation comprises four-bed dorms and en-suite rooms, all with fan. The place is well kept and the amicable female proprietor speaks excellent English. A good choice; small discounts available when things are quiet. Dorm beds RM10, rooms ❹

Teresek View Motel ☎ 09/266 9744. Once a modest array of chalets, but now dominated by a pale pink new building with a café below. Chalets and stuffy, spartan A-frames survive, all with bathroom inside, but it's the comfy en-suite rooms (some with a/c) on two floors that are most worth shelling out for, especially if you get an off-season discount. There's also a large dorm. Well run – staff persevere unenviably to try to keep the place free of muddy prints. Dorm beds RM10, A-frames ❸, chalets & rooms ❹

Woodland Resort Reached not off the main road but by heading a short distance southeast from the *Teresek View* ☎ 09/2661111, ⓦ www.woodland.com.my. The least annoying of a handful of substantial new tourist developments just south of the village, this is not so much characterless as just plain incongruous, with chalet units somewhere in between kampung house and Alpine hut, surrounded not by woodland but by a rubber plantation. The rooms are utterly bland but do pack in the creature comforts – a/c, TV, fridge and modern bathroom. The indigo-tiled swimming pool is probably the best feature. ❻

The park headquarters and resort

On the hill above the park jetty is the sprawling *Mutiara Taman Negara Resort* and, above it, the offices of the **park headquarters** (☎ 09/266 1122, ℱ 266 4110), belonging to the Wildlife Department. Their **information desk** (daily 8am–10pm, except Ramadan until 6.30pm) should be your first port of call: here you can pay the nominal park entry fees, buy any licences you may need, book **hides** and **activity packages**, charter **boats** or hire **guides**. There is a **left luggage** service, costing roughly RM5 per item per day, with a deposit sometimes required. It's worth putting any questions you have about the park to the staff, many of whom are Wildlife Department guides and may be local to the area. For a list of park fees and charges, see p.256. Close by is a pricey convenience store.

The Wildlife Department puts on a free **video screening** about the park every evening at around 8.30pm in the Exhibition Hall nearby. It's informative and worth attending if you're at a loose end – even if everyone does snigger when **tigers** get mentioned: they're down to around two hundred within the park and seldom spotted, though droppings or prints are sometimes seen.

The Taman Negara Resort

Though pricey, the three-star *Mutiara Taman Negara Resort* (☏09/266 2200 or 3500, Ⓦwww.mutiarahotels.com; chalets from RM380) can be busy, and it's worth booking a couple of months ahead to stay during the peak season or local school holidays. Most of the accommodation comprises fairly plush air-conditioned chalets, with a spacious bathroom, woven bamboo walls and cane furniture, though no TV, for which you'll need to take one of their two extortionately priced self-contained bungalows, each with two bedrooms and a small kitchen. They also have institutional eight-bed **dorms** with bunk beds (at an astounding RM60). The *Resort* has two- or three-night **packages**, but these are worthwhile mainly for the convenience: a three-day, two-night Explorer deal, with some meals and guided activities thrown in, costs around RM1500 for two people – rather more than the sum of its parts (Malaysians and Singaporeans should enquire about separate packages, costing around a third less). Transfers to and from the park aren't included either, but the *Resort* operates a Tembeling jetty bus for guests, leaving from the *Crowne Plaza Mutiara Hotel* in KL (daily at 8.45am; RM40) and arriving in time for the afternoon boat sailing, for which the usual fare applies.

The resort runs the park headquarters' **campsite** (RM5 per person per day), which is signposted uphill from the information desk, at the start of the trail to Lubok Lesong; guitars and radios are forbidden, and monkey feeding is discouraged (it's wise not to leave any food lying around). There are toilets and showers here, and tents can be rented (two-person RM14, four-person RM20).

Wherever you're staying, the resort's *Seri Mutiara* **restaurant** is worth a splurge, serving mouthwatering fare at eyewatering prices. They have a great range of pizzas and sandwiches, including good *quesadillas*, plus steaks and slick Asian specialities, such as beef *rendang*. Main courses start at RM15, but ribeye steak will set you back at least RM35, and the admittedly generous *eis kacang* weighs in at a shocking RM15. Still, the occasional lunch and dinner buffets can be good value. This is also the only spot in Kuala Tahan where alcohol can be consumed.

Inside the park

The account of the park below is divided into three sections: **day-trips** that you can make from Kuala Tahan, trips made from the **upriver sites** at Trenggan and Keniam, and **longer trails** – the Rentis Tenor and Gunung Tahan – which require a certain commitment. Getting well away from the park headquarters to boost your wildlife-spotting prospects is worth the time and expense; you'll never forget the first time you saw an elephant in the forest. For some treks you'll require specific equipment and resources, which are detailed where appropriate. None of the trails themselves, however, require any special skills, nor do they demand anything beyond an average level of fitness. There's a **map** showing the area around Kuala Tahan on p.258 and a map of the whole park on p.248.

Most people in the park for just a few days also sign up for one or two of the little **activity packages** offered by the Wildlife Department and by the *Mutiara Taman Negara Resort* (their bookings counter is next to the resort's reception). The prices charged by each are broadly similar, as are the activities: the resort has a night jungle walk (1hr–1hr 30min; RM30) and night safari (2hr; RM40), plus cave exploration (2hr; RM45) and "rapids-shooting" trips (1hr; RM40).

Taman Negara fees and charges

Park entry	RM1 per person
Camping permit	RM1 per person per night
Camera licence	RM5
Fishing licence	RM10
Use of fishing lodges to fish	RM8 per person
Use of fishing lodges for overnighting	RM1 per person
Hides	RM5 per person
Guide hire	RM150 per day, plus RM100 for overnighting

Boat excursions

The sample prices below are to charter a boat to your destination and back – the boatman may wait for you at the destination or, more likely, return to collect you at an arranged time.

Destination	Four-seater	Ten-seater
Canopy walkway	RM40	RM60
Gua Telinga	RM40	RM60
Kuala Keniam	RM180	–
Kuala Keniam Kecil	RM300	–
Kuala Perkai (for *Perkai Lodge*)	RM280	–
Kuala Trenggan	RM90	RM120
Lata Berkoh	RM120	–
Lubok Lesong	RM80	–
Tabing/Cegar Anjing hides	RM40	–

The **night jungle walks** are fun if you like insects and flora – the park staff escort a chain of groups of about ten on a spooky hike, pointing out the odd scorpion, luminous worm and medicinal plant on a circuit of the area around the resort. The **night safaris** actually take place outside the park; you're driven around a plantation in a 4WD, and may get to see leopard cats or the occasional snake. Neither the cave exploration or rapids trips are especially challenging; they're designed to appeal to families and can be good fun.

Beyond these possibilities, you can think about doing a guided forest walk, or spending a night in one of several **hides.** These are positioned deep in the jungle overlooking salt licks, where you can espy animals drinking the brackish water, or indulge in a spot of **birdwatching at** dawn. If you're into **fishing**, your best bet is probably the Sungai Keniam, northeast of Kuala Tahan, where you might hope to catch catfish or snakehead. You may also want to ask the Wildlife Department about the *ikan kelah* (zoological name *Tor tambroides*) sanctuary at Lubok Tenor, where a project is underway to stock a deep part of the river with these fish; angling isn't allowed here, but you can watch the fish being fed.

To get into truly undisturbed forest you really need to stay for a week or more. On a week's visit, you could start with the thirty-kilometre **Rentis Tenor trail**, a lasso-shaped trek leading west from Kuala Tahan to Gua Telinga, then northwest into deep forest to the campsite at Sungai Tenor. Having returned to Kuala Tahan, you could then go upriver to Kuala Keniam, walk along the wild **Keniam trail** (where elephants are sometimes spotted), and spend the night in a hide before taking a sampan from Kuala Trenggan back to park headquarters. Unless the park is very busy, you're unlikely to see more than a handful of people on these trails. The most challenging thing you could do in a week is the 55-kilometre trek northwest to **Gunung Tahan** (a shorter, quicker approach is from Merapoh; see p.247); allow a day extra either side of the trek to sort out arrangements.

If you have a **specialist interest**, in particular types of fauna, for example, it's worth calling the park headquarters a week in advance of your visit to see if a guide with matching knowledge can be arranged. Being trained by the Wildlife Department, the guides are in fact generally much better on fauna than flora.

To keep **leeches** at bay, which can be a serious problem after rain, wear walking boots or sports shoes, with your trousers tucked into heavy-duty socks and spray on insect repellent liberally every hour or so. Many of the park guides prefer to wear shorts as they say it's easier to deal with leeches if you can see them – but this approach requires an advanced jungle temperament. Except on the very simplest day hikes, you should **inform park staff** of your plans so they know where to look if you get into difficulty; you won't be able to phone for help, as the cell-phone signal dies out just a little way from Kuala Tahan.

Hides and campsites

Spending a night in one of the park's six **hides** (known as *bumbun*s) doesn't guarantee sightings of large mammals, especially in the dry season when the **salt licks** – where plant-eating animals come to supplement their mineral intake – are often so waterless that there's little reason for deer, tapir, elephant, leopard or *seladang* (wild ox) to visit, but it's an experience you're unlikely to forget.

The hides are basic, featuring only wooden beds without mattresses, and a simple chemical toilet; bring sleeping bags, food that doesn't require heating, and water. As well as a torch, take rain gear, hat and sleeping bag, and all the food and drink you will need – and bring all your rubbish back for proper disposal at the resort. It's best to go in a group and take turns keeping watch, listening hard and occasionally shining the **torch** (these can be rented at the park information desk) at the salt lick – if an animal is present its eyes will reflect brightly in the beam. Many people leave scraps of food below the hide, although environmentalists disapprove of this, as it interferes with the animals' naturally balanced diet. You have to book your bunk in the hide at the Wildlife Department office. All the hides sleep twelve people, except for Bumbun Tabing, which sleeps eight.

There are four hides north of the *Taman Negara Resort* and two to the south. Of the northern ones, the closest is **Bumbun Tahan**, which is situated just south of the junction with the Bukit Teresek trail. Deeper in the park and thus more promising are **Bumbun Tabing**, on the east bank of Sungai Tahan (see "Bukit Teresek", p.258, for directions), and **Bumbun Cegar Anjing**, an hour further and slightly to the south, on the west bank of Sungai Tahan, beside an old airstrip. It's reached by fording the river, but in the wet season is only accessible by boat, as the river's too powerful to wade across. The most distant hide to the north of the resort is the **Bumbun Kumbang**, which can be a good place to catch sight of animals such as elephants. It's an eleven-kilometre walk from Kuala Tahan, but can be reached by taking a boat to Kuala Trenggan (45min from the resort), followed by a 45-minute hike.

To the south, **Bumbun Blau** is on the Gua Telinga trail, and beyond the cave, **Bumbun Yong**, at either of which there's only a small chance of spotting wildlife as the hides are quite close both to the traffic on Sungai Tembeling and the resort's vast electricity generator.

Although you don't need to book to use the park's various **campsites**, check with the Wildlife Department as to which are open and their current condition. All the campsites, with the exception of the one at Kuala Tahan, have no facilities whatsoever, though most are close to rivers where you can wash.

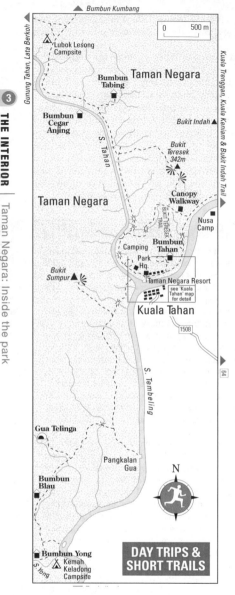

Boats can be chartered like a taxi service to get around the park, and are useful for day-trips as well as longer treks if you're short on time; book boats at the Wildlife Department's information desk (see the box on p.256 for fares). It can be cheaper to use SPKG's **river bus** service, on which fares are per passenger; their boats run at fixed times to a few locations around the park, for example to the Yong hide (RM10 return) and Kuala Trenggan (RM20). For more details and tickets, ask at the *Nusa Holiday Village* office, moored among the floating restaurants.

Day-trips

Popular and easy places to visit close to the park headquarters are **Bukit Teresek**; the **canopy walkway**, where you might be able to observe treetop jungle life close up; the large limestone **Telinga** cave; and the **Berkoh Falls** (the first part of the trail there is a good way to kill a couple of spare hours). You could feasibly tackle two, perhaps three, of these in a day.

Bukit Teresek

Although it's the most heavily used trail in the park, the route to **Bukit Teresek** is an excellent starter trek. You start by following the path which weaves between the chalets east of the resort office, beyond which a trail heads northeast away from the river. It's wide and easy to follow, hitting primary jungle almost immediately; most of the tree types for around 500m along the way have been labelled.

The climb up Bukit Teresek – a 342-metre hill – is best negotiated early in the morning, before 8am, while it's still relatively cool. Along the trail you might hear **gibbons** or **hill squirrels** in the trees; the **monkeys** are relentless pursuers of any type of food, so keep it out of sight. It takes about one hour at an even pace to reach the top, where there's a shelter set on exposed sandstone. The views from here north over the valley to Gunung Tahan (2187m) and Gunung Perlis (1279m) are marvellous. Back at the base of the hill, the canopy walkway is just 300m to the south along a clearly marked, springy path crisscrossed by slippery tree roots.

The canopy walkway and the Bukit Indah trail

About thirty minutes' walk northeast from the resort, along the riverside Bukit Indah trail, is the **canopy walkway** (take the second turning, signed, to the left; daily 9am–3pm, except Fri until noon; RM5). At any one time only a small group of people can gain access to the walkway, so you're likely to have to wait at the start. Taking around thirty minutes to negotiate, the walkway is a five-hundred-metre-long swaying bridge made from aluminium ladders bound by rope, supported at twenty- to sixty-metre intervals by 250-year-old *tualang* trees. Set 30m above the ground, it's reached by climbing a sturdy wooden tower; you return to terra firma by another wooden stairwell at the end of the third section. Once you've got used to the walkway's swaying, you can take in the views of Sungai Tembeling and, if you're lucky, observe the geckoes, cicadas, crickets and grasshoppers which live at this height. Other species you may see include the grey-banded leaf monkey, with a call that sounds like a rattling tin can, and the white-eyed dusky leaf monkey, with its deep, nasal "ha-haw" cry; both lope about in groups of six to eight.

Past the canopy the route divides, with one branch leading north and slightly uphill to the Tabing hide, another 1km further on. The other goes northeast, heading marginally downhill and cutting back towards Sungai Tembeling along the lovely **Bukit Indah trail**. Initially, this follows the riverbank and you're bound to see monkeys, plenty of bird life, squirrels, shrews, a multitude of insects and (if it's early or late in the day) perhaps tapir or *seladang* (wild ox). The path to Bukit Indah itself leaves the main riverside trail (which continues to Kuala Trenggan, 6km away) and climbs at a slight gradient for 200m; the top of the hill offers a lovely view over Sungai Tembeling. It's a three-kilometre, three-hour return trip from the resort office.

Gua Telinga and Kemah Keladong

Another major trail leads south not far from the Tembeling River, with branches off to the limestone outcrop of Gua Telinga, the Blau and Yong hides, and the campsite at Kemah Keladong. The quickest way to tackle this is by chartering a boat five minutes downriver to the jetty more or less due east of the cave. A short, steep path leads up from here to the top of the riverbank, where the trail levels out and veers right almost immediately. Close by you may come across a semi-permanent **Batek settlement**, comprising several *atap*-thatch shelters around a clearing. You may spy women cooking meals in little woks and plenty of children at play, but be discreet about photography; the headman speaks some English and may ask you to pay a small sum for the privilege.

Continuing along the trail, you'll find what looks like a side trail on your left after just a few minutes. Take this and after twenty or thirty minutes you'll come to a rope bridge over a stream and, another fifteen minutes from here, a signpost for Gua Telinga, now just 500m away, and Bumbun Blau. To reach the cave, simply carry on in the direction signed, ignoring a side trail that soon presents itself. **Gua Telinga** looks small and unassuming, but it's deceptively deep – something you only discover when you slide through it. Although in theory it's possible to follow a guide rope through the eighty-metre cave, in practice only small adults or children will be able to tug themselves through the narrow cavities – most people will have to crawl along dark narrow passages in places and negotiate areas of deep, squishy guano. Thousands of tiny roundleaf and fruit bats reside in the cave, as well as giant toads, black-striped frogs and whip spiders (which aren't poisonous). You're most likely to see the roundleaf bats, so called because of the shape of the "leaves" of skin around their nostrils, which help direct the sound signals transmitted to assist the bat in navigation.

Back at the signpost, it's another 1km to the Blau hide through beautiful tall forest, and another kilometre to that at Yong, where the trail divides, north to Kemah Rentis (see p.264) and southeast to the tranquil Kemah **Keladong campsite**, 500m further on, on the terraced bank of Sungai Yong. With an early start, it's quite possible to reach this point, have a swim in the river, and get back to the resort before dusk.

There's an alternative, longer approach to Gua Telinga, starting from the Sungai Tahan just across from the park headquarters. Having crossed the river by sampan (ask staff at the information desk to arrange this), on the opposite bank you follow the trail through a small kampung into the trees. The undulating trail ultimately leads to the jetty east of the cave, but you'll need to turn off to the right after 2km or so, for Gua Telinga and Blau.

Lata Berkoh

Most people visit the "roaring rapids" of **Lata Berkoh** by boat, as it's an eight-kilometre, three-hour trip on foot. You could, however, walk the trail there and arrange for a boat to pick you up for the return journey – or vice versa – getting the best of both worlds. Whilst it's possible to hike all the way to Lata Berkoh, if water levels are high you're likely to face a swim across the river close to the end; it's best to ask the Wildlife Department about current conditions. If you only have a morning left to fill, you could walk the trail as far as Lubok Simpon, where there's a popular swimming spot, then turn back.

Sampans to the rapids head upstream on Sungai Tahan, the busiest of the park's tributaries. The jetty at the other end is just 100m from the simple **Berkoh Lodge**, a small shelter with toilets, set back from the river in a clearing; there's also a **campsite** here.

The **waterfall** itself is 50m north of the lodge. There's a deep pool with surprisingly clear water for swimming (tread carefully around the large rocks on the river bed) and you can picnic here too, overlooking the swirling water. If you ask the boatman to cut his engine, you'll improve your chances of hearing the sounds of the forest and of seeing kingfishers with their yellow-and-red wings and white beaks, large grey-and-green fish eagles, melodious *bulbul* birds and, on the rocks, camouflaged monitor lizards.

The **trail** from the resort to Lata Berkoh starts at the park headquarters' campsite and leads gently downhill, past the turning for the Tabing hide to the east. After around 3km you reach the campsite at **Lubok Simpon**, just to the left of which there's a broad, pebbled beach leading down to a deep pool in Sungai Tahan. The route to the waterfall veers west from the main trail around thirty minutes' walk beyond the campsite, crossing gullies and steep ridges before reaching the river, which must be forded. The final part of the trail runs north along the west side of Sungai Tahan before reaching the falls.

Kuala Trenggan, Kuala Keniam and the Perkai Lodge

Two sites up the Sungai Tembeling from the park headquarters, Kuala Trenggan and Kuala Keniam, offer interesting day hikes, and there's a simple lodge not far from the latter where you can base yourself. In fact, both sites once had pretty slick **Lodges** of their own, but these were disused at the time of writing (the *Trenggan Lodge* may yet reopen; enquire at the *Taman Negara Resort*).

KUALA TRENGGAN, 11km up the Sungai Tembeling from the park head-quarters, can be reached either by boat, which takes less than an hour, or by one of two trails, which take between six and eight hours. The shorter and more direct trail (9km) runs alongside Sungai Tembeling on a well-trodden, lowland forest path which can be quite hard-going; the easier inland route (12km) runs north past the campsite at Lubok Lesong, bearing right into dense forest where elephant tracks may be seen, and then crosses the narrow Sungai Trenggan 500m to the north, to reach the lodge.

A further 20km up Sungai Tembeling is **KUALA KENIAM** (2hr by boat from Kuala Tahan. From here, you could hike two hours down the **Perkai trail** alongside Sungai Perkai (which cuts away from Sungai Tembeling 200m north of the lodge). The trail, which runs roughly parallel to the river, leads to the **Perkai Lodge** (also reachable by boat from Kuala Tahan), a popular spot for fishing and bird-spotting; in places it's possible to leave the main path and find a way down to the water. This far from Kuala Tahan, the region is rich in **wildlife**, including banded and dusky leaf monkeys, long-tailed macaques and white-handed gibbons, all of which are relatively easy to spot, especially with binoculars. As for big mammals, elephants certainly roam in these parts; smaller animals like tapirs, civets and deer are best seen at night or early in the morning. The lodge itself (RM8 per person per night) is a basic shelter with beds but no mattresses (bring sleeping bags), toilets and simple cooking facilities. The water supply can be a problem, in which case you'll need to wash with river water, which is clear here and fine for cooking with, too. There's also a space to **camp** nearby.

The Keniam–Trenggan trail

Hiking the 13km between Kuala Keniam and Kuala Trenggan is a great high-light of the park, combining the possibility of seeing elephants with visits to three caves, one of which is big enough for an army to camp in. The trail is a tough one, with innumerable streams to wade through, hills to circumvent, and trees blocking the path. Usually a full day's hike in dry conditions, it can be covered in around six hours and you should probably hire a guide. Some people take two days instead, overnighting either in the Kepayang Besar cave (conveniently, no tent is needed here), in one of the caves en route, or on a stretch of clear ground near a stream.

The trail cuts southwest from Kuala Keniam along a narrow, winding path through dense forest dominated by huge *meranti* trees with red-brown fissured bark. It's two hours before you enter limestone-cave country, first reaching **Gua Luas** which, though it doesn't have a large internal cavity, is impressive nonetheless. One hundred metres south is **Gua Daun Menari** ("Cave of the Dancing Leaves"), which does have a large chamber through which the wind blows leaves and other jungle debris. Climb up the side of the cave and you'll see small dark holes leading into the cave chamber where, in the pitch darkness, thousands of roundleaf bats live.

To regain the main trail, go back 50m towards Gua Luas and look for an indis-tinct path on the left; follow this for another 30m, at which point you should see the main trail ahead. Bear left here – the third cave, **Kepayang Besar,** is around ten minutes' walk further on. This has a very large chamber at the east-ern side of the outcrop, which is easy to enter and an excellent place to spend the night. The fourth cave, **Kepayang Kecil**, is the last limestone outcrop on the trail. Here, a line of fig trees drops a curtain of roots down the rock, behind which lies a small chamber, with a slightly larger one to the right, containing stalactites and stalagmites.

After passing Kepayang Kecil you're about halfway along the trail, but there are plenty more streams to cross, with armies of ants, flies and leeches. The trail is illuminated in places by patches of sunlight highlighting tropical fungi on the trees and plants, though you're soon back in the gloom again. Parts of the path are wide and easy to follow, while other sections are far narrower, passing through tunnels of bamboo. The final two hours comprise more boggy crossings as the trail descends slightly to Kuala Trenggan. Rather than be collected by boat and heading back to Kuala Tahan, you can prolong the excursion by overnighting near here in the **Kumbang hide**.

Longer trails

The two main long trails in the park are the trek to **Gunung Tahan** and back, requiring a week, and the four-day, circular **Rentis Tenor** trail, which reaches the beautiful Sungai Tenor before dipping back east. For either, you'll need loose-fitting, lightweight cotton clothing with long sleeves, long trousers to keep insects at bay, a raincoat or waterproof poncho, and a litre bottle of water (plus water-purifying equipment or tablets). Also take a tent, a powerful torch, cooking equipment and a compass, all of which can be rented from the Wildlife Department, from whom you can also buy spare batteries; check with your guide or the resort office as to how much food you'll need to take. For Gunung Tahan you also need a sleeping bag for the two nights spent at a high-altitude camp.

Perhaps the most important advice on all long-distance trails is to know your limitations and not run out of time. Slipping and sliding along in the dark is no fun and can be dangerous – it's easy to fall at night and impossible to spot snakes or other forest-floor creatures which might be on the path.

The Gunung Tahan trail

To the Batek Orang Asli, **Gunung Tahan** is the Forbidden Mountain, its summit the home of a vast monkey, who stands guard over magic stones. The Batek venture to the foothills on hunting expeditions but rarely head further up the mountain, because of this belief. Reaching the summit, Peninsular Malaysia's highest peak at 2187m, is the highlight of any adventurous visitor's stay in Taman Negara. Although in high season hundreds of people trudge along the trail every week, the sense of individual achievement after fording Sungai Tahan dozens of times, hauling yourself up and down innumerable hills and camping out every night – let alone the arduous ascent – is supreme. Not for nothing do successful hikers proudly display their "I climbed Gunung Tahan" T-shirts.

One of the chief thrills of the route is that it passes through various types of terrain, from lowland jungle to cloudforest, before reaching the summit. Attaining the summit involves following precarious ridges which weave around the back of the mountain, since the most obvious approach from Sungai Tahan would mean scaling the almost sheer one-thousand-metre-high Teku Gorge – which the first expedition to attempt this route, organized by the Sultan of Pahang, tried and failed to do in 1863. The summit was finally reached in 1905 by a combined British–Malay team, led by the explorer Leonard Wray.

The Gunung Tahan trail must be booked one month in advance, and is the only one in the park on which you must be accompanied by a **guide** (for which a flat fee of RM500 applies, for a group of up to twelve). The first day involves an easy six-hour walk to **Melantai**, the campsite on the east bank of Sungai Tahan, across the river from Lata Berkoh. On the second day more ground is covered, the route taking eight hours and crossing 27 hills, including a long trudge up Bukit Malang ("Unlucky Hill"). This section culminates at **Gunung Rajah** (576m), before descending to Sungai Puteh, a tiny tributary of the Tahan. Before the campsite at **Kuala Teku** you'll ford the Tahan half a dozen times – if the river's high, extra time and energy is spent following paths along the edge of the river, crossing at shallower spots.

On the third day you climb from 168m to 1100m in seven hours of steady, unrelenting trekking which takes you up onto a ridge. Prominent among the large trees along the ridge is *seraya*, with a reddish-brown trunk, as well as oaks and conifers, but the *seraya* thin out when the ridge turns to the west. Here, the character of the landscape changes dramatically to montane oak forest, where elephant tracks are common. Park experts believe that elephants live around this point, where the forest is more open and less dense than lower down, but still rich enough in foliage to provide food. The night is spent at the Gunung Tahan base camp, **Wray's Camp**, named after Leonard Wray.

The fourth day's trek consists of six hours of hard climbing along steep gullies, ending up at **Padang Camp**, on the Tangga Lima Belas Ridge, sited on a plateau sheltered by tall trees. The summit is now only two and a half hours away, through open, hilly ground with knee-high plants, exposed rocks and peaty streams, which support thick shrubs and small trees. Weather conditions up the mountain can't be relied upon: the moss forest, which ranges from 1500m to 2000m, is often shrouded in cloud, which can be present even at the top. The trail follows a ridge into the moss forest and soon reaches the **summit** where, provided it's clear, there's a stupendous view, around 50km in all directions. It's a pristine environment: pitcher plants, orchids and other rare plants grow in the crevices and gullies of the summit.

On the return trip, the fifth night is spent back at the padang, the sixth at Sungai Puteh, and by the end of day seven you're back at Kuala Tahan. If you don't fancy retracing your steps, you can continue more quickly westwards and exit the park at **Merapoh**.

Four-Steps Waterfall

The seven-day (50km) trail to **Four-Steps Waterfall**, east of Gunung Tahan, follows the same route as that described above for the first three days. At **Kuala Teku**, hikers take the right fork instead, which after eight hours of following the course of the Sungai Tahan reaches the foot of the falls. Although the falls are only 30m high, their gorgeous setting makes the trek worthwhile: flat stones by the path are a good point to rest, listen to the sound of the water and look out for birds and monkeys. You can camp below the falls at **Pasir Panjang**, which can be reached in around three hours along a clear path to the right of the falls.

The Rentis Tenor trail

The other major long-distance trail is the four-day, thirty-kilometre, circular **Rentis Tenor**, which leads south to Sungai Yong, then northwest to the campsite at Kemah Rentis and southeast back to Kuala Tahan. A guide isn't compulsory, but in practice hardly anyone goes without hiring one.

The initial route is the same as that to Gua Telinga, bearing north at the Yong hide (2hr from the resort), before following the course of Sungai Yong and reaching the campsite at **Kemah Yong**, just under 10km from the resort. Two hundred metres south of the campsite a side trail leads off to the left to **Bukit Guling Gendang** (570m), a steep, ninety-minute climb best undertaken in the morning, after a good night's rest. From the top, there's a lovely view north to Gunung Tahan, west to Gua Siput and beyond that to Bukit Penyengat (713m), the highest limestone outcrop in Peninsular Malaysia. Towards the summit the terrain changes from lowland tropical to montane forest, where tall conifer trees allow light to penetrate to the forest floor and **squirrels** predominate, with the black giant and cream giant the main species. Both are as big as a domestic cat, their call varying from a grunt to a machine-gun burst of small squeaks.

On day three the main trail continues on into the upper catchment of Sungai Yong, then over a low saddle into the catchment of Sungai Rentis. The path narrows through thick forest alongside the river, crossing it several times, until it joins Sungai Tenor three hours later. Here there is a remote and beautiful clearing, **Kemah Rentis**, beside the river, where you camp. It's a fifteen-kilometre hike back to the resort from here; some trekkers take it easy and spend a fourth night at **Kemah Lameh** (4km from Kemah Rentis) or the **Lubok Lesong** campsite (8km from Kemah Rentis) on Sungai Tahan.

As for the trail itself from Sungai Tenor, follow the river downstream through undulating terrain to the rapids at **Lata Keitiah** (which takes around 1hr), beyond which another tributary stream, Sungai Lameh, enters the Tenor. You're now in lowland open forest where walking is fairly easy; after four hours the trail leads to **Bumbun Cegar Anjing** (another possible overnight stop) from where it's 3km back to the resort.

From KL northeast to Kuala Krai

Two routes cut across the interior from KL to the northeast coast: the jungle railway and Route 8. The main points of interest are **Fraser's Hill**, 100km north of KL; **Kuala Lipis**, the former tin-mining town and erstwhile capital of Pahang, 170km northeast of KL; the state park at **Kenong Rimba**; the caves at **Gua Musang**; and **Stong State Park**. But the chief reason for making the trip to the northeast coast is to spend time in the region's forests and limestone hills, an environment even now somewhat removed from the economic expansion of much of the rest of the Peninsula.

In this lush and rugged region, **Senoi** Orang Asli still lead semi-nomadic lives along inaccessible river basins and in the wide catchment area of the ponderous **jungle railway**. The lifestyles of the two main groups, the Temiar and the Semiar, revolve around a combination of shifting cultivation (where there is still enough accessible land left for this to be feasible), the trading of forest products, fishing and animal trapping. The **Temiar** are mountain dwellers, though the Temiar of southern Kelantan sometimes raft timber down Sungai Kelantan to Kuala Krai, selling the wood on to Chinese middlemen. Although the Temiar are increasingly exploiting the forest for timber, their logging practices are marginal compared to those of the State Forestry Department. The **Semiar**, in contrast, prefer to live in lowland jungle or flat open country, and there are several Semiar communities close to Merapoh, at the northern edge of Pahang.

On the final section of the jungle railway – the 75km from Kuala Krai to Tumpat on the northeast coast – the geography changes from mountainous, river-gashed jungle to plantations of rubber, pepper and oil palm. This is also **cattle country**, where cows grazing along the railway sidings are a constant problem for train drivers; there are occasional collisions. For Kota Bharu, get off at the penultimate stop, Wakaf Bharu, 7km away.

Fraser's Hill (Bukit Fraser)

The development at **FRASER'S HILL** (actually seven hills), 1500m up in the Titiwangsa mountain range, was built to provide welcome relief for the British expatriate community from the humidity of Kuala Lumpur, 75km to the south as the crow flies. The hills were originally known as Ulu Tras, until the arrival in the 1890s of a solitary British pioneer, called James Fraser. An accountant by profession, he travelled to Australia at the peak of its gold rush and then came to Malaya. Although gold wasn't found in any quantity in the hills here, Fraser did find plentiful **tin** deposits. The tin was excavated by Chinese miners and hauled by mule along a perilous hill route down through thick jungle, to the nearest town, Raub, where Fraser set up a camp and a gambling den for his workers. After 25 years, Fraser mysteriously disappeared, and when a search party trekked up into the area to look for him in 1917, the camp and mines were deserted. However, the excellent location recommended itself to the party, who soon convinced the British authorities that it would make a perfect **hill station**.

Just on the Pahang side of the Pahang and Selangor border, Fraser's Hill was never as popular as the much larger Cameron Highlands to the north, and feels remote even today. During the Emergency in the 1950s, the surrounding mountainous jungle provided perfect cover for some of the communist guerrillas' secret camps, from where they launched strikes on British-owned

△ *Ye Olde Smokehouse*, Fraser's Hill

plantations and neighbouring towns. If you approach Fraser's Hill via Kuala Kubu Bharu, due north of KL, roughly halfway up you'll see a sign, "Emergency Historical Site", marking the spot where Sir Henry Gurney, the British High Commissioner for Malaya at the height of the communist insurgency in 1951, was ambushed and killed. The guerrillas hadn't known how important their quarry was: their aim had been only to steal guns, ammunition and food, but when Gurney strode towards them demanding that they put down their weapons, they opened fire.

Today, Fraser's Hill is a sleepy, well-tended settlement, its streets planted with flowering rhododendrons, ageratums and daylilies. The chief attraction is the chance to tackle a network of nature **trails** in relatively cool conditions, but **birdwatching** is also a draw, with long-tailed sibias and silver-eared mesias among the birds potentially on view. Every June, the Fraser's Hill International Bird Race has teams competing to sight as many species of bird as they can. While there's nothing especially compelling about the place, Fraser's makes a good getaway from the heat and hubbub of KL, and at weekends (when accommodation prices shoot up) it draws local families from both there and as far away as Singapore. A day-trip from KL is feasible only with a car; in any case, it's far preferable to spend a restful night at the hill station.

Travel practicalities

Fraser's Hill lies on the road between **Kuala Kubu Bharu** (KKB), on Route 1 (the old north–south main road on the Peninsula), and **Raub** on Route 8. If you're driving to Fraser's Hill from KL, it's best to head there via KKB (either using Route 1 itself or the North–South Expressway initially), which you leave at the Rawang exit. The only **public transport** is a battered old bus, run by the Pahang Lin Siong bus company, that shuttles a few times a day between Raub and KKB (2hr), though note that on only one of these runs does the bus get all the way up to the hill station itself. At other times, the bus stops 8km short of the hill station, at the Gap (see p.268), from where you'll have to hike up. Departures from Raub are at 8am and 1.30pm, while departures from KKB are at 10.30am and 4pm; the 10.30am bus from KKB reaches the Gap around 11.15am and then climbs to the hill station itself, arriving half an hour later and descending for Raub at noon. The fare from KKB to Fraser's Hill is around RM4.

Connecting onto this bus **from KL** means getting to KKB, one of those journeys that, confusingly, can be done in several ways. The route given here avoids the capital's traffic snarl-ups by using the KTM Komuter service to **Rawang** (50min from KL Sentral; RM4). Head out of the lane from the station and left into a one-way road that's one of Rawang's two main thoroughfares. You'll need to cross the road and continue in the same direction for a minute or so, looking for a lane on the right where buses are parked. A blue-and-yellow KKB bus departs roughly hourly from here (there are Chinese *kedai kopis* in the lane for a bite while you wait), getting you to KKB's bus station in an hour. Given the slight uncertainty over bus timings from Rawang, aim to be in Rawang at least two hours before the Fraser's bus leaves KKB. To hook up with the morning Fraser's bus, for example, you need to take the train which passes through KL Sentral at 7.30am, and then catch the 9am Rawang–KKB bus. If you somehow arrive in KKB too late for the Fraser's bus, you may be able to charter a taxi to take you up (RM60).

Raub is the place to aim for if you're travelling **from the interior**. There are plenty of Raub buses from Kuala Lipis during daylight hours (1hr 30min; RM5), and several buses a day from Temerloh and **Kuantan** as well.

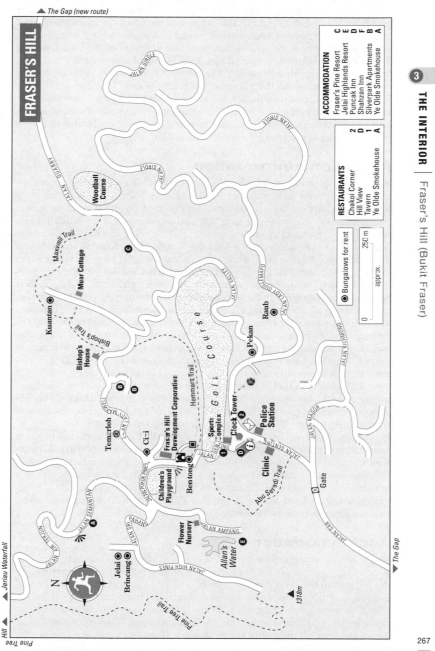

FRASER'S HILL

▲ The Gap (new route)

Jalan Girdle

Jalan Girdle

Woodball Course

Jalan Quarry

Maxwell Trail

Muar Cottage ■ C

Kuantan ◉

Bishop's Trail

Bishop's House

B ■

B

Jalan Maxwell

Temerloh

Cili

Fraser's Hill
Development Corporation

Children's
Playground

Bentong

Jalan Genting

Henmart Trail

Golf Course

Pekan ◉

Raub ◉

Jalan Valley

Jalan Lady Maxwell

Sports
Complex

Clock Tower

2

1

D

i

Police
Station

Clinic

Jalan Genting

Jalan Mager

Gate

Jalan Richmond

Abu Seradi Trail

Jalan Bukit

The Gap ▼

Jalan Pokok Pines

Jalan Semantan

Air Terjun

Jalan BB

Pahang

Flower
Nursery ■

Jalan Ampang

Allan's
Water

E

Jelai ◉
Brincang ◉

Jalan High Pines

1318m ▲

Pine Tree Trail

N

Jeriau Waterfall ◀

Hill ◀

Pine Tree ◀

RESTAURANTS

Chakoi Corner	2
Hill View	D
Tavern	1
Ye Olde Smokehouse	A

ACCOMMODATION

Fraser's Pine Resort	C
Jelai Highlands Resort	E
Puncak Inn	D
Shahzan Inn	F
Silverpark Apartments	B
Ye Olde Smokehouse	A

◉ Bungalows for rent

0   250 m
approx.

The hill station is reached by a single-lane road which branches off the KKB–Raub road at a spot called **the Gap**, where there's a colonial-style lodge, the *Gap Rest House* (☎09/362 2227; RM50), with a restaurant for refreshments, and pleasant rooms. The road takes summit-bound traffic only, with downhill traffic using a road that joins the KKB–Raub road 1km northeast of the Gap. **Leaving Fraser's** by bus presents no special problems, though if you need to catch a bus from the Gap (roughly 8.45am & 2.15pm for KKB, noon & 4.15pm for Raub), be sure to descend from the hill station in plenty of time. If you're heading for KL, you'll find local buses from KKB all the way to Puduraya bus station (the main bus station in the city), or you can travel via Rawang as described earlier. Heading for the interior or east coast, as ever, travel early in the day to have a reasonable number of onward connections to choose from.

Arrival and information

If you head up to Fraser's Hill from KKB, you'll pass a considerable depression filled by a lake and surrounded by denuded slopes – the result of the recently built **KKB dam** on Sungai Selangor. A project of this scale, creating a new reservoir for the burgeoning Klang Valley, naturally couldn't be realized without major environmental consequences, and there was controversy over the destruction of the rainforest here and the transfer of Orang Asli from one of their traditional areas to new settlements. As the road climbs, you begin to take in vistas of the surrounding forested hills (the left-hand side of the bus gives the best views), while on the road itself, epiphytic wild orchids dangle their blooms gorgeously from the woodland shrubs. Unfortunately you may not feel like savouring all this natural beauty as the road, while in good condition, is one of those whose twists and turns somehow conspire to amplify the slightest propensity to motion sickness. This doesn't stop the hill road being a popular, moderately demanding test for **mountain bikers**, but unfortunately there are no outlets in the area renting bikes; the people you may see pedalling determinedly uphill have driven here with all their gear.

An old-fashioned **clock tower** marks the centre of the hill station. Nearby, in the large block containing the *Puncak Inn*, is a helpful **tourist office** (Mon–Fri 8am–5pm, Sat & Sun 8am–10pm; ☎09/362 2201). A local guide, the knowledgeable Mr Durai (☎013/983 1633, ✉ durefh@hotmail.com), can often be found here. More or less opposite, in the so-called sports complex (really a basic clubhouse for the golf course), is the WWF-sponsored **Nature Education Centre** (Wed–Sun roughly 9am–5pm; ☎09/362 2517), which also offers information on the trails, and on the bird species of the area (much of which is available in the "Fraser's Hill" section of ⓦ www.fmalaysia.org).

Outside the *Shahzan Inn* (see opposite) is a small branch of Maybank where you can **change money** (there are no ATMs at Fraser's Hill).

Accommodation

Much of the accommodation in Fraser's Hill is motel-like, and geared to families and groups. It's also possible to stay in a number of **bungalows** (at the hill station the term applies to both detached single-storey houses as well as small apartment blocks); most once had terribly Anglo-Saxon monikers, but have now been given Malay ones. Many belong to large corporations and are rarely let to the public, but several (including *Bentong*, *Cini* and *Kuantan*) can be booked through the tourist office (apartments and rooms in houses from ❺). A few, much slicker bungalows and houses with a hint of mock Tudor about them (*Brinchang*, *Jelai*, *Raub* and *Temerloh*) are let by Highland Rest House

Holding (their office is in the *Pekan* bungalow; ℡09/362 2645 or 03/2163 2816, ✉highlands_rh@myjaring.net; doubles in *Pekan* from ●, three-bedroom houses from RM450), but note that their rates can as much as double at weekends. Finally, the tourist office also has a few units to let in the substantial, modern *Silverpark Apartments* complex, crowning a nearby ridge (●).

Fraser's Pine Resort Jalan Quarry ℡09/362 2122, reservations ℡03/7804 3422, ⓦwww .thepines.com.my. One of the largest developments in the area, unobtrusively positioned in a valley between two hills; on offer are modern one- to three-bedroom apartments with basic kitchen facilities. Rates go stratospheric at weekends and during school holidays (the "Calendar" section of the website lists variations through the year). Breakfast is included. Low season ●, high ●

Jelai Highlands Resort Jalan Ampang ℡09/362 2600, ℻362 2604. Spacious en-suite rooms with green carpets and a small amount of cane furniture, but all slightly tatty. The rate includes breakfast, which, unusually, is a cooked Western one (rice or noodles are an option on weekends only). Prices rise by twenty percent at weekends. Weekdays ●

Puncak Inn Jalan Genting; bookings through the tourist office. The only budget place up here, in a decidedly institutional block. Rooms are basic but in reasonable condition, and have their own bathroom with hot water. ●

Shahzan Inn Jalan Lady Guillemard ℡09/362 2300, ✉shahzan8@tm.net.my. Located next to the golf course, this recently renovated hotel comprises tiers of rooms ascending a terraced hillside. It's largely bland and modern, but everything's in good shape; rooms are en suite and have satellite TV. Breakfast is included. Good value during the week; at weekends, rates rise by fifty percent. Weekdays ●

Ye Olde Smokehouse Jalan Semantan ℡09/362 2226, ⓦwww.thesmokehouse .com.my. The most characterful lodging in Fraser's Hill by a mile, quaintly decorated throughout in the style of a stereotypical English country inn. You can lounge by the fire in the evenings and then retire to your room's four-poster bed, guaranteed to make the cool nights pass all the more blissfully; rooms are very spacious and the bathrooms have been sympathetically renovated. The restaurant serves some of the most delightfully bland food you might have in Malaysia. Rates (it doesn't hurt to ask about weekday discounts) include a full English breakfast. ●

The hill station

As is apparent the moment you arrive, the hill station comprises several wooded hills, with named trails snaking off on all sides. If you don't fancy wandering through the undergrowth, you can enjoy some pleasant walks just by following the roads, which are seldom steep. The easiest target is a small lake, **Allan's Water**, along Jalan Ampang, where you can rent a rowing boat (RM6 for 15min). Another possibility is to head to **Jeriau Waterfall**, around 4km north of the clock tower on foot; on the way you'll pass *Ye Olde Smokehouse*, where, if you time it right, the **cream teas** (daily 3.30–6pm) are a very strong inducement to pause for a breather. Another reason to drop by is to survey the reasonably convincing English country decor – some of which might have rubbed off from its origins, in 1924, as a sort of club for British personnel in Malaya who'd fought in World War I. Yet another good walk involves taking Jalan Lady Guillemard east to the loop road, Jalan Girdle; this leads to the most remote section of the hill station, bordering **Ulu Tramin Forest Reserve**. Completing the circle, all the way round and back to the tourist office, takes around ninety minutes.

Most of the **trails** can be covered in less than two hours (indeed it would only take a couple of days to cover them all), but they aren't signposted and aren't always easy to follow; there have been a couple of major scares in recent years when a British biologist and some unsupervised boys from Singapore separately got lost up here for days. Both incidents were highly atypical, so you shouldn't be paranoid about losing your way, but it doesn't hurt to talk through your route with the tourist office before you set out, and you may want to engage Mr Durei as a guide. The trails can get quite slippery in wet weather, so be sure to wear proper footgear and take the standard precautions against leeches (see p.44).

The **Abu Suradi trail** begins on Jalan Genting close to the mosque, and takes about twenty minutes to reach its southern end, also on Jalan Genting, near the clinic. The **Hemmant trail** also starts from near the mosque and snakes along the edge of the golf course just within the jungle. At the far end of the trail, you can turn left and either walk on to Jalan Lady Maxwell, or continue as far as the Bishop's House, where you can pick up the **Bishop's trail**. After about 45 minutes, this route joins the **Maxwell trail**, at which point you can either leave the trail by turning right up the hill and returning to town via Jalan Lady Maxwell, or continue another hour on the Maxwell trail until it reaches Jalan Quarry. Here there's a course for **woodball** – a hybrid of croquet and golf, played with long mallets – with equipment available to rent. The longest trail is the **Pine Tree trail** (4km), which starts at the end of Jalan High Pines and winds up to Pine Tree Hill.

Eating and drinking

Culinary pride of place on Fraser's Hill goes to the **restaurant** at *Ye Olde Smokehouse*. It's pricey (main courses start at RM40), but is well worth the expense for a slap-up meal: the classic English fare – beef Wellington, oxtail stew with dumplings, bread-and-butter pudding and the like – is pretty convincing, and the service suitably reserved and unhurried. They also do **cream teas** (daily 3.30–6pm), as well as a good range of beers and whiskeys, plus shandy, all of which go down especially well in the country-pub-style lounge. Things are fairly informal during the day, but don't turn up in a T-shirt and shorts in the evening.

Clustered around the clock tower are two inexpensive restaurants – *Chakoi Corner* for *mee bandung* (their speciality), *lontong* and other Malay fare; and the *Hill View*, next to the tourist office, serving Chinese food. Also here is the *Tavern*, for American breakfasts (RM8), steaks and burgers, as well as expensive scones (RM12). Both the *Tavern* and the *Hill View* serve alcohol.

Kuala Lipis and Kenong Rimba

It's hard to believe that **KUALA LIPIS**, about 100km northeast of Fraser's Hill by road, was the state capital of Pahang from 1898 to 1955. Today, it's a sleepy, inconsequential place, situated at the confluence of Sungai Lipis and Sungai Jelai (a tributary of the Pahang), dwarfed by steep hills and surrounded by forest and plantations, though it still has frontier-town charm.

Kuala Lipis started life as a small riverside settlement in the early nineteenth century; the population grew from a few dozen to around two thousand by the 1890s. By then it was a **trading centre** for *gaharu* (a fragrant aloe wood used to make joss sticks) and other jungle products, collected by the Semiar and traded with Chinese *towkays*. Until the first road was built from Kuala Lumpur in the 1890s – allowing the 170-kilometre journey here from the capital to be made by bullock cart – the river was the only means of transport; the trip from Singapore by ship and then sampan upriver took over two weeks. Nevertheless, because of its central geographical position and early importance as a transit point on Sungai Pahang for locally mined tin, Kuala Lipis was where the colonial government set up its state administrative headquarters. However, the tin deposits soon evaporated, and while today Kuala Lipis benefits to a degree from nearby gold-mining, it has long since been eclipsed by the rise of Kuantan on the east coast.

For a town whose main street is only 400m long, Kuala Lipis boasts a disproportionate number of colonial-era buildings, which could keep you pleasantly occupied for half a day. But the reason most travellers stop here is nearby **Kenong Rimba State Park**, promising rainforest hikes without the crowds that frequent Taman Negara's headquarters.

The Town

The old core of Kuala Lipis comprises just a few streets of shophouses, squeezed into a sliver of land between the railway line and the Jelai River. The railway forms a divide in more ways than one, for to the south of the line is an altogether different landscape of wooded hillsides and playing fields, nestled among which are the town's surviving colonial buildings. An elevated pedestrian walkway and a road bridge are practically all that connect the old centre with the town's hinterland, which is small enough to cover on foot in two or three hours.

From the complex traffic intersection by the Centrepoint development, a road leads east along a small ridge, past the town's hospital, to the **Pahang Club** (1867). Though once the archetypal colonial club in the tropics, it's not at all grand – indeed there's something of the English rural train station about the building, all white wooden slats and grilles. The club was the first building constructed by the British in the town, later serving as a temporary residence for Pahang's most famous Resident, Hugh Clifford. Recently refurbished, it's now a meeting place and sports venue for the town's small business community, and is restricted to members, though if you ask nicely you may be allowed to look around.

The buildings you can see across the fields to the south of the Pahang Club belong to the town's historic Clifford School. Don't head across the fields to get there, but instead take the road that descends southwest from the club, joining

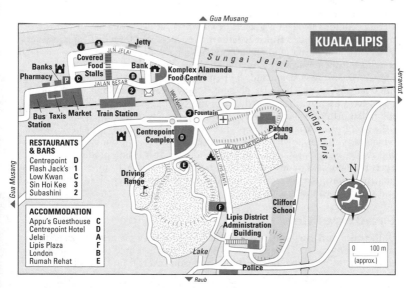

△ The Lipis District Administration Building

the town's north–south artery close to an Indian temple, where you turn left. Further on, just before the major T-junction, you'll spot a flight of steps up to the top of a hillock crowned by the town's largest colonial structure, the crimson-and-white **Lipis District Administration Building**. Dating from 1919, it's been beautifully maintained and now serves as the local law court. Below here is the access road for **Clifford School**, built in 1913 and part-funded by Hugh Clifford; the original buildings are at the far end of the compound. The school is still one of a select group where the country's leaders and royalty are educated – though these days it's perhaps equally known for having been attended by Malaysia's biggest-selling pop songstress, Siti Nurhaliza. There's not a lot to see, but you may be able to have a discreet look around.

Hugh Clifford lived in a graceful two-storey house atop one of the town's highest hills, now called **Bukit Residen**, the access road for which coils upwards from just south of the *Lipis Plaza* hotel. It's a pleasant, none too taxing stroll to the top, but the rewards are slim: the building is now the somewhat disappointing *Government Rest House*, and the marvellous views of the Pahang jungles the hill once offered have been largely screened by trees. Not so long ago the house could have been reached directly from the centre by a steep flight of steps on the hill's north side, but this is now so overgrown as to be impassable.

A vibrant **pasar malam** takes place around the bus station every Friday night, when everybody in town turns out. Stalls sell everything from cleaning utensils and digital watches to pet birds, fruits and river fish (some produce may have been brought by Orang Asli from as far away as Kuala Krai), while hawkers prepare massive trays of cooked noodles, seafood, pies, deep-fried prawn cakes and superb cornmeal puddings.

Practicalities

Both **train and bus stations** are on the old town's main street, Jalan Besar, where you'll find a few **banks**, the post office and a couple of pharmacies. The easiest way to reach the **Taman Negara** headquarters from here is to charter a taxi to the Tembeling jetty (RM40), though it's also possible to get a local bus to Mela, where you change for a Kerambit bus, which passes the jetty. Alternatively, hop on a train for Jerantut and get the Kuala Tahan bus from there.

Kuala Lipis has no tourist office, though on one of the two lanes to the train station is a **travel agency**, run by Hassan Tuah (℡09/312 3277, ⓔkenongrimba@hotmail.com), who can dispense general information and offers packages to Kenong Rimba State Park, as well as to the **Jeram Besu** rapids, a popular rafting spot near Raub. The Centrepoint Complex – promoted as "Seven Levels of Splendour" but actually several concrete floors of dreary shops around a central courtyard, positively spooky at night – has a couple of places for **Internet** access, including Best Modern Computing on Level 3; there's also a terminal at *Appu's Guesthouse*.

Accommodation

There are plenty of budget and mid-range places to stay, though avoid the cheapest places you'll see in the centre, as they tend to be seedy.

Appu's Guesthouse 63 Jalan Besar ℡09/312 2619, ⓔjungleappu@yahoo.com. Appu leads trips to Kenong Rimba and has put his affection for the forest into the jungle mural that adorns one wall here. His guesthouse is a homely affair and popular with travellers, with a range of basic rooms (including a quad room with a/c) which share facilities. The sign outside reads *Lipis Hotel*. Dorm beds RM10, rooms ❶

Centrepoint Hotel ℡09/312 2688, ℻312 2699, ⓔlcphotel@tm.net.my. The Centrepoint Complex's saving grace, this hotel is one of the best deals in town. It boasts a vast range of rooms, all with a/c, satellite TV and tiled bathrooms; the cheapest rooms are rather poky and some are windowless, but they're good value nonetheless. There's a decent restaurant too (rates include breakfast). Reception is on level 5 of the complex. ❸

Jelai 44 Jalan Jelai ℡09/312 1192, ℻315 1050. First impressions here aren't promising: the receptionists are barricaded behind glass like bank tellers, and the corridors are bare. Somehow, though, the rooms are immaculate – spotless, with a/c, bathroom, and TV. They have a second hotel

near the Centrepoint Complex but it's nowhere near as good. ❸

Lipis Plaza Komplek Taipan, Jalan Benta–Lipis ℡&℻09/312 5588. This modern hotel, in a leafy area at the base of Bukit Resident, is a bit of a let-down, with rather musty rooms. A fallback in the unlikely event that the *Centrepoint* is full. Rates include breakfast. ❹

London 82 Jalan Besar ℡09/312 1618. Staff aren't particularly welcoming and don't speak much English, but the rooms are tolerable for a night, and the basic ones with fan are very affordable (if you want a/c and TV you'd do much better elsewhere). ❶

Rumah Rehat (Government Rest House) Bukit Residen ℡09/312 2784, ℻312 3953. Not to be confused with a second *Rumah Rehat* to the southeast of town, Clifford's former home has been jazzed up with a coat of scarlet paint, but the interior is rather bland. Still, the rooms – all with a/c and TV – are well kept if a little spartan, and the attached bathrooms are huge, dwarfing rooms in many cheap hotels. It's easiest to drive up. ❸

Eating and drinking

The best place to **eat** in town is the lively *Sin Hoi Kee*, just across from the Centrepoint Complex, with a wide-ranging Chinese menu at reasonable prices. The restaurant at the *Centrepoint Hotel* comes a close second, offering a great seafood platter with chips and tartare sauce, plus steaks and sandwiches. Unusual, locally caught river fish is the speciality of the *Low Kwan* **restaurant** underneath *Appu's Guesthouse*, but doesn't come cheap – you could end up paying RM40 for one dish. For an inexpensive meal, head along Jalan Besar to *Subashini*, an agreeable Tamil curry house which has the usual spread of fiery fare as well as *nasi lemak* and *mee goreng* at breakfast, and great orange and mango yoghurt drinks; get there early if you want dinner, as it can shut around 8.30pm. Otherwise, there are plenty of **food stalls** in the Alamanda food centre and Centrepoint Complex for Malay and Chinese fare, while the alley connecting Jalan Besar and Jalan Jelai has a collection of Chinese *kedai kopi*s and bakeries.

There are a few somewhat tacky Chinese **beer gardens** in the lanes around the Centrepoint Complex, but the best place in town for a drink is *Flash Jack's* at 55 Jalan Jelai. It's predictably Chinese in some ways – as the racy posters of Hong Kong nymphets on the walls bear out – but in other respects is quite distinct from the competition, with cowboy saloon-style swing doors, a collection of hats on the walls and a laid-back atmosphere. At the time of writing they were talking of moving north across the Jelai River, where a new suburb of Kuala Lipis is beginning to appear; in this event, any hotel in town should be able to let you know the new location.

Kenong Rimba State Park

Coupled with a visit to Kuala Lipis, **Kenong Rimba State Park** makes for a nicely varied three- to five-day stop-off en route from KL to Kota Bharu. Rimba's main attraction is that it offers a compact version of the Taman Negara experience – jungle trails, riverside camping, mammal-spotting and excellent birdwatching – at much reduced prices and without the hype which characterizes the larger park on its northeastern border. One-tenth of the size of Taman Negara, Kenong Rimba stretches over 128 square kilometres of the Kenong Valley, east of Banjaran Titiwangsa. It's dotted with limestone hills, which are riddled with caves of varying sizes, and crossed by trails which snake along the forest floor. The park is also a promising place to spot big mammals, though it's still unlikely you'll catch sight of a tiger or elephant.

As Rimba is small, you can see most of its main sights within four days. You could check out the caves for a day, spend another trekking to the waterfall, and two or three days walking back through the jungle, where you may chance upon a village of the nomadic Batek people. The main trail in the park, the nine-kilometre Kesong trail, heads north from park headquarters along the Sungai Kesong to the Lata Kenong (Seven Steps Waterfall). Here you are surrounded by lowland forest, through which little sunlight penetrates. Over the years, the Batek have cleared portions of forest around this trail for agricultural purposes, which could account for the jungle's impenetrability – secondary forest tends to grow back more thickly than primary. Returning on the southeastern loop of the trail takes longer and is harder going as it traverses several small hills – Gunung Putih (884m) is the largest. If you only have time for a brief visit to the park, you could make straight for the waterfall and camp there for a night, leaving the park by the same route the next day.

The caves

The first of the six **caves** in Rimba is outside the park proper, close to the Tanjung Kiara jetty. About ten minutes' walk from the jetty along the road, look out for a path on your left which leads west to **Gua Batu Tinggi,** a small cave just big enough to clamber into. Inside, there's a surprising variety of plant life, including orchids and fig trees.

Gua Batu Tangga (Cave of Rock Steps) is a twenty-minute walk direct from the camp at Gunung Kesong, though you can also get there from the Batu Tinggi cave by returning along the trail leading to it and crossing the road, following the path to the left of a house – a sign points to the cave, which lies twenty minutes' walk further on. Shaped like an inverted wok, the large limestone cave has a wide, deep chamber, in whose northwest corner a

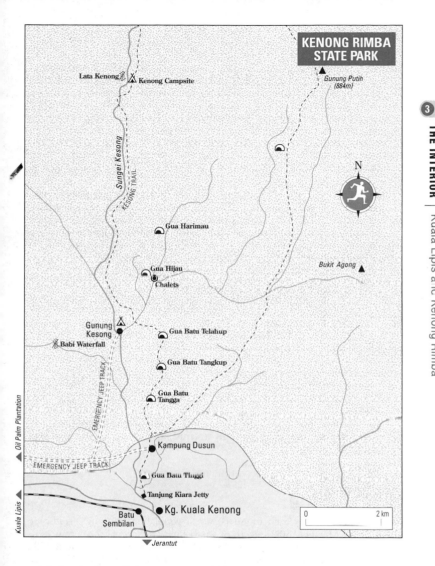

row of rocks forms ledges or steps, which give the cave its name. The cave is sometimes occupied by elephants – the trail through it narrows between rocks rubbed smooth over time, probably by the passage of the great creatures – but you're more likely to catch sight of mousedeer or porcupine scurrying away. Two smaller caves, **Gua Batu Tangkup** and **Gua Batu Telahup**, are just a few hundred metres beyond Tangga on the same trail.

Two more caves lie close to the park headquarters: **Gua Hijau** (Green Cave), just five minutes' walk east over two bridges, is home to thousands of bats, while **Gua Harimau** (Tiger Cave), a little further along on the right, is scarcely more than an overhang and reputedly the lair of tigers.

Practicalities

As there's no scheduled transport to the park, it's best to go on a package trip or hire a guide who can make the necessary arrangements. The most straightforward option is to go with Green Park Adventure (☎012/688 8314, ⓦwww .my-greenpark.com), who are based at their guesthouse in Jerantut (see p.251). Their package trips (roughly RM250 per person for three days and two nights, depending on group size) depart from either Jerantut or Kuala Lipis, with the choice of four-wheel-drive or boat transfers. In Kuala Lipis, Appu at *Appu's Guesthouse* has done plenty of Kenong Rimba treks in his time, and charges RM60 per person per day, including food, plus RM250 per group to cover the boat trip there and back. You'll also need to pay a camping fee of RM5 per person per night. Hassan Tuah offers three-day, two-night packages for groups of four, costing RM250 per person.

Boat journeys into the park usually begin at the **Kuala Lipis jetty**, where you take a sampan down the Jelai River. The journey to Tanjung Kiara jetty, the entry point to the park, takes approximately an hour and fifteen minutes. It's also possible to take a local **train** journey to **Batu Sembilan**, near to the jetty; you might be able to find a sampan to Tanjung Kiara from here (RM50 per boat), but don't count on it. About ten minutes' walk from the jetty is the village of Kampung Dusun, from where it's another half-hour walk to reach the park proper.

The only proper **accommodation** in the park is the chalets (RM40) and dorms (RM10) near Gua Hijau, run by Green Park Adventure. If you're here on one of their packages, you'll spend one night here and another in the cave itself. There are shared bathrooms on site, but there's no electricity – though paraffin lamps help keep the jungle soundscape from getting a little too eerie when night closes in. A small **café** here serves breakfast (RM6), meals and snacks into the early part of the evening.

No special **equipment** is needed in the park, but be sure to take sturdy walking shoes and a decent quantity of drinking water on the trails. Lots of mosquito repellent is also worth having on hand, and make sure to take precautions against leeches (see p.44). It's also worth bringing a torch, swimsuit, sandals (for wading through streams), a rain poncho and a change of clothing.

Gua Musang

As you head north by train or on Route 8 you'll find the jungle landscape altering near Merapoh, 80km north of Kuala Lipis (and one of the entrances to Taman Negara), where there's a predominance of large, round limestone hills. From Merapoh, it's another half-hour by local train to **GUA MUSANG**, just off Route 8. As in Kuala Lipis, there's a distinct frontier spirit here, but that's about the only parallel. Gua Musang being in Kelantan, it has relatively few Malaysians of Indian extraction compared to towns in Pahang; the Malay used in its streets shows signs of the distinctive Kelantanese twang – and alcohol is practically unavailable. For more on Kelantan society and politics, see p.293. After the arrival of Route 8, Gua Musang expanded quickly as logging money flowed in, the new road having made remote tracts of forest accessible to the timber saws. While logging appears to have tailed off, Gua Musang's development is proceeding apace, and a whole **new town** is springing up a couple of kilometres south of the original settlement.

Gua Musang is fairly close to the Taman Negara entrances at Merapoh and Kuala Koh, but the main reason visitors stop off is to explore the **caves** that riddle the mass of limestone above the town. Both the caves and the town are named after a small creature, the *musang*, which looks like a civet and used to live up in the caves; it's now almost extinct. To get to the caves, cross the railway track at the station and walk through the small kampung in the shadow of the rock behind the station. Here you'll have to ask one of the villagers to guide you (it's usual to pay around RM10 for this); it is possible to reach the caves on your own, but the trail – which is directly at the back of the huts – is difficult to negotiate after rain, when it's likely to be extremely slippery. Wear strong shoes and take a torch to use inside the cave.

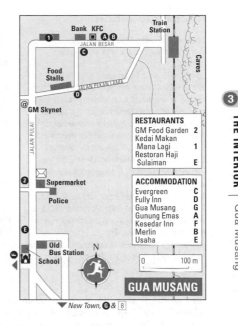

Once you've climbed steeply up 20m of rock face you'll see a narrow ledge; turn left and edge carefully along until you see a long slit in the rock which leads into a cave – you'll need to be fairly thin to negotiate this. The inside of the cave is enormous, 60m long and 30m high in places, and well lit by sunlight from holes above. The main cave leads to lesser ones, which have rock formations jutting out from the walls and ceilings. The only way out is by the same route, which you'll need to take very carefully, especially the near-vertical descent off the ledge and back down to the kampung.

Practicalities

Gua Musang's **train station** is at one end of the old town, while the main **bus station** is 2km to the south in the new town. The old bus station along Jalan Pulai is still called at by buses to and from points north, though these start and end their journeys in the new town. Both bus stations have taxis available to charter for destinations such as Kuala Besut (for the Perhentians), Kuala Lipis and Kota Bharu (prices for these three are roughly RM100 per car), the Taman Negara Kuala Koh entrance (RM100) or even the Cameron Highlands (RM120). A taxi ride between old town and new costs RM5.

There are a few **banks** in the old town on Jalan Besar, close to the train station. Jalan Pulai, the road leading towards the new town, has GM Skynet for **Internet** access, and a **supermarket** close to the **post office**. A helpful local **travel agent** is Kesedar Travel (℡09/912 6366, ⓦ www.kesedartravel.com.my); they arrange rafting trips on the nearby Nenggiri River, homestays in Malay kampungs, visits to an Orang Asli settlement and trips to Taman Negara via the nearby Merapoh gate. Given a few weeks' notice, they may be able to organize trips to Taman Negara via Kuala Koh, or Stong State Park.

Accommodation

Evergreen 57 Jalan Besar ☎09/912 2273. A simple affair, but popular, with a/c en-suite rooms. ❸

Fully Inn 75 Jalan Pekan Lama ☎09/912 3311, ℱ912 3322. Chinese-run hotel that's the grandest in town, with a thing for ostentatious marble stairways. Rooms are slickly furnished, with satellite TV, a/c and bathroom. The restaurant serves largely Asian fare with a few Western dishes thrown in, at slightly inflated places. Rates include breakfast. ❺

Gua Musang In the new town, close to the bus station ☎09/912 2121. A decent hotel with a/c en-suite rooms. ❸

Gunung Emas 20 Jalan Besar, ☎09/912 6843. Fine for a night, with en-suite a/c rooms, plus a few slightly shabby single and double rooms with fan and shared facilities. ❶

Kesedar Inn 400m west of the Jalan Pulai Mosque ☎09/912 1229, ℮ekes_inn@tm.net.my. Quite a contrast to the long lane on which it lies, lined with wooden stilt houses and fruit trees, the *Kesedar Inn* is a complex of new buildings with hints of colonial styling. Rooms are a tad stale, but they do have mod cons and modern furnishings, and can be taken for day use at a keen rate. Breakfast included. ❹

Merlin ☎09/912 1813. This spartan hotel isn't signed, but can be found above the newsagent/café on Jalan Besar. Rooms are separated from one another by thin partitions and share bathrooms with *mandis*. There's a choice of fan or a/c rooms. ❶

Usaha 187 Jalan Pulai, across from the old bus station ☎09/912 4003, ℱ912 4002. A friendly Malay-run hotel with a popular restaurant below. Not quite as well kept as it should be, but the simple rooms, en-suite with TV and a/c, are more than acceptable. ❸

Eating

One of the few eating places in town to really advertise its presence is *Kedai Makan Mana Lagi*, a converted open-air food court on Jalan Besar that's festooned with coloured lights in the evening. This simple, lively Malay restaurant serves food with a Thai twist, as is often the case in Kelantan; even the humble fried *kangkung* with squid has a lemongrass kick to it. They have a good range of *tom yam* and *kerabu*-style dishes, plus quite a lot of seafood, including *ikan tiga rasa*, one of the house specialities – though none of the staff can explain what the three flavours of the name derive from. *Restoran Haji Sulaiman*, below the *Usaha* hotel, is also a good bet, busy well into the night and serving both Malay and Chinese food. Otherwise, for Chinese food, there's the rather spartan pavilion of the *GM Food Garden* on Jalan Pulai, and plenty of stalls and *kedai kopis* on and around Jalan Pekan Lama.

Dabong and around

Around 55km north of Gua Musang, **DABONG** is a Malay village sited on the east bank of the wide Sungai Galas and surrounded by flat-topped limestone peaks and dark-green forest. The main reason to come here is to visit the **Stong State Park** (often referred to by its old name, **Jelawang Park**) around Gunung Stong to the south of town, offering good hiking. However, it can be tricky to organize a trek there independently, so it's not a bad idea to arrive on a package trip. Guesthouses and travel agencies in Kota Bharu are a good place to enquire, with prices from around RM60 per person per day for a group of four; it may also be possible to organize a trip in Kuala Terengganu or with Kesedar Travel in Gua Musang (see p.277).

Bypassed by Route 8, tiny Dabong has been very much a backwater, its main links to the outside world being the river, the rail line (Dabong is an express-train stop) and the Gua Musang–Jeli road, which passes to the west of the village. Until recently villagers had to get a boat west across the Galas to the access road for Stong State Park and the Gua Musang road, but by the time you read this, a major new bridge will have dealt with this hassle. There's also a very minor road west to Gua Musang from Kampung Tembeling on Route 8. If you're heading here independently from Kota Bharu to the north, an alternative to the train is a combination of bus and boat: take the 7.20am SKMK bus #5 to **Kuala Krai** (RM6; 1hr 30min), from where you can catch the morning boat to Dabong (see p.280).

Dabong is not quite the classic Malay kampung these days, its older, wooden houses now overshadowed by brick and concrete constructions. There's only one **place to stay** here, *Rumah Rehat Dabong* (☎019/960 6789; ❷), run by the friendly Din, who speaks some English (ask around for Abang Din if he's not there when you arrive). To reach it from the **train station**, head along the station road, past the school on the right, and immediately turn left into Jalan Pejabat; the resthouse is the long, largely yellow bungalow 50m further along on the right. From the **jetty**, take the single path up to the mosque, and you'll see the back of the resthouse. The building looks a little dilapidated on the outside, but the rooms (some with a/c) are totally serviceable, with a *mandi* and a squat toilet. The walls are thin though, and with the mosque just across the road, interrupted sleep is a distinct possibility. You might prefer to stay in Stong State Park, but if the resort there is closed, the only other possibility is to camp. For **food**, there's nothing more than a *kedai kopi* or two and a couple of shops on the station road.

Gua Ikan

A minor attraction near Dabong is **Gua Ikan**, one of several limestone caves a little way south of the village. It's an hour's walk away along a modern road lined with monotonous *belukar*: from the station, cross the railway track, turn right (south), and continue for 4km. Better is to try to ask around for a taxi or pay one of the locals to give you a ride there on the back of a motorbike. The caves are clearly signposted off to the right of the road, set in a small, unmaintained park. In the main cave, 40m long and 20m high, you can follow the course of a stream which runs along the cave floor; make sure to bring a torch and sturdy sandals (the rocks are too slippery to go barefoot and the stream may be knee-high at times, making shoes impractical). Any locals present may be able to point out a few rock formations, including a structure shaped vaguely like an upright piano, which people like to say would be suitable for *bersanding* – the part of the Malay wedding ceremony during which bride and groom are presented on a dais to the guests. The stream leads out to the other side of the cave to a small rock-enclosed area, a lovely spot to rest and listen to the birds and monkeys.

Stong State Park

Stong State Park offers the prospect of hiking alongside Peninsular Malaysia's highest waterfall (variously called Lata Jelawang or Air Terjun Stong) and heading up to the top of **Gunung Stong**, one of Kelantan's highest peaks at over 1400m. The three-hour **Seven Waterfalls** circuit takes you up the west side of the waterfall to a simple campsite, then heads down the east side. The uphill part of the trek takes around ninety minutes and is fairly gruelling, involving some sheer, muddy sections, though rocks at the side of the trail allow you to rest and look back over the forest. The **Elephant trek**, the longer of the two trails here, follows the main path up the mountain for two hours to the top of Gunung Stong, before winding along the ridge and crossing over onto neighbouring

Gunung Ayam. Although it's possible to return to the waterfall campsite the same day on this trek, it's preferable to camp for the night at a clearing along the trail, near a small stream – you'll need some warm clothing and a sleeping bag. People have seen elephants here, and there's a chance of encountering **tapir** and **deer** in the early morning or early evening.

If you're not visiting on an organized trip, you can ask Din at the *Rumah Rehat* to help you find a local guide. The park is at least ninety minutes' trudge southwest along the Dabong access road, with little shade for the first hour; save your energies for the trek up and find someone to drive you to the foot of Gunung Stong (a few locals operate an informal taxi service). The *KPK Stong Hill Resort* here was intended to be an ecotourism development, but is shut more often than not for one reason or another. Otherwise, you could stay up at **Baha Adventure Camp** (☎019/959 1020; RM10 per person), an hour's steep hike away (store most of your gear at the resthouse in Dabong); cross the bridge at the base of the falls, go past the last few chalets and take the track up through the forest. If you haven't arranged to be met, you may want to pay someone from the nearby village to guide you up. Baha was responsible for pioneering tourism at Jelawang but died suddenly a few years ago; his family now carries on the enterprise. The camp has simple bamboo huts plus space to camp (nominal fee charged; bring your own tents), and there are two chemical toilets close by, but no showers, so most visitors make good use of the waterfall's small rock pools instead. Guides can be hired for RM50 per day, and full-board packages are available at around RM200 per person for three days; contact the camp for prices appropriate to the size of your party.

Kuala Krai

Close to the confluence of the Kelantan and Galas rivers, **KUALA KRAI** (just "Krai" on rail timetables) is a busy commercial centre serving inland Kelantan; before the arrival of the road, great barges laden with goods were floated from here down to the coast. Despite Krai's regional importance, the pace of life here remains slow. With a few decent *kedai kopi*s, Kuala Krai is a reasonable place for a break if you're driving, but otherwise the only reason to come here is if you fancy taking the boat to Dabong (for the Stong State Park; see p.279) over the train.

The **train station** is at the eastern end of Jalan Ah Sang, with the **bus station** a hundred metres or so west along the road. For the **jetty**, continue west for a couple of minutes, then take the small road on the left and go past the blue-and-white police barracks. Look out for signs for Tangga Krai, indicating the ruled post at the steps down to the jetty (the post allowed flood levels on the Sungai Kelantan, an impressive 200m wide here, to be measured). Everyone has different ideas as to when the Dabong *penambang* leaves, but it's unlikely to be before 10am or after 11.30am. The jetty consists of a floating pavilion connected to the riverbank by a bowed plank – traverse it with care if you're encumbered with luggage. If the lone boatman doesn't show up from Dabong, you'll have to hang around for the mid-afternoon local train.

Close to the stations are two **hotels**, the cheaper option being the *Hotel Krai* at 190 Jalan Ah Song (☎09/966 6301; ❷), which has rooms with fans and shared bathrooms. For en-suite rooms, some with air-conditioning, go to the *Hotel Seri Maju* on Jalan Chun Hua (☎09/966 6000; ❷); it's reached by taking the turning opposite the fire station ("Bomba"), then the first left. Opposite the hotel is a **Maybank**, and opposite the bus station there's an Internet café.

There are plenty of reasonable Chinese **kedai kopis** plus a few Malay places along Jalan Ah Song. One of these, on the south side of the road between the bus station and the *Krai* hotel, is that unusual culinary entity, a Chinese curry house. Called the *Pokok Tanjung*, it mainly does rice with a choice of excellent curry toppings, and is popular with all sections of the community.

The southern interior

The main tourist interest in the southern part of the interior, along or south of the East Coast Highway, lies in its two lake systems, **Tasik Chini** and **Tasik Bera**, both beautiful areas where Orang Asli groups live and work. Both lakes have opportunities for trips out on the water and various activities (including excellent fishing at Bera), plus small, inexpensive resorts for accommodation – which is just as well, as day-trips are largely ruled out by the fact that it's time-consuming to reach the lakes by public transport. Chini, by far the smaller of the two, is also the more developed, with a large agricultural new town at its northern end, whereas the lake system at Bera, the most extensive in Malaysia, is a swampy area and sparsely populated. If you want somewhere to hole up for a couple of days of rest and reflection, with the odd boat trip as a distraction, choose Bera; Chini, for its part, is a more sociable experience.

The best time to visit either lake is from June to September, when their khaki waters are brightened by shimmering pink and white **lotus** blossoms. Both lakes also feature striking clumps of *rasau*, a tall aquatic variety of screwpine (*Pandanus helicopus*) with crowns of toothed leaves, which boat passengers at Bera in particular have to keep dodging. There's very little cover out on the lakes, so a hat and **sun protection** are vital.

Tasik Bera is close enough to the small town of Triang, on the rail network, that you can be collected from there by the lake's resort; otherwise access is via **Temerloh**, the largest town between KL and Kuantan. Chini can be reached by bus from Kuantan and, with your own car, from Temerloh or Segamat.

If you're driving to the lakes using the East Coast Highway, consider a diversion at **Lanchang**, 70km northeast of KL, where you turn north off the highway for the twenty-minute drive to the admirable **Kuala Gandah National Elephant Conservation Centre** (daily roughly 8am–12.30pm & 2–4.30pm; donations appreciated; Ⓦ www.wildlife.gov.my). Here, they care for elephants being relocated to reserves from areas of habitat destruction, or which had to be subdued while *mengamuk* – a Malay term that would be untranslatable were it not the source of the English word "amok". The best time to turn up is 2pm, when for an hour and a half visitors have the chance to get hands-on with the elephants, riding or even bathing with them (bring a change of clothes for the latter). Without your own transport, you'll have to charter a taxi here from Temerloh (roughly RM150 return, including a wait), or come on a pricey day-tour from KL (the travel agent at MTC sells these for RM180 per person, including a visit to a nearby deer farm; ☏03/2163 0162).

Tasik Chini

Spanning an area of around twenty square kilometres, **Tasik Chini** is a conglomerate of twelve connecting lakes of varying sizes. The Orang Asli population here are the **Jakun**, living in settled communities and occasionally doing seasonal work. Their creation legend has it that they were planting crops one day when an old woman with a walking stick appeared and said that the group should have sought her permission before clearing the land. But she allowed them to stay, and to legitimize their right she stabbed her stick into the centre of the clearing and told them never to pull it out. Years later, during a particularly ferocious rainstorm, a tribe member accidentally pulled out the stick, leaving a huge hole which immediately filled with water, creating the lake. Another legend tells of an ancient city which, when threatened with external attack, was flooded by its inhabitants using a system of aqueducts, with the intention of draining it later. Some Jakun believe a serpent – or *naga* – guards the lakes, but it has remained as elusive as the lost city.

Sadly, with development encroaching on the area, Tasik Chini hasn't been exempt from **enviromental problems**. In 2004 the lake was tainted by high levels of *E. coli* bacteria, which some blamed on the Jakun, though a more likely cause was the leaking of sewage from a new military camp nearby. The damming of the lake's outflow to the Sungai Pahang several years earlier has impeded circulation and badly reduced oxygen levels in the water. Even the lake's trademark lotuses can come under pressure, from vigorous water weeds.

Boat trips and activities

Various boat tours are on offer at the *Chini Resort* (from RM25). Longer trips are a better value, such as going west and south to **Laut Melai**, the lake where the lotuses are most plentiful, or to **Laut Babi**, the biggest lake in the system. A more peaceful alternative to the resort's motorboat trips is to hire a **canoe** at **Kampung Gumum** (RM15 per hour), a modernish Jakun village that's also the destination of the most popular **trail** from the resort. The two-kilometre lakeside track between the resort and the village can be hard to follow after heavy rain, and may involve wading through water. A longer, four-hour trail from the resort goes to a **campsite** at **Laut Terembau**, the path weaving in and out of mangroves, oil-palm plantations and forest. The trail continues beyond the camp and after 5km leads to a secondary road; travel east along this for 20km and you arrive at the Segamat–Kuantan road (Route 12).

When the lake is at its busiest – usually coinciding with the flowering of the lotuses – there are enough visitors around to support a small-scale tourist industry, including a number of Orang Asli **carvers** who live and display their work at the lake's *Chini Resort*.

Practicalities

The most straightforward way to get onto the lake is from the south, where the *Chini Resort* and Kampung Gumum are located. If you're relying on public transport, it's easiest to start from **Kuantan**, from where you catch a local bus to Felda Chini (1hr 30min; RM6), a vast agglomeration of numbered settlements belonging to the state-owned oil-palm cooperative, FELDA. The driver will tell you where to get off in **Felda Chini Dua**, around 20km short of the lake, after which you shouldn't have trouble finding a local with a car or motorbike to take you on to the resort or Kampung Gumum (RM15–20). The last bus back to Kuantan leaves at 5pm. Easier, naturally, is to book a place on a **tour**; Kuantan's tourist office offers day-trips at around RM110 per person. There are two ways to get to the resort if you're **driving**. One is Route 12, which links the East Coast Highway near Kuantan with Segamat much further south; follow signs for Felda Chini, from where the lake is signposted. The other is to reach the lake from the north: turn off Route 2 (the old KL–Kuantan road) to **Kampung Belimbing** and make for the Belimbing jetty on the Pahang River. Here you charter a boat to take you to the dam near the mouth of the Sungai Chini tributary (RM15), and from there another (RM60) to the lake itself.

The **Chini Resort** (☎09/477 8037, ℱ477 8036; dorm beds RM15, rooms ❸) is an unsophisticated affair built on a hillock on the edge of the main lake. The wooden chalets are homely and come in two grades, both with their own bathroom and a corrugated iron roof. The reception shares premises with the simple **restaurant** (daily 8am–10pm), serving the usual mix of rice and noodle dishes and light Western meals. The resort can get busy at weekends when large groups arrive, so it's best to go in the week – although during the wet season, you may have the place to yourself. Inexpensive tents, gas stoves and sleeping bags are available to rent. If you've booked to stay at the resort, ask if they'll collect you from Felda Chini.

For a much more rustic experience focused on trekking, stay at the excellent **Rajan Jones Guesthouse** in Kampung Gumum (☎017/913 5089, ℰjones_rajan@hotmail.com; half board ❶). Rajan, a Tamil, is also something of an honorary Jakun; he's been living in this community for two decades, encouraging the Jakun to cling on to their culture. His guesthouse, about five minutes' walk from the lakeshore, is a timber bungalow partitioned into ten rooms, each with a fan, mosquito net and mattresses on the floor; toilets and showers are in very clean shacks below the main building. Slightly more expensive Jakun-style huts on the lakeshore are also available to stay in. Rajan leads a variety of **treks** around the lake, from day walks to forays involving two nights' camping (tents and food are provided), on which he demonstrates the uses of various plants on view. In the village itself, you needn't feel too cut off from the outside world: there's a Chinese store for general supplies, and boat trips around the lake or across to the resort can be organized.

Tasik Bera

Tasik Bera was the first area in Malaysia to be listed under the international Ramsar Convention on Wetlands, in recognition of the lake's environmental importance. Apart from supporting a superb range of freshwater fish, the lake has endemic flora that's unique to the area, plus an array of mammal and reptile life, including rare crocodiles and turtles.

The crocodiles have a particular significance for the local **Semelai** Orang Asli, who believe their ancestors forged a relationship of mutual respect with the mythic supreme crocodile of the lake. Though few Semelai now undertake shifting cultivation, it was this practice which over the centuries helped create a forest of great diversity in the area, one in which large trees have been thinned and a wide variety of edible plants, such as pepper and root vegetables, have been sown. Now living in kampung-style houses, the Semelai subsist on cultivated vegetables, tapioca and other crops, and collect forest products, including latex, for a living. They use boats made from hollowed-out tree trunks, although these days they tend to buy them rather than build them. One recent development has been the opportunity for visitors to **stay** with the Semelai on the lake's southern fringe.

The main lake, in the northern part of the system, is over 16km wide and incredibly beautiful, its peat-edged watercourse and peat-floored bed rendering the waters almost black in places. A warren of channels leads from one lake to another, through waterways where strands of *rasau* grow with abandon. The plants can be almost submerged when the water level is high, but their sharp crowns are revealed when it's low; mind your head if you're on a boat traversing a particularly narrow channel between clumps. At times you may find great stretches of *rasau* burnt brown, an alarming sight; there's some dispute as to who is responsible for starting the fires that lead to this destruction, but it's actually a useful control measure for what would otherwise be an invasive species.

A variety of **boat trips**, in small craft for four people, are available at Tasik Bera's only formal accommodation, the *Tasik Bera Resort*. The most appealing of these is the so-called river cruise (RM60 per boat), in which the boat traverses narrow water courses on the lake fringes, overhung by forest growth and with opportunities to spot kingfishers and other birds. You see much more diverse vegetation on these trips than on the standard lake excursions (RM30 per boat), on which you may rapidly tire of pandanus. **Fishing** is a favourite activity here (if you're interested but have no gear, you can arrange rental with the resort in advance); the lake has stocks of *ikan toman* (snakehead) and *ikan tenggalan*, among others, and anything you catch can be nicely cooked up for you by the resort's restaurant. Various fishing huts and platforms are available for free (you pay for the boat transfer, a nominal sum). Otherwise, there's also kayaking (RM10 for an hour) and guided trekking (from RM50 per group of eight).

Practicalities

The compact *Tasik Bera Resort* (bookings on ☎03/2692 8049 or at Ⓦwww .journeymalaysia.com; dorm beds RM30, chalets ❷; closed Ramadan), on the northern lakeshore, is comfortable but fairly simple. There are a couple of inexpensive chalets, but most of the accommodation comprises rooms and fancier chalets (❺). Various full-board packages – including some activities – are available, and can be good value. The resort's simple restaurant, unsurprisingly, has lake fish as the star item on the menu. Close to the resort is the Ramsar office, a base for Wildlife Department rangers, with some **information** displays.

Driving to the northern part of the lake, turn east off **Route 10** (the Gemas–Temerloh road) at Bandar Bera, from where the lake is around 30km away, and signposted. The little-visited **southern sections** of Tasik Bera can be reached via Route 11 (which links Route 10 and Route 12 from Segamat). This gives access to the southernmost point on the lake, a kampung called **Pos Iskandar**, one of the places to which the Semelai were resettled during the Emergency. **Homestays** can be arranged here, either directly (☎013/286 5367) or through the NGO Wetlands International (☎03/7804 6770), who are backing a small-scale tourism initiative in the area to give the Semelai experience of project management and other business skills.

If you're staying at the resort – day-trips here are barely worthwhile without your own transport – you can arrange for their staff to collect you from **Triang** (aka Teriang) on Route 10 west of the lake, and served by local trains; expect to pay around RM40 per car for this. Triang is also served by local buses from Temerloh (every 45min–1hr). If you really want to head to the lake independently, your best bet is to get off the Triang bus at the bus station in **Bandar Bera** (a new town, and the only sizeable place the bus passes through, 1hr from

Temerloh) and charter a taxi the rest of the way (RM40). Simpler is to charter a taxi in Temerloh for the whole journey (RM60).

Temerloh

TEMERLOH is the starting point for the main part of Tasik Bera if you're using the bus, and you may well find yourself overnighting here on the way to the lake. The town has two **bus stations**. The main station ("*terminal utama*"), used by long-distance services and taxis, is on the little Jalan Sudirman, off the main street, Jalan Ahmad Shah, which has several **banks**. Local buses arriving in Temerloh let some passengers off at Jalan Sudirman before proceeding 250m to the end of the main street, where it veers to the right and down into a little depression containing the local bus station.

The budget **hotels**, run-down though functional enough, are all on or very near to Jalan Tengku Bakar, a lane leading off the main street where it swings downwards. A good bet here is the *New Ban Hin Hotel*, 40 Jalan Tengku Bakar (⑦09/296 7331; ❶), which has rooms with fan and shared bathrooms, as well as slicker rooms with air-conditioning and TV. The best value in town is the well-kept *Rumah Rehat Temerloh* (⑦09/296 3218, ⑤296 3431; ❺), which is old-fashioned like many resthouses, but features very spacious en-suite rooms with air-conditioning and TV. To reach it, turn right at the end of Jalan Tengku Bakar and continue a short way to the mosque, where you turn left onto a road that almost doubles back along the far side of an overgrown valley.

For **eating**, *Ali's* is a bright new restaurant at the start of Jalan Sudirman, with better-than-average *mamak* fare. There are a few more restaurants along the main street, plus plenty of Malay stalls close to the local bus station, and Malay and Chinese *kedai kopis* on or close to Jalan Tengku Bakar. The complex containing the main bus station has a swish **supermarket**.

Travel details

Trains

Express services through the interior run once daily in each direction between KL and Tumpat, and between Singapore and Tumpat. They're supplemented by slow local services (stopping at almost every minor station, and denoted "Mel" on timetables) between Singapore and Gua Musang, between Gua Musang and Tumpat, and between Gemas and Tumpat. While the frequencies given here are for the two types of service combined, the journey times are for express services (unless the station is served by local trains only, indicated by *); local trains take roughly half again as long.
Gua Musang to: Dabong (5 daily; 1hr); Gemas (4 daily; 6hr 30min); Jerantut (4 daily; 2hr 45min); Johor Bahru (2 daily; 10hr); Kota Bharu (Wakaf Bharu station; 5 daily; 3hr 30min); Kuala Krai (5 daily; 2hr 15min); Kuala Lipis (4 daily; 1hr 45min); Kuala Lumpur (1 daily; 9hr 45min); Merapoh* (2 daily; 40min); Seremban (1 daily;

8hr 30min); Singapore (2 daily; 11hr); Tembeling* (2 daily; 4hr); Triang* (2 daily; 6hr 45min).
Jerantut to: Dabong (3 daily; 3hr 45min); Gemas (4 daily; 4hr); Gua Musang (4 daily; 2hr 45min); Johor Bahru (3 daily; 7hr); Kota Bharu (Wakaf Bharu station; 3 daily; 6hr); Kuala Krai (3 daily; 4hr 45min); Kuala Lipis (4 daily; 1hr); Kuala Lumpur (1 daily; 7hr 30min); Merapoh* (2 daily; 3hr 30min); Seremban (1 daily; 6hr); Singapore (3 daily; 8hr); Tembeling* (2 daily; 15min); Triang* (2 daily; 2hr 45min).

Buses

Many intercity buses depart only during daylight hours.
Gua Musang to: Kota Bharu (4 daily; 4hr); Kuala Krai (hourly; 2hr 30min); Kuala Lipis (2 daily; 2hr 30min); Kuala Lumpur (2–4 daily; 6hr).
Jerantut to: Kuala Lipis (hourly; 1hr 30min); Kuala Tahan (4 daily; 1hr 45min); Kuantan (3 daily; 3hr); Tembeling jetty (4 daily; 40min), Temerloh (10 daily; 1hr).

Kuala Krai to: Gua Musang (hourly; 2hr 30min); Kota Bharu (every 30min; 2hr 30min); Kuala Lumpur (1 daily; 8hr).

Kuala Lipis to: Gua Musang (2 daily; 2hr); Kuala Lumpur (6 daily; 4hr); Kuantan (2 daily; 6hr); Raub (several daily; 1hr 30min).

Kuala Lumpur to: Gua Musang (4 daily; 6hr); Kota Bharu (6 daily; 10hr); Kuala Krai (4 daily; 8hr); Kuala Lipis (6 daily; 3hr); Mentakab (hourly; 1hr 15min); Raub (10 daily; 1hr 30min); Temerloh (every 30min; 1hr 30min).

Temerloh to: Jerantut (10 daily; 1hr); Johor Bahru (4 daily; 7hr); Kota Bharu (2 daily; 8hr); Kuala Lipis (4 daily; 4hr); Kuala Lumpur (every 30min–1hr; 2hr); Kuala Terengganu (2 daily; 5hr); Kuantan (hourly; 2hr); Melaka (4 daily; 4hr); Triang (every 45min–1hr; 1hr 30min).

Boats

Kuala Krai to: Dabong (1 daily; 2hr).

Kuala Tembeling jetty to: Kuala Tahan (daily at 9am & 2pm except Fri 9am & 2.30pm; 2hr 30min).

The east coast

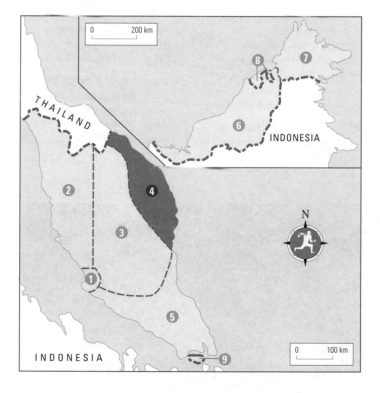

CHAPTER 4 # Highlights

✳ **Kota Bharu** One of the Peninsula's most characterful cities, offering a glimpse of Kelantanese Malay culture; come here to see traditional crafts being made and traditional art forms staged. See p.293

✳ **Pulau Perhentian** Two of the most enticing islands the Peninsula has to offer, with excellent snorkelling and accommodation ranging from backpacker chalets to slick resorts. See p.306

✳ **The Terengganu State Museum** A whirlwind trip through Malaysia's history, culture and crafts at one of the country's most interesting cultural complexes, in Kuala Terengganu. See p.324

✳ **Pulau Kapas** A small island with some decent sands and opportunities for snorkelling and kayaking – perfect for a couple of days' relaxation, with some watersports thrown in. See p.330

✳ **Cherating** Chill by the beach or enjoy the amiable, low-key nightlife at the east coast's long-established travellers' hangout. See p.334

△ A typical Perhentians scene

4

The east coast

T he four-hundred-kilometre stretch from the northeastern corner of the Peninsula to Kuantan, roughly halfway down the east coast, displays a quite different cultural legacy to the more populous, commercial western seaboard. For hundreds of years, the Malay rulers of the northern states of **Kelantan** and **Terengganu** were vassals of the Thai kingdom of **Ayuthaya**, suffering repeated invasions as well as the unruly squabbles of their own princes. Nevertheless, the relationship forged with the Thais allowed the Malays a great deal of autonomy, which, together with the adoption of Islam in the seventeenth century, gave the region a strong sense of identity and independence. Remaining free of British control until 1909, Kelantan and Terengganu escaped the economic and social changes that rocked the western Malay Peninsula during the nineteenth century. Furthermore, these two states, as well as eastern **Pahang**, were insulated from developments elsewhere in the Peninsula by the mountainous, jungled interior. It was not until 1931 that the railway arrived in Kelantan; prior to that, the journey here from KL involved thirteen river crossings. While immigrants poured into the tin and rubber towns of the west, the east remained rural and, as a result, Kelantan and Terengganu are still very much **Malay heartland** states; both do have prominent Chinese minorities, but people of Indian extraction are somewhat underrepresented. The east coast still has a rustic feel today, the economy being largely based on agriculture and fishing, apart from the very obvious exception of Terengganu's oil industry.

Given all this, it's two things that sum up the east coast for most visitors: the natural beauty of its many **beaches and islands**, especially those belonging to Terengganu; and traditional **Malay culture**, a good taste of which – political restrictions notwithstanding (see p.301) – can still be had in Kelantan in particular. The greatest appeal arguably lies in the casuarina-fringed beaches and coral reefs of **Pulau Perhentian**, **Pulau Redang** and **Pulau Kapas**, some of the most beautiful islands in the South China Sea, all three with great opportunities for diving and snorkelling. Further south along the coast, the backpackers' enclave of **Cherating** is a deservedly popular place to simply chill out for a few days. All along the east coast, there are a handful of beaches where, between May and September, it's possible to view marine **turtles** coming ashore to lay their eggs. Among the cities, it's vibrant **Kota Bharu**, close to the Thai border, that stands out for its opportunities to glimpse the gradually disappearing worlds of Malay crafts and performing arts. **Kuala Terengganu**, 140km to the south, is more downbeat, though it does have an atmospheric old Chinese quarter, a traditional boat-building industry and an excellent museum. Both are infinitely preferable to the sheer mundanity

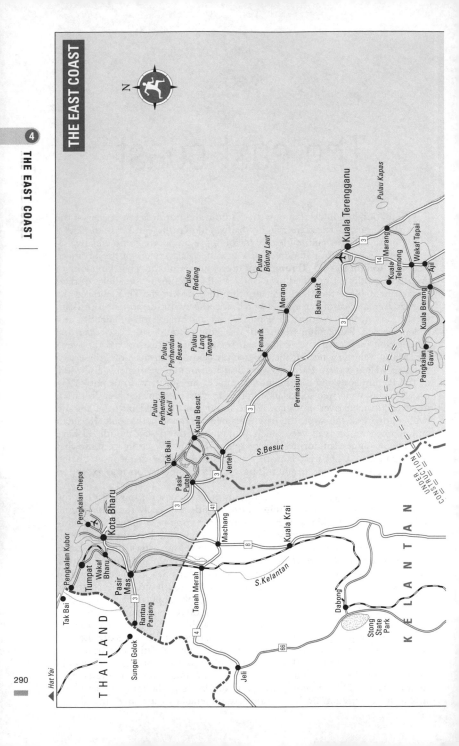

THE EAST COAST

N

▲ Hat Yai

THAILAND

Tak Bai
Pengkalan Kubor
Tumpat
Wakaf Bharu
Pasir Mas
Rantau Panjang
Sungei Golok
Pengkalan Chepa
Kota Bharu
Tanah Merah
Jeli
Machang
Kuala Krai
Dabong
Stong State Park
S.Kelantan

K E L A N T A N

Pasir Puteh
Tok Bali
Jerteh
S.Besut
Kuala Besut
Pulau Perhentian Kecil
Pulau Perhentian Besar
Penarik
Permaisuri
Merang
Batu Rakit
Pulau Lang Tengah
Pulau Redang
Pulau Bidung Laut
Kuala Terengganu
Kuala Telemong
Kuala Marang
Wakaf Tapai
Ajil
Kuala Berang
Pangkalan Gavi
Pulau Kapas

UNDER CONSTRUCTION

3
3
3
3
3
41
8
4
66
14

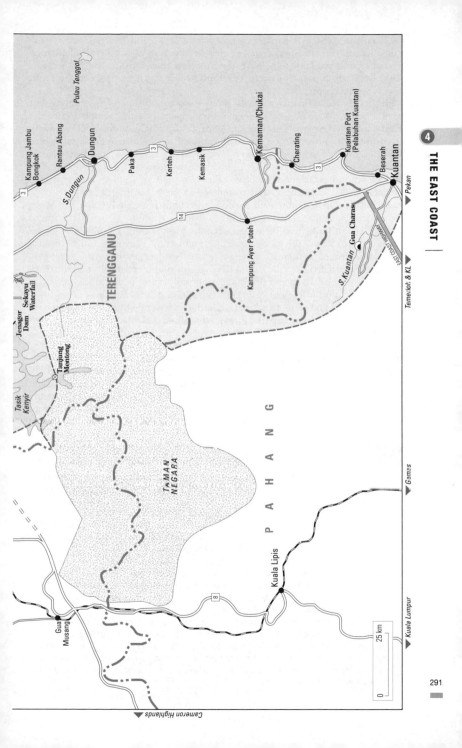

of **Kuantan**, which is partly redeemed by a few good beaches and restaurants. Kuantan is the southernmost city on this side of the Peninsula, which perhaps partly explains why locals tend to view the continuation of the coast from here not as part of eastern Peninsular Malaysia, but as part of the south – covered in chapter 5.

Flights to Kota Bharu or Kuala Terengganu can be useful time-savers, but road access to the east coast has really opened up with the completion of the **East Coast Highway**. This links up with the E8 Highway from KL to Karak in the interior, and arrives on the coast just north of Kuantan, reducing the drive from KL to the east coast to a three-hour whiz. The highway has already led to improved bus links between KL and much of the coast, and its impact will soon be felt even more directly when phase two of the highway, leading due north from Kuantan to Kuala Terengganu, is completed in 2009. Meanwhile, the backbone roads through the region remain the coast road (which is called Route 3 between Kuala Terengganu and Kuantan) and its shadow, running 10 to 20km inland (Route 14 south of Kuala Terengganu, Route 3 to the north). Unsurprisingly, it's the coastal road that's the more interesting, connecting a string of laid-back small towns and fishing kampungs. One more new road bears mentioning, slipping across the northern interior to put Terengganu within relatively easy reach of the Cameron Highlands and Perak. The only **rail** service is the atmospheric one through the interior (see box, p.243) to Tumpat, near Kota Bharu.

Visitors should be aware that Kelantan and (to a lesser degree) Terengganu have a reputation for **conservatism**. It was, after all, in Kelantan that the country's religious opposition party, **PAS** (an acronym of sorts for Parti Islam SeMalaysia), was born in the middle of the last century. The party, which sees itself as very much focused on Islam (as opposed to Malay nationalism or economic development), has governed its home state for two lengthy spells, including from 1990 to the time of writing. PAS has managed to attract support from non-Muslim voters by allying itself with other opposition parties, and – more importantly – by not being stridently anti-business. However, PAS's momentum was set into reverse in the wake of 9/11 and the arrival of Abdullah Badawi at the helm of

The east coast in the off-season

Many visitors give the east coast a wide berth during the especially wet **northeast monsoon**, which sets in during late October and continues until February. It's certainly true that heavy rains and sea swells put paid to most boat services to the islands off the east coast at this time, and most beach accommodation, whether on the mainland or offshore, is shut anyway. However, this isn't to say you can't have a decent beach holiday on the east coast during the rainy season. This being the tropics, the wet season shouldn't be taken too literally – the rains may well be interspersed with good sunny spells, just as the so-called dry season can bring its share of torrential downpours. With luck, and a flexible schedule, you will find boats heading sporadically to and from the islands during the northeast monsoon, while enquiries will turn up a handful of beach resorts and chalets that are open (island accommodation that's likely to be open year-round is highlighted in this chapter). While diving and snorkelling aren't much good at this time of year thanks to reduced visibility, at the same time the east coast comes into own for **windsurfing**, possible at Kuantan and the Perhentians. Away from the beaches, there's always reasonable sightseeing to take advantage of in Kota Bharu and Kuala Terengganu – though be prepared to take lengthy refuge in cafés or on recessed shophouse walkways when yet another thunderstorm breaks.

UMNO, the mainstream Malay party. In the 2003 elections, PAS relinquished Terengganu, which it had held for one term, while in Kelantan it failed for the first time in years to gain a majority in parliamentary seats, and clung on to the state assembly only by its fingertips.

For foreign visitors, this political backdrop distils down to the simple truth that the **social climate** of Kelantan and Terengganu is not that of Melaka, Penang or, for that matter, Pahang. **Alcohol** is relatively hard to obtain; most restaurants, whatever cuisine they serve, are **halal**; and **dress** – for both men and women – needs to be circumspect (see p.79 for more), except at heavily touristed beaches. You may also find that **English** is less understood in Kelantan and Terengganu than in most other parts of the Peninsula.

Kota Bharu and around

The capital of Kelantan, **KOTA BHARU** sits at the very northeastern corner of the Peninsula, on the east bank of the broad, muddy Sungai Kelantan. Many of the visitors who make it here arrive from across the nearby Thai border, and for most of them the city is simply a half-decent place to rest up, get their Malaysian bearings and pop into a museum or two for a dabble in the region's history; their real goal is to head out of Kelantan altogether – either to Taman Negara and KL, or to Kuala Besut and the delights of the Perhentian islands. But to breeze through Kota Bharu and the rest of Kelantan would be to gloss over one of the most characterful states in the country. **Kelantan** has historically been something of a crucible for **Malay culture**, fostering a range of art forms that drew on influences from around Southeast Asia and as far away as India. Kota Bharu is the ideal place to witness this distinctive heritage, on show at its **Cultural Centre** and at the various **cottage industries** that thrive in its hinterland – among them kite-making, batik printing and woodcarving. The city also boasts its share of historical buildings, now largely **museums**, plus some excellent **markets** and a few **temples** in the surrounding countryside.

The wholehearted embrace of Islam that's so evident in Kelantan was facilitated by its long coastline, which encouraged trading contacts with the Arab world, enabling a free flow of new ideas and customs from as early as the 1600s. Travel to Mecca was common by the nineteenth century and, unlike elsewhere in the country, Kelantan's legal system operated according to Islamic law – an important factor in the maintenance of national pride under Thai overlordship. It should come as no surprise that one of Kota Bharu's most famous sons is **To' Kenali**, who was a renowned religious teacher; after some years of study in Cairo, he returned to his home town at the beginning of the twentieth century to establish *sekolah pondok* – huts functioning as religious schools to spread Islamic doctrine. This strategy was mirrored in the early years of PAS, when religious schools were a useful way of spreading support for the party in the community.

Kelantan retains its regional identity today, to the extent that it has regulations making it difficult for anyone from outside the state to buy property here. It also remains a fascinating crucible – not the cultural hothouse of past centuries, but one in which the arts are at odds with the Islamic precepts of the state's religious authorities, and where PAS and UMNO are locked in a bitter political battle. The latter tussle is producing some dramatic changes in Kota Bharu, for after years of stagnation under PAS and abstemious handouts by UMNO from federal coffers, both parties have simultaneously decided that development is the avenue to political glory. As a result, the city now boasts a major shopping mall and a sprinkling of fancy riverside apartments – all of which would have been unthinkable here until recently.

While some foreign women can find Kelantan's conservatism uncomfortable, especially if they've arrived from Thailand, by and large Kota Bharu comes across as a bustling, pragmatic sort of place (and indeed Kelantanese men and women alike have a deserved reputation in Malaysia for entrepreneurial talent). One additional thing that strikes those visitors with some knowledge of Malay is the unique **dialect** (*kecek Kelate*) heard in Kota Bharu and all over the state. So odd it's confusing even to many Malays, broad Kelantanese will have your head spinning: it's about as singsong as Malay gets; features various contractions, changes to consonant clusters and twists to word endings, such as the conversion of -*an* to -*ay* (Kelantan is actually rendered here as "Kelatay"); and boasts a few words all of its own, such as *gwano* instead of *bagaimana* for "how", and – worth noting – **ria** sometimes instead of ringgit, when prices are given.

Arrival, information and transport

Long-distance **buses** arrive at one of the two bus stations, inconveniently situated on the southern outskirts of the city: the state bus company, SKMK, operates out of the **Langgar bus station** on Jalan Pasir Puteh, as do Transnasional and MARA; other companies use the **Hamzah bus station**, 600m west. A taxi into the centre should cost around RM7; unlicensed taxis (basically, private cars) charge double that and may be all you can find, particularly at night. Many long-distance services call at the **local bus station**, off Jalan Padang Garong in the centre, on their way to one of the other stations. **Long-distance taxis** park up in various spaces on Jalan Doktor, south of the local bus station. The nearest **train station** to Kota Bharu is 7km to the west at Wakaf Bharu. From here it's a twenty-minute ride into town on bus #19 or #27 – they run to and from Kota Bharu's local bus station.

The **airport** is 9km northeast of the centre, from where a taxi into town costs RM20 – buy a coupon from the airport's taxi counter. A couple of agencies with desks at the airport operate transport to the Perhentians.

The **tourist office** (Mon–Thurs & Sun 8am–4.45pm; ☏09/748 5534, ☏748 6652), close to the clock tower on Jalan Sultan Ibrahim, is very helpful; **tours** of various local craft workshops, cookery courses and homestays can be booked here. They can also tell you about various **cultural festivals** held throughout the year, celebrating traditional kites, or drumming, or other facets of local life.

Local taxis (which can be booked on ☏09/744 7104) operate from the same general area as long-distance taxis. The city still has a few **trishaws**, which can be found along the roads around the local bus station; the normal fare for a ten-minute journey around the centre is RM5 – make sure you agree the price beforehand.

Accommodation

For a fairly small city, Kota Bharu has an excellent range of accommodation, and budget travellers especially will appreciate the choice of good-value **guesthouses**, many of which can arrange tickets for onward travel, and offer packages to Stong State Park (aka Jelawang; see p.279) and sometimes to Taman Negara via Kuala Koh (see p.247). Most of the hotels and guesthouses below represent the cream of the crop for each budget; there are plenty more places to stay scattered about the city centre.

Moving on from Kota Bharu

For most **long-distance buses**, you simply need to turn up at Hamzah or Langgar bus stations, as both serve a variety of destinations. However, Transnasional buses to Kuala Terengganu and Kuantan, plus SKMK buses to places within or just outside Kelantan – notably Wakaf Bharu (for trains), Kuala Krai (for the Dabong boat), Rantau Panjang (to cross into Thailand) and **Kuala Besut** (for the Perhentians; RM5) – operate from the **local bus station**. SKMK has an information counter here (daily 8am–9pm, closed Fri 12.45–2pm; ☏09/744 0114). Long-distance taxi fares are around RM35 per vehicle to Kuala Besut, RM100 to Kuala Terengganu or Gua Musang, RM220 to Kuantan; the taxi stand on Jalan Doktor (☏09/744 7104) can give fares for other destinations.

At the time of writing, the **express train** to KL leaves Wakaf Bharu at 6.46pm (be sure to allow for rush-hour congestion on the roads out of Kota Bharu), with the Singapore-bound express following at 8.31pm. Train information can be obtained from Wakaf Bharu station on ☏09/719 6986.

MAS, at Komplek Yakin, Jalan Gajah Mati (☏09/748 3477), very near the clock tower, has flights to KL only; AirAsia operates to KL and Johor Bharu, but its ticket office is at the airport. For **flight information**, call the airport on ☏09/743 7000.

Crossing the Thai border

There are two designated crossings into Thailand near Kota Bharu, one inland, the other at the mouth of the Golok River. Both of these **border posts** are open daily between 6am and 10pm – but remember that Thailand is one hour behind Malaysia. **Visas** for Thailand can be obtained from the consulate in Kota Bharu (see "Listings", p.303).

The more used of the two crossings is at **Rantau Panjang**, 30km southwest of Kota Bharu. Bus #29 departs from the local bus station in Kota Bharu every thirty minutes (6.45am–6.30pm; RM4) for the 45-minute trip there, or you can take a shared taxi from Kota Bharu for RM4 per person. Once at Rantau Panjang, it's a short walk across the border to **Sungai Golok** on the Thai side. Trains from here to Bangkok (22hr), via Hat Yai and Surat Thani, leave at 11.30am and 1.35pm (timetables can be checked on ⓦwww.railway.co.th), and buses to Hat Yai (4hr) are frequent. The coastal crossing is at **Pengkalan Kubor**, 20km northwest of Kota Bharu, which connects with the small town of Tak Bai on the Thai side. Take bus #27 or #43 from the local bus station for the thirty-minute journey, then the car ferry. On the Thai side, the closest large town to either crossing is **Narathiwat**, from where there are buses to other parts of southern Thailand, plus flights to Bangkok.

Roselan Hanafiah at the tourist office runs a **homestay programme** offering the chance to stay with a family, often expert in a particular craft which you can be taught; for a minimum of two people staying for two nights, expect to pay around RM320 per person, including all meals and craft materials.

Hotels

Azam 1782A & B Jalan Padang Garong, ☏09/7478800, ☏7477780. Beyond the irksome peach facade is a newish hotel with predictably bland, modern twins and doubles, more substantially furnished than others in the same class, each with a pleasant tiled bathroom, a/c and satellite TV. Reasonable value, though rates don't include breakfast. ❺

Crystal Lodge 124 Jalan Che Su ☏09/747 0888, ⓦwww.crystallodge.com.my. Two enormous Chinese porcelain vases in the lobby set the tone at this sleek new hotel. Facilities include a café-restaurant and plenty of satellite TV channels. A good deal, with especially keen rates for single rooms, and breakfast included. ❻

Grand Riverview Jalan Post Office Lama ☏09/743 9988, ⓦwww.grh.com.my. The river views aren't anything to write home about, but still,

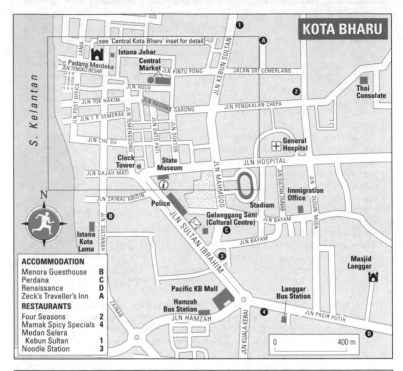

KOTA BHARU

see 'Central Kota Bharu' inset for detail

Istana Jahar
Central Market
Padang Merdeka
Thai Consulate
General Hospital
Clock Tower
State Museum
Immigration Office
Stadium
Police
Gelanggang Seni (Cultural Centre)
Istana Kota Lama
Masjid Langgar
Pacific KB Mall
Langgar Bus Station
Hamzah Bus Station

ACCOMMODATION

Menora Guesthouse	B
Perdana	C
Renaissance	D
Zeck's Traveller's Inn	A

RESTAURANTS

Four Seasons	2
Mamak Spicy Specials	4
Medan Selera Kebun Sultan	1
Noodle Station	3

0 — 400 m

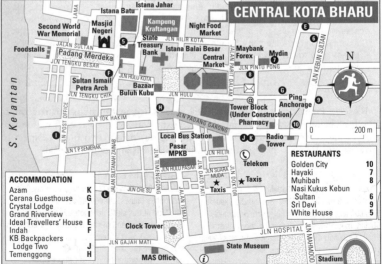

CENTRAL KOTA BHARU

Istana Jahar
Istana Batu
Second World War Memorial
Masjid Negeri
Kampung Kraftangan
Night Food Market
Foodstalls
Padang Merdeka
State Treasury Bank
Istana Balai Besar
Central Market
Maybank Forex
Mydin
Sultan Ismail Petra Arch
Bazaar Buluh Kubu
Tower Block (Under Construction)
Pharmacy
Ping Anchorage
Local Bus Station
Pasar MPKB
Radio Tower
Telekom
Taxis
Clock Tower
State Museum
MAS Office
Stadium

0 — 200 m

ACCOMMODATION

Azam	K
Cerana Guesthouse	G
Crystal Lodge	L
Grand Riverview	I
Ideal Travellers' House	E
Indah	F
KB Backpackers Lodge Two	J
Temenggong	H

RESTAURANTS

Golden City	10
Hayaki	7
Muhibah	8
Nasi Kukus Kebun Sultan	6
Sri Devi	9
White House	5

this substantial hotel is modern and comfortable, and the rooms are spacious, en suite and offer a/c and terrestrial TV. Not a sensible option if they stick to the rack rate, but discounts are available most of the time. Rate includes breakfast. ⑥

Indah 236A & B Jalan Tengku Besar ☎09/748 5081, ⓕ748 2788. This simple hotel is showing its age, but remains more than tolerable. The rooms, arranged around a shabby rectangular shaft, all have a/c, TV and bathroom. Below is an inexpensive restaurant serving mainly Malay food, with the odd Chinese and Western dish thrown in. Not bad for the price. ❸

Perdana Jalan Mahmood ☎09/748 5000, ⓦwww.hotelperdana.com.my. A cold concrete box on the outside, but the rooms are comfy (if even blander than average), the bathrooms have proper baths, and there's satellite TV and a pool. Guests get concessionary rates on racket sports and bowling at the adjacent municipal sports centre. ⑥

🏃 **Renaissance** Jalan Sultan Yahya Petra ☎09/746 2233, ⓦwww.http://marriott .com. The only five-star hotel in Kota Bharu, as locals invariably describe it – and a real bargain. There's a range of rooms, some with great views over the city, and all featuring a bathroom with an actual bath and plenty of marble, plus a fridge and satellite TV. Among the amenities are a couple of restaurants, a gorgeous blue-tiled pool, a gym and, at the time of writing, the only hotel bar in the city with alcohol. Rates include breakfast. ⑦

Temenggong Jalan Tok Hakim ☎09/748 3844, ⓕ744 1481. Rather dull a/c en-suite rooms, in need of refreshing, with TV and fridge – okay for the price. If they're full, steer clear of the Suria, their similarly priced sister establishment nearby, which isn't as good. ❹

Guesthouses

🏃 **Cerana Guesthouse** First floor, 39521 Jalan Padang Garong ☎019/943 3599, ⓔewan_76@hotmail.com. A tiptop Malay-run place, very sociable, with well-kept a/c singles and doubles (one of which is en suite), plus a family room sleeping five. The lounge is plastered with soccer posters and has satellite TV for world matches, plus a range of DVDs to while away rainy days. Staff are particularly big on packages to Stong State Park – for which they can also offer useful practical advice – and can also arrange homestays on a fishing island 12km offshore. ❷

🏃 **Ideal Travellers' House** 3954F & G Jalan Kebun Sultan ☎09/744 2246. At the end of

a quiet lane off Jalan Kebun Sultan, this excellent guesthouse is just like staying in a middle-class Chinese home dating back around thirty years – as that's exactly what it is. There's a dorm and a range of rooms, all with fan; one room is especially spacious, with its own bathroom and a balcony for views over the pleasant garden, which is dominated by a mature *jambu* fruit tree. Transport ticket bookings and Internet access are available. Dorm beds RM8, rooms ❶

KB Backpackers Lodge One First floor, 1872 Jalan Padang Garong ☎09/748 8841, ⓔbackpackerslodge2@yahoo.co.uk. A friendly travellers' haunt with the customary facilities – rooms and a dorm, lounge, roof garden, Internet access and packages to Stong State Park. Rooms have fan, with the option of a/c in some. Dorm beds RM8, rooms ❶

Menora Guesthouse First floor, 3338D Jalan Sultanah Zainab ☎09/748 1669. A laid-back, old-fangled residence with an English-speaking Chinese owner, simple rooms and bathrooms, parquet flooring, plenty of sofas and chairs to lounge in, and orchids and allamandas in the roof garden. Unfortunately, the road outside is often too noisy for comfort, and if business is slow, the place can get pretty soporific inside. ❶

🏃 **Rumah Rakit Nik Ismail** On the Sungai Kelantan, close to the *Grand Riverview Hotel* ☎09/747 5794, ⓕ712 9294. Pretty much unique in Malaysia is this accommodation on a floating platform (hence *rumah rakit*, meaning "raft house"), featuring a cosy lounge kitted out with antique furniture, a veranda that's great for views of the sunset across the river, and just four rooms, with four-poster beds and sharing three sets of facilities. Simply one of the most characterful places to stay on the east coast; to find it, head 25m south along a track close to the corner where Jalan Che Su turns into Jalan Post Office Lama, then veer right to reach steps heading down to river, where the smart Malay-style timber bungalow is unmistakable. Reservations essential. ❺

Zeck's Travellers' Inn On a lane off Jalan Sri Cemerlang ☎09/743 1613, ⓔztraveller _inn@hotmail.com. A simple, family-run Malay guesthouse, slightly marooned in a residential area. There's a dorm and a handful of rooms, including one that's en suite and has a/c. They offer ticket reservations and Perhentians transfers. Not quite as slick as the competition. Dorm beds RM7, rooms ❶

The City

To wander around Kota Bharu is to be at the heart of PAS's fiefdom: there are images of the party's turbanned leader – and Kelantan chief minister – Nik Aziz bin Nik Mat everywhere, and banners proclaiming Kota Bharu an "**Islamic City**", part of an international marketing exercise by PAS. The reality, though, is that Kota Bharu is like every other Malaysian city in being a multi-ethnic jigsaw, with plenty of Chinese and a few Indian businesses on show in the centre. You may spot the odd poster in large stores indicating separate checkouts for men and women, part of an abortive drive by PAS to impose gender segregation on everyone; the measure ultimately flopped because most shop owners and shoppers didn't see any reason to change the habits of a lifetime and, in a victory for Malaysian common sense, simply ignored it.

The city centre is compact and easily negotiated on foot. Useful **reference points** include the curious rocket-like clock tower marking the junction of the town's three major roads, Jalan Hospital, Jalan Sultan Ibrahim and Jalan Temenggong; the towering radio mast off Jalan Doktor, a handy landmark when it's illuminated at night; and, in the south of town, the gleaming Pacific KB Mall complex. Most of the city's **markets** and many of the **banks** and the biggest stores lie between Jalan Hospital and Jalan Pintu Pong, a few blocks to the north.

Around Padang Merdeka

West of the markets, and close to the river, the quiet oasis of **Padang Merdeka** marks Kota Bharu's historical centre. It was here that the British displayed the body of the defeated Tok Janggut (Father Long Beard), a peasant spiritual leader who spearheaded a revolt against the colonial system of land taxes and tenancy regulations in 1915, one of the few specifically anti-colonial incidents to occur on the east coast. The four **museums** that occupy the vicinity today are open daily, except on Friday, between 8.45am and 4.45pm.

Dominating the eastern end of the square is the immense **Sultan Ismail Petra Arch**, a recent structure built to mark Kota Bharu being declared a showcase for Malay culture. To the east of the arch, and half-hidden behind high walls and entrance gates, the single-storey **Istana Balai Besar** dates from 1844; containing the Throne Room and State Legislative Assembly, it's now used primarily for ceremonial functions and is closed to the public. To the right of its gates is the former Kelantan **State Treasury Bank**, whose presence gave the square its unofficial name of "Padang Bank". An unobtrusive stone bunker no more than two metres high, it remained in use until well into the twentieth century.

However, it's the **Istana Jahar**, to the north of the arch, which really draws your attention, an impressively styled traditional structure built in 1887, with a timber portico and polished decorative panels adorning the exterior. Extensive renovations carried out by Sultan Mohammed IV in 1911 added an Italian marble floor, which cools the interior, and two wrought-iron spiral staircases. The palace is now a museum housing an exhibition on **royal ceremonies** (RM2), which can reasonably be seen in an hour. In fact, many of the ceremonies in question – depicted using life-sized dioramas – would have been practised by commoners as well, though obviously not with the same level of opulence. The ground floor is given over to displays concerning weddings, including a bridal suite boasting a striking four-poster with linen and canopy, all in royal golden yellow. Exhibits upstairs illustrate how infants had to undergo rites prior to the most mundane of life experiences, such as the *istiadat naik* *endoi*, a ritual haircut before their first doze in a cradle; and the *istiadat pijak tanah*, before their first footstep on bare earth.

A stone's throw further north is the sky-blue **Istana Batu** (RM2), an incongruous 1930s villa built as the sultan's residence. One of the first concrete constructions in the state (its name means "stone palace"), it's now the Kelantan Royal Museum, the rooms furnished largely as they would have been originally. A brief wander through is worthwhile if only to survey the tat which royals the world over seem to feel obliged to accumulate – here including stacks of crystal glassware and English crockery. Directly opposite to the east is the **Kampung Kraftangan** or "Handicraft Village" (same times as the museums), largely a collection of gift shops.

West of Jalan Sultanah Zainab

The padang is bordered on its northern side by the white **Masjid Negeri**, completed in 1925; it's been referred to as Serambi Mekah, "veranda of Mecca", because of its prominent role in the spread of Islam throughout Kelantan. Close by, west along Jalan Sultan, is the **Islamic Museum** (free), of interest only for the building itself, a pastel blue-green echo of the Istana Jahar, built in the 1910s as a residence for the chief minister.

The adjacent **Second World War Memorial** (RM2), a squat, pale yellow building, was originally the Mercantile Bank of India, but became known locally as *bank kerapu*, literally "frequent bank", for the odd reason that there are numerous bumps and pits on the roughly rendered exterior. The war museum inside is pertinent; it was Kelantan's beaches where Japanese troops first set foot in Malaya, capturing all of the state in December 1941, with Singapore falling just two months later – during the occupation, the bank became the local base for the Japanese secret police. While the war artefacts are largely desultory (bits of old ordnance, ration pouches and the like), the commentaries give some useful insight into the swiftness of the Japanese advance and the British collapse.

The markets

Just east of the historical centre is Kota Bharu's humming **central market** (aka Pasar Besar Siti Khadijah; daily roughly 8am–6pm), one of the focal points of the city. The main building, an octagonal hall, has a perspex roof casting a soft light over the multicoloured patchwork filling most of the main trading floor – a mass of vegetables, dried goods and, sadly, turtle eggs (on sale all down the east coast, and laid by the moderately threatened green turtle). The whole scene is worth contemplating at length from one of the upper floors – the vantage point of many a tourist-brochure snap. Trading continues east of here in a new extension to the market, with more stalls to be found spilling out onto the surrounding pavements.

Though lacking in atmosphere, the **Bazaar Buluh Kubu**, a couple of minutes' walk west of the central market, does have a good range of batik items, *songkets* and other crafts on sale. A few blocks to the south is the still more humdrum **Pasar MPKB**, a municipal-run mix of wet market and food stalls.

More exciting than any of these is the informal, morning-only **Friday market** which, accompanied by a major Islamic gathering and sermon, sets up in the streets just south of Pasar MPKB. To visit the market is to witness the rustic heart of Kelantan laid bare, as traders and shoppers pour in from the surrounding kampungs on their weekend day out in the city. Amid the mundane household merchandise you may spot oddities such as fearsome knives reminiscent of traditional Arab daggers – except that the blades turn out to be stamped "JAPAN". Most striking of all is the emphasis on folk remedies and general quackery, ranging from herbal products whose labels proclaim them beneficial to both men and women, to little blue pills dispensed – invariably to elderly men in traditional garb – by youths in baseball caps and jeans, who don surgical gloves to count out the required quantity.

The State Museum and the Cultural Centre

Situated on the corner of Jalan Hospital and Jalan Sultan Ibrahim, the **State Museum** (Thurs–Sat 8am–4.45pm; RM2) houses an odd collection including romantic rural Malay paintings and lots of earthenware pots. Better is the

△ *Gasing* (spinning tops), Kota Bharu

The performing arts in Kelantan

Kelantan has one of the richest artistic traditions of any state in Peninsular Malaysia, boasting two costumed dance/drama forms, **mak yong** and the Thai-influenced **Menora**, as well as **wayang kulit**, or shadow puppetry, which, for visitors lucky enough to see a performance, is one of the most striking entertainments available in Malaysia. Traditionally, *wayang kulit* is staged on a dais screened from the audience by a large cloth sheet, illuminated from behind by a dangling light bulb. The cast is a set of stencils, made of hide in the shapes of the various characters, which are manipulated against the screen by a sole puppeteer, who also improvises and voices all the dialogue. Reflecting the long history of Indian influence in the region, the tales thus enacted are taken from the Hindu epic, the Ramayana; in the past, *wayang kulit* would function as a sort of *kampung* soap opera, serializing Ramayana instalments nightly during the months after the rice harvest. Performances are gripping affairs, as the puppets (comprising royalty, demons, clowns and a monkey god, often painted in translucent colours which come through on the screen) inveigle, romance and fight to a hypnotic soundtrack provided by an ensemble of drums, gongs and the oboe-like *serunai*, seated behind the puppeteer.

Sadly, all three of the above traditional art forms were **banned** in Kelantan, for reasons various and sometimes vague, when PAS returned to power in the state in the 1990s. PAS has cited issues of public morality – which could mean they object to the fact that both *mak yong* and *menora* can involve an element of cross-dressing, the male lead in *mak yong* traditionally being played by a woman, while a *menora* troupe usually consists of three men, who take female roles as necessary. PAS also objects to the non-Islamic nature of these performances, since they involve folk tales or, in the case of *wayang kulit*, Hindu mythology. Finally, the party also has a problem with the strong **spiritualist** element permeating the traditional arts. A *wayang kulit* performance always begins with a *buka panggung* ceremony, in which the puppeteer readies the stage by reciting mantras and making offerings of food to the spirits; *mak yong* can be staged as part of a folk-healing tradition called *main puteri*, in which the performers enter a trance to remove a spirit believed to be affecting the "patient" for whom the performance is held.

Whatever the main reason for the ban, the effect has been akin to cultural hari kiri, depriving a generation of Kelantanese of their own cultural traditions. Dozens of *wayang kulit* troupes have been reduced to a mere handful, performing largely outside Kelantan or, thanks to one concession from PAS, for the benefit of the mainly tourist audience at Kota Bharu's Cultural Centre. On a brighter note, *menora* can sometimes be seen in Kedah, and all three forms mentioned here are being passed on to a new generation, and sometimes staged, at the National Arts Academy in KL (ⓦwww.ask.edu.my), far from their traditional heartland.

collection of musical instruments on the first floor, among which is the *kertok*, a large coconut with its top sliced off and a piece of wood fastened across the opening to form a sounding board. Decorated with colourful pennants and hit with a cloth beater, it's one of the percussion instruments peculiar to Kelantan.

You can see these in action (and possibly try your hand at them), and watch many other Malay artistic and recreational activities, at the excellent **cultural centre** (Gelanggang Seni; open Jan–Aug) on Jalan Mahmood, southeast of the museum. Free demonstrations here (Mon, Wed & Sat; check times with the tourist office) feature many of the traditional **pastimes** of the Peninsula, such as *gasing* (spinning tops) and *congkak* (a mancala game like those found in West Africa and the Middle East, involving the strategic movement of seeds around the holes on a wooden board). Best of all, on Wednesday evenings there are *wayang kulit* (shadow puppetry) performances from 9pm until around midnight, though the action doesn't begin until around 9.30pm when the instrumental prelude is over. A visit to the centre is the easiest way to see many of the arts that are dying out elsewhere in Malaysia, and the standard here is consistently high.

Eating and drinking

Kota Bharu has a few Malay restaurants dotted around the centre, but for many locals, the Malay culinary scene in the city is dominated by the outdoor **night food market** (aka *Medan Selera MPKB*), on the nondescript northern fringes of the centre. Until recently, when it occupied a prime site at the heart of the Jalan Padang Garong shopping area (now being turned into a towering office building), the market was the hub of Kota Bharu nightlife and one of the most atmospheric in the country; notwithstanding its new location, however, the food remains a big draw. Other than the expected Malay specialities, such as excellent **nasi kerabu** (quintessentially Kelantanese rice, tinted blue using flower petals – though these days additives may be used instead – and typically served with fish curry), the few dozen stalls here also offer a great range of *murtabaks*; just watching the sellers stretch, fold and flip the dough on their griddles is mouthwatering. You might want to wash your meal down with *sup ekor* (essentially oxtail soup) or *sup tulang* (made from beef bones), or round it off by sampling the colourful *kuihs* on offer, including *jala emas*, looking like saffron-coloured vermicelli. The whole thing gets going daily around 6pm and stays open till midnight, with a brief break around 8pm for the *maghrib* prayer. Note that the market may well move again in the near future, so you may have to ask around for its location. If the market has a Chinese counterpart, it's the *Medan Selera Kebun Sultan*, housed in a cavernous hall on Jalan Kebun Sultan and offering a wide range of Chinese street food.

For another very Malaysian eating experience, join the throngs at the humble pushcart operation signed *Nasi Kukus Kebun Sultan*, also on Jalan Kebun Sultan. Part of a small row of Malay stalls, this attracts locals of all creeds with its freshly prepared *sambal* fish, okra curry, *ikan bakar (grilled fish)* and the like. Point at your preferred toppings and they will be poured over the rice, on a banana leaf, which is then folded into a pyramid shape and wrapped up in newspaper for you to take away.

This brilliant street food apart, the city has a decent selection of low-key **restaurants**. The Chinese eating places on Jalan Kebun Sultan are among the few that aren't halal, and these are also your best bet for **alcohol**, along with the swish bar at the *Renaissance* hotel. To combine eating with shopping, head to the **Pacific KB Mall**: aside from a couple of Western cafés, it has a handy food court on the top floor.

Restaurants and kedai kopis

Four Seasons Jalan Dusun Raja ☎ 09/743 6666. A modern Chinese restaurant with a varied menu, particularly strong on seafood, including reliable winners like steamed fish in soya sauce. Their oyster omelette and steamboat are also recommended. Meals are priced according to the amount ordered – almost any four dishes from the menu, plus rice, Chinese tea and fresh fruit for dessert, will come to around RM50. Packed at weekends. Daily noon–2.30pm & 6–10pm.

Golden City Jalan Padang Garong. Lively, brightly lit *kedai kopi* serving decent Chinese food, including *curry mee* and other spicy noodle dishes for around RM5. Along with the upstairs drinking area, it stays open until 11pm.

Hayaki Jalan Pintu Pong. As close as the centre gets to a Western-style café, and one of very few venues in Kota Bharu where twenty-somethings can chill out at. The menu features both Western and Asian snacks and light meals.

Mamak Spicy Specials Jalan Sultan Yahya Petra. The usual *mamak* favourites in modern surroundings, well placed for both long-distance bus stations and the Pacific KB Mall. A popular meeting place well into the evening.

Muhibah Jalan Pintu Pong. Excellent, inexpensive Chinese-owned vegetarian establishment with plenty of Malay staff and patrons, as befits a place whose name means "harmony". Downstairs comprises a bakery and café, serving local and Western pastries and ice-blended shakes; upstairs is a small restaurant with a great spread of stir-fries and stew toppings for rice, plus a menu of more involved dishes. You really don't have to be veggie to enjoy it, and it's a haven on hot days – both floors have a/c. Daily early until 9pm or so.

Noodle Station Jalan Ismail. A small restaurant serving up numerous tasty wonton noodle permutations – fried or in soup, with prawn or chicken in various guises, costing up to RM5. There's a

culinary gear change after the main course, when a range of sorbets and coffees become the chief temptations. Daily 8am till late.

Sri Devi Jalan Kebun Sultan. Topnotch South Indian *kedai kopi* with excellent *mee goreng* and banana-leaf curries. Daily roughly 7.30am–8.30pm.

White House Jalan Sultanah Zainab. No grand mansion, but a tiny white bungalow housing the most mundane-looking *kedai kopi*. In fact, it's a city institution and social nexus, attracting Malay worshippers at the Masjid Negeri opposite, as well as Chinese professionals. The trademark dish is humble *telur setengah masak* – softboiled eggs cracked into a saucer, seasoned with soy sauce and white pepper, and delicious scooped up with buttered toast, all washed down with *teh* or *kopi tarek*. A great place for breakfast or a late snack. Daily 8am–1.30pm & 9pm–1am.

Listings

Banks and exchange There are several banks in and around the rectangle bounded by Jalan Pintu Pong, Jalan Padang Garong, and Jalan Kebun Sultan (on the last of these, you'll find both Maybank and Bumiputra Commerce Bank). Maybank operates a convenient foreign exchange office on the corner of Jalan Pintu Pong and Jalan Parit Dalam (daily 10am–6pm).

Car rental Avis, *Hotel Perdana* lobby ☏09/748 4457; Hawk, at the airport ☏09/773 3824.

Hospital Jalan Hospital ☏09/748 5533.

Internet access Quite a few small Internet cafés lurk, usually in upstairs premises, on the lanes between Jalan Pintu Pong and Jalan Padang Garong.

Left luggage At the bus station on Jalan Hamzah (daily 8am–10pm).

Pharmacies There are several centrally located pharmacies, including a Guardian pharmacy on Jalan Padang Garong and a Watsons outlet in the Pacific KB Mall.

Police Headquarters on Jalan Sultan Ibrahim (☏09/748 5522).

Post office The GPO is on Jalan Sultan Ibrahim (closed Fri); there's also a convenient branch post office on the lane just south of Jalan Pintu Pong (also closed Fri).

Shopping The Pacific KB Mall is a good place for most requirements, and has a Maybank ATM on the

ground floor. Here you'll also find the huge Pacific supermarket and a Popular Bookstore outlet. More centrally, on Jalan Pintu Pong there's a Mydin supermarket and the old-fashioned Pantai Timur complex, a collection of assorted shops, while on Jalan Padang Garong, next to the *Suria* hotel, you'll find the Muda Osman bookshop.

Thai visas Many nationalities can get a one-month visa stamped in at the border. Visas can be obtained in advance from the Thai Consulate, 4426 Jalan Pengkalan Chepa (☏09/748 2545; Mon–Thurs & Sun 9am–noon & 2–3.30pm); it helps to be smartly dressed when you apply, as they have been known to refuse entry to people wearing shorts.

Travel agents Kota Bharu has a dearth of good travel agents, though the city's guesthouses help plug the gap by arranging trips to the most obvious nearby attractions, the Perhentians and Stong State Park. Otherwise, try Sampugita Holidays at the *Perdana* hotel (☏09/743 2178), or Ping Anchorage, the very efficient Kuala Terengganu-based tour operator, who have a branch office on Jalan Padang Garong (☏09/744 2020).

Visa extensions At the Immigration Department, second floor, Wisma Persekutuan, Jalan Bayam (Mon–Wed & Sun 8am–4pm, Thurs 8am–12.45pm; ☏09/748 2120).

Around Kota Bharu

While there's plenty in Kota Bharu itself to keep you occupied for a couple of days, the surrounding areas offer a look at the **cottage industries** producing local crafts, a few **temples**, and relaxation at the **beaches** to the north and east of town. Compared to what's on offer in Terengganu, the sands here are nothing special, despite their wistfully romantic names, and the prevailing conservatism may not be conducive to relaxed sunbathing (though a few locals, especially Chinese, can be seen in Western swimwear). That said, if you're continuing on to the interior, a seaside outing does provide a nice contrast to the jungles that prevail there, and outside the weekend you may be able to find a quiet stretch of beach for a little privacy.

The craft workshops and PCB

As every guidebook will tell you, Kota Bharu's best-known beach, 11km north of the city, was once known as Pantai Cinta Berahi (**PCB** for short), the "Beach of Passionate Love", until the PAS-controlled state assembly changed its name to the placid **Pantai Cahaya Bulan**, or "Moonlight Beach". Unfortunately, flooding caused by very occasional freak tides has led to a defence being hastily put in place on the section of the beach where the road arrives. This stretch is now not so much a beach as a mosaic of large rocks strewn over the sand, whose efficacy in the face of the next ultra-high tide is somewhat doubtful.

While the southern part of PCB, a little further along, remains in reasonable condition, for many visitors the attraction is not so much the beach but the traditional **craft workshops** on the way there. The area is one of the few places

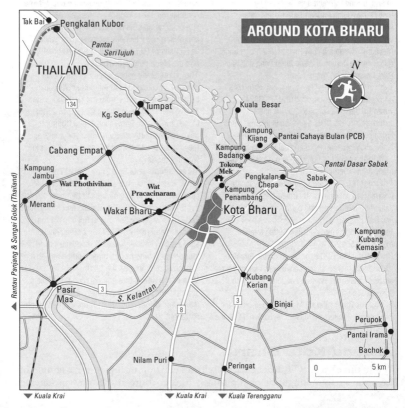

▼ *Kuala Krai* ▼ *Kuala Krai* ▼ *Kuala Terengganu*

in Malaysia where these have survived in any number, and it's a great place to see the craftsmen in action and make a purchase or two.

The production of **batik** and *songkets* are among the commonest crafts in Malaysia, and there are several outlets specializing in these, including Pantas Batek (☎09/744 1616) in Kampung Penambang, just over 4km from Kota Bharu, and Sabihah Batek (☎09/774 2350), close to Kampung Kijang, 8km from town. Also in Kampung Kijang is KB Craft Trading (☎09/774 2680), home to skilled **silversmiths** who produce a variety of elegant filigree brooches (from RM40), including depictions of Kelantan kites. You can see actual **kites** being made at the Sapi'e Wau workshop (no phone) in Kampung Pauh Badang (between Penambang and Kijang villages); the little building is opposite Balai Polis Badang, the police post. The kites are painstakingly assembled over a period of about two weeks; the decorations are unique to the craftsman, although tradition dictates that leaf patterns and a pair of birds are the principal elements in the design. The most unusual aspect of the kite's structure is the long projection above its head, supporting a large bow that hums when the kite is flying.

One of the most impressive examples of artisanship in the Kota Bharu area is the **woodcarving** at May Kris (☎09/747 3760) in Banggol, just before Kampung Pauh Badang. Here, in a workshop within his home, Rosman bin Ramli turns out some stunning examples of hilts and scabbards in *kemuning* wood for the *kris*, the traditional Malay dagger. The hilts feature stylized birds' heads, usually fiendishly detailed; simple, abstract versions are available to buy with blades or as paperweights for around RM150, while the ornate versions, which can take two months to finish, will set you back at least ten times as much. Visits are by appointment only, and you'll need to ask directions as Rosman's house is a little way off the main road.

It's also possible to observe the making of **gasing** (spinning tops). The tops resemble a discus except for a short steel spike inserted in one side; producing them involves carefully selecting the wood, which must be delicately planed and shaped, and the precise balancing of the metal spike – the whole process can take anything up to three weeks. If you want to watch this, or the manufacture of the hide puppets used in *wayang kulit*, it's best to contact Roselan Hanefiah at the tourist office to make arrangements.

An unrelated diversion on the way to PCB is **Tokong Mek**, just off the main road about 6km outside Kota Bharu (look for it on the left if you're heading out to the beach). With some unusually dramatic wall reliefs featuring tigers and dragons, this Chinese temple dates all the way back to 1780, proof of the long Chinese presence in Kelantan, in turn the reason why the community here has acquired a distinctive identity. Unlike Chinese everywhere else in Malaysia and in Singapore, they identify only weakly with their ancestral province or city in China, preferring to see themselves as Cina Bandar or Cina Kampung – town or country Chinese. The very use of Malay to categorize themselves underlines the fact that local Chinese are proudly integrated; many are effectively native speakers of the tricky Kelantanese dialect.

Practicalities

If you want to see the craft workshops and outlets, it's best to drive or charter a city taxi, either in the taxi parks close to the local bus station, or through your accommodation. For a group of six or more, Roselan Hanefiah at the tourist office can arrange customized half-day tours of some workshops, with an interpreter, some demonstrations and lunch thrown in, all for around RM200 per person. Otherwise, you could just get on the PCB **bus** (#10), which passes through Kampung Penambang and Kampung Kijang, and close by Tokong Mek. Ask the driver or conductor to tell you where to alight; you'll be able to pick up another bus on to PCB or back to town easily enough.

If you make it to the **beach** itself, you'll want to head down past the rocky breakwater for some decent sands, adjoining (but not exclusive to) the *PCB Resort* (☏09/773 2307; RM100), a slightly dated complex with reasonable **chalets**. There are a few cheaper places along the main road just before the beach itself, including the bland *Ekonomi Guesthouse* (☏09/773 7791; RM60), whose air-conditioned en-suite rooms are, ironically, overpriced. The resort has a **restaurant**, and a handful of stalls selling food and fresh coconuts can be found on or just before the beach.

The temples

Buses #19 and #43 depart Kota Bharu regularly for the trip northwest to **Pantai Seri Tujuh**, a two-kilometre stretch of coastline that looks far more idyllic on the map than it actually is – its lagoons have now become muddy puddles. The bus passes several Thai temples en route, in various states of disrepair. One of the most glamorous is **Wat Pracacinaram**, easily spotted just outside **Wakaf Bharu**, on the road to Cabang Empat. It's a brand new building, with an elaborate triple-layered roof decorated in gold, sapphire and red. **Wakaf Bharu** itself is home to the nearest train station to Kota Bharu, but is otherwise a nondescript little town.

At the **Wat Phothivihan**, 15km west of Kota Bharu, a forty-metre-long Reclining Buddha is said to be the second largest in the world (not a unique claim in these parts). The colossal, if rather insipid, plaster statue contains ashes of the deceased, laid to rest here according to custom (though a popular rumour says that it is actually a secret cache for the temple's funds). Other pavilions within the complex, somewhat dwarfed by the central structure, are of little interest, except for a small shrine to the left which honours a statue of a rather wasted-looking hermit. You can reach Wat Phothivihan by **bus** from Kota Bharu – the #19 or #27 from the local bus station brings you to Cabang Empat, from where it's a three-and-a-half-kilometre walk or a short taxi ride away.

Pantai Dasar Sabak and Pantai Irama

Back on the coast, **Pantai Dasar Sabak**, 13km northeast of Kota Bharu, is of historical interest – it was the first landing place of the Japanese in 1941, during their invasion of the Peninsula. It's a desolate place, a rough, windswept stretch of coast with a crumbling World War II bunker.

Pantai Irama, a further 12km south, strikes a less solemn note – its name literally means "Rhythm Beach". Despite a little rubbish along the water's edge, it's the nicest beach within easy reach of Kota Bharu, a quiet, tree-fringed stretch of white sand, freshened by the sea breeze. Unless you visit on a Friday, you should have the place to yourself. To get there, take the #23 or #39 **bus** or minibus #2a or #2b (every 30min; 45min) to Bachok from Kota Bharu's local bus station; the beach is about 500m north of the bus terminus.

Pulau Perhentian

The name **Pulau Perhentian** actually covers two islands, **Perhentian Besar** and **Perhentian Kecil** (their names meaning large and small stopping places, respectively; Big Island and Small Island are sometimes used instead), both

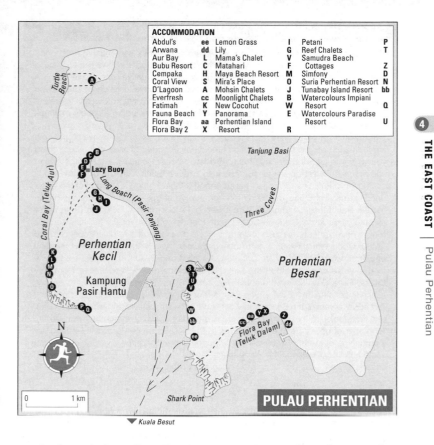

ACCOMMODATION

Abdul's	**ee**	Lemon Grass	**I**
Arwana	**dd**	Lily	**G**
Aur Bay	**L**	Mama's Chalet	**V**
Bubu Resort	**C**	Matahari	**F**
Cempaka	**H**	Maya Beach Resort	**M**
Coral View	**S**	Mira's Place	**O**
D'Lagoon	**A**	Mohsin Chalets	**J**
Everfresh	**cc**	Moonlight Chalets	**B**
Fatimah	**K**	New Cocohut	**W**
Fauna Beach	**Y**	Panorama	**E**
Flora Bay	**aa**	Perhentian Island	
Flora Bay 2	**X**	Resort	**R**

Petani	**P**
Reef Chalets	**T**
Samudra Beach	
Cottages	**Z**
Simfony	**D**
Suria Perhentian Resort	**N**
Tunabay Island Resort	**bb**
Watercolours Impiani	
Resort	**Q**
Watercolours Paradise	
Resort	**U**

Turtle Beach

Ⓐ

Coral Bay (Teluk Aur)

Ⓒ Ⓑ
Ⓓ
Ⓔ Ⓕ **Lazy Buoy**

Long Beach (Pasir Panjang)

Ⓖ Ⓗ Ⓘ
Ⓙ

Tanjung Basi

Three Coves

Perhentian Kecil

Ⓚ
Ⓛ
Ⓜ
Ⓝ
Ⓞ

Kampung Pasir Hantu

Ⓟ Ⓠ

Perhentian Besar

Ⓢ Ⓡ
Ⓣ
Ⓤ
Ⓥ

Ⓦ
bb

Ⓨ Ⓧ
aa Ⓩ
Cc dd
ee

Flora Bay (Teluk Dalam)

N

0   1 km

Shark Point

PULAU PERHENTIAN

▼ *Kuala Besut*

textbook tropical paradises. Despite an increasing number of visitors, they retain considerable appeal, and the essentials of any idyllic island holiday – fantastic sandy beaches, and great **snorkelling** and **diving** – are all in place. An outing with local **fishermen**, easily arranged at your accommodation for a modest fee, offers a chance to see the way of life that sustains most island-ers (though bear in mind that the smell of the landed fish and the swells can combine to make you queasy). Away from the beach and marine pursuits, both islands have jungly hills in their interior, with a few paths for some chal-lenging **walks** and opportunities to spot flying foxes, monkeys and monitor lizards. All this is capped by a laid-back atmosphere both rare and refreshing among popular island destinations, thanks partly, it must be said, to the austere attitude towards alcohol here in Terengganu.

Much of the **accommodation** on the islands comprises low-priced chalets and resorts, the most basic of which are pretty rustic; a few places still use hurricane lamps rather than electric lighting. Perhentian Kecil caters more to the backpacker scene, epitomized by **Long Beach**, while Besar, the more developed of the two, has most of the mid-range accommodation and is popular with families, package tourists and better-heeled independent travellers. **Peak season** is roughly June until the end of August, outside of which rates fall by at least 25 percent (the price codes given in our reviews

Snorkelling and diving around the Perhentians

Outside the monsoon, conditions in the waters around the Perhentians are superb: currents are gentle, and visibility is up to 20m (although the sea lice can be a problem, inflicting an unpleasant but harmless sting not unlike that of a jellyfish). A **snorkelling** foray around the rocks at the ends of most bays turns up an astonishing array of brightly coloured fish and live coral. For the more adventurous still, there are some spectacular **dive sites** a short boat ride offshore, including a couple of wreck dives open to those with Advanced Open Water qualifications.

Snorkelling **trips** to undeveloped coves around either island, with five stops, cost around RM30 per person; your accommodation can either charter you a boat or tell you where to join one of these trips. At a few places, including the *Arwana Resort* and *Mama's Chalet* on Besar, you can also arrange a snorkelling trip further afield, southeast to Pulau Lang Tengah, for around RM60 per person in a group of ten or so. Snorkel, mask and fins can be rented from a **dive shop** – every Perhentians beach has several of these, and also offer a variety of **PADI courses**, including Open Water and the introductory Discover Scuba; a couple also offer specialist facilities such as Nitrox. Prices are pretty much uniform: a single dive for qualified divers costs around RM80, Open Water RM850, and Advanced Open Water RM700. Among the many operators worth talking to are Coral Sky Divers (Long Beach; their website, ⓦwww .coralskydiver.com, includes descriptions of various choice dive sites), Flora Bay Divers (Flora Bay; ⓦwww.florabaydivers.com), Spice Divers (Long Beach; ⓦwww .spicedivers.com.my); Steffen Sea Sports (Coral Bay; ⓦwww.steffenseasports.com); Turtle Bay Divers (Long Beach and west shore of Besar; ⓦwww.turtlebaydivers.com); and Watercolours Dive Centre (west shore of Besar; ⓦwww.watercoloursworld.com). A number of operators offer diving trips to Pulau Lang Tengah or Pulau Redang, for a surcharge of around RM60 or RM100 per person respectively over the cost of the same number of dives at the Perhentians.

For a few do's and don'ts of snorkelling and diving, see Basics, p.81.

represent peak rates). Many resorts begin closing in late October, sometimes earlier, and don't open again until the following February or March, but it is possible to find a few places to stay during the northeast monsoon, for a truly isolated island experience.

It's well worth **booking** in advance for the peak season, particularly if you want to stay at Long Beach, where travellers without reservations sometimes spend their first night sleeping out on the sands. As a couple of the cheaper places on the islands have a habit of changing their (usually cellular) phone numbers, it can be worth talking to travel agents, particularly those at Kuala Besut (see opposite); the best of these firms can not only book accommodation but also give impartial advice on the latest accommodation picture. Most of the pricier resorts do their own full-board packages, which can be good value, typically for three days and two nights, and including boat transfers and some snorkelling (pricier diving packages are also available).

Many of the resorts (certainly most of the few which have a cove to themselves) run a **restaurant**, open to all-comers. A handful of these serve up moderately elaborate Asian cuisine, or a range of pizzas, steaks and pasta, but the vast majority offer the usual rice and noodle variations, plus simple Western fare such as omelettes, pancakes, and occasionally even baked potatoes; seafood is, unsurprisingly, also usually a feature.

Note that there are **no banks** on the islands, nor at either of the two locations from which Perhentians boats depart. While plastic can be used to pay for accommodation and food at some mid-range places, it obviously makes sense to arrive with enough cash to last the duration of your island stay. There's no problem with using **cell phones** on both islands, and you may well prefer texting to getting **on line** at the lunatic rate charged by Internet centres here – at least RM5 for fifteen minutes.

While PAS was in charge of Terengganu, the party's lukewarm attitude to commercialization helped keep large-scale development on the Perhentians to a minimum. This is just as well, given that both islands are home to several protected **turtle nesting** sites, and that the impact of the existing resorts on the environment isn't negligible, with shortages of **water** (much of which comes from wells) a hassle during the tourist peak. Things have loosened slightly with UMNO back in the driving seat: at least one major new resort has since been completed, and **alcohol** is sold less furtively these days at a handful of restaurants. Few restaurants seem to mind if you bring your own booze from the mainland.

Travel to and around the Perhentians

Nearly all Perhentians boats depart from the little town of Kuala Besut on the northern Terengganu coast, off Route 3. The exception is boats run by Simfony (one of the chalet operators on Long Beach), who operate from **Tok Bali**, just inside Kelantan; Simfony, plus the two Kuala Besut-based agencies mentioned below, have desks just outside arrivals at Kota Bharu airport, where you can arrange taxis to the departure points (RM60 for four people) and boat tickets. Note that visiting the Perhentians incurs a marine parks **conservation fee** of RM5, valid for three days' stay, which you pay at the jetty before setting off (keep the ticket/receipt in case you need to produce it later).

Kuala Besut

KUALA BESUT is easily reached by chartering a **taxi** from Kota Bharu (RM32), Kota Bharu airport (RM50), or Kuala Terengganu (RM60). You may also be able to find a taxi here from Gua Musang (RM140), Cherating (RM200) or even the Cameron Highlands or Jerantut (RM300). **Local buses** operated by S P Bumi run to Kuala Besut from Kuala Terengganu around eight times daily (RM6). Travelling by bus from Kota Bharu, catch bus #3, departing the local bus station frequently throughout the day for the hour's ride to Pasir Puteh, from where bus #96 (every 30min) makes the remaining half-hour journey to Kuala Besut.

Kuala Besut itself is practically a one-street affair, the street in question running past the **boat terminal** (on the right as you arrive) to terminate just beyond the **bus and taxi station**, which is just a few seconds' drive further on. Several **agents** selling boat tickets and Perhentians packages can be found in the lanes along this street or in the boat terminal. Many taxis will drop you at a firm called Perhentian Pelangi Travel & Tours so the driver can earn a commission, and if you bought your ticket in advance from a guesthouse in Kota Bharu it will quite probably be with them. There are other agencies without the hard-sell approach, in particular the excellent Anjung Holidays (☏09/697 4095, ⓦwww.anjungholidays.com) in the boat terminal. Besides selling boat tickets most of the year (during the northeast monsoon, you can pay the boatmen directly), Terengganu island packages and transfers to other locations in the Peninsula, such as the Cameron Highlands, they can give you advice on most of the accommodation on the islands, which is particularly useful in the busier months. Another reasonable agent is Perhentian Trans Holiday (☏09/690 3269, ⓦwww.perhentiantrans.com), on the lane opposite the ferry terminal.

There's always a chance that unfavourable weather conditions may force you to spend the night in town. On the lane directly opposite the boat terminal, the *Nan Hotel* has a range of simple en-suite **rooms** (☎019/985 3414; RM30), including a few with air-conditioning and TV. Also worth considering is the more basic *Yaudin*, upstairs in the building just beyond the bus station (☎09/697 4677; RM20), where the rooms have a fan and shared facilities.

Around the boat terminal are a number of decent stalls and restaurants with a particular emphasis on **seafood**, including the Chinese-run *Sakura*, practically opposite the terminal. For Malay food, you could do worse than head to *Unjang*, next to the bus station. The most humble of *kedai kopis*, in the popularity stakes it nonetheless wipes the floor with the competition thanks to its brilliant self-service *nasi campur* spread, which often feature *ayam bakar* and a rich *sayur lodeh*, plus more unusual concoctions, such as a pineapple curry.

Perhentians boats

Once at Kuala Besut, you'll find that the most efficient way to get to the islands is to use the **fast boats** (RM30 one-way), which set off for the Perhentians typically at 9am, 11am and 2pm, taking just over half an hour. There are also **slow boats** (RM20) setting off a couple of times between 10am and 2pm, and taking up to three times as long. All boats drop you at the bay of your choice, though at those bays without a jetty (notably Long Beach), you'll need to pay another RM2 to get ashore on a taxi boat. **Return tickets** are available for the price of two one-way tickets, and you don't need to know exactly when or from which bit of the islands you're going to come back from; the day before your departure, show your accommodation your ticket, and they'll arrange for you to be picked up at the required time (boats typically depart at 8am, noon and also at 4pm if there's demand). Note that the boat service to the islands is regular only between March and October; at other times services are much reduced thanks to the harsh northeast monsoon, although there is usually at least one boat a day to the fishing village on Perhentian Kecil.

A so-called **water taxi** service operates around the Perhentians, provided by plenty of small speedboats. **Fares** start at RM4 per person for a journey between adjacent bays (walking is often not an option thanks to rocky obstructions), and rise to up to RM12 to travel from one side of Besar to the other, or from one island to the other. When you need a boat taxi, just inform the management of the accommodation or restaurant where you happen to be, and they'll usually be able to rustle up one of the boatmen within a few minutes. The exception to this is after dark, when the water taxis can become scarce; at this time you may have to pay double the usual fare if there are few other passengers to share the ride. If you simply need to get across either island, you may be able to use one of the **footpaths** instead (after dark a **torch** is essential for these, and handy for beach walks too).

Perhentian Kecil

In the southeast of **Perhentian Kecil** is the island's only village, the spookily named **Kampung Pasir Hantu** (the name means "Sand of Ghosts") – there's no reason to go there unless you need to avail yourself of the clinic or police station. For many visitors, its the east-facing **Long Beach** that's the prime attraction, boasting a wide stretch of glistening-white, deep, soft sand. It does lack a view of the sunset, which is lost behind the island's hilly spine, but somehow that really doesn't matter: the light simply does a long, slow fade, leaving the illumination from the beach restaurants and their CDs of Bob Marley or generic, pumping house to dominate the senses. This is backpackerdom by the beach, and there's a genuinely infectious buzz about the place; during the peak season there are fairly frequent **beach parties** which, while in no way comparable to the moonlit raves across the Thai border at Ko Pha Ngan, can be enormous fun. Things can all be a bit too intense at the height of the season, when you might prefer to stay on the quieter west-facing coves, such as **Coral Bay**. The western shore is appealing in its own right, of course, with sheltered waters (which make it a better bet than Long Beach during the northeast monsoon), good snorkelling and, of course, sunset views. As Coral Bay and Long Beach are only a ten-minute walk apart, via a footpath, shuttling between them to sample different hangouts is straightforward (though bring a torch at night).

For **eating**, standouts include *Mohsin Chalets*, which ploughs its own furrow with tempting offerings like roast beef and mashed potatoes, and Indian veggie platters, while the restaurant at *Lily* is pretty popular for Chinese food.

Internet access is available at two shops, Lazy Buoy and the Gen Mini Mart, in the middle of Long Beach. The latter also changes traveller's cheques, while the former offers a range of **water sports** during the northeast monsoon, including windsurfing and bodyboarding.

Western-shore accommodation, including Coral Bay

Aur Bay ⓣ013/995 0817. Fairly basic but popular chalets with mosquito nets and private facilities. They also have verandas, but each faces the chalet opposite rather than the beach. Rates can halve outside the peak season. ❸

Fatimah No phone. Rooms here are two to a chalet, and hardly sophisticated, with fan and plasticky floor lining, but the en-suite facilities are quite reasonable. As at the adjacent *Aur Beach*, of which this is an offshoot, the chalets face each other. Not bad for the price. ❷

Maya Beach Resort ⓣ019/924 1044, ⓔmayabeachresort@yahoo.com. A handful of newish en-suite fan chalets, with a dive shop and café. Good discounts outside the peak season. ❸

Mira's Place ⓣ019/967 2349. A small cluster of charmingly rustic chalets on their own immaculate cove, a half-hour walk south of Coral Bay. The friendly woman proprietor speaks some English. A great choice for that *Robinson Crusoe* experience you always wanted. Open all year. ❷

Petani ⓣ019/426 7100. Five airy en-suite chalets with mosquito nets and walls of woven *mengkuang*, with a terrace restaurant offering vistas of glorious blue sea. It's secluded on its own cove, from where it's a rough 45min hike up and over the headland to the adjacent beach and *Mira's Place*; water taxis are a much better way to get around. Open all year. ❸

Suria Perhentian Resort ⓣ09/697 7960, reservations ⓣ03/7806 4752, ⓦwww.suriaresorts.com. En-suite chalets, sturdily built but quite simply furnished, well placed on the southern end of the bay, with its own dive shop. ❻

Watercolours Impiani Resort ⓣ019/981 1852, ⓦwww.watercoloursworld.com. Relaunched in 2006, this is a mid-range development offering fancy a/c en-suite chalets in a wooded setting. You can pay for accommodation alone, or take one of various full-board packages, which start at RM300 in a double. For a premium you can add snorkelling or canoeing, or various dive options (they have their own dive shop); guided jungle treks can also be arranged. The restaurant offers à la carte and buffet meals. ❼

Eastern-shore accommodation, including Long Beach

Bubu Resort ⓣ03/2142 6688 or 09/697 8888, ⓦwww.buburesort.com.my. Catering mainly for package holidaymakers, this is a motel-like complex of en-suite a/c rooms, with its own restaurant and bar. All perfectly decent, but jars a little on unassuming Long Beach. ❽

Cempaka No phone. A mishmash of A-frames, a tad run-down, and rather better en-suite chalets in a longhouse-type block. ❷

D'Lagoon ⓣ019/985 7089, ⓦwww.geocities.com/d_lagoon_my. Set in a tiny, isolated cove at the very northeastern tip of the island, this place offers en-suite chalets as well as rooms with shared facilities. It gets mixed reports, but has a trump card, namely that it presides over some of the very best snorkelling and diving on Kecil, with a fantastic coral garden offshore. It's also possible to clamber across the narrow neck of the island to the turtle-spotting beach on the other side. ❷

Lemon Grass ⓣ012/956 2393 or 019/938 3893. Spartan chalets up a little slope, with fan and mosquito net; toilets and showers are in a separate shack. The good views compensate for the less-than-wonderful facilities. ❷

Lily ☎019/222 4365. An odd assortment of half-wooden, half-brick chalets, each with a small attached bathroom. It could do with a new lick of paint, though, and is certainly overpriced. **❼**

Matahari ☎019/987 5002. Set a little way back from the beach and reached via a concrete walkway, this is a jumble of wooden chalets with faded blue roofs – generally a little rough around the edges, but pretty good value and thus popular. Cheapest are the twin rooms which share facilities, but there's also a longhouse block with en-suite rooms. **❷**

Mohsin Chalets ☎019/913 2525 or (off-season only) ☎019/381 6747, ⓔmohsinchalets@yahoo.com. Four tiers of long-house-style wooden buildings on a hillside behind Long Beach. Rooms are en suite, and a couple have a/c as well. The homely restaurant pavilion enjoys views over the beach, which is only a couple of minutes' walk away, and is a great spot to watch international football matches on big-screen TV. Rates rise with the quality of the view – basically, the higher up you are. Usually open year round, but call to check. **❹**

Moonlight Chalets ☎019/985 8222. A wide range of chalets set at the northern end of the beach, ranging from dirt-cheap A-frames to en-suite doubles (the best deal); four of the latter have a/c for a hefty RM150 a night, though that rate does include breakfast. The restaurant has a good view across the beach and some interesting culinary offerings, including barbecued stingray and a "special shake" containing mashed-up Mars bars and M&Ms. A-frames **❶**, rooms with fan **❸**

Panorama ☎09/697 7542. Set back from the beach in the shady jungle, this place has some basic en-suite cabins with fan, and a few plusher ones, plus some family chalets. Has a restaurant with Western and local dishes, though the setting is not quite up to the *Matahari*'s next door. **❸**

Simfony ☎09/778 2189. Nothing but fairly basic A-frames with shared facilities, but there are beach views and it's smack in the heart of Long Beach. They run the sole Perhentians boat service to and from Tok Bali in Kelantan. **❶**

Perhentian Besar

The **beaches** on the western shore of Perhentian Besar and at Flora Bay on the southern shore remain relaxed, despite a nearly continuous string of resorts. Flora Bay is less cramped but also tends to be slightly institutional in feel, whereas the western shore is packed in a pleasingly organic way; the latter also has a good vibe after dark when the restaurants get very busy, though the sunset is predictably lost behind Kecil. From the western shore, a steep **trail** (45min) to the western end of Flora Bay begins just past the second jetty south of *Abdul's*, behind some villas intended for visiting politicians. Another trail links Flora Bay with the *Perhentian Island Resort* (30min), passing the island's waterworks close to the bay.

For the very best beaches on Besar, get a water taxi to **Three Coves Bay** on the north of the island, a stunning conglomeration of three beaches separated from the western shore by rocky outcrops. This area also provides a secluded haven between May and September for green and hawksbill turtles to come ashore and lay their eggs, during which period it's off-limits to tourists.

The best **eating** on the island is on the western shore. Here, the restaurant at *Tunabay Resort* serves a tempting range of fare, from steaks through the odd fusion item, such as spicy Thai tuna pasta, to veggie burgers. Equally recommended is the atmospheric restaurant at *Coral View*, with a variety of "sizzlings" (basically grills – choose from fish or mixed seafood or meat), plus Malay specialities like *masak merah* (spicy beef), and a range of nonalcoholic "mocktails". Otherwise, you can't go far wrong at *New Cocohut* for Chinese fare, *Mama's Chalet* for Malay food, or *Watercolours* for first-rate pizzas. **Internet access** is available at the *Perhentian Island Resort* and *Flora Bay*, among others.

Western shore accommodation

Abdul's ☎09/697 7058 or 019/912 7303. Sturdy en-suite chalets with fan, the better, roomier ones fronting the beach. They're a little sparsely furnished but at the price, they're a sound choice. **❸**

Coral View ☎09/697 4943, ⓕ09/690 2600. A range of comfortable rooms, mainly in smart,

Malay life

The Malays, who comprise just over half the population of Malaysia, around fifteen percent of Singaporeans and nearly three-quarters of the people of Brunei, tend to be something of an unknown quantity for visitors. To get you up to speed, this section gives you a whirlwind tour of some distinctive aspects of Malay life you may encounter on your travels. Bear in mind that many Malays are giving up their traditional, rural existence, and the urban Malays you meet may well be keener on, say, partying to Western R&B than doing folk dances. Still, you've a good chance of seeing the customs mentioned here in cultural centres and during festivals; ask at tourist offices for details. For more on Malay history and ethnic groups see our "Contexts" section.

Traditional kite making, Kota Bharu

Traditional dress

A fact immediately apparent to visitors is that Malay traditional dress remains fairly common – the **baju Melayu** for men, and the **baju kurung** for women. In line with the Islamic dress code, the **tudung** (headscarf) is commonly worn by women, though it's sometimes substituted with a **selendang** (shawl), draped around the head and shoulders. For men, standard accessories include the **songkok**, a flattish oval cap made of stiff card lined with black velvet, and the **samping**, a knee-length sarong, which is sometimes worn over trousers. The finest *sampings*, which you'll see sported during festivals and other special occasions, are made of **songket**, hand-woven brocade featuring beautiful geometrical patterns in gold thread.

Bright colours are popular with Malay women

Sports and pastimes

Flying **kites** is still quite a popular Malay pastime, the kites in question being substantial affairs (as large as 2m in length and 1.5m across), colourfully decorated with floral motifs. They come in various elaborate shapes, most strikingly that of the Kelantanese *wau bulan*, a stylized outline of which is used as Malaysia Airlines' logo. Once upon a time, enthusiasts would compete to cut the strings of each other's kites, using dangerously sharpened strings coated with ground glass. Nowadays participants are judged on their kite-handling skills or on how melodiously their kite hums in the wind – the sound, produced by a rattan strip attached to the kite, is sometimes the first clue that someone is flying a kite in the vicinity.

Like kite-flying, **top-spinning** is both an amusement and a competitive sport for Malays, with none of the childish connotations it has in the West. There are two types of competition: the straightforward spin, in which the winner is simply the one whose top spins the longest; and the striking match, where one top has to knock out the other. Players launch the tops from shoulder height rather like a shot put – no mean feat with the bigger tops intended for endurance spinning, which can be in several kilos in weight and keep going for an hour or more.

More obviously recognizable as a sport is **silat**, the Malay martial art, demonstrations of which are fairly common at cultural

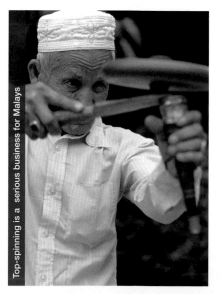

Top-spinning is a serious business for Malays

Traditional kampung house, Pulau Pangkor

Kampung houses

One of the most memorable sights in rural areas is that of charming **kampung houses**, generally made of **timber** (though plaited bamboo strips are sometimes used for the walls) and raised on stilts or posts to afford protection from floods and wild animals. They're traditionally roofed with *atap* (palm thatch), though these days corrugated iron or tiles are just as common. Inside, the layout is open-plan – a large rectangular room acts as the principal living area and as a reception room for guests, with bedrooms behind, separated by screens or drapes. The kitchen is often separate from the main part of the house, to which it's connected by an open courtyard.

Malay carpenters excel at decorative **woodcarving**, and the fancier kampung houses feature plenty of examples, in the form of patterned fanlights, tracery in veranda railings and repeated motifs at the edges of roofs. In another sign of the artisans' prowess, these houses were traditionally built without nails; instead, an elaborate jointing system was used to bind all the timbers together. It's not unknown for someone to buy an old house and then have it dismantled and reassembled, like a gigantic jigsaw puzzle, in a new location. Unfortunately, termites and the elements do take their toll, so it's almost impossible to find kampung houses over 200 years old.

contros. But often more gripping to watch, if you happen to stumble upon a game in a kampung or town, is **sepak raga** (also called *sepak takraw*, or *takraw* in Thailand and other Southeast Asian countries where it's played). A close cousin to volleyball, the game involves keeping a rattan ball in the air using just about every area of the body apart from the arms – a restriction which leads to some spectacular acrobatics and leaps as players try to the put the ball away on the opposing team's side of the net.

Young Malays practising silat

Music and dance

Among the many traditional musical genres, **dikir barat** is probably the one to look out for. It involves a chorus led by a *tukang karut*, whose role is to improvise

Traditional dance shows are fun for all concerned

rhyming lines, not unlike that of the MC in hip-hop; the chorus then echoes these lines, over an instrumental accompaniment provided by a frame drum, gong and the oboe-like *serunai*. *Dikir barat* is often staged in a competitive atmosphere, with two contingents trying to outdo each other by producing the most pleasing and witty lines, sometimes taking verbal potshots at each other in the process. Even if you don't understand Malay, the spectacle is well worth a brief look; performances are sometimes organized by cultural centres and are advertised on flyposters.

The most common of the many folk dance forms is the **joget**, which you may well come across if you're invited to a Malay function; it's also featured at touristy dance shows, where the finale is often a *joget* session with audience participation actively encouraged. Thought to be derived from dance forms introduced by the Portuguese in Melaka, *joget* is a lively affair danced by couples. Should you get involved, though, resist the urge to take your partner by the hand: men and women doing *joget* weave in and out of each other's way, alternately dancing face-to-face or side-by-side, but they never touch.

Wayang kulit

If there is one must-see piece of Malay entertainment, it's the **wayang kulit**, its name literally meaning "skin show", after the fact that this piece of village theatre involves puppets made of hide. More significant is that these are **shadow puppets**, only their silhouettes appearing on a screen before the audience. Sadly, *wayang kulit* is currently banned in its heartland, the northeastern Peninsular state of Kelantan, but tourists have special privileges to view shows in the state capital, Kota Bharu; for more on *wayang kulit* and the complex reasons behind its suppression, see the box on p.301.

A puppeteer performing *wayang kulit*

steep-roofed chalets with small attached bathrooms. They're all connected by various walkways taking you through a pleasant garden that's magical at night, when subtle lighting comes into play. Great restaurant and dive shop too. A good deal in general, especially for fan chalets (a/c comes at a premium). **⑤**

Mama's Chalet ☎ 09/690 4600 or 019/985 3359, ⓦ www.mamaschalet.com. Prim, very decent chalets, including a few seafacing ones with a touch of the kampung house, in the fanlights of multicoloured glass. All rooms have private facilities, and there's a popular Malay restaurant, too. **③**

New Cocohut ☎ 09/697 7988, ⓦ www .cocohuttravel.com. Chinese-run establishment with comfortable en-suite, a/c rooms and chalets. Cheapest are the rooms, in two-storey blocks; the chalets have the bonus of TV, hot water, armchair and fridge. The popular restaurant scores points too. **⑤**

Perhentian Island Resort ☎ 09/697 7775 or 03/2144 8350, ⓦ www.perhentianresort.com. my. A veritable campus of bungalows and chalets containing various grades of room, all spacious and boasting modern furnishings and verandas. Well-placed wooden wind chimes add atmosphere, but the lighting in parts of the grounds is inadequate at night, and staff can seem out of their depth; all in all, you'd expect much better for the price. The lovely beach here doesn't belong to them, despite what the signs would have you believe. **⑧**

Reef Chalets ☎ 09/697 7991 or 019/981 6762, ⓔ thereefpp@hotmail.com. Simple chalets arranged in a semicircle under a shady clump of trees, set back from the beach. **④**

🏃 **Tunabay Island Resort** ☎ 09/697 7779, ⓦ www.tunabay.com.my. This well-managed collection of chalets gets it just right – all the comforts of a good mid-range city hotel, with a cool informality that's perfect for a laid-back beach holiday. The restaurant and bar are deservedly popular, and breakfast is included the rate. **⑥**

Watercolours Paradise Resort ☎ 019/981 1852, ⓦ www.watercoloursworld.com. Simply furnished en-suite chalet rooms with fan and a small veranda, some with a seaview. There's also a dive shop and a popular restaurant. Open year-round. **③**

Flora Bay accommodation

Arwana ☎ 09/752 1741, ⓦ www .arwanaperhentian.com.my. This sizeable, recently built resort sneaked into the last gap on Flora Bay, behind the only bit of indifferent pebbley sand. The nicest rooms are in the row of chalets with verandas facing the beach, but most rooms are in three-storey blocks built around the resort's best feature, the fantastic freeform swimming pool. The large pavilion restaurant serves buffet meals plus some à la carte Western and Asian dishes, and has football on satellite TV plus karaoke nights; the resort also has its own dive shop. It's all a bit of a mixed bag – not as well run as the facilities deserve, but reasonably priced, and its packages can be good value. **⑥**

Everfresh ☎ 09/697 7620. A mix of A-frames and two-room chalets with matted walls, fraying slightly at the edges, but all set in a particularly lush garden. **②**

Fauna Beach ☎ 09/697 7607, ⓕ 697 7507. Pleasant, unremarkable chalets with fan (plus a couple with a/c), facing the beach and set in a neat garden. **③**

Flora Bay & Flora Bay 2 ☎ 09/697 7266, ⓦ www .florabayresort.com. A huge range of options, from inexpensive rooms with fan in institutional two-storey blocks, to beachfront chalets, some of which have a/c, though these are overpriced. All rooms are en suite. *Flora Bay*, with its garden of frangipanis and oleanders, is marginally preferable. **③**

Samudra Beach Cottages ☎ 09/697 7608 or 019/969 0957. Fairly standard chalets, three rooms to a unit, plus cheaper A-frames. Not bad at all, though fraying a little at the edges. **②**

Merang, Pulau Redang and Pulau Lang Tengah

A tiny coastal kampung some 35km northwest of Kuala Terengganu, **Merang** began to attract foreign travellers in the 1970s, when opportunities to stay with local families became something of a tourist draw. Nowadays, while Merang (not to be confused with Marang, south of Kuala Terengganu) does boast a reasonable beach, a few simple guesthouses and, incongruously, one stratospherically pricey spa resort, the homestays have all but dried up. The reason visitors come to Merang these days is usually to catch a boat for the one-hour trip out to **Pulau Redang** (also served by flights from KL and Singapore) or **Pulau Lang Tengah**, both of which have great snorkelling and diving, though hardly any inexpensive accommodation. Practically all visitors to these islands arrive on resort-based package trips, but if it's chiefly the underwater attractions that tempt you, then consider a side trip here with one of the dive operators on the Perhentians (see p.308). Note that the resorts on both islands shut up shop during the northeast monsoon.

Merang

Most travellers who make it to **MERANG**, along the coastal road just south of the creek that is the Sungai Merang, only glimpse the back of the village, which the road swings past. The beach, which can be reached along a couple of side roads, is not exceptional, the sand strewn in places with sea morning glories. Still, the village is usually quiet, there's reasonable swimming, and the beach gives a memorable view of the quartet of islands offshore – from left to right, the Perhentians, Lang Tengah, Redang and finally Bidung Laut, once the site of a refugee camp for Vietnamese boat people.

S P Bumi operates a convenient daytime **bus** service between Kuala Besut and Kuala Terengganu via Merang, with around eight departures daily in each direction; fares to Merang from either starting point are around RM4. Chartering a taxi here costs RM50 from Kuala Besut, and RM35 from Kuala Terengganu. Approaching from Kota Bharu, it's simplest just to charter a taxi (RM80), though you could always get the bus to Kuala Besut and change for the S P Bumi bus.

The buses stop at or opposite Merang's school, where a turning off the coast road leads to the riverside, ten minutes' walk away, and a succession of **jetties** for the islands. Most jetties serve specific resorts, so you may need to ask around to find the boat you want; tickets (around RM45 one-way to either Redang or Lang Tengah) are available from booths or from the boatmen, though most people on packages have their transfers included.

To reach Merang's beachfront **accommodation**, head down the side road from the bus stop on the east (southbound) side of the road, and you come to a T-junction. Turn left here to reach the simple *PN Chalet & Restaurant* (℡09/653 1229; ❸), which has air-conditioned rooms with a spacious attached bathroom, and its own restaurant. In the opposite direction from the T-junction is the friendly *Kenbara Resort* (℡ & ℻09/653 1770, ⓦkembararesort.tripod.com; dorm beds RM10, rooms ❷), set in a large garden with tables shaded by palms. They have a variety of rooms (a few with a/c), cooking facilities – handy as there are only basic dining-out options in Merang – and Internet access, and arrange all-day snorkelling trips to Redang (RM100 per person). A little further along, but in another domain of comfort altogether, is the *Aryani* (℡09/653 2111, ⓦwww .thearyani.com; ❾), an immaculate Malay-styled spa resort of just twenty luxurious rooms and suites, most of which have a sunken outdoor bath to lounge in. Besides a range of treatments, many of which involve lotions and cleansers derived from tropical herbs and flowers, there's a sumptuous pool area and fine Malay, Thai and Western fare in the slick restaurant. For a mere RM1055 per night, you can sleep in their Heritage Suite, a century-old Malay stilt house which once belonged to a Terengganu Sultan – it was moved here piece by piece.

Pulau Redang

Just 5km by 8km in size, **PULAU REDANG** is very much a resort enclave, with more than fifteen establishments having set up here over the past few years, and a few more on the way. For most visitors, the chief attraction is the abundant marine life, sustained by the **coral reefs** which thrive around the island. The house reefs have had to endure a lot over recent decades – a large-scale attack by the crown-of-thorns starfish in the mid-1970s and, more recently, silt deposition caused by development all over the island. Forests have been felled and hillsides levelled to make way for a **golf course**; new roads and a freshwater pipeline from the mainland have been laid; a kampung has been built inland for the two-thousand-strong fishing community who used to live in a traditional floating village, removed to make way for a jetty and even more tourist development.

Thankfully, coral reefs have remarkable properties of self-renewal, and Redang's marine environment appears to have stabilized in a reasonable state. Conservation has certainly been helped by Redang's designation as one of Malaysia's **marine parks**, and by the regulation of certain activities, such as spear-fishing, trawling and water sports, in the vicinity. The best **snorkelling** is off the southern coast around the islets of Pulau Pinang and Pulau Ekor Tibu, while most of the **dive sites** are located off Redang's eastern shore, which, as it happens, is where almost all the resorts are located (most have their own dive shops). Among the most common fish are batfish, angel fish, box fish and butterfly fish, which feed off the many anemone, sponges and bivalves to be found around the rocks. The highlight of the island's social calendar is arguably the **candat sotong** festival in April, celebrating a pastime popular all along the east coast, involving the catching of squid by dipping small hand-held lures with hooks on one end into the sea.

Practicalities

There's regular transport to Redang from March to October only, when the resorts are open. Almost all **boats** to Redang depart from Merang, except for those to the island's *Berjaya Beach* resort, which use Kuala Terengganu's Shahbandar jetty. In addition, Berjaya Air (ⓦ www.berjaya-air.com) operates daily **flights** to Redang's airstrip from KL (Subang airport; RM500 return) and Singapore (Seletar airport; S$300), with boats ferrying arrivals from the airstrip to the various resorts. Note that visitors to Redang are, in theory, liable to pay a RM5 marine parks **conservation fee** covering three days' stay, though in practice you may find it's levied only if you're on a snorkelling or diving package; your accommodation may collect the fee just before taking you to one of the most popular snorkelling areas, around Pulau Pinang just south of Redang (which, as it happens, is also the site of the Marine Park Centre, which administers the park).

The best source for the latest **information** on Redang is the terrific ⓦ www.redang.org, run by a Singapore-based couple who are passionate about the island. The website includes sections on all the practical aspects of visiting Redang, plus coverage of dive sites and conservation, as well as tons of photos and a worthwhile user forum.

It's usually cheaper to book a **package** to Redang than to visit independently. Standard packages typically include accommodation, boat transfers, some or all meals, and at least one snorkelling excursion (but normally exclude equipment rental); some resorts also offer diving packages. Packages are available through travel agents or the resorts themselves – practically all of them have booking offices in Kuala Terengganu, and a few have offices in KL as well.

Accommodation

Most **accommodation** on Redang is located on the island's eastern shore, either on **Pasir Panjang** (Long Beach) and the adjacent Shark Bay, or just to the south at another bay, **Teluk Kalung**. Pasir Panjang features a particularly gorgeous stretch of fine white sand that, appropriately, seems to go on forever; Teluk Kalung's beach is narrower and pebbley in places, but is largely inviting nonetheless. The beaches on the north of the island, at **Teluk Dalam**, home of the *Berjaya Beach* resort, rival those at Pasir Panjang. The resorts themselves, all of which have en-suite, air-conditioned rooms and their own restaurants, tend to be small and humdrum at the cheaper end of the market, while at the other end of the scale there are a few elaborate complexes with plenty of mod cons; the selection below gives an idea of what to expect.

Given the predominance of packages at Redang, and the fact that some resorts don't have accommodation-only rates, some reviews include the price *per night* of a three-day, two-night **package** for two people (indicated by "FBP", for full-board package). Where rates rise during the height of the season (July & Aug) or at weekends, the prices or codes apply to the higher rate. "B&B" denotes a room-only rate, with breakfast included; "KT" next to a phone number indicates a sales office in Kuala Terengganu.

Southern Redang

Redang Kalong Teluk Kalung ☎09/622 1591, reservations ☎03/7960 7163, ⓦwww .redangkalong.com. A single-storey timber development comprising rather sparsely furnished rooms, with its own dive shop. FBP RM370

Pasir Panjang/Shark Bay

Coral Redang ☎09/630 7110 or (KT) ☎623 6200, ⓦwww.coralredang.com.my. A bit more characterful than most places on Redang, with rooms boasting cane furniture, a veranda, bamboo matting on the walls and a touch of marble in the bathroom. There's also a small swimming pool with a poolside bar. FBP RM540 including snorkelling gear, B&B ❽

Laguna Redang ☎09/630 7888 or (KT) ☎631 0888, ⓦwww.lagunaredang.com.my. One of the largest and slickest establishments on Redang, with over two hundred rooms all set around the enormous freeform pool. Rooms are very cosy and have their own fridge and a safe. Internet access available (RM10/hr). FBP RM400, B&B ❽

Redang Beach (KT) ☎09/623 8188, ⓦwww .redang.com.my. A sizeable collection of two-storey blocks with red-tiled roofs and comfortable, modern rooms. FBP including three snorkelling trips RM450, B&B ❽

Redang Lagoon (KT) ☎09/666 5020, ⓦwww .redanglagoon.com. Along with *Redang Reef*, one of the best-value places on the island, though the vaguely Malay-themed chalets aren't anything special. FBP RM280, room only ❺

Redang Pelangi ☎09/624 2158, ⓦwww .redangpelangi.com. Unremarkable two- and four-bed rooms, each with their own safe. Rates fall by at least fifteen percent outside peak season. FBP RM360

Redang Reef ☎09/630 2181 or (KT) 622 6181, ⓦwww.redangreefresort.com.my. Perched on the headland at the southern end of Shark Bay, and reached by a long wooden walkway, this is one of the cheaper options on Redang, with simply furnished rooms. Discounts may be available early and late in the season. FBP RM360

Teluk Dalam

Berjaya Beach ☎09/697 3988 or (KT) 630 8866, ⓦwww.berjayaresorts.com.my. The one place which tends to stay open all year, and certainly a cut above most of the rest, with its own swimming pool and tennis facilities. In addition to snorkelling, offered on their packages, they also have optional round-island boat trips on which you can snorkel and feed the fish by hand, and can organize jungle walks. Standard packages are half board and include one snorkelling trip for RM500, B&B ❾

Pulau Lang Tengah

A chip off the old Redang block, **Lang Tengah** island offers a much more low-key version of the Redang experience, being only a fraction the size of its near neighbour, and with only a handful of places to stay. As at Redang, there's a RM5 **conservation charge** to pay, and **packages** are the norm. The *Redang Lang* (☎09/623 9911, ⓦwww.redanglangresort.com.my; packages RM340) and *Square Point* (☎09/697 7035 or 623 5333, ⓦwww.squarepoint.com.my;

packages RM348) resorts both have full-board deals, covering two nights' accommodation, meals, some snorkelling and transfers from Merang; naturally, diving packages are also available.

Kuala Terengganu

Only thirty years ago, **KUALA TERENGGANU**, 140km southeast of Kota Bharu as the crow flies, and 170km north of Kuantan, was little more than an oversized fishing village that just happened to be the capital of Terengganu and the seat of its sultanate, founded in the early eighteenth century by one Zainal Abidin, of the royal house of Johor. The town enjoyed a long spell as an

The Terengganu Peasants' Revolt

In the first three decades of the twentieth century, major changes were wrought on the **Terengganu peasantry**. The introduction by the Malay rulers of the system of *cap kurnia*, or royal gifts of land, created a new class of absentee landlords, and reduced farmers who had previously been able to sell or mortgage their land to the status of mere tenant cultivators. Furthermore, the installation of the **British Advisory system** sought to consolidate colonial power by imposing new land taxes, a costly registration of births, deaths and marriages, and permits for everyday things like collecting wood to repair houses. These ploys were greatly resented by the peasantry, whose religious perceptions framed their reaction – to the faithful, the deterioration in their living conditions signalled the imminent coming of the Mahdi, who would restore true faith. Consequently, their response was directed against all *kafir* (unbelievers), including the Malay rulers who were seen to be in collusion with the colonists.

The campaign of resistance began in 1922 with a series of anti-tax protests, organized by the village imams and spearheaded by two charismatic *ulama*s (Islamic scholars), Sayyid Sagap and Haji Drahman. As the peasants' militancy increased, so relations with the government deteriorated, until one incident in April 1928 triggered a full-scale revolt. A group of around five hundred armed men angrily confronted three British officials investigating an illegal tree-felling near Tergat, deep in the Terengganu interior. This was an attempt to provoke the British, but as it turned out, it was Sultan Sulaiman himself who travelled upstream to hear the crowd's grievances, which he promised to consider. The resulting legislation failed to satisfy the peasantry, who decided on a major assault on Kuala Terengganu. Moving upriver, they first captured the District Office at Kuala Berang and then proceeded to Kuala Telemong, where they were to join forces with a local band of rebels. But the rendezvous never happened: impatient to capitalize on previous successes, the group at Kuala Telemong, a motley crew by comparison with the well-armed band at Kuala Berang, decided to attack the government installation on their own, walking straight into the line of fire. Many of their leaders, who had been believed to be invulnerable, were killed, taking the wind out of the sails of the peasants.

However, it was the behaviour of the two *ulama*s that dealt the most powerful blow to the rebellion. Sayyid Sagap denied that he had ever been involved, claiming to be a loyal subject of the sultan; luckily for him, he had remained too far in the background to be firmly implicated. Haji Drahman had fled on hearing of the Kuala Telemong shooting, although he eventually returned voluntarily to face trial. He was too influential a figure to imprison, and so he was persuaded to call off hostilities in return for comfortable exile to Mecca, with a healthy stipend from the government to keep him there. The peasants, having been deserted by their leaders, were then subject to the unfettered and strangling effects of British bureaucracy.

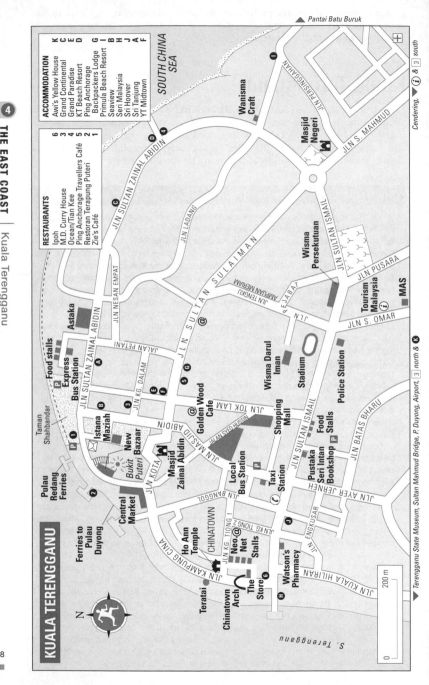

▲ *Pantai Batu Buruk*

KUALA TERENGGANU

N

S. Terengganu

Ferries to
Pulau Duyong

Pulau
Redang
Ferries

Taman
Shahbandar

Food stalls

Express
Bus Station

Central
Market

Istana
Maziah

*Bukit
Puteri*

New
Bazaar

Masjid
Zainal Abidin

Ho Ann
Temple

CHINATOWN

Teratai

Chinatown
Arch

The
Store

Watson's
Pharmacy

Neo.@
Net Stalls

Astaka

Golden Wood
Cafe

Local
Bus Station

Taxi
Station

Shopping
Mall

Pustaka
Seri Intan
Bookshop

Food
Stalls

Police Station

Wisma Darul
Iman

Stadium

Tourism
Malaysia

MAS

Wisma
Persekutuan

Masjid
Negeri

Wanisma
Craft

*SOUTH CHINA
SEA*

JLN SULTAN ZAINAL ABIDIN
JLN SULTAN ZAINAL ABIDIN
JLN NESAN EMPAT
JALAN PETANI
JLN KG. DALAM
JLN MASJID ABIDIN
JLN KOTA
JLN KAMPUNG CINA
JLN KG. TIONG 1
JLN KG. TIONG 1
JLN BANGGOL
JLN SYED HUSSIN
JLN TOK LAM
JLN SULTAN SULAIMAN
JLN TENGKU AMPUAN MARIAM
JLN ILADANG
JLN SULTAN ISMAIL
JLN SULTAN ISMAIL
JLN BATAS BHARU
JLN AYER JERNEH
JLN ENGKUSAR
JLN KUALA HILIRAN
JLN PEJABAT
JLN S. OMAR
JLN PUSARA
JLN S. MAHMUD
JLN PERSINGGAHAN

200 m

▼ *Terengganu State Museum, Sultan Mahmud Bridge, P. Duyong, Airport,* 3 *south*

Cendering, **i** & 3 *south*

RESTAURANTS
Ipoh
M.D. Curry House   6
Ocean/Tian Kee   3
Ping Anchorage Travellers Café 4
Restoran Terapung Puteri 5
Zie's Café   2

ACCOMMODATION
Awi's Yellow House   K
Grand Continental   C
Grand Paradise   E
KT Beach Resort   D
Ping Anchorage   G
Backpackers Lodge   I
Primula Beach Resort   B
Seaview   J
Seri Malaysia   H
Sri Hoover   A
Sri Tanjung   F
YT Midtown

important port, exporting gold and pepper to China during the eighteenth and nineteenth centuries, but by the late nineteenth century it had been eclipsed by the rise of Singapore and other new ports in the Melaka Straits.

Following the transfer of Terengganu from Siamese to British control in the early twentieth century, the state become the very last in the Peninsula to take a British Adviser, in 1919. Economic development remained slow, and Terengganu languished as a rural state with the atypical feature of having most of its settlements at river mouths, rather than inland on the lower reaches of rivers as is the usual pattern in Peninsular Malaysia. Over fifty years on, the discovery of **oil** off the Terengganu coast dramatically altered the outlook for the state; thanks to petroleum and the attendant petrochemicals industry, Terengganu's economy now rivals that of Penang, as is hinted at everywhere in road building and other infrastructure projects.

For the visitor, however, this activity is belied by a certain austerity about Terengganu that's most noticeable in Kuala Terengganu itself, which lacks the commercial buzz of Kuantan and can seem a little downbeat compared even to Kota Bharu. This is partly because oil revenues haven't much trickled down to the man or woman in the street, but also down to the fact that Terengganu remains at heart a conservative, strongly Islamic state. It was here that the only rebellion in the Peninsula led by religious scholars occurred, in the 1920s (see box on p.317), and the state's present-day Islamic credentials are proclaimed in religious messages on billboards, as well as by a huge hillside sign on the main western approach road into the capital, translating as "God protect Terengganu".

While it's no surprise, then, that Kuala Terengganu is far from being a shrine to urban consumption, at the time of writing the city was entering the throes of a giddy **revamp**, aimed at transforming it into a major centre for tourism on the east coast. A new bazaar is being built opposite the present Central Market; there's also talk of demolishing several old Chinese shophouses dating back to the nineteenth century (age-old by Malaysian architectural standards) to make way for new retail outlets. It remains to be seen if these schemes will add more to the city's character than they take away.

In the meantime, Kuala Terengganu's hotels, restaurants and shopping are nothing to write home about, and many visitors use the city simply as a transit point for Terengganu's best-known attractions – the pleasant **beaches** that line most of the coastline, and sparkling **islands**, from the Perhentians (see p.306) to Kapas (see p.330). Using the city as a base, you can also venture inland to **Tasik Kenyir** (see p.327) to experience something of the outdoor life for which the state's interior is renowned. However, there's enough in Kuala Terengganu itself to reward a day or two's sightseeing, in particular the lively **Central Market** and the adjacent old **Chinatown** quarter; the **State Museum**, which is one of the best cultural complexes in Malaysia; and **Pulau Duyong**, in the estuary of Sungai Terengganu, where the city's maritime heritage survives in the island's traditional **boat-building trade**.

Arrival, information and city transport

Kuala Terengganu's compact centre is built on a semicircular parcel of land that bulges north into the very mouth of the Terengganu River, which flows past the western half of the city, the eastern half being flanked by the South China Sea. If you arrive by road from any of the numerous coastal towns to the south, chances are you'll enter the city from the southeast, along Jalan Sultan Mahmud; but if you use the inland Route 14 from Kuantan, your approach to the city may be from the southwest. The latter is also true if you're arriving along Route

Moving on from Kuala Terengganu

Transport options from Kuala Terengganu are uncomplicated. The only **flights** from Kuala Terengganu airport are to KL, with either MAS (℡09/622 1415), whose office is at 13 Jalan Sultan Omar, or AirAsia, in the Menara Yayasan Islam Terengganu (the building where the Tourism Malaysia office is located; ℡09/631 3122). For flight information, call ℡09/667 0080.

Buses operate to major destinations on the Peninsula from the express bus station (aka Terminal Tanjung) and, in most cases, the local bus station as well, whose focus is towns within Terengganu as far afield as Kemaman/Chukai; tickets can be booked at the bus-company booths at either station. Long-distance **taxis** park up just to the south of the local bus station, and can be chartered to destinations across the Peninsula, including Kota Bharu (RM100) and Kuantan (RM140).

The **Shahbandar jetty** on the seafront is used by boats to Pulau Redang, serving the *Berjaya Beach* resort. You could, in principle, use these to head to Redang independently (RM80 return), but might well then have to charter another boat to reach the resort of your choice; in any case, package trips to Redang – which are the best way to visit – usually include boat transfers in the price.

3 from points north, in which case the penultimate bit of the approach involves heading across the impressive **Sultan Mahmud Bridge**, built over the river and Pulau Duyong.

The **airport** is 18km north of the city, from where a taxi into the centre costs around RM20. The **local bus station** on Jalan Masjid Abidin is a sizeable, modern affair, much more impressive than the assorted sheds and bays comprising the **long-distance bus station** at the northern end of town, on Jalan Sultan Zainal Abidin; in fact, many intercity buses call at the local station on their way into or out of the city.

As a result of building work for the new bazaar, the city's **tourist office** has moved all the way out to Padang Negara, on the coast road nearly 6km south of town (daily except Fri 9am–5pm; ℡09/617 3553, Ⓦwww.tourism .terengganu.gov.my), though it's possible that a new central tourist office will be created some time in 2007. An alternative source of information is **Tourism Malaysia**, whose office is south of the centre in Jalan S. Omar, on the fifth floor of the Yayasan Islam Terengganu building (Mon–Thurs & Sun 8am–4.30pm; ℡09/622 1433).

Kuala Terengganu is small enough to walk around, which is just as well as the city has fairly limited public transport. **Taxis** are found easily enough at the taxi station close to the local bus station, and around the Central Market and express bus station, but you'd have to be pretty lucky to flag one down. Hotels can usually summon up a taxi or a car with a driver, if requested. Trishaws ply along Jalan Sultan Zainal Abidin, and there are often a couple parked up near the Central Market.

Accommodation

Kuala Terengganu has plenty of **mid-range** places to stay, including a couple of hotels slightly out from the centre overlooking the South China Sea, though at the time of writing the merits of a seaside location were negated by an ongoing municipal project to widen and improve several kilometres of beach from the city centre southwards. With your own transport, and a taste for pricey, traditionally-styled accommodation, you could consider basing yourself out of town at the *Aryani* in Merang (see p.314) or at *Pura Tanjung Sabtu* (see p.323).

Unfortunately, the lower mid-range and **budget** places don't offer much by way of choice or quality; the cheap places around the long-distance bus station are largely downright seedy. At least there is a decent backpackers' **hostel**, run by the city's largest travel agency, and over on Pulau Duyong there's a gem of a rustic getaway in *Awi's Yellow House*.

Awi's Yellow House Pulau Duyong ℡09/624 5046. A delightful timber complex built on stilts over the water on the eastern shore. Accommodation is mostly in huts (not actually yellow) with walls of matted bamboo and thatched roofs, batik drapes instead of doors, and a solitary ceiling light. Rooms all have mosquito nets and their own shower and toilet – a square hole in the floor. There's also a spacious dorm, a kitchen (provisions can be bought from a nearby minimarket), and a shady garden brimming with ferns. The only two snags with staying here are that access by public transport can seem a little forbidding after dark, and that the place is occasionally booked by student groups, which can make the place a little more lively than you'd like. The best way to reach *Awi's* is to arrive by boat, then follow the track south from the jetty for around five minutes (you may need to ask directions); for more on transport to Duyong and the island itself, see p.324. Dorm beds RM6, huts ➊

Grand Continental Jalan Sultan Zainal Abidin ℡09/625 1888, ⓦwww.ghihotels.com. The biggest and best place in town, part of a national chain, in a good beachfront location. Predictably modern, with a swimming pool and a coffee house licensed to serve beer. Rate includes breakfast. ➐

Grand Paradise 20 & 20A Jalan Tok Lam ℡09/622 8888, ⓦwww.paradisegroup.com.my. Not quite as its name would have you believe, this representative of a budget hotel chain has a tacky waterfall feature in the tiny lobby, and poky a/c, en-suite rooms, the cheapest ones windowless. Still, it's more than okay for the price, and a good fallback, though note that they don't take bookings. ➌

KT Beach Resort 548-E Jalan Sultan Zainal Abidin ℡09/631 5555, Ⓕ 631 6666. A motel-like complex on a humdrum stretch of public beach. It's pleasant enough, with appealing Chinese-style wooden benches and vases in the reception area, and jumbo-sized TVs in the rooms. Good value. ➍

Ping Anchorage Backpackers Lodge 77A Jalan Sultan Sulaiman ℡09/626 2020, ⓦwww .pinganchorage.com.my. A range of basic rooms with fan, louvred internal windows and cement flooring, all sharing facilities, plus one dorm and one a/c en-suite room. There's also a rooftop garden to lounge in and use of a washing machine, and the management – the travel agency whose premises are below – also run a great café with satellite TV a couple of doors away. The only niggle

is that as this is a basically a sideline of the firm's burgeoning tour-booking business, it can occasionally feel as though you're left to your own devices while staff get on with their work. Still, a very good deal. Dorm beds RM9, rooms ➊

Primula Beach Resort Jalan Persinggahan ℡09/622 2100, ⓦwww.primulahotels.com. Beyond the slightly shabby concrete facade is a large, well-run hotel complete with swimming pool, a tennis court and three restaurants, including the poolside *Mumbai* – basically a glorified *mamak* joint. Rooms are spacious, with TV and a/c, and the bathrooms have proper bathtubs. A good choice, potentially a great one once the works along the beach come to an end. Rate includes breakfast. ➏

Seaview 18a Jalan Masjid Abidin ℡09/622 1911, Ⓕ622 3048. With helpful staff, this place has comfortable a/c rooms, though they're a bit musty and sparsely furnished for the asking price – and the sea views are not going to be etched into memory. ➍

Seri Malaysia Jalan Hiliran, on the riverside ℡09/623 6454, ⓦwww.serimalaysia.com.my. Unexciting but sound chain hotel with views of Pulau Duyong from west-facing rooms, though what appear to be balconies are in fact just parapets masking the a/c units. Rate includes breakfast. ➏

Sri Hoover 49 Jalan Sultan Ismail ℡09/623 3833, Ⓕ622 5975. It's hard to make a more unfavourable first impression – the concrete exterior is ghastly, and the corridors are bare but for sickly green astroturf-like carpeting. That said, the rooms are adequate for the price, with TV, a/c and bathroom, though very plain; there's also free parking, but no breakfast. ➍

Sri Tanjung Jalan Sultan Zainal Abidin ℡09/626 2636. Pretty much the only cheap place close to the bus station that's worth considering. It's predictably spartan, though rooms do have a/c, and the pricier ones have TV. Toilets and showers are located at the end of each corridor. ➋

YT Midtown 30 Jalan Tok Lam ℡09/622 3088, Ⓔ ythotel@streamyx.com. In a city not noted for bustling efficiency, this slick multi-storey hotel, with some 140 rooms, actually hits the right note. All rooms have functional modern fittings and decor, plus TV and bathroom, and there's a decent restaurant. The very central location is an added bonus, as is the buffet breakfast included in the rate. ➎

The City

The main artery through the commercial sector is Jalan Sultan Ismail, where you'll find the banks and government offices, while the **old town**, including **Chinatown**, is the sector west of Jalan Masjid Abidin. Most places of interest in the centre can be covered easily on foot. The outskirts hold various **craft workshops** and the excellent **Terengganu State Museum**, while only 500m west across Sungai Terengganu from the centre are the boatyards of **Pulau Duyong**.

The old town

Set back from the sea in manicured gardens on Jalan Sultan Zainal Abidin, the neat and precise **Istana Maziah** (closed to the public) is one of Kuala Terengganu's few historic monuments. Now used only for official royal functions, it's reminiscent of a French chateau, with a steeply inclined red-tile roof and tall, shuttered windows.

Further west along the pedestrianized promenade, **Bukit Puteri** (literally "Princess Hill"; daily except Fri 9am–5pm; RM1), rises high above the town. Relics of its time as a stronghold during the early nineteenth century – when the sultans Mohammed and Umar were fighting each other for the Terengganu throne – include a fort, supposedly built using honey to bind the bricks, and several cannons imported from Spain and Portugal. The lighthouse at the top is still in use. Turn to your left after you've descended the steps from Bukit Puteri and you'll come across Terengganu's **Central Market** (aka Pasar Payang; daily 6am–6pm), a modern multi-storey building backing onto the river, and airier and tidier than its better-known counterpart in Kota Bharu. The ground floor is taken up by a thriving wet market, plus plenty of stalls selling a marvellous range of Malay confections in just about every conceivable hue. The upper floors comprise a maze of food stalls and outlets where you can seek out batik, *songkets* and brassware.

Heading south from the market takes you along Jalan Kampung Cina (aka Jalan Bandar) which, true to its name, gives access to **Chinatown**, established as long ago as the eighteenth century, when the trading links between

△ Fishing boats, Kuala Terengganu

Terengganu and China drew Chinese to settle here. Efforts are being made to revitalize the area, as is evident from a sprinkling of refurbished shophouses, and there are some excellent shops here, such as Teratai at no. 151 (daily except Fri 10am–5.30pm), selling Terengganu batik as well arts and crafts from around Southeast Asia.

Arts and crafts workshops

Kuala Terengganu is famed for its high-quality **arts and crafts**, and it's a great place to watch traditional production methods and pick up some souvenirs. In particular, local artisans have long been known for their **brassware**, working in an alloy called "white brass", unique to the state. Formerly the preserve of the sultans, white brass – a brass containing at least forty percent zinc, with added nickel to make the colour less yellow – is now used to make decorative articles such as candlesticks and large gourd-shaped vases. At **Wanisma Craft** (daily: showroom 9am–6.30pm, workshop until 4pm), close to the junction of Jalan Sultan Zainal Abidin and Jalan Ladang in the east of the centre, you can observe the traditional "lost wax" technique, whereby a wax maquette is covered with clay, then fired in a kiln to melt the wax and leave behind a mould into which to pour molten brass. When the metal hardens, the clay is chipped off and the metal surface is polished and decorated.

The weaving of *mengkuang* (pandanus) is also practised in Terengganu: using the long, slender leaves, women fashion delicate but functional items like bags, floor mats and fans. Ky Enterprises, about 3km due south of the centre on Jalan Panji Alam, is a good place to watch the process; take minibus #12, #13c, #15 or #26 there from the local bus station.

There are several other craft workshops in neighbouring Pasir Panjang, about 500m west of Jalan Panji Alam. Perhaps the most famous is that belonging to Abu Bakar bin Mohammed Amin, a **kris** maker on Lorong Saga (call to make an appointment; ☏09/622 7968). Here you can watch the two-edged dagger and its wooden sheath (for more on the *kris*, see box on p.324) being decorated with fine artwork, a process which, together with the forging, can take several weeks to complete. To get to the workshops, take minibus #12 from the local bus station and get off at the sign marked "Sekolah Kebangsaan Psr. Panjang".

Close to the coast 7km south of the city, one of Malaysia's largest **batik** producers, Noor Arfa, stays close to its Kuala Terengganu roots by maintaining a factory and showroom (daily except Fri 9am–5pm; Ⓦwww.noor-arfa.com .my) where you can watch batik artists at work, and choose from an impressive display of garments and fabrics, including *songkets* (from RM120) and psychedelically rainbowy shirts (from RM80). The factory is in the Cendering Industrial Area, just north of the coastal village of **Cendering**; minibus #13 goes directly there from the local bus station. If you're driving out there along the coast road, it's worth pausing briefly en route at the unmistakable **Tengku Tengah Zaharah Mosque**, built on piles just above the surface of an artificial lake, hence its local epithet, the "Floating Mosque".

Finally, if you've a particular interest in **songkets**, you can watch these fabrics being woven at *Pura Tanjung Sabtu*, a complex of classic Malay wooden houses along Sungai Nerus, west of Kuala Terengganu (☏09/615 3655, Ⓦwww .puratanjungsabtu.com). A former country estate of the sultan's, the site is managed by Tengku Ismail, himself a member of the royal family and a *songket* designer. **Day visits** (call to arrange a few days in advance; RM20, or RM35 with tea and *kuih*) feature an architectural tour in addition to the weaving demonstration. Getting here is half the fun, as you can take advantage of the

The kris

The **kris** occupies a treasured position in Malay culture, a symbol of manhood and honour believed to harbour protective spirits. Traditionally, all young men crossing the barrier of puberty receive one, which remains with them for the rest of their lives, tucked into the folds of a sarong; for an enemy to relieve someone of a *kris* is tantamount to stripping him of his virility.

The weapon itself is intended to deliver a horizontal thrust rather than the more usual downward stab. When a sultan executed a treacherous subject, he did so by sliding a long *kris* through his windpipe, just above the collar bone, thereby inflicting a swift – though bloody – death. The distinguishing feature of the dagger is the hilt, shaped like the butt of a gun to facilitate a sure grip. The hilt can be used to inflict a damaging blow to the head in combat, especially if there isn't time to unsheath the weapon.

The daggers can be highly decorative: the iron blade is often embellished with fingerprint patterns or the body of a snake, while the hilt can be made from ivory, wood or metal; the designs are usually based on the theme of a bird's head.

old-fashioned boat (*bot penambang*), usually packed with women returning to their kampungs with their weekly food shop, that leaves for Jeram from the area by the *Restoran Terapung* (daily at 10.30am; RM1.50; 1hr 15min). The boat passes innumerable riverside hamlets en route, including Tanjung Sabtu itself, where it's a two-minute walk up from the river to the estate (the gate isn't the first one you come to but the next one along the road, on the left). Buses run by S P Bumi head back to Kuala Terengganu until around 4.30pm. Pricey accommodation is available on the estate; contact Tengku Ismail for details of rates and packages.

Pulau Duyong

Pulau Duyong ("Mermaid Island") is the largest of the islets dotting the Terengganu estuary. For now the island remains tranquil, though it hasn't escaped unscathed from change: the boss of Ferrari is building a villa here, and the northern section of Duyong was levelled in double-quick time to build a prestige yacht club for the international **Monsoon Cup** competition (Ⓦwww .monsooncup.com.my), first staged here during the northeast monsoon of 2005 and intended to be an annual event. The rest of the island, however, still features a delightful kampung of brightly painted houses nestling among stands of mature, impossibly tall coconut palms, a great place for a hour's stroll. The island is also the proud home of a venerable **boat-building** tradition, which you can observe from the sidelines at any of the boatyards (ask any villager for directions; if you've a special interest in the industry but don't speak Malay, you can arrange a visit with an interpreter through the tourist office in Kuala Terengganu or a travel agent such as Ping Anchorage, p.327).

The island is a five-minute ferry ride (RM1; last boats around 8pm) from the jetty near the central market. Buses that use the Sultan Mahmud Bridge (#17 and #20) can drop you on the island.

The Terengganu State Museum

Arriving at the **Terengganu State Museum** (daily except Fri 9am–5pm; RM5, or RM2 for Malaysians; ☏09/622 1444 for information on special exhibitions), 5km west of the town centre, you might think you've chanced upon an *Alice in Wonderland* realm that's somehow appeared by the Sungai Terengganu,

Boat-building on Pulau Duyong

The shipwrights of Pulau Duyong work mostly from memory rather than set plans. For hulls, their preferred material is **cengal**, a wood whose toughness and imperviousness to termite attack make it prized not only for boats but also kampung houses. The hull planking is fastened with strong hardwood pegs, and then a special sealant – derived from swampland trees, and resistant to rot – is applied. Unusually, the frame is fitted afterwards, giving the whole structure strength and flexibility. As construction takes place in **dry docks**, the finished boats have to manoeuvre on rollers into the water, an effort that often requires local villagers to pitch in en masse.

Historically, the boatyards produced a variety of **schooners**, from humble fishing craft to the hulking *perahu besar*, a class of vessels which could be up to 30m in length. These days however, motorized, modern alternatives to the old-fashioned wooden boats, the increasing cost of timber, plus the lure of other careers in Malaysia's modernizing economy, have all contributed to a steep decline in boat-building on the island. Today fewer than five boatyards are still engaged in the business, compared to more than three dozen twenty years ago.

With the fall in local demand for working boats of the traditional kind, any salvation for Duyong's boat-building looks to lie in clients from around the world, who have been placing orders for all manner of bespoke craft. One of the most impressive commissions at the time of writing is for the **Naga Pelangi II**, a pleasure craft taking the form of a 21-metre-long *perahu besar*, in the best tradition of the old Malay sailboats. The German instigator of the project has a commitment to the survival of boat-building here that transcends the *Naga Pelangi II* itself, and has actually moved to Duyong for the three years that the work is expected to last. See ⓦ www.naga-pelangi.de for the latest on the project, how to **charter** the vessel (available upon completion in late 2006) and lots of interesting background on the boat-building process.

for confronting you are a series of proud buildings modelled on the archetypal Terengganu village house, but absolutely gargantuan in scale. Somehow the dislocation in size is fitting though, for at its best the museum far outstrips most of its provincial counterparts in the quality and extent of its exhibits.

The main building, **Bangunan Utama**, houses displays of exquisite fabrics at its lowest level, while the second floor has displays on various crafts and the third details the history of Terengganu. In the attached building to the left is the **Petronas Oil Gallery**, and behind this the **Islamic Gallery**, with fine examples of Koranic calligraphy, sometimes executed on local artefacts – copper jars, trays and so forth. Beside the river are two examples of the **sailing boats** for which Kuala Terengganu is famed – unique blends, which you can climb into, of European ships and Chinese junks. A small **Maritime Museum** is close by, as is an excellent outdoor gallery of smaller, beautifully decorated fishing boats.

The landscaped gardens feature imposing modern interpretations of the triple-roofed houses common to the area. Also within the grounds are ancient timber palaces which have been rebuilt, the supreme example being the **Istana Tengku Long**, originally built in 1888 entirely without nails (to Malays, these signify death, because of their use in coffins). Like the majority of traditional east-coast houses, the hardwood rectangular building has a high, pointed roof and a pair of slightly curved wooden gables at either end. Each gable is fitted with twenty gilded screens, intricately carved with verses from the Koran and designed to not only admit air but also provide protection from driving rain.

The museum is easily reached by a twenty-minute journey on minibus #19. En route to or from the museum, you could stop over in the Losong district of town if you've a particular interest in matters culinary, for this is the nerve centre for the production of one of the city's trademark comestibles, *keropok lekor* (see below).

Eating and drinking

Like Kelantan, Terengganu has its own signature rice dish, **nasi dagang** (actually not uncommon in Kelantan), which, like Kelantan's *nasi kerabu*, is usually served with a fish curry. There the resemblance ends, for while *nasi kerabu* is essentially ordinary rice tinted unusual colours with flower petals, *nasi dagang* is a slightly sticky rice, steamed with a little coconut milk and chopped shallots, and often eaten for breakfast. Another delicacy that locals rave about is **keropok lekor**, basically a dumpling made with fish and sago flour, and unappetizingly resembling giant brown slugs when first prepared, but very tasty once sliced and boiled or fried, and served with a chilli dip. There's a cottage industry producing the stuff in the Losong area, southwest of the centre, where you can drop by at any of the factories – little more than exaggerated kitchens – to watch workers moulding and kneading the dough by hand, then boiling the dumplings in humongous woks.

Both *keropok lekor* and *nasi dagang* are easy enough to find around town, but as is often the case with Malay food, discovering the best offerings is much more about serendipity at nondescript stalls than dining at the few proper restaurants. One of the bigger clusters of Malay stalls in town can be found just south of the junction of Jalan Sultan Ismail and Jalan Tok Lam, and the stalls at the central market are also worth trying. Chinatown is the obvious focus for **Chinese fare**, with a bunch of busy food stalls along Jalan Kampung Tiong 1 (where there's also a little row of Malay stalls) and several excellent restaurants, though the two seaside places close to the *KT Beach Resort* are also worthwhile.

It can be worth taking advantage of the **buffet breakfasts** at the *YT Midtown* hotel, good value (RM11) though unremarkable – except on Friday mornings, when they roll out delicious Malay specialities such as *sayur lodeh* made with *tempeh* (slightly nutty, fermented bean curd), or *sambal ikan bilis*, sometimes even with *ketupat* (glutinous rice wrapped in palm leaves) as a foil to eat with them.

It's no surprise that Kuala Terengganu is largely dry; your best bets for **alcohol** are the Chinese restaurants and stalls, the coffee house at the *Grand Continental* hotel, which serves beer, or the travellers' café run by Ping Anchorage.

Ipoh Jalan Kampung Cina. One of several busy Cantonese *kedai kopis* on Chinatown's main street, majoring on seafood, including classics like fish-head curry and steamed garoupa, plus more unusual items like butter crabs and even frogs' legs. Daily 3–11.30pm.

M.D. Curry House Jalan Kampung Dalam. Tiny, humble South Indian *kedai kopi* run by a friendly Tamil guy from Penang. There's a terrific range of curries and rotis, including banana-leaf meals, biryanis and a few non-Indian standbys to keep the multicultural clientele happy, such as Chinese-style chicken in soy sauce and good *acar* (pickles) for the Malays.

Ocean Just along from the *KT Beach Resort*, Jalan Sultan Zainal Abidin. Well-regarded Chinese restaurant specializing in seafood, with steamboats another popular choice. The adjacent *Tian Kee*

(eves only) is just as good and pork-free. Daily noon–2.30pm & 5.30–11.30pm.

Ping Anchorage Travellers Café Jalan Sultan Sulaiman. Backpackers' mecca serving Western café food with some local dishes thrown in. There's also satellite TV with live football matches and good films, and beer. Daily 7am–11pm.

Restoran Terapung Puteri Jalan Sultan Zainal Abidin. Not actually floating as its name translates, but built on stanchions at the waterfront, this airy, relaxed affair is in essence a very smartly turned-out *kedai kopi*, popular with Malay families on an evening out. While the food's decent if not spectacular, at least there are plenty of Malay selections, from *ayam bakar* (grilled chicken) to tangy mango *kerabu* – unripe mango shreds laced with dried shrimp and some fiery green chilli – and they do a great *kobis goreng kampung*, stir-fried cabbage with turmeric and plenty of rich coconut milk. Also worth trying is the Pattani-style *nasi goreng*, in which the rice is parcelled up inside a square omelette.

Zie's Café On the waterfront promenade, close to the Shahbandar jetty. A workaday, open-air place that's as close as Kuala Terengganu gets to a trendy hangout for young people. There's the usual range of Western snacks, though predictably it's the *nasi lemak* that most locals plump for. They also do good slushy milk shakes – the one based on soursop is a great way to get acquainted with one of the odder local fruits. Less successful is their take on *ais krim goreng*, the fried ice-cream dessert that's a mainstay of the Batu Burok beach south of town; here it's frighteningly like a chicken Kiev with ice cream where the butter should be. Daily 5.30pm till late.

Listings

Banks and exchange All the major banks have offices on Jalan Sultan Ismail, west of the junction with Jalan Tok Lam; the Maybank here is your best for changing money.

Car rental Two local agencies have counters at the airport: Elite City (℡013/960 4145) and SCP (℡013/921 2801).

Hospitals and clinics The state hospital is on Jalan Sultan Mahmud (℡09/623 3355 or 621 2121), 1km southeast of the centre. There are plenty of privately run walk in clinics and the odd dentist's surgery along Jalan Tok Lam, some staying open well into the evening.

Internet access There are a few Internet shops round town, including Golden Wood on Jalan Tok Lam, and Neo.Net on Jalan Kampung Tiong 1 in Chinatown.

Left luggage Available at the express bus station on Jalan Sultan Zainal Abidin and at the local bus station on Jalan Masjid Abidin (both RM1 a day).

Pharmacy There's a branch of Watson's on Jalan Sultan Ismail.

Police The main police station is on Jalan Sultan Ismail (℡09/624 6222).

Post office The GPO on Jalan Sultan Zainal Abidin has poste restante.

Shopping As in Kota Bharu, the modern shopping development has been very late in coming to Kuala Terengganu, but the city's first mall should be open on Jalan Tok Lam, just east of the local bus station, by the time you read this. Otherwise, try the small Astaka shopping complex next to the long-distance bus station, or the Store, a general emporium and supermarket in Chinatown. The western section of Jalan Sultan Ismail and the southern part of Jalan Kampung Cina both feature a variety of shops large and small; camera shops cluster on Jalan Syed Hussin, just north of the local bus station. For crafts, try the outlets at the Central Market. The best bookshop is Pustaka Seri Intan, on the south side of Jalan Sultan Ismail (opposite the Maybank); it only has a limited range of English novels, but does sell an excellent selection of Western magazines.

Travel agents Ping Anchorage Travel and Tours, 77A Jalan Sultan Sulaiman (℡09/626 2020, ⊛www.pinganchorage.com.my), is one of the country's most successful travel agents; efficient and well organized, they offer numerous packages and plenty of information on sights throughout the east coast and the interior. The tourist office has information on visiting most places in the vicinity, and can also recommend travel agencies.

Visa extensions The Immigration Department is in Wisma Persekutuan on Jalan Sultan Ismail (Mon–Wed & Sat 8am–4.15pm, Thurs 8.30am–1pm; ℡09/622 1424).

Tasik Kenyir and Sekayu Waterfall

More than three hundred square kilometres in size, with 340 islands within it, **Tasik Kenyir** was created in 1985, when the Kenyir hydroelectric dam across Sungai Terengganu was completed. The whole area was once lush jungle (partially submerged trees still jut out of the clear waters), and while you're here you may find it impossible to blot out the thought that the lake somehow isn't quite meant to exist. Though the site of a large hydroelectric dam may not seem a promising place for a back-to-nature experience, the lake offers scope for **fishing** and waterborne excursions – there are many **waterfalls** on the lake periphery, with cool plunge pools for swimming, and in the hills to the south of the lake you can visit the limestone **Bewah and**

Taat caves. The lake is also Terengganu's gateway to **Taman Negara**, thanks to the park entrance at Tanjung Mentong in the south of the lake (covered on p.247). Unfortunately, the substantial cost of boat charters and the fact that the attractions are scattered around the lake makes extensive exploring uneconomical unless you're in a group of four or more, though this situation is partly alleviated by the possibility of **houseboat stays**, some of which have cruises to popular sites included in the price.

Practicalities

One of the Terengganu state government's websites (ⓦwww.ketengah.gov .my/kenyir) has useful general **information** on visiting the lake, and there's a **tourist office** at Pangkalan Gawi (daily 8am–4pm; ⓣ09/626 7788), the jetty at the northeast of the lake, which serves as the focal point for tourism.

Chartering a **taxi** to the jetty from Kuala Terengganu costs around RM70. There are no **buses** to the lake from here, but ironically there is a bus service all the way from KL, the Tasik Kenyir Express (ⓣ03/4044 4276; RM35), which leaves from Putra bus station at 9am and 9pm daily, taking eight hours to get to Pangkalan Gawi (runs back to KL leave at 8am and 8pm). You can drive to the lake using **Route 3** west of Kuala Terengganu (accessible from Jertih, not far southwest of Kota Bharu, or from Kuala Terengganu via the Sultan Mahmud Bridge), following signs for the lake; alternatively, get onto **Route 14** (accessible by heading southwest out of Kuala Terengganu, or north from Kuantan and the East Coast Highway from KL) and turn off 30km from Kuala Terengganu at Ajil, heading west along Route 106 for **Kuala Berang**, then northwest, all the while following intermittent signage for the lake. Eventually it will also be possible to reach the jetty from **Route 8** through the interior, as a new lake road starting a little way east of Gua Musang is in the works.

The classiest **accommodation** on the lake is the *Kenyir Lakeview Resort* (ⓣ09/666 8888 or 03/2052 7766, ⓦwww.lakekenyir.com; ⑨), an elegant collection of buildings with Terengganu-style pitched roofs, steep at the top and gently sloping below. Besides a swimming pool and a tennis court, it offers the usual range of lake trips, including an outing to the dam itself. Promotions can knock a third off the steep rack rate, and they also offer various full-board packages, which can be good value.

Much more appealing, however, is the prospect of staying one of the lake's **houseboats** and **floating lodges**, all of which offer simple rooms with shared facilities. Packages for a two-day, one-night stay cost RM180–280 per person depending on the grade of accommodation provided, and include a lake cruise plus transfers from Kuala Terengganu; contact Ping Anchorage (ⓦwww .pinganchorage.com.my) for more details and bookings. They also offer a day-trip to the lake from Kuala Terengganu (from RM100 per person), starting with a look at the dam, followed by a cruise to the Lasir Waterfall.

Sekayu Waterfall

If you can't face the hassle or expense of visiting Tasik Kenyir, then a trip to **Sekayu Waterfall**, part of a forest park complex known as **Hutan Lipur Sekayu** (daily 9am–6pm; free) is a reasonable alternative. It's a busy weekend picnic spot, thanks to the environment here being somewhat tamed, with rustic shelters, a bird park, mini-zoo and a fruit farm, along with opportunities for some pleasant hikes.

Unfortunately, lack of public **transport** makes it awkward to visit the falls from Kuala Terengganu. You can take a local bus to Kuala Berang (1hr), then a taxi for the fifteen-minute drive to the park, but don't forget to arrange a pick-up time with your driver as there's no taxi stand at the park, and note that the last bus back to Kuala Terengganu leaves around 4pm. Ping Anchorage can arrange a day-trip here from Kuala Terengganu, costing RM70 per person for a group of four.

Marang and Pulau Kapas

The coastal village of **MARANG**, 17km south of Kuala Terengganu (and not to be confused with Merang, the transit point for Pulau Redang, north of Kuala Terengganu), was once nicknamed "cowboy town" because of its dusty one-horse feel, with ramshackle wooden shops and houses. This was the Marang that drew a steady trickle of foreign visitors, attracted by the promise of "old Malaysia"; these days, however, the place has had a complete facelift – many residents have been relocated to a new settlement just inland, while at the waterfront a new jetty complex and landscaped parks have been built. While Marang now offers slim pickings, it remains a target for tourists as it's the departure point for the delightful **Pulau Kapas**, just 6km offshore. Regular buses mean you're unlikely to get stuck in Marang en route to or from the island, but there's decent mainland accommodation to choose from should the need arise, and to be fair Marang isn't a bad place to while away half a day or so, with a relaxed air and a good beach 2km to the south at **Rhu Muda**.

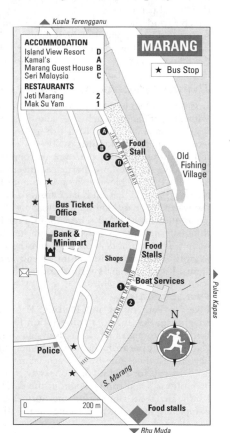

▲ Kuala Terengganu

MARANG
★ Bus Stop

ACCOMMODATION
Island View Resort   D
Kamal's   A
Marang Guest House   B
Seri Malaysia   C
RESTAURANTS
Jeti Marang   2
Mak Su Yam   1

Food Stall
Old Fishing Village
JALAN BATU MERAH
Bus Ticket Office
Market
Bank & Minimart
Shops
Food Stalls
Boat Services
JALAN BANTAI MATANG
N
Police
S. Marang
0   200 m
Food stalls
▶ Pulau Kapas
▼ Rhu Muda

Practicalities

There are local **buses** at least hourly between Kuala Terengganu and Marang during the daytime, or you could charter a **taxi** for the journey (around RM30). It's also possible to reach Marang on several daily long-distance Kuantan–Kuala Terengganu buses that travel the coast road, via Cherating, Dungun and Rantau Abang. To move on from Marang, you can either flag down local buses (note that southbound services go no further than Dungun; see p.333) or arrange pick-up by an express bus; tickets for express services can be bought at the **bus ticket office** close to the main road (closed Fri).

There is a bank with an **ATM** on the main road close to the bus stops (though you may find that the machine doesn't take foreign cards), and a post office towards the southern end of the village. Most **accommodation** in Marang is on or around the hillock north of the jetty area, a ten-minute walk from the jetty or the main road. There's not much to choose between *Kamal's* (☎09/618 2181; ❷) and the *Marang Guesthouse* (☎09/618 1976; ❷), both of which have a range of simple, well-kept rooms with fan and attached bathroom, and the option of air-conditioning. The cheaper rooms at *Kamal's* are marginally better than those at the *Marang*, though the latter also has family rooms for RM100, a simple restaurant and good views. Also worth considering is the *Island View Resort* (☎09/618 1707; RM25), a mishmash of chalets, some with air-conditioning, sleeping up to four. The only mid-range place to stay is the *Seri Malaysia* (☎09/618 2889, ⓦwww.serimalaysia.com.my; ❻), with a swimming pool and restaurant, though it's overpriced unless discounts happen to be available. On the beach at Rhu Muda (at the 20km marker out of Kuala Terengganu), a great, homely choice is the *Angullia Beach House Resort* (☎09/618 1322, ⓦwww.geocities.com/angullia_resort; ❹), with variously priced en-suite chalets, some with air-conditioning, plus a restaurant; they also organize fun trips up the Marang River (RM35 per person), on which you get to see monkeys and lizards, and glimpse village activities like the making of *atap* thatch and palm sugar.

As for **food**, there's a large, reasonable seafood restaurant, the *Jeti Marang* (daily 4.30pm till late), opposite which there's *Mak Su Yam*, a simple place with inexpensive rice and noodle dishes. Up the road, there are plenty of **food stalls** at the market, where on Sundays you'll also find a good **pasar malam**.

Pulau Kapas and Pulau Gemia

Less than half an hour from Marang by speedboat is diminutive **Pulau Kapas**, with arcs of sandy beach the colour of pale brown sugar, and aquamarine waters that visibly teem with fish as close to the shore as at the island's sole jetty. Naturally, **snorkelling** is a draw, particularly round rocky **Pulau Gemia**, just northwest of Kapas; there are also opportunities for **diving**, with a Japanese wreck dive suitable for experienced divers half an hour away by boat. Back on dry land, it's possible to take a 45-minute **hike** to the remote eastern side of Kapas via a track that leads back from the jetty, with sheer cliffs plummeting to the water's edge making for a dramatic walk. All these combine to make Kapas a very pleasant island to retreat to for a spell; the only time of the season when things are not quite so idyllic is from June to August, when the island is at its busiest. The one notable highlight in the island's slim social calendar happens in April, when your visit might be enlivened – or slightly disrupted – by the annual Kapas–Marang **swimathon**.

Practicalities

Like the Perhentians and Redang, Kapas is one of Terengganu's designated **marine parks**, and so a conservation fee of RM5 applies for a stay of up to three days, though there isn't always an official at Marang to levy the fee. The Kapas **boat operators**, including the helpful Suria Link (☎ & ⓕ09/618 3754), have their offices side-by-side at Marang's jetty, and all offer the same deal of a return trip for RM30, or a one-way trip for RM15. Boats usually run from 9am onwards and run throughout the day, leaving when full, though note that hardly any boats run during the northeast monsoon, when the island almost completely shuts down. Arriving on the island, the boats don't necessarily use its sole jetty, as they may be heading for a particular resort or stretch of beach elsewhere; in this event the boats anchor in the shallows up to 5m from the beach, to which you'll have to wade – given the small size of the island though, you don't need to be fussy as to which boat you use, unless you've got tons of luggage. You could in principle tackle the island as a **day-trip**, catching one of the early boats out and returning late in the afternoon (check with the boat operator as to where you should wait for the boat back), but this does entail having to make the most of the potentially blistering heat of midday.

Most places to stay on Kapas can arrange **snorkelling** – either just rental of gear (from RM10), or with a boat trip out to a choice site (from RM18). There's one **dive shop** on the island, namely Aqua-Sport (☎019/983 5879, ✉azamaqua@time.net.my), offering PADI Open Water and Discover Scuba courses (RM950 and RM180

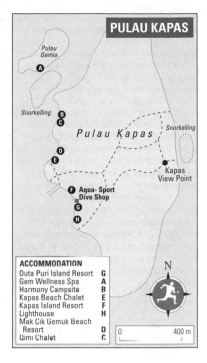

respectively), as well as regular dives (RM90 for one, with slightly cheaper rates for multiple dives). They also have **kayaks** available for an invigorating but none too strenuous paddle around the coves (RM15/hr), as does the *Harmony* campsite (RM7/hr).

Accommodation and eating

For such a tiny island, Kapas has a surprising range of **accommodation** options, including a friendly **campsite**, *Harmony* (☎ & ☎09/618 6179; RM8 per person per night, RM15 for tent rental), with washing and cooking facilities. All the places to stay are on the western shore, facing the mainland. As at the Perhentians, those places which have cellular phones have a nasty habit of changing their number from one season to the next; Suria Link can usually provide the latest details. On **Pulau Gemia**, there's the *Gem Wellness Spa and Island Resort* (☎09/618 3310 or 03/7727 0252), a well-designed place with all the chalets built on stilts at the water's edge. They offer a variety of snorkelling packages, from day-trips, including lunch and boat transfers, for RM100 per person, to three-day, two-night deals for RM600 per person, including meals and transfers.

All the Kapas resorts have their own **restaurants**, of varying degrees of sophistication. There's also an amicable Malay-run restaurant close to the jetty, with a range of fruit juices and the usual rice and noodle concoctions.

Duta Puri Island Resort ☎09/624 6090 or 012/684 8760. A large complex with a range of vaguely Balinese-style en-suite rooms and chalets, most with a/c. Full-board snorkelling packages start at around RM275 for two nights' stay, including boat transfers. **⑤**

Kapas Beach Chalet ☎017/936 0750 or 019/968 2331. Malay/Dutch-run establishment with nine decent A-frame chalets, plus more basic rooms in a long bungalow. Popular – actually a little too busy during peak periods. The food can be a little overpriced. Rooms RM25, chalets ❸

Kapas Island Resort ☎09/631 6468, ✆www .kapas-island-resort.com. Very neat Malay-style bungalows, all en suite, plus a couple of single-sex dorms. All have a/c, and the place also boasts its own swimming pool. Western and Malay food is served in an airy pavilion restaurant, diving and snorkelling can be arranged, and kayaks and fishing gear are available to rent. Rate includes breakfast; promotions can shave a fifth off regular prices. Dorm beds RM23, bungalows ❺

Lighthouse ☎012/972 1470. In an attractive, relatively secluded spot at the far southern end of the bay, this is an attractive elevated longhouse of dark timber, with rooms and dorm beds, all sharing facilities. Not the most sophisticated place, but the chilled-out atmosphere compensates. Dorm beds RM15, rooms ❷

Mak Cik Gemuk Beach Resort ☎09/624 5120. A cluster of en-suite chalets painted a vibrant orange, with the option of a/c in some. There are also much cheaper rooms in a long, low block, with tolerable toilets and showers in a separate building. Institutional, but still popular with locals in particular. Rooms RM25, chalets ❸

🏃 Qimi Chalet ☎019/648 1714, ✉qimichalet@yahoo.com. Just three well-kept, characterful chalets, one of bamboo, the second made from *nibung* palm logs, the third of *tembusu* wood. All feature a double bed, fan, mosquito nets, shower and toilet, and louvred windows with bamboo blinds. The place is brilliantly kept by the friendly Rosmawati, who does fantastic food too – with a couple of hours' notice, she can whip up a *tom-yam* steamboat or a beach barbecue. During the northeast monsoon, you can have the island virtually to yourself if you notify her in advance of your plans; she'll keep the chalets open and arrange a boat to the island. ❸

Southern Terengganu

The stretch of Terengganu between Marang and the Pahang border offers fairly slim pickings for travellers. Pleasant **beaches** aplenty are the main draw, any of which makes for a great way to break a drive along the coast road, though facilities at most amount to a mere straggle of food stalls. One stretch of beach with accommodation lies some 40km south of Marang at the village of **Rantau Abang**, where a Turtle Information Centre serves as a somewhat forlorn reminder of the importance of Malaysia's east coast as a nesting site for many of the world's severely threatened marine turtles. The only other point of note is the extremely upmarket resort at Tanjung Jara.

Rantau Abang

No more than a handful of guesthouses strung out along a couple of kilometres of dusty road, **RANTAU ABANG** used to reap a rich reward from its status as one of a handful of places in the world where the giant **leatherback turtle** comes to lay its eggs. The village retains a small **Turtle Information Centre** (hours variable but open at least Mon–Thurs & Sun 8am–4pm; free), with informative displays on turtle biology and conservation, but with the collapse in leatherback turtle populations in the Pacific Ocean at least, so Rantau Abang has drifted back into relative obscurity. It's still a pleasant way station though, offering a beach with fine sand and, being on a straight stretch of coast, superb 180-degree views of blue-green sea. If you want to spot turtles, your best bets are elsewhere along the east coast; see the box on pp.336–337 for more on marine turtles and their conservation.

Practicalities

Local **buses** from Kuala Terengganu and Marang run at least hourly during daylight hours to Rantau Abang. Coming by local bus from the south, you have to change at Dungun, 13km away (see below), from where you can easily get another local bus for the remainder of the journey. Buses drop you on the main road, at the Petronas petrol station, just a short walk from all the accommodation and the Turtle Information Centre.

All the **accommodation** is close to the beach. Prices rise a little when the turtles might theoretically arrive to nest (May–Sept), though they're not high to begin with; the price codes in this section refer to the high-season rate. Close to the information centre are two well-kept places: the friendly, long-established *Awang's* (℡09/844 3500, ℮awangs_resort@hotmail.com; ❷), with a variety of simple en-suite rooms, some overpriced air-conditioned chalets and a pair of amazing caged mynas chirruping incessantly in Malay; and the awkwardly named *Turtles De' Village Inn* (℡09/845 6001, ℱ848 3210; ❸), where all the rooms are spacious affairs with two beds, air-conditioning, a bathroom and a small veranda. Around a kilometre south of the information centre, *Dahimah's Guesthouse* (℡09/845 2843, ℮dahimahs@hotmail.com; ❷) is slightly back from the beach and has a wide range of accommodation, from simple doubles with fan to family rooms with TV, air-conditioning and a proper bath (RM120).

Both *Awang's* and *Dahimah's* have simple **restaurants**, but by far the best eating in the area is at the venerable *C.B. Wee*, close to the *Tanjong Jara Resort*; either guesthouse should be able to arrange a taxi there if requested.

Tanjung Jara

The contrast between the unprepossessing guesthouses of Rantau Abang and the super-luxurious **Tanjong Jara Resort** (℡09/845 1100 or 03/2145 9000, ℹwww.tanjongjararesort.com; ❾) could not be greater. Four kilometres south of Rantau Abang and north of Dungun, this is one of the priciest resorts on the east coast, a Malay-themed spa complex of timber pavilions and houses fit for a sultan, where doubles start at RM800 a night. The expected range of traditional treatments are on offer, there's a diving and watersports centre on site (the reefs of the **Pulau Tenggul** marine park are only a short boat ride offshore), and when your system has been suitably reinvigorated by expert pampering or marine exertions, you can assuage your appetite at their *Nelayan* seafood restaurant, at which there's no menu – the chef cooks everything to order in consultation with guests. The resort also offers a range of activities and hikes, from waterfall treks led by the their very own intrepid naturalist, Captain Mok, to demonstrations of traditional Malay pastimes.

On the west (northbound) side of the coast road, just south of the signed turning for the resort, a sense of normality is restored at the excellent *C.B. Wee* (daily 9am–3pm & 6–10pm; ℡09/844 3515), a halal Chinese restaurant housed in a mundane pavilion that's become a popular port of call for drivers, tour-group buses and occasional resort guests. Seafood, including great butter prawns, is the natural thing to go for, but they also do a limited range of Western fare, including steak and chips, and whatever you order, it'll be freshly prepared and worth the wait.

Dungun to the Pahang border

The backwater town of **Dungun**, a little further south of Tanjung Jara, is predominantly Chinese, with a handful of shophouses and a night market each Thursday; there's no reason to spend much time here, though. The **local bus station** (for services to Rantau Abang or south to Kemaman/Chukai) is on the west side of the padang; if you're arriving by local bus and need to change for a long-distance service, ask the driver for "Kaunter Transnasional", and you should be let off the bus at the start of the access road for Dungun, where there's an office selling tickets for Transnasional and several other long-distance operators.

South of Dungun, the highway swerves suddenly inland, bypassing a small promontory, before rejoining the coast at **Paka**, a small fishing village nestling uncomfortably amid a sprawling new town. Both are in marked contrast to **Kerteh**, just a few minutes' drive further on, where a veritable forest of gleaming metal towers and piping marks the nucleus of Terengganu's petrochemicals industry. **Kemasik**, 20km south, has a decent stretch of beach, its sands sliced in two by a small creek, with a tiny fishing village just behind the beach. A couple of steep rocky outcrops, standing sentinel at the front of the beach, offer a good panorama if you make the climb, though you may find that picking your way back down is a lot trickier than clambering up.

Kemaman/Chukai

More or less midway between Dungun and Kuantan, the southernmost settlement of significance in Terengganu is the nondescript fusion of **Kemaman** and neighboring **Chukai**, no longer distinguishable as separate towns; you'll probably need to change buses here if you're using local services in either direction. This is also where you'll find the closest **banks** to Cherating – Maybank, best for foreign exchange, is five minutes' walk from the bus station in the direction of the river – and one of the best **cafés** on the east coast, in the shape of ⚘ *Hai Peng*, 3753 Jalan Sulaimani (daily except Fri 6.30am–6.30pm; ☎09/859 7810). Determinedly kept going by Elaine, whose father started the business in 1940, this Hainanese coffee shop roasts its own delicious coffee, using Indonesian beans. Besides fantastic ice-blended coffees, they do various lattes and a good range of snacks – peanut-butter-and-banana sandwiches, *kuih*, great *roti kahwin* (buttered toast with *kaya*), curry puffs and so forth. It's a popular hangout for locals of all creeds, who come here to chat around the old-fashioned marble-topped tables, beneath walls plastered with vintage film posters and photographs. The only snag is finding the place – Jalan Sulaimani runs roughly parallel to Sungai Kemaman, with Maybank at the southeastern end, and *Hai Peng* is in a nondescript four-storey building around ten minutes' walk away to the northwest, close to the traffic lights.

Cherating

At first it can be hard to discern the appeal of **CHERATING**, a laid-back village of sorts, dominated by a strip of tourist accommodation, 45km north of Kuantan. Many of the locals have long since moved out, to a new settlement a little way to the south, and the beach, hugging the northern end of a windswept bay, is pleasant but not outstanding, and pebbley in places. Nevertheless, once you've settled in, the quiet charm of this stalwart travellers' hangout begins to work its magic. Chilled out, yet warm-spirited, Cherating is simply an outstanding little community, a place to share quality time with old companions and, chances are, to end up with a whole bunch of new acquaintances too.

Part of the attraction here is the range of activities away from the beach itself, all of which are conducive both to unwinding and to socializing. For a back-to-nature experience, most of the guesthouses and chalets offer Sungai Cherating **boat trips**, on which you have a chance to spot long-tailed macaques (admittedly, hard to miss in the village itself), black-and-white hornbills, plus otters, tree snakes and, just possibly, the odd crocodile. Nighttime trips

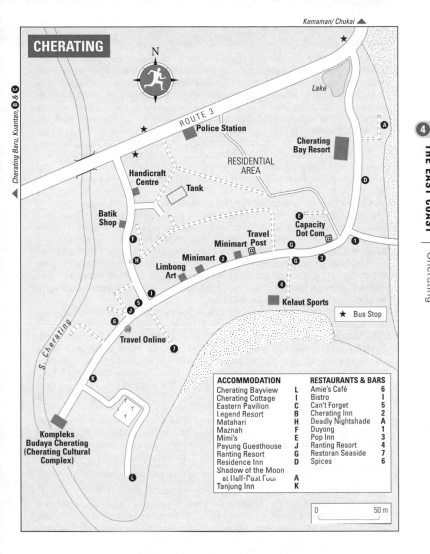

CHERATING

Kemaman/ Chukai ▲

Cherating Baru, Kuantan, B & C

N

ROUTE 3

Police Station

Lake

Cherating
Bay Resort

RESIDENTIAL
AREA

Ⓐ

Ⓓ

Handicraft
Centre

Tank

Ⓔ
Capacity
Dot Com

Batik
Shop

Ⓕ

Travel
Minimart Post
@

Ⓖ

Ⓘ

Minimart ❷

Ⓖ ❸

Ⓗ

Limbong
Art

S. Cherating

Ⓘ

❹

Ⓙ

Kelaut Sports

❺

Ⓖ

★ Bus Stop

@
Travel Online

❼

Ⓚ

ACCOMMODATION		RESTAURANTS & BARS	
Cherating Bayview	L	Amie's Café	6
Cherating Cottage	I	Bistro	I
Eastern Pavilion	C	Can't Forget	5
Legend Resort	B	Cherating Inn	2
Matahari	H	Deadly Nightshade	A
Maznah	F	Duyong	1
Mimi's	E	Pop Inn	3
Payung Guesthouse	J	Ranting Resort	4
Ranting Resort	G	Restoran Seaside	7
Residence Inn	D	Spices	6
Shadow of the Moon			
at Half-Past Four	A		
Tanjung Inn	K		

Kompleks
Budaya Cherating
(Cherating Cultural
Complex)

Ⓛ

0   50 m

are also run, with fireflies the main attraction. A couple of kilometres from the village, around the rocky headland at the eastern end of the bay, and close to the exclusive *Club Med* development, Cherating has its very own **turtle sanctuary** (daily 9am–6pm & 9pm–5am; ☎09/581 9078), where hatchlings are released into the sea nightly at 10.30pm, and where, if you're lucky, you'll see green turtles come ashore during the egg-laying season.

In the village itself, three **batik** outlets offer worthwhile classes in which you learn how to slap your own designs onto fabric or T-shirts, perhaps mixing the dyes yourself to achieve the hues you want. There's also the **Kompleks Budaya**, which puts on Malay cultural shows (usually third Sat or Sun of the month; free; ☎09/581 9446 for details), featuring dancing, traditional hobbies

While four types of marine turtle lay their eggs on Malaysia's east coast, for years it was the sight of the largest of these, the giant **leatherbacks**, with their unusual black, rubbery skin, that was the star attraction, drawing visitors from far and wide to Rantau Abang in Terengganu. This has made the survival of the endangered leatherback turtle a particularly emotive cause for concern, but in fact all other kinds of marine turtle – **green** (Malaysian nesting sites include the Perhentians; Pulau Redang; Cherating; Ma'Daerah, see opposite; and the Turtle Islands National Park in Sabah, see p.570), **hawksbill** (Pulau Redang; Paka, south of Dungun; Penarek, north of Merang; Turtle Islands National Park; and Melaka), **Olive Ridley** (Paka and Penarek), and **Kemp's Ridley** and **loggerhead** (neither of which nest in Malaysia) – are also at risk. Harmful fishing methods, such as the use of **trawl nets**, are responsible for the deaths of thousands of marine turtles each year, which helps to explain the dramatic reduction in leatherbacks nesting on the Terengganu coast. In 1956, more than ten thousand were recorded; in 2000, just three; in 2002, there were no sightings of leatherbacks in Rantau Abang for the first time since records began; in 2005, sightings of leatherbacks, hawksbills and Olive Ridley's in Terengganu were all at zero, and green turtle figures were significantly down. Even allowing for the fact that nesting turtle numbers vary cyclically, these statistics could hardly be more disheartening. On the rare occasions when leatherback eggs are turned up, they often fail to hatch, probably because of the increasing rarity of male–female turtle encounters when populations are dwindling.

In Southeast Asia in particular, the turtles have a predator far more menacing than any in the wild – human beings. For Chinese in Malaysia and Singapore, turtle soup is a classic delicacy, and while Muslims in Malaysia eschew turtle meat, forbidden by their religious law, they do consume **turtle eggs**, which are easy to find on sale at markets throughout the east coast; the eggs, which look not unlike ping-pong balls, are laid by the green turtle and collected under license from particular Malaysian beaches. For the moment, there appears to be no political will to outlaw this traditional food, a sad irony given Malaysia's otherwise laudable efforts towards saving the turtles. At least the deliberate slaughter of thousands of turtles for their shells, once fashioned into ornaments, such as bowls and earrings, primarily for the Japanese market, has been banned since 1992. With a survival rate of only fifty percent among hatchlings under ordinary conditions, any additional pressure on turtle populations exerted by man has drastic consequences for their survival.

The leatherback life cycle

Among leatherback turtles, only the female – measuring 150cm in length and weighing 400kg on average – comes ashore. She heaves herself out of the water at night with her enormous front flippers until she reaches dry sand; she then uses her rear flippers to make digging movements, creating a narrow hole 50–80cm deep in which she deposits up to a hundred eggs. The turtle then covers the hole

such as top-spinning and, for a bit of a diversion, trained monkeys retrieving coconuts from the tops of the palms.

Of course a trip here wouldn't be complete without some time spent on the **beach**. While there are far whiter stretches of sand a little further north in Terengganu, at least the shelter of the bay here ensures calm waters, suitable for children. If you want a swim, it's best to avoid low tide, when the sea recedes 100m or more, requiring you to plod over soft, wet sand to reach it, still further to get deep enough to swim. The headland obliterates any sunrise views, but in good weather it's still worth taking a dawn stroll on the beach, when the with her hind flippers, while disguising the whole nest site by churning up more sand with the front ones.

Although a single turtle never lays eggs in consecutive seasons, she can nest three or four times within the same season at two-weekly intervals. The eggs incubate for around sixty days, after which the hatchlings, no more than a hand-span in length, crawl to the surface of the sand, leaving their broken shells at the bottom of the pit. The first few hours of a hatchling's life are particularly hazardous, for even if it doesn't get destroyed by larvae or fungi in the sand, it can be picked off by crabs, birds and other predators before even reaching the sea. Usually emerging under the cover of night, hatchlings seem to know in which direction the sea lies, even if it can't be seen from where they hatched, and propel themselves rapidly towards the water using their outsize flippers. Years later, the mature females perform another baffling feat: swimming in waters as far away as South America, they somehow manage to find their way back to nest on the very Malaysian beach where they themselves hatched.

Turtle-spotting and conservation

Turtle-spotting was once something of a sport, with participants taking outrageous liberties, such as riding the creatures for the sake of a photograph. Nowadays, humans are excluded from various sites on Malaysia's east coast that have been designated as **sanctuaries** for nesting turtles, including stretches of mainland beach, as well as locations on the Perhentian islands and Pulau Redang. Also off-limits in general are the sanctuary's **hatcheries**, set up to protect the eggs from theft or damage. The eggs are dug up immediately after the turtle has laid them and reburied in sealed-off sections of the beach, surrounded by a wire pen tagged with a date marker. Burying the eggs in sand of the correct temperature is crucial – warm sand produces more females, while cooler sand favours males. When the hatchlings have broken out of their shells, they are released at the top of the beach, and their scurry to the sea is supervised to ensure their safe progress.

On the east coast, it's only at two of these sanctuaries – **Cherating** and **Ma'Daerah** – where the public is allowed to watch the nesting turtles, and only under scrutiny of rangers. Observers are asked to keep at least 5m away and refrain from making noise and using torches or camera flashes (unfortunately, not everyone obeys the rules). The sanctuary at Cherating (see p.335) is open to the general public, but the WWF-supported Ma'Daerah (May to mid-Aug; Ⓦ madaerah-turtle-sanctuary.org) is only open by prior arrangement. The latter, does, however, offer a great way to get hands-on experience of turtle conservation, through their three-day **Weekend with Turtles** volunteer programme, on which you might be involved in anything from updating their records of nesting turtles to moving eggs into the hatchery and patrolling the beach with their rangers. The fee (RM250) covers dorm accommodation at the sanctuary for Friday and Saturday night, and meals; staff will collect you from **Kerteh**, roughly midway between Kuala Terengganu and Kuantan, and easily accessible by bus from either.

headland looms darkly against a glowing eastern sky, and the only activity to disturb the stillness is a few fishing boats. At any time of day, look out for lacework patterns in the sand where it's been disturbed by little crabs that scuttle down into burrows marked by small, telltale surface holes. For something rather more stimulating, **windsurfing** and **kayaking** (the latter not just on the bay, but also upriver if you're so minded) are both available, and during the off-peak northeast monsoon in particular, **surfing** becomes a possibility. Horse-riding on the beach is also an option.

△ Turtle eggs on sale at an east-coast market

Practicalities

Any express **bus** plying the coast road between Kuala Terengganu and Kuantan will drop you off at Cherating (RM15 from Kuala Terengganu), either in **Cherating Lama** (the old village) or in the new settlement at **Cherating Baru**. If you're on a local bus from Kuantan (at RM3.50 much better value than the express bus, since discounts aren't given for short hops on express services; 1hr 30min) and want to be let off in Cherating Lama, be sure to press the buzzer when you see the 168-kilometre marker on the left. Chartering a **taxi** here from Kuantan is worth considering, at RM40. If you're driving here from KL, simply follow the East Coast Highway all the way to Pelabuhan Kuantan, the port 25km north of Kuantan, where you pick up the coast road.

On Cherating Lama's main drag there are a few offices for bus-ticket bookings and other travel arrangements, such as transfers to Taman Negara or islands off the east coast. Among these agencies are Travelpost, Capacity Dot Com and Travel Online, all of which have **Internet access** and **tours** to nearby attractions such as Tasik Chini (see p.270); Capacity Dot Com also runs a useful little **library** and book exchange. For windsurfing (RM35/hr), kayaking (RM15/hr), surfing (RM15/hr) and **snorkelling** trips to nearby Snake Island (RM35 per person), talk to the guys from Kelaut Sports (☎09/581 9658 or 019/917 1934), who can be found either at their premises close to the *Ranting Resort* bar, or at the *Payung Guesthouse*. They and the two travel agencies above also offer Cherating river trips (RM35 per person). **Bike rental** – useful for the turtle sanctuary as well as general wandering around Cherating's environs – is available at the *Payung Guesthouse* (RM5 for 3hr, or RM10 per day). Riding will set you back RM50 for a half-hour canter on the beach, or RM10 if you want a beginner's lesson, in which case you'll be taken around the paddock at the stables, near the *Duyong* restaurant.

With no banks or ATMs in Cherating, if you run short of ringgit, you'll have to change **cash** (not at great rates) with Travelpost or Capacity Dot Com, or make the short trip north to Kemaman/Chukai (see p.334) to use the banks there. Either travel agent can arrange a **taxi**, as can most of Cherating's accommodation and restaurants.

Accommodation

There's no shortage of **places to stay** in old Cherating, the best of which are listed below. Many of these don't provide food, but given the plethora of cafés and restaurants in the village, this hardly presents a problem.

With your own transport, you could consider staying in Cherating Baru, which boasts several modern, family-oriented resort developments (all signposted off the coast road), while nipping across to Cherating Lama to dip into the old village's community feel – though if this is what you're really after, it makes much more sense to compromise on a mid-range place in Cherating Lama itself.

While discounts are available during the northeast monsoon, prices can rise by a third or more at weekends and on public holidays throughout the year; the price codes in the reviews represent weekday rates in the peak season.

Cherating Lama

Cherating Bayview ⊤09/581 9248, Ⓕ581 9415. At the quieter end of the bay, this newly extended and renovated complex is decent enough, if a little unexciting. It has its own swimming pool, with some chalets clustered around; seafront chalets are also available, though somewhat overpriced (from RM120). All units are en suite, and most have a/c. ❹

Cherating Cottage ⊤09/581 9273, Ⓦcherating-cottage.com. A range of options, cheapest of which are the rooms in a two-storey block, their so-called "travellers' longhouse". Also packed into the grounds are a range of chalets (billed as "bungalows") and family bungalows, the latter sleeping five and with the bonus of a/c and TV. All accommodation is en suite. Rooms and chalets ❷, family bungalows RM85.

Matahari ⊤09/581 9835. Basic rooms, each with a fan, solitary light bulb, mosquito net and fridge, with a communal kitchen, TV room and shared bathrooms and showers. There's also a batik workshop on site. Good value. ❷

Maznah ⊤09/581 9359. Even more rustic than the *Matahari*, but quite acceptable as a fallback. A few of the chalets have their own bathroom. ❶

Mimi's Popular with surfers during the monsoon, this place has a tight cluster of well-kept chalets, each with slightly different decor, though all have bathrooms painted in vivid shades, as well as a TV; a couple have a/c as well. They have an odd attitude towards bookings though – they don't give out their phone number as they prefer people to just turn up. Discounts available for longer stays. ❸

Payung Guesthouse ⊤019/917 1934 or 09/581 9658. A deservedly popular collection of ten chalets set in a small but very tidy garden. All are en suite, with fan and mosquito net; most have a double bed, though there are a few two-bed permutations. The place is efficiently run, and the friendly owners can arrange plenty of activities and provide general information on the area. An excellent choice. ❷

Ranting Resort ⊤09/581 9068. Decent en-suite chalets, roomier than some offered by the competition, and with the option of a/c; plus a bunch of much pricier new chalets pretty much on the beach, including some units sleeping four. Chalets ❸, with a/c ❹, beachfront chalets ❻

Residence Inn ⊤09/581 9333, Ⓦwww.ric.com.my. If you prefer resort-style accommodation and want to stay in old Cherating, this complex of tidy en-suite rooms with a/c and TV, built around a collection of swimming pools, is the place to come. The only drawback is that the beach is a five-minute walk away. ❻

Shadow of the Moon at Half-Past Four ⊤09/581 9186. Deliberately set on a wooded hillside well away from the beachside community, this unreconstructed hippy retreat has an airy reception lounge/bar area that's like a cross between a not-quite-there safari lodge and a pre-punk rock rag, the walls plastered with psychedelic art. There are shelves of countless old paperbacks to read, with a faded copy of M.M. Kaye's 1950s novel *Shadow of the Moon* given pride of place by the bar. The chalets themselves aren't bad, each with their own bathroom, and can be treated as two-bed dorms. The promotional leaflet correctly notes that the atmosphere here "is not meant to appeal to everyone". Dorm beds RM20, chalets ❷

Tanjung Inn ⊤09/581 9081. A range of timber-built en-suite accommodation, from simple chalets with fan to rooms in brilliant traditionally styled kampung houses, each boasting a/c, four-poster beds and a slate-tiled bathroom with hot water. They're all set around two vast ponds in a pretty garden, with the occasional monitor lizard for added company. Were the management not somewhat hands-off, and there not noise some nights from a nearby karaoke bar, this would without doubt represent the best value in Cherating; it's still a great option though. Fan chalets ❷, a/c rooms ❺, four-bed family units RM130.

Cherating Baru

Eastern Pavilion ☎09/581 9500, reservations ☎03/2162 2922, ⓦwww.holidayvilla.com.my. Each of the twelve "villas" here is actually a luxurious elaboration of the kampung house, supposedly deriving from every state of the Federation. They all come with one or two beautifully appointed bedrooms, a lounge and a small outdoor pool and Jacuzzi, discreetly screened from prying eyes; a great place to pamper yourself. By comparison, the neighboring *Holiday Villa*, sharing the same management, is pretty mundane. Rate (RM600) excludes breakfast. ❾

Legend Resort ☎09/581 9818, ⓦwww .legendsgroup.com. A series of interlinked pools with a central waterfall feature lies at the heart of this sprawling, popular development, which also adjoins a stretch of (public) beach. The expansive central lounge and lobby area has a small stage where karaoke and a Filipino house band provide the evening entertainment; otherwise, pool tables and squash courts should help keep you occupied. The rooms themselves are modern and unremarkable. Packages and discounts often available. ❼

Eating and drinking

The old village boasts a string of inexpensive beach **restaurants**, several of which are Chinese affairs, all much of a muchness, emphasizing seafood – including the oddly named *lala*, a sort of clam, which turns up in a variety of sauces – but there are also a couple of places for decent Western food, and just about everywhere does a few Western snacks. A good number of these places serve **alcohol**, which often leads to some gentle carousing well into the night. Make the most of Cherating if you're intending to continue into Terengganu and Kelantan; opportunities to sample relatively unformulaic Western fare and quaff beer are few and far between further north. Malay fare isn't much in evidence, though there is a *kedai kopi* opposite *Amie's Café* where you can get a passable *roti canai* in the morning and *nasi campur* at lunchtime, and an only marginally more elaborate operation, the *Cherating Inn*, for evening meals.

Amie's Café ⓦwww.amiescafe.com. A humble pavilion belies one of the nicest cafés in the country, offering more interesting and generally healthier Western fare than many comparable places in KL. For breakfast there's a great range of omelettes and pancakes, and terrific brown bread with Vegemite, chocolate spread or butter and jam; lunchtime ushers in a new set of delights – sandwiches on white or brown bread, tasty beef brisket cheeseburgers and spicy Bollywood chips. The choice of beverages is just as diverse – a selection of teas, great coffee (supplied by *Hai Peng* in Chukai; see p.334) and luscious shakes. Newspapers and board games are provided. Unmissable. Daily 8am–4pm.

Bistro At the *Cherating Cottage*. A combination of Asian and Western fare, with decent pizzas the most notable offering.

Can't Forget An extensive menu featuring Thai, Chinese and Western dishes, and an emphasis on seafood. Not unforgettable, but not at all bad.

Deadly Nightshade At the *Shadow of the Moon* at *Half-Past Four*. Of interest mainly as a boozing den, if you enjoy downing your beer or whisky to the sounds of Rod Stewart and other hoary rockers of yesteryear.

Duyong Tasty, good-value Chinese and Thai food, and beach views; often busy.

Pop Inn Definitely *the* place to be of an evening, with a couple of Swiss specialities, including *wiener schnitzel* and *rösti*, among the main courses (RM20–35), plus a range of snacks, soups and salads, and decent wine. Stays open late, with a house band, led by local batik personage Brian, churning out covers of rock standards Thurs–Sat.

Ranting Beach Resort The little beach bar here is a laid-back place, and often has good happy-hour prices.

Restoran Seaside Fairly standard Cantonese restaurant set just back from the beach, with a few tables actually encroaching upon it. Claypot dishes are a speciality, standbys such as *kangkung belancan* (crunchy convolvolus greens fried with pungent prawn paste) are available, and there's the tempting prospect of satay some evenings. A safe bet. Open lunchtime till midnight or later.

Spices Sharing premises with *Amie's Café*, this serves up a largely north Indian menu with a few Malay items for good measure. The menu basically comprises fish, prawns, squid, mutton, chicken and tofu, served up in your choice of curry sauce (masala or vindaloo) or in a sweet-and-sour or chilli base. Unfortunately, as we went to press it appeared that they might either be changing hands or be closing for an extended period; for the latest, ask at the *Payung Guesthouse*.

Kuantan and around

KUANTAN is one of those Malaysian cities that offer little to capture the imagination. The state capital of **Pahang** since the 1955, the city is an undistinguished agglomeration of concrete, commercial buildings built around a tiny, older core of shophouses close to Sungai Kuantan. While there's very little by way of historical or cultural interest in the city itself, Kuantan can be a breath of fresh air after a sojourn in Kelantan or Terengganu – it's closer in feel to the cities of the west coast than to Kuala Terengganu or Kota Bharu, and, for the time being, offers better shopping and eating prospects than either of its two austere counterparts further north. If you're arriving from elsewhere in the country, however, Kuantan's lack of attractions and a proper centre can make it seem mundane in the extreme. With the creation of the **East Coast Highway** to Pelabuhan Kuantan, the port 40km north of the city, it's straightforward to bypass Kuantan altogether if you're travelling between KL and the east coast.

If you do choose to hang around for a night or two in Kuantan, it's worth making a visit to **Gua Charas**, a limestone cave temple within easy reach of the town. The trip here is worth it for the stunning setting alone – dramatic outcrops in virtually deserted plantation country. You might also want to head south to the rural town of **Pekan**, which, as the capital of the state until 1898, boasts the cultural heritage so obviously absent from Kuantan, with two museums, including a surprisingly good display devoted to Malay **boat-building**. Finally, Kuantan is a possible base for a foray into the interior to **Tasik Chini** (see p.270).

Arrival, information and accommodation

If Kuantan has a focus of sorts, it's the **padang**, between which and the river are the oldest streets in the city, where you'll also find quite a few of the hotels and restaurants. However, plenty of the city's amenities are scattered in all directions from the padang, including the **express bus station**, several blocks to the north close to Jalan Tun Ismail. The **local bus station** amounts to little more than a car park on Jalan Besar, close to the river. **Taxis** can be found between Jalan Besar and Jalan Mahkota, whereas long-distance taxis arrive at the express bus station. A taxi to the centre from the Sultan Ahmad Shah **airport**, 15km west of town, costs RM20.

The **tourist office** on Jalan Mahkota (Mon–Sat 9am–1pm & 2–5pm, closed Fri 12.30–2.45pm; ☎09/516 1007, ⓦwww.pahangtourism.com.my) has plenty of useful material on attractions within Pahang, and can advise on local buses. They also supply a handy free **map** of Kuantan and its environs.

Accommodation

The accommodation picture in Kuantan is a little strange: there's no shortage of places to stay, so much so that many establishments offer **discounts** off their published prices – yet occupancy rates can be fairly high, especially in the

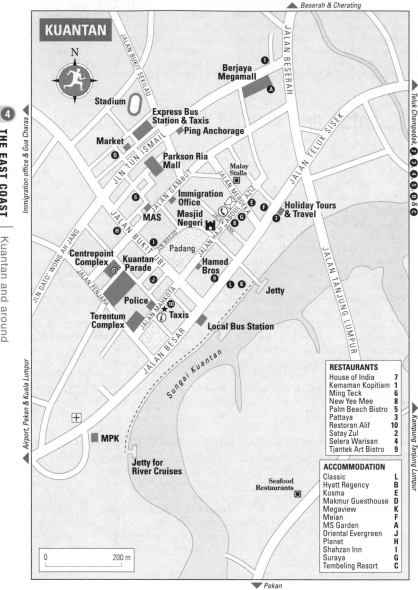

KUANTAN

N

▲ Beserah & Cherating

Berjaya
Megamall

❶

Ⓐ

Stadium

Express Bus
Station & Taxis

Ping Anchorage

Market

Ⓓ

Parkson Ria
Mall

Malay
Stalls

Immigration
Office

Ⓔ

Ⓕ

❻

MAS

Masjid
Negeri

Holiday Tours
& Travel

Ⓗ

❼

Ⓖ

Ⓘ

❽

Centrepoint
Complex

Kuantan
Parade

Padang

Hamed
Bros

Ⓙ

❾

Ⓛ Ⓚ

Jetty

Police

❿

Terentum
Complex

ⓘ Taxis

Local Bus Station

JALAN BESAR

Sungai Kuantan

MPK

Jetty for
River Cruises

Seafood
Restaurants

▼ Pekan

◀ Immigration office & Gua Charas

◀ Airport, Pekan & Kuala Lumpur

Teluk Chempedak, ❷, ❸, ❹, ❺, Ⓑ & Ⓒ ▶

Kampung Tanjung Lumpur ▶

0   200 m

RESTAURANTS

House of India	7
Kemaman Kopitiam	1
Ming Teck	6
New Yee Mee	8
Palm Beach Bistro	5
Pattaya	3
Restoran Alif	10
Satay Zul	2
Selera Warisan	4
Tjantek Art Bistro	9

ACCOMMODATION

Classic	L
Hyatt Regency	B
Kosma	E
Makmur Guesthouse	D
Megaview	K
Meian	F
MS Garden	A
Oriental Evergreen	J
Planet	H
Shahzan Inn	I
Suraya	G
Tembeling Resort	C

mid-range hotels, so it's a good idea not to turn up without a **reservation**. Mid-range places are certainly better value than the cheap boarding houses, which here are often pretty basic, charmless and not really geared up to travellers. If you're in the market for something classy, there's no need to base yourself in the city centre – fronting the South China Sea are the five-star *Hyatt* and an excellent **apartment** complex at Teluk Chempedak, only a short taxi ride east of the centre; you could even stay at the very pleasant *Swiss Garden* resort at Balok Beach (℡09/544 7333, ⓦwww.swissgarden.com; B&B RM180), boasting balconied rooms overlooking either a landscaped garden or the South China Sea, and the customary swimming pool, tennis courts and gym. The beach, 30km north of Kuantan, can be reached by taxi (around RM20) or on a Cherating-bound bus from the local bus station (45min).

Central Kuantan

Classic 7 Jalan Besar ℡09/516 4599, ⓔchotel@tm.net.my. The rooms here look as though they've not been redecorated since the 1980s, but still, they're en suite (with actual bathtubs), have TV and a/c, and are pretty comfortable; some rooms also have river views. A good deal. ❻

Kosma 59 Jalan Haji Abdul Aziz ℡09/516 2214. A friendly Malay-run hotel with rather poky en-suite doubles and more spacious family rooms. Not quite as good as *Oriental Evergreen*, but okay for the price. ❷

Makmur Guesthouse B16, second floor, Jalan Pasar Baru ℡09/514 1363. Of the cheapies close to the bus station, this is just about the best bet, with a range of fairly basic rooms. ❷

Megaview Jalan Besar ℡09/517 1888, ⓦwww.megaviewhotel.com. Business-oriented, efficient high-rise hotel on the river, with good, if not mega, views. Regular promotions make it good value, particularly during the week. There's also a popular bar on the terrace with football on widescreen TV. Rate includes breakfast. ❻

Meian 78 Jalan Teluk Sisek ℡09/552 0949 or 012/952 8213. Old-fashioned Chinese flophouse offering spartan fan rooms – some of the cheapest in town – with shared facilities; a bit noisy, but okay for a night or two. ❶

MS Garden Lorong Gambut, off Jalan Beserah ℡09/517 7899, ⓦwww.msgarden.com.my. From the palatial lobby on up, this really is the slickest hotel in the city centre, with spacious rooms, a coffee house and popular Cantonese restaurant, a fitness centre and a swimming pool complete with waterfall. ❼

Oriental Evergreen 157 Jalan Haji Abdul Rahman ℡09/513 0168, ⓕ513 0368. Marooned in an area undergoing redevelopment, and thus flanked by derelict shophouses, this 1980s five-storey hotel looks decidedly plain and older than its age from the outside. Inside, however, the rooms are very serviceable, with a/c that's almost too effective, plus TV and en-suite facilities. Excellent value;

places that are only slightly better charge almost double the rate here. ❷

Shahzan Inn Jalan Bukit Ubi ℡09/513 6688. A mundane tower block of a hotel, but with comfortable en-suite rooms, some with great views of the State Mosque across the padang, and its own swimming pool. Rate includes breakfast. ❻

Suraya 55–57 Jalan Haji Abdul Aziz ℡09/516 4266, ⓕ516 2028. Not dissimilar in price and facilities to the *Classic*, but rooms here aren't quite as dated. No breakfast though. ❹

Teluk Chempedak

Hyatt Regency ℡09/566 1234, ⓦwww.kuantan .regency.hyatt.com. A long-established beach retreat for well-heeled folks from KL and Singapore, and deservedly so. Emerging from the breezy reception pavilion, you'll find a complex that just seems to go on and on, with two swimming pools (one with a built-in bar), a gym, tennis and squash courts, childcare facilities, three restaurants and two bars, one of which is a converted ship that once carried Vietnamese boat people. The only thing it lacks is a private beach – the sands it's set just back from are open to the public. ❽

Tembeling Resort Jalan Padang Golf ℡09/567 6688, ⓕ567 9988. A huge condominium development on the wooded headland just south of Teluk Chempedak, popular with expats based in the industrial area around Kuantan's port. The one-bedroom apartments face landward, but the larger apartments have gorgeous views over the South China Sea; all have a dining area and kitchen, though it's much simpler to eat at their coffee house. The only beach to speak of is a rocky bit of public sand below, but there's no point tramping down there when you can head up to the resort's great swimming pool. Recreational facilities also include billiard tables and a gym. RM30 discount outside weekends; good monthly rates. Weekends: one-bedroom apartments RM180, two-bed RM280, three-bed RM380.

The City

The old commercial part of Kuantan is relatively small, squeezed between the padang and the river. On the northeastern edge of the padang is the town's one real sight, the **Masjid Negeri**, built in 1991, with a pastel exterior – green for Islam, blue for peace and white for purity. It's distinctly Turkish in appearance, thanks to the pencil minarets at all four corners of the sturdy square prayer hall, topped with a looming central dome; non-Muslims can visit in the morning by permission of the caretaker. At night, the sound of prayer calls and sermons don't exactly contribute to the serenity of the padang, while the mosque itself – now subtly lit – takes on a whole new complexion, as the minarets, tipped with red points of light, look for all the world like rockets primed for launch.

Down by the river, starting at the *Megaview Hotel*, a smart promenade feels slightly out of place clinging to the banks of Sungai Kuantan. Early evening is a good time to take a stroll here, to see fishing boats returning with the day's catch and perhaps the occasional red eagle swooping on its prey. The walkway continues south to the new jetty, from where the **Kuantan River Cruise** departs (daily except Fri 11am & 2.30pm, Fri 10am & 3pm, Sat also 8pm; 1hr 30min; RM10); it heads downstream alongside the town and under the Tanjung Lumpur bridge, before turning around and navigating back upstream past the fishing villages of Tanjung Lumpur and Peramu. The highlight (omitted on the Saturday evening outing) is a stop at Taman Bakau, a **mangrove forest reserve** where a 250-metre raised wooden walkway has been built for easy viewing. Commentary during the trip is a recorded retelling, in Malay, of the history of Kuantan, though you may be able to get some information in English if a tour guide is present. Tickets for the cruise are available at the MPK (town council) office near the jetty, from an hour before departure.

The riverside villages

Just a short hop south of the river from the commotion of central Kuantan are the village suburbs of Kampung Tanjung Lumpur and Peramu. Reached by local bus, **Kampung Tanjung Lumpur**, about a kilometre east of the centre, is by night the lively **seafood** restaurant capital of Kuantan. It was also once an impoverished fishing community, though with easy access to the centre – thanks to the newish Tanjung Lumpur bridge – land prices have skyrocketed, and new residential areas have sprung up. The largest and most popular of the eating places here is the *Phuket Seafood Restaurant* on the main road, Jalan Tanjung Lumpur, serving up mainly Thai seafood for RM10–15 per dish. **Peramu**, a couple of kilometres up the road, and also reached by bus from the local bus station, is changing visibly too. However, if you follow one of the tracks east from the main road, you'll find a flotilla of brightly painted fishing boats moored to tumbledown wooden jetties on the riverbank. In contrast, the modern city skyscrapers of Kuantan can be seen just downriver.

The coastline to the south of the town is in many ways more appealing than the **beach** at Teluk Chempedak to the north, not least because it is still relatively undeveloped. **Pantai Sepat**, about 3km south of Kampung Tanjung Lumpur, is particularly good, a wide sweeping expanse of sand and shallow sea, whose currents are a whole lot safer than the buffeting waves further north. To get here, take one of the regular buses from the local bus station or a taxi (RM15).

Teluk Chempedak

East of the centre, Jalan Besar becomes Jalan Teluk Sisek, which swings east, parallel to the coastline, and transforms into Jalan Teluk Chempedak. This terminates 5km from the centre, around the corner from a wooded headland, at an east-facing stretch of coast where **Teluk Chempedak** has long been a popular evening and weekend hangout for Kuantan families and young people alike. The sands of the bay are encouragingly white, and though undertows can render the sea off-limits for swimming (in which event, watch out for hoisted red flags), there is an appealing liveliness about the place, quite at variance from the langourous mood on the otherwise even better sands of rural Terengganu. With a few decent restaurants and stalls to boot, Teluk Chempedak makes a relaxing place to spend a half-day or evening away from the blandness of the city centre.

Bus #39 runs regularly from outside the mosque on Jalan Haji Abdul Aziz to Teluk Chempedak – the last bus back is around 10pm. The bus terminates near where the road ends, close to a welter of stalls and inexpensive restaurants (to the left as you face the sea), the pricey *Hyatt* hotel complex (to the right), and the beach itself. A taxi here costs around RM10 from the centre; other than late at night, it's usually not hard to find a taxi back to town from the main road.

Among the stalls you'll find the open-air *Pattaya* and *Selera Warisan* **restaurants**, both doing good seafood for around RM12 a head. Rather smarter is the *Palm Beach Bistro* (daily except Mon 5pm till late; ☎09/566 9969), more or less where the road ends, close to the *Hyatt* and just back from the beach itself; it does a mixture of Western fare such as rib-eye steak and pasta dishes, plus local rice and noodle dishes. For something really upmarket, you could avail yourself of the restaurants at the *Hyatt* – one Chinese, one Italian, and one offering both local and Western fare. **Nightlife** revolves around a handful of bars interspersed between the souvenir and batik shops on the main road just before the beach; if you like karaoke bars, *Lips TC* is the place to head.

Eating, drinking and nightlife

Kuantan's eating scene isn't too bad for a provincial city. There are plenty of reasonable **kedai kopis**, particularly in the old streets between the padang and the river, where you'll find a sprinkling of Malay cafés on and around the northern end of Jalan Haji Abdul Aziz, plus Chinese and Indian places scattered about. At the other end of the scale, the better hotels have reliable restaurants, with the *MS Garden* as good a place for a blowout as any (the Chinese restaurant here does good *dim sum* at lunchtime). Both the Berjaya Megamall and Kuantan Parade have reliable **food courts**. Out from the centre, there's always the prospect of seaside eating at Teluk Chempedak, or you could join the hordes of locals at *Satay Zul*, halfway to Teluk Chempedak at the junction of Jalan Teluk Sisek and Jalan Alor Akar (daily 6pm till late, but closed every other Mon; ☎09/568 7859); a taxi ride out here costs around RM6. A two-storey place, they serve a full range of satay, made not just from the usual meats but also from liver or beef tripe; also available are local favourites like *mee kari* and *nasi dagang*. Most of the satay costs around RM0.50 a stick, with venison the priciest of all at around RM0.80 a stick.

The most atmospheric place in town for an evening **drink** is down by the river at the *Megaview Hotel*. For a spot of **entertainment**, you might be lucky enough to catch a trio of brilliant Malay musicians playing traditional *asli* music, increasingly rarely heard these days, on accordion, guitar and frame drum; they perform at around 8pm (except on Mondays) at the coffee house in the *MS Garden* hotel.

House of India 61 Jalan Teluk Sisek. Mid-priced a/c restaurant serving good banana-leaf curries and tasty lassis.

Kemaman Kopitiam Lorong Tun Ismail, off Jalan Tun Ismail. A breakaway from the long-established

Hai Peng in Chukai (see p.334), and offering a very similar range of hot and cold coffees and shakes, excellent light bites (from *mee goreng* to fried mackerel – *ikan kembong* – stuffed with *belacan*), pastries (*kuih*, custard tarts) and decor that's meant to recall Chinese cafés of yesteryear. Not as proficient as the original, but enjoyable all the same. There are a few other vintage-style cafés nearby, too. Daily 7am till late.

Ming Teck On an unnamed lane between Jalan Tun Ismail and Jalan Gambut, this Chinese veggie *kedai kopi* puts a mock-meat spin on local street food – hence serving up meatless and fishless *nasi lemak*, fishball noodles (in soup or fried), *bee hoon* (vermicelli) and so forth. There's a good range of *pow* too. Daily 7.30am–6.30pm, though hours may be reduced at weekends.

New Yee Mee Jalan Haji Abdul Aziz. Well-established Chinese *kedai kopi*, particularly busy at lunchtime when there's an excellent spread of toppings for rice. They also do various dishes to order, including favourites like lemon chicken, fish-head curry and beef served sizzling on a hot plate.

Restoran Alif 91 Jalan Mahkota. Good a/c *mamak* establishment with a range of curries served on banana leaves, plus South Indian staples like *idli* and *thosai*, and fish-head curry. Various fruit juices and home-made barley water are available. Daily 7.30am till late.

Tjantek Art Bistro 46 Jalan Besar ☏09/516 4144. The classiest stand-alone restaurant in downtown Kuantan, with elegant modern furniture and artwork plastering the walls, though no a/c – the place, on the ground floor of a restored shophouse, is open to the busy street, which adds a pleasingly incongruous touch to the dining experience. They use NZ beef for their steaks (properly rare if requested) and also serve pasta dishes (al dente) and sandwiches aplenty. They have a variety of coffees, teas and shakes too, including a scrumptious iced almond mocha shake. Not pricey either – main courses are around the RM15 mark. Mon–Sat 4pm till late.

Listings

Banks Standard Chartered Bank and Maybank are situated around the intersection of the aptly named Jalan Bank and Jalan Besar; other banks are to be found on Jalan Mahkota and Jalan Tun Ismail.

Bookshops Hamed Bros on Jalan Haji Abdul Aziz, midway along the padang, has a limited range of English language books, plus various maps of Malaysia. The Parkson Ria Mall on Jalan Tun Ismail has a branch of Popular Bookstore, while tucked away on level 1 of the Berjaya Megamall is the MBS Bookstore.

Car rental Avis (☏09/538 3843) and Mayflower (☏09/538 3490) are both at the airport; Orix is at the *Grand Continental Hotel* (☏09/515 7488), Jalan Gambut.

Cinemas Golden Screen Cinemas Multiplex (☏09/508 8188) on the top floor of Berjaya Megamall shows some English-language films.

Internet access There's an Internet café in the Centrepoint Complex, opposite the Kuantan Parade mall, and another, Zoom Prime Technology, hidden away on level 2 of the Berjaya Megamall.

Post and communications The GPO, with poste restante, is on Jalan Haji Abdul Aziz; the Telekom office is next door.

Shopping Both the Berjaya Megamall on Jalan Tun Ismail, close to the intersection with Jalan Beserah, and Kuantan Parade, Jalan Penjara, have supermarkets, pharmacies and a range of other outlets. On Saturday evenings there's a *pasar malam* on Jalan Gambut, close to the junction with Jalan Bukit Ubi.

Travel agents Holiday Tours and Travel in the Wisma Pan Global, Jalan Teluk Sisek (☏09/516 4051, ⊛www.holidaytours.com.my), does a range of day-trips to the attractions in the vicinity, such as Tasik Chini (RM110 per person), and Gua Charas combined with the waterfalls at Sungai Pandan (RM95 per person); they also offer Taman Negara packages and can help sort out air tickets and other travel needs. Ping Anchorage, the Kuala Terengganu-based travel agent, sells its extensive range of east-coast packages from its branch on Jalan Tun Ismail (☏09/514 2020, ⊛www .pinganchorage.com.my).

Visa extensions The immigration office is just over 2km northwest of the centre in the state government's offices at Kompleks KHEDM, Bandar Indra Mahkota (Mon–Fri 8am–1pm & 2–5pm, Sat 8am–1pm; ☏09/573 2200); buses (signed "Jabatan Imigresen") head out here from the local bus station.

Watersports Balok Beach, 30km north of town, is home to a simple water sports centre (Pusat Rekreasi Balok; daily 8am–5pm; ☏09/544 8371), which can be reached on the same local bus that heads to Cherating and Kemaman; the centre is just beyond the *Swiss Garden Hotel*, and around ten minutes' walk from the main road. Facilities are limited to canoeing (RM7 for use of a two-seater) and fishing (RM50 for the boat trip, but you'll need your own gear), though there's also a pleasant stretch of beach to enjoy.

Gua Charas

One of the great limestone outcrops surrounding Kuantan is home to **Gua Charas** (aka Gua Charah), 25km northwest of the town. A temple built into the cave can be seen as a leisurely day-trip: bus #48 departs the local bus station every hour for the thirty-minute journey to the village of **Panching**, where a sign to the caves points you down a four-kilometre track through overgrown rubber plantations and rows upon rows of palm-oil trees – agricultural legacies responsible for the large numbers of Tamils living in the area, descendants of the indentured workers brought from southern India in the nineteenth century. It's a long, hot walk to the cave, so take plenty of water with you. Alternatively, charter a taxi (around RM100, including a wait) for a combined trip to the caves (the taxi can take you right up to the steps for the caves) and the nearby Sungai Pandan **waterfall**, where you can splash around in various pools, though there are few facilities other than the odd food stall.

Once you've reached the outcrop and paid your RM1 donation, you're faced with a steep climb to the Thai Buddhist **cave temple** itself. About halfway up, a rudimentary path strikes off to the right, leading to the entrance of the main cave. Descending into the eerie darkness is not for the faint-hearted, even though the damp mud path is dimly lit by fluorescent tubes. Inside the echoing cavern, with its algae-stained vaulted roof and squeaking bats, illuminated shrines gleam from gloomy corners, guiding you to the main shrine deep in the cave, where a nine-metre sleeping Buddha is almost dwarfed by its giant surroundings. Back through the cave, steps lead to another, lighter hollow. It's nothing special, but if you go as far as you can to the back, the wall opens out to give a great view of the surrounding countryside, stubby oil palms in regimented rows stretching towards the horizon.

Pekan

Just 45km south of Kuantan lies the unassuming royal town of **PEKAN**, whose name actually means "small town". The state capital of Pahang until 1898, Pekan has a meagre modern centre backing onto a sprawling, peaceful kampung, but its neat and sober streets also boast a variety of **royal residences**, some modest, some vulgar – all products of the state's rapid turnover of sultans – and a handful of colonial buildings which, though reasonably maintained by the state, feel somehow out of place and unloved.

At the edge of the tiny commercial sector, Jalan Sultan Ahmad faces the languid riverfront. Down the street, past a row of shophouses dating from the beginning of the twentieth century and shaded by huge rain trees, is the **Muzium Sultan Abu Bakar** (Tues–Sun 9.30am–5pm, closed Fri 12.15–2.45pm; RM1), the State Museum of Pahang. It's housed in a well-proportioned Straits colonial building that has been used for various purposes down the years: as the sultan's *istana*, as the centre of British administration, and as the headquarters of the Japanese army during the occupation. Today it houses a collection which includes splendid Chinese ceramics salvaged from the wreck of a junk in the South China Sea, and an impressive display of royal regalia in the new east wing. There's also a collection of regional musical instruments including the xylophone-like *gambang kayu*, and a number of *kenong*s, large pot-shaped gongs set horizontally on a rack. If it's not too busy, the friendly curators will let you have a go.

Opposite the museum, a footbridge leads to the **Watercraft Gallery** (same hours as State Museum; free), an innovatively designed museum comprising four pavilions topped by pyramidal roofs of multicoloured glass, on an island

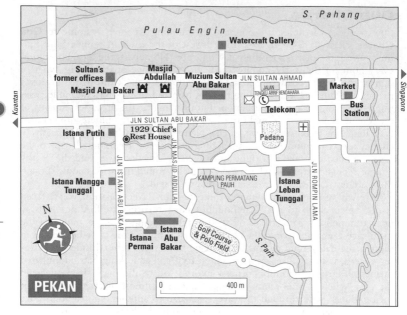

in the middle of the Sungai Pahang. The displays here, labelled in Malay and English, are genuinely worthwhile, tracing the history of local boat-building. Besides a reconstruction of an ancient boat whose 1500-year-old hull was found submerged in murky water in 1926, you can also see some fine examples of the *perahu kulit kayu*, a boat fashioned from a single sheet of bark, favoured by the Orang Asli in the upper reaches of the Sungai Rompin and Sungai Endau, and a beautifully painted *perahu payang*, used for fishing.

Further west along Jalan Sultan Ahmad is the unusual **Masjid Abdullah**, built during the reign of Sultan Abdullah (1917–32). No longer used for active worship, this Art Deco structure, whose blue domes look more Turkish than Southeast Asian, is now home to the Pusat Dakwah Islamiah, the state centre for the administration of religious affairs. Next door, the current mosque, **Masjid Abu Bakar**, is more conventional, with bulbous golden domes.

Round the corner at the end of the road, past the unremarkable former offices of the sultan, is a crossroads. An archway built to resemble elephants' tusks marks your way ahead to the royal quarter of the town, past the fresh, white **Istana Putih** on the corner. A few minutes' walk south is the sky-blue **Istana Mangga Tunggal**, and the **Istana Permai** (closed to the public), a tiny blue-roofed subsidiary palace that is home to the Regent of Pahang. Here you'll also see the rectangular facade of the **Istana Abu Bakar**, the palace currently occupied by the royal family, its garish opulence untypical of the buildings in Pekan; the expansive grounds are now a royal golf course and polo ground.

North of the nearby sports field, a narrow winding lane brings you into **Kampung Permatang Pauh**, the secluded village area of Pekan with simple wooden houses built on stilts. A ten-minute walk across Sungai Parit (the paths through the kampung are confusing, so it's best to ask for directions) leads to the most impressive of Pekan's royal buildings, the **Istana Leban**

Tunggal – a refined wooden structure fronted by a pillared portico, with an unusual symmetrical hexagonal tower.

Practicalities

From Kuantan, bus #31 leaves at least hourly from the local **bus station** for Pekan (RM4), an hour's journey on. If you're arriving from the south by bus, you can ask the driver to drop you off in town – all buses pass through Pekan on their way to Kuantan. If you want to head south from Pekan, you can either backtrack to Kuantan to pick up one of the many express buses leaving there, or be picked up by Transnasional here (you'll need to buy a ticket in advance from their agent at 18 Jalan Sultan Ahmad; ☎09/422 2340), close to Pekan's **bus station**.

Pekan has one gem of a **place to stay**, the *1929 Chief's Rest House* on Jalan Istana Permai (☎09/422 6941; dorm beds RM10, rooms ➍). This would simply be a humdrum rural guesthouse were it not for the building it occupies, a spacious timber bungalow raised off the ground, with a terrace all around the exterior. Accommodation comprises nine high-ceilinged rooms with suitably old-fangled four-poster beds and bamboo blinds, brought up to date only by air-conditioning and TV; there are also a couple of four-bed dorms. The only drawback is that you're fifteen minutes' walk from the bus station and the humdrum **restaurants** of the centre, but the tranquil atmosphere more than compensates. If you're arriving on the #31 bus, getting off just after the "Daulat Tuanku" archway at the western edge of town leaves you with just a short walk to the *Rest House*. It's also possible to find **homestays** in the area; contact the Kuantan tourist office for details.

Travel details

Trains

The rail terminus is at Tumpat, on the coast 12km north of Kota Bharu, though Wakaf Bharu is the closest station to the city. Express services run once daily in each direction between Tumpat and KL, and between Tumpat and Singapore. They're supplemented by slow local services (stopping at almost every minor station, and denoted "Mel" on timetables) between Tumpat and Gua Musang. While the frequencies given here are for the two types of service combined, the journey times are for express services unless otherwise stated; local trains take roughly half again as long.
Kota Bharu (Wakaf Bharu station) to: Dabong (5 daily; 2hr); Gemas (3 daily; 8hr); Gua Musang (5 daily; 3hr 30min); Jerantut (3 daily; 6hr); Johor Bahru (1 daily; 13hr 30min); Kuala Krai (5 daily; 1hr 15min); Kuala Lipis (3 daily; 5hr); Kuala Lumpur (1 daily; 13hr 15min); Merapoh (for Taman Negara's Merapoh gate; local; 1 daily; 6hr 15min); Seremban (1 daily; 11hr 45min); Singapore (1 daily; 14hr 30min).

Buses

Kota Bharu to: Alor Setar (2 daily; 8hr); Butterworth (2 daily; 8hr); Johor Bahru (3 daily; 12hr); Kuala Lumpur (several daily; 9hr); Kuala Terengganu (at least 8 daily; 3–4hr); Kuantan (at least 10 daily; 7hr); Melaka (1 daily; 10hr). For details of buses into Thailand, see p.295.
Kuala Terengganu to: Alor Setar (2 daily; 9hr 30min); Butterworth (2 daily; 12hr); Cherating (at least 10 daily; 3hr 30min); Ipoh (2 daily; 10hr); Johor Bahru (5 daily; 9hr); Kemaman/Chukai (10 daily; 3hr); Kota Bharu (at least 8 daily; 3–4hr); Kuala Besut (8 daily; 2hr 30min); Kuala Lumpur (every 1–2hr; 8hr 30min); Kuantan (at least 10 daily; 4–5hr); Marang (at least hourly; 30min); Melaka (3 daily; 10hr); Merang (8 daily; 1hr); Mersing (5 daily; 7hr); Rantau Abang (at least hourly; 1hr 30min); Singapore (2 daily; 10hr 30min).
Kuantan to: Alor Setar (4 daily; 10hr); Butterworth (4 daily; 9hr); Cherating (every 30min–1hr; 1hr–1hr 30min); Felda Chini (for Tasik Chini; 5–6 daily; 1hr

30min); Ipoh (4 daily; 6hr); Jerantut (3 daily; 3hr); Johor Bahru (at least 6 daily; 5hr 30min); Kota Bharu (at least 10 daily; 7hr); Kuala Lipis (3 daily; 5hr); Kuala Lumpur (at least hourly; 3hr); Marang (several daily; 3hr 30min); Kuala Terengganu (at least 12 daily; 4–5hr); Melaka (1 daily; 6hr); Mersing (6 daily; 3hr); Pekan (hourly; 1hr); Singapore (4 daily; 6hr 30min); Taiping (4 daily; 7hr); Temerloh (hourly; 2hr).

Tasik Kenyir (Pangkalan Gawi) to: Kuala Lumpur (2 daily; 8hr).

Flights

Kota Bharu to: Johor Bahru (3 weekly; 1hr 10min); Kuala Lumpur (at least 8 daily; 1hr).

Kuala Terengganu to: Kuala Lumpur (at least 6 daily; 45min).

Kuantan to: Kuala Lumpur (at least 5 daily; 40min).

Pulau Redang to: Kuala Lumpur (Subang airport; March–Oct daily; 45min); Singapore (Seletar airport; March–Oct 4 weekly; 1hr).

The south

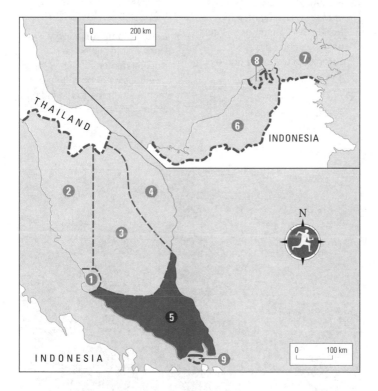

CHAPTER 5

Highlights

✳ **Minangkabau architecture** The towns of Seremban and Sri Menanti are home to the spectacular and distinctive architecture of the Minangkabau, an ancient Sumatran tribe. See p.356

✳ **Melaka** The historic heritage of Melaka is evident in its Portuguese, Dutch and British buildings and unique Peranakan ancestral homes. See p.360

✳ **Pulau Tioman** Palm-fringed, scenic and with great diving, this has been named one of the ten most beautiful islands in the world. See p.395

✳ **Seribuat Archipelago** Tioman may attract all the attention, but it's the other islands of the Seribuat Archipelago that offer the best beaches and real seclusion. See p.407

✳ **Endau Rompin National Park** A little-visited lush tropical rainforest, rich with rare species of both flora and fauna and home to the indigenous Orang Ulu. See p.411

△ The Istana Lama, Sri Menanti

The south

The south of the Malay Peninsula, below Kuala Lumpur and Kuantan, has some of the most historically and culturally significant towns in the country. In the fifteenth century, the foundation of the west-coast city of **Melaka** led to a Malay "golden age" under the Muslim Melaka Sultanate, during which period the concept of *Melayu* (Malayness), still current in Malaysia, was established. For all its influence, the sultanate was surprisingly short-lived, its fall in the early sixteenth century to the Portuguese marking the start of centuries of **colonial involvement** in Malaysia. The Dutch and British followed the Portuguese in Melaka; indeed, British colonial rule was an essential part of the eighteenth- and nineteenth-century development of the country. Melaka also boasts the unique culture of the Peranakan community (also called Baba-Nonya), the society that resulted from the intermarriage of early Chinese immigrant traders and Malay women.

Just two hours by bus from KL, Melaka, in the centre of a small state of the same name, makes a logical starting point for exploring the south. While its sights will keep you absorbed for several days, other local destinations make good day-trips: the easy-going towns of **Muar** and **Segamat**, **Pulau Besar**, and the coastal villages of **Tanjung Bidara** and **Tanjung Kling**. Between KL and Melaka, the region that's now the state of Negeri Sembilan is where the intrepid **Minangkabau** tribes from Sumatra settled, making their mark in the spectacular architecture of **Seremban** and **Sri Menanti**, both just over an hour south of the capital by road.

At the tip of the Peninsula, the town of **Johor Bahru** (or JB) dates back only to 1855, its origins in the establishment of a settlement, Tanjung Puteri, across the Johor Straits from Singapore. Visitors tend to travel along the east or west coasts, from KL and Kuantan to JB, avoiding the mountainous interior where the road network is poor. Along with the train line, the North–South Expressway (NSE) connects KL with Singapore via the west coast; its counterpart, the narrow Route 3 on the east coast, is a good deal more varied, winding for 300km through oil-palm country and past luxuriant beaches. Most people head for the active little seaport of **Mersing** in order to reach **Pulau Tioman** and the other islands of the **Seribuat Archipelago** – a draw for divers and snorkellers as well as those who simply like the idea of sandy beaches and transparent waters. Increasingly, visitors are also getting off the beaten track to see the primeval **Endau Rompin National Park**, the southernmost tropical rainforest in the Peninsula. It's a worthy and more rugged alternative to the much-visited Taman Negara further north.

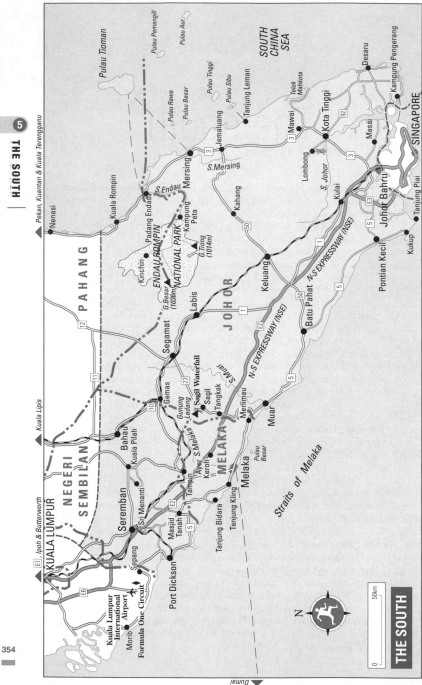

THE SOUTH

0   50km

N

Negeri Sembilan

In the fifteenth century, the Minangkabau tribes from Sumatra established themselves in the Malay state of **Negeri Sembilan**, whose modern-day capital is the town of **Seremban**, 67km south of Kuala Lumpur. The cultural heart of the state though, is the royal town of **Sri Menanti**, 30km east of Seremban. Centres of **Minangkabau** civilization (see box on pp.356–357) since the early years of the Melaka Sultanate, both towns showcase traditional Minangkabau architecture, typified by distinctive, saddle-shaped roofs.

The modern state of Negeri Sembilan is based on an old confederacy of nine districts (hence its name – *sembilan* being Malay for "nine"). By the middle of the nineteenth century, the thriving **tin trade** and British control over the area were well established, with colonial authority administered from Sungai Ujong (today's Seremban). Wars between rival Malay and Minangkabau groups for control over the mining and transportation of tin were commonplace, most notably between the Dato' Kelana, the chief of Sungai Ujong, and the Dato' Bandar, who controlled the middle part of Sungai Linggi, further to the south.

The heavy influx of Chinese immigrants – who numbered about half the total population of Negeri Sembilan by the time of the first official census in 1891 – only had the effect of prolonging the feuds, since their secret societies, or Triads, attempted to manipulate the situation to gain local influence. The most significant figure to emerge from this period was **Yap Ah Loy**, a charismatic leader who helped orchestrate clan rivalry through a series of violent skirmishes, one of which resulted in the sacking of Sri Menanti. He later moved to the newly established tin-mining town of Kuala Lumpur, where he quickly became an influential figure (see p.93). In an attempt to control a situation that was rapidly sliding out of control, British Governor Jervois installed Abu Bakar of Johor as overlord, a man not only respected by the Malays but also apparently sympathetic to the colonists' aims. However, two prominent British officials, Frank Swettenham (later Resident in Selangor at the time of KL's early meteoric expansion) and Frederick Weld, weren't convinced about Abu Bakar's loyalty and bypassed his authority with the use of local British officials. Learning from their mistakes in Perak, where the hurried appointment of a British advisor had caused local uproar (see p.177), the British adopted a cautious approach. A treaty was eventually signed in 1895, narrowing the divide between the British colonial authorities and the Minangkabaus that had been the cause of so much strife.

The state runs its own tourism website, ⓦ www.tourismnegerisembilan.com.

Seremban

An hour south of the capital and just twenty minutes from KL International Airport, **SEREMBAN** is a bustling town whose commercial centre is a mixture of decorative Chinese shophouses and faceless concrete structures, while further out, imposing colonial mansions line its streets. However, by far the best reason to come to Seremban is to visit the **Taman Seni Budaya Negeri** (State Arts & Culture Park; Tues, Wed, Sat & Sun 10am–6pm, Thurs 8.15am–1pm, Fri 10am–noon & 2.45–6pm; free), 3km northwest of the centre, close to the North–South Expressway. The best introduction that you could have to the principles of Minangkabau architecture, the new museum building is of traditional construction, and the grounds contain three original timber houses, reconstructed here in the 1950s. The first of these, the **Istana Ampang Tinggi**, built forty years before the palace at Sri Menanti (see p.359), was passed

The Minangkabau

The old adat, ancient heritage,
Neither rots in the rain,
Nor cracks in the sun.

Old Minangkabau proverb

The **Minangkabau people**, whose cultural heartland is in the mountainous region west of central Sumatra (Indonesia), established a community in Malaysia in the early fifteenth century. As they had no written language until the arrival of Islam, their origins are somewhat sketchy; their own oral accounts trace their ancestry to Alexander the Great, while the *Sejarah Melayu* (see p.727) talks of a mysterious leader, Nila Pahlawan, who was pronounced king of the Palembang natives by a man who was magically transformed from the spittle of an ox. Oxen feature prominently, too, in the legend surrounding the origins of the name "Minangkabau". When their original home in Sumatra came under attack from the Javanese, the native people agreed to a contest whereby the outcome of a battle fought between a tiger (representing the Javanese) and a buffalo (representing the locals) would determine who controlled the land. Against all the odds, the buffalo killed the tiger, and henceforth the inhabitants called themselves Minangkabau, meaning "the victorious buffalo".

In early times the Minangkabau were ruled in Sumatra by their own overlords or *rajas*, though political centralization never really rivalled the role of the strongly autonomous *nagari* (Sumatran for village). Each *nagari* consisted of numerous **matrilineal clans** (*suku*), each of which took the name of the mother and lived in the *adat* house, the ancestral home. The *adat* household was also in control of ancestral property, which was passed down the maternal line. The *sumando* (husband) stayed in his wife's house at night but was a constituent member of his mother's house, where most of his day was spent. But although the idea that the house and clan name belonged to the woman remained uppermost, and women dominated the domestic sphere, political and ceremonial power was in the hands of men; it was the *mamak*

down through successive generations of royalty until 1930, after which it began to fall into disrepair. The interior of the veranda, where male guests were entertained, displays a wealth of exuberant and intricate leaf carvings, with a pair of unusual heavy timber doors. The two other houses nearby are similar, though less elaborate, their gloomy interiors only relieved by shutters in the narrow front rooms. Inside the museum proper, the lower floor contains an exhibition of village handicrafts, as well as some moth-eaten stuffed animals; considerably more lively are the old photographs on show, though little of the labelling is in English. The easiest way to get here is to take a taxi from town (RM5).

North of the river from the bus and taxi stations, past the **Wesley Church** of 1920, is the business district where most of the hotels, restaurants and banks are located, including the hulking Oriental Bank with its Minangkabau-inspired roof. East along Jalan Dato' Sheikh Ahmad, a right turn leads to the recreation ground, across which the nine pillars supporting the scalloped roof of the grey concrete **Masjid Negeri** come into view. Each pillar, topped by a crescent and star, symbols of Muslim enlightenment, represents one of the nine districts of the state. Beyond this lies the artificial **Lake Garden**.

Head north along Jalan Dato' Hamzah beside the park and after a ten-minute walk you'll see the white-stuccoed Neoclassical **State Library** – once the centre of colonial administration – with its graceful columns and portico. Past the black-and-gilt wrought-iron gates of the Istana (closed to the public) just to the north, a left turn leads to the current **State Secretariat**, whose architecture (mother's brother) who took responsibility for the continued prosperity of the lineage (he was the administrative figurehead and the authority for the proper distribution of ancestral property).

While population growth and land shortage encouraged **migration**, it was the *sumando*'s lack of ties to his wife's family, and his traditional role as an entrepreneur, that facilitated his wanderlust. The society encouraged a man's desire to further his fame, fortune and knowledge, and, when Islam became more established, this was achieved by undertaking religious studies under famous teachers or visits to Mecca.

When and why the Minangkabaus initially emigrated to what is now **Negeri Sembilan** in Malaysia is uncertain. Their subsequent history is closely bound up with that of Melaka and Johor, with the Minangkabau frequently called upon to supplement the armies of ambitious Malay princes and sultans. Little is known of their interaction with the native Malay population, although evidence of intermarriage with the region's predominant tribal group, the Sakai, indicates acceptance by the Malays of the matrilineal system. What is certain is that the Minangkabaus were a political force to be reckoned with. Their dominance in domestic affairs was aided by their reputation for supernatural powers, rumours of which were so widespread that the early eighteenth-century trader Alexander Hamilton noted, "Malays consider the Minangkabau to have the character of great sorcerers, who by their spells can tame wild tigers and make them carry them whither they order on their backs."

Although migration remained standard practice, after the mid-nineteenth century the drift was towards urban centres, and communal living in the *adat* house became relatively rare. In the twentieth century, two important adaptations to the matrilineal system were documented: the tendency for families from the various clans to migrate rather than just the husband; and a change in the hereditary customs, whereby individually earned property can be given to a son, becoming ancestral property only in the next generation. Today, the Minangkabau are very much integrated with the Malays, and their dialect is almost indistinguishable from standard *Bahasa Melayu*.

reflects the Minangkabau tradition. Its hillside position ensures that the layered, buffalo horn roof is one of the first sights you see in the town.

Practicalities

Seremban has regular train connections with Kuala Lumpur and is linked with both Melaka and KL by express buses. The **bus** and **taxi stations** are about five minutes' walk from the centre of town across the river, while the **train station** is just south of the centre. To get to town from KLIA, either take the bus (every 30min 7am–7pm; RM5) or get the KLIA Transit to Nilai station, than a Komuter train.

The town has a chronic shortage of decent, inexpensive **hotels** (indeed, many of the cheaper ones are brothels; the places we've listed below are all above board). There's no shortage of **places to eat**, however. The *Bilal*, at 100 Jalan Dato' Bandar Tunggal, serves reliable Indian dishes; the nearby *Suntory* restaurant on the same road, has a reasonably priced, wide-ranging Chinese menu and an air-conditioned lounge. Good Thai food is available at *Restoran Indra Rina Thai*, 4 Jalan Dato' Lee Fong Yee. There are **food stalls** along Jalan Tuanku Munawir, Jalan Dato' Lee Fong Yee, Jalan Lee Sam and close to the train station; any of the bakeries on Jalan Dato' Sheikh Ahmad is a good spot for breakfast.

Seremban is well supplied with **Internet** cafés, most of which can be found in the giant Terminal One shopping centre (next to the bus station) which also has a **cinema** on the top floor.

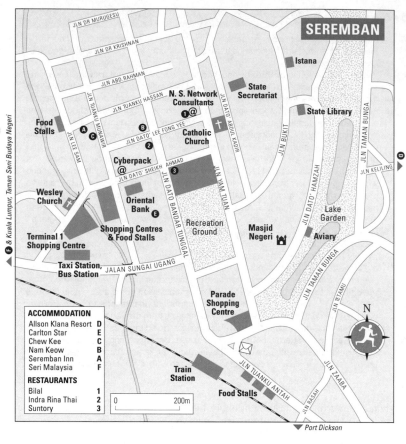

& Kuala Lumpur, Taman Seni Budaya Negeri

Port Dickson

Accommodation

Allson Klana Resort Jalan Penghula Cantik
☎06/762 9600, ⊛www.allsonklana.com.my. Set
500m east of the lake gardens, this is *the* top spot
in Seremban, with everything you'd expect from a
high-class resort hotel, including a swimming pool,
gym and restaurant. ❽

Carlton Star 47 Jalan Dato' Sheikh Ahmad
☎06/762 5336, ☎762 0040. Reasonably neat
and clean rooms with a/c and TVs, but not as good
value as the *Seremban Inn*. ❹

Chew Kee 41 Jalan Tuanku Munawir ☎06/762
2095. Cheap, uninspiring partitioned rooms, but
clean by Seremban standards. Hidden away on the
first floor of a poorly signposted building, it's just

before the *Seremban Inn* signs as you head north
from the bus or train stations. ❷

Nam Keow 61–62 Jalan Dato' Bandar Tunggal
☎06/763 5578. Seedy but passable budget option.
The large, cheap rooms here all have attached
bathrooms. ❷

Seremban Inn 39 Jalan Tuanku Munawir
☎06/761 7777, ☎763 7777. The cleanest, best
value mid-range hotel in town with helpful staff
and well-equipped rooms. ❹

Seri Malaysia Jalan Sungai Ujung ☎06/764
4181, ⊛www.serimalaysia.com.my. One kilometre
away from the bus station, on the road to Taman
Seni Budaya Negeri. A comfortable option, with
large, nicely furnished rooms; breakfast is included
in the price. ❺

Sri Menanti

Thirty kilometres east of Seremban lies the former royal capital of Negeri Sembilan, **SRI MENANTI**, its palaces, ancient and modern, set in lush, mountainous landscape. The only reason to visit this little town, however, is to see a jewel of Minangkabau architecture, the **Istana Lama** (Mon–Wed & Sat 10am–6pm, Thurs 8.30am–1pm; free). A timber palace set in geometric gardens, it was the seat of the Minangkabau rulers, whose migration to the Malay Peninsula began in the fifteenth century during the early years of the Melaka Sultanate. The sacking of Sri Menanti during the Sungei Ujong tin wars destroyed the original palace; the four-storey version that stands here now was designed and built in 1902 by two Malay master craftsmen who, as the tradition dictates, used no nails or screws in its construction. Until 1931, the palace was used as a royal residence, with the ground floor functioning as a reception area, the second as family quarters, and the third as the sultan's private apartments. The tower, once used as the treasury and royal archives, can only be reached by ladder from the sultan's private rooms and is not open to the public. At its apex is a forked projection of a type known as "open scissors", now very rarely seen (though it's reproduced in the roof of the Muzium Negara in Kuala Lumpur).

The whole rectangular building is raised nearly 2m off the ground by 99 pillars, 26 of which have been carved in low relief with complex foliated designs. Though the main doors and windows are plain, a long external veranda is covered with a design of leaves and branches known as *awan larat*, or "driving clouds". Above the front porch is the most elaborate decoration, a pair of fantastic creatures with lions' heads, horses' legs and long feathery tails, its style suggesting that the craftsmen responsible were Chinese.

Inside, the Istana Lama is of little or no decorative interest. The palace now houses the lacklustre **Muzium Di Raja** (Tues, Wed, Sat & Sun 10am–12.45pm & 2–6pm, Thurs 8am–12.45pm, Fri 10am–12.15pm & 2.45–6pm; free), a rather stuffy commemoration of local royalty, its reconstructed state rooms bedecked in yellow (the royal colour) lacking atmosphere. There are old costumes, ceremonial *keris*, golfing memorabilia and photographs of past sultans and British administrators, all of which fail to excite.

Reaching Sri Menanti is relatively straightforward. From Seremban, take a United **bus** for the 45-minute journey to Kuala Pilah. There, you can either wait for an infrequent local bus to Sri Menanti, or take a shared taxi, a ten-minute ride costing no more than RM5 per person. Tell the driver where you are going and he'll drop you off in front of the Istana Lama. Don't be misled by the sign for the Istana Besar, the rather imposing current royal palace, topped by a startling blue roof.

Port Dickson

The rather dismal strip of the **coast** stretching south of the capital to Melaka is a major draw for KL weekenders who, attracted by the populous resort of **PORT DICKSON**, turn a blind eye to its polluted sea. It's hard to see why the town, 34km southwest of Seremban, is so popular: it's not much more than a few shops and banks. Port Dickson's beach, stretching as far as the Cape Rachado (Tanjung Tuan) lighthouse, 16km to the south, is marred by passing oil tankers, sludgy brown sand, dishwater-grey sea and an enormous sewage pipe spilling out into the north of the bay. Yet it attracts a growing number of regular weekenders, to whom the town is affectionately known as PD.

Whatever the reason for the town's popularity, its hoteliers are rubbing their hands with glee. To cope with the increasing demand, new hotels and condominiums are constantly springing up along the length of the coastline – most of the developers involved have, sensibly, built swimming pools too.

Regular **bus** connections with KL ensure ease of access to all points along this stretch of coast. The coastal road, Route 5, branches west off the North–South Expressway south of KL and reaches the west coast at Morib; a little tortuous in places, the road at least makes for a more varied journey than travelling the monotonous expressway.

Practicalities

Buses from KL stop at the **bus station** in the commercial part of town, about 2km north of the beach. The best **places to stay** are strung out along Jalan Pantai (part of Route 5), which runs south of Port Dickson. Locations along the road are usually specified according to milestones – the number of which are painted on lampposts along the way, prefaced by *batu* (stone). It's easy enough to hop on any Melaka-bound bus until you reach the hotel of your choice; coming from Melaka, you can get off the buses at any point on the coastal road before reaching town. **Watersports** facilities are available at most of the hotels or at Sea Sun Water Sports (T06/647 0580) near the three-mile marker.

Most chalets and hotels have their own **restaurants**, and many other eating places line the road, of which the nicest is the Muslim *Pantai Ria*, near the seven-mile marker; it specializes in seafood and Chinese cuisine at around RM8 a dish. The food court just north of the *Regency* is also worth a visit for its range of foods and pleasant outdoor seating. The **food stalls** around the four- and five-mile markers offer everything from burgers to freshly caught fish.

Accommodation

Asrama Belia T06/647 2188. Behind a row of shops and restaurants, north of the Petronas service station at the four-mile marker. Affiliated to the IYHF (as the only sign attests), this slightly worn place has cooking facilities, clean chalets for up to four people (❷) and dorms (RM10).

Bayu Beach Resort T06/647 3703, Wwww .bayu.com. Halfway between the fourth- and fifth-mile marker. A pleasant complex of apartments offering very good-value deals for parties of four. To either side of the resort lies the best stretch of beach for a long way. ❼

Corus Paradise Resort T06/647 7600, Wwww .corusparadisepd.com. The nearest resort to PD town, near the two-mile marker. Spacious, luxury beach-front hotel with a small lagoon. As one of the newer resorts on this stretch, it's a good option at the upper end of the scale. ❻

Regency T06/647 4090, F647 4792. PD's most upmarket hotel, located near the five-mile marker. Built in striking Minangkabau style, it has facilities for watersports and tennis, along with a popular Thai restaurant. Good value. ❼

Rotary Sunshine Camp T06/647 3798. On a hill south of the three-mile marker. The cheapest accommodation in PD, a cheerful turquoise- and yellow-painted complex of basic chalets, with dorm beds only (RM6).

Seri Malaysia T06/647 6070, Wwww.serimalaysia .com.my. Just 100m south of *Rotary Sunshine Camp*, this is another in the reliable national chain of luxury hotels, although it doesn't match up to some of the extravagant resorts here in PD. ❻

Melaka and around

When Penang was known only for its oysters and Singapore was just a fishing village, **MELAKA** (formerly "Malacca") had already achieved worldwide fame. Under the auspices of the Melaka Sultanate, founded in the early fifteenth century, political and cultural life flourished, helping to define what it means to be Malay. Yet, beginning in 1511, Melaka suffered a series of takeovers and botched administrations involving the Portuguese, Dutch and British, causing the humiliating subjugation of the Malay people.

Because of its cultural legacy, there's something about Melaka that smacks of over-preservation, all too easily apparent in the brick-red paint wash that covers everything in the so-called "historical centre". At its core, the **Dutch Square** sports a fake windmill and an early twentieth-century fountain, bordering on pastiche. For a more authentic encounter with the past, it's better to strike out into **Chinatown**, where the rich Baba-Nonya (see p.374) heritage is displayed in the opulent merchants' houses and elegant restaurants that line the narrow thoroughfares. There have been attempts to sanitize and tourist-package even this area, to the extent that some traditional businesses have been forced out, but for now its character remains mostly intact. There are reminders of the human costs of empire building in the many churches and graveyards scattered around the town, where tombstones tell of whole families struck down by fever and of young men killed in battle. The **Portuguese Settlement** to the east of the centre has something of the synthetic colonial heritage that typifies Melaka, while land reclamation in the new town area, **Taman Melaka Raya**, southeast of the centre, points to the urban regeneration that the city badly needs. Out of the centre, there are a couple of places of interest, including the green-belt area of **Ayer Keroh**, 14km north of the city, and the beach resort at **Pulau Besar**.

At a push you could get around the colonial core in a day (an RM5 **ticket** can be purchased at any of the town's public museums, for entry to them all). It's better, however, to spend three days in Melaka, taking things at a more leisurely pace and seeing Chinatown and the outskirts, as many visitors find that the city grows on them the longer they stay.

Some history

The foundation of Melaka had its roots in the fourteenth-century struggles between Java and the Thai kingdom of Ayuthaya for control of the Malay Peninsula. The *Sejarah Melayu* (Malay Annals) records that when the Sumatran prince Paramesvara (from Palembang in the Srivijaya Empire; see p.729) could no longer tolerate subservience to Java, he fled to the island of Temasek (later renamed Singapore), where he set himself up as ruler. The Javanese subsequently forced him to flee north to Bertam, where he was welcomed by the local community. While his son, Iskandar Shah, was out hunting near modern-day Melaka Hill, a mousedeer turned on the pursuing hunting dogs, driving them into the sea. Taking this courageous act to be a good omen, Shah asked his father to build a new settlement there and, in searching for a name for it, he remembered the *melaka* tree, which he had been sitting under.

Melaka rapidly became a cosmopolitan market town, **trading spices** from the Moluccas in the eastern Indonesian archipelago and textiles from Gujarat in northwest India; a levy exacted on all imported goods made Melaka one of the wealthiest kingdoms in the world. With the adoption of **Islam** in the early fifteenth century, Melaka consolidated its influence; it was said that to become a Muslim was to enter the society of Melaka Malays. Melaka's meteoric rise was initially assisted by its powerful neighbours, Ayuthaya and Java, who made good use of its trading facilities. But they soon had a serious rival, as Melaka started a campaign of **territorial expansion**. By the time of the reign of its last ruler, Sultan Mahmud Shah (1488–1530), Melaka's territory included the west coast of the Peninsula as far as Perak, the whole of Pahang, Singapore and most of east-coast Sumatra. By the beginning of the sixteenth century, Melaka's population had increased to one hundred thousand, and it would not have been unusual to count as many as two thousand ships in its port.

Culturally, too, Melaka was supreme – its sophisticated language, literature and dances were all benchmarks in the Malay world. The establishment of a court structure (see box below) defined the nature of the Melaka state and the role of the individuals within it, a social system which remained virtually unchanged until the nineteenth century.

But a sea change was occurring in Europe which was to end Melaka's supremacy. The Portuguese were seeking to establish links in Asia by dominating key ports in the region and, led by Alfonso de Albuquerque, conquered Melaka in 1511. Eight hundred officers were left to administer the new colony; although subject to constant attack, the Portuguese – or "white Bengalis" as they were known by the Malays – maintained their hold on Melaka for the next 130 years, introducing Catholicism to the region through the efforts of St Francis Xavier, the "Apostle of the East". Little tangible evidence of the Portuguese remains in Melaka today (bar the Eurasian community to the east of town), a reflection of the fairly tenuous nature of their rule, which relied on the internal squabbles of local leaders to dissolve any threats to the Portuguese position.

However, the formation of the Vereenigde Oostindische Compagnie (VOC), or **Dutch East India Company**, in 1602 spelled the end of the Portuguese.

Malay court structures

One of the most outstanding achievements of the Melaka Sultanate was to create a **court structure**, setting a pattern of government that was to last for the next five hundred years, and whose prominent figures are still reflected in the street names of most towns in the country. At the top of the hierarchy was the **sultan** who, by virtue of his ancestry (which could be traced back to the mighty empire of Srivijaya), embodied the mystique which set Melaka apart from its rivals. He was far from being an autocratic tyrant: a form of social contract evolved whereby the ruler could expect undying loyalty from his subjects in return for a fair and wise dispensation of justice (this was the crux of the confrontation between Hang Tuah and Hang Jebat; see box, p.370). Nor were sultans remote ceremonial figures; many supervised the planting of new crops, for instance, or wandered freely in the streets among the people, a style of behaviour that may explain the relative humility of the palaces they occupied.

Below the ruler was a clutch of **ministers**, who undertook the day-to-day administration of government. The most important of these was the **Bendahara**, who dealt with disputes among traders and among the Malays themselves. In effect, he was the public face of the regime, wielding a great deal of power, backed by his closest subordinate, the **Penghulu Bendahari**, who supervised the syahbandars (harbour masters) and the sultan's domestic staff. Potential bendaharas were trained at the office of the **Temenggung**, who was responsible for law and order, working in close partnership with the **Laksamana**, the military commander, whose strongest armed force was the navy. Wide-ranging consultation regarding new measures took place in a **council of nobles**, who had earned their titles either through land ownership or from blood ties with royalty. Little is known of the **common people** of Melaka, though it is certain that they had no part in the decision-making process; the Sejarah Melayu nevertheless speaks of them with some respect: "Subjects are like roots and the ruler is like the tree; without roots the tree cannot stand upright."

To reinforce the status of the royal family, the colour yellow was only allowed to be used by royalty and no one but the ruler was permitted to wear gold – unless it was a royal gift. In addition, commoners could not have pillars or enclosed verandas in their houses, or windows and reception rooms in their boats. Despite these methods of distinction, threats to the throne were commonplace – particularly from the Bendahara.

Having already founded Batavia (modern-day Jakarta), the VOC set its sights on Melaka, for the saying was, "Whoever controls Melaka has his hands on the throat of Venice". The ascendancy of Johor, an enemy of the Portuguese, gave the Dutch a natural ally, but although they made several attempts on Melaka from 1606 onwards, it wasn't until January 14, 1641, after a five-month siege, that they finally captured the city.

Where the Portuguese had tried to impose rule on the Malays, the Dutch sought to integrate them, finding them useful on matters of etiquette when negotiating with other Malay rulers. The Protestant Dutch made half-hearted attempts at religious conversion, including translating the Bible into Malay, but on the whole their attitude to the Catholic Melakans was tolerant. Chinese immigrants were drawn to the city in large numbers, often becoming more successful in business than their European rulers; many of the Chinese married Malay women, creating a new racial mix known as **Peranakan** or Baba-Nonya. However, the settlement never really expanded in the way the VOC had hoped. High taxes drove merchants away to more profitable ports such as the newly founded Penang, and the Dutch relied ever more on force to maintain their position in the Straits – which lost them the respect of their Malay subjects. A ditty put about by their British rivals at that time had it that, "In matters of commerce, the fault of the Dutch/Is offering too little and asking too much".

The superior maritime skills and commercial adroitness of the British East India Company (EIC) provided serious competition for the control of Melaka. Weakened by French threats on their posts in the Indies, the Dutch were not prepared to put up a fight and handed Melaka over to the British on August 15, 1795, initially on the understanding that the EIC was to act as a caretaker administration until such time as the Dutch were able to resume control. For a while Melaka flew two flags and little seemed to have changed: the language, the legal system and even some of the officials remained the same as before. But the EIC was determined that Penang be the principal settlement on the coast and against the advice of the Resident, William Farquhar, ordered the destruction of Melaka's magnificent fort to deter future settlers. In fact, the whole population of Melaka would have been forcibly moved to Penang had it not been for Thomas Stamford Raffles, convalescing there at the time, who managed to impress upon the London office the impracticality – not to mention the cruelty – of such a measure.

Despite the liberalizing of trade by Farquhar, the colony continued to decline, and with the establishment of the free-trade port of Singapore in 1819, looked set to disintegrate. British administrators – just thirty in number, though this rose slowly to around 330 by 1931 – attempted to revitalize Melaka, introducing progressive agricultural and mining concerns, while the **Chinese** continued to flock to the town, taking over former Dutch mansions. However, investment in new hospitals, schools and a railway did little to improve Melaka's spiralling deficit. It wasn't until a Chinese entrepreneur, Tan Chay Yan, began to plant **rubber** that Melaka's problems were alleviated for a time; the industry boomed during the early years of the twentieth century. After World War I, though, even this commodity faced mixed fortunes – when the **Japanese occupied** Melaka in 1942, they found a town exhausted by the interwar depression.

Modern-day developments, such as the land reclamation in Taman Melaka Raya and the reorganization of the chaotic road network, are still working to reverse Melaka's long-term decline. Whatever damage was wrought during its centuries of colonial mismanagement, nothing can take away the enduring

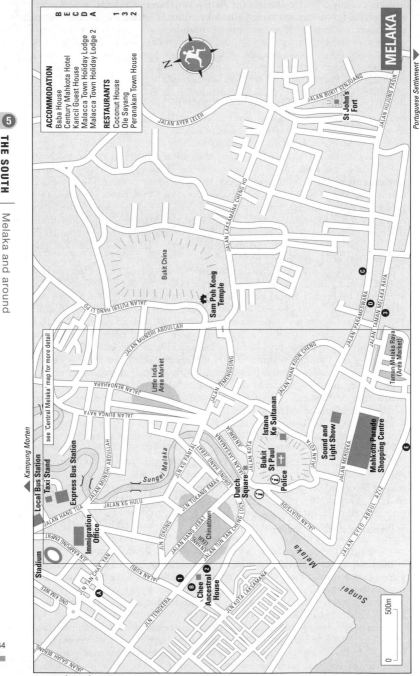

◄ Kampung Morten

◄ Masjid Tranquerah

ACCOMMODATION
Baba House   B
Century Mahkota Hotel   E
Kancil Guest House   C
Malacca Town Holiday Lodge   D
Malacca Town Holiday Lodge 2   A

RESTAURANTS
Coconut House   1
Ole Sayang   3
Peranakan Town House   2

MELAKA

Portuguese Settlement ►

JALAN AYER LELEH

Bukit China

Sam Poh Kong Temple

JALAN MUNSHI ABDULLAH

JALAN PUTERI HANG LI PO

Little India
Area Market

JALAN BENDAHARA

JALAN BUNGA RAYA

JALAN LAKSAMANA CHENG HO

St John's Fort

JALAN BUKIT SENJUANG

JALAN HUJUNG PASIR

JALAN PARAMESWARA

JALAN TAMAN MELAKA RAYA

Taman Melaka Raya
(Area Market)

JALAN CHAN KOON CHENG

JALAN KEMENGGONG

Istana
Ke Sultanan

Bukit
St Paul

Police

Sound and
Light Show

Mahkota Parade
Shopping Centre

JALAN KOTA

JALAN MERDEKA

JALAN QUAYSIDE

JALAN SYED ABDUL AZIZ

Sungei Melaka

Dutch
Square

JALAN LAKSAMANA

JALAN KOTA

JALAN HANG TUA

JALAN MUNSHI ABDULLAH

Local Bus Station

Taxi Stand

Express Bus Station

Immigration
Office

see 'Central Melaka' map for more detail

JALAN KAMPUNG EMPAT

JALAN KG HULU

JLN KG PANTAI

JLN TUKANG EMAS

LORONG HANG JEBAT

JALAN HANG JEBAT

JALAN TUN TAN CHENG LOCK

Chinatown

Chee Ancestral
House

JLN TOKONG

JALAN HANG LEKIR

Stadium

JLN CHAY YAN

ONG KIM WEE

JALAN KUBU

JLN TENGKERA

JLN KOTA LAKSAMANA

Sungei Melaka

JALAN GAJAH BERANG

500m

0

influence of Melaka's creation of a Malay language, court system and royal lineage – a powerful legacy established in a mere hundred years that was to permanently affect development in the Peninsula.

Arrival, information and city transport

Both bus stations are located on the northern outskirts of the city, off Jalan Hang Tuah. In a tiny square by the river is the chaotic **express bus station**, just south of the **taxi stand**. The **local bus station** just north of the taxi stand operates services to and from most destinations within the conurbation, as well as Singapore. From either, it's just a ten-minute walk to the town centre. Many of the streets are very narrow and the one-way system is awkward, so **drivers** should park their cars at the first possible opportunity and get around the city by bus, trishaw or taxi.

Many people arrive by **ferry** on the two-hour daily service from Dumai in Sumatra, which docks at the Shah Bandar jetty near Jalan Quayside, within easy walking distance of both the historical centre and the budget hostel area. Melaka's **airport**, Batu Berendam, is 9km north of the city and handles a small number of Merpati Air services from Sumatra. The no. 56 bus from the airport into the centre is irregular, so it's best to take a taxi into town (around RM25). There's no **train station** in Melaka itself, the nearest being at Tampin, 38km away; buses from there drop you at the local bus station.

The very helpful **tourist office** is on Jalan Kota (Mon–Sat 9am–5pm, Sun 9am–4.30pm; ☏06/283 6538), 400m from the Shah Bandar jetty. The information board outside displays the times of the river trips to Kampung Morten (see p.375).

City transport

Most of the places of interest are located within the compact historical centre, and so are best visited **on foot**. For longer journeys, **taxis** or **trishaws** are

Moving on from Melaka

By air

From Batu Berendam airport, which caters only for small aircraft, Merpati Air (☏06/317 4175) runs a service to Padang in Sumatra. For tickets, contact Asfora Travel & Tours (☏06/282 9888).

By bus

There are frequent departures from the express bus station to KL, Ipoh, Butterworth, Alor Setar, Mersing, Singapore and other points on the Peninsula. There's rarely any need to book in advance: just turn up before departure and buy a ticket from one of the booths at the bus station.

By ferry

There are two services daily to Dumai in Sumatra at 9am and 3pm (RM80 one-way; 2hr): for tickets and information contact Tunas Rupat at 17a Jalan Merdeka (☏06/283 2506).

By train

From Tampin train station, 38km to the north of town (☏06/341 1034), there's a daily train service to Singapore via JB. There are regular buses to Tampin (40 min) from the local bus station.

the best bet, both costing roughly the same (though trishaw drivers are more difficult to negotiate with); a sightseeing tour by trishaw, covering all the major sights including the Portuguese Settlement, costs RM40–50 per hour for two people. You should be able to get a trishaw around the Dutch Square and outside the Mahkota Parade shopping centre. Taxis are quite hard to find on the street, but you can always get one from the taxi stand; a trip from the bus station to the centre costs around RM8–10.

The **town bus service** has several useful routes for visitors, departing the local bus station: #17 runs to Taman Melaka Raya and the Portuguese Settlement (50 sen to either), and #19 out to Ayer Keroh (RM1.20).

Accommodation

Melaka has a huge selection of **hotels**, although prices are a little higher than in other Malaysian towns. Most in the lower price bracket are located in the noisiest areas, around the bus stations or main shopping streets. Standards are generally high though, compared to those in KL or Georgetown. In the Taman Melaka Raya area (bus #17 from the local bus station; a taxi or trishaw there costs RM5) there's a rapidly growing number of budget **hostels**, all offering broadly the same facilities. Amiable guesthouse reps wait at the local bus station armed with photos to help you decide on your accommodation. Most work on a fee rather than commission and are a good source of information.

Baba House 125 Jalan Tun Tan Cheng Lock ☎06/281 1216, ⊛www.melaka.net /babahouse. These beautifully restored Peranakan houses have been turned into an atmospheric hotel, though the lobby area is better than the rooms themselves, which are a little small. ❹

Century Mahkota Hotel Jalan Merdeka ☎06/281 2828. The newest five-star hotel in Melaka, with swimming pool, poolside pizza terrace and regular price-promotions. ❼

Chong Hoe 26 Jalan Tukong Emas ☎06/282 6102. A well-looked-after hotel in Chinatown offering smallish rooms with a/c and showers, though the lobby – within earshot of the temple and mosque – can be noisy. ❷

Eastern Heritage 8 Jalan Bukit China ☎06/283 3026, ⊛www.eastern-heritage .com. One of the best budget hostels in Melaka, set in an imaginatively decorated house that makes the best of its original architectural features. The dorms and rooms are spotless, and there are nice touches such as a plunge pool and a batik workshop. The sole drawback is that there's only one bathroom. Dorm beds RM8, rooms ❷

Equatorial Jalan Bandar Hilir ☎06/628 28333, ⊛www.equatorial.com. With brightly decorated rooms boasting huge beds, and a wide range of restaurants, this comes a close second to the *Renaissance* in terms of grandeur. Recommended. ❻

Heeren House Jalan Tun Tan Cheng Lock ☎06/281 4241, ✉herenhse@tm.net.my. An ideal location in Chinatown and tasteful rooms – some with four-poster beds – make this a good choice for a small, upmarket hotel. Prices, which include breakfast, are slightly higher at weekends. ❻

Hotel Puri Jalan Tun Tan Cheng Lock ☎06/282 5588, ⊛www.hotelpuri.com. Set in a beautifully restored Peranakan shophouse, this is one of the best-value options in town. Rooms are decorated in a contemporary style and make good use of space. Breakfast is included in the rates. ❻

Kancil Guest House 177 Jalan Parameswara ☎06/281 4044, ⊛www .machinta.com.sg/kancil/. Lovely guesthouse in an old Chinese ancestral home with a small garden and terrace. Facilities include library, email, bicycles for hire and plenty of information. ❷

Malacca 27a Jalan Munshi Abdullah ☎06/282 2252. Housed in a crumbling old building, this hotel boasts large rooms full of substantial old wooden furniture. The noisy road is a drawback, though it's otherwise good value and handy for the bus station just over the bridge. ❷

Malacca Town Holiday Lodge 148b Jalan Taman Melaka Raya 1 ☎06/284 8830. Above the large *Kingdom* restaurant. Run by the Lee family, who now have another guesthouse west of the bus station, this is a friendly place, a shade less expensive than its partner establishment. There's a choice of rooms, with or without attached showers. ❶

Malacca Town Holiday Lodge 2 52a Kampong Empat ☎06/284 6905. Occupying the three floors of the Wine and Spirit Association building, this slightly tired-looking hostel's rooms are all named after famous brands of liquor. Apart from being in a quiet area, there's some antique Chinese furniture to add to the atmosphere, plus bicycle rental (RM10 a day) and a wide choice of rooms. Very popular with Japanese backpackers. ❷

May Chiang 59 Jalan Munshi Abdullah ☎06/282 2101. Modest Chinese-style hotel with small rooms which, though not quite as large as the *Malacca's*, are relatively clean. ❷

Renaissance Melaka Jalan Bendahara ☎06/284 8888, ⓦwww.renaissancehotels.com/mkzrn. The town's foremost luxury hotel, with an imposing lobby – complete with huge chandeliers – and elegant, well-furnished rooms. ❾

Robin's Nest 205b Jalan Melaka Raya 1 ☎06/282 9142. This friendly hostel has dorms and small but clean rooms. There are hot showers, kitchen facilities and a pleasant lounge. Dorm beds RM9, rooms ❷

Traveller's Lodge 214b Jalan Melaka Raya 1 ☎06/226 5709. As pleasant a hostel as you'll find in Malaysia. Spotlessly clean and efficiently maintained, this family-run place boasts a shady roof terrace, handy cafeteria and traditional Malay-style lounge area complete with books and board games. ❷

The City

The centre of Melaka is split in two by the murky **Sungai Melaka**, the western bank of which is occupied by **Chinatown** and, 2km to the north, **Kampung Morten**, a small collection of stilted houses. On the eastern side of the river lies the colonial core – the main area of interest – with **Bukit St Paul** at its centre, encircled by Jalan Kota. Southeast of here is a section of reclaimed land known as **Taman Melaka Raya**, a new town that's home to a giant shopping centre and many of the budget hotels, restaurants and bars. There are a few sights further east of the centre, a little too far flung to be comfortably covered on foot: the **Portuguese Settlement**, **St John's Fort** and **Bukit China**, the last of these being the Chinese community's ancestral burial ground. Town bus #17 runs regularly to the Portuguese Settlement, 3km from town, from where St John's Fort is only about a kilometre's walk; you can take a taxi or trishaw from the latter to Bukit China (around RM10 for a trishaw).

Central Melaka's historic buildings are denoted as such by being painted a uniform brick-red. Intended to symbolize the red laterite from which many of Melaka's original structures were constructed, this practice has, sadly, destroyed the individual character of each building. That said, it has at least meant that the area has been kept in reasonable condition.

The Istana to the Islamic Museum

On Jalan Kota, the **Istana ke Sultanan** (daily 9am–6pm, closed Fri 12.15–2.45pm; RM2), in the geographical centre of town, has played a central role in Malaysian history. The imposing dark-timber palace, in neatly manicured gardens, is a contemporary reconstruction, based on a description in the *Sejarah Melayu*, of the original fifteenth-century istana. In the best Malay architectural tradition, its multilayered, sharply sloping roofs contain no nails. It was here that the administrative duties of the state were carried out, and also where the sultan resided when in the city (for the most part he lived further upriver at Bertam, safe from possible attacks on Melaka). Inside – remove your shoes to ascend the wide staircase to the verandaed first floor – is a cultural museum which houses an interesting and colourful display of life-sized re-creations of scenes from Malay court life, including the epic duel of Melaka's most famous warriors, Hang Tuah and Hang Jebat (see box, p.370), as well as costumes and local crafts. The building alone, though, is worth the entrance fee.

At the time of their conquest of Melaka, the Portuguese used the forced labour of fifteen hundred slaves to construct the mighty **A Famosa** fort. All that's left

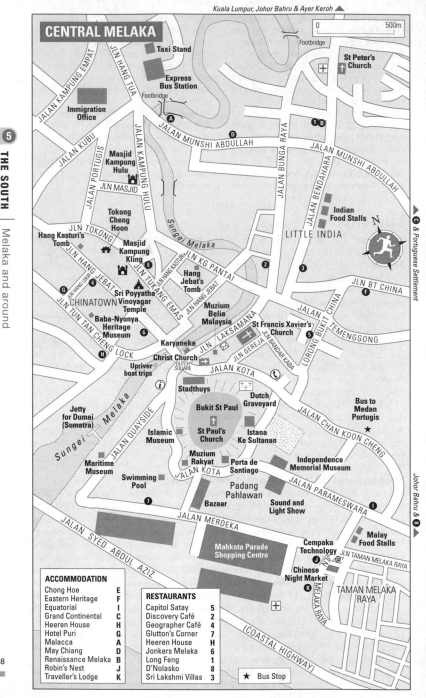

Kuala Lumpur, Johor Bahru & Ayer Keroh ▲

CENTRAL MELAKA

0   500m

Footbridge

Taxi Stand

Express
Bus Station

Footbridge

Immigration
Office

St Peter's
Church

Ⓐ   Ⓓ   Ⓑ

JALAN MUNSHI ABDULLAH

JLN HANG TUA

JALAN KAMPUNG EMPAT

JALAN KUBU

JALAN PORTUGIS

Masjid
Kampung
Hulu

JLN MASJID

JALAN KAMPUNG HULU

Sungei Melaka

JALAN MUNSHI ABDULLAH

JALAN BENDAHARA

JALAN BUNGA RAYA

Indian
Food Stalls

LITTLE INDIA

N

Tokong
Cheng
Hoon

JLN TOKONG

Hang Kasturi's
Tomb

Masjid
Kampung
Kling

JLN KG PANTAI

JLN KASTURI

Ⓔ

Hang
Jebat's
Tomb

Ⓒ

Ⓖ & Portuguese Settlement

Ⓖ   Ⓕ

Ⓖ

CHINATOWN

JLN HANG LEKIR

JLN HANG JEBAT

Ⓔ

Sri Poyyatha
Vinoyagar
Temple

JLN TUKANG EMAS

JLN HANG JEBAT

Muzium
Belia
Malaysia

St Francis Xavier's
Church

Ⓔ

JLN BT CHINA

JALAN TEMENGGONG

Ⓕ

Baba-Nyonya
Heritage
Museum

Ⓗ

JLN TUN TAN CHENG LOCK

Ⓖ

Karyaneka

JLN LAKSAMANA

JLN BANDAR KABA

LORONG BUKIT CHINA

JALAN BUKIT CHINA

Ⓖ

Christ Church

Upriver
boat trips

DUTCH
SQUARE

JLN GEREJA

Ⓒ

JALAN KOTA

ⓘ

Stadthuys

Dutch
Graveyard

Bus to
Medan
Portugis

★

Jetty
for Dumai
(Sumatra)

Bukit St Paul

St Paul's
Church

Istana
Ke Sultanan

JALAN CHAN KOON CHENG

JALAN QUAYSIDE

Sungei Melaka

Islamic
Museum

Muzium
Rakyat

Porta de
Santiago

Independence
Memorial Museum

Maritime
Museum

Swimming
Pool

Ⓖ

JALAN KOTA

Padang
Pahlawan

JALAN PARAMESWARA

Ⓘ

Johor Bahru & 8 ▲

Bazaar

Sound and
Light Show

JALAN MERDEKA

Malay
Food Stalls

JALAN SYED ABDUL AZIZ

Mahkota Parade
Shopping Centre

Cempaka
Technology

Ⓙ

JLN TAMAN MELAKA RAYA

@

Chinese
Night Market

Ⓚ

TAMAN MELAKA
RAYA

MELAKA RAYA

(COASTAL HIGHWAY)

ACCOMMODATION

Chong Hoe	E
Eastern Heritage	F
Equatorial	I
Grand Continental	C
Heeren House	G
Hotel Puri	H
Malacca	A
May Chiang	D
Renaissance Melaka	B
Robin's Nest	J
Traveller's Lodge	K

RESTAURANTS

Capitol Satay	5
Discovery Café	2
Geographer Café	4
Glutton's Corner	7
Heeren House	H
Jonkers Melaka	6
Long Feng	1
D'Nolasko	8
Sri Lakshmi Villas	3

★ Bus Stop

of it today is a single gate, the crumbling whitewashed **Porta de Santiago**, just to the right as you leave the palace museum. The hillside site was chosen not only for its strategic position but also because it was where the sultan's istana was located – its replacement by the Portuguese stronghold a firm reminder of who was now in charge. Square in plan, with walls nearly 3m thick, the fort's most striking feature was the keep in the northwestern corner, which loomed 40m and four storeys high over the rest of the garrison. This was no mean feat of engineering, even if the design of the fort as a whole was considered old-fashioned by contemporary European observers. When it defeated the Portuguese in 1641, the Dutch East India Company used the fort as its head-

△ Porta de Santiago, Melaka

quarters, later modifying it, adding the company crest and the date 1670 to the Porta de Santiago – features which are just about distinguishable today.

The fort stood steadfast for 296 years and probably would have survived, were it not for the arrival of the British in 1795. With their decision to relocate to Penang, orders were given in 1807 to destroy the fort in case it was later used against them. The task of demolition fell to Resident William Farquhar, who reluctantly set about the task with gangs of labourers armed with spades and pickaxes. Failing to make an impression on its solid bulk, he resorted to gunpowder, blowing sky-high pieces that were "as large as elephants and even some as large as houses". Munshi Abdullah wrote that the fort "was the pride of Melaka and after its destruction the place lost its glory, like a woman bereaved of her husband, the lustre gone from her face".

In 2003 the construction of a shopping mall at the northern edge of Padang Pahlawan uncovered walls of the fort five metres below ground – walls that had previously been thought to have been destroyed by the British. The laterite bricks are believed by local archeologists to be the foundation and walls of Santiago Bastion, part of the original Portuguese fort.

Turning your back on the gate, you'll see the **Independence Memorial Museum** (Tues–Thurs, Sat & Sun 9am–6pm, Fri 9am–noon & 3–6pm; free). Built in 1912, this elegant mansion of classic white stucco, with two golden onion domes on either side of its portico, formerly housed the colonial **Malacca Club**, whose most famous guest was the novelist Somerset Maugham. This is where he was told the tale which was the basis of his short story, *Footprints in the Jungle*, in which both the Club and Melaka itself (which he calls

If any ruler puts a single one of his subjects to shame, that shall be a sign that his kingdom will be destroyed by Almighty God. Similarly it has been granted by Almighty God to Malay subjects that they shall never be disloyal or treacherous to their rulers, even if their rulers behave evilly or inflict injustice on them.

From the *Sejarah Melayu*

Recounted in the seventeenth-century epic *Hikayat Hang Tuah*, the tale of the duel between **Hang Tuah** and **Hang Jebat** symbolizes the conflict between absolute loyalty to the sovereign and the love of a friend. These two characters, together with Hang Kasturi, Hang Lekir and Hang Lekiu, formed a band known as "The Five Companions" (because of their close relationship since birth), and were highly trained in the martial arts. When they saved the life of Bendahara Paduka Raja, the highest official in the Malay court, Sultan Mansur Shah was so impressed by their skill that he appointed them court attendants. Hang Tuah rapidly became the sultan's favourite and was honoured with a beautiful *kris*, **Taming Sari**, which was said to have supernatural powers. This overt favouritism rankled with other long-serving officials who, in the absence from court of the rest of the companions, conspired to cast a slur on Hang Tuah's reputation by spreading the rumour that he had seduced one of the sultan's consorts. On hearing the accusation, the sultan was so enraged that he ordered the immediate execution of Hang Tuah. But the bendahara, knowing the charge to be false, hid Hang Tuah to repay his debt to him, reporting back to the sultan that the deed had been carried out.

When Hang Jebat returned to the palace, he was shocked to discover Hang Tuah's supposed death and rampaged through Melaka, killing everyone in sight as retribution for the life of his treasured friend. The sultan, in fear of his own life, soon began to regret his decision, at which point the bendahara revealed the truth and Hang Tuah was brought back to protect the sultan from Hang Jebat's fury and to exact justice for the murders committed. Hang Tuah wrestled hard with his conscience before deciding that the sultan had the absolute right to dispose of his subjects how he wished. So, with a heavy heart, Hang Tuah drew his *kris* against Hang Jebat and, after a protracted fight, killed him, a much-recounted tale whose moral – of deference to the sovereign – is seen by some as setting the seal on the Malay system of government.

Tanah Merah) feature prominently. The museum depicts the fascinating events surrounding the run-up to independence in 1957 and showcases the proud achievements of modern Malaysia.

The Muzium Rakyat and the Islamic Museum

Skirting west round the base of the hill from Porta de Santiago brings you to the **Muzium Rakyat** (People's Museum; daily 9am–6pm; Fri closed 12.15–2.45pm; RM2) on Jalan Kota. Its ground and first floors house exhibits showing the development and successes of Melaka during the last decade – fine if you're into housing policy and the structure of local government. The third floor contains the much more interesting – and at times gruesome – **Museum of Enduring Beauty** (covered by Muzium Rakyat ticket). Taking "endure" in the sense of "to suffer", the exhibits show how people have always sought to alter their appearance, no matter how painful the process might be: head deformation, dental mutilations, tattooing, scarification and foot-binding are just some of the "beautifying" processes on display. For some light relief, the top floor here has a display of **kites** from Malaysia and around the world.

Continuing north along Jalan Kota brings you to the **Islamic Museum** (daily 9am–6pm; Fri closed 12.15–2.45pm; RM1) housed in a renovated Dutch building. Billed as an introduction to Islam and the Muslim way of life, the displays focus on Islamic culture as is practised by ethnic Malays from Sumatra to Mindinao.

Bukit St Paul

If you double back through the Porta de Santiago and climb up the steps behind, past the trinket and picture sellers, you reach **Bukit St Paul**. An alternative route from Jalan Kota is up a steep set of steps near the museum. On the summit stands the shell – roofless, desolate and smothered in ferns – of **St Paul's Church**, a ruin for almost as long as it was a functioning church. Constructed in 1521 by the Portuguese, who named it "Our Lady of the Mount", the church was visited by the Jesuit missionary **St Francis Xavier** between 1545 and 1552. On his death in 1553 his body was brought here for burial – a brass plaque on the south wall of the chancel marks the spot where he was laid. A grisly story surrounds the exhumation of the saint's body in 1554 for transfer to its final resting place in Goa in India. In response to a request for his canonization, the Vatican demanded his right arm which, when severed from his body – which allegedly showed very few signs of decay after nine months of burial – appeared to drip blood. A related tale concerns the marble statue of St Francis that has stood in front of the church since 1952: on the morning following its consecration ceremony, a large *casuarina* tree was found to have fallen on the statue, severing the right arm.

The Dutch Calvinists changed the denomination of the church when they took over in 1641, renaming it St Paul's Church, and it remained in use for a further 112 years until the construction of Christ Church at the foot of the hill. The British found St Paul's more useful for military than for religious purposes, storing their gunpowder here during successive wars, and building the light-house that guards the church's entrance. The tombstones that lie against the interior walls, together with those further down the hill in the **graveyard** itself, are worth studying. Being the only major port in the Straits until the nineteenth century, Melaka received many visitors, some of whom were buried here (including Bishop Peter of Japan, who was a missionary in Melaka in 1598), as well as large numbers of Portuguese, Dutch and British notables, whose epitaphs have long been partly obscured by lichen. In the graveyard on the slopes below, note the tomb of the Velge family, five members of which died within twenty days of one another during the diphtheria epidemic of 1756.

Dutch Square and around

A winding path beside St Paul's Church brings you down into the so-called **Dutch Square**, one of the oldest surviving parts of Melaka, although two of its main features date from much later times: the Victorian marble fountain was built in 1904 to commemorate Queen Victoria's Diamond Jubilee, and the clock tower erected in 1886 in honour of Tan Beng Swee, a rich Chinese merchant. Even more recent is the twee miniature windmill, installed by tourist officials in the 1980s, a quirky nod to the town's Dutch heritage.

Presiding over the entire south side of the square is the sturdy **Stadthuys**, now housing the **Museum of Ethnography** (Mon & Wed–Sun 9am–6pm, Fri closed 12.15–2.45pm; RM2). The simple, robust structure – more accurately a collection of buildings dating from between 1660 and 1700 – was used as a town hall throughout the whole period of Dutch and British administration. Although the long wing of warehouses projecting to the east is the oldest of the buildings here, recent renovations have revealed the remains of a Portuguese well and drainage system, suggesting that this was not the first development on the site. The wide, monumental interior staircases, together with the high windows that run the length of the Stadthuys, are typical of seventeenth-century Dutch municipal buildings, though they are less suited to the tropical climate than European winters. Look out of the back windows onto the whitewashed, mould-encrusted houses that line the courtyard, and you could be in a Vermeer scene. The museum itself displays an array of Malay and Chinese ceramics and weaponry, though there's also a reconstruction of a seventeenth-century Dutch dining room. The rooms upstairs have endless paintings giving a blow-by-blow account of Melakan history.

Turn to the right as you leave the Stadthuys and you can't miss **Christ Church** (Tues–Sun 9am–5pm; free), also facing the fountain. Built in 1753 to commemorate the centenary of the Dutch occupation of Melaka, its simple design, with neither aisles nor chancel, is typically Dutch; its porch and vestry were nineteenth-century afterthoughts. The cool, whitewashed interior has decorative fanlights high up on the walls and elaborate, 200-year-old hand-carved pews, while the roof features heavy timber beams, each cut from a single tree. The plaques on the walls tell a sorry tale of early deaths in epidemics, and a wooden plaque to the rear of the western wall of the church commemorates local planters who were killed in World War II. There is a service in English every Sunday at 8.30am; at other times, the spiritual atmosphere is diluted by the postcards, pictures and trinkets being pedalled inside the church.

East of the church, along Jalan Kota, lie the overgrown remains of the **Dutch Graveyard**. This was first used in the late seventeenth century, when the VOC was still in control (hence the name), though British graves easily outnumber those of their predecessors. The tall column towards the centre of the tiny cemetery is a memorial to two of the many officers killed in the Naning War in 1831, a costly attempt to include the nearby Naning region as part of Melaka's territory under the new Straits Settlements.

North to St Peter's Church

Back at Christ Church, head north up Jalan Laksamana, moving quickly past the **Muzium Belia Malaysia** (Museum of Youth; daily 9am–6pm, closed Fri 12.30–2.45pm; RM2), replete with pictures of smiling, wholesome youths shaking hands with Dr Mahathir, Malaysia's former strongman. The road leads to **St Francis Xavier's Church**, a twin-towered, nineteenth-century, Neo-Gothic structure. Further up from here, skirting the busy junction with Jalan Temenggong and taking Jalan Bendahara directly ahead, you're in the centre of Melaka's tumbledown **Little India**, a rather desultory line of incense and saree shops, interspersed with a few eating houses. After about five minutes' walk, you come to a sizeable crossroads with Jalan Munshi Abdullah, beyond which is **St Peter's Church**, set back from the road on the right. The oldest Roman Catholic church in Malaysia, built by a Dutch convert in 1710 as a gift to the Portuguese Catholics, it has an unusual barrel-vaulted ceiling. The church really comes into its own at Easter as the centre of the Catholic community's celebrations.

The river and docks

If you feel like a rest from pavement pounding, take one of the **boat trips** up Sungai Melaka. These leave from the small jetty behind the tourist office (hourly from 10am–2pm, depending on the tide; 45min; RM8); buy your tickets on the boat. The trip takes you past "Little Amsterdam", the old Dutch quarter of red-roofed godowns, which backs directly onto the water. Look out for the slothful monitor lizards that hang out on either side of the bank, soaking up the sun, and the local fishermen who line the route, mending boats and nets. The boat turns round without stopping at Kampung Morten (see p.375), opposite which, on the east bank, you can just make out a few columns and a crumbling aisle – all that remains of the late-sixteenth-century Portuguese church of St Lawrence – poking out from beneath the undergrowth. On the return journey, you're taken beyond the jetty to the **docks** along Jalan Quayside, crowded with low-slung Sumatran boats bringing in charcoal and timber which they trade for rice; these heavy wooden craft are still sailed without the aid of a compass or charts. The best time to catch the activity at the docks is around 4.30pm, when the multicoloured fishing boats leave for the night's work.

From here, you can also see the new **Maritime Museum** (daily 9am–9pm, closed Fri 12.15–2.45pm; RM2) on the quayside, housed in a towering replica of the Portuguese cargo ship, the *Flor De La Mar*, which sank in Melaka's harbour in the sixteenth century. Inside its hull, lots of model ships and paintings chart Melaka's maritime history from the time of the Malay Sultanate to the arrival of the British in the eighteenth century. Across the road, another section of the museum houses a drab display about the Malaysian navy and, much more interestingly, some of the recovered items from the wreck of the *Diana*, which sank in the Straits of Melaka while en route to Madras in 1817. The salvage operation, which began in 1993, eventually yielded eighteen tonnes of chinaware.

Chinatown and Masjid Tranquerah

Melaka owed a great deal of its nineteenth-century economic recovery to its Chinese community: it was one Tan Chay Yan who first planted rubber here, and a certain Tan Kim Seng who established a steamer company early on, which later became the basis of the region's great Straits Steam Ship Company. Most of these entrepreneurs settled in what became known as Chinatown, across Sungai Melaka from the colonial district. Turn left after the bridge by the tourist office, then take the first right to follow the one-way system, and you come to Jalan Tun Tan Cheng Lock, formerly Heeren Street. The elegant townhouses that line the narrow road are the ancestral homes of the Baba-Nonya community (see box, p.374). The wealthiest and most successful of these merchants built long, narrow-fronted houses, and minimized the "window tax" by incorporating several internal courtyards, designed also for ventilation and the collection of rainwater. A **shophouse** at no.8, dating back to the seventeenth century, has been lovingly restored and includes an interpretation centre (Tues–Sat 11am–4pm; free).

At nos. 48–50, the **Baba-Nonya Heritage Museum** (daily 10am–12.30pm & 2–4pm; RM8; not covered by Melaka museum day-pass ticket) is an amalgam of three adjacent houses belonging to one family, and an excellent example of the Chinese Palladian style. Typically connected by a common covered footway, decorated with hand-painted tiles, each front entrance has an outer swing door of elaborately carved teak, while a heavier internal door provides extra security at night. Two red lanterns, one bearing the household name, the other messages of good luck, hang either side of the doorway, framed by heavy Greco-Roman columns. But the upper level of the building is the most eye-catching: a canopy of Chinese tiles over the porch frames the shuttered windows, almost Venetian in character, their glass protected by intricate wrought-iron grilles, with eaves and fascias covered in painted floral designs. Inside, the homes are filled with gold-leaf fittings, blackwood furniture inlaid with mother-of-pearl, delicately carved lacquer screens and Victorian chandeliers.

Tales of Melaka's burgeoning success brought vast numbers of merchants and entrepreneurs to its shores, eager to benefit from the city's status and wealth. The Chinese, in particular, came to the Malay Peninsula in droves, to escape Manchu rule – a trend that began in the sixteenth century, but continued well into the nineteenth. Many Chinese married Malay women; descendants of these marriages were known as **Peranakan** or sometimes "Straits-born Chinese". While their European counterparts were content to while away their time until retirement, when they could return home, the expatriate Chinese merchants had no such option, becoming the principal wealth-generators of the thriving city. The **Babas** (male Sino-Malays) were unashamed of flaunting their new-found prosperity in the lavish townhouses which they appropriated from the Dutch, transforming these homes into veritable palaces filled with Italian marble, mother-of-pearl inlay blackwood furniture, hand-painted tiles and Victorian lamps. The women, known as **Nonyas** (sometimes spelt Nyonya), held sway in the domestic realm and were responsible for Peranakan society's most lasting legacy – the **cuisine**. Taking the best of both Malay and Chinese traditions, its dishes rely heavily on sour sauces and coconut milk; its eating etiquette is Malay – using fingers, not chopsticks.

Further up the road, at no. 107, the **Restoran Peranakan Town House** is another former mansion, now a restaurant specializing in Nonya cuisine (see p.378). Beyond, at no. 117, you can't fail to notice the **Chee Ancestral House**, an imperious Dutch building of pale-green stucco topped by a gold dome, and home to one of Melaka's wealthiest families, who made their fortune from tapioca and rubber. Continuing northwest from here, up Jalan Tengkera, you pass through Melaka's suburbs of picturesque Peranakan mansions and come to the **Masjid Tranquerah**, about 2km from the town centre on the right. A pagoda-like Melakan mosque dating from the eighteenth century, it's where Sultan Hussein, who ceded Singapore to Stamford Raffles in 1819, is buried. You can also get here from the local bus station on bus #51, which continues on to Tanjung Kling.

Back in Chinatown, **Jalan Hang Jebat** – formerly named **Jonkers Street** or "Junk Street" – runs parallel to Jalan Tun Tan Cheng Lock. Melaka's antiques centre (see "Shopping", p.378), it's worth a wander even if you don't intend to buy. The street is closed to vehicular traffic on Friday and Saturday nights, when you'll find all the shops stay open late. Most of the antique shops are selling handicrafts these days – much of it from Bali – and what few antiques are left are almost insultingly expensive. Crammed between the Chinese temples and shophouses here is the small, whitewashed tomb of Hang Kasturi, one of the "Five Companions" (see box, p.370). A short way east up Jalan Tokong is **Tokong Cheng Hoon** (Merciful Cloud Temple), reputed to be the oldest Chinese temple in the country – though several others would dispute the title. Dedicated to the goddess of mercy, the main prayer hall has a heavy saddled roof and oppressive dark-timber beams, reminiscent of the Khoo Kongsi in Georgetown (see p.207). Smaller chambers devoted to ancestor worship are filled with small tablets bearing a photograph of the deceased and strewn with wads of fake money and papier-mâché models of luxury items, symbolizing creature comforts for the dead. The temple authorities here act as the trustees for Bukit China, the ancestral burial ground to the northeast of town (see p.376).

A little further down the road is the 1748 **Masjid Kampung Kling**, displaying an unusual blend of styles: the minaret looks like a pagoda, there are English and Portuguese glazed tiles, and a Victorian chandelier hangs over a pulpit carved with Hindu and Chinese designs. Next door, the Hindu **Sri Poyyatha Vinoyagar Temple** also has a minaret, decorated with red cows, but its gloomy interior is disappointing. From the temple, head north for Jalan Kampung Hulu and **Masjid Kampung Hulu**, thought to be the oldest mosque in Malaysia. Constructed around 1728 in typical Melakan style, it's a solid-looking structure, surmounted by a bell-shaped roof with red Chinese tiles and, again, has more than a hint of pagoda in its minaret. Such architecture has its origins in Sumatra, perhaps brought over by the Minangkabaus (see box, p.356) who settled in nearby Negeri Sembilan.

From here, an alternative route back to the centre of town is to walk south down Jalan Kampung Hulu as it follows the river and merges into Jalan Kampung Pantai. At the junction with Jalan Hang Kasturi, a couple of minutes further on, you can pause for a moment at **Hang Jebat's Tomb**, another tiny mausoleum to one of the great warriors of the Malay "golden age".

Kampung Morten

The village of **Kampung Morten**, named after the British district officer who donated RM10,000 to buy the land, is a surprising find in the heart of the city. It's easiest to explore this community on foot: take the footbridge down a small path off Jalan Bunga Raya, one of the principal roads leading north out of town (you can also reach the village by heading east from the local bus station). The wooden stilted houses here are distinctively Melakan, with their long, rectangular living rooms and kitchens, and narrow verandas approached by ornamental steps. On the left as you cross the footbridge, the **Villa Sentosa** (daily 9am–5pm, closed Fri noon–3pm; voluntary donation), with its miniature kampung house and mini-lighthouse, is a 70-year-old family home that now functions as a museum. The warm and welcoming family will gladly show you artefacts and heirlooms handed down by the old patriarch, Tuan Haji Hashim Hadi Abdul Ghani, who died at the age of 98.

The Portuguese Settlement and St John's Fort

The road east of Jalan Taman Melaka Raya leads, after about 3km, to Melaka's Portuguese Settlement; turn right into Jalan Albuquerque, clearly signposted off the main road, and you enter its heart. You can also get here on bus #17 from Jalan Parameswara, just outside Jalan Taman Melaka Raya, or the local bus station.

In 1933, the colonial administration, prompted by increasing levels of poverty and the depletion of the Portuguese community (which was barely any larger than the two thousand recorded in the first census in 1871), established this village on the historic site of their original community. Today you're likely to recognize the descendants of the original Portuguese settlers only by hearing their language, **Kristao**, a unique blend of Malay and old Portuguese, or by seeing their surnames – Fernandez, Rodriguez and Dominguez all feature as street names.

Medan Portugis (Portuguese Square), at the end of the road, is European to the hilt – you could be forgiven for thinking that its whitewashed edifice, worn by the salty winds, was a remnant from colonial times. Through the archway, the souvenir shop and tourist-oriented restaurants surrounding the central courtyard soon make it clear that this is a purpose-built "relic", dating only from 1985. That said, the square, cooled by the sea breeze, is a good place for a quiet beer at sunset, and the local restaurateurs make an effort to conjure up a Portuguese atmosphere, though the food is Malay in character. A three-day

fiesta – the feast of St Pedro – is held in the square, commencing on June 29 every year, with traditional Portuguese food, live music and dancing.

Heading back into town, you can make a brief detour to **St John's Fort**, up Bukit Senjuang. The fort, a relic of the Dutch occupation, is not terribly exciting, and somewhat dwarfed by the adjacent water tower, but does offer good views over the town and the Straits of Melaka.

Bukit China

Northeast of the colonial heart of Melaka is **Bukit China**, the ancestral burial ground of the town's Chinese community, indeed the oldest and largest such graveyard outside China. Although Chinese contacts with the Malay Peninsula probably began in the first century BC, it wasn't until the Ming Emperor Yung-Lo sent his envoy Admiral Cheng Ho here in 1409 that commercial relations with Melaka were formally established, according the burgeoning settlement with vassal status. At the foot of the hill, at the eastern end of Jalan Temenggong is the **Sam Poh Kong**, a working temple dedicated to Cheng Ho, upon whom the title of "Sam Poh" or "Three Jewels" was conferred in 1431. Accounts of the time are vague about the arrival of the first Chinese settlers, though the *Sejarah Melayu* recounts that on the marriage of Sultan Mansur Shah (1458–77) to the daughter of the emperor, Princess Hang Liu, the five hundred nobles accompanying her stayed to set up home on Bukit China. It was supposedly these early pioneers who dug the well behind the temple; also known as the **Sultan's Well**, it has been of such importance to the local inhabitants as a source of fresh water that successive invading armies all sought to poison it. The Dutch enclosed it in a protective wall, the ruins of which still remain.

At the top of Bukit China, horseshoe-shaped **graves** stretch as far as the eye can see. On the way up, you'll pass one of the oldest graves in the cemetery, belonging to Lee Kup who died in 1688. He was the first Chinese *kapitan*, a mediatory position created by the VOC, which made it possible for them to rule the various ethnic communities. His successor was Captain Li, whose grave on the other side of the cemetery is the subject of local myth: a fortune teller, asked to advise on the location and construction of the grave, prophesied that if it were to be dug three feet deep, Li's son would benefit; any deeper and all profit would go to his son-in-law. Whether by accident or design, the grave was made three-and-a-half feet deep, and the son-in-law, Chan Lak Koa, went on to found the elaborate Tokong Cheng Hoon as an expression of gratitude for his prosperity.

In the 1980s the burial ground was the subject of a bitter legal battle between its trustees and the civil authorities. Competing plans to develop the area into a cultural and sports centre provoked a claim by the government for a RM2 million bill for rent arrears, stating that the exemption over the previous centuries had been a "clerical error". This outraged the Chinese community, who flatly refused to pay. The controversy was only settled in the early 1990s when the decision was made to develop Melaka's waterfront area instead. Today, Bukit China is more an inner-city park than burial ground, where you're likely to encounter locals jogging, practising martial arts or simply admiring the view.

Eating and drinking

Surprisingly, there are very few quality restaurants in the centre of town – in fact, aside from a few places in Chinatown, it's hard to find much open at all at night. Instead, **Taman Melaka Raya** is fast becoming the favoured food centre, featuring Chinese, Nonya, Malay, Indian and seafood restaurants. Budget meals are not as common as elsewhere in Malaysia – even the city's principal **food stalls** on Jalan Merdeka, known as "Gluttons' Corner", are overpriced; it's far better to try the stalls just off Jalan Parameswara. Sampling **Nonya cuisine** is a must at some stage during your stay, though it's generally more expensive than other types of food. The emphasis is on spicy dishes, using sour herbs like tamarind, tempered by sweeter, creamy coconut milk; some specialities are mentioned below. By contrast, the city's few remaining **Portuguese** restaurants are generally disappointing, pricier still and tourist-oriented (a notable exception is *Heeren House*).

Usual restaurant **opening hours** are daily 9am–11pm, unless otherwise stated; phone numbers are given where it's necessary to book (usually only on Saturday nights).

Markets and food malls

Chinese night market Taman Melaka Raya. A blur of chopping cleavers and furiously boiling woks make for great entertainment while you sample from the many stalls. Dishes can be made to order if you can make yourself understood. Very inexpensive and open 24hr

Gluttons' Corner Jalan Merdeka. More a collection of permanent restaurants than food stalls, the city's highest-profile eating area also has high prices and impersonal service. One of the better places is *Bunga Raya*, whose local seafood is popular with the locals. A full meal at any of the restaurants costs at least RM12 a head.

Jalan Bendahara Indian food stalls *Roti canai* and other South Indian favourites are served here from early morning till well into the night.

Jalan Parameswara Malay food stalls Quick, tasty fare can be had from these stalls along the road linking Jalan Merdeka with Jalan Parameswara, south of the *Equatorial* hotel.

Mahkota Parade/Parkson Grand Jalan Merdeka. The Merdeka Grand shopping mall has a decent a/c food court with dishes for around RM5, while the adjacent mall, the Parkson Grand, has a full range of Western fast-food outlets and a supermarket.

Cafés and restaurants

Capitol Satay Jalan Bukit China. Experience the Melaka version of fondue – *satay celup* – at this lively café, where you take your pick of assorted fish, meat and vegetables skewered on sticks and cook them in a spicy peanut sauce before eating. Each stick is around 50 sen; you'd be hard pressed to spend more than RM8 per person. Daily 7pm–midnight.

Coconut House 128 Jalan Tun Tan Cheng Lock. Art gallery, bookshop, art-film venue and woodfire pizzeria, all in a tastefully renovated Chinese townhouse. Mid-range prices, good atmosphere and great pizzas.

Discovery Café 3 Jalan Bunga Raya. Traveller-oriented café-bar with inexpensive local and Western cuisine, a riverside terrace, plus Internet facilities and a library.

Geographer Café 83 Jalan Hang Jebat. One of a new breed of trendy café-bars, this airy pre-war shophouse on a busy corner in Chinatown is a good place to have a drink and watch the world go by. Simple dishes from RM5, pizzas from RM10.

Heeren House 1 Jalan Tun Tan Cheng Lock. This trendy a/c café and gift shop, beneath the hotel, offers Nonya lunches at weekends for RM15 and very reasonably priced local Portuguese fare. Daily 8am–6pm.

Galeri Café *Hotel Puri*, Jalan Tun Tan Cheng Lock. Located in a faithfully restored Peranakan shophouse, *Galeri Café* is an excellent choice if your party can't make up its mind – there is Nonya cuisine as well as European and even some Malay dishes. This is also a decent place for light Western breakfasts at around RM12. Daily 7am–10pm.

Jonkers Melaka 17 Jalan Hang Jebat. In a beautiful Peranakan house, this café is also a gift shop and art gallery. Set meals, including Nonya cuisine, start at RM16. There are also some good vegetarian choices. There are home-made desserts too. Daily 10am–5pm.

Long Feng Chinese Restaurant *Renaissance Melaka Hotel*, Jalan Bendahara ☎06/284 8888. Excellent Cantonese and Szechuan dishes in a classy setting, but not cheap at around RM25 per dish.

D'Nolasco Medan Portugis. A Mediterranean atmosphere accompanies the oriental food, such as crabs in tomato and chilli sauce with soy. Around RM20 a head.

Ole Sayang 198–199 Jalan Taman Melaka Raya ☎06/283 4384. A moderately priced Nonya restaurant with re-created Peranakan decor. Try the beef *goreng lada*, in a rich soya-based sauce, or the *ayam lemak pulut*, a spicy, creamy chicken dish. Dinner for two costs about RM50. Daily 11.30am–9.30pm.

Peranakan Town House 107 Jalan Tun Tan Cheng Lock ☎06/284 5001. Marble tables with white-lace tablecloths, and a reasonably priced Nonya menu in a picture-book Chinatown setting; try the

spicy *rendang* dishes or claypot *ayam*. Dishes average around RM15. Daily 11am–9pm.

Sri Lakshmi Villas 2 Jalan Bendahara. Both this and *Sri Krishna Bavan* next door have reliable South Indian *thalis* with as many top-ups as you can eat for RM5.50 a go. Good for vegetarians. Daily 7am–9.30pm.

Nightlife and entertainment

At night, while the centre of town is dead – except for the discos in the top hotels and a couple of the newer café-bars – **Taman Melaka Raya** comes alive. There's no shortage of karaoke bars (usually 8pm–2am), though both these and the discos are expensive and somewhat lacking in character. For a straight-forward drink at a reasonable price, you're better off eschewing the Western-style bars in favour of one of the grotty Chinese bottle shops in the centre of town. *Restoran de Lisboa*, at Medan Portugis, has a live band on most nights, and cultural dance shows on Saturdays.

Mahkota Parade includes a 24-lane bowling alley, an amusement arcade and a three-screen cineplex. Otherwise the only source of entertainment is the nightly **Sound and Light Show** on Padang Pahlawan. A must for fans of high drama ("Something is rotten in the state of Melaka" intones the soundtrack), it drags a bit at an hour in length, but provides a one-stop introduction to the city's history. The buildings are well lit and the sound system is used imagi-natively; take lots of mosquito repellent. Shows are in English (daily 8.30pm; RM10) and you can buy tickets from the booths at each end of the padang.

Shopping

Melaka is famed for its **antiques**, but these days you'll find cheaper Asian antiques anywhere but in Asia. Among the handicraft outlets along Jalan Hang Jebat and Jalan Tun Tan Cheng Lock, you will find a handful of antiques – mostly Chinese – but the prices are nothing short of heartbreaking. If the item you're thinking of buying is a genuine antique (most shops fill their windows with colourful but inauthentic clutter), check that it can be exported legally and fill in an official clearance form; the dealer should provide you with this. Jalan Bunga Raya and Jalan Munshi Abdullah comprise the modern shopping centre, where you'll find a variety of Western and local goods.

Abdul Co 79 Jalan Hang Jebat. A good place for china and glass.

Dragon House 65 Jalan Hang Jebat. The best value for old coins and banknotes, with helpful staff.

Jehan Chan Art Gallery 10 Jalan Tun Tan Cheng Lock ☎06/286 1615. Jehan Chan, a former teacher, has achieved considerable fame nationally for his paintings in watercolour and oil. They can be viewed and purchased at his small gallery.

Koo Fatt Hong 92 Jalan Tun Tan Cheng Lock. Specialists in "Asia Spiritual and Buddha images" – various deities carved in stone and wood.

Orang Utan 59 Lorong Hang Jebat. Here, local artist Charles Chan sells his paintings, and T-shirts printed with witty cartoons and sayings.

Parkson Grand Jalan Merdeka. A huge a/c department store, connected to the Mahkota Parade shopping mall, with fast food and a supermarket in the basement.

Ringo 12 Jalan Hang Jebat. British bikes and old biker artefacts, as well as unusual toys; pricey.

Tribal Arts Gallery, 10 Jalan Hang Jebat. Specialists in Sarawakian crafts, including wood-work and weaving.

Wah Aik 103 Jalan Kubu. Renowned for making silk shoes for bound feet. With foot binding no longer practised, the shoes are now lined up in the window as souvenirs, at a mere RM75 per pair.

Listings

Airlines MAS, *Century Melaka Hotel*, Jalan Merdeka ☎06/283 5722; Merpati Air ☎06/317 4175.

Banks and exchange Bank Bumiputra, Jalan Melaka Raya; Hong Kong Bank & Maybank, Jalan Hang Tuah, near the bus station. Often more convenient, with rates as good as the banks', are the moneychangers, including Malaccan Souvenir House and Trading, 22 Jalan Tokong, and SPAK, 31 Jalan Laksamana.

Bookshops Estee Book Exchange, Jalan Taman Melaka Raya, has a good selection of English-language classics and other fiction. MPH, on the ground floor of Mahkota Parade, also has an excellent range of books, as does Tai Khuang upstairs on the second level.

Car rental Hawk, Jalan Laksamana ☎06/283 7878; Annah Car Rental, 27 Jalan Laksamana, ☎06/283 5626.

Cinema The Cineplex in Mahkota Parade shows English-language films; check in the newspapers for what's on when.

Hospital The Malacca Hospital is in the north of town on Jalan Mufti Hj Khalil (☎06/282 2344). The Southern Hospital is nearer the centre of town at 169 Jalan Bendahara (☎06/283 5888). The well-equipped Mahkota Medical Centre is at 3 Mahkota Melaka, Jalan Merdeka (☎06/281 3333).

Internet access There are plenty of places around town to go online, usually costing around RM4 per hour. Try the *Discovery Café* (see p.377) or the east end of Jalan Merdeka.

Police The Tourist Police office (☎06/282 2222) on Jalan Kota is open 24hr.

Post office The GPO is inconveniently situated on the way to Ayer Keroh on Jalan Bukit Baru – take town bus #19 from the local bus station. A minor branch on Jalan Laksamana sells stamps and aerograms.

Sport The Merlin Melaka sports centre on Jalan Munshi Abdullah offers ten-pin bowling, snooker, squash and roller-skating.

Swimming There's a public swimming pool on Jalan Kota (daily 10am–1pm, 2–4.15pm & 6–8pm; RM1.80).

Telephones The Telekom building is on Jalan Kota (daily 8am–5pm). The quietest and most efficient place to make international calls, though, is the Cempaka Technology Shop at 155 Jalan Taman Melaka Raya.

Travel agents Try Atlas Travel at 5 Jalan Hang Jebat (☎06/282 0777) for plane tickets.

Visa extensions Visas can be extended on the spot at the immigration office on the second floor of the Bangunan Persekutuan, Jalan Hang Tuah (☎06/282 4958).

Around Melaka

While there's more than enough to keep you occupied in Melaka itself, you may well fancy a break from sightseeing for more relaxed pleasures, using the city as a base. The nearby town of **Ayer Keroh** is a popular excursion, with recreation parks, tame wildlife and frequent cultural displays, while the beach resorts of **Tanjung Kling** and **Pulau Besar** provide an opportunity to feel some sand between your toes.

Ayer Keroh

Fourteen kilometres north of the centre, **AYER KEROH** – despite its position adjacent to the North–South Expressway – is a leafy recreational area that provides a pleasant alternative to staying in the city itself. Town buses #19 and #105 run here every thirty minutes from Melaka's local bus station.

The major attractions are all within a few hundred metres or so of one another. Apart from the **Hutan Rekreasi** (daily 7am–6pm; free), an area of woodland set aside for walking and picnicking, all the attractions – the **Taman Buaya** (Crocodile Park; Mon–Fri 9am–6pm, Sat & Sun 9.30am–7pm; RM5); the **Melaka Zoo** (Mon–Fri 9am–6pm, Sat & Sun 9.30am–6.30pm; RM5), purportedly the oldest and second largest in the country; and the **Taman Rama Rama** (Butterfly Park; daily 8.30am–5.30pm; RM5), with its walk-through aviary and small marine centre – are somewhat contrived. The only thing that demands more than fleeting attention is the **Taman**

Mini Malaysia and **Mini ASEAN** (☎06/232 0422; daily 9am–9pm; RM4), a large park fifteen minutes' walk north of the Crocodile Park, with full-sized reconstructions of typical houses from all thirteen Malay states and the other members of the Association of Southeast Asian Nations, an economic alliance of the region's states. The specially constructed timber buildings are frequently used as sets for Malaysian films and soap operas, and cultural shows featuring local music and dance are staged at the park's open-air arena – ask at the ticket office for details.

The area around the lake, just off the main road, is where you'll find most of the **places to stay**, limited exclusively to upmarket resort accommodation. The best of the bunch is the *INB Resort* (☎06/553 3023, ℱ553 3022; ⑥), with comfortable chalet-style accommodation and a swimming pool. Nearby, *D'Village Resort* (☎06/232 8000; ⑤) is the least attractive option, with blue-roofed chalets crammed together, though it does have the cheapest rooms. **Places to eat** are more or less limited to those in the resorts, save for a few tourist-oriented food stalls at the main attractions.

Tanjung Kling

The village and beach resort of **TANJUNG KLING** ("kling" being a term – now considered derogatory – for the Tamil immigrants who first populated this village) lies on Route 5, around 9km west of Melaka and 18km southeast of the turn-off to Tanjung Bidara. New developments are popping up all around this area, despite the fact that the dingy beach is less than inviting, and the village itself lacks amenities.

A right turn at the mosque, following the signpost to the Malacca Club, brings you to **Makam Hang Tuah**, the grave of the famous fifteenth-century warrior. It was formerly known locally only as *Makam Tua* or "Old Grave" in order to conceal its presence from the Portuguese, who went about destroying all buildings connected with the Melaka Sultanate on their takeover in 1511.

There's a string of small **resorts** back on the main road, of which the most appealing is the homely ⚵ *Shah's Beach Resort* (☎06/315 3121, ⓦwww.shahsresorts.com; ⑤). Its intriguingly designed wooden chalets incorporate elements of Portuguese architecture, as well as genuine antique furniture; the facilities here include an open-air *atap*-roofed restaurant, tennis courts and a pool. Next door, in stark contrast, the *Riviera Bay Resort* (☎06/315 1111, ⓦwww.meritus-hotels.com; ⑥) is an enormous 450-room complex with an arched entrance, boasting large, comfortable rooms. It also has a decent range of restaurants and – fortunately – a good pool, since the beach is narrow and litter-strewn. The hotel's "leisure club", open to non-residents, offers wind-surfing, tennis and squash.

Pulau Besar

Long before it was turned into an exclusive beach resort, **PULAU BESAR** (literally "Big Island", though it covers just sixteen square kilometres), about 5km off the coast of Melaka, was known as the burial ground of passing Muslim traders and missionaries, tales of whom live on in distorted local legends. Although vigorously promoted by the tourist authorities, its historic sites consist of little more than a few ancient graves, several wells, and remnants of the Japanese occupation, such as a bunker and dynamite store. However, the island's beaches and hilly scenery are pleasant enough, and its compact size makes it easy to stroll around in a day.

Pulau Besar is easily reached by **ferry**, departing from the Anjung Batu jetty in Melaka (6 daily starting 8.30am, last boat out 6.30pm; RM11 return).

You can also get there by fishing boat from the **Pengkalan Pernu jetty** in Umbai (on request; RM8 return for a group of 12, otherwise RM50 to hire the whole boat one-way), 6km southeast of Melaka (bus #2; 20min). The only available **accommodation** on the island is the campsite (℡06/281 8007, ℱ281 5941; RM20 per person including tent rental), next to a resort now only used for conventions. As for **eating**, there are a couple of local *kedai kopis* serving rice and noodle dishes.

Gunung Ledang and around

Inland from Melaka, east of the North–South Expressway, a maze of minor roads covers the sparsely populated lowland, the only feature on the horizon being the conical **Gunung Ledang**. Further inland still, you'll meet up with the sweep of Route 1, connecting a string of lifeless towns.

Gemas, 25km northwest of Segamat, is a grubby little place whose merit is its importance to the train network – you may have to change here if you want to venture into the interior by train. Transport connections throughout inland Johor are uncomplicated, with a good network of buses serving all destinations.

Gunung Ledang

Formerly called Mount Ophir by the British, **Gunung Ledang** (1276m), the highest mountain in the state of Johor, is believed by the animist Orang Asli to be inhabited by spirits. The best-known legend associated with Gunung Ledang concerns the betrothal of Sultan Mansur Shah to the mountain's beautiful fairy princess. A lengthy list of requirements was presented to the sultan, on fulfilment of which the princess would consent to marry him; while the sultan was not daunted by such items as trays of mosquito hearts and a vat of tears, he drew the line at a cup of his son's blood, and withdrew his proposal.

Gunung Ledang features a **waterfall** – an impressive cataract after the rains, but disappointing in the dry season – and challenging **treks**, though the latter are restricted to experienced climbers with their own camping equipment. Once you're past the hotel and clutter of food and souvenir stalls at the approach to the waterfall, the surroundings gradually become more leafy and refreshing, leading to the start of the trail to the summit. A series of rapids, which the main path follows closely, form natural pools, ideal for a cooling dip, though the water is a bit murky in places. Reaching the waterfall's source, a 45-minute hike, requires stamina.

Practicalities

To drive here, turn off the North–South Expressway at Tangkak, from where you take Route 23 northeast, passing **Sagil** after 11km. After a further 3km, you'll see the waterfall clearly signposted ("Air Terjun") off the road, from which point it's 1500m to the beginning of the rapids. The mountain is easily reached by any Kuantan-bound express bus from Melaka – though the driver may tell you to get off in Sagil, the best place to leave the bus is actually at the stop a couple of kilometres beyond, signposted "Gunung Ledang Resort"; from here, you simply take the turning opposite. You can also get to Sagil on cheaper local buses; take a bus from Melaka to Tangkak (40 mins), then change for Sagil.

You pay the RM1 entrance fee at the *Gunung Ledang Resort*, a combination of park administration offices and hotel (℡06/977 2888, ℗www.ledang.com; ⑥), with comfortable, en-suite **rooms**. Also here is the *Kem Rimba Tamu Nature Camp*, including an obstacle course adjoined by thirty huts, which each sleep up to four people (RM40 a night). If you're on a tight budget, there's also a dorm with beds for RM15. An even cheaper way to see the mountain is to **camp** at one of the many sites along the trail; the resort charges a nominal RM10 a week per person for this but all trekkers must be accompanied by a **guide** these days too, as climbers have been known to get lost on the mountain for days. Local guides can be booked through the resort (one day RM200, two days RM250, three days RM300). Inexpensive **food** is available at the market stalls outside the gate. There are various **packages** on offer that combine a stay at the resort with expeditions up the mountain, from around RM150 – contact the resort (✉kemrimba@yahoo.com) for details.

From Melaka to Johor Bahru

The journey from Melaka southeast along **Route 5** to Johor Bahru covers a distance of 206km, the first 45km of which – to the Malay town of **Muar** – is through verdant countryside dotted with neatly kept timber stilted houses with double roofs. These houses, in some of the prettiest kampungs in Malaysia, are especially numerous along Route 5 and worth a stop if you have time. One of the best is the striking **Penghulu's House**; heading south, you find it to your right, just off the main road 2km south of the village of **Merlimau**. The house, built in 1894 for a local chieftain, has elaborate woodcarvings adorning the veranda and eaves, and the front steps are covered in colourful Art Nouveau hand-painted tiles. It's still inhabited by the chieftain's descendants, who will show you around for a voluntary donation. The house has fallen into disrepair in recent years, with birds nesting in the roof and the wooden structure deteriorating rapidly, but for now, its character remains. Further south, the towns of **Batu Pahat** and **Pontian Kecil** are of scant interest (the former, slightly inland, has a reputation as a red-light resort for Singaporeans). If you do want to stop anywhere else before Johor Bahru and Singapore, aim for **Kukup**, right at the southern end of the west coast, and terrific for seafood.

To get to Johor Bahru in a hurry, skip the scenery of Route 5 and use the North–South Expressway instead. From Melaka, you can head north to the expressway via Ayer Keroh; it's also straightforward to join the expressway from Muar (take the Bukit Pasir road for about 20km) and Batu Pahat (take Route 50 northeast off Route 5). On **public transport**, hourly express buses from Melaka (RM12) and Muar (RM8) are faster than the convoluted train journey south from Tampin.

Muar

The old port town of **MUAR** – also known as Bandar Maharani – exudes an elegance and calm that attracts surprisingly few tourists. Legend has it that Paramesvara, the fifteenth-century founder of Melaka, fled here from Singapore to establish his kingdom on the southern bank of Sungei Muar, before being persuaded to choose Melaka. Although rejected by the Sumatran prince, Muar later became an important port in the Johor Empire (see p.731), as well as a centre for **ghazal music** (see p.770) and the place whose **dialect** is considered the purest Bahasa Malaysia in the Peninsula.

Today, Muar's commercial centre looks like any other, with Chinese shop-houses and *kedai kopi*s lining its parallel streets, Jalan Maharani, Jalan Abdullah and Jalan Meriam. But if you turn right out of the **bus station** on Jalan Maharani, following the river as the road turns into Jalan Petri, you'll see an altogether different part of town. Under the shade of huge rain trees, Muar's **Neoclassical colonial buildings** – the Custom House and Government Offices (Bangunan Sultan Abu Bakar) on your right, and the District Police Office and Courthouse on your left – still have an air of confidence and prosperity from the town's days as a British administrative centre. The graceful **Masjid Jamek Sultan Ibrahim**, completed in 1930, successfully combines Western and Moorish styles of architecture, in a design that was duplicated for the Masjid Jamek Kedua, built in 1999 on the opposite bank of the Sungai Muar. Further along Jalan Petri you'll pass a jetty on your right, from where irregular **river cruises** depart.

Practicalities

Bus #2 runs frequently here from Melaka's local bus station, taking less than ninety minutes to arrive in Muar at the **bus station** on Jalan Maharani. There are plenty of reasonable **hotels** in town, a selection of which appears below. Aside from **eating** houses in the commercial centre of town, none of which can be particularly recommended, the *Medan Selera* near the bridge on Jalan Maharani serves Malay snacks, while the *Classic Hotel* has a good ground-floor restaurant with great Chinese food – to get there, head down Jalan Sulaiman, which leads away from the river from a point about 100m southwest of the bridge, and turn left into Jalan Ali. A bit further out is the *Heritage Garden*, a decent mid-range Chinese restaurant on Jalan Bakri, the road leading east from the bridge.

Accommodation

Kingdom 158 Jalan Meriam ☎06/952 1921. Walk southeast away from the river along Jalan Sulaiman and take the second left onto Jalan Meriam. This clean, inexpensive Chinese-run hotel has simple but functional rooms with attached bathrooms. Good value. ❷

Riverview 29 Jalan Bentayan ☎06/951 3313, ⓕ951 8139. Walk along Jalan Maharani from the bus stop, keeping the river on your left, and turn right onto Jalan Bentayan. This central hotel has large, comfortable rooms with decent attached bathrooms. ❹

Rumah Persingghan Muar Jalan Sultanah ☎06/952 7744, ⓕ953 7933. A ten-minute taxi ride away from the town centre in a countryside setting. This place has the quietest, most upmarket accommodation in town, with huge rooms complete with TV and telephone, a children's play area, as well as some family chalets sleeping four. ❸

Townview Hotel 60 Jalan Sisi ☎06/951 1788, ⓕ953 7236. Jalan Sisi leads off from the waterfront, a short walk northeast of the bus stop. Under the same management as the *Riverview*, this place is a little smarter, with comfortable en-suite rooms with TV. ❹

Batu Pahat and Pontian Kecil

Continuing south, Route 5 hugs the palm-fringed coast as far as **BATU PAHAT** (also called Bandar Penggaram), where the Art Deco **Masjid Jamek** and Straits Chinese **Chamber of Commerce** are the only buildings of note. The town has a reputation as a venue for "dirty weekends", though a more noteworthy association is with a couple of important political events. The governing party, UMNO, initially a coalition of organizations opposed to the British-inspired Malayan Union, had its origins here in 1946. Years later, during the constitutional crisis of 1983, Prime Minister Dr Mahathir held a mass rally in the town to protest against the position taken by the sultans urging the people to assert their constitutional rights and elect him. The choice of Batu Pahat as the venue for this conscience-stirring symbolized Dr Mahathir's desire to remind the rulers of UMNO's role in reversing their original acquiescence with the Malayan Union many years before (see p.738).

Batu Pahat is a convenient point to cut across to the **east coast**: Route 50 links the town with Mersing, 140km away. To the south of Batu Pahat lies plantation country – the crop in this case being pineapples, piled high on roadside stalls in season, filling the air with their sweet smell. Over a hundred species of pineapple are grown in the region, including the Josapine, an aromatic hybrid of Johor and Sarawak pineapples. The next place of any consequence is the unassuming town of **PONTIAN KECIL**, 70km southeast of Batu Pahat. It's low on sights other than the fishing boats on the river and a lacklustre market, but the grubby little *Hotel Campbell* (☏07/687 9907; ❷) can put you up if you get stuck. There are regular **bus** services from the bus station to JB (RM3.30; 1 hr).

Kukup

The signs flanking the roadside at **KUKUP** feature giant king prawns waving their tentacles – in eager expectation, no doubt, at the money you're about to part with. This small fishing community, just 19km south along Route 5 from Pontian Kecil, has opened its doors to the Singapore package-tour trade, whose clients come to see the ancient, stilted houses built over the murky river and to sample Kukup's real attraction, the **seafood**: the town's single tumbledown street is packed with restaurants. Tours usually include an appetite-inducing trip to the offshore **kelong**, a huge fish trap with rickety wooden platforms. The nets cast from here float on their moorings rather than being anchored to the sea bed. The agency right by the jetty or any of the restaurants can sell you a ticket for the 45-minute tour (RM5).

Kukup is a little-known exit point from Malaysia to Tanjung Balai in **Indonesia**, a 45-minute ferry ride from the jetty (daily except Fri; regular boats between 8.30am & 5.30pm; RM40 one-way). The problem with **arriving** in Kukup from Indonesia is that onward travel connections are sketchy – you'll have to catch a taxi from Kukup to Pontian Kecil and then catch a bus on from there. You don't need to arrange a visa in advance for this trip

Practicalities

There's a dearth of transport from Pontian Kecil to Kukup, so you're better off catching a **taxi** between the two for around RM5 per person or RM15 to hire the taxi outright. There are at least a dozen **places to eat** on the town's small street; a popular place is the enormous *Makanan Laut*, closest to the jetty, where you can sit on the large wooden waterfront deck and watch the fishermen and tourists floating around on the river. Immediately opposite is the more modest *Restoran Zaiton Hussin*, where the emphasis is on Malay rather than Chinese-style seafood. The influx of visitors has pushed prices up; expect to pay RM18 for fish, RM16 for prawns and RM8 for mussels.

A kilometre back towards Pontian Kecil from Kukup, you'll see a turn-off for **Tanjung Piai**. A gradually narrowing road through lush tropical fruit plantations takes you to the "southernmost tip of the mainland Asia continent" as the advertising for the *Tanjung Piai Resort* (☏ & ℱ07/696 9000; ❹) puts it. This string of large wooden bungalows, on concrete stilts at the edge of the mangrove swamps and connected by causeways, commands a dramatic vista of the ships coming to and from Singapore, clearly visible on the horizon; there's also a seafood restaurant and friendly management. Apart from eating, there's little to do here other than chill out, watch the fireflies at night and enjoy the view.

Johor Bahru

The southernmost Malaysian city of any size, **JOHOR BAHRU** – or simply **JB** – is the main gateway into **Singapore**, linked to the city-state by a 1056-metre **causeway** carrying a road, a railway, and the pipes through which Singapore imports its fresh water. Around fifty thousand people a day travel across the causeway (the newer **second crossing** from Geylang Patah, 20km west of JB, to Tuas in Singapore is much less used because of its tolls), and the ensuing traffic, noise and smog affects most of unsightly downtown Johor Bahru. Despite the lack of sights, JB does have the air of both a border town and a boomtown. This is where all of Singapore comes to shop for cheap everything, from shark's fin soup to sex. And while the goods on offer may not always constitute an attraction in themselves, the city's feverish buy-and-sell vibe is worth experiencing. The past half decade saw a burst of construction that begat huge indoor malls – some with the expected brand-name outlets like Nike, and others filled with booth-sized shops selling every conceivable piece of women's clothing and accessories. The unending stream of visitors from Singapore also means an impressive amount of food on offer. Restaurants do a thriving business, and supermarkets are stacked high with Malaysian produce; probably nowhere else in Malaysia will you see so much tropical fruit being prodded and sniffed. By far the vast majority of visitors to the city are daytrippers, but there seems to be no shortage of night-time guests. Johor Bahru's nightlife is, however, aimed squarely at Singaporean men, whose appetite for liquor, hostesses and karaoke is more than adequately provided for.

Besides the commercial scene, Johor Bahru's only real attraction is the royal **Istana Besar**, but for most the city is merely a hurdle to jump on the way to the North–South Expressway and the more noteworthy sights of Melaka and Kuala Lumpur. **Historically** though, JB stands with Melaka as one of the most important sites in the country. Chased out of its seat of power by the Portuguese in 1511, the Melakan court decamped to the Riau Archipelago, south of modern-day Singapore, before upping sticks again in the 1530s and shifting to the upper reaches of the Johor River. A century of uncertainty followed for the infant kingdom of Johor, with persistent offensives by both the Portuguese and the Acehnese of northern Sumatra, forcing the court to shift its capital regularly. Stability was finally achieved by courting the friendship of the Dutch in the 1640s; the rest of the seventeenth century saw the kingdom of Johor blossom into a thriving trading **entrepôt**. By the end of the century, though, the rule of the wayward and tyrannical Sultan Mahmud had halted Johor's pre-eminence among the Malay kingdoms, and piracy was causing a decline in trade. In 1699, Sultan Mahmud was killed by his own nobles and, with the Melaka-Johor Dynasty finally finished, successive power struggles crippled the kingdom.

Bugis immigrants to Johor, escaping the civil wars in their native Sulawesi, eventually eclipsed the power of the sultans (see p.389), and though the Bugis were finally chased out by the Dutch in 1784, the kingdom was now a shadow of its former self. The Johor-Riau Empire – and the Malay world – was split in two, with the Melaka Straits forming the dividing line following the Anglo-Dutch Treaty of 1824. As links with the court in Riau faded, Sultan Ibrahim assumed power, amassing a fortune based upon hefty profits culled from plantations in Johor. The process was continued by his son Abu Bakar, named Sultan of Johor in 1885 and widely regarded as the father of modern Johor; it was he who, in 1866, named the new port across the Johor Straits Johor Bahru, or "New Johor".

Arrival and information

The Larkin **bus station** is on Jalan Geruda, 3km north from the centre of JB; the **train station** is to the east of the city centre, off Jalan Tun Abdul Razak. Flights to JB land at **Senai airport**, 28km north of the city, from where a regular bus service (RM2.70) runs to the bus station; alternatively, you can get a taxi to the city for about RM30. Heading out to the airport, there's a shuttle bus (RM4) from outside Waterfront City, which connects with all major MAS flights. The MAS office is at Level 1, Menara Pelangi, Jalan Kuning Taman Pelangi (☎07/334 1001). **Ferries** from Tanjung Pinang and Pulau Batam in Indonesia and Changi and Tanah Merah in Singapore arrive at the terminal in the Bebas Cukai shopping centre, 2km east of the causeway; tickets for these services can be booked directly through the ferry company Tenggara Senandung (☎07/221 1677) or at Sriwani Tours and Travel (☎07/221 1677).

The main **tourist office** (JOTIC) (Mon–Fri 8am–4.15pm, Sat 8am–12.45pm, Sun 10am–4pm; ☎07/223 4935, ⓦwww.johortourism.com.my) is on Jalan Air Molek. There are moneychangers in the main shopping centres, or try Maybank, 11 Jalan Selat Tebrau; Bank Bumiputra, 51 Jalan Segget; Hong Kong Bank, 1 Jalan Bukit Timbalan; or OCBC, Jalan Ibrahim. A brace of cashpoints can be found on the south side of the Merlin Tower. **Internet** access is available at the *Pussat Internet Café* (daily 10am–9pm) on the second floor of the Kotaraya shopping centre. You can **rent a car** by contacting either Avis, at the *Tropical Inn* (☎07/224 4824); or Hertz at JOTIC, Jalan Ayer Molek (☎07/223 7570).

Accommodation

JB's manufacturing boom means the city attracts more businessmen than tourists, so **hotel** prices tend to be a little higher than elsewhere in mainland Malaysia. Moreover, since the city's nightlife continues to appeal to Singaporeans, some of its budget hotels charge double as brothels. The majority of JB's lower-priced hotels are on or around Jalan Meldrum, right in the centre of town, but most of them are extremely unappealing. The best budget option is the good **homestay** listed opposite.

Travel between JB and Singapore

Two frequent **bus** services run between JB and Singapore throughout the day from Larkin station: the air-conditioned Singapore–JB Express (daily 6.30am–11pm; every 15min; RM2.40) is the more comfortable, though the #170 is cheaper (RM1.60) and runs every ten minutes from 5.20am to 12.10am. It's also possible to board buses to Singapore at the causeway terminal, which is much closer to the centre of JB than the bus station. The buses drop passengers outside the immigration checkpoints at each end of the causeway; retain your bus ticket as you'll need it for the onward journey. Once you're through immigration (the formalities take about ten minutes to complete), you continue into Singapore on any bus of the same type as the one that you took to the causeway, though not necessarily on the very same vehicle. There's also an MAS bus service (RM10) from Waterfront City in town or from JB's Senai airport to Singapore's *Novotel Orchid* on Dunearn Road – buses connect with all MAS departures and arrivals.

The **train** journey to Singapore costs RM8 for a second-class seat; you have to be cleared by Malaysian immigration on board, and then again by the Singapore authorities at the Woodlands checkpoint in the north of the island. **Taxis** between Singapore and JB (RM7 per person) depart from Jalan Trus near Johor Temple and leave only when they are full.

Causeway Inn 6A–FJalan Meldrum. Passable hotel with good-sized en-suite rooms offering a/c and TVs, but it's more expensive than the better *Meldrum*. ❹

Compact Hotel 18 Jalan Wong Ah Fook ☎07/221 3000, ⓦ www.compacthotel.com.my. Stylish hotel – all wooden floors, soft lighting and designer furniture – whose higher floors command good views across JB and Singapore. Recommended. ❻

Footloose Homestay 4H Jalan Ismail ☎07/224 2881, ⓔ footloose_jb2000@yahoo.com. Friendly budget homestay to the northwest of the town centre. It's clean, tidy and characterful, and evening meals can be arranged. Easily the best of the cheaper places in JB, but with just two double rooms and a dorm, it pays to book ahead. Dorm beds RM15, rooms ❷

Hawaii 21 Jalan Meldrum ☎07/224 0633. This Chinese standard is a bit worn around the edges, but it's the cheapest place in the centre of town. ❷

Hotel JB 80A Jalan Wong Ah Fook ☎07/2234788. Noisy, grubby, but cheap place with basic fan rooms without bathrooms (❷) and cleaner, nicer a/c rooms (❸).

Meldrum Hotel 1 Jalan Sui Nam ☎07/ 227 8988. This mid-range hotel is the best choice in this price range. All rooms have a/c, bathrooms and TV. ❸

Puteri Pan Pacific The Kotaraya, Jalan Trus ☎07/223 3333, ⓦ www.panpacific.com. Central JB's most opulent address, with five hundred sumptuous rooms including huge corner suites, and five restaurants. Prices halve during the seemingly random promotions. ❽

Rasa Sayang Jalan Datok Dalam ☎07/224 8600, ⓕ 224 8612. Comfortable though characterless mid-priced hotel, with comfortable but smallish rooms, in a quiet spot a short walk from the centre of JB. The rate includes breakfast at the hotel's coffee house. ❹

Tropical Inn 15 Jalan Gereja ☎07/224 7888, ⓔ tropicalinn@hotmail.com. Older three-star hotel, with well-equipped but slightly shabby rooms, decent restaurants, a coffee bar and a gym. Rates include breakfast. ❻

The City

JB is a sprawling city, with most places of interest located close to the causeway. Hilly downtown JB is undeniably scruffy, a fact born out by a stroll through the claustrophobic alleys of the sprawling market, below the KOMTAR building on Jalan Wong Ah Fook, where machetes, silk and "one-thousand-year-old eggs" (actually preserved for a year in lime, ash and tea leaves) are sold. Although KOMTAR is an enduring favourite for cheap shopping, the retail epicentre has shifted a block to the south with the arrival of City Square, a huge, glitzy shopping and office complex. A little way further south, the **Sri Mariamman Temple** lends a welcome splash of primary colours to the cityscape. Underneath its *gopuram*, and beyond the two gatekeepers on horseback who guard the temple, is the usual collection of vividly depicted figures from the Hindu pantheon. Just west of the Sri Mariamman is JB's oldest temple, the nineteenth-century **Johor Temple** on Jalan Trus, its murals of Chinese life darkened by years of incense smoke.

From here, it's a short walk to the western seafront. Take Jalan Trus south, past weathered shophouses and the occasional stray ladyboy, turn right at the end of the street, and follow this feeder road as it leads on to Jalan Ibrahim. After the cramped streets of the city centre, the open waterfront comes as a great relief. There are good views of distant Singapore, and of the slow snake of traffic labouring across the causeway. Turning your back on Singapore and looking towards JB, the view is dominated by the austere, grey-bricked **Sultan Ibrahim Building** on Jalan Bukit Timbalan, which today houses the state government offices. Completed in 1940, it was used by the Japanese to command their assault on Singapore in February 1942.

Continuing west along the water, past the garlanded facade of the **City Council**, you soon reach the grey arch marking the entrance into the expansive gardens of the **Istana Besar** – the former residence of Johor's royal family. Ornate golden lamps line the path to the istana, a magnificent building with chalk-white walls and a low, blue roof, set on a hillock overlooking the Johor

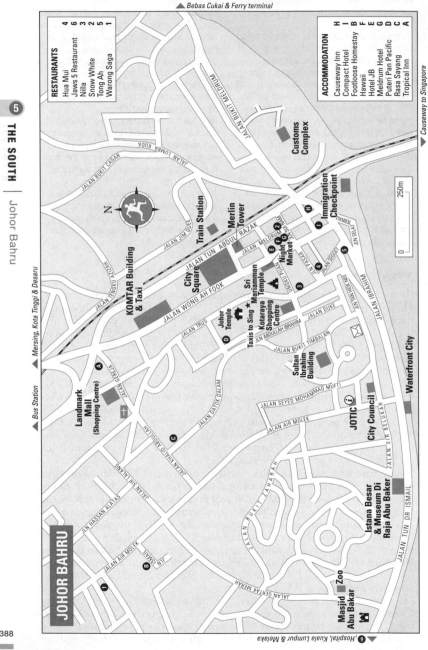

⑤

▲ *Bebas Cukai & Ferry terminal*

RESTAURANTS	
Hua Mui	4
Jaws 5 Restaurant	6
Nilla	3
Snow White	2
Tong Ah	5
Warong Saga	1

ACCOMMODATION	
Causeway Inn	H
Compact Hotel	I
Footloose Homestay	B
Hawaii	F
Hotel JB	E
Meldrum Hotel	G
Puteri Pan Pacific	D
Rasa Sayang	C
Tropical Inn	A

▼ *Causeway to Singapore*

JOHOR BAHRU

Customs Complex

Immigration Checkpoint

N

Train Station

Merlin Tower

City Square

KOMTAR Building & Taxi

Sri Mariamman Temple

Night Market

Johor Temple

Taxis to Sing

Kotaraya Shopping Centre

Sultan Ibrahim Building

Landmark Mall (Shopping Centre)

JOTIC ℹ

City Council

Waterfront City

Istana Besar & Museum Di Raja Abu Bakar

Zoo

Masjid Abu Bakar

JALAN BUKIT MELDRUM
JALAN LUMBA KUDA
JALAN BUKIT CAGAR
JALAN TUN ABDUL RAZAK
JALAN JIM DUYE
JALAN TENGKU AZIAH
JALAN WONG AH FOOK
JALAN TRUS
JALAN MELDRUM
JLN PASAR
JLN ABDULLAH IBRAHIM
JALAN DUKE
JALAN BUKIT TIMBALAN
JALAN DATOK DALAM
JALAN KHALID ABDULLAH
JALAN GEREJA
JALAN SEYED MOHAMMAD MUFTI
JALAN AIR MOLEK
JALAN SIR BELUKAR
JALAN IBRAHIM
JALAN TUN DR ISMAIL
JALAN GERTAK MERAH
JALAN BUKIT ZAHARAH
JLN SIR TALANG
JLN HASSAN ALATAS
JALAN AIR MOLEK
JLN ISMAIL
JLN SELAT
JALAN SEGGET
JALAN HOCK NEE
UNGKU PUTAH
TERBRAU

0   250m

▲ *Bus Station*   ▲ *Mersing, Kota Tinggi & Desaru*

▼ *Hospital, Kuala Lumpur & Melaka* **⑥**

The sultans and the law

The antics of the British royal family are nothing compared to what some of the nine royal families in Malaysia get up to. Nepotism, meddling in state politics and flagrant breaches of their exemption from import duties are among their lesser misdemeanours, which generally go unreported in the circumspect local press. But the most notorious of them all is Johor's Sultan Iskandar ibni Al-Marhum Sultan Ismail – along with his son, the Tunku Ibrahim Ismail. The former is alleged to have beaten his golf caddy to death in the Cameron Highlands after the unfortunate man made the mistake of laughing at a bad shot. Tunku Ibrahim, for his part, was convicted of shooting dead a man in a JB nightclub, though the prince was immediately pardoned because of who his father was. Such behaviour had long incensed Prime Minister Dr Mahathir, who was itching to bring the lawless royals into line. He got his chance in 1993 when yet another beating incident involving the sultan of Johor was brought up in the federal parliament along with 23 other similar assaults since 1972. As a result, the federal parliament voted in the Constitutional Amendment Bill, removing the sultans' personal immunity from prosecution. Naturally, the royal families were not too happy about this, but following a stand-off with Mahathir, they agreed to a compromise – no ruler would be taken to court without the attorney general's approval. To underline his victory against the sultans, Mahathir introduced another constitutional amendment in 1994, to the effect that the sultans could only act on the advice of the government. Despite this, the sultan of Johor retains considerable influence in the state and is the only one of the Malay royals to have a private army.

Straits. Nowadays, the royal family lives in the Istana Bukit Serene, a little further west of the city, and the Istana Besar is open to the public as the **Museum Diraja Abu Bakar** (Sat–Thurs 9am–5pm, last entry 4pm; RM20). The bulk of the pieces on show here are gifts – some exquisite, some tacky – from foreign dignitaries, including ceramics from Japan, crystal from France and furniture from England, as well as Southeast Asian items like stuffed tigers, ornate daggers and an umbrella stand crafted from an elephant's foot.

Five minutes' walk further west, the four rounded towers of the **Masjid Abu Bakar** make it the most elegant building in town. Completed in 1900, the mosque can accommodate two thousand worshippers; as at the istana, Sultan Abu Bakar himself laid the first stone, though he died before the mosque was completed.

Eating

There are scores of **restaurants** in JB, serving everything from Pakistani to Japanese dishes. The liveliest place to eat is the large **night market**, beside the Sri Mariamman Temple. A smaller night market takes place on the waterfront in front of the General Hospital on Jalan Skudai, about 500m west of the Abu Bakar Mosque.

Food markets and malls

City Square Jalan Wong Ah Fook. Popular top-floor food court plus various Western fast-food establishments at this huge shopping centre.

Kotoraya Shopping Centre Jalan Trus. On the top floor, there are several Western fast-food outlets and a good range of hawker stalls which stay open till 8.30pm.

Pasar Malam Jalan Wong Ah Fook. Colourful and vibrant night market with a mouth-watering array of goodies. Try the local speciality *mee rebus* – noodles in a thick sauce garnished with bean curd, sliced egg, green chillies and shallots.

Restaurants

Hua Mui 131 Jalan Trus. Western and Chinese dishes are on the menu in this two-floored restaurant. Daily 7am–9.30pm.

Jaws 5 *Straits View Hotel*, 1d Jalan Skudai. Open-air restaurant with backdrop of traditional

Malay houses, whose inexpensive menu includes
fish and shark's-fin dishes. Daily 11.30am–
midnight.

Nilla 109 Jalan Trus. "The best banana leaf food in
town" boasts the sign and it's certainly tasty and
inexpensive. Daily 7am–10pm.

Snow White 9A & 11A Jalan Siu Nam. Affordable, open-sided restaurant up above the thrum of
JB's traffic; specializes in Cantonese seafood and
steamboats, though it also serves Malay food. Daily
11am–2am.

Tong Ah 14 Jalan Ibrahim. No-frills *nasi padang*
restaurant where it's clear that the food and
not the decor is what keeps them coming. Daily
7am–9pm.

Warong Saga 5 Jalan Mahmudiah. This amiable
and extremely popular restaurant serves Chinese
and Nonya cuisine with a rotating menu of daily
specials, so if you stay in JB a week, you get a
crash course on the local cuisine. Especially good
are Saturdays (*laksa johor*) and Tuesdays (*laksa
nonya*). Daily 7am–12.30am.

△ *pasar malam*, Johor Bahru

Up the east coast from Johor Bahru

Without the patronage of neighbouring Singapore, the area around Johor Bahru
would have quietly nodded off into a peaceful slumber. Not that it's exactly a
thrilling region even now: places like the desultory seaside resort of **Desaru** on
the east coast have flourished, one suspects, more for their geographical than
their aesthetic merits. Most people heading east beat a hasty path along Route
3 to **Mersing**, neglecting to stop even at **Kota Tinggi**, whose waterfall constitutes the region's most enduring sight. Mersing itself is an attractive little town
that is the departure point for boats to Pulau Tioman.

Kota Tinggi and around

KOTA TINGGI, 40km northeast of JB, clings to the wide and fast-flowing
Sungai Johor. Although the town's not worth a visit in its own right,
you may want to stop at the **waterfall** (daily 8am–6.30pm, and until 7pm
Sat; RM2.50) at **LOMBONG**, 15km northwest. Of the two falls here,
the pool at the bottom of the farther one is the bigger and the better for
swimming, being deep and unobstructed by boulders. If you remain on land,
you'll still be soaked by the fine spray given off by the pounding water.
There's chalet accommodation and a couple of restaurants here but it's best
to avoid the falls at weekends and holidays when they become extremely
overcrowded.

Another minor diversion can be found about 15km northeast of Kota
Tinggi en route to Mersing: the road east off Route 3 here leads past the
forgotten royal mausoleums, at **Mawai**, of previous Johor sultans, to the uninspiring resort bay of **Teluk Mahkota**, amid bleak and desolate marshland.
If you choose instead to head southeast from Kota Tinggi, you come to the
resort of Desaru, 50km away.

Practicalities

Buses from JB's Larkin bus station run every twenty minutes on the one-hour trip to Kota Tinggi (RM5), stopping at the centrally situated **bus station**, which caters for both express and local services. Bus #41 leaves hourly from Kota Tinggi for the waterfall (daily 7am–7pm; RM2), winding up through rubber-plantation country on the way.

Several decent **hotels** are located around Kota Tinggi's bus station. The modern and spotless *Sin May Chun*, 26 Jalan Tambatan (☎07/883 3573; ❷), offers the best value, while the *Bunga Raya* further along at 12 Jalan Jaafar (☎07/883 3023; ❷) is also well kept. Top of the line is the *Hotel Seri Kota*, 47–49 Jalan Jaafar (☎07/883 8111, ℻883 8115; ❸), with comfortable, well-maintained air-conditioned doubles and nice bathrooms. All three are close to each other, a two-minute walk southwest from the bus stand. Seafood is a speciality in the town, with a number of good **restaurants** close to the river, including the *Sin Mei Lee* and the *Restoran New Mui Tou*, near the junction of Jalan Jaafar and the riverside Jalan Tepi Sungai. This is the place to try out crab, lobster and prawns – prices are reasonable at around RM10 per dish.

You can stay by the Lombong **falls** in the air-conditioned chalets at the *Kota Tinggi Waterfalls Resort* (☎07/883 6222, ℻883 1146; ❻). Despite the unattractive concrete buildings, the rooms are modern and the setting is wonderful, with jungle creepers trailing down to the tumultuous water. The Chinese *Restoran Air Terjun*, just by the entrance, has a good menu, though the resort's restaurant has the best view of the falls.

Desaru

As beaches go, **DESARU**, 50km southeast of Kota Tinggi, isn't that bad, with its sheltered, *casuarina*-fringed bay. It's the nearest major resort to Singapore, and as a result, weekends and holidays are busy. Despite its popularity, there are better places further up the coast, and the wide, well-kept but rather soulless streets here don't inspire lengthy stays.

With the road route here from JB covering nearly 100km (via Kota Tinggi, then southeast along Route 92), most visitors from Singapore come by sea from Changi Point (see p.629), arriving at the Malaysian port of **Kampung Pengerang**. Shuttle buses make the 45-minute journey from the port to Desaru itself. From JB, catch a local bus to Kota Tinggi, from where there are regular buses to Desaru.

The five **places to stay**, listed below, are all strung in a row along the beach, but be warned that room rates rise by about fifty percent at weekends and holidays. All have **restaurants** – predominantly Chinese and Japanese – where a very average meal costs a bare minimum of RM20 a head. There are a handful of cheap **food stalls** on the beach near the car park just north of the *Golden Beach Hotel*, which has a watersports centre – also the place to find go-karting and quad bikes.

Accommodation

Desaru Holiday Chalet ☎07/822 1211, ℻822 1245. Next to the *Desaru Leisure Camp*, 1km from the *Perdana* and *Impean*, with large and comfortable cabins set on the beach. ❻
Desaru Impean Resort ☎07/838 9911, ℻838 9922. At the northern end of the beach, this is the largest of the hotels here, modern though rather kitsch, with a miniature railway, theme park and well-kitted-out rooms. ❽

Desaru Leisure Camp ☎07/822 2888, ℻822 2666. A kilometre or so beyond the *Desaru Perdana*. This is the only option if you're avoiding the rates charged at the big hotels, and has tents (RM40), spartan, box-like rooms and slightly better "mini huts". You can also bring your own tent and camp for RM10 per person. There is also an "entrance fee" to the camp: adults RM2, kids RM1. ❸
Golden Beach Hotel ☎07/822 1101, ✉hotel@desaruresort.com. At the southeastern

end of the strip, this hotel is passable, its swimming pool and golf course offering some compensation for the small, rather uninspiring cheaper rooms ; better are the luxurious beachfront villas ❼–❾.

Pulai Desaru Beach Resort ☎07/822 2222, ☏822 2223. A little less grand than the *Desaru Impean* next door, but more tasteful. ❽

Mersing and around

The fishing port of **MERSING**, 130km north of Johor Bahru, lies on the languid Sungai Mersing. You're unlikely to stay more than one night in this bustling and industrious little town, which is the main gateway to **Pulau Tioman** and the smaller islands of the Seribuat Archipelago. Hotels, restaurants and travel agencies have sprung up to cater for the seasonal flood of tourists – it pays to work out exactly what you want to do before arriving in Mersing, or you may be swamped by the touts that hang around the jetty.

Mersing is grouped around two main streets, Jalan Abu Bakar and Jalan Ismail, fanning out from a roundabout on Route 3. The town's Chinese and Indian temples, just south of the roundabout, are unremarkable; the only real sight is the square **Masjid Jamek**, on a nearby hilltop, its cool, pastel-green-tiled dome and minaret lit to spectacular effect at night, when it appears to hang in the sky. In the centre of town, by a mini-roundabout on Jalan Abu Bakar, is a historic Chinese **shophouse**, built by a Mersing pioneer named Poh Keh.

Due to the number of tourists passing through Mersing, a few enterprising guesthouses have put together worthwhile **tours** that offer a glimpse of local life. A typical itinerary might include a batik workshop, an orchid farm, a rubber plantation and a stop at a rural kampung. **River cruises** are also available, cruising upriver through the jungle to see monkeys, iguanas and the odd eagle swooping into the water to catch its prey. Ask at the *New East Coast Hotel* or *Omar's* for more information.

Practicalities

The **jetty** is about five minutes' walk east along Jalan Abu Bakar from the roundabout. **Express buses** from Singapore, JB or Kuantan drop you off just before the roundabout, handy for the town's accommodation, and at the R&R Plaza near the jetty, where you should alight if heading straight out to Tioman. Close to the river bank on Jalan Sulaiman is the **local bus station**, used by services from Kota Tinggi, Padang Endau and elsewhere; **taxis** can be picked up here too.

Mersing's **tourist office** (METIC, Mon–Fri 8am–12.45pm & 2–6.30pm, Sat 8am–12.30pm; ☎07/799 1979) is in a new building on Jalan Abu Bakar, with helpful staff who offer impartial advice on the many different island deals. The **post office** is further southwest on the opposite side of the street. Mersing is well supplied with **cyber cafés**, most of which can be found along Jalan Abu Bakar. You can **change money** at the Maybank or Bank Bumiputra on Jalan Ismail.

It can be problematic **leaving Mersing** by bus; few services originate here, so there can be a scramble for seats in the peak season. Express-bus tickets can be bought in advance from R&R Plaza or from Island Connection Travel & Tours (☎07/799 2535; ❷ Jalan Jemaluang). Buses out of Mersing depart from the R&R Plaza near the jetty.

Getting to the islands

Mersing is the main departure point for Tioman and the other islands of the **Seribuat Archipelago** (for details of departures from Tanjung Gemuk, see

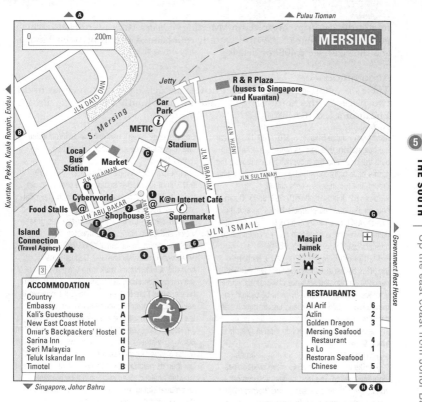

p.395). At the jetty there's a secure **car park** (RM7 per day) and a cluster of agency booths representing various islands, boats and resorts, known collectively as the **Tourist Centre**. For impartial information you're better off going to METIC. It's sensible to change money in Mersing before you head out to the islands, as the exchange rates there are lousy.

Many companies operate **express boats to Tioman**; the journey takes two hours or less, depending on the tide. Inside the nearby R&R Plaza – a collection of restaurants, moneychangers and more resort offices – you'll find a large signboard giving details of the day's sailings, including departure times and the name of the company operating each service – the last departure is normally no later than about 3pm, depending on the tide. Once you've found out which company operates the boat you want to catch, buy your ticket from the corresponding booth (RM30–35 for the one-way trip, though Mersing travel agents may offer discounts if you buy an open-return ticket). You can also take a speedboat to any part of Tioman (1hr 30min; RM45 per person one way) from the same jetty. As with the ferries, you can buy a ticket at the jetty or at a travel agent.

To get to the **other islands**, it's better to book a day or two in advance at the office representing that particular island (all the offices are based around the jetty), or at one of the many **travel agencies** in town (mostly found along Jalan Abu Bakar and, to a lesser degree, Jalan Ismail), since boat services are less regular and accommodation more at a premium. Another possibility is taking one of the day-trips, organized by Mersing's *Omar's Backpackers' Hostel*, which go to three or four of the small, mostly uninhabited islands between Tioman and the coast; see p.408 for details.

Accommodation

There's no shortage of low-budget **hotels** in Mersing. To get to either of the two places to the north of town, take the half-hourly local bus to Padang Endau or a taxi (RM3).

Country 11 Jalan Sulaiman ☎07/799 1799. Near the bus station, this hotel is more upmarket than both the price and the reception area suggest; the rooms have bathrooms and some have balconies, though the furniture is a little old. **②**

Embassy 2 Jalan Ismail ☎07/799 3545. Clean enough, but dull and characterless. Some of the rooms smell a bit musty and could use a lick of paint. Two or three beds to a room, in addition to ordinary doubles, some with a/c. **②**

Kali's Guesthouse ☎07/799 3613. A charming place by the sea 2km north of town, with a peaceful garden and a choice of A-frames, chalets or dearer cottages. Phone them to be picked up from town, or take the Padang Endau-bound bus. If you're staying in Mersing a while, this is an altogether more relaxing option than staying in town. **②–③**

🏃 **New East Coast Hotel** 43A Jalan Abu Bakar ☎07/799 3546, ⓦwww.geocities .com/anwarkinin. The best budget accommodation in town, boasting clean rooms, dorms (RM10), helpful, informative staff, Internet access, and great pizzas. They also organize sightseeing tours around Mersing, island-hopping trips and tours to Endau Rompin National Park. **①**

🏃 **Omar's Backpackers' Hostel** Jalan Abu Bakar ☎07/799 5096, ⓔeo_bentris @hotmail.com. Opposite the GPO, this small, basic hostel has clean dorm beds and two double rooms.

Omar himself is very useful for local information and runs island-hopping tours. Dorm beds RM8, rooms **①**

Sarina Inn Lot 956, Jalan Sekakap ☎07/799 6012. Four kilometres south of the centre; to get there, turn left off Jalan Ismail before the hospital and keep the sea to your left along the shore road. A small, family-run affair by the sea, it has great views and three comfortable doubles. **③**

Seri Malaysia Jalan Ismail ☎07/799 1876, ⓦwww.serimalaysia.com.my. Opposite the hospital, a ten-minute walk from the jetty. Part of the nationwide chain of reasonably priced quality hotels, rates here include breakfast; it's also worth asking about promotional offers which can lower the price by a third in low season. **⑤**

Teluk Iskandar Inn 1456 Jalan Sekakap ☎07/799 6037, ⓔkrisma14@tm.net.my. A few doors south of the *Sarina Inn*, the *Iskandar* is even more pleasant than its neighbour, with several well-constructed wooden chalets, all en suite, and a comfortable communal sitting area. They're priced according to the quality of their sea views. **③–⑤**

Timotel 839 Jalan Endau ☎07/799 5888, ⓕ799 5333. Despite its unpleasant facade this new hotel, on the main road is in fact the plushest place in town, with huge double beds and breakfast included in the rate; there's also an attached karaoke pub and a decent, though unatmospheric, restaurant. **⑤**

Eating

Mersing is a great place for **eating** out, with seafood topping the menu. The **food stalls** near the roundabout at the southern end of the bridge are particularly good – try the satay and the banana fritters. The **market** is a good place for the popular local breakfast dish *nasi dagang*; glutinous rice cooked in coconut milk, served with *sambal* and fish curry; you'll have to be quick, as they usually sell out by 9am.

Al Arif Jalan Ismail. Opposite the Tops supermarket, this Indian café serves good-quality food, though it's a little overpriced.

Azlin Jalan Abu Bakar. If you can get a table, this extremely popular Indian eatery makes a good spot for a *roti canai* breakfast or a *teh tarik*.

Golden Dragon *Embassy Hotel*, 2 Jalan Ismail. Has the widest-ranging Chinese and seafood menu

in town, though it's a touch more expensive than some. Averages RM8 per dish.

Mersing Seafood Restaurant 56 Jalan Ismail. A variety of delicious seafood dishes at reasonable prices; try the chilli crab – RM18 gets you three to share.

Restoran Ee Lo Jalan Dato' Md. Ali, on the Jalan Abu Bakar mini-roundabout. A variety of Chinese and Malay dishes, as well as a limited range of seafood. Inexpensive.

Restoran Seafood Chinese Jalan Ismail. One of the best seafood restaurants in town, with a/c and a good selection of crab, prawn and mussel dishes at around RM10 each.

North of Mersing

About 35km north of Mersing along Route 3, past **Kampung Air Papan** (reputed to have the best beach in the locality), is the village of **Padang Endau**, on the Johor side of the Sungai Endau. Across the bridge in Pahang state, 3km from the village centre, is the **Tanjung Gemuk ferry terminal**, from where there are daily services to Tioman at 10am and 2pm (RM30 one-way; ☎09/413 1997). The journey is slightly faster than from Mersing, taking just over an hour to reach the *Berjaya Tioman Beach Resort*, the first stop on the island. The jetty consists of a largely empty development of shops and the *Seri Malaysia Hotel* (☎09/413 2725, ⓦ www.serimalaysia.com.my; ❹), which organizes trips into the Endau Rompin National Park. Heading further north up Route 3 brings you eventually to the former state capital of Pahang, Pekan, served by hourly buses from Mersing.

Pulau Tioman

Shaped like a giant apostrophe in the South China Sea, **PULAU TIOMAN**, 30km northeast of Mersing, has long been one of Malaysia's most popular holiday islands. Thirty-eight kilometres in length and nineteen kilometres at its widest point, it is the largest of the 64 volcanic islands that form the **Scribuat Archipelago**. According to legend, the origins of Pulau Tioman lie in the flight of a dragon princess on her way to China. She fell in love with the surrounding waters and decided to settle here permanently by transforming her body into an island. The first mention of the island in official records dates back to 1403, when a Chinese trading expedition to Southeast Asia and Mecca found Tioman, with its abundant supplies of fresh water, a handy stopping place. Shipping charts called it Zhumaskan, though local inhabitants believe the island to be named after the *tiong* (hill mynah bird) that is commonly found here.

Ever since the 1970s, when Tioman was voted one of the ten most beautiful islands in the world by *Time* magazine, crowds have been flocking to its palm-fringed shores, in search of the mythical Bali H'ai (for which it was the chosen film location in the Hollywood musical, *South Pacific*). But thirty years is a long time in tourism; where slow fishing vessels used to ply the seas for the arduous five-hour journey to Tioman, noisy express boats now complete the trip in less than two hours. These services, and the several daily flights from Singapore and other parts of the Peninsula, have helped destroy the sense of romantic isolation that once made the island so popular. However, Pulau Tioman displays a remarkable resilience, and to fail to visit it is to miss out – the greater part of the island has still not lost its intimate, village atmosphere. Those in search of unspoilt beaches will on the whole be disappointed, though there are some superb exceptions. The island was designated a "**duty-free island**" by Malaysian Customs, meaning visitors from both Singapore and the Malaysian mainland can combine sunshine and shopping in one neat package. With grand duty-free shopping plazas already in the planning stages, it remains to be seen whether this initiative will revitalize the island, as intended, or signal the final nail in the coffin for this once tranquil island paradise.

As you approach, Tioman's mountains loom above you, shrouded in cloud; the two peculiar granite pinnacles of Bukit Nenek Semukut on the southern part of the island are known as *chula naga* (dragon's horns). The sheer size and inaccessibility of its mountainous spine has preserved its most valuable asset – the dense **jungle**; you can go **wildlife-spotting** on its few easy hikes, which afford a high chance of seeing mousedeer, tree snakes, flying lemur, long-tailed macaques and monitor lizards, some upwards of six feet long. There are also plenty of opportunities for **outdoor activities**, particularly diving (see box, below) and watersports. Look out for the clusters of greater frigate birds that gather on the surrounding islands and rocks; occasionally you'll even see Christmas Island frigate **birds**, which breed only on the island after which they are named, more than 2000km south of Tioman. The island's ridge of mountains culminates in an impressive cluster of peaks in the south, of which the highest, **Gunung Kajang** (1038m), is inaccessible to all but the most experienced and well-equipped climbers.

Like the rest of the Peninsula's east coast, Tioman is affected by the **monsoon** between November and February, when the whole island winds down dramatically and many places close. July and August are the busiest months, when prices increase and accommodation is best booked in advance. Even in the dry season (March to October), it rains almost daily here; cloud seems to hang permanently around the island's mountainous ridge.

Accommodation possibilities range from the island's one international-standard resort, through to chalet developments and simple beachfront A-frames – the latter being gradually edged out by tin-roofed box chalets. The standard and pricing of each type of accommodation – A-frames, box chalets with shower, air-conditioned chalets – hardly varies from place to place on the same beach, so it's a good idea to pick your spot according to atmosphere and view as much as anything else. Most of the places to stay on Tioman are along the west coast, with the largest concentration of popular budget establishments being in the bay of Air Batang, just north of the island's grotty main village, Tekek. The east coast's sole settlement, Juara, is very quiet – you'll easily find a place to stay here or in Air Batang for under RM20 per head. Genting and

---

Snorkelling and diving around Pulau Tioman

With such abundant **marine life** in waters around Tioman, it's unlikely that you'll want to be island-bound the whole time. Many of the nearby islets provide excellent opportunities for **snorkelling**, and most of the chalet operations offer **day-trips** for the purpose, costing around RM25 (excluding equipment). The relatively untouched coral and huge biodiversity in these temperate waters make for some world-class **dive sites**. Many dive centres on Tioman offer a full range of PADI certificates, from an intensive four-day "Open Water" course which includes three days of theory and seven to nine dives (around RM750), through to the fourteen-day "Dive Master" (RM1300); check that qualified English-speaking instructors are employed, and that the cost includes all the necessary equipment. For the already qualified, two dives cost RM160 per person. Of the dive shops, B&J's in Air Batang is the best established (☎09/419 1218) with a second shop in Salang (☎09/419 5555).

Golden Reef (typical depth 10–20m). Fifteen minutes off the northwestern coast; rocks provide a breeding ground for marine life, as well as producing many soft corals.

Salang are smaller, slightly more upmarket resorts though both have budget outlets, while Paya and Nipah, together with Mukut on the island's southern coast, are just opening up to tourism. Long gone are the days when you had to resort to a hurricane lamp at night – everywhere has an electricity supply now, albeit from a local generator. **Nightlife** has still to take off, however, though beer is available everywhere on the island.

Arrival and information

Arriving by express boat or speedboat **from Mersing**, it's important to decide in advance which bay or village you want to stay in, since the express boats generally make drops only at the major resorts of Genting, Paya, Tekek, Air Batang and Salang (in that order). There are only occasional express boats from Mersing to Juara on the east coast, though you could get a speedboat here. The two daily ferries here **from Tanjung Gemuk** stop first at the *Berjaya Tioman Beach Resort*. The on again, off again ferry **from Singapore** was off at the time of writing, though you can contact the *Berjaya Tioman Beach Resort* to see if the service has started anew. The **tourist office** (daily 7.30–11.30am & 2–4.30pm), situated right beside the jetty at Air Batang, can help with boat tickets or day-trips.

Arriving **by air**, you land at the airstrip in Tekek, from where there's a half-hourly shuttle bus to the *Berjaya Tioman Beach Resort*, 2km to the south. To reach the other beaches, you will have to rent a boat, or walk.

Getting around the island

The road between Tekek and the *Berjaya Tioman Beach Resort*, used by the airport bus, is the only one on the island wide enough for vehicles other than motorbikes. A two-metre-wide concrete path, used by motorbikes and walkers, runs north from Tekek to the headland marking the end of the beach, a twenty-minute walk; the path commences again on the other side of the rocks for the length of Air Batang. The network of **trails** is limited, though crossing the island has been made a lot easier by the building of cement steps beginning around ten minutes' walk north from Tekek jetty and running intermittently as far as Juara (see p.404 for

Pulau Chebeh (15–25m). In the northwestern waters, this is a massive volcanic labyrinth of caves and channels. Napoleon fish, trigger fish and turtles are present in abundance.

Pulau Labas (5–15m). South of Pulau Tulai, tunnels and caves provide a home for puffer fish, moray eels and corals such as fan and sweet-lip nudibranch.

Pulau Renggis (5–13m). Near the *Berjaya Tioman*, this sheltered spot is suitable for training and night dives. Good for spotting barracuda, stingray, angel fish and buffalo fish, as well as two resident, harmless black-tip sharks.

Tiger Reef (10–25m). Southwest of Pulau Tulai, and deservedly the most popular site, with yellow-tail snappers, trevally and tuna, spectacular soft coral and gorgonian fans.

Tokong Magicienne (10–25m). Due north of Pulau Tioman, this colourful, sponge-layered coral pinnacle is a feeding station for larger fish – silver snappers, golden-striped trevally, jacks and groupers.

Tokong Malang (5–15m). Just off the southeastern tip of Pulau Tulai, this shallow reef traversed by sand channels is full of sponges. Watch out for barracuda, large cuttlefish, yellow-spotted stingray and leopard shark.

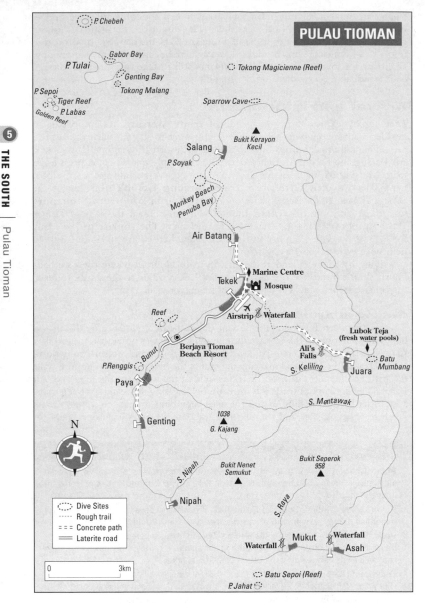

details of the route). During the dry season a 4WD jeep "taxi" plies the dirt track between Tekek and Juara. The trip costs RM75 and can take up to three passengers. Less obvious trails connect Genting with Paya, and Air Batang with Penuba Bay, Monkey Beach and Salang – details are given in the respective sections.

Transport around the shore of the island is via hired boats; these are very expensive by Malaysian standards, the cheapest hops costing RM50–75. To get

Although many of the travel agencies in Mersing may try to sell you an open-return boat ticket to Tioman, tickets are readily available from outlets at any of the bays on the island. **Express boats** all leave at around 7 or 8am daily, making their pick-ups from each jetty. Slower boats usually leave before noon, picking up from every bay – check with your chalet-owner. The ferry to Tanjung Gemuk (12 noon & 4pm) leaves from the *Berjaya Tioman Beach Resort*. If you are planning to leave Tioman during a full or new moon, ask ahead of time if the tidal conditions will affect departure times. There are also **flights** to Kuala Lumpur (daily; RM214) and Singapore (daily; RM240) with Berjaya Air (℡09/419 1303, ℗www.berjaya-air.com). You can make reservations for Berjaya Air at the *Berjaya Tioman Beach Resort* (℡09/414 1000).

from one side of the island to the other will cost anywhere from RM150 to RM250. You could also hop onto one of the **round-the-island boat trips** (RM70) which run from the various chalets, but they tend to spend an hour or so in each spot. Since so much of the west coast is paved, **bicycle rental** – at RM4 an hour from several outlets in Tekek and Air Batang – seems a sensible option, but you can't go far without having to carry the bike over the headlands at some point.

Tekek

The sprawling village of **TEKEK**, the main settlement on the island, isn't really a place you'd want to stay for long. Years of over-development have been followed by an economic slump, and much of the seafront is now run-down or fenced off. The incessant stream of chugging ferries, the roar of aeroplanes and the churning of concrete mixers all combine to make Tekek the least inspiring part of Tioman.

The shabby central beach has yet to get a face-lift, and the whole area suffers from an unpleasant litter problem, though things start to get better well south of the main jetty where, apart from a few high-end resorts, the shore is relatively unspoilt. For a break from the beach, pop into the **Tioman Island Museum** (daily 9.30am–5pm; RM2) on the first floor of the airstrip's terminal complex. Apart from displaying some twelfth- to fourteenth-century Chinese ceramics, which were lost overboard from early trading vessels, it also outlines the facts and myths concerning the island. North of the main jetty, at the very end of the bay, is the government-sponsored **Marine Centre**, its hefty concrete jetty and dazzlingly blue roofs making it hard to miss. Set up to protect the coral and marine life around the island, and to patrol the fishing taking place in its waters, the centre also contains an aquarium and displays of coral (daily 9.30am–4.30pm; free).

Practicalities

You'll find the **post office**, moneychangers and TM Mart **Internet** (daily 9.30am–10pm; RM7 per hour) in the new terminal complex next to the airstrip. The police station is a five-minute walk south from here. Most of the **places to eat** are attached to the chalet operations; the best are those with beachside settings, such as *Sri Tioman Chalets*. One of Tekek's nicest restaurants, *Liza*, is at the far southern end of the bay, with a wide-ranging menu specializing in seafood and Western snacks – the average meal here costs in the neighbourhood of RM20.

There are lots of **places to stay** in Tekek, though most are dilapidated and located next to piles of rubbish and the ever-present building materials. However, the high-end options well south of the main beach can be a good choice, especially the *Berjaya Tioman Beach Resort*, the only place of an international standard here. With Air Batang just a little way north, though, it's hard to see why anyone would want to stay in Tekek proper.

Berjaya Tioman Beach Resort ☎09/419 1000, Ⓦ www.berjaya resorts.com. A village-sized complex set in impeccably manicured grounds 1500m south of Tekek, with everything from double rooms to deluxe apartments; other facilities include two pools, tennis courts, horse riding, water sports and a golf course. Occasional promotions offer good value. ❾

Monté Chalet ☎09/419 1648. The simple wooden chalets here, some right on the beach, are nice enough from the outside, but the interiors are not up to much. There's a branch of Eco-Divers on site. ❸

Persona Island Resort ☎09/419 6215, Ⓔ pesonahotelresort@hotmail.com. A pleasant, upmarket operation with sturdy hotel-style rooms and an airy restaurant set around a courtyard. The management offer island-hopping tours to more remote parts of the archipelago. If occupancy is high, a seafood barbecue is usually arranged for RM10 per person. ❺

Sri Tioman Chalets ☎09/419 1189. Good atmosphere and value, with a reasonable seafood restaurant and chalets set on the beach in front of the *Persona*. ❷

Swiss Cottage Beach Resort ☎09/419 1642. Just north of the *Berjaya Tioman* resort in a shady jungle setting, the beach here is among the best in Tekek, and its bamboo-weave huts, set in a garden, are good value. There's also a dive shop and small restaurant. ❸

Air Batang and Penuba Bay

Despite its ever-increasing popularity, **AIR BATANG**, 2km north of Tekek from jetty to jetty, is still one of the best areas on Tioman, competing with Juara for the budget market. Larger than Salang or Juara, far less developed than Tekek and well connected by boat services, Air Batang, or ABC as it's often called, is a happy medium as far as many visitors are concerned; what development there is here tends to be relatively tasteful and low-key.

A jetty divides the bay roughly in half; the beach is better at the southern end of the bay, close to the promontory, though the shallow northern end is safer for children. The cement path that runs the length of the beach is interrupted by little wooden bridges over streams, overhung with greenery. A fifteen-minute **trail** leads over the headland to the north which, after an initial scramble, flattens out into an easy walk, ending up at **Penuba Bay**. This secluded cove is littered with dead coral right up to the sea's edge, which makes it hard to swim comfortably, though the snorkelling is good; many people prefer the peace and quiet here to the beach at Air Batang. From Penuba Bay, it's an hour's walk to Monkey Beach, beyond which is Salang.

Accommodation

As you get off the boat, a signpost helpfully lists the direction of the numerous **places to stay** in the bay. All but the most basic A-frames have fans and their own bathrooms, and mosquito nets are usually provided. Anything costing more than about RM50 a night should have a hot shower. Unless specified otherwise, all accommodation below sleeps two people. **Internet** facilities are available at *ABC*, *Nazri's* and *Bamboo Hill*, but they're uniformly expensive (around RM10 an hour).

ABC ☎09/419 1154. At the far northern end of the bay, and therefore a little quieter than most, this long-established operation is still among the best in Air Batang. The pretty chalets are set in a well-tended garden with its own freshwater stream. In addition to basic huts (❷) there are five newer, more sturdy chalets (❻) furnished much like those at *Bamboo* next door.

Bamboo Hill Chalets ☎09/419 1339, ✉bamboosu@tm.net.my. Six beautiful wooden chalets on stilts, perched on the northern headland of Air Batang, with stunning views. The rooms are well equipped, with bathrooms, fridges, mosquito screens and bedside lamps. Excellent value – the best accommodation in Air Batang. ❻

Johan's ☎09/419 1359, ✉jjohan@goplay.com. A good choice, with well-spaced standard chalets and larger ones up the hill on a pleasant lawn, although staff can be surly. There's also a dorm (RM10–12); some rooms have a/c. ❷–❹

Mawar Beach Chalet ☎09/419 1153. Simple, well-run chalets with a good location right on the beach; rooms are smallish but have a veranda. There's also a restaurant and resident monitor lizard. ❷

Mokhtar's Place ☎09/419 1148. South of the jetty, this place is more comfortable than most, though the chalets are a little close together and face inwards, rather than out to sea. ❷

Nazri's II ☎09/419 1375, ✉cabnora@tm.net .my. Located at the northern end of Air Batang, this elaborate outfit boasts large, a/c cottages set in spacious grounds, as well as some ordinary, cheaper chalets at the back. The lively restaurant offers a good selection of travellers' fare with a few local dishes. ❷–❹

Nazri's Place ☎09/419 1329, ✉bungur@tm.net .my. At the southern end of the bay, this has the best bit of beach on the strip and offers the same range of rooms as the affiliated *Nazri's II*, as well as massage and reflexology. The twelve new luxury rooms have a/c. ❷–❹

Penuba Inn Resort ☎013/772 0454. The only accommodation at Penuba Bay, with a quieter beach than at Air Batang. If you stay here, you're committed to eating here every night too, unless you fancy a scramble over the headland in the dark. Its chalets, on stilts and high up on the rocks, have fantastic views out to sea. ❷

Rinda Resort ☎09/419 1157. A good spot in a neat, shaded setting at the northern end of Air Batang, perfect for lying in one of their hammocks and watching the sun go down. One of the friendliest and lowest-priced hostels on Tioman, with simple, clean en-suite huts. ❷

South Pacific ☎09/419 1176. Close to the jetty. Clean chalets with attached bathrooms, some right on the beach. This place offers long-term stays at less than half the normal rate. ❷

Eating, drinking and nightlife

Air Batang keeps its **nightlife** low-key, unlike Salang, which can get rowdy during the season. Most of the chalets have their own **restaurants**, open to non-residents. Menus, which tend to reflect Western tastes, have fish as a staple feature.

🏃 **ABC** Good-quality food – chicken and fish dishes average RM10 – and fresh fruit juices. The informal bar and good sound system mean this friendly joint is always rocking.

Mokhtar's Place Serves traditional Malay food; you won't need to part with more than about RM7 per person.

Nazri's II The food is slightly more expensive than elsewhere – chicken-in-a-basket or burgers

average RM8. The balcony is great for a sunset beer, and there's a lively atmosphere.

🏃 **Nazri's Place** Recently rebuilt after a fire, and in the same great location on the beach, Nazri's once again does a very hearty breakfast for RM8.50 and lots of Western-style food for lunch and dinner (around RM10 a dish).

Salang and Monkey Beach

Just over 4km north of Air Batang, **SALANG** is a smaller bay with a better beach. Nevertheless, there has been a lot of development and every suitable inch of land has been built on. In fact, even unsuitable land has been used – the large *Nadia Inn Resort* built on Salang's southern headland has never opened because the steep ground on which it is built has been deemed unsafe. The crowded accommodation here makes for a busy and vibrant atmosphere, and with a couple of lively bars, Salang is the only place on the island with much **nightlife** to speak of.

Though most accommodation here costs a shade more than at Air Batang, there are still lots of budget choices. The southern end of the beach is the more scenic, while swimming is a bit of an ordeal at the northern end, where sharp rocks and coral make the water difficult to approach. Just off the southern headland is a small island, Pulau Soyak, with a pretty reef for snorkelling.

A rough trail takes you over the headland to the south for the 45-minute scramble to **Monkey Beach**. There are few monkeys around these days, but the well-hidden cove is more than adequate compensation. It's a popular spot for

trainee divers because of its clear, calm waters, and you may want to base yourself here to take advantage of the two good **dive schools**, Dive Asia and Ben's Diving Centre, both of which run daily courses (RM725–1200), with instruction in English and German.

Practicalities

On the right (south) as you leave the jetty are a little cluster of budget **places to stay**, listed opposite. You can get **online** at the *Salang Beach Resort* and *Salang Huts* if you can stomach the hefty charge. There is a two-level choice when it comes to **eating**: the expensive restaurants at *Salang Dream* and *Salang Beach Resort*, where the emphasis is on Malay

△ Seaside accommodation, Salang

cuisine and seafood at around RM10 per dish, and the more informal cafés around town, serving excellent Western and Malay dishes for no more than RM3. For **nightlife**, there are several choices: *Na Café* next to B&J Diving Centre and, further north, the *Sunset Boulevard*, which has the best views of the bay.

Accommodation

Nora's Chalet ☎09/419 5003. A friendly family operation, whose well-kept chalets with bathroom, fan and mosquito nets make them the best value here, set behind the little lagoon

where the local monitor lizards are getting on to alligator size. ❷

Pak Long Chalet ☎09/419 5000. Set in a shady garden with a range of chalets starting at RM20, the accommodation here is good value. ❶–❷

Salang Beach Resort ☎09/419 5022,
ⓔnatureholiday@hotmail.com. A variety of rooms
all packed together including fan and a/c chalets,
all with wall-to-wall carpets. ❷

Salang Huts ☎09/419 5027. These tumbledown
huts at the far end of the bay are considerably
quieter than others along the stretch, though they
overlook unattractive piles of rocks and there's no
beach to speak of. ❷

Salang Indah ☎09/419 5015, ⓕ419 5024.
The largest outfit in Salang, towards the centre
of the bay, with well-appointed chalets to suit
every budget, from run-of-the-mill box rooms
(❷) to sea-facing family chalets with a/c and hot

shower (❻); they also arrange snorkelling and
diving trips.

Salang Pusaka Resort ☎09/419 5317,
ⓔsalangpusaka@yahoo.com. With friendly
management, this place is set back from the
beach in landscaped gardens. Some of the rooms
have a/c. ❸

Salang Sayang Resort ☎09/415 5020,
ⓔsalangsayang@hotmail.com. At the southern
end of the beach, this well-located resort has
comfortable, hillside chalets (❸) and more
expensive sea-facing ones (❹). There are also
some family rooms (❺).

Juara

As Tioman's western shore becomes more and more developed, many people
are making their way to **JUARA**, the only settlement on the east coast. Life
is simpler here; the locals speak less English and are much more conservative than elsewhere on the island (officially, alcohol isn't served in Juara).
Although Juara's seclusion may have saved it so far from the excesses all too
apparent on the west coast, plenty of simple chalet resorts have already been
built – any more, and the village might begin to lose its peaceful appeal. For
the time being, however, Juara has fewer speedboats and motorbikes buzzing
around, while its lovely wide sweep of beach is far cleaner and less crowded
than anywhere on the other side of the island. The constant sea breeze means
that fans aren't necessary, though the downside to this is that the water is
always choppy, and the bay, facing out to the open sea, is the most susceptible
on the island to bad weather.

There are a couple of very easy **walks** from Juara; a 45-minute stroll to Ali's
Fall, a big freshwater pond good for swimming, and a slightly harder hour-long
jungle trek to Lubok Teja, another good spot for a dip. Maps (RM2) are available at the sea bus ticket counter at the jetty.

Practicalities

An old trail from Tekek to Juara, said to be a leftover from the days during World
War II when the Japanese occupied the island, has been widened enough so that
4WD vehicles can make the trip. The only one on the island for hire belongs
to a friendly guy named Kennet (☎013/780 9543) who will make the one-
way trip for RM75, which can be split three ways. There are also a number of
motorcycle "taxis" that can do the trip for RM25 each way, but it is more than
a little dangerous, especially if you have a pack – hang around long enough and
you'll see some sorry limper who tried it but couldn't hang on. The cheapest
way to get to Juara is on foot through the jungle, a steep trek that takes about
two hours from Tekek, not counting rest stops. The start of the trail (a five-
minute walk from the airstrip) is easy enough to identify, since it's the only
concrete path that heads off in that direction. The path passes the local mosque
but the paved section ends soon after. Continue in the same direction into the
jungle; a rocky path and intermittent sections of concrete steps guide you uphill
through the greenery, tapering off into a smooth, downhill path once you're
over the ridge. En route there are unusual blue ferns, and some of the rarer trees
are labelled. After 45 minutes, there's a **waterfall**, where it's forbidden to bathe
– it supplies Tekek with water. From this spot, it's another hour or so to Juara

village, which consists of two bays; the path emerges at the northern one, opposite the **jetty**.

Accommodation

Most of the **accommodation** is on the northern bay (along with the restaurants), within a five-minute walk of the jetty. Although the southern bay does have a few chalets, to get to the nearest restaurants from here you'll face a long scramble over the rocks or a dark walk along the concrete path that runs behind all the developments. Most of the places of accommodation have no phones, and would probably not bother with taking reservations even if you could call; simply turn up and hope for a vacancy.

Among the places to stay, *Paradise Point* (❶) is the only one north of the jetty, about 200m away along the beach; it has the cheapest chalets here, with attached bathrooms. *Atan's* (❷), just south of the jetty and the path, boasts two interesting, two-storey guesthouses, rather like Swiss chalets. The biggest operation here, though, is *Mutiara* (☎09/419 3159, ℱ419 3160; ❶–❸), with a wide variety of rooms and prices including dorms for RM8 – these are also the people to see if you want to arrange a boat trip for fishing or **snorkelling**. They have more chalets behind their shop, a little way north along the beach. A little further south, *Basir* has good sea-facing chalets (❷) and some cheaper huts as well, while at the southern end of the strip, ⚓ *Bushman Huts* (☎09/419 3109; ❶), *Sunrise* (❶) and *Rainbow* (❶) have characterful, painted A-frames right on the beach.

If you follow the path round to the even quieter southern bay, you'll find that the beach here is even better than that of its northern counterpart; there are several cheap places to stay, including *Mizani Chalet* (☎09/547 8445; ❷), which boasts clean huts and its own restaurant.

Eating

While there's less choice for **eating** than on the west coast, portions here tend, on the whole, to be larger, and the menus more imaginative. The restaurant at *Paradise Point* does good *rotis*, as well as unusual dishes such as fish with peanut sauce and fried rice with coconut, averaging around RM5. Two simple places, *Ali Putra* and *Beach Café*, nestle side by side at the jetty; both have a huge range of local and Western dishes. South of the jetty, *Happy Café* is always busy, has good music and is one of the few places where you can get ice cream, among other things, while the restaurant at *Sunrise* is open for breakfast and lunch only, offering muesli, home-baked bread and cakes, as well as the usual rice and noodle fare. At night, try *Bushman's*, next to *Sunrise*, and the only place serving alcohol at Juara.

Asah and Mukut

On the southeast corner of the island are the deserted remains of the village at **ASAH**; you can get here on the round-the-island boat trip, or take a sea taxi from Genting (RM60 per person), the nearest point of access. These days, the only signs of life are the trails of litter left by day-trippers dropping by to visit the famous **waterfall**, the setting for the *Happy Talk* sequence from the film version of *South Pacific*. A fifteen-minute walk from the ramshackle jetty, the twenty-metre-high cascade is barely recognizable as the one in the film, though certainly photogenic enough. Though the deep-plunge pool at the foot of the waterfall provides a refreshing dip, there's not much else to detain you in Asah, except for the stunning view of the dramatic, insurmountable twin peaks of **Bukit Nenet Semukut**.

Mukut

It's far better to spend time at nearby **MUKUT**, a tiny fishing village just five minutes from Asah by sea taxi, in the shadow of granite outcrops. Shrouded by dense forest, and connected to the outside world by a solitary cardphone, it's a wonderfully peaceful and friendly spot to unwind, though be warned that this is still a conservative place, unused to Western sunbathing habits.

Having paid handsomely to get here, you'll probably want to make it worth your while by **staying** for some time. The nicest position is occupied by *Chalets Park* (❸), with secluded chalets shaded by trees. The accommodation at *Sri Tanjung Chalets* (❷), at the far western end of the cove, overlooks a patch of beach – book at the house in the village where the name is painted on a tyre. Places to eat are few and basic; the *Sri Sentosa* is a bit on the dingy side, though popular with the locals, while the views from *Mukut Coral Resort* (☎09/412 0392 ❶) just by the jetty make up for their lack of variety menu-wise.

South of Tekek: Paya, Genting and Nipah

The western beaches south of Tekek are rarely frequented by foreign tourists, though they're popular with local holiday-makers. There also seems to be more of a sense of local kampung life here, despite the concrete resorts. Just 5km south of Tekek, the understated developments at **PAYA**, in contrast to those at Genting a little further south, seem relatively peaceful. Once again, package tours are the norm, and individual travellers turning up at this narrow stretch of pristine beach will find their options somewhat limited.

Jungle walks are worth exploring here, as the island's greenery is at its most lush, despite the minor inroads made by the resorts. The thirty-minute trail north to Bunut ends up at a fantastic, deserted beach. From here it's a hot 45-minute walk through the golf course back to the *Berjaya Tioman Beach Resort* and a further half-hour to Tekek. You can also walk between Paya and Genting, a pretty thirty-minute route along a concrete coastal path.

The *Paya Holiday* (☎09/4197090; ❹), right in the centre of the small bay, is quite serviceable. A little further to the north, the *Paya Beach Resort* (☎07/799 1432, ⓦwww.payabeach.com; ❼) has comfortable chalets, and offers seasports and snooker. By far the best operation is the *Paya Tioman Resort* (☎09/419 7073, ⓔtiomanpr@tm.net.my; ❹), set back in the woodland, with an open-air restaurant and barbecue facilities. The best place **to eat** in Paya is the *NR Seafood Restaurant* in the centre of the beachfront, which has a good selection of tasty, hot Malay specials and some Chinese dishes.

Genting

Usually the first stop for boats from the mainland, the ugly blot of **GENTING**, at the western extremity of the island, hardly offers a heartening welcome. The settlement, its cramped developments catering largely for Singaporean tour groups, is awash with discos and karaoke bars. Except during weekends and holidays (when prices rise by about fifty percent), it has a rather gloomy feel.

The southern end of the beach is the best, and where most of the low-budget **accommodation** is situated. There's little to choose between *Genting Jaya* (℡07/799 4811; ❷) and the many similar, unnamed places nearby, all offering wooden bedrooms. *Sun Beach* (℡07/799 4918; ❸), the largest enterprise just north of the jetty, has the widest variety of rooms and a large balcony restaurant. **Places to eat** are generally limited to big, open-plan restaurants attached to the resorts; the emphasis is on catering for large numbers rather than providing interesting, quality meals. Prices are predictably inflated, though the *Yonghwa Restaurant* in front of the jetty has more moderately priced dishes on its Chinese-based menu.

Nipah

For almost total isolation, head to **NIPAH** on Tioman's southwest coast. This is the closest you'll get to an idyllic beach hideaway on the island, comprising a clean, empty beach of coarse, yellow sand, and a landlocked lagoon. It has no village to speak of, though there is a **Dive Centre** and canoeing. You might be lucky enough to get a ferry from the mainland to drop you here since there's an adequate jetty, but it's more likely that you'll have to come by sea taxi from Genting, costing around RM30 per person.

There's only one **place to stay**: the *Nipah Chalets* (book through Island Connection in Mersing, ℡07/799 2535, who will organize a free sea taxi from Genting; ❷), offering basic chalets and more expensive A-frames, as well as a nicely designed restaurant; the food can get a little monotonous though. The air-conditioned longhouse, *Nipah Paradise*, at the far end, caters only for pre-booked packages from Singapore.

The other Seribuat islands

Though Pulau Tioman is the best known and most visited of the 64 volcanic islands which form the **SERIBUAT ARCHIPELAGO**, there are a handful of other accessible islands whose beaches and opportunities for seclusion outstrip those of their larger rival. For archetypal azure waters and table-salt sand, four in particular stand out: Pulau Besar, Pulau Tinggi, Pulau Sibu and Pulau Rawa – though none of them are particularly geared to a tight budget. All the islands

---

Sandflies

Sandflies can be a real problem on all of the Seribuat islands, though reputedly Juara, on the east coast of Tioman, is the worst place, especially in summer. These little pests, looking like tiny fruit flies, with black bodies and white wings, suck blood and so cause an extremely itchy lump, which can sometimes become a nasty blister if scratched. The effectiveness of various treatments and deterrents is much debated; the general feeling is that short of dousing yourself all over with insect repellent or hiding out in the sea all day long, there's not much you can do to avoid the insects, although using suntan oil rather than lotion or cream is supposed to help. Urine (your own) is among the more esoteric remedies for the itching. The closest thing to a consensus, though, seems to be that Tiger Balm, available at any chemist, can reduce the maddening itch and help you get a night's sleep.

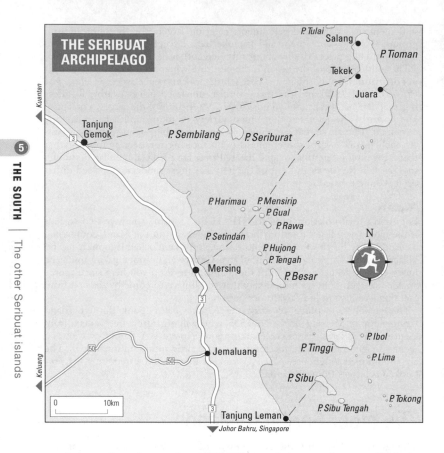

THE SERIBUAT
ARCHIPELAGO

P. Tulai Salang
P. Tioman
Tekek
Juara

Tanjung
Gemok
P. Sembilang *P. Seriburat*

3

P. Harimau *P. Mensirip*
  P. Gual
    P. Rawa
P. Setindan

P. Hujong
P. Tengah
Mersing

P. Besar

N

3

P. Ibol
P. Tinggi *P. Lima*

50 Jemaluang
50

P. Sibu
P. Tokong
0   10km
3 Tanjung Leman *P. Sibu Tengah*
▼ Johor Bahru, Singapore

are designated **marine parks** and, like Tioman, belong to the state of Pahang, unlike their port of access, Mersing, which lies in Johor.

Omar's Backpackers' Hostel and the *New East Coast Hotel* in Mersing (see p.394) both offer one-day island-hopping trips, the only cheap way of seeing several islands at the same time. The trips (Feb–Nov daily 10am; 7hr; RM70) usually take in either three islands to the south of Mersing (Pulau Hujung, Tengah and Besar) or four to the north (Pulau Harimau, Mensirip, Gual and Rawa). The use of snorkelling equipment, together with a packed lunch and boat transport from one splendid coral reef to another, is included in the price.

Pulau Rawa

The privately owned island of **Pulau Rawa** is only a 30-minute boat ride from Mersing (1 departure daily, noon; RM35 one-way). Although the island's sugary sands and transparent waters get rave reviews, the sandflies are unavoidable, and you're not allowed to bring your own food and drink. There's only one **place to stay** on the island, the deluxe *Rawa Safaris Island Resort* (☎07/799 1204, ⓦwww.rawasfr.com; ❺), where there are cheaper *atap*-roofed A-frames as well as comfortable, well-equipped chalets with air conditioning and proper bathrooms, and every facility for watersports. Try to book in advance, especially at weekends.

Pulau Besar

The long and narrow **PULAU BESAR**, 4km by 1km in size, is also known as Pulau Babi Besar, or "Big Pig Island". About half an hour's ride from Mersing by ferry (1 daily around noon; RM50 one-way), it's one of the most developed islands, with a variety of resorts and chalets, but despite this, you're still likely to have the place to yourself outside the main holiday periods.

Topped by two peaks, Bukit Atap Zink (225m) and Bukit Berot (275m), the island is crossed by three relatively easy **trails**: a ten-minute stroll from behind the *Hillside Chalet Island Resort*, at the northern end of the island, brings you to the Beach of Passionate Love; while an hour's walk starting either from behind the central jetty or from just beyond the *Nirvana Resort* leads to secluded bays. The island is supposedly sheltered from the worst of the monsoon, but there's a strong undertow and constant sea breeze even in the dry season.

Accommodation and eating

With one exception, the resorts are all located at intervals on the west-facing beach, the best on the island. Top among them is the *Aseania Island Resort* (☎07/799 4152, ☞799 1413; ❻), more or less in the middle of the bay, with superbly designed chalets and a swimming pool. To the north of the *Aseania* is the *D'Coconut Island Resort* (☎07/799 2381, ✉dcoconut@tm.net.my; ❼) with twenty comfortable bungalows offering air conditioning, hot showers and TVs. The only budget-oriented place is a set of four A-frames (❷) right by the sea, not far from the *Aseania* – ask at the small shop by the phone and post box. The *Niwana Resort* (☎07/799 5979, ☞799 5978; ❺), at the far southern end of the bay, has its own jetty and the best bit of beach on the island; its clapboard buildings look a bit motley at first sight, but they're quite comfortable inside. Right at the far northern end of the island, the exclusive *Hillside Chalet Island Resort* (☎07/799 4831; ❻) has an isolated setting, a good thirty-minute walk from the rest of the developments. Its beach isn't that special, but the chalets are comfortable, arranged in flourishing green gardens; breakfast is included in the rate.

All the places to stay have their own **restaurants**, open to non-residents; the *Aseania* has an elegant open-air restaurant designed to catch the sea breezes, with dishes at RM10–15, while the one at the *Hillside* is the most expensive at around RM30 per head.

Pulau Sibu

Closest to the mainland, **PULAU SIBU** is the most popular of the islands after Tioman. Though it's also the least scenically interesting, the huge monitor lizards and the butterflies here make up for the lack of mountains and jungle. The island's narrow waist can be crossed in only a few minutes, revealing a double bay known as Twin Beach. Like the rest of the islands, Sibu boasts fine beaches, though the sand is yellower and the current more turbulent here than at some others; most of the coves have good offshore coral.

Practicalities

The majority of the resorts on Sibu operate their own boats from **Tanjung Leman**, a tiny mainland coastal village clearly signposted off Route 3, about 30km south of Mersing. These boats, which take an hour to reach the island, need to be arranged in advance, apart from the *Black Pudding*, a daily boat run by the *O&H Kampung Huts* (see below). Secure parking is available at the jetty for RM7 per day.

Tanjung Leman is awkward to get to without your own transport. If you're taking *O&H*'s boat, a free bus ride from Mersing is included – if not you pay RM10 for the journey. A taxi to the village from Johor Bahru or Mersing costs around RM60, but since there is no stand at Tanjung Leman, you must arrange to be picked up when you return.

Accommodation and eating

Halfway along Sibu's eastern coast, *O&H Kampung Huts* (☎07/799 3125) is a friendly and relaxed set-up of A-frames and some dearer, though still fairly basic, chalets. Also on the eastern side, the *Sea Gypsy Village Resort* (☎07/222 8642, ⓦwww.siburesort.com; ❻) is much more exclusive, aiming for the diving market, with all-inclusive packages costing around RM400 per night for two people. It's a tasteful place, with simple chalets and an attractive lounge and dining area. For something unusual, try *Rimba Resort* (☎012/7106855, ⓦwww .resortmalaysia.com; ❼) on the north coast, whose simply furnished, cosy two-bed cottages have an African theme and whose communal areas are scattered with floor cushions; they offer a package including boat transfers and all meals. ✚ *Sibu Island Cabanas* (☎07/861 4473, ⓦwww.sibuisland.com; ❻) is one of the lower-priced options – its chalets are shabby, though the stretch of beach is good. Head back from the *Cabanas*, over the small ridge in the centre of the island, to get to *Twin Beach Resort* (☎07/799 1268; ❸), the only place with views of both sunrises and sunsets; its A-frames and pricier chalets are run-down, but you can also camp here for free.

Eating on Pulau Sibu is a pleasure. The *O&H* has excellent fish and chicken curries with rice, vegetables and salad, as well as Western dishes, at around RM15 for a full meal. *Sea Gypsy* also offers great cuisine, including grilled fish, though for residents only. The restaurant at *Twin Beach* specializes in Chinese food at reasonable prices. As with most places offering accommodation along Malaysia's beaches, the dining facilities are open to all, whether a resident or not.

Pulau Tinggi

One of the largest islands of the group, **PULAU TINGGI**, a ninety-minute boat ride from Tanjung Leman (see p.409), is also the most distinctive, with its towering dormant volcanic peak sticking up like a giant upturned funnel (*tinggi* means "tall" or "high"). The mountain can be climbed, an arduous four-hour trip, though you need a local guide as the route can be quite dangerous. A gentler excursion is to the **waterfall**, about thirty minutes over the headland along a well-worn path; although it's pretty disappointing outside the rainy season, it has a splendid beach a little way downstream.

Accommodation is limited to a few resorts. *Nadia's Inn* (☎03/242 9506; ❷–❽) has comfortable chalets to suit every budget, as well as a bar and a good swimming pool. The friendly *Tinggi Island Resort* (☎019/775 0184; ❻), on a hillside overlooking the beach, is a little less plush, but has an extensive range of watersports facilities. You can **eat** at both of the resorts for about RM15 per person a meal, and at the food stalls by the jetty, which serve *nasi goreng*.

Endau Rompin National Park

One of the few remaining areas of lowland tropical rainforest left in Peninsular Malaysia, the **ENDAU ROMPIN NATIONAL PARK** covers approximately 870 square kilometres – about one and a half times the area of Singapore. Despite being valued by conservationists for the richness of both **flora and fauna** (see box below), the area was the site of damaging logging in the 1970s, and it wasn't until its designation as a national park in 1989 that adequate protective measures were finally put in place. This dense, lush habitat has nurtured several species new to science, including at least three trees, eight herbs and two mosses, documented by the Malaysian Nature Society during its 1985–86 expedition, which itself helped to establish the need for a properly controlled park here. There's plenty on offer for the less specialized nature-lover, from gentle **trekking** to more strenuous mountain-climbing and **rafting**; although gradually becoming accustomed to tourists, Endau Rompin still has a long way to go before it suffers the overuse that afflicts Taman Negara, and for the time being at least, its trails remain refreshingly untrampled.

Surrounding the headwaters of the lengthy Sungai Endau and sitting astride the Johor–Pahang state border, the region was shaped by volcanic eruptions more than 150 million years ago. The force of the explosions sent up huge clouds of ash, creating the quartz crystal ignimbrite that's still very much in evidence along the park's trails and rivers, its glassy shards glinting in the light. Endau Rompin's steeply sloped mountains level out into sandstone plateaux, and the park is watered by three **river systems** based around the main tributaries of Sungai Marong, Sungai Jasin and Sungai Endau, reaching out to the south and east. At the confluence of the latter two rivers, at the eastern end

---

Flora and fauna in Endau Rompin

There are at least seven species of **hornbill** (see box on p.509) in the park, which are hard to miss, particularly in flight, when their oversized, white-tipped wings counterbalance their enormous curved orange bills. Early in the morning, the hooting of the male **gibbon** joins the dawn chorus of insects, cuckoos and babblers. This is the time of day when the wildlife is most active; by noon all the action has died down. The late afternoon cool heralds a second burst of activity, and is a particularly good time for bird-watching, and at night, owls, frogs, rats and pythons are about. If you're on a tour with a guide, you've a better chance of spotting tiger or elephant **footprints**, though wild pigs, mousedeer and colourful toads are far more usual sightings. The park is also the habitat of the increasingly rare **Sumatran rhinoceros**, though this hides out in the far western area of the park, off-limits to visitors.

At the upper levels of the jungle, **epiphytes** are common: these non-parasitic plant take advantage of their position on tree branches to get the light they need for photosynthesis. Massive palms are found here too, but it's mostly orchids and ferns that flourish. Lower down in the forest shade, moths and spiders camouflage themselves among the greyish brown lichen that covers the barks, and squirrels and lizards scurry up and down. Much closer to eye level, where most of the light is cut out by the virtually impenetrable canopy, are **birds** like babblers and woodpeckers. You'll also see **tree frogs**, whose expanded disc-like toes and finger tips, sticky with mucus, help them cling to leaves and branches. The forest floor is mostly covered by **ferns and mosses**, as well as tree seedlings struggling to find sunlight from a chink in the canopy.

of the park, lies Endau Rompin's base camp at **Kuala Jasin**. Although the park's boundaries lie some distance before the rivers, it is only in these river valleys before Kuala Jasin that you can roam freely. The aboriginal people of the area are commonly referred to by the generic term **Orang Ulu**, meaning "upriver people" – their lives revolve around the rivers (you can still see them using dugouts made from a single tree trunk and canoes made of lengths of bark sewn together with twine). In recent years, these nomadic peoples, traditionally collectors of forest products such as resins, rattan and camphor wood, have become more settled, living in permanent villages such as Kampung Peta, accessible only by an old logging track two hours' drive from the nearest sealed road.

Acquiring a permit for the park can require a certain degree of determination and given that conditions inside the park are fairly primitive, it's best to book yourself on a tour; see "Practicalities" opposite for thorough information on visiting the park.

Hikes and trails

Near base camp, the **Janing Barat plateau** (710m) can be reached by a relatively easy four-hour trail which leads southeast from Kuala Jasin. Topped by a giant sandstone slab, the outcrop marks an abrupt change from the lush growth of wild ginger, characterized by its bright crimson flowers, and the ever-present betel-nut palm, in favour of tough fan palms above. On the ridge of the mountain, at around 450m, is a boggy, waterlogged area, producing a small patch of heath forest, though it is in the taller forest that most of the wild animals can be found – look out for the occasional group of pigs, or a solitary tapir chewing at the bark of the trees.

Each river boasts a major **waterfall**, the best of which is along Sungai Jasin, southwest of base camp. Two routes lead from the base camp to the head of the river, where the spectacular **Buaya Sangkut** cascades in a forty-metre torrent, almost as wide as it is high. A track along the northern bank leads directly to the falls, a six-hour hike across the multiple ridges of Bukit Segongong (765m). An Orang Ulu legend tells of an old crocodile who lived in the pools above the waterfall, and one day got stuck between some rocks, its body transforming itself into the whitewater rapids – the translation of the waterfall's name in fact means "trapped crocodile". A longer, less-defined trail branches off south, about ten minutes' walk out of base camp, crossing Sungai Jasin to reach the estuary, Kuala Marong, about 45 minutes later. From here, you can head east along Sungai Marong as far as Kuala Bunuh Sawa (2hr), or continue along Sungai Jasin to the **Upeh Guling** waterfall, ten minutes further on. Although initially less impressive than Buaya Sangkut, it has one striking feature: the collection of deep potholes just upstream of the falls. Here, the river's steep sides have been eroded by the water into smooth, natural bathtubs – a good place to soothe aching feet. Following the river closely for a further two hours brings you to **Batu Hampar** waterfall, where you can either pitch a tent, or continue the additional three hours to Buaya Sangkut.

Practicalities

The best time to visit Endau Rompin is between February and October, while the paths are dry and the rivers calm. During the monsoon, however, the park is completely inaccessible, since many of its waterways are swollen and the trails are too boggy to use. Further **information** on current conditions in the park can be obtained from the tourist office in Kuantan (see p.341). Take loose-fitting, lightweight cotton clothing that dries quickly – even in the dry season you're bound to get wet from crossing rivers – and helps to protect you from scratches and bites. Waterproofs will come in handy, and you'll need tons of insect repellent – and a lighter to burn off leeches.

There are two road routes to the park. From **Kuala Rompin** in Pahang, there's a paved road 26km to Selanding, followed by a dirt road for the remaining 24km to Kinchin, on the park boundary. From the **south**, you need to approach on **Route 50**: at the signpost for the Kahang oil-palm mill, 5km east of Kahang, turn north and continue for 48km along logging tracks (passable in an ordinary car unless it's very wet) until you reach the Orang Asli settlement of Kampung Peta, the site of the Visitor Control Centre; here you leave your car and register with the park rangers. To reach Route 50 from Mersing, take Route 3 south as far as Jemaluang, where you head west along Route 50 for a further 42km until you reach the turning for the park. From the Visitor Control Centre, it's another 15km to the base camp at Kuala Jasin, taking close to three hours on foot, though by boat it takes just 45 minutes (departures on request; RM20 per person). **By boat**, you can reach the park by making a trip upriver from **Endau**, 33km north of Mersing – a six-hour trip on a motorboat as far as Kampung Peta, costing around RM200 one way.

The only way to stay in the park is to book an **organized tour** through a travel agency, which will arrange permits and travel. Packages for non-Malaysians start at RM499 for a four-day/three-night package that includes meals at the park's A-frame bungalows. Packages can be booked at travel agents in Mersing or online (Ⓦ www.journeymalaysia.com /rainforestendaucamp.htm). In Mersing, either *Omar's* or the *New East Coast Hotel* (see p.394) can arrange packages. Ask at the Visitor Control Centre at Kampung Peta for advice on arranging a **rafting** trip; rafting down the peaty Sungai Endau is a possibility, with short stretches of stony bed and relatively sluggish flow interspersed by whitewater rapids and huge boulders. After the river merges with Sungai Kinchin, the flow becomes slower and the scenery generally less exciting.

Travel details

Trains

Gemas to: Kuala Lumpur (5 daily; 3hr 40min–4hr 15min).

Johor Bahru to: Gemas (5–6 daily; 3–5hr); Kuala Lipis (2 daily; 7hr); Kuala Lumpur (3 daily; 5hr 40min); Seremban (3 daily; 4hr 20min); Singapore (6 daily; 25min); Tumpat (1 daily; 12hr).

Segamat to: Kuala Lumpur (5 daily; 3hr 35min–5hr 10min).

Seremban to: Gemas (3 daily; 2hr); Johor Bahru (3 daily; 5–7hr); Kuala Lumpur (5 daily; 2hr); Singapore (3 daily; 6hr).

Buses

Johor Bahru to: Alor Setar (2 daily; 12hr); Butterworth (at least 2 daily; 9hr); Ipoh (4 daily; 6hr); Kota Bahru (2 daily; 10hr); Kuala Lumpur (hourly; 5hr); Kuala Terengganu (2 daily; 8hr); Kuantan (4 daily; 6hr); Melaka (6 daily; 3hr); Mersing (at least 3 daily; 2hr 30min); Singapore (every 10min; 1hr).

Melaka to: Alor Setar (6 daily; 12hr); Butterworth (14 daily; 9hr); Ipoh (14 daily; 4hr); Johor Bahru (6 daily; 3hr); Kota Bharu (3 daily; 10hr); Kuala Lumpur (hourly; 2hr); Kuala Terengganu (3 daily; 9hr); Kuantan (1 daily; 5hr); Mersing (2 daily; 5hr); Singapore (9 daily; 5hr).

Mersing to: Johor Bahru (at least 3 daily; 2hr 30min); Kluang (every 45min; 2hr); Kuala Lumpur (4 daily; 7hr); Kuantan (5 daily; 4hr); Melaka (2 daily; 5hr); Singapore (4 daily; 3hr 30min).
Seremban to: Butterworth (4 daily; 9hr); Ipoh (2 daily; 5hr); Johor Bahru (3 daily; 4hr); Kota Bharu (4 daily; 10hr); Kuala Lumpur (every 45min; 1hr); Melaka (every hour; 1hr); Mersing (2 daily; 5hr).

Ferries

Kukup to: Tanjung Balai (Indonesia; 2 daily; 45 min).
Melaka to: Dumai (Sumatra; 2 daily; 2hr).
Mersing to: Pulau Rawa (1 daily; 1hr 20min); Pulau Tioman (at least 2 daily; 1–4hr).

Pulau Tioman to: Singapore (daily; 4hr 30min).
Tanjung Leman to: Pulau Sibu (1 daily; 1hr); Pulau Tinggi (1 daily; 1hr 30min).

Flights

Johor Bahru to: Ipoh (8 weekly; 1hr); Kota Bharu (6 weekly; 1hr 10min); Kota Kinabalu (2–3 daily; 2hr 20min); Kuala Lumpur (at least 8 daily; 45min); Kuching (4–5 daily; 1hr 25min); Miri (8 weekly; 2hr); Penang (2–3 daily; 1hr); Sandakan (6 weekly; 2hr 40min); Sibu (6 weekly; 1hr 30min); Tawau (8 weekly; 2hr 45min).
Melaka to: Padang (3 weekly; 1hr 50min).
Pulau Tioman to: Kuala Lumpur (2 daily; 45min); Singapore (1 daily; 30min).

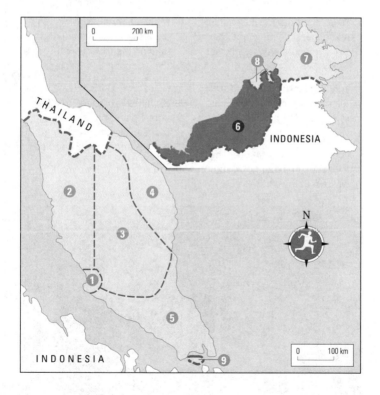

6

Sarawak

CHAPTER 6 # Highlights

* **Kuching** A great city, with sensational cuisine, buzzy bars and nightlife and captivating historic sites. See p.426

* **Santubong/Damai** Lovely beaches hosting chilled resort hotels and back-to-nature camps below Gunung Santubong. See p.445

* **Bako National Park** Beautiful and accessible park, with easy trekking and plenty of wildlife. See p.448

* **Tanjung Datu National Park** Simply the top beach in East Malaysia. See p.455

* **Iban longhouses** Traditional communities dot the rivers near the Kalimantan border in south-western Sarawak. See p.457

* **Sibu and the Rajang** Vibrant upriver city, the launching pad for visits to longhouses on Batang Rajang. See p.462

* **Niah Park** Enormous cave chamber within a well-resourced state park, where archeologists found evidence of early man. See p.484

* **Mulu National Park** Visit this extensive cave system and take on the tough climb to see the astounding Pinnacles. See p.501

* **Kelabit Highlands** Trek this cool, upland paradise, visiting traditionally designed long-houses and friendly people. See p.510

△ Longhouse, Kampung Tellian

Sarawak

Six hundred kilometres across the South China Sea from Peninsular Malaysia, the two East Malaysian states of Sarawak and Sabah occupy most of the northwest flank of the island of Borneo, the rest of which, save the enclave of Brunei, is Kalimantan, part of Indonesia. **SARAWAK** is the larger of the two states, and a more different place to Peninsular Malaysia is hard to imagine. Rivers spill down the jungle-covered mountains to become wide, muddy arteries nearer the sea, while the surviving rainforest, highland plateaux and river communities combine to form one of the most complex and diverse ecosystems on earth. Monkeys, deer and lizards abound, although **deforestation**, caused by both the logging industry and indigenous farming, has led to diminishing wildlife as well as impacting on indigenous communities. Ironically, even Sarawak's official state emblem, the eccentric-looking hornbill, whose beak has been used for centuries by tribespeople to carve images from the natural and supernatural worlds, is at risk as numbers have been substantially reduced as a result of logging practices. Sarawak has its fair share, too, of beautiful **national parks**, including the mountainous Mulu, ornithologist's paradise Bako, the cave-riddled Niah and the sublime littoral paradise, Tanjung Datu.

Another convincing reason for hopping across the sea to Sarawak is for its culture. Visitors can't fail to meet locals – Iban, Kayan or Melenau – while enjoying a drink in a pumping Kuching nightspot or visiting the traditional upriver communities. Making up around half the state's population, they fall into groups known historically as Land Dyaks (who live up in the hills – the Bidayuh of southwestern Sarawak are the chief example), Sea Dyaks (such as the Iban and Melenau, who dwell along river valleys) and Orang Ulu (like the Kenyah, Kelabit and Kayan, who live along rivers in the remote, often highland regions of the northern interior. The indigenous peoples have for centuries lived in multi-doored **longhouses**, visits to which are among the highlight of many travellers' trips to Sarawak. It is still possible to see longhouses made out of local hardwoods but most nowadays are smaller, concrete buildings. Just about all longhouse communities have joined the twenty-first century too with electricity supply, efficient hydrology and snappy couture. Although the inhabitants seldom wear traditional dress, this takes nothing away from the enjoyment of being among these people; their warmth, hospitality and humour remain legendary despite the passing of many traditions. Although any time is right for a visit, the dry season festival period (late May to early June), when harvest and fertility rituals are enacted, is particularly enjoyable (see *Longhouse culture* colour section). Unfortunately, the number of longhouses is slowly decreasing as communities move into more conventional kampung-style housing. Such changes reflect the fact that government policies, economic changes, and contemporary patterns of social mobility, have conspired to make moving away from traditional lands (and accommodation) more appealing to native peoples. But although many of the younger men and women head for the cities and towns for work, a good many also return to the longhouses or kampungs at weekends, when they help with myriad seasonal jobs like rubber tapping, pepper picking and the rice harvest, and at festival times for parties.

Some tour operators based in Kuching and Miri pay certain longhouses an annual stipend in exchange for bringing in travellers, both Malay and foreign,

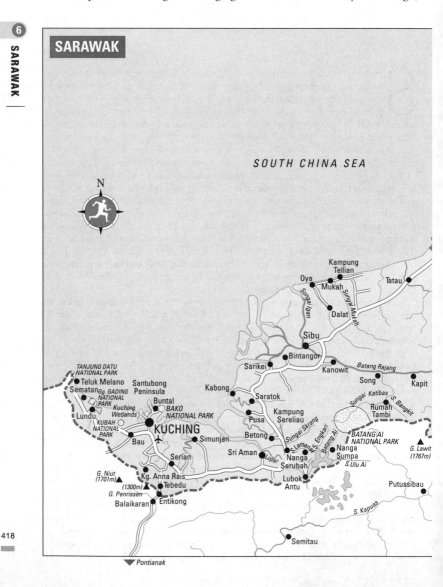

SARAWAK

SOUTH CHINA SEA

N

Kampung
Tellian
Oya
Mukah
Tatau
Sungai Igan
Sungai Mukah
Dalat
Sibu
Bintangor
Sarikei
Kanowit
Batang Rajang
TANJUNG DATU
NATIONAL PARK
Teluk Melano
Santubong
Kabong
Song
Kapit
Sematan
Gg. GADING
NATIONAL
PARK
Peninsula
Saratok
Sungai Katibas
S. Bangkit
Kuching
Wetlands
Buntal
BAKO
NATIONAL PARK
Pusa
Kampung
Sereliau
Rumah
Tambi
Lundu
KUBAH
NATIONAL
PARK
KUCHING
Betong
Sungai Skrang
Engkari
BATANG AI
NATIONAL PARK
Bau
Simunjan
Sri Aman
Sungai Lemanak
Batang Ai
Nanga
Sumpa
G. Lawit
(1767m)
Serian
Lupar
Nanga
Serubah
S.Ulu Ai
G. Niut
(1701m)
(1300m)
Kg. Anna Rais
Lubok
Antu
Putussibau
G. Penrissen
Tebedu
Balaikaran
Entikong
S. Kapuas

Pontianak

sums which pay for structural renovations, medical expenses, and travel and education costs for longhouse children. The majority of visits to longhouse communities are made in the **Batang Ai National Park**, through a tour operator (there are many excellent outfits to choose from in Kuching), most notably. However, the relatively unexplored, but still accessible, communities along **Sungai Katibas**, off Batang Rajang near Kapit, offer promising possibilities for the independent-minded traveller. State-wide, resistance to logging concessions – once the main point of controversy – is now dying down as timber production itself is scaled back, but the unsustainable timber industry remains a major

Flights from Peninsular Malaysia to Sarawak have over recent years become much more competitive with the advent of AirAsia but accommodation and travel within the state cost a little more than on the mainland. However, food and drinks are always a bargain (though as in Sabah beer is pricier than on the Peninsula), and ethnic artefacts bought along the way are excellent value too, as well as often being unique to the region. Note that Sarawak has different rules on **entry permits** to the rest of Malaysia; see p.37.

Getting there

Flights to **Kuching** are the most straightforward way into Sarawak. The prices listed below are approximate one-way fares unless otherwise stated. From: **KL** (7 direct flights daily with AirAsia from RM100; 10 flights daily with MAS, RM260); **Johor Bahru** (4 daily with AirAsia, from RM40; 3 daily with MAS, RM170); **Kota Kinabalu** in Sabah (3 daily with AirAsia from RM50; 3 daily with MAS, RM230). There are also non-stop flights to **Miri**, in the north of the state, from KL (3 daily with AirAsia, from RM20; 4 daily with MAS, RM164); to **Bintulu** (1–2 daily with AirAsia, from RM10; 2 daily with MAS, RM117), and to **Sibu** (1–2 daily with AirAsia from RM10; 3 daily with MAS, RM72).

The main overland route into Sarawak is by bus from Kuala Belait in Brunei to Miri, though this involves a time-consuming ferry ride across the Belait River and often slow passage through border stations (and avoid the weekend log jams if at all possible; see p.518 for full travel details). A second crossing is via Sipitang in Sabah (see p.552) to Lawas, one of Sarawak's two northern divisions. The Lawas Express coach originates in Sabah's capital Kota Kinabalu, and will get you to Lawas before nightfall. From Lawas you can get onward travel by bus to the Brunei capital, or there are flights to Miri. More straightforward is the southern overland route, with daily buses leaving from Pontianak, the capital of Kalimantan, crossing from Entikong to Tebedu in southwest Sarawak, around 100km from Kuching.

There are daily boat services from Brunei to both Lawas and the other of Sarawak's northern divisions, Limbang. Note that Limbang is only connected to the rest of Sarawak by air.

Getting around

Boats, often the only mode of transport in the interior, nearly always run to a reliable timetable, and come in three main types: sea-going **launches**, which ply the busy stretch from Kuching to Sarikei, at the mouth of Batang Rajang; express **boats**, which shoot up and down the main rivers; and smaller **longboats**, which provide transport along the tributaries.

If you need to **rent a longboat** to get along more remote tributaries, note that this can be prohibitively expensive if you aren't travelling in a group. It's common to pay in excess of RM150 a day per person for a boat ride to visit distant longhouses as diesel goes up in price substantially the further you are away from a filling station. In

bone of contention, notably in remote inland regions such as Belaga division, where unscrupulous financiers clear land and pollute rivers, acting outside the letter of the law. Meanwhile, pressure groups have shifted their attention more towards the massively expanding oil palm cultivation, which requires ever more land clearance and encroaches on indigenous people's customary land as well as nature reserves. Many issues remain surrounding indigenous peoples' **land rights** but there have been a number of landmark court cases that have helped establish the parameters of *adat* (tribal law) and led to a degree of improved protection for the environment.

addition, although the distances travelled from one longhouse to another are often not great (around 2–5km on average), travelling upstream against the current, in shallow waters (in the dry season) and through rapids, can be hard going, placing a major strain on outdoor motors and the craft's underbelly. You may have to get out of the boat and help pull it over the rocks.

In northern Sarawak, an essential way of getting around is by **Twin Otter** and **Fokker planes**, a service formerly run by MAS and now run by Fly Asian Xpress (FAX; ⓦwww.flyairasianxpress.com), a subsidiary of AirAsia, which seat around eighteen and fifty people respectively. These small aircraft service a great many remote communities, most significantly Bario and Ba Kelalan in the Kelabit Highlands, Marudi and Mulu National Park. It's best to book up to a month in advance for both legs of your journey, if your schedule permits, as the planes can fill up fast. The standard baggage allowance on these planes is only 10kg per person, with excess baggage, if room, charged at high rates.

Accommodation

Most towns in Sarawak have a good spread of accommodation in all price brackets. High standard, and often very reasonably priced **hotels,** are located in Kuching, Miri, Bintulu and Sibu. Resorts, catering for higher-end travellers, are starting to appear too – some large, like the magnificent *Royal Mulu Resort* (see p.505), others smaller and more bespoke. At the budget end of the scale, avoid the cut-price *rumah tumpangan* (the local term for hostel) as these are aimed at contract workers and local travellers. The middle tier of accommodation – Chinese-run cheap hotels and guesthouses – tends to be the most popular choice for travellers, offering low-cost rooms which are usually well run and clean, though can sometimes be a little squalid. Don't expect to save funds by **camping**: although it is sometimes possible in national parks, towns never provide this option (with one exception – see p.446) and locals seldom, if ever, sleep out in the open – to do so would at the very least invite much curiosity, and at worst attract unfriendly wildlife.

Visiting **longhouses** is usually only possible as part of a tour, though on the plus side most are of a very high standard. At some Longhouses, you may sleep in lodges built especially for tourists, at most you will sleep dormitory-style on the veranda, either on a thin mat or a (not much thicker) mattress. For longhouses off the tour operators' routes, such as those of the Iban on Sungai Katibas or the Kelabit Highland communities, the custom is that guests contribute to the cost of the food but do not pay for lodging – you will find out on arrival from the *tuai* (chief) if a donation is required – but bear in mind that gifts of any sort are appreciated. For information on longhouse design, and more details on arranging a visit to one, see the *Longhouse culture* colour section. The best times to visit are during the Iban *Gawai Dayak* period (see p.459) and the Bidayuh *Gawai Padi* (see p.453), when you can see traditional costumes and festivities.

This is not to say that heavy-handed practices by private enterprise and government are a thing of the past. Following the badly-managed **transmigration** in the late 1980s of a few thousand Iban from ancestral communities around Batang Ai near Kuching to make way for a dam, the late 1990s saw a much larger transmigration project from river communities in Belaga – the largest, but remotest division in Sarawak – which caused over ten thousand Orang Ulu peoples to be displaced and moved to Asap, two or more hours drive away. The resulting, massive hydroelectric dam at **Bakun**, which is slated for completion in 2007, is the subject of a vociferous and sometimes bitter campaign which has mobilized the likes of Survival International (as recounted in James Ritchie's book *Who Give A Dam*, see "Books", p.780). For more on indigenous rights, politics and the timber industry, see pp.758–761.

Most people start their exploration of Sarawak in the capital **Kuching**, in the southwest. A beautiful and lively small city, it's the starting point for visiting the Bidayuh dwellings beyond Bau and a base from which to explore **Bako National Park**. Often underestimated by travellers, this is one of Asia's most perfect nature parks with a wild shoreline of mangrove swamp and a hinterland of *kerangas* bush bustling with proboscis monkeys and birdlife. Although Sarawak is not noted for its **beaches**, there are beautiful ones in Bako, and further west along the state's southwestern seaboard at **Tanjung Datu National Park**, accessible from the capital in the dry season only (March–Sept), and even then with some difficulty by bus and boat.

A four-hour boat ride northeast of Kuching, the city of **Sibu** marks the start of the popular route along **Batang Rajang**, Sarawak's longest river (*batang* means "big river" or "river system"). Upriver beyond Sibu, it's worth stopping at the bazaars of **Song** and **Kapit**, and using these lively little places as bases for travel along the Katibas and Baleh tributaries. From Kapit, it is five hours by express boat, running the Pelagus Rapids, to **Belaga**, a remote settlement fronting the upper section of the Rajang. Tribal peoples still come to this bazaar to sell goods but the area is much changed by the devastation caused by the Bakun development, and visitors wishing to visit longhouses close to Belaga must negotiate with care. One advantage of reaching Belaga, though, is that you can travel quickly by Land Cruiser to **Bintulu** on the coast, first along logging trails, and then paved road.

The road route north from Sibu to Bintulu makes for a quick, largely comfortable trip; increasingly travellers are inclined to stop briefly at the river-side town of **Mukah**, itself rather nondescript but close to the Melenau base of **Kampung Tellian**, a colourful traditional community. Beyond Bintulu the main drag passes close to the littoral national park, **Similajau** before reaching **Niah National Park**, with its vast cave system and accessible forest hikes. The road snakes north to the Brunei border through **Miri**, a busy, vibrant town built on oil money, and noted for its excellent fish restaurants.

Southeast of Miri, tons of hardwood logs are floated down the **Batang Baram** from forests upstream. Express boats go upriver via **Marudi**, where a proud fort, housing a museum, overlooks the majestic river. Travellers switch to small longboats for the stunningly picturesque ride deeper into the forested interior to **Mulu National Park**. Sarawak's chief natural attraction, Mulu, features astonishing limestone Pinnacles and numerous extraordinary caves and passageways under its three mountains. Another way in is by Twin Otter plane to Mulu airport and then, one stop further on by air, to **Bario** in the northeastern **Kelabit Highlands**, a forested plateau from where you can visit Kelabit longhouses, witness ancient megaliths and encounter some of the few remaining semi-nomadic Penan.

Some history

Sarawak's first inhabitants were cave-dwelling **hunter-gatherers** who lived here forty thousand years ago. Evidence of the existence of early humans was discovered in 1958 at Niah Caves, by a team from the Sarawak Museum headed by its curator, Tom Harrisson. The various tribes lived fairly isolated lives and there was little contact with the wider world until the first trading boats from Sumatra and Java arrived in around 3000 BC, exchanging cloth and pottery for jungle produce. Mainly Hindu merchants later settled in the Santubong region of Sarawak, while a larger group of Muslim Malays from Java and Sumatra founded the city of Vijayapura in northern Borneo, close to Brunei, in the eleventh century AD.

As the Srivijaya Empire collapsed at the end of the thirteenth century, so regional trading patterns changed and Chinese merchants became dominant, bartering beads and porcelain with the coastal Melenau people for bezoar stones (from the gall bladders of monkeys) and birds' nests, both considered aphrodisiacs by the Chinese. In time, the traders were forced to deal with the rising power of the Malay sultans, who by the fifteenth century controlled the northwest of Borneo. Paramount was the Sultan of Brunei, at the height of whose power even the indigenous peoples of Sarawak, based on the coast and in the headwaters of the large rivers in the southwest, were being taxed heavily. Meanwhile, Sarawak was attracting interest in Europe. Pigafetta, the chronicler of Magellan's voyage in the sixteenth century, described meeting Sea Dyak groups near Brunei Bay, while in the seventeenth century the Dutch and English established short-lived trading posts near Kuching in order to extract pepper and other spices.

With the eventual decline in power of the Brunei sultanate, the region became impossible to administrate. At the beginning of the eighteenth century civil war erupted as a result of feuding between various local sultans, while piracy threatened to destroy what was left of the trade in spices, animals and minerals. In addition, the indigenous groups' predilection for **head-hunting** had led to a number of deaths among the traders and the sultan's officials, and violent territorial confrontations involving the more powerful ethnic groups were increasing.

Matters were at their most explosive when the Englishman **James Brooke** took an interest in the area. Born in India, Brooke joined the Indian army and, after being wounded in the First Anglo–Burmese War, was sent to his family home in Devon to convalesce. Returning to the East, he arrived in Singapore in the 1830s, where he learned of the Sultan of Brunei's troubles in Sarawak. The sultan's uncle, Has Him, had recruited Dyak workers to mine high-grade antimony ore in a valley of the Sarawak River (near present-day Kuching), but conditions were intolerable and the Dyaks, with the support of local Malays, rebelled. Brooke – having chartered a schooner in Singapore and gathered together a small but well-armed force – quelled the rebellion and, as a reward, demanded sovereignty over the area around Kuching. The sultan had little choice but to relinquish control of the difficult territory and in 1841 Brooke was installed as the first White Rajah of Sarawak, launching a dynastic rule which lasted for a century.

Brooke signed treaties with the sultan and tolerated the business dealings of the Chinese, though his initial concern was to stamp out piracy and pacify the warring tribal groups. He built a network of **forts** to strengthen his rule, and sent officials into the malarial swamps and mountainous interior to make contact with the Orang Ulu (upriver tribes). Displaying an early environmental awareness, Brooke also opposed calls from British- and Singapore-based businessmen to exploit the region commercially which, he believed, would have been to the detriment of the ethnic groups, whom he found fascinating. In the 1840s he wrote, "Sarawak belongs to all her peoples and not to us. It is for them we labour, not for ourselves." Despite these laudable words, Brooke's administration was not without its troubles. In one incident his men killed dozens of marauding Dyaks, while in 1857 Hakka Chinese **gold-miners**, based in the settlement of Bau on Sungai Sarawak, opposed Brooke's attempts to eliminate their trade in opium and suppress their secret societies. They attacked Kuching and killed a number of officials – Brooke got away by the skin of his teeth. His nephew, **Charles Brooke**, assembled a massive force of warrior Dyaks and followed the miners; in the ensuing battle over a thousand Chinese were killed.

In 1863 Charles Brooke took over and continued the acquisition of territory from the sultan of Brunei. River valleys – known as **divisions** – were bought for a few thousand pounds, the Dyaks living there either persuaded to enter into deals or crushed if they resisted. Elsewhere, Brooke set the warrior Iban against the Kayan, whose stronghold was in the central and northern interior, and by 1905 his fiefdom encompassed almost all of the land traditionally occupied by the coastal Malays, as well as that of the Sea Dyaks along the rivers and the Land Dyaks in the mountains. Brunei itself had shrunk so much it was now surrounded on all three sides by Brooke's Sarawak, establishing the geographical parameters that still define the sultanate today.

During the 1890s Charles Brooke encouraged Chinese **immigration** into the area around Sibu and along Batang Rajang, where pepper, and later rubber, farms were established. Bazaars were set up and traders travelled the rivers bartering with the ethnic groups. Charles Brooke thought that these few intrepid Chinese traders – mostly poor men forever in debt to the *towkays* (merchants) in the towns who had advanced them goods on credit – might undermine the indigenous way of life, so he banned them from staying in longhouses and insisted they report regularly to his officials.

The third and last rajah, **Vyner Brooke**, consolidated the gains of his father, Charles, but was less concerned with indigenous matters, although the new constitution that he proposed in 1941 would have helped bring the sub-colonial backwater of Sarawak into the twentieth century. The **Japanese invasion**, however, effectively put an end to his control. Brooke escaped, but most of his officials were interned and some subsequently executed. With the Japanese surrender in 1945, Australian forces temporarily ran the state; Vyner returned the next year and ceded Sarawak to the British government. Many Malays opposed this, believing that **British rule** was a backward step, and their protest reached its peak in 1949 when the British governor was murdered. With Malaysian independence in 1957, attempts were made to include Sarawak, Sabah and Brunei in the **Malaysian Federation**, inaugurated in 1963, but Brunei exited at the last minute. Sarawak's inclusion in the federation was opposed by Indonesia, and skirmishes broke out along the Sarawak–Kalimantan border, with Indonesia arming communist guerrillas inside Sarawak, who opposed both British and Malay rule. During this insurgency, known as the **Konfrontasi**, the small Sarawak army needed to call upon British military aid to help defend the bazaar towns in the interior; the conflict continued for three years, but was eventually put down by Malaysian troops aided by the British.

Throughout the 1960s and 1970s, reconstruction programmes strengthened regional communities and provided housing, resources and jobs. These days, Sarawak is a peaceful, multiracial state, though social tensions, triggered by the government's economic strategy, sometimes rise to the surface. Over the last few years the question of land rights has become paramount, with small non-governmental organizations like Rengah Sarawak (Ⓦ www.rengah.c2o .org) and a few concerned lawyers assisting rural communities in conflicts with **oil-palm estates** and (rather less now than in the 1990s) the timber industry, over encroachment on community lands.

Sarawak has a history of sparring with Kuala Lumpur over national funding and political loyalties but in recent years the dominant parties have tied their flags to the Barisan Nasional mast, invariably taking longhouse constituencies with them. But the state's coffers are lower now than at the turn of the millennium: timber royalty income, which used to represent 30 to 35 percent of state revenues, has now fallen to around 20 percent. Over the next decade it it likely to contribute less and less to the state finances as there is not much easily extractable timber left. Moreover, the government has spent US$2 billion on a new technology plant, a robust attempt to enter the global microelectronic processing industry, but so far this investment isn't bringing in any returns. On the plus side, state revenue from oil is going up and contributes about RM1 billion.

The southwest

The most densely populated part of the state, **southwest Sarawak** supports around two million people. It's also the only part of the state to be well served by road, a reflection of its long-standing trading importance. Malays from Sumatra and Java first arrived five thousand years ago, Chinese traders have been visiting the region since the eighth century AD, while Iban tribes migrated here from the Kapuas River basin in present-day Kalimantan around three hundred years ago, supplanting the original Bidayuh population. A second wave of Chinese immigrants settled here in the eighteenth century, initially to mine gold and antimony, the latter then in great demand in Europe for use in medicines and dyes. Later, when the bottom dropped out of the antimony market, the Chinese switched their endeavours to growing pepper and rubber and more recently timber extraction, pulp mills and palm-oil cultivation for export.

Located upriver from the swamp-ridden coastline, **Kuching** is on most people's itinerary both as a captivating place in itself and as a starting point for travel around the southwest and onwards to Sibu, reachable by air, bus and boat. The city and environs certainly contain enough to occupy up to a week or more's sightseeing: Kuching's **Sarawak Museum** holds the state's best collection of ethnic artefacts, while easy half-day trips can be made to **Semenggoh Orang-utan Rehabilitation Centre** and **Jong's Crocodile Farm**, to the south of the city and the **Sarawak Cultural Village**, on Santubong Peninsula to the north. You'll need more time for **Bako National Park** – preferably a couple of days – although at a pinch you can go on a day return. Some travellers also choose to overnight at either of two small parks to the west of Kuching, **Gunung Gading** and **Kubah**, although with a vehicle either can be visited in a single day. More challenging are visits to the **Bidayuh communities** near the Kalimantan border or the far-away, languid coastal village of **Sematan**, access point for the spectacular and little-visited **Tanjung Datu Park** to the west on the maritime border with Kalimantan. Experiencing the **Iban longhouses** east of the capital around Batang Ai National Park, especially on Batang Ai itself, Sungai Engkari and Sungai Lemanak, is best done as part of a tour, but is well worth the effort and relative expense.

Kuching

With its many period attractions and zestful energy **KUCHING** is one of the most pleasant cities in the whole of Malaysia. Occupying the southern bank of Sungai Sarawak, its centre is easy to traverse on foot, and distinctive. It's rather surprising that the city has a population of over half a million – only on weekend evenings or at festivals does it ever appear to get crowded. But, despite the prevalence of colonial architecture and the occasional echo of a bygone era, Kuching very much lives in the present: techno beats boom from boutiques, fashionable cafés serve health drinks and fusion food while Internet cafés provide hot-wiring to the world.

In the heart of the old town, the commercial district is a warren of crowded lanes in which Kuching's Chinese community run cafés, hotels, general stores and laundries. Main Bazaar, the city's oldest street, sports the remains of its original godowns – now converted into shops – overlooking the integral watercourse, Sungai Sarawak, Kuching's main supply route since the city's earliest days for Iban war parties and White Rajahs alike. In recent years much of the city's highly visible youthful energy has moved to the eastern hotel quarter, sometimes called the Golden Triangle, especially along Jalan Padungan, where Western-style cafés, bars and restaurants have sprung up. All this adds up to a newfound confidence, imbuing Kuching with an atmosphere that's at once

Moving on from Kuching

By air
A taxi from the town centre to the airport is RM17 (airport information: ☎082/457373 or 454242). Alternatively, take #12a bus from the Lebuh Jawa terminus (6.30am–7.30pm; every 50min; RM1.60) to the airport stop, 100m from departures. There are daily flights on AirAsia to Peninsular cities KL and Johor Bahru, and daily MAS flights to KL, Johor Bahru, plus Sibu, Bintulu and Miri in Sarawak, and Kota Kinabalu in Sabah.

By boat
Express Bahagia, 50 Jalan Padungan (☎013/820 3702), runs a daily service to **Sarikei** (RM32) and **Sibu** (RM40), departing at 8.30am from Pending wharf. It's best to book in advance from the Kuching Visitors' Information Centre and get there at least twenty minutes before the boat departs. Note that if the weather is inclement the boat may well not leave and tickets will be held over for the next day's departure or you can get a full refund. The wharf is 6km from the city centre: buses #17 and #19 (30min; 60 sen) leave from the Lebuh Jawa terminus, stopping outside the post office on Jalan Tuan Haji Openg; a taxi from anywhere in the city centre costs RM10.

By bus
Long-distance **buses** to points north in Sarawak depart from the regional express terminal on Jalan Penrissen, 5km out of town (twice-hourly buses from 6am to 6pm run there from the post office stop, and once an hour thereafter until 10pm; RM1) There is generally little need to buy tickets for express buses in advance – just turn up at least thirty minutes before departure – although it is advisable if a national holiday is approaching. A current bus timetable is printed daily in the *Borneo Post* newspaper. More local buses to Kuching and Bau division destinations, Anna Rais, Serian, Sri Aman and Lubok Antu, depart from the Lebuh Jawa terminus. For details of departures to sights in the vicinity of Kuching, see p.443.

both exciting and laid-back. But then the city has always been an ethnic melting pot, its inhabitants divided between Chinese, Malays, Indians and the various Dyak and Orang Ulu groups (mainly Iban and Bidayuh, but also Melenau, Kayan and Kenyah).

The city is culturally of interest too, with attractions including the **Sarawak Museum**, one of the finest in Malaysia, and the new **Textile Museum**, a fascinating insight into cultural history and dapper dress sense. Whenever there's an auspicious date in the Chinese calender, keep an eye on Lebuh China's **Chinese temple**, where there's always a frenzy of celebration and activity.

Some history

In 1841, James Brooke came up the river, arriving at a village, known as Sarawak, which lay on a small stream called Sungai Mata Kuching (cat's eye), adjoining the main river; it seems likely that the stream's name was shortened by Brooke and came to refer to the fast-expanding settlement. However, a much-repeated tale has it that the first rajah pointed to the village and asked its name. The locals, thinking Brooke was pointing to a cat, replied – reasonably enough – "kucing" (cat). Either way, it wasn't until 1872 that Charles Brooke officially changed the settlement's name from Sarawak to Kuching.

Until the 1920s, the capital was largely confined to the south bank of Sungai Sarawak, stretching only from the Chinese heartland around Lebuh Temple east of today's centre, to the Malay kampung around the mosque to the west. On the north bank, activity revolved around the fort and a few dozen houses reserved for British officials. It was the pre-war **rubber boom** that financed the town's expansion, with the elegant tree-lined avenue Jalan Padungan, 1km east of the centre, becoming the smart place in which to live and work. The kampung areas increased in size, too, as the population was swollen by the arrival of a new bureaucracy of Malay civil servants, as well as by Dyaks from the interior and immigrants from Hokkien province in mainland China looking for work. The city escaped serious destruction during World War II, since Japanese bombing raids were mainly intent on destroying the oil wells in the north of Sarawak – the few bombs that were dropped on Kuching missed the military base at Fort Margherita and set fire to a fuel store.

Since independence, business has boomed, and though many of the impressive nineteenth-century buildings have been restored, others have been destroyed to make way for new roads and office developments. However, the planners cast a sympathetic eye over perhaps the most important part of Kuching. Following large-scale renovation, a pedestrianized riverside area, referred to now as the **waterfront**, once again integrates the city with the waters that have shaped its growth. Another sensible decision has been to close busy Jalan India to traffic, better highlighting a glittering concentration of shops and cafés.

Arrival, information and transport

Kuching's glistening and modern international **airport** (☏082/457373) is 14km south of the city; the arrivals hall contains shops and cafés and a taxi kiosk. To reach the city centre, it's best to take a taxi (RM17). There is no direct bus from the airport into the city centre although the #12a runs along the highway, 100m from the arrivals hall, arriving at the centre's Lebuh Jawa terminus by an indirect route (7am–3pm; every 1hr 15min; 30min; RM1.60). For buying or changing MAS tickets, the large, glass-fronted MAS office is located on Jalan Song Thian Cheok (Mon–Fri 8am–5pm, Sat 8am–1pm; ☏082/244144 or 246622 or 24hr number ☏1300 883 000). It's advisable to

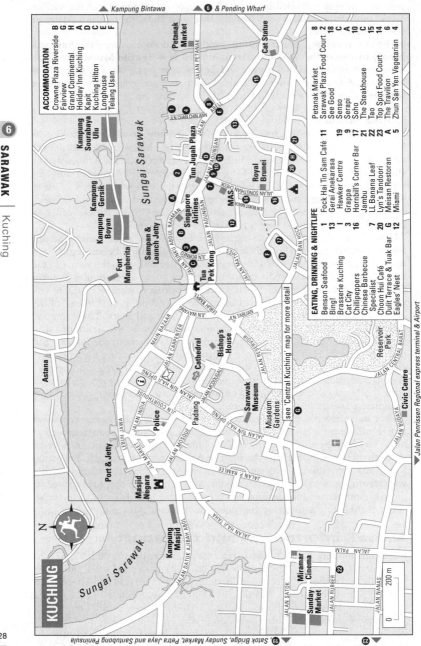

KUCHING

▲ Kampung Bintawa   ▲ ❻ & Pending Wharf

ACCOMMODATION
Crowne Plaza Riverside	B
Fairview	G
Grand Continental	H
Holiday Inn Kuching	A
Kapit	D
Kuching Hilton	C
Longhouse	E
Telang Usan	F

EATING, DRINKING & NIGHTLIFE
Benson Seafood	1	Fock Hai Tin Sam Café	11	Petanak Market	8
Bing!	13	Gerai Anekarasa	I	Sarawak Plaza Food Court	2
Brasserie Kuching	3	Hawker Centre	9	See Good	18
Cat City	I	Hornbill's Corner Bar	17	Senso	C
Chillipeppers	16	Grappa	19	Serapi	A
Chinese Barbecue	7	Jambu	21	Soho	10
Specialist		LL Banana Leaf	22	The Steakhouse	C
Choon Hui Café	20	Lyn's Tandoori	20	Tao	15
Dulit Terrace & Tuak Bar	G	Meisan Restoran	12	Top Spot Food Court	14
Eagles' Nest		Miami	A	The Travillon	6
				Zhun San Yen Vegetarian	4

Kampung Sourabaya Ulu

Kampung Gersik

Kampung Boyan

Fort Margherita

Sampan & Launch Jetty

Singapore Airlines

Tua Pek Kong

Tun Jugah Plaza

Royal Brunei

MAS

Petanak Market

Cat Statue

Sungai Sarawak

Astana

Port & Jetty

Masjid Negara

Kampung Masjid

Sunday Market

Miramar Cinema

Cathedral

Bishop's House

Police

Padang

Sarawak Museum

Museum Gardens

Reservoir Park

Civic Centre

see 'Central Kuching' map for more detail

▼ Jalan Penrissen Regional express terminal & Airport

▼ ❶❾ ▲ Satok Bridge, Sunday Market, Petra Jaya and Santubong Peninsula

0 — 200 m

N

visit this office first thing as long queues form by 10am, usually taking thirty minutes to an hour to clear.

The **long-distance bus station** is at Jalan Penrissen, 5km south of town, from where buses #3 and #3a (daily 6.30am–6pm; every 30min) run to the town station, Lebuh Jawa; a taxi into town from Jalan Penrissen costs RM10. **Boats** from Sibu and Sarikei dock at Bintawa, 5km east of the city centre. For information on getting into town from here, see "Moving on from Kuching", p.426.

Information

There is a small **Sarawak Tourist Association** (STA) desk in the airport (daily 8am–5pm; ☎082/456266), but the main place for tourism information and enquiries is the new **Kuching Visitors' Information Centre**, located in the Old Courthouse, Jalan Tun Haji Openg, on the western edge of the waterfront (Mon–Fri 8am–6pm, Sat, Sun & public hols 9am–3pm; ☎082/410944 or 410942, Ⓦwww.sarawaktourism.com). The centre has plenty of maps (including a free city map), bus timetables, hotel listings and dozens of glossy leaflets on everything from weaving to tattooing. Ask for the Handicrafts Directory put out by the Sarawak Craft Council (Ⓦwww.sarawakhandicraft.com). The centre also contains the booking desk of the National Parks and Wildlife Office, where accommodation in the parks can be organized (☎082/248088).

For the latest and most comprehensive listings of hotels and restaurants in and around the city, pick up a copy of Mike Reed and Wayne Tarman's excellent and free annually updated *Official Kuching Guide*, available from the above offices and most city hotel lobbies; the booklet also gives insights into visiting longhouses and national parks. The English-language *Borneo Post*, *Sarawak Gazette* and *The Star*, available at newsagents, contain small sections on cultural events in town and around the state.

City transport

You can **walk** around much of downtown Kuching with ease and so will have little use for the city buses. A few of the local **bus** routes are handy, including the blue-and-white buses run by the Chin Lian Long company that trundle out from Jalan Mosque to the Indonesian Consulate, the immigration office and Pending wharf (for the Sarikei/Sibu boat).

The main **taxi rank** is at the western end of Jalan Gambier. You can usually flag down a taxi in front of the hotels along Jalan Tunku Abdul Rahman too, though be aware though that the fixed price charged by these taxis is steeper than at other points, starting from RM10 for most places in the city rather than the RM6 charged at the taxi ranks or on the road. You should always negotiate the price before starting the trip – often this high "fixed rate" will lower after a bit of haggling. Note that fares increase after midnight.

Diesel-powered **sampan** boats (daily 6am–10pm; every 15min) depart from the jetty opposite the visitors' centre on the western end of the waterfront, crossing Sungai Sarawak to reach Fort Margherita in the northern part of Kuching. The boat trip only takes a few minutes. A slightly longer boat trip (RM2) takes you one kilometre upstream to the jetty at Kampung Bintawa, a small Malay suburb few travellers visit. Should you wish to take in more of the river, go on a river cruise – the best are organised by CPH Travel (see p.442). You can choose between a morning cruise (9am) and a sunset one (5pm) – both cost RM40. The journey, usually taking around two hours, is a revealing introduction to Kuching life, even if the river is used socially and commercially far less nowadays. It is not necessary to book ahead, just turn up at the jetty, mid-way along the waterfront, twenty minutes before departure.

Accommodation

Kuching has a wide and excellent range of **accommodation**, though prices tend though to be a little higher than elsewhere in Sarawak: be prepared to pay at least RM40–50 for a double room if the budget places are full. The big hotels, with swimming pools and 24-hour service, are mostly clustered on or near the waterfront, often offering great views. Promotional rates which slash the published price are often available and are sometimes there for the asking. The appealing guesthouses and mid-range hotels are mostly located back from the river, but still close to the main restaurant and café area, Jalan Padungan and the historic quarter, which is enclosed between Main Bazaar and Jalan Carpenter.

As an alternative to staying in the city, head for Damai on the coast (see p.445). All the hotels below are marked on either the map of greater Kuching on p.428 or central Kuching on p.432.

Upmarket hotels

Crowne Plaza Riverside Jalan Tunku Abdul Rahman ☎ 082/247777, ⊛ www.holidayinn -sarawak.com. One of Kuching's priciest and most opulent hotels, this ten-floor marble extravaganza offers all the comforts and amenities you could wish for: several classy restaurants and bars, full sporting facilities, a business centre and an adjoining shopping complex. The rooms aren't very large but are sumptuously appointed, and the views from those that face the river are breathtaking. ❽

Grand Continental 46 Jalan Ban Hock ☎ 082/230399, ⊛ www.ghihotels.com/malaysia. Slightly away for the centre, the *Grand* is an excellent deal, with regular promotional rates. Rooms are immaculately appointed, as expected from a business-class hotel, and there's a swimming pool on the second floor. ❻

Harbour View Lorong Temple ☎ 082/274666, ⊛ www.harbourview.com.my. Slick, business-orientated, relatively new addition to the city's hotel scene, in a lively location. The en-suite rooms are competitively priced – often promotional rates can get down close to RM100 – but smallish. ❻

Holiday Inn Kuching Jalan Tunku Abdul Rahman ☎ 082/423111, ⊛ www.ichotelsgroup.com. Overlooking the river, with some of its superbly appointed rooms looking directly out across to the fort on the opposite bank (for an extra RM20), this hotel has an inviting little pool to cool off in, two restaurants, two cafés and a well-stocked book-shop among its amenities. ❽

Kuching Hilton Jalan Tunku Abdul Rahman ☎ 082/248200, ⊛ www.kuching.hilton.com. Another top-class hotel, whose front rooms have a great view of the river. There's a pool and a mouth-watering range of food and drink outlets. ❽

Merdeka Palace Jalan Tun Haji Openg ☎ 082/258000, ⊛ www.merdekapalace.com. This excellent place boasts large rooms with satellite TV and elegant bathrooms, plus a fine Italian restaurant with pizza to die for. The rooms at the front overlook the padang; there are sometimes reductions on rooms at the back. ❽

Mid-range hotels and lodges

Borneo 30 Jalan Tabuan ☎ 082/244122, ⓔ bidasbuan@yahoo.com. Superb, comfortable hotel, one of Kuching's oldest, where the lovely rooms have polished wooden floors, a/c, bath or shower, and TVs. There's an excellent café/restaurant beside the foyer. ❺

Fata Jalan McDougall ☎ 082/248111. In a busy location, 100m from Reservoir Park, this hotel has small, rather shabby rooms with a/c, showers and TVs. The plain-looking café of the same name alongside serves delicious local food at incredibly low prices. ❹

Kapit 59 Jalan Padungan ☎ 082/420961. Away from the centre, this hotel is popular with Iban visitors from out of town. The good-value rooms have a/c, shower and TV, and the hotel staff are friendly and helpful.

Longhouse Jalan Abell ☎ 082/419333. East of the centre, this hotel is frequented mainly by visiting business people. Rooms are large and good value, if a bit down-at-heel, with a/c, showers and TV. ❸

Mandarin 6 Jalan Green Hill ☎ 082/418269. A good option in this cramped thoroughfare. Full facilities include a/c, shower, toilet and TV, but the rooms are a little on the shabby side. The back of the hotel aligns a jungle-thick hill. ❸

🏃 Singgahsana Lodge 3 Lorong Temple ☎ 082/429277, ⊛ www.singgahsana.com. Stylishly renovated by young owners Donald and Marina Tan from a crumbling Chinese godown 30m from the waterfront, this recently opened boutique backpacker lodge packs in dozens of themed and tastefully decorated rooms, including some with dorm beds at RM30, set around a central sitting and eating area. It has quickly become a mecca for travellers visiting southwestern Sarawak. Excellent value. ❹–❻.

🏃 **Telang Usan** off Jalan Ban Hock ☎082/415588, ⓦwww.telangusan.com. Friendly, Kayan-run place, located in a quiet compound, and an easy walk from the centre. Its wall and stairs are adorned with art by the late Kenyah artist Tusan Padan, and facilities include an excellent restaurant and veranda-style bar. Rooms range in size and shape but are generally cosy, comfortable and clean, and the bathrooms have tubs. ❺

Guesthouses

Anglican Rest House Jalan McDougall ☎082/414027. Set in a tranquil location away from the main street in the Anglican Cathedral gardens, this guesthouse comprises the main two-storey, wooden, colonial building with comfortable, twin-bedded rooms with high ceilings and shared bathrooms, and two self-contained apartments with bedroom, veranda and bathroom (RM35). The resthouse has had a few security problems, so don't leave valuables unattended. Booking ahead is essential as it's often full of people on church business. ❷

B&B Inn First floor, 30–31 Jalan Tabuan ☎082/237366. Utilitarian backpacker spot with simple, rather cramped dorms and a handful of bare but tidy private rooms, both ranges sharing common facilities. A basic but unlimited tea-and-toast breakfast is included. Dorm beds RM14; ❶

🏃 **Fairview** 6 Jalan Taman Budaya (beside Reservoir Park), ☎082/240017, ⓔthefairview@yahoo.com. Welcome addition to the city's accommodation options, located 200m behind the Sarawak Museum. A heritage site set in a lush, secluded garden, Eric's perfectly restored house includes two massive en-suite rooms with period touches, and a number of four-bed en-suite dorms (RM25). Guests can make their own meals in the house kitchen. ❹

The City

The central area of the city, sandwiched between Jalan Courthouse to the west, Jalan Wayang to the east and Reservoir Park to the south, is usually referred to as **colonial Kuching** The Old Courthouse, the post office and the Sarawak Museum are the most impressive buildings here, with the museum itself the city's most absorbing cultural attraction; aside from the museum, the buildings will occupy just a few hours of your time. Set within this small area is **Chinatown**, which incorporates the main shopping streets Main Bazaar and Jalan Carpenter. To the east of Jalan Wayang lie Jalan Green Hill, Jalan Tunku Abdul Rahman and Jalan Padungan, the principal hotel districts. The area around Jalan Tunku Abdul Rahman and Jalan Padungan has become the new town centre, with bars, pubs and plazas galore. Further south from the old town's narrow, busy street – yet only fifteen minutes' walk from the river – is **Reservoir Park**; while bordering the colonial area, on the western edge of the centre, is the pedestrianized Jalan India, another shopping hotspot and home, as the name suggests, to several of the city's top Indian cafés. A short hop further west is the state **mosque** and main Malay residential area, dominated by detached kampung-style dwellings with sloping roofs, intricate carvings around the windows and elevated verandas. Southwest of here, Satok Bridge leads to Kuching new town, the Timber Museum and the city's famous Saturday night market, while north, across the river, is **Fort Margherita** and the **Astana**, still one of the residences of Sarawak's head of state.

The waterfront and Old Courthouse

Fronting the city for almost a kilometre – from the Jalan Gambier markets in the west to the Triangle's *Holiday Inn* – the waterfront is a lovely spot to begin a city tour. For locals, the walkway is *the* place to go in the evening, its manicured lawns enlivened by sculptures, seating areas and a dozen little soft-drink and snack stalls. Several of the godowns that once fronted onto the river were sacrificed during the development, but two fine buildings – the lovingly restored **Sarawak Steamship Building**, which now houses a multimedia centre with

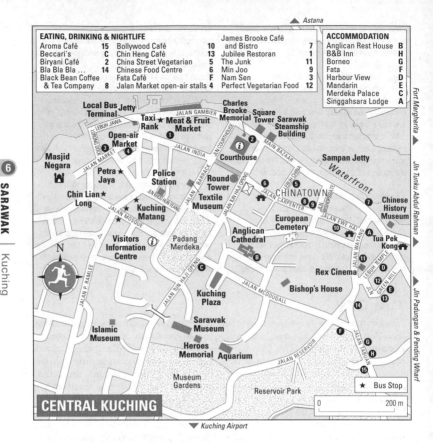

▲ *Astana*

EATING, DRINKING & NIGHTLIFE

Aroma Café	15	Bollywood Café	10	James Brooke Café
Beccari's	C	Chin Heng Café	13	and Bistro	7
Biryani Café	2	China Street Vegetarian	5	Jubilee Restoran	1
Bla Bla Bla ...	14	Chinese Food Centre	6	The Junk	11
Black Bean Coffee		Fata Café	F	Min Joo	9
& Tea Company	8	Jalan Market open-air stalls	4	Nam Sen	3
				Perfect Vegetarian Food	12

ACCOMMODATION

Anglican Rest House	B
B&B Inn	H
Borneo	G
Fata	F
Harbour View	D
Mandarin	E
Merdeka Palace	C
Singgahsara Lodge	A

Fort Margherita ▶

Jln Tunku Abdul Rahman ▶

Jln Padungan & Pending Wharf ▶

CENTRAL KUCHING

0 ——— 200 m

★ Bus Stop

▼ *Kuching Airport*

Internet terminals and a theatre, plus a café, and the former Chinese General Chamber of Commerce – have survived. Early-morning strollers here may see enthusiasts going about their daily Tai chi routines.

At the western end of the waterfront, at the junction of Main Bazaar and Jalan Tun Haji Openg, lies the recently renovated **Old Courthouse**, now housing the Visitors' Information Centre. Built in 1874, and sporting impressive Romanesque columns and a balcony, the Courthouse is fronted by the **Charles Brooke Memorial**, a six-metre-high granite obelisk erected in 1924, at whose four corners are stone figures representing the four largest ethnic groups in Sarawak: the Chinese, Dyaks, Malays and Orang Ulu. Close by, the single-turreted **Square Tower** is all that's left of a fortress that was built in 1879. An earlier wooden construction was burnt down in the 1857 gold-miners' rebellion.

The post office, Textile Museum and south to the Bishop's House

Opposite the Courthouse, across Jalan Tun Haji Openg, is the excessively grand **post office**, whose massive ornamental columns, semicircular arches and decorative friezes were outmoded almost as soon as they were completed in 1931. Nearby, housed in the immaculately restored Pavilion Building, a lovely example of colonial baroque architecture on Jalan Barrack, lies the city's

△ The Old Courthouse, Kuching

newest cultural attraction, the **Textile Museum** (daily 9am–5.30pm; free). The three-floor collection is a cornucopia of dazzling costume and artefacts from the region across the centuries. The first floor's photographic display covers all the state's races, including one mesmerizing shot of a young Iban couple, just married, in the early years of the century. Their heavy adornment is described in the caption: "Any textile can be embellished with surface decoration, either purely for ornamentation or to show the wearer's social status." On the second floor are headdresses, belts and traditionally weaved fabrics, known as *pua kumba*, from the upriver peoples, displayed alongside models of Iban and Malay traditional weddings.

Continuing south, skirt the well-groomed grassland known as **Padang Merdeka**, turn east onto Jalan McDougall and you'll see the modern Anglican **Cathedral**. A walk through its grounds leads to the oldest consecrated plot in Borneo, the European **cemetery**. An unassuming patch of land, and very easily missed, it nevertheless manages to conjure up the ghosts of old Kuching. Of the few stones still legible, one recalls Charles James Fox and Henry Steel, "officers of the Sarawak Government, who were treacherously murdered at Kanowit" in 1859. "Justice", the stone reassures us, "was done". A few steps further east stands another Kuching landmark, the large, two-storey wooden **Bishop's House**, built in 1849, making it the oldest surviving building in the city.

The Sarawak Museum

Return to the padang, and head a little way south along Jalan Tun Haji Openg to reach Kuching's prime tourist attraction, the **Sarawak Museum** (daily 9am–6pm; free; free 1hr guided tour Fri 9.30am; ☎082/244232), set back from the road in lovely gardens. Built in the 1890s, it's the largest colonial structure in Kuching. It was Charles Brooke who conceived the idea of a museum in Kuching, prompted by the nineteenth-century naturalist Alfred Russell Wallace, who spent two years in Sarawak in the 1850s. Wallace's natural-history exhibits now

Sarawak's ceramic jars

The status and wealth of members of Sarawak's indigenous tribes depended on how many **ceramic jars** they possessed, and you can still see impressive models in longhouses, as well as in the Sarawak Museum, today. Ranging in size from tiny, elegantly detailed bowls to much larger vessels, over a metre in height, the jars were used for a range of purposes including storage, brewing rice wine and making payments – dowries and fines for adultery and divorce settlements. The most valuable jars were only used for ceremonies like the *Gawai Kenyalang* (the rite of passage for a mature, prosperous man, involving the recitation of stories by the longhouse bard); or for funerary purposes: when a member of northern Sarawak's Berawan died, the corpse was packed into a jar in a squatting position. As decomposition took place, the liquid from the body was drained away through a bamboo pipe, leaving the individual's bones or clothing, which would subsequently be removed, placed in a canister and hoisted on to an ossuary above the riverbank. It's said that the jars can also be used to foretell the future, and can summon spirits through the sounds they emit when struck.

form the basis of the collection on show. The museum's best-known curator was **Tom Harrisson** (1911–76), whose discovery of a 39,000-year-old skull in the caves at Niah in 1957 prompted a radical reappraisal of the origins of early man in Southeast Asia. Under the museum's auspices, Harrisson frequently visited remote Orang Ulu tribes, bringing back the ceremonial artefacts that comprise some of the museum's greatest assets.

There's an information desk at the main entrance, beyond which is the **natural science** section, whose varied exhibits include a massive ball of dried hair from a crocodile's stomach and fairly pedestrian displays highlighting the diverse range of plant, animal and bird species in Borneo. The **ethnographic** section on the upper floor is of an altogether different standard, despite the occasionally vague labelling. Here you can walk into an authentic wooden Iban longhouse (for more on longhouses, see *Longhouse culture* colour section) and climb up into the rafters of the *sadau* (loft), which is used to store bamboo fish baskets, ironwork and sleeping mats; you're also free to finger the intricately glazed, sturdy Chinese ceramic jars (see box above) and fine woven *pua kumbu* cloth. The Penan hut here is a much simpler affair, constructed of bamboo and rattan, within which are blowpipes and *parang*s (machetes), animal hides, coconut husks used as drinking vessels, and hardy back-baskets, made from the pandanus palm and the *bemban* reed. At the other end of the floor, there's a collection of fearsome Iban war totems, and woodcarvings from the Kayan and Kenyah ethnic groups who live in the headwaters of the Rajang, Baram and Balui rivers. One carving – a ten-metre-high ceremonial pole made of hardwood – sports a pattern of grimacing heads and kneeling bodies stretching up in supplication. Towering above all of this, on one of the walls, is a massive mural of images from longhouse culture: sowing and reaping rice, hunting, fishing, dancing and playing music. Cabinets lining the walls close by showcase **musical instruments** used by the various tribes: the Bidayuh's heavy copper gongs, Iban drums and the Kayan *sape*, a stringed instrument looking a little like a lute. Also, keep an eye out for the small collection of Iban *palangs* – two-centimetre-long rhinoceros-bone penis pins – which were once a popular method of re-energizing a wilting love life in the longhouse: inserted horizontally through the foreskin by the longhouse "doctor", in case you were wondering.

From the Sarawak Museum to Reservoir Park

Ten minutes' walk west, the other side of Jalan Tun Haji Openg, the **Islamic Museum** (daily except public hols: 9am–6am; free) is housed in the tastefully restored Madrasah Melayu Building, a former religious school, painted in brilliant white and with a cool tiled interior. The museum's seven galleries represent diverse aspects of Islamic culture, from architecture to weaponry, history to coinage, and textiles to prayer.

Back across Jalan Tun Haji Openg, a path leads across the Sarawak Museum's sloping gardens to the **Heroes' Memorial**, commemorating the dead of World War II and the Konfrontasi (see p.741), just five minutes' walk. You will pass the Kuching **aquarium** (daily 9am–6pm; free) on the way, which contains a small collection of marine life, including turtles from Sipadan in Sabah. Following the path past the memorial takes you to the corner of the museum gardens and out onto narrow Jalan Reservoir, across which lies **Reservoir Park**, a beautiful, if artificial, tropical environment with many resident bird species and wildlife. There's a café (daily 8am–6pm), a drinks kiosk, boats for rent, a playground and stretching frames for workout enthusiasts. The other road bordering the park, Lorong Park, leads up to the **civic centre** on Jalan Budaya, an ultramodern building with a **planetarium** (Tues only) and space for temporary exhibitions.

Chinatown and further east

Back at Jalan Tun Haji Openg, the grid of streets behind the waterfront, running eastwards to the main Chinese temple, Tua Pek Kong, constitutes Kuching's **Chinatown**. On busy Main Bazaar and, one block south, on Jalan Carpenter, there are numerous cafés, restaurants, and stores operating out of two-storey shophouses, built by Hokkien and Teochew immigrants who arrived in the 1890s. The shophouses were originally divided into three sections: the front room was where the merchant conducted business and stored his goods (salt, flour, jungle products collected by indigenous peoples, and salted fish caught and prepared by Malay fishermen), the back room was the family quarters, and the loft was where the business partners would sleep.

Sandwiched between the western ends of Jalan Tunku Abdul Rahman and Jalan Padungan, overlooking the river, stands **Tua Pek Kong**, the oldest (it was built in 1876) Taoist temple in Sarawak; in accordance with Chinese tradition, its position was carefully divined through geomancy. Supplicants burn paper money and joss sticks, and pray for good fortune to the temple deity, Tua Pek Kong. The temple maintains an immensely busy cultural life, especially during Chinese New Year, when it plays host to theatrical and musical performances.

Tua Pek Kong may have been taking care of all matters spiritual in the Chinese community, but matters temporal were long the domain of the squat, cream-coloured edifice below on the waterfront, once the Chinese General Chamber of Commerce. The building now houses the **Chinese History Museum** (daily except Fri 9am–6pm; free), which makes use of paintings, black-and-white photographs and a modest selection of artefacts to chart the arrival and subsequent integration of Sarawak's Chinese community.

Jalan Tunku Abdul Rahman heads east from the Tua Pek Kong, past several of the swankier hotels and the Sarawak Plaza. Also leading east from the temple, a little way south of Jalan Tunku Abdul Rahman, is **Jalan Padungan**, which runs eastwards out to the edge of the city. The 1.5-kilometre walk along this tree-lined avenue takes you past Western-style bars and fusion restaurants, and splendidly ornate shophouses (whose elaborate decor was paid for by the rubber boom of the 1930s). At its eastern end, you can't fail to spot the **cat statue**, a 1.5-metre-high white-plaster effigy, her paw raised in welcome. Created by local artist Yong Kee Yet as a nod to the supposed derivation of the city's name, it's a popular spot for family photos.

North across Sungai Sarawak

Cross Sungai Sarawak in a sampan to visit a number of interesting buildings. Sampans leave from a number of Waterfront jetties, including the one opposite the Courthouse (daily 6am–10pm; every 15min). The first buildings constructed on the north side of the river here were small dwellings, part of the earlier Malay kampung, but following the arrival of the British in Kuching, Charles Brooke had two of the city's most important buildings constructed here. The **Astana**, built by Charles Brooke in 1869 and still the official home of Sarawak's governor, is the first of these, and accessible along a marked path from the jetty. An elegant, stately building with a distinctive shingle roof, it's set in a long, sloping garden with an excellent view of the Courthouse on the opposite bank. Various pieces of Brooke memorabilia and other relics are kept in one of the rooms, but unfortunately you can only visit the Astana on two days of the year, over the *Hari Raya Puasa* holiday at the end of Ramadan.

Along the riverbank, 1km to the east, is **Fort Margherita**; retrace your steps back to the jetty and you can follow a marked path there through a narrow slice of parkland. The first fort built on this site was James Brooke's most important defensive installation, commanding the view along Sungai Sarawak. However, the fort was burned to the ground in 1857 by rebel Chinese gold-miners and was rebuilt by Charles Brooke in 1879, who named it after his wife. It is the finest example of the Brookes' system of fortifications, and renovations have ensured that it looks much as it did in the nineteenth century. There are around twenty other river forts of humbler construction throughout Sarawak, strategically placed to repel pirates and Dyak or Kayan war parties. Looking for all the world like a defensive English castle, Fort Margherita is one of only a few forts that are open to the public. It's situated within the city's police barracks so bring along ID with you.

From the fort, it's easy to thread your way eastwards and down to the Malay kampungs over which it stands guard: **Kampung Boyan** shades into **Kampung Gersik**, which in turn is assimilated by **Kampung Sourabaya Ulu**. All three feature wonderful clapboard stilt houses, some in cheery pastel blues and greens, others gloriously dilapidated, teetering on knock-kneed stilts and accessed by bowed promenades. From this side of the fort, boats will deposit you near the *Crowne Plaza Riverside Hotel* on the east side of the city centre.

Jalan Gambier and the markets

Back at the waterfront on the south bank, head west from the Old Courthouse along Jalan Gambier and to reach the **cargo port** and **market area**. In the late afternoon you'll see boats from Kalimantan unload tons of tropical fruits and vegetables to be sold in the warren of shops and stalls surrounding the jetty. Walk around and you will soon be drawn by the allure of spices. Kuching's **spice market**, like much else at Jalan Gambier, is open 24 hours – a popular place with nighthawks before dawn for a warm beverage and snack.

One block back on Jalan Market, there's a stream of open-air food stalls which are very much the focal point for the port workers, who tuck into noodle soups and stir fries, *roti canai* and dhal throughout the day and night. East of here, hopping over a concourse congested with taxis and through a handsome arch leads into **Jalan India**, the busiest pedestrian thoroughfare in Kuching and the best place in the city to buy shoes and cheap clothing. The street is named after the Indian coolies who arrived in the early part of the twentieth century to work at the docks.

Masjid Negara, Kampung Masjid and Jalan Satok

About 100m west of the Jalan Market food stalls is the **Masjid Negara** (9am–3pm; closed Fri), standing on a steep hill, topped with gold cupolas. There's been a mosque on this site for around two hundred years, though this one only dates from the 1960s. Male visitors must wear long trousers and women skirts and a headscarf (this is provided by the mosque at the entrance).

From here, following the curve of the river southwest for 300m or so along Jalan Datuk Ajibah Abol, you reach the Malay enclave of **Kampung Masjid**. The area retains many well-preserved family houses, built at the start of the twentieth century by well-to-do government officials and boasting traditional features such as floor-level windows fronted by carved railings.

To the south of Kampung Masjid is the wide, traffic-clogged **Jalan Satok**. At its junction with Jalan Palm, opposite the Miramar Cinema, lies the site of Kuching's **Sunday market**, which actually kicks off late Saturday afternoon; it continues until about midnight, picks up again at 7am on Sunday and finally ends around noon. Buses #4a and #4b get you there from the stop on Jalan P. Ramlee or from outside the post office, in around fifteen minutes, or it's about a 25-minute walk. This is the place for picking up supplies of everything from rabbits to knives; other stalls sell satay, curry pie, sweets and *lycheesank*, a soft drink – Iban in origin – made with puréed beans, rice pellets, sugar and lychees. Amid the congested confusion, look out for the alley where Dyaks sell fruit, vegetables and handicrafts – a good place to pick up inexpensive baskets and textiles.

Petra Jaya

Across Satok Bridge, southwest of the centre, the road careers round to the northern part of Kuching and the new town, known as **Petra Jaya**. This is a busy, but generally uninteresting area, but you will find two contrasting museums that might make it worth a visit.

The appropriately log-shaped **Timber Museum** (Mon–Fri 8.30am–5pm; free) is next to the stadium on Jalan Wisma Sumbar Alam, the main thoroughfare in Petra Jaya; bus #8 runs here from the stop on Jalan P. Ramlee. Built in 1985 for the express purpose of putting across the timber industry's point of view in the increasingly acrimonious debate on tropical deforestation, the museum does its job well, with informative displays and exhibits, and plenty of facts and figures about tree types and the economic case for logging. The other side of the argument, specifically that the land farmed for generations by the tribal groups is often devastated in the process, isn't squarely addressed.

There's some light relief in the **Cat Museum** (Tues–Sun 9am–5pm; free) in Petra Jaya's DBKU Building, visible from just about all over Kuching. Claiming to be the only such museum in the world, the exhibits take as their starting point the supposed derivation of the city's name from the Malay word for "cat" – which means photos of cats from around the world, *Garfield* comic strips, feline-related art and folklore that's strictly for cat freaks. To get here, take bus #2b from the Petra Jaya bus stand at Jalan Market.

Eating

Kuching is a fantastic city to eat out in, a competitive environment where new places are opening – and shutting – monthly. The day of the week makes little difference to Kuching-ites: only when the monsoon is heavy and the city is awash with rain do people opt to scuttle back early to eat at home. The culinary range is wide too: the mainstays – Malay, Chinese and Indian – still pull in the crowds but in recent years many Western-style cafés and bars have opened up, broadening the offering to include a form of East Malaysian/Western fusion cuisine. There are also a trio of vegetarian cafés rivalling anywhere else in Southeast Asia.

Local **specialities** such as wild boar and deer sometimes crop up on Chinese menus; seafood favourites include steamed pomfret fish and *umai*; jungle fern vegetables, *midin* and *paku*, are available throughout the city; and delicious rubbery little vegetables, *ambal* (sometimes called "bamboo clam" and known locally as "monkeys' penises"), are a delicacy, collected wild amongst the mangrove swamps lining the coast and rivers. In addition, Kuching has its own versions of *kuey teow* (thick rice "Shanghai" noodles, with meat and vegetables in gravy), and *laksa*, the coconut-laced thick soup often slurped down by Sarawakians for breakfast, though some prefer *kolok mee*, an oily, tasty dish featuring dry noodles.

With such a rich range of dishes to sample, it's worth noting that many of the **cafés** and **hawker stalls**, especially those along Jalan Carpenter and Jalan India, close around sunset; even the top **restaurants** can close quite early, with last orders around 10pm. As a general rule, locals eat in the Main Bazaar and Jalan Gambier/Jalan India quartiers in the daytime and at the Triangle and Jalan Padungan later on in the evening and at night.

Food centres and hawker stalls

Chinese Food Centre Jalan Carpenter. Opposite the Chinese temple, this atmospheric centre offers a range of dishes, including Taniwah's superb *laksa* from RM2.

Gerai Anekarasa Hawker Centre Jalan Satok, under the bridge; you can take any Petra Jaya bus there. Famous for its barbecued chicken and steaks; a whole chicken plus rice and vegetables only costs around RM10 for two here. From 6pm.

Jalan Market open-air stalls Dozens of tiny stalls, very cheap and popular with dock workers, serving basic rice, noodle and curry dishes. A few sell seafood and beer into the early hours. Look out for the line of outlets selling fresh madeira cake and strong tea.

Petanak Market Jalan Petanak. Opposite the *Longhouse Hotel*, this early-morning market has a food centre that kicks off at 5am, making it an excellent option at the end of a very late night out; all regional cuisines are represented.

Sarawak Plaza Food Court Basement fast-food mall with an array of Malay and Chinese options, and very popular with Kuching youth.

Top Spot Food Court Jalan Bukit Mata Kuching. The top floor of the car park is devoted to seafood and fish, with claypot a speciality. The vegetables are very fresh too and other culinary styles, including Malay and Western, are available. Open daily 2pm–midnight.

Chinese restaurants and cafés

Benson Seafood Waterfront end of Jalan Chan Chin Ann. Massive warehouse-style seafood place with the freshest grilled and steamed fish and seafood. Daily 6–11pm.

Black Bean Coffee and Tea Company 87 Jalan Carpenter. One of the few cafés in East Malaysia serving coffee made from locally harvested beans – *liberica* and *robustica* from Bau district. Daily except Wed 10.30am–11pm.

Chin Heng Café 5 Jalan Green Hill. Taxi drivers' haven and local café for those who stay at the nearby hotels. Breakfast is served until 11am, after which delicious chilled beans, sweet and sour dishes and stir-fries appear for around RM3–5 a portion.

Chinese Barbecue Specialist Jalan Padungan. Takeaway meals of barbecued duck, chicken and back cuts of pork are hacked up unceremoniously and laid on rice at the front of this bustling, rough-and-ready shophouse; a Cantonese kitchen with a sitting area operates at the back.

Choon Hui Café 34 Jalan Ban Hock. Fiery *laksa* and filling *kolok mee* make this stylish coffee shop, just beyond Kuching's Hindu temple, a huge breakfast-time hit with locals and visitors in the know.

Fata Café Jalan McDougall. Plain looking place serving delicious Malaysian–Chinese home food. Daily except Sun 8am–2pm & 6–9pm.

Fock Hai Tin Sam Café 52 Jalan Padungan (Triangle end). Busy coffee shop with scrumptious noodles, a breakfast-size portion setting you back just RM3.

Hornbill Corner *Telang Usan* compound, off Jalan Ban Hock. Outdoor seafood restaurant well known for steamboat, where you grill stingray and marinated meats on a barbecue plate yourself. There's a popular bar behind (see p.440).

Meisan Restoran Ground floor, *Holiday Inn Kuching*, Jalan Tunku Abdul Rahman. Spicy Szechuan food. Although the Sunday-lunchtime dim sum is reasonably priced, evening meals are expensive – RM50 for two including beer – but worth splashing out for.

Min Joo Corner of Jalan Carpenter and Jalan Bishopsgate. Usually packed with Chinese–Malaysian locals and famous for the *kolok kosong* (plain noodles) that comes with a soup of pork, kidney and seaweed. Don't be put off by the gruff man taking the orders – it's worth the treatment and the wait.

Nam Sen 17 Jalan Market. Highly cool, old coffee shop, complete with varnished chairs, marble tables and "No spitting" signs. Popular with workers from the nearby docks and handy for snatching an early-morning coffee or noodle soup before catching a bus.

See Good Jalan Ban Hock (in front of the *Telang Usan* hotel and beside the *Hornbill*). Don't be fooled by this seafood eating-house's inauspicious surrounds: standards of cooking are the very highest here. Slipper lobster in pepper, bamboo clams, steamed pomfret, *ambal* and *midin* make for a fine dinner. Two can eat heartily for RM60, including beer, or more if you make a selection from the wine menu. Evenings only; closed on the 14th and 18th of every month and for a long spell over Chinese New Year.

Malay, Indian and indigenous

Aroma Café Jalan Tabuan. Set back from the street in an office block, this outlet for Bidayuh cuisine is extremely good – classic Land Dyak food, with the spicy fish out of this world. The lunch buffet (11am–2pm) is particularly good, although food is served until late. Daily except Sun 6am–midnight.

Biryani Café 16 Main Bazaar. Busy traditional place opposite the waterfront with mouthwatering *rojak* and *roti canai* for around RM5. 8am–7pm.

Bollywood Café, 66 Jalan Carpenter (Jalan Ewe Hai end). Super-friendly Naraindas and family serve up vegetarian and non-vegetarian savoury dishes, but excel with their Indian sweets. 8am–8pm.

Chillipeppers Jalan Song Thian Cheok, close to junction with Jalan Ban Hock. Very good value a/c place with a wide menu including Malay, Chinese and Indonesian dishes; RM15 per head for a full meal. Daily 10am–11pm.

Jubilee Restoran 49 Jalan India. Malay restaurant set amid busy textile stores. The *kacang goreng* (peanuts in fish paste), *sayur* (green beans in chilli and lemon) and *tahu* (bean curd) are tasty house specials. Full meals from RM8 for two. Closes at 7pm.

LL Banana Leaf 7 Lorong Rubber 1, Jalan Rubber, off Jalan Satok. Lucy Lingam's simple and delicious traditional South Indian place with dosai, banana leaf and vegetarian thali, plus meat and fish curries. Worth the trek out; could be combined with a visit to nearby Satok Market (Sat night and Sun morning). Daily 9am–9pm.

Lyn's Tandoori Lot 62, Lorong 4, Jalan Nanas ☎082/234934. Tandoori specialist, a short taxi ride from the town centre (RM10), but worth seeking out for its excellent North Indian menu. Closed Sun.

Serapi *Holiday Inn*, Jalan Tunku Abdul Rahman. Top-drawer authentic North Indian food courtesy of an Indian chef. Try to make the buffet lunch (RM25 each person) on Wed for a wide range of Western, Malay, Chinese and Indian dishes.

Western and fusion

Beccari's *Merdeka Palace Hotel*. Probably the best Italian restaurant in East Malaysia with fine wines and great pizzas and lasagne – expect to pay RM60–80 per person. Daily noon–11pm.

Bing! 84 Jalan Padungan. Comfortable, Western-style coffee lounge with all the usual range of brews, plus delicious cakes. Mon–Thurs noon–midnight & Fri–Sun noon–1am.

Bla Bla Bla… 27 Jalan Tabuan, Jalan Wayang end ☎082/233944. Like *Tao*, a beautifully-designed world of exotic water features, luscious art and Balinese wall hangings. The main dishes, especially the prawn and chicken curries, are inventive, delicious and pricey (main dishes RM25–35). Daily except Tues 11am–11.30pm.

Brasserie Kuching *Hotel Grand Continental* ☎082/230399. Specializes in excellent value all-you-can-eat buffets (RM50), with a range of Western and Malaysian dishes. Main meals from RM25, and there's a good pizza corner.

Jambu 32 Jalan Crookshank, a 15min walk from centre ☎082/235292. New addition to the city's inventive culinary landscape, with a constantly evolving menu combining Western and Malaysian elements and much else besides into "modern Borneo cuisine". Quite pricey at RM25–35 per main, but exceptional, with puddings like Moroccan date tart to die for. Also has a superb garden terrace bar out the back where you can catch owner Chris chilling most nights. Daily except Mon 6pm–12.30am.

The Junk 80 Jalan Wayang. Chef George's house favourites, including lamb with mashed potatoes, come in massive portions; an essential spot to visit, with its topsy-turvy decor of elegant multicultural bric-a-brac. Prices around RM15–20 for main courses.

James Brooke Café and Bistro Waterfront eastern end. Perfect part-open spot to sit back over a pot of tea and watch the waterfront's comings and goings with the Tua Pek Kong Temple at your back. The main dishes, although good, are quite pricey (RM12–20). Daily 10am–midnight; last order 10.30pm.

The Steakhouse *Kuching Hilton*, Jalan Tunku Abdul Rahman. One of Kuching's best; an excellent restaurant of a high international standard. The three-course special in the evening for RM79 is a memorable event, if you are into steaks or similar cuts.

Tao 175 Jalan Padungan. Coined a lifestyle café and gallery, *Tao* is as stylish as they come, serving health and energy drinks, lattes, beer and wine, while the food covers Malaysian tapas and fusion. Global chill out and funky pop is played on the sound system and the Balinese decor, including lovely water features, is stunning. Daily 10am–midnight.

Vegetarian

China Street Vegetarian Lebuh China, off Main Bazaar. Coffee shop offering a range of tofu dishes cooked to taste (and convincingly like fish and meat dishes). Daily 7.30am–2.30pm.

Perfect Vegetarian Food Jalan Green Hill. Paired with the *Zhun San*, this Chinese vegetarian buffet offers slightly less choice, but is still delicious and excellent value. Mon–Sat 7am–5pm.

Zhun San Yen Vegetarian Jalan Chan Chin Ann. Quite exceptional Chinese-run café with dozens of delicious, exclusively vegetarian and vegan dishes sold from a buffet by weight. Also excellent juices, including watermelon and carrot. The overall cost hardly ever comes in at more than RM20 for two. Mon–Sat 8am–2.30pm & 5–8.30pm.

Drinking and nightlife

Although the city's nightlife scene is tiny by Kuala Lumpur's standards, and some bars and clubs come and go with the seasons, Kuching, the only city in East Malaysia with a club scene, has a standard set of great venues doing the biz. Expect an excitable but polite crowd and a music mix of international pop, R&B, hip-hop, house and the odd Cantonese tune, usually remixed with a techno throb. As with the exciting new cuisine, head straight to the Triangle end of Jalan Padungan where most of the bars and nightclubs stay open until 4am, Friday and Saturday nights and up to 1am the rest of the week.

Bars

Cat City Taman Sri Sarawak Plaza (opposite *Kuching Hilton* hotel). Renovated pub-style bar with a balcony. Happy hour is from 4.30–9.30pm, and there are karaoke, DJs and occasionally live music.

Dulit Terrace and Tuak Bar *Telang Usan Hotel*, Jalan Ban Hock. Mostly quietish bar at the Kenyah-run hotel where you can develop a taste for local rice wine, *tuak* or sample good Kenyah home cooking. A good place to meet local characters.

Eagles' Nest 20 Jalan Bukit Mata Kuching. Kuching hangout where you can dance to Sarawakian hits, play pool and guzzle Tiger beer. Daily 7pm–3am.

Hornbill's Corner Bar *Telang Usan* compound, off Jalan Ban Hock. Local bar popular with soccer lovers, who gather to watch games on satellite TV. Noon–midnight.

Miami Taman Sri Sarawak, opposite *Kuching Hilton*. Though the beer is often just Tiger and the music a touch kitsch, this is a classic, not-to-be-missed, very friendly watering hole – the kind of place where the Kuching hardcore go for their last drink (and one more). Open 6pm–early hours.

Soho 64 Jalan Padungan. Located next to *Grappa*, this ultra-fashionable two-floor bar absolutely heaves at weekends, when the DJ plays international funky pop. The veranda isn't quite Ibiza, but is pretty good nonetheless. Come early if you want to eat (local tapas-style small plates). 6pm–early hours.

Clubs

Grappa Jalan Padungan. Cutting-edge, often packed nightspot attracting a young crowd. Local DJs play Western house music and dance-music flavoured pop. Mon–Thurs 7pm–midnight, Fri & Sat 7pm–early hours.

Senso Ground floor, *Kuching Hilton*. The city's leading music nightspot, with top DJ Ian Teo spinning house and techno expertly to an often-packed dance floor. The hitch lies in the staggeringly high price of drinks, including water. Fri & Sat only 10pm–3am.

The Travilion Jalan Petanak. New plaza at the end of Jalan Padungan full of bars and clubs. The best is *Zing*, with its eclectic soundtrack of local and international pop and dance. Thurs–Sat 8pm–early hours.

Longhouse *culture*

The traditional longhouse is, in many ways, a testament to the cultural survival of Sarawak's ethnic groups. On the one hand it serves as a graceful reminder of customs that have gradually faded away in the face of modern technology; yet it also continues to support a way of life for entire communities that even now couldn't be any further removed from most travellers' experiences. Staying in a longhouse, however briefly, and participating in the daily routines of the people who live in them, is a captivating experience that will leave a lasting impression. For information on tour operators that run trips to Sarawak's longhouses, see p.441.

Drying rice on the veranda

Community dwelling

Longhouses are built first and foremost with practical considerations, designed to sustain entire communities under a single roof. As such, these dwellings can reach impressive sizes: deep in the Sarawak interior, they are still sometimes built up to 1km in length. **Traditional longhouses** are usually built of hardwoods and bamboo with ironwood shingles on the roof; they comprise three levels that are usually elevated on stilts so as to provide shelter for livestock.

The house itself is split into several sections, each with its own specific function. On approach, you will see a **long open veranda** (*tanju*) where rice, pepper or rubber is laid out to dry. You enter the longhouse via a ladder through to a **roofed veranda** (*ruai*), the area in which the community's social life is conducted. Here women weave magnificently patterned textiles and boys are taught to construct rattan baskets and mats. On the opposite side of the *ruai* from the *tanju*, through closed doors, lies each family's **apartment**, or *bilik*. Directly above the *ruai* is the **loft**, where rattan baskets and sleeping mats are kept.

Location, location, location

Longhouses are often found in truly spectacular **settings** – usually on the bends or at the confluences of rivers. While aesthetically pleasing, these locations were actually selected for strategic reasons, as a **good defensive position** was essential until well into the twentieth century when inter-tribal warfare died down. In keeping with their concerns about defence, longhouse tribes would also consider their combative strength when choosing a location. Larger groups might build big longhouses in open locations as a show of strength, while smaller ones might opt for more modest homesteads deeper in the forest.

Iban longhouse

Visiting longhouses

Melenau longhouse

Longhouses are working buildings where a traditional way of life continues to this day, and a visit will incorporate all sorts of age-old practices and rituals. On **arrival** – usually after a long and exhilarating journey through the forest – your first experience of longhouse life will be an **introduction to the chief** (*tuai*). In order to avoid giving offence, be sure to shake hands with everyone who wants to shake yours and don't ascend the longhouse ladder to the veranda until invited to do so by an older member of the community. After the formalities, you'll be led onto the *ruai* and offered a glass of *tuak* (rice wine), or orange squash if you are visiting a more strict Christian community. Longhouse dwellers in Sarawak are originally **animist** but now the majority are **Christian**; there are some **Muslim** groups too.

The grand annual Iban party

The most social time to visit an Iban longhouse is the end of May and early June, when the **Gawai Dayak** (harvest festival celebrations) get into full swing. It is a time for relaxing, hunting and merrymaking, and also the season for celebrations and rituals such as weddings, christenings and circumcisions. Many Iban who work or study in the cities return over this period for their annual holiday, and parents hope that their coming-of-age sons and daughters will return from *bejalai* (a kind of gap year where young Iban find work elsewhere) to rejoice in the old ways. Proceedings can last up to two full days and involve dancing, singing and storytelling; participants wear traditional garments and, sometimes, centuries-old heirlooms are taken down from the rafters – you may even catch a glimpse of a **shrunken head** or two. To find out where and when one is being held, ask at Kuching's Visitor Information Centre (see p.429), or in cafés in Sri Aman (see p.457) or Lubok Antu (see p.460). Each longhouse hosts at least one open weekend during a *gawai* when visitors are welcome, though it's customary to bring **gifts**.

Girl at Gawai Dayak

Dried skulls

During your stay, there are various **activities** you can partake in. In the daytime, you may be shown the pepper and fruit orchards that have been maintained over generations by the longhouse families. If harvesting is imminent you can often join a visit to check on the rubber trees. In the evening you may be given the opportunity to join a hunt for wild boar. **Food** will usually be taken with the chief's family, and you should feel free to eat as much as you like. Following the meal there are often shows of dancing and traditional singing performed to please the ancestors. In recent years, some of the larger longhouses have built lodges close by to house visitors; otherwise, you will **sleep** on the longhouse veranda.

Where to visit longhouses in Sarawak

➤ **Bidayuh of the southwest/Kalimantan border** The Bidayuh are a small, shy community, which seldom see visitors and live a very traditional lifestyle, celebrating the seasons and still respecting age-old animist traditions. Their longhouses, notably around Gunung Penrissen, are customarily built away from rivers on high ground.

➤ **Iban of the Southwest** The longhouses on the Skrang, Lemanok, Delok, Ai and Lemanak rivers, belonging to the Iban, are the most popular with tourists. They are lively, vibrant places where musical ensembles often perform, hunting is plentiful and modern entertainment (radio, television, DVD) is encouraged and enjoyed.

➤ **The Ulu Kayan and Kenyah of the north** These tribes are known for their spectacular longhouses and their prowess as fine weavers and wood carvers. Expect to see lovely decorative touches and the odd dried skull, for old time's sake.

➤ **The Kelabit of the Kelabit Highlands** Living around Bario, Long Dano and Ba Kelalan, in smaller longhouses often beside beautiful freshwater streams, the Kelabit are gregarious, well-educated people with a great sense of humour. Visiting these communities is popular with independent travellers.

Basket making

Shopping

Kuching is the best place in Sarawak to buy just about anything, especially tribal textiles, pottery, Iban *pua kumbu* (hand-woven rugs), lovely rattan mats of various sizes, and other handicrafts. However, if you are offered a locally made item that you like in a longhouse at a price that seems reasonable, snap it up and don't wait for Kuching, as some of the admittedly lovely products on Main Bazaar, Jalan Temple and Jalan Wayang are produced in factories and aren't bespoke.

The city is well known especially for its locally produced Chinese pottery, whose decoration bears local Dyak influences. There are some ceramics stalls on the road to the airport, but it's better to visit the **potteries** (daily 8am–noon & 2–6pm) themselves, where you can walk around and watch the potters in action at the wheel and firing kilns; each pottery also has a shop on site. They're clustered together on Jalan Penrissen, around 8km from town – take Sarawak Transport Company bus #3, #3a, #9a or #9b from Lebuh Jawa.

Artrageously Ramsey Ong 94 Main Bazaar. Ong is a leading modernist Malaysian painter, specializing in nature and rural culture. His gallery/shop includes work from other artists, including silk paintings.

Arts of Asia 68 Main Bazaar. One of the most comprehensive private galleries in town, it sells naturalistic paintings and sculpture, which tend to be expensive.

Atelier Galley 104 Main Bazaar. Collection of handicrafts, *objets d'art*, furniture and antiques.

Boonia 73 Jalan Padungan Gallery displaying new work by mostly naturalistic Sarawakian artists which doubles as a picture frame store.

Edric Ong 20 Main Bazaar. Lovely fabrics, textiles and sculpture.

Galeri M *Kuching Hilton* and Main Bazaar. Besides beadwork, hornbill carvings and Sarawakian antiques, you can find a massive range of contemporary local art here.

Nelsons' Antiques and Jewellery 14 Main Bazaar. Cornucopia of Sarawakian crafts from mats to pottery, furniture to jewellery.

Ngee Tai Pottery Factory Eighth mile, Jalan Penrissen. Located on the right-hand side of the

road as you head out of town, this is probably the best of the potteries. The master potter, Ng Hua Ann, shows visitors a wide range of ceramic wares ranging from huge pots to small souvenir items such as coffee mugs and flower vases.

Sarakraf 78 Jalan Tabuan. Decent stock of baskets, textiles and ironwork.

Sarawak Handicraft Centre Round Tower, Waterfront. Showroom plus stalls outside displaying locally made handicrafts.

Sarawak House 67 Main Bazaar. Flashy and expensive but usually worth a look for textiles and longhouse artefacts.

Sarawak Plaza Jalan Tunku Abdul Rahman. This mall is the major focus for Western products – fashion accessories, shirts and designer shoes, and Malay and Western music – plus a few handicraft stores with a good range of bags, T-shirts and ethnic jewellery.

Tan Brothers Jalan Padungan, close to the junction with Jalan Mathies. Baskets, carvings and bags.

Yeo Hing Chuan 46 Main Bazaar. Interesting carvings and other handicrafts; a quality 30cm carved hardwood figure costs about RM300.

Tour operators

Tour operators in Sarawak, like in Sabah, have grown into a vital resource for adventure travel in the state. Essential for **longhouse** visits, many travellers also use operators for trips to national parks, bespoke treks and even town visits. Standards, particularly around the Ai, Lemanak and Skrang rivers, 300km east of Kuching, are usually high. The Iban longhouses here are vibrant, fascinating places, and always welcoming. The tours themselves have changed over the years, evolving to show more sensitivity to longhouse culture – for example, a tour will be postponed if there has been a death in the community, as by custom, a private, grieving period must be respected.

As always, shop around to see what is on offer, although prices are largely uniform – the standard fee is RM100–150 per person per day. All operators listed here have a proven record in quality, and highly enjoyable, trips.

Asian Overland 286a first floor, Westwood Park, Jalan Tuban ☏082/251163. Good longhouse trips in the Kuching vicinity and on the Batang Ai river system. Also arranges trips north to Mulu National Park and on the "Head-hunters' Trail" from Mulu to Limbang.

Borneo Adventure 55 Main Bazaar ☏082/245175, ⊛www.borneoadventure.com. Award-winning operation running excellent trips throughout Sarawak and Sabah. Its jungle lodge (❼), beside the Nanga Sumpa longhouse, along the Ulu Ai, is a fine example of best practice and a beacon for ecotourism in Malaysia.

Borneo Exploration Tours and Travel 76 Wayang St ☏082/413472, ⓔckkc@tm.net.my. Popular, small outfit with a guide, Desmond Kon, who comes highly recommended.

Borneo Interland 63 first floor, Main Bazaar ☏082/426328. Also has tour desk at *Merdeka Palace Hotel* (☏082/258000, ext. 8018). Specializes in local trips, including Gunung Gading Park, Bau's Fairy and Wind caves and Anna Rais longhouse.

Borneo Transverse 15 Jalan Green Hill ☏082/257784, ⊛www.borneotransverse.com.my.

Excellent, veteran outfit which offers, amongst others, culturally fascinating tours to Iban longhouses on Sungai Lemanak.

CPH Travel 70 Jalan Padungan ☏082/243708. Waterbound experts offering Sungai Sarawak cruises (2 daily; 2hr; RM40 from the waterfront jetty) and, when the sea isn't too rough, cruises to the newly open, fascinating Kuching Wetlands National Park, close to Santubong, to view Irrawaddy dolphins, proboscis monkeys and birds (5hr; RM200). Alternatively, the company offers a mangrove cruise off Buntal (3hr; RM140).

Diethelm Travel Second floor, Lot 168, Jalan Chan Chin Ann ☏082/412778, ⊛www.diethelmtravel .com. Directly opposite *Zhun San Yen*, this experienced outfit has excellent contacts on Sungai Lemanak. Assistant Director Panch is a mine of information on the region's longhouse culture. Also organize trips along Batang Rajang and northwards to Mulu National Park.

Interworld 161 Jalan Temple ☏082/252344. Organizes expeditions up the Skrang and Batang Ai rivers. The three-day/two-night "Head-hunters of Borneo" trip costs RM500–600 per person; plus Niah and Mulu trips too.

Listings

Airlines AirAsia, Wisma Ho Ho Lim, ground floor, 291, Lot 4, Jalan Abell (☏082/283222, 24-hour call centre ☏03/8775 4000); MAS, Lot 215, Jalan Song Thian Cheok (☏082/246622 or 244144; Mon–Fri 8.30am–5pm, Sat 8.30am–1pm); Royal Brunei Airlines, first floor, Rugayah, Jalan Song Thian Cheok (☏082/243344); Singapore Airlines, Wisma Bukit Maja Kuching, Jalan Tunku Abdul Rahman (☏082/240267).

Airport Flight enquiries on ☏082/457373 or 454242.

Banks and exchange Reliable ATM at Maybank, 13 Jalan Tunku Abdul Rahman. Overseas Union Bank, Jalan Tun Haji Openg; Standard Chartered, Wisma Bukit Mata Kuching, Jalan Tunku Abdul Rahman. Moneychangers: Majid & Sons, 45 Jalan India; Mohamad Yahia & Sons, basement, Sarawak Plaza, Jalan Abell. Both offer OK rates.

Boat Express Bahagia's 8.30am daily Kuching–Sibu launch, ☏013/820 3702. It's useful to check the boat is running during the monsoon period when the sea is high before going to the jetty.

Bookshops Popular Books, third floor, Tun Jegah Mall and Premier Books, first floor, Sarawak Plaza, both have a reasonable range of English-language books including travel, cookery and fiction. Mohamad Yahia & Sons – with branches in the *Holiday Inn* and the basement of the Sarawak Plaza – offers the best range of books in the city, and also stock the best maps of the state. In addition, they sell the English-language *Borneo Post*, which features international news and a small section on events in the state. Sky Book Store, 57 Jalan Padungan, and Star Books, 30 Main Bazaar, are good for geography, culture and anthropology.

Car rental Expect to pay around RH140 for day hire, though this drops the longer you hire for. Borneo Interland, 63 Main Bazaar ☏082/413595 (24-hour line ☏082/426328), ⊛www.bitravel.com.my; Mayflower Car Rental, first floor, Wisma Bukit Mata Kuching, Jalan Tunku Abdul Rahman ☏082/410110 (evenings and weekends ☏019/8160553), ⊛www .start.com.my/wiki/index.php/Car_rentals; Pronto Car Rental, first floor, 98 Jalan Padungan ☏082/237889, 24-hour ☏013/811 6778.

Consulates Australia ☎082/233350; Indonesia, 111 Jalan Tun Haji Openg ☎082/241734 (Mon–Thurs 8.30am–noon & 2–4pm); New Zealand ☎082/482177; UK and Ireland ☎082/250950.
Hospitals Sarawak General Hospital, Jalan Ong Kee Hui (☎082/276666), charges RM50 for consultations. For private treatment, go to Normah Medical Centre, Jalan Tun Datuk Patinggi (☎082/440055). For holistic treatment try Akita Foot Reflexology, 51 Jalan Padungan (☎082/230239).
Internet Cyber City, Taman Sri Sarawak, off Jalan Borneo (☎082/257555 daily 10am–10pm), is not the only Internet café in town but is the most reliable, central and inexpensive (RM3 per hour). Kuching connection speeds are generally excellent – much faster than most other towns in Sarawak.
Laundry Easy Wash, corner of Jalan Ban Hock, and Mr Dobi, Jalan Abell (next block along from *Pizza Hut*). Both excellent value as you pay by weight. Both open daily 8am–6pm.
Massage The Blind Health Massage Centre in the Timberland Medical Centre, Jalan Ong Tiang Swee, situated 2km from the city centre, offers excellent massage from blind people at very reasonable prices (RM40 for 1hr; 10am–7pm).
Motorbike rental Teck Hua Motor, 31 Jalan Tabuan ☎082/417068. The cost is RM35–60 per day depending on the size of bike.
Pharmacy Apex Pharmacy, first floor, Sarawak Plaza.
Police Central Police Station (Tourist Police Unit), opposite Pandang Merdeka (☎082/241222). Come here to report stolen and lost property.
Post office The main post office is on Jalan Tun Haji Openg (Mon–Sat 8am–6pm, Sun 10am–1pm); post restante/general delivery can be collected here – take your passport.
Swimming There's a pool at MBKS Building, Jalan Pending (Mon–Fri 2.30–9pm, Sat 6.45–8.45pm, Sun 9.30am–9pm; ☎082/426915); RM3 adults, RM1 children. Closed on public holidays.
Taxi Contact the ever-reliable and reasonable Chris Khoo (☎013/822 0133) for taxi trips around the city and for the airport hop; 24-hour services ☎082/480000 and 348898.
Visa extensions Immigration Office, first floor, Bangunan Sultan Iskandar, Jalan Simpang Tiga (Mon–Fri 8am–noon & 2–4.30pm; ☎082/245661); take Chin Lian Long bus #11. Get there by 3pm to have your application processed on the day.

Day-trips around Kuching

The area **around Kuching** is well served by road, and at least a week's worth of interesting excursions can be made by bus or car without the trouble of hiring guides and porters. Within an hour's bus ride from the city are the kampungs, beaches and resorts of the **Santubong Peninsula**, also known as **Damai**. Some people stay out at the peninsula's stylish accommodation or at *Camp Permai*, more a budget choice, near to which is the **Sarawak Cultural Village**, a show-piece community where model longhouses are staffed by guides from each of the ethnic groups. A visit to **Jong's Crocodile Farm** is not a highlight, but on balance just about worth a visit, while trekking around **Kubah National Park** is a sweaty but worthwhile experience. If you're travelling outside the rainy season (March–Oct), then **Kuching Wetlands National Park** is worth a visit, although this must be done through a tour operator (such as CPH Travel, see "Tour operators", opposite). Also enjoyable is a morning or afternoon in the **Orang-utan Rehabilitation Centre**.

Three Kuching **bus** companies operate useful services within the area. From the western end of Lebuh Jawa, Sarawak Transport Company (STC) buses depart for Bau and Lundu to the west, and Semenggoh and Jong's Crocodile Farm to the south. To head north to Santubong and Bako (see p.448), use Petra Jaya Transport buses, which leave from below the open-air market on Jalan Market, or for Santubong, the shuttle service which runs from *Crowne Plaza Hotel* and the *Holiday Inn* twelve times daily (RM10, check with hotels for times). Finally, for Kubah, take Matang Transport Company buses from the stop on Jalan P. Ramlee.

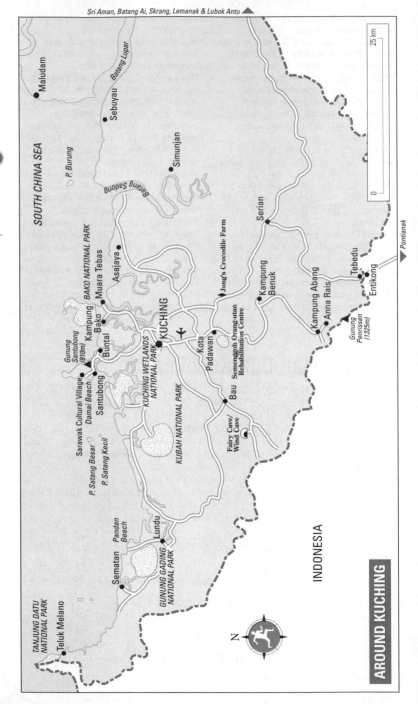

AROUND KUCHING

Sri Aman, Batang Ai, Skrang, Lemanak & Lubok Antu

SOUTH CHINA SEA

25 km

0

Maludam

Sebuyau

Batang Lupar

Simunjan

P. Burung

Batang Sadong

Serian

Asajaya

Muara Tebas

BAKO NATIONAL PARK

Kampung
Bako

Buntal

*Gunung
Santubong
(810m)*

Sarawak Cultural Village
Dama Beach

Santubong

P. Satang Besar

P. Satang Kecil

*KUCHING WETLANDS
NATIONAL PARK*

KUCHING

Kota
Padawan

Jong's Crocodile Farm

Kampung
Benuk

Semenggoh Orang-utan
Rehabilitation Centre

Kampung Abang

Anna Rais

Tebedu

Entikong

*Gunung
Penrissen
(1325m)*

Pontianak

KUBAH NATIONAL PARK

Bau

Fairy Cave/
Wind Cave

Pandan
Beach

Lundu

Sematan

*GUNUNG GADING
NATIONAL PARK*

*TANJUNG DATU
NATIONAL PARK*

Teluk Melano

INDONESIA

N

Santubong Peninsula

Located 25km north of Kuching and bordered by the Sarawak River to the south, the **Santubong Peninsula** (also called Damai) is dominated by the densely forested 810-metre Gunung Santubong. It is a fascinating area, its inhabitation going back to pre-history. During excavation in the 1960s and 1970s tens of thousands of objects, including digging implements, were found across six neighbouring sites here, and were dated back to 3000 BC when the Indian/Javanese Empire reached this far, probably its furthest extent. Little can be seen today – a possible tantric shrine at Bongkissah, 2km from Kampung Santubong, is covered by grass and jungle ferns. In the eighth century, the peninsula was the location for a larger trading settlement. The region is also dotted with spectacular formations – besides Gunung Santubong, they include strangely shaped rocks amongst the patches of thick forest.

Since the 1980s, stretches of the river and coastline have been rapidly developed as retreats for tourists, curious travellers and city-weary locals, though thankfully the resorts don't disturb the tranquil, almost lonesome nature of the area, which is among the most beautiful in Sarawak. Pleasures are simple: sitting on the peninsula's golden sand, watching a spectacular sunset with Sarawak's lush green hills to one side and the sea on the other, and eating delicious fish in the riverside villages. An added attraction – and worth a half-day trip itself – is the informative and entertaining **Sarawak Cultural Village**, a collection of traditionally built dwellings which showcase the lifestyles of the state's indigenous peoples. It's here too that the Rainforest Music Festival takes place in July/August (see box on p.447).

Buntal and Kampung Santubong

The #2b bus (daily 6.40am–6pm; every 40min) from Kuching's Jalan Market heads north for the forty-minute trip through the city's ever-expanding suburbs and small rubber and pepper plantations, leaving the main road and running along the edge of the river to **BUNTAL**. This quiet riverside kampung, bordered by forest, is famed for its **seafood restaurants**, which stand on stilts in the seaside shallows; *Lim Hok An* is the pick of the bunch. There's a small beach, too, with the locals offering short boat trips along Sungai Sarawak, but no accommodation.

From Buntal, the bus returns to the main road and runs alongside Gunung Santubong, before turning east down a narrow road for 2km to **KAMPUNG SANTUBONG**, a very pretty place set on an inlet with fishing boats hauled up onto the beach. Just visible in the hills above the kampung is a wooden bungalow where the famous scientist Alfred Russell Wallace lived on his arrival in Sarawak, at the invitation of Rajah James Brooke, in 1854 – Wallace penned his theory on speciation and biogeography here. There are plans to restore the bungalow, currently a ruin, over the next few years and convert it into a museum and/or guesthouse. Two Chinese **cafés**, *Son Hong* and the *Santubong*, in the centre of the kampung, can whip up tasty stir-fry and rice dishes.

There are some interesting **rock carvings** near Santubong – head back along the Kuching road for 200m and turn left just before the 6km sign onto a track. Thirty metres along, to the left of a house, follow on overgrown path between two rocks – this leads to some curiously carved boulders, one featuring a prone human figure, though the other forms are hard to decipher. There hasn't been an exact dating yet, although archeologists think the images could be a thousand or more years old.

Accommodation

Five hundred metres from Kampung Santubong, *Nanga Damai* (☎82/257330 or 010/887 1017; ❹–❾) is a four-storey house which both has its own private beach just a few hundred metres away and rubs shoulders with untouched jungle. Beautifully designed, the house has a large, semi-open dining terrace with a bar and pool, and large rooms, either en-suite or with adjacent bathrooms, with an open feel and panoramic views. The owner, Polycarp Teo Sebom, will pick you up from Kuching given a bit of warning and can drive you in and out of the city most days.

However, most visitors head straight to the resorts, snugly located below Gunung Santubong. The *Holiday Inn Resort Damai Beach* (☎082/846999, ⓦ www.holidayinn-sarawak.com; ❼, although promotional discounts are often available) nestles in a natural hollow and has two swimming pools, an outdoor massage centre and a private palm-fringed, pebbled beach. Its best feature however is its Bidayuh-style Baruk chalets (RM350 a night for two people), poised 300 metres up on the hill among casuarina trees overlooking the main body of the resort. Hopelessly romantic, it's not surprising that they are a favourite among honeymooners. The hotel also offers a lavish all-you-can-eat buffet breakfast (included in price), and it is possible to book a van (RM10) to and from Kuching here. Next door, the *Holiday Inn Resort Damai Lagoon* (☎082/846900, ⓦ www.holidayinn-sarawak.com; ❼) is slightly pricier; sculpted around a few lagoon-style swimming pools, one with a sunken bar, this compact resort has lovely rooms, most of them with balconies.

Right at the end of Jalan Gunung Santubong, and 300m from the *Holiday Inn, Camp Permai* (☎082/846490) is a kind of camouflaged burrow dug into the leafy side of the mountain. It has a dozen magnificent en-suite tree houses (❹–❺) only a few metres from the water's edge, and two more functional and budget-aware longhouses (❷), plus there's a **campsite**, with tents included (RM5). The café, built on stilts above the sea, offers good meals at reasonable prices and the view is magnificent.

Trails

The **trail** that loops uphill from the entrance to the *Holiday Inn* and returns to the road close to the entrance of the Cultural Village makes for a pleasant ninety-minute forest stroll. The resort's entrance is also the starting point for the much more demanding **Gunung Santubong Trek**, for whose final ascent you need to rely upon ropes and rope ladders; it's well marked, however, and you don't need a guide. Allow at least three hours for your ascent, plus a couple more to return to sea level.

Sarawak Cultural Village

Beside the entrance to the *Holiday Inn Resort Damai Beach* is the **Sarawak Cultural Village** (daily 9am–5.15pm, stage shows 11.30am & 4.30pm; RM45; ☎082/846411, ⓦ www.scv.com.my). It comprises seven authentically built traditional dwellings which stand in a dramatic setting, the sea to one side, a lake in the middle of the site and the jungle escarpment of Gunung Santubong looming behind. As well as Iban, Orang Ulu and Bidayuh longhouses, there's a Malay townhouse, a Chinese farmhouse, a Melenau "tall house" (*rumah tinggi*), a Penan jungle settlement and the latest addition, a Kenyah/Kayan longhouse where you can watch local craftsmen make the *sape*, the Sarawakian harp-cum-lute. A café offers light and full meals and a wide range of beverages.

When it was opened in the early 1990s, the village was a kind of theme park for the state's varied ethnic groups, though today the set-piece houses and facilities feel like a real community, and many of the people you come across in the houses,

The Rainforest Music Festival

Held annually at the Sarawak Cultural Village since 1998, the **Rainforest Music Festival** (day-tickets RM60; see ⓦ www.rainforestmusic-borneo.com or contact the Sarawak Tourist Board, ☎ 082/423 600, for line-up and festival pass details) takes place annually in July, with seminars and workshops in the afternoons, and an outdoor stage providing the setting for the main performances in the evenings. While a variety of Western artists have performed here, the festival is especially worthwhile for the opportunity it affords to watch performers from various parts of Malaysia, some rarely seen outside their own communities. At the very first festival, for example, Mak Minah, a Temuan Orang Asli singer from the Peninsula, brought the house down with her powerful voice; East Malaysian artists you're likely to see here every year include the Sape Ulu Quartet (the *sape* being a traditional bamboo lute) from the upriver division, Belaga; and Usun Apau, a Penan vocal group that sings **sinui** (ancestral) tunes. The festival also features artists from across Southeast Asia, and is made all the more appealing by its atmospheric setting in the Sarawak Cultural Village. Locally based author Heidi Munan described one night this way: "Musicians and audience move from one Damai longhouse to the next for concerts, workshops, flute-offs, drum-outs and sing-ins. Gongs and drums pulse from the dimly lit spaces into the jungle darkness and the rhythmic stomp of many feet reverberates through the sturdy structures."

most notably the Iban and Bidayuh, live there a lot of the time. In the daytime, there are demonstrations of weaving, cooking and instrument-playing, along with more idiosyncratic pursuits like top-spinning (in the Malay townhouse), blowpipe-drilling (in the Penan settlement) and sago-processing (at the Melenau tall house). The shows put on twice daily are, however, rather too touristy, and some visitors have complained at their trivialization of ancient forest skills. However, for a brief overview of the costumes, traditions and daily lives of Sarawak's peoples, the Cultural Village is a worthwhile experience. A particularly good time to visit is July over the Rainforest Music Festival (see box, above).

Jong's Crocodile Farm

Jong's Crocodile Farm (daily 9am–5pm; RM5; ☎082/242790), 29km south of Kuching on the Serian Highway, is hardly an essential attraction but is worth a quick look in if you haven't got time to head upriver into Sarawak's interior, where you might glimpse crocodiles in the wild. Various types of crocodiles (an endangered species in Sarawak) breed on the premises, and some are killed at a tender age and their skins sold. There isn't a great deal to see apart from at feeding times (daily 9am & 3pm) and a few grisly photographic reminders that people are frequently attacked by crocodiles: one photo shows a dead croc whose stomach has been cut open, revealing an assortment of masticated animals. To get to the farm, take STC bus #3 or #3a to Siruban village (4 daily; 40min; RM2.50).

Semenggoh Orang-utan Rehabilitation Centre

The **Semenggoh Orang-utan Rehabilitation Centre** (daily 8am–12.30pm & 2–4.30pm; free) is a 25-year old success story, with dozens of orang-utans now roaming freely in the surrounding forest. The best time to visit is at feeding times (9–9.30am & 1pm–3.30pm) when some of the largely solitary primates gather to gorge on a meal of seasonal fruit including over-ripe bananas and watermelons, though note that during the fruit season (April–May) very few orang-utan will bother to come to the feeding stands as they will find their food elsewhere. The Centre is 32km south of Kuching; take #6, an STC bus from Lebuh Jawa (8 daily; 7am–2pm; 40min; RM1.70). The last bus back to the city leaves at 4pm.

Kubah National Park

Located just 20km west of Kuching, the dipterocarp forest of **Kubah National Park** (RM10) offers a pleasing and manageable day-trip out of Kuching. Matang Transport Company bus #11 leaves from Kuching's Lebuh Jawa terminus hourly from 6.30am to 4.30pm (RM1.80; 35min) and drops you a three-hundred-metre walk from the park entrance. (To get back to Kuching hail a bus on the other side of the road; the last one passes at 5pm.)

Situated on a sandstone plateau, the small park contains crystal-clear streams, waterfalls created out of hardened limestone and a wide selection of palms and orchids. Indeed Kubah is considered one of the richest sites for **palm** species in the world: 95 types have been found there, including coconut, sago and many rattans, with eighteen of these species endemic to the region (among Sarawak's other parks, only Mulu has more types of native palm).

Three modest mountains, **Selang**, **Sendok** and **Serapi**, emerge out of the lush forest; they're crisscrossed by trails, waterfalls and streams. Staff at the park headquarters will point you in the direction of Kubah's marked hikes, among them: the three-hour **Ulu Raya Trail**, a good walk to catch sight of the palms; the **Waterfall Trail**, a ninety-minute uphill hike to impressive, split-level falls; and the **Bukit Selang Trail**, less than an hour's walk from headquarters and boasting some grand views. Kubah's best views, however, are from the three-hour **Gunung Serapi (Summit) Trail** – from the mountain's summit, you can see Kuching and much of southwestern Sarawak. There's **accommodation** (RM5 campsite; RM15 for a dorm bed; RM150 for a four-bed lodge) but no canteen or places to eat nearby, so bring your own **provisions** – the main park building has a small kitchen. The parks desk at Kuching's Visitors' Information Centre (see p.429) handles bookings.

Kuching Wetlands National Park

Located just 15km from Kuching and 5km from Damai the newly created estuarine **Kuching Wetlands National Park** contains a mangrove system with an intricate system of marine waterways. The site has value especially as a breeding and nursery ground for fish and prawn species – over forty families of fishes and eleven species of prawns have been found here – and is particularly well worth visiting for its marine wildlife, most notably Irrawaddy dolphins. It is only accessible on a tour and by a sturdy boat or launch; the main company accessing the region is Kuching-based CPH Travel (see p.442); trips leave at around 4pm, getting onto the water at 5pm, the best time to view the dolphins. A van will take you to the Santubong Boat Club (30min from Kuching), where you get on the launch.

Bako National Park

Though no further away from Kuching than the Santubong Peninsula, **BAKO NATIONAL PARK** (☏082/248088; RM10) a two-hour bus and boat journey northeast of the city, is too much of a gem to try to pack into one

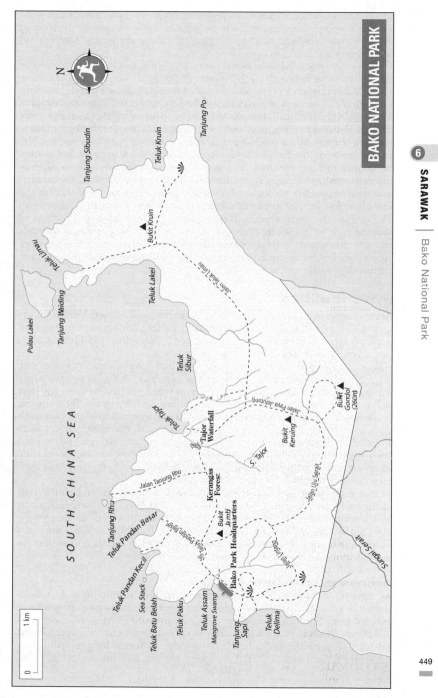

BAKO NATIONAL PARK

SOUTH CHINA SEA

Pulau Lakei

Teluk Limau

Tanjung Waiding

Tanjung Sibudin

Teluk Kruin

Tanjung Po

Bukit Kruin

Teluk Lakei

Jalan Teluk Limau

Teluk Sibur

Teluk Tajor

Tajor Waterfall

S. Tajor

Jalan Paya Jelutong

Bukit Keruing

Bukit Gondol (260m)

Jalan Ulu Serait

Sungai Serait

Kerangas Forest

Jalan Tanjung Rhu

Teluk Tanjung Rhu

Sea Stack

Teluk Pandan Besar

Teluk Pandan Kecil

Teluk Batu Belah

Teluk Paku

Teluk Assam

Mangrove Swamp

Bukit Jambi

Jln Teluk Pandan Besar

Bako Park Headquarters

Jalan Lintang

Tanjung Sapi

Teluk Delima

N

0   1 km

day. The park's ecology, wildlife, views and atmosphere make it feel like a place which time forgot, where proboscis monkeys swing from trees to the roofs of the park's few buildings, and beaches that are among the best in Sarawak can be reached on short hikes.

Bako is Sarawak's oldest national park, occupying the northern section of the Muara Tebas Peninsula at the mouth of Sungai Bako. The area was once part of a forest reserve – a region set aside for timber growing and extraction – but in 1957 was made a national park, fully protected from exploitation. Although relatively small, Bako is spectacular in its own way: its steep rocky cliffs, punctuated by deep bays and lovely sandy beaches, are thrillingly different from the rest of the predominantly flat and muddy Sarawak coastline. The peninsula is composed of sandstone which, over the years, has been worn down to produce delicate pink iron patterns on cliff faces, honeycomb weathering and contorted rock arches rising from the sea. Access to some of the beaches is difficult, requiring tricky descents down nearly vertical paths. Above, the forest contains various species of wildlife, and rivers and waterfalls for bathing. The hike to the highest point, Bukit Gondol (260m), offering a wide view over the park to the South China Sea, is among the most popular of the trails that crisscross the park. Bako's **plant life** is varied and stunning, ranging from looming eighty-metre dipterocarp trees to dense mangrove forest, with pitcher plants easily visible on many of the trails.

Practicalities

Accommodation must be booked at the parks desk at Kuching's Visitors' Information Centre (see p.429); you can pay the park fee (RM10) there too or wait until you arrive at the park. Note, if you're not booking in advance, that it tends to get very busy at weekends and during holidays.

To get to the park, take the Petra Jaya #6 **bus** (every 50min 6.30am–6pm; RM1.50, 45min) from Jalan Market, or a **minibus** (daily 7am–4pm; RM3; 40min) from the same location, which leaves when full. Both run to the jetty at **Kampung Bako**, where longboats are on hand for the lovely thirty-minute cruise beside mangrove swamps to the park headquarters (RM40 per boat; each takes up to five people). By **car** from Kuching, the 37-kilometre journey takes around forty minutes, and there's a car park at Kampung Bako where you can safely leave your vehicle. There is rarely a delay in catching a longboat at the kampung, unless a large tour group is being relayed out to the park, and even then the wait shouldn't be more than an hour.

Once at the **park headquarters** the ranger will supply an informative **map** of the park and take you to your accommodation. You may want an hour to look around the excellent displays and exhibits at the Information Centre; these identify the flora and fauna in the park as well as describing in detail the park's history and unique characteristics. In the evening, films and slide shows on the park's ecology are shown in the Centre.

Accommodation and eating

At the park headquarters, various types of accommodation have been built along the edge of the forest, divided from the beach 50m away by a row of coconut trees. For budget travellers there's a **campsite** (RM5) and snug, four-bed dorms (RM15.75), with reasonably equipped shared kitchens, in the **forest hostel**. Going up the scale, there's also a range of **forest lodges**: two rooms with three beds in each (RM105 per room) and two en-suite rooms, each with two single beds (RM52.50 per room).

△ Proboscis monkeys, Bako National Park

The **café** (daily 8am–9pm) at the park headquarters is very simple, with a daily menu of rice with vegetables, meat or fish and egg dishes, all at budget prices. The park **shop** has a limited range of goods but can keep you supplied with tinned provisions, rice, fruit and a few vegetables, so there's no need to lug food out from Kuching.

Around the park

Given the easy access from Kuching and cheap accommodation within the park, many people stay a few days longer than planned at Bako, taking picnics to one of the seven **beaches**, relaxing at the park headquarters itself, or going slow on the trails to observe the flora and fauna. In all, you'll come across seven different types of **vegetation**, including peat bog, scrub and mangrove; most of the sixteen trails run through an attractive mixture of primary dipterocarp forest and *kerangas* (in Iban, "poor soil"), a sparser type of forest characterized by much thinner tree cover, stubbier plants and more open pathways. On top of the low hill on the Lintang trail, the strange landscape is covered in rock plates, where, among the shrubs, you'll find **pitcher plants**, whose deep, mouth-shaped lids open to trap water and insects which are then digested in the soupy liquid. On the cliffs, delicate plants cling to vertical rock faces or manage to eke out an existence in little pockets of soil, while closer to the headquarters the coastline is thick with mangrove trees.

One of the great pluses of Bako is the near-certainty that you will see wildlife, either while lazing at the chalets or out on the trails. Monkeys are always lurking around on the lookout for food, so it's important to keep the kitchen and dormitory doors locked. Even the rare flying lemur has been sighted swinging from the trees around the park headquarters. Although the best time to see wildlife on the trails is undoubtedly in the early morning and dusk – the rare proboscis monkey as well as macaque and silver-leaf monkeys will make sure they are heard if not easily seen – even in the raw heat of the day, animal activity is usually assured. Snakes, wild boar, giant monitor lizards, squirrels, bearded pigs, otters and mouse deer can be sighted, especially if you're quiet and observant. The park headquarters and the open paths in the *kerangas* are the best places for birdwatching: 150 species have been recorded in Bako, including two rare species of hornbills (for more on which see p.509).

The trails

The park map you receive when you first sign in clearly shows the **trails**, which all start from park headquarters. The sixteen trails are all colour-coded, with splashes of paint, denoting the trail, clearly marked every 20m on trees and rocks. It's best to get an early start, taking much-needed rests at the strategically positioned viewpoint huts along the way. You'll need to carry a litre of water per person (you can safely refill your bottle from the streams), a light rainproof jacket, mosquito repellent and sunscreen. Wear comfortable shoes with a good grip (there's no need for heavy-duty walking boots), light clothing like a T-shirt and shorts, and take a sun hat. Don't forget your swimming gear either, as cool streams cut across the trails, and beaches and waterfalls are never far away.

Probably the most popular trail is the 3.5-kilometre hike to **Tajor Waterfall**, a hike lasting around two and a half hours, though it can easily be done in ninety minutes if you don't linger too long for rests or plant study. The initial half-hour climb from the jetty, on a steep and circuitous path up the forested cliff is the hardest section. At the top you move swiftly through scrub and into *kerangas*, where pitcher plants abound. The path leads to a simple wooden hut with a fine prospect of the peninsula. Moving on, you return to sun-shielded forest, where the dry, sandy path gives way to a muddy trail through peat bog, leading eventually to the waterfall itself, a lovely spot for swimming and eating your picnic.

Leaving the Tajor trail at the wooden hut and viewpoint, a path descends west to two beautiful **beaches**, Teluk Pandan Kecil and Teluk Pandan Besar, each around a thirty-minute hike from the viewpoint, with Kecil in particular involving a steep, rugged descent down sandstone rocks to reach the refreshingly clean water. During the week you'll probably be the only person at either. The other two main beaches at Bako – teluks Sibur and Limau – are much harder to reach, but enjoyable once you've got there. To find **Teluk Sibur** Beach, continue past Tajor Waterfall, following the main trail for around forty minutes, before turning west on the black-and-red trail. The demanding descent to the beach takes anything from twenty minutes to an hour to accomplish. You'll have to drop down the cliff face using creepers and roots to help you, and your troubles aren't over when you reach the bottom either, since you're then in a mangrove swamp and must tread carefully so as not to lose your footing among the stones. After wading across a shallow stream you reach the beach – the longest on the peninsula and, not surprisingly, seldom visited. It is at once stunningly beautiful and desolate, a perfect spot for swimming, picnicking and daydreaming; watch out, though, for sand flies, which have a small but irritating bite.

The hike to **Teluk Limau**, estimated at seven hours, can be done in five at a push, especially if you get an early start. The terrain alternates between swampland and scrub, giving an exhilarating variety of environments on one trail, and provides fabulous views round the whole peninsula. It's not really feasible to get to the beach, which marks the most northerly point in the park, and return the same day; either bring a **tent** and **food** and camp on the beach – as perfect a spot to lay your head as you will ever find – or arrange with park headquarters for a boat to pick you up for the trip back, which costs around RM200. Once out at Limau you could detour on the way back along the marked trail to

Kruin, at the eastern end of the park – an area where you're very likely to spot wildlife. There is a secluded freshwater pond on the way and, from the top of the nearby hill, a grand view of the park's eastern edges.

Far western Sarawak

Far western Sarawak has become an increasingly popular region on Sarawak's tourism trail largely due to the development of facilities in the national parks and other attractive locations. A visit to the region would be best spent over a few days, visiting the caves near **Bau**, **Gunung Gading National Park**, located just north of the small town of Lundu; the beach village of **Sematan**; and the stunning **Tanjung Datu National Park**; further west along the coast, which is only accessible outside the monsoon period (Nov–Feb), when the sea is too rough.

Bau and its Caves

To reach the small market town of **BAU**, take an STC #2 bus (every 30min 6.20am–6pm; 1hr; RM3.30) from Kuching's Lebuh Jawa. Nineteenth-century prospectors were drawn here by the gold that veined the surrounding countryside, but modern-day Bau doesn't live up to its romantic past and it's only worth visiting really as a stepping stone to the nearby caves. There is no accommodation in Bau although there are a number of *kedai kopis*.

Wind Cave, 3km from Bau, meanders through a rocky outcrop on the banks of Sungai Sarawak; a plank walk makes it possible to wander from one side of the outcrop to the other. **Fairy Cave**, 5km further south, is larger with a flight of concrete steps leading up to a cave high in a limestone cliff. As at Wind Cave, plank walks are accessible so visitors can explore the passage. The cliff face also holds some outdoor adventure; **Batman Wall** is popular with rock climbers, with routes of varying degrees of difficulty. From Bau take the #3 bus (every 30min 6.30am–6pm; 20min; 70sen) and ask to be let off at the junction, from where the route to the caves is marked. It is a 500-metre signposted walk to Wind Cave, and a 1.5-kilometre one further on to Fairy Cave.

It's also worth visiting Bau around *Gawai Padi* time, in June, when the Bidayuh communities of the area celebrate the **festival** throughout the month. The celebration is centred on seven shamanistic rituals in which the Bidayuhs give thanks to the rice goddess for an abundant harvest. The final ritual is a celebration involving the whole community and comprises singing and dancing to the traditional *sape* and hand drums. Everyone is welcome to the celebrations, which differ slightly from village to village, but you'll need to stay in Kuching or nearby as the communities have no room to put travellers up. For food and drink look no further than the festivities themselves where every manner of local delicacy, plus rice wine and soft drinks, are on offer.

Lundu and the Gunung Gading National Park

STC bus EP07 leaves Kuching's regional express bus terminal on Jalan Penrissen for **LUNDU** at 8am, 11am, 2pm and 4pm (RM10), clattering through a landscape which gradually transforms from plantation into forest, with jungle-clad hills close by. A dozy and enchanting upcountry place reaching out from the banks of Sungai Lundu, the town comprises a few blocks of shophouses, a large, new two-storey market and some government buildings. Along the signposted road out towards the park lie attractive kampung houses within lush gardens where pineapples and papaya and mango trees compete for space. If you're merely waiting for an onward connection, take a walk around the small **market**, where you can buy fresh fruit, or go into one of the busy *kedai kopis* that border the town square, selling excellent *roti canai* and *nasi campur* throughout the day; the *Jouee* serves tasty noodles. There are a couple of **places to stay**: the *Lundu Gading Hotel*, Lot 174, Jalan Lundu (❸) and the *Cheng Hak Boarding House*, 51 Jalan Bazaar (☎082/735018; ❷) nearby.

Beyond the entrance for Gunung Gading National Park, the road from Lundu continues northward until it reaches the coast, some 8km later, at **Pandan Beach**, which you can reach on the same bus that heads to the park. Considered by many locals to be the best in the area, Pandan is a half-kilometre-long stretch of white sand near a beachfront kampung. A campsite at Pandan is slated to open in late summer 2006, with basic facilities including toilets, showers, lights and a canteen. A little way out to the east of Pandan lies the shorter **Siar Beach**, another pleasing spot. Siar does not have eating or accommodation facilities.

Gunung Gading National Park

From Lundu's central bus terminal, the regular STC #17 "Pandan" bus (every 2hr; daily 8am–4pm; 40sen) covers the 2km up the road north of town to the headquarters of **Gunung Gading National Park** (RM10), although it's a pleasant walk if you don't want to wait for the bus. The park, which mostly clings to the sides of four small mountains, was used solely as a conservation zone for the vast, parasitic **rafflesia** plant until it received full national park status in 1994. The emphasis, however, is still on conservation, with visitors only allowed to view the spectacular plant, with its enormous, smelly blooms, from plankways that stop anyone treading on the young buds. If you call Kuching's park desk (☎082/240888) first thing in the morning, you can ask the warden what chance there is of viewing one that day, and when you arrive, a ranger may lead you out to the plant in bloom, if you are in luck.

Besides Gunung Gading itself, the park has three other mountains, Perigi, Lundu, and Sebuloh. It's possible to climb both Gading and Perigi on the colour-coded trails that trace the forest. Both are full-on hikes, not to be undertaken lightly; the first is a seven-hour round trip, the second, eight hours. It's best to aim to camp on the summit where you'll be rewarded with a sublime sunrise. From there you can follow a trail back to Batu Bakubu, a former communist camp during the insurgency. For lesser mortals, the two-hour round trip offered by the Waterfall Trail is a more sedate alternative. Waterfall 7, where it ends, offers good, refreshing swimming.

For **accommodation** the park has a campsite (RM5), a hostel (four rooms with dorm beds at RM15, or RM40 for a four-bed room) and a lodge (six-bed chalets for RM150). It's likely that during the week there'll be empty beds, though the usual form is to book at the Visitors' Information Centre in Kuching, which can also advise you on whether a *rafflesia* is in bloom.

Sematan and Tanjung Datu National Park

Some 25km northwest of Lundu lies **SEMATAN**, at the end of the road from Kuching, about 100km west of the state capital. **Buses** (RM2.50) head to Sematan from Lundu at 10am, 2pm and 3.30pm, returning at 11am, 3.30pm and 4.30pm. The town has few facilities and no stand-out café, and most people come to walk on the long, picturesque **beach** with its reasonably clean yellow sand backed by coconut palms. Be aware though that sand flies are notoriously bad here, and the water is shallow. A coastal track runs for several miles northwest of Sematan; an hour's walk from town is rugged **Cape Belinsah**, where you can clamber around on the rocks.

For **accommodation** in the village, there's the *Sematan Palm Beach Resort* (☎082/711112) at 12 Sematan Bazaar, comprising two four-bed chalets (④) and other rooms (⑤) inside a building with a terrace. More picturesque though is the *Sematan Resort* (☎082/451188), a kilometre away from the village. A new development, the resort offers both three-room chalets (RM200 per chalet) and two ten-room longhouse terraces (RM120 per six-bedded room), surrounded by palm and pine trees, with access to a private beach (RM3 for day visitors). A **homestay** program has also just started up near the town – contact Mohamad Abdullah (☎013/8041404) for vacancies in nearby Trusan Jaya, Teluk Melano and Sungai Kilong kampungs. The tour operator Borneo Inbound (☎082/237287, ⊜inbound@po.jaring .my) has a hand also in coordinating the program and can help with advice and bookings. The programme is part of a locally funded activities project which also offers river cruises (RM80) or the opportunity to go out fishing with a local (RM120 for 2–4 persons).

The Sematan area also has several local **trails**, starting from the wood just 200m away across the bay from town. Ask one of the boatmen at the small central jetty to take you over; it should only cost a few dollars and take a couple of minutes. Once across the water, the boatman can point out the start of a circular trail, which runs through plantations and a tiny kampung, before winding around to join the road on which the bus comes in. All in all, it's a two-hour trip.

Another excursion from Sematan is to **TELUK MELANO**, a picturesque Malay fishing village sitting in a beautiful bay. This is only possible in the dry season (March–Oct), as the rest of the time the seas are often too high for boats to safely negotiate. There are two ways to get there – by speedboat (RM200 to hire, maximum six passengers; 40min) or by local fishing boat (around RM20 per person; the boats normally arrive at around 10am daily at Sematan jetty; 2hr). Teluk Melano is a pretty place, home to around forty families who live in traditional wooden Malay houses scattered around the bay. It's possible to stay with one of these families via the local homestay programme.

Tanjung Datu National Park

Further along the coast is **Tanjung Datu National Park** (RM10). The only way to get there is by boat from the jetties at Sematan (40min; RM60) and at Teluk Melano (10min; RM20), though they can only negotiate the large swell and difficult currents between March and October. Situated in a mountainous region around a coastal spur close to the Kalimantan border, with peaks towering above, the tiny park offers splendid rainforest, swift, clean rivers and isolated bays. The main draws though are its dazzling beaches, the best in East Malaysia, and shallow, unspoilt coral reefs perfect for snorkelling, only a short distance from the shore; further out there are a number of artificial reefs, begun in 1986 and now starting to take shape, with marine life establishing itself alongside. The park is also one of the few destinations in Sarawak where ocean turtles come to lay eggs. There are no visitor facilities as yet at the park, though once at Sematan or Teluk Melano a visit is quite feasible and certainly worth the effort.

Anna Rais and south to the border

One hundred kilometres south of Kuching, near the mountains straddling the border with Kalimantan, lies **ANNA RAIS**, the largest Bidayuh settlement in the area and the only significant one easily accessible by road. Here in the south of Samarahan division, the **Bidayuh longhouses** offer a fascinating insight into the culture of the only remaining Land Dyaks in Sarawak still living a semi-authentic lifestyle.

Unlike other ethnic groups, the Bidayuh built their multi-levelled, elevated longhouses at the bases of hills rather than on rivers and, as a consequence, endured violent attacks during the nineteenth century from other more aggressive groups, especially the Iban. But the Bidayuh weren't exactly passive victims: traditional communities always had a **head-house**, where the heads of their enemies were kept and which served as a focus for male activities and rituals. Although quite an introverted group, the Bidayuh in Anna Rais welcome sympathetic visitors as much as the more demonstrative Iban or Kelabit. The community is used to visitors so everybody is greeted warmly at any time of year.

From Kuching's Lebuh Jawa, STC bus #9A (daily at 9am; 2hr; RM6) heads to Anna Rais along a bumpy uphill road heading towards the cloud-enveloped mountains which snake along the Kalimantan border. When visitors arrive, they are greeted by locals at the car park and escorted around the settlement, which consists of two massive longhouses on either side of a river, Sungai Penrissen, and many separate dwellings. The best time to go is at the weekend when the women are finished with their farming duties, the children are in from school and the wage-earners back from working in the oil-palm plantations or in Kuching. As you wander around, you'll be offered food and drink, possibly even betel nut to chew – a traditional way of making someone welcome – and invited to watch and participate in craft demonstrations. Most visitors stay a couple of hours, returning to Kuching the same day. Alternatively, ask at the longhouse if you can sleep in the community hall at **Kampung Abang**, a ten-minute drive beyond Anna Rais, and a useful overnight stop if you want to trek up nearby Gunung Penrissen the next day.

Gunung Penrissen

The most accessible of the mountains on the Sarawak/Kalimantan border is the spectacular 1300-metre-high **Gunung Penrissen**, located a few kilometres from and west of Anna Rais. The Penrissen hike involves tough walking along narrow paths and crossing fast-flowing streams which descend from the source of Sungai Sarawak; vertical ladders help you on the last section. As the trails aren't easy to follow, you must hire a guide in Anna Rais (expect to pay RM150–200 for a group of up to five people). Although the ascent and descent of Penrissen can be done in one hard day, you may prefer to set up camp at the foot of the summit, in which case bring a **tent** and **food**. Gunung Penrissen was strategically important in the 1950s border skirmishes between the Malaysian and Indonesian armies, and there's still a partially-manned Malaysian **military post** close to the summit, from where you can gaze over the rainforest into Kalimantan to the south and east, and to the South China Sea over the forests to the north.

Serian and the border crossing

Some 20km southeast of Anna Rais is the **border crossing** at **Tebedu**, 120km from Kuching. Buses to Tebedu leave from **Serian**, a workaday town on the main Kuching–Sri Aman road, although most people get the through coaches from Kuching to Pontianak which leave at 7am, 8am, 10.30am and 12.30pm (RM45). If you're not on the through coach then make sure you get to Tebedu in time to catch one of the local buses that go to the Indonesian town of **Entikong** and on to Pontianak; these stop running in the early afternoon. Tebedu is little more than an administrative centre, with a couple of dispiriting hotels. The border crossing at Entikong is opens 6am–6pm; ask at the Indonesian Consulate in Kuching about information on **visas**.

Sri Aman and Batang Ai river system

Sri Aman, 150km southeast of Kuching, is the closest sizeable town to the Iban longhouses of the Batang Ai region, though tour operators tend to bypass it, heading to the longhouses straight from Kuching. Taking a tour is an ideal way to visit the upriver longhouses, though check that the size of the tour group doesn't exceed twenty, and ideally it shouldn't be more than ten. Though nondescript, Sri Aman can be a useful base if you're travelling independently. To the south of Batang Ai, and close to the Indonesian border, is **Lubok Antu**, another access point for a visit to the longhouses.

Many tours to the longhouses start from **Batang Ai river system** jetty, 50km east of Sri Aman, from where you can visit some of the few dozen **longhouses** on Batang Ai and sungais Delok and Engkari. There are also many popular longhouses on two other rivers, sungais Lemanak and Skrang – the jetty for the Lemanak longhouses is 20km northwest from the park jetty; that for Skrang 10km further north.

Sri Aman

SRI AMAN is the second biggest town in southwest Sarawak and the administrative capital of this part of the state. It sits near the mouth of Sungai Lupar, whose lower reaches are over 1500m wide, though the river narrows dramatically further up the flat alluvial plain. Just before Sri Aman, a small island in the river obstructs the flow of the incoming tide, producing the town's renowned tidal bore: once or twice a year, when enough water has accumulated, a billowing wave rushes by with some force – longboats are hauled up onto the muddy bank and large vessels head for mid-stream in an attempt to ride the bore as evenly as possible. At its most impressive, the bore rolls up like a mini-tidal wave, rocking boats and reaching as far as the new Chinese temple, set back from the pier. Somerset Maugham was caught by the wave in 1929 and nearly drowned, a tale he recounted in "Yellow Streak" in his *Borneo Tales*.

The town itself has a central defensive fort, **Fort Alice**, more compact than the forts in the capital and the only one of its kind still to have its original turrets, drawbridge and parts of its period spiked fence. It was built by Charles Brooke in 1864, thus predating Fort Margherita in Kuching, and so-called after Ranee Margaret Alice Brooke. Charles Brooke based himself in this region for many years, heading a small force which repelled the advances of pirates and intervened in the upriver conflicts between warring Iban factions.

Practicalities

Buses to Sri Aman leave from the Kuching regional bus terminus at Jalan Penrissen (daily at 7.30am, 9.45am, noon, 3.15pm & 7.45pm; 3hr; RM19).

The **Iban** – one of the ethnic groups categorized as Sea Dyaks – comprise nearly one-third of the population of Sarawak, making them easily the most numerous of Sarawak's indigenous peoples. They originated in the Kapuas river basin of west Kalimantan, on the other side of the mountains that separate Kalimantan and Sarawak, but having outgrown their lands they migrated to Sungai Lupar in southwest Sarawak in the early sixteenth century. Once in Sarawak, the Iban clashed with the coastal Melenau, and by the eighteenth century they had moved up the Rajang into the interior, into areas that were traditionally Kayan. Inevitably, great battles were waged between these two powerful groups, with one contemporary source recording seeing "a mass of boats drifting along the stream, while the Dyaks were spearing and stabbing each other; decapitated trunks and heads without bodies, scattered about in ghastly profusion".

The practice of **head-hunting** became established during the Iban migrations: the more heads in a longhouse, the more it would be feared by outsiders and so be less likely to be attacked. It generally didn't matter how the head was taken or to whom it belonged – though revenge occasionally played a part. An account in the *Sarawak Gazette* in 1909 – just when Charles Brooke hoped his policy of stopping head-hunting was at last becoming effective – reported that:

Justly are the Dyaks called head-hunters, for during the whole of their life, from early youth till their death, all their thoughts are fixed on the hunting of heads. The women, in their cruelty and blood-thirstiness, are the cause. At every festival the old trophies are taken from the fireplace and carried through the house by the women who sing a monotonous song in honour of the hero who cut off the head, and in derision of the poor victims whose skulls are carried around. Everywhere, the infernal chorus, "Bring us more of them", is heard.

Although conflict between the various ethnic groups stopped as migration itself slowed down, heads were still being taken as recently as the 1960s during the Konfrontasi skirmishes, when Indonesian army units came up against Iban fighters in the Malaysian army.

Along with the Melenau, the Iban are the most "modernized" of Sarawak's ethnic groups. Nowadays more than half live in towns – mostly Kuching, Sri Aman, Kapit and Sibu – and these days work in most sectors of the state's economy, from handicrafts and tour-guiding to manufacturing and white-collar positions in banking and law. Indeed, many Iban hold positions of power – some of Sarawak's best-known politicians have been drawn from their ranks. Even the bulk of the rural Iban, the vast majority of whom still live in longhouses, undertake seasonal work in the rubber and oil industries, and it is no small irony that logging – the business that most devastated their own customary lands – has in the past supplied much plentiful and lucrative work; these days oil-palm cultivation and production provide more employment. As a consequence, some longhouses have become occasional homes, with many families living close to their work for much of the year. You may visit one week and see few people, and return at the weekend to find the place is buzzing, though not at harvest time – June to August – when all hands are on deck. Traditionally, young men would have left the longhouse to go on **bejalai** (the activity of joining a warring party); nowadays though, youths on *bejalai* are more likely to be found trying to get work on oil rigs offshore in Brunei or on the oil-palm plantations. The central premise through history has been for a young man to establish his independence and social position before getting married.

Unlike other ethnic groups, the Iban are a very egalitarian people – the longhouse *tuai* (headman) is more a figurehead than someone who wields great power. Women in the community have different duties from men; they never go hunting or work in logging, but are great weavers; indeed, traditionally it's been an Iban woman's weaving prowess that has determined her status in the community. The women are most renowned for their beautiful **pua kumbu** (blanket or coverlet) work, a cloth of intricate design and colour. The *pua kumbu* once played an integral part in Iban rituals, when they were hung up prominently during harvest festivals and weddings, or used to cover structures containing charms and offerings to the gods. Inevitably too they would have a role in the head-hunting rituals: the women would wear the *pua kumbu* to receive the "prize" brought home by their men-folk. The cloth is generally made by using the *ikat* technique, which involves binding, tying and then dyeing the material to build up complex patterns.

Of all the customs maintained by the Iban, perhaps the most singular is their style of **tattooing**, which is not just a form of ornamentation, but also an indication of personal wealth and other achievements. Many designs are used, from a simple circular outline for the shoulder, chest or outer side of the wrists, to more elaborate designs (dogs, scorpions or dragons) for the inner and outer thigh. The two most important places for tattoos are considered to be the hand and the throat. A tattoo on the hand indicates that you have "taken a head" – some elders still have these – while one on the throat means that you are a fully mature man, with wealth, possessions, land and family. Tattooing is usually carried out by an experienced artist – either a longhouse resident or a travelling tattooist who arrives just prior to the festival season, though it is not the custom these days for young Iban to receive their tattoos locally; rather, it is more impressive to have gone further abroad and *earnt* them. A carved design on a block of wood is smeared with ink and pressed to the skin; the resulting outline is then punctured with needles dipped in dark ink, made from a mixture of sugar-cane juice, water and soot. For the actual tattooing a hammer-like instrument with two or three needles protruding from its head is used. These are dipped in ink, the hammer placed against the skin and hit repeatedly with a wooden block, after which rice is smeared over the inflamed area to prevent infection.

The best time for visiting the Iban is during *Gawai Dayak* at the end of May or early June (see *Longhouse culture* section), though another festival, the *Gawai Antu* (festival for the departed souls), is sometimes celebrated in November or December; it's the Iban equivalent of the Christian All Souls' Day or the Taoist Hungry Ghost Festival.

△ *pua kumba* cloth

There are several **hotels** in Sri Aman: the *Champion Inn*, 1248 Main Bazaar (T083/320140; ❷), is the most central, with small, comfortable rooms; and the *Hoover Hotel*, 139 Jalan Club (T083/321985; ❸), the best in town, with larger rooms than the *Champion Inn*. You can **eat** at the *Hoover's* café, or at *Chuan Hong*, a Chinese *kedai kopi* in the centre of town at 1 Jalan Council.

Lubok Antu

South from Batang Ai River System, **Lubok Antu** is the last town before the Kalimantan border; there are no customs, and it's a crossing-point only for Sarawak Malaysians and Kalimantan Indonesians. The small town has a number of stores where the small predominantly Iban population can buy basic provisions. Buses and vans plying the stretch to Sri Aman and Betong gather beside the morning market, which expands into a colourful spectacle on Saturdays. There are decent rooms at the only hotel in town, the *Kelingkang Inn* (T083/584331; ❷). Filling meals are served up beside the bus station in the *Oriental Café*. There are no buses to Batang Ai jetty from Lubok Antu; a taxi costs RM10.

Batang Ai region and the longhouses

The **Batang Ai river system** consists of various rivers which feed into Batang Ai reservoir. Along these rivers lie a few dozen longhouses, the main spots for travellers to experience traditional Iban life. The majority of the longhouses in the river system – including all the ones discussed below – are outside the boundaries of Batang Ai National Park, part of Lanjak Entimau Wildlife Sanctuary (LEWS), an immense region of dipterocarp forest and rivers bordering Kalimantan. There are no facilities in the park and tourists only visit whilst staying at some of the longhouses below.

Practicalities

There is no direct public **transport** to the Batang Ai river system jetty from Sri Aman or Kuching, but buses do run from Sri Aman to Lubok Antu, 10km from the jetty (twice daily; 1hr; RM10). Ask to be let off at the Batang Ai turn-off, from which you will have to walk the remaining few kilometres. Alternatively, if you're staying in Lubok Antu, it is possible to ride pillion on a motorbike taxi up to the jetty (around RM5) or take a taxi (around RM15).

The only **accommodation** on the reservoir is at the sprawling *Hilton Batang Ai* (T082/248200, W www.batang.hilton.com; ❽). The hotel only fills to capacity a few times a year, when tourist groups or conference delegates descend; the rest of the time it is possible to get significant discounts. With small but highly luxurious rooms, housed in four 200-metre longhouses, it's a relaxing place to while away your time and a good place to stay for a night before visiting the authentic longhouses upstream. There's also a large swimming pool, reasonably priced guided activities, such as fishing, trekking and longhouse visits, and high-quality local cuisine.

Sungai Delok and Batang Ai

After crossing the reservoir, the scenery becomes quite spectacular, the forest mass reaching down to the water's edge as the longboat snakes along dodging driftwood. The closest upriver longhouse to the Batang Ai jetty and the *Hilton* is

Rumah Ipang on Sungai Delok (40min by motorized longboat), a traditional thirty-door structure, rebuilt in 1988 after a massive fire. It's home to thirty Iban families and is built largely from traditional materials.

Beyond Ipang, Batang Ai branches off from Sungai Delok. One hour upstream along the steadily narrowing Ai lies **Nanga Sumpa**, another lively and busy Iban community. The tour operator Borneo Adventure (see p.442) has built a lodge a few metres from the longhouse, where visitors regularly stay, allowing them to be independent but still able to join in longhouse culture. Though basic, the ten-bedroom lodge is large, and has a kitchen, hot showers and toilets. The Sumpa longhouse itself is a breathtaking place to visit: it's a beautiful, traditionally-built dwelling with an outer first-floor veranda, invariably covered by drying crops, and a communal inner space running the building's length, where people come and go all the time; beyond here are the private family rooms.

A local trek with Borneo Adventure takes visitors to a lovely waterfall (1hr), while other activities include trips further up the river, fishing and visiting the nearby communities. The evenings are usually spent in the longhouse, drinking, chatting and playing games with one of the families and perhaps the chief.

Sungai Engkari

Starting back from the reservoir, one hour upstream on Sungai Engkari, is **Nanga Spaya**, where 52 families inhabit two longhouses. Reputed to be a great place to visit at *gawai* (harvest festival), Spaya is a lovely, authentic design combining local wood and bamboo with concrete and iron, longer-lasting materials. A little further along Sungai Engkari, and with a commanding view of the landscape, is **Nanga Ukon**, a 25-door longhouse, whose chief, Jarau, is most welcoming.

Sungais Lemanak and Skrang

The jetty from which boats leave to visit the longhouses on Sungai Lemanak is at Kampung Sereliau, 15km northeast of Batang Ai river system jetty on the road to Betong. Most tour operators however access the most popular and well-resourced longhouse on the river, **Nanga Serubah**, by a road that was opened a few years ago. With greater ease of access to the community has come a new building programme by the longhouse residents nearby, and Serubah also now has a small lodge where visitors can stay; these are frequently used by Diethelm Travel and Borneo Tranverse (see p.442). Serubah's chief and shaman are well-respected Iban elders who are happy to meet visitors and answer questions through an interpreter about their culture. The longhouse itself is a spectacular design, built in 1999 to authentic specifications: the roof is made from *belian* (ironwood) shingle, and locally sourced timber, including the *ankabang* tree, is used for the main structure. Elegantly engraved motifs adorn the bamboo hallway in the inner veranda. Twenty minutes further up Sungai Lemanak is a smaller, more modern longhouse, Nanga Kesit, and beyond that, Nanga Ngemah Ili.

There are also longhouses on Sungai Skrang, some of which are very regularly used by the tour operators. To reach Sungai Skrang's jetty, continue on the road north to Betong from Kampung Sereliau to reach the kampung at Entaban.

Sibu and the Rajang Basin

At the very heart of Sarawak stretches the 560-kilometre-long **Batang Rajang**, Malaysia's longest river. Already over two hundred metres across downsteam at the inland bazaar town of Kapit, by the time the Rajang reaches the busy port of **Sibu**, the largest town on the river, it is eight times as wide. At the height of the timber boom, massive quantities of logs journeyed down the river strapped to huge barges, sometimes clogging up parts the of the great waterway, and causing hazards, erosion and other environmental damage. At Sibu, your initial impressions of the Rajang will be of a wide, dirty channel, but in fact its soupy, brown appearance these days is caused by ecological erosion and landslides generated by forest clearance.

Although Sibu's importance in the timber trade has made it a prosperous and energetic place, in many ways it's changed little since the late nineteenth century, when Chinese and Malay adventurers took boats from its wharf to **Kapit**. Between Sibu and Kapit, the little town of **Song** is a jumping-off point for **Iban longhouses** along the Katibas tributary of the Rajang; there are also Iban communities along the Baleh tributary, east of Kapit. Beyond here, through the Pelagus Rapids and onwards to the remote settlement of **Belaga**, the Batang Rajang becomes wild and unpredictable and the scenery spectacular. This is a world of isolated colonial forts, longboat trips and thriving Iban and Orang Ulu communities, people living on the cusp of the traditional and modern worlds. Guides can lead you on jungle treks to **Kayan longhouses** or visits to **Penan** communities in the upper Rajang region (Belaga division), though the social dislocation caused by the Bakun Dam (see p.476) has had a detrimental effect on longhouse tourism.

Some history

For centuries, the Rajang was rife with tribal conflict. In the fifteenth century, when the Malay sultanates were at their height, Malays living in the estuaries of southern Sarawak pushed the immigrant Iban up the rivers towards present-day Sibu. This antagonized the indigenous people of those regions, especially the Baleh and upper Rajang Kayan, and throughout the seventeenth and eighteenth centuries they and the Iban fought amongst themselves for territory and heads. Occasionally, when they felt threatened, the Malays and the Iban would form an uneasy alliance to attack inland Kayan tribes and carry out piratical raids on passing Indonesian and Chinese ships.

With the arrival of the British, it was clear that no serious opening up of the interior could go ahead until the region was made relatively safe – which meant controlling the land and subjugating, or displacing, many of the indigenous inhabitants. To this end, James Brooke bought a section of Batang Rajang from the sultan of Brunei in 1853, while his successor, Charles, asserted his authority over the Iban and Kayan tribes, and encouraged **Chinese pioneers** to move into the interior. Some of the more intrepid among these started to trade upriver with the Iban and, with support from the Malay business community and Brooke's officials, built settlements at Kanowit and Sibu in the late nineteenth century, hacking out farms in the jungle, on which, with varying degrees of success, they grew rice, vegetables, pepper and rubber. Indeed, Sibu's early growth was largely financed by the proceeds of rubber cultivation. But the pioneers faced numerous disputes with the Iban who, having come here after being pushed out of their river valleys by the Malays, resented the Chinese for clearing and growing crops on land the Iban believed now belonged to them.

The traders among the pioneers would spend a month or more plying the tributaries, leaving cloth, salt and shotgun cartridges on credit with the Dyaks and then returning to pick up **jungle produce** in exchange, like birds' nests, camphor, beeswax, honey and bezoar stones. But it was a risky life for these pioneers, especially when faced with an Iban tribesman whose only way out of a credit impasse was to do away with the trader. Most of the traders lived on their *atap*-roofed boats, never leaving them, even while doing business with the Iban. Some, however, learned the tribal languages and customs and, although banned from doing so by Brooke, spent nights in the longhouses, a few marrying Dyak women.

Sibu

SIBU, sixty kilometres upriver from the South China Sea, began life in the 1850s as a tiny Melenau encampment, and has grown into Sarawak's second largest city, with a population of over 200,000, and its biggest port. It seethes with activity, much of the action taking place on the riverfront, with its separate jetties for passenger boats, commercial craft and logging barges, although the attractive esplanade, a 300-metre stretch of park along part of the waterfront just south of the commercial area, offers some respite from all this bustle. Most of the local population are Foochow Chinese (the town is known locally as New Foochow); indeed, the town's speedy modern growth is largely attributed to these industrious and enterprising immigrants. Sibu, unlike Kuching or Miri, never retained a large contingent of Brooke's officials, which means its Chinese character has never really been diluted. Following the success of the early rubber plantations, manufacturing industries (largely textiles and consumer items) were established here, while later, after independence, Chinese businessmen moved into the lucrative trade in **timber**. But it wasn't all unimpeded expansion: in 1889 a fire razed the embryonic town to ashes, and in 1928 the Chinese godowns along the wharf and many of the cramped lodging houses and cafés were destroyed by another fire. The town was devastated again in World War II by advancing Japanese forces, who occupied it for three years, during which time much of the Chinese population was forced into slave labour.

There is still a wild edge to Sibu, and the traders are louder and more persuasive than their like in Kuching and Miri. Everywhere are signs of the city's wealth: stores packed with TV sets, multi-storey commercial buildings enveloping the outskirts of town, and Toyota pick-ups muscling their way along the city centre's narrow *lebuh*s. The town's most striking landmark is the towering, seven-storey Tua Pek Kong Temple, north of which is the old **Chinatown**, its warren of narrow streets home to most of the cheap hotels, hawker stalls and cramped fish, meat and vegetable markets. Beyond simply soaking up the town's vibrant atmosphere, there's little for visitors to do in Sibu, though you'll want to check out the bustling day market and **pasar malam**, and the small **museum** on the edge of town, which focuses on the Chinese migration and the displaced ethnic communities. Most people come here as a starting-point for an expedition upriver – though don't be surprised if you end up liking its gregarious vitality and don't want to leave.

Arrival and information

The **airport** is 25km east of the city centre; to reach the city most visitors take a taxi (RM20) – collect a chit from the taxi desk in arrivals. To get into Sibu by bus, walk from the terminal to the main road (200m) where you can hail the #3a (daily 7am–6pm; every 40min), which will take you to the local terminus and taxi station on Jalan Khoo Peng Loong. Buses from Sarikei, Kuching and points north arrive at the long distance **bus station**, 10km northwest of the centre and only reachable by taxi (RM10). The new express boat wharf, **Terminal Penumpang**, is at the western end of the esplanade, Jalan Maju, from which boats arrive from Kuching downriver and Kanowit, Song, Kapit and Belaga upriver.

Sibu's enthusiastically staffed **Visitors' Information Centre** is centrally located at 16 Jalan Tukang Besi (Mon–Fri 8am–4.30pm, Sat 8am–12.45pm; ☎084/340980), from where you can pick up tourist leaflets, an accommodation list and a map of the town.

Accommodation

It is usually easy to find good-quality, reasonably-priced **accommodation** in Sibu, with most places to stay located within a ten-minute walk of the terminal. There are a number of budget places, but like elsewhere watch out for promotional cuts at some of the city's leading hotels.

Bahagia 21 Jalan Wong Nai Siong ☎084/331131. Located in a good central position close to the *pasar malam*, though the rooms are quite small and bathrooms cramped. ❸

Garden 1 Jalan Hoe Ping ☎084/317888. Likeable 40-room hotel just a stone's throw from the city centre, with a coffee shop and business centre. ❹

Hoover Guesthouse Jalan Pulau ☎084/345334. This church-run guesthouse is the best deal in town. Set back from the street, it has simple, spotless rooms with bathrooms attached, plus others with communal bathrooms. To reach the guesthouse office (open Mon–Fri 8am–4.30pm, Sat 8am–noon; it's not possible to check in outside these times), go round the back of the main building to the annex. ❶

Kingwood 12 Lorong Lanang ☎084/335888, ✉kingwood@tm.net.my. Sibu's biggest hotel, with a grand foyer and huge, lovely rooms overlooking the river. Check if they have any promotions on – these can slash the price by around RM70. ❺

Malaysia Jalan Kampung Nyabor ☎084/332299. A popular, though fairly shabby place, located on a busy main road, with small rooms, shared toilet and shower; it's family-run and friendly. ❷

Phoenix 1–3 Jalan Ki Peng, off Jalan Kampung Nyabor ☎084/313877. Smart and friendly, this is one of the best upmarket hotels, with spacious modern rooms, some with bath and TV, though it can be a little noisy. ❸

Premier Jalan Kampung Nyabor ☎084/323222. Large-scale hotel with high central atrium; rooms are spacious and smartly decorated. ❼

River Park Hotel 51 Jalan Maju ☎084/316688. Tucked away on the eastern part of the esplanade, and close to the riverside café, the *River Park* is a superb, mid-range hotel with comfortable beds, spacious bathrooms and friendly service. ❹

Tanahmas Lorong Bengkel ☎084/333188, ✉tanamas@po.jaring.my. A fine, top-quality hotel in the *Premier* mould with a vast lobby and large, a/c rooms. The ground floor café, *Peppers*, has a wide-ranging menu and is often packed until midnight at weekends. ❼

Villa Hotel 2 Jalan Central ☎084/337833. Always busy, this Chinese-run first-floor place is clean and friendly, with small rooms and communal bathrooms. ❷

Zuhra Jalan Kampung Nyabor ☎084/310711. This quality hotel has clean, neat rooms with a/c, TV and tastefully tiled bathrooms. ❺

The Town

The centre of Sibu has recently been engulfed by a surge of civic pride, with the new Sibu Gateway, a futuristic-looking car park and various landscaping

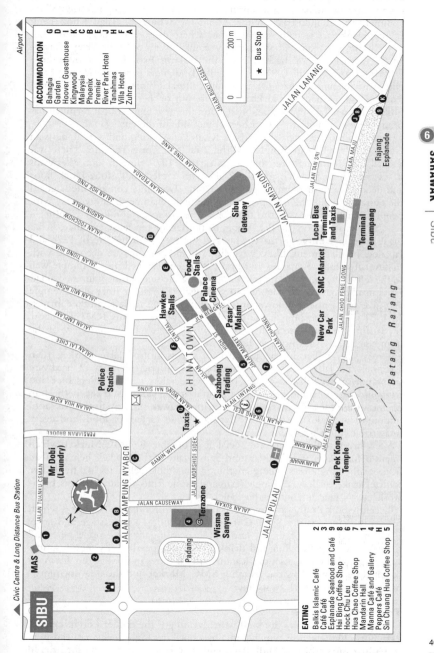

SIBU

ACCOMMODATION
Bahagia   G
Garden   D
Hoover Guesthouse I
Kingwood   K
Malaysia   C
Phoenix   B
Premier   E
River Park Hotel J
Tanahmas   H
Villa Hotel   F
Zuhra   A

0 _____ 200 m

★ Bus Stop

▲ Civic Centre & Long Distance Bus Station

▲ Airport

JALAN TUANKU OSMAN

MAS

JALAN KAMPUNG NYABOR

PERSIARAN BROOKE

JALAN HUA KIEW

JALAN TAI CHEE

JALAN EMPLAM

JALAN MUI HONG

JALAN TIONG HUA

HARDIN WALK

JALAN LOOCHOW

JALAN HOE PING

JALAN TONG SANG

JALAN PEDADA

JALAN BUKIT ASSEK

JALAN LANANG

JALAN MAJU

JALAN TAN SRI

JALAN MISSION

JALAN KHOO PENG LOONG

Police Station

Mr Dobi (Laundry)

RAMIN WAY

JALAN MORSHIDI SIDEK

JALAN CAUSEWAY

Terazone

Wisma Sanyan

Padang

JALAN PULAU

JALAN SUKAN

JALAN BANK

JALAN WHARF

Tua Pek Kong Temple

JALAN TEMPLE

JALAN TUKANG BESI

JALAN WONG NAI SIONG

JALAN LINTANG

CHINATOWN

HIGH ST

JALAN CENTRAL

JLN BENGKEL

JALAN MARKET

JALAN CHANNEL

JALAN KAMPANG

Taxis

Sazhoong Trading

Hawker Stalls

Palace Cinema

Pasar Malam

Food Stalls

Sibu Gateway

New Car Park

SMC Market

Local Bus Terminus and Taxis

Terminal Penumpang

Rajang Esplanade

Batang Rajang

6 SARAWAK | Sibu

EATING
Baikis Islamic Café   2
Café Café   3
Esplanade Seafood and Café   9
Hai Bing Coffee Shop   8
Hock Chu Leu   6
Hua Chao Coffee Shop   7
Mandarin Hall   1
Manna Café and Gallery   4
Peppers Café   H
Sin Chuang Hua Coffee Shop   5

465

projects all helping to make the town altogether more modern and less grubby than in the past. For a century or more, Batang Rajang has been Sibu's commercial and industrial lifeline. Along the **wharf**, on Jalan Khoo Peng Loong, plankways lead to several points where cargo boats dock, while the stores lining the road sell everything you may ever need for a river journey. At the eastern edge of the harbour is the **Rajang Esplanade**, a lovely little waterfront park built in 1987 on reclaimed land and a popular place to sit and enjoy the evening breeze. Occasionally cultural events, too, like traditional dancing and Chinese firework displays, are put on here, and the park is also host to a dawn Tai chi routine. Next door, the new express boat terminal has brought more activity to this hitherto quiet side of the city.

Head along to the other end of Jalan Khoo Peng Loong, and west along Jalan Channel to reach Jalan Temple and the **Tua Pek Kong Temple**. There was a small, wooden temple on this site as early as 1870, though soon afterwards it was rebuilt on a much grander scale, with a tiled roof, stone block floor and decorative fixtures imported from China. Two large concrete lions guard the entrance, while the fifteen-metre-wide main chamber is always busy with people paying respects to the deity, Tua Pek Kong, a prominent Confucian scholar. The statue of Tua Pek Kong, to the left of the front entrance, is the most important image in the temple and survived both the fire of 1928 and Japanese bombardment. Elsewhere, the roof and columns are decorated with traditional statues of dragons and birds, while emblazoned on the temple wall to the left of the entrance are murals depicting the signs of the Chinese zodiac. For a small donation, the friendly caretaker will tell you the story of the temple and give you a brief rundown on the significance of these and other images. In 1987 the rear section of the temple was replaced by the RM1.5-million, seven-storey **pagoda**, from the top of which there's a splendid view of the immense Rajang snaking away below.

Across Jalan Pulau, in the network of streets around Jalan Market, Jalan Channel and Jalan Central is **Chinatown**, with its plethora of hardware shops, newspaper stalls, busy cafés, textile wholesalers, cassette sellers, food and fruit-juice vendors and hotels. The central artery, **Jalan Market**, is the hub of one of the most vibrant *pasar malam*s in Sarawak (nightly from dusk until midnight) with dozens of stalls offering a wide variety of foods and every imaginable household item.

A few streets to the south is the social heart of Sibu, the **SMC Market**, which opens before dawn and closes around 5pm. Many of the hawkers here are Iban from nearby longhouses, selling anything from edible delicacies like flying fox, squirrel, snake, turtle, snail, jungle ferns and exotic fruits, to rattan baskets, bead-work, charm bracelets and leather belts.

Recently built on the southwestern side of Jalan Kampung Nyabor – which bisects the city – is the **Sibu Gateway**, comprising a large stage and lawn. Civic performances of drama and music occasionally take place here and there's a row of stalls selling soft drinks and snacks nearby. Fifty metres south-west of the Gateway is a set of pleasant water features in front of the *Tanahmas* hotel, close by which is the teeming **SMC Market** and the new, incongruously gleaming car park to its left.

The civic centre

On the outskirts of Sibu but well worth visiting is the modern **civic centre**, 2km north of the centre, which contains a small but high-quality collection in its **Cultural Exhibition Hall** (Tues–Sun 10am–5.30pm; free) on the ground floor. To get there, take bus #3 from the local bus station and ask for the civic centre. In a series of display chambers, the hall details the varied peoples of Batang Rajang by means of well-chosen photographs, artefacts and paraphernalia. Among the costumes, backpacks and instruments in the Orang Ulu chamber, look out for some evocative old snaps of headmen, and an amazing photograph of a peace-making ceremony between Kayan and Iban tribespeople on November 16, 1924, at which representatives from both tribes killed pigs to authenticate their truce. There are more atmospheric pictures – of tattooing and cockfighting – in the adjacent Iban chamber, plus a scale model of an Iban longhouse that was made using bark, ironwood and bamboo. The mocked-up Malay wedding room falls somewhere short of interesting, but the Chinese display makes a good stab at charting the history of the Foochow migration to the region – a bust of Wong Nai Siong, the Methodist minister who led the original pioneers, takes centre stage. There are also records of numerous cultural associations, the immigrants' first port of call when they disembarked; in exchange for voluntary labour, the associations would find the new arrivals paid work and lodgings and induct them into the business and cultural life of the city.

Eating

Throughout town there are Chinese **cafés** selling Sibu's most famous dish, **Foochow noodles** – steamed and then served in a soy and oyster sauce with spring onions, chilli, garlic and dried fish. Other local favourites include *midin* (a type of wild fern), *kang puan mee* (noodles cooked in lard) and *kong bian* (oriental bagels, sprinkled with sesame seed). Prawn and crab are of a high quality and, in season, tropical fruit like star fruit, rambutan, durian, papaya and guava are available from market stalls.

Although Sibu has some fine air-conditioned **restaurants**, most people prefer to be outside at the **hawker stalls** when the weather's good, or to head to one of many superior Chinese **coffee shops**. Busiest in the morning are those on the first floor of the **SMC Market**, while in the evening everyone congregates at the **pasar malam** one hundred metres north, which serves up, besides dim sum and snacks, specific Sibu delicacies like stuffed dumplings, grilled fish in shrimp sauce and chicken wings in peanut oil, as well as a range of offal and pigs' and ducks' heads. The pasar malam's only drawback is that there's nowhere to sit and eat the delicacies you've bought most people wander down to the esplanade to eat. Also popular are the stalls in the block on Jalan Bengkel, west of the *Premier Hotel*, and those in the two-storey, circular building just to the south, where the stalls specialize in Malay food – crisp green beans with soy sauce and ginger, and curried chicken and beef dishes – with plenty of tables protected from the elements.

Cafés are **open** throughout the day, from around 7am to 8pm, with the Chinese coffee shops staying open until midnight. Restaurants open from around 11am until 11pm.

Balkis Islamic Café 69 Jalan Osman. Near the MAS office, this excellent-value café offers a buffet from RM3 per head, with very good North Indian staples like *roti canai*, *murtabak* and curries. Open daily 7am–8pm.

Café Café 93 Jalan Kampung Nyabor. Cool, clean café, popular with students, offering Western and Malaysian meals, coffee and beer.

Esplanade Seafood and Café In a superb position on the esplanade, this café serves coffee (RM3) and a fine range of Western and Chinese meals (RM12).

Hai Bing Coffee Shop 31 Jalan Maju. A stone's throw from the *River Park Hotel*, this is an atmospheric Chinese eatery with excellent seafood and typical pork and chicken dishes, and also serves beer. You can choose between a/c and pavement tables.

Hock Chu Leu 28 Jalan Tukang Besi. Well-known Foochow restaurant with great baked fish and fresh vegetables. Around RM25 for two, including beer.

Hua Chao Coffee Shop Jalan Market, 20m from the night market. A venerable establishment, the *Hua* is frequented by a colourful cross-section of Sibu locals – plus a few visitors coming by for a beer or tea. Food is tasty Chinese fare, quickly delivered, with the musical rhythms coming courtesy of the brightly-lit CD store across the road.

Mandarin Hall Wisma See Hua, Jalan Tuanku Osman. Excellent Foochow restaurant that turns its hand to breakfast each morning, when stalls serving *bubor cha cha*, dim sum, *laksa*

and *kang puan mee* do a roaring trade in the dining room.

Manna Café and Gallery Top floor, Wisma Sanyan. Large café in a new plaza selling soft drinks and a wide variety of local dishes. It's worth resting here awhile if only to admire the bird's-eye view of the city and Batang Rajang. Books and local artwork are also on show.

Peppers Café *Tanahmas Hotel*, Jalan Kampung Nyabor. The wide-ranging menu here – from Western dishes to Malay fish curries – is very popular but doesn't come cheap at around RM60 for two.

Sin Chuang Hua Coffee Shop Jalan Market. Like the *Hua*, a very busy Chinese café where over a beer, noodles or rice, you can watch market life revolve.

Listings

Airlines The MAS office is a 30min walk northwest from the centre at 61 Jalan Tunku Osman (☎084/326166).

Airport For flight information call ☎084/307082.

Banks Bumiputra, Lot 6 & 7, Jalan Kampung Nyabor; Public Bank, 2–6 Jalan Tunku Osman.

Handicrafts Chai Chiang Store, 5 Jalan Central, for woodcarvings, beadwork, bamboo and rattan baskets, and mats; prices are cheaper than in Kuching. There are also stalls selling basketware where Jalan Channel hits the wharf. There are several ceramics factories close to Sibu: buses

leave every hour from Jalan Khoo Peng Loong to Toh Brothers, Jalan Ulu Oya.

Hospital Jalan Ulu Oya ☎084/343333.

Internet access Terazone, fifth floor, Wisma Sanyan (10am–10pm, RM4 per hr).

Laundry Mr Dobi Sibu, Jalan Tuanku Osman (Mon–Sat 7.45am–6pm).

Police Jalan Kampung Nyabor ☎084/336144.

Post office The main office is on Jalan Kampung Nyabor (Mon–Fri 8am–6pm, Sat 8am–noon).

Taxis Sibu Taxis ☎084/320773.

Moving on from Sibu

By air

From Sibu's airport, there are daily flights to Bintulu (MAS 3 daily, RM64), Johor Bahru (AirAsia 1 daily, from RM40), KK (MAS 1 daily, RM180), KL (AirAsia 2 daily from RM90; MAS 1 daily, RM320), Kuching (AirAsia 3 daily, from RM40; MAS 8 daily, RM720), and Miri (MAS 2 daily, RM112). Bus #3a runs out to the airport (RM2) from the foot of the esplanade, on Jalan Maju.

By boat

Express launches depart from the new **Terminal Penumpang** up Batang Rajang to Kanowit (1hr 30min; RM12), Song (2hr; RM17) and Kapit (3hr; RM20), leaving half-hourly or hourly from 5.45am to 4.30pm. If you want to reach Belaga in one day (where you can stay for a night before travelling onward to Bintulu), you must catch the 6.15am or 6.45am express (8hr; RM50). The daily service downriver to Kuching leaves at 11.30am (4hr; RM40).

By bus

There are departures to Kuching (8hr; RM40), Mukah (3hr 30min; RM15.30), Bintulu (3hr 30min; RM20) and Miri (7hr; RM40) throughout the day from the long-distance bus station, 10km out of town. Some of the Kuching-bound buses travel onwards to Pontianak, in Kalimantan.

Along the Rajang: Kanowit, Song and Sungai Katibas

From Sibu, express launches head up the Rajang, stopping first at **Kanowit**, and then **Song**, from where it's possible to explore **Sungai Katibas**. Many then terminate at Kapit, a three-hour journey from Sibu, whereas others – those that leave early – continue further upsteam to Belaga, the last stop. As the river narrows, tiny Iban boats can be seen hugging the sides of the river to get as far away as possible from the swell the speeding launches create. Wood-reprocessing plants – a frequent sight on the stretch from Sarikei to Sibu – thankfully become less common as you head upriver, so the weight and mass of the jungle on either side becomes more apparent.

The first Sibu–Kapit boat sets off before dawn at 5.45am, after which launches leave once or twice an hour until 2.30pm. You need to get the 5.45am to be sure of getting to Belaga the same day, although in the dry season boats don't go beyond the Pelagus Rapids, near Kapit. Boats seldom sell any provisions, so bring your own water and food.

Kanowit

An hour from Sibu, the boat reaches the sleepy settlement of **KANOWIT**. The only real reason to get out here is to see **Fort Emma**, one of the first defensive structures built by James Brooke. It's just a couple of hundred metres to the west of the jetty in front of the town's two hotels – en route you'll pass the lurid-green mosque and a gaily flowered waterfront park. Built in 1859 of timber and bamboo, the fort took its name from James's beloved sister, its presence intended to inhibit the numerous raids by the local Iban on the remaining Rajang Melenau tribes. However, soon after the fort was built it was overrun by an Iban warring party; future attacks were only repelled by stationing a platoon here, mostly comprising Iban and Malays in the pay of Brooke's officials. Up until the Japanese occupation, Fort Emma was the nerve centre of the entire district, but with the passing of colonial rule the building fell into disuse as there were no more pirates to repulse, head-hunters to pursue, or rebellious Chinese miners to suppress. Despite years of neglect, the fort, perched on raised ground, is still impressive.

Practicalities

The two **hotels**, both on the waterfront Jalan Kubu, are the *Kanowit Air Con* (☏084/752155; ❷) which, despite its name, only has a/c in some of its rooms; and the *Harbour View Inn* (☏084/753188; ❷), whose rooms can be noisy in the early morning due to its proximity to the jetty. There are also a few waterfront **cafés**, serving basic Chinese rice dishes and the odd Malay dish in the mornings.

Song and Sungai Katibas

The small Iban settlement of **Song** is an hour upstream from Kanowit. It lies close to the junction of one of the Rajang's major tributaries, **Sungai Katibas**, which winds and narrows south towards the mountainous border region with Kalimantan.

Song

There's not much to **SONG**, which is little more than a few blocks of water-front shophouses (some of them 1920s wooden affairs, their shutters painted in cheery blues and greens), a jetty, a small Chinese temple and two water-front **hotels**. The *Capital Hotel* (☏084/777264; ❷) has dark corridors, small, stuffy rooms and shared bathrooms, but the *Katibas Inn* (☏084/777323; ❷) is much more jolly, with neat rooms and acceptable bathrooms. A third option, the *Mesra Inn* (☏013/8280477, ❷), is one block back from the river, with a pleasant lobby and airy, neatly decorated and clean rooms. Along the riverside are the usual Chinese stores, plus several **coffee shops** serving simple noodle dishes. In addition, stalls on the upper floor of the market facing the *Capital* offer *nasi lemak* and other Malay staples; you have to head up to the nearby *Happy Garden Seafood Restaurant* for a meal of any sophistication. But Song does have a helpful **guide**, Richard Kho (☏084/777228 or 013 567 5480), who can arrange visits to Iban longhouses on the Katibas. He has no office but can usually be found selling produce on the waterfront; if not, ask the manager of the *Capital Hotel*, Simon Low, for him.

Sungai Katibas

To explore **Sungai Katibas**, you need to catch the passenger longboat that leaves Song daily at 9.30am from the jetty. On the Katibas are several Iban longhouses well worth visiting. It takes between two and three hours to reach **Rumah Tambi**, a small settlement comprising a longhouse and other houses, where Sungai Bangkit branches away from Sungai Katibas. This is the boat's final port of call, so most of your fellow passengers will get off here. The settlement's longhouse women here are excellent **weavers**, and you can buy a wall hanging or thin rug for around RM300. There are another twelve or so Iban longhouses along the banks of Sungai Bangkit, each with their own rice fields and orchards, clinging to the inclines, but there's no formal transport beyond Rumah Tambi, only small private longboats that it may be possible to travel in, if room. The boat back to Song leaves at 6am the next morning – note that it's impossible to visit Rumah Tambi as a day-trip.

Despite their proximity to big-town Sibu, these river communities still hold their customs dear. Along the banks of the Katibas and the Bangkit you may catch sight of small **burial houses** set back on the banks. For a good 100m either side of the burial spots, the jungle is left undisturbed; these areas are strictly out of bounds to locals from neighbouring longhouses and other visitors. The surrounding areas also remain uncultivated out of respect to the ancestors. In contrast to the longhouses in southwestern Sarawak, those here see few overseas visitors. If you are offered an overnight stay, you are not likely to be charged anything, so have some **presents** with you as a contribution.

Kapit and around

The riverside bazaar town of **KAPIT** – around three hours east of Sibu – is the centre for buying and selling in the middle Rajang. It started life as a remote settlement for a small community of British officials and Chinese *towkays* trading with the region's indigenous population, but these days, the signs of rapid expansion are easily visible: machine parts and provisions are unloaded from the tops of express boats while, like in Sibu, new municipal buildings are fast changing the character of the town. As well as its remote location and usefulness as a base for onward travel and longhouse visits, Kapit offers an opportunity to visit Fort Sylvia, one of the splendid wooden structures erected by the Brooke dynasty, now converted into an informative museum, redolent of the upriver colonial era.

Although most travellers stay just one night in Kapit – waiting for boats either way along **Sungai Rajang** – it's easy to reserve a soft spot for the town. Though the place is little more than a smallish grid hacked out from the luxuriant forest, there are lots of good cafés in which to while away the time. Moving on from here, there's the nearby **Pelagus Rapids** and some Iban longhouses that welcome overnight visits.

The Town

Close to the jetty is Kapit's main landmark, the imposing white **Fort Sylvia**. Renamed after Vyner Brooke's wife in 1925, it was built in 1880 in an attempt to prevent the warring Iban attacking smaller and more peaceable groups such as the upriver Ukit and Bukitan. The fort also served to limit Iban migration along the nearby Sungai Baleh, and confine them to the section of the Rajang below Kapit. Its most famous administrator, **Domingo de Rozario**, was the son of James Brooke's Portuguese chef. De Rozario's memoirs record that life in Kapit was pleasant and that he got on well with the natives, but he found it most troublesome when dealing with "cases of heads taken on raids". Now the fort houses an intriguing **museum** (Tues–Sun 10am–noon and 2–5pm; free), spread over two floors. There are evocative photographs of great moments in the history of the upriver divisions, including the 1924 peacemaking ceremony in Kapit between Brooke officials and the warring Iban and Kayan tribal representatives. In addition, there are spectacular carvings, ceramic jars, *pua kumba* textiles, small cannons and precious stones on display.

Leading away from Fort Sylvia is Kapit's main street, **Jalan Temenggong Koh**, whose rows of simple shophouses that once nestled between patches of jungle are now giving way to stores and cafés housed in concrete buildings, which can better withstand the deluges of rain that regularly occur here. The **jetties** in front are a hive of activity, too, with longboats bobbing up and down and scores of people with bulky bundles of goods making their way back and forth between the express boats and smaller craft. Merchants, timber employers and visitors watch the goings-on from marble-topped tables in the *Chuong Hin* café, opposite the jetty.

Kapit's main square – simply called **Kapit Square** – is surrounded by shops selling everything from noodles to rope. The walk westwards along Jalan Temenggong, which forms the square's northern edge, leads to the **day market** where tribespeople urge you to buy clusters of tropical fruit, and other traders point out boxes of wriggling eels and shrimps. There are textile and shoe stalls upstairs in the main building, and the stalls in front of the market sell great fast food – prawn cakes, *pau* (Chinese buns), curry puffs and sweet pastries.

Back from the jetty along Jalan Hospital, near the pond, is the **Civic Museum** (Mon–Thurs & Sat 9am–noon & 2–4pm; free), which has a collection of interesting exhibits on the tribes in the Rajang region, including a well-constructed longhouse and a mural painted by local Iban. The sketches and watercolours of Kapit, Belaga and Song on display, by Timothy Chua, portray a life that is slowly disappearing. The museum also describes the lives of the Hokkien traders who were early pioneers in the region.

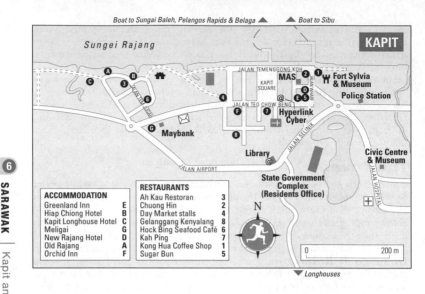

ACCOMMODATION		RESTAURANTS	
Greenland Inn	E	Ah Kau Restoran	3
Hiap Chiong Hotel	B	Chuong Hin	2
Kapit Longhouse Hotel	C	Day Market stalls	4
Meligai	G	Gelanggang Kenyalang	8
New Rajang Hotel	D	Hock Bing Seafood Café	6
Old Rajang	A	Kah Ping	7
Orchid Inn	F	Kong Hua Coffee Shop	1
		Sugar Bun	5

0 ──── 200 m

Practicalities

Kapit is only accessible by water – express **boats** dock at the town jetty, from where it is a few minutes' walk to anywhere in town. Three **banks** can change traveller's cheques: the Maybank, beside the *Hotel Meligai*, which also has an ATM; MBF, beside the *Kapit Longhouse Hotel*; and Bank Simpanan Nasional on the riverfront. **Internet cafés** are popular in Kapit; besides the one in the town library on Jalan Selinik (Mon–Fri 9am–5pm, Sat 9am–12.30pm), there's Hyperlink Cyber on Jalan Teo Chow Beng. A useful contact in Kapit is Iban **tour guide**, Joshua Muda (℡019/467 6004), based at the *New Rajang Hotel*, who, given advance notice, can arrange interesting two to four-day trekking trips at reasonable rates (around RM150 per person per day), staying in Iban longhouses.

To travel beyond Kapit by river you need a **permit**, available from the Residents Office (℡084/796963; Mon–Fri 8am–12.30pm & 2.15–4.15pm) on the first floor of the State Government Complex, 80m north of the jetty on Jalan Selinik. Take your **passport** with you; the process can take up to an hour to complete. Express boats leave from the jetty for Belaga twice a day at 8.45am and 9.45am (4–5hr; RM25) and hourly from 6.30am to 3.30pm for the trip to Sibu (3hr; RM20).

Accommodation

Greenland Inn Jalan Teo Chow Beng ℡084/796388. Near the waterfront, Kapit's best hotel has small but clean rooms, all with a/c and attached bathroom. The view over the Rajang is worth the high price. ❺
Hiap Chiong Hotel, 33 Jalan Temenggong Jugah ℡084/796314. Good value with clean, simple rooms and small bathrooms. ❷
Kapit Longhouse Hotel 21 Jalan Berjaya ℡084/796415. Although a bit grubby, it's second

only to the *Old Rajang* for popularity with travellers. The rooms are small, with chugging fans; bathrooms are shared. ❷
Meligai Jalan Airport ℡084/796817, ✉aswee@tm.net.my. A quiet, upmarket hotel, five minutes' walk from the waterfront. Rooms are large with tiled floors and attached bathrooms. ❹
New Rajang Hotel 104 Jalan Wharf ℡084/796600. Popular place, close to the waterfront, and more upmarket than its sister

establishment, the *Old Rajang*. Small but clean rooms with attached bathrooms. ❶
Old Rajang 28 Jalan Temenggong Jugah ☎084/796700. Classic Kapit dive – the best deal in town. Watch out for the scalding water in some of the bathrooms. Don't expect luxury and you'll be content. ❶–❷
Orchid Inn 64 Jalan Teo Chow Beng ☎084/796325. Adequate rooms with a/c, showers and TV. ❸

Eating

Kapit is a reasonable town for food although there is not much choice beyond regular Chinese and Malaysian fare. The food from the **hawker stalls** and **markets** is usually plentiful and tasty, and you can always get fresh meat and vegetables in the sit-down **coffee shops** and **restaurants**.

Ah Kau Restoran Jalan Temenggoh Jugah. Specializes in local recipes: wild boar, steamed fish, jungle vegetables, and as much rice as you can eat, with beer, at RM25 for two.
Chuong Hin Jalan Temenggong Koh. The best of the cafés in the morning: savoury cakes, curry puffs and hard-boiled eggs will set you up for the day. The staff are rather surly with travellers, but there's no better place to watch the comings and goings at the wharf.
Day Market stalls Jalan Teo Chow Beng. Sarawak fast-food like curry puffs, prawn cakes, cornmeal cake and tofu buns. Open 7am–5pm.
Gelanggang Kenyalang Two blocks back from Kapit Square, this covered market's dozen separate stalls serve Chinese, Malay and Dyak dishes, including *roti canai* and various noodle dishes with local vegetables, seafood and meat. The optimum time to eat here is between noon and 3pm, after which the food may not be so fresh.
Hock Bing Seafood Café Jalan Temenggong Koh. With some pavement tables, this bustling café serves the best prawn, wild-boar and fern dishes in Kapit. Friendly, atmospheric and excellent value at around RM20 for two people, including beer.
Kah Ping Jalan Teo Chow Beng. A good spot to watch Kapit life go by; the best options here are the excellently priced Chinese noodle and rice dishes at RM4–6 for a full plate of great food.
Kong Hua Coffee Shop 1 Jalan Wharf. One block back from the waterfront, and beside the *New Rajang*, this stylish little place has great eggs, toast and noodles plus strong coffee and beers.
Sugar Bun Jalan Teo Chow Beng. Not the town's finest food but a good place to watch Kapit's youth culture congregate.

Pelagus Rapids

Forty minutes' upriver from Kapit churn the waters of the **Pelagus Rapids**, an 800 metre-long, deceptively shallow stretch of the Rajang where large, submerged stones make your through passage treacherous. According to local belief, the rapids' seven sections represent the seven segments of an enormous serpent which was chopped up and floated downriver by villagers to the north. It's only in the last ten years that running the rapids has become safe, thanks to the new express boats, which have reinforced steel hulls and immense thrust.

Tucked in between the rapids and the jungle-covered Bukit Pelagus behind is the *Regency Pelagus Rapids Resort* (☎084/799050; ⓦwww.theregencyhotel .com.my/Pelagus; ❻), a beautiful longhouse-shaped hideaway whose exquisite double rooms, with attached bathroom and a veranda, look out either over the beautiful stretch of river or west over the swimming pool towards the profuse, jungle-hugging hills. Its riverfront dining room is exemplary, serving three meals a day, the menu running to exotic local dishes like *pangsoh* (chicken baked in bamboo) and various exotic takes on steamed fish.

The resort's resident guide, Nyaring Bandar, leads day-trips (around RM100) to the Iban longhouse nearby where he was raised, as well as a fascinating two-hour boat trip to visit a **Punan** community (a small subgroup of the Orang Ulu); on the latter, you can see *klirieng* burial poles of elaborate design with a dug-out chamber on top for storing the bones of aristocrats – these are rare nowadays as the practice was discontinued a long time ago.

△ Punan tribesman

Also on offer are night-time hikes into the surrounding rainforest and a rewarding half-day trek (guide not required). The latter follows a trail up the hill behind the resort to an old forest track and back down towards the river, offering fabulous views of the surrounding undisturbed forest, accompanied by a cacophony of birdsong, before meandering back along a path running beside the river (a three-hour round trip).

In order to get to the resort, most people call them in advance to arrange a speedboat from Kapit (RM50–60 return). Express boats to and from Belaga can use the landing bay 300m along the river from the resort's jetty, but you'll need to arrange for the resort's boat to drop you at this bay as there's no path there from the resort.

Sungai Baleh

Sungai Baleh branches off from the Rajang east of Kapit, at the point where the main river twists north towards the Pelagus Rapids. If you want to explore the Baleh in any depth, you will need to charter a longboat from Kapit (around RM200 a day), or, better, discuss a tailor-made tour with Joshua Muda (see p.442). **Sungai Gaat**, a tributary of the Baleh, also offers some fascinating longhouses.

If you have the time and money, it is worth making the effort to get to this inaccessible and seldom visited part of upland Borneo. Wherever you head, the **scenery** is magnificent – the land is covered in dense jungle, with the mountains on the Sarawak–Kalimantan border, to the south, peeping out of the morning mist. Occasionally you'll hear sounds of conversation or splashing as you round a corner and catch sight of an Iban family pulling their bamboo fish traps out of the water, or cooking their catch over an open fire. The river brims with fish, while the surrounding forest supports deer, buffalo and wild boar. Here, you're within sight of the remote peak, **Batu Tiban**, reached by explorer Redmond O'Hanlon, and described in his book *Into the Heart of Borneo*.

To Belaga

In the nineteenth century, the 150-kilometre trip from Kapit to **Belaga** (see opposite), on the furthest reaches of the Rajang, took two weeks in a longboat; a treacherous journey which involved negotiating rapids and dodging Iban raids on longhouses that belonged to the original inhabitants of the **upper Rajang** – the **Kenyah** and the **Kayan**. These days the trip takes between five and six hours from Kapit, depending on the river level. Occasionally the boat companies cancel departures: if the water level is very low, the Pelagus Rapids can be particularly hazardous, but if the level is high, the Rajang becomes a raging torrent. However, if the conditions are right, it's an excellent trip. Deep in the centre of Sarawak, wispy clouds cloak the hills and the screech of rainforest monkeys and birds can be heard.

Longhouses are dotted along the riverbank. As far as **Long Pila**, ninety minutes from Kapit, the people are mostly Iban, though between here and Belaga there are many other tribes, including the Ukit, Bukitan, Tanjong and Sekapan. Before the 1860s, the Kayan were numerous here, too, but when they protected the killers of two government officials, Charles Brooke led a punitive expedition against them, driving them back to Sungai Belaga, upstream from Belaga itself.

Belaga

BELAGA, which lies 40km west of the confluence of the Rajang and Sungai Balui, is as remote as you can get in the Sarawak interior. However, it's not uncharted territory by any means. The town started life as a small bazaar, after Charles Brooke had purchased the region from the sultan of Brunei in 1853. As early as 1900, pioneering Chinese *towkay*s arrived to open up Belaga to

The Kayan and Kenyah

The **Kayan** and the **Kenyah** are the most numerous and powerful of the Orang Ulu groups who have been living for centuries in the upper Rajang, along the Batang Baram and the Sungai Balui and their tributaries. The Kayan are the more numerous, at around forty thousand, while the Kenyah population is around ten thousand (though there are substantially more Kenyah over the mountains in Kalimantan). Both groups migrated from East Kalimantan into Sarawak approximately six hundred years ago, although during the nineteenth century, when Iban migration led to clashes between the groups, they were pushed back to the lands they occupy today.

The Kayan and the Kenyah have a lot in common: their language, with Malay–Polynesian roots, is completely different to those of the other groups, and they have a well-defined social hierarchy (unlike the Iban or Penan). Traditionally, the **social order** was topped by the **tuai rumah** (chief) of the longhouse, followed by a group of three or four lesser aristocrats or **payin**, lay families and slaves (slavery no longer exists).

Both groups take great pride in the construction of their **longhouses**, which are very impressive. Tom Harrisson, of the Sarawak Museum, learned in the 1950s of a longhouse on the upper Baleh which was nearly one kilometre long.

Artistic expression plays an important role in longhouse culture, the Kayan especially maintaining a wide range of **musical traditions** including the lute-like **sape**, which is used to accompany long voice epics. **Textiles** are woven by traditional techniques in the upriver longhouses, and Kayan and Kenyah **woodcarvings**, which are among the most spectacular in Southeast Asia, are produced both for sale and for ceremonial uses. One artist, Tusau Padan, originally from Kalimantan, became much revered as one of the finest Malaysian artists of his time. He used a mixed media of vibrant colours to create the flowing motifs he applied to painting and textiles – adorning burial poles, longboats and the walls of many Ulu Sarawak chiefs' homes.

Potent **rice wine** is still drunk by some Kayan, although nearly all the communities have now converted to Christianity, as a result of which alcohol is less in evidence.

trade and were supplying the tribespeople – both the Kayan and the nomadic Punan and Penan, who roamed over a wide swath of forest – with kerosene, cooking oil and cartridges, in exchange for beadwork and mats, beeswax, ebony and tree gums. The British presence in this region was nominal – officials would occasionally brave the trip from Kapit, but no fort was built this far up the river.

In recent years, logging roads have snaked their way across the interior, and there is now a highway (of sorts) linking Belaga with the main Bintulu–Miri road, 100km away. Until the **Bakun dam** (see box below) diversion tunnel made river travel beyond Belaga impossible, visitors would use Belaga as a jumping-off point for visits to longhouses along Sungai Balui. Now the express boats go no further than Bakun logging camp, which holds no appeal at all. But even with little opportunity to travel farther northeast Belaga still holds interest, if only because of its exquisite remoteness.

The Town

The chief activity in Belaga is just watching the comings and goings of the colourful characters that make up the area's wide ethnic mix. Occasionally the Penan come by offering metalwork like their uniquely carved knives, which can be picked up here for far less than you would pay for them in Sibu. A seasonal appearance is also made by the **wild-honey collectors** from Kalimantan, who arrive in March and again in September to trade their

The Bakun dam

The controversial **hydroelectric dam** at **Bakun** was given the go-ahead by Malaysian Prime Minister Dr Mahathir in 1993. It promised 2,400 MW of electricity but in the process would flood 69,000 hectares of rainforest and river channels displacing up to 11,000 indigenous people, mostly Penan who for hundreds of years had lived off the jungle. The forest also included indigenous agricultural lands and many thriving longhouse communities. The 200-metre-high, concrete-faced dam, one hour upstream on Batang Rajang from Belaga, was designed to generate much more than just Sarawak's power needs, and environmentalists, already red in the face about the social displacement and inevitable ecological degradation, pointed out that the task of exporting power to Peninsular Malaysia was nigh on technically unfeasible.

The economic crisis of 1997 put paid to the original plans for the dam, but they re-surfaced in 2000. By then, the social damage had already been done: the vast majority of the local communities had already been displaced to Asap, two hours' drive along logging roads north from Belaga. Only small groups of Kayan and Kenyah families held on in the most isolated of the longhouses furthest along Sungai Balui.

The Sarawak State Government now expects construction at Bakun to be completed by 2007, and power generation to commence the following year. The revived Bakun dam, according to developers Sime Darby, will benefit from the modifications to the project following seventeen environmental impact assessments, but it is of course too late for the traditional communities. The Asap communities have received **compensation**, but their representatives continue to argue that the sums agreed upon have not been nearly enough, and while all groups are finding it hardgoing at Asap, it is feared that the smaller groups, like the Ukit, who have found it particularly tough to adapt to the alien conditions, will lose the remaining traditional elements of their culture. Recent reports indicate that conditions at Asap have gone from bad to worse, and some critics have suggested that the "new town" has deteriorated into Sarawak's first slum, bedevilled with the problems of majority unemployment and social dislocation.

jungle produce for supplies. Other faces on Belaga's small network of streets include Kayan and Kenyah, with their fantastic tattoos and elongated ear lobes, wandering through the bazaar and eating wild boar and fried ferns in the Chinese cafés. Belaga is fairly compact, comprising a market, some shops selling provisions, a few nondescript houses and, beyond, a small track snaking towards the formidably dense forest, a few hundred metres away. Twenty minutes' walk along a riverside path there's a pretty kampung where the **Kejaman** (a small ethnic group related to the Kayan, and now almost extinct) burial pole that's on display outside the Sarawak Museum in Kuching was found in the early years of the twentieth century. Just beyond the kampung and before the playing field, as you look out over the river, you see a Kayan *salong* or **burial tomb** on the opposite bank; it's a small wooden construction with a multicoloured wooden sculpture sporting the image of a face.

Practicalities

Boats terminate at the jetty directly in front of the town's main street. Belaga's three **hotels** all offer similar rooms, which are of quite a high standard considering the isolation. *Belaga Hotel*, 14 Main Bazaar (☎086/461244; ❷), is the favourite – the rooms have bathrooms and fans. Owner Andrew Tiong and his family run a **café** downstairs, which is the best place to eat in town. The *Bee Lian Hotel*, 11 Main Bazaar (☎086/461439; ❷), and *Sing Soon Huat Hotel*, 27 New Bazaar (☎086/461307; ❸), are the alternatives, both offering small, basic rooms with external bathrooms.

Note that a number of **unlicensed travel guides** operate in Belaga – names include Daniel Levoh and John Belarik – and it is best to **avoid** trips offered by these men as some travellers have complained about their behaviour. As a rule of thumb, only visit longhouses at the invitation of locals you meet on the express boats.

Moving on from Belaga, there are two boats daily downstream: the 6am express boat, via Kapit, goes all the way to Sibu (RM50), while the 9am express only travels as far as Kapit (RM30). Most days a 4WD vehicle drives to Bintulu (3hr; RM60). There is no way of booking this trip in advance; see Andrew Tiong for the latest information or ask around town.

The coast from Sibu to Lawas

The route along the western flank of Sarawak from Sibu towards the Bruneian border is one of the most travelled in the state. Although dense mangrove swamp deprives the 150km of inland road linking Sibu with Bintulu of a clear view of the South China Sea, a lone chink in the vegetation leads to the busy bazaar town of **Mukah**, close to which lies the charming Melenau village of Kampung Tellian, with its appealing museum-cum-guesthouse.

Further northeast, the Sibu–Brunei road offers diversions into some of Sarawak's – indeed Malaysia's – best national parks. **Similajau National Park**, 20km northeast of the industrial town of **Bintulu**, is a long, isolated strip of beach and forest with a windswept beauty all of its own; the small forest enclave, **Lambir Hills National Park**, has easily covered trails and excellent accommodation; and Sarawak's most-visited natural wonder, **Niah National Park**, halfway between Bintulu and Miri, is noted for its formidable **limestone caves** – Deer Cave includes the largest chamber in the world. Niah was put on the map in the mid-1950s when the curator of the Sarawak Museum, Tom Harrisson, discovered human remains and rock graffiti inside the caves; subsequent work has suggested that Southeast Asia's earliest inhabitants were living in Sarawak as long as forty thousand years ago.

Northeast of Niah, it's another two hours to **Miri**, which, like Sibu, is predominantly a Chinese town and an important administrative centre. The town has benefited from the discovery of massive oil reserves in the vicinity, though in the energy stakes, Miri has recently been rivalled by Bintulu, which has specialized in the tapping of abundant pockets of natural gas on its doorstep. Both towns have a smaller percentage of indigenous inhabitants than Sarawak's other main settlements, and although some Iban and Melenau live in the area, there are very few longhouses to visit.

Northwards beyond Kuala Baram (the mouth of Batang Baram), the highway reaches Kuala Belait and the **Brunei border**. East of here, tucked into the folds of Brunei, are two peculiar "divisions" of Sarawak: finger-shaped **Limbang**, and **Lawas**, the most northerly strip of Sarawak, stretching north to meet Sabah.

Mukah and around

MUKAH, lying on **Sungai Mukah** a few kilometres inland from the South China Sea, is a three-hour bus journey from either Sibu or Bintulu. The last ninety kilometres of the trip, north from the Sibu–Bintulu highway, is a real bone-shaker, though the discomfort is somewhat alleviated by the views of lush sago palms as you pass through.

Mukah comprises a congested but atmospheric **old town**, a simple grid of streets running roughly east–west along the south bank of Sungai Mukah, and a new section two kilometres away from the river. Old Mukah's most defining image is its *casuarina*-lined waterfront, which contains both new shophouses and older, more charismatic wooden versions, some of which are brightened by striped screens. The town's main sights are the **Sago Furnace**, a simple brick construction unobtrusively sited beside the waterfront and a reminder of the region's importance in the collection and processing of the vitamin-rich sago palm, and, close by, **Tua Pek Kong Chinese Temple**, from whose veranda you can view the river's stilt houses and boats. The bearded Tua Pek Kong, patron saint of businessmen, sits at the head of the temple's main hall, while on its walls are finely painted murals of Buddhist and Taoist deities.

Practicalities

Mukah's **airport** lies five kilometres west of town with FAX flights to Kuching (2 daily; 1hr 10min; RM76), Miri (1–2 daily; 50min; RM55), Sibu (1 daily; 40min; RM30) and Bintulu (2 weekly; 35min; RM44). There are no buses from the airport into Mukah; a taxi costs around RM10. The **bus station** lies on the eastern edge of the old town on Jalan Sedia Raja, although still walking distance from the centre. Tickets for outbound flights can be purchased at MAS, on the waterfront at 6 Jalan Pasar or in the departures room of the airport itself.

Most of the **accommodation** in Mukah is to be found in the old town, either on or just south of Jalan Pasar. On Main Bazaar, the *Sri Umpang* (☎084/872415; ❸) is the town's best choice, bright and appealing, with clean, a/c rooms and sizeable bathrooms. Alternatively, the *Weiming Hotel* (☎084/872278; ❸), directly across the road, and the *King Ing Hotel* (☎084/871400; ❸), on Jalan Boyan opposite the temple, both have modern rooms and satisfactory bathrooms.

To **eat** during daytime head for the *Melenau Food Court* on the western edge of the market facing the river. Any one of the stalls here sells delicious fresh local cuisine, including the area's speciality, *umai*, a delicious raw fish and lime dish. One block back from the river, on Jalan Oya, *Arwa Café*, another daytime place, sells excellent *nasi campur* and fresh noodles. In the evening, head to the *Nibong House*, a five-minute walk from the old town on Jalan Orang Kaya Sedia Raja for a wide choice of Chinese dishes.

Kampung Tellian

Three kilometres east of Mukah on Sungai Misan, a tributary of Sungai Mukah, lies the Melenau water village of **Kampung Tellian**. Buses here are few and far between; taxis from Mukah's bus terminus will charge RM5. The kampung is a veritable spaghetti junction of winding paths, precarious crisscrossing board-walks and bridges. Some of the Melenau residents of its many stilt houses still work at processing sago the traditional way – by pulverizing the pith in large troughs and squeezing the pulp through a sieve, then leaving it to dry.

Aside from its picturesque appeal, Tellian's main attraction is its little museum and guesthouse, **Lamin Dana** (Mon–Sat 9am–5pm for non-residents; RM3; ☎084/871543, ⓦwww.lamindana.com), centred around a traditional Melenau tall house, a thin form of a longhouse hoisted on a platform high off the ground. It is the first of its kind to be built in over a hundred years. Exhibits include a collection of betel nut jars, traditionally used to store heirlooms, finely woven textiles for ceremonial occasions, musical instruments including a medley of gongs, and handicrafts such as hand-woven ratten baskets for which the Melenau are renowned across Sarawak. A short walk along the plankway to the front of the tall house reveals a Melenau burial ground, or *bakut*, amidst a clump of bare, ancient trees.

Lamin Dana also offers **accommodation**, in the form of eight airy rooms (❸) – all with shared bathrooms – off a central corridor on the building's first floor. The views are lovely, overlooking the kampung's colourful stilt houses and Sungai Misan. Directly outside the tall house is the kitchen and eating area – food is made to order and includes Melenau, Malay and Western dishes. *Lamin Dana* can also arrange short **boat trips** along the river (RM60; 2hr), which include a visit to a sago-making house and birdwatching.

Bintulu and around

BINTULU is at the centre of Sarawak's fast-growing industrial area. Up until thirty years ago, the settlement was little more than a convenient resting point on the route from Sibu to Miri, but when large **natural gas** reserves were discovered offshore in the 1960s, speedy expansion began. Since then Bintulu has followed in Miri's footsteps as a primary resources boom town, a far cry from the town's origins. The name Bintulu is, in fact, derived from the Malay

Menta Ulau – "the place for gathering heads"; before Bintulu was bought by Charles Brooke from the sultan of Brunei in 1853, Melenau pirates preyed on the local coast, attacking passing ships and decapitating their crews.

Modern Bintulu is a flat, compact rectangle of streets bordered by the old airfield to the east and Sungai Kemena to the west, with dense lines of shops and cafés in between. Despite its functional look Bintulu is a vibrant, friendly town. Inexpensive accommodation is easy to find, the restaurants and cafés are excellent and the flourishing day and night markets, which sell local delicacies like fresh fish grilled with *belacan* (shrimp paste), a delight. Although most people just stay overnight to await a bus connection to Sibu one way, or Niah National Park the other, staying a little longer will give you time to take in **Taman Tumbina Park**, a few kilometres north of the centre, and the beautiful, seldom-visited **Similajau National Park**.

Arrival

The international **airport** is 25km from the town, a taxi-ride that will set you back RM27 for the forty-minute journey; there are no buses. The **long-distance bus station** is, however, just a modest 5km out of town at Medan Jaya, from where you can get into the town centre on local bus #29 (RM1.50) or by taxi (RM10). Bintulu's main **taxi rank** is on Main Bazaar, just behind the day market. There is no tourist office.

Accommodation

There's quite a wide range of **accommodation** in Bintulu with the mid-priced choices offering particularly good value for money.

City Inn 149 Jalan Masjid ℡086/337711, ℻086/336529. The rooms here are small but do come with a/c, TV and shower; after dark, the din from the nearby *La Bamba* karaoke joint can make sleeping difficult. ❷

Fata Inn 113 Jalan Masjid ℡086/332998. Amiable staff and pleasant a/c rooms with attached bathrooms make the *Fata* an appealing choice; ask for a room with hot water. ❸

Hoover Jalan Abang Galau ℡086/337166. Acceptable rooms equipped with a/c and shower. ❹

Kemena Inn 78 Jalan Keppel ℡086/331533. Excellent small-scale place with decent en-suite rooms, run by a friendly family. Ask for rooms at the back, away from the main road. ❸

National Inn Jalan Abang Galau ℡086/337222. Small rooms with powerful a/c but showers and toilets are out in the passage. ❷

Regency Plaza Jalan Abang Galau ℡086/335111, ℅hotel@plazabintulu.com.my. Friendly, business-oriented hotel with an opulent lobby, rooftop swimming pool, massive rooms boasting enormous beds and full facilities. ❻

Riverfront Inn 256 Taman Sri Dagang ℡086/333111. Superb, very popular, mid-range hotel bang opposite the river, offering comfortable rooms with spacious bathrooms, satellite TV, mini-bar; some also have lovely views. There is also an excellent, popular restaurant serving Chinese and Malay dishes. ❺

Sea View Inn 254 Taman Sri Dagang ℡086/339118. Tucked on the edge of the town centre and gazing out over the river, the friendly *Sea View* has small, but rather shabby en-suite rooms. ❸

The Town and around

Bintulu's main commercial streets, **Main Bazaar**, **Jalan Masjid** and **Jalan Keppel** (the latter named after an early British official who did a long stint here), are lined with cafés and stores full of shoes, clothes and electrical equipment. A couple of blocks to the west of the commercial hub, Main Bazaar passes the **Kuan Yin Tong**, a less impressive Chinese temple than those at

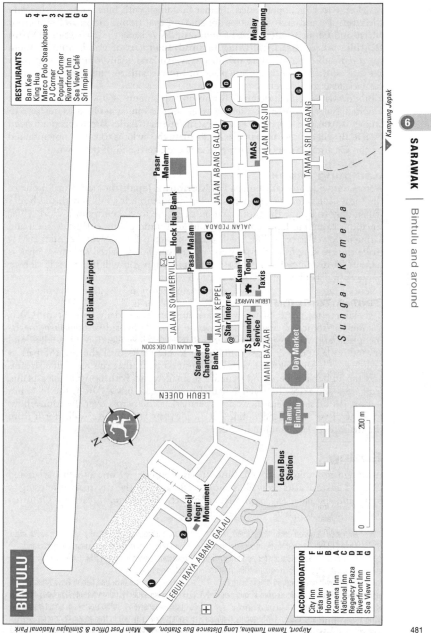

BINTULU

RESTAURANTS

Ban Kee	5
King Hua	4
Marco Polo Steakhouse	1
PJ Corner	3
Popular Corner	2
Riverfront Inn	H
Sea View Café	G
Sri Impian	6

ACCOMMODATION

City Inn	F
Fata Inn	E
Hoover	B
Kemena Inn	A
National Inn	C
Regency Plaza	D
Riverfront Inn	H
Sea View Inn	G

Old Bintulu Airport

Council Negri Monument

LEBUH RAYA ABANG GALAU

Standard Chartered Bank

LEBUH QUEEN

JALAN LEU GEK SOON

JALAN SOMMERVILLE

Hock Hua Bank

Pasar Malam

Pasar Malam

JALAN KEPPEL

@Star Internet

TS Laundry Service

LEBUH MARKET

MAIN BAZAAR

Kuan Yin Tong

Taxis

JALAN PEDADA

JALAN ABANG GALAU

MAS

JALAN MASJID

TAMAN SRI DAGANG

Malay Kampung

Day Market

Tamu Bintulu

Local Bus Station

Sungai Kemena

200 m

Kampung Jepak

Airport, Taman Tumbina, Long Distance Bus Station, Main Post Office & Similajau National Park

Kuching or Sibu but still a rallying point for the town's Hokkien-descended population in the evening. Fifty metres west, across Main Bazaar, is the **day market**, two large, open-sided circular buildings with blue roofs overlooking the river; seafood and vegetables are sold on the ground floor, and numerous Malay and Chinese cafés can be found upstairs. Adjacent is the outdoor **Tamu Bintulu**, where locals still bring in small quantities of goods and lay them on rough tables to sell. The town's **pasar malam** (daily 6pm–midnight), to the east of the centre, is a great place to browse, and to tuck into grilled fish, pastries, *umai* and sweets.

Bintulu witnessed a little bit of history in September 1867, when the first ever Council Negri (legislative assembly meeting) of the states that were later to comprise Malaysia was convened here. Chaired by Charles Brooke, and attended by five British officers and sixteen local chiefs, the event is today commemorated by the **Council Negri Monument**, at the western end of the town.

Kampung Jepak

Across the wide Sungai Kemena lies **Kampung Jepak**, the traditional home of the local Malay and Melenau-descended population. It's well worth the hour's trip, if only to escape the hustle and bustle of the town centre for a short while, since the kampung has a completely different atmosphere to Bintulu itself and a much slower pace of life. Small diesel-powered boats (every 20min; RM1) make the crossing from the jetty. As well as its *cencaluk* (salted shrimps), Jepak is famous for its pungent shrimp paste, *belacan*, which you will find on sale all over Sarawak and Peninsular Malaysia.

Taman Tumbina

Two kilometres north of town is **Taman Tumbina** (daily 9am–6pm; RM3), a compact tropical recreation area, whose name (a hybrid of *tumbuhan*, meaning plant, and *binatang*, animal) reflects its sizeable collection of wildlife and vegetation. Extending across a hill, with lovely views over the sea, the park is crisscrossed with walkways, wooden steps and paths that run alongside streams and dip under creepers, and contains a small wood with bougainvillea plants, fruit trees and ferns. To reach Taman Tumbina, take bus #1 from the local bus station, get off at the Sing Kwong supermarket, then cross over the roundabout in front of you and head uphill – it's a pleasant five-minute walk north from the main road, Jalan Tanjung Batu.

Eating

Although no culinary capital, Bintulu has a number of fine North Indian and Chinese **restaurants** as well as **food stalls** at both the day market (closing at 5pm) and the *pasar malam*, the latter in particular serving great fish. Unfortunately there is nowhere to sit here though.

Ban Kee Between Jalan Masjid and Jalan Abang Galau. Tucked away in a pedestrianized area, this daytime café transforms at night into one of Sarawak's top seafood restaurants. There's room for well over one hundred diners here to enjoy superb fish and seafood from a long Chinese menu. A town institution not to be missed.

King Hua Jalan Abang Galau. High-quality Chinese café with lavish portions of *umai*, roasted pork, chicken in chilli, seafood dishes, fresh vegetable options including *kalian* (baby spinach), *sayur masi* (aubergine), *midin* and long beans in garlic and *belacan*. Expect to spend RM30 per person including beer.

Marco Polo Steakhouse Lebuh Raya Abang Galau. High-quality, upmarket steakhouse, though quite expensive at RM50 per head. Local bands sometimes play in the upper-floor room.

PJ Corner Jalan Abang Galau. Daytime Indian café with tasty inexpensive curries and *roti canai*.

Moving on from Bintulu

By air

Bintulu is served by non-stop **flights** from KK (FAX 2 daily, RM127), KL (AirAsia 1 daily, from RM40; MAS 2 daily, RM379), Kuching (AirAsia 2 daily, from RM10; MAS 6 daily, RM117), Miri (FAX 4 daily, from RM69), Mukah (FAX 1 daily, from RM44) and Sibu (FAX 3 daily, from RM64).

By bus

A dozen or so daily **bus** services run the arterial route north from Bintulu to Miri (RM20), passing Niah National Park (RM18). There are buses three times a day to Mukah, and many more to Sibu (RM19). To reach the long-distance bus terminal in Medan Jaya, take a local bus from Lebuh Market (hourly: 7am–9pm).

Popular Corner Lebuh Raya Abang Galau. Several outlets under one roof, selling claypot dishes, seafood, chicken rice and juices; out front is a capacious forecourt where you can sit.
Riverfront Inn 256 Taman Sri Dagang. High-quality Chinese restaurant with a/c and a menu covering local Bintulu favourites like shark-fin soup with scrambled egg, plus Western, Thai and Malay dishes. Expect to pay around RM20 per person.

Sea View Café 254 Taman Sri Dagang. Excellent Chinese coffee shop in a pleasant position over-looking Sungai Kemena and away from the traffic. Exquisite noodle dishes are served until mid-morning, after which equally good rice dishes take over.
Sri Impian Jalan Abang Galau. Café offering an expansive spread of Malay food at reasonable prices (RM5 per plate). There's also an in-house *murtabak* and *roti canai* stall.

Listings

Airlines MAS is at 129 Jalan Masjid (open Mon–Fri 8.30am–4.30pm, Sat 8.30am–12.30pm; ☎086/331554).
Airport Call ☎086/331073 for flight information.
Banks Standard Chartered Bank, 89 Jalan Keppel; Hock Hua Bank, Jalan Sommerville.
Hospital Lebuh Raya Abang Galau ☎086/331455.
Internet Star, Jalan Leu Gek Soon.
Laundry TS Laundry Service, Lebuh Market, for same day service which costs around RM5.

Pharmacies There are two directly opposite the main jetty.
Police Branch on Jalan Sommerville ☎086/332113.
Post office Main office is on Jalan Tun Razak (☎086/339450), while a smaller branch is on Jalan Sommerville.
Taxis Thian Sek Chong ☎086/252133.
Visa extensions The Immigration Department (☎086/312211) is on Jalan Tun Razak, 3km north of the town centre.

Similajau National Park

Thirty kilometres northeast along the coast from Bintulu, **Similajau National Park** (RM10) is well worth a day-visit, or, even better, an overnight stop. The seventy-square-kilometre park has a lot in common with Bako, near Kuching, with its long, unspoiled sandy beaches broken only by rocky headlands and freshwater streams. Beach walks and short hikes are possible here, either along its 30km of coastline or following the **trails** which run alongside small rivers winding through the forest, down from the undulating hills that rise only a few hundred metres from the beach. Shrubs grow on the cliff faces, pitcher plants can be found in the ridges and orchids hang from the trees and rocks. Two dozen or so species of mammal have been recorded in the park, including gibbons and long-tailed macaques, mouse deer, wild boar, porcupines, civets and squirrels. The monkeys are quite friendly but sightings of anything else are quite rare unless you're very patient. Saltwater crocodiles are found occasionally wallowing in some of the rivers, especially after rain – one good reason for not swimming in the river close to the park centre – and there have even been sightings of dolphins and porpoises out in the waves.

The trails

By far the greatest attractions are the beaches, on which turtles occasionally nest in April and May. The two-and-a-half-hour walk north to the two **turtle beaches** starts from the park headquarters, the first stage involving crossing Sungai Likau in a motorized longboat. The trail ascends into the forest and soon reaches the turning to the **Viewpoint Trail** which, some forty minutes from the headquarters, delivers superb views of the South China Sea. Meanwhile the main trail follows the coastline to the turtle beaches, an hour beyond which is **Golden Beach**, noted for its fine sand. Walk north along Golden Beach for ten minutes, and you reach the trail that runs inland along the side of Sungai Sebubong. It is possible to reach this point by boat from headquarters (trips are offered by the park authorities) but the forest route is much more enjoyable. After fifteen minutes the trail reaches **Kolam Sebubong**, a freshwater pool whose waters are stained a remarkable ruby red by the (harmless) tannin from the nearby peat swamp.

The other worthwhile trail leads to the **Selansur Rapids**. Follow the Turtle Beach trail for one hour and look for a marked trail which heads into the forest parallel to a small river, Sungai Kabalak. It passes through forests of sparse *kerangas* and towering dipterocarp trees before climbing the sides of hills, where you'll hear monkeys high up in the trees and the omnipresent chainsaw-like call of the cicadas. After around ninety minutes you reach the rapids, a pleasant place to rest and take a dip.

Though the trails aren't particularly arduous, it's as well to **wear** light boots, a long-sleeved shirt and long trousers, as well as a hat to protect against the sun. It's also useful to have a water bottle, although the river water is quite drinkable.

Practicalities

The only feasible way to get to the park, as there are no buses, is by taxi from Bintulu (a one-way trip costs RM40). The road to the park leaves the Bintulu–Miri highway after 15km and bears left, signposted to the small kampung of Kuala Likau, 3km further on. The park entrance is a few hundred metres beyond the village. In the dry season it is possible to access the park by speedboat from the jetty on Taman Sri Dagang in Bintulu, though this is likely to cost as much as RM200 one way. The park's headquarters, the starting point for the short trail north to the beach, are just by the jetty where you alight.

Accommodation at the park (☎086/391284) ranges from two forest hostels with dorm beds (RM15) and two-bed rooms (❷) with bathrooms outside, to four-bed, en-suite chalets (RM50) and a **campsite** (RM5) although camping equipment is not provided. The park headquarters has a **canteen** that serves simple rice and noodle dishes, and an **information centre** (both daily 8am–6pm), with a small display on the local flora and fauna, and it is also here you pay the **entrance fee** (RM10).

Niah National Park

NIAH NATIONAL PARK (☎085/73745; RM10), 130km northeast of Bintulu, consists of 31 square kilometres of lowland forest and limestone massifs, the highest of which is the cave-riddled **Gunung Subis**, rising to nearly 400m. A visit to the park is a highly rewarding experience – in less than a day you can explore a **cave** that's among the world's largest, see prehistoric rock paintings in the remarkable Painted Cave, and hike along trails through primary forest. Although the region wasn't designated a national park until 1975, it has been a National Historic Monument since 1958, when Tom Harrisson discovered evidence that early man had been using Niah as a cemetery. In the outer area of the present park, deep excavations revealed **human remains**, including skulls which dated back forty thousand years and artefacts like flake stone tools, bone points and shell ornaments – the first evidence that people had lived in Southeast Asia that long ago.

Practicalities

Roughly halfway between Bintulu and Miri, the park is 11km off the main highway and 5km from the small town of **Batu Niah**. There are currently no direct buses from either Bintulu or Miri to the park, but from Batu Niah you can take a boat along Sungai Niah (20min; RM15), hitch-hike, or walk (1–2hr).

If you need to **stay** in Batu Niah, try the *Niah Cave Inn* (☎085/737333; ❹), a smart, modern hotel with adequate, if overpriced, rooms. Below the inn is a good café, offering Chinese noodle and rice dishes. The park itself has the best range of accommodation of any park in the state, offering: lovely forest hostels with dorm beds (RM15); four-bed lodges (RM105) with veranda, communal sitting area and shared bathrooms; two forest lodges (RM158), each consisting of two simple but spacious en-suite double rooms (❸) and a campsite (RM5), for which you need to bring your own equipment. It's advisable to **book** accommodation in advance at the parks desks in Miri or Kuching, especially over weekends and public holidays.

The park's **canteen** (daily 7.30am–10pm) is very good, with tables both outside, overlooking Sungai Niah, and inside. A range of dishes, such as stir-fries, noodles

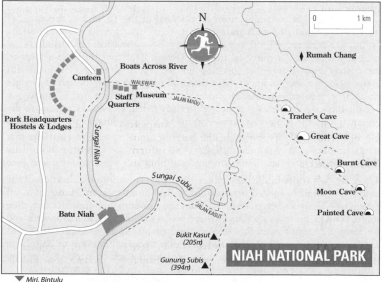

NIAH NATIONAL PARK

and omelettes, is available at very reasonable prices, and drinks include fine fruit juices. The **Display Room** (free), beside the park headquarters, offers a good account of the history of the caves, as well as geological and archeological information. There is also a recently opened **museum** (daily except public holidays 9am–5pm; free), with just a few exhibits and photographs of the caves, located on the eastern side of Sungei Niah; the crossing costs RM1).

The caves

The path uphill from the museum continues along a wooden walkway through dense rainforest where you are likely to see monkeys, hornbills, bird-wing butterflies, tree squirrels and flying lizards. A clearly marked path on the left leaves the walkway after forty minutes, running to a small longhouse, **Rumah Chang**, where you can buy soft drinks and snacks.

Further along the main walkway, a rock- and creeper-encrusted jungle wall looms up ahead and the path takes you up through the **Trader's Cave** (so called because early nest-gatherers would congregate here to sell their harvests to merchants) to the mind-blowing, 60m by 250m, west mouth of the **Great Cave**. The smell of bat guano intensifies as the path leads around extraordinary rock formations, and the sounds – of your voice, of dripping water, of bat-chatter and the nest-collectors' scraping – are magnified considerably. As the walkway worms deeper into the darkness, the light through the cave mouth ebbs and artificial lighting takes over. As the planks are often slippery with guano, it's best to wear shoes with a grip and take a **torch**.

After a thirty-minute walk through the cave you exit briefly into the light before entering the **Painted Cave**, in which early Sarawak communities buried their dead in **boat-shaped coffins**, or "death ships", arranged around the cave walls; when Harrisson first entered, the cave had partially collapsed, and the contents were spilled all around. Subsequent dating proved that the caves had been used as a cemetery for tens of thousands of years. One of these wooden coffins is still perched on an incline, as though beached after a monumental journey, its contents long since removed to the Sarawak Museum for safekeeping.

Despite the light streaming from an opening at the far end of the cave, it's hard to distinguish the **wall paintings** that give the cave its name (especially as they are now fenced off), but they stretch from the dark right-hand corner behind the coffin – a thirty-metre-long tableau depicting boats on a journey, the figures apparently either jumping on and off, or dancing. This image fits various Borneo mythologies where the dead undergo water-bound challenges on their way to the afterlife. The markings, although crude, can be made out, but the brown paint strokes are now extremely faded. The only way back to the entrance is by the route you came – try to be there at dusk to see the swiftlets return and the bats swarm out for the night.

The trails

There are two **trails** in the park which, after the claustrophobic darkness of the caves, offer a much-needed breath of fresh air. The first, **Jalan Madu**, splits off a little way along the caves walkway from the museum and cuts first east, then south, across a peat swamp forest, where you see wild orchids, mushrooms and *pandanus*. The trail crosses Sungai Subis and then follows its south bank to its confluence with Sungai Niah, from where may find a passing boat to Batu Niah (RM5), 400m away. A three-kilometre trail leads back to park HQ, or you can pick up a boat en route; there is no trail on Batu Niah's eastern bank.

The other trail, **Jalan Kasut**, takes you to Bukit Kasut, winding through *kerangas* forest, round the foot of the hill and up to the summit. It is a hard one-hour slog, but at the end there's a fine view both of the impenetrable forest canopy and of Batu Niah.

Lambir Hills National Park

Three-quarters of the way from Bintulu to Miri, and slap bang on the highway, is **Lambir Hills National Park** (RM10), which has some pleasant trails and is particularly popular with Miri day-trippers at weekends. Lambir Hills offers good accommodation, making an overnight stay a tempting option, though half of the park has been closed since flooding in 2004; check with Miri's Visitors' Information Centre if this section has re-opened.

The contours of the region comprising the park were formed sixty million years ago, when a vast area of sedimentary rock was laid down, stretching from present-day western Sarawak to Sabah. There is limestone and clay at lower levels, and sandstone and shale closer to the surface. Subsequent upheavals created the hills and the rich soil substrata, and gave rise to the local rainforest, with its distinctive vegetation types. Mixed dipterocarp forest makes up over half the area with the vast hardwood trees – *meranti, kapur* and *keruing* – creating deep shadows on the forest floor; the *kerangas* forest, with its peat soils, low-lying vegetation and smaller trees, is lighter and drier.

Fourteen well-marked **trails** crisscross the south part of the park, several leading to **waterfalls**. The longest trail – the four-hour trek to the summit of **Bukit Lambir** – is tough but rewarding, with a wonderful view across the park, the sounds of insects and birds echoing below. The trail cuts across deceptively steep hills, where gnarled roots are often the only helping hand up an almost vertical incline – you may well catch sight of monkeys, lizards or snakes on the trail.

To reach the three **Latak waterfalls**, 1.5km from park headquarters, follow the trail marked "Latak", which branches off north from the Bukit Lambir trail. The furthest of the falls (Latak itself) is the best, its 25-metre cascade feeding an alluring pool, but given its proximity to park headquarters, it is inevitably overrun at the weekends. There are more spectacular falls further afield, past Latak; it takes two and a half hours to reach the **Pantu** and **Pancur** waterfalls – watch for the narrow paths which lead down to the rivers from the main Bukit Lambir trail. These are fine places to stop and eat, and take a deliciously cool swim. The most remote waterfall, **Tengkorong**, is a further thirty minutes' walk from Pancur.

Practicalities

Lambir Hills is clearly signposted from the Bintulu–Miri highway but make it clear to the bus driver that you want to be dropped off there as the park is not a registered stop. All Bintulu–Miri and Miri–Bintulu coaches, which leave hourly from 6.30am to 4.30pm from both towns, pass by.

As at other parks, it's best to book **accommodation** at the parks desk at the nearest Visitors' Information Centre. At Lambir you can choose between the recently built and immaculately clean three-bed chalets (RM60) or the campsite (RM5), although for this you'll need to bring your own tent. A **canteen** (daily 7am–6pm) has a limited menu comprising simple Malay and Chinese dishes. Note that if you intend to go on the longer trails, bring hiking boots, water bottle, torch, sun hat and insect repellent.

Miri

With a population of well over 300,000, **MIRI** has well and truly burst out of its early geographic confines – the narrow streets of the old town – and in recent years has seen major development eastwards including the sprouting of plazas crammed with stores and eateries, and expanded office space, car parks and so on. But despite historic links with Western businesses – specifically the **oil** producer Shell – and a significant expatriate community, it retains a strong Chinese character. Most visits to northern Sarawak's natural wonders, including Mulu and Loagan Bunut national parks and the Kelabit Highlands, require a pit stop in Miri, and, although the centre of the city is noisy and polluted, after a week or two spent trekking in wild northeastern Sarawak, the place will grow on you, especially as the food and accommodaton on offer is extremely good.

Some of Miri's earliest inhabitants were pioneering **Chinese** merchants who set up shops to trade with the Kayan longhouses to the northeast along Batang Baram. But Miri remained a tiny, unimportant settlement up until the time oil was discovered in 1882, though it wasn't until 1910 that the black gold was drilled in any quantity. Since then, over six hundred wells have been drilled in the Miri area, onshore and offshore, and the main refineries are just 5km up the coast at Lutong.

Miri boasts a number of superb **hotels** – one, the *Miri Marriott*, is Sarawak's only five-star – and the city's seafood **restaurants** are internationally renowned. The town's authorities are also trying to boost the area's offshore tourism potential – there are some fine coral reefs currently little explored by divers.

Arrival and information

Miri International Airport is 10km west of the town centre, with a taxi (15min; RM20) the most reliable form of transport into town. Alternatively, the infrequent #9 bus (daily 6.15am–8pm; every 1hr 10min) runs from outside the terminal to Miri's **local bus station**, located next to the town's first shopping centre, Wisma Pelita. It's a five-minute walk from this bus station east to Jalan China and the old town. The **long-distance bus station** is 4km southeast of the centre along Jalan Miri Pujut; buses #30 and #28 run there hourly from the local bus station, or a taxi costs RM10 (in either direction). Next to the local bus station, the **Visitors' Information Centre**, 452 Jalan Melayu (Mon–Thurs 8am–4.30pm, Fri 8am–4.45pm, Sat 8pm–12.45pm; ☏085/434181), has maps and leaflets, and is also the place to go if you need to **book accommodation** at the local national parks.

Accommodation

Miri has a good array of accommodation in the mid-range and top-end categories, but a disappointing selection of budget options.

Centre of town

Cosy Inn Jalan South Yu Seng ☏085/415522. Well positioned close to the MAS office and a string of excellent Indian cafés. The rooms, though small, all have a/c, TV and bathroom. ❸

Dynasty Jalan Miri Pujut ☏085/421111, ⊚www.dynastyhotelmiri.com. Beautiful rooms with sea view and full amenities plus large bathrooms (in muted yellow). ❻

Fairland Inn Jalan Raja, at Raja Square ☏085/413981. Average but well-priced and popular hostel with basic en-suite rooms run by a rather unfriendly man. ❷

Gloria 27 Jalan Brooke ☏085/416699. Very reasonable if rather soulless hotel with adequate, functional rooms. ❹

Kingwood Inn Lot 826, North Yu Seng Rd ☏085/415888. Upmarket place which is

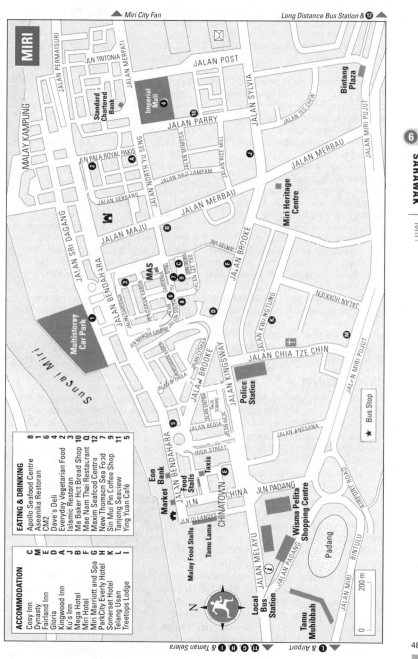

MIRI

ACCOMMODATION
Cosy Inn	**C**
Dynasty	**M**
Fairland Inn	**E**
Gloria	**D**
Kingwood Inn	**A**
Ku's Inn	**J**
Mega Hotel	**B**
Miri Hotel	**F**
Miri Marriott and Spa	**G**
ParkCity Everly Hotel	**H**
Somerset Hotel	**K**
Telang Usan	**L**
Treetops Lodge	**I**

EATING & DRINKING
Apollo Seafood Centre	8
Aseanika Restoran	1
CM2	6
Dave's Deli	4
Everyday Vegetarian Food	2
Islamic Restoran	3
Ma Baker Hot Bread Shop	10
Mae Nam Thai Restaurant	Q
Maxim Seafood Centre	12
New Thomson Sea Food	7
Sin Mui Pin Coffee Shop	9
Tanjong Seaview	11
Ying Yuan Café	5

JALAN PERMAISURI
JLN TRITONIA
JALAN MERPATI
MALAY KAMPUNG
Standard Chartered Bank
JLN PALA ROYAL PAKIS
JALAN SERDANG
JALAN SRI DAGANG
JALAN MAJU
JALAN BENDAHARA
JALAN NAKHODA GAMPAR
JLN PERSIARAN KABOR
Multistorey Car Park
Sungai Miri

JALAN POST
Imperial Mall
JALAN PARRY
JALAN NORTH YU SENG
JALAN MIMOSA
JALAN HAJI LAMPAM
JALAN MERBAU
JALAN GARDENIA
JALAN SOUTH YU SENG
JALAN LEE TAK
JALAN BROOKE

Bintang Plaza
JALAN SYLVIA
JALAN TEO CHEW
JALAN MERBAU
JALAN RICE MILL
JALAN MIRI PUJUT
Miri Heritage Centre
JALAN KWONGTUNG
JALAN HOKKIEN
JAL-N MIRI PUJUT

JALAN CHIA TZE CHIN
JALAN KINGSWAY
Police Station
JALAN CYNTHIA
JALAN ENTIBA
JALAN D'THULIA
PADA SQUARE
JALAN BEGIA
JALAN RAJA
JALAN ANGSANA

HIGH STREET
Eon Bank
Market
Food Stalls
Taxis
JLN
JALAN BENDAHARA
JLN OLEANDES
CHINATOWN
CHINA
Tamu Lama
Malay Food Stalls

JLN PADANG
Wisma Pelita Shopping Centre
JALAN MELAYU
JALAN PADANG
Padang
Tamu Muhibbah
Local Bus Station
JALAN MIRI
BINTULU
AIRPORT ROAD

★ Bus Stop

N

0   200 m

popular with business people. The rooms are large with full facilities – a/c, showers and TV. Good value. ❹

Ku's Inn 3 Jalan Sylvia ☎085/413733. Located on a busy street, the rooms here are small but cosy, with a/c and shower. ❷

Mega Hotel 907 Jalan Merbau ☎085/432432, ⓦwww.megahotel.net. Highly popular with Chinese families; the rooms are faultless, the restaurant top class, and the a/c extremely efficient. ❼

Miri Hotel 47 Jalan Brooke ☎085/421212. Opposite the *Brooke Inn*, this is a good choice with pleasant rooms and neat bathrooms. Central for both parts of town. ❹

Somerset Hotel 12 Jalan Kwangtung ☎085/422777, ⓔsohotel@po.jaring.my. A discreet and stylish place, with small but perfectly formed rooms and quite the most exquisite foyer of any Miri hotel. ❺

Outside the centre

Miri Marriott and Spa Jalan Temenggong Datuk Oyong Lawai ☎085/421121, ⓦwww .marriotthotels.com/myymc. Three kilometres along the coast road, this five-star resort is one of the best hotels in Malaysia, with a few hundred sumptuous rooms, some with balconies facing the sea. The giant swimming pool is a joy, the spa options are plentiful, with massage, reflexology and aromatherapy all available, and there's a wide range of restaurants and bars. Promotional rates are often available, especially during the week. ❼

ParkCity Everly Hotel Jalan Temenggong Datuk Oyong Lawai ☎085/440288, ⓦwww.vhhotels .com. With immaculate rooms, first-class service and a snug, shaded swimming pool, this hotel, formerly the *Holiday Inn*, is almost up with its neighbour the *Marriott*, but with far cheaper rates than next door. ❻

Telang Usan Block 1, 2.5km, Jalan Airport ☎085/411433. Three kilometres from the centre, on the airport road and easily reachable on airport bus #9. The rooms here are spacious, with a/c and TV, and the breakfasts are of the traditional Kayan variety with fresh tropical fruit. Sister to the Kuching hotel of the same name. ❺

Treetops Lodge Lot 210, Siwa Jaya Kampung, off Jalan Bakam ☎085/482449, ⓦwww .treetops-borneo.com. A top-of-the-range hideaway, run by an Englishman and his Kayan wife, *Treetops* is a large, comfortable house nestling on the edge of the jungle, 20km south of Miri. It features small, en-suite rooms built of locally sourced wood, a paddling pool, and delicious Kayan, food available on request. Guests can use a private beach 15min walk away too. Owner Mike is happy to pick up guests from Miri's airport or bus station as long as you give him plenty of notice; alternatively, catch bus #13 from Miri's local bus station. ❸

The Town and around

The **old town** around Jalan China teems with cafés and shops, and remains Miri's social hub and the most enjoyable area of the town to wander around. There's a wet fish, spice and vegetable **market** at the north end of Jalan China, next to which is the **Chinese temple**, a simple red-and-yellow building whose bottle-green roof is patrolled by fearsome dragons. From its small, river-facing forecourt, where devotees burn joss sticks, you can watch the boats being unloaded at the fish market next door. The wide road running parallel to the river, **Jalan Bendahara**, is the simplest route into the **new town** area, where you find most of the Miri's tour operators and plazas. Many of the town's best restaurants can be found along **Jalan North Yu Seng**, one block south of Jalan Bendahara, and at Imperial Mall, where hundreds of stalls and boutiques vie for trade. Four hundred metres further east, along Jalan Merpati, on the city's outskirts, is a vast open-air theatre, the under-used **Miri City Fan**, which has capacity for a few thousand people.

Directly south of the local bus station next to Wisma Pelita is the padang, on the edge of which lies **Tamu Muhibbah** (daily 6am–2pm), the town's jungle-produce market, where Orang Ulu come downriver to sell rattan mats, tropical fruits, rice wine and even jungle animals. Just east of the bus station is the oldest of Miri's many shopping malls, **Wisma Pelita**, with a good range of stalls and boutiques and two reliable Internet cafés.

Taman Selera, 4km west of town and just past the *ParkCity Everly* and *Marriott* hotels, has a tranquil beach one kilometre long; it's a fine place to watch

By air

There are non-stop **flights** from Miri to Bario (FAX 2 daily, RM70), KK (AirAsia 2 daily, from RM10; 4 daily from RM95), KL (AirAsia 2 daily, from RM109; MAS 3 daily, RM422), Kuching (AirAsia 1 daily, from RM20; MAS 4 daily, RM164), Labuan (FAX 3 daily, from RM66), Lawas (FAX 5 daily, RM55), Limbang (FAX 3 daily, RM68), Marudi (FAX 4 daily, from RM29), Mukah (FAX 1 daily, RM55), Mulu (FAX 2 daily, from RM84) and Sibu (FAX 2 daily, RM112); and weekly FAX flights to Kelabit Highland destinations Ba Kelalan, Long Akah, Long Banga, Long Lellang, Long Seridan from RM50.

By bus

All long-distance buses leading south to Lambir Hills National Park, Bintulu and beyond leave from the long-distance bus terminal, 4km from the town centre on Jalan Miri Pujut. Buses #1 and #1A north to Kuala Baram and Kuala Belait (for Brunei) leave from the local bus station, Wisma Pelita. The last departure from Kuala Belait to Bandar Seri Begawan in Brunei is at 3.30pm, so it's best to leave Miri early, ideally on the 7.30am service, if you want to be sure of getting to the Brunei capital the same day.

the sun go down, eat satay and drink beer from the hawker stalls. Buses #11, #13 and #15 (RM1) head out here from the Wisma Pelita bus station.

Eating and drinking

You can hardly go wrong for food in Miri, although **restaurants** *Apollo*, *Maxim's* and *New Thomson* are a cut above the rest for value and quality. More informal, beside Jalan China's markets there is a set of **Malay stalls** serving delicious *laksa* and Malay nasi buffets. Vegetable dishes include *sayur kacang* (green beans) and *sayur nangaka* (a grey root vegetable) served in *sambal*. For breakfast, one block east of Jalan China, check out the Central Market **breakfast food court** (daily 6.30–11am) where you'll find the best wet noodles in town; vegetables and fruit are also sold here.

The **bar** scene has quietened down in recent years with many expats preferring to drink in hotel bars or at home. Most of the places listed below serve beer.

Apollo Seafood Centre 4 Jalan South Yu Seng Highly popular place, and with good reason – the grilled stingray and pineapple rice is exquisite, and just about any other seafood option excels – though meals are not cheap at around RM80 for two (including beer). Open daily 6–11pm, except public holidays; no bookings so turn up before 9pm.
Aseanika Restoran Jalan Sri Dagang. Popular Malay café serving excellent *rotis* and curries. Daily 10am–10pm.
CM2 Jalan South Yu Seng. Specializes in Western food like burgers and chicken wings, with Thai fish, satay and *obor-obor* (jellyfish) as well. Daily 3pm–2am.
Dave's Deli Ground floor, Imperial Mall, Jalan Parry. Western-style deli with a scrumptious range of pies, soups, roast chicken (RM10) and desserts.
Everyday Vegetarian Food Jalan Pala Royal Pakis. Excellent if nondescript-looking Chinese

café offering tofu dishes (with the texture of meat and fish) in tasty sauces. Prices range from RM8 for a basic soya-based dish to RM15 for the café's finest vegetarian fish in *belacan* sauce. Daily 10am–11pm.
Islamic Restoran 233 Jalan Maju. This busy place specializes in spicy Malay dishes for RM6 each.
Ma Baker Hot Bread Shop Lot 1286, ground floor, Jalan Parry. Clean Western-style daytime café with superlative cakes as well as Malay staples.
Mae Nam Thai Restaurant *Dynasty Hotel*, Jalan Miri Pujut. Authentic Thai cuisine at around RM40 a head for a full meal.
Maxim Seafood Centre Lot 342, Block 7, Jalan Miri Pujut. Three kilometres out of town but worth the RM10 taxi ride, *Maxim's* is Miri's top restaurant, serving a superb array of grilled fish with *belacan*, and delicious vegetable dishes

with chilli, herbs and garlic; meals cost roughly RM80 for two, including beer. It's not possible to book, but it's best to arrive early – preferably before 8.30pm.

New Thomson Sea Food Lot 382, Jalan South Yu Seng. Close to *Apollo*, the *New Thompson* is less flashy but just as good, with tremendous fish, seafood and vegetable dishes served up in a trice by the friendly, harmonious team. Outstanding house specials include preserved green mustard and beancurd soup. Expect to pay around RM60 for two. Open daily 6pm–2am.

Sin Mui Pin Coffee Shop 5 South Yu Seng Rd. High-quality fish restaurant (the stingray is excellent) with a vibrant atmosphere. Order your rice and vegetables from the people at the back, and get there before 8pm to avoid a long wait.

Tanjong Seaview Taman Selera Beach. Food centre very popular with local families, offering superb satay at low prices.

Ying Yuan Café Lot 55, Jalan Bendahara. Busy Chinese café noted for its *nasi campur*, which includes: filling and delicious prawns, chicken, baby sweet corn and okra at RM10 per portion.

Listings

Airlines AirAsia, ground floor, 661 Unify Centre Block, 7 Jalan Miri Pujut ☎085/438022; MAS, Jalan South Yu Seng ☎085/414144, 24hr number ☎1300 883000.
Airport For flight enquiries call ☎085/414242.
Banks and exchange Standard Chartered, Jalan Merpati; Eon Bank, Jalan Bendahara (11am–3pm only). There is a moneychanger in the Magnum 4-digit shop at 12 Jalan China.
Car rental Mega Services, 3, Lorong 1, Sungai Krokop ☎085/427436.
Hospital Miri's General Hospital is on the airport road (☎085/420033).
Internet access Cyber Corner.biz and Cyberworld, first floor, Wisma Pelita (daily 9am–9pm); *Planet Café*, 1st floor, Bintang Plaza (RM6 each hour, fast connection); DC Enterprise, third floor, Imperial Mall (daily 10am–10pm).
Laundry Tally Laundry Service, Lot 514, Jalan Merbau (daily 8am–6pm). Excellent deal as you pay by weight.

Pharmacy First floor, Wisma Pelita.
Police headquarters On Jalan Kingsway (☎085/433677).
Post office On Jalan Post.
Shopping Borneo Arts, 548 Jalan Yu Seng Selatan (☎085/422373) for handicrafts, textiles and pottery; Imperial Mall, Jalan Parry, is Miri's latest upmarket plaza with a wide range of shops including the well-stocked Kwan bookshop; Miri Heritage Centre, Jalan Merbua, sells tourist-oriented crafts and textiles; Pelita Book Centre, first floor, Wisma Pelita, has a wide selection of English-language books on Sarawak culture and geography; Syarikat Unique Arts and Handicrafts Centre, Lot 2994, Jalan Airport, 4km out of Miri, sells local crafts at lower prices than in town.
Taxis Miri Taxis ☎019 8151093.
Tour operators Tropical Adventure, ground floor, *Mega Hotel*, Jalan Merbau (☎082/419337, ✉info@asiabudgetholidays.com) specializes in treks to the Baram, Mulu National Park and the

---

The Miri Reef

It is only recently that the exquisite **reefs** off Miri's coastline have begun to be appreciated by divers, who for decades have been flocking to other East Malaysian dive sites like Sipidan and Mabul. Miri's **coral** can be viewed on reefs varying in depth from 10 to 30m, with an average visibility of 15 to 30m, making diving conditions very good indeed. The most visually exciting reefs are Batu Mass, Siwa and VHK, none of which is more than forty minutes by speedboat from the city. Marine wildlife includes anemones while reef fish such as groupers, stingray and wrasses are also abundant. Diving is generally good all year round but busiest in the peak tourist season, between December and February.

A number of specialist dive operators have begun to promote diving here; try Dive Borneo (⊛www.diveborneo.com) for trips ranging from half-day dives (RM150) to full three- or four-day packages (from RM1300, including accommodation). Miri-based operators include the ever-dependable Seridan Mulu (see "Tour operators", opposite), who offer a one-day dive for RM280, including dive equipment, transfers, two dives and lunch.

Kelabit Highlands; expect to pay around RM800 for two people to go on a three to five day trek. Seridan Mulu, ground floor, *Miri Marriott and Spa* (☎085/414300, ⓦ www.seridanmulu.com) runs trips into the little-visited Loagan Bunut National Park as well as Mulu Park visits. Its five-day trip, incorporating both parks, a night in a longhouse and a visit to Marudi, is excellent value at around RM400 per person. They also run diving trips.

Visa extensions The Immigration Office is at Jalan Kipas (Room 3; Mon–Fri 8am–noon & 2–4.15pm).

North of Miri: the border with Brunei

The trip by **road** from Sarawak **to Brunei** is quite straightforward, though heading on **to Sabah** can take up to two days from Miri; many people prefer either to fly direct to Kota Kinabalu, or to take a flight to Labuan and a boat from there to KK. The only advantage – and not a particularly compelling one at that – of the overland route through Brunei is that you can visit the territorial divisions of **Limbang** and **Lawas**, which contrast greatly with the land around Miri as they are comparatively sparsely populated with an ethnic mix of Iban, Murut, Berawan and Kelabit. This is a difficult area to get around, though, as there are few boats and roads.

To Kuala Baram and Brunei

The trunk road north of Miri runs a few kilometres in from the coast to **Kuala Baram**, 20km away, a small town situated at the mouth of Batang Baram – you can catch the express boat to Marudi here. Buses #1 and 1A leave Miri's long distance bus station regularly between 7am and 3pm for Kuala Baram (40min; RM2.20).

There are also direct buses from Miri to the Bruneian border town of **Kuala Belait** (3hr; RM12.20), leaving at 7am, 10am, 1pm and 3.30pm – to reach Bandar Seri Begawan the same day you need to catch the first bus. The bus crosses Batang Baram by ferry (daily 6am–8pm; every 20min), before arriving at Kuala Belait another 6km further on. From here you can catch a Bruneian bus to Seria, where you need to change again for BSB. The last bus from Seria to the Bruneian capital leaves at around 3.30pm.

Limbang

To the south of Bandar Seri Begawan is **Limbang**, a strip of Sarawak roughly 30km wide and 50km deep, sandwiched between the two parts of Brunei. It's an inaccessible and thus seldom-visited district, though travel here is possible along Sungai Limbang, which snakes into the interior from the mangrove-cloaked coast, and provides access to Mulu National Park by an adventurous river trip along Sungai Medalam. For centuries, Limbang Town was a trading centre run by Malays, who bartered the jungle produce collected by the Berawan, Kelabit, Besayak and Murut peoples with fellow Malay and Chinese merchants. Although the White Rajahs never actually bought Limbang from the sultan of Brunei, as they did the areas to the south, Charles Brooke occupied the region in 1890, following demonstrations by the ethnic groups against the increasingly decadent rule of the sultan. However, Brooke's main reason for interceding was to acquire as large a slice of what was left of Brunei as possible, before his Sabah-based rivals in the British North Borneo Chartered Company overran it.

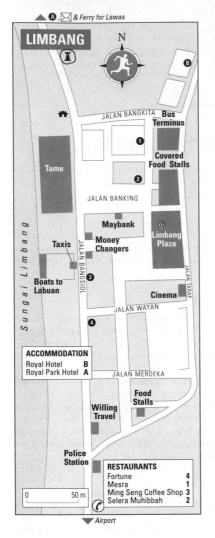

Limbang Town

The only building of note in the division's only settlement, **LIMBANG TOWN**, is the riverbank **fort**, the most northerly of Charles Brooke's defensive structures. Constructed in 1897, it was renovated in 1966 when much of the woodwork was replaced by more durable materials like concrete and *belian* (ironwood). The fort was originally designed to serve as an administrative centre, but was instead used to monitor native insurgency in the early years of the twentieth century. The rest of the small town is composed of a few streets set back from the river; the main street, Jalan Bangsiol, leads to the **tamu** (market), which is at its busiest on Friday when fruit, animals and vegetables are brought in from the forest to be sold.

Practicalities

The **airport** is 2km south of the town; a taxi into the centre (there are no buses on this route) costs around RM6. The jetty used by **express boats** to Labuan in Sabah (leaves 7.30am; 2hr; RM25) and to Muara, Brunei's port (30min; RM20), is south of the fort on Jalan Bangsiol; the daily Lawas boat (leaves 7.30am; 40min; RM20) uses the jetty a few hundred metres north of the old town. The bus terminus is five minutes' walk along Jalan Bangkita from the Labuan/Brunei jetty. **Buses** go to Nanga Medamit, first stop for the overland "Head-hunters' Trail" into Mulu National Park (see p.508) but there is no published schedule for the ninety-minute trip, so check at the bus station. There are no buses to the Bruneian border but it is possible to hire a taxi to Bangar, the only town in Brunei's Temburong district (RM100), from where boats for onward travel to Bandar Seri Begawan are plentiful. There are also AirAsia **flights** from Miri to Limbang and Kota Kinabalu. **Internet access** is available at *Media Cybercafé*, second floor, Limbang Plaza, close to the bus station.

There's no budget **accommodation** in town but there are a couple of mid-range options that are serviceable, including the *Royal Hotel* (☎085/215690; ③) on Jalan Tarap, which has large, clean, en-suite rooms, and the *Royal Park Hotel* (☎085/212155; ③), opposite the Lawas jetty some 400m north of the old town, with small but tidy rooms.

The hawker **stalls** on the breezy first floor of the **tamu** offer the most afford-able **food** in town, as well as good views of the water village across the river. There are more stalls in the covered building south of the bus station, and still more on the open ground below Jalan Merdeka. The pick of Limbang's **restau-rants** are the friendly Malay ones, the *Mesra* and the *Selera Muhibbah*, both good for *rotis* and *biriyanis*; the *Fortune*, serving quality Chinese food; and the plain *Ming Seng Coffee Shop*, with a smaller range of Chinese fare.

Lawas

Boxed in between Brunei's sparsely inhabited Temburong district and Sabah is Sarawak's most northwesterly district, **Lawas**. Bought by Charles Brooke from the sultan of Brunei in 1905, the division is a little larger than Limbang, and has more coastline. From its origins as a remote bazaar and trading centre for Berawan, Kelabit and Chinese pioneers, **LAWAS TOWN** – the only settlement of any size in the area – has grown into a bustling centre on Sungai Lawas, becoming prosperous from its timber industry. Above the river is a large new market which has become the town's main focal point, selling tropical fruits and vegetables, and with several food stalls upstairs. On the other side of the street is another produce market situated underneath a massive *ara*, a tropical hardwood tree, providing much-needed shade for the traders. Saturdays are the busiest days at both markets, when traders from Sabah sometimes arrive to sell clothes and textiles. The only other diversion in town is the **Chinese temple** five minutes' north of the market on Jalan Bunga Teratai, remarkable only for the unusual fact that a large portion of it is open to the elements.

North of town, Jalan Punang leads, after around 7km, to **Punang** itself, the site of a reasonably attractive beach – minibuses (RM3) make the trip from the bus station.

Practicalities

Lawas **airport** is around 3km south of town, from where you will need to get a taxi (RM5) into town. There are daily FAX flights back and forth from KK, Limbang, Bario and Ba Kelalan in the Kelabit Highlands. **Boats** arrive and depart from the jetty beside the old mosque, 400m east of the town; there are numerous services to Brunei daily (from 7am; RM20) and a single boat each day to to Limbang (9am; RM20). Tickets are sold at the jetty just before depar-ture. The **bus station** is in the centre of town, 50m north of the markets. Buses leave daily at 7am for Kota Kinabalu (4hr; RM20) and there are occasional minivans to Beaufort, south of KK (4hr; 15min).

The *Soon Seng Lodging House* at 18 Jalan Dato Taie (☎085/285490; ❶), ten minutes' walk north from the bus station, is the town's most inexpensive **place to stay**, with tiny, dusty, poky rooms and communal bathrooms. Higher up the scale are the *Mega Inn*, 1 Jalan Muhibbah (☎085/283888; ❸), with modern a/c, en-suite rooms, though they can be noisy in the mornings. The most opulent choice is the vast *Hotel Perdana*, 365 Jalan Punang (☎085/285888; ❹), fifteen minutes' walk north out of town, with large, en-suite rooms.

For inexpensive **food**, try the upper floor of the market, with the usual selection of Malay and Chinese stalls. There's no menu at the tidy *Soon Seng* **restaurant** below the hotel of the same name, but the Chinese food there is good. Alternatively, try the Malay restaurant, *Hj Narudin Bin Matusop*, which has tasty buffets, or the *Bee Hiong* restaurant, which specializes in dim sum. The Chinese coffee shop, *Ho Peng*, serves up ample noodle dishes.

The northern interior

The **northern interior**, loosely defined as the watershed of **Batang Baram** – the major river to the northeast of Miri – incorporates both some of the wildest, most untouched parts of Sarawak, and areas of the most environmentally degraded. At the northernmost point of the White Rajahs' reach, Batang Baram had a number of imposing military fortifications, but the tribal groups living along the river's reaches were largely left to their own devices. From the 1960s, though, the Baram was the first part of Sarawak to be systematically logged, though now timber clearance has given way to wood and oil-palm processing plants, which operate at the edge of the wide, soupy artery. Many of the **Kayan** and **Kenyah longhouses** in this beautiful part of the state have in fact gained economically from the new industries, though the ecological damage is obvious – soil erosion has damaged their lands, water catchments are murky and often unfit for drinking, and the food supply – both forest game and agricultural produce – is diminishing. The semi-nomadic Penan are the worst affected because, as former hunters and gatherers, they are less able to rely on the forest for survival.

Despite the despoliation, the northern interior holds many of Sarawak's most renowned natural delights. Beyond the delightful gateway town of **Marudi**, one of Batang Baram's tributaries, **Sungai Tutoh**, branches off east

△ Batang Baram

to **Mulu National Park**, now a UNESCO World Heritage Site, with its famous limestone Pinnacles and vast cave systems. Further east still, straddling the border with Kalimantan and only accessible by plane, lies the lush and magnificent sparsely populated mountain plateau of the **Kelabit Highlands**. The pleasing climate and low humidity makes it the best place in the state for long treks in the rainforest. Now accessible by bus from Miri, **Loagan Bunut National Park** boasts an exquisite lake, the home to a large population of tropical birdlife, while beyond, on the banks of the Baram, it's possible to visit the fascinating community of **Long San**.

Travel in the region is surprisingly efficient, thanks to the FAX connections and reliable river travel. In a seven-day trip you could easily, for example, visit Mulu National Park, the Kelabit Highlands and the bazaar town of Marudi. Bear in mind, however, that it's difficult to get a seat on some of the Fokker and Twin Otter flights, particularly from Miri and Marudi to either Mulu or Bario, unless you book a few weeks in advance.

Marudi and around

On Batang Baram 80km southeast of Miri, **MARUDI** is the only sizeable bazaar town in the whole Baram watershed, supplying the interior with consumer items, from packaged food to outboard engines. Round the small town's jetty, where express boats dock, stalls and cafés do a brisk trade especially when the boats from Kuala Baram dock. There's little to do here except watch small-town life – timber magnates in jeans and dark glasses drive by in brand-new Toyota vans while groups of young men wait for work in the nearby estates and processing yards.

Marudi was acquired from the sultan of Brunei by Charles Brooke in 1882. He renamed it Claudetown, after the first official sent by James Brooke to administer the area. Charles Brooke encouraged Iban tribespeople from the middle Rajang to migrate here, to act as a bulwark against Kayan war parties who, at their peak in the mid-nineteenth century, amassed up to three thousand warriors on expeditions downriver in search of human trophies.

The town is dominated by two features, the jetty and the hilltop **Fort Hose**, now a museum, which is reached by following Jalan Fort from the main Bazaar Square, west of the jetty, to the top of the hill. Built in 1901, the fort was named after the best known of Sarawak's colonial officials, the naturalist Charles Hose; its ironwood tiles are still in perfect condition, as are the ceremonial brass cannons at the front. The fort's exhibits include photographs of colonial officials and longhouse communities through the years, plus textiles and ceremonial handicrafts. Five minutes further along the hilltop road is the old **Resident's house**, which, though sturdy and quite habitable, is abandoned and becoming increasingly tatty in the tropical climate.

Practicalities

It is ten minutes' walk from Marudi's **airport** into town; a taxi costs RM3. Flights arrive from and depart for Mulu National Park, locations in the Kelabit Highlands and Miri. The boat **jetty**, where boats go back and forth to Kuala Baram for Miri (leaving at 7.30 and 8.30am, then hourly from 10am until 3pm; RM20), to the north, and Long Lama, to the south (see p.499), is north of the centre and only five minutes' walk from the main hotel, the massive *Grand* (T085/755711; **3**). Just off the airport road, Jalan Cinema, on Lorong Lima, it provides far and away the best **accommodation** in town, with clean, quiet rooms; the reception also has details of Mulu tours and visits to longhouses. Other options include the *Hotel Zola*, a stone's throw from the jetty on Jalan Cinema (T085/755311; **2**), and the *Victoria Hotel*, Lot 961, Bazaar Square (T085/756067; **2**), which has good views over the river.

There are two good **restaurants**: the Indian *Restoran Koperselara* on Jalan Cinema, which sells *roti canai*, curries and refreshing *teh tarek* (a full meal here costs around RM4) and *Boon Kee Restoran*, set behind the main street in Jalan Newshop, which is a great place for dinner. A favourite meal here is sweet and sour prawns, greens in garlic, and rice – all for around RM15 a head, including beer. Otherwise, a couple of the **cafés** beside the jetty and on the square do adequate rice and noodle dishes.

River trips from Marudi

The downriver express boat to Kuala Baram leaves hourly between 7.30am and 2.30pm (3hr; RM20). Upriver, boats leave daily at noon for **Long Terawan**, on Sungei Tutoh (4hr; RM20), where there's a connection for **Mulu National Park**, returning the following day at 7.30am. Although most people travel this route specifically to go to the park, on the way you pass a number of traditional Kayan longhouses. An hour from Marudi along the Tutoh, you reach the periphery of the loggers' activities; from here on, the river is clear and the jungle closes in around the riverbanks.

Loagan Bunut National Park

Loagan Bunut National Park (RM10) is an ornithologist's paradise, boasting many species of **birds**, including bittern, stork-billed kingfishers and hornbills. The 100-square-kilometre park, focused around the compact **Tasik Bunut**, is still seldom visited despite having opened in 1991, but the undisturbed forest around the lake promises fine hikes. The accommodation is rudimentary, which may explain why so few people are visiting this inaccessible but quite magical place.

Tucked away on the upper reaches of **Sungai Teru**, a tributary of Sungai Tinjar, Tasik Bunut is no ordinary lake. In the dry-spell months of February, May and June the water level drops drastically, and it's then that a peculiar form of fishing, which the local **Berawan** people call *selambau*, is carried out. Just prior to the whole lake becoming one expanse of dry cracked mud, the fish that haven't escaped down the lake's two watercourses are scooped up into giant spoon-shaped wooden frames in a spectacular action; they even jump into the boats in a lame attempt at escaping their fate. For birds, these months are a perfect time to feed too, and in May and June the surrounding peat-swamp forest supports breeding colonies of many avian species, particularly darters, egrets and herons.

The lake

After only a short while on the lake it's clear how profuse the **birdlife** is, with herons and kingfishers swooping across the tributaries, calling out in flight. Initially the lake can appear huge, its edges hard to detect as the sunlight is often hazy; however, it's only around 500m in width and 1km in length. On the lake are a number of rafts with small cabins built on them, housing Berawan fishermen. Around these homes lie an intricate network of fishing plots, with underwater nets and lines tied to stakes pushed into the lake bed; boats move slowly and carefully around here so as not to get entangled with them. At the southeast corner of the lake is the privately run lodge (see opposite).

The best times to drift by boat across the lake are **early morning** and **dusk** when the birds are at their most active. It's then that you may well see the lumbering gait of a **hornbill** and hear its characteristic, guttural squawk. You can also go **fishing** along Sungai Teru, just east of the lodge, when the river is high. A short **trail** leads from the back of the lodge into the dense jungle, though it very soon becomes hard to follow and it's best not to venture any further without Meran, the lodge owner, as guide. Beyond these activities there is little to do in the park; most visitors adapt to Berawan ways quickly and simply relax, taking in the tranquillity of this beautiful spot which remains a sanctuary of calm in Sarawak's frenzy of development.

Practicalities

Most people get to the park on a **tour** from Miri or by their own transport. Seridan Mulu, one of the two top operators in Miri (see p.493), runs day-trips (RM150) and a three-day, two-night excursion (RM400); the latter gives ample time to explore the lake and its environs.

To get to Loagan Bunut by **public transport**, take the Lapok bus (every 2hr from 7am until 3pm; 2hr 30min; RM10) from the local bus station in Miri (see p.488). The bus terminates in **LAPOK**, a small bazaar town at the junction of Sungai Tinjar and Sungai Teru, 80km south of Miri; on the main street, where the bus drops you, there are a few cafés offering simple **meals** and drinks. From Lapok, the last bus back to Miri leaves at 4pm. To get to the park from Marudi, get the daily 8am boat to Lapok via **Long Lama** (3hr; RM15). Buy any provisions you need in Lapok, as there are no shops in the park; also bring mosquito repellent, as the mosquitoes at the lake are particularly voracious. The remaining 25km of the journey from Lapok to the park cannot be covered by public transport, and you must charter a motorbike or jeep; the cost one-way for the former is RM20 while four-wheel transport is around RM40 per person, but negotiable. Alternatively, contact the parks desk in Miri (☎085/434184) to arrange a pick-up in Lapok.

Once at the park there's just one type of **accommodation**, the forest hostel, which has dorm beds in four seven-bed rooms (RM15 with fan). For reservations, again contact the Miri's parks desk.

Long San and around

LONG SAN, 250km southeast of Miri, is one of the largest **Kenyah** communities on the Baram. It was just 55 years ago that the settlement was established by the Kenyah, who moved here from Long Tikan, 20km upstream, when the agricultural lands there became exhausted. Though not a repository of traditional rituals and beliefs, the Kenyah here are a strong, unified, mostly forward-looking community who are keen to develop a small, manageable tourist industry. Not especially bothered that the rainforest is being stripped around them, they are only too pleased to be no longer isolated from mainstream social and economic development. As well as vastly improved links with other towns (ten years ago it took three days to get to Marudi by longboat; now Lapok is just three hours away by four-wheel-drive, making Marudi easily accessible), they now have a good clinic and an excellent school.

The region around Long San constitutes another compelling reason to travel so far upcountry. Only a few minutes away by longboat is the historic bazaar of **Long Akah**, the shell of its fort somehow highly atmospheric, as if colonial soldiers had only just left. Also nearby, the settled **Penan** community at **Long Beku** offers an insight into the world of Borneo's last hunter-gatherers.

The settlement

There are dozens of longhouse communities on the river, but Long San is in fact more of a small town, which can surprise those who believe Sarawak's indigenous peoples live either just in longhouses or have exchanged traditional life for the modernity and anonymity of the city. In fact, it's a busy, thriving community where you are just as likely to hear dance music blasting from a window as watch an old-timer deliver a long prose poem at a night's revelry. It has a variety of dwellings, including shops, an art gallery and a prominent Catholic church. The village, with around a thousand people, has two distinct sections, one on each side of a small river, Sungai San, a tributary of Batang Baram. Tragically, the community's main living area, a forty-door longhouse, was burnt to the ground. They hope that a replacement will be built by late 2007.

Practicalities

The only way to get to the settlement directly is a five to six-hour drive by Land Cruiser (4WD) along rough logging roads; the *Telang Usan* hotel in Miri offers trips (℡085/411433 for details; RM80 per passenger). You can also take the Miri–Lapok bus (see p.499) and arrange to be picked up from Lapok (2hr; RM50 per passenger when arranged with *Telang Usan*).

There is just one **place to stay** at Long San: an attractive wooden guesthouse close to the river, which serves inclusive meals (❶). Opposite is a shop where you can buy snacks, essential items, cold beer and local firewater. Staff at both the guesthouse and the shop speak some English and can help with arrangements.

Around Long San

A **day-trip** (RM150 per person), booked at the guesthouse in Long San, takes in a nearby **Kayan longhouse**, a **Penan community**, and **Long Akah** and its **fort**, finishing with a **swim** in the rapids upstream. It's also possible to visit isolated longhouses further afield, though this is expensive – around RM200 per day per person – owing to the high cost of buying diesel upriver. The best places to make for are: **Long Mekaba**; a Kayan longhouse two hours upriver, where resident musicians play the lute-like *sape* and traditional dances are sometimes performed; and **Long Moh** and **Long Pallai** (4–5hr away by boat) where the accoutrements of longhouse culture – firewood, chickens, pigs and longboats – are still housed underneath the traditional *belian* building.

The logging road from Lapok continues beyond the turning for Long San, heading east for another 100km or so as far as **Lio Matoh** (see p.516), where it's possible to trek to Bario in the Kelabit Highlands. To charter a Land Cruiser from Long San to Lio Matoh costs RM250.

Long Liam and Long Beku

Twenty minutes down Batang Baram from Long San is the thirty-door Kayan longhouse of **LONG LIAM**. Along the way, the longboat passes *laran* trees whose large white flowers drop into the water and are eaten by the fish which the Kenyah and Kayan net. The longhouse, which houses 150 people, is 50 years old; its inhabitants, many of whom originally came from Sungai Akah, near Long Akah, grow rice, tapioca, maize and sweetcorn in fields close by Long Liam. Their diet is supplemented with wild fruits from the jungle, and *kuman babi* (wild pig), which is plentiful in the forest. The only other building of note here is a small school staffed by three teachers giving lessons in Malay and Kayan.

Another two hours along the river is the **Penan** community at **LONG BEKU**. The Penan here – who are extremely poor in stark contrast to the nearby Kayan and Kenyah – have been in the area for around 55 years, using

Beku as a base while they hunt wild boar and cut sago. Some members of the community derive an income from making *parang*s (machetes), and you may well see them smelting the iron, then slotting the blade into a wooden handle before sharpening it on a lathe.

Long Akah

In the nineteenth century, **LONG AKAH** was a vital trading post supplying the whole of the upriver region. Sarawak's Resident was once based here, the settlement's fort permanently garrisoned, and its pretty little cottages, with their well-tended gardens, once used by colonial officers and civil servants on missions into the territory. Now, Long Akah is decaying, the superb *belian* shingle roof of the vast barn-like centrepiece building – the former storehouse – seemingly collapsing a little more with every tropical storm. Still, the place is redolent of history: to walk along its overgrown concrete path alongside white, wooden bungalows is to revisit a tropical outpost of Empire. Nowadays employees of Sarawak's Agricultural Department reside here, supplying farmers with pesticides, fertilizers, seeds and know-how.

Accessible now only by a five-minute river trip is Long Akah's once-impressive **fort**, overlooking a spur on Batang Baram. Now dilapidated, this spacious building started life as the furthest outpost of the Brookes' security apparatus. Unless funds are put aside to preserve this magnificent, whitewashed wooden structure the place will soon collapse.

Mulu National Park

Located deep in the rainforest, **MULU** is Sarawak's premier **national park** and largest conservation zone, and is now listed as a UNESCO World Heritage Site. Featuring thousands of animal and plant species encased in spectacular scenery with extensive cave systems, some little explored, it is a must on everyone's Sarawak itinerary. Until 1992, when commercial flights began, Mulu was accessible only by a full-day journey from Marudi along the Baram, Tutoh and Melinau rivers. The region has been a magnet for explorers and scientists since the nineteenth century. Quite apart from the park's primary rainforest, which is characterized by clear rivers and high-altitude vegetation, there are three mountains dominated by dramatically eroded features, including dozens of fifty-metre-high razor-sharp limestone spikes – known as the **Pinnacles** – on Gunung Api; there's also the largest limestone **cave system** in the world, much of which is still being explored. The two major hikes, to the Pinnacles and to the summit of **Gunung Mulu**, are daunting, but the reward is stupendous views of the rainforest, stretching as far as Brunei.

Most of the world's limestone landscapes have been modified by glaciation within the last two million years. Mulu predates this period considerably (the region was formed over twenty million years ago) and has been weathered by a combination of rainfall, rivers and high temperatures, but never by ice. The caves, which penetrate deep into the mountains, were formed by running water and are ancient: the oldest formed around five million years ago, the youngest during the last fifty thousand years. The surface water driving down the slopes of Mulu has eroded vast amounts of material, shaping the landscape outside, as well as carving cave passages within, dividing the great chunks of limestone into separate mountains.

Modern **explorers** have been coming to Mulu for a century and a half, starting in the 1850s with Spenser St John, who wrote inspiringly about the region in his book *Life in the Forests of the Far East*, though he didn't reach the summit of Gunung Mulu. A more successful bid was launched in 1932 when the explorer Lord Edward Shackleton got to the top during a research trip organized by Tom Harrisson, who would later become the curator of the Sarawak Museum. After his successful ascent, Shackleton wrote that:

Although it was steep, the going during the first day or two was comparatively good, for the forest still consisted of big timber rising to a height of over one hundred feet. But it grew colder and soon we entered at around four thousand feet that extraordinary phenomenon, the moss forest. Sometimes we found ourselves plunging deeper and deeper, not knowing whether we were walking on the top of the wood or on the forest floor and occasionally having to cut tunnels through the squelching moss.

In 1976, a Royal Geographical Society expedition put forward a quite overwhelming case for designating the region a national park, based on studies of the flora, fauna, caves, rivers and overall tourist potential. Over 250km of the caves have now been explored, yet experts believe this is only around thirty percent of the total.

Practicalities

Many people visit Mulu National Park (RM10; ℡085/432561, ⓌWww .mulupark.com) as part of a package offered by **tour operators** such as Miri's Seridan Mulu (see p.493) or one of the Kuching-based companies (see p.441). These can be quite reasonable (RM500 for three days/two nights) but shop around as prices differ. If you are travelling to the park independently remember that with improved accessibility it has now become essential to **book accommodation** at Park Headquarters (HQ) well ahead, whether direct with the parks management or at the main parks desks at the Visitors' Information Centres in Miri, Kuching or Sibu. If you need to share costs you may choose to join a group, in which case the useful noticeboard and helpful staff at the parks office should be your first port of call. As a rule of thumb, if you visit independently as a group of two to four people, you will pay less than on an organized tour arranged with an operator, but allow yourself an extra day at the beginning of the visit to explore options and prices. Try to avoid arriving at the weekend or on a public holiday when the park is at its busiest; if you do, it's absolutely vital to have secured accommodation before coming.

Whether you're here independently or as part of a group, you won't be able to avoid shelling out for **boat travel** within the park. For a group of up to four people prices range from RM25 per person for the return trip from HQ to Clearwater and Wind caves; and up to RM85 for the return trip to Kuala Birar, for the Pinnacles.

Equipment

Among the **equipment** you will need are: comfortable walking shoes with a good tread; sun hat; swimming gear; a poncho/rain sheet; torch; mosquito repellent; headache pills; salt solution; ointment for bites; and a basic first-aid kit. Check with the park office if you'll need a sleeping bag and mat for any trek you intend to do. On the trails it's best to wear light clothing – shorts or loose trousers and T-shirts – rather than fully cover the body; this way, if the conditions are wet, it'll be easier to see any leeches that might be

Guiding costs

Although guide fees below look steep, it is important to note that quality guiding is essential as the park lies over a vast area and weather can change very quickly and dramatically. Guides can be picked up at Park Headquarters.

The minimum **guiding costs** for a group of up to five people (more for each extra person) are as follows:

The Pinnacles
3 days/2 nights; RM400

Mulu summit
4 days/3 nights; RM1000

Garden of Eden
Half-day; RM200

Adventure caving
Clearwater Cave; RM300
Lang's Caves; RM100 per person

As well as the **park fee** (RM10), there is an extra charge of RM10 for staying at any of Camps 1, 3, 4 or 5, and a RM4 fee for visiting the Deer/Lang's Caves and the Wind/Clearwater Caves.

clinging to you. For the Pinnacles, Gunung Mulu and Head-hunters' Trail, bring long trousers and long-sleeved shirts for the dusk insect assault, and for the occasional cool nights.

Getting to the park

There are twice-daily Twin Otter and Fokker **flights** to Mulu from Miri (RM84) and one daily back and forth from KK (RM179). It's essential to **book** well ahead, as flights get full far in advance.

Reaching Mulu by **boat from Marudi** involves a number of stages and takes much of the day, but is a pleasant trip nonetheless. The express boat leaves at noon for Long Terawan (RM20) on Sungai Tutoh. When the river is low, this may only go as far as Long Panai (RM12), from where you can take a shallower longboat (RM10) to Long Terawan. It takes about three hours to reach Long Terawan where you switch to a longboat (RM55) for the final two-hour trip into Tutoh's tributary, Sungai Melinau, and then on to the park headquarters. It is along the Melinau that the scenery really becomes breathtaking, the multiple greens of the forest deepening in the early-evening light, the peaks of Gunung Mulu and Api peeping through a whirl of mist. The return trip requires getting up at 5am to get the boat to Long Terawan in time for the next stage on to Marudi at 7.30am. Give the Berawan boatmen at Park HQ ample warning (two days) that you want to be on the early morning ride.

Another way of accessing the park by boat is from the north, setting off from **Nanga Medamit** and travelling up the Sungai Medalan, a tributary of the Limbang, a route known as the **Head-hunters' Trail**. Along the way, you pass Iban longhouses at Melaban and Bala, as well as the rangers' lodge at Mentawai. The boat trip from Nanga Medamit costs around RM100 to **Kuala Terikan**, from which it's a one-hour hike into the park. For details of getting to Nanga Medamit from Limbang Town, see p.494; for information on leaving the park by this route, see p.508.

Arrival

The **airstrip** is 500m east of Park HQ. Vans ferry people either to the HQ or to the *Royal Mulu Resort* (RM3 for each; RM5 from HQ back to airport). **Longboats** from Long Terawan drop you straight at HQ. Upon

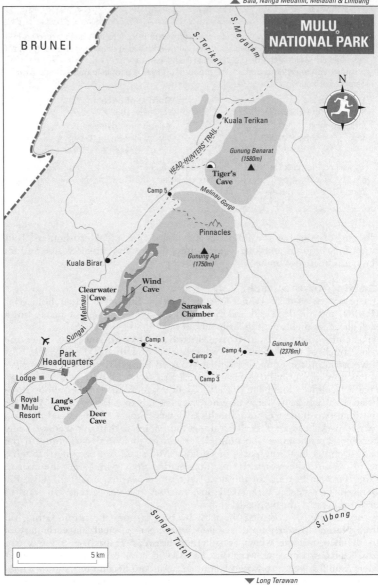

arrival at the HQ (office open daily 7am–8pm) you must sign in and pay the RM10 park fee.

Accommodation and eating

Accommodation must be booked ahead, either at the Visitors' Information Centre in Miri or with the Park HQ directly, by email or preferably telephone. Opposite the park headquarters, on the other side of the padang, you'll find various lodges, offering a range from dorm beds (RM18) to two-bed en-suite rooms (❸). Also within the main building, with a large veranda sitting area, is the *Mulu Café* (daily 8am–11pm), serving a wide range of **meals**, with good vegetarian options, fresh fish, rice and noodles. Breakfasts are particularly enticing with eggs and pancakes the standout options. Beside the canteen a small **shop** sells just the sort of foodstuffs you'll want while trekking – nuts, chocolate, fruit and biscuits. Across the bridge stretching from the park headquarters are a few other places which undercut the park café and have the added attraction of selling beer (the park is dry): *Sipan Café* and *Mulu Canteen,* which both serve Western and Asian meals (RM8), breakfasts, packed lunches and drinks; and *Jowels'*, 50m further back on the road towards the airport, which has some of the best retail *tuak* in Sarawak, at knockout prices too (RM20 for a large bottle), as well as simple meals (RM8).

The other main place to stay is a chic jungle hideaway, the lavish *Royal Mulu Resort* (☎085/790100, ⓦwww.royalmuluresort.com; ❽) situated 2km further down the road from the airport, and like the PH, on the banks of the Melinau – it can also be reached on a five-minute boat ride. Elevated on stilts to protect it from flooding during the lashing monsoon rains, the resort has a stylish, longhouse-style entrance, small swimming pool and large coffee house which serves decent Western and Malaysian food, though at rather inflated prices, while its hundreds of self-contained chalets all have balconies, large bathrooms, TVs and minibars.

The Park

Everyone's itinerary at Mulu includes visits to the **show caves**, and if you're fit and have time to stay for more than two days in the park, it should include scaling the **Pinnacles** as well. More specialist are the four-day trek to **Gunung Mulu** itself, and **adventure caving**, both of which will push out the budget significantly.

The show caves

Only four of the 25 caves so far explored in Mulu are open to visitors – Deer Cave, Lang's Cave, Wind Cave and Clearwater Cave. As these so-called **show caves** are Mulu's most popular attractions, they can sometimes get quite crowded, and there's the occasional log jam along the plankway to the two closest to park headquarters, Deer Cave and Lang's Cave.

Deer and Lang's Caves

The most immediately impressive cave in the park is **Deer Cave**, the nearest to the headquarters, which contains the largest cave passage in the world. Once inhabited by deer, which used to shelter in its cavernous reaches, Deer Cave would have been known to the Berawan and Penan but was never used for burial purposes, unlike the smaller caves dotted around the park. From the headquarters, there's a well-marked three-kilometre plankway to the cave, which runs through a peat-swamp forest and passes an ancient Penan burial cave in which were found fragmented skulls, now in the Sarawak Museum. Inside, the cave passage is over 2km long and 174m high, while up above, hundreds of thousands of bats live in the cave's nooks and crannies. Also numerous are the cave's swiftlets, who navigate and identify their nests – cup-shaped homes made from threads of saliva – using the cave's echoes. Birds'-nest gatherers climb up the cave shafts to extract the nests, which sell in the outside world for the same price per kg as silver.

After an hour, the path through the cave leads to an area where a large hole in the roof allows light to penetrate. Here, in the so-called **Garden of Eden**, scientists of the 1976 Royal Geographical Society expedition discovered luxuriant vegetation that had been undisturbed for centuries; the leader, Robin Hanbury-Tenison, noted that "even the fish were tame and gathered in shoals around a hand dipped in the water". It's an incredible spot: plants battle for the light, birds and insects celebrate the warm air, giant ferns grow in clusters around rocks and families of grey-leaf monkeys scuttle about unafraid.

The best – and the busiest – time to visit Deer Cave is in the late afternoon: wait around the cave entrance at dusk and you'll usually see the vast swarms of bats – up to three million – streaming out in a protective doughnut-shaped formation into the darkening skies, off in search of food.

Close to the Deer Cave entrance is the entrance to **Lang's Cave** (named after the local guide who first found it), the smallest of the show caves; its weird and wonderful rock formations, most spectacularly the curtain stalactites and coral-like growths – helictites – gripping the curved walls. Although a round trip to Deer and Lang can easily be accomplished in under three hours, if you have time, an extra one or two hours should be added on for the Garden of Eden.

Clearwater and Wind Caves

Probing some 107km through Mulu's substratum, the **Clearwater Cave system**, thought to be the longest in Southeast Asia, is reached by a fifteen-minute longboat journey along Sungai Melinau from the park headquarters. The longboats moor at a small jungle pool, after which the cave is named, at the base of the two-hundred-step climb to the cave mouth. Discovered in 1988, the cave tunnels here weave deep into the mountain; ordinary visitors can only explore the small section close to the entrance, where lighting has been installed along a walkway leading 300m on to **Young Lady's Cave**, which ends abruptly in a fifty-metre-deep pothole. Deep inside the main body of the cave is the subterranean **Clearwater River**, which flows through a five-kilometre passage reaching heights and widths of as much as 90m. En route to Clearwater Cave, most visitors halt at the comparatively small **Wind Cave**, which contains a great variety of golden, contorted

△ Deer Cave

rock shapes, stalactites and stalagmites, best appreciated in the subtly illuminated King's Room. It's another five minutes from Wind Cave to Clearwater Cave, whether by boat or via the walkway joining them; the alternative is to indulge in some adventure-caving and trek between them, an exhausting and muddy five-hour trip involving lots of wading and swimming in the icy Clearwater River. Wind Cave and Clearwater Cave can be combined with a trip to or from the Pinnacles.

Batu Bungan

Most tour operators' show cave itineraries include a stop at a nearby Penan settlement, **Batu Bungan**, where handicrafts are available. The Penan here have been forcibly settled by the government and have been equipped with a school to help the youngsters at least adjust to non-nomadic modernity. Although some of the crafts are beautifully made, the short stop is unlikely to be a highlight of any trip to Mulu as the whole experience feels rather forced.

The Pinnacles and around

Five million years ago, a constant splatter of raindrops dissolved Gunung Api's limestone and carved out the **Pinnacles** – 50-metre high shards, with the sharpness of Samurai swords – from a solid block of rock. The erosion is still continuing and the entire region is pockmarked with deep shafts penetrating far into the heart of the mountain: one-third of Gunung Api has already been washed away and in perhaps another ten million years the whole of it will disappear. Getting a good view of the Pinnacles requires an almost masochistically demanding **ascent** up the south face of Gunung Api to a ridge 1200m up the mountain. Once there, it's impossible not to be over-awed by the sheer size and grandeur of the Pinnacles. At that height in such a volatile jungle climate, conditions can alter within minutes – piercing sun can be replaced by billowing clouds, and tumultuous rain can follow moments later. Most treks reach the top in late morning as the weather is more prone to change in the afternoon. Beware that the climb is tough and must not be underestimated. Some tour operators are being economical with the truth when they describe the climb as "moderate" – to the less than fully fit, climbing to the Pinnacles can be extraordinarily taxing, if not quite on a par with Gunung Kinabalu in Sabah. Your guide will recommend that you bring at least two litres of water each; other than snacks, carry little else or you'll be too weighed down. Wear light clothing, a hat, and waterproof shoes or boots with grip.

Day 1: To Camp 5

From the park headquarters, the first part of the trip to the Pinnacles is an hour-long journey by longboat upstream along Sungai Melinau; you may have to help pull the boat through the rapids if the water level is very low. After mooring at Kuala Birar, there's a two-and-a-half-hour trek through lowland forest to reach **Camp 5**, which is beautifully situated on the edge of the river. The large, open-plan one-storey building has around half a dozen rooms with raised platforms for sleeping and a communal eating area at one end with a kitchen behind.

Here you're close to the Melinau Gorge, across which nearby **Gunung Api** (1750m) and **Gunung Benarat** (1580m) cast long shadows in the fading afternoon light. A bridge straddles the river here – the path that disappears into the jungle on the other side is the first stage of the Headhunters' Trail (see p.508).

Day 2: The ascent

The next morning, trekkers retrace their steps 50m along the track and turn left onto a path at the base of the mountain which at times nearly disappears among tree roots and slippery limestone debris. The trail is honeycombed with holes and passages through which rainwater immediately disappears. After two hours' uphill climb, during which you will have rested on numerous occasions, a striking vista opens up: the rainforest stretches below as far as the eye can see, and wispy clouds drift along your line of vision. The climb gets even tougher as you scramble between sharp rocks at steeper gradients, but fatigue will give way to appreciation when the high trees give way to **moss forest**, where pitcher plants feed on insects, and ants and squirrels dart in and out among the roots of trees.

The last thirty minutes of the climb is almost a sheer vertical manoeuvre, painful and exhausting. Nineteen ladders, thick pegs and ropes help you on this final ascent; just when your limbs are finally giving way, you arrive at the top of the **ridge** that overlooks the Pinnacles. The ridge is itself a pinnacle, although sited across a ravine from the main cluster, and if you tap the rocks around you, they reverberate because of the large holes in the limestone underneath. The vegetation here is sparse, but includes the balsam plant, which has pale pink flowers, and pitcher plants. After taking in the stunning sight of the dozens of fifty-metre-high grey-limestone shapes, jutting out from their perch in an unreachable hollow on the side of the mountain, it's time for the return slog, which many people find harder on the legs and nerves – it takes three to four hours, or even longer when the route is particularly slippery. Once back at the camp, most people rest, swim, eat and sleep, preferring to start the return trip to park headquarters the following day, though it's possible to stay longer and explore the area.

Days 3 & 4: Walks from Camp 5

Some people opt to leave early on day three for the return journey back to camp but others prefer to go on a few undemanding treks from Camp 5. From the camp, a two-hour round-trip takes you along the path that follows the river further upstream and ends below the **Melinau Gorge**, where two vertical walls of rock rise 100m above the river, which emerges from a crevice. There's nowhere other than slippery rocks to rest and admire this beautiful spot before you return to Camp 5.

Another short trail leads to the base of **Gunung Benarat** and to the lower shaft of **Tiger's Cave**, a return trip of around three hours. Once across the bridge, turn left to get onto the so-called **Head-hunters' Trail**, from which the trail to the cave branches off after about a kilometre. A third, much longer option is to follow the Head-hunters' Trail all the way out of the park to **Limbang**, a route supposedly traced by Kayan war parties in days gone by. Once over the bridge you turn left and walk along a wide trail passing a large rock, Batu Rikan, after around 4km. From here the trail is clearly marked to **Kuala Terikan**, two hours (5km) away, a small Berawan settlement on the banks of Sungai Terikan, where you'll find basic hut accommodation. The trail continues for three hours to Sungai Medalam, where you can stay at an Iban longhouse, Rumah Bala Lesong. The next day, you take a longboat (2hr; RM50) to Nanga Medamit, where buses go to Limbang Town, arriving in the late afternoon. This is a particularly good route for those wanting to get to Brunei from Mulu, as boats run frequently from Limbang to Muara port in the sultanate.

The trek to Gunung Mulu

The route to the summit of **Gunung Mulu** (2376m) was first discovered in the 1920s by Tama Nilong, a Berawan rhinoceros-hunter. Earlier explorers hadn't been able to find a way around the huge surrounding cliffs, but Nilong discovered the southwest ridge trail by following rhinoceros tracks, enabling Lord Shackleton in 1932 to become the first mountaineer to reach the summit. It's still an arduous climb, as much of the route is very steep, and few visitors to Mulu Park undertake it. Park guides will argue against setting out if the weather is very wet; **book** ahead by email or telephone if you are thinking of undertaking it.

Day 1: To Camp 1

The first stage is from park headquarters to Camp 1, an easy three-hour walk on a flat trail which crosses from the park's prevalent limestone plain to the

Hornbills

Hornbills are those bizarre, almost prehistoric-looking, inhabitants of tropical forests, whose presence (or absence) is an important ecological indicator of the health of the forest. You should have little difficulty in identifying hornbills: they are large, black-and-white birds with disproportionately huge bills (often bent downwards), topped with an ornamental **casque** – a generally hollow structure attached to the upper mandible. The function of the casque is unknown, though it's thought it may play a role in attracting a mate and in courtship ceremonies. In addition to this, the birds have a long tail and broad wings which produce a loud whooshing sound as they glide and flap across the forest canopy.

Hornbills are heavily dependent upon large forest trees for **nesting**, using natural tree cavities as nest sites. The female seals herself into the cavity by plastering up the entrance to the nest hole with a combination of mud, tree bark and wood dust. This prevents snakes, civets, squirrels and other potential predators from raiding the nest. She spends up to three months here, totally dependent on the male bird to provide her and her offspring with a diet of fruit (mainly figs), insects and small forest animals by means of a narrow slit in the plaster wall. When the young bird (there's only one per brood) is old enough to fly, the female breaks open the mud wall to emerge back into the forest. Given the hornbill's nesting habits, it is essential that large, undisturbed, good-quality tracts of forest are retained in order to secure their future. Sadly, hornbill populations in many parts of Asia have declined or been driven to the point of extinction by human encroachment, over hunting and deforestation.

Ten of the world's 46 species of hornbill are found in Malaysia, many of them endangered or present only in small, isolated populations. Two of the most commonly seen species are the pied hornbill and the black hornbill. The **pied hornbill** can be identified by its white abdomen and tail, and white wingtips in flight. Apparently more tolerant of forest degradation than other species, it's the smallest hornbill you're likely to see, reaching only 75cm in length. Outside breeding season, it gathers in noisy flocks which are generally heard well before they are seen. The **black hornbill** is only slightly larger and black, save for the white tips of the outer tail feathers (some individuals also show a white patch behind the eye). Among the larger species of hornbill found in Malaysia are the **helmeted hornbill** and the **rhinoceros hornbill**, both over 120cm in length, mainly black, but with white tails and bellies. The rhinoceros hornbill has a bright orange rhino-horn-shaped casque (hence the name), whereas the helmeted hornbill has a bright red head, neck and helmet-shaped casque. The call of the helmeted hornbill is a remarkable series of "took" notes which start off slowly and then accelerate to reach a ringing crescendo of cackles.

Good places to spot hornbills in East Malaysia are Mulu National Park, Sabah's Danum Valley and Mount Kinabalu National Park.

sandstone terrain of Gunung Mulu. En route, hornbills fly low over the jungle canopy and, if you watch the trail carefully, you may see wild boar and mouse-deer tracks. The first night is usually spent at Camp 1, which is no more than a hut in poor condition; sleeping bags are placed on raised wooden platforms and your guide prepares food.

Day 2: Into the moss forest

Day two comprises a hard, ten-hour, uphill slog; there are two resting places, referred to rather confusedly as Camps 1 & 2, on the way where you can wash your tired limbs in small rock pools. From here onwards you're in a moss forest, where small openings in the canopy reveal lovely views of the park. The next part of the trail is along Nilong's southwest ridge, a series of small hills manoeuvred via a narrow, twisting path. When the rain has been heavy, there are lots of little swamps to negotiate; one known as "Rhino's Lake" because it was here that what was thought to be the last rhinoceros in the area was shot in the 1950s. You will stay the night at Camp 4's hut, 1800m up, which can be cool so you'll need a sleeping bag.

Day 3: To the summit

Most climbers set off well before dawn for the hard ninety-minute trek from Camp 4 to the **summit**, if possible timing their arrival to coincide with sunrise. At dawn itself, the forest wakes up, the insect and bird chorus reverberating in the thin, high-altitude air. After an hour's climb you pass an overgrown heli-copter pad. On the final stretch there are big clumps of pitcher plants, though it's easy to miss them as by this point you are hauling yourself up by ropes onto the cold, windswept, craggy peak. From here, the view is exhilarating, looking down on Gunung Api and, on a clear day, far across the forest to Brunei Bay. Sungai Melinau can also just be made out, a pencil-thin wavy light-brown line, bisecting the deep-green density of the forest carpet.

Day 4: Back to Camp 1

In good conditions it's just about possible to do the **return leg** from the summit to park headquarters in one day, omitting a return night at Camp 3; but the trip, which can't be done in less than twelve hours, is exhausting. The red-and-white marks on the trees at least make the trail easier to follow in fading light.

The Kelabit Highlands

Along the border with Kalimantan and 100km southeast of Gunung Mulu, the long, high plateau of the **Kelabit Highlands** has been the home of the Kelabit people for hundreds of years. Western explorers had no idea of the existence of this self-sufficient mountain community until the beginning of the twentieth century, when Brooke officials made a few brief visits. But the Highlands were (literally) not put on the map until World War II, when British and Austral-ian commandos, led by Major Tom Harrisson (who later became curator of the Sarawak Museum in Kuching), used a number of Kelabit settlements as bases for waging a guerrilla war against the occupying Japanese forces. After parachuting into the forest, Harrisson and his team were taken to the largest longhouse in the area, in the village of **Bario**, to meet the chief, with whose help Harrisson set out to contact the region's other ethnic groups. Within twelve months, Harrisson was in a position to convince the Allied Command in Manila that the tribes were thirsty for retaliation against their occupiers.

Before Harrisson's men built the airstrip at Bario, trekking over the inhospitable terrain was the only way to get here – it took two weeks from Marudi to the west, which required hacking through moss forests and circumnavigating sharp limestone hills and savage gorges. It was another seven days through similar conditions to the furthest navigable point on Batang Baram, **Lio Matoh**, just off the edge of the plateau. After the war, missionaries arrived and converted the animist Kelabit to Christianity, with the consequence that many of their traditions, like burial rituals and wild parties called *iraus* (where Chinese jars full of rice wine were consumed) disappeared. What's more, the magnificent Kelabit **megaliths** associated with these traditions were soon swallowed by the jungle: the dolmens, along with urns, rock carvings and ossuaries used in funereal processes, were mostly lost to the elements. Among the carvings, those of human faces celebrated feats of valour, like a successful head-hunting expedition, and birds were also popular images – a motif that still survives in the bead- and craftwork of neighbouring ethnic groups. Now the four most populous Kelabit settlements – Bario, **Long Lellang** to the southwest, **Long Banga** to the south and **Ba Kelalan** to the north – have regular air service in Twin Otter and Fokker planes, giving the highland people the chance of daily contact with the world beyond, and curious tourists the opportunity to visit them with relative ease.

For all the recent contact, the highlands remain a gloriously unspoiled region, with dazzlingly vivid flora, abundant game and a cool refreshing

climate. Not surprisingly, these factors have made it a popular target for walkers, attracted by jungle **treks** and the prospect of encountering friendly local people, many of whom live in sturdy **longhouses** (a visit to which is an unmissable part of any trip here) surrounded by their livestock, fruit trees and wet paddy fields. The Kelabit aren't as concerned as the Iban or Kayan with formality; when you turn up at a longhouse and attract the attention of an adult inhabitant, you're inevitably invited in, soon after which the chief will arrive and take charge, urging you to eat with his family and (probably) insisting that you stay in his rooms. If you're here to stay with prior acquaintances, no harm is done by turning the chief down and staying with them. However, it's essential to hire a **guide** (see opposite) for any trip longer than the overnight treks from Bario centre to nearby longhouses and settlements. Guides are usually related to members of the longhouses, solving the matter of where and with whom to stay, and can be hired in the centres of Bario and Ba Kelalan.

Bario and around

The centre of the Kelabit Highlands is the village of **BARIO**, approximately 15km west of the border with Indonesian Kalimantan, and a few days' hard hike from Long Lellang to the south or Ba Kelalan to the north. It's a small, widely dispersed but busy community with a number of distinct settlements, set among the plateau's rolling hills and surrounded by rice fields. With no land-line telephones – though there is irregular mobile reception – and few motorized vehicles, the pace of life is slow, the tranquillity disturbed only by arriving planes. The isolated mountain region is now online, however – the E-Bario project, based in Bario's new Telecentre block receives its satellite connection from solar panel; visit Ⓦwww.ebario.com or Ⓦwww.kelabit.net for information on Kelabit culture and the region. Also in the Telecentre is an Internet café (daily except Sun noon–5pm; RM10 per hr).

Practicalities

There are two daily FAX **flights** from Miri (RM70), one from Marudi (RM55) and twice-weekly flights to Ba Kelalan. The planes bring in a slow drip of new arrivals, most of whom are returning locals that have been working away or have collected goods and provisions. The planes don't land when the weather's bad so it's entirely possible to get stuck in Bario; so bring funds to stay a day or two longer than you intended, as there are no banks. Trying to get on the flight from Miri in the first place can be hard, as Kelabits tend to book ahead and the 18-seat Twin Otter flights fill up quickly: if you can't get a seat, the best practice currently is to ask to be put on the reserve list and call back regularly the day before you want to fly. If you're still unsuccessful, go to Miri or Marudi airport early, and queue for standby. The same applies on leaving Bario. This system may change as AirAsia takes up MAS's old routes – check the airline's website or contact the Miri office for up-to-date information.

Bario's **airport** is 2km away to the east of Bario, at **Padang Pasir**. There is a paved road, built in 2004, which goes from town to the airport, but no taxis; most visitors ride pillion on a motorbike (RM3) to get into town. As well as the airport road there are some unpaved tracks to six nearby villages, though these are accessible only by 4WD. The furthest village accessible by road is just six kilometres away; all the other arteries hacked out of the highland forest and shrub are jungle trails, used by locals, trekkers and buffalo alike.

Accommodation

Bario region now has several places to stay, all very cheap and of a high standard. Most are in the dispersed settlement's centre, but a couple are along lanes in the bush. See also below for the beautiful *Gem's Lodge.*

Bariew Guesthouse Reddish Place, Jalan Bario ℰ reddisharan@hotmail.com. Three hundred metres past the shops away from the airport, this recently opened guesthouse is the best option in town, with twenty clean rooms with mosquito nets, a shared sitting room, and communal showers and toilets. The price includes breakfast, lunch and dinner – the food is delicious – and owner Reddish is a great Kelabit enthusiast. ❷

Bario Asal Homestay Bario Asal ⓦ www.kelabit .net. Located in a village 2km west of Bario centre, this place offers the opportunity to sleep in a Kelabit longhouse and eat communally (the price includes food) with guide Peter Matu's family; send email though the website to book. ❸

De Plateau Lodge ℰ deplateau@hotmail.com. Three kilometres east of Bario centre, on the way to Pa Umor, lies Douglas Munney's compound which comprises seven rooms. Munney specializes in birdwatching trips nearby, and is a fount of knowledge on Kelabit culture and lands. Meals cost RM10. ❶

Labang's Longhouse ☎ 016/895 2102, ℰ ncbario@yahoo.com. One kilometre east of Bario centre, this 17-room longhouse has been built for use by visitors instead of local Kelabits, and is well suited to groups; three daily meals available for RM40. ❷

Tarawe's Jalan Bario ℰ jtarawe@bario.net. Very chilled place where you'll awake to the sounds of cockerels and pigs. Its four rooms have three beds in each, with extra mats to accommodate bigger groups if necessary. Inexpensive, hearty meals are available too, including wild boar (occasionally), ferns in garlic, rice and other seasonal dishes (around RM10 per meal); Coffee, Milo, tea crackers, peanut butter and jam always available. ❶

Eating

Most visitors eat in the guesthouses listed above, although there are three **cafés** in Bario centre, if you want to eat out. The best, *Café Batu Lawi* sells acceptable noodle and rice dishes. There is also a small café in the airport at Padang Pasir which sells hot and soft drinks, biscuits and cakes; everyone ends up going here when the flights are inevitably delayed because of weather conditions.

Guides

Guides are vital for any trip of longer than two days, and are usually attached to the guesthouses. At *Tarawe's* you'll find Wilson Bala (ℰ wilsonbala@hotmail .com), an expert in jungle survival, while another exceptional guide is Jaman Riboh, a former high-school teacher who specializes in nature trips where he'll point out plants and wildlife. Riboh also runs *Gem's Lodge*, a guesthouse on the river at Pa Umor. Good guides will estimate the fitness of those in the group and set the trekking pace accordingly. The trips should involve, whenever possible, gathering wild vegetables, catching fish and cooking, Kelabit-style, on the campfire. The usual rate to hire a guide is from RM80 per day for one person down to RM60 each if a larger group.

Day-trips from Bario

A good way to acclimatize to the high-altitude conditions is to embark on short treks from Bario – the two-and-a-half hour stroll to the longhouse at **Pa Umor** is especially rewarding. Go back towards the airport and after 600m fork left up a hill. A kilometre along here, at the point where the road snakes away downhill, take a narrow track to your left. Two kilometres down this buffalo track – look out for the small boulder marking the spot halfway along on the right – and off to your right is the *Gem's Lodge*, seemingly magically tucked away in a small wood. The large wooden building has four double bedrooms and a chalet with an additional two en-suite bedrooms (☎019/8553546, ✉gems_lodge@yahoo.com food RM20 a day; ❸).

Just 100m past the *Gem's* turning you reach the settlement **Pa Umor**. The village is centred on a longhouse with a neat, tiny church beside it. These days most visitors stay in *Gem's* rather than the longhouse, but it used to be a very popular stopover with a reputation for great food and parties. No one should pass through without stopping in to say hello – the best time to call being early evening when everyone's back from the fields. From here the path leads past the fork to the Kalimantan frontier post at **Lembudud** (four hours' walk away) and over a precarious bridge, past remnants of an earlier longhouse, into a lovely copse, from where there are fine views of the lush highlands. Watch out for a right fork along a buffalo track, which leads into a thick, aromatic forest. At the end of this path is one of only two functioning **salt licks**, a natural spot where salt is in abundance making it a good spot to watch animals. Extracting fine, grey salt from the muddy water at the bottom of the small well is a traditional Kelabit industry which goes back centuries, (though with imported salt readily available, it's seldom practised nowadays). The salt is then cooked and dried, and heaved back on the narrow trail to the longhouses.

Another longhouse, **Pa Ukat**, lies a pleasant forty-minute walk along the main buffalo track past Pa Umor. A twenty-minute stroll west of Bario, along the road adjacent to the airstrip, will take you to one of the larger longhouses in the area, the hilltop **Ullong Pallang**. The residents' grandparents decamped here from Pa Main (see opposite) during the Konfrontasi.

South of Bario

The Kelabit longhouses of **Ramudu, Pa Dalih** and **Long Dano**, where it's possible to stay, can be linked up in the **Bario Loop**, a demanding four- or five-day trek through secondary forest that starts and finishes in Bario. From Ramudu, it's possible to continue for the gruelling six- to eight-day trip south on the **Harrisson trail** to the Batang Baram settlement of **Lio Matoh**.

The Bario Loop

Tracing the **Bario Loop** is the perfect way to experience the natural beauty and attractive longhouses of the Kelabit Highlands. The clockwise loop described below takes you in a rough oval through the settlements of Kampung Baru, Long Dano, Pa Dalih, Ramudu and Pa Berang. All walkers stop over in Long Dano, Ramudu and Pa Berang, and many also spend an extra night at Pa Dalih. Although some sections of the journey (Long Dano to Pa Dalih, for instance) are easier to follow than others you must still hire a **guide**. The cost shouldn't be more than RM400 for five days – check with your guide if it's the form to pay RM10–20 courtesy charge at the longhouses you stay at in order to cover food and lodging. Comfortable shoes with a good grip are essential, as are waterproofs and a light pack.

The first leg is the nine-hour slog from Bario to Long Dano. The initial route is across the airfield and along a wide, stream-side track to the long-house settlement of **Kampung Baru**, which appears some 45 minutes later. One kilometre beyond the settlement, you follow a path to the left over a wobbly steel-and-bamboo bridge, which leads onto a narrow, undulating buffalo path. If it's been raining, mud will have collected in troughs along the route; on occasions you may have to wade through the mud. The path weaves up and down the sides of the hills and occasionally drops into the mud pools which provide bathing holes for the buffalo, the most valuable livestock of the Kelabit. There are several resting places en route; you'll see Kelabit families carrying produce back and forth to Bario, including generators and rolls of wire to bring electricity to isolated longhouses. Four or five hours out of Kampung Baru, you'll pass through the area where the longhouse of **Pa Main** used to stand, until its residents relocated to the Bario settlements of Pa Ramapuh and Ullong Pallang during the uncertain times of the Konfrontasi. Your guide should be able to lead you to the hillside site of the British Army outpost that oversaw Pa Main, where empty shell canisters and other such detritus remain to this day.

Long Dano

From here, another three hours' walking brings you to the Kelabit longhouse community of **Long Dano**, which nestles in fields beside a small brook, with the forest crowding in around. Visitors spend most of their time on the communal bamboo veranda, from where you can see tiny apartments, one for each family. Below the veranda are storerooms for the stocks of rice, other grains and fried fish. A Christian community, Long Dano incorporates a Methodist church and even a tiny shop. The settlement is surrounded by tended fields, the river nearby is full of fish and game is abundant. Jobs like rice harvesting, mat-making and textile-weaving are dictated by the time of year – the rice-growing cycle starts in August with the clearing and planting of the fields and the crop is harvested in February. After the hard labour required in processing the rice, the Kelabit women turn their attention to crafts and the men to hunting or fishing, going on trips to other longhouses or to big towns like Miri and Marudi. Some Long Dano Kelabits leave to work in Miri but most return for the *iraus*, which centre on massive feasts of wild boar, crackers and rice and traditional games. The conversion to Christianity since the war has meant that rice wine has been banned – there are copious jugs of lemonade and chocolate drinks to slake the thirst instead.

Pa Dalih

The track from Long Dano to **Pa Dalih** is in reasonable condition, and the journey takes just two hours. It's tempting to push on to Ramudu, but since this next leg is arguably the most exacting of the loop, you might want to catch your breath before the rigours of the five-hour hike. Comprising three longhouses, a school and a football field, Pa Dalih is a springboard to several highland adventures, among them the half-day hike to see the village's huge stone drums, once used as caskets for the dead.

Ramudu

The journey from Pa Dalih to **Ramudu** kicks off by skirting Pa Dalih's paddy fields. Shortly after you emerge into buffalo pasture, where to your left is a large rock in whose carved niches the remains of the village's dead were once left in jars; one collapsed example is still apparent. Four or five hours of steep rises and drops follow, before you reach the ten-door Ramudu longhouse, set behind groves of pineapple trees and sugar cane, vegetable gardens and a grassy airstrip. The people of Ramudu are famed for their skilfully woven rattan baskets, worn on the back, and they may have a surplus of stock and thus some on sale. They also make delicious *gula tapur*, or sugar-cane candy. Ten minutes before you reach Ramudu is a **carved boulder** with intriguing representations of a face, a buffalo and a human figure. *Gem's Lodge*'s Jaman Riboh is the man to speak to if you intend to push south, off the Bario loop, to Long Beruang and beyond.

Pa Berang is seven and a half hours away from Ramudu, along a path that sets off past Ramudu's rice-mill shed and across a hanging bridge spanning Sungai Kelapang. The trail follows the Kelapang for an hour, then plunges into the forest for several hours, finally reaching Pa Berang after splashing through swampland. The settlement is home to eight Penan families, who live in somewhat poorer conditions than those enjoyed by the residents of the loop's other longhouses. Food isn't forthcoming here, so you'll need to have brought rice and tinned food with you from Bario, which you'll be able to prepare in the kitchen of the chief, Tama Simun. Tama doesn't speak English, though the local teacher, Balang Ibun, does.

The last section of the loop, which takes between four and five hours, threads around a few gentle slopes and crosses a half-sunk bridge over Sungai Drapur, before coming to a lengthy stretch of swamp forest that becomes a quagmire in the rainy season. The going is made fractionally easier by the lengths of bamboo that locals have laid along portions of the path, but you'll still be glad to surface in the pastures that border Bario.

Further south: Lio Matoh and Long Banga

From Ramudu, a southerly trail runs right the way down to the head of Batang Baram at Lio Matoh. The trail follows the watershed of Sungai Kelapung, taking a full day to reach the jungle shelter at **Long Okan**, which hasn't any facilities, so you'll need a light blanket for sleeping. The next day, it's four more hours along a hard, hilly trail to **Long Beruang**, a large Penan settlement whose inhabitants are semi-nomadic, preferring sago-collecting and hunting to the settled rice-growing of the Kelabit. It's worth having a few little **gifts**, like food or tobacco, at hand. At Long Peluan the path forks, west to Ba Lai and **Long Lellang** and south to Lio Matoh. A homestay has recently been set up at Long Lellang. Run by Pedrus Raja, the lodge (RM20 per day for food; ❶) welcomes visitors and is a marvellous new addition to the accommodation options in the highlands.

Four hours' walk on from Long Peluan gets you to the longhouse at **Long Banga**, from where it is now possible to get back to Marudi (Tuesday) and Miri (Tuesday and Saturday) on morning flights. From Banga it's a two-hour walk downhill off the plateau to the timber camp and longhouse at **Lio Matoh**, the most easterly settlement on Batang Baram. For the Kelabit especially, this is a thriving, busy community, much in contrast with the jungle longhouses up the track. From Lio Matoh, longboats travel downriver along Batang Baram to Long San (and onwards to Marudi). If you need to move on more quickly you can get to Lapok in two days, though you'll need to charter a boat, for which the price will be high (around RM1000) unless you join a group of locals already heading downriver. From Lapok, express boats go to Marudi (RM20), for onwards travel to Kuala Baram and Miri.

North of Bario

The other main excursion from Bario is the four-day trail due north through the villages of Pa Lungan and Pa Rupai to the large Kelabit village of **Ba Kelalan**, which has an airstrip, and from where it's possible to travel overland to Lawas (see p.495). A side trip to climb **Gunung Murud** (2423m) is possible from Ba Kelalan too, though there is no organized trip to this peak, so ask in Ba Kelalan for trained **guides**.

To Ba Kelalan via Pa Lungan

The time required for this difficult trek depends on fitness: although a Kelabit could pull it off in twelve hours, it's best to allow three days – this is some of the richest, thickest forest in Borneo. Bring a sleeping mat as some nights are spent in extremely basic shelters, and if you're attempting it in the rainy season beware of heavy mud, leeches and mosquitoes.

The route from Bario heads past the longhouse at Pa Ukat (see p.514); watch out for the **trailside boulder** a few kilometres along the trail, on which human faces are carved, the only known example of funerary art remaining in the highlands. After about eight hours you reach **Pa Lungan**, which consists of detached family units around a large rectangular field for pigs and buffalo. Visitors stay in the longhouse, usually in the chief's quarters.

On the second very long day, it takes from four to six hours to get to the abandoned village of **Long Rapung**. On the way, before the forest closes in around you, look out for Gunung Murud on your left, if it's not shrouded in mist. There is just a small shelter at Long Rapung – little more than an inter-section of paths and a place to rest – but it's a very beautiful place nonetheless, with a small clean river running gently past, and most guides opt to spend the night here, allowing for a less strenuous third day. Four more hours on a hard and narrow trail – infamous for its leeches – are needed to reach **Pa Rupai**. The long downward slope passes through irrigated rice fields to the village. You're now in Kalimantan, although there are no signs to prove it. Two hours further and you pass through the village of **Long Medang** and on up a short, steep hill which marks the frontier with Kalimantan. A path alongside rice fields leads to an army outpost where you need to show your **passport**, as your route has taken you inadvertently back and forth across the border. The trail leads after a short walk to Ba Kelalan.

Ba Kelalan and around

Ba Kelalan is smaller and more compact than Bario, with a smattering of single dwellings, one large longhouse, two coffee shops, and a few shops selling basic provisions. There are two places to stay: the *Green Apple Inn* is the premier spot, with neat and clean rooms and en-suite shower and toilet (❷), and has the added advantage that the owner speaks English. The other, *Ba Kelalan Inn* (❷), is very basic with none-too-clean rooms with communal toilet and shower. There is no way of contacting these two places in advance – just turn up.

There are twice-weekly, morning FAX flights from Bario (around RM23) and Lawas (around RM46), the airport is close to the town centre. There is also a road from Ba Kelalan to Lawas; it's a hard, six-hour trip by Land Cruiser on logging roads through largely deforested but sometimes quite spectacular scenery.

The trek to Gunung Murud

From Ba Kelalan, **Gunung Murud** presents a quite challenging but highly rewarding trek with spectacular views across the highlands. The two-day hike requires a guide (RM80 per day) – ask at the *Green Apple Inn* for guide availability – and proper equipment. The first day involves a five-hour hike along logging roads, during the latter stages of which you'll be walking through primary jungle. At an abandoned shelter a rough trail leaves the road and snakes slowly up the mountain's foothills. An hour later you arrive at an unnamed deserted village, which is used by the local Lun Bawang just once a year – for a Christian meeting. Here, you'll spend the night in a shelter, leaving early in the morning for the two-hour, increasingly tough haul onto the Murud ridge, where for some distance you intermittently follow a plankway. You follow this onto a large rock, dubbed the "Rock Garden", which, although not technically the summit, constitutes the most accessible high point on Murud. After returning to the shelter and resting, you return to tackle the long haul back down and along the logging road to Ba Kelalan.

Travel details

Buses

Bintulu to: Miri (12 daily; 3hr); Mukah (3 daily; 3hr); Sibu (8 daily; 4hr).

Kuching to: Anna Rais (every 30min; 2hr); Bako (12 daily; 1hr); Damai Beach (every 40min; 1hr); Lundu (4 daily; 2hr); Pontianak, Indonesia (6 daily; 8–10hr); Sarikei (3 daily; 5–6hr); Serian (1 daily; 1hr); Sibu (10 daily, 8hr); Sri Aman (6 daily; 3hr); Tebedu (1 daily; 10hr).

Limbang to: Lawas (1 daily; 5hr); Miri (1 daily; 5hr); Nanga Medamit (1 daily; 1hr 30min).

Miri to: Bintulu (12 daily; 3hr); Kuala Baram (every 15min; 45min); Kuala Belait (6 daily; 3hr); Lambir Hills (every 30min; 40min), Sibu (10 daily; 7hr).

Mukah to: Bintulu (3 daily; 3hr); Sibu (3 daily, 3hr 30min).

Sarikei to: Bintulu (4 daily; 4hr); Kuching (3 daily; 5–6hr).

Sibu to: Bintulu (8 daily; 4hr); Kuching (10 daily; 8 hr); Miri (10 daily; 7hr); Mukah (3 daily; 3hr 30min).

Boats

Belaga to: Kapit (2 daily; 5hr).

Kapit to: Belaga (2 daily; 4–5hr); Kanowit (12 daily; 1hr 30min); Sibu (12 daily; 3hr); Song (12 daily; 1hr),

Kuala Baram to: Marudi (7 daily; 3hr).

Kuching to: Sarikei (1 daily; 2–3hr); Sibu (1 daily; 4hr).

Limbang to: Bandar Seri Begawan, Brunei (10 daily; 30min); Labuan (2 daily; 1–2hr); Lawas (1 daily; 30min).

Long Lama to: Marudi (3 daily; 3hr); Long Terewan (1 daily; 4hr).

Marudi to: Kuala Baram (7 daily; 3hr); Lapok (1 daily; 2hr); Long Lama (3 daily; 3hr) Long Terewan (1 daily; 4hr).

Sarikei to: Kuching (2 daily; 2–3hr); Sibu (2 daily; 1–2hr).

Sibu to: Kapit (12 daily; 3hr); Kuching (1 daily; 4hr).

Flights

Ba Kelalan to: Bario (2 weekly, 40min); Lawas (2 weekly; 35min).

Bario to: Ba Kelalan (2 weekly, 40min); Marudi (1 daily; 40min); Miri (2 daily; 50min).

Bintulu to: Kota Kinabalu (2 daily; 1hr 15min); Kuala Lumpur (1 daily; 2hr 10min); Kuching (2 daily; 1hr); Miri (4 daily; 35min); Mukah (1 daily; 35min); Sibu (3 daily; 1hr).

Kuala Lumpur to: Bintulu (1 daily; 2hr–2hr 15min); Kuching (17 daily; 1hr 40min); Miri (7 daily; 2hr 15min); Sibu (4–5 daily; 1hr 45min–2hr).

Kuching to: Bintulu (1–2 daily; 1hr); Johor Bahru (4 daily; 1hr 20min); Kota Kinabalu (6 daily; 2hr 20min); Kuala Lumpur (17 daily; 1hr 40min); Miri (7 daily; 1hr); Mukah (2 daily; 1hr 10min); Sibu (10 daily; 40min).

Lawas to: Ba Kalalan (2 weekly; 35min); Limbang (2 weekly; 20min); Miri (5 daily; 45min).

Limbang to: Lawas (2 weekly; 20min); Miri (3 daily; 35min).

Long Banga to: Marudi (1 weekly; 50min); Miri (2 weekly; 1hr).

Long Lellang to: Marudi (1 weekly; 30min); Miri (2 weekly; 1hr).

Long Seridan to: Marudi (1 weekly; 30min); Miri (2 weekly; 1hr).

Marudi to: Bario (1 daily; 40min); Long Banga (1 weekly; 1hr); Long Lelland (1 weekly; 1hr); Long Seridan (1 weekly; 1hr); Miri (4 daily; 20min).

Miri to: Bintulu (4 daily; 35min); Johor Bahru (8 weekly; 2hr); Kota Kinabalu (6 daily; 1hr 40min); Kuala Lumpur (5 daily; 2hr 15min); Kuching (5 daily; 1hr); Lawas (5 daily; 45min); Limbang (3 daily; 35min); Long Banga (2 weekly; 1hr); Long Lellang (2 weekly; 1hr); Long Seridan (2 weekly; 1hr); Marudi (4 daily; 20min); Mukah (1–2 daily; 1hr); Mulu (1–2 daily; 40min); Sibu (2 daily; 1hr).

Mukah to: Bintulu (1 daily; 35min); Kuching (2 daily; 1hr 10min); Miri (1–2 daily, 1hr); Sibu (1 daily; 25min).

Mulu to: Miri (1–2 daily; 40min).

Sibu to: Bintulu (4 daily; 35min); Johor Bahru (6 weekly; 1hr 30min); Kota Kinabalu (2 daily; 1hr 40min); Kuching (10 daily; 40min); Miri (2 daily; 1hr); Mukah (1 daily; 25min).

Sabah

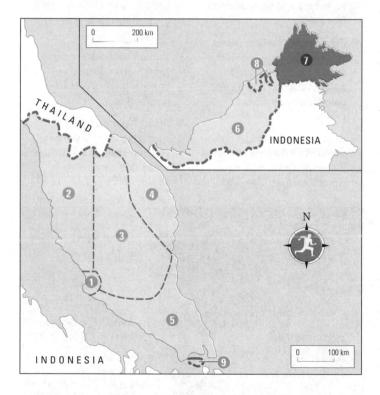

CHAPTER 7 # Highlights

* **Kota Kinabalu** Sabah's capital has a vibrant atmosphere and a laid back bar and café culture. See p.526

* **Pulau Gaya** Perfectly formed little island close to Kota Kinabalu, with trekking, swimming and tasty seafood. See p.537

* **Pulau Tiga** "Survivor Island" is a veritable paradise with amazing beaches, good accommodation and a mud bath for good measure. See p.547

* **Gunung Kinabalu** The arduous climb to see dawn over the South China Sea is well worth the effort. See p.556

* **Sandakan** An ethnic melting pot, Sandakan is a perfect jumping-off spot for nearby attractions. See p.564

* **Sungai Kinabatangan** Tributaries off this river are home to a great diversity of bird and animal life including the solitary orang-utan. See p.574

* **Danum Valley** Stunning stretch of untouched rainforest with treks and wildlife galore. See p.579

* **Pulau Sipadan** Spectacular marine life and stunning beaches make it a must for divers and snorkellers. See p.583

△ Snorkelling off Pulau Sipadan

Sabah

U ntil European powers began to gain a foothold here in the nineteenth century, **SABAH**, at the northern tip of Borneo, was inhabited by tribal peoples who only had minimal contact with the outside world, thus preserving their unique costumes, traditions and languages. But since joining the Malaysian Federation at its foundation in 1963, Sabah has undergone rapid modernization, its various peoples largely exchanging traditional indigenous ways for a collective Malaysian identity. As the state's cultural landscape has changed, so has its environment; the **logging** industry has decimated much of the state's natural forests, the cleared regions often used to plant thousands of acres of oil palm, a monoculture which has little truck with ecological diversity. This agro-industry, however, offers thousands work and much-needed income into the state coffers.

Thankfully, this bleak picture neglects the natural riches on view in a fertile region, whose name – according to some sources – goes back to biblical times and means "the land below the wind" (Sabah's 72,500 square kilometres falling just south of the typhoon belt). Within the state are a variety of **terrains**, from wild, swampy, mangrove-tangled coastal areas, through the dazzling greens of paddy fields, pristine rainforests to the dizzy heights of the Crocker Mountain Range – home to the highest mountain peak between the Himalayas and New Guinea, **Gunung Kinabalu** (Mount Kinabalu). Further east, Sabah encompasses many great spots for **wildlife**; at Sungai Kinabatangan you can see forest-dwelling proboscis monkeys, orang-utans, bearded pigs, elephants and hornbills, while on Pulau Selingan (Turtle Island) you'll be bewitched by mother turtles laying their eggs. Then, at the islands surrounding Semporna, on the wild east coast, lie some of the world's great **diving spots**, rich with marine life.

Many varieties of dialect are spoken by Sabah's ethnic groups, which number over a dozen, though with traditional costumes increasingly losing out to T-shirts and shorts, it's now hard to distinguish one tribe from another. The peoples of the **Kadazan/Dusun** tribes constitute the largest indigenous racial group, then there are the **Murut** of the southwest, and Sabah's so-called "sea gypsies", the **Bajau**. More recently, Sabah has seen a huge influx of Filipino and Indonesian immigrants, particularly on its east coast. One of the few annual events when indigenous culture is celebrated is the Sabah Fest, a week-long celebration, held in May, the climax of Pesta Kaamatan, the Kadazan/Dusun harvest festival. **Tamus**, or market fairs, usually held weekly in towns and villages across the state are a wonderful opportunity for visitors to take in the colourful mixture of cultures. Two such large fairs are held on Sundays, one at Jalan Gaya, in the capital Kota Kinabalu, the other in the small town of Kota Belud, two hours north by bus. The latter *tamu* has long been an important social focal point of

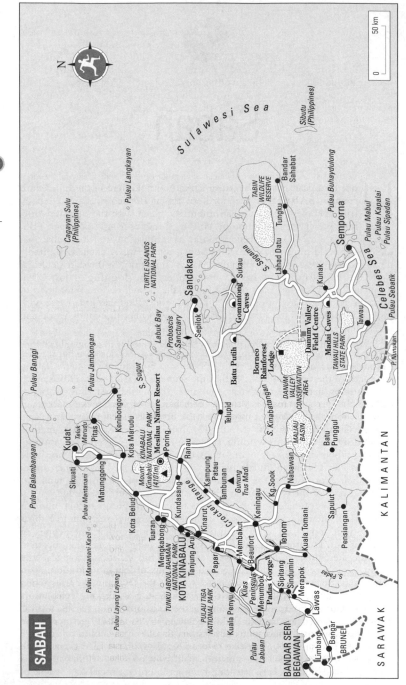

SABAH

Sulawesi Sea

Sibutu (Philippines)

Cagayan Sulu (Philippines)

0   50 km

Pulau Langkayan

Pulau Banggi

TURTLE ISLANDS NATIONAL PARK

Sandakan

Labuk Bay

Proboscis Sanctuary

Sepilok

Gomantong Caves

Sukau

S. Segama

TABIN WILDLIFE RESERVE

Bandar Sahabat

Tungku

Lahad Datu

Pulau Buhaydulong

Semporna

Pulau Mabul
Pulau Kapalai
Pulau Sipadan

Kunak

Batu Putih

Borneo Rainforest Lodge

DANUM VALLEY CONSERVATION AREA

Danum Valley Field Centre

Madai Caves

Tawau

Pulau Sebatik

Celebes Sea

Pulau Nunukan

Pulau Balambangan

Kudat

Teluk Marudu

Pitas

Kenibongan

Sikuati

Matunggong

Kota Marudu

Mesilau Nature Resort

Poring

S. Sugut

Telupid

Ranau

Pulau Jambongan

Pulau Mantanani

Pulau Mantanani Kecil

Kota Belud

Mount Kinabalu (4101m)

KINABALU NATIONAL PARK

Kundasang

Kampung Patau

Tambunan

Gunung Trus Madi

MALIAU BASIN

Batu Punggul

KALIMANTAN

Pulau Layang Layang

Tuaran

Mengkabong

TUNKU ABDUL RAHMAN NATIONAL PARK

KOTA KINABALU

Tanjung Aru

Papar

Kinarut

Crocker Range

Keningau

Kg.Sook

Nabawan

Sapulut

Pensiangan

PULAU TIGA NATIONAL PARK

Klias Peninsula

Menumbok

Kuala Penyu

Membakut

Beaufort

Padas Gorge

Sipitang

Sindumin

Tenom

Kuala Tomani

Merapok

S. Padas

Lawas

Pulau Labuan

BANDAR SERI BEGAWAN

Limbang

Bangar

BRUNEI

SARAWAK

S. Sugut

S. Kinabatangan

S. Kinabatangan

TAWAU HILLS STATE PARK

Proboscis Sanctuary

tribal life in Sabah, and draws crowds of people from the surrounding region, who come to gossip as much as to buy and sell produce.

Sabah's **urban centres** are not very attractive or historically rich places: World War II bombs and hurried urban redevelopment have conspired to produce a capital city and a chain of towns devoid of much architectural worth. But what places like **Kota Kinabalu** (usually shortened to KK) and **Sandakan** lack in notable buildings they make for in atmosphere and energy. A walk through their streets is always an event; whether just watching harbour-side life in Sandakan's renowned fish market or choosing where to eat along KK's Jalan Pantai, or browsing in the busy malls, probably the most user-friendly in Malaysia.

Sabah practicalities

Sabah is 600km away from the Peninsula. Prices are on a par with Sarawak, but if you want to take advantage of the region's unique wildlife and nature, it can take a large chunk out of your budget.

Getting there
Kota Kinabalu (KK) is almost certain to be your first port of call in Sabah. From the Peninsula, MAS flies there from **KL** (around RM435) and AirAsia from KL and **Johor Bahru** (from RM80). Note that AirAsia also flies directly to KK from Bangkok and Manila. There are also numerous MAS departures from **Kuching** in Sarawak (around RM228) and, on Royal Brunei Airlines, a daily flight from **Bandar Seri Begawan** (around B$80).

A regular boat service runs from Muara in **Brunei**, and from **Lawas** and **Limbang** in northern Sarawak, to Pulau Labuan, from where there are fast, sea connections to KK. There's a daily ferry from northeastern **Kalimantan** to Tawau and a weekly ferry from Zamboanga in the **Philippines** to Sandakan. The only **overland route** into Sabah is from Lawas which is a short bus ride away from the border at Merapok; see p.495 for more.

Getting around
Sabah has the poorest **roads** in Malaysia – perhaps a quarter aren't sealed and many are little more than dirt tracks, impassable in the rainy season. That said, most roads between the main towns are fine.

The most common form of public transport on both local and long-distance routes are the **minivans**, whose drivers have their own way of doing things – either going the straightest way between two points at breakneck speed or languidly following a circuitous path, picking up and dropping customers off seemingly at whim. Travellers who aren't in a hurry will gain fascinating insights into everyday life – whether you are going the wrong way up a human tide heading for Friday prayers or depositing an elderly couple miles along a track at a farm.

Minivans travel at all times but in contrast, **buses** are most plentiful early in the morning. They are worth catching for trips between the main towns especially from KK to Sandakan, passing Kinabalu National Park on the way, and to points south of KK including Beaufort and Tenom.

Landcruisers, or **4WDs**, are the most comfortable means of travel, though appreciably more expensive than the other options, and just used for travelling upcountry, for example from Keningau to Sapulut in the south or for the Tawau-Keningau loop.

Taking **internal flights** makes sense and is inexpensive. For example, the route from KK to Lahad Datu – for onward travel to Semporna – costs RM96 and takes just 50 minutes by plane compared to twelve by bus. Sabah is criss-crossed by a good plane network, operated by **Fly Asian Xpress** (FAX; ⓦ www.flyasianxpress.com) with daily flights between Kota Kinabalu, Kudat, Lahad Datu, Sandakan and Tawau.

Many visit Sabah with a specific purpose in mind, the classic reason being to climb 4101-metre Gunung Kinabalu while others come to trek uninhabited areas like the isolated **Maliau Basin**, or the more accessible but equally rewarding rainforest sanctuary, **Danum Valley**.

Whatever your itinerary, most trips start in the capital **Kota Kinabalu**, from where Sabah's main road heads south to **Beaufort**, where the state's only railway heads into the rural **interior**, its route taking advantage of the swathe cut through the Padas Gorge by the broad Sungai Padas, which snakes southwards through rainforest to the Sarawak border – the river has recently become popular for whitewater rafting, just beyond or through the breathtaking gorge. The train line terminates midway between the towns of **Tenom** and **Keningau**, to the southwest of which is Murut territory, isolated enough to allow a taste of the adventures that travelling in Sabah once entailed.

North of KK, the trunk road climbs into Bajau country, then eastwards through **dipterocarp forest** onto the huge granite shelves of Gunung Kinabalu. The mountain is an awesome sight but climbing it is quite a challenging proposition, harder than often supposed. From the jagged summit there are staggering views of Sabah's west coast below. Further north are the beaches and coconut groves of the tranquil **Kudat**, where the few remaining longhouses of the Rungus tribe can be visited.

Eastwards towards the early capital, Sandakan, a kind of frontier feel pervades, given the proximity of the lawless islands off the southern Philippines. **Sandakan** however is a safe and enjoyable town to visit, its vibrant commercial modernity juxtaposing neatly with a sense of old-world colonial charm. This clammy, noisy place is also the jumping-off point for visits to the small dive site **Pulau Lankayan**, located in a recently protected marine reserve, and the offshore Pulau Selingan in the **Turtle Islands National Park**, where you're likely to see a turtle laying her eggs, but you won't be alone; many tourists flock here daily.

Indeed, if wildlife is your main reason for coming to Sabah, you'll be keen to visit the nearby **Sepilok Orang-utan Rehabilitation Centre**, as well as the wondrous region around **Sukau**, on the lower reaches of **Sungai Kinabatangan**, which support families of proboscis monkeys, elephants and the solitary orang-utan. Further south, the **Danum Valley Conservation Area** has embarked on a programme of ecotourism, its *Borneo Rainforest Lodge* offering visitors a luxurious environment from which to enjoy a spectacular canopy walkway revealing the splendours of the rainforest. Also in this region, close to the wild town of **Lahud Datu**, lies **Tabin Wildlife Reserve**, with its mud volcano and often-spotted elephant colony.

For divers, the islands of **Sipadan**, **Kapalai** and **Mabul** off Semporna on the southeastern coast are the jewel in Sabah's crown. Sipadan is Sabah's only oceanic island (it's not part of the Bornean continental shelf), and offers superb deep diving off a coral wall. With its muddy sea, neighbour Pulau Mabul is rated as one of the world's top muck dives and on Pulau Kapalai, a snorkeller's paradise, shallow waters lap pure white sand bars, close to one of Malaysia's best, and most discreet, resort hotels.

Some history

Little is known of Sabah's **early history**, though archeological finds in limestone caves in the east of the state indicate that the northern tip of Borneo has been inhabited for well over ten thousand years. Chinese merchants were trading with local settlements by 700 AD, and by the fourteenth century, the tract of land now known as Sabah came under the sway of the sultans of Brunei and

Sulu, though its isolated communities of hunter-gatherers would generally have been unaware of this fact. Europe's superpowers first arrived in 1521, when the ships of the Portuguese navigator Ferdinand Magellan stopped off at Brunei and later sailed northwards. But it was to be nearly 250 years before any colonial settlement occurred, when – in 1763 – one Captain Cowley established a short-lived trading post on Pulau Balambangan, an island north of Kudat, on behalf of the **British East India Company**. Further colonial involvement came in 1846, when Pulau Labuan (at the mouth of Brunei Bay) was ceded to the British by the Sultan of Brunei and by 1881 the **British North Borneo Chartered Company** had full sovereignty over northern Borneo.

First steps were then taken towards making the territory pay its way: rubber, tobacco and, after 1885, timber, were commercially harvested. By 1905 a **railway** linked the coastal town of **Jesselton** (later called Kota Kinabalu) with the resource-rich interior. When the company introduced taxes the locals were understandably ill-pleased and native resistance followed – **Mat Salleh**, the son of a Bajau chief, and his followers sacked the company's settlement on Pulau Gaya in 1897. Another uprising, in **Rundum** in 1915, resulted in the slaughter of hundreds of Murut tribespeople by British forces.

No other major disturbances troubled the Chartered Company until New Year's Day, 1942, when the Japanese Imperial forces invaded Pulau Labuan; less than three weeks later Sandakan fell. The years of **World War II** were devastating ones for Japanese-occupied Sabah, which was bombed by Allied forces eager to neutralize its harbours. By the time of the Japanese surrender on September 9, 1945, next to nothing of Jesselton and Sandakan remained standing. Even worse were the hardships that the captured Allied troops and civilians endured – culminating in the infamous Death March of 1945, see p.572.

Unable to finance the rebuilding of North Borneo, the Chartered Company sold the territory to the British Crown in 1946, and Jesselton was declared the new capital of the **Crown Colony of North Borneo**. However, within fifteen years, plans had been laid for an independent federation consisting of Malaya, Singapore, Sarawak, North Borneo and Brunei. Although Brunei pulled out at the last minute, the **Federation** was still proclaimed at midnight on September 15, 1963, with North Borneo quickly being renamed Sabah. Objecting to the inclusion of Sarawak and Sabah in the Federation, Indonesia's President Sukarno initiated his anti-Malaysian Konfrontasi policy (see p.741), and sporadic skirmishes broke out along the Sabah–Kalimantan border for the next three years. The decade that followed saw Sabah's **timber industry**, begun in the nineteenth century, reach its destructive peak (for more on this issue, see p.759).

It's only recently that relations with Kuala Lumpur, strained since the mid-1980s, have taken a turn for the better. Sabah had toed the line of the federal ruling party, the Barisan Nasional (BN), until 1985, but then the opposition **Parti Bersatu Sabah** (PBS), led by the Christian Joseph Pairin Kitingan, was returned to office in the state elections – the first time a non-Muslim had attained power in a Malaysian state. Anti-federal feelings were worsened by the fact that much of the profits from Sabah's flourishing **crude oil** exports were being siphoned off to KL. Pairin held power in the 1994 **state elections** but in those of 1999 the trend towards local BN-aligned parties holding power across East Malaysia was further consolidated and by 2004 only one seat was held by an opposition politician.

Although the PBS remains a strong force in Sabah's political firmament, its days of voicing independent policies are clearly numbered. For reasons of political survival it continues to grow strategically closer to the BN. Central government is sticking by the policy of patching up long-running, cross-state disunity to further realize Malaysia's vision of a multi-ethnic, but Muslim-dominated nation.

Kota Kinabalu and around

Since 1946, Sabah's seat of government has been based at **KOTA KINABALU** (KK), halfway up the state's western seaboard. First impressions are of a rather utilitarian concrete sprawl, but KK usually manages to charm visitors with the friendliness of its citizens; the lively buzz which characterizes its bars, cafés and markets; and its proximity to a clutch of idyllic islands. It also has excellent tranpsort links whether by air, sea or road.

Modern-day KK can trace its history back to 1882, the year the British North Borneo Chartered Company first established an outpost on nearby **Pulau Gaya**. After this was burned down by followers of the Bajau rebel, Mat Salleh, in 1897, the Company chose a mainland site for a new town which was known to locals as *Api Api*, or "Fire, Fire". One explanation for the name was that it referred to the firing of the original settlement; another, that it reflected the abundance of fireflies inhabiting its swamps. Renamed **Jesselton**, after Sir Charles Jessel, the vice-chairman of the Chartered Company, the town prospered. By 1905, the Trans-Borneo Railway reached from Jesselton to Beaufort, meaning that for the first time, rubber could be transported efficiently from the interior to the coast.

The Japanese invasion of North Borneo in 1942 marked the start of three and a half years of **military occupation**: of old Jesselton, only the Atkinson Clock Tower, the red-roofed Land and Surveys Building and the post office (today's tourist office) survived the resulting Allied bombing. In 1967 the name was changed again to Kota Kinabalu (meaning simply Kinabalu City). Progress in the second part of the twentieth century was startling and today, with a population of quarter of a million, KK is a beehive of activity once again.

Most of downtown KK was reclaimed from the sea during the twentieth century – so ruthlessly in some places that pockets of stilt houses have been left stranded in stagnant lakes. On the resulting new patches of land, large complexes of interconnecting concrete buildings have been constructed – the Sinsuran and Segama complexes and Asia City are three – their ground floors taken up by shops, restaurants and businesses, the upper floors turned into apartments. In addition, the Sutera Harbour project (2km south of the city centre) has added two big-name hotels and a flash marina. The most recent development is a waterfront stretch of cafés, bars and restaurants, popular with young KK-ites and tourists alike.

The city has a small number of reasonable sights, the best of which are its markets, the **State Museum** and the **Bird Sanctuary**, 3km north of the city centre at Likas Bay. The highlight of any extended stay is, without doubt, the offshore **Tunku Abdul Rahman Park**, whose five unspoilt islands (including the exquisite Pulau Gaya), are a short trip away by boat.

Arrival

KK has two **airports**, the new **KK International**, 8km south of the centre close to the kampung Tanjung Aru, and **KK Terminal Two**, used exclusively by AirAsia/FAX for their international and domestic flights, 7km, again south, on the road to *Shangri-La Tanjung Aru Resort*. From KK International, **buses** #17A, #17B and #17C leave for the town centre (every 30min 7am–7pm, daily; RM1.50); from Terminal Two, #16 leaves from outside the terminal on the main Tanjung Aru Road (every 30min 7am–7pm, daily; RM1.50). Most travellers, though, opt for a **taxi** (RM17; coupon from taxi kiosk in arrivals; RM20 after 10pm). It is also possible to walk onto either of the main roads and

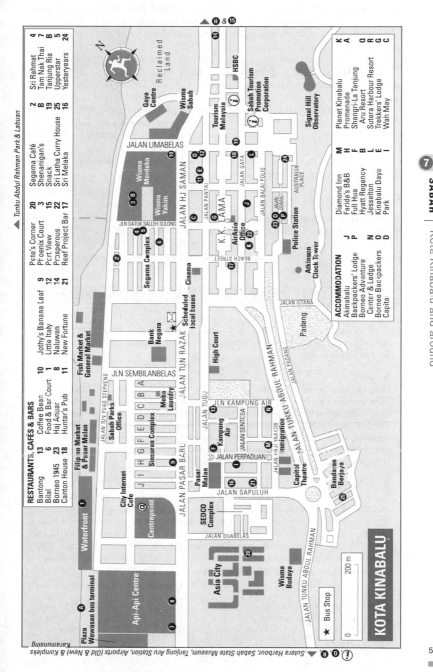

KOTA KINABALU

RESTAURANTS, CAFÉS & BARS					
Bantong	13	Jothy's Banana Leaf	9	Pete's Corner	20
Bilal	6	Coffee Bean	10	Phoenix Court	3
Borneo 1945	23	Little Italy	1	Prct View	15
Canton House	18	Food & Bar Court	12	Prosperous	22
		Haj Anuar	8	Reef Project Bar	17
		Hunter's Pub	11		
Filip no Market & Pesar Malan		Naluwan	14	Segama Café	2
Fish Market & General Market		New Fortune	11	Shenanigan's	3
				Snack	19
Sri Rahmat	4			Sri Latha Curry House	25
Tam Nak Thai	7			Sri Melaka	16
Tanjung Ria	5				
Upperstar	19				
Yesteryears	24				

ACCOMMODATION					
Akinabalu	J	Diamond Inn	M	Planet Kinabalu	K
Backpackers' Lodge	P	Farida's B&B	H	Promenade	A
Borneo Adventure Center & Lodge	N	Full Hua	B	Shangri-La Tanjung Aru Resort	Q
Borneo Backpackers	O	Hyatt Regency	L	Sutera Harbour Resort	R
Capita	D	Jesselton	E	Trekker's Lodge	G
		Kinabalu Daya Park	I	Wah May	C

▲ Tunku Abdul Rahman Park & Labuan

JALAN LIMABELAS

JALAN HJ SAMAN

JLN DATUK SALLEH SULONG

JLN SEMBILANBELAS

JALAN TUN FUAD STEPHENS

Sabah Parks Office

JALAN TUN RAZAK

JALAN TUGU

JLN KAMPUNG AIR

JALAN PASAR BARU

JALAN SENTOSA

JALAN PERPADUAN

JALAN HAJI YAACOB

JALAN SAPULUH

JALAN DUABELAS

JALAN TUNKU ABDUL RAHMAN

JALAN ISTANA

JALAN PADANG

JALAN TUNKU ABDUL RAHMAN

K.K. LAMA

BEACH STREET

JALAN PANTAI

JALAN GAYA

JALAN BALAI POLIS

JALAN DEWAN

AUSTRALIA PLACE

Reclaimed Land

Gaya Centre

Wisma Sabah

Wisma Merdeka

Wisma Yakim

Segama Complex

Cinema

Scheduled local buses

Bank Negara

High Court

Kampung Air

Immigration

Capitol Theatre

Bandaran Berjaya

Padang

Atkinson Clock Tower

Police Station

AirAsia Office

Tourism Malaysia

Sabah Tourism Promotion Corporation

HSBC

Signal Hill Observatory

Waterfront

City Internet Cafe

Centrepoint

SEDCO Complex

Asia City

Wisma Budaya

Api-Api Centre

Plaza Wawasan bus terminal

Pasar Malan

Meba Laundry

Sinsuran Complex

★ Bus Stop

0   200 m

N

Karamunsing ◀ ⓘ 🅗 🅞 🅑 ◀ Sutera Harbour, Sabah State Museum, Tanjung Aru Station, Airports (Old & New) & Kompleks hail a **minivan** (RM1); but this is hardly viable if you have much luggage. Most minivans and the airport buses terminate in the city centre at the local bus stand, Jalan Tugu, close to the GPO from where, armed with a map, you can locate your accommodation, or take a city taxi (RM6).

 Trains from Tenom and Beaufort pull in close to the international airport at **Tanjung Aru station** on Jalan Kepayan. Long-distance **buses** from Sandakan and elsewhere north of KK arrive at the new City Bus Terminal North (CBTN), 8km east of the city centre in the suburb, Inanam. Short hop buses between CBTN and KK's Padang, run every twenty minutes (6am–8pm; RM1.50; 20min). Arriving at CBTN outside these hours requires a taxi (RM10) from directly outside the terminal. **Buses** from southern Sabah arrive at the Jalan Kemajuan terminus, near Plaza Wawasan on the southwestern edge of the city centre. **Ferries** from Labuan and the Tunku Addul Rahman Islands arrive at the Port Authority jetty, east of the centre, on Jalan Haji Sarnan.

Information

The **Sabah Tourism Board** (STB; Mon–Fri 8am–5pm, Sat & Sun 8am–4pm, ℡088/212121, Ⓦwww.sabahtourism.com) is in the old GPO at 51 Jalan Gaya. The friendly staff can help with just about anything – ask for the excellent tourist **map** of KK available free. **Tourism Malaysia** (Mon–Fri 8.30am–4.30pm, Sat

---

Moving on from KK

By air
From KK's **airports** there are regular, nonstop, MAS and AirAsia/FAX flights to points across Sabah, Sarawak and the Peninsula. In addition, Royal Brunei flies daily to Bandar Seri Begawan.

By bus
Long-distance buses for destinations including **Sandakan**, **Kudat** and **Tawau** leave from the new City Bus Terminal North (CBTN) at Inanam, on the outskirts of KK. Bus tickets are now easy to buy thanks to a computerized booking system. Buses heading **south of KK**, to Beaufort, Tenom, for Pulau Tiga, or onwards to Brunei and Sarawak, leave from the Wawasan Plaza terminal, on the western edge of the city centre (20min walk from centre; RM6 taxi ride). This is also where minivans plying stretches both south and north leave from.

By train
Sabah's only train line runs from Tanjung Aru station due south to **Papar**, **Beaufort** and **Tenom**. Trains leave twice a day for Beaufort (9.50am & 1.40pm; 2hr 30min) and once a day to Tenom (7.45am; 5hr). Additionally, Sutera Harbour Hotels have renovated an old **North Borneo Railway** train for a pricey, weekly trip to Papar (℡088/263933, Ⓦwww.northborneorailway.com.my; Sat 10am–2am; RM160, tiffin lunch included), a trip unashamedly aimed at tourists, many of whom will have been staying at the two Sutera hotels in KK.

By ferry
There are four daily services to **Labuan** (RM31; 3 hr), the first leaving at 8am and the last at 3pm. All tickets are sold at the Port Authority building on Jalan Haji Saman, close to the jetty. It's worth booking ahead if you plan to travel at the weekend or over a public holiday. Speedboats go hourly to the **Tunku Abdul Rahman Park** islands a few kilometres offshore; prices from RM10.

8.30am–noon; ☎088/211732), across Jalan Gaya in the EON CMG Building, is also fully stocked with leaflets on Sabah, but better at answering questions about Peninsular Malaysia or Sarawak.

For information about the environment and ecology of Sabah's National Parks, visit the **Sabah Parks office** (Mon–Fri 8.30am–5pm, Sat 8.30am–12.30pm; ☎088/240309, Ⓦwww.sabahparks.org.my), which faces the South China Sea at Block K of the Sinsuran Complex, Jalan Tun Fuad Stephens, opposite the General Market. The website has an excellent overview of Sabah's protected areas, facilities and ecology.

What's on information is in relatively short supply in KK, though details of cultural events can be found in any of Sabah's English-language newspapers – the *Borneo Mail*, *Sabah Times*, *Morning Post* and *Daily Express*. Otherwise, the **noticeboards** at guesthouses are valuable sources of information on matters as diverse as discovering the Maliau Basin or the tastiest hawker stalls to eat at in KK.

City transport

The city centre is compact enough to traverse on foot inside an hour. **Taxis** are inexpensive – it costs no more than RM5–6 to travel right across the city centre. There are taxi ranks outside the *Hyatt Hotel* on Jalan Datuk Salleh Sulong; at the GPO, on Jalan Tun Razak; along Jalan Perpaduan (close to the spot used by the long-distance buses) in Kampung Air; and at Centrepoint Mall on Jalan Pasar Baru.

Taking a local **bus** is more complicated, since there's no central station in KK. The bus stops beside and opposite the GPO on Jalan Tun Razak and nearby Jalan Tugu are the starting point for buses travelling through KK's suburbs – as far as Tuaran in the north and Penampang in the south. Marginally cheaper than minivans, these leave at set times, empty or full, but take longer to reach their destinations. **Minivans** for the suburbs and the airport leave when full from the Wawasan Plaza terminus.

Accommodation

Facilities for backpackers have improved significantly in recent years, with a good range of **hostels** now up and running in the centre and on the outskirts. The bulk of the mid-range **hotels** – most of them Chinese-run – are evenly spread across the city, although the best-positioned and most popular quarter is around jalans Pantai and Gaya and in nearby Australia Place. If you want to spoil yourself, there are a number of excellent-value, high-end hotels and resorts both in, and close to, the city; the *Shangri-La Tanjung Aru Resort*, 4km south of the centre, is the most exclusive and priciest.

Hostels

Akinabalu Floors 1–4, 133 Jalan Gaya ☎088/272188, ⓔakinabaluyh@yahoo.com. New, chic, but inexpensive hostel, proving very popular. Clean, fairly spacious four- to six-bed dorms, compact double rooms and an airy communal area. Dorm beds RM20, ❸

Backpacker's Lodge Lot 25, Lorong Dewan, Australia Place ☎088/261495, ⓔbackpackerkk @yahoo.com. Small, homely and very popular with small four- and six-bed dorms, TV, library and washing facilities. Dorm beds RM18, ❷

Borneo Adventure Center & Lodge 2, Lorong 1, Kampung Air ☎088/241515, ⓔborneoadventurecenter@yahoo.com. Just opened in 2006, this large complex has tidy doubles and small dorms. Centrally located and run by a friendly staff, this is a good choice if *BB*, *BL* and *Akinabalu* are full. Dorm beds RM18, ❸

🏃 **Borneo Backpackers** Lorong Dewan ☎088/234009; Ⓦwww.borneobackpackers .com. Small, recently opened lodge, set up by the man behind the excellent, Borneo Eco Tours, Albert Teo. Managed by Ali, this is a great place, tucked away on a side street in Australia Place, backing onto the jungle. As well as one double room and a number of four- to ten-bed dorms, there is a communal area, with TV and Internet, plus an interesting museum/coffee shop downstairs. Dorm beds RM20, ❸

Farida's B&B 413 Jalan Saga, Mile 4.5, Kampung Likas ☎088/428733, ⓔfaridabb@hotmail.com. Perfect if you want a quiet life, this delightful family-run concern is fifteen minutes away by bus or minivan from the minvan terminal – catch a "Kg Likas" minvan. The double rooms and various six-bed dorms are wonderfully airy, fitted out in varnished wood and the food excellent. Dorms RM12, ❷

Planet Kinabalu 98 & 100 Jalan Gaya ☎088/319168, ⓔplanetkinabalu@hotmail.com. Friendly, student-orientated, two-floor complex consisting mostly of four-bed dormitories; fairly basic and unadorned. Has a noticeboard and good information on KK and around. Breakfast is included. Dorms RM20, ❶

Trekkers Lodge 3rd & 4th floors, 46 Jalan Pantai ☎088/213888; ⓦwww.trekkerslodge .com. A popular and reliable choice with dorms and very small single/double rooms. Also includes laundry facilities and Internet access. Dorms RM20, ❷

Hotels

Capital 23 Jalan Haji Saman ☎088/231999. Light and comfortable rooms with a/c and terrestrial TV; though the hotel has few other amenities. ❻

Diamond Inn Block 37, Kampung Air ☎088/213222. Centrally placed, this competitively priced, comfortable and friendly hotel is not as clean as it once was, but still a bargain. ❸

Full Hua 14 Jalan Tugu, Kampung Air ☎088/234950, ⓔhotelfh@hotmail.com. Superbly positioned for Kampung Air's vibrant atmosphere, this popular, friendly place has small, neat en-suite rooms with a/c and TV. ❸

Hyatt Regency Jalan Salleh Sulong ☎088/221234, ⓦwww.kinabaluregency.hyatt.com. Modern hotel with over two hundred rooms and all the comforts you might imagine – swimming pool, business centre and brilliant buffet restaurant. (See "Eating"). ❽

Jesselton 69 Jalan Gaya ☎088/223333, ⓔjesshtl@po.jaring.my. Lady Mountbatten and Muhammad Ali are just two of the illustrious guests to have sampled the old-world charm of KK's most famous hotel. Run by an ebullient Texan lady, it's set on the city's most elegant street. A good

Western grill, convivial coffee shop and nightly chanteuse performances complement the sophisticated rooms. ❻

Kinabalu Daya Lot 3, 9 Jalan Pantai ☎088/240000, ⓦwww.kinabaluhotel .com. Excellent mid-range establishment, perfectly placed in the busy northern section of town, opposite shoppers' paradise Wisma Merdeka. The rooms are snug and en suite and the first-floor breakfast-room-cum-bar a KK legend. ❺

Park Lot 11, Block 39, Jalan Sentosa, Jampung Air ☎088/235666. Although the rooms and en-suite bathrooms are small, the air conditioning works a treat and the service is top class. ❸

Promenade 4 Lorong Api Api, Api Ai Centre ☎088/265555; ⓦwww.promenade.com.my. New addition with a spectacular beachfront location, lavish foyer and sumptuous rooms. With promotional prices often available it can be a top-end bargain. ❻

Wah May 36 Jalan Haji Saman ☎088/266118; ⓦwww.wahmayhotel.com. Smaller but quite similar to the *Daya*, this is a friendly place with compact rooms and neat bathrooms in a central location. ❺

Resort hotels

Shangri-La Rasa Ria Dalit Bay, Tuaran ☎088/792888, ⓦwww.shangri-la.com. Thirty kilometres north of KK, this resort is set on a gorgeous bay in an idyllic location. Swimming pools, excellent buffets and a relaxed atmosphere make it close to paradise. The grounds include a slab of hilltop jungle where macaque monkeys can be spotted. Shuttle bus to/from KK available (RM10). Although prices are high, good-value promotional rates are often available on inquiry. ❽

Shangri-La Tanjung Aru Resort Tanjung Aru Beach ☎088/225800, ⓦwww.shangri-la.com. Five kilometres southwest of the centre and set in rolling, landscaped grounds, this luxury hotel boasts two pools, watersports and fitness centres, several food outlets – and prices to match. Hourly shuttle buses ensure easy access into the city. ❾

Sutera Harbour Resort (*Pacific* & *Magellan* wings) 1 Sutera Harbour Boulevard, Sutera Harbour ☎088/317777, ⓦwww.suteraharbour.com.my. Opened in 1999 and 2000 respectively, KK's spectacular shore-side development boasts two contrasting venues: *Pacific* (❼) is more functional – designed with business and family needs to the fore – whereas *Magellan* (❽) adopts a more luxurious longhouse design. There's a marina park squeezed between the two and no less than 17 swimming pools.

The City

Downtown KK was almost totally obliterated by World War II bombs. Only in the Australia Place quarter, in the southeastern corner of the city centre, is there anything left of its colonial past. A fascinating place to start a stroll around the city is at the **Borneo 1945** coffee house (part of *Borneo Backpackers*) which doubles as a tiny museum, its walls displaying wartime photographs of Australian and British soldiers, local unsung heroes as well as replicas of war memorial plaques in Sabah.

A block east, under the shadow of Bukit Bendera (Signal Hill), stands the **Atkinson Clock Tower**, a robust wooden landmark built in 1905 in memory of a district officer in the Chartered Company who died of Borneo fever. From here, a set of steps leads up to Jalan Bukit Bendera which leads to **Signal Hill Observatory**, a fifteen-minute walk away. The vantage point provides a stunning view of KK's matrix of functional buildings and of the infinitely more attractive bay beyond. Early photographs of the city show colonial officers playing cricket on the **padang** below.

One block north of Australia Place, across the busy artery Jalan Belai Polis, lies **Jalan Gaya**, KK's most elegant street lined with stylish Chinese *kedai kopis*; its chief landmarks the city's oldest and most beautiful hotel, the *Jesselton* and, a few metres away, the wood-boarded, *belian*-tiled, old post office, now housing the Sarawak Tourism Board. A lively **street market** is held along Jalan Gaya every Sunday morning, with stalls selling herbal teas, handicrafts, orchids and rabbits, and street-side coffee shops doing a roaring trade in dim sum and noodles.

It's a ten-minute stroll from Jalan Gaya across town to KK's waterfront markets, the most diverting of which is the **Filipino Market,** opposite blocks K and M of the Sinsuran Complex. The warren of stalls are run by Indonesian and Filipino immigrants, who stock Sabahian ethnic wares beside their own baskets, shells and trinkets. Next door is the dark and labyrinthine **general market** – the first floor has dozens of daytime food stalls – and, behind that, the manic waterfront **fish market** – worth investigating if you can stomach the smell.

△ Kota Kinabalu from Signal Hill

To the Sabah State Museum

The **Sabah State Museum** (daily except Fri 9am–5pm; RM5), KK's most rewarding sight, can be reached on the State Museum bus from opposite the GPO or by taxi (RM8); however, the twenty-minute walk there is interesting enough, taking you southwest along Jalan Tunku Abdul Rahman, past the pyramidal Catholic **Sacred Heart Cathedral**, turning left at a roundabout before the **Sabah State Mosque**, whose eye-catching dome sits, like a Fabergé egg, on top of the main body of the complex.

The museum buildings are styled after Murut and Rungus longhouses and set in exotic grounds that are home to several splendid steam engines. Its highlight is the **ethnographic collection** which features a *bangkaran*, or cluster of human skulls, dating from Sabah's head-hunting days; and a *sininggazanak*, a totemic wooden figurine which would have been placed in the field of a Kadazan man who had died leaving no heirs. Photographs in the history gallery trace the development of Kota Kinabalu – look out for an intriguing picture of Jesselton at a time when Jalan Gaya still constituted the waterfront, lined with lean-tos thatched with *nipah*-palm leaves. There are old snaps of Chartered Company officials, Sabahian natives and Chinese pioneers, while beyond, in the Merdeka Gallery, newspaper cuttings trace the story of Malaysia's path to independence. Most of the Islamic Civilization Gallery comprises photographs of objects from other museums around the world, though it does boast an exquisite nineteenth-century Ottoman chessboard crafted from mother-of-pearl, ebony and ivory, and several antique Korans. Beside the museum entrance is a souvenir shop selling handicrafts and postcards.

The **Science and Technology Centre** (same hours as museum; free), next door to the museum, houses less-than-gripping exhibitions on oil-drilling and broadcasting technology, so head upstairs to the **Art Gallery** (same hours) instead. Its centrepiece is a giant string of Rungus beads, created by Chee Sing Teck, hanging from the ceiling.

Fronting the museum is a **botanical garden** (daily 8am–6pm; free), whose range of tropical plants is best experienced on one of the free guided tours (daily except Fri at 9am & 2pm). Finely crafted traditional houses representing all Sabah's major tribes border the garden, in the Kampung Warisan, or Heritage Village.

Past the museum, Jalan Tunku Abdul Rahman continues on for another 3km (becoming Jalan Mat Salleh) to the beach at **Tanjung Aru**, site of the swanky and sprawling *Shangri-La Resort* beyond. The long, narrow beach itself isn't spectacular, and given that there are so many beautiful islands just off the coast, there's no great incentive to visit other than at weekends, when large numbers of locals come for satay and barbecued seafood sold at the **food and drink stalls**. To reach Tanjung Aru direct from the centre, take a red Luen Thung Company bus from the GPO.

Kota Kinabalu City Botanical Park

Designated as a bird sanctuary in 1996, **Kota Kinabalu City Botanical Park**, Jalan Bukit Bendahara Upper (☎088/262420; ✉likaswetlands@hotmail.com; 8am–6pm, Tues–Sun; RM10), comprises 24 hectares of mangrove forest, 3km north of the city centre; the only remaining patch of an extensive mangrove system that once covered this coastline. The site is an important refuge and feeding ground for many species of resident birds, as well as several migratory species from northern Asia.

There are a number of marked trails on **boardwalks** where you may catch sight of various herons, egrets, sandpipers, pigeon and doves, but come quite early in the morning or late in the afternoon for optimum viewing conditions. Other mangrove wildlife here includes fiddler crabs, mudskippers, monitor lizards, weaver ants, water snakes and mud lobsters.

To get there its possible to take the Likas bus (half hourly; RM1) from the Wawasan Plaza terminal, west of the city centre. It won't go right into the park though; ask to be dropped at the turn-off before Likas where you must walk for twenty minutes to reach the park reception. Given this, it is clearly more convenient to get a taxi from the centre (RM10–15).

Eating, drinking and nightlife

There's a good range of Malay and Indian **restaurants** in KK, but the city excels in its no-frills, Chinese **kedai kopis**, where you find excellent-value noodle breakfasts, seafood and stir-fries; also highly dependable are the numerous **hawker stalls** (daily 7am–6pm), usually offering satay and barbecues. Sabahian cuisine is, unfortunately, harder to find – rather a disappointment considering the state's indigenous peoples all have their own tasty dishes. Bear in mind that locals tend to eat quite early and many restaurants require last orders by 9pm. There are a few good **bars**, listed below, but generally KK is not noted for its nightlife

Hawker stalls & food courts

Beach Street (between Jalan Pantai and Jalan Gaya). Pedestrianized area made more welcoming and atmospheric by a judicious assortment of plants and flowers. The various outlets include *Sugar Bun*'s cakes and juices, *Pizza Hut*'s mediocre pizzas, a hawker selling excellent *roti canai* (closed 6pm) and more substantial Malay *nasi campur*. A performance area in the centre hosts bands and karaoke 7pm onwards.

General Market Jalan Tun Fuad Stephens. The *nasi campur* stalls on the upper floor provide filling, good-value meals during the day but it all closes up around 6pm.

Night Market Behind the Filipino Market, Jalan Tun Fuad Stephens. Fried chicken and barbecue fish are the specialities here, 6pm–2am.

SEDCO Square SEDCO Complex (between Jalan Sepuluh and Jalan Duabelas). Restaurant-lined square, with outdoor tables; a fine spot for satay, chicken wings and barbecued fish (try *Kam Bah Seafood Restoran*). Prices vary from RM3 for satay sticks to RM50 for king prawns and fresh red snapper.

Waterfront Food and Bar Court Jalan Tun Fuad Stephens. New development in the north-western corner of the city overlooking the South China Sea where two dozen restaurants and cafés compete for business; it's best for a beer or juice enjoying the cool night air on the long communal boarwalk, picking at fresh salad or satay. Daily 6pm–2am.

Cafés

Bantong Jalan Kampung Air 1. Cheap, cheerful and topnotch café. Cooks David and Ian churn out enticing *iyam goring* (lemon chicken), *nasi* and the KK speciality *bonga* – greens in shrimp sauce, ginger, garlic and soy. Daily 8am–11pm (dinner menu begins at 7pm).

Borneo 1945 24 Lorong Dewan, Australia Place ☎088/272945. A fascinating new addition to KK's café scene, this coffee shop, located on the ground floor of *Borneo Backpackers*, doubles as a tiny World War II museum. Smoked chicken and beef stew – in memory of wartime ration packs – are the trademark dishes. Daily 7.30am–10pm.

Coffee Bean Ground floor, Wisma Merdeka ☎088/232333. Popular but pricey Western-style coffee shop with scrumptious cakes and excellent coffee. Daily 9am–9.30pm.

New Fortune Block 36, Jalan Laiman Diki, Kampung Air. A busy local favourite, it houses several stalls, the best of which serves superb dim sum at breakfast and later. Daily 6am–7pm.

Pete's Corner Block B, Asia City. Neatly tiled, open-fronted corner shop serving egg, sausage and baked-bean breakfasts, omelettes and sandwiches, as well as more substantial Western meals such as steaks and chops plus Malaysian favourites, all at very affordable prices (RM10 for lamb chops). Daily 8am–6pm.

Snack 63 Jalan Gaya ☎016/806 8686. Narrow, neat little juice bar run by sophisticated young KK-ites. Mon–Sat 8am–6pm, Sun 8am–2pm.

Restaurants

Bilal Block B, Segama Complex. A classic North Indian Muslim eating house, with a buffet-style range of tasty and inexpensive curries. Daily 6am–9pm.

Haj Anuar Block H, Sinsuran Complex. Cosy, open-fronted place opposite the *Sinsuran Inn*, with a Malay menu including *mee soto*, *nasi lemak* and *nasi campur*. Daily 7am–7pm.

Hyatt Hotel The all-you-can-eat evening buffet (6.30–9.30pm) in the *Tanjung Ria* café is a great bargain at RM49 per person (RM25 for vegetarian). The range of dishes is mind-boggling, especially at Wednesday's Malaysian food night. (Each evening has a different theme.)

Jothy's Banana Leaf 1/G9, Api-Api Centre. Excellent South Indian establishments with immaculate *dosai* and a variety of flavoursome curries including vegetarian banana leaf. Daily 10am–11pm.

Little Italy Jalan Pantai/Jalan Limabelas ☎088/232231. Although setting you back around RM80 plus for two, this is a most welcome addition to KK's culinary landscape; superb pizzas, fresh salads and acceptable house wine. Daily 10am–11pm.

Naluwan 16–17 Jalan Haji Saman. A huge, cavernous place, which for a modest outlay (RM10 lunch, RM18 dinner) buys you all you can eat from a buffet that's constantly replenished with all manner of tasty pan-Asian dishes. Daily 9am–11.30pm.

Sri Latha Curry House 33 Jalan Bandaran Berjaya. The banana-leaf curry in this simple South Indian restaurant west of the Padang is one of the best deals in KK (RM3.50 for vegetarian, RM6 for meat), accompanied by an informed and friendly staff. There's chicken biriyani on a Saturday (RM2), and *masala dosai* on Sunday (RM1.20). Daily 8am–11pm.

Sri Melaka 9 Jalan Laiman Diki, Kampung Air. Popular spot, best for Malay and Nonya food; try the excellent *asam* fish-head (RM10 portion feeds two) and *ulang ulang*, the in-season vegetable

platter, which at RM6 is enough for two. Daily 11am–10pm.

Sri Rahmat Lot 7, Block D, Segama Complex. A basic, no-frills, Malay restaurant (though with a/c) that's worth frequenting for the delicious *laksa* alone. Mon–Sat 7am–9pm, Sun 7am–5pm.

Tam Nak Thai Y/G5, Api-Api Centre ☎088/257328. Fine Thai cuisine and a pleasing ambience. Best to book, especially if you to intend to eat after 8pm. Daily 11.30am–3pm & 6–10pm.

Yesteryears 9 Lorong Dewan, Australia Place ☎088/239257. Funky little pizza house frequented by locals, tucked away down a quiet street. Reasonable prices – RM7 for a Margarita – and cheap beer make this a top spot. Daily 10am–10.30pm.

Bars and clubs

Hunter's Pub On the first floor of KK's most popular hotel, the *Kinabalu Daya*, this is the place where all the characters – locals and travellers alike – congregate from 10pm onwards. The karaoke can get a bit shrill but the atmosphere is great. Free entry.

Reef Project Dance Bar Beach Street. First-floor club/bar with nightly live music and a funky terrace overlooking the busy pedestrianized street's comings and goings. The only downsides are the expensive beer and average food. Daily 11am–2pm. Occasional entry charge.

Shenanigan's *Hyatt Hotel* (entrance on Jalan Datuk Salleh Sulong). KK's top town-centre bar whose staff pull English pints as well as local lagers. Features live Filipino bands nightly and a rather good DJ mix from 10pm including Sarawak hits, R&B and hip hop. Mon–Thurs 6pm–1am, Fri & Sat 6pm–3am, Sun 4pm–midnight. Free entry.

Upperstar Café & Bar Jalan Saleh Sulong (opposite the *Hyatt*). Youthful bar with a cracking balcony on KK's hippest street; eclectic soundtrack, friendly service, competitively priced beers and tasty tapas-style dishes, Daily noon–2am. Free entry.

Tour operators

KK has plenty of reliable and reasonably priced **tour operators** offering an immense array of trekking, rafting, diving and wildlife-watching packages. Many are based in the Wisma Sabah plaza at the eastern end of the city centre (opposite the *Kinabalu Daya Hotel*). Note that many of the locations on offer are only possible on a tour and these are often tailor-made to travellers' requirements; for this reason it's best to contact operators as far **in advance** as possible. Expect to pay around RM50 for a half-day KK city tour, or RM80 for a half-day dive; RM120 for day-trips to Tunku Abdul Rahman; RM180 for a day's whitewater rafting; RM300 upwards for extended tours into the forested interior and RM1000 plus for two days diving off Semporna. We've listed some of the best operators below; for a complete rundown visit the Sabah Tourism Board or check their website at Ⓦ www.sabahtourism.com.

Borneo Divers and Sea Sports 9th floor, Menara Jubili, 53, Jalan Gaya ☎ 088/222226; Ⓦ www .borneodivers.info. Diving specialists with a resort on Mabul for Sipidan dives. RM1000 for two-night stay plus dives.

🏃 **Borneo Eco Tours** Lot 1, Pusat Perindustrian, Kolombong Jaya, Mile 5.5, Jalan Kolombong; ☎ 088/438300; Ⓦ www .borneoecotours.com. Run by Sabah ecotourism pioneer and nature photographer, Albert Teo, tours include the Sabah Wildlife Safari, a seven-day trip around the state taking in the Tunku Rahman and Turtle Islands, and Sepilok orangutan sanctuary (all around RM100). But the jewel in this award-winning operation's crown is its *Sukau Rainforest Lodge* on Sungai Kinabatangan, the very best place to view wildlife in Sabah.

Borneo Nature Tours Lot 10, Ground floor, Sadong Jaya Complex ☎ 088/267637; Ⓦ www.brl .com.my. BNT runs the luxurious *Borneo Rainforest Lodge* (RM250 a night), in Danum Valley (nearest town Lahud Datu); it's also the only operator with a licence to take groups into the inaccessible Maliau Basin, Sabah's "lost world".

Borneo Sea Adventures First floor, 8A, Karamunsing Warehouse, PO Box 10134 ☎ 088/230000, Ⓦ www.bornsea.com. Arranges dive tours in Cipadan and Kota Delud.

Borneo Ultimate Lot G29, Ground floor, Wisma Sabah ☎ 088/225188;

Ⓦ www.borneoultimate.com.my. Offers a heart-racing day whitewater rafting on Sungai Padas for RM180 including lunch.

Sabah Divers G27 Ground floor, Wisma Sabah ☎ 088/256433; Ⓦ www.sabahdivers.com. Specialist diving outfit offering SSI courses (as industry-acceptable as PADI) and dives off Tunku Abdul Rahman island, close to KK.

Seaventures Tours and Travel Fourth floor, Wisma Sabah ☎ 088/422423, Ⓦ mattasabah.com /seaventures/index.asp. Leading, well-resourced operator offering Sipadan and Mabul diving packages from around RM1200 for three nights with morning and afternoon dives.

Sipadan Dive Centre A1 103, 11th floor, Wisma Merdeka ☎ 088/240584, Ⓔ sipadan@po.jaring.my. Offers a three-day diving excursion to Sipadan for around RM1300 per person; prices include return transfer from KK to Sipadan by air, land and sea, daily boat dives plus unlimited shore dives. The company also runs the *Pulau Tiga Resort* where the TV series *Survivor* was shot.

Wildlife Expeditions Ground floor, Tanjung Wing, *Shangri-la Tanjung Aru Resort* ☎ 088/246000, Ⓦ www.wildlife-expeditions.com. Wildlife specialists with a lodge near Sukau on the Sungai Kinabatangan, where a two-day/one-night visit, plus transport from Sandakan costs around RM400–500 (more if including flight from KK).

Listings

Airlines AirAsia, 94 Jalan Gaya ☎ 088/284669, Mon–Sat 8.30am–5pm; MAS, 10th floor, Kompleks Karamunsing, Jalan Tuaran ☎ 088/213555 or 290600, Mon–Fri 8.30am–5pm, Sat 8.30am–midday (24hr number: ☎ 1300883000), and 11th floor, Gaya Centre, beside Wisma Sabah ☎ 088/213555; Mon–Fri 9am–5pm. British Airways, Jalan Haji Sam ☎ 088/428057, Royal Brunei, ☎ 088/242193, Singapore Airlines ☎ 088/255444 and Thai Airways ☎ 088/232896 are all on the ground floor of Kompleks Kuwasa.
Airport information ☎ 088/238555.
American Express Lot 3.50 and 3.51, 3rd floor, Kompleks Karamunsing, Jalan Tuaran ☎ 088/241200 (Mon–Fri 8.30am–5.30pm).
Banks and exchange HSBC, 56 Jalan Gaya; Sabah Bank, Block K, Sinsuran Complex; Standard

Chartered Bank, 20 Jalan Haji Saman. Money-changers (Mon–Sat 10am–7pm) include Ban Loong Money Changer and Travellers' Money Changer, both on the ground floor of Wisma Merdeka; there's also an office in the Taiping Goldsmith, Block A, Sinsuran Complex.
Bookshops Iwase Bookshop (Wisma Merdeka), Tung Nam, 129 Jalan Gaya, and the Yaohan bookstore (2nd floor, Centrepoint) have a few shelves of English-language novels. For an unparalleled array of books on Southeast Asia, head for Borneo Books, (ground floor and 2nd floor Wisma Merdeka, Ⓦ www.borneobooks.com) and Borneo Crafts (1st floor, Wisma Merdeka), or the latter's branch at the Sabah State Museum; the *Hyatt's* bookshop stocks a modest range of international newspapers and magazines.

Car rental Kinabalu Rent-A-Car, Lot 3.60, 3rd floor, Kompleks Karamunsing ☎ 088/232602, ✉ rentcar@po.jaring.my; Hertz, Level 1, Lot 39, KK International Airport ☎ 088/317740, ✉ kk@hertz.simenet.com. Rates start from around RM150 per day, though four-wheel-drives (from RM230) are advisable if you plan to get off the beaten track.

Cinemas The Poring and Kilan Cinema, and the Capitol Theatre, below the SEDCO Centre at the western edge of downtown KK, both have regular screenings of English-language movies. Programme listings are in the *Borneo Mail* or *Daily Express*.

Consulates Konsulat Jenderal Indonesia, Jalan Kemajuan ☎ 088/218600, issues visas for Kalimantan. The nearest consular representation for most nationalities is in KL; see p.146.

Hospital Queen Elizabeth Hospital is beyond the Sabah State Museum, on Jalan Penampang ☎ 088/218166. In an emergency, dial ☎ 999.

Internet access *The Net*, 6th floor, Wisma Merdeka, also branches at Lot D-50, 4th floor, Wisma Sabah and 3rd floor, Centrepoint (1RM for 30min); *City Internet Café*, Lot 41, ground floor, City Parade, Jalan Centrepoint (3RM per hour)

Laundry Meba Laundry Services, Block B, Sinsuran Complex (daily 8.30am–7pm). Very reasonable prices (cheaper than hotel services).

Pharmacies Centrepoint Pharmacy, Centrepoint; Farmasi Gaya, 122 Jalan Gaya; Metropharm, Block A, Sinsuran Complex.

Police The main police station, Balai Polis KK ☎ 088/247111, is below Atkinson Clock Tower on Jalan Padang. In an emergency dial ☎ 999.

Post Office The GPO (Mon–Sat 8am–5pm, Sun 10am–1pm) lies between the Sinsuran and Segama complexes, on Jalan Tun Razak; poste restante/general delivery is just inside the front doors.

Shopping Borneo Handicraft, first floor, Wisma Merdeka, has a good choice of woodwork, basketry and gongs; Borneo Handicraft & Ceramic Shop (ground floor, Centrepoint) stocks ceramics, antiques and primitive sculptures. Also good are the souvenir shops at the Sabah State Museum and the STB, while the Filipino Market's scores of stalls sell both local and Filipino wares. Sri Pelancongan Lot 4, ground floor, Block L, Sinsuran Complex (☎ 088/232121; located behind Sabah Parks) has a small but quality selection of baskets, artwork and textiles.

Spas and massage H.T. Reflexology Centre, Lot 49, Shoplot 11, ground floor, Block F, Raun inggah Mata 3, Asia City ☎ 5088/270273 (daily 8am–6.30pm); Ka'andaman Traditional Healing Garden, KM8, Hongkod Kolsam, Jalan Penam-pang (on the road to Donggongon from KK) ☎ 088/721008, ⓦ www.kaandamanspa.com.my (daily 11am–11pm).

Taxis Book a taxi on either ☎ 088/252113 or 251863.

Telephones There are IDD facilities at Kedai Telekom (daily 8am–10pm), in Centrepoint. Phonecards, available at the GPO and any shops displaying the "Uniphone Kad" sign, can be used for international calls from orange public phone booths; yellow booths are for local calls only.

Train information ☎ 088/254611.

Visa Extensions Immigration Department, 4th floor, Wisma Dana Na Bandang, Jalan Tunku Abdul Rahman (Mon–Thurs 8am–1pm & 2–4.30pm, Fri 8am–1pm & 2–3.30pm, Sat 8am–1pm; ☎ 088/216711). Visa extensions of up to a month are available.

Around Kota Kinabalu

The main attraction around KK is undoubtedly the beaches and wildlife of **Tunku Abdul Rahman Park**. It's also worth considering a day-trip south to the **Monsopiad Cultural Village** and on to **Kinarut**, a quaint village nestling below the Crocker Mountain Range.

Tunku Abdul Rahman Park

Named after Malaysia's first prime minister, and situated just a short boat trip from Kota Kinabalu, the five islands of **Tunku Abdul Rahman Park** (sometimes written "TAR Park") represent the most westerly ripples of the undulating Crocker Mountain Range. The islands' forests, beaches and coral reefs lie within just an eight-kilometre radius of downtown KK, with park territory as close as 3km off the mainland. They constitute West Sabah's most-visited site and are well worth visiting; try to avoid the weekends and public holidays when facilities can get overstretched.

The site of the British North Borneo Chartered Company's first outpost in the region, **Pulau Gaya** is the closest of the islands to KK and also the largest, its name derived from *goyoh*, the Bajau word for "big". Although a native chief granted the island's timber rights to a certain Mr White in 1879, they were never fully exploited, and so lowland rainforest still blankets Gaya, a seven-kilometre trail snaking across it. The island's premier trail starts on the southern side of the island at **Camp Bay**, which is adjacent to a mangrove forest where crabs and mudskippers can be viewed from the boardwalk that intersects it. The easy-going three-hour jungle trail starts at quite a gradient, climbing to 1750m at its highest point, providing glimpses of the emerald sea through the trees. Lizards flicker across your path and there is abundant birdlife, depending on the time of day. The path drops back to the shoreline, close to the resort, where a boat can ferry you back (RM10), although plan to leave this no later than 6pm as boatmen are harder to catch after then. As the boatmen have a small office on the beach, there is no need to book their services earlier.

While Camp Bay offers pleasant enough swimming, a more secluded and alluring alternative is **Polis Beach**, 500m south. Boatmen demand extra for the trip but it's money well spent: the bay is idyllic, its white-sand beach, running gently down to the water, lined by trees. The wildlife on Gaya includes hornbills, wild pigs, lizards, snakes and macaques – which have been known to swim over to nearby **Pulau Sapi** (Cow Island), an islet just northwest of Gaya. Though far smaller than Gaya, Sapi too has trails and is home to macaques and hornbills; with the best beaches of any of the islands, it's popular with swimmers, snorkellers and picnickers.

The park's three other islands cluster together a few kilometres west of Gaya. The park headquarters are situated on crescent-shaped **Pulau Manukan** – site of a former stone quarry and now the most developed of all the park's islands. Manukan's sandy beaches and coral have led to the construction of chalets, a restaurant, swimming pool and tennis courts, which draw large numbers of locals. Across a narrow channel from Manukan is tiny **Pulau Mamutik**, which can be crossed on foot in fifteen minutes in low tide and has excellent sands on either side of its jetty. The last of the group, **Pulau Sulug**, is the most remote and consequently the quietest, though its good coral makes it popular with divers.

Practicalities

There are frequent **boat services** to the islands from the Port Authority jetty, east of the city centre, on Jalan Haji Sarnan. To Pulau Manukan, ten-seater launches leave when full (RM15 return; 20min); this usually involves little more than a thirty-minute wait. It's best to book your return trip when you buy your outbound ticket. A visit to Manukan can also be part of an island hop, taking in Sapi, Sulug and Gaya; check at the jetty booking office for prices.

Accommodation is fairly limited on the islands; it is only possible to stay the night at the resorts in Manukan and Gaya. No camping is permitted anywhere in the park. *Manukan Island Resort*, has twenty chalets (RM200 for four occupants, RM10 for every extra person) and is the only accommodation on that island. Most of the chalets are under trees close to the beach but a few – the best ones – are further uphill on the island's only road. Each one, which must be reserved as a whole, contains two double rooms, a spacious living area, bathroom and kitchen; **book** in advance in KK through the Sutera Sanctuary Lodges, G15 ground floor, Wisma Sabah (Mon–Fri 8am–5pm, Sat 8am–2pm;

☎088/243629; ⓦwww.suterasanctuarylodges.com. The resort **restaurant** (daily 7am–10pm) is the only one on the island and offers tasty buffet lunches and dinners for RM15 each.

A little pricier but with more elegant, airy, chalets is the 🥢 *Gayana Island Eco Resort* (☎088/245158, ⓦwww.gayana-resort.com/info.html; ⑥) on Pulau Gaya; the launch from the jetty costs RM15 one way. As resorts in Sabah go it's small-scale, rustic and unpretentious, with spacious bathrooms in the lovely, airy two-bed chalets, located on stilts over the lapping waves. The resort also contains a fabulous fish **restaurant**, a marine conservation centre with various tanks containing eels, lobsters and strange-looking flora and fauna as well as numerous activities from kayaking to trekking.

⑦ South to Donggongon and Monsopiad Cultural Village

Regular minivans from Jalan Tun Fuad Stephens leave the city for the suburb of **Donggongon**, around 10km to the south. From the bus station here, it's a ten-minute local bus ride past rice fields and winding streams to **KAMPUNG MONSOPIAD's Cultural Village** (daily 9am–6pm; RM50; guided tours 10am, noon, 3pm & 5pm; ⓦwww.monsopiad.com), a Kadazan theme park nestled in a rustic setting. It's arguable whether the village is really worth the effort given the high entrance price, although the interesting exhibits might just swing the balance.

Founded in memory of the Kadazan head-hunter Monsopiad, the village comprises a museum, handicraft workshop, granary and main hall, in which cultural performances and native feasts are held (the latter by prior arrangement). Monsopiad's grisly harvest of 42 skulls are displayed in a row along a rafter in his ancestral house and decked with *hisad* (palm) leaves signifying the victims' hair. Among them is a thigh bone, attesting to one of several legends about the great man. Monsopiad eventually grew too fond of harvesting heads and constituted a public menace; killed by a group of friends, he was buried beneath a stone that still stands near the house, with his own head left intact out of respect. Once a year (usually in May), a Kadazan priestess, or *bobohizan*, is called in to communicate with the spirits, whose job it is to watch over Monsopiad's descendants.

Once you're out in Donggongon, take the opportunity to see Sabah's oldest church, **St Michael's Catholic Church**, only a twenty-minute walk (or short bus ride) beyond the bus terminus and along the main road. Built in 1897, the sturdy granite building stands on a hillock above peaceful Kampung Dabak, its red roof topped by a simple stone cross. Inside, the church is undecorated, save a mural depicting the Last Supper and framed paintings of the Stations of the Cross.

On to Kinarut and Papar

Further down the main road south, KK's suburbs yield to a carpet of paddy fields that stretches away to the foothills of the Crocker Mountain Range. From the minivan terminal in KK there are frequent departures to the village of **KINARUT**, 21km away, the starting point for an enjoyable half-hour stroll along a quiet road to **Kampung Tampasak**, where there's a replica of the *sininggazanak* in the State Museum in KK. From the two faded old shophouses that form the centre of Kinarut, walk across the train line, cross the bridge to your left and turn right – the turning to the kampung is signposted by an overgrown tyre. On your way, you'll see two or three mysterious *menhirs*, upright stones, thought to have been erected centuries ago either as status symbols or boundary stones, or to mark the burial places of shamans.

Two to three kilometres away at **KINARUT LAUT** (take a Papar minivan from KK), the *Seaside Travellers' Inn* (T088/750313; W www.infosabah.com.my /seaside; ❸) has become a popular retreat for KK weekenders, with neat, clean dorms (RM20) and airy, pleasant rooms with communal shower and toilet. A balcony off the dining room looks out to the nearby islands of Dinawan and Muntukat, and over the inn's own stretch of beach. Close to the inn is the equally appealing, small-scale beachfront resort, *Langkah Syabas*, PO Box 451, Kinarut (T088/752000, E lsr@po.jaring.my; ❺), managed by environmentally focused Australians. The fourteen detached and semi-detached chalets here are set in a nice garden and encircle a swimming pool. Activities on offer include boat trips to nearby islands, horse riding and short treks; shuttle bus available. With notice, you can get picked up from town or the Inanam coach terminal.

The one town of any size between KK and Beaufort, **Papar**, is another 20km or so further south; minivans run here all through the day from KK's Wawasan Plaza terminal. Unless you're in Papar on Sunday for the decent weekly market, the only reason to break your journey here is to visit the nearby beach – **Pantai Manis** – reached by minivan (RM1), from the small town's centre.

Southwestern Sabah and the interior

Sabah's **southwestern** reaches are dominated first by the long, hard haul up to the cloud forest of the **Sinsuron Pass** before the highway folds out onto the ridges of the **Crocker Mountain Range**, which divides the state's west coast and swampy Klias Peninsula from the area christened the **interior** in the days of the Chartered Company. At one time, this sparsely populated region was effectively isolated from the west coast by the mountains. This changed at the turn of the twentieth century, when a railway was built between Jesselton (modern-day KK) and Tenom in order to transport the raw materials being produced by the region's thriving rubber industry. Today, oil palm cultivation takes precedence, though the Kadazan/Dusun and Murut peoples still look to the interior's fertile soils for their living, cultivating rice, maize and cocoa. Despite the prevalence of oil palm there is a wild beauty to the scenery with premier features, the **Padas Gorge** and the **Maliau Basin**, spectacular and well worth visiting. Traditionally only accessible to the most independent of travellers, the terrain is now opening up thanks to trekking and adventure trips run by tour operators.

Travelling by bus, train or car/4WD, it is possible to circumnavigate the region from KK, starting with a drive southeast over the mountains to the Kadazan/ Dusun town of **Tambunan**, which sits on a plain chequered with paddy fields. From Tambunan, the road continues further south to **Keningau**, the launch pad for more adventurous detours deeper into the heart of the interior. Following the circular route to KK entails travelling south on to **Tenom** which, along with Keningau, marks the start of Murut territory, which stretches down to the Kalimantan border. For the most adventurous travellers this is one of the embarkation points to the Maliau Basin; a route only negotiated by four-wheel-drive vehicles.

Tenom itself sits on the bank of the Sungai Padas, whose turbulent waters you have to negotiate if you sign up for a **whitewater rafting** tour (see KK tour operators). The train line connects Tenom with **Beaufort**, from where you can head one of three ways: north to KK; south to Sipitang, the terminus for buses and taxis into Sarawak; or west into the **Klias Penin-sula**, an infertile former swamp forest that forms the northeastern reach of Brunei Bay. From Kuala Penyu, in the northern corner of the peninsula, boats travel to the tiny **Pulau Tiga National Park**, one of East Malaysia's most gorgeous spots.

Sinsuron Pass

Unless you take a Tenom-bound train from Beaufort, the only way to reach the interior of Sabah is to follow the 80km of road from KK southeast to Tambunan; buses plying this route leave regularly from the CBTN terminal at Inanam, on the outskirts of KK. Ten kilometres out of the city, paddy fields give way to the rolling foothills of the **Crocker Mountain Range**, and cars and buses start the long, twisting haul up to the 1649-metre-high **Sinsuron Pass**. From here, there are views of mighty Gunung Kinabalu, weather permitting. The occasional lean-to shack squats by the side of the road, piled with in-season produce like pineapples, mangoes, rambutans, bananas and vegetables.

Tambunan and around

Seventeen kilometres short of Tambunan, a kink in the road reveals the gleaming emerald paddy fields of **Tambunan Plain** below. **Gunung Trus Madi**, Sabah's second highest mountain (2642m), towers above the plain's east-ern flank; climbing it is an exciting alternative to ascending Gunung Kinabalu.

After such a pretty approach, the bustling little town of **TAMBUNAN**, centred on an ugly square of modern shophouses, is bound to disappoint. The best thing about the place (the administrative centre of Tambunan District) is its lively *tamu*, held on Thursday mornings close to the town centre.

Although now a sleepy agricultural district, Tambunan featured in one of the more turbulent periods in Sabah's history, when it witnessed the demise of folk hero and rebel, **Mat Salleh**. In 1897, he burned down the British settlement on Pulau Gaya in protest at taxes being levied by the Chartered Company; branded an outlaw, with a price on his head, Salleh finally negoti-ated a deal with William Clarke Cowie of the Chartered Company that allowed him and his men to settle in Tambunan. The outcome outraged other members of the company and Salleh hurriedly withdrew to Tambunan Plain, where he erected a fort of bamboo and stone. Sure enough, British forces descended into the plain at the beginning of 1900 and besieged Salleh's fort; by the end of January, Salleh was dead, killed by a stray bullet. It's said that had Salleh been wearing his "invulnerable jacket", inscribed with verses from the Koran (it's exhibited at the Sabah State Museum), he would have lived to fight another day. At Kampung Tibabar, a few kilometres north of Tambunan, a stone memorial marks the site of his fort.

Practicalities

Buses to and from KK, Ranau and Keningau stop in the main square, around which are a number of nondescript cafés. The only reasonable **place to stay** is the *Tambunan Village Resort Centre* (TVRC; ☎087/774076, ⓦ www.tvrc.net), 1km north of town, with ten rooms (❸) and twin-bed chalets (❹). To get there, catch a minivan (RM1) from the town square going along the KK road and ask to be dropped at the TVRC turning to the right. The centre, in a lovely location beside a fast-running river, has a **restaurant** serving basic Chinese and Malay dishes. Staff there seasonally produce *lihing* – the rice wine for which

Tambunan is locally renowned. Kayaking and buffalo riding are available here too, though for residents only.

Around Tambunan: Mawar Waterfall and Gunung Trus Madi

The *Tambunan Village Resort Centre* arranges tours to the beautiful **Mawar Waterfall**, located in dense forest at Kampung Patau, though it's possible to get there by catching the Ranau bus, for the 7km ride from Tambunan to **Kampung Patau** (hourly; RM3). Here there's a wide gravel trail leading to the waterfall, a two-hour hike away through an idyllic bowl of hills stepped with groves of fern and bamboo.

The centre also arranges treks up **Gunung Trus Madi**, the second highest mountain in Sabah. It's renowned as a good place to catch sight of the rare, insectivorous pitcher plant (*Nepenthes*) close to the summit, and also offers fabulous views across the Crocker Range towards Tambunan and Gunung Kinabalu. The climb, however, is a demanding overnight trip, the first part involving a one-hour journey by van to **Kampung Kengaran**, at the base of the mountain. The climb up to the summit, where you camp in cool conditions for the night, takes five hours up a rough, and oftentimes steep, path, which shouldn't be attempted without a guide. To get an update on local **weather conditions** and to hire a **guide** contact the Sabah Parks office in KK (see p.529), the Forestry Department in Tambunan (☏087/774691) or talk it over with the staff at the TVRC.

Crocker Range National Park

Due west of Tambunan, within eyeshot, lies the deep green, enfolding ridges of Sabah's largest single protected area, the 140,000-hectare **Crocker Range National Park**. A giant backbone of greenclad ridges that stretch from Gunung Kinabalu's granite peaks down to the gorge of Sungai Padas, the park is largely inaccessible and has as yet no visitor facilities or public transport to its gates. Visiting the park will be of particular interest to those who enjoy trekking in lower montane and dipterocarp forest; it's also possible to catch sight of the world's largest flower, the spectacular *Rafflesia* which blooms at various points on the edge of the park. Contact Sabah Parks for further information (@www.sabahparks.org.my).

Keningau

A fifty-kilometre bruising journey south from Tambunan down one of the worst roads in the state brings you to the busy town of **KENINGAU**. It's a hectic, noisy place, streets crammed with tooting buses and taxis, pavements lined with locals hawking all manner of goods. Keningau's single attraction is its **Chinese temple**, situated right beside the bus terminus. The brightly painted murals that cover its walls and ceilings are more reminiscent of those in a Hindu temple, while in the forecourt is a statue of a fat, smiling Buddha, resplendent in red-and-yellow gown. If you're in town on a Thursday morning, check out Keningau's weekly *tamu*, a short walk up the main Keningau–Tambunan road. The only other distraction is the minivan ride twenty minutes northeast of town, through paddy fields and small kampungs, to **Taman Bandukan**. This pleasant riverside park is packed with picnicking locals on Sundays, but at other times, grazing cows and scores of butterflies are your only company; the river is clean and good for swimming, while from above its far banks – reached by a wobbly suspension bridge – there's a good view of the surrounding hills. To get to the park, take a Bingkor-bound minivan from the central square; tell the driver where you're headed.

Rather than moving on, to either Tenom or Tambunan, a more exciting alternative is to head for **Sapulut** to explore Sabah's Murut heartland. This remote region is effectively a dead end and accessible only from Keningau, to which you'll have to backtrack afterwards, although it's possible to take a 4WD and strike east along the logging roads which connect the interior with Tawau, the largest town in southern Sabah. The trip will take longer than a day unless you ask around for a vehicle to leave no later than 6.30am.

Practicalities

There are **minivans** to Keningau from Tambunan (RM8) and from KK (RM16), with buses and taxis terminating in and around the town's central square. It isn't possible to reserve a seat on a 4WD to Tawau (RM80–120 depending on number of passengers), so turn up early – around 6.30am – if you want to head out on this route.

An adequate **hotel**, *Hotel Hiap Soon* (☎087/331541; ❷), with small, simple air-conditioned rooms, lies close to the centre, though the majority are found in the new part of town, five minutes' walk behind the Chinese temple, up Jalan Masuk Spur. It's here that you'll find Keningau's friendliest budget choice, *Wah Hin* (☎087/332506; ❶), whose rooms are small and have fans and shared bathrooms; and the town's high-end spot, *Hotel Perkasa* (☎087/331045, ❹), which boasts an in-house fitness centre and restaurants, 1km out of town on the Tambunan road.

Locals congregate at the *Yung On* coffee shop, which serves cakes and pastries; it's at the northeastern edge of town, a five-minute walk to the east of the Chinese temple's neighbour, the Yuk Yin School. Nearby are *Restoran Shahrizal*, which serves fine *rotis* and curries behind its bamboo facade; and Keningau's best **restaurant**, the *Mandarin*, where one of the specialities is freshwater fish. For more economical food, try the cluster of **food stalls** beside the bus stop, bearing in mind that most are closed by dusk, or the stalls at the Thursday market.

The interior: Sapulut, Batu Punggul and the Maliau Basin

Two buses (RM20) a day make the 116-kilometre journey from Keningau southeast to **Sapulut**, deep in the heart of Murut country – the departure point for some exhilarating **river expeditions**. The time-honoured customs of Sabah's indigenous peoples are slowly dying out, but along the rivers around Sapulut you can still witness **traditional community life**. Moreover, the experience of sitting at the prow of a boat that's inching up a churning river under a dense canopy of forest is one that's hard to beat. If you do make the trip, bear in mind that it takes a few days and that you'll have to retrace your steps to Keningau, as the road runs out at Sapulut.

The trip starts inauspiciously: the terrain towards Sapulut has been so scarred by logging that, for much of the journey, you wonder why you bothered coming. Around an hour out of Keningau is tiny **Kampung Sook**, barely more than a wide stretch of the road, with a few stalls and split bamboo houses and a huge district office.

Sapulut

From Keningau, it takes three to four hours to reach **SAPULUT**, situated at the convergence of the Sapulut and Talankai rivers, and hemmed in by densely forested hills. It remains an appealing place in spite of its ugly tapioca mill, and though the main reason for coming here is to continue up- or downriver, there's enough of interest to warrant a day in the village itself. Across the pedestrian suspension bridge that spans Sungai Talankai is Sapulut's former schoolhouse (dating back to the Japanese occupation, and now overgrown) and its **Mahkamah**, or native court building. A two-hour climb through the secondary forest above the mill brings you to a panoramic view of the surrounding kampungs and countryside. The only snag with Sapulut is that there's nowhere **to stay**, so unless you're on a tour or befriend a local, you will have to return to Keningau.

Beyond Sapulut

With no accommodation in Sapulut, getting to **Batu Punggul** presents a number of problems which is a shame as the 400-metre-high limestone cliff is worth visiting. The short but steep climb to the summit is rewarded by outstanding views of the forest, while another few minutes' walk brings you to the impressive **Tinahas Caves**, whose walls are lined with swifts' nests and roosting bats. Again, there is **no accommodation** available here, a shame given the tremendous potential for ecotourism.

The **boat** trip from Sapulut to Batu Punggul (around RM200 to charter a boat for six passengers) takes around two and a half hours, though it can take twice as long, depending on the weather, passing isolated riverside kampungs and longhouses on the way.

The going gets tougher – and pricier – if you travel downriver from Sapulut to visit one of the kampungs, some of which have longhouses, towards the Kalimantan border. The first settlement of any size, forty minutes south of Sapulut, is **Pagalongan**, a surprisingly large community. It's another ten minutes to the bend in the river commanded by **Kampung Silungai**'s huge 120-metre long-house. Despite its jarring zinc roof, the longhouse is an appealing construction of green-and-white wooden slats, centring on a ceremonial hall, and home to a few hundred villagers.

Maliau Basin Conservation Area

Sabah's last wildlife wilderness, the 39,000-hectare **MALIAU BASIN CONSERVATION AREA** (🌐 www.ysnet.org.my/maliau/index.html), was originally part of a one-million-hectare timber concession belonging to the Sabah Foundation. In 1981 the Foundation designated Maliau Basin – along with Danum Valley 50km to its east – a Conservation Area for the purposes of research, education and training, thus ensuring the protection of the forest from further logging or oil-palm exploitation. The area is still hardly explored, with most visitors scientists or researchers. The basin features various types of forest including lower montane, heath and dipterocarp and is known to be home to an impressive range of large mammals, notably the Asian elephant and the Malayan sun bear, while the variety of birds include rare species found otherwise only at Gunung Kinabalu and Trus Mardi. There are around 60km of **marked trails**, a 30m high canopy and an **observation platform** at the Camel Trophy Camp. To visit, you must be on a **tour** and, at the time of writing, only Borneo Nature Tours (see KK tour operators), owners of the *Borneo Rainforest Lodge* in Danum Valley, offers trips there.

Practicalities

There is no public transport to the Maliau Basin Conservation Area; on a tour you travel the 190-kilometre journey by 4WD from Keningau. The headquarters is at Agathis Camp, from where it's a six-hour walk over the southern rim of the basin to a second base, the Camel Trophy Camp. Both have have basic facilities, including rudimentary **accommodation** currently being upgraded. From Camel camp its a hard day's hike to the region's top draw – the Maliau Falls. There are no roads in the Maliau Basin Conservation Area.

Tenom and around

After Keningau, the small town of **TENOM**, 42km to the southwest, comes as some relief. The heady days when Tenom was the bustling headquarters of the Interior District of British North Borneo are now long gone, and today it's a peaceful backwater with its fair share of simple hotels and good cafés. Lying within a mantle of forested hills, the town boasts a selection of charismatic wooden shophouses and a blue-domed mosque. The surroundings are extremely fertile, supporting maize, cocoa and soybean – predominantly cultivated by the indigenous Murut people.

The **Sabah Agricultural Park** (✆087/737952; Ⓦwww.sabah.net.my /agripark/facilities.htm; Mon–Thurs 8am–2pm, Fri & Sat 8–11am) in Lagud Sebrang, a 25-minute bus ride (RM2) from Tenom, is where the state's Agricultural Department carries out studies on a wide range of crops. The research station is renowned for its **Orchid Centre**, where a profusion of orchids cascade from trees and tree trunks. Less tempting, though actually much better than it sounds, is the nearby **Crop Museum** (free), where you can easily spend an hour strolling through the groves of exotic fruit trees and tropical plants, such as durian, rambutan, jackfruit, coffee and okra – all tended by women in wide-brimmed hats.

Practicalities

Tenom marks the furthest point south for Sabah's railway system, the track skirting the southeast edge of town. The **train station** (✆087/735514) is on the southern edge of the padang. The route from Tenom to Beaufort (one daily; 2hr 30min; RM2.80) passes through the Sungai Padas Valley, a region previously devastated by fire, but as is often the case in a lush tropical zone like southern Sabah, re-growth has been fast. Although the bus is almost twice as quick and the line is prone to delays, it is well worth taking the train and sitting back and enjoying the view.

Minivans congregate on the town's main street, Jalan Padas, which runs along the north side of the padang. The journey northwest back to KK via Beaufort is best done by train though it's possible – and faster - to get a minivan there. Minivans north to Keningau (RM6) circle around Tenom all day, looking for passengers; you can always pick a bus up on the main street, at the western edge of the padang. **Shared taxis** to Keningau cost RM10 and leave from the main street whenever they've assembled enough passengers.

Accommodation here includes the reliable *Hotel Sri Perdana*, on Jalan Tun Mustapha (✆087/734001; ❷) and the *Hotel Kim San* (✆087/735485; ❷), one street north of Jalan Tun Mustapha, about 500m southwest of the padang. The classiest place in town though, is the *Hotel Perkasa* (✆087/735811; ❹), a RM3 taxi ride (or strenuous short hike) up the hill above town, its pleasing rooms affording great views of the surrounding countryside. **Places to eat** are plentiful, with a clutch of coffee shops and restaurants in the area around the *Hotel Kim San*. For a tasty *mee* soup, try the *Restoran Double Happiness*, below the padang; or, for something a bit more lavish, head 2km south of town along the Tomani road to the cavernous *YNL Restaurant* (daily 6pm–midnight), where the speciality is fresh fish caught in the nearby Sungai Padas. The *Perkasa* has decent Chinese food and on Saturday evenings, hawker stalls are set out on the hotel's front lawn.

Beaufort

Named after Leicester P. Beaufort, one of the early governors of British North Borneo, **BEAUFORT** is a quiet, uneventful town whose commerical significance has declined markedly since the laying of a sealed road from KK into the interior lessened the importance of its rail link with Tenom. The town's position on the banks of the Sungai Padas leaves it prone to flooding, which explains why its shophouses are raised on steps – early photographs show Beaufort looking like a sort of Southeast Asian Venice. But once you've poked around in the town market, inspected angular **St Paul's Church** at the top of town and taken a walk past the stilt houses on the river bank, you've exhausted its sights; tourists normally only stop by as part of the train ride to Tenom, or on their way to the whitewater rafting on the Sungai Padas (see KK Tour Operators).

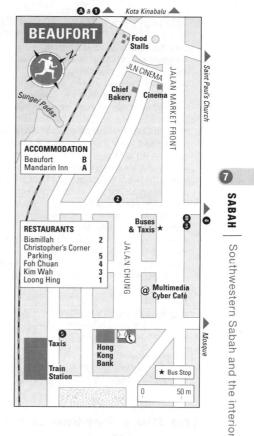

Practicalities

The **train station** is on the southern side of town, next to the river. Buses stop in the centre itself, beside the market, while **taxis** congregate outside the train station. **Internet** access is available at the *Multimedia Cyber Café*, first floor, Lot 9, Lo Chung Park.

Beaufort's two **hotels** are the *Beaufort* (☎087/211911; ❸), east of the market, and the *Mandarin Inn* (☎087/212798; ❷), five minutes' walk across the river – they're practically identical, each with basic rooms. The *Beaufort* has en-suite bathrooms to its credit, though the *Mandarin* has the edge in terms of freshness. When it comes to **eating**, you could do a lot worse than *Christopher's Corner Parking*, across from the train station, whose friendly owner will rustle you up a really good Western breakfast – toast, marmalade, sausage, beans and egg. *Restoran Kim Wah*, a sizeable establishment below the *Hotel Beaufort*, serves simple Chinese food, though better is to be found at the *Foh Chuan*, sited in one of the new blocks just north of the *Beaufort*, which is famed locally for its noodle dishes. The *Loong Hing*, 250m over the bridge and out of town, is another establishment that comes highly recommended, though if it's curry and *roti*s you're after, the *Bismillah* in the town centre is hard to beat. There are also hawker stalls next to the bridge.

Sabah's railway line

Over the metals all rusted brown,
Thunders the "Mail" to Jesselton Town;
Tearing on madly, reck'ning not fate,
Making up time – she's two days late
See how the sparks from her smokestack shower,
Swaying on wildly at three miles an hour.

As this 1922 rhyme illustrates, Sabah's main **railway line** (information on ☏088/254611)
is more a curiosity than a practical mode of transport. Although the line runs all the
way from KK to Tenom, travel between Beaufort and the capital is far quicker by **bus**,
and it's only the journey from **Beaufort to Tenom** (2hr 30min) – a bone-shaking ride
tracing the twists and turns of the Sungai Padas – that's worth making. Here, the train
passes tiny stations and winds through dramatic jungle that at times arches right over
the track – but in many places the scars left by a devastating fire in 2000 remain.
Three types of train – diesel, cargo and railcar – ply this part of the route daily; the
fastest, most comfortable and most expensive option is the compact **railcar** (RM8.50
one-way; on the other types of train, the one-way fare is RM3), whose front windows
afford an unimpeded view of the oncoming countryside; it only holds a handful of
passengers, so phone or call in at the station to book ahead.
  See also p.528 for information on the North Borneo Railway.

Timetable

Beaufort–Tenom
Mon–Sat: 8.30am (railcar); 10.00am (diesel); 12.30pm (cargo); 3.55pm (cargo).
Sun: 6.45am (diesel); 10.50am (diesel); 2.30pm (diesel); 4.05pm (railcar).

Tenom–Beaufort
Mon–Sat: 6.40am (railcar); 8am (cargo); 10.15am (diesel); 2.50pm (cargo).
Sun: 7.20am (railcar); 7.55am (diesel); 12.10pm (diesel); 3.05pm (diesel).

The Klias Peninsula and Pulau Tiga National Park

Immediately west of Beaufort, and served by regular minivans from the centre
of town, is the **Klias Peninsula**, from whose most westerly settlement, tiny
Menumbok, several ferries depart daily for Pulau Labuan (see p.548). Alternatively, it's a jarring, hour-plus bus ride from Beaufort northwest to **KUALA
PENYU**, at the northern point of the peninsula, the departure point for **Pulau
Tiga National Park**. The only place to stay near Kuala Penyu is the *Tempurong
Seaside Lodge* 🏊 (☏088/773066; ✉info@borneoauthenticadventure.com; ➎) a
few kilometers out of town along a bumpy track. The owners are happy to pick
you up, though, given some warning. The chalets are snug and comfortable,
the views over the sea panoramic and the home-cooking, available on request,
superb. The lodge has a private beach too, a short trek down a cliff path.
  Leaving Kuala Penyu, you can either get a direct bus to Beaufort, or take a
local bus 5km to **Kampung Kayul** and, at the junction of two equally dusty
– or muddy – unpaved roads, wave down a bus coming from Menumbok heading either for KK or Beaufort.

Pulau Tiga National Park

In the South China Sea, north of Kuala Penyu, **Pulau Tiga National Park**
once comprised three islands, but wave erosion has reduced one of them, Pulau

Kalampunian Besar, to a sand bar. The remaining two, Tiga and Kalampunian Damit, offer good **snorkelling** around the 7km coral reef that surrounds Tiga and the chance to see some unusual **wildlife**. Most people visiting stay at the *Pulau Tiga Resort*, a magical retreat in a gorgeous tropical marine location, or the newly opened *Borneo Survivor Resort*, although the Sabah Parks headquarters has some basic rooms too. The island acquired notoriety – and fame – as the location of the first *Survivor* reality TV series.

Pulau Tiga itself was formed by erupting mud volcanoes; indeed one of the most popular activities is to trek for 30 minutes to one in the centre of the island, whereupon you are urged to wade into the mud for an invigorating cleanse. While walking the network of trails, keep an eye out for the island's most famous inhabitants, its megapodes – rotund incubator birds, so called because they lay their eggs in mounds of sand and leaves. Most people, however, are simply happy to relax on the fine-sand beaches (Pagong-Pagong on the north side is certainly one to write home about) and swim in the azure sea.

Pulau Kalampunian Damit, 1km northeast of Pulau Tiga, is known locally as Pulau Ular, or "Snake Island", as it attracts a species of sea snake called the yellow-lipped sea krait in huge numbers – on an average day, dozens of these metallic-grey and black creatures come ashore to rest, mate and lay their eggs. Though dozy in the heat of the day, the sea kraits are poisonous, and you can only visit them with a park ranger or guide from one of the resorts.

Practicalities

To arrange boat transport **to the park**, call the Sabah Parks officer at the park itself (☏011/810636 or, for general enquiries, ☏088/211881). The return journey costs RM50 per passenger as long as there are no less than five people travelling. From Tiga, except to pay RM30 more for a boat to visit Kalampunian Damit. Even if you are staying in the Sabah Parks budget accommodation it may be possible to get on a launch run by the resorts from Penyu which leave at around 11am and 4pm daily (RM50 return). Be cautioned though that you can't fully rely on this mode of transport as, if the boat is already full, you won't get on it. It's best then to call the resorts ahead to find out if there is room.

There are three **accommodation** options on Tiga. The park authorities run a hostel (dorm beds RM30) and also twin-bed cabins (⑤) bookable through the KK Sabah Parks office (☏088/211881); note that there is no restaurant but you can use the kitchens provided to cook your own food. Alternatively, the *Pulau Tiga Resort* ⚓ (☏088/240584, ⓦwww.pulau-tiga.com; ⑥) run by the Sipadan Dive Centre, has dozens of twin-bed chalets attractively nestling on a short beach; there's also a shop, bar and a fine café/restaurant open to non-residents, with tasty buffets for all tastes (RM30). The resort's package (RM500 for three days/two nights' accommodation), includes the two-hour trip by minivan from KK to Kuala Penya and the thirty-minute boat ride to the resort. The dive store is equipped for shallow dives and snorkelling with prices from RM200 for a half day's dive plus equipment. Divers report viewing parrotfish, lionfish, clownfish and jacks attracted by the soft and hard coral. The recently opened *Borneo Survivor Resort* (☏088/919686; ⓦwww.borneosurvivor.com.my; ⑥) is still in the process of building chalets and is more of a budget operation than the *Tiga Resort*. It only has two double rooms; although the six-bed dorms (RM30) are clean and adequate. It is also possible to camp (RM10), with the resort providing the tents.

To Sarawak: Sipitang

On the bumpy gravel road 47km southwest of Beaufort, **SIPITANG** is a sleepy seafront town worth bearing in mind if you need a place to stay en route to Sarawak. As you approach from the north, a bridge marks the start of town – look out for the pretty stilt houses to your left as you cross. Just over the bridge, there's a **jetty** from where a boat leaves (daily 7.30am; RM20) for Labuan; 250m beyond that, you're in the town centre. **Buses** from Beaufort, KK and Lawas (see p.495) congregate at the terminus in the centre of town, right next door to which is the **taxi** stand. Except for a trip to Taman Negara – a beachside picnic spot a few kilometres south of town, and favoured by locals at the weekend when there'll probably be a minvan service – there's nothing to do in Sipitang. On the bright side there are a few decent **places to eat**. Across the main road, *Restoran Bismillah* does delicious curries and breakfast *rotis*; a minute or so further south, the *Asandong* puts on a good Malay buffet every night. Also, a number of satay and fried-chicken sellers set up stalls on the waterfront at dusk. Of the **hotels** along the main road, the *Hotel Asanol* (☎087/821506; ❷), just 200m from the centre, is the friendliest and most affordable with compact, en-suite rooms; the similar *Hotel Shangsan* (☎087/821800; ❸) nearby has air conditioning to boot, while the *SFI Motel* (☎087/802097; ❺), at 31 Jalan Jeti, is on a grander scale with spacious, en-suite rooms and facilities including a bar and Chinese restaurant.

Pulau Labuan

A short distance west of the Klias Peninsula, **PULAU LABUAN** is a small, arrowhead-shaped island whose size bears no relation to its significance. Its fine anchorage and **coal deposits** – the northern tip is still called Tanjung Kubong, or Coal Point – made it an attractive trading post and the island fell into the hands of the British in 1846, long before neighbouring Sabah was procured. The British administration made Labuan a free port in 1848, and by 1889, it had been incorporated into British North Borneo, a state of affairs that lasted until it joined the Straits Settlements a few years into the twentieth century.

World War II brought the focus of the world upon Labuan. Less than a month after the bombing of Pearl Harbour, the island was occupied by the invading **Japanese** army; it was through Labuan that the Japanese forces penetrated British North Borneo. In June 1945, the men of the Ninth Australian Infantry Division landed on the island and three and a half years of occupation came to an end. Labuan, along with Sabah, reverted to the British Crown in July 1946, though it was a further seventeen years before it actually became part of Sabah. Then, in 1984, the island was declared part of Malaysian Federal Territory, governed directly by Kuala Lumpur.

Today, Labuan, with a population of nearly eighty thousand, is still a duty-free port, popular for shopping with middle-market Sabahians, Bruneians and a steady expat population. Given that ferries from KK and Brunei interconnect at Labuan, you may well end up overnighting here, wishing to benefit, perhaps, from the lower alcohol prices. The main settlement, **Labuan Town**, is well laid out and clean and there are diving opportunities nearby. It's also worth considering visiting Labuan Marine Park on Pulau Kuraman, 20km offshore, which has reasonable beaches.

The island

The centre of Labuan, previously known as Victoria but now referred to simply as **LABUAN TOWN**, lies on the southeastern side of the island. The *gerai*, or general **market**, at the western end of town, is small in comparison with other Sabah markets though its upper level affords good views of Kampung Patau Patau, the modest **water village** northwest of town. Below the market is a gathering of tin shacks, where Filipinos sell seashell models, leather bags, brassware, cloth and silks. Replacing the cramped, chaotic bays of old, the town now has a gleaming new ferry terminal on Jalan Merdeka, which, along with the just completed international airport, attests to the island's relative prosperity and geographic importance.

Scuba divers will find more to entertain them offshore: there are several World War II and postwar **shipwrecks** in the waters off Labuan's southern coast, among them the USS *Salute* (scuppered by a mine in 1945); a freighter which was transporting cement to Brunei in the mid-fifties when it hit another ship; and the *Semerang*, a passenger steamer commandeered by the Japanese and sunk by the Australian air force in 1945. Borneo Divers (see p.551), charge around RM200 for one wreck dive (half day), RM350 for two dives (full day), and RM100 for a reef dive off Pulau Kuraman, one of several islands off Labuan's southern coast.

The recently designated **Labuan Marine Park** has its base on Kuraman where accommodation is available in chalets (❹) and at a camping ground (RM15), to the western end of the island. Beginners' courses in **diving** are on offer and other activities include snorkelling, sailing, fishing, short jungle walks as well as the opportunity to enjoy the island's unspoilt beaches. Contact the tourist office for boat transport times (RM50 return) and to arrange accommodation.

Practicalities

Labuan's **airport** is 5km north of town; the only way into the cente is by taxi (RM8). **Ferries** from Kota Kinabalu, Limbang and Lawas in Sarawak, and Bandar Seri Begawan in Brunei, dock at the **new terminal** on Jalan Merdeka, which runs along the seafront below the town centre, forming the spine of Labuan Town. Close to the ferry terminal you'll find the **tourist office** (☎087/423445), on Jalan Merkeka after a branch of HSBC. The local MAS office is situated in the *Federal Hotel*, on Jalan Bunga Kesuma (☎087/412263) while AirAsia can be found at Level 1, Labuan airport.

Moving on from Labuan

By air

There are daily **flights** to KL, KK and Kuching operated by MAS and Air Asia. There are also daily flights to Miri operated by FAX.

By boat

There are numerous departures per day to **KK** (8.30am–3pm, RM28, 90min); four to **Brunei** (9am, noon, 2pm & 4pm, RM35, 1hr 15min); two to **Limbang** (12.30pm & 2.30pm, RM22, 2hr) and one daily to **Lawas**, except on Tuesday and Thursday (12.30pm, RM22, 2hr). For **Menumbok**, there are three daily car ferries (8am, 4pm & 8pm; RM10 for foot passengers), and smaller ferries leave hourly from 8am to 4pm (RM10; 30min). Tickets for ferries are sold at the new terminal.

Pulau Labuan

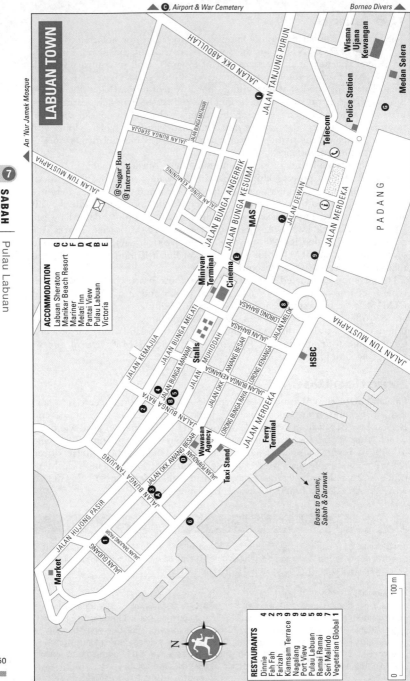

LABUAN TOWN

▲ *An 'Nur Jamek Mosque*

▲ **C**, *Airport & War Cemetery*

Borneo Divers ▲

ACCOMMODATION

Labuan Sheraton	G
Manikar Beach Resort	C
Mariner	F
Melati Inn	D
Pantai View	A
Pulau Labuan	B
Victoria	E

RESTAURANTS

Dinnie	4
Fah Fah	2
Farizah	3
Kiamsam Terrace	9
Nagalang	9
Port View	6
Pulau Labuan	5
Ramai Ramai	8
Seri Malindo	7
Vegetarian Global	1

Wisma Ujana Kewangan

Police Station

Medan Selera

Telecom

PADANG

MAS

Minivan Terminal

Cinema

Stalls

Market

Taxi Stand

Wawasan Agency

Ferry Terminal

Boats to Brunei, Sabah & Sarawak

HSBC

@ Sugar Bun
@ Internet

JALAN OKK ABDULLAH

JALAN TANJUNG PURUN

JALAN TUN MUSTAPHA

JALAN BUNGA SEROJA

JALAN BUNGA KEMUNING

JALAN BUNGA ANGGERIK

JALAN BUNGA KESUMA

JALAN DEWAN

JALAN MERDEKA

JALAN KEMAJUA

JALAN BUNGA MELATI

JALAN BUNGA MAWAR

JALAN BUNGA RAYA

JALAN MUHIDDAH

JALAN BAHASA

ORONG BAHASA

JALAN MELOK

JALAN OKK AWANG BESAR

JALAN OKK AWANG BESAR

JALAN PERPADUAN

JALAN BUNGA TANJUNG

JALAN HUJONG PASIR

JALAN TANJUNG PASIR

JALAN GUDANG

JALAN TUN MUSTAPHA

JALAN OKK

LORONG BUNGA RAYA

LORONG BUNGA KENANGA

JALAN BUNGA KENANGA

JALAN MERDEKA

N

100 m

0

Running north from the middle of Jalan Merdeka, and effectively splitting the town in two, is Jalan Tun Mustapha, home to the new post office building and, near the waterfront, the local office of the **diving specialist**, Borneo Divers, at 1 Jalan Wawasan, Watefront Labuan(☎087/415867). The best places for **Internet** access are Tawau Internet, next door to *Sugar Bun* on Jalan Tun Mustapha, and The Net (daily 10am–8pm; 3RM for 30min), on the first floor in the mall on Wisma Ujana Kewangan, 300m east on Jalan Merdeka, past the tourist office.

Accommodation

There are plenty of **places to stay** in Labuan although few budget options. The best deal for a room with a fan is at the *Pantai View Hotel*, while the out-of-town *Manikar Beach Resort* has good offers.

Labuan Sheraton Jalan Merdeka ☎087/422000. Fine rooms with three restaurants and a bar to keep you busy. Price includes breakfast and there's a nice pool to wallow in too. ❼

Manikar Beach Resort ☎087/418700. You have to find your own way to this waterfront resort, which is 20min by taxi from the town centre. Set in fifteen acres of private beach and gardens up on the northwestern tip of the island, this 250-room hulk constitutes a fine deal – especially if a promotional price is available. ❸

Mariner Jalan Tanjung Purun ☎087/418822, ✉mhlabuan@tm.net.my. Well-appointed rooms, with TVs and a/c, near the centre of town, represent excellent value. ❸

Melati Inn Jalan OKK Awang Besar ☎087/416307. Right opposite the ferry terminal, *Melati*'s double rooms come with TVs, a/c and en-suite bathroom. ❸

Pantai View Jalan Bunga Tanjung ☎087/411339. Good-value Indian-run hotel perfectly positioned for onward boat travel and the town's eating spots; the fan-cooled rooms are small and quite basic with shared bathrooms. ❸

Pulau Labuan Jalan Muhibbah ☎087/416288. Comfortable but somewhat over-priced option, with large a/c, en-suite rooms. ❺

Victoria 360 Jalan Tun Mustapha ☎087/412411. Large, comfortable hotel that's well positioned between the old and new sides of town with neat, clean rooms and adequate, en-suite bathrooms. ❺

Eating and drinking

Along Jalan Merdeka and Jalan OKK Awang Besar you'll find lots of entirely adequate, no-frills, Chinese and Indian restaurants while a cluster of popular, and very good cafés can be found two blocks back on Jalan Bunga Mawar.

Dinnie Jalan Bunga Mawar. Reasonable café with buffet-style meals. Daily 8am–10pm.

Fah Fah Jalan Bunga Mawar. Relaxed café which is popular with expats and locals for/after a few beers. Daily 8am–midnight.

Farizah Jalan Bunga Tanjung. Good, very inexpensive choice for Indian *rotis*, *murtabaks* and curries; located beside the budget accommodation, *Pantai View*. Daily 7.30am–9pm.

Kiamsam Terrace Jalan Merdeka. Small coffee shop beside the *Nagalang*. Daily, 8am–6pm.

Nagalang Chinese & Japanese *Hotel Labuan*, Jalan Merdeka. Situated in the *Hotel Labuan* this is an upmarket restaurant serving Chinese and Japanese staples. RM30–40 per person; daily midday–10pm.

Port View Jalan Merdeka ☎087/422999. Tasty Chinese dishes including fried rice, fresh greens and stir-fries; situated on the waterfront with fine sea views. Around RM20 per person; daily 11am–11pm.

Pulau Labuan Coffee House Jalan Bunga Mawar ☎087/416288. Air-conditioned restaurant with a wide range of Malay and Western Chinese dishes. RM15–25 per person; daily 7.30am–11pm.

Ramai Ramai Jalan Merdeka. Chinese café with good dim sum in the mornings and delicious Chinese tea.

Seri Malindo Jalan Dewan ☎087/416072. Busy, outdoor restaurant with a wide range including breakfast, Malay and Chinese buffets and set meals. RM10–15 per person; daily 8.30am–11.30pm.

Vegetarian Global Jalan OKK Awang Besar ☎087/426206. Excellent, relaxed vegetarian restaurant with delicious buffet-style Malay dishes; stir-fries and banana-leaf curries available too. RM10 per person; daily 7.30am–3.30pm.

Crossing into Sarawak

To travel from Sipitang **to Sarawak** get the local bus to Merapok just across the Sarawak border (daily, every hour, RM3) and then catch a bus onwards to Lawas town. Alternatively the Lawas Express bus (RM10), which leaves KK daily at 1pm, passes through Sipitang at around 4pm, getting to **Lawas** around 6pm, border hassles permitting. Whichever you choose, the driver will wait while you pass through the passport controls flanking the border – one in Sindumin and the other a couple of hundred metres further on, at the edge of Merapok – where your passport's stamped entitling you to remain in Sarawak for a month.

North of Kota Kinabalu

North of KK, Sabah's trunk highway hurries through the capital's suburbs to the more pastoral environs of **Tuaran**. From here, the *atap* houses of the Bajau water villages, **Mengkabong** and **Penambawang**, are both a stone's throw away. Just outside Tuaran the main road forks, with the eastern branch heading towards Kinabalu National Park, Ranau and onwards to Sandakan. Continuing north the main road quickly reaches **Kota Belud**, the site of a weekly *tamu* that attracts tribespeople from all over the region. Beyond here the landscape becomes more exciting: jewel-bright paddy fields, and colourful stilted wooden houses line the road for much of the way up to the **Kudat Peninsula**, with Gunung Kinabalu dominating the far distance. Journey's end is signalled by the coconut groves and beaches of **Kudat**, formerly capital of British North Borneo, and now a focal point for the Rungus people who dwell in modernized longhouses in the surrounding countryside.

Buses for Tuaran, Kota Belud and Kudat leave KK's Inanam terminal through the day, with the first two destinations perfect for enjoyable day-trips out of the capital. Kudat requires an overnight stay, although note that the pretty beaches are very inaccessible and the Rungus longhouses can be a bit of a disappointment.

Tuaran, Mengkabong and Penambawang

It takes just under an hour to travel the 34km from Kota Kinabalu to **TUARAN**, from where it's possible to visit two water villages. **MENGKABONG**, ten minutes out of Tuaran on a local bus from the town centre, is the most accessible and a favourite destination with some KK tour operators. The sight of a village built out over the sea on stilts is usually a compelling one, but Mengkabong is a noisy, charmless example, and you'd do well to make the extra effort to reach **PENAMBAWANG**. Minivans to Kampung Surusup – the tiny settlement from where you can catch a boat to Penambawang – leave from the road west of Tuaran's brown clock tower; it's a twenty-minute drive (on a rough road) through idyllic paddy fields. Once in Surusup, you need to ask around at the jetty for a boat (RM20 return) – Penambawang is fifteen minutes northeast, across a wide bay skirted with mangroves. The Muslim Bajau people's houses are made of *atap*, bamboo and wood interconnected by labyrinthine boardwalks – called *jambatan* – along which fish are laid out to dry.

While **hotels** in Tuaran are nothing to write home about, the *Shangri-La Rasa Ria Resort* (see p.530), 5km west on Dalit Bay, is as classy a place to stay as any in Sabah, and worth considering if you want to splash out. Several shuttle buses leave daily from the *Tanjung Aru Resort*, taking around 45 minutes to reach Dalit Bay, and there's also a bus service to the bay from Tuaran's centre (9am & 2pm), and back again.

Kota Belud

For six days of the week, **KOTA BELUD**, 75km northeast of KK on the road to Kudat, is a busy but undistinguished town. Each Sunday, however, it springs to life as hordes of villagers from the surrounding countryside congregate at its weekly **tamu**, undoubtedly the biggest in Sabah. The market, ten minutes' walk out of town along Jalan Hasbollah, fulfils a social, as much as a commercial, role, and draws – among others – Rungus, Kadazan/Dusun and Bajau indigenous groups. Though Kota Belud's popularity among KK's tour operators means there are always tourists here, you're far more likely to see dried fish, chains of yeast beads (used to make rice wine), buffalo, betel nut and *tudung saji* (colourful food covers used to keep flies at bay) for sale, than souvenirs. Arrive early – if heading here from KK, plan to leave the city by 8am at the latest.

At Kota Belud's annual *tamu besar*, or "big market", usually held in November, there are cultural performances, traditional horseback games and handicraft demonstrations in addition to the more typical stalls. For specific details each year, ask at the STB office in KK.

Practicalities

Buses for Kota Belud (RM5) leave from the CBTN at Inanam, near KK – the same spot as Kudat-bound ones – for the ninety-minute trip. Buses from KK drop and pick up passengers at the district office in the centre of town, from where it's a twenty-minute walk to the *tamu*; it's a better bet to hail one of the minivans (RM1) which ply the stretch on market days. There are plenty of good **cafés** in Kota Belud – the Malay food at *Restoran Rahmat* below the district office has particularly varied and appetizing meals. Of the coffee shops over in the newer part of Kota Belud (to the west of the Kudat road), the *Restoran Zam Zam*, 50m north of the main street and on the edge of the old market, does good curries and fried chicken. Besides some *rumah tumpangan*, which are best avoided, the only place to stay in Kota Belud is the modern *SIU Motel*, Km 1, Jalan Kuala Abai (T088/976617, ❸), 1km north on the Kudat road, with clean rooms, most with communal bathrooms.

On to Kudat

The journey from Kota Belud to Kudat takes in some of Sabah's most dramatic scenery, with, early in the journey, Gunung Kinabalu's peaks reflected – rice harvest allowing – in the still waters of the paddy fields to the east. At the base of Marudu Bay, the road forks, turn right for **Kota Marudu** – a town with two hotels and several restaurants, but with nothing else to entice you to stop. Continuing along the main road to the left takes you past coconut groves and paddy fields; many of the coconuts end up at the desiccated-coconut factory 9km out of Kudat, right on Borneo's northern tip – piles of discarded husks can be seen, resembling bleached skulls on the roadside.

The Kudat Peninsula is home to the Rungus people, some of whom still live in longhouses. Today though, most of the dwellings are made from sheets of corrugated zinc, whose durability makes it preferable to the traditional materials like timber, tree bark, rattan and *nipah* leaves. Set back from the

△ Women selling fish at the *tamu*, Kota Belud

main road, 37km short of Kudat, **Kampung Tinanggol** consists of three 25-door longhouses and a quaint white church. The STB has helped construct a longhouse in the village, allowing visitors to stay in a traditional Rungus environment with locals cooking tasty, inexpensive meals when required (RM40 plus meals).

Kudat and around

The natural harbour at **KUDAT**, on the western shore of Marudu Bay, led to it being declared the administrative capital of British North Borneo in 1881, though two years later the capital was switched to Sandakan. Although Kudat is lively and indisputably friendly, there's not much to bring you here, except perhaps Sabah's oldest **golf club**, opened in 1906 (T088/611002, non-members can play Mon–Thurs; RM50).

The town's main thoroughfare, Jalan Lo Thien Chock, is dominated by classic shophouses, among the oldest in Sabah. During a visit, leave time to peek at the town centre's orange-hued **Chinese temple** and stroll around the busy harbour. A short excursion worth making is to the adjacent **stilt village** at the southern end of town, only fifteen-minutes' walk away.

Kudat's most famous **beach** is **Bak Bak**, 12km north of town, though **Tajau**, a few kilometres further on, is favoured by locals. It's hard to get to either by public transport though as Kudat's buses are so erratic. Taking a taxi is the only practical solution (prices start at around RM20 for the return journey). Across on the west coast, there's **Bangau Beach**, near the town of **Sikuati** – any bus headed for KK can drop you at the turning. After that you'll need to wait for a Kudat-based minivan plying the last 6km stretch (RM4).

It's also possible to take a ferry to **Pulau Banggi**, off Sabah's north coast, though only if you've got a few days to spare, as departures are unpredictable, and the only way to get around the island once you're there is to get talking to local boatmen. The island has lovely forest and beaches, and there's a small government **resthouse** (T088/612511; ❷) at **Kampung Kalaki**, the main settlement. It is necessary to take food and drink with you as there are no shops on the island.

Practicalities

Downtown Kudat centres on the intersection of Jalan Ibrahim Arshad and Jalan Lo Thien Chock – the latter is Kudat's main street, with most of its shops and a Standard Chartered Bank. **Minivans** to and from Kota Belud and KK congregate a few metres east of the intersection, as do the town's **taxis**, though KK **buses** (outward journey daily at 7.30am and noon) stop along Lorong Empat west of Jalan Lo Thien Chock. For **ferries** to Pulau Banggi, head for the jetty at the southern end of Jalan Lo Thien Chock. Kudat's **airstrip** handles FAX flights from KK and Sandakan.

For **accommodation** there's *Hotel Sunrise* (T088/611517; ❸) on the main drag, Jalan Lo Thien Chock, a good bet with small, neat rooms with fans and shared bathrooms. Another quite acceptable, mid-priced option is *Hotel Kinabalu* (T088/613888; ❸), with neat rooms, on Jalan Melor, close to the junction with Thien Chock. For a bit more comfort, opt for the *Hotel Greenland* (T088/613211; ❸), five minutes' walk east of the town centre, in Block E of the SEDCO shophouse development on Jalan Lo Thien Chock, or the new *Upper Deck Hotel* (❹), ten minutes west along Jalan Lintas, which commands a fine view over Marudu Bay.

The best **restaurant** in town is the *Sungai Wang*, two minutes beyond the *Greenland Hotel*, serving such delights as scallops in black-bean sauce and tofu with crabmeat for around RM6 each; there are tables outside on the wooden patio, which is strung with fairy lights. Back in the town centre, *Sri Mutiara*, opposite the *Sunrise* on Jalan Lo Thien Chock, is a spruce joint that serves tasty Malay food and fried chicken, while the *Sayang*, on the junction of Lo Thien and Ibrahim Arshad, is a typical clean and inexpensive Malay café with lovely *pari*, a tangy dish comprising slivers of marrow.

Kinabalu National Park

Eighty-five kilometres northeast of KK and plainly visible from Sabah's west coast, there's no more impressive sight than **Gunung Kinabalu** (Mount Kinabalu), whether it's poking dramatically through the clouds or, looming serenely over the Crocker Range and valley below. At 4101 metres high, it totally dominates the 750 square-kilometres of **KINABALU NATIONAL PARK**, a World Heritage Site renowed for its varied ecology and geology.

Climbing the mountain has become one of the must-dos of a Malaysian itinerary and for the twenty thousand who come here annually to haul themselves up, the process is made a little easier by a well-defined, 8.5-kilometre-long path which weaves up the southern side to the bare granite of the summit. Despite its popularity, it's a very tough trek and not to be undertaken lightly. Even given perfect weather conditions, there's the remorseless, freezing, final ascent

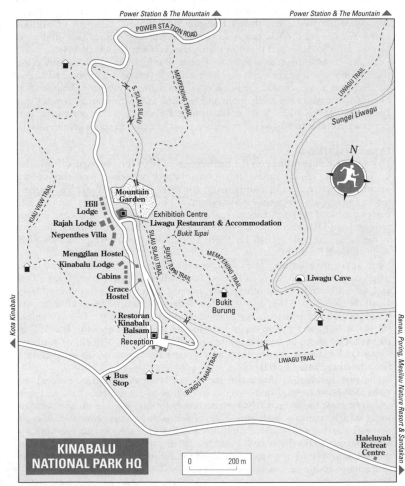

Power Station & The Mountain ▲

Power Station & The Mountain ▲

POWER STATION ROAD

MEMPENING TRAIL

S. SILAU SILAU

LIWAGU TRAIL

Sungei Liwagu

N

KIAU VIEW TRAIL

Mountain Garden

Exhibition Centre

Hill Lodge

Liwagu Restaurant & Accommodation

Rajah Lodge

Bukit Tupai

Nepenthes Villa

SILAU SILAU TRAIL

BUKIT TUPAI TRAIL

Menggilan Hostel

MEMPENING TRAIL

Kinabalu Lodge

Cabins

Liwagu Cave

Grace Hostel

Bukit Burung

Restoran Kinabalu Balsam

Reception

LIWAGU TRAIL

★ Bus Stop

BUNDU TUHAN TRAIL

◀ Kota Kinabalu

Ranau, Poring, Mesilau Nature Resort & Sandakan

Haleluyah Retreat Centre

KINABALU NATIONAL PARK HQ

0   200 m

to contend with and it's quite possible to suffer from altitude sickness and not get to the top. Climbers shouldn't undertake the challenge unless fully prepared with suitable clothing (see p.560) and in good general health; they should also keep close to their mandatory guide at all points in the trek.

Limbs that are weary from the climb will welcome the warm, sulphurous waters of the **Poring Hot Springs**, around 40km away, just outside the park's southeastern border. Between these two sites is the small, nondescript town of **Ranau**, which has a couple of places to stay and transport links to KK.

Some history

Conquering Gunung Kinabalu today is far easier than it was in 1858, when Spenser St John, British consul-general to the native states of Borneo, found his progress blocked by Kadazan "shaking their spears and giving us other hostile signs". Hugh Low, at the time British colonial secretary on Pulau Labuan, had made the first recorded ascent of the mountain seven years earlier, though he baulked at climbing its highest peak, considering it "inaccessible to any but winged animals". The peak – subsequently named after Low – was finally conquered in 1888 by John Whitehead. The mile-deep **Low's Gully** (see box, p.560) splits the summit into a U shape, which led early explorers to conclude that Kinabalu was volcanic; in fact, the mountain is a granite pluton – an enormous ball of molten rock which has forced its way through the Crocker Mountain Range over millions of years, solidifying at the surface. This process continues today, with the mountain gaining a few millimetres annually.

The origin of the mountain's name is uncertain; one legend tells how a Chinese prince travelled to Borneo to seek out a huge pearl, guarded by a dragon at the summit of the mountain. Having slain the dragon and claimed the pearl, the prince married a Kadazan girl, only to desert her and return to China. His wife was left to mourn him on the slopes of the mountain – hence *Kina* (China) and *balu* (widow) – where she eventually turned to stone. Another idea is that the name derives from the Kadazan words *Aki Nabalu* – "the revered place of the dead". Nineteenth-century climbers had to take into account the superstitions of local porters, who believed the mountain to be a sacred ancestral home. When Low climbed it, his guides brought along charms, quartz crystals and human teeth to protect the party, and Kadazan porters still offer up chickens, eggs, cigars, betel nut and rice to the mountain's spirits at an annual ceremony.

Practicalities

You need at least **two days** to ascend and descend Gunung Kinabalu. Most climbers spend their first night at park headquarters, leaving for the mountain from around 8am the next morning. The second night is spent in huts on the mountain itself before the final dawn ascent. It's worth factoring in an extra day or two, in the event of cloud cover spoiling the view from the summit, whereupon you may decide to postpone the climb (in the case of very poor weather conditions, the park officials stop people setting out from park headquarters, full stop). Also, allow an extra day in the park's vicinity if you want to recuperate at Poring.

Hourly **buses** leave KK's Inanam terminus for Sandakan and Ranau from 7am and take around two hours (RM15) to get to the park entrance. A good ploy is to arrive in the early afternoon the previous day, giving you time to **acclimatize** on the short trails beginning from park headquarters. That said, it is possible to take an early-morning **taxi** from KK to the park (RM60) in order to begin your ascent that very morning. If you are going to do this you will

If you dash headlong up and down Gunung Kinabalu and then depart, as some visitors do, you'll miss out on many of the region's natural riches. The national park's diverse terrains have spawned an incredible variety of **plants** and **animals**, and you are far more likely to glimpse some of them by walking its trails at a leisurely pace. Remember, you do not need to hire a guide to trek below Panar Laban so if you're able to stay in the park for a few more days you may wish to return to the mountain trails for a less hurried meander through the rich nature.

Plants
Around a third of the park's area is covered by **lowland dipterocarp forest**, characterized by massive, buttressed trees, allowing only sparse growth at ground level. The **world's largest flower**, the parasitic – and very elusive – *rafflesia*, occasionally blooms in the lowland forest around Poring Hot Springs. Between 900m and 1800m, you'll come across the oaks, chestnuts, ferns and mosses (including the *Dawsonia* – the world's tallest moss) of the **montane forest**.

Higher up (1800–2600m), the **cloudforest** supports a huge range of flowering plants: around a thousand orchids and 26 varieties of rhododendron are known to grow in the forest, including Low's rhododendron, with its enormous yellow flowers. The hanging lichen that drapes across branches of stunted trees lends a magical feel to the landscape at this height. It's at this altitude, too, that you're most likely to see the park's most famous plants – its nine species of insectivorous **pitcher plants** (*nepenthes*) whose cups secrete a nectar that first attracts insects and then drowns them, as they are unable to escape the slippery sides of the pitcher. Early climber Spenser St John is alleged to have seen one such plant digesting a rat.

Higher still, above 2600m, only the most tenacious plantlife can survive – like the agonizingly gnarled *sayat-sayat* tree, and the heath rhododendron found only on Mount Kinabalu – while beyond 3300m, soil gives way to granite. Here, grasses, sedges and the elegant blooms of Low's buttercup are all that flourish.

Animals
Although orang-utans, Bornean gibbons and tarsiers are among the **mammals** which dwell in the park, you're unlikely to see anything more exotic than squirrels, rats and tree shrews – you might just catch sight of a mouse deer or a bearded pig, if you're lucky. The higher reaches of Gunung Kinabalu boast two types of **birds** seen nowhere else in the world – the Kinabalu friendly warbler and Kinabalu mountain blackbird. Lower down, look out for hornbills and eagles, as well as the Malaysian tree pie, identifiable by its foot-long tail. You're bound to see plenty of **insects**: butterflies and moths flit through the trees, while down on the forest floor are creatures like the trilobite beetle, whose orange-and-black armour plating lend it a fearsome aspect.

---

need to call ahead to **reserve** your place in a climbing group (the last group usually sets off by 11am).

Arrival and information
Buses drop you opposite the park gates (RM15 entrance fee) on the KK–Ranau road. Directly inside are an extended cluster of lodgings, restaurants and offices including park **reception** (daily 7am–7.30pm), where you confirm your accommodation with Sutera Sanctuary Lodges (see opposite). This is also where you fix up the details of your climb with Sabah Parks staff. Information sheets and a **map** are available at reception and at the Sabah Parks office the next door along.

Twenty kilometres of **trails** loop the montane forest around the headquarters, with a guided walk (RM3) leaving daily from the reception office at 11am. A ten-minute walk up the road from reception, the **Exhibit Centre** contains a number of facilities including the *Liwagu* restaurant on the ground floor and, upstairs, an exhibition with photographs and mounted exhibits of park flora and fauna (look out, in particular, for the monster stick insect). There is also a video show daily at 2pm (RM2). There are more plants on show at the **Mountain Garden** (Mon–Fri 8am–4.30pm, Sat & Sun 9am–5pm; RM5) just to the rear of the Exhibit Centre.

Accommodation and eating

Park **accommodation** is run by Sutera Sanctuary Lodges (SSL), Lot 330, third floor, Wisma Sabah, KK (Mon–Fri 8am–5pm, Sat 8am–2pm; ☎088/248629, Ⓦwww.suterasanctuarylodges.com). It is essential to book this **before arriving at the park** so contact them as far in advance as possible (either at their office in KK or via their website). SSL also run the chalets and hostels at Poring as well as the *Mesilau Nature Resort*, on the eastern fringes of the park, around 50km away; again, **book** some way in advance to avoid disappointment.

There is a good choice of hostels and chalets/lodges around **park headquarters**; note that the latter are usually booked on a group basis and the prices below refer to hiring the whole unit for a night. For those on tight budgets, the *Menggilan* and *Grace* **hostels** are the places to head for (dorm beds RM46); both are equipped with basic cooking facilities. Going up the scale, the next options are the *Hill Lodge*'s snug, twin-bed cabins (RM135), the *Liwagu Suite* in the Exhibit Centre which sleeps four (one double and two singles; RM255), and the *Nepenthes Villa* which sleeps four in a similar configuration (RM380). Top of the scale are the eight-bed *Kinabalu Lodge* (RM540) and the ten-bed *Rajah Lodge* (RM1500) both commanding great views of the mountain.

The accommodation on the mountain itself at the **Laban Rata** complex comprises the basic, unheated *Panar Laban* and *Waras* huts (eight beds in each; RM46), the 60-bed *Gunting Lagadan* hut (also unheated; same price), and the more upmarket (and heated) *Laban Rata Resthouse* which has 52 dorm beds (RM69) as well as two private units, one with a double and two single beds (RM300) and the other with one double bed (RM180).

There are two **restaurants** around park headquarters: the recently upgraded *Kinabalu Balsam* (daily 7am–10pm, Sat & Sun until 11pm) offering good-value lunch and dinner buffets (RM25) with Chinese, Malay, Indian and Western dishes; and the slightly more expensive *Liwagu* (daily 11am–11pm), with more nuanced, à la carte fare. There is also a basic restaurant at Laban Rata serving noodles and rice dishes which opens for one hour at 2am (for climbers making the final ascent) and then from 7am–10pm daily.

Outside the park

A cluster of hotels and resthouses has sprung up along the main road **outside the park** towards Ranau; the only budget choice is the Christian-run *Haleluyah Retreat Centre*, fifteen minutes' walk from the park headquarters (☎088/223443, Ⓔkandiu@tm.netmy, dorm beds RM30). More upmarket is *Kinabalu Rose Cabin*, Km 18, Ranau Road (☎088/889233, Ⓦwww.kinabalurosecabin.8m .com; ❼) with lovely en-suite rooms and a fine restaurant; alternatively, the large *Kinabalu Pine Resort*, 10km further along the road on the outskirts of Kundasang (☎088/889388; Ⓔpatrvl@tm.net.my; ❻) is good value and extremely comfortable.

Mesilau Nature Resort

Seventeen kilometres east of the headquarters, the **Mesilau Nature Resort** 🜨 is located slightly higher up in the moutain's foothills than Park HQ. The advantage of being based here is that it's a lot quieter than at headquarters, with far fewer people starting the climb from this point. There's not much to see or do, with just one rather average **café** to eat at, but the place has a special atmosphere, with a gushing river running through the resort and abundant bird life. Accommodation consists of various dorms (RM46 per bed) and around twenty two-bedroom, spacious chalets, equipped with all mod cons (RM450 per chalet).

Note that the climb takes a little longer from here – a narrow path curls up the slope before joining the main trail at Carson's Camp. Along the route are some of the best spots in Sabah to see the largest *Nepenthes* plants in the world – ask your guide to point them out.

The easiest way to reach the *Mesilau* resort is to charter a minivan from park reception (RM60).

Guides, porters and equipment

Unless you're starting the climb from the *Mesilau Nature Resort*, aim to be at the park reception by 8am, where, besides the **climbing permit** (RM100) and compulsory **insurance** (RM7), you must pay for a **guide** (RM70 per group of one to three people; RM74 for four to six and RM80 for seven or eight). Some climbers opt to pay for a **porter**, costed by the weight he carries (RM66 per 10 kg). Note that **lockers** and a safe room are available at reception to deposit valuables or even your pack. Extra costs include **camera and video permits**, (RM5 and RM30).

Essential items to take with you are a torch, headache tablets (for altitude sickness), suntan lotion, energy boosters like nuts, fruit and muesli bars and adequate drinking water. You should also wear waterproof shoes or hiking boots with a good tread and bring warm clothes to combat the bracing cold on the summit – raincoats are sold at the park's souvenir shop. Also, most guides do not carry first-aid kits, so it might be worth investing in one.

Low's Gully

Gunung Kinabalu grabbed the world's headlines in March 1993, when two British army officers and three Hong Kong soldiers went missing on a training exercise down **Low's Gully** – described by Spenser St John as "a deep chasm, surrounded on three sides by precipices, so deep that the eye could not reach the bottom. ... There was no descending here." Defeated by impassable waterfalls and boulders, the men set up camp in a mountain cave and left out an SOS marked out with white pebbles. Treacherous weather conditions and inhospitable terrain repeatedly thwarted rescue attempts, but the men were finally found, on day thirty of what should have been a ten-day mission – by which time they were surviving on a diet of Polo mints.

Five years later another British expedition, in perfect weather conditions, succeeded in abseiling down the gully and finding their way out. Climber Steve Long remembers tackling Commando Cauldron, part of the vertical wall of the gully: "We were in a boulder-choked gully only 5m wide, dwarfed by one-thousand-metre high cliffs towering back towards the summit rim. It was an awe-inspiring place. We spoke in whispers, anxious to avoid triggering rock falls. All around us pulverized granite and uprooted trees bore stark and silent witness to the devastation this would wreak. A final abseil, a leap into the last lagoon, and we were out."

The climb

The summit route begins for most with a minivan ride (RM2; 25min) as it's over an hour's uneventful walk from the reception, along Power Station Road, to the beginning of the mountain path at Timpohon Gate. The climb to the mountain huts at **Laban Rata** takes between five and six hours, depending on your fitness and trail conditions. Roots and stones along the trail serve as steps,

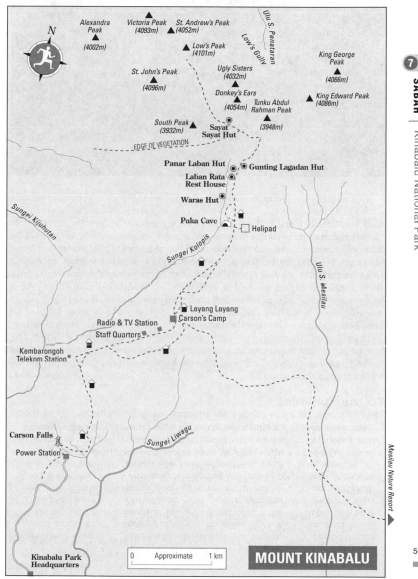

△ Climbers descending from Gunung Kinabalu

with wooden "ladders" laid up the muddier stretches. The air gets progressively cooler as you climb, but the walk is still a hard and sweaty one, and you'll be glad of the water tanks and rest point at Layang Layang (2621m) around three hours into the climb. At around this point, if the weather is kind, incredible views of the hills, sea and clouds below you start to unfold; higher up, at just above 3000m, a detour to the left brings you to **Pondok Paka**; Paka Cave is little more than a large overhanging rock, and was the site of overnight camps on early expeditions. It's a further 6km to Laban Rata, which lies at 3272m, the final 2km dominated by large boulders and steep slippery rock surfaces which, combined with lower oxygen levels, are demanding even for the fittest. The benefit as the first day draws to a close is witnessing the mighty granite slopes of the Panar Laban rock face, veined by trickling waterfalls, and the promise of reaching your accommodation.

To the summit

Most climbers get up at 2.30am for the final ascent, crossing the sheer **Panar Laban** rock face, past the Sayat Sayat hut and onwards to the summit at Low's Peak. Although ropes, handrails and wooden steps help in places, this is at the very least a stiff climb, in pitch darkness – head lamps are an advantage and a powerful torch a must. Vegetation is shrub height and offers little protection against the biting cold. Climbers should also be aware of the symptoms of altitude sickness – headaches, nausea and breathlessness – setting in. Some believe that it's fruitless leaving so early as you get to the summit as much as an hour before sunrise – you can always ask your guide if your group can leave a little later.

After the final push, the beautiful spectacle of sunrise at **Low's Peak** will rob you of any remaining breath. Then, after all that toil, it's back to Laban Rata for a hearty breakfast before the return journey to park headquarters, usually covered in four to six hours. When you finally get back and start to feel the delayed rebellion of your leg muscles, reflect on the fact that the Nepalese Kusang Gurung, the winner of the annual **Kinabalu Climbathon** in 1991, ran up *and* down the mountain in a staggering 2 hours, 42 minutes and 33 seconds.

Poring Hot Springs

Located 43km from park headquarters, on the southeastern side of Kinabalu National Park, are the **Poring Hot Springs** (RM15 conservation fee; camera permit RM5, video RM30). The springs were developed by the Japanese during World War II, though the wooden tubs they installed have since been replaced by outdoor cement versions, large enough to seat two people at a time.

After a few days' hiking up the mountain, a soak in Poring's hot (48–60°C), sulphurous waters is just the ticket. The baths (daily 7am–6pm, free) are a couple of minutes from the main gates, across a suspension bridge that spans Sungai Mamut; here there are two enclosed baths with jacuzzi and an adjacent plunge pool. Unfortunately many of the tubs are in poor condition, chipped and with a film of grime and the staff appear uninterested and generally unhelpful. Even the **café** close to the tubs is inefficiently run although the food is acceptable.

A fifteen-minute walk beyond the baths brings you to Poring's **canopy walkway**, affording a monkey's-eye view of the surrounding lowland rainforest. If you're set on witnessing some wildlife, go in the early morning, when it's cooler and quieter.

Another trail strikes off to the east of the baths, reaching the 150-metre-high **Langanan Waterfall** about an hour and a half later. On its way, the trail passes the smaller **Kepungit Waterfall** – whose icy pool is ideal for swimming – and a cave lined with squealing, fluttering bats, as well as groves of towering bamboo. Be warned: if it's been raining, there'll be leeches on the trail.

Practicalities

To get to Poring from park headquarters, you'll need to charter a minivan (RM60) for the one-hour trip (RM80 from the *Mesilau Nature Resort*). For **accommodation**, there's a large campsite (RM5 per tent) and the *Kelapit* and *Serindit* hostels (dorm beds RM46 in each), as well as a range of cabins and chalets, each of which must be booked as a whole: the *Tempua* (RM100 and *Enggang* (RM135) cabins sleep four while the *Rajawali* lodge (RM380) sleeps six. As at park headquarters and the *Mesilau Nature Resort*, **book** accommodation in advance through SSL (see p.559).

Besides the café by the hot tubs, there are two **eating** options outside the gates: the *Poring Restoran* (daily 8am–8pm), which serves average Chinese food; and the *Kedai Makanan Melayu* (daily 8am–6pm), next door, offering simple Malay dishes.

To Ranau

If you stay at the *Mesilau Nature Resort* or Poring it's impossible to get direct transport to Sandakan or back to KK; instead take a minivan to the small town of **RANAU**, where buses stop on trips across the state. Set in a pleasant valley, Ranau huddles around a square on the south side of the main KK–Sandakan road, 20km from Kinabalu National Park. En route to Ranau from the park, after 10km you come to **Kundasang**, little more than a junction with simple stalls selling fruit and vegetables. The only reason to stop is to see the **war memorial** signposted 150m off the main road. It commemorates the victims of the "Death March" of September 1944, when Japanese troops marched 2400 POWs from Sandakan to Ranau (see p.572).

Ranau is based around a grid of ugly, lettered blocks, with street names in short supply, though one exception is Jalan Kibarambang – the first turning on the right if you're coming from KK, and home to both a rickety old market and a new **Chinese temple**, its pale-cream walls striped by red pillars. The first day of every month sees a lively *tamu*, around one kilometre out of town towards Sandakan.

Practicalities

Long-distance **buses** (Sandakan RM23; KK RM15), stop on the trunk road beside the turning into the town whereas **minivans** arrive at the eastern edge of town. There's **Internet access** at Cyber City Centre, Lot 4, Wisma Budaya, right in the centre (daily 9am–9pm; RM2.50 an hour).

Ranau has quite a few **hotels**, the best of which is the quiet, six-room *View Motel* (☎088/876445; ❷) in Block L, with good-sized en-suite rooms. The *Hotel Ranau* (☎088/875661; ❷), next to the Bank Bumiputra on the north side of the square, has a range of rooms, from box-like singles to more spacious air-conditioned doubles with bathrooms. The *Kinabalu Hotel* (☎088/876028; ❸), south of the square in Block A, is a smartly painted place with cosy rooms and shared bathrooms.

Eating options include the cheerful *Restoran Muslim* (daily 8am–10pm), where you can feast on great fried chicken to the strains of wrestling videos on the TV; the next-door *Yeong Hing* does good *pow*. For Malay food, make for the *Sugut* (daily 7am–10pm), below the *View Motel*.

Sandakan and around

Sandwiched between sea and cliffs, **SANDAKAN**, like KK, was all but destroyed during World War II, and postwar reconstruction worked around an unimaginative – and, in Sabah, all too familiar – grid system of indistinguishable concrete blocks, without the sense of space you find in KK. That said, the town does have some good attractions including the boisterous fish market, the recently opened Agnes Keith House and the stylish *English Tea House* in a renovated colonial villa on the cliffs, where afternoon tea is served on a croquet lawn with spectacular views overlooking Sandakan Bay. The former capital of Sabah, the town is more notably a springboard to several fascinating destinations, including the offshore **Turtle Islands Park**, the divers' paradise **Pulau Lankayan**, **Sepilok Orangutan Rehabilitation Centre** and **Sungai Kinabatangan**.

Some history

Although there are eighteenth-century accounts of a trading outpost called Sandakan within the Sultanate of Sulu (whose centre was in what's now the Philippines), the town's modern history began in the late 1870s. The area of northeast Borneo between Brunei Bay and Sungai Kinabatangan had been leased by the Sultan of Brunei to the American Trading Company in 1865 but its attempt to establish a settlement here failed, and in 1877 an Anglo-American partnership took up the lease, naming Englishman **William Pryer** as the first Resident (the most senior administrative official) of the east coast.

By 1885, Sandakan was the **capital** of British North Borneo, its natural harbour and proximity to sources of timber, beeswax, rattan and edible birds' nests transforming it into a thriving commercial centre. Sabahian timber was used in the construction of Beijing's Temple of Heaven, and much of Sandakan's early trade was with Hong Kong; there's still a strong Cantonese influence in the town.

In January 1942 the Japanese army took control, establishing a POW camp from where the infamous Death March to Ranau commenced (see p.572). What little of the town was left standing after intensive Allied bombing was burned down by the Japanese, and the end of the war saw the administration of Sabah shift to KK. Nevertheless, by the 1950s a rebuilt Sandakan profited from the **timber** boom and by the 1970s generated such wealth that the town was reputed to have the world's greatest concentration of millionaires. Once the region's decent timber had been exhausted in the early 1980s, Sandakan looked to **oil palm** and cocoa, crops which now dominate the surrounding landscape.

Arrival, information and transport

The **long-distance bus station** is 5km west of town; flag down a minivan (RM1) or taxi (RM8–10) from the main road outside. There are no buses into town from the **airport**, 11km north of Sandakan, although minivans sometimes appear outside arrivals (RM2) going to the southern end of Jalan Pelabuhan; otherwise you're dependent on a taxi into the centre (RM15). The **ferry** from Zamboanga, in the Philippines, docks at **Karamunting Jetty**, 5km west of town – there are usually minivans awaiting the new arrivals.

Sandakan has an excellent **tourist office** (Mon–Fri 8am–12.30pm & 1.30–4.30pm, Sat 8am–noon; ☏089/229751, ✆esong02@tm.net.my), housed in Wisma Warisan, the old government building of the British administration. The centre's coordinator, Elvina Ong, is highly knowledgeable and has good local contacts. To get there, walk up the steps from Third Avenue (Lebuh Tiga).

It's best to contact Crystal Quest, Sabah Parks jetty, Jalan Buli Sim-Sim, 400m west of the town centre (☏089/212711, ✆cquest@tm.net.my) ahead of time if you want to stay at **Pulau Selingan** unless you are arranging the trip through another tour operator (see p.570). Quest's prices, given that all you are doing is heading out to the island, staying the night and then coming back, are the most reasonable.

To arrange a stay at the divers' haunt **Pulau Lankayan** contact Ken Cheung at Pulau Sipadan Resort and Tours, 1st floor, Lot 7, Block A, Bandar Pasaray, Mile 4, North Rd, Sandakan (☏089/228081, ✆sepilok@po.jaring.my).

Note that Sandakan **addresses** take a little getting used to, as they rely on numbers rather than street names; indeed less central addresses are pinpointed according to their distances out of the downtown area, hence "Mile 1 and a half", "Mile 3" and so on.

Transport

Local **buses** vie for space on the busy waterfront area: the only ones of importance are the red, yellow and green striped ones bound for points west, travelling up Jalan Leila to the night market and out to Sepilok Orang-utan Rehabilitation Centre.

A short walk west along Jalan Pryer brings you to the local **minivan** area, while **taxis** gather at the southern end of Fourth Street (useful for visiting the *English Tea House* and the Agnes Keith House).

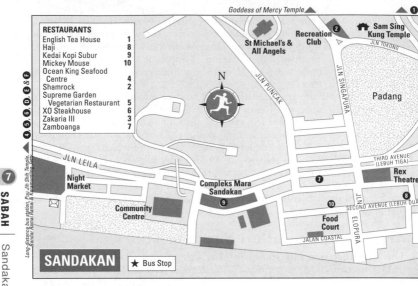

RESTAURANTS

English Tea House	1
Haji	8
Kedai Kopi Subur	9
Mickey Mouse	10
Ocean King Seafood Centre	4
Shamrock	2
Supreme Garden Vegetarian Restaurant	5
XO Steakhouse	6
Zakaria III	3
Zamboanga	7

St Michael's & All Angels
Recreation Club
Sam Sing Kung Temple
JLN TOKONG
JLN PUNCAK
JLN SINGAPURA
Padang
N

JLN LEILA
THIRD AVENUE (LEBUH TIGA)
Rex Theatre
Night Market
Compleks Mara Sandakan
Community Centre
JLN ELOPURA
SECOND AVENUE (LEBUH DUA)
Food Court
JALAN COASTAL

Long-distance bus station, Puu Jih Shih Temple, Bandar Ramai Ramai & Karamunting Jetty

SANDAKAN ★ Bus Stop

Accommodation

The majority of town **hotels** are in the utilitarian blocks comprising the centre but the most colourful – and best value accommodation – is out at **Sepilok**, 20km from Sandakan, close by the Orang-utan Rehabilitation Centre (see p.573).

City View Lot 1, Block 23, Third Ave ☎089/271122. Clean, quite adequate place with small rooms and en-suite bathrooms. ⑤

Mayfair First floor, 24 Jalan Pryer ☎089/219855. This is a treat of a place: a superbly positioned, wonderfully airy guesthouse which is the pride and joy of its Chinese owner. All rooms are equipped with DVD players (guests can borrow DVDs for free from the owner's huge collection) and the a/c is extremely cooling. ②

Moving on from Sandakan

By air
AirAsia fly daily to KL and Johor Bahru with MAS providing a service from KL. There are also daily non-stop **flights** from Sandakan to KK on MAS and FAX. FAX also fly daily to Kudat and Tawau.

By boat
The passenger **ferry** (18hr; cabin beds RM130; RM150 with a/c), to Zamboanga in the Philippines leaves twice a week from the Karamunting jetty – check with operator Timarine (☎089/212063) for current timetable. Tickets should be bought at the jetty (which can be reached on a Pasir Puteh bus) at least a day before departure. Tourists are currently issued a three-week visa upon arrival.

By bus
There are six **buses** per day to KK (first departure 6.30am, last depature 2pm; RM34, 6hr); two to Lahad Datu (7.15 & 7.30am; RM18, 3hr) and five to Tawau (first departure 6am, last departure 10am; RM50, 6hr). However, **minivans** and **4WDs** fill in the schedule gaps, leaving also from the long-distance bus station when full.

A, Labuk Road, Airport, Agnes Keith House & Sepilok

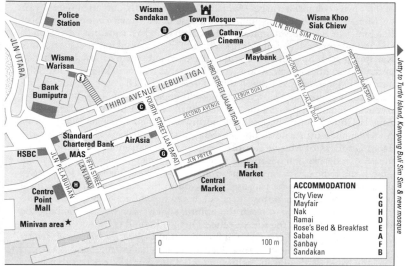

Jetty to Turtle Island, Kampung Buli Sim Sim & new mosque

ACCOMMODATION	
City View	C
Mayfair	G
Nak	H
Ramai	D
Rose's Bed & Breakfast	E
Sabah	A
Sanbay	F
Sandakan	B

Nak Jalan Pelahuban ☏089/272988; ✉info@nakhotel.com. Facing the harbour, this is in the heart of old Sandakan's frenetic merchandising district. The rooms are in need of sprucing up and the bathrooms a bit grubby but it's a solid place nevertheless. **④**

Ramai Mile 1 1/2 Jalan Leila ☏089/273222. Real effort has been made in this excellent mid-range hotel, whose 40ish spacious rooms, complete with splendid bathrooms, TV and a/c, are 2km west of the city centre on the main drag into town. Minivans pass every few minutes (RM1) and taxis arrive in a jiffy (RM6). **④**

Rose's Bed and Breakfast Block C, Lot 6, 2nd & 3rd floors, Bandar Ramai Ramai ☏089/223582, ✉rosebb@tm.net.my. Friendly and functional hostel (close to the Ramai), with a communal living room, Internet access and kitchen. Dorm beds RM15; **②**

🏃 **Sabah** Kilometre 1, Jalan Utara ☏089/213299, ⓦwww.sabahhotel.com.my. Sandakan's five-star finest, located 2km north of town (taxi RM5), with swish restaurants, business centre, swimming pool and sports facilities. **⑧**

Sanbay Mile 1 1/2 Jalan Leila ☏089/275000, ✉sanbay@po.jaring.my. Smart new hotel west of the centre, with spacious en-suite rooms. **④**

Sandakan Wisma Sandakan ☏089/221122; ⓦwww.hotelsandakan.com.my. The town's most popular hotel for business folk and visiting local families. It is quite good value, given the fine service, large rooms and excellent restaurant. **⑤**

The Town

Despite its lively colonial history, Sandakan's main attraction is its hot, steamy **waterfront** – a teeming, chaotic multi-purpose place where the fish and central **market** (daily 7am–6pm), hawker stalls and transport all seem to combine in a profusion of colour and activity. In the market's dark aisles can be found conches and turtle eggs, illegally imported from the Philippines, and fish bigger than shovels. From before dawn to late-morning, fruit and vegetable sellers line the front of the general market and, on the top floor, food stalls sell innumerable noodle dishes and seafood delicacies. The next building eastwards is the anarchic **fish market**, Sabah's largest, just behind which a row of weather-beaten old fishing boats are moored.

The streets set back from the sea are a little more serene, lined with simple coffee shops and garment stalls. To the west of the centre lies the **padang** – a reminder of the town's colonial heritage – which is, extraordinarily, only used once a year on Merdeka Day. A fifteen-minute walk east of the town centre, along Jalan Buli Sim-Sim, deposits you in front of Sandakan's modern **mosque**, which stands on a promontory and commands fine views of the bay. Flanking its eastern side is **Kampung Buli Sim-Sim**, the water village around which Sandakan expanded in the nineteenth century, whose countless photogenic shacks spread like lilies into the bay, crisscrossed by walkways. There's a marked contrast between the dilapidation of the water village and the well-tended surroundings of Sandakan's colonial remnants, especially the quintessentially English **St Michael's and All Angels Church**, a five-minute walk northwest of the Padang, up Jalan Puncak. A few minutes further north up Jalan Singapura is Sandakan's oldest temple, the Taoist **Goddess of Mercy Temple**, set in a grove of magnificent palms; unfortunately modernization has robbed it of any character.

From the temple, a sweaty, twenty-minute walk north up Jalan Utara, across on the eastern side of the padang, brings you to the foot of Jalan Astana, from where an **observation point** offers good views of the town, boats and islands below. It is also possible to reach the point a rather faster way by climbing the 100 steps from behind the tourist office. Directly behind the observation point is a beautifully restored colonial building, now the *English Tea House and Restaurant* and, next door, the 🏛 **Agnes Keith House** (daily 9am–5pm; RM15), a museum based on the life and achievements of the World War II British novelist (see box below).

The house on the hill

The house on the hill was where **Agnes Newton Keith** lived in the 1930s, writing evocative and descriptive books on Sabah like *Land Below the Wind* and *White Man Returns*. But her most famous novel, *Three Came Home*, was written during World War II while she and her infant son were interned at Pulau Berhala in terrible conditions along with other European women. These works had been selling Sabah to the rest of the world long before detailed guidebooks came about. Now, after many years as a ruin, the house's restoration has been overseen in a joint project by the Museums and Antiquities Department in KL and the Sabah Museum in KK. In 2005 the house opened, largely to highlight Sabah's colonial heritage.

Downstairs, reproductions of colonial furniture decorate the rooms while the staircase landing is adorned with imitation skulls and other artefacts including Murut blowpipes; upstairs is a study room with a collection of guns and knives and ceramics from the Sung and Ming dynasties (on loan from the Sabah Museum collection). There is also an area displaying first editions of Agnes Keith's seven books, all in their original jackets, and exhibits featuring photographs, quotations and texts of the Keith family. The end room has been converted into a small cinema where the movie version of *Three Came Home* and the documentary, *Sandakan 1950,* a vivid testimony to the era that's well worth watching, are both screened.

Keith was one of only twenty Caucasian women living in Sandakan on the eve of World War II but her writings indicate that she didn't identify much with the rest of the Europeans, preferring to describe the indigenous peoples – especially the servants she had regular dealings with – the country and local architecture. She loved Sandakan's friendly, inviting people and atmospheric, warren of godowns. In *Barefeet in the Palace* she wrote "We knew that we could walk into any ramshackle, threadbare, war-salvaged dwelling or shop of any prewar Sandakan inhabitant, and ask, and receive, whatever we needed." It seems she was less enamoured of the lifestyle of the British of the time. "The significance attached to doing and saying the right thing irked me", she wrote, but adapted to it because her husband, Harry, was an administrative officer.

Turn right down the road beyond the observation point, and bear left after Sandakan's half-Tudor, half-kampung-like **Astana**, and you're in the huge town **cemetery**, its thousands of green and sky-blue gravestones banked impressively up a hillside. You can continue along the path to the **Japanese cemetery** where, besides the graves of Japanese soldiers killed in action in World War II, are those of Japanese girls sold into prostitution in the late nineteenth and early twentieth centuries. There's another pleasing view of Sandakan Bay from the **Puu Jih Shih Temple**, a new complex high up on the cliffs, 4km west of town; a Sibuga bus from the the waterfront drops you off nearby. Inside, three tall statues of Buddha, carved from imported teak and embellished with gold leaf, stand on the altar, ringed by 32 dragon-entwined pillars – also of teak. Come early in the morning and your visit will be accompanied by the songs of scores of birds that swoop around the temple's rafters.

Speedboats from below Jalan Pryer run across to **Pulau Berhala**, 4km offshore, below whose vertical sandstone cliffs is a decent beach; with a lot of bargaining, the return fare should come to RM30. Berhala once housed a leper colony, and in World War II was used as a POW camp by the Japanese, housing author Agnes Keith and her son George, among others.

Eating and drinking

Sandakan may not be able to match KK's variety of **restaurants**, but there's still enough choice here to suit most people, with Malay, Chinese, Indian and Western food all well represented. Most places are in the town centre or along Jalan Leila, though several renowned **seafood** restaurants open every evening on Trig Hill, high up above the town. Also, take time to visit the *English Tea House* which attracts Sabahian cognoscenti through to tourists grateful for a quality cuppa. The *Tea House* garden commands a wonderful view at sunset out to sea and has the added attractions of a croquet lawn and Pimm's on request as well as more substantial fare.

For **hawker stalls**, head first for the market on Jalan Pryer, where stalls open during the day are particularly great for breakfast, or the night market on Jalan Leila, ten minutes' walk west of the centre, where Malay *nasi*, including mango salad in lime dressing and *lanka* – bamboo shoots in curry sauce – as well as chicken wings and *pisang goreng* (fried bananas) are of the highest standard but at the customary low prices.

Restaurants

English Tea House Jalan Istana ☎089/222544, ⓦwww.asiaextreme.biz/eth. British favourites including pies, both savoury and sweet, and baked potatoes are firm favourites although quality Malay and Indian food is also available. Most important perhaps – you can get the best pot of tea in Sabah here. Prices range from RM5 for tea, RM15 for the pies and RM25 for full meals. Daily 10am–midnight.

Haji One of several restaurants just south of the Rex Cinema. The fresh juices and *rotis* at this popular Muslim Indian place are memorable, as is the creamy chicken korma. There's an a/c dining room upstairs. Daily 8am–9pm.

Kedai Kopi Subur Kompleks Mara Sandakan, Jalan Leila. No-frills coffee shop specializing in

coto makassar – a tasty, meaty broth with chunks of rice cake. Daily 8am–9pm.

Ocean King Seafood Centre Batu 2 1/2 Jalan Baut Sapi ☎089/618111. A RM6–8 taxi ride west of town, this premier seafood spot is pricey but atmospheric; around RM60 for two. Daily 6pm–midnight.

Supreme Garden Vegetarian Restaurant Block 30, Jalan Leila, Bandar Leila. Affordable and welcoming establishment, two blocks back from the main drag and 2km from town centre. The imaginative menu runs to mock-meat dishes such as "fried frog with black-bean sauce", with the usual tasty tofu and green vegetables. A vegetarian steamboat (RM3.50 per person) is available Mon–Sat. Daily 8.30am–1.45pm & 5.30–8.45pm.

XO Steakhouse Hsiang Garden Estate, Mile 1
1/2 Jalan Leila. Sandakan's premier Western food
restaurant, serving fish and seafood as well as
Australian steaks. Daily 11am–2pm & 6–11pm.
Zakaria 111 Corner of Jalan Buli Sim-Sim and
Third Street (opposite the *Sandakan* hotel).
Inexpensive and highly popular locals' eaterie

specializing in fiery *dhal* and South Indian curries;
softer Malay dishes are available too.
Zamboanga Jalan Leila, between Jalan Puncak
and Jalan Singapore. Nondescript coffee shop
that's enlivened by the arrival of a Filipino chef
after 7pm, when the menu widens to include
Philippine seafood dishes. Daily 10am–10pm.

Bars

Beer is widely available in Chinese restaurants and coffee shops. **Bars** include
Cowboy City on Jalan Lelia, a big, bare, air-conditioned place which doesn't
get started until after 10pm and *Fatman* and *Mickey Mouse* – close to the Rex
Cinema at the western end of Second Avenue; but for the best atmosphere, head
to the no-frills *Shamrock*, on the junction of Third Avenue and First Street. This
is where Sandakan's most weathered locals mix with expats and well-heeled
Filipinos on the spend.

Listings

Airlines AirAsia, Lot 11A, Ground floor, Block 25,
Second Ave ☏089/222737; also a branch at the
airport. MAS, Sabah Building, Jalan Pelabuhan
☏089/273966 (Mon–Fri 8am–4.30pm, Sat
8am–3pm, Sun 8am–noon).
Banks and exchange Bank Bumiputra, opposite
Standard Chartered Bank, Third Ave; HSBC, corner
of Third Ave and Jalan Pelabuhan Maybank, Third
Ave; Standard Chartered Bank, Sabah Building,
Jalan Pelabuhan.
Car rental M B Pertmai Tours (☏089/219534
Ⓔmbpermaitours@yahoo.com), Lot 3, Termi-
nal Building, Sandakan Airport; *Sabah Hotel*
(☏089/213299, Ⓦwww.sabahhotel.com.my).
Hospital Duchess of Kent, Jalan Leila (2km west
of the centre, ☏089/212111).
Internet access Cyberjazz.net & Komputer Jazz,
Lot 1, second floor, Centre Point, Jalan Edinburgh;
InternetKaf, Lot 301, third floor, Wisma Sandakan.
Laundry Sandakan Laundry, Third Ave, between
Third St and Fourth St.
Pharmacy Borneo Dispensary, corner of Fifth St
and Second Ave.
Police The main police station is on Jalan Buliu
Sim-Sim (☏089/211222).
Post office Sandakan's GPO is five minutes' walk
west of town, on Jalan Leila (Mon–Fri 8am–5pm,
Sat 10am–1pm).

Telephones At the Telekom office, sixth floor,
Wisma Khoo Siak Chiew, Jalan Buli Sim-Sim (daily
8.30am–4.45pm); IDD calls can presently only be
made on cardphones.
Tour operators Borneo Eco Tours, c/o *Hotel
Hsiang Garden*, Jalan Leila, PO Box 82
☏089/220210, Ⓔinfo@borneoecotours
.com for *Sukau Lodge*, Gomantong Caves and
Turtle Island; SI Tours, Lot 1002, I0th floor,
Wisma Khoo Siak Chiew ☏089/213502;
Ⓔinfo@sitoursborneo.com for Turtle Island,
Sukau, Sepilok and Labuk Bay; Wildlife
Expeditions, Level 2, *Sabah Hotel* ☏089/273093,
Ⓦwww.wildlife-expeditions.com for Sukau,
Sepilok, Turtle Island and Labuk Bay. For
Sepilok Nature Resort and accommodation
at *Lankayan Island Dive Resort* contact Pulau
Sipadan Resort and Tours, 1st floor, Lot 7,
Block A, Bandar Pasaraya, Mile 4, North Rd
☏089/228081, Ⓔsepilok@po.jaring.my. To
arrange accommodation on Turtle Island, contact
Crystal Quest (see p.565). For Tabin Wildlife
Reserve (see p.581): Intra Travel Services,
Ground floor, Lot 13, Block B, Bandar Pasaraya,
Mile 4, North Road, PO Box 1459, ☏089/274988,
Ⓦwww.intra-travel.com.my.
Visa extensions Immigration Office, Wisma
Secretariat, Batu 7, Ranau Rd ☏089/666552.

Turtle Islands National Park

Peeping out of the Sulu Sea some 40km north of Sandakan, three tiny islands
comprise Sabah's **TURTLE ISLANDS NATIONAL PARK.** They are the
favoured egg-laying sites of the green and hawksbill turtles, varying numbers
of which haul themselves laboriously above the high-tide mark to bury their

7

clutches of eggs almost every night of the year. Malaysia's first turtle hatchery was established here to help protect them and, today, all three of the park's islands (Pulau Selingan, Pulau Bakkungan Kecil and Pulau Gulisaan) have hatcheries – though only **Selingan** can be visited by tourists. It's an extraordinary experience – as well as seeing a mother turtle laying her eggs, you can watch as the the park wardens release newly hatched turtles, which waddle, Chaplin-like, into the sea to face an uncertain future. Those on a tight schedule, however, may have to give Turtle Island a miss as it involves hanging around for a day before the evening's action takes place.

Turtles of both species don't begin to come ashore until after 7pm – rangers scout the island after dark and alert you once a sighting has been made. Typically, it takes a few hours for a female to lurch up the sand, dig a nesting pit and lay her slimy, ping-pong-ball-sized eggs – an average clutch will contain between thirty and eighty. All the egg-laying turtles are tagged, to aid research into the size and distribution of Southeast Asia's turtle population; their eggs, meanwhile, are taken for reburial to the hatchery, where they are safeguarded from hungry rats and birds.

There's plenty of time for **swimming** and **sunbathing** on Selingan before the turtle-watching (but watch out for sandflies which can be voracious, especially when it rains); alternatively, you can go **snorkelling** off nearby Bakkungan Kecil (RM60 per person, minimum four people; details from reception). On your way to Turtle Islands Park, you pass scores of **bagang**, or fish traps. At night, the light of the kerosene lamps hung from their bamboo frames attracts shoals of anchovies, which are then caught in nets – though on certain days of the month the moon is too full and bright for the process to work. The *bagang* are washed away by the annual storms of the November monsoon and rebuilt early the next year.

Practicalities

You can only visit the park as part of a **tour** with accommodation inclusive of the package price (for example, RM160 with Crystal Quest, see p.565). Although you need a **permit** to visit the island, the tour group you are with will organise that for you. The package is pretty much the same whichever operator you go with – **boats** leave the Crystal Quest jetty, 300m east of Sandakan town centre at 8am (operators will pick you up from your hotel or hostel a little earlier) and arrive at the island an hour later. Note that the day is then yours to stroll around the tiny island, swim or chill out in your room before the turtle viewing. There are beds for around fifty visitors a night, all of whom are put up in the island's comfortable, although fairly basic, **chalets**. Everyone eats in the same **café** – the rather average buffet spread is included in the package. Boats leave next moring at 7am after breakfast.

Pulau Lankayan

An hour-and-a-half's boat ride north of Sandakan in the Sulu Sea lies the Sugud Islands Marine Conservation Area, comprising three islands: Lankayan, Billiean and Tegaipil. Designated a protected area in December 2001, only **PULAU LANKAYAN** is visitable, following a deal struck between the eco-friendly Pulau Sipadan Tours and Resorts, which has opened a resort there, and the Sabah state government. Although the island itself is beautiful – its lush tropical vegetation stretching down to the coastline's pure white sandy beaches – it's the diving which is the real pull. The dive sites compare well with the better known Pulau Sipadan. The island is surrounded by hard and soft corals which offer an array of macro fauna, while during March through to May, sightings of whale sharks are frequent.

Practicalities

Pulau Lankayan itself can only be visited on a tour with Pulau Sipadan Tours and Resorts, 1st floor, Lot 7, Block A, Bandar Pasaraya, Mile 4, North Rd, Sandakan (℡089/228081, ⊛www.lankayan-island.com) and although all packages include transport from Sandakan to the island, prices vary depending on the amount of diving you want to do. A two-day, one-night stay including transport from Sandakan and food costs around RM500 (minus dives). Other firms, including Borneo Divers (see p.535), offer day-trips from Sandakan to dive off Lankayan.

Sandakan Memorial Park

Twelve kilometres west of Sandakan on Jalan Rimba, on the way back to Ranau, is **Sandakan Memorial Park** (9am–5pm; free). The park marks the site of the World War II POW camp where the **Death March** of 1945 originated. In 1942, 2700 British and Australian soldiers were transported from Singapore to Sandakan and set to work building an airstrip. By early 1945 many had died, but the surviving 1800 Australians and 600 British troops were force-marched to Ranau, where they were to start work on a new project. Just six soldiers, all Australian, survived the 240-kilometre march through mud and jungle. Dominating the park is a simple white block dedicated to the Allies who fought in North Borneo, as well as the locals who helped POWs and those involved in the Sandakan underground movement. Remnants of the camp are scattered around the sadly neglected grounds of the park. To get there take a Batu 8 bus to the Esso petrol station at the airport roundabout, then walk along Jalan Rimba for five to ten minutes – the park is on your right; taxis cost RM12 from central Sandakan.

Sepilok Orang-utan Rehabilitation Centre

Orang-utans – tailless, red-haired apes (their name means "man of the forest" in Malay) – can reach a height of around 1.65m, and can live to over thirty years old. Solitary but not aggressively territorial, these primates live a largely arboreal existence, eating fruit, leaves, bark and the occasional insect. There are just four designated sanctuaries for these creatures in the world, one of which, the **Sepilok Orang-utan Rehabilitation Centre** (daily 9am–12.30pm & 2–4.30pm; feeding times 10am & 3pm; RM30, photographic pass RM10; ℡089/531180, ⊜soutan@po.jaring.my), occupies a 43-square-kilometre patch of lowland rainforest 25km west of Sandakan. At the centre, young, traumatised and domesticated orang-utans whose survival instincts are undeveloped are trained to fend for themselves in the wild. When the centre was established in 1964, the orang-utans it trained had been liberated by a law prohibiting keeping them as pets, though nowadays the creatures are more often given to the centre by oil-palm planters or others responsible for clearing the forest. Although not always successful, the training process has so far seen more than a hundred orang-utans reintroduced to their natural habitat. To aid the integration process, there's a **feeding station** where those still finding their forest feet can find bananas and milk; the diet is never varied, as a way of encouraging orangutans to forage for other food in the trees.

At the **information centre** there's an exhibition on forest preservation and a useful video outlining the work carried out here is shown three times daily

(8.40am, 10.40am & 3.30pm). Close to feeding time, a warden leads you for ten minutes along a wooden boardwalk, passing the nursery, where baby orang-utans are taught elementary climbing skills on ropes and branches, to the feeding station. There are usually at least two orang-utans waiting for their meal and they immediately cluster round the warden as he sets out the fruit. Others may soon come along, swinging, shimmying and strolling towards their breakfast (or lunch), jealously watched by gangs of macaques that loiter around for scraps. The more cunning orang-utans take away enough bananas for a less public meal in the surrounding trees.

Practicalities

The blue Sepilok Batu 14 **bus** (RM2, 30min) leaves for the centre from 8am, hourly, from Sandakan's waterfront. If you want an earlier start, take a "Batu 14" minivan (RM2.50) from the same place. The last bus leaves the centre at 4.30pm; any later and you'll need to hitch or walk the 1.5km to the main road and flag down a bus or minivan.

Many visitors choose **to stay** in and around Sepilok as the accommodation is rather better, or at least more stylish, than what's on offer in Sandakan. Most of the **guesthouses** below are on the Sepilok Road which leads from the trunk road to the centre. Most offer food but there is also a **café** at the centre itself.

Accommodation

Sepilok B&B Lorong Sepilok ☎089/532288. Rather more basic than the others with small, pleasant rooms and acceptable dorms. Dorm beds RM25, ❸

Sepilok Jungle Resort, Lorong Sepilok ☎089/533031, ✉sepilokjr@yahoo.com. Rustic cabins and a campsite (RM10), nestling under trees. Its *Banana Café* serves good Malay cuisine and snacks. ❷

Sepilok Nature Resort Lorong Sepilok ☎89/765200, ⓦsepilok.com. Plush, eco-aware chalets nestling in lush jungle; the in-house restaurant serves the best food in Sepilok (around RM25 for a full meal). ❼

Sepilok Resthouse Lorong Sepilok (☎089/534900, ✉imejbs@tm.net.my). Located a little further down the lane but still only 5min walk

from the centre, this one has spacious en-suite rooms and Internet access. ❸

Uncle Tan's B&B Lot 8, SUDC Shoplots, Mile 16, Jalan Gum Gum ☎089-531639, ⓦwww.uncletan .com. Popular budget hostel nearly 4km from Sepilok on the way back to KK. Most visitors are on a package tour which includes a trip to the orang-utan centre and a night at *Uncle Tan's Wildlife Camp* on Sungai Kinabatangam, (RM280 for three days/two nights including three meals a day). To get to *Uncle Tan's B&B* take the Batu 16 bus from Sandakan's Labuk Road station and ask the driver to tell you when you get there – but often Tan's son Eugene will arrange to pick you up. Dorm beds RM25.

Wildlife Lodge Lorong Sepilok ☎089/533031. A welcoming, family-run operation set in delightful grounds. Dorm beds RM25, ❸

Labuk Bay Proboscis Monkey Sanctuary

The **Labuk Bay Proboscis Monkey Sanctuary**, Mile 8, Jalan Lintas (☎089/672133; ⓦwww.proboscis.cc), is 20km west of Sepilok near Kampung Samawang, Labuk Bay. The sanctuary is set in an area of mangrove forest teeming with wild proboscis monkeys (see box, p.574). An observation platform offers a perfect vantage point to view them (there are set feeding times at 10am and 3pm), and there are also plenty of marked trails to wander around. The sanctuary's **information centre** shows a video on the monkeys twice daily (11.30am & 2.30pm).

One area of mangrove, a five-minute walk from the information centre, is good for **swimming**. It's possible to view sea birds diving for fish and eagles circling here; hornbills and kingfishers can also be sighted in the park.

Proboscis monkeys

For many, a trip to Borneo would not be complete without an encounter with a **proboscis monkey**, a shy animal found nowhere except the riverine forests and mangrove swamps of the Bornean coast. The monkey derives its name from the enlarged, drooping, red nose of the adult male monkey; females and young animals are snub-nosed. The role of the drooping nose, which seems to straighten out when the animal is issuing its curious honking call, is unclear, although it is likely that it helps in attracting a mate. The monkeys are reddish-brown in colour, with a dark red cap, long, thick, white tails and white rumps; in addition, the adult males have a cream-white collar and large bellies, giving them a rather portly, "old gentleman" appearance. Males are significantly heavier than females, weighing up to 23kg, compared with the female's maximum weight of around 10kg. All in all, this combination of features has earned male proboscis monkeys the (not necessarily complimentary) name of *orang Belanda*, or "Dutchman", in parts of Borneo.

The monkeys live in loose groups, spending their days in trees close to the water, though they will walk across open areas when necessary, and can swim proficiently, aided by their partly webbed feet. The creatures are most active at dawn and dusk, when moving to and from feeding sites. Feeding on young leaves, shoots and fruit, they are quite choosy eaters, preferring the leaves of the *Sonneraita* mangrove tree, a rather specialist diet which means that large areas of forest need to be protected to provide groups of monkeys with sufficient food. This fact, coupled with the restricted range of the proboscis monkey, makes the species vulnerable to habitat loss and hunters.

Visitors can hope to see proboscis monkeys in several of the national parks in Sabah and Sarawak, most notably in the Kinabatangan area, the Labuk Bay Proboscis Monkey Sanctuary and in Sarawak's Bako National Park.

Practicalities

It is possible to travel independently to the sanctuary but access is not straightforward: **buses** (every 20min, 6am–6pm; RM2.60) from Sandakan waterfront stop by the Mile 19 junction, from where it may be possible to flag down a **minivan** or a motorbike taxi (both RM 15) for the remaining forty-minute journey. A **taxi** from Sandakan will set you back RM45 one way (RM80 return), the trip taking ninety minutes. Alternatively the sanctuary offers **day trips** from Sandakan (hotel pick up 9.30am) for RM150 (minimum two people), or RM200 if alone. This price includes transport and a guided tour of the sanctuary.

Accommodation is in two buildings, the *Bangkatan House*, which has twin rooms (⑤) and the *Nipah Lodge* with dorms (RM30); both are bookable through the sanctuary's website.

Sungai Kinabatangan and Sukau

South of Sandakan Bay, Sabah's longest river, the 560-kilometre **Kinabatangan**, ends its northeasterly journey from the interior to the Sulu Sea. Whereas logging has had an adverse impact on the river's ecology upstream, the dual threats of piracy and flooding have kept its lower reaches largely free of development, and the area is therefore rich in **wildlife**. It is the largest forested flood plain in Malaysia, laden with oxbow lakes, mangrove and grass swamps and distinctive vegetation including massive fig trees overhanging the water's edge.

△ View from a river safari boat, Sungai Kinabatangan

Despite Sabah's rather haphazard approach to making the most of its superb natural resources, the designation of the Kinabatangan as a **wildlife sanctuary** in 1999 was a brilliant move. That said, sanctuary status is one level below that of a national park, and so villages and agricultural development have been allowed to crisscross the protected sections. The area where birds and animals are most easily viewed is close to the small village of **Sukau** (134km from Sandakan). The sanctuary takes the form of a wildlife corridor along the river, with primary and mature secondary forest only a few kilometres deep on either bank, yet teeming with activity. Asian elephants, orang-utans, proboscis and macaque monkeys and gibbons all dwell in the forest flanking the river, and the resident **birdlife** is equally impressive. With luck, visitors get glimpses of hornbills, brahminy kites, crested serpent eagles, egrets, exquisite blue-banded and stork-billed kingfishers, and oriental darters, which dive underwater to find food and then sit on the shore, their wings stretched out to dry. In the river itself are freshwater sharks, (small) crocodiles, rays, even the occasional irrawaddy dolphin, and a great variety of fish species too.

The most effective way to view the wildlife is on a tour (see below) with each operator offering similar activities: boat trips along the river and its tributaries in the early morning, early evening or at night. Visitors can also go on short hikes away from the river on narrow paths in search of **orang-utan** nests – catching sight of a new nest usually means the orang-utan isn't far behind, as the solitary animal builds a different one each day.

Practicalities

Although tour operators arrange transport to their lodges and camps, it's relatively easy to get to **Sukau** (10km from the river mouth) by public transport. Either take a **minivan** (3 daily: 8am, 10am & 2 pm; 3hr; RM12) from Sandakan's waterfront or a Lahad Datu **bus** (7.15 & 7.30am; RM8), from Sandakan bus station; ask to be dropped at the Sukau junction, then flag down a minivan for the final 25km to Sukau (RM5). Returning from Sukau to Sandakan, minivans leave daily at 6.30am and noon from the tiny kampung.

Most visitors stay in the operators' comfortable **jungle lodges** or, in the case of veteran Kinabatangan operator, *Uncle Tan's*, in more basic **hut** accommodation. The cheapest option, however, is to head to Sukau independently (most of the jungle lodges are only a few hundred metres upstream for here), check into a **B&B** and hire a boat and guide in the village.

Kampung Sukau

In **KAMPUNG SUKAU** there are two excellent places to stay: *Sukau B&B* (☎089/230269; ❶), run by Esri Masri, has a few twin-bed rooms with communal bathrooms in a homestay arrangement. His family offers lunch and dinner for RM25 per day. Hiring a boat (plus guide) costs from RM70 to RM100 depending on the intended destination. Then there's *Temonggoh B&B*, located 2km along the river bank and run by the brothers Udik and Udin. They offer treks into the surrounding forest (RM50 for three hours; minimum two people) and can arrange boat trips along the river (same prices as *Sukau B&B*). Watch out for Sukau's weekly *tamu* on Fridays where locally made sarongs are piled beside chickens, kitchenware and jungle produce; there's also a smaller daily market.

Jungle lodges

There are now quite a few **lodges** around the Sukau stretch of the river, all of which can only be visited on a pre-booked package (the best are listed below). Expect to pay around RM400–500 for a one night stay (including transport from Sandakan) or RM600-700 for two nights.

The *Sukau Rainforest Lodge* run by Borneo Eco Tours (see KK tour operators or Sandakan listings) comprises twenty twin-bed chalets on stilts just 200m upstream from the kampung. This lodge is a fine example of ecotourism in practice, using only solar energy, and is well worth a visit. The three square meals a day, included in the price, are of a superb standard and the guided trips at dawn and dusk organized by Joseph "Sumo" Chung are fascinating and inspiring. Another tour operator, Sipadan Dive Centre (☎088/240584), runs the *Proboscis Lodge* which is closer to the Sukau jetty, a little further away from the tributaries the boats snake down. Downstream from Sukau, the new budget operation, *Kinabatangan Jungle Camp* (☎089/220299; ✉singmata@streamyx .com), has the added advantage of trails in the surrounding forest. A one-night stay here (plus transport and meals) costs around RM350.

Further upriver, away from the sometimes rather congested waterways around Sukau, you'll find *Uncle Tan's Wildlife Camp* (☎089/531639; ⓦwww.uncletan .com) twinned with the hostel of the same name between Sandakan and Sepilok. Although the **camp** is more basic than the hostel, it has an excellent location, and has been a hit with the backpacker market for many years. The package (RM280 for three nights, two spent on the river) includes accommodation in four-to-six berth huts, three meals a day and river safaris and jungle treks. *Uncle Tan's* is now run by his son Eugene, followng the sad death of his father, a towering figure in Sabah nature conservation.

River safaris

A usual river safari goes along the Kinabatangan tributary, **Sungai Menanggul**, catching sight of gibbons, proboscis monkeys and the occasional orang-utan, and takes around three hours, while a visit to Kelenanap and Kelandaun **oxbow lakes**, a most relaxing trip, good for birdwatching and perhaps for a sighting of a napping crocodile, usually takes four hours in total. Longer rides to kampungs **Bilet** and **Abai**, close to quieter tributaries, are an adventurous alternative but will take all day and are likely to cost at least RM150. One option is to base yourself at the *Trekkers Lodge Kinabatangan* (☎088/252263, 🌐www.trekkerslodge.com), Kampung Bilet (its sister operation is the renowed *Trekker, Lodge* in KK). A package from KK is equivalent to *Uncle Tan's* at around RM290 for three days/two nights, with accommodation in clean and functional dorms built out of recycled wood.

Batu Putih and Gomantong Caves

Within the limestone outcrop of **Batu Putih** (known locally as Batu Tulug), 1km north of the Kinabatangan Bridge on the road between Sandakan and Lahad Datu, small **caves**, visible from the road, contain wooden coffins well over a hundred years old. When the former curator of the Sarawak Museum, Tom Harrisson, explored the caves in the 1950s, he found many hardwood coffin troughs and lids, as well as a wooden upright, grooved with notches that were thought to represent a genealogical record. It was from here that the two-hundred-year-old coffin lid with a buffalo's head carved into handles, displayed at the Sabah State Museum, was taken; other coffins are still in their original spots, though unless archeology is your passion, think twice about making the detour to see them. All buses running between Sandakan and Lahad Datu pass by the caves (no admission charge).

Gomantong Caves

Off the Sukau road, the **Gomantong Caves** are vast limestone cavities with a strange claim to fame: deep in the main cave, there is the largest pile of *guano* (bat's droppings) in the world which was filmed in a remarkably tricky sequence for the 2006 BBC programme, *Planet Earth*. The bats, like at Deer Cave in Sarawak, vacate the caves at sundown to forage for food, before returning before morning. The caves' other chirpy residents are an equally large number of **swiftlets** whose nests are harvested for the bird's nest soup trade (see box below). Outside the caves there's a picnic site and canteen, and an **information centre** that will fill you in on the caves' ecosystem.

Of the two major caves, **Simud Hitam** is easiest to visit, reached by following the trail that runs off behind the staff quarters to the right of the reception building, taking a right fork after five minutes, and continuing on for a further ten minutes – the stench of ammonia will tell you when you are

---

Bird's nest soup

Chinese merchants have been coming to Borneo to trade for **swiftlets' nests** for at least twelve centuries. The nests – made of dried saliva – are cleaned and mixed with chicken broth to make **bird's nest soup**, a Chinese culinary speciality popular throughout Asia, especially in Hong Kong and Taiwan. Nests of the white-nest swiftlet, made of pure dried saliva, can fetch prices of over RM500 a kilogram whereas those of the black-nest swiflet, a mixture of saliva and feathers, fetch around RM100.

Harvesting the nests is a dangerous business involving scaling precarious rattan ladders and ropes – some up to 60m high. Sabah's Wildlife Department, which administers the caves, permits just two harvests a year – one between February and April, allowing the birds time to rebuild before the egg-laying season, the other between July and September, when the young have hatched and left. Bird's nests harvests also take place at Niah Caves in Sarawak (see p.486), and the trade also uses boarded-up shophouses in some towns as artificial nesting sites.

getting near. Reaching a height of 90m, with bug-ridden piles of compacted guano on the floor, Simud Hitam supports a colony of black-nest swiftlets. Above Simud Hitam is the larger but less accessible **Simud Putih**, home to the white-nest swiftlet. To reach Simud Putih, take the left fork, five minutes along the trail originating from the reception building, and start climbing. If you travel here independently, be sure to bring a torch, so that you can experience the full effect of the caves. Ringing the whole area is a patch of virgin jungle supporting orang-utans and elephants – neither of which you're very likely to see.

It's easiest to visit the caves as part of a **tour**; *Uncle Tan's*, for example, will include a detour to the caves as part of their tours around Sungai Kinabatangan for an extra RM30–50 per person. To get to the caves under your own steam **from Sandakan**, get a Sukau-bound minivan and ask to be dropped at the junction for Gomantong (20km before Sukau), from where it's a five-kilometre hike to the caves. Alternatively, if you're on a bus to or from Lahad Datu (see opposite), get off at the turning for Sukau, and catch a minivan or motorbike taxi (both RM5) for the 20km to the Gomantong junction. There is nowhere to stay in and around Gomantong, so plan to leave the caves well before dark if you are not on a tour.

South to Semporna

Below Sandakan Bay, the horseshoe of Sabah's main road continues southwards over the Kinabatangan Bridge to the towns of **Lahad Datu** and **Tawau**. This far east, the state's central mountain ranges taper away, to be replaced by lowland – and sometimes swampy – coastal regions lapped by the **Sulu** and **Celebes** seas, and dominated by oil-palm plantations. Archeological finds around **Madai**, off the road between Lahad Datu and Tawau, prove that this area of Borneo has been inhabited for over three thousand years. Nowadays, this is Sabah's "wild east": historically, pirates working out of islands in the nearby Filipino waters pose a real threat to fishermen and the separatist Filipino organization, Abu Sayyaf operates from the Mindanao islands, only twenty minutes by speedboat from Semporna. There are estimates that more than three quarters of a million illegal immigrants from the Philippines and Indonesia now call Sabah home, eking out a living on the streets. The influx began in the 1950s, when they were drawn by the prospect of work on Sabah's plantations, and rose sharply in the 1970s as a result of the civil unrest in Mindanao.

The lowland dipterocarp rainforest runs riot at the **Danum Valley Conservation Area**, which is reached via Lahad Datu. This is also the route to the mostly secondary-forested **Tabin Wildlife Reserve**. Closer to Kalimantan, and around the southern lip of wide **Darvel Bay**, the oceanic islands off Semporna, **Sipadan, Mabul** and **Kapalai**, are acclaimed **diving** spots, their reefs ablaze with exotic fishes and sea creatures.

If you're heading back to KK, there is an alternative to retracing your steps around the crown of the state. From **Tawau**, 4WDs depart daily for Keningau, travelling on rough roads that complete a **ring road** of sorts around Sabah. Many also choose to fly from Tawau to KK, a trip of 45 minutes compared with twelve hours by bus.

Tawau also has transport links to northeastern Kalimantan in **Indonesia**: MAS flies to Tarakan twice weekly and there are daily ferries (RM25) to Nunakan.

Lahad Datu

LAHAD DATU, 175km south of Sandakan, has something of a frontier feel, the conspicuous consumption in the town resulting from the oil-palm and timber industry money which has underpinned its growth. In the 1990s, this boom town was flooded by immigrants – many of whom have found gainful, if illegal, employment on the plantations and in town. The Celebes Sea coastline is famous for a certain degree of lawlessness. In 1986 a mob of heavily armed pirates stormed the Standard Chartered Bank and MAS office on Jalan Teratai, Lahad Datu's main street, and made off with RM100,000. More recently, in April 2000, a group of tourists on Pulau Sipadan were kidnapped and held for two months by the Filipino Muslim separatists before being released unharmed, no ransom having been paid. The incident appears to have been a one-off, thankfully, and has not profoundly affected the tourist industry in the region. The town itself is nondescript, just a jumping off point for Danum Valley Conservation Area and Tabin Wildlife Reserve.

Practicalities

Buses from Sandakan, Semporna and Tawau stop at the **bus terminus** on Jalan Bunga Raya, a couple of minutes' walk east of the town centre. From the **airport**, north of town, it's only a short taxi ride (RM5) into the centre (there are no buses on this route). If you are heading out to the *Borneo Rainforest Lodge* in Danum Valley your first port of call is likely to be the **Borneo Nature Tours office**, Lot 20, Block 3 (ground floor), Fajar Centre (℡089/880207, ⓦwww .borneorainforestlodge.com/indexg.asp.

You can find just about acceptable **accommodation** at *Ocean Hotel* (℡089/881700; ❸) which has simple rooms with attached bathrooms. The best hotel, though, is the *Executive* (℡089/881333; ❺), a smart, welcoming place in an otherwise dull and boring town. The *Executive* also has an excellent **restaurant** with a mostly Chinese menu.

Danum Valley Conservation Area

Spanning 438 square kilometres of primary dipertocarp rainforest 65km west of Lahad Datu, the **Danum Valley Conservation Area** (DVCA) is contained within a sprawling logging concession owned by the Sabah Foundation (Yayasan Sabah HQ, PO Box 11623, KK; ℡088/422211, ⓦwww.ysnet .org.my). The logging work has helped fund the foundation's charitable works across the state. Established in 1981 for the purpose of rainforest-related "conservation, research, education and recreation", the DVCA is a meeting place for naturalists worldwide. The valley supports a wealth of wildlife including bearded pigs, orang-utans, elephants, proboscis monkeys, as well as 250 bird species, reptiles, fish and insects. Short hiking **trails** are limited to the eastern side, where the tourist accommodation is located. The remainder is pristine forest, out of bounds to all but researchers on well-resourced and long scientific expeditions.

Practicalities

The valley has two **places to stay**: the Field Studies Centre and, nine kilometres further into the area, the *Borneo Rainforest Lodge*, sited on a bend in Sungai Danum – the latter can only be visited as part of a package tour with Borneo Nature Tours. For many years the **Field Studies Centre** was used exclusively by scientists but it's been recently opened up to tourists. Facilities include twin-bed chalet accommodation (❸), an excellent café, a library of academic

△ Canopy walkway, Danum Valley Conservation Area

standards and Internet access. There are two observation towers for wildlife-watching and **excursions** include treks to two waterfalls and a Dusun burial site, as well as night safaris by jeep (available on request, RM40 per person). For **booking** and transport details, contact their head office in KK (☎088/243245, ⓦwww.ysnet.org.my/maliau).

The *Borneo Rainforest Lodge* (☎088/243245) is a luxurious network of hardwood **chalets** situated in a beautiful spot on the Sungai Danum with the multi-layered sound of the rainforest reverberating around. The lodge has a cavernous communal hall, a bar and a little library. The high prices (around RM500 per night) include excellent buffet **meals** – usually a mix of Western and Asian dishes. **Activities** include braving the sixty-metre-high canopy walkway (where, given patience and luck, you may glimpse orang-utans), guided night safaris (in an open-backed truck) and jungle walks.

Guests are picked up either from the airport or the Borneo Nature Tours office in Lahud Datu for the two-hour trip to the lodge by jeep or minivan. **Bookings** are taken at both their Lahud Datu (see p.535) and KK offices.

Tabin Wildlife Reserve

One-and-a-half hours' drive northeast of Lahad Datu lies **Tabin Wildlife Reserve** (🌐 www.tabinwildlife.com.my). Although just eleven percent primary dipterocarp forest – the rest is secondary forest – Tabin is another place to visit in this remote part of Sabah where you are very likely to see wildlife. Either by **trekking** or **night drives** along the edge of the nearby oil-palm plantation there are opportunities to come across elephant, *banter-ing* (Asian cattle), *tembedau* (deer) or wild boar as they cross the tracks from the forest to the plantations in search of food. Endemic species like the red giant-flying squirrel and birds including hornbills are easy to spot too. There are also several interesting treks inside Tabin including a one hour's walk to a splendid **waterfall** and lake for bathing in. A small number of Sumatran rhinos have been sighted by researchers, and baby tracks were photographed in 2002; however, it is extremely unlikely you might catch sight of one these quintessentially shy animals. A highly endangered sub-species, the rhinos are being monitored by SOS Rhino (🌐 www.sosrhino.org) which has a base 400m from the park headquarters. Under-visited at present, the reserve has excellent facilities, including stunning **chalets** overlooking Sungai Lipad and sleeping platforms for hire lower down the river valley.

Practicalities

From central Lahad Datu a **minivan** (daily noon 1pm; RM20) makes the 1hr 15min journey to the reserve, returning to the town at 8.30am. That said, currently the reserve's managers, Intra Travel Services (☎089/274988, 🌐 www.intra-travel.com.my), only offer all-inclusive packages combining travel, accommodation and activities. Prices range from RM200 for a two-night stay on an **eco-platform** in tents provided by the company, to more than double to stay in a **chalet**. Food at the *Lipad Café* is excellent, and is included in the package price, as are visits to a waterfall and a mud volcano.

Madai Caves

Roughly midway between Lahad Datu and Semporna, the **Madai Caves**, 13km west of the unremarkable coastal town of Kunak, are worth a stop, particularly if you aren't able to get to Gomantong Caves. **Minivans** between Tawau and Lahad Datu will drop you in the Madai area for RM8, though with the caves 3km off the main road, it's worth paying a taxi an extra RM2 to be driven all the way.

Although humans have dwelt in them for over ten thousand years, the caves of the Madai limestone massif are most remarkable for the birdlife they support; here, as at Gomantong, the **nests** of swiftlets are harvested for bird's nest soup. The entrance to the cave system is marked by a few fragile stilt huts – home, in season, to nest-harvesters. Once beyond the front aperture, you'll discover a succession of vast chambers in which swiftlets dive, bats squeak and guano lies ankle-deep. In season, harvesters will offer to show you the remnants of old Idahan coffins in the caves – at a price. The caves are pitch-black, so a **torch** is essential.

Semporna and around

The sleepy fishing village of **SEMPORNA**, is usually only visited in passing by travellers on their way to **Pulau Sipadan** and the other Celebes islands, **Mabul** and **Kapalai**, where **scuba diving** is the main activity. However, it's an atmospheric place – seemingly in danger of spilling into the pure blue waves of its shoreline – and there is a growing backpacker scene, with many visitors arranging diving tours from here rather than paying the higher prices for dive packages.

For generations Muslim Bajau and Suluk peoples have farmed the surrounding seas for fish, sea cucumbers, shells and other marine products. Often dubbed "sea gypsies", these people were originally nomads who lived aboard their intricately carved wooden boats, called *lipa-lipa*. Although they are now mostly settled in and around Semporna, their love of, and dependence upon, the sea remains strong today and the characteristic white sails of the Bajau boats can still be seen, billowing in the breeze across the bay and around the Celebes Sea's picture-postcard islands.

Practicalities

Though not served by long-distance buses, Semporna is linked by hourly **minivans** with Lahad Datu (RM25), Sandakan (RM40) and Tawau (RM15). The terminus is 100m east of the waterfront. There is no official tourist office, though the Semporna Ocean Tourism Centre (SOTC; ☎089/769950; ⓦwww.northborneo.net), dangling out from the harbour, can provide some information on the area.

Accommodation

Darmai Lodge One block back from seafront ☎089/782011. A good bet with clean en-suite rooms and small dorms. Dorm beds RM20, ❸
Dragon Inn Jalan Kastam ☎089/781088. Semporna staple with quite expensive doubles. Dorms RM15, ❻
Mabul Backpackers Lodge One block back from seafront ☎089/781002, ⓦwww.mabulbackpackerslodge.blogspot.com. Run by Uncle Chang, it sleeps fourteen in seven twin rooms. Chang also arranges competitively-priced dives off Sipidan and Mabul. ❸

Scuba Junkie Lot 45–46, Semporna Seafront ☎089/785372, ⓦwww.scuba-junkie.com. Owned by dive-mad British marine biologist Ric Owen, this new place with doubles and dorms, has become the focal point for budget travellers after reasonably priced dives (around RM200 a day). Dorm beds RM20, ❸
Seafest Hotel Semporna Seafront ☎089/782333, ⓔseafast@tm.net.my. Imposing concrete block with smart en-suite doubles. ❼

Eating

Most visitors **eat** at their hotels; although the classy *Pearl City Restaurant* in the *Dragon Inn* has views out to sea and good seafood, as does the flimsy but atmospheric *Floating Restaurant*, which bobs in the water in between the inn and the harbour.

The islands off Semporna

The islands off Semporna – also Bajau territory – are exquisitely beautiful and, with the exception of **Sipadan** and **Mabul**, rarely visited. **Sibuon**, for example, on the edge of the chain and just over half an hour by boat from Semporna, has a breathtaking beach and shallow coral reefs and **Sabangkat**, twenty minutes from town, likewise has coral, as well as small villages and a seaweed farm. A lovely spot for diving and snorkelling, Sabangkat remains almost solely the preserve of the local Bajaus. **Mataking** and **Boheian** have some coral too and are renowned for their turtles and magnificent rays. For some terrestrial wildlife, the large island of **Timbun Mata** has a population of birds, deer, monkeys, wild boar and bats. But these jewels are often overlooked by visitors who are impatient to get out to the dive meccas of Sipadan, Mabul and Kapalai. To get to these outlying islands, go to the SOTC causeway. The cost of chartering a boat for four passengers is RM150–300; more if snorkelling equipment is included.

Pulau Sipadan

For some years, visiting **Pulau Sipadan** – 30km south of Semporna in the Celebes Sea – has become de rigueur for the hardcore scuba-diving fraternity. Acclaimed by the late marine biologist Jacques Cousteau as "an untouched piece of art", Sipadan is a cornucopia of marine life, its waters teeming with turtles, moray eels, sharks, barracuda, vast schools of gaily coloured tropical fish, and a diversity of coral that's been compared to that at Australia's Great Barrier Reef. Tragically, a serious accident in May 2006, where a dredger ripped a large amount of the reef's coral away, seriously threatens the area's ecological riches.

The island, carpeted by lush forest and fringed by flawless white-sand **beaches**, up which green **turtles** drag themselves to lay their eggs, is at the crown of a limestone spire, which rises 600m from the seabed and widens at the top to form a coral shelf shaped like an artist's palette. Among the highlights for divers here is a network of marine caves, the most eerie of which is Turtle Cavern, a watery grave for the skeletal remains of turtles which have strayed in and become lost. There's also White-tip Avenue and Barracuda Point, frequented respectively by white-tip sharks and spiralling shoals of slender barracuda, and the Hanging Gardens, an extraordinarily elegant profusion of soft coral hanging from the underside of the reef ledge. Snorkellers accompanying divers to the island can expect to see reef sharks, lion fish, barracudas and scores of turtles, without having to leave the surface; the drop-off, just beyond the jetty, is a good place to wade out and don goggles.

Since 2004, **accommodation** has been banned on Sipidan after a state ruling which judged that conserving the island's fragile ecology was more important than the tourism industry.

Pulau Mabul

Following the accommodation ban on Sipadan, the big dive resorts moved to **Mabul**, the largest island in the chain. Although visibility is poor compared with Sipadan, the silted waters around Mabul are perfect for "**muck dives**", popular perhaps for the shock element – you can't see the fish, or other marine life, until they suddenly loom up in front of you. Mabul is also distinct from Sipadan ecologically – it's predominantly made up of coconut trees; almost every one is numbered and associated with an individual who cares for the tree and harvests its coconuts. Apart from diving, there is little else to do except stroll between the resorts or visit the island's sole fishing village.

△ Pulau Kapalai

The following operators have all received good feedback and all have fully equipped dive centres. Room **prices** are always part of a package deal; expect to pay around RM600 for a two-night stay including dives.

Resorts

Borneo Divers Mabul Resort ☎088/222226, ⓦwww.borneodivers.info. Dozens of lavish two-room chalets and an excellent restaurant close to a lovely beach.

Sipadan Water Village ☎089-752996, ⓦwww .swvresort.com. Top-of-the-range kampung-style resort arranged around a stilted water village, built to Bajau architectural design. It includes a bar, reception area and a large circular restaurant.

Sipadan-Mabul Resort (SMART) ☎088/230006 ⓦwww.sipadan-mabul.com.my. Located on the south-east side of the island overlooking nearby Pulau Sipadan, this resort boasts over forty wooden en-suite chalets and a top class restaurant.

Pulau Kapalai

Little more than a sandbar, tiny **Kapalai** is exquisite and otherwordly – an ever-changing kaleidoscope of sand, sky and water. There is only room for one resort, the *Sipadan-Kapalai Resort* run by Pulau Sipadan Resort and Tours, 484 Bandar Sabindo, Tawau (☎089/765200, ⓦwww.sipadan-kapalai.com). The two dozen chalets are spectacular, and appear to hover above the shallow azure water, which is perfect for snorkelling. The resort also runs regular dives off nearby Sipadan and Mabul.

Tawau and around

Sabah's southernmost town of any size, **TAWAU**, is 150km southwest of Lahad Datu and 70km west of Semporna, making its tiny airport the closest one for people heading for Sipadan. Indeed, most travellers don't even give the town a nod, they just head straight from the airport to the islands.

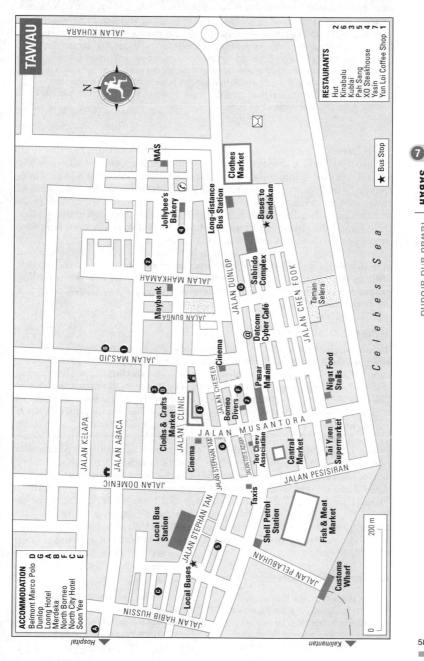

TAWAU

JALAN KUHARA

N

RESTAURANTS

Hut	2
Kinabalu	6
Kublai	3
Pah Sang	5
XO Steakhouse	4
Yasin	7
Yun Loi Coffee Shop	1

★ Bus Stop

Celebes Sea

MAS

Jollybee's Bakery

Clothes Market

Long-distance Bus Station

Buses to Sandakan ★

JALAN MAKKAMAH

Maybank

JALAN BUNGA

JALAN DUNLOP

Sabindo Complex

JALAN CHEN FOOK

Taman Selera

JALAN MASJID

Datcom Cyber Café @

JALAN KELAPA

JALAN ABACA

Cloths & Crafts Market

JALAN CLINIC

Cinema

Cinema

JALAN CHESTER

Borneo Divers

Pasar Malam

Night Food Stalls

JALAN CATHY KAM

Teo Chew Association

JALAN MUSANTORA

Central Market

Tai Yien Supermarket

JALAN DOMENIC

JALAN STEPHAN TAN

Taxis

JALAN PESISIRAN

Shell Petrol Station

Fish & Meat Market

Local Bus Station

JALAN STEPHAN TAN

Local Buses ★

JALAN HABIB HUSSIN

JALAN PELABUHAN

Customs Wharf

▼ Hospital

▼ Kalimantan

0   200 m

AirAsia **flies** from Tawau to KL and Johor Bahru, while their subsidiary, FAX, flies daily to Sandakan. MAS also flies here from KL. Tawau is also the stepping stone for **boat travel** to Kalimantan, with daily departures to Pulau Nunukan (1hr 30min; RM25). Note that from Nunukan boats go further round the coast to Tarakan (3hr; RM75). **Long-distance buses** to KK, Lahad Datu and Semporna leave from the station at the eastern end of Jalan Dunlop; **4WDs** to Keningau leave from the same site. However, the four, daily buses to and from Sandakan have their own stop, one block south from here, just in front of Jalan Chen Fook.

The town was originally a small Bajau settlement, until the British North Borneo Chartered Company, attracted by its fine harbour and rich volcanic soil, transformed it into a thriving commercial port, a role which it continues to fulfil today. While the town's prosperity relied at first upon the cultivation of cacao, then timber, nowadays oil-palm plantations are in the ascendancy (as in so many parts of Sabah), attracting many Filipino and Indonesian immigrants. As Tawau is the major departure point for the **Kalimantan** port Nunakan, hundreds of Indonesians arrive daily on the ferry.

Central Tawau in contrast is an orderly blend of wooden shophouses and concrete buildings. There are numerous **markets**: the clothes and trinket stalls in the crowded building beside the *Soon Yee Hotel* and the sprawling produce market on the square of reclaimed land in front of Jalan Chen Fook are both worth a browse.

Practicalities

Tawau's **airport** is located 3km northwest of the town centre (there's an AirAsia office on the first floor). There are no buses from the airport – a taxi into town costs RM10. **Long-distance buses** arrive at the **station** below the eastern end of Tawau's main street, Jalan Dunlop. **Ferries** from Kalimantan arrive at Customs Wharf, Jalan Pelabuhan, 150m south of Jalan Dunlop's Shell petrol station. The **local bus station** is on Jalan Stephen Tan, in the centre of town, while **shared taxis** park at the southern end of Jalan Domenic.

As well as several **banks**, the commercial estate known as the Fajar Centre, east of Jalan Masjid, houses both the Telekom building in Block 35, and the MAS office in Wisma Sasco; you'll find the **post office** across the southern side of Jalan Dunlop. One of provincial Sabah's busiest **Internet** cafés, *Datcom Cyber Café*, is right in the centre of town on the second floor of Suhindo Plaza, Jalan Dunlop. Pulau Sipadan Resort and Tours, who run the resort on Pulau Kapalai (see p.584), have an office on the first floor of 484 Bandar Sabindo (☎089/765200), as does Sipadan Water Village, who run dive trips and accommodation on Pulau Mabul (226, first floor, Lot 3, Wisma MAA, ☎089/752996).

Accommodation

Belmont Marco Polo Jalan Stephen Tan ☎089/777988. The classiest address in town is still this swish place above the mosque, with large a/c rooms, a friendly bar equipped with piano and karaoke, a fitness centre and a reasonable restaurant (RM25 for Chinese dishes). **7**

Dunlop Jalan Dunlop ☎089/770733. Average Chinese-run place with small, adequate rooms. **2**

Loong Hotel Jalan Abaca ☎089/765308. Good choice with large, clean rooms with small and neat bathrooms. ❹
Merdeka Jalan Masjid ☎089/776655. Smart, mid-range hotel with, good-value a/c rooms. ❹
North Borneo Jalan Dunlop ☎089/763060. A mid-range establishment located behind Tawau's cinema, with neat en-suite rooms. ❺

North City Hotel 175 Jalan Belia Tawau ☎089/773100. Medium-sized functional place close to the local bus and minivan stands with acceptable clean rooms. ❸
Soon Yee 1362 Jalan Stephen Tan ☎089/772447. The best of the budget spots in town; with most rooms with communal bathrooms but a few en suite (RM50). ❷

Eating

As well as the cafés and restaurants listed below, Tawau has a **pasar malam** on Jalan Nusantaras selling good Malay and Indian food (daily 6–11pm). There's also a stretch of open-air restaurants and stalls collectively known as **Taman Selera** which sets up in the Sabindo Complex, south of Jalan Dunlop (daily 7.30am–6pm).

The Hut Block 29, Fajar Centre. Generous Western set meals including decent steaks. Daily 6–11pm.
Kinabalu Jalan Kong Fah. Good Muslim restaurant with a buffet and set meals. Daily 10am–8pm.
Kublai Restaurant *Belmont Marco Polo Hotel*. Rather overpriced hotel eatery but with a great dim sum breakfast on Sunday mornings. Daily 6.30am–10pm.
Loong Hotel Restaurant Jalan Abaca. Serves good claypot dishes within an international menu.

In the evenings there's a BBQ seafood stall out on the covered forecourt. Daily noon–10pm.
Pah Sang Jalan Cole Adam. Chinese café specializing in good noodle dishes. Daily 9am–8pm.
XO Steakhouse Fajar Centre. Good spot for a protein fix. Daily 6–11pm.
Yasin Jalan Dunlop. Indian café with curries, *rotis* and *murtabak*. Daily 8am–8pm.
Yun Loi Coffee Shop Jalan Masjid. Probably the best sit-down café in town with delicious noodles and dumplings. Also stocks beer and fruit juices. Daily 8am–10pm.

Tawau Hills State Park

Out of town, an hour's drive north, is the 270-square-kilometre **Tawau Hills State Park** (☎089/753564; RM10), a lovely stretch of lowland rainforest with one major trail leading up 1000m through thick, damp, mossy forest and another, easier hike to a waterfall on Sungai Tawau where the park has built shelters, toilets and changing rooms. It is three hours further into the forest to the hot springs where there is another waterfall. Reaching the park, however, is tricky – no buses come here and most taxi drivers aren't familiar with the maze of roads crisscrossing the Borneo Abaca Ltd agricultural estate in which the park is situated. Dorm-bed **accommodation** (RM20) is in a large block and, like the food in the canteen, basic, but there also are four-bed chalets to hire at RM200 each.

West into the interior

A network of **logging roads** spanning the southern portion of Sabah makes it possible to travel back to KK overland, without having to retrace your steps. While not cheap, the journey by **4WD** (vehicles leave when full; RM80), from Tawau to Keningau, along a track that parallels the Kalimantan border, is worth taking for excitement value alone.

The journey is comfortable enough as you leave Tawau but at **Merotai**, some 20km out, the sealed road ends and the jolting ride begins, taking you past cocoa and palm plantations, lush forest and vast timber mills. You should reach Keningau in the early evening as long as you leave Tawau before 9am.

Travel details

Trains

See box on p.546

Beaufort to: KK (2 daily; 2hr 30min); Tenom (2 daily; 2hr 30min).
KK to: Beaufort (2 daily; 2hr 20min); Papar (1 weekly; 2hr); Tenom (1daily; 5hr).
Tenom to: Beaufort (2 daily; 2hr 30mins); KK (1 daily; 5hr).

Buses

Beaufort to: KK (hourly; 2hr); Kuala Penyu (8 daily; 1hr); Menumbok (8 daily; 1hr 30min); Sipitang (hourly; 50min); Tenom (hourly; 50min).
Keningau to: KK (hourly; 2hr 30min); Tambunan (hourly daily; 1hr); Tawau (2 daily; 10hr); Tenom (3 daily; 1hr).
KK to: Beaufort (hourly; 2hr); Keningau (hourly; 2hr 30min); Kinabalu National Park (hourly; 2hr 30min); Kota Belud (every 30min; 1hr 30min); Kudat (hourly; 3hr); Lawas, Sarawak (1 daily; 4hr); Menumbok (6 daily; 2hr 30min); Papar (20 daily; 40min); Ranau (10 daily; 2hr); Sandakan (12 daily; 6hr); Tambunan (hourly; 1hr 30min); Tawau (2 daily; 10hr); Tenom (3 daily; 1hr 30min).
Sandakan to: KK (hourly; 6hr); Lahad Datu (6 daily; 2hr 30min); Ranau (8 daily; 3hr 30min); Tawau (8 daily; 4hr 30min).
Tawau to: KK (3 daily; 10hr); Lahad Datu (hourly; 2hr); Sandakan (8 daily; 4hr 30min); Semporna (twice hourly; 1hr 30min).

Tenom to: Beaufort (hourly; 50min); Keningau (3 daily; 1hr); KK (3 daily, 1hr 30min).

Ferries

KK to: Labuan (4 daily; 3hr).
Labuan to: Brunei (4 daily; 1hr 30min); KK (4–6 daily; 2hr); Menumbok (hourly; 25min).
Tawau to: Nunakan (Indonesia; 2 daily; 1hr 30min).

Flights

KK to: Bandar Seri Begawan (12 weekly; 40min); Johor Bahru (2 daily; 2hr 15min); Kuala Lumpur (numerous daily; 2hr 30min); Kuching (3 daily; 2hr); Kudat (2 daily; 30min); Labuan (4 daily; 30min); Lahad Datu (4 daily; 50min); Sandakan (7 daily; 50min); Singapore (5 daily; 2hr 15min); Tawau (7 daily; 45min).
Kudat to: KK (2 daily; 30min); Sandakan (4 daily; 50min)
Labuan to KK (4 daily; 30min); Kuala Lumpur (5 daily; 2hr 25min); Kuching (1 daily; 2hr 15min); Miri (3 daily; 40min)
Lahad Datu to: KK (4 daily; 50min).
Sandakan to: Johor Bahru (6 weekly; 2hr 40min); KK (7 daily; 50min); Kuala Lumpur (2 daily; 2hr 45min); Kudat (4 daily; 50min); Tawau (2 daily; 30min).
Tawau to: Johor Bahru (8 weekly; 2hr 45min); KK (7 daily; 45min); Kuala Lumpur (3 daily; 2hr 45min); Sandakan (2 daily, 30min).

Brunei

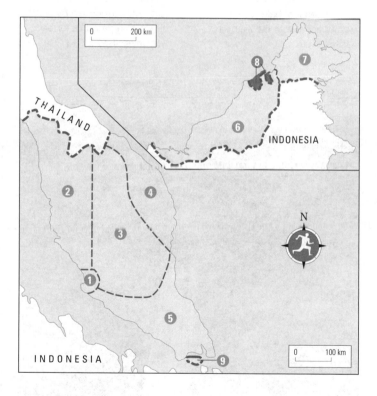

CHAPTER 8

Highlights

✴ **Omar Ali Saifuddien Mosque** The centre of Brunei's capital is dominated by this magnificent mosque. See p.601

✴ **Water village, Bandar Seri Begawan** The stilt village of Kampung Ayer is picturesque, balancing the traditional with the modern. See p.602

✴ **Ulu Temburong National Park** Brunei's premier park with a heart-stopping canopy walkway, exhilarating boat rides and short treks. See p.611

✴ **Tasek Merimbun** This majestic lake in Tutong District, surrounded by rice fields, is a paradise for bird-watching. See p.613

△ Canopy walkway, Ulu Temburong National Park

Brunei

T he tiny Islamic sultanate of **BRUNEI** perches on the northwestern coast of Borneo, surrounded and split in two by the meandering border of Sarawak. Officially titled Negara Brunei Darussalam, the name translates as "Abode of Peace"; and tranquil it certainly is with virtually no crime and a general sense of calm bolstered by high employment levels and a commensurate standard of living, all driven by its massive offshore oil and gas deposits which have produced an economy that is the envy of surrounding states. Its 374,000 inhabitants (of which Malays account for seventy percent, the rest being Chinese, Indians, indigenous tribes and expatriates) enjoy a quality of life almost unparalleled in Southeast Asia – education and healthcare are free; houses, cars, and even pilgrimages to Mecca are subsidized.

Brunei, however, is virtually an absolute monarchy with **Sultan Hassanal Bolkiah** (see box, p.596), combining the dual roles of prime minister and defence minister, and his extended family, the Bolkiahs, in control of virtually all of the government departments and the vast majority of the nation's wealth; it's said that nothing of any real importance is done without the thumbs up from a family member. The sultan rules by decree but, perhaps surprisingly, in 2004 he made the first moves in the direction of political reform by appointing a parliament – but there's been no word on a date for elections.

Brunei has an illustrious past: at its height in the sixteenth century, it was the seat of the proudest **empire** in Borneo, its sultans receiving tribute from as far away as Manila; elephants imported from India patrolled its jungle pathways from the South China to the Sulu seas. But Brunei's glory days were long past by the end of the nineteenth century, when the country feared for its very existence, European adventurers having methodically chipped away at its territory, absorbing it into their new colonies.

Geographically, Brunei lies on a slim coastal plain threaded by several substantial rivers. Most of the country is less than 150m above sea level, its rainforest, peat swamp and heath forest running down to sandy beaches and mangrove swamps. The country is divided into four districts: **Brunei Muara**, which contains the capital, **Bandar Seri Begawan** (known locally simply as BSB); agricultural **Tutong**; oil-rich **Belait**; and **Temburong**, a sparsely populated backwater severed from the rest of Brunei by Sarawak's Limbang district. Thanks to its oil, Brunei has never needed to exploit its forestry to any great degree, with the result that primary and secondary tropical forest still covers around seventy percent of the total land area.

However, despite its natural riches, the sultanate's massive tourist potential has been largely overlooked by the Bolkiahs; indeed officials at times avowedly discouraged the backpacker market. Now, though, with the expansion of the

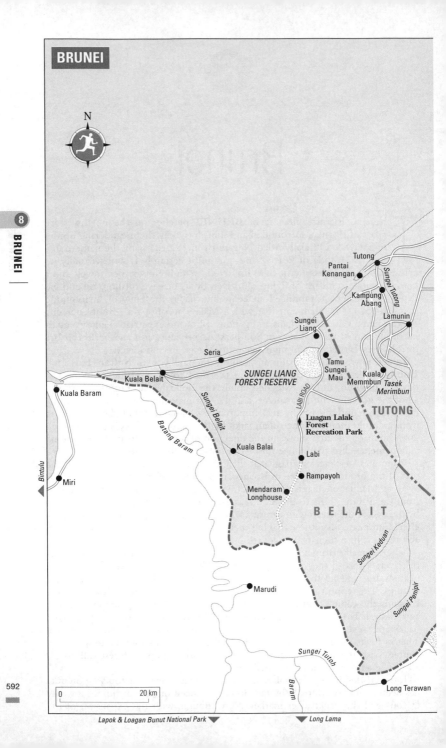

BRUNEI

N

Tutong
Pantai
Kenangan
Sungei Tutong
Kampung
Abang
Lamunin
Sungei
Liang
Seria
Tamu
Sungei
Mau
Kuala
Memmbun
Tasek
Merimbun
Kuala Belait
SUNGEI LIANG
FOREST RESERVE
LABI ROAD
TUTONG
Kuala Baram
Luagan Lalak
Forest
Recreation Park
Batang Baram
Sungei Belait
Bintulu
Kuala Balai
Labi
Miri
Rampayoh
Mendaram
Longhouse
B E L A I T
Sungei Keduan
Marudi
Sungei Penipir
Sungei Tutoh
Baram
Long Terawan

0   20 km

Lapok & Loagan Bunut National Park ▼   ▼ Long Lama

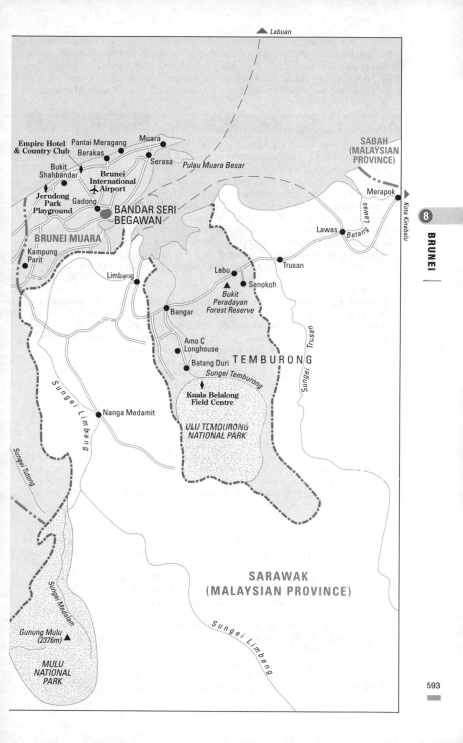

international airport, the sultanate is witnessing a steady increase in arrivals – backpackers included – even if most visitors merely overnight between flights or linger just for one or two days. Many are drawn to the pristine rainforest of **Ulu Temburong National Park** in the eastern section of the country. Also now accessible for visitors with a car is the magical lake, **Tasek Merimbun**.

Brunei practicalities

Following the growth in the number of **flights** to Brunei, more tourists are coming to the sultanate as a holiday destination. However, the international airport's most common visitors are transit passengers. Previously, visitors tended to use the sultanate as a stepping stone to either Sabah or Sarawak but numbers going overland are diminishing largely because the route is fiddly and time consuming.

Accommodation is quite pricey in Brunei, although of a very high quality; food is reasonably priced and excellent, and public transport slowly improving. This all makes a few days' stopover both feasible and enjoyable. A further practical point to remember is that although Brunei is dry you are permitted to bring into the kingdom up to two bottles of hard liquor and twelve cans of beer. It is against the law to consume this alcohol in a public place so getting slightly pickled in your hotel room is the norm.

Getting there
There are regular **flights** from Malaysia to Brunei; the prices given here are approximate one-way fares. Both Royal Brunei and MAS fly daily from **Kuala Lumpur** (around RM550; B$410), **Kota Kinabalu** (RM100; B$80) and **Kuching** (RM320; B$250). The budget airline AirAsia also flies daily from Kuala Lumpur (from RM130). From Singapore, there are daily Singapore Airlines and Royal Brunei flights (S$400; B$389).

Boats to Brunei depart daily from **Lawas** and **Limbang** in northern Sarawak, and from **Pulau Labuan** in Sabah. From **Miri** in Sarawak, several **buses** travel daily to Kuala Belait, in the far western corner of Brunei.

Getting around
If you intend to explore Brunei in some depth, you have little option but to **rent a car**. Car rental is not overly expensive, starting at B$80 a day (or B$400 a week; see p.608 for agencies). Beyond a few main, mostly coastal, roads, **bus** services are non-existent, while **taxis** are expensive if you want to cover much ground outside the capital. Apart from short hops across Sungai Brunei in BSB's river taxis, the only time you're likely to use a **boat** is to get to Temburong District (see p.610), which is cut off from the rest of Brunei by the Limbang area of Sarawak, or for leaving Brunei from the launch jetty at Muara.

Accommodation
All **hotels** in Brunei are up in the mid- to upper-range price brackets (B$60 upwards); there is little accommodation outside of this price range, though BSB has three hostels, two of which are quite cheap and popular with independent travellers. Although a few **longhouses** still exist in the interior, it is not possible to stay in them. However, **homestays** in rural areas, where visitors stay in a kampung house with a local family, are occasionally useful; here you pay substantially less for a room than in a hotel.

Throughout the Brunei chapter we've used the following **price codes** to denote the cheapest available room for two people. Single occupancy should cost less than double, though this is not always the case. Some guesthouses provide dormitory beds, for which the dollar price is given.

❶ B$25 and under   ❹ B$61–100   ❼ B$201–300
❷ B$26–40   ❺ B$101–150   ❽ B$301–400
❸ B$41–60   ❻ B$151–200   ❾ B$401 and above

City sights in and around BSB include two exquisite **mosques**, the Kampung Ayer **stilt village** and a steady flow of ambitious building developments including plazas and hotels, the most impressive of which is the *Empire and Country Club*, one of the world's most opulent hotels.

Some history

Contemporary Brunei's modest size belies its pivotal role in the formative centuries of Borneo's history. Little is known of the sultanate's **early history**, though trade was always the powerhouse behind the growth of its empire. Tang and Sung dynasty coins and ceramics, found in the Kota Batu area, a few kilometres from Bandar Seri Begawan, suggest that China was trading with Brunei as long ago as the seventh century, while allusions in ninth-century Chinese records to tributary payments to China by the ruler of an Asian city called Puni are thought to refer to Brunei. In subsequent centuries, Brunei benefited from its strategic position on the trade route between India, Melaka and China, and exercised a lucrative control over merchant traffic in the South China Sea. As well as being a staging post, where traders could stock up on supplies and off-load some of their cargo, Brunei was commercially active in its own right; local produce such as beeswax, camphor, rattan and brassware was traded by the *nakhoda*, or Bruneian sea traders, for ceramics, spices, woods and fabrics. By the fourteenth century, this commercial clout led to Brunei being brought under the sway of the Majapahit Empire, though by the end of that century the first sultan had taken the reins of independent power.

Islam had begun to make inroads into Bruneian society by the mid-fifteenth century, as the sultanate courted the business of foreign Muslim merchants. The religion's presence was accelerated by the decamping to Brunei of wealthy Muslim merchant families after the fall of Melaka to the Portuguese in 1511. Brunei was certainly an Islamic sultanate by the time it received its first **European visitors** in 1521. When Antonio Pigafetta, travelling to Southeast Asia with Ferdinand Magellan, he found a thriving city ruled over by a splendid and sophisticated royal court. Pigafetta and his companions were taken by elephant to an audience with the sultan, whom they met in a hall "all hung with silk stuffs" – though not before they were taught "to make three obeisances to the king, with hands joined above the head, raising first one then the other foot, and then to kiss the hands to him".

Pigafetta's sojourn in Brunei coincided with the sultanate's golden age. In the first half of the sixteenth century, Brunei was Borneo's foremost kingdom, its influence stretching along the island's northern and western coasts and even as far as territory belonging to the modern-day Philippines. The word "Borneo", in fact, is thought to be no more than a European corruption of Brunei. However, by the close of the sixteenth century, things were beginning to turn sour for the sultanate. Trouble with Catholic Spain, now sniffing around the South China and Sulu seas with a view to colonization, led to a sea battle off the coast at Muara in 1578; the battle was won by Spain, whose forces took the capital, only to be chased out days later by a cholera epidemic. The threat of piracy caused more problems, scaring off passing trade. Worse still, at home the sultan's control waned with factional struggles loosening his grip.

Western entrepreneurs arrived in this self-destructive climate, keen to take advantage of trade gaps left by Brunei's decline. One such fortune-seeker was **James Brooke**, whose arrival off the coast of Kuching in August 1839 was to change the face of Borneo forever. For helping the sultan quell a Dyak uprising, Brooke demanded and was given the governorship of Sarawak; Brunei's contraction had begun. Over subsequent decades, the state was to shrink steadily,

Brunei's head of state, **Sultan Hassanal Bolkiah** (whose full title is 31 words long), is the 29th in a line stretching back six hundred years. Educated in Malaysia and Britain, he was the world's richest man before high-tech moguls such as Bill Gates rapidly climbed the tree. Scandals involving a number of financial blunders – blamed on Hassanil's younger brother Jefri – also chipped away at the pot and eroded stock confidence. However, the sultan's wealth is still estimated at around US$7 billion and his nuanced extravagance is legendary: once, while playing polo with Britain's Prince Charles, he had his polo shoes delivered by helicopter onto the palace field. Interestingly, though, Hassanil is not out of touch with his people; perhaps like a ruler from a bygone era, anyone can meet him. For two days a year, on *Hari Raya Aidilfitri*, the populus – and any visitors in town – can queue at the palace for a handshake.

In 1991 the sultan introduced a conservative ideology called **Malay Muslim Monarchy**, which presented the monarchy as the defender of the faith. Apparently aimed at pre-empting calls for democratization, it is said to have alienated Brunei's large Chinese and expatriate communities. However, in September 2004 the sultan revived Brunei's **parliament**, two decades after it was suspended. With the constitution allowing up to fifteen elected MPs – although elections are still to take place – some observers feel that it was a tentative step towards giving some political power to the country's citizens, who may become more vocal as oil and gas reserves start to dwindle in 2015. Another intriguing move came in 2005 when the Sultan sacked four members of his cabinet, replacing them with ministers with private sector experience for the first time.

as Brooke and his successors used the suppression of piracy as the excuse they needed to siphon off more and more territory into the familial fiefdom. This trend culminated in the cession of the Limbang region – a move which literally split Brunei in two.

Elsewhere, more Bruneian land was being lost to other powers. In January 1846, a court faction unsympathetic to foreign land-grabbing seized power in Brunei and the chief minister was murdered. British gunboats quelled the coup and Pulau Labuan was ceded to the British Crown. A **treaty** signed the following year, forbidding the sultanate from ceding any of its territories without the British Crown's consent, underlined the decline of Brunei's power. In 1865, American consul Charles Lee Moses negotiated a treaty granting a ten-year lease to the American Trading Company of the portion of northeast Borneo that was later to become Sabah. By 1888, the British had declared Brunei a **protected state**, which meant the responsibility for its foreign affairs lay with London.

The start of the twentieth century was marked by the **discovery of oil**: given what little remained of Bruneian territory, it could hardly have been altruism that spurred the British to set up a Residency here in 1906. Initially, though, profits from the fledgling oil industry were slow to come, and the early decades of the century saw rubber estates springing up at Berakas, Gadong and Temburong. However, by 1931, the Seria Oil Field was on stream and profits were soon such that, despite the British appropriating a hefty slice, the sultanate was able to pay off debts from the lean years of the late nineteenth century.

The Japanese invasion of December 1941 temporarily halted Brunei's path to recovery. As in Sabah, Allied bombing over the three and a half years of occupation that followed left much rebuilding to be done. While Sabah, Sarawak and Pulau Labuan became Crown Colonies in the early postwar years, Brunei remained a British protectorate and retained its British Resident. Only in

1959 was the Residency finally withdrawn and a new constitution established, with provisions for a democratically elected legislative council. At the same time, Sultan Omar Ali Saifuddien (the present sultan's father) was careful to retain British involvement in matters of defence and foreign affairs – a move whose sagacity was made apparent when, in 1962, an armed coup led by Sheik Azahari's pro-democratic **Brunei People's Party** was crushed by British Army Gurkhas. Ever since the attempted coup, which resulted from Sultan Omar's refusal to convene the first sitting of the legislative council, the sultan has ruled by decree in his role as non-elected prime minister, and emergency powers – including provisions for detention without trial – have been in place. Despite showing interest in joining the planned Malaysian Federation in 1963, Brunei suffered a last-minute attack of cold feet, choosing to opt out rather than risk losing its new-found oil wealth and compromise the pre-eminence of its monarchy. Instead, Brunei remained a British protectorate until January 1, 1984, when it attained full independence.

While the **economy** remains booming, oil revenues having exceeded all expectations, the Bolkiah family have over the past two decades controlled the country and the economy in tandem with a steady rise in living standards. The troubles with Jefri aside, Bruneians seems pretty content with their lot – visitors, though, may note the alarming disparities between the substantial legions of unskilled foreign workers (mostly Bangladeshi) and the locals; occasionally there are murmurs of concern over the foreign workers' low pay and often squalid domestic arrangements.

Bandar Seri Begawan

The capital of Brunei, **BANDAR SERI BEGAWAN (BSB)** is the sultanate's only settlement of any real size. Until 1970, BSB was known simply as Brunei Town; the present name means "Town of the Seri Begawan", Seri Begawan being the title Sultan Omar Ali Saifuddien took after abdicating in favour of his son Hassanal Bolkiah in October 1967. Straddling the northern bank of a twist in the Sungai Brunei, the city is characterized by its unlikely juxtaposition of striking modern buildings – such as its two grand **mosques** and the twin malls of the Yayasan Sultan Haji Hassanal Bolkiah (YSB) shopping complex – with its traditional stilt houses, which hug and expand outwards from the attractive waterfront.

This water village, **Kampung Ayer**, was Brunei's original seat of power and is still home to around a quarter of BSB's population. After the arrival of the British Residency in 1906, the streets which form downtown BSB were laid out on reclaimed land, but the kampung dwellers stayed put, preferring to retain their traditional way of life despite an attempt to coax them onto dry land. As recently as the middle of the twentieth century, Brunei's capital was still a sleepy water village; the novelist Anthony Burgess, posted here as a teacher in the late 1950s, observed that onshore BSB comprised "a single street of shops, run by Chinese, which sold long-playing records and old copies of the *Daily Mirror Weekly*".

That contemporary BSB has become the attractive, clean and modern waterfront city it is today is due, inevitably, to oil. With the new-found wealth of the 1970s came large-scale urbanization north of the Sungai Brunei, resulting in housing schemes, shopping centres and, more obviously, the magnificent **Omar Ali Saifuddien Mosque**, which dominates the skyline of BSB.

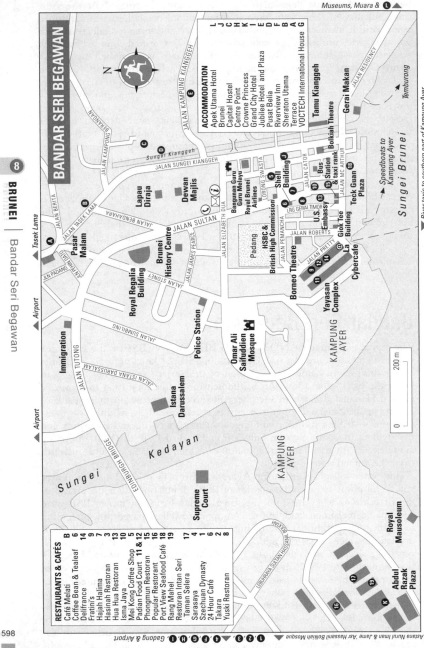

BANDAR SERI BEGAWAN

N

ACCOMMODATION
Apek Utama Hotel   L
Brunei   J
Capital Hostel   C
Centre Point   H
Crowne Princess   K
Grand City Hotel   I
Jubilee Hotel and Plaza   E
Pusat Belia   D
Riverview Inn   F
Sheraton Utama   B
Terrace   A
VOCTECH International House G

RESTAURANTS & CAFÉS
Café Melati   B
Coffee Bean & Tealeaf   6
Delifrance   14
Fratini's   9
Hajah Halima   7
Hasinah Restoran   3
Hua Hua Restoran   13
Isma Jaya   10
Mei Kong Coffee Shop   5
Padian Food Court   11 & 12
Phongmun Restoran   15
Popular Restorant   16
Port View Seafood Café   18
Rang Mahel   19
Restoran Intan Seri   17
Taman Selera   4
Sarasaya   1
Szechuan Dynasty   6
24 Hour Café   2
Takara   8
Yuski Restoran

0   200 m

First-time visitors to BSB are pleasantly surprised by a sense of space and tranquility that is quite rare among Southeast Asia's leading cities. Unfortunately, though, BSB isn't cheap to visit; the fact that most visitors to Brunei are business people means most room prices are quite high. Nevertheless, the sights of BSB are interesting enough to warrant a day or two's stopover.

Arrival, information and city transport

Flying into BSB, you land at **Brunei International Airport**, 8km north of the city; buses run hourly (7am–6pm B$1), from directly outside the terminal to BSB's only bus station on Jalan Cator. A **taxi** into town from the airport costs B$30.

Small speedboats from Bangar in Temburong District arrive 300m to the east along Jalan Residency (hourly; 7.30am–3.30pm), the main street which runs along the city's waterfront, and **ferries** from Labuan and smaller craft from Limbang and Lawas dock at the **ferry terminal** at Muara, 25km northeast of the city, from where you will need to take a taxi to town (B$35).

Moving on from BSB

By air

Central and Northern line buses (B$1) run to the airport from the bus station hourly between 6am and 6pm; you can also get a taxi there (B$25) from the bus station – although most visitors take one from their hotel which usually works out a little cheaper. The **airport tax** is B$5 for flights to Malaysia and Singapore, B$12 for all other destinations.

By boat

Boats for **Limbang**, **Lawas** and **Labuan** leave from the **ferry terminal** at Muara, 25km northeast of BSB. To get there, take the Muara express bus from BSB's bus station (every 30min; 6.50am–4.50pm; 30min; B$2). Express boats leave for Labuan (regular daily departures 7.30am–4.10pm; 1hr, B$15) and Lawas (one daily at 11.30am; 2hr; B$10); tickets bought at the terminal. **Limbang** boats (frequent departures between 6am–6pm; 30min; B$10) leave from the Jalan Roberts jetty; tickets for this route are sold at the stalls on Jalan MacArthur, just beside the entrance to the jetty. From Labuan, there are daily connections on to KK and Menumbok in Sabah, though to ensure you catch one, it's wise to leave BSB early in the day. Note that the schedule can change, so double-check departure times to all destinations at Ⓦ www.bruneibay.net.

Boats to **Bangar** in Temburong (hourly; 6.30am–4.30pm; 40min; B$7) depart from the Temburong jetty, 300m east of the centre on Jalan Residency; tickets are sold beside the jetty. From Bangar, it's possible to travel overland to both Lawas and Limbang (see p.611).

By bus

Given how skimpy the **bus network** is, if you want to make a day-trip out of BSB, you have to start early in the morning. Among the main routes from the bus station, there are buses north to Muara (B$2), and west to Tutong (B$4) and Seria (B$6) – here you can change for Kuala Belait, from where there are departures for Miri in Sarawak. If you're heading for Miri, it's best to catch the 7.15am BSB–Seria bus which connects with the 9.30am Seria–Kuala Belait service. This arrives in KB in easy time to catch the 11am to the Sarawak border. It is necessary however to go through a small rigmarole at the bus station office where you buy the onward ticket to Miri where you need to show your passport.

You will find the **tourist office** (Mon–Thurs & Sat 8am–noon & 2–4.30pm, 8am–noon Sat; ☎02/382807, ⊛www.tourismbrunei.com), in the old Post Office Building, Jalan Sultan (corner with Jalan Elizabeth Dua). Here you can pick up lists for hotels, car rental companies, the *Explore Brunei* booklet, and information on tour operators and local sights.

City transport

With much of BSB's population living in the villages that make up Kampung Ayer, it makes sense that the most common form of **public transport** in the city should be **water taxis**. A veritable armada of these skinny speedboats ply Sungai Brunei night and day, charging only B$1–2 for a short hop – pay your fare on board. You can hire a water taxi for a longer tour of the water villages, or to see the sultan's palace from the river; a half-hour round trip costs B$15-20 per person. The jetty below the intersection of Jalan Roberts and Jalan McArthur is the best place to catch a water taxi, though it's also possible to hail one from Jalan Residency or opposite the Apek Utama Hotel, 3km east of the centre (B$1, 5min to Jalan McArthur).

Though user-friendly and inexpensive, BSB's local **bus** network has the drawback of closing down at 6.30pm (it's largely geared to getting people to and from work). The bus terminal on Jalan Cator is very well organized though, with maps alongside each bay. The bus services largely ply the roads in and around the capital: the most useful for tourists are Central Line buses, which run between the airport and the Brunei and Malay Technology museums, crossing the city en route; and Circle Line services, which do a loop taking in the Jame 'Asr Hassanal Bolkiah Mosque and the suburb of Gadong. For destinations outside the capital, bus details are given throughout the chapter; services leave from Jalan Cator too.

BSB has two distinct types of **taxi**: the CTS service, whose purple cars run within the city only, are useful for districts like Gadong and Batu 1 but don't go as far as the museums or the airport. They charge a flat B$3 for a trip under 1km, with an extra B$1 tacked on for each kilometre after that. The rate goes up to B$4.50 after 9pm. The other type are the regular, metered, yellow taxis which congregate beside the bus station and outside shopping centres and hotels. Fares start from B$3, and a short journey – say, from the city centre to the Brunei Museum – costs B$5–7, with a B$2 surcharge between 9pm and 6am. For longer journeys, out to Seria or Kuala Belait for instance, you can haggle with drivers and fix a price. **Car rental** agencies are listed on p.608.

Accommodation

Brunei is slowly waking up to the need for budget **accommodation**. There are a number of main locations: downtown, in the suburb of Gadong and along the river. As well as a number of **budget places** there's a fair selection of comfortable **hotels** to choose from slightly higher up the price scale. For the top bracket, opt for the **Sheraton** or even the *Empire* (see p.609).

Downtown

Brunei 95 Jalan Pemancha ☎02/242372, ⊛www .bruneihotel.com.bn. Comfortable, with spacious, a/c en-suite rooms, this is BSB's most central hotel. ❼

Capital Hostel Jalan Kampung Berangan ☎02/223561. Has small, clean en-suite rooms and is popular with government officials. ❸

Centre Point Centre Point Plaza, Jalan Kuilap, Gadong ☎02/430430, ⊛www.arhbrunei.com. Glamorous hotel on Gadong's main street with massive rooms and oversized bathrooms. ❽

Jubilee Hotel and Plaza Jalan Kampung Kianggeh ☎02/228070. East of Sungai Kiangggeh, but still downtown, this mid-range hotel has large en-suite rooms with TV and a/c. It's set opposite a patch of traditional kampung houses, giving it a pleasant neighbourhood feel. ❹

Pusat Belia Jalan Sungai Kianggeh ☎02/222900. Brunei's youth hostel, and the cheapest option downtown. The dorms sleep four, and there's a massive swimming pool (B$1) downstairs. ❶

Sheraton Utama Jalan Tasek Lama ☎02/244272, ⓦwww.sheraton.com. Brunei's earliest international-standard hotel, with over 150 swanky rooms and suites, plus a well-equipped business centre with Internet access. ❽

🏃 Terrace Jalan Tasek Lama ☎02/243554, ⓦwww.terracebrunei.com. Popular, well-positioned hotel with small, comfortable rooms and good bathrooms. Ask for a room overlooking the lovely little swimming pool, set by the breakfast terrace and an exquisite rockery. Has very good Internet access (5B$ a half hour). ❹

Gadong and west of centre

Crowne Princess Jalan Tutong ☎02/241128, ⒺLteph@brunet.bn. Situated away over Edinburgh Bridge; regular shuttle buses run between here and the city centre. With over a hundred well-appointed rooms, this place also has a restaurant serving decent Asian cuisine. ❹

Grand City Hotel Block G, Kampung Pengkalan Gadong ☎02/452188, Ⓔgrandcity@brunet.bn. Good-value modern hotel with large en-suite rooms, in the pleasant suburb of Gadong. ❹

Riverview Inn Km 1, Jalan Gadong ☎02/238238, Ⓔriverview_htl@brunet.bn. A very good option if the equally comfortable *Brunei* is full; large, pleasant, airy rooms equipped with TV, a/c and attached bathrooms. ❻

VOCTECH International House Jalan Pasar Baharu, take the Circle Line bus from the Jalan Cator terminal ☎02/447992, Ⓔvoctech@brunet .bn. This large hostel, ostensibly set up for international student groups, is now increasingly used by tour groups and independent travellers. Rooms are large and simply decorated, with balconies and attached bathrooms. It's got a well-priced café, a kitchen, which can be used by guests and a library with Internet access. Five minutes' walk away is an excellent night market serving cheap, tasty food. ❸

Along the river

🏃 **Apek Utama Hotel** Simpang 229, Kampung Pintu Malim, Jalan Kota Batu ☎02/220808. The *Apek* has quickly become BSB's main traveller haven in recent years with its dozens of neat, light rooms (with communal bathrooms) spread over three floors, set in a modern complex 3km from town. Take the museum bus #39, which goes right by. An alternative way to get to and from the centre is to jump on a water taxi (1B$) from the jetty opposite the hotel entrance. ❷

The City and around

Downtown BSB's most obvious point of reference is the **Omar Ali Saifuddien Mosque**, overlooking the compact knot of central streets and sitting in a cradle formed by **Kampung Ayer** (Water Village), a collection of settlements protruding from the river. Over Edinburgh Bridge, **Jalan Tutong** runs westwards and past the Batu 1 area (a grid of shopping complexes and hotels), reaching Astana Nurul Iman 3km later; branching off to the northwest is **Lebuhraya Sultan Hassanal Bolkiah**, one of several routes for the plazas of the commercial suburb of **Gadong** and for the airport. On the eastern end of the centre, **Jalan Residency** hugs the river bank on its way to the **Brunei Museum** and its neighbouring attractions.

The Omar Ali Saifuddien Mosque

At the very heart of both the city and the sultanate's Muslim faith is the magnificent **Omar Ali Saifuddien Mosque** (Mon–Wed, Sat & Sun 8am–noon, 1–3pm & 4.30–5.30pm, Thurs open to Muslims only, Fri 4.30–5.30pm). Built in classical Islamic style, and mirrored in the circular lagoon surrounding it, it's a breathtaking sight, whether viewed dazzling in the sun or seen illuminated a lurid green at night. Commissioned by and named after the father of the present sultan, the mosque was completed in 1958 and makes splendid use of opulent yet tasteful fittings – Italian marble, granite from

Shanghai, Arabian and Belgian carpets, and English chandeliers and stained glass. Topping the cream-coloured building is a 52-metre-high golden dome whose curved surface is adorned with a mosaic comprising over three million pieces of Venetian glass. Anthony Burgess described the mosque's construction in his autobiography, *Little Wilson and Big God*: "The dome had been covered with gold leaf," he wrote, "which, owing to the contraction and expansion of the structure with comparative cool and large heat, fell to the ground in flakes and splinters which were taken by the fisher-folk to be a gift from Allah." In the lagoon is a replica of a sixteenth-century royal barge, or *mahligai*, used on special religious occasions. The usual dress codes – modest attire, and shoes to be left at the entrance – apply when entering the mosque.

Kampung Ayer

Stilt villages have occupied this stretch of the Sungai Brunei for hundreds of years: Antonio Pigafetta, visiting Borneo in 1521, described a city, "entirely built on foundations in the salt water ... it contains twenty-five thousand fires or families. The houses are all of wood, placed on great piles to raise them high up". Today, an estimated thirty thousand people live in the scores of sprawling villages that compose **Kampung Ayer**, their dwellings connected by a maze of wooden promenades. These villages now feature their own clinics, mosques, schools, a fire brigade and even a police station; homes here have piped water, electricity and TV. There's a strong sense of community, as a result of which government attempts to move the inhabitants into modern housing schemes on dry land have met with little success.

The meandering plank walkways of Kampung Ayer make it an intriguing place to explore on foot, especially late on Friday afternoons when, following prayers, the fashion is to visit one another's homes. For a more panoramic impression of its dimensions though, it's best to charter one of the water taxis that zip around the river. A handful of traditional **cottage industries** continue to turn out copperware and brassware (at Kampung Ujong Bukit), and exquisite sarongs and boats (Kampung Saba Darat); ask a boatman the way to these.

Jalan Sultan and north to Tasek Lama

A short walk east of the Omar Ali Saifuddien Mosque, BSB's main drag, the broad **Jalan Sultan**, runs north past several of the city's lesser sights. First is the **Brunei History Centre** (℡02/238368; Mon–Thurs & Sat 7.45am–12.15pm & 1.30–4.30pm; free), a research institution whose dull displays – maps showing Brunei's changing shape over the centuries, and tables outlining the genealogy of past sultans – will have you hurrying next door to the **Royal Regalia Building** (Mon–Thurs 8.30am–5pm, Fri 9–11.30am & 2.30–5pm, Sat & Sun 8.30am–5pm; free), which is a little more inviting. Opened in 1992 as part of the sultan's silver jubilee celebrations, this magnificent semicircular building, fitted out with lavish carpets and marble, contains an exhibition charting the life of the present sultan. There's some quite interesting stuff here, including a surprisingly happy, smiling shot of the sultan taken during his circumcision ceremony, as well as a golden hand and forearm used to support his chin during the coronation, and a beautifully ornate crown. The **Constitutional Gallery** in the same building is inevitably drier, but its documents and treaties are worth a scan. Fronting the whole collection is the **coronation carriage**, or *usungan*, ringed by regalia from the coronation ceremony – which took place just across Jalan Sultan in the **Lapau Diraja** (Royal Ceremonial Hall) on August 1, 1968. The hall's slightly tacky exterior belies the grandeur of its huge inner chamber, whose western side is approached by a mini escalator. Beyond this, rows of red,

△ Kampung Ayer with Omar Ali Saifudden Mosque in the background

black, pink and white pillars run up to the golden *patarana*, or royal throne. Although the hall is not officially open to the public, it's usually possible to take a peek at its lavish interior. Next door is the parliament building, the **Dewan Majlis**, which used to house the Legislative Assembly.

East of the Lapau Diraja and parallel to Jalan Sultan is **Jalan Sungai Kianggeh**, which runs past the daily produce market, **Tamu Kianggeh** and BSB's most central **Chinese temple**, before arriving at Jalan Tasek Lama, the turning to tranquil **Tasek Lama Park** which is five minutes' walk from the main road. Bear left and you pass through the pretty gardens to a small waterfall; bear right along the sealed road and right again at the fork and you end up at a bottle-green reservoir.

East to the Brunei Museum

Jalan Residency runs eastwards from Sungai Kianggeh, bordered to the south by the Sungai Brunei and to the north by a hillside Muslim cemetery whose scores of decrepit stones are shaded by an orchard of frangipani trees. After a little less than a kilometre, the road reaches the **Arts & Handicrafts Centre** (Mon–Thurs 8am–5pm, Fri & Sat 8–11.30am & 2–5pm; free; ⓦwww.museums.gov.bn), an organization dedicated to perpetuating the sultanate's cultural heritage. Here, young Bruneians are taught traditional skills, such as weaving, basketry and bamboo-working, brass casting and the crafting of the *kris* (traditional dagger). Apart from the occasional weaving demonstration though, you can't watch the proceedings unless you've sought permission to do so in advance. You'll probably have to make do with browsing through the **craft shop**'s decent selection of reasonably priced basketry, silverware and spinning tops.

From here it's a further 3km to the **Brunei Museum** (ⓣ02/226495, ⓦwww.museums.gov.bn; Mon–Sat 9.30am–5pm, Fri 9–11.30am & 2.30-5pm; free), shortly before which is the **tomb of Sultan Bolkiah** (1473–1521), Brunei's fifth sultan, who held sway at the very peak of the state's power. It's worth setting aside an hour or two for the museum, which has several outstanding galleries. In the inevitable Oil and Gas Gallery, set up by Brunei Shell Petroleum, exhibits, graphics and captions recount the story of Brunei's oil reserves, from the drilling of the first well in 1928, to current extraction and refining techniques. Also interesting, though tantalizingly sketchy, is the **Muslim Life Gallery**, whose dioramas allow glimpses of social traditions such as the sweetening of a newborn baby's mouth with honey or dates, and the disposal of its placenta in a *bayung*, a palm-leaf basket either hung on a tree or floated downriver. At the back of the gallery, a small collection of early photographs shows riverine hawkers trading from their boats in Kampung Ayer. The museum's undoubted highlight, though, is its superb **Islamic Art Gallery** (ground floor) where, among the riches on display are beautifully illuminated antique Korans from India, Iran, Egypt and Turkey, and exquisite prayer mats. Circle Line **buses** run to the museum from Jalan Cator, passing the *Apek Utuma* hotel.

Steps around the back of the museum drop down to the riverside **Malay Technology Museum** (daily 9am–5pm except Fri 9–11.30am & 2.30–5pm, closed Tues; free), whose three galleries provide a mildly engaging insight into traditional Malay life. Of greatest interest is Gallery Three, whose exhibits include the *pelarik gasing*, a machine which evenly cuts spinning tops; the *lamin keleput*, used for boring blowpipes; and other devices worked from forest materials by Brunei's indigenous people. In the same gallery are authentic examples of Kedayan, Murut and Dusun dwellings, while elsewhere in the building you see dioramas highlighting stilt-house and *atap*-roof construction, boat-making and fishing methods. Also worth a look is the extensive betel box collection on the ground floor. The boxes, some shaped like boats and others representing animals including turtles, traditionally contain mixtures which avert bad spirits and witchcraft as well as more prosaic ointments to alleviate the irritation caused by mosquito bites and flatulence. There are also some intriguing works of modern Brunei and Southeast Asian sculpture dotted around the museum. To catch the **bus** back to the city centre, return to the Brunei Museum, as there are no buses along the lower road where the Technology Museum is located.

The Jame 'Asr Hassanal Bolkiah Mosque

Visiting the **Jame 'Asr Hassanal Bolkiah Mosque** (Mon–Wed, Sat & Sun 8am–noon, 1–3.30pm & 4.30–5.30pm; Thurs & Fri open to Muslims only), is a wonderfully serene experience. Constructed to commemorate the silver jubilee of the sultan's reign in 1992 and located northwest from the city centre in a large compound, the building has immense style and grandeur. Teams of Bangladeshi workers busily clip and sweep outside, below the mosque's sea-blue roof, golden domes and slender minarets, while silk-clad Bruneians go about their prayers. The mosque, Brunei's largest, is referred to by locals as the Kiarong Mosque (after a neighbouring kampung), who find its full name rather a mouthful. Circle Line **buses** skirt the grounds of the mosque en route to Gadong. Directly across from the mosque in Kampung Kiarong is a useful **Internet café** and a couple of cafés.

The Istana Nurul Iman

The **Istana Nurul Iman**, the official residence of the sultan, is sited at a superb riverside spot 4km west of the centre. Bigger than London's Buckingham Palace, the istana is a monument to self-indulgence. Its design, by Filipino architect Leandro Locsin, is a sinuous blend of traditional and modern, with Islamic motifs such as arches and domes, and sloping roofs fashioned on traditional longhouse designs, combined with all the mod cons you'd expect of a house whose owner is estimated to earn millions of dollars a day. James Bartholomew's book, *The Richest Man in the World*, lists some of the mind-boggling figures relating to the palace which, over half a kilometre long, contains a grand total of 1778 rooms, including 257 toilets. Illuminating these rooms requires 51,000 light bulbs, many of which are consumed by the palace's 564 chandeliers; simply getting around the rooms requires 18 lifts and 44 staircases. The throne room is said to be particularly sumptuous: 12 one-tonne chandeliers hang from its ceiling, while its 4 grand thrones stand against the backdrop of an 18-metre arch, tiled in 22-carat gold. In addition to the throne room, there's a royal banquet hall that seats 4000 diners, a prayer hall where 1500 people can worship at any one time, an underground car park for the sultan's hundreds of vehicles, a state-of-the-art sports complex and a helipad.

Inevitably, the palace is not open to the general public, apart from two days every year during *Hari Raya Aidilfitri*, at the end of Ramadan (see p.76). Otherwise, nearby **Taman Persiaran Damuan**, a kilometre-long park sandwiched between Jalan Tutong and Sungai Brunei, offers the best view, or you can fork out for a boat trip (B$30) and see the palace lit up at night from the water. Opposite the park is **Pulau Ranggu**, where monkeys congregate on the shore towards dusk.

All westbound buses travel along Jalan Tutong, over the Edinburgh Bridge and past the *istana*, though it is possible to walk there. En route you'll pass the city's **Batu 1** area, in the southwestern corner of which the **Royal Mausoleum and Graveyard** are tucked away. Brunei's sultans have been buried at this site since 1786, though only the last four were laid to rest in the mausoleum.

Gadong

The suburb of **Gadong**, 3km northwest of the centre of BSB, is worth visiting largely for shopping and eating. Gadong's Centre Point Plaza contains the *Centre Point Hotel* and a variety of outlets including jewellery, bargain clothing retailers, fast food and restaurants. In 2004, The Mall, a much larger, five-floor plaza opened next to Centre Point on the suburb's main street, Jalan Kuilap. This lavish plaza has a vast central atrium, lovely murals and elegant decorative touches. On the ground floor, there's a good bookshop, Best Eastern, some expensive boutiques, a homeopathic store, Nature's Farm, and the pricey *Ringum Coffee House*. On the first floor you can find the city's top Indonesian restaurant, *Sanur* (11.30am–2.30pm & 5.30–9.30pm, daily) as well as the Japanese eatery, *Ku Ra* (same times). Numerous stores lead off the atrium across all the floors, while the top floor is dominated by a massive food court, selling local and Western fast food, and a cinema with three screens showing Western and Asian movies (some dubbed into Malay).

Eating

BSB's **restaurants** are reasonably priced and there's an increasingly good range of places to eat, reflecting the multicultural make-up of the city's population with numerous, excellent Indian and Malay cafés, as well as Chinese and Western options. If you're on a tight budget, it's worth heading to either of the **pasar malams**, one on Jalan Tasek Lama (opposite the *Terrace Hotel*), the other situated in a car park across the road from *VOCTECH* (both 6–11pm). Here delicious Malay favourites are laid out buffet-style but food has to be taken away as there are no tables and chairs. There are also cheap stalls behind the Chinese temple on Jalan Sungai Kianggeh, where the bursting flames and billowing smoke of chicken being cooked over charcoal fires have a rather dramatic aspect. A further option is the *Tamu Kianggeh*, the other side of Jalan Sultan, a large open market with some food stalls and the small food court behind the Temburong jetty on Jalan Residency, which has good and cheap *soto ayam* (rice cubes served with shredded chicken and broth), *nasi campur* and other Malay staples. These stalls close in the early evening.

One thing you won't find in BSB, or for that matter in Brunei, is a bar. Drinking **alcohol** in public has been outlawed in Brunei since New Year's Day, 1991. The substantial expat community, though, are allowed to bring alcohol to certain restaurants where beer or wine can be consumed, with food. If you aren't Muslim and find yourself in such an establishment there is no reason why you can't ask to do the same. In most hotels it is acceptable to drink alcohol (which you have brought into the country), with or without food, but it is important to inform the staff each time you wish to do so.

Downtown

Café Melati *Sheraton Utama*, Jalan Sungai Kianggeh. The generous buffet lunch (B$25) in this bright and breezy establishment fills you up for the day; their buffet dinner (B$35) features a different international culinary theme every night. Mon–Sat noon–2pm & 7–10pm, Sun 7–11pm.

Coffee Bean & Tealeaf Jalan Pemancha/Jalan Sultan ☎02/454270. Western-style coffee shop with tasty cakes, great coffee and high prices. Also has an outlet in Gadong's Centre Point mall. Daily 8am–11.30pm.

Delifrance Ground floor, Yayasan Complex, Jalan Kumbang Pasang. Slick, French-style coffee and croissant joint. Very popular with Brunei's well-heeled crowd. Daily 9am–9pm.

Fratini's Ground floor, Yayasan Complex, Jalan Kumbang Pasang ☎02/232892. Italian-run expat oasis, adding a dash of sophistication to BSB's dining scene; choose from a decent range of pizzas and pastas (B$15), then round things off with a cappuccino. Daily 11.30am–2pm & 6–10pm.

Hajah Halima Jalan Sultan ☎02/234803. Friendly North Indian café with a *nasi campur*-style buffet with chicken and lamb options, prawn curry and vegetable side dishes. Daily 6am–9pm.

Hua Hua Restoran 48 Jalan Sultan ☎02/225396. Steamed chicken with sausage is one of the highlights in this simple, no-frills Chinese establishment, where B$15 feeds two people. Daily 7am–9pm.

Isma Jaya 27 Jalan Sultan. One of several good Indian restaurants along Jalan Sultan; lip-smacking korma and biriyani sell well here. Daily 6am–8pm.

Mei Kong Coffee Shop 108 Jalan Pemancha. Fronted by a chicken and rice bar, this unmarked coffee shop, right beside the HSBC Bank, also serves noodles, *rotis* and *panggang* (rice and prawns cooked in banana leaves). Daily 5am–8pm.

Padian Food Court First floor, Yayasan Complex, Jalan Kumbang Pasang. Snow-bright, a/c food court whose spotless stalls serve Thai, Middle Eastern, Japanese and Indian fare and several other regional cuisines. Daily 9am–10pm.

Phongmun Restoran Second floor, Teck Guan Plaza, Jalan Sultan. Classy and centrally located Cantonese restaurant serving dim sum, with wall panels depicting roses and dragons. Daily 6.30am–11pm; dim sum served 6.30am–4pm.

Popular Restorant Shop 5, Block 1, Putri Anak Norain Complex, Batu 1, Jalan Tutong. Bare but clean Indian restaurant, serving lovely *dosai*, tandoori breads and curries. Mon 4–10pm, Tues–Sun 8am–10pm.

Port View Seafood Café Jalan McArthur. Quite expensive Western and Asian fare in a relaxing setting overlooking the harbour and Kampung Ayer. The pasta dishes are usually tasty and filling, and the rice-based Malay and Chinese food is good as well. Bands play Fri & Sat from 10pm–2am.

Rang Mahel First floor, 3a Bangunan Mas Panchawarna, Batu 1, Jalan Tutong. Cosy and well respected North Indian place; below is the *Regent's Den*, where cheaper Indian snacks are available. Both open daily 7.30am–10.30pm.

Restoran Intan Seri Taman Selera 1–2 Bangunan Mas Panchawarna, Batu 1, Jalan Tutong. Popular, buffet-style Malay restaurant with a satay stall outside at night. Daily 9am–9.30pm.

24 Hour Café, Jalan Sultan (beside *Coffee Bean & Tealeaf*). Like its neighbour, an expensive Western-orientated coffee with cakes, muffins, full meals (B$15) and coffee.

Yuski Restoran Jalan Sultan. Excellent Indian café renowned for its biriyanis, chicken and mutton curries.

Gadong

Hasinah Restoran Block 1, Unit 9, Abdul Razak Complex, Gadong. Excellent, inexpensive Malay and South Indian daytime café. With nine types of *dosai* and a mouthwatering *nasi campur* spread.

Sarasaya Block C, Abdul Razak Complex, Gadong. Excellent Japanese restaurant, owned by and popular with Japanese expatriates.

Szechuan Dynasty Centre Point, Abdul Razak Complex, Gadong. A truly elegant dining experience, though not necessarily to all tastes – the prevalence of chilli, pepper and ginger means the emphasis here is firmly on hot, spicy Chinese food. Daily noon–2.30pm & 6–10pm.

Takara Centre Point, Abdul Razak Complex, Gadong. Top-notch Japanese restaurant serving classics such as sashimi and teppanyaki; groups might consider dining the authentic Japanese way – cross-legged on the floor, in a tatami room. Daily 11.30am–2.30pm & 6–10pm.

Tour operators

In the absence of the government developing and expanding tourism infrastructure, it has been left to **tour operators** to lead the way. Below is a short list of operators offering rewarding, well-priced trips in the sultanate, ranging from the enjoyable two-hour cruise in Brunei Bay's **mangrove area** (around B$65) to a three-day, two-night visit to **Ulu Temburong Park** including rafting (B$250). Note that although Brunei is more expensive to visit than Malaysia, tours are competitively priced when compared with equivalent ones in Sabah or Sarawak.

Freme Travel 403B Wisma Jaya, Jalan Pemancha ☎02/234280, ⍟www.freme.com. Highly professional outfit with an exciting rafting option along Sungai Temburong (as part of their Temburong Park visit). Also offers trips to Tasek Merimbun and BSB city and Kumpung Ayer tours.

Golden Touch Holidays Royal Brunei Airlines ☎02/343314, ⍟www.bruneiair.com/gth. Tour offshoot of the government-owned airline with a wide range of short trips around BSB or day-trips to sights including Labi and Ulu Temburong.

Mona Florafauna Tours G07, Ground floor, Block A, Yayasan Complex ☎02/230762;

⍟mft@brunet.bn. Run by Dave "Jungle" Coleman, this operator currently leads the field in Brunei with competitively priced trips ranging from the 2hr cruise along BSB's mangrove forests in search of playful proboscis monkeys, to the full-day visit to Tasek Merimbun (B$95) and overnight visits to Ulu Temburong Park (B$180 plus) and Kuala Belai (email for details). Expect excellent guides and top of the range service.

Sunshine Borneo ☎02/441791, ⍟www .sunshineborneo.com. The first operator offering tours into Ulu Temburong, it still arranges day visits to the park and a heritage tour around BSB.

Listings

Airlines British Airways, Lot 100, Jalan McArthur/ Jalan Kianggeh ☏02/225871; Garuda Indonesia, 49 Wisma Jaya, Jalan Pemancha ☏02/235870; MAS, 144 Jalan Pemancha ☏02/224141; Philippine Airlines, first floor, Wisma Haji Fatimah, Jalan Sultan ☏02/244075, Royal Brunei Airlines, RBA Plaza, Jalan Sultan ☏02/242222; Singapore Airlines, 49–50 Jalan Sultan ☏02/244901; Thai Airways, fourth floor, Komplek Jalan Sultan, 51–55 Jalan Sultan ☏02/242991.

Airport For flight information call ☏02/331747.

American Express Unit 401–03, fourth floor, Shell Building, Jalan Sultan ☏02/228314 (Mon–Fri 8.30am–5pm, Sat 8.30am–1pm).

Banks and exchange HSBC, Jalan Sultan; International Bank of Brunei, Jalan Roberts; Overseas Union Bank, RBA Plaza, Jalan Sultan; Standard Chartered Bank, Jalan Sultan. Banking hours are Mon–Fri 9am–3pm, Sat 9–11am.

Bookshops Best Eastern Books, first floor, The Mall, Gadong & G4 Teck Guan Plaza, Jalan Sultan, stocks a modest range of English-language books and magazines; Times Bookshop, first floor, Yayasan Complex, isn't bad either.

Car rental Avis 16 Haji Daud Complex, Jalan Gadong ☏02/426345; Ellis 3a Gadong Proprietors Building, Jalan Gadong ☏02/427238; Hertz Unit 6, ground floor, Badiah Building, Jalan Tutong ☏02/390300.

Cinemas Borneo Theatre, on Jalan Roberts, and Bolkiah Theatre, on Jalan Sungai Kianggeh, both screen English-language movies; tickets around B\$4.

Embassies and consulates Australia, Dar Takaful IBB Utama, Jalan Pemancha ☏02/229435; Indonesia, Lot 4498, Simpang 528, Sungai Hanching Baru, Jalan Muara ☏02/330180; Malaysia, 61 Simpang 336, Kampong Sungai Akar, Jalan Kebangsaan ☏02/381095; Philippines, 17 Simpang 126, Mile 2, Jalan Tutong ☏02/241465; Singapore, 8 Simpang 74, Jalan Subok ☏02/262741; Thailand, no. 2, Simpang 682, Kampung Bunut, Jalan Tutong ☏02/653108; UK, Unit 2.01, Block D, Complex Yayasan Sultan Hassanil Bolkiah ☏02/222231; US, third floor, Teck Guan Plaza, Jalan Sultan ☏02/225293.

Hospital The Raja Isteri Pengiran Anak Saleha Hospital (RIPAS) Jalan Tutong ☏02/242424; or there's the 24hr Katong Clinic, 6, first floor, Block B, Abdul Razak Complex, Jalan Gadong (☏02/428715). For an ambulance, call ☏991.

Internet access *Cyberstar Café*, opposite the *Apek Utama* hotel (daily 9am–10pm); *Cyber Café*, 8, Block A, Kiarong Complex, opposite the Kiarong Mosque (daily noon–10pm); LA Ling *Cybercafé*, second floor, Yayasan Complex (Mon–Sat 9.30am–9.30pm, Sun 10am–6pm).

Pharmacies Khong Lin Dispensary, G3A, Wisma Jaya, Jalan Pemancha; Sentosa Dispensary, 42 Jalan Sultan.

Police Central Police Station, Jalan Stoney ☏02/222333/993, or call ☏993.

Post office The GPO (Mon–Thurs 8am–4.30pm & Sat 8am–12.30pm) is at the intersection of Jalan Elizabeth Dua and Jalan Sultan. Poste restante is at the Money Order counter.

Taxis ☏02/394949; airport taxis ☏02/343671.

Telephones Telekom (daily 8am–midnight) is next to the GPO on Jalan Sultan; international calls can be made from here, or else buy a phonecard (in B\$5, B\$10, B\$20 or B\$50 denominations) and use a public phone.

Visa extensions At the Immigration Office, Jalan Menteri Besar ☏02/383106 (Mon–Thurs & Sat 7.45am–12.15pm & 1.45–4.30pm).

Brunei Muara

As most of Brunei's nature attractions are in Temburong and Tutong there's little to detain you in the capital's district, **Brunei Muara**. However, no visit to Brunei would be complete without checking out the **Empire Hotel & Country Club**. Also worth a visit is **Muara Beach** and the **Jerudong Park Playground** theme park. Of rather less interest are the **Bukit Shahbandar Forest Recreation Park**, a medium-sized nature reserve but lacking even the most basic facilities for visitors and **Kampung Parit**, an evocation of how Bruneians lived in the days before oil and concrete. Although Muara Beach and Jerudong Park can be reached with some struggle by bus, the easiest way to get to all these places is by car, either rental, or taxi, unless you are travelling on a tour.

North to Muara

Northeast of BSB, beyond the Brunei Museum, Jalan Kota Batu stretches all the way up to **MUARA**, an oil town and Brunei's main port. The town was originally established to serve the now-defunct Brooketon Coal Mine, which was situated a few kilometres to the west. While there's nothing to bring you to Muara itself, nearby **Muara Beach** boasts a perfectly pleasant stretch of sand, although food stalls or cafés are thin on the ground outside the weekend when, in good weather, locals often descend. At **Serasa Beach**, a few kilometres south of Muara, a recently built watersports complex has facilities for sailing, windsurfing, water-skiing and fishing. **Buses** (B\$2) to Muara from BSB's Jalan Cator pass along Jalan Kota Batu, skirting Sungai Brunei's north bank, but don't go to either beach. You will need to change in Muara town; the local bus to the beaches is, however, extremely infrequent, around every two hours (B\$1).

The Empire Hotel & Country Club

A favourite stop on the global circuit for celebrities, the **Empire Hotel & Country Club** (T02/418888, W www.theempirehotel.com; 9) at Jerudong BG3122, is situated on the Muara–Tutong highway, around ten kilometres northwest of BSB. One of the world's few seven-star hotels, it's a massively expensive, opulent work of architecture and a top attraction for Bruneians and visitors alike.

Apart from the hotel itself – the best place in Asia to take tea outside of *Raffles* in Singapore – the complex includes one of the world's top golf courses, a number of restaurants, a bowling alley, cinema, a beach, three swimming pools and a vast semi-covered, air-conditioned café/bar/restaurant. Visitors who aren't hotel guests can explore most of the complex, although there's a B\$100 levy applied for pool use.

A pet project of Prince Jefri, the sultan's discredited brother, the *Empire* is reputed to have cost over a billion US dollars; thousands of craftsmen from a number of nations pooled their skills and the result is jaw-dropping. Just to walk in the 25 metre-high central atrium with its marble columns, covered with complex Islamic designs in shimmering gold leaf is striking enough. Then there's the lobby staircase's gold-plated balusters laden with 370 tiger's eye gemstones and the handrails coated with mother-of-pearl and semi-precious stones from the Philippines. If your budget stretches to tea (B\$10) or something more substantial then you'll experience the hotel's famed top-class service.

Practicalities

The *Empire* has 360 opulently appointed rooms, 63 suites and 16 secluded villas, the least expensive room hardly a pinch at over B\$500. However, promotions cutting the price substantially are sometimes available through the website. There is no public transport serving the hotel so taxis (B\$10) from BSB, or renting a car (see "Listings"), are the options.

Bukit Shahbandar Park & Jerudong Park Playground

Around 20km west of Muara is the **Bukit Shahbandar Forest Recreation Park** (daily 8am–6pm; free), a compact area of acacia, pine and heath forest scored by unchallenging trails, and dotted with shelters and lookout points over BSB and the South China Sea. Marking the entrance to the park is an information centre with displays on the surrounding terrain; it's also possible to **camp** here (free). Unfortunately, Bukit Shahbandar is tricky to reach; unless you're prepared to pay for a taxi, you'll have to take the bus to Berakas (B$2) and try to hitch from there.

Several kilometres west of Bukit Shah, and on the road to Tutong, Jerudong has long been known as the playground of the sultan, whose polo stadium and stables are located here. The **Jerudong Park Playground** (grounds daily 2pm–2am; games and rides Mon, Tues & Wed 5pm–midnight, Thurs & Sat 5pm–2am, Fri & Sun 2pm–midnight; during Ramadan daily 8pm–2am; free) was conceived as a "lasting testimony to His Majesty's generosity to his rakyat (people)"; the park has since expanded into a funfair/adventure park whose scores of rides make it a fun half-day out. Unless you come at the weekend, there's little queuing for rides, and you'll find enough of interest to keep you amused for quite a few hours; there's also a good food court beside the park's yellow towers.

To get to Jerudong Park Playground, catch the Jerudong **bus** from BSB's bus station (daily: outward services 8am–5pm, return buses 8.30am–5.30pm; every 2hr; B$3). To get back once buses have stopped in the early evening, you have to take a taxi (around B$30) or try to share one with locals to cut the cost. There is no bus to Jerudong via Muara or Berakas.

Selirong Recreation Park

A final attraction near BSB is Brunei Bay's recently opened **Selirong Recreation Park**, only approachable by a one-hour boat journey from the capital, where plank walkways have been built across swamp and mangrove forest. It is possible to see waterbirds like storks, egrets, plovers, herons and kingfishers and, less frequently, mammals including monkeys, flying foxes, lemurs, snakes and turtles. The park currently lacks any facilities and visitors can only go by arranging a visit through the Forestry Department (☎02/381687, ✉jphq@brunet.bn).

Kampung Parit

Some 15km west of BSB along the inland highway to Tutong, a mosque marks the turning southwards onto **Jalan Mulaut**. From here, it's a further 10km to the **Kampung Parit Heritage Park** (daily 8am–6pm; free), where a number of old-style Bornean dwellings have been erected to shed light on traditional Bruneian village life. Among the exhibits, which were built by local artisans using only forest materials, is a replica of Kampung Ayer, the way it was before the advent of zinc and manufactured timber. The park's playground, picnic site and cluster of food stalls make it popular with Bruneian weekenders. Even so, access is only by taxi or rented car.

Temburong District

Hilly **Temburong District** has been isolated from the rest of Brunei since 1884, when the strip of land to its west was ceded to Sarawak. Sparsely populated by Malay, Iban and Murut groups, this rainforest-dominated region is worth a visit to see the 500-square-kilometre **Ulu Temburong National Park**, with its canopy walkway and trails. While in the region, you may choose to make use of the homestays available in the **kampung** at **Labu**. Temburong has over 60km of good roads, providing links into Sarawak – with **Limbang** (see p.493) to the west and **Lawas** (p.495) to the east.

Bangar

The starting point for all the above trips in Temburong is the district's only town, **BANGAR**. Standing on the Sungai Temburong, Bangar can only be reached by a rapid speedboat journey from BSB (daily 6.30am to 4.30pm; every 45min; 40min; B$6). The boats, known as flying coffins because of their shape, scream through narrow mangrove estuaries that are home to crocodiles and proboscis monkeys, swooping around corners and narrowly missing vessels travelling the opposite way, before shooting off down Sungai Temburong. After all that, you'll find the town of Bangar is nothing much to write home about; its main street, which runs west from the jetty to the town mosque, is lined mainly by a handful of coffee shops and provisions stores. Also on the main road, across the bridge from the jetty, is Bangar's grandest building, the District Office, whose waterfront **café** is one of the few places to eat in the town.

The main street has a small **tourist office** (☏03/5221439), where it may be possible to organize trips into Temburong Park for a lower price than those offered by the BSB-based operators. For **accommodation**, there is one guesthouse, the *Likut Intan* (☏03/5221078; ❷) in the centre of town. Note that no local bus operates in or out of Bangar; except the daily Lawas Express (see box below).

Amo C longhouse

From Bangar, a short taxi ride (20min; B$15) brings you to **Amo C**, a five-door Iban **longhouse** (no phone), where it's possible to visit but not stay overnight. There are usually people around to invite you in (most of the young ones speak some English). It's as well to take some small gifts, like pens and notebooks, for the children although this isn't expected. The longhouse is just a few kilometres north of **Batang Duri** from where boats leave for Ulu Temburong National Park.

Around the longhouse are some pleasant forest trails which the Brunei Ibans use for hunting; you need to hire a local as a guide if you want to explore these (day-trip B$30).

Ulu Temburong National Park

Constituting a tenth of the area of Brunei, the 500-square-kilometre **Ulu Temburong National Park** (park fee inclusive in tour price), is the finest example of the sultanate's successful forest protection policy (although the border region, to the south of the park, suffers some illegal logging). The park is reached via longboat from the jetty at **Kampung Batang Duri**, 15km south of Bangar, but only visitors on tours run by registered operators (see p.607) can visit. Most trips begin in BSB although it is possible to join the tour group in Bangar.

The one-hour boat journey traverses mangrove forests on the way to the *nipah*-lined Sungai Temburong and the park's headquarters. En route, dense

---

Crossing into Sarawak from Temburong

Crossing from Temburong into Sarawak, either to **Limbang** or **Lawas**, is a fiddly process. First you have to make for the immigration post a few metres from the border beside the turning for Kampung Puni, 5km west of Bangar. Here your passport is checked and stamped; you then return to Bangar and await buses either way, which leave from the main road 200m from Bangar jetty. The eastbound **Lawas Express** bus (B$12) leaves at 8.30am, getting to the Senokoh junction at 9am and arriving at Lawas – after a B$1 river crossing – at around 10am. Going west towards Limbang, the bus leaves Bangar at around 2pm, arriving at Limbang an hour later.

jungle cloaks the hills on either side and birds and monkeys abound in the trees, an atmospheric journey that sets the tone for the park itself. Just before you reach the headquarters is the **Kuala Belalong Field Centre** (not open to the public), established in 1991 to house the Brunei Rainforest Project. The primary goal of the project has been to document the biodiversity of the forest; the results show that the park contains many hitherto unknown species among its 170 different types of ferns, 700 tree species and tens of thousands of types of insect.

The main attraction of the park is the **canopy walkway**, reached by an hour-long trek taking in two hanging bridges and a plank-way, followed by a giddy-ing climb up the stairs around a near-vertical, sixty-metre-high aluminium structure. The view from the top, of Brunei Bay to the north and Sarawak's Gunung Mulu Park to the south, is quite breathtaking. At this height, on a good day you can see four types of hornbill and gibbon in the trees, as well as numerous kinds of squirrels and small birds. According to a University of Brunei Darussalam survey, fifty species of birds have been sighted on the netting around the walkway, and flying lizards, frogs and snakes feed regularly at ground level. Other activities in the park include chartering a small **longboat** (around B$50 return) to go further upstream to a tree house where a few trails weave for short distances into the surrounding jungle, and **night walks**, conducted from time to time by the park office staff.

Practicalities

From Batang Duri, longboats take around ninety minutes to reach park **headquarters** (daily 8am–6.30pm) set on a spit of land at the junction of Sungai Temburong and a tributary. Ten minutes' walk from the headquarters along a plankway above the river is the park's **accommodation**, seven wooden cabins (❹) nestling in the forest, comprising small rooms and simple bathrooms with cold showers. Contact the tourist office in BSB for accommodation vacancy details.

To Labu

Twenty kilometres east of Bangar, on the road to Lawas in Sarawak, is the **Labu** region of Temburong. The area used to be largely comprised of rubber plantations until the bottom dropped out of the rubber market in the 1950s; today, paddy fields line the road on the north side, while the forest creeps down to the road on the other. Fifteen kilometres out of Bangar, you come to the **Bukit Peradayan Forest Reserve**, a small park featuring a strenu-ous three-hour trek along an uphill plankway to the **Bukit Patoi** (310m), passing unusual rock formations and caves on the way. From the top of the hill there are great views across Brunei's spectacular and largely undisturbed rainforests, south towards Sarawak. There are no amenities in the park, so bring your own food and drink.

Five kilometres further east, a signposted road to the right leads to **SENOKOH**, a Malay and Murut village comprising a few dozen stilt dwell-ings. While there's little to do besides walking around the kampung, meeting people and having local fruit trees pointed out, a visit can offer a rare insight into the lifestyle of traditional, rural Bruneians; it's well worth making the effort to get here for that alone.

The only **bus** service through Labu is the Lawas Express, which stops on request at the forest reserve and 2km from Senokoh on the main highway.

Tutong District

West of Brunei Muara District is wedge-shaped **Tutong District**, whose main settlement, **Tutong**, is a little over 40km west of BSB. Tutong is slowly becoming an agricultural zone as the government prepares for the eventual demise of the oil reserves. The district contains coffee, tapioca and cinnamon plantations and a research station, at **Birau**, which develops new strains of cereal crops.

Though a coastal highway connects Tutong with Muara District, buses (daily from 8.30am–3pm; every 2hr; B$3) from BSB's Jalan Cator terminal only travel along the inland route along Jalan Tutong, which is skirted by scrublands and grasslands.

Tutong and around

Bruneian settlements don't come any sleeper than **TUTONG** town, which has witnessed none of the oil-related development seen further west. Though it makes no real demands upon tourists' time, Tutong is an amiable enough place to break the trip between Sarawak and BSB. The one street of any size, Jalan Enche Awang (buses drop you at the end beside the river), is flanked by rows of shophouses on one side, and on the other by the broad Sungai Tutong, its far bank massed with palm trees. Tutong has no places to stay, though it does have several **restaurants**: try the *Haji K-K-Koya* at Jalan Enche Awang 14, or the Chinese *Ho Yuen* at no. 12.

If you're in town on a Friday morning, you should visit the animated **Tamu Tutong**, which draws fruit and vegetable vendors from the interior of Brunei. The market takes place on a patch of land 1km south of central Tutong at Kampung Serambagaun, and is reached by walking out of town along Jalan Enche Awang and taking a left turn at the fork in the road. Ignoring this fork and continuing on across the coastal highway brings you, after fifteen minutes, to the best stretch of beach in the area, the peninsula **Pantai Seri Kenangan**, whose yellow sands divide Sungai Tutong from the South China Sea. Its name translates as "Memorable Beach", and though this may be rather stretching the point, the beach is pleasant enough, with a basic café. The royal family have a house nearby, which is less opulent than you may expect. If you want to take a peek at it, turn off at Tamu Tutong.

Tasek Merimbun

Tutong District's most impressive geographical feature is the 7,800-hectare **Tasek Merimbun**, the largest lake in Brunei. Declared an ASEAN National Heritage site in 1984, and Brunei's fastest-growing nature attraction, it's home to a variety of fauna and and flora and facilities include walkways and newly opened chalet accommodation. Wooden boardwalks run from the attractively landscaped lake shore across to Pulau Jelandung, a tiny wooded island which has a profusion of **birdlife** (ask the staff for boat availability), and pathways and picnic spots are to be found around the lake itself. Bird species easily spotted in the vicinity include egrets, falcons and eagles and a host of smaller ones.

Practicalities

Unfortunately, there's no public transport to the park, so you will have to rent a car or go on a **tour** (see p.607 for BSB-based tour operators). To get there from BSB follow Jalan Tutong and after around 30km take the left turn to Lamunin. From there, signposts lead you to Tasek Merimbun, along roads that traverse glistening paddy fields. **Accommodation** is limited, consisting of one chalet with three rooms (B$100 for one three-bed room). Camping inside the chalet hall is also available for groups. To reserve accommodation contact Samhan Nyawa, Brunei Museum administrative offices, Jalan Menteri Besar, BSB (☎3/2244545, ✉bndir@brunet.com.bn).

Belait District

Belait District, to the west of Tutong, is oil and gas country, and has been the economic heart of the sultanate ever since the Seria Oil Field was established in 1931. The oil boom led directly to the rise of the region's two main coastal towns, **Seria** and **Kuala Belait**. Inland, though, it's a different story: down the fifty-kilometre-long **Labi Road**, a few Iban **longhouses** and tiny kampungs survive in the face of the tremendous changes brought about by the sultanate's wealth and the substantial population shift to the coast. Along with Temburong, this is the most serene and attractive part of Brunei to visit.

The coastal road west from Tutong is lined with flat scrubland, the sands along this stretch of Brunei's coast a brilliant white due to their high silica content (in time, as Brunei looks for moneymaking alternatives to its finite oil reserves, these sands could well spawn a glass industry). Around 20km west of Tutong at Kampung Sungai Liang, a turning south marks the start of **Labi Road**, which offers the chance to explore the interior (though there's no public transport along this road); continue west along the coast however, and you end up at Seria. Brunei tour operators are hoping to open out new areas in the south of the district by establishing trips which will take you down two rivers, Sungai Keduan and Sungai Penipir.

The Labi Road

Just 500m from the northern end of Labi Road is the **Sungai Liang Forest Reserve**, whose thick lowland forest can be explored by following one of the well-kept walking trails leading from the lakes, information centre and picnic shelters clustered around the entrance. Several kilometres south is the site of the bustling **Tamu Sungai Mau**, held on Sundays, while another 15km further along is the **Luagan Lalak Forestry Recreation Park**, whose freshwater swamp swells into a lake with the onset of the monsoon rains, flooding the area around it.

Some 35km south of Sungai Liang is **LABI** itself, a small agricultural settlement relying on harvests of durian and rambutan for its livelihood. Despite much speculative drilling, its surrounding hills have so far refused to yield any oil, though it was Labi's oil potential which led to the construction of the road here in the first place. There's nowhere to stay or eat in Labi. Shortly after Labi, the roads turns into a laterite track; around 300m along, a trail off to the east leads, after two hours' walk, to **Wasai Rampayoh**, a large waterfall. Back on the track, continue south and you reach **Mendaram Longhouse**, the first of several Iban communities here, where around a hundred people live. Like most Iban architecture in Brunei, this is a modern structure with electricity and running water. The people here are very friendly and happy to guide you along the trail to **Wasai Mendaram**, a small waterfall twenty minutes' walk away with a rock pool perfect for swimming.

A few kilometres further on, and around half-an-hour's drive from Labi, there is another longhouse, **Teraja**, which marks the end of Labi Road, with only swamp forest beyond. The locals can point out a trail, which runs alongside a stream eastwards, to another small waterfall and on up to the largest hill in the region, Bukit Teraja, where there are spectacular **views** across Brunei and Sarawak; this route takes around 45 minutes.

Seria

At the very centre of Brunei's oil and gas wealth is **SERIA**, 65km west of BSB. Until oil was first discovered here at the start of the twentieth century, the area where the town now stands was nothing more than a malarial swamp, known locally as Padang Berawa, or "Wild Pigeon's Field"; an oil prospector in the area in 1926 reported that "walking here means really climbing and jumping over naked roots, and struggling and cutting through air roots of mangroves of more than man's height". It took until 1931 for S1, the sultanate's first oil well, to deliver commercially, after which Seria expanded rapidly, followed by offshore drilling in the 1950s. Despite its mineral wealth, Seria remained an isolated settlement for several decades, unlinked by road with the capital.

As you approach from Tutong, you see numbers of small oil wells called "nodding donkeys" because of their rocking motion, though they actually bear a closer resemblance to praying mantises. Around the town are green-roofed housing units and bungalows, constructed by Brunei Shell for their employees, while on the waterfront is the **Billionth Barrel Monument**, whose interlocking arches celebrate the huge productivity of the first well.

Practicalities

Seria town centre is a congested place, dominated by the Plaza Seria shopping mall, across from the **bus terminus** where the regular buses from BSB (hourly 7am–3pm) terminate. Though there are no places to stay, budget **restaurants** and coffee shops abound. On Jalan Sultan Omar Ali (left of the plaza when viewed from the bus station), you'll find the *Universal Café* at no. 11, a sleepy retreat that's good for coffee. Next door, the air-conditioned *Restoran Sayang Merah* sells Asian and Western dishes such as spaghetti, Spanish omelettes and T-bone steaks. For a more upmarket meal, try the *New China Restaurant* in Plaza Seria.

Kuala Belait

It's a little under 20km from Seria to the neighbouring oil town of **KUALA BELAIT**. There's nothing very enticing about the place, but with all buses to and from Miri in Sarawak stopping here, it's a spot you may have to visit. The town is ringed by suburban development that caters for the expat community, while central Kuala Belait is characterized by the many workshops and businesses that the local oil industry has spawned.

Buses stop at the intersection of Jalan Bunga Raya and Jalan McKerron, across which is the town's **taxi** stand. There are just two **hotels**, one of which, *Hotel Sentosa* (☎03/334341; ●) at 93 Jalan McKerron, has 36 capacious, well-appointed and welcoming rooms. The alternative is the slightly less expensive *Seaview Hotel* (☎03/332651; ●), 3–4km back along the coastal road towards Seria. You can **change money** in town at HSBC (Mon–Fri 9am–3pm, Sat 9–11am).

Jalan McKerron houses several good **restaurants**, the best of which are the tastefully decorated *Buccaneer Steakhouse* at no. 94, whose mid-priced international food is aimed squarely at the expat market; and the *Akhbar Restaurant*, at no. 99a, with a Malay and North Indian menu which includes excellent *dosai*. Of Kuala Belait's handful of other restaurants, two in particular, the first-floor *Healthy Way Tandoori* at 30 Jalan Pretty (the town's main drag, a block east of McKerron), and Jalan Bunga Raya's *Orchid Room*, are worth a visit – the former for its naans, tikka masalas and lassis, the latter for its good-value three-course Western set lunches (Mon–Fri; B$5).

Kuala Balai

Another up-country location worth a visit is **KUALA BALAI,** a Malay community which has become a kind of show village. You can only visit as part of a tour and attractions include trekking and participating in village life. Once a thriving centre for sago processing, Kuala Balai has seen its population dwindle but the hope is that more visitors will be attracted by the promise of experiencing the slower pace of kampung life. The longhouse at Balai remains uninhabited but is the locus for culture shows put on by the villagers for tour groups. Mona FloraFauna Tours (see p.607) can arrange for visitors to stay overnight with a kampung family.

Kuala Balai is around a 90-minute-drive from BSB, initially along the Tutong-Belait coastal road, then south on the Labi Road at Sungai Liang, and a further unpaved road leading west off the Labi Road.

Travel details

Buses

BSB to: Berakas (5 daily; 20min); Jerudong (5 daily; 40min); Muara town (every 30min until 4.30pm; 30min) with a connection to Muara beach; Seria (hourly until 3pm; 2hr); Tutong (hourly until 3pm; 1hr).
Kuala Belait to: Miri (5 daily; 2hr 30min); Seria (every 30min until 6.30pm; 45min).
Muara to: Berakas (5 daily; 20min).
Seria to: BSB (every 45min until 3pm; 1hr 45min); Kuala Belait (every hour; 30min); Miri (5 daily; 2hr).

Ferries

BSB to: Bangar (11 daily; 40min), Limbang (1 daily, 30min).
Muara to: Labuan (numerous daily; 1hr 30min); Lawas (1 daily; 2hr); Limbang (numerous daily; 30min).

Flights

BSB to: Kota Kinabalu (12 weekly; 40min); Kuala Lumpur (2–3 daily; 2hr 30min); Singapore (3 daily; 2hr).

Singapore

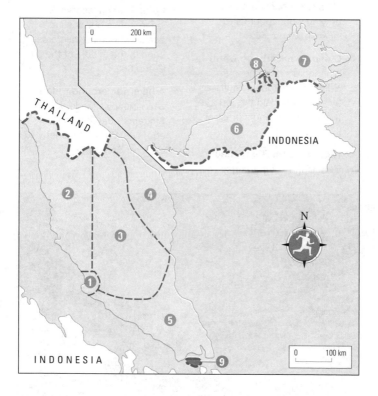

CHAPTER 9 **Highlights**

✳ **A Singapore Sling at Raffles**
No trip is complete without
a glass of the hotel's famous
cherry brandy cocktail. See
p.651

✳ **Thian Hock Keng Temple**
Drink in the atmosphere of the
gilt altars, chanting monks,
praying worshippers and
incense. See p.662

✳ **Chinatown Heritage Centre**
Singapore's best museum
tells of the hardships suffered
by those who laid the foundations for the island's prosperity. See p.667

✳ **Night time on Boat Quay**
Bars and restaurants galore

alongside the Singapore River.
See p.670

✳ **Serangoon Road** A sensual
overload of fortune-telling
parrots, colourful sarees
and aromatic spice-grinding
shops. See p.674

✳ **Bukit Timah Reserve** An
incongruous but pristine
pocket of primary rainforest
bang in the middle of the city.
See p.682

✳ **A bike ride around Pulau
Ubin** Sleepy Ubin looks like
Singapore did fifty years
ago; hire a bike at the jetty to
explore. See p.692

△ Sri Mariamman Temple

Singapore

Singapore is certainly the handiest city I ever saw, as well planned and carefully executed as though built entirely by one man. It is like a big desk, full of drawers and pigeon-holes, where everything has its place, and can always be found in it.

William Hornaday, 1885

Despite the immense changes the past century has wrought upon the tiny island of Singapore, natural historian William Hornaday's succinct appraisal is as valid today as it was in 1885. Since gaining full independence from Malaysia in 1965, this absorbing city-state, just 580 square kilometres in size and linked by two causeways to the southern tip of Malaysia, has been transformed from a sleepy colonial backwater to a pristine, futuristic shrine to consumerism. It's one of Southeast Asia's most accessible destinations, its downtown areas dense with towering skyscrapers and gleaming shopping malls, while sprawling new towns ring the centre, with their own separate communities and well-planned facilities. Yet visitors prepared to peer beneath the state's squeaky-clean surface will discover a profusion of age-old buildings, values and traditions that have survived in the face of profound social and geographical change. The island has not been overwhelmed by development – as you make your way around the island, you're struck immediately by Singapore's abundance of parks, nature reserves, and lush, tropical greenery. Inevitably, given its geographical position, the state is seen by most people as a mere stopover and its compactness means you can gain an impression of the place in just a few hours. However, a lengthier stay is easily justified. Quite apart from enjoying its cultural highlights, you'll find several days spent in Singapore invaluable for arranging financial transfers, seeing to medical problems and generally gathering strength before continuing on to the region's less affluent – and often more demanding – areas.

Singapore's progress over the past three decades has been remarkable. Lacking any noteworthy natural resources, its early prosperity was based on a vigorous **free trade** policy, put in place in 1819 when Sir Stamford Raffles first set up a British trading post here. In the twentieth century, mass industrialization bolstered the economy, and today the state boasts the world's second busiest port after Rotterdam, minimal unemployment and a super-efficient infrastructure. Almost the entire population has been moved from unsanitary kampungs into swish new apartments, and the average per capita income is around US\$28,000.

Yet none of this was achieved without considerable compromise – indeed, the state's detractors claim it has sold its soul in return for prosperity. Put simply, at the core of the Singapore success story is an unwritten bargain between its government and population, which stipulates the loss of a certain amount

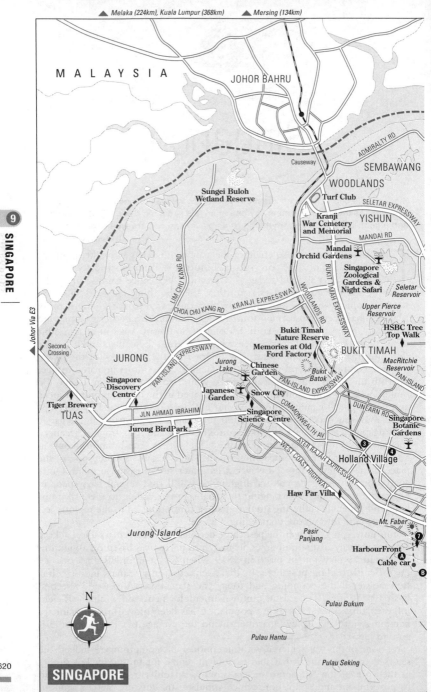

▲ Melaka (224km), Kuala Lumpur (368km)   ▲ Mersing (134km)

MALAYSIA

JOHOR BAHRU

ADMIRALTY RD

Causeway

SEMBAWANG

WOODLANDS

Sungei Buloh
Wetland Reserve

Turf Club

SELETAR EXPRESSWAY

Kranji
War Cemetery
and Memorial

YISHUN

MANDAI RD

Mandai
Orchid Gardens

Singapore
Zoological
Gardens &
Night Safari

Seletar
Reservoir

LIM CHU KANG RD

BUKIT TIMAH EXPRESSWAY

WOODLANDS RD

Upper Pierce
Reservoir

CHOA CHU KANG RD

KRANJI EXPRESSWAY

HSBC Tree
Top Walk

Bukit Timah
Nature Reserve

BUKIT TIMAH

MacRitchie
Reservoir

Second
Crossing

Memories at Old
Ford Factory

PAN-ISLAND

JURONG

PAN-ISLAND EXPRESSWAY

Jurong
Lake

Chinese
Garden

Bukit
Batok

PAN-ISLAND EXPRESSWAY

Singapore
Discovery
Centre

Japanese
Garden

Snow City

DUNEARN RD

Singapore
Botanic
Gardens

Tiger Brewery

TUAS

JLN AHMAD IBRAHIM

Singapore
Science Centre

COMMONWEALTH AV

3

4

Jurong BirdPark

AYER RAJAH EXPRESSWAY

Holland Village

WEST COAST HIGHWAY

Haw Par Villa

Jurong Island

Pasir
Panjang

Mt. Faber

1

HarbourFront

A

Cable car

B

N

Pulau Bukum

Pulau Hantu

Pulau Seking

Johor Via E3

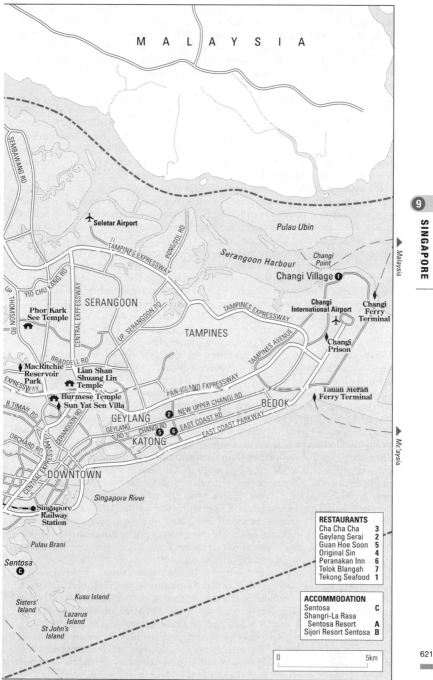

MALAYSIA

Seletar Airport

Pulau Ubin

Serangoon Harbour

Changi Point

Changi Village ❶

SEMBAWANG RD

TAMPINES EXPRESSWAY

PONGGOL RD

YIO CHU KANG RD

UP. THOMSON RD

SERANGOON

UP. SERANGOON RD

CENTRAL EXPRESSWAY

Phor Kark
See Temple

TAMPINES

TAMPINES EXPRESSWAY

Changi
International Airport

Changi
Ferry
Terminal

BRADDELL RD

TAMPINES AVENUE

Changi
Prison

MacRitchie
Reservoir
Park

Lian Shan
Shuang Lin
Temple

EXPRESSWAY

PAN-ISLAND EXPRESSWAY

Tanah Merah
Ferry Terminal

B. TIMAH RD

Burmese Temple
Sun Yat Sen Villa

Serangoon Rd

NEW UPPER CHANGI RD

BEDOK

GEYLANG

❷

GEYLANG
RD

CHANGI RD

EAST COAST RD

ORCHARD RD

CENTRAL EXPRESSWAY

KATONG

❺ ❻

EAST COAST PARKWAY

DOWNTOWN

Singapore River

Singapore
Railway
Station

Pulau Brani

Sentosa ❸

Sisters'
Island

Kusu Island

Lazarus
Island

St John's
Island

RESTAURANTS

Cha Cha Cha	3
Geylang Serai	2
Guan Hoe Soon	5
Original Sin	4
Peranakan Inn	6
Telok Blangah	7
Tekong Seafood	1

ACCOMMODATION

Sentosa	C
Shangri-La Rasa Sentosa Resort	A
Sijori Resort Sentosa	B

0   5km

▼ Batam (Indonesia)

of personal freedom, with the government orchestrating the economy and society, in return for levels of affluence and comfort that would have seemed unimaginable thirty years ago. Lee Kuan Yew (the long-serving former prime minister) has gone on record as saying, "When you are hungry, when you lack basic services, freedom, human rights and democracy do not add up to much." Outsiders often bridle at these sentiments, and it's true that some of the regulations in force here can seem extreme: neglecting to flush a public toilet, jaywalking and eating on the subway all carry sizeable fines, while chewing gum has been outlawed. The case of American teenager, Michael Fay, caught the world's headlines in early 1994, when he was given four strokes of the *rotan* (cane) for vandalizing cars. But far more telling is the fact that these punishments are rarely, if ever, inflicted, as Singaporeans have learned not to break the law. The population, trusting the wisdom of its leaders, seems generally content to acquiesce to a **paternalistic** form of government that critics describe as soft authoritarianism. Consequently, Singaporeans have earned a reputation for cowed, unquestioning subservience, a view that can be overstated, but which isn't without an element of truth. The past has taught Singaporeans that, if they follow their government's lead, they reap the benefits. In addition, they take a pride in their country that occasionally extends to smugness – witness the huge celebrations that accompany National Day, Singapore's annual collective pat on the back. Yet there is good reason to be proud: Singapore is a clean, safe place to visit, its amenities are second to none and its public places are smoke-free and hygienic. And as the nation's youth (who don't remember a time before the improvements they take for granted) begin to find a voice, public life should become increasingly, if gradually, more liberal and democratic.

Whatever the political ramifications of the state's economic success, of more relevance to its millions of annual visitors is the fact that improvements in living conditions have been shadowed by a steady loss of the state's **heritage**, as historic buildings and streets are bulldozed to make way for shopping centres. Singapore undoubtedly lacks the personality of some Southeast Asian cities, but its reputation for being sterile and sanitized is unfair. Shopping on state-of-the-art Orchard Road is undoubtedly a major draw for many tourists, but under the long shadows cast by giddy towers and spires you still find the dusty temples, fragrant medicinal shops and colonial buildings of old Singapore, neatly divided into enclaves, each home to a distinct ethnic culture. Much of Singapore's fascination springs from its **multicultural population**: of the 3.5 million permanent residents, 77 percent are Chinese (a figure reflected in the predominance of Chinese shops, restaurants and temples across the island), 14 percent Malay, and 8 percent Indian, with the remainder made up of other ethnic groups. This diverse ethnic mix textures the whole island, and often turns a ten-minute walk into what seems like a hop from one country to another. One intriguing by-product of this ethnic melting pot is **Singlish** (see p.786), or Singaporean English, a patois which blends English with the speech patterns, exclamations and vocabulary of Chinese and Malay.

The entire state is compact enough to be explored exhaustively in just a few days. Forming the core of downtown Singapore is the **Colonial District**, around whose public buildings and lofty cathedral the island's British residents used to promenade. The bug-eye beauty of the **Theatres on the Bay** project, just to the east, hauls the Colonial District into the twenty-first century.

Each surrounding enclave has its own distinct flavour, from the aromatic spice stores of **Little India**, to the tumbledown backstreets of **Chinatown**, where it's still possible to find calligraphers and fortune-tellers, or the **Arab Quarter**, whose cluttered stores sell fine cloths and silks. **North** of the city, you'll find the country's last pocket of primary rainforest at **Bukit Timah Nature Reserve**, and the splendid **Singapore Zoological Gardens**. In addition to Singapore's industrial zone and port, the west of the island boasts fascinating **Jurong Bird Park**, and **Haw Par Villas** – a mind-boggling hybrid of eastern mythology and Disneyland kitsch. Aside from the infamous former jail near **Changi** Village, where so many soldiers lost their lives in World War II, the **east** of Singapore features some of the island's best seafood restaurants, set behind long stretches of sandy beach. In addition, over fifty islands and islets lie within Singaporean waters, all of which can be reached with varying degrees of ease. The best offshore day-trips, however, are to **Sentosa**, the island amusement arcade which is linked to the south coast by a short causeway (and cable car), and to **Pulau Ubin**, off the east coast, where the inhabitants continue to live a kampung life long since eradicated from the mainland.

Some history

What little is known of Singapore's ancient history relies heavily upon legend and supposition. Third-century Chinese sailors could have been referring to Singapore in their account of a place called Pu-Luo-Chung, or "island at the end of a peninsula". In the late thirteenth century, Marco Polo reported seeing a place called Chiamassie, which could also have been Singapore. by then the island was known locally as Temasek – "sea town" – and was a minor trading outpost of the Sumatran Srivijaya Empire. The island's present name – from the Sanskrit **Singapura**, meaning "Lion City" – was first recorded in the sixteenth century, when a legend narrated in the Malay annals, the *Sejarah Melayu*, told how a Sumatran prince saw a lion while sheltering on the island from a storm; the annals reported that the name had been in common use since the end of the fourteenth century.

Throughout the fourteenth century, Singapura felt the squeeze as the Ayuthaya and Majapahit empires of Thailand and Java struggled for control of the Malay Peninsula. Around 1390, a Sumatran prince called **Paramesvara** threw off his allegiance to the Javanese Majapahit Empire and fled from Palembang to present-day Singapore. There, he murdered his host and ruled the island until a Javanese offensive forced him to flee north, up the Peninsula, where he and his son, **Iskandar Shah**, subsequently founded the Melaka Sultanate. A grave on Fort Canning Hill (see p.656) is said to be that of Iskandar Shah, though its authenticity is doubtful. With the rise of the Melaka Sultanate, Singapore devolved into a peripheral fishing settlement of little consequence; a century or so later, the arrival of the Portuguese in Melaka forced Malay leaders to flee southwards to modern-day Johor Bahru for sanctuary. A Portuguese account of 1613 described the razing of an unnamed Malay outpost at the mouth of Sungai Johor to the ground, after which began two centuries of historical limbo for Singapore.

By the late eighteenth century, with China opening up for trade with the West, the British East India Company felt the need to establish outposts along the Straits of Melaka to protect its interests. Penang was secured in 1786, but with the Dutch expanding their rule in the East Indies (Indonesia), a port was needed further south. Enter **Thomas Stamford Raffles** (see p.652) who, in 1818 was authorized by the governor-general of India, then lieutenant-governor of Bencoolen (in Sumatra), to establish a **British colony** at the southern tip of the Malay Peninsula. Early the following year, Raffles stepped ashore on the northern bank of the Singapore River accompanied by Colonel William Farquhar, former Resident of Melaka and fluent in Malay. At the time, inhospitable swampland and tiger-infested jungle covered Singapore, and its population is generally thought to have numbered around 150, although some historians suggest it could have been as high as a thousand. Raffles recognized the island's potential for providing a deep-water harbour, and immediately struck a treaty with **Abdul Rahman**, *temenggong* (chieftain) of Singapore, establishing a British trading station there. The Dutch were furious at this British incursion into what they considered their territory, but Raffles – who still needed the approval of the Sultan of Johor for his outpost, as Abdul Rahman was only an underling – disregarded Dutch sensibilities. Realizing that the Sultan's loyalties to the Dutch would make such approval impossible, Raffles approached the sultan's brother, **Hussein**, recognized him as the true sultan, and concluded a second treaty with both the *temenggong* and His Highness the Sultan Hussein Mohammed Shah. The Union Jack was raised, and Singapore's future as a free trading post was set.

With its **strategic position** at the foot of the Straits of Melaka and below the South China Sea, and with no customs duties on imported or exported goods, Singapore's expansion was meteoric. The population had reached ten thousand by the time of the first census in 1824, with Malays, Chinese, Indians and Europeans arriving in search of work as coolies and merchants. In 1822, Raffles set about drawing up the demarcation lines that divide present-day Singapore. The area south of the Singapore River was earmarked for the Chinese; a swamp at the mouth of the river was filled and the commercial district established there. Muslims were settled around the Sultan's Palace in today's Arab Quarter. The Singapore of those times was a far cry from the pristine city of the present. "There were thousands of rats all over the district", wrote Abdullah bin Kadir, scribe to Stamford Raffles, "some almost as large as cats. They were so big that they used to attack us if we went out walking at night and many people were knocked over."

In 1824, Sultan Hussein and the *temenggong* were bought out, and Singapore ceded outright to the British. Three years later, the fledgling state united with Penang and Melaka (now under British rule) to form the **Straits Settlements**, which became a British Crown Colony in 1867. For forty years the island's *laissez-faire* economy boomed, though life was chaotic, and disease rife. More and more immigrants poured into the island; by 1860 the population had reached eighty thousand, with each ethnic community bringing its attendant cuisines, languages and architecture. Arabs, Indians, Javanese and Bugis all came, but most populous of all were the **Chinese** from the southern provinces of China, who settled quickly, helped by the clan societies (*kongsis*) already establishing footholds on the island. The British, for their part, erected impressive Neoclassical theatres, courts and assembly halls, and in 1887 Singapore's most quintessentially British establishment, the *Raffles Hotel*, opened for business.

In 1877, Henry Ridley began his one-man crusade to introduce the **rubber plant** into Southeast Asia, a move which further bolstered Singapore's importance as the island soon became the world centre of rubber exporting. By the end of the nineteenth century, the opening of the Suez Canal and the advent of the steamship had consolidated Singapore's position at the hub of international trade in the region, with the port becoming a major staging post on the Europe–East Asia route. This status was further enhanced by the slow but steady drawing of the Malay Peninsula under British control – a process begun with the Treaty of Pangkor (see p.188) in 1874 and completed in 1914 – which meant that Singapore gained further from the mainland's tin- and rubber-based economy. Between 1873 and 1913 trade increased eightfold, a trend which continued well into the twentieth century.

Singapore's **Asian communities** found their political voice in the 1920s. In 1926, the Singapore Malay Union was established, and four years later, the

Malayan Communist Party (MCP), backed by local Chinese. But grumblings of independence had risen to no more than a faint whisper before an altogether more immediate problem reared its head.

In December 1941, the Japanese had bombed Pearl Harbour and invaded the Malay Peninsula. Less than two months later they were at the northern end of the causeway, a direction from which "Fortress Singapore" had not been prepared for an attack – Singapore's artillery were pointed south from what is now Sentosa Island. On February 15, 1942, the **fall of Singapore** (which the Japanese then renamed Syonan, or "Light of the South") was complete. Winston Churchill called the British surrender "the worst disaster and the largest capitulation in British history"; ironically, it later transpired that the Japanese forces had been outnumbered and their supplies hopelessly stretched immediately prior to the surrender.

Three and a half years of brutal **Japanese** rule ensued, during which thousands of civilians were executed in vicious anti-Chinese purges and Europeans were either herded into **Changi Prison** or marched up the Peninsula to work on Thailand's infamous "Death Railway". Less well known is the vicious campaign, known as Operation Sook Ching, mounted by the military police force, or *Kempeitai*, during which upwards of 25,000 Chinese males between 18 and 50 years of age were shot dead at Punggol and Changi beaches as enemies to the Japanese. Following the destruction of Hiroshima and Nagasaki in 1945, Singapore was passed back into British hands, but things were never to be the same. Singaporeans now wanted a say in the government of the island, and in 1957 the British government agreed to the establishment of an elected, 51-member legislative assembly. Full internal **self-government** was achieved in May 1959, when the **People's Action Party** (PAP), led by Cambridge law graduate **Lee Kuan Yew**, won 43 of the 51 seats. Lee became Singapore's first prime minister, and quickly looked for the security of a merger with neighbouring Malaya (what's now called Peninsular Malaysia). For its part (despite reservations about aligning with Singapore's predominantly Chinese population), anti-Communist Malaya feared that extremists within the PAP would turn Singapore into a Communist base, and accordingly preferred to have the state under its wing.

In 1963, Singapore combined with Malaya, Sarawak and British North Borneo (modern-day Sabah) to form the **Federation of Malaysia**. The alliance, though, was an uneasy one, and within two years Singapore was asked to leave the federation, in the face of outrage in Kuala Lumpur at the PAP's attempts to break into Peninsular politics in 1964. Hours after announcing Singapore's **full independence**, on August 9, 1965, a tearful Lee Kuan Yew went on national TV and described the event as "a moment of anguish". One hundred and forty-six years after Sir Stamford Raffles had set Singapore on the world map, the tiny island, with no natural resources of its own, faced the prospect of being consigned to history's bottom drawer of crumbling colonial ports.

Instead, Lee's personal vision and drive transformed Singapore into an Asian economic heavyweight, though this position was achieved at a price. Heavy-handed **censorship** of the media was introduced, and even more disturbing was the government's attitude towards **political opposition**. When the opposition Workers' Party won a by-election in 1981, the candidate, J.B. Jeyaretham, found himself charged with several criminal offences, and chased through the Singaporean law courts for the next decade. The archaic **Internal Security Act**, which grants the power to detain without trial anyone the government deems a threat to the nation, kept political prisoner Chia Thye Poh under lock and key from 1966 until 1989 for allegedly advocating violence. Singapore's population policies, too, have brought charges of social engineering from foreign critics. These measures began in the early 1970s, with a **birth-control campaign** which proved so successful that it had to be reversed: the 1980s saw the introduction of the "Go For Three" project, which offered tax incentives for those having more than two children in an attempt to boost the national – and some say, more specifically the Chinese Singaporean – birth rate. Lee Kuan Yew also made clear his conviction that Singapore's educated elite should intermarry in order that they might create highly intelligent future generations.

At other times, Singapore tries so hard to reshape itself that it falls into self-parody. "We have to pursue this subject of fun very seriously if we want to stay competitive in the twenty-first century" was the reaction of government minister George Yeo, when confronted with the fact that some foreigners find Singapore dull. The government's annual courtesy campaign, which in 1996 urged the population to hold lift doors open for neighbours and prevent their washing from dripping onto passers-by below, appears equally risible to outsiders. Whether Singaporeans will continue to suffer their government's foibles remains to be seen. Adults beyond a certain age remember how things were before independence and, more importantly, before the existence of the island's metro system, housing projects and saving schemes, and so particularly appreciate how the standard of living has improved. But their children and grandchildren have no such perspective, and telltale signs – presently nothing more extreme than putting one's feet up on metro train seats and jaywalking – suggest that the government can expect more **dissent** in future years. Already a substantial brain drain is afflicting the country, as skilled Singaporeans choose to move abroad in the pursuit of heightened civil liberties.

The man who led Singapore into the new millennium was **Goh Chok Tong**, who became prime minister upon Lee's retirement in 1990, although many felt that Lee still called the shots in his role as senior minister. In August of 2004 Goh was replaced by **Lee Hsien Loong**, Lee Kuan Yew's son. On the same day that the younger Lee took office, the elder Lee was named "minister mentor", a newly-created cabinet position that seemingly gave him an official high horse from which to oversee Singaporean affairs.

△ Theatres on the Bay

More recently, plans are afoot to make the island self-sufficient in water by building an enormous **coastal reservoir** at Marina Bay, and there is continuing investment in biotechnology. Tussles with Malaysia over various issues seem ongoing, most recently over Malaysian plans to build a crooked bridge over the Straits of Johor, which they eventually backed down on. Politics apart, Singapore is considering plans to turn itself into Southeast Asia's Las Vegas by building a huge **casino** in a prime location. Despite some domestic opposition it looks set to go ahead, and will probably have a huge impact on the area's tourism.

Arrival

The diamond-shaped island of Singapore is 42km from east to west at its widest points, and 23km from north to south. The downtown city areas huddle at the southern tip of the diamond, radiating out from the mouth of the **Singapore River**. Two northeast–southwest roads form a dual spine to the central area, both of them traversing the river. One starts out as **North Bridge Road**, crosses the river and becomes **South Bridge Road**; the other begins as **Victoria Street**, becomes Hill Street and skirts Chinatown as **New Bridge Road**.

The island has developed a system of expressways, of which the main ones are the east–west **Pan Island Expressway** and the **East Coast Parkway/Ayer Rajah Expressway**, both of which run from Changi to Jurong, and the **Bukit Timah Expressway**, which branches off north from the Pan Island Expressway at Bukit Timah new town, running north to Woodlands. At Woodlands, the road (shadowed by the train from the railway station near Chinatown) crosses the 1056-metre **causeway** linking Singapore with Johor Bahru in Malaysia. A **second crossing**, at Singapore's far western end, links Johor with the Ayer Rajah Expressway.

Most people's first glimpse of Singapore is of Changi International Airport in the east of the island, and a telling glimpse it is. Its two main terminals, plus the low-cost terminal for budget flights, connected by the Skytrain monorail, are modern, efficient and air-conditioned – a Singapore in microcosm. A third terminal is set to be completed in 2008. Flights from the Malaysian resort island of Tioman set down at smaller Seletar airport, up to the north of the island. Other arrivals are from over the causeway from the Malaysian city of Johor Bahru, or by boat from the Indonesian archipelago. Wherever you arrive, the well-oiled public transport infrastructure, including a **bus** network and **MRT** metro **trains**, means that you'll have no problem getting into the centre. See the map on p.645 for Singapore's arrival points.

By air

Changi airport is at the far eastern end of Singapore, 16km from the city centre. As well as duty-free shops, moneychanging and left-luggage facilities, the airport boasts a 24-hour post office and telephone service, hotel reservation counters, day rooms for a quick snooze, saunas, business centres and Internet cafés. There are also **car rental agencies** at the airport (see "Listings", p.723), though you'd be advised not to drive around Singapore (see "Transport" p.621, for other alternatives). For **food**, there are several fast-food outlets and, in Terminal One's basement, a food centre – the cheapest and most authentically Singaporean option – for a bite. That said, the likelihood is that you'll barely get the chance to take in the place at all – baggage comes through so quickly at Changi that you can be on a bus or in a taxi within fifteen minutes of arrival.

If you're planning to travel overland into Malaysia, note that Singapore dollar ticket prices on Transnasional Buses and KTM are massively inflated compared to what they would be in Malaysia; KTM actually adopts the pretence that the Singapore dollar is worth the same as the ringgit – an exchange rate that hasn't applied since the 1970s. If you're counting every cent, it's best to take advantage of ringgit fares by catching a bus to Johor Bahru and continuing your journey from the train station there or the Larkin Terminal.

For Changi airport flight enquiries, and the contact details of airlines, travel agencies and the Malay, Indonesian and Thai consulates in Singapore, see "Listings", p.723.

By train

There are air-conditioned trains to KL via JB from Singapore's train station at 8.20am, 1pm and 10.15pm. You can make seat reservations up to one month in advance of departure at the station's information kiosk (daily 8.30am–2.30pm & 3–7pm; ☏62225165). Check the Malaysian Railway (KTM) website to get up-to-the-minute schedule information for all Malaysian trains: ⓦwww.ktmb.com.my.

By bus and taxi

To Malaysia: If you just want to get to Johor Bahru, the easiest way across the causeway is to get the **#170** JB-bound bus from the Ban San Terminal (every 10min; daily 5.30am–midnight; S$1.20) or the plusher air-con **Singapore–Johor Express** (every 10min; 6.30am–midnight; S$2.40), both of which leave every ten minutes or so and take around an hour (including border formalities) to reach their destination. If you're on the #170 bus, hang on to your ticket at immigration so you can use it to resume your journey (not necessarily on the same vehicle) once you're through. These buses terminate at JB's bus station, though it's easier to reach the town centre by leaving the bus at the causeway. From the taxi stand next to the Ban San Terminal, a shared taxi to JB (seating 4) costs S$28, or S$7 a head if you share. Long-distance buses to Peninsular Malaysia are operated by Transnasional (☏62947035) and the Singapore–KL Express (☏62928254), the latter leaving from the Ban San Terminal daily at 9am, 1pm, 5pm and 10pm (6hr; S$23). There are also a handful of luxury bus companies, including Transtar (for KL, Melaka and Penang; ☏62999009, ⓦwww.transtar.com.sg) and Plusliner (for KL; ☏62565755, ⓦwww.plusliner.com). For other destinations in West Malaysia, go to the Lavender Street Terminal or the Golden Mile Complex.

To Thailand: Buses leave early morning from Beach Road's Golden Mile Complex. You can buy a ticket all the way to Bangkok (though it may be cheaper just to buy

---

Before you leave the building, be sure to pick up one of the free **maps** and weekly *This Week Singapore* guides that the Singapore Tourism Board leaves at the airport, plus a copy of the excellent what's on magazine, *Where Singapore*.

Singapore's underground train system extends as far as the airport, and is the most affordable means of getting into the city centre. A single to downtown City Hall station is S$1.40, and shouldn't take more than half an hour. From City Hall interchange you can move on to any part of the island.

The **bus** departure points in the basements of both terminals are well signposted – but make sure you've got the right money before you leave the concourse, as Singapore bus drivers don't give change; take the #36 (daily 6am–midnight, every 10min; S$1.60). The bus heads west to Stamford Road, before skirting the southern side of Orchard Road. Ask the driver to give you a shout at the Capitol Building stop for Beach Road, or at the *YMCA* stop, where you need to cross over Bras Basah Park if you are staying in Bencoolen Street.

one as far as Hat Yai and pay for the rest of the journey in Thai currency once there). Fares to Hat Yai start at around S$30, while Bangkok will set you back around S$80. Try Gunung Raya Travel (☎62947911) or Grassland Express (☎62931166), and don't forget to allow two working days for securing a Thai visa (needed for stays of over fifteen days).

By boat

To Malaysia: From Changi Point (bus #2 to Changi Village), bumboats run to **Kampung Pengerang**, on the southeastern tip of Johor (for access to the beach resort of Desaru, see p.391); boats leave when they're full (daily 7am–4pm; S$6 one-way). A newer, more reliable service departs three times daily for **Tanjung Belungkor**, also in Johor, from the Changi Ferry Terminal (bus #2 to Changi Village, and then a taxi). Run by Cruise Ferries (☎65468518), the service costs S$22 return and takes 45 minutes; check in one hour before departure. Finally, from the Tanah Merah Ferry Terminal (bus #35 from Bedok MRT), there's an 8.35am service (March–Oct daily except Tues & Thurs; Sun–Thurs S$154 return, Fri & Sat S$190 return) to **Tioman Island** (p.395). Penguin Ferry Services (☎62714866). Again, check in one hour before departure.

To Indonesia: Boats to **Batam** in the Riau archipelago depart throughout the day from the HarbourFront Centre (7.30am–10.30pm; S$16 one-way), docking at Sekupang, from where you take a taxi to Hangnadim airport for internal Indonesian flights. There are also several boats a day from the Tanah Merah Ferry Terminal (S$25 one way) to **Tanjung Pinang** on Pulau Bintan, from where cargo boats leave three times a week for Pekanbaru in Sumatra. There are also boat services from Kijang Port, south of Tanjung Pinang, to Jakarta. Information and tickets are available from either Dino Shipping (☎62760668), Bintan Resort Ferries (☎65424369, ⓦwww.brf .com.sg) or Penguin Ferry Services (☎62714866, ⓦwww.penguin.com.sg).

By air

There are direct **flights** from Changi airport to KL, Penang, Langkawi, Kota Kinabalu, Kuching and Bandar Seri Begawan. A departure tax of $15 dollars is levied on all flights out of the island. There are also flights from Seletar airport to Redang and Tiomann islands with Berjaya Air (☎62273688, ⓦwww.berjaya -air.com). If you're planning to head for either Malaysia or Indonesia, it's often quite a bit cheaper to fly from, respectively, **Senai airport** beyond JB (set off in plenty of time to clear immigration formalities and get to the airport) or **Batam** (the nearest Indonesian island).

Taxis from the airport levy a S$3 surcharge on top of the fare, rising to S$5 at the weekend. Again, the taxi rank is well signposted; a trip into downtown Singapore costs around S$15 and takes twenty minutes or so. Another option is to take a **MaxiCab** shuttle into town. These six-seater taxis, equipped to take wheelchairs, depart every fifteen minutes or when full, and will take you to any hotel in the city for a flat fare of S$7 (children S$5).

From **Seletar airport**, in the north of the island, a taxi into town will cost around S$15, plus S$3 airport surcharge, but be prepared to have to make a phone booking upon landing.

By road

Drivers and a few luxury buses using the second causeway from Johor arrive in Singapore along the Ayer Rajah Expressway in the west of the island. But most vehicles, and all trains from Malaysia use the old causeway from JB into Woodlands town in the north, with the **buses** stopping at one of three terminals in Singapore. Local buses from JB arrive at **Ban San Terminal** at the junction of Queen and Arab streets, from where a two-minute walk along Queen Street, followed by a left along Rochor Road, takes you to Bugis MRT station. Buses from elsewhere in **Malaysia** and **from Thailand** terminate at one of two sites, Lavender Street Terminal and the Golden Mile Complex. **Lavender Street Terminal**, at the corner of Lavender Street and Kallang Bahru, is around five minutes' walk from Lavender MRT; bus #145 passes the Lavender Street Terminal on its way down North Bridge Road and South Bridge Road. From outside the **Golden Mile Complex**, take any bus along Beach Road to Raffles City to connect with the MRT system. You'll have no trouble hailing a cab at any of the terminals.

By train

Trains from Malaysia end their journey at the **Singapore Railway Station** on Keppel Road, southwest of Chinatown. Oddly, you haven't officially arrived in Singapore until you step out of the station – the train line is Malaysian territory – and into the street, as a sign above the main station entrance saying "Welcome to Malaysia" testifies. The grounds of Singapore's railway system were sold lock, stock and barrel to the Federated Malay States in 1918, though recently the Singapore government has been buying back segments of it piecemeal. From Keppel Road, bus #97 travels past Tanjong Pagar, Raffles Place and City Hall MRT stations and on to Selegie and Serangoon roads, or you can usually find a cab in the forecourt.

By sea

Boats **from Batam**, in the Indonesian archipelago of Riau (through which travellers from Sumatra approach Singapore) dock at the **HarbourFront Centre**, off Telok Blangah Road, roughly 5km east of the centre. From the adjacent HarbourFront MRT, the city centre is just a few stops away. From Telok

---

The Eastern & Oriental Express

There's no more luxurious way to cover the 1900km from **Singapore to Bangkok** than on the sumptuous **Eastern & Oriental Express** (ⓦ www.orient-express.com), a fairy-tale trip that unashamedly re-creates the pampered days of the region's colonial past. Departing once or twice weekly from Singapore, the Express takes approximately 41 hours to wend its unhurried way to Bangkok's Hualamphong station, stopping at Kuala Lumpur, Ipoh and Butterworth en route. At Butterworth, passengers disembark for a whistle-stop **tour of Penang** by bus and trishaw. On board, guests enjoy breakfast in bed, lunch, tea and dinner, all served by attentive Thai and Malaysian staff in traditional or period garb. There are two bars – one is in the observation carriage at the rear of the train – as well as two luxurious restaurant cars serving Western and Oriental cuisine of a high standard; fortune-tellers, Chinese opera singers and musicians keep you entertained. A word of warning: many guests dress up lavishly for the occasion, so be sure to have suitably **smart clothes** with you or you'll feel decidedly uncomfortable.

The two-night Singapore–Bangkok experience costs from US$600 per person. **Bookings** can be made in Singapore at E&O Services, #32-01/3 Shaw Towers, 100 Beach Rd (ⓣ 63923500), or in Bangkok through Sea Tours Co Ltd, eighth floor, Payatai Plaza, 128 Phyathai Rd (ⓣ 2/2165783).

Blangah Road, bus #97 runs to Tanjong Pagar MRT, bus #65 goes to Selegie and Serangoon roads via Orchard Road, or take bus #166 for Chinatown. Boats from Indonesian **Bintan** dock at the **Tanah Merah Ferry Terminal**, linked by bus #35 to Bedok MRT station.

It's also possible to reach Singapore by boat **from Malaysia**. Bumboats from Kampung Pengerang on the southeastern coast of Johor moor at Changi Village, beyond the airport, from where bus #2 travels into the centre, via Geylang, Victoria and New Bridge roads. Swisher ferries from Tanjung Belungkor, also in Johor, dock at the Changi Ferry Terminal a little way east of Changi Village; from here you'll have to take a taxi, either all the way into town, or into Changi Village to connect with bus #2. Finally, ferries from Tioman Island dock at the Tanah Merah Ferry Terminal.

Information

The Singapore Tourism Board (toll-free ☎1-800/736-2000, ⓦwww .visitsingapore.com) maintains several **Visitors' Centres**, including offices at terminals 1 and 2 at Changi Airport. The main downtown office is at Tourism Court, at the junction of Cairnhill and Orchard roads (daily 9.30am–10.30pm). Other locations include level 1 of Liang Court Shopping Centre, 177 River Valley Road (daily 10.30am–9.30pm), just across the river from Chinatown; #01-35 Suntec City Mall (daily 10am–6pm), close to Beach Road and the Colonial District; and 73 Dunlop Street in Little India (daily 10am–10pm). It's worth dropping in to pick up their free hand-outs and **maps**. The best map of the island is the 1:22,500 Nelles Singapore map, though the *Singapore Street Directory* (with an online version at ⓦwww.streetdirectory.com; S$12.90) is invaluable if you're going to rent a car.

A number of publications offer listings of **events**. Two of these, *Where Singapore* and *This Week Singapore* are available free at hotels all over the island. The "Life!" section of the *Straits Times* has a decent listings section, but best of all are *8 Days* magazine, published weekly (S$1.50), and *I-S*, a free paper published fortnightly.

For information on costs and currency in Singapore see p.46.

Useful websites

ⓦafterdark.hotspots.com Ratings and reviews of Singapore's latest nightspots.
ⓦwww.ehotelsingapore.com Good hotel reservation service with lots of travel information.
ⓦwww.expatsingapore.com A definitive guide to expat life in Singapore.
ⓦwww.getforme.com An excellent portal to all things Singaporean, from local cuisine to info for backpackers.
ⓦwww.visitsingapore.com The Singapore Tourism Board's official site, featuring tour planner, attractions, current events, a virtual tour of the island and an accommodation search by price range.

Transport

All parts of the island are accessible by bus or MRT – the metro train network – and fares are reasonable; consequently, there's little to be gained by renting a car. However you travel, it's best to avoid rush hour (8–9.30am & 5–7pm) if at all possible; outside these times, things are relatively uncongested. The

Transitlink Guide (S$1.50), available from bus interchanges, MRT stations and major bookshops, outlines every bus and MRT route on the island in exhaustive detail. Singapore also has thousands of **taxis** which are affordable and easily available. Though getting around **on foot** is the best way to do justice to the central areas, bear in mind, that you are in the tropics: apply sunscreen if you're fair-skinned, and stay out of the midday sun. Strolling through the remaining pockets of old Singapore entails negotiating uneven five-foot ways (the covered pavements that front Singapore's old shophouses) and yawning storm drains, so watch where you walk.

On a tourist visit you're unlikely to make use of the **LRT** (Light Rail Transit) loop line that links Bukit Panjang New Town to Choa Chu Kang MRT station. It's a suburban feeder line and doesn't serve any of Singapore's tourist attractions.

Most Singaporeans avoid the rigmarole of buying tickets for each bus or MRT journey by purchasing an **ez-link Farecard** – a stored-value card that's valid on all MRT and bus journeys in Singapore, is sold at MRT stations and bus interchanges, and shaves a few cents off the cost of each journey. There's a minimum purchase of S$10 credit and a maximum of S$100; a S$5 deposit is also collected. The cost of each journey you make is automatically deducted from the card when you hold it over a reader as you pass through an MRT barrier or step onto a bus; any credit on the card when you leave Singapore will be reimbursed if you take it to a Farecard outlet at an MRT station. The **Tourist Day Ticket**, available for S$10 from most MRT stations, allows you to take up to twelve bus or MRT rides a day, regardless of distance travelled – though you'd have to do an awful lot of travelling to make this ticket pay.

The MRT (Mass Rapid Transit) System

In terms of cleanliness, efficiency and value for money, the system is second to none – compared to London's tubes or New York's subways, a trip on the MRT is a joy.

The system has three main lines: the north–south line, which runs a vaguely horseshoe-shaped route from Marina Bay up to the north of the island and then southwest to Jurong, the east–west line, connecting Boon Lay in the west to Changi airport in the east; and the new north-east line, linking the HarbourFront Centre on the south coast, to Ponggol in the northeast of the island. Trains run every four to five minutes on average, daily from 6am until midnight. For **information**, enquire at the station control room on any ticket concourse, or call the **MRT Information Centre** toll-free line ☎1-800/336 8900. A **no-smoking** rule applies on all trains, and eating and drinking is also outlawed. Signs in the ticket concourse appear to ban hedgehogs from the MRT; in fact, they signify "no durians" – not an unreasonable request if you've ever spent any time in a confined space with one of these pungent fruits. **Tickets** cost between 60¢ and S$1.80 for a one-way journey. You need coins for the ticket machines, found inside the main hall at each station; adjacent change machines break S$1 and S$2 notes, while larger notes can be changed at the station control room.

Buses

Singapore's **bus** network is slightly cheaper to use than the MRT system, and far more comprehensive – you'll probably spend more time on buses than on trains, and there are several routes that are particularly useful for sightseeing (see box, p.634). Two bus companies operate on the roads of Singapore, both

THE MRT SYSTEM

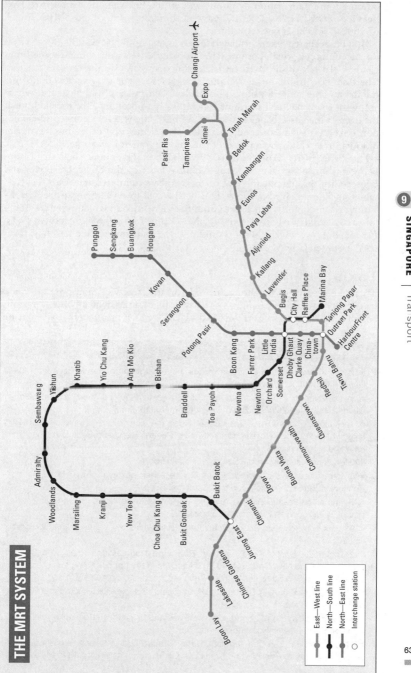

Changi Airport ✈
Expo
Pasir Ris
Tampines
Simei
Tanah Merah
Bedok
Kembangan
Eunos
Paya Lebar
Aljunied
Kallang
Lavender
Bugis
City Hall
Raffles Place
Marina Bay
Tanjong Pagar
Outram Park
HarbourFront Centre
China-town
Clarke Quay
Dhoby Ghaut
Somerset
Orchard
Newton
Little India
Farrer Park
Boon Keng
Potong Pasir
Serangoon
Kovan
Hougang
Buangkok
Sengkang
Punggol
Tiong Bahru
Redhill
Queenstown
Commonwealth
Buona Vista
Dover
Clementi
Jurong East
Chinese Garden
Lakeside
Boon Lay
Bukit Batok
Bukit Gombak
Choa Chu Kang
Yew Tee
Kranji
Marsiling
Woodlands
Admiralty
Sembawang
Yishun
Khatib
Yio Chu Kang
Ang Mo Kio
Bishan
Braddell
Toa Payoh
Novena

East—West line
North—South line
North—East line
○ Interchange station

633

SINGAPORE | Transport

9

offering route information by phone and on the Internet: the **Singapore Bus Service** (SBS; ☎1800-2872727, ⓦwww.sbstransit.com.sg) and SMRT Buses (☎1800-7674333, ⓦwww.smrtbuses.com.sg).

Most buses charge distance-related **fares** ranging from 70¢–S$1.30 (80¢–S$1.60 for air-con buses, which comprise the majority of services), though some buses charge a flat fare as displayed on the destination plates on the front of the bus. There are now **night buses** running along a few major routes across the island; call the hotlines above for more information. Once you've told the driver where you want to go, he'll tell you how much money to drop into the metal chute at the front of the bus. Change isn't given, so make sure you have coins. Some buses don't take cash payments at all; check for signs at the front of the bus. If you are in town for a while, buy an ez-link Farecard or Tourist Day Ticket.

The **Singapore Trolley** (☎63396833), a mock-antique bus that loops between the Botanic Gardens, the Colonial District, the Singapore River and Suntec City throughout the day, offers one day's unlimited travel for S$14.90, which includes a riverboat tour. Finally, kids will love the **Singapore Duck-Tour**, an amphibious craft dating from the Vietnam War, which provides hour-long, land- and sea-bound tours (daily 9.30am–7.30pm; S$33, children S$17; ☎63333825, ⓦwww.ducktours.com.sg) of the civic district and harbour; tours start at Suntec City Mall.

Taxis

There are over eighteen thousand **taxis** on the streets of Singapore, so you'll hardly ever have trouble hailing a cab, day or night. Taxis, which come in various colours and are always clearly marked "TAXI", are all metered, the fare starting

---

Useful bus routes

Below is a selection of handy **bus routes**; note that many of the services from the Orchard Road area actually leave from Penang Road or Somerset Road.

#2 passes along Eu Tong Sen Street (in Chinatown) and Victoria Street (past the Arab Quarter) en route to Changi Prison and Changi Village.

#7 runs along Orchard Road, Bras Basah Road and Victoria Street; its return journey takes in North Bridge Road, Stamford Road, Penang Road and Somerset Road en route to Holland Village.

#36 loops between Orchard Road and Changi airport.

#65 terminates at the HarbourFront Centre, after passing down Jalan Besar, Bencoolen Street, Penang Road and Somerset Road.

#97 runs along Stamford Road to Little India, then on to Upper Serangoon Road; returns via Bencoolen Street and Collyer Quay.

#103 runs between New Bridge Road Terminal (in Chinatown) and Serangoon Road (in Little India).

#124 connects Scotts Road, Orchard Road and North Bridge Road with South Bridge Road and New Bridge Road in Chinatown; in the opposite direction, it travels along Eu Tong Sen Street, Hill Street, Stamford Road and Somerset Road.

#139 heads past Tai Gin Road, via Dhoby Ghaut, Selegie Road, Serangoon Road and Balestier Road.

#167 passes down Scotts Road, Orchard Road and Bras Basah Road, Collyer Quay, Shenton Way and Neil Road (for Chinatown).

#170 starts at the Ban San Terminal at the northern end of Queen Street, passing Bukit Timah Nature Reserve and Kranji War Cemetery on its way to JB in Malaysia.

at S$2.40 for the first kilometre, after which it rises 10¢ for every 225m. However, there are **surcharges** to bear in mind, most notably the fifty percent extra charged on journeys between midnight and 6am. Journeys from Changi airport incur a S$5 surcharge and there's a S$6–8 surcharge for taxis booked over the phone. Electronic tolls levied on journeys along expressways and within the CBD (see below) are also reflected in taxi fares.

On the whole, Singaporean taxi drivers are a friendly enough bunch, but their English isn't always good, so it's a good idea to have your destination written down on a piece of paper if you are heading off the beaten track. If a taxi displays a red destination sign on its dashboard, it means the driver is changing shift and will accept customers only if they are going in his direction. Finally, tourists confined to **wheelchairs** should note that SMRT Taxis (☎65558888) has ten wheelchair-accessible cabs in its fleet.

Driving and cycling

The Singapore government has introduced huge disincentives to driving in order to combat traffic congestion. One of these measures is an Electronic Road Pricing (ERP) programme within the city's Central Business District (**CBD**) – encompassing Chinatown, Orchard Road and the financial zone – between 7.30am and 7pm. If you want to drive into the CBD during these hours, you have to buy a stored-value **CashCard**, available at petrol stations, to cover the electronic tolls that are now automatically levied. Parking, too, is expensive and requires that you purchase coupons from a licence booth, post office or shop.

With all these charges, and given the efficiency of public transport, the only worthwhile reason for **renting a car** in Singapore is to travel up into Malaysia – and even then it's far cheaper to rent in JB, as Singaporean firms levy a S$25 Malaysia surcharge (though note that you can't drive a Malaysian vehicle into the CBD without having an In-Vehicle Unit for CashCards installed at the causeway, an expensive task). If you're still keen on driving in Singapore itself, see the list of rental companies on p.72.

Bike rental is offered by Wheelpower at #01-09 Sunshine Plaza, 91 Bencoolen St (daily 9.30am–7pm; S$28 per day; ☎1800-2382388). There are more rental firms along the East Coast Parkway, where the cycle track that skirts the seashore is always crowded with Singaporeans zooming around in full cycling gear. Expect to pay around S$4–8 an hour for a mountain bike, and bring some form of ID to leave at the office. There are **cycling trails** at Bukit Timah Nature Reserve; Bike & Hike (☎67638382) at 382 Upper Bukit Timah Rd rent out mountain bikes at S$6 an hour. The dirt tracks that criss-cross Pulau Ubin, off Changi Point at the eastern tip of the island, are ideal for biking – a day's rental at one of the cluster of shops near the jetty again costs S$4–8, though the price doubles in school holidays (June, Nov & Dec). Finally, there's a range of bikes – including tandems – available for rent next to the ferry terminal on Sentosa Island (S$2–5 an hour), providing by far the best way to see the island.

Organized tours

Usefully, if you're pushed for time, several reputable operators in Singapore offer **sightseeing tours**. A couple are listed on p.724, or ask at your hotel or the tourist office. Tours vary from one operator to the next, but four-hour city tours typically take in Orchard Road, Chinatown and Little India, and cost around S$30. **Specialist tours** are also available – on such themes as Singapore

Singapore River, island and harbour cruises

A fleet of **cruise boats** ply Singapore's southern waters every day and night. Singapore River Cruise boats (daily 9am–11pm; ☎63366111, ⓦwww.rivercruise.com.sg) cast off from Clark Quay for a S$12 cruise (children S$6) on a traditional bumboat, passing the old godowns upriver where traders once stored their merchandise. A slightly longer cruise that begins at Robertson Quay costs S$15 (children S$8).

Several other cruise companies operate out of Clifford Pier, offering everything from luxury catamaran trips around Singapore's southern isles to dinner on a *tongkang* (Chinese sailing boat). A straightforward cruise will set you back around S$20, and a dinner special S$35–50. If you don't relish the idea of an organized cruise, you can haggle with a bumboat man on Clifford Pier; if you're lucky, he'll take a group up and down the river for S$50 an hour.

Cruise companies
Eastwind Organization ☎63333432
Singapore River Boat ☎63389205
Singapore River Cruises ☎63366111
Watertours ☎65339811

by night, World War II sights, Chinese opera, Asian cuisines and even Feng Shui – costing S$30–80 per person; for details on these, contact the STB.

Members of the Registered Tourist Guides Association (☎63392114) charge S$25–50 an hour (minimum 4hr) for a **personalized tour** – as do the guides of Geraldene's Tours (☎67375250).

Trishaws – three-wheeled bicycles with a carriage on the back – were once a practical transport option in Singapore, though they're a bit of an anachronism these days. You'll still see a few trishaws providing a genuine service around Little India and Chinatown, but most drivers now congregate on the open land opposite the *Summer View Hotel* on Bencoolen Street, from where they'll give you a 45-minute sightseeing ride for S$50.

Accommodation

Room rates take a noticeable leap when you cross the causeway from Malaysia into Singapore, but good deals still abound if your expectations aren't too high or, at the budget end of the scale, if you don't mind sharing. Singapore's status as one of the main gateways to Southeast Asia means that occupancy rates are permanently high. Even so, you shouldn't encounter too many difficulties in finding a room, and advance booking isn't really necessary unless your visit coincides with Chinese New Year or one of the Hari Raya festivals (see p.76).

The **Singapore Hotel Association** (ⓦwww.sha.org.sg) has a booking counter at each of Changi airport's two terminals (Terminal One counter Sat–Thurs 7am–6am, Fri 7am–11.30pm; ☎65426966. Terminal Two counter daily 7am–3am except Mon 7am–11.30pm; ☎65459789); these counters will find you a room in the city for a S$10 deposit that's deducted from your bill at the end of your stay, though they only represent Singapore's official hotels, all of which are listed in two free STB booklets, *Hotels Singapore* and *Budget Hotels Singapore*. Touts at the airport hand out flyers advertising rooms in guesthouses and hostels. It's also possible to book a room online through ⓦwww.singaporehotelbooking.com,

Ⓦwww.stayinsingapore.com.sg or Ⓦwww.hostelworld.com, the last of which is particularly good on backpacker accommodation.

The cheapest beds are in the **dormitories** of Singapore's resthouses, where you'll pay S$10 or less a night. Bedbugs can be a problem and the lights are left burning all night and with a number of cheap decent hostels it's not really worth bothering with one of these. The next best deals are at **guesthouses**, most of which are situated in the Beach Road and Little India areas, with some also south of the river, in Chinatown. A recent makeover of the Bencoolen area has seen most of its guesthouses closed down to make way for new hotels and commercial premises.

Guesthouses aren't nearly as cosy as their name suggests: costing S$20–30, the rooms are tiny, bare, and divided by paper-thin partitions; toilets are shared and showers are cold. However, another S$10–20 secures a bigger, air-con room, and often TV, laundry and cooking facilities, lockers and breakfast are included. Always check that the room is clean and secure, and that the shower and air-con work before you hand over any money. It's always worth asking for a discount, too, and you stand a better chance of a reduction if you are staying a few days. Finally, since guesthouses aren't subject to the same safety checks as official hotels, it's a good idea – without sounding alarmist – to check for a fire escape.

The appeal of Singapore's **Chinese-owned hotels**, similar in price to guesthouses, is their air of faded grandeur – some haven't changed in forty years. Sadly, faded grandeur is something the government frowns upon, with the result that there are precious few left. In more modern, **mid-range hotels**, a room for two with air-con, private bathroom and TV will set you back around S$60–90 a night. From there, prices rise steadily; at the top end of the scale, Singapore boasts some extraordinarily opulent hotels, ranging from the colonial splendour of *Raffles* to the awesome spectacle of the *Swissôtel The Stamford* – until recently the world's tallest hotel. Though you'll find the greatest concentration of upmarket hotels around Orchard Road, most of the new breed of **boutique hotels** – mid-range places that use antique furniture and fittings to create an air of Oriental nostalgia – are based in Chinatown.

Finding an address

With so many of Singapore's shops, restaurants and offices located in vast high-rise buildings and shopping centres, deciphering **addresses** can sometimes be tricky. The numbering system generally adhered to is as follows: #02-15 means room number 15 on the second storey; #10-08 is room number 8 on the tenth storey; ground level is referred to as #01.

Most mid-range and upmarket hotels in Singapore make no charge for children under 12 years old if they are occupying existing spare beds in rooms. However, if you require an extra bed to be put in your room, there's usually an additional charge of ten to fifteen percent of the room rate, though cots are provided free.

Bencoolen Street and around

Bencoolen Street has long been the mainstay of Singapore's backpacker industry. Times are changing, though, and many of the decrepit hotels that once housed the lion's share of Singapore's budget guesthouses have already fallen to the demolition ball and been replaced by posher hotels. *Peony Mansion*, the classic Singapore crash pad, is still limping along, despite news of its imminent demise having floated around for the past half decade.

Although there's no longer the concentration of backpacker-targeted places this area once boasted, for the moment you'll still find dorm beds and rooms as cheap as any in Singapore. Bencoolen Street is a five-minute walk southeast from Dhoby Ghaut MRT station. See the "Little India & the Arab Quarter" map on pp.672–673.

Albert Court Hotel 180 Albert St ☎63393939, ⓦwww.albertcourt.com.sg. This charming boutique hotel, designed around the restaurants of lively Albert Court Mall, is just a short walk from both Bugis Village and Little India; rooms have all the standard embellishments. **❼**

Bencoolen Hotel 47 Bencoolen St ☎63360822, ⓦwww.hotelbencoolen.com. Great-value, fairly upmarket option, with business centre, laundry service, flight-booking facilities and smart rooms equipped with all mod cons. **❹**

City Bayview 30 Bencoolen St ☎67372882, ⓦwww.bayviewintl.com. Following recent renovations, there are comfortable rooms, a compact rooftop swimming pool and a friendly, modern café in this pleasing, mid-range hotel. **❺**

Hawaii Hostel Second floor, 171b Bencoolen St ☎63384187. Small, tidy enough air-con rooms with breakfast included, plus dorm beds for S$12. **❷**

Lee Boarding House Seventh floor, *Peony Mansions*, 46–52 Bencoolen St ☎63383149. *Peony Mansions*' last remaining guesthouse, with bare but clean enough rooms, a breakfast area and laundry facilities. If you want a dorm bed you'll need to go to the *Hawaii Hostel* or one of the *Lee* branches on Beach Road. **❷**

South East Asia Hotel 190 Waterloo St ☎63382394, ⓦwww.seahotel.com.sg. Behind a yellow and white 1950s facade, spotless doubles with air-con, TV and phone for those yearning for a few creature comforts. Downstairs is a vegetarian restaurant serving Western breakfasts, and right next door is Singapore's liveliest Buddhist temple. **❹**

Strand Hotel 25 Bencoolen St ☎63381866, ⓦwww.strandhotel.com.sg. Excellent-value hotel with clean, welcoming rooms, a café serving Western and local dishes and a variety of services. **❹**

Summer View Hotel 173 Bencoolen St ☎63381122, ⓦwww.summerviewhotel.com.sg. The future face of Bencoolen Street: a smart but unpretentious 100-room hotel with all the facilities the budget-minded traveller might need (café, car rental, valet services, currency exchange and tour desk), but none of the needless frills that push up prices. **❺**

Waterloo Hostel Fourth floor, Catholic Centre Building, 55 Waterloo St ☎63366555, ⓦwww .waterloohostel.com.sg. Catholic-run hostel, centrally located, spick-and-span, and boasting rooms with air-con, TV and phone. Complementary breakfast is thrown in. The mixed and single-sex dorms (S$15–20) are as welcoming as any in Singapore. **❹**

Beach Road to Victoria Street

A few blocks east of Bencoolen Street, **Beach Road** boasts a full range of accommodation options, from charismatic old Chinese hotels to swish, new, five-star affairs. What's more, you can brag about having stayed down the road from the *Raffles Hotel* – or even in it – when you get home. See the "Little India & the Arab Quarter" map on pp.672–673.

Ah Chew Hotel 496 North Bridge Rd ☎68370356. Simple but charismatic rooms with "Wild West" swing doors, crammed with period furniture, and run by T-shirted old men lounging on antique opium couches. There are also fan and air-con dorms (S$8–12), baggage storage and self-service laundry facilities. Try and get a room at the front of the building – despite its address, the *Ah Chew* is just around the corner from North Bridge Road, on buzzing Liang Seah Street. ❷

Aliwal Park Hotel 77 Aliwal St ☎62939022, ✉aliwal@pacific.net.sg. One of the few hotels in the Arab Street district, the *Aliwal* has spruce doubles with TV, air-con and attached bathrooms, at competitive prices. ❸

Beach Hotel 95 Beach Rd ☎63367712, ⓦwww.beachhotel.com.sg. The Lee Empire's most salubrious address is professionally run and very tidy. The location in the CBD is not quite as atmospheric as a Chinatown or Colonial District address, but central nonetheless. ❹

Golden Landmark Hotel 390 Victoria St ☎62972828, ⓦwww.goldenlandmark.com.sg. Very pleasant and well appointed, once you get past the dated shopping centre downstairs. Also handy for Bugis MRT station and Arab Street. ❺

Intercontinental 80 Middle Rd ☎63387600, ⓦwww.intercontinental.com. Opulent hotel within the thriving Bugis Junction development, convenient and sumptuously furnished, with swimming pool, health club and an array of excellent restaurants. ❽

Lee Home Stay Third floor, 490a North Bridge Rd ☎63041000. Bare but adequate rooms and dorms (S$10), whose rates include free flow of hot drinks – but no breakfast or hot showers. All rooms share common facilities. The rooftop terrace makes a pleasant place to relax. To enter, walk to the back of the curry house below, and up the stairs to your left. ❷

Lee Traveller's Club Sixth floor, Fu Yuen Building, 75 Beach Rd ☎63395490. A bright and breezy common room overlooking Middle Road sets this place a cut above the other *Lee* addresses in the area. All rooms have air-con, but private facilities cost an extra S$10. Laundry service is available. Dorm beds are S$12. ❷

Metropole Hotel 41 Seah St ☎63363611, ⓦwww.metrohotel.com. Friendly, great-value establishment, just across the road from *Raffles Hotel* and home to the recommended *Imperial Herbal Restaurant* (see p.709). ❺

New 7th Storey Hotel 229 Rochor Rd ☎63370251, ⓦwww.nsshotel.com. Despite its rather old-fashioned exterior, this is a clean and characterful hotel with perfectly respectable rooms, all with TV. Rooms with bathrooms en suite are available, though the communal ones are fine. Booking online saves a few dollars; dorm beds are S$17. ❹

Oxford Hotel 218 Queen St ☎63322222, ⓦwww.oxfordhotel.com.sg. Terrific well-run 135-room hotel, centrally sited, well-serviced, friendly and affordable; prices are inclusive of breakfast. Recommended. ❹

Plaza Park Royal 7500 Beach Rd ☎62980011, ⓦwww.plaza.singapore.parkroyalhotels.com. Luxurious, eye-catching hotel whose amenities include restaurants, and a business centre. Slightly off the beaten track, though there is a free shuttle service into town. ❼

Raffles Hotel 1 Beach Rd ☎63371886. ⓦwww.raffleshotel.com. The flagship of Singapore's tourism industry, *Raffles* is a beautiful place, dotted with frangipani trees and palms, and the suites (there are no rooms) are as tasteful as you would expect at these prices. See p.650 for more details. ❾

△ *Raffles Hotel*

The Colonial District

A handful of expensive hotels stand at the edges of the Padang, just north of the Singapore River. Several of them – including the *Marina Mandarin* and *Oriental* – stand on the reclaimed land which robbed Beach Road of its beach. See maps on pp.660–661 and pp.672–673.

Conrad Centennial Singapore 2 Temasek Blvd ⊕63348888, ⓦwww.conradhotels.com. This relatively recent arrival has elbowed its way into the very top ranks of the island's hotels; all imaginable comforts can be found within its monolithic structure. ❽

Fullerton Hotel 1 Fullerton Sq ⊕67338388, ⓦwww.fullertonhotel.com. Chic, harmonious rooms that show an awareness of the *Fullerton's* heritage (see p.670). Luxury extras include in-room Playstations and Net access on the TVs. An expensive treat. ❾

Marina Mandarin Hotel 6 Raffles Blvd ⊕63383388, ⓦmarina-mandarin.com.sg. Top-flight hotel, architecturally interesting and affording great harbour views; the atrium is particularly impressive. ❽

Oriental Singapore 5 Raffles Ave ⊕63380066, ⓦwww.mandarinoriental.com. Housed, likethe *Marina Mandarin*, in what's claimed to be Southeast Asia's largest shopping centre and hotel complex, Marina Square, the *Oriental* is one of Singapore's priciest hotels, but with very good reason: the rooms are exquisitely furnished, the views out over Marina Bay are breathtaking and all the luxuries you could want are on hand. ❾

Peninsular Excelsior Hotel 5 Coleman St ⊕63372200, ⓦwww.ytchotels.com.sg/sp-ytcexcel. Really two hotels merged together – hence the name – this place is as handy for the Financial District as for Orchard Road's shopping centres. There are several food outlets (best is the excellent *Annalakshmi* Indian vegetarian restaurant), and a swimming pool whose glass walls abut the lobby lounge. ❼

Summer Tavern 31 Carpenter St ⊕65366601, ⓦwww.summertavern.com. Justifiably popular hostel in a prime location near the quays. The best feature is the relaxed ground-floor lounge stuffed with leatherette sofas and serving beer, but the dorms are comfy and there are several double rooms too. Free Internet access. Dorms are large and comfy, and there are several double rooms as well; all have a/c and share well-maintained facilities. Prices include breakfast. Dorm beds S$22, ❹

Swissôtel The Stamford 2 Stamford Rd ⊕63388585, ⓦwww.singapore-stamford .swissotel.com. Upper-floor rooms aren't for those with vertigo, though the views are as splendid as you'd expect from the second tallest hotel in the world. There are over a thousand classy rooms here, oodles of restaurants and bars, and an MRT station downstairs. ❾

Orchard Road and around

Sumptuous hotels abound in and around **Orchard Road**; at all except a handful, you should be prepared to spend at least S$90 a double. You can multiply that figure by four or five, though, if you decide to treat yourself. See the map on pp.680–681.

The Elizabeth 24 Mount Elizabeth ⊕67381188, ⓦwww.theelizabeth.com .sg. Within its toy-town exterior, this boutique hotel oozes panache; the rooms are delightful and well appointed. ❼

Goodwood Park Hotel 22 Scotts Rd ⊕67377411, ⓦwww.goodwoodparkhotel.com.sg. Don't be surprised if this opulent hotel reminds you of *Raffles* – both were designed by the same architect. The building is a study in elegance, its arching facades fronting exquisitely appointed rooms. ❾

Holiday Inn Park View 11 Cavenagh Rd ⊕67338333, ⓦwww.singapore.holiday-inn.com. Guests of this smart hotel with all the trimmings

are next-door neighbours of Singapore's president for the duration of their stay as the Istana is just across the road. ❼

Lloyd's Inn 2 Lloyd Rd ⊕67377309, ⓦwww .lloydinn.com. Motel-style building with attractive rooms and a fine location, just five minutes' walk up Killiney Road from Orchard Road. ❹

Meritus Mandarin Hotel 333 Orchard Rd ⊕67374411, ⓦwww.mandarin-singapore.com. Every luxury you could hope for; even if you don't stay, take a trip up to the top floors for the magnificent view of central Singapore. ❽

Metropolitan Y 60 Stevens Rd ⊕67377755, ⓦwww.mymca.org.sg. Not as central as the *Y* on

Orchard Road, but perfectly adequate rooms with air-con, bathroom, TV and minibar. Suitable for travellers in wheelchairs. **5**

🏃 **New Sandy's Place** 3c Sarkies Rd ☏ 67341431, ⓦ www.geocities.com /sandysplacesingapore. Rooms are all very tidy in this friendly, laid-back place, set across a field from Newton MRT. Expect to pay S$15 over the basic rate for air-con. The price includes a fruit breakfast. It's best to phone ahead. **3**

The Regent Singapore 1 Cuscaden Rd ☏ 67338888, ⓦ www.regenthotels.com. At the western end of Orchard Road, the elegant rooms of this sumptuous hotel are a short stroll from the Botanic Gardens. **8**

Shangri-La Hotel 22 Orange Grove Rd ☏ 67373644, ⓦ www.shangri-la.com. Top-flight hotel whose 700-plus rooms are set in six hectares of landscaped greenery, only five minutes from Orchard Road. **9**

Singapore Marriott 320 Orchard Rd ☏ 67355800, ⓦ www.marriotthotels.com/SINDT. A superior hotel and a Singapore landmark, housed in a 33-storey pagoda-style building next to the C.K.Tang department store. **8**

Sloane Court Hotel 17 Balmoral Rd ☏ 62353311, ⓔ sloane@singnet.com.sg. As close to a Tudor house as Singapore gets, the *Sloane Court* is tucked away in a prime residential area, near Newton MRT. Rooms are cosy and well appointed. **4**

Hotel Supreme 15 Kramat Rd ☏ 67378333, ⓔ supremeh@starhub.net.sg. A great-value budget hotel, well placed at the eastern end of Orchard Road, offering laundry and room service among its many facilities. **4**

YMCA International House 1 Orchard Rd ☏ 63366000, ⓦ www.ymcai.org.sg. Smack-bang in the middle of town, and looking all the jollier for a recent lick of paint, the *YMCA* offers lush but overpriced rooms, excellent sports facilities (including rooftop pool) and free room service from the *McDonald's* downstairs. The dorm beds (S$25) are the most expensive in town, though. Bus #36 from the airport stops right outside. **4**

YWCA Fort Canning Lodge 6 Fort Canning Road ☏ 63384222, ⓦ www.ywcafclodge.org.sg. Not women-only, as you might imagine, but still a secure and friendly place with pool and tennis courts – and just a stone's throw from Dhoby Ghaut MRT. Pass up the dorm beds, though, which are a rip-off at S$45 a head. **5**

Little India

Little India, along with Chinatown, has become the budget hotel centre of Singapore. What's more, the Little India and Farrer Park MRT stations mean this colourful enclave is very accessible. All the places below are marked on the map on pp.672–673.

Ali's Nest 23 Roberts Lane (☏ 62912938). Grubby, shambolic, but undeniably welcoming homestay, one minute from Farrer Park MRT, where rooms and dorm beds (S$10) share common bathrooms. Prices include breakfast and free flow of hot drinks. **2**

Dickson Court 3 Dickson Rd ☏ 62977811, ⓦ www.dicksoncourthotel.com.sg. With smart, well-furnished rooms off tight courtyard corridors, the *Dickson Court* is pretty good value; most corners of central Singapore are accessible from the bus stop across the road on Jalan Besar. **4**

Fortuna Hotel 2 Owen Rd ☏ 62953577, ⓔ fortunac@singnet.com.sg. Mid-range hotel offering brilliant value for money; facilities include a health centre and secretarial services. **4**–**5**

Haising Hotel 37 Jalan Besar ☏ 62981223. Set between Dunlop and Dickson roads, the *Haising* offers plain but spotless rooms and air-con dorms (S$20). Ask the friendly front desk staff about self-service laundry (S$10). **3**–**4**

🏃 **Inn Crowd Hostel I** 35 Campbell Lane ☏ 62969169, ⓦ www.the-inncrowd.com. Singapore's best guesthouse, thanks to scrupulous cleanliness, its peerless facilities and the warm welcome extended by owners, Ping and Hui. Guests have free use of the kitchen and free Net access, and lockers are available for long-term rental. If the one double room is taken you'll have to take a dorm bed (S$18). Highly recommended. **2**

Inn Crowd Hostel II 73 Dunlop St ☏ 62969169, ⓦ www.the-inncrowd.com. Just around the corner from the original, this place is just as well run, with spotless common areas and comfortable dorm beds for S$18.

Julia's Guesthouse Zaman Centre, 1–5a Roberts Lane ☏ 98534790. Friendly, clean, carpeted joint with ten rooms, but not a patch on the *Inn Crowd*. Dorm beds are S$10. **2**

Kerbau Hotel 54–62 Kerbau Rd ☏ 62976668, ⓔ kerbauinn@pacific.net.sg. Friendly place, if rather dark, with spruce and welcoming rooms; discounts for stays of three days or more. **4**

Perak Lodge 12 Perak Rd ☏ 62997733, @www.peraklodge.net. One of the new breed of upper-bracket guesthouses, set within an atmospheric blue-and-white shophouse in a back street behind the Little India Arcade and run by friendly staff. The rooms are secure, well appointed and welcoming, and the price includes a continental breakfast. Downstairs is an airy, residents-only living area. Recommended. ❹

Sleepy Sam's 55 Bussorah St ☏ 92774988, @www.sleepysams.com. Welcoming and surprisingly stylish hostel, located in a row of traditional houses round the corner from the Sultan Mosque. *Sam's* offers a kitchen for self-caterers and a decent café for anyone else; laundry service, free Internet access and safe deposit box facilities. Dorms (mixed and female-only) from S$25. ❹

Chinatown and around

The range of budget and mid-range accommodation in **Chinatown** has grown in inverse proportion to that of Bencoolen Street's. Whatever your budget, you're sure to find an address to suit you in this most charismatic of enclaves, which contains a mass of upmarket hotels that benefit from their proximity to the Financial District. The following places are all shown on the map on pp.660–661.

Backpacker Hotel 11a Mosque St ☏ 62246859. Unremarkable rooms in an equally unremarkable place that nevertheless locates you bang in the middle of Chinatown. ❷

Chinatown Hotel 12–16 Teck Lim Rd ☏ 62255166, @www.chinatownhotel .com. Intimate boutique hotel with smart rooms and a well-stocked business centre. The remodelled facade gives a hint at what this original shophouse building looked like. Inside, everything is clean and new. ❹

Damenlou Hotel 12 Ann Siang Rd ☏ 62211900 @www.damenlou.com. Given its lovingly restored 1925 facade, the twelve compact but well-appointed rooms in this friendly hotel are surprisingly modern. After a pre-dinner drink overlooking Chinatown on the rooftop garden, head down to the excellent *Swee Kee* restaurant on the ground floor (see p.707). ❺

Dragon Inn 18 Mosque St ☏ 62227227, ☏ 62226116. Sizeable, comfortable double rooms in the middle of Chinatown, all with a/c, TV, fridge and bathroom, and set in attractive shophouses. Try to avoid rooms backing onto the central air shaft, which houses many noisy a/c units. ❹

Gallery Hotel 76 Robertson Quay ☏ 68498686, @www.galleryhotel.com .sg. Extravagantly lit with neon stripes at night, and boasting striking modern architecture, the *Gallery* is getting listed in the trendy "hip hotel" coffee-table books. The pool is to die for, some of Singapore's coolest nightspots are onsite, and all the urban-chic rooms offer free broadband access. Recommended. ❽

Grand Copthorne Waterfront 392 Havelock Rd ☏ 67330880, @www.millenniumhotels.com. The *Grand Copthorne* demands consideration: its

500-plus rooms are piled up above a selection of riverfront restaurants, a short stroll along the river from the nightspots of Clarke Quay. ❽

Hotel 1929 50 Keong Saik Rd ☏ 62223377, @www.hotel1929.com. This old shophouse building looks very 1929 on the outside, but the interior has been renovated to look like a twenty-first century version of the early 1960s; it's very retro chic and all tastefully done with a hip, boutique feel about it. Recommended. ❽

The Inn at Temple Street 36 Temple St ☏ 62215333, @www.theinn.com.sg. Glossy and grand inside, this boutique hotel has been sculpted out of a row of Chinatown shop-houses. Its owners have filled it to bursting with furnishings and curios from old Singapore. Recommended. ❺–❻

New Majestic Hotel 31–37 Bukit Pasoh Rd ☏ 62223377, @www .newmajestichotel.com. This Chinatown classic has recently undergone major renovations, giving the interior a stylish, modern makeover that would not be out of place in New York or London. If you're looking for a hip boutique hotel, this is probably it. ❼

Robertson Quay Hotel 15 Merbau Rd ☏ 67353333, @www.robertsonquayhotel .sg. Cylindrical riverside hotel, whose compact but inviting rooms off circular corridors yield great views of the river and city skyline. There's a cute circular pool with slide and waterfall on the third floor terrace. Can't be faulted. ❺

Royal Peacock Hotel 55 Keong Saik Rd ☏ 62233522, @www.royalpeacockhotel.com. The silky, sassy elegance of this place recalls the days when Keong Saik Road was a red-light district. Sculpted from ten shophouses, it's a superb boutique hotel, with great rooms, a bar, café and business services. ⑤

Traveller's Rest Stop 5 Teck Lim St, ☎62254812, ⓕ62254813. In a wedge-shaped building with some palpable Chinatown atmosphere, this place has clean rooms and brightly lit corridors, and benefits from nice touches like watercolours of old Chinatown, TVs and fridges. ④

The East Coast: Geylang and Katong

Geylang and Katong, along Singapore's southeastern coast, have traditionally both been Malay-dominated areas. If you can't face the noise and the bustle of central Singapore, this region might appeal – certainly its cool sea breezes and Malay markets are an advantage. MRT and buses connect you quickly with downtown Singapore.

Century Roxy Park Singapore 50 East Coast Rd ☎63448000, ⓦwww.centuryhotels.com. One of the east Coast's more upmarket options, located midway between the city and Changi airport. The design theme is contemporary Asian, the rooms sophisticated, and the choice of restaurants varied. ⑦

Fragrance Hotel 219 Joo Chiat Rd ☎63449888, ⓦwww.fragrancehotel.com. Behind its chocolate-box exterior, a bright and cheery place whose clean rooms boast fresh sheets, sparkling bathrooms, TV, air-con and fridge. One of a chain of hotels in this part of Singapore. ④–⑤

Hotel 81 Joo Chiat 305 Joo Chiat Rd ☎63488181, ⓦwww.hotel81.com.sg. Housed in a beautifully restored Peranakan building in cream and burgundy, *Hotel 81* offers rooms pleasant enough for any self-respecting businessperson, but at a fraction of the prices of the heavyweights downtown. Check out their website for details of the chain's many other properties. ④

Sing Hoe Hotel 759 Mountbatten Rd ☎64400602, ⓕ63465996. Beautifully kept colonial house, with attractive reliefs on its external walls. Rooms are air-con but be sure to ask for one facing the side or back gardens for a leafy view. ③

Sentosa

Three luxury hotels on the island of **Sentosa** allow you to bypass the bustle of downtown Singapore. You can get a taxi direct from the airport to Sentosa (though note that from 7am to 10pm a S$3 surcharge is levied). For details of public transport to the island, see p.700.

Sentosa 2 Bukit Manis Rd ☎62750331, ⓦwww.beaufort.com.sg. A swanky hotel, elegantly appointed and fitted out in varnished wood and bounded by two 18-hole golf courses and a beach. Prices go up by S$40 on Fri and Sat. The Spa Botanica makes it the perfect place for a pampering getaway. ⑧

Shangri-La Rasa Sentosa Resort ☎62750100, ⓦwww.shangri-la.com. Opened in 1993, the *Rasa Sentosa* is the first hotel in Singapore to have its own beachfront, and its situation on Sentosa Island makes it a good option if you've got kids to amuse. Adults might prefer to check out the spa or seasports centre. Prices take a S$21 hike on Friday and Saturday, and rooms with sea view cost extra. ⑧

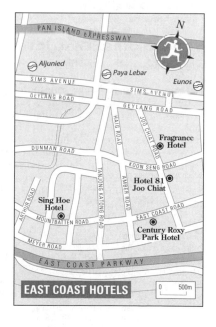

EAST COAST HOTELS

0   500m

Sijori Resort Sentosa 23 Beach View ☎62712002, ⓦwww.sijoriresort.com.sg. Sentosa's latest accommodation option, the *Sijori* is slap-bang in the middle of the island, making it an ideal base for exploring. There's a lovely pool, should you tire of theme parks and adventure rides. ⑥–⑦

Camping

Changi Beach Camping at Changi and East Coast Parkway is free, but you'll need to be issued a permit on weekdays. Park rangers make the rounds and issue the permits to campers, checking up on things daily. This is done to keep people from squatting in the park. At weekends and on public holidays rangers don't bother to register campers.

East Coast Parkway Free camping for up to three consecutive nights, once you've obtained a permit from the bicycle kiosk near car park C3 near *McDonald's* (Mon–Sat 10am–7pm, Sun 11am–2pm; ☎64487120).

Downtown Singapore

Ever since Sir Stamford Raffles first landed on its northern bank, in 1819, the area around the Singapore River, which strikes into the heart of the island from the south coast, has formed the hub of Singapore. All of Singapore's central districts lie within a three-kilometre radius of the mouth of the river – which makes **downtown Singapore** an extremely convenient place to tour. Although buses and MRT trains do run between these districts, you might find that you prefer to explore the whole central region on foot. You need at least two days to do full justice to the main areas: the **Colonial District**, **Chinatown** and the **Central Business District**, **Little India** and the **Arab Quarter**; while Singapore's commercial mecca, **Orchard Road**, can occupy a single morning, or several days, depending on how much you enjoy shopping.

The Colonial District

The Padang, north of the Singapore River, is the very nexus of the **Colonial District**, flanked by dignified reminders of British rule. The view from here is a panorama that defines Singapore's past and present. In the foreground is the Singapore Cricket Club – the epitome of colonial man's stubborn refusal to adapt to his surroundings. Behind that, the river snakes westwards and inland, passing the last few surviving godowns from Singapore's original trade boom. Towering high above all this are the spires of the modern business district; also to the south are Empress Place Building and the Old Parliament House. To the north is the grand old *Raffles Hotel*, beyond which a string of nineteenth- and twentieth-century churches leads to Singapore's famous entertainment centre, Bugis Village. Heading west, you pass City Hall and the former Supreme Court before climbing the slopes of Fort Canning Hill, ten minutes' walk from the Padang, and one of the few hills in Singapore not yet lost to land reclamation. If it sounds as if the twenty-first century is totally absent amid all these echoes of the past, then think again; the district's more modern buildings don't do things by half – the *Swissôtel*, on Stamford Road, was until recently the world's tallest hotel, while the Theatres on the Bay complex is as spectacular and contemporary an arts centre as you'll find anywhere in the world.

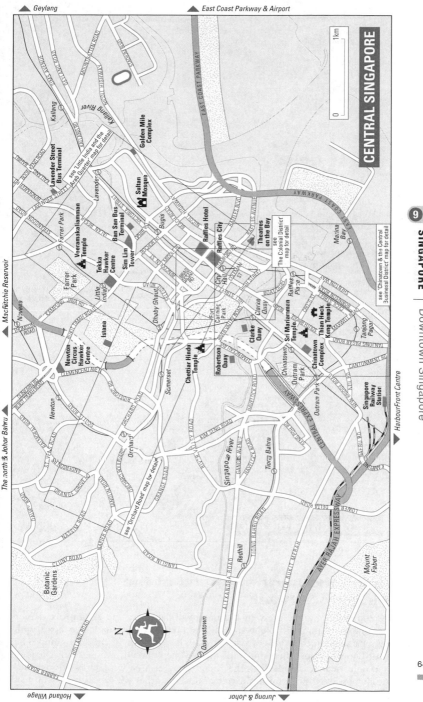

CENTRAL SINGAPORE

▲ Geylang

▲ East Coast Parkway & Airport

▲ The north & Johor Bahru

▲ MacRitchie Reservoir

▲ Holland Village

▲ Jurong & Johor

▼ HarbourFront Centre

Kallang River

Kallang

Golden Mile Complex

Lavender Street Bus Terminal

Farrer Park

Sultan Mosque

see Little India and the Arab Quarter map for detail

Veerasamakaliamman Temple

Ban San Bus Terminal

Tekka Hawker Centre

Sim Lim Tower

Little India

Raffles Hotel

Raffles City

Bugis

Theatres on the Bay

Marina Bay

see The Colonial District map for detail

see 'Chinatown & the Central Business District' map for detail

Dhoby Ghaut

City Hall

Farrer Park

Istana

Newton Circus Hawker Centre

Newton

Fort Canning Park

Chettiar Hindu Temple

Clarke Quay

Robertson Quay

Clarke Quay

Sri Mariamman Temple

Chinatown Complex

Raffles Place

Thian Hock Keng Temple

Chinatown

Outram Park

Tanjong Pagar

Cantonment

Orchard

Somerset

see 'Orchard Road' map for detail

Singapore River

Tiong Bahru

Outram Park

Singapore Railway Station

Central Expressway

Botanic Gardens

Redhill

Queenstown

Ayer Rajah Expressway

Mount Faber

N

0   1km

SINGAPORE | Downtown Singapore

9

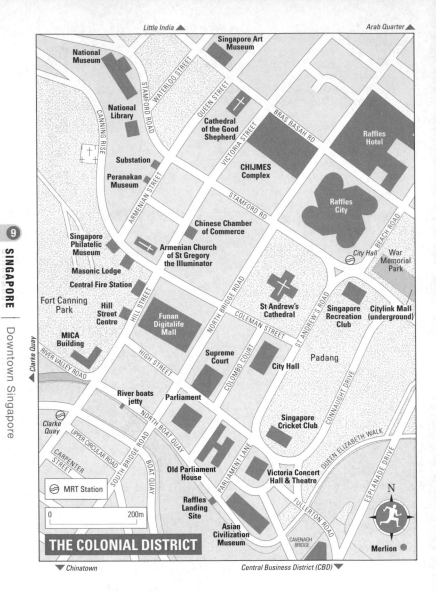

Little India ▲

Arab Quarter ▲

National Museum

Singapore Art Museum

STAMFORD ROAD

WATERLOO STREET

QUEEN STREET

BRAS BASAH RD

Raffles Hotel

CANNING RISE

National Library

VICTORIA STREET

Cathedral of the Good Shepherd

CHIJMES Complex

Raffles City

BEACH ROAD

Substation

ARMENIAN STREET

Peranakan Museum

STAMFORD RD

Chinese Chamber of Commerce

City Hall

War Memorial Park

Singapore Philatelic Museum

Armenian Church of St Gregory the Illuminator

NORTH BRIDGE ROAD

Masonic Lodge

Central Fire Station

HILL STREET

St Andrew's Cathedral

ST ANDREW'S ROAD

Singapore Recreation Club

Citylink Mall (underground)

Fort Canning Park

Hill Street Centre

Funan Digitalife Mall

COLEMAN STREET

MICA Building

HIGH STREET

COLOMBO COURT

Supreme Court

City Hall

Padang

▲ Clarke Quay

RIVER VALLEY ROAD

CONNAUGHT DRIVE

⊖ **Clarke Quay**

UPPER CIRCULAR ROAD

NORTH BOAT QUAY

River boats jetty

Parliament

Singapore Cricket Club

QUEEN ELIZABETH WALK

CARPENTER STREET

SOUTH BRIDGE ROAD

BOAT QUAY

PARLIAMENT LANE

Old Parliament House

Victoria Concert Hall & Theatre

ESPLANADE DRIVE

⊖ **MRT Station**

0   200m

Raffles Landing Site

FULLERTON ROAD

N

Asian Civilization Museum

CAVENAGH BRIDGE

Merlion ●

THE COLONIAL DISTRICT

▼ Chinatown

Central Business District (CBD) ▼

Along the northern bank of the Singapore River

As the colony's trade grew in the nineteenth century, the **Singapore River** became its main artery, clogged with bumboats – traditional cargo boats with eyes painted on their prows, as if they are looking where they are going. The boat pilots ferried coffee, sugar and rice to the godowns, where coolies loaded and unloaded sacks. Indeed, in the 1880s the river itself was so busy it was practically possible to walk from one side of it to the other without getting your feet wet. These days, with most of the bumboats gone (a few remain to offer trips upriver), the river is quieter, cleaner and inevitably less charismatic, though parts of both banks have undergone a profound commercial revitalization as new restaurants and bars move into the formerly abandoned buildings.

From the Raffles Place MRT station, it's just a couple of minutes' walk past the former GPO, to the elegant suspension struts of **Cavenagh Bridge** – a good place to start a tour of Singapore's colonial centre. Named after Major General Orfeur Cavenagh, governor of the Straits Settlements from 1859 to 1867, the bridge was constructed in 1869 by Indian convict labourers using imported Glasgow steel. Times change, but not necessarily on the bridge, where a police sign still maintains: "The use of this bridge is prohibited to any vehicle of which the laden weight exceeds 3cwt and to all cattle and horses."

Stepping off the bridge, you're confronted by **Empress Place Building**, a robust Neoclassical structure named after Queen Victoria and completed in 1865. It served for ten years as a courthouse before the Registry of Births and Deaths and the Immigration Department moved in. Today it houses the **Asian Civilization Museum** (Mon 1–7pm, Tues–Thurs, Sat & Sun 9am–7pm, Fri 9am–9pm; S\$5/2.50 including free guided tour Mon 2pm, Tues-Fri 11am & 2pm, Sat & Sun 11am, 2pm & 3.30pm; ✆63327798, ⓦwww.nhb.gov.sg/acm). The ACM traces the origins and growth of Asia's many and varied cultures. Its ten themed galleries hold nearly two thousand artefacts bringing to life the religions, history and cultures of every corner of Asia, from South Asia to Southeast Asia, and from Islamic West Asia to China. Temporary exhibitions in the Special Exhibitions Gallery allow the curator to drill down further into specific facets of Asian life and culture. There is also an engaging Singapore River Interpretive Gallery, featuring oral history accounts of the river delivered by individuals from generations that lived beside it and worked it all their lives.

The time capsule in the grounds in front of the building was sealed in 1990 as part of Singapore's silver jubilee celebrations. It contains "significant items" from Singapore's first 25 years of independence: the clever money says that when opened it will yield a Lee Kuan Yew speech or two. The southern flank of the Empress Place Building has been appropriated by the all-conquering *Indochine* bar and restaurant chain. Its string of Khmer-influenced outlets afford peerless views of the Singapore River.

Next door to the Empress Place Building, stand two fine examples of colonial architecture, the **Victoria Concert Hall** and adjoining **Victoria Theatre**, still the venues for some of Singapore's most prestigious cultural events. The theatre was originally completed in 1862 as Singapore's town hall, while the concert hall was added in 1905 as a tribute to the monarch's reign. During the Japanese occupation, the clock tower here was altered to Tokyo time, while the statue of Raffles that once stood in front of the tower only narrowly escaped being melted down. The newly installed Japanese curator of the National Museum (where the statue was sent) valued it sufficiently to hide it and report it destroyed.

Further inland, along North Bank Quay, a copy of the statue marks the **landing site** where, in January 1819, the great man apparently took his first steps on Singaporean soil. Sir Stamford now stares contemplatively across the river towards the business district. Singapore River Cruise boats (see p.636) depart from a tiny jetty a few steps along from Raffles' statue.

North of the statue up Parliament Lane, the dignified white Victorian building on the left ringed by fencing is **Old Parliament House**, built as a private dwelling for a rich merchant by Singapore's pre-eminent colonial architect, the Irishman George Drumgould Coleman, who was named the settlement's superintendent of public works in 1833. Relieved of its legislative duties, the building now goes under the name of the **Arts House** and is home to cafés, shops, galleries and film/theatre space. The bronze elephant in front of Parliament House was a gift to Singapore from King Rama V of Thailand (upon whose father *The King and I* was based) after his trip to the island in 1871 – the first foreign visit ever made by a Thai monarch. It is sometimes possible to watch Singapore's parliament in session in the new Parliament House, across Parliament Lane from its predecessor; call ℗63368811 or 63326666 for details, or check out Ⓦwww.parliament.gov.sg.

The Padang

The **Padang**, earmarked by Raffles as a recreation ground shortly after his arrival, is the very essence of colonial Singapore. Such is its symbolic significance that its borders have never been encroached upon by speculators and so it remains much as it was in 1907, when G.M. Reith wrote in his *Handbook to Singapore*, "Cricket, tennis, hockey, football and bowls are played on the plain … beyond the carriage drive on the other side, is a strip of green along the sea-wall, with a foot-path, which affords a cool and pleasant walk in the early morning and afternoon." Once the last over of the day had been bowled, the Padang would have assumed a more social role: the image of Singapore's European community hastening to the corner once known as Scandal Point to catch up on the latest gossip is pure Somerset Maugham. As an April Fool's Day joke in 1982, the *Straits Times* reported that the Padang was to be sold off for development; the ensuing public outcry jammed the newspaper's switchboard. Today the Padang is still kept pristine by a bevy of gardeners on state-of-the-art lawnmowers.

The brown-tiled roof, whitewashed walls and dark green blinds of the **Singapore Cricket Club**, at the southwestern end of the Padang, have a nostalgic charm. Founded in the 1850s, the club was the hub of colonial British society and still operates a "members only" rule, though there's nothing to stop you watching the action from outside on the Padang. The Singapore Rugby Sevens are played here, as well as a plethora of other big sporting events and parades; a timetable of forthcoming events is available at the club's reception. Eurasians who were formerly ineligible for membership of the cricket club founded their own establishment instead in 1883: the **Singapore Recreation Club**, which lies across on the north side of the Padang. The current grandiose, colonnaded clubhouse dates back to a S$65 million overhaul completed in 1997.

Just to the west of the cricket club, Singapore's erstwhile **Supreme Court** (formerly the site of the exclusive *Hotel de L'Europe*, whose drawing rooms allegedly provided Somerset Maugham with inspiration for many of his Southeast Asian short stories) was built in Neoclassical style between 1937 and 1939, and sports a domed roof of green lead and a splendid, wood-panelled entrance hall. Since its replacement opened a block back, on Northbridge Road, early in the new millennium, the building has sat idle, awaiting a fresh purpose. The Sir Norman Forster-designed **New Supreme Court** is also worthy of note, though more for its impressive, flying saucer-shaped upper tier than for its lumpen, marble and glass main body.

Next door to the former Supreme Court is the older **City Hall**, whose uniform rows of grandiose Corinthian columns lend it the austere air of a mausoleum and reflect its role in recent Singaporean history. It was on the steps of this building that Lord Louis Mountbatten (then supreme allied commander

The Sepoy Mutiny

Plaques on the west wall of St Andrew's Cathedral commemorate the victims of one of Singapore's bloodiest episodes, the **Sepoy Mutiny** of 1915. The mutiny began when a German warship, the *Emden*, was sunk by an Australian ship off the Cocos Islands: its survivors were brought to Singapore and imprisoned at Tanglin Barracks, at the western end of Orchard Road. With almost all of Singapore's troop contingent away in Europe fighting the Kaiser, soldiers of the Fifth Light Infantry, called **sepoys** – whose members were all Muslim Punjabis – were sent to guard the prisoners. Unfortunately, these men's allegiance to the British had recently been strained by the news that Muslim Turkey had come out against the Allies in Europe. A rumour that they were soon to be sent to Turkey to fight fellow Muslims upset them still further, and the German prisoners were able to incite the sepoys to mutiny. In the ensuing rampage through the city on February 15, 1915, the sepoys killed forty soldiers and civilians before they were finally rounded up by some remaining European sailors and a band of men led by the Sultan of Johor. All were court-martialled and 36 sepoys were executed before huge crowds. As for the Germans, they took the opportunity to effect an escape. Nine of them finally got back to Germany via Jakarta and one, Julius Lauterbach, received an Iron Cross in recognition of his daring and rather convoluted flight home through China and North America.

in Southeast Asia) announced Japan's surrender to the British in 1945; fourteen years later, Lee Kuan Yew chose the same spot from which to address his electorate at a victory rally celebrating self-government for Singapore. Nowadays, rather less dramatic photographs are taken on the steps as newlyweds line up to have their big day captured in front of one of Singapore's most imposing buildings. Like the old Supreme Court, City Hall currently lies empty – presumably awaiting rebirth as a museum or arts space.

The final building on the west side of the Padang, **St Andrew's Cathedral** on Coleman Street, gleams even brighter than the rest. The third church on this site, the cathedral was built in high-vaulted, Neo-Gothic style, using Indian convict labour, and was consecrated by Bishop Cotton of Calcutta on January 25, 1862. Its exterior walls were plastered using Madras *chunam* – an unlikely composite of eggs, lime, sugar and shredded coconut husks which shines brightly when smoothed – while the small cross behind the pulpit, a later addition, was crafted from two fourteenth-century nails salvaged from the ruins of England's Coventry Cathedral after it was razed to the ground during World War II. Closed-circuit TVs allow the whole congregation to view proceedings up at the altar – a reflection of the Chinese fascination with all things hi-tech, since the cathedral's size hardly requires it.

Esplanade – Theatres on the Bay

Singapore's skyline seems to change almost by the day, but rarely has a building caused such ripples as the new, S\$600 million **Esplanade – Theatres on the Bay** project (www.esplanade.com), which occupies six hectares of waterfront land in the downtown Civil District. Esplanade boasts a concert hall, theatre, recital studio, theatre studio, gallery space and outdoor theatre. The Esplanade Mall threads round these various auditoria, offering shopping, eating and drinking and making the complex as much a social hub as a cultural landmark. From the waterfront restaurants and bars on the south side of the complex, there are peerless views across the bay. On the third floor is **library@esplanade**, a performing arts library with a wide range of arts-related resources.

Opinion is split on whether the two huge, spiked shells that roof the complex are peerless modernistic architecture or plain indulgent kitsch. They have variously been compared to hedgehogs, kitchen sieves, golf balls, huge microphones, even mating aardvarks; locals have taken to calling them "the durians", though they are perhaps best described as resembling two giant insects' eyes.

The idea for an integrated national arts centre was first mooted in the 1970s. The project's radical architecture was unveiled to the Singaporean public in 1994, and work began officially in 1996. The gala opening night, in October 2002, saw thousands of Singaporeans turn out for a spectacular fireworks display. In giving this ambitious project a green light, the government has upped the ante in its attempts to nurture a unified Singaporean culture. The authorities are viewing Esplanade as an iconic statement of Singapore's developing nationhood.

Should you decide to investigate Esplanade's monthly schedule, you'll find a varied programme of events spanning jazz, Asian dance, pipe organ recitals, classical ballet, Broadway musicals and contemporary drama. Real theatre buffs might enjoy the 45-minute **guided tours** (Mon–Fri 11am & 2pm, Sat & Sun 11am; S$8/5; ☎68288377) of the area that start from the Concourse Information Counter.

Raffles City and Raffles Hotel

North of the Theatres on the Bay is **Raffles City**, a huge development that sits beside the intersection of Bras Basah and North Bridge roads and comprises two hotels – one of which is the 73-storey *Swissôtel* – as well as a multilevel shopping centre and floor upon floor of offices. Completed in 1985, the complex was designed by Chinese-American architect I.M. Pei – the man behind the glass pyramid which fronts the Louvre in Paris – and required the highly contentious demolition of the venerable Raffles Institution, a school established by Raffles himself and built in 1835 by George Drumgould Coleman. The **Swissôtel** holds an annual vertical marathon, in which hardy athletes attempt to run up to the top floor in as short a time as possible: the current record stands at under seven minutes. Elevators transport lesser mortals to admire the view from the sumptuous bars and restaurants on the top floor. The open land east of Raffles City is home to the imposing **Civilian War Memorial**, comprising four seventy-metre-high white columns; it's known locally as "the chopsticks".

If the *Swissôtel* is one of the tallest hotels in the world, across the way is perhaps the most famous. The lofty halls, restaurants, bars, and peaceful gardens of the legendary **Raffles Hotel**, almost a byword for colonialism, prompted Somerset Maugham to remark that it "stood for all the fables of the exotic East". Oddly, this inherently British hotel started life as a modest seafront bungalow belonging to an Arab trader, Mohamed Alsagoff. After a spell as a tiffin house run by an Englishman called Captain Dare, the property was bought in 1886 by the Sarkies brothers, enterprising Armenians who eventually controlled a triumvirate of quintessentially colonial lodgings: the *Raffles* in Singapore, the *Eastern & Oriental* in Penang, and the *Strand* in Rangoon.

Raffles Hotel opened for business on December 1, 1887, and quickly began to attract an impressive list of guests. It is thought that Joseph Conrad stayed in the late 1880s, and certainly Rudyard Kipling visited soon after, though at that stage the hotel couldn't, it seems, boast such sumptuous rooms as in later years. "Let the traveller take note," wrote Kipling, "feed at *Raffles* and stay at the *Hotel de l'Europe*". The hotel had its heyday during the first three decades of the twentieth century, a time which saw it firmly establish its reputation for luxury and elegance – it was the first building in Singapore with electric lights and fans. In 1902, a little piece of Singaporean history was made at the hotel, according to an apocryphal tale, when the last tiger to be killed on the island was shot inside the building. Thirteen years later, bartender Ngiam Tong Boon created another *Raffles* legend, the "Singapore Sling" cocktail. The rich, famous and influential have always patronized the hotel, but despite a guest list heavy with politicians and film stars, the hotel is proudest of its literary connections. Herman Hesse, Somerset Maugham, Noel Coward and Günter Grass all stayed at *Raffles* at some time – Maugham is said to have written many of his Asian tales under a frangipani tree in the garden.

During World War II, British expatriates who had gathered in *Raffles* as the Japanese swept through the island in 1942 were quickly made POWs, and the hotel became a Japanese officers' quarters. After the Japanese surrender in 1945, *Raffles* became a transit camp for liberated Allied prisoners. Postwar deterioration earned it the affectionate but melancholy soubriquet, "grand old lady of the East", and the hotel was little more than a shabby tourist diversion when the government finally declared it a national monument in 1987. A S$160-million facelift followed and the hotel reopened on September 16, 1991.

The new-look *Raffles* gets a very mixed reception. Though the hotel retains much of its colonial grace, the shopping arcade which now curves around the back of the building lacks class, selling *Raffles*-related souvenirs, exclusive garments, leatherware and perfume. Still, if you're in Singapore, there's no missing *Raffles* and, assuming you can't afford to stay here, there are other ways to soak up the atmosphere. A free **museum** (daily 10am–9pm), located upstairs, at the back of the hotel complex, is crammed with memorabilia, much of which was recovered in a nationwide heritage search which encouraged Singaporeans to turn in souvenirs that had found their way up sleeves and into handbags over the years. Otherwise, a Singapore Sling in the Bar and Billiards Room – one of thirteen food and beverage outlets in the hotel – will cost you around S$20.

Bras Basah Road and the Singapore Art Museum

Bras Basah Road cuts northwest from *Raffles*, crossing North Bridge Road and then passing one of Singapore's most aesthetically pleasing eating venues, the **CHIJMES** complex. The many bars and restaurants are based around the Neo-Gothic husk of the former Convent of the Holy Infant Jesus (from whose name the acronym for the complex is derived). Its lawns, courtyards, waterfalls, fountains and sunken forecourt give a sense of spatial dynamics that is rare indeed in Singapore. A relic from CHIJMES' convent days survives on its Victoria Street flank, where local families left unwanted babies at the **Gate of Hope**, to be taken in by the convent. Many were "Tiger Girls", so called because they were born in a year of the tiger and were therefore thought to bring bad luck to their families. CHIJMES' shops and boutiques open between 9am and 10pm, the restaurants and bars from 11am to 1am.

Beyond CHIJMES, Bras Basah crosses Victoria and Queen streets, where elderly trishaw drivers in yellow T-shirts tout for custom, before arriving at the **Singapore Art Museum** (daily 10am–7pm, Fri til 9pm; S$3 including free tour, Mon 2pm, Tues-Thurs 11am & 2pm, Fri 11am, 2pm & 7pm, Sat & Sun 11am, 2pm & 3.30pm; ☎63323222, ⓦwww.singart.com) at 71 Bras Basah Road. A long-overdue replacement for the tired art wing of the National History Museum, the Art Museum has a peerless location in the former St

Let it still be the boast of Britain
to write her name in characters of light;
let her not be remembered as the tempest
whose course was desolation,
but as the gale of spring reviving
the slumbering seeds of mind and
calling them to life
from the winter of ignorance and oppression.
If the time shall come
when her empire shall have passed away,
these monuments will endure when her triumphs
shall have become an empty name.

This verse, written by **Sir Stamford Raffles** himself, speaks volumes about the man whom history remembers as the founder of modern Singapore. Despite living and working in a period of imperial arrogance and self-motivated land-grabbing, Raffles maintained an unfailing concern for the welfare of the people under his governorship, and a conviction that British colonial expansion was for the general good – that his country was, as Jan Morris says in her introduction to Maurice Collis's biography *Raffles*, "the chief agent of human progress . . . the example of fair Government."

Fittingly for a man who was to spend his life roaming the globe, Thomas Stamford Raffles was born at sea on July 6, 1781, on the *Ann*, whose master was his father Captain Benjamin Raffles. By his fourteenth birthday, the young Raffles was working as a clerk for the **East India Company** in London, his schooling curtailed due to his father's debts. Even at this early age, Raffles' ambition and self-motivation was evident as, faced with a lifetime as a clerk, he resolved to educate himself, staying up through the night to study and developing a hunger for knowledge which would later spur him to learn Malay, amass a vast treasure trove of natural-history artefacts, and write his two-volume *History of Java*.

Abdullah bin Kadir, Raffles' clerk while in Southeast Asia, described him in his autobiography, the *Hikayat Abdullah*: "He was broad of brow, a sign of his care and thoroughness; round-headed with a projecting forehead, showing his intelligence. He had light brown hair, indicative of bravery; large ears, the mark of a ready listener. . . He was solicitous of the feelings of others, and open-handed with the poor. He spoke in smiles. He took the most active interest in historical research. Whatever he found to do he adopted no half-measures, but saw it through to the finish."

Raffles' diligence and hard work showed through in 1805, when he was chosen to join a team going out to Penang, then being developed as a British entrepôt; overnight, his annual salary leapt from £70 to £1500. Once in Southeast Asia, Raffles' rise was meteoric: by 1807 he was named chief secretary to the governor in Penang.

Joseph's Institution, Singapore's first Catholic school, whose impressive semicircular front and silvery dome rang to the sounds of school bells and rote learning until 1987. Though extensions have been necessary, many of the original rooms survive, among them the school chapel (now an auditorium), whose Stations of the Cross and mosaic floor remain intact. The school quad, the former gymnasium, periodically displays statues and sculptures such as the tuberous glassworks of American designer Dale Chihuly.

The Art Museum's rolling schedule of visiting collections brings work by such acclaimed artists as Marc Chagall and the sculptor Carl Milles. But

Soon Lord Minto, the governor-general of the East India Company in India, was alerted to Raffles' Oriental expertise. Meeting Minto on a trip to Calcutta in 1810, Raffles was appointed secretary to the governor-general in Malaya; this promotion was quickly followed by his appointment as governor of Java in 1811. Raffles' rule of Java was wise, libertarian and compassionate, his economic, judicial and social reforms transforming an island bowed by Dutch rule.

Post-Waterloo European rebuilding saw the East Indies returned to the Dutch in 1816 – to the chagrin of Raffles, who foresaw problems for British trade should the Dutch regain their hold on the area. From Java, Raffles transferred to the governorship of Bencoolen, on the southern coast of Sumatra, but not before he had returned home for a break, stopping at St Helena en route to meet Napoleon ("a monster"). While in England he met his second wife, Sophia Hull (his first, Olivia, had died in 1814), and was knighted.

Raffles and Sophia sailed to Bencoolen in early 1818, Sophia reporting that her husband spent the four-month journey deep in study. Once in Sumatra, Raffles found the time to study the region's flora and fauna as tirelessly as ever, discovering the *Rafflesia arnoldi* – "perhaps the largest and most magnificent flower in the world" – on a jungle field trip. By now, Raffles felt strongly that Britain should establish a base in the Straits of Melaka; meeting Hastings – Minto's successor – in late 1818, he was given leave to pursue this possibility and in 1819 duly sailed to the southern tip of the Malay Peninsula, where his securing of Singapore early that year was a daring masterstroke of diplomacy.

For a man whose name is inextricably linked with Singapore, Raffles spent a remarkably short time on the island. His first stay was for one week, the second for three weeks, during which time he helped delineate the new settlement. Subsequent sojourns in Bencoolen ended tragically with the loss of four of his five children to tropical illnesses, and his own health began to deteriorate. Raffles visited Singapore one last time in late 1822, his final public duty there being to lay the foundation stone of the Singapore Institution (later the Raffles Institution), an establishment created to educate local Malays, albeit upper-class ones.

By August 1824, he was back in England. Awaiting news of a possible pension award from the East India Company, Raffles spent his free time founding the **London Zoo** and setting up a farm in Hendon. But the new life he had planned for Sophia and himself never materialized. Days after hearing that a Calcutta bank holding £16,000 of his capital had folded, his pension application was refused; worse still, the company was demanding £22,000 for overpayment. Three months later, on July 4, 1826, the brain tumour that had caused him headaches for several years took his life. Buried at Hendon, he was honoured by no memorial tablet – the vicar had investments in slave plantations in the West Indies and was unimpressed by Raffles' friendship with William Wilberforce. Only in 1832 was Raffles commemorated, by a statue in Westminster Abbey.

greater emphasis is placed on contemporary local and Southeast Asian artists and artwork. Indeed, the museum's real strength lies in its mapping of the Asian experience. Only a selection from the collection is displayed at any one time, but works you may be lucky enough to catch include Bui Xuian Phai's *Coalmine*, an unremittingly desolate memory of his labour in a Vietnam re-education camp, and Srihadi Sudarsono's *Horizon Dan Prahu*, in which traditional Indonesian fishing boats ply a Rothkoesque canvas. Look out, too, for local artist, Liu Kang's sketches and paintings of postwar kampung life in Singapore.

Outside the museum, the souvenir shop stocks prints and postcards, and there's a classy branch of *Dôme*, where you can have a coffee under the watchful gaze of a statue of the seventeenth-century saint, John Baptist de la Salle, which stands over the museum's porch.

Waterloo Street and Bugis Village

Semi-pedestrianized **Waterloo Street** is at its best on Sundays, springing to life as worshippers throng to its temples and churches. Thanks to an expansion and modernization project back in 1982, **Kuan Yim Temple**, named after the Buddhist goddess of mercy, may not have the cluttered altars, dusty rafters and elaborate roofs of Chinatown's temples, but it remains one of Singapore's most popular. Thousands of devotees flock to the temple every day, and all along the pavement outside, old ladies in floppy, wide-brimmed hats sell them fresh flowers from baskets. Religious artefact shops on the ground floor of the apartment building opposite are well placed to catch worshippers on their way out – one shop specializes in small shrines for the house: the deluxe model boasts flashing lights and an extractor fan to expel unwanted incense smoke. **Fortune-tellers** and street traders operate along this stretch of the road, too, and look out for the cage containing turtles and a sleepy old snake: make a donation, touch one of the creatures inside, and it's said that good luck will come your way.

Sri Krishnan Temple, next door, began life in 1870, when it amounted to nothing more than a thatched hut containing a statue of Lord Krishna under a banyan tree. Nearing a century and a half later, it is a popular venue for Hindu weddings. Now called **Sculpture Square**, the unassuming church across Middle Road from the temple was erected in the 1870s as the Christian Institute, where residents could debate and read about their faith. After a short stint as the focal point of Singapore's Methodist missionaries, the building became a girls' school in 1894, before transforming into a Malay church. Today, its grounds and interior gallery space feature modernist works by local artists. The courtyard café out back makes a peaceful place to break up a day's sightseeing.

One block east of Waterloo Street's shops and temples, at the junction of Rochor Road and Victoria Street sits **Bugis Village** – a rather tame manifestation of infamous Bugis Street. Until it was demolished to make way for an MRT station, Bugis Street embodied old Singapore: after dark it was a chaotic place, crawling with rowdy sailors, transvestites and prostitutes – anathema to a Singapore government keen to clean up its country's reputation. Singaporean public opinion demanded a replacement, though when Bugis Village opened in 1991, it was revealed as a shadow of its former self, its beer gardens, restaurants and stalls drawing a largely negative local reaction and only a modest stream of tourists. Today, Bugis Village is reduced to little more than a dull crossroads of market stalls and snack sellers. The transvestites are noticeable only by their absence, and even the weak cabaret shows of the *Boom Boom Room* nightclub have gone.

Hill Street and Armenian Street

From Stamford Road, **Hill Street** heads south to the river, flanking the eastern side of Fort Canning Park. The **Singapore Chinese Chamber of Commerce**, at 47 Hill Street, a brash, Chinese-style building from 1964 featuring a striking pagoda roof, lies 30m down on the left. Along its facade are two large panels, each depicting nine intricately crafted porcelain dragons flying from the sea up to the sky. By way of contrast, the tiny Armenian **Church of St Gregory the Illuminator**, across the road and next to the former American Embassy, was designed by George Drumgould Coleman in 1835 (which makes it one of the oldest buildings in Singapore). Inside is a single, circular chamber, fronted by a marble altar and a painting of the Last Supper. Among the white gravestones and statues in the church's frangipani-scented gardens is the tombstone of Agnes Joaquim, a nineteenth-century Armenian resident of Singapore, after whom the national flower, the delicate, purple Vanda Miss Joaquim orchid is named; she discovered the orchid in her garden, and had it registered at the Botanic Gardens.

The **Central Fire Station**, a stone's throw from the Armenian Church, across Coleman Street at 62 Hill Street, is a splendid red and white striped edifice. When it was first built in 1908, the watchtower was the tallest building in the region, making it easy for firemen to scan the downtown area for fires. Though the station remains operational, part of it is now taken up by the Civil Defence Heritage Galleries (Tues–Sun 10am–5pm, free), which trace the history of fire fighting in Singapore from the formation of the first Voluntary Fire Brigade in 1869. The galleries display old helmets, extinguishers, hand-drawn escape ladders and steam fire engines, all beautifully restored and buffed up; and upstairs there are explanations of current equipment and practices. Of most interest, though, are the accounts of the island's two most destructive fires. The first of these was the Bukit Ho Swee fire of 1961, which claimed four lives and sixteen thousand homes when it ripped through a district of atap thatched huts and timber yards. This led directly to a public housing scheme that spawned today's network of new towns and HDB blocks. The second was the blaze in Robinson's department store in Raffles Place, in 1972, when a short circuit in old wires led to the deaths of nine people.

Directly behind the Central Fire Station on Coleman Street, Singapore's **Masonic Lodge** with its colonial facade of moulded garlands and protractors, sits beside the cream walls of the **Singapore Philatelic Museum** (Mon 1–7pm, Tues–Sun 9am–7pm; S$3/2; ℡63373888; Ⓦwww.spm.org.sg). The museum occupies Singapore's former Methodist Book Room, which date back to 1906. Although clearly a niche destination, it manages to use its stamp collection imaginatively to highlight facets of the multicultural history and heritage of Singapore. The **National Archives Building** (Mon–Fri 9am–5.30pm, Sat 9am–1.30pm; free; ℡63327973; Ⓦwww.nhb.gov.sg/NAS), next door at 1 Fort Canning Rise, houses enough records, documents, maps and photographs to keep the most committed amateur historian busy for weeks. Much of the NAS collection of over three thousand audio-visual history accounts is available to the public, allowing access to fascinating interviews on such subjects as vanishing Singaporean trades, the Japanese occupation and traditional performing arts.

Given its past, it seems appropriate that the spectacular colonial-era mansion, fronted by two black eagles, around the corner on Armenian Street, should house a museum. Dating from 1910, the building was once home to the Tao Nan School, the first school in Singapore to cater for new arrivals from the Hokkien region of China. The old school gates are displayed upstairs. When it reopens in 2008, the museum's galleries will provide a cultural and historical context to Singapore's Peranakan community.

Adjacent to the museum, the **Substation**, a disused power station, has been converted into a multimedia arts centre. Even if you don't have the time to check out its classes, discussions and performances, the coffee shop is a pleasant place to hang out for a while. A market takes place in the courtyard every Sunday afternoon, with stalls selling anything from local crafts to secondhand Russian watches.

National Museum

Turning left at the end of Armenian Street, you'll see the eye-catching dome of stained glass that tops the entrance to the **National Museum** on Stamford Road (T63323659, Wwww.nationalmuseum.sg). As this book went to press, the museum was due to reopen after a three-year, top-to-bottom overhaul that added a gallery theatre and a public sculpture garden. The museum's forerunner, the Raffles Museum and Library, was opened in 1887 and soon acquired a reputation for the excellence of its natural history collection. In 1969, the place was renamed the National Museum in recognition of Singapore's independence, and subsequently altered its bias towards local history and culture. Out front, a stack of silver triangles marks the site of the "Singapore at the turn of the millennium" capsule, to be opened in January 2050; near it stands a chunky slate statue of Tai chi boxers by Taiwanese sculptor, Ju Ming.

Fort Canning Park and around

When Raffles first caught sight of Singapore, **Fort Canning Park** was known locally as Bukit Larangan (Forbidden Hill). Malay annals tell of the five ancient kings of Singapura, said to have ruled the island from here six hundred years ago, and archeological digs have unearthed artefacts that prove it was inhabited as early as the fourteenth century. The last of the kings, Sultan Iskandar Shah, reputedly lies here, and a *keramat*, or auspicious place, on the eastern slope of the hill marks the supposed site of his grave – though the simple stone tomb doesn't look very auspicious. It was out of respect for – and fear of – his spirit that the Malays decreed the hill forbidden, and these days the *keramat* still attracts a trickle of Singaporean Muslims, as well as childless couples who offer prayers here for fertility.

However, when the British arrived, Singapore's first British Resident, William Farquhar, displayed typical colonial tact by promptly having the hill – then named Government Hill – cleared and building a bungalow, Government House, on the summit. The bungalow was subsequently replaced in 1859 by a fort named after Viscount George Canning, governor-general of India, but of this only a gateway, guardhouse and adjoining wall remain today. An early European **cemetery** survives, however, upon whose stones are engraved intriguing epitaphs to nineteenth-century sailors, traders and residents, among them pioneering colonial architect George Coleman. In colonial times, the report of a 68-pound artillery gun fired at Fort Canning Hill marked the hours of 5am, noon and 7pm.

History apart, Fort Canning Park is spacious and breezy and offers respite from, as well as fine views of, Singapore's crowded streets. Most visitors approach the park from Stamford Road, to the north, but there's a "back entrance" to the park, which involves climbing the exhausting flight of steps that runs from beside the MICA Building on Hill Street. Once you reach Raffles Terrace at the top, there's a brilliant view along High Street towards the mouth of the river.

The hill, which houses two theatres, cannons, the colonial flagstaff and a lighthouse, is ringed by two walks, signs along which illuminate aspects of the park's fourteenth- and nineteenth-century history. If you circumnavigate the park, look out for some truly magnificent **old trees** on the western (River Valley) side. There's also a nod to more recent wartime history.

The Battle Box

On the northwest flank of Fort Canning Hill lies the **Battle Box** (Tues–Sun 10am–6pm; S$8/5), the underground operations complex from which the

Allied war effort in Singapore was masterminded. The exhibition uses audio and video effects and animatronics to bring to life the events leading up to the decision by British officers to surrender Singapore to Japanese occupation, on February 15, 1942. Authentic, if a little clunky, it provides an engaging enough context to Singapore's darkest hour.

Conceived as a gas- and bomb-proof operations chamber, the Battle Box was completed in October 1939, and became a part of the Malaya Command World War II Headquarters. Following faithful restoration of its 26 rooms, the complex now conveys a palpable sense of the claustrophobia and tension suffered by the British as the Japanese bore down upon Singapore.

The experience gets off to a low-key start, with a history lesson on a small TV set whose muddy sound is barely audible over the buzzing air-con unit. Thankfully, things look up once you proceed to the chambers themselves. First stop is the switchboard and exchange room, where an animatronic signalman is hard at work patching through messages from bases at Changi, Pulau Bukum and Pulau Blakang Mati (modern-day Sentosa). Next door, in the cipher rooms, the air crackles with the rat-tat-tat of Morse sets and the furious tapping of typewriters, cipher machines and coding machines. Meanwhile, soldiers shift Jap fighter planes around a huge map of Malaya in the operations room, like croupiers raking up chips in a casino.

The Battle Box reaches a theatrical climax in the conference room, where more life-sized figures act out the debate that convinced Lieutenant-General Arthur Percival that surrender was the only option open to him.

River Valley Road

Fort Canning Park's southern boundary is defined by **River Valley Road**, which skirts below the park from Hill Street. At its eastern end is the **MICA Building** – formerly the Hill Street Police Station, but now home to the Ministry of Information, Communications and the Arts. The MICA Building's rows of shuttered windows are painted a rainbow of colours, making it a

△ Sandal shop on Arab Street

vibrant addition to the riverfront area; its central atrium houses several galleries majoring in Asian artworks. Further west, River Valley sweeps past **Clarke Quay**, a chain of nineteenth-century godowns, or warehouses, renovated into a shopping and eating complex. Unless a mooted makeover is successful, nearby Boat Quay (see p.670) will remain the better bet for evening drinks and fine dining. Clarke Quay's problem is that it touts itself as a riverside dining experience, yet its geography means that most of its outlets have no sightline of the water. The mushroomy rain canopies that have recently sprouted, and the gaudy banquette-style seating that have been laid out along the riverside have done nothing to help the ambience. The arrival of *Hooters* bar and the topless shows at *Crazy Horse* nightclub hint at a more adult-oriented future for Clarke Quay. **GMAX**, Singapore's first ever bungie jump (Mon–Fri 3pm–12am, Sat & Sun noon–12am; S\$50; ☎63381146; ⓦ www.gmax.com.sg) is probably best sampled before, rather than after, you settle into one of Clarke Quay's many bars and restaurants. River taxis for Clarke Quay (daily 11am–11pm; S\$3) depart every five minutes from several quays further down the river (see p.636).

Robertson Quay, further inland from Clarke Quay, is extending the gentrifications of the Singapore River. Already, restaurants, bars and hotels are amassing beside its banks – though one or two pleasingly tumbledown godowns still survive, inland of Pulau Saigon Bridge.

The **Chettiar Hindu Temple** (daily 8am–noon & 5.30–8.30pm), a minute's walk further west at the intersection of River Valley and Tank roads, is the goal of every participant in Singapore's annual *Thaipusam* festival (see p.676). This large temple is dedicated to Lord Subramaniam and boasts a wonderful *gopuram* or bank of sculpted gods and goddesses. Built in 1984, it replaced a nineteenth-century temple built by Indian *chettiars* (moneylenders); inside, 48 glass panels etched with Hindu deities line the roof.

Chinatown

The two square kilometres of **Chinatown**, bounded by New Bridge Road to the west, Neil and Maxwell roads to the south, Cecil Street to the east and the Singapore River to the north, once constituted the focal point of Chinese life and culture in Singapore. Nowadays the area is on its last traditional legs, scarred by the wounds of demolition and dwarfed by the Central Business District, where the island's city slickers oversee the machinations of one of Asia's most dynamic money markets. Even so, a wander through the surviving nineteenth-century streets still unearths musty and atmospheric temples, traditional craft shops, clan associations and old-style coffee shops and restaurants. Provision stores crammed with birds' nests, dried cuttlefish, ginger, chillies, mushrooms and salted fish do a brisk trade, and you might still hear the rattle of a game of mahjong being played.

The area was first earmarked for settlement by the Chinese community by Sir Stamford Raffles himself, who decided that the ethnic communities should live separately on his second visit to the island in June 1819. As increasing numbers of immigrants poured into Singapore, Chinatown became just that – a Chinese town, where new arrivals from the mainland – mostly from the Kwangtong (Canton) and Fujian (Fukien) provinces – would have been pleased to find temples, shops, and most importantly, *kongsi* (clan associations), which helped them to find food, lodgings and work, mainly as small traders and coolies. The prevalent architectural form was the **shophouse**, a shuttered building whose moulded facade fronted living rooms upstairs and a shop on the ground floor. By the mid-twentieth century, the area southwest of the Singapore River was

Songbirds

One of the most enduringly popular of Singaporean hobbies is the keeping and train-ing of **songbirds,** and every Sunday morning scores of enthusiasts – and their birds – congregate at an unnamed nondescript coffee shop on the corner of Tiong Bahru and Seng Poh roads, just west of Chinatown. Songbird competitions are common-place in Singapore, but this gathering is an informal affair with bird owners coming to show off their pets and admire those of fellow collectors. The exquisite cages that house the birds are hung on a metal frame that fronts the coffee shop. Birds are grouped according to their breed, lest they pick up the distinctive songs of other breeds. The various types of bird you'll see include the delicate green mata puteh, or "white-eye bird"; the jambul, with its showy black crest and red eye-patches; and the sharma, which has beautiful, long tail feathers. You can have toast and coffee at the café while watching and listening to the proceedings, which start around 6am – a good early-morning start to a tour around nearby Chinatown. To get there, catch bus #851, which passes along Tiong Bahru Road, from North Bridge Road, or hop in a cab. The other central Sunday songbird venue is Sturdee Road, off Petain Road, which lies between Serangoon Road and Jalan Besar in Little India.

rich with the imported cultural heritage of China; but with independence came ambition: the government regarded the tumbledown slums of Chinatown as an eyesore and embarked upon a catastrophic **redevelopment** campaign that saw whole roads bulldozed to make way for new shopping centres, and street traders relocated into organized complexes.

Only in the last decade has public opinion finally convinced the Singaporean authorities to restore rather than redevelop Chinatown. There are some reno-vated buildings that remain faithful to their original designs, though there's a tendency to render once characterful shophouses improbably perfect. The latest problem to threaten the fabric of Chinatown is spiralling rents, which have driven out all but a last few remaining families and traditional businesses, leaving the area open for full exploitation by bistros, advertising agencies and souvenir shops. Ironically, if you want to get a taste of the old ways of Chinatown, you'll need to spurn its central streets and head into the surrounding housing blocks.

Along Telok Ayer Street

Follow the signs for Maxwell Road out of Tanjong Pagar MRT and you'll surface on the southern edge of Chinatown. Cross Maxwell Road and cut through Telok Ayer Park and you'll quickly hit **Telok Ayer Street**, whose Malay name – meaning "Watery Bay" – recalls a time when the street would have run along the shoreline of the Straits of Singapore. Nowadays, thanks to land reclamation, it's no closer to a beach than is Beach Road, but alongside the shops and stores there are still a number of temples and mosques that have survived from the time when immigrants and sailors stepping ashore wanted to thank the gods for their safe passage.

Facing you as you approach Telok Ayer Street is the square **Chinese Methodist Church**, established in 1889, whose design – portholes and windows adorned with white crosses and capped by a Chinese pagoda-style roof – is a pleasing blend of East and West. The Muslim faith holds sway a short walk up the street and beyond McCallum Street, where the simple lines of the sky-blue **Al-Abrar Mosque** mark the spot where Chulia worshippers from the coast of southern India first set up a thatched *kuchu palli* (in Tamil, small mosque), in 1827.

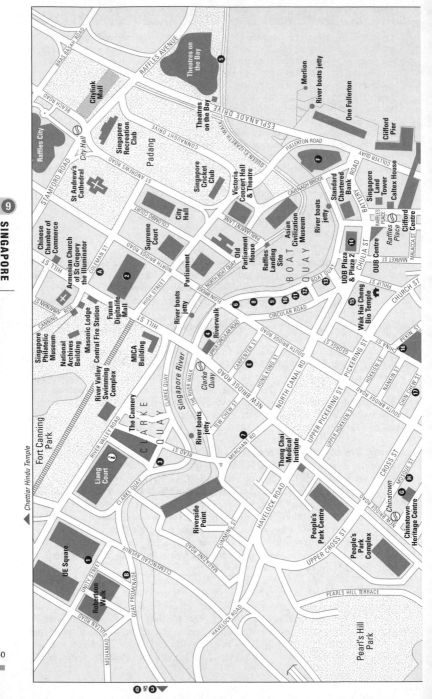

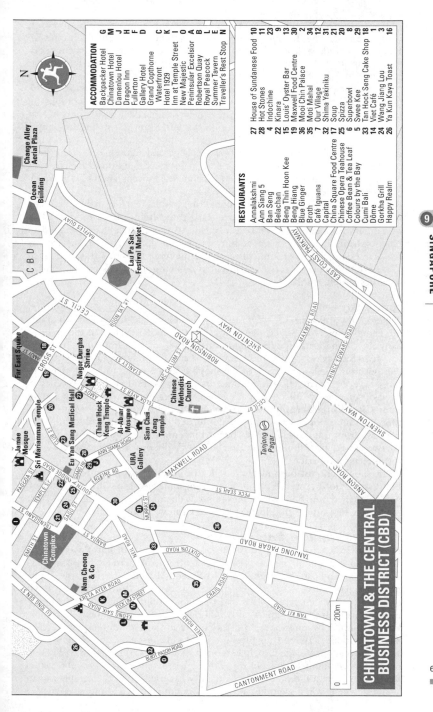

CHINATOWN & THE CENTRAL BUSINESS DISTRICT (CBD)

ACCOMMODATION
Backpacker Hotel	G
Chinatown Hotel	M
Camenlou Hotel	J
Dragon Inn	H
Fullerton	F
Gallery Hotel	D
Grand Copthorne Waterfront	C
Hotel 1929	K
Inn at Temple Street	I
New Majestic	O
Peninsular Excelsior	A
Robertson Quay	B
Royal Peacock	L
Summer Tavern	E
Traveller's Rest Stop	N

RESTAURANTS
Annalakshmi	27
Ann Siang 5	28
Ban Seng	4
Belachan	22
Beng Thin Hoon Kee	15
Beng Hiang	19
Blue Ginger	36
Broth	35
Café Iguana	7
Capital	32
China Square Food Centre	17
Chinese Opera Teahouse	25
Coffee Bean & Tea Leaf	6
Colours by the Bay	5
Cumi Bali	33
Dôme	14
Gorkha Grill	24
Happy Realm	26
House of Sundanese Food	10
Hot Stones	11
Indochine	23
Kinara	9
Louis' Oyster Bar	13
Maxwell Food Centre	30
Mooi Chin Palace	2
Moti Mahal	34
Our Village	12
Shima Yakiniku	31
Soup	21
Spizza	20
Superbowl	8
Swee Kee	29
Tan Hock Seng Cake Shop	18
Viet Café	1
Wang Jiang Lou	3
Ya Kun Kaya Toast	16

9

SINGAPORE

Further up, shortly beyond McCallum Street, the enormous **Thian Hock Keng Temple**, the Temple of Heavenly Happiness, is a hugely impressive Hokkien building, and sprucer than ever after a recent makeover. Its construction began in 1839 using materials imported from China, and the temple was built on the site of a small joss house where immigrants made offerings to Ma Chu Por (also known as Tian Hou), the queen of heaven. A statue of the goddess, shipped in from southern China in time for the temple's completion in 1842, still stands in the centre of the main hall, flanked by the god of war on the right and the protector of life on the left. From the street, the temple looks spectacular: dragons stalk its broad roofs, while the entrance to the temple compound bristles with ceramic flowers, foliage and figures. Two stone lions stand guard at the entrance, and door gods, painted on the front doors, prevent evil spirits from entering. Look out, too, for the huge ovens, always lit, in which offerings to either gods or ancestors are burnt.

It's a testament to Singapore's multicultural nature that Thian Hock Keng's next-door neighbour is the **Nagore Durgha Shrine**, built in the 1820s by Chulias from southern India as a shrine to the ascetic, Shahul Hamid of Nagore. Sadly the shrine's tiered minarets, onion domes and Islamic facades are currently in a state of some disrepair. **Telok Ayer Green**, a tranquil, paved garden dotted with life-sized metal statues depicting the area's earliest settlers, separates temple and shrine.

Amoy Street

A block west of Telok Ayer Street is **Amoy Street**, which – together with China Street and Telok Ayer Street, was designated a Hokkien enclave in the colony's early days. Long terraces of shophouses flank the street, all featuring characteristic **five-foot ways**, or covered verandas, so called simply because they jut five feet out from the house. A few of the shophouses are in a ramshackle state, but most have been marvellously renovated, only to be bought by companies in need of some fancy office space. It's worth walking down to mustard-coloured **Sian Chai Kang Temple**, at 66 Amoy Street. Below the fiery dragons on its roof, it's a musty, open-fronted place dominated by huge urns, full to the brim with ash from untold numbers of burned incense sticks. Guarding the temple are two carved stone lions whose fancy red neck ribbons are said to attract good fortune and prosperity.

The shophouse just beyond the temple and across the path up to Ann Siang Hill Park, at no.70, was the first home of Singapore's **Anglo-Chinese School**, which opened in 1886 when Reverend William Oldham, Singapore's first missionary, began teaching thirteen sons of Chinese businessmen.

Far East Square and around

North of Cross Street, Amoy Street strikes into the heart of **Far East Square**, a shopping-cum-dining centre which taps Chinatown's heritage for its inspiration, and which boasts the **Fuk Tak Chi Street Museum** (daily 10am–10pm; free) as its party piece. It's the surest sign yet of the gentrification of Chinatown that one of its oldest temples has had to suffer the ignominy of being turned into a tourist attraction – and a fairly dull one at that. The Fuk Tak Chi Temple was established by Singapore's Hakka and Cantonese communities in 1824. The temple has scrubbed up nicely – too nicely, in fact: none of the musty ambience that once made it such an interesting place has survived its S$200,000 renovation. A model junk of the kind that would have brought across Singapore's earliest Chinese settlers sits on what used to be the temple's main altar. Elsewhere, you'll see odds and ends – opium pillows and pipes, Peranakan jewellery, an instrument from old Singapore once used by food hawkers to drum up trade, though the most arresting exhibit is a diorama depicting how Telok Ayer Street would have appeared when it was still a waterfront street in the nineteenth century. The recent addition of tables and chairs means you can now take Chinese tea in the temple, but you'd be better advised to head for nearby **Ya Kun** (see p.705) for a cup of strong, sweet coffee and a plate of melt-in-the-mouth *kaya* toast.

On Philip Street, the **Wak Hai Cheng Bio Temple** completes Chinatown's string of former waterfront temples, fronted by an ugly concrete courtyard crisscrossed by a web of ropes supporting numerous spiralled incense sticks. Its name means "Temple of the Calm Sea", which made it a logical choice for early worshippers who had arrived safely in Singapore; an effigy of Tian Hou, the queen of heaven and protector of seafarers, is housed in the temple's right-hand chamber. This temple, too, has an incredibly ornate roof, crammed with tiny models of Chinese village scenes. The temple cat meanders across here sometimes, dwarfing the tableaux like a creature from a Godzilla movie.

From China Street to Ann Siang Hill

Far East Square has subsumed China Street and its offshoots, meaning another slice of residential Chinatown has been lost forever. To get a flavour of the old ways that survived in these streets until the turn of the millennium you'll have to push on across South Bridge Road into the **Hong Lim Complex**, a modern housing estate where old men sit chewing the cud in walkways lined with medical halls, chop makers (seals) and stores selling birds' nests, pork floss, dried mushrooms and gold jewellery.

At the southern end of China Street, Club Street rises up steeply, a thoroughfare once noted for its **temple-carving shops**, though these too have fallen to the demolition ball and been replaced by swish apartment blocks and swanky bars and restaurants. An impromptu **flea market** still takes place on the far side of the car park opposite, where traders squat on their haunches surrounded by catalogues, old coins, sleeveless records and phonecards.

Even the **clan associations** and **guilds** that gave Club Street its name are fast disappearing, though there are still a few to be seen, higher up the hill. These are easy to spot; black-and-white photos of old members cover the walls, and behind the screens, which almost invariably span the doorway, old men sit and chat. From upstairs, the clacking sound of mahjong tiles reaches the street. Most notable of all, is the **Chinese Weekly Entertainment Club**, at no.76 – flanked by roaring lion heads, it's an imposing, 1891-built mansion that was established by a Peranakan millionaire.

Along South Bridge Road

During the Japanese occupation, roadblocks were set up at the point where **South Bridge Road** meets Cross Street, and Singaporeans were vetted at an interrogation post for signs of anti-Japanese feeling in the infamous Sook Ching campaign (see p.625). Those whose answers failed to satisfy the guards and their hooded local informants either ended up as POWs or were never seen again. Today South Bridge Road is fast becoming antiques-central, as more and more of the dingy shophouses that line it are turned into Asian arts curiosity shops.

Turn right (east) out of Ann Siang Hill and you'll see the beautifully renovated **Eu Yan Sang Medical Hall** (Mon–Sat 8.30am–6pm), at 267–271 South Bridge Road. First opened in 1910, the shop is reasonably well geared up for the tourist trade – some of the staff speak good English. The smell is the first thing you'll notice (a little like a compost heap on a hot day), the second, the weird assortment of ingredients on the shelves, which to the uninitiated look more likely to kill than cure. Besides the usual herbs and roots favoured by the Chinese, there are various dubious remedies derived from exotic and endangered species. Blood circulation problems and external injuries are eased with centipedes and insects, crushed into a "rubbing liquor"; the ground-up gall bladders of snakes or bears apparently work wonders on pimples; monkey's gallstones aid asthmatics; while deer penis is supposed to provide a lift to any sexual problem. Antlers, sea horses, scorpions and turtle shells also feature regularly in Chinese prescriptions, though the greatest cure-all of Oriental medicine is said to be **ginseng**, a clever little root that will combat anything from weakness of the heart to acne and jet lag. If you need a pick-me-up, or are just curious, the shop administers free glasses of ginseng tea.

Above the hall is the small but engaging **Birds' Nest Gallery** (Mon–Sat 10am–5.30pm; S$5), which casts light on the history, harvesting and processing of this most famous of Chinese delicacies, which can command prices to its weight in gold. Birds' nests emerged as a prized supplement among China's royal and noble classes during the Ming Dynasty, and today they are still valued for their high glycoprotein, calcium, iron and vitamin B1 content, and for their efficacy in boosting the immune system and curing bronchial ailments. Produced by swiftlets in the limestone and coastal caves of Southeast Asia, birds' nests are a mixture of saliva, moss and grass. It's the painstaking process of picking out this moss and grass by hand that makes the product so expensive - that, and the slow and precarious business of initial harvesting. A screen presentation in English shows nest harvesters or "spidermen" scaling bamboo poles as long as 25 metres in the caves of Borneo, with only the torches attached to the poles to guide them. To visit the gallery, ask a member of staff in Eu Yan Sang.

The egg tarts, walnut cookies, buns and other Chinese cakes at the Tong Heng Chinese pastry shop just up the road at 285 South Bridge Road offer a great way to top up your blood-sugar level before pressing on to further sights.

Across the road from the front doors of Eu Yan Sang, the compound of the **Sri Mariamman Hindu Temple** bursts with primary-coloured, wild-looking statues of deities and animals, and there's always some ritual or other being attended to by one of the temple's priests, drafted in from the subcontinent and dressed in simple loincloths. A wood and *atap* hut was first erected here in 1827, on land belonging to Naraina Pillay – a government clerk who arrived on the same ship as Stamford Raffles, when Raffles first came ashore at Singapore. The present temple was completed in around 1843 and boasts a superb *gopuram* over the front entrance. Once inside the temple, look up at the roof and you'll see splendidly vivid friezes depicting a host of Hindu deities, including the three manifestations of the supreme being: Brahma the creator (with three of his four heads showing), Vishnu the preserver, and Shiva the destroyer (holding one of his sons). The main sanctum, facing you as you walk inside, is devoted to the goddess Mariamman, who's worshipped for her powers to cure disease. Smaller sanctums, dotted about the open walkway circumnavigating the temple, honour a host of other deities. In that dedicated to the goddess Periachi Amman, a sculpture portrays her with a queen lying on her lap, whose evil child she has ripped from her womb; it's odd, then, that the Periachi Amman is the protector of children, to whom babies are brought when one month old. Sri Aravan, with his bushy moustache and big ears, is far less intimidating; his sanctum is at the back on the right-hand side of the complex.

To the left of the main sanctum there's an unassuming patch of sand which, once a year during the festival of **Thimithi** (see p.74), is covered in red-hot coals, which male Hindus run across to prove the strength of their faith. The participants, who line up all the way along South Bridge Road waiting for their turn, are supposedly protected from the heat of the coals by the power of prayer, though the presence of an ambulance parked round the back of the temple suggests that some aren't praying quite hard enough.

Hanging a left out of the temple quickly brings you to the twin octagonal minarets of the **Jamae Mosque**, at 218 South Bridge Road. Established by southern Indian Muslims in 1826, the mosque has barely changed since it was completed four years later.

URA Gallery

A skip around the **URA Gallery** (Mon–Fri 9am–4.30pm, Sat 9am–12.30pm; free; ☎63218321, ⓦwww.ura.gov.sg) at the URA Centre, 45 Maxwell Road, offers a fascinating insight into the grand designs of Singapore's Urban Redevelopment Authority. Town planning may not sound the most inspiring premise for a gallery; but, then again, no other nation plans with such extravagant ambition as Singapore, whose land architects continue to remould their island like a ball of putty, erasing roads here and reclaiming land there. You need only consider the distance between downtown Beach Road and the shoreline it used to abut, to appreciate the extent of change that Singapore has undergone up to now. At the URA Gallery, you can view the blueprint for the island's future.

Interactive exhibits, touch screen terminals and scale models trace Singapore's progress from sleepy backwater to modern metropolis and chart ongoing efforts to reshape and redefine specific regions of the island. The URA has rightly been criticized in the past for its disregard for Singapore's architectural heritage, so it is heartening to see displays making such reassuring noises about the future of the venerable shophouses and colonial villas that remain in such districts as Balestier Road, Tanjong Katong and Joo Chiat. But the gallery's emphasis is more upon the future than the past. A vast model of the downtown area of Singapore – which highlights areas currently under development and offers new arrivals to the island the chance to get their bearings – is best scrutinized through one of the telescopes set up on the floor above. Elsewhere on the upper floor, there is the chance to control a sky cam high above the city, try your hand at a little municipal planning and learn more about Singapore's state-of-the-art MRT system.

Tanjong Pagar

The district of **Tanjong Pagar**, at the southern tip of South Bridge Road and between Neil and Tanjong Pagar roads, is another area that's changed beyond recognition in recent years. Once a veritable sewer of brothels and opium dens, it was earmarked by the authorities as a conservation area, following which over two hundred shophouses were painstakingly restored, painted in sickly pastel hues and converted into bars, restaurants and shops. The emergence of other entertainment hubs such as Boat Quay and CHIJMES has seen the area's star wane in the new millennium, though there are plans – as the URA Gallery will attest – to reinvent it and bring back the revellers. Curiously, Tanjong Pagar Road is now the site of many bridal shops.

While touring Tanjong Pagar, it's worth making time for a stop at one of the traditional **teahouses** along Neil Road. At *Tea Chapter* at no. 9a–11a (daily 11am–11pm), you can have tea in the very chair in which Queen Elizabeth sat when she visited in 1989; the shop is plastered with photographs of the occasion. The Chinese take tea drinking very seriously. Buy a bag of tea here and one of the staff will teach you all the attached rituals (see box, p.666); 100g bags cost from S$5 to over S$65 and tea sets are also on sale, though they don't come cheap.

Taking Chinese tea

If you're in need of a quick, thirst-quenching drink, avoid **Chinese teahouses**: the art of tea-making is heavily bound up in ritual, and the unhurried preparation time is crucial to the production of a pleasing brew. What's more, when you do get a cup, it's barely more than a mouthful and then the whole process kicks off again.

Tea drinking in China goes back thousands of years. Legend has it that the first cuppa was drunk by Emperor Shen Nong, who was pleasantly surprised by the aroma produced by some dried tea leaves falling into the water he was boiling; he was even more pleased when he tasted the brew. By the eighth century, making tea was such a complex art that Chinese scholar Lu Yu produced a three-volume tome on the processes involved.

Teahouses normally have conventional tables and chairs, but the authentic experience involves kneeling at a much lower traditional table. The basic procedure is as follows: the server places a towel in front of himself and his guest, with the folded edge facing the guest, and stuffs leaves into the pot with a bamboo scoop. Water, boiled over a flame, has to reach an optimum temperature, depending on which type of tea is being made; experts can tell its heat by the size of the bubbles rising, which are described variously, and rather confusingly, as "sand eyes", "prawn eyes", "fish eyes", etc. Once the pot has been warmed inside and out, the first pot of tea is made, transferred into the pouring jar and then, frustratingly, poured back over the pot – the thinking being that over a period of time, the porous clay of the pot becomes infused with the fragrance of the tea. Once a second pot is ready, a draught is poured into the sniffing cup, from which the aroma of the brew is savoured. Only now is it time to actually drink the tea and if you want a second cup, the complete procedure starts again.

Sago Street to Mosque Street

Today, the tight knot of streets west of South Bridge Road between Sago Street and Mosque Street is tour-bus Chinatown, heaving with gangs of holiday-makers plundering souvenir shops. But in days gone by these streets formed Chinatown's nucleus, their shophouses harbouring opium dens and brothels, their streets teeming with trishaw drivers, peddlers and food hawkers.

Until as recently as the 1950s, **Sago Street**, across South Bridge Road from Ann Siang Hill, was home to several death houses – rudimentary hospices where skeletal citizens saw out their final hours on rattan camp beds. These houses were finally deemed indecent and have all now gone, replaced by restaurants, bakeries, medicine halls and shops stacked to the rafters with Chinese vases, teapots and jade. Sago, Smith, Temple and Pagoda streets only really recapture their youth around Chinese New Year, when they're crammed to bursting with stalls selling festive branches of blossom, oranges, sausages and waxed chickens – which look as if they have melted to reveal a handful of bones inside.

Sago Street skirts to the right of the Chinatown Complex, and its name changes to **Trengannu Street**. Despite the hordes of tourists, and the shops selling Singapore Airlines uniforms, presentation chopstick sets and silk hats with false pony tails, there are occasional glimpses of Chinatown's **old trades** and industries, such as Nam's Supplies at 22 Smith Street, which offers shirts, Rolex watches, Nokia mobile phones, money, laptops and passports – all made out of paper – which the Chinese burn to ensure their ancestors don't want for creature comforts in the next life. They even have "Otherworld Bank" credit cards, "Hell Airlines" air tickets and "Hell City" cigarettes. Nam Cheong and Co, off nearby Kreta Ayer Street, takes this industry to its logical conclusion, producing huge houses and near-life-size safes, servants and Mercedes for the self-respecting ghost about town; the shop is at #01-04, Block 334, Keong Saik Road, between Chinatown Complex and New Bridge Road.

The Chinatown Complex

The hideous concrete exterior of the **Chinatown Complex**, at the end of Sago Street, belies the charm of the teeming market it houses. Walk up the front steps, past the garlic, fruit and nut hawkers, and once inside, the market's many twists and turns reveal stalls selling silk, kimonos, rattan, leather and clothes. There are no fixed prices, so you'll need to haggle. Deep in the market's belly is shop 01-K3, selling Buddhist amulets; while the Capitol Plastics stall (#01-16) specializes in **mahjong sets**. There's a food centre on the second floor, while the wet market within the complex gets pretty packed early in the morning, when locals come to buy fresh fish or meat. Here, abacuses are still used to tally bills, and sugar canes lean like spears against the wall.

The Chinatown Heritage Centre

Chinatown may long ago have been stripped of much of its life, colour and history, but at least the excellent **Chinatown Heritage Centre** (daily 10am–7pm; S$8/4.80), at 48 Pagoda Street, offers a window upon the district's past. If you go to just one museum in Singapore, this should be it. Housed in three superbly restored shophouses, the centre is an invaluable social document, where the history, culture, pastimes and employments of Singapore's Chinese settlers spring vividly to life. The museum is crammed with displays, artefacts and information boards; but its masterstroke is to give voice to former local residents, whose first-hand accounts of Chinatown life, projected onto walls at every turn, form a unique oral history of the Chinese in Singapore.

A model junk (*singkeh*), like those on which early immigrants came in search of work, sets the scene at the start of the tour. Accounts on the wall tell the story of their perilous journeys across the South China Sea. Once ashore at Bullock Cart Water (the contemporary name for the area that would become Chinatown), settlers quickly formed clan associations, or less savoury secret societies, and looked for employment. As you move through the centre's narrow shophouse corridors, these associations and societies, and every other facet of Chinatown life, work and leisure, are made flesh. All the while, you progress to a soundtrack of crashing gongs and cymbals, age-old songs of mourning and 1950s crooners on scratchy 78s.

The genius of the centre lies in its detail, from the mock up of the shabby flourishes of a prostitute's boudoir, and the marble table of a traditional coffee shop, to the pictures and footage of thin and haunted addicts seeking escape from the pain of their backbreaking work through opium, their "devastating master". Among the many artefacts, look out for an example of an original hawker stall – a charcoal burner and a collection of ingredients yoked over the shoulders and carried from street to street, and a million miles away from the air-con luxury of today's incarnations. Look out, too, for the section focusing upon the death houses of Sago Street, where the sick and old went to die. Trishaw riders collecting the dead would, one Chinatown veteran recounts, "put a hat on the corpse, put it onto the trishaw, and cycle all the way back to the coffin shop".

The tour climaxes with a superb recreation of the unbearable living quarters that settlers endured in the shophouses of Chinatown. Landlords were known to shoehorn as many as forty tenants into a single floor, and their cramped cubicles, cooking and bathing facilities are reproduced in all their grisly squalor. Plumbing was non-existent in these times. One former resident tells of an

As well as the markets and stores covered in the text, look out for the following, all either on or near to New Bridge Road and Eu Tong Sen Street. Opening hours are generally 10am–9.30pm.

Chinatown Point 133 New Bridge Rd. One of its two buildings houses bright, fashionable, Orchard Road-style shop units; the other is a handicraft centre, with scores of tourist-oriented businesses.

Hong Lim Complex 531–531a Upper Cross St. Several Chinese provisions stores, fronted by sackfuls of dried mushrooms, cuttlefish, chillies, garlic cloves, onions, fritters and crackers. Other shops sell products ranging from acupuncture accessories to birds' nests.

Lucky Chinatown Complex 11 New Bridge Rd. Fairly upmarket place with lots of jewellery shops.

New Bridge Centre 336 Smith St. The Da You Department Store (second floor) sells Chinese religious artefacts, tea sets and crockery.

Pearl's Centre 100 Eu Tong Sen St. A centre for Chinese medicine. Sinchong Traditional Medicine at 03-19 and TCM Chinese Medicines at 02-20 both have a Chinese clinic, where a consultation will cost you S$5.

People's Park Centre 101 Upper Cross St. Stall-like shop units selling Chinese handicrafts, CDs, electronics, jade and gold.

People's Park Complex 1 Park Rd. The Overseas Emporium is at 02-70 and sells Chinese instruments, calligraphy pens, lacquer work and jade. Cobblers set up stall in the courtyard beside the complex, behind which is a market and food centre.

occasion when a tenant knocked a full bucket of human waste down a staircase, and was forced to burn incense for days afterwards, to mask the stench. The absence of any air-conditioning goes some way towards conveying the stifling heat that residents suffered daily.

Back on the ground floor is a tailor's shop, the mercantile element of the shophouse. Beside that, a traditional **kopitiam** – featuring old metal signs advertising Horlicks, Brylcreem, and huge biscuit boxes on the counter – is a good place to grab a coffee and reflect on what you've seen. There are sometimes **walking tours** of Chinatown based out of the centre; call ☎63252878 for more details.

New Bridge Road and Eu Tong Sen Street

Chinatown's main shopping drag comprises southbound **New Bridge Road** and northbound **Eu Tong Sen Street**, along which are a handful of large malls. Try to pop into one of the *bak kwa* barbecue pork vendors around the intersection of Smith, Temple and Pagoda streets with New Bridge Road – the flat squares of red, fatty, delicious meat that they cook on wire meshes over fires produce a rich, smoky odour that is pure Chinatown. As you eat your *bak kwa*, check out two striking buildings across the road. Nearest is the flat-fronted **Majestic Opera House**, which no longer hosts performances but still boasts five images of Chinese opera stars over its doors. Just beside it, the Yue Hwa Chinese Products Emporium occupies the former **Great Southern Hotel**, which was built in 1927 by the son of Eu Yan Sang, Eu Tong Sen. In its fifth floor nightclub, *Southern Cabaret*, wealthy locals would drink liquor, smoke opium and pay to dance with so-called local "taxi girls".

The **Thong Chai Medical Institute** has been sited at the top of Eu Tong Sen Street since 1892, when it first opened its doors with the avowed intention of dispensing free medical help regardless of race, colour or creed. Listed as a national monument, this beautiful southern Chinese-style building is now used as commercial premises.

The Central Business District

Until an early exercise in land reclamation in the mid-1820s rendered the zone fit for building, the patch of land south of the mouth of the Singapore River, where Raffles Place now stands, was swampland. However, within just a few years Commercial Square (later renamed Raffles Place) was the colony's busiest business address, boasting the banks, ships' chandlers and warehouses of a burgeoning trading port. The square now forms the nucleus of the **Central Business District** (see map, pp.660–661) – the commercial heart of the state, home to many of its banks and financial institutions. Cutting through the district is **Battery Road**, whose name recalls the days when Fort Fullerton (named after Robert Fullerton, first governor of the Straits Settlements) and its attendant battery of guns used to stand on the site of the *Fullerton* hotel.

Raffles Place and the south riverbank

Until superseded by Orchard Road in the late 1960s, **Raffles Place** was Singapore's central shopping area. Two department stores, Robinsons and John Little, dominated the area until then, but subsequent development turned Raffles Place into Singapore's financial epicentre, ringed by buildings so tall that pedestrians crossing the square feel like ants in a canyon. The most

---

The Barings Bank scandal

Singapore hit the international headlines in early 1995 when the City of London's oldest merchant bank, **Barings**, collapsed as a result of what the London *Evening Standard* called "massive unauthorized dealings" in derivatives on the Japanese stock market. The supposed culprit – "the man who broke the bank", as the press dubbed him – was named as Nick Leeson, an Englishman dealing out of the bank's offices in the Financial District of Singapore. Leeson, it was alleged, had gambled huge funds in the hope of recouping losses made through ill-judged trading, only calling it a day when the bank's losses were approaching £1 billion. One of his colleagues claimed that Leeson made "other fraudsters look like Walt Disney", although many have questioned the quality of Barings' management and financial controls which allowed such a catastrophe to happen.

By the time the scandal broke, Leeson was missing, and a manhunt across Southeast Asia was in full swing when he finally turned up – and was promptly arrested – six days later in Frankfurt. News of his capture was greeted with cheers from dealers in the Singapore Stock Exchange when it flashed across their screens. In the weeks that followed, Dutch bank ING bought Barings for one pound sterling, while Nick Leeson languished in a Frankfurt jail. In time, Singapore's application for extradition was duly granted, and less than two weeks after being passed into Singaporean custody, on December 2, 1995, Leeson pleaded guilty to two charges of deceit, receiving a six-and-a-half-year sentence, three and a half years of which he served out before he was released. In 1999, Leeson's story formed the basis of the movie *Rogue Trader*, in which he was played by Ewan McGregor.

The new millennium has been kinder to Leeson than the last one. Since returning to the UK, he has fully recovered from cancer, gained a psychology degree, remarried and forged a fresh career on the after-dinner speaking circuit.

striking way to experience the giddy heights of the Financial District is by surfacing from Raffles Place MRT, following the signs for Raffles Place itself out of the station, and looking up to gleaming towers, blue skies and racing clouds. To your left is the soaring metallic triangle of the **OUB Centre** (home to the Overseas Union Bank), and to its right, the rocket-shaped **UOB Plaza 2** (United Overseas Bank); in front of you are the rich brown walls of the **Standard Chartered Bank**, and to your right rise sturdy **Singapore Land Tower** and the almost Art Deco **Caltex House**. A smallish statue, entitled *Progress and Advancement*, stands at the northern end of Raffles Place. Erected in 1988, it's a miniature version of what was then the skyline of central Singapore. Inevitably, the very progress and advancement it celebrates has already rendered it out of date – not featured is the **UOB Plaza**, a vast monolith of a building only recently built beside its twin, the UOB Plaza 2. The three roads that run southwest from Raffles Place – Cecil Street, Robinson Road and Shenton Way – are all chock-a-block with more high-rise banks and financial houses; to the west is Chinatown.

Just north of Raffles Place, and beneath the "elephant's trunk" curve of the Singapore River, the pedestrianized row of shophouses known as **Boat Quay** has enjoyed an upturn in fortunes. Derelict until the early 1990s, it's currently one of Singapore's most fashionable hangouts, sporting a huge collection of thriving restaurants and bars. There are those around the Singapore restaurant scene that think the authorities aren't vetting tenants of Boat Quay's units rigorously enough, and that rowdier venues have been allowed to open, to the detriment of the sophistication the area. Certainly, some stretches of the quay are noisier than others, so it's worth taking a stroll before you pick a spot for dinner, in case you find yourself beside a bar specializing in heavy rock or dance music.

East of Raffles Place

Branching off the second floor of the Clifford Centre, on the eastern side of Raffles Place, is **Change Alley Aerial Plaza**. The original Change Alley was a cheap, bustling street-level bazaar, wiped off the face of Singapore by redevelopment; all that remains is a sanitized, modern-day version, housed on a covered footbridge across Collyer Quay. The tailors here have a persuasive line in patter – you have to be very determined if you aren't going to waste half an hour being convinced that you need a new suit.

Walking east through Change Alley Aerial Plaza deposits you at **Clifford Pier**, long the departure point for trips on the Singapore River and to the southern islands. There are still a few bumboats tied up here, though these days they're rented out for cruises rather than as cargo boats. Just north of Clifford Pier, **One Fullerton** is a new entertainment venue that has been constructed on land reclaimed from Marina Bay. Its bars, restaurants and nightclub share peerless views out over the bay. Just above One Fullerton a statue of Singapore's national symbol, the **Merlion**, guards the mouth of the Singapore River. Half-lion, half-fish and wholly ugly, the creature reflects Singapore's name – in Sanskrit, *Singapura* means "Lion City" – and its historical links with the sea. Across the road stands the elegant **Fullerton Building**, fronted by sturdy pillars. Built in 1928 as the headquarters for the General Post Office (a role it fulfilled until the mid-1990s), remarkably this was once one of Singapore's tallest buildings. Old photographs of Singapore depict Japanese soldiers marching past it after the surrender of the Allied forces during World War II. These days, the building is a luxury hotel, and the lighthouse that used to flash up on the roof is a swanky restaurant.

Back at Clifford Pier, it's just a short walk to the south along Raffles Quay to Telok Ayer Market, recently renamed **Lau Pa Sat Festival Market**. Originally built in 1894 on land reclaimed from the sea, its octagonal cast-iron frame has been turned into Singapore's most tasteful food centre (daily 24hr), which offers a range of Southeast Asian cuisines, as well as laying on free entertainment such as local bands and Chinese opera performances. After 7pm Boon Tat Street, on the south side of the market, is closed to traffic between Robinson Road and Shenton Way, and traditional satay stalls and other hawker stalls take over the street.

One of Singapore's most ambitious land reclamation projects, **Marina South**, is plainly visible from Raffles Quay and Shenton Way to the south of the Financial District. For years, the project has shown all the makings of a splendid folly – the entertainment and recreation park which was built on it during the 1980s has gone bankrupt and the large patch of land now seems to serve no other purpose than to carry the East Coast Parkway on its journey west. For now, Marina South is a ghost town, its only real asset an imaginative children's playground within a pleasant park. But plans are afoot to extend Singapore's downtown area into this space. Construction starts soon on an integrated **resort** with casino, entertainment and shops due to open on its northern tip, from where city planners intend to run a helix-shaped, glass and steel bridge to the waterfront east of the Theatres on the Bay complex (see p.649).

Below Marina South, Singapore's port begins its sprawl westwards. Singapore is the world's busiest container port (the second busiest port overall after Rotterdam), and hundreds of ships are at anchor south of the island at any one time, waiting for permission from the Port of Singapore Authority to enter one of the state's seven terminals.

Little India

A tour around **Little India** amounts to an all-out assault on the senses: Indian pop music blares out from gargantuan speakers outside cassette shops, the air is heavily perfumed with sweet incense, curry powder and jasmine garlands; Hindu women promenade in bright saris; and a wealth of "hole-in-the-wall" restaurants serve up superior curries. The district's backbone is the north–south **Serangoon Road**, whose southern end is alive with shops, restaurants and fortune-tellers. To the east, stretching as far as Jalan Besar, is a tight knot of roads that's ripe for exploration, while parallel to Serangoon Road, **Race Course Road** boasts a clutch of fine restaurants and some temples.

Indians did not always dominate this convenient central niche of Singapore, just fifteen minutes from the Colonial District. The original occupants were Europeans and Eurasians who established country houses here, and for whom a racecourse was built (on the site of modern-day Farrer Park) in the 1840s. Only when Indian-run **brick kilns** began to operate here did an Indian community start to take shape. The enclave grew when a number of **cattle and buffalo yards** opened in the area in the latter half of the nineteenth century, and more Hindus were drawn in, in search of work. Street names hark back to this trade: side by side off the southern end of Serangoon Road are Buffalo Road and Kerbau (confusingly, "buffalo" in Malay) Road, along both of which cattle were kept in slaughter pens. Indians featured prominently in the development of Singapore, though not always out of choice: from 1825 onwards, convicts were transported from the subcontinent and by the 1840s there were over a thousand Indian prisoners labouring on buildings such as St Andrew's Cathedral and the Istana.

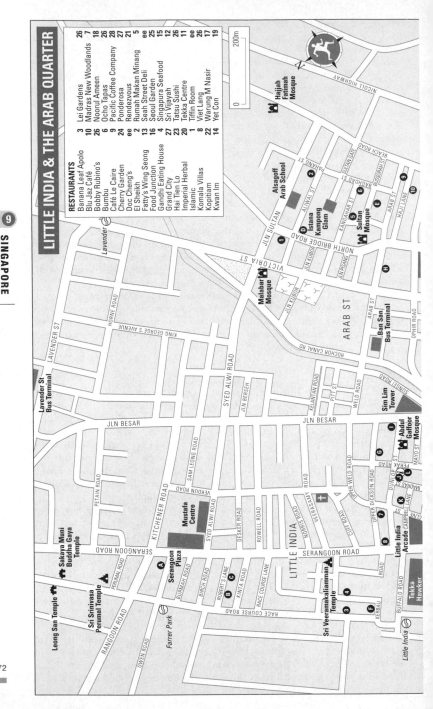

LITTLE INDIA & THE ARAB QUARTER

RESTAURANTS		Lei Gardens	3
Banana Leaf Apolo	26	Madras New Woodlands	10
Blu Jaz Café	7	Noorul Ameen	26
Bobby Rubino's	18	Ocho Tapas	6
Bumbu	26	Pacific Coffee Company	9
Café Le Caire	28	Ponderosa	24
Cherry Garden	27	Rendezvous	ee
Doc Cheng's	21	Rumah Makan Minang	2
El Sheikh	5	Seah Street Deli	13
Fatty's Wing Seong	ee	Seoul Garden	16
Food Junction	25	Singapura Seafood	4
Gandhi Eating House	15	Sri Vijayah	27
Grand City	12	Tatsu Sushi	23
Hai Tien Lo	26	Tekka Centre	20
Imperial Herbal	11	Tiffin Room	1
Islamic	ee	Viet Lang	8
Komala Villas	17	Warung M Nasir	22
Kopitiam	19	Yet Con	14

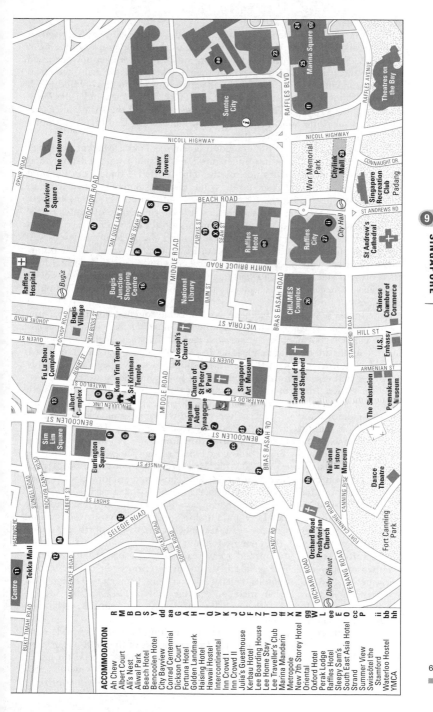

ACCOMMODATION

Ah Chew	R
Albert Court	M
Ali's Nest	B
Aliwal Park	D
Beach Hotel	S
Bencoolen Hotel	Y
City Bayview	dd
Conrad Centennial	aa
Dickson Court	G
Fortuna Hotel	A
Golden Landmark	H
Haising Hotel	I
Hawaii Hostel	Q
Intercontinental	V
Inn Crowd I	K
Inn Crowd II	J
Julia's Guesthouse	C
Kerbau Hotel	F
Lee Boarding House	Z
Lee Home Stay	T
Lee Traveller's Club	U
Marina Mandarin	ff
Metropole	X
New 7th Storey Hotel	N
Oriental	gg
Oxford Hotel	W
Perak Lodge	L
Raffles Hotel	ee
Sleepy Sam's	E
South East Asia Hotel	O
Strand	cc
Summer View	P
Swissôtel the Stamford	ii
Waterloo Hostel the	bb
YMCA	hh

Along Serangoon Road

Dating from 1822 and hence one of the island's oldest roadways, **Serangoon Road** is a kaleidoscopic whirl of Indian life, its shops selling everything from nostril studs and ankle bracelets to incense sticks and *kum kum* powder (used to make the red dot Hindus wear on their foreheads). Little stalls, set up in doorways and under "five-foot ways", sell garlands, gaudy posters of Hindu gods and gurus, movie soundtracks and newspapers like *The Hindu* and *India Today*. Look out for parrot-wielding **fortune-tellers** – you tell the man your name, he passes your name on to his feathered partner, and the bird then picks out a card with your fortune on it.

At the southwestern end of Serangoon Road, the **Tekka Market** combines many of Little India's ventures under one roof. Beyond its ground-floor food centre is a wet market that's not for the faint-hearted – traders push around trolleys piled high with goats' heads, while the halal butchers go to work in full view of the customers. Elsewhere, live crabs shuffle busily in buckets, their claws tied together, and there's a mouthwatering range of fruits on sale, including whole branches of bananas. Upstairs, on the second floor, you'll find Indian fabrics, leatherware, footwear, watches and cheap electronic goods. On Sunday, the forecourt of the centre becomes an ad hoc social club for immigrant labourers working in Singapore, most of whom are Bangladeshi. Along the northern side of the Zhu Jiao Centre, **Buffalo Road** sports a cluster of provisions stores with sacks of spices and fresh coconut, ground using primitive machines out on the road.

Little India's remaining shophouses are fast being touched up from the same pastel paintbox as that which has "restored" Chinatown to its present doll's-house cuteness. Fortunately the colours work far better in an Indian context, and the results are really quite pleasing. In particular, check out **Kerbau Road**, one block north of Buffalo Road, whose shophouses have been meticulously renovated and now harbour a proliferation of Indian produce stores and a pleasant beer garden. If the mood takes you, you can get your hands painted with intricate henna patterns at Traditional Body Charm, at no. 9; while Ansa, at no. 27, is a traditional Indian framer's shop, packed with images of colourful Hindu deities. Look out, too, for the curving staircase, dragon-headed banisters and carved shutters of the old **Chinese mansion** at no.37 – pop into TM Silks on the ground floor, and you can still see Chinese scenes painted high up on the walls and oriental beams finished with floral motifs. A right turn from Kerbau Road takes you onto **Race Course Road**, whose fine restaurants serve both North and South Indian food; several specialize in fish-head curry.

The little braid of roads across Serangoon Road from the Tekka Market – Hastings Road, Campbell Lane and Dunlop Street – also merits investigation. Bounded by Serangoon to the west, Campbell Lane to the north and Hastings Road to the south, the lovingly restored block of shophouses comprising **Little India Arcade** was opened a few years back as a sort of Little India in microcosm: behind its lime walls and green shutters you can purchase textiles and tapestries, bangles, religious statuary, Indian sweets, tapes and CDs, and even traditional ayurvedic (herbal) medicines. At the time of *Deepavali*, the arcade's narrow ways are choked with locals buying decorations, garlands, traditional confectionery and fine clothes.

The roads nearby are also worth exploring. Exiting Little India Arcade onto Campbell Lane leaves you opposite the riot of colours of the Jothi flower shop where staff thread jasmine, roses and marigolds into garlands, or *jothi*, for prayer offerings. Campbell Lane is a good place for buying Indian sandals, while walking along Clive Street towards Upper Dickson Road you'll find on your right a batch of junk dealers patiently tinkering with ancient cookers, air-con units and TVs. Left along Upper Dickson Road – past an old barber's shop where a short back and sides is followed by a crunching head yank to "relieve tension" – are the *Madras New Woodlands Restaurant*, at no. 12–14 and, around the corner, *Komala Vilas*, 76 Serangoon Road, two of Little India's best southern Indian restaurants (see p.710). Chances are that they make their delicious curries with spices bought nearby at Cuff Road, where **traditional spice grinders** still ply their trade at no.2.

Dunlop Street has become something of a backpacker enclave in the past few years, but it remains defined by beautiful **Abdul Gaffoor Mosque** (at no. 41; daily 8.30am–noon & 2.30–4pm), whose green dome and bristling minarets have enjoyed a comprehensive and sympathetic renovation in the last few years. Set amid gardens of palms and bougainvillea and within cream walls decorated with stars and crescent moons, the mosque features an unusual sundial whose face is ringed by elaborate Arabic script denoting the names of 25 Islamic prophets. Staff will give you a sarong or headdress to enable you to enter the prayer hall and see the mihrab, or arched niche, where the imam sits; and the *mimbar*, or raised pulpit, from where he preaches. Traditionally, the imam always preaches from the second step of the *mimbar* as the top step is symbolically reserved for the prophet Mohammed. Renovated shop houses to the left of the mosque as you enter the grounds, have been converted into a *madrasah*, or Islamic school. From the Abdul Gaffoor Mosque, it's just a short walk to 13 Upper Dickson Road, where you can buy a cooling *kulfi* (Indian ice cream).

In the heart of Little India on Serangoon Road opposite the turning to Veerasamy Road, the **Veeramakaliamman Temple** – dedicated to the ferocious Hindu goddess, Kali – features a fanciful *gopuram* that's flanked by majestic lions on the temple walls. Worshippers ring the bells hanging on the temple doors as they enter, so that their prayers are answered. Inside, the *mandapam*, or worship hall, holds a jet-black image of Kali, the goddess of power and incarnation of Lord Shiva's wife, depicted with a club in hand. Flanking her are her sons, Ganesh and Murugan. Each year over *Deepavali* (see p.76), a pulsating market takes place on the open land just above the temple.

△ Flower stall, Serangoon Road

You won't find **Pink Street** – one of the most incongruous and sordid spots in the whole of clean, shiny Singapore – on any city map. The entire length of the "street" (in fact it's merely an alley between the backs of Rowell and Desker roads) is punctuated by open doorways, inside which gaggles of bored-looking prostitutes sit knitting or watching TV, oblivious to the gawping crowds of local men who accumulate outside. Stalls along the alley sell distinctly un-Singaporean merchandise such as sex toys, blue videos and potency pills, while con-men work the "three cups and a ball" routine on unwary passers-by.

North of Desker Road

Beyond Desker Road, a five-minute walk north takes you to the edge of Little India, a diversion worth making to see three very different temples. Each year, on the day of the *Thaipusam* festival (in late January), the courtyard of the **Sri Srinivasa Perumal Temple**, at 397 Serangoon Rd, witnesses a gruesome melee of activity, as Hindu devotees don huge metal frames (*kavadis*) topped with peacock feathers, which are fastened to their flesh with hooks and prongs. The devotees then leave the temple, stopping only while a coconut is smashed at their feet for good luck, and parade all the way to the Chettiar Temple on Tank Road, off Orchard Road. Even if you miss the festival, it's worth a trip to see the five-tiered *gopuram* with its sculptures of the various manifestations of Lord Vishnu the preserver. On the wall to the right of the front gate, a sculpted elephant, its leg caught in a crocodile's mouth, trumpets silently.

Just beyond the Sri Srinivasa Temple complex, a small path leads northwest to Race Course Road, where the **Sakaya Muni Buddha Gaya Temple** (also called the Temple of the Thousand Lights) is on the right at no. 366. Slightly kitsch, the temple betrays a strong Thai influence – which isn't surprising as it was built entirely by a Thai monk, Vutthisasala. On the left of the temple as you enter is a huge replica of Buddha's footprint, inlaid with mother-of-pearl; beyond sits a huge Buddha ringed by the thousand electric lights from which the temple takes its alternative name; while 25 scenes from the Buddha's life decorate the pedestal on which he sits. It is possible to walk inside the Buddha, through a door in his back; inside is a smaller representation, this time of Buddha reclining. The left wall of the temple features a sort of wheel of fortune – to discover your fortune, spin it (for 30¢) and take the numbered sheet of paper that corresponds to the number at which the wheel stops. Further along the left wall, a small donation entitles you to shake a tin full of numbered sticks, after which, again, you get a corresponding sheet of forecasts.

Back on Serangoon Road, a five-minute walk southeast along Petain Road towards Jalan Besar takes in some immaculate examples of **Peranakan shophouses**, their facades covered with elegant ceramic tiles reminiscent of Portuguese *azulejos*. There's more Peranakan architecture on display on Jalan Besar itself – turn right at the end of Petain Road – and along Sam Leong Road, where the shophouse facades are decorated with depictions of stags, lotuses and egrets. Further south, a daily **flea market** takes place around Pitt Street, Weld Road, Kelantan Lane and Pasar Lane – secondhand tools, odd shoes and foreign currency are all laid out for sale on plastic sheets at the side of the road by citizens whom Singapore's economic miracle has passed by.

The Arab Quarter and and around

Before the arrival of Raffles, the area of Singapore west of the Rochor River housed a Malay village known as Kampong Glam, after the Gelam tribe of sea gypsies who lived there. After signing a dubious treaty with the newly installed "Sultan" Hussein Mohammed Shah (see p.624), Raffles allotted the area to the sultan and designated the land around it as a Muslim settlement. Soon the zone was attracting Malays, Sumatrans and Javanese, as well as Hadhrami Arab traders from the region of southern Arabia that is now Yemen, as the road names in today's **Arab Quarter** – Baghdad Street, Muscat Street and Haji Lane – suggest. Until it was redeveloped as a heritage centre a few years ago, descendants of Sultan Hussein lived in the grounds of the Istana Kampong Glam, a palace right in the centre of the district, bounded by Arab Street, Beach Road, Jalan Sultan and Rochor Canal Road.

Arab Street to North Bridge Road

While Little India is memorable for its fragrances, it's the vibrant colours of the shops of **Arab Street** and its environs that stick in the memory. The street boasts the highest concentration of shops in the Arab Quarter; its pavements are an obstacle course of carpets, cloths, baskets and bags. Most of the shops have been modernized, though one or two (like Bamadhaj Brothers at no. 97, and Aik Bee at no. 73) still retain their original dark wood and glass cabinets, and wide wooden benches where the shopkeepers sit. Textile stores are most prominent, their walls, ceilings and doorways draped with cloths and batiks. Elsewhere you'll see leather, basketware, gold, gemstones and jewellery for sale, while the most impressive range of basketware and rattan work – fans, hats and walking sticks – is found at Rishi Handicrafts, at no. 58. It's easy to spend a couple of hours weaving in and out of the stores, but don't expect a quiet window-shopping session – the traders here are masters of the forced sale, and will have you loaded with sarongs, baskets and leather bags before you know it.

The quarter's most evocative patch is the stretch of **North Bridge Road** between Arab Street and Jalan Sultan. Here, the men sport long sarongs and Abe Lincoln beards, and the women fantastically colourful shawls and robes, while the shops and restaurants are geared more towards locals than tourists: Kazura Aromatics at 705 North Bridge Road, for instance, sells alcohol-free perfumes while neighbouring stores stock prayer beads, mats, the *songkok* hats worn by Muslim males in mosques, and *miswak* sticks – twigs the width of a finger used by some locals to clean their teeth. A gaggle of superb Muslim Indian restaurants operates along this stretch of North Bridge Road: see p.710 for details.

Several roads run off the western side of North Bridge Road, including Jalan Pisang (Banana Street), on which a street barber works under a tarpaulin. A walk up Jalan Kubor (Grave Street) and across Victoria Street takes you to an unkempt Muslim **cemetery** where, it is said, Malay royalty are buried. On Sundays, Victoria Street throngs with children in full Muslim garb on their way to study scripture at the religious school, **Madrasah Aljunied Al-Islamiah**, on North Bridge Road.

Sultan Mosque and Istana Kampong Glam

Along the eastern side of North Bridge Road (though the best initial views of its golden domes are from palm-tree-lined, pedestrianized Bussorah Street to the east) is the **Sultan Mosque** or Masjid Sultan (Mon–Thurs & Sat 9am–1pm & 2–4pm, Fri 9–11.30am & 2.30–4pm), the beating heart of the Muslim faith in Singapore. An earlier mosque stood on this site, finished in 1825 and constructed with the help of a S$3000 donation from the East India Company. The present building was completed a century later, according to a design by colonial architects Swan and MacLaren; if you look carefully at the necks of the domes, you can see that the glistening effect is created by the bases of thousands of ordinary glass bottles attached flush against the surface, an incongruity which sets the tone for the rest of the building. Steps at the top of Bussorah Street lead past papaya and palm trees into a wide lobby, where a digital display lists current prayer times. Beyond, and out of bounds to non-Muslims, is the main prayer hall, a large, bare chamber fronted by two more digital clocks which enable the faithful to time their prayers to the exact second. An exhaustive set of rules applies to visitors wishing to enter the lobby: shoes must be taken off and shoulders and legs covered; no video cameras are allowed inside the mosque and entry is not permitted during the Friday mass congregation (11.30am–2.30pm). The best time to come is in the Muslim fasting month of **Ramadan** (see p.75) – when the faithful can only eat after dusk, and Muscat and Kandahar streets are awash with stalls selling biriyani, barbecued chicken and cakes.

Bussorah Street itself has undergone quite a transformation in recent years, and efforts to morph it into the heart of a busier, buzzier Arab quarter have brought various businesses into its restored shophouses including cafés, shops selling Islamic books, music and aromatics, and even, at no. 61, a Balinese spa. A renewed interest in the Arabic roots of this district has resulted in a handful of middle-eastern restaurants and cafés that make pleasing venues for a drink, a snack or a *shisha*.

Squatting between Kandahar and Aliwal streets, the **Istana Kampong Glam** was built as the royal palace of Sultan Ali Iskandar Shah, son of Sultan Hussein who negotiated with Raffles to hand over Singapore to the British; the sultan's descendants lived here until just a few years ago. Today, this modest, colonial building houses the **Malay Heritage Centre** (Mon 1–6pm, Tues–Sun 10am–6pm, S$3/2; cultural show Wed 3.30pm & Sun 11.30am, S$10/5), a mixed bag of history and culture spanning maps, model boats, cannons, ceremonial drums and daggers from around the Malay archipelago. The most engaging exhibits are upstairs, where touch screens cast light on Malay community life in the pre-war years of the twentieth century, and where a mock-up kampong house allows you to peek inside a traditional Malay dwelling. The twice-weekly **cultural show** offers a passable blend of Malay music, dance and costumes.

Beach Road

It's only a five-minute walk on to the **Hajjah Fatimah Mosque** on **Beach Road**, just outside the quarter proper, where a collection of photographs in the entrance porch show the mosque through the years following its construction in 1846 – first surrounded by shophouses, then by open land, and finally by huge housing projects. The mosque is named after a wealthy Malaccan businesswoman who amassed a fortune through her mercantile vessels, and whose family home formerly stood here. After two break-ins and an arson attack on her home, Hajjah Fatimah decided to move elsewhere, then underwrote the construction of a mosque on the site. The minaret looks strangely like a church steeple (perhaps because its architect was European) and is beautifully illuminated at night. Its 6-degree list – locals call the mosque Singapore's Leaning Tower of Pisa – is barely noticeable. Across from the mosque, the **Golden Mile Complex** at 5001 Beach Rd attracts so many Thai nationals that locals refer to it as "Thai Village". Numerous bus firms selling tickets to Thailand operate out of here, while inside, the shops sell Thai foodstuffs, cafés sell Singha beer and Mekong whisky, and authentic restaurants serve up old favourites. On a Sunday, Thais come down here in hordes to meet up with their compatriots, listen to Thai pop music, and have a few drinks.

Beach Road still maintains shops – ships' chandlers and fishing-tackle specialists – which betray its former proximity to the sea. It's worth taking the time to walk southwest along Beach Road to see the two logic-defying office buildings that together comprise **The Gateway**. Designed by I.M. Pei, they rise magnificently into the air like vast razor blades, appearing two-dimensional when viewed from certain angles. When **Parkview Square**, the huge, Gotham-esque building across Beach Road was built, much care was taken to site it dead between The Gateway's sharp points, so as to ward off bad feng shui. To be on the safe side its developers placed four giant figures carrying good-luck pearls along the top of the tower.

Orchard Road and around

It would be hard to conjure an image more diametrically opposed to the reality of modern-day **Orchard Road** than C.M. Turnbull's description of it during early colonial times as "a country lane lined with bamboo hedges and shrubbery, with trees meeting overhead for its whole length". One hundred years ago, a stroll down Orchard Road would have passed row upon row of nutmeg trees, and would have been enjoyed in the company of merchants taking their daily constitutionals, followed at a discreet distance by their trusty manservants. Today, Orchard Road is synonymous with **shopping** – indeed, tourist brochures refer to it as the "Fifth Avenue, the Regent Street, the Champs Élysées, the Via Veneto and the Ginza of Singapore". Huge malls, selling everything you can imagine, line the road, though don't expect shopping here to be relaxing; hordes of dawdling tourists from the numerous hotels along the road make browsing difficult. The road runs northwest from Fort Canning Park and is served by three MRT stations, Dhoby Ghaut, Somerset and Orchard, of which the last is the most central for shopping expeditions.

The coming years will see Orchard Road morph into a more **tourist-oriented district** than it is now. Mindful that several of its older shopping centres are looking a little on the shabby side, the Singapore Tourism Board recently unveiled grand, S$1.6bn plans to revamp the area into what it calls "a giant events stage…a dynamic, vibrant and vital urban centre for overseas visitors and locals".

From Dhoby Ghaut to the Istana

In the **Dhoby Ghaut** area (at the eastern tip of Orchard Road), Indian *dhobies*, or laundrymen, used to wash clothes in the Stamford Canal, which once ran along Orchard and Stamford roads. Those days are long gone, and today the area is ringed by shopping centres, though there is a remnant of old Singapore in the **Hotel Rendezvous**, on the corner of Selegie and Bras Basah roads, where the venerable *Rendezvous* restaurant is once again cooking up its famous curries (see p.711). Three minutes' walk west along Orchard Road from Dhoby Ghaut MRT takes you past Plaza Singapura, beyond which stern-looking soldiers guard the gate of the **Istana Negara Singapura**. Built in 1869, the istana, with its ornate cornices, elegant louvred shutters and high mansard roof, was originally the official residence of Singapore's British governors, though on independence it became the residence of the president of Singapore – currently S.R. Nathan, whose portrait you'll see in banks, post offices and shops across the state. The shuttered istana is only open to visitors on public holidays and is probably worth a visit if your trip coincides with one – the president goes walkabout at some point during every open day as thousands of Singaporeans flock to picnic on the well-landscaped sweeps and dips of its lawns, and brass bands belt out jaunty tunes. There's also a **changing of the guard** ceremony, which takes place at the gates onto Orchard Road (first Sun of every month at 5.45pm).

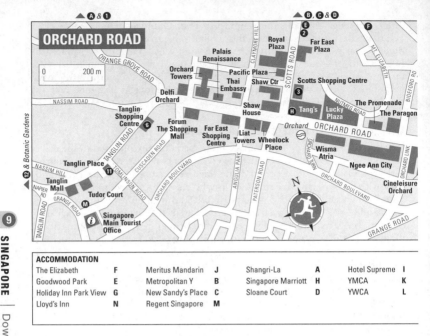

The **Tan Yeok Nee Mansion**, across the road at 207 Clemenceau Ave, is now home to the Chicago Graduate School of Business. Built in traditional southern Chinese style for a wealthy Teochew merchant who traded in pepper and gambier (a resin used in tanning), and featuring ornate roofs and massive granite pillars, the mid-1880s mansion served as headquarters to the Singapore Salvation Army from 1940 until 1991.

Cuppage Road, Emerald Hill and the Goodwood Hotel

Further along Orchard Road, most of **Cuppage Road** has been pedestrianized, making it a great place to sit out and have a beer or a meal. **Cuppage Terrace**, halfway along on the left, is an unusually (for Orchard Road) old row of shophouses, where a burgeoning restaurant and bar scene has developed. A number of even more architecturally notable houses have also survived the bulldozers in Emerald Hill Road, parallel to Cuppage Road. **Emerald Hill** was granted to Englishman William Cuppage in 1845 and for some years afterwards was the site of a large nutmeg plantation. After Cuppage's death in 1872, the land was subdivided and sold off, much of it bought by members of the Peranakan community. A walk up Emerald Hill Road takes you past a number of exquisitely crafted houses dating from this period, built in a decorative architectural style known as Chinese Baroque, typified by highly coloured ceramic tiles, carved swing doors, shuttered windows and pastel-shaded walls with fine plaster mouldings.

West of Emerald Hill Road, the **shopping centres** of Orchard Road begin to come thick and fast. Once you reach Orchard MRT station, a couple of minutes' walk north up Scotts Road brings you to the gleaming white walls of the impressive **Goodwood Hotel**, which started life in 1900 as the Teutonia Club for German expats. With the start of war across Europe in 1914, the club was commandeered by the British Custodian of Enemy Property and didn't

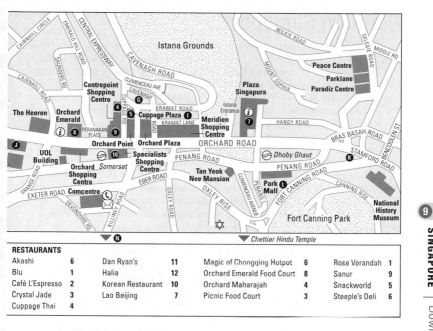

RESTAURANTS							
Akashi	6	Dan Ryan's	11	Magic of Chongqing Hotpot	6	Rose Verandah	1
Blu	1	Halia	12	Orchard Emerald Food Court	8	Sanur	9
Café L'Espresso	2	Korean Restaurant	10	Orchard Maharajah	4	Snackworld	5
Crystal Jade	3	Lao Beijing	7	Picnic Food Court	3	Steeple's Deli	6
Cuppage Thai	4						

open again until 1918, after which it served for several years as a function hall. In 1929 it became a hotel, though by 1942 the *Goodwood* – like *Raffles* – was lodging Japanese officers. It's fitting, then, that the hotel was chosen, after the war, as one of the venues for a war crimes court.

The Botanic Gardens

A ten-minute walk from the western end of Orchard Road are the open spaces of the **Singapore Botanic Gardens** (daily 5am–midnight; free) on Cluny Road. Founded in 1859, it was where the Brazilian seeds that gave rise to the great **rubber plantations** of Malaysia were first nurtured in 1877. Henry Ridley, named director of the botanic gardens the following year, recognized the financial potential of rubber and spent the next twenty years of his life persuading Malayan plantation-owners to convert to this new crop, an obsession which earned him the nickname "Mad" Ridley. The spacious gardens feature a mini-jungle, rose garden, topiary, fernery, palm valley, and lakes that are home to turtles and swans. There's also the **National Orchid Garden** (daily 8.30am–7pm; S$5/1) with one thousand species and two thousand hybrids; orchid jewellery, made by plating real flowers with gold, is on sale here – pieces start from around S$30. At dawn and dusk, joggers and students of Tai chi haunt the lawns and paths of the gardens, while at the weekend, newlyweds bundle down from church for their photos to be taken – a ritual recalled in Lee Tzu Pheng's poem, *Bridal Party at the Botanics*, whose bride's "two hundred dollar face/is melting in the sun", while beside her is her groom, "black-stuffed, oil-slicked, fainting/in his finery, by the shrubbery". You can pick up a free **map** of the grounds at the ranger's office, a little to the right of the main gate.

Northern Singapore

While land reclamation has radically altered the east coast and industrialization the west, the **northern** expanses of the island up to the Straits of Johor still retain pockets of the **rainforest** and mangrove swamp which blanketed Singapore on Raffles' arrival in 1819. Today, these are interspersed with sprawling **new towns** like Toa Payoh, maze-like Bishan and Ang Mo Kio, built in the 1970s. The name of the last, meaning "red-haired one's bridge" refers to the nineteenth-century British surveyor, John Turnbull Thomson, under whose supervision the transport network of Singapore began to penetrate the interior of the island. Man-eating tigers roamed these parts well into the twentieth century, and it was here that Allied forces confronted the invading Japanese army in 1942, a period of Singaporean history movingly recalled by the **Kranji War Memorial** on Woodlands Road and the new Memories at Old Ford Factory gallery in Bukit Timah. What remains of Singapore's agricultural past still clings tenaciously to the far northern sweep of the island: you'll see prawn and poultry farms, orchards and vegetable gardens when travelling in these parts.

Dominating the central northern region are two nature reserves, divided by the Bukit Timah Expressway, the main road route to Malaysia. West of the expressway is **Bukit Timah Nature Reserve**, an accessible slice of primary rainforest, while to the east, the four reservoirs of the Central Catchment Area are one of Singapore's main sources of water. North of here, the principal tourist attractions are the excellent **Singapore Zoological Gardens** and the adjacent **Night Safari**, sited on a finger of land pointing into the Seletar Reservoir. To the east are two of Singapore's most eye-catching Buddhist temples – **Lian Shan Shuang Lin Temple** and the **Kong Meng San Phor Kark See Temple** complex – as well as tiny Tai Gin Road, where the occasional residence of Chinese nationalist leader Dr Sun Yat Sen, and Singapore's Burmese Temple are found.

Exploring the north is a matter of pinpointing the particular sight you want to see and heading straight for it; the bus trip to the zoo, for instance, takes around 45 minutes from downtown Singapore. Travel between all these places can be tricky unless you are driving or in a cab, so don't expect to take in everything in a day. However, Lian Shan Shuang Lin Temple, Sun Yat Sen Villa and the Burmese Temple all nestle around the outskirts of Toa Payoh New Town and could be incorporated into a single expedition; as could the zoo, Mandai Orchid Gardens and the Kranji cemetery and memorial. The Kong Meng San Phor Kark See Temple complex really requires a separate journey.

Bukit Timah

Bukit Timah Road shoots northwest from the junction of Selegie and Serangoon roads, arriving at the faceless suburb of **Bukit Timah** 8km later. Bukit Timah boasts Singapore's last remaining pocket of primary rainforest, which now comprises **Bukit Timah Nature Reserve** (daily 6.30am–7.30pm; free; ☎1800-4685736, ⓦwww.nparks.gov.sg). **Bus** #171 passes along Somerset and Scotts roads en route to Bukit Timah Reserve; a second option is to take the #170 from the Ban San Terminal on Queen Street. Both buses drop you beside a row of shops on Upper Bukit Timah Road, where you can pick up **light snacks** and bottled water to take into the reserve.

Visiting this area of Singapore in the mid-eighteenth century, natural historian Alfred Russell Wallace found Bukit Timah's vegetation "most luxuriant…in about two months I obtained no less than 700 species of beetles…in all my subsequent travels in the East I rarely if ever met with so productive a spot".

Wallace reported "tiger pits, carefully covered with sticks and leaves and so well concealed, that in several cases I had a narrow escape from falling into them...Formerly a sharp stake was stuck erect in the bottom," he continued, "but after an unfortunate traveller had been killed by falling into one, its use was forbidden." Today the 81-hectare reserve, established in 1883 by Nathaniel Cantley, then superintendent of the Botanic Gardens, yields no such hazards and provides a refuge for the dwindling numbers of species still extant in Singapore – only 25 types of mammal now inhabit the island. Creatures you're most likely to see in Bukit Timah are long-tailed macaques, butterflies, insects, and birds like the dark-necked tailorbird, which builds its nest by sewing together leaves. Scorpions, snakes, flying lemurs and pangolins (anteaters, whose name is derived from the Malay word *peng-goling*, meaning "roller", a reference to the animal's habit of rolling into a ball when threatened) still roam here too.

Alterations over the last few years have vastly improved the reserve, which now has an informative visitor centre (daily 8.30am–6pm) full of displays, specimens and photos relating to the wildlife beyond. Several paths from the centre twist and turn through the forest around and up to the top of **Bukit Timah** itself, a hill which – at a paltry 163m – is actually Singapore's highest. The paths are all well signposted, colour-coded and dotted with rest and shelter points, and clearly mapped on the free leaflet handed out to all visitors. Two bike tracks have also been added recently. You'd do best to visit in the early morning (when it's cooler) and during the week (when there are fewer visitors).

Across Upper Bukit Timah Road from the reserve, another forested hill, **Bukit Batok**, is where British and Australian POWs were forced to erect a fifteen-metre-high wooden shrine, the Syonan Tyureito, for their Japanese captors. Only the steps at its base now remain, and the hill is now topped by a telecoms transmitter. Legend has it that the shrine itself was destroyed by termites which the prisoners secretly introduced to the structure. Gone, too, is the wooden cross erected by the POWs to honour their dead. The hill is located at the end of Lorong Sesuai, a left turn opposite Bukit Timah fire station, 500m further up the road from the entrance to Bukit Timah Reserve. Lorong Sesuai was laid by the same prisoners who constructed the shrine. The surrender that consigned them to such labours took place 400m further up Upper Bukit Timah Road, at the Art Deco old Ford Factory; a new gallery, **Memories at Old Ford Factory** (Mon–Fri 9am–5.30pm, Sat 9am–1.30pm; free), tells the story of that surrender, and of the dark years of Japanese occupation from 1942 to 1945. The exhibition uses period newspapers, first-hand audio accounts and relics such as Morse coders, anti-tank guns, signal lamps and grenades to fascinating effect. Details of life as a POW are kept to a minimum (this facet of Singaporean history is well covered at Changi Prison Museum); instead, it's the civilian experience of Japanese occupation that comes to life. When the factory opened in October 1941, it was the first car assembly plant in Southeast Asia. During the Malayan campaign, its assembly equipment was used by the RAF to assemble fighter planes. But by February 1942, Japanese forces had advanced into Singapore, and on February 15, Lt Gen Percival, head of the Allied forces in Singapore, surrendered to Japan's General Yamashita in the Ford Motor Company Board Room. While Percival was taken to Changi prison as a POW (he would fly to Tokyo Bay three years later to witness the Japanese surrender), the Japanese commanders gathered for a ritual ceremony of thanks, ate their emperor's gifts of dried cuttlefish and chestnuts and drank a silent *sake* toast.

Then it was down to business. Stung by overseas Chinese efforts to raise funds for China's defence against Japan, Japanese troops launched *Sook Ching*, a brutal purge of anti-Japanese Chinese in Singapore. *Kempaitei* (military police) officers established screening centres, to which Chinese men had to report. Even the most tenuous of evidence – tattoos, a Chinese education, wearing glasses or having the soft hands of the educated – could result in individuals being loaded onto lorries and taken to massacre grounds around the island. The Japanese estimated the number of dead around five thousand; Singapore's Chinese Chamber of Commerce thought it was eight times that many.

Concurrently, the occupying army began a mass "Japanisation" process. Locals were urged to learn Japanese and celebrate imperial birthdays; the press was controlled by the Japanese Propaganda Department; and Japanese cultural shows were held at Victoria Theatre and Memorial Hall. The new currency introduced by the Japanese came to be known as 'banana money', as the S$10 note featured a banana plant. The gallery ends with images of General Seishiro, commander in chief of the Japanese 7th area army, surrendering to Admiral Lord Louis Mountbatten, supreme allied commander of southeast Asia, on September 12th, 1945. At the ceremony, Allied troops raised the same Union Jack that had been handed over at the Ford Factory three years earlier. Oil palm, tapioca, sweet potato, papaya and other food crops grown during the occupation have been planted in the **wartime garden** outside the factory, but the garden's location amongst the air-con units behind the building is puzzling.

The MacRitchie Trails

East of Bukit Timah, the shoreline and environs of MacRitchie Reservoir play host to the **MacRitchie Trails** (daily 6.30am–7.30pm; free), a network of six colour-coded tracks and boardwalks that allow you to experience Singapore's lowland tropical dipterocarp forest. Bisecting lush vegetation and skirting the reservoir's glassy waters, the trails offer the chance to see macaques, monitor lizards, terrapins, squirrels, eagles and kingfishers in the wild. If you happen to be in town on the second Sunday of the month, you can join the free nature appreciation walk that starts from the head of the Prunus Trail at 9.30am (ⓣ65545127 to pre-book). One of the longer trails, MacRitchie Nature Trail, leads to the **HSBC TreeTop Walk** (Tues–Fri 9am–5pm, Sat & Sun 8.30am–5pm; free), a free-standing, 25m-high, 250m-long suspension bridge that gives you a monkey's-eye view of the forest canopy. As long as there are no noisy school parties bustling across, you've got a pretty good chance of spotting some colourful fauna and birdlife. The MacRitchie Trails all start at MacRitchie Reservoir Park, where there are rest rooms, a café and information boards. To reach the park, take bus #132, 166 or 167 from downtown, and alight at Thomson Road. If you don't fancy the 4km hike to the TreeTop Walk, stay on any of the buses listed above and at the turning to the Singapore Island Country Club, on Upper Thomson Road.

The zoo and Mandai Orchid Gardens

On Mandai Lake Road off the Bukit Timah Expressway, the **Singapore Zoological Gardens** (daily 8.30am–6pm; S$15, kids S$7.50, S$28/14 incl. Night Safari, S$35/17.50 incl. Night Safari and Bird Park; ⓦwww.zoo.com .sg) are spread over a promontory jutting into peaceful Seletar Reservoir. The gardens attract 1.2 million visitors a year – a fact perhaps explained by their status as one of the world's few open zoos, where moats are preferred to cages. The zoo manages to approximate the natural habitats of the animals it holds, and though leopards, pumas and jaguars still have to be kept behind bars, this is a thoughtful, humane place, described as "one of the really beautiful zoos" by no less an authority than conservationist Sir Peter Scott.

There are some 3200 animals here, representing more than 330 species, so it's best to allow a whole day for your visit. A **tram** circles the grounds on a one-way circuit, but as it won't always be going your way, be prepared for a lot of legwork. Highlights include orang-utans, komodo dragons, polar bears (which you view underwater from a gallery), and Primate Kingdom; also worth checking out is the **special loan enclosure**, which has recently played host to a giant panda, an Indian white tiger and a golden monkey. No exhibit lets you get any closer to the resident animals than the **Fragile Forest** biodome, a magical zone where you can walk amid ring-tailed lemurs, tree kangeroos, sloths and fruit bats. Various **animal shows** and **feeding shows** run throughout the day from 10am until 5pm, featuring sea lions, elephants, polar bears and other exotic creatures. There are also elephant (S$6/3) and pony rides (S$4) and, in **Children's World**, there's the chance to hold young chicks and watch a milking demonstration. At 9am daily, you can even share breakfast with a selection of the zoo's residents, including orang-utans and snakes (see p.704 for details).

The opening of the **Night Safari** (daily 7.30pm–midnight; S$20, kids S$10, S$28/14 including zoo, S$35/17.50 including zoo and Bird Park; ⓦwww.zoo.com.sg) a few years back substantially increased the grounds of the zoo. Here, a thousand animals representing well over a hundred species – among them elephants, rhinos, giraffes, leopards, hyenas and otters – play out their nocturnal routines under a forest of standard lamps. Three **walking trails**, geared around forest giants, leopards and the incredibly cute fishing cats, respectively, wind through the safari. However, only five of the safari's eight zones are walkable – to see the rest you'll need to take a 45-minute Jurassic Park-style tram ride, and tolerate the intrusive chattering of its taped guide.

Practicalities

To get to the zoo, take **bus** #171 from Stamford Road, Orchard Boulevard or Bukit Timah to Mandai Road, then transfer to the #927; or take the MRT to Ang Mo Kio station and catch the #138 from there. Upon **arrival**, pick up the leaflet with details of riding and feeding times and the helpful map, which suggests itineraries taking in all the major shows and attractions. At the other end of your trip, you might care to drop by the **gift shop** next to the exit, which stocks the usual cuddly toys, key rings and pencil cases. Several food and drink kiosks are dotted around the zoo, or you can head for *Jungle Flavours*, bang in the centre of the grounds, and offering a range of local dishes.

Mandai Orchid Gardens

It's only a ten-minute walk from the zoo down Mandai Lake Road to the **Mandai Orchid Gardens** (daily 8.30am–5.30pm; S$3; ⓣ62691036, ⓦwww.singaporeorchids.com.sg), or you can take the #138 bus from the zoo, which stops right outside. Orchids are big business in Singapore. Here, four hectares of flowers are cultivated on a gentle slope, tended by old ladies in wide-brimmed hats. Unless you are a keen horticulturist, the place will be of only limited interest, since little effort has been taken to make it instructive. Still, the gardens make a colourful detour, and the cost of a gift box of orchids (starting from S$20) compares favourably with prices charged by central flower shops.

North to Woodlands and the Sungei Buloh Nature Park

Five kilometres north of the zoo is the bustling town of **WOODLANDS**, from where the **causeway** spanning the Strait of Johor links Singapore to Johor Bahru in Malaysia – for the moment, at least. The causeway has become a bone of contention between the governments of Singapore and Malaysia in recent years, with Malaysia pressing hard for its demolition and replacement with a new, crooked bridge. It cites an untenable increase in traffic volume and dangerous levels of pollution in the Straits of Johor as its reasons. At peak hours (6.30–9.30am & 5.30–7.30pm) and at weekends, the roads leading to the causeway seethe with cars and trucks – all full of petrol, after a law passed in the early 1990s banned Singaporeans from driving out of the country on an empty tank. Previously, people crossed into Malaysia, filled up with cut-price fuel and then headed home; now, signs line the roads approaching the causeway requesting that "Singapore cars please top up to 3/4 tank" – or risk a S$500 fine.

Kranji War Memorial

Bus #170 from Ban San Terminal on Queen Street heads towards Woodlands on its way to JB, passing the **Kranji War Cemetery and Memorial** on Woodlands Road, where only the sound of birds and insects breaks the silence in the immaculate grounds. (You can also get here by alighting at Kranji MRT Station, from where it's a 500m walk.) The cemetery is the resting place of the many Allied troops who died in the defence of Singapore; as you enter, row upon row of graves slope up the landscaped hill in front of you, some identified only as "known unto God". The graves are bare: placing flowers is banned because still water encourages mosquitoes to breed. Above the simple stone cross which stands over the cemetery is the **memorial**, around which are recorded the names of more than twenty thousand soldiers (including personnel from Britain, Canada, Australia, New Zealand, Malay and South Asia) who died in this region during World War II. Two unassuming **tombs** stand on the wide lawns below the cemetery, belonging to Yusof bin Ishak and Dr Benjamin Henry Sheares, independent Singapore's first two presidents.

Singapore Turf Club

Singapore's only racecourse (adjacent to Kranji MRT Station, or passed by bus #170) is at **Singapore Turf Club**, a short way beyond the war memorial. As gambling in Singapore outside the course is restricted, the annual racing calendar here is very popular. The most prestigious events include the Lion City Cup, the Singapore Gold Cup and the Singapore Derby. Race dates change from year to year, so it's worth calling the information hotline or checking the club website (℡68791000, ⓦwww.turfclub.com.sg) if you want to time your visit to coincide with a big race day. When there's no racing in Singapore, a giant video screen links the racecourse to various courses across the causeway in Malaysia. There's a fairly strict dress code – sandals, jeans, shorts and T-shirts are out – and foreign visitors have to take their passports with them. Friday cards begin at 6.30pm, Saturday's and Sunday's after lunch, and tickets cost from S$3 to S$20. A day's racing viewed from the grandstand's posher upper tiers can be booked in advance, but you'd do far better to just turn up, eat at the lower grandstand's decent food court and soak up the atmosphere in the stands.

Sungei Buloh Wetland Reserve

The 130-hectare swathe of **Sungei Buloh Wetland Reserve** (Mon–Sat 7.30am–7pm, Sun 7am–7pm; S$1/50¢, free Sat & Sun; ℡67941401, ⓦwww .sbwr.org.sg), 4km northwest of Kranji Cemetery on the north coast of Singapore, is the island's only protected wetland nature park. Beyond its visitor centre, café and video theatre (shows Mon–Sat 9am, 11am, 1pm, 3pm & 5pm,

Sun hourly 9am–5pm) walking routes and boardwalks thread through and over an expanse of mangrove, mud flats, orchards and grassland, home to kingfishers, herons, sandpipers, kites and sea eagles and, in the waters, mudskippers, needlefish and archerfish – which squirt water into the air to knock insects into devouring range. The reserve's 500m-long mangrove boardwalk offers an easy means of getting a sense of the shoreline environment. You'll take your stroll to the accompaniment of cicadas and birdsong. En route, you'll spot tortoises, crabs and mudskippers among the reaching fingers of the mangrove swamp. From here you can graduate to walks ranging from three to seven kilometres into the guts of the reserve. Visit between September and March, and you're likely to catch sight of migratory birds from around Asia roosting and feeding. Come on a Saturday and you can join a free guided tour (9am, 10am, 3pm & 4pm); at other times you'll need to pre-book a tour (S$50 per group).

To reach the park, take the MRT to Kranji station, then transfer to bus #925, which stops at Kranji Reservoir car park from Monday to Saturday, and at the park's entrance on Sundays.

Tai Gin Road: the Sun Yat Sen Villa and Burmese Temple

Between Jalan Toa Payoh to the north and Balestier Road to the south is the **Sun Yat Sen Villa** (Tues–Fri & Sun 9am–5pm, Sat 10am–10pm; S$3; ☎62567377, ⓦwanqingyuan.com.sg), on tiny Tai Gin Road. Built to house the mistress of a wealthy Chinese businessman, this attractive Palladian-style bungalow changed hands in 1905, when one Teo Eng Hock bought it for his mother. Chinese nationalist leader Dr Sun Yat Sen paid the first of several visits to Singapore the following year, and was invited by Teo to stay at Tai Gin Road, where he quickly established a Singapore branch of the Tong Meng Hui – a society dedicated to replacing the Manchu Dynasty in China with a modern republic. After serving as a communications camp for the Japanese during World War II, the villa fell into disrepair until 1966, when it was opened to the public. A recent renovation has added an extra wing to the building, allowing space for six **galleries**, whose displays, artefacts and visuals variously focus upon the villa's history, the life of Dr Sun, and the historical context to the Chinese revolution in which he played such a substantial part. There's also a gallery celebrating the role of Southeast Asia's overseas Chinese in supporting the revolution – a huge painting of Dr Sun rallying support from tin miners and rubber tappers in Malaya dominates it. There's enough here to engage the mind for a while, but realistically this is best left to visitors with an active interest in Chinese history. Around the villa's attractive gardens, stretches the 58m-long "Common Memories" **mural**, which portrays the multiracial, multicultural existence of the Singaporeans from the early nineteenth century to World War II.

Next door is the **Sasanaramsi Burmese Buddhist Temple** (daily 6am–10pm; ☎62511717, ⓦwww.bbt.org.sg), reconstructed in just two years having been moved from its previous site at Kinta Road because of redevelopment. Decorated by craftsmen from Burma, the temple's ground floor is dominated by a large, white-marble statue of the Buddha brought over from Burma in the 1920s – a series of **murals** on the top floor depict the statue's journey by ship, train, barge, truck, elephant and fork-lift from Sagyin Hill in Burma to Singapore. Upstairs is another Buddha statue, this time standing, and ringed by blue skies painted on the wall behind.

To reach Tai Gin Road's attractions, take bus #139 from outside Dhoby Ghaut MRT station.

The Lian Shan Shuang Lin and
Phor Kark See temples

Two of Singapore's largest Chinese temples are situated in the island's central region, east of the Central Catchment Area. Both are rather isolated, but have plenty to interest temple enthusiasts, and buzz with activity at festival times.

The name of the popular **Lian Shan Shuang Lin Temple**, at 184e Jalan Toa Payoh (a ten-minute walk from Toa Payoh MRT station), means "Twin Groves of the Lotus Mountain" – a reference to the Buddha's birth in a grove of trees and his death under a bodhi tree. The Chinese abbot, Sek Hean Wei, established the temple at the start of the twentieth century when, passing through Singapore on his way home after a pilgrimage to Sri Lanka, he was waylaid by wealthy Hokkien merchant and philanthropist, Low Kim Pong, who supplied both the land and finances for the venture. Several renovations have failed to rob the temple of its grandeur: set behind a half-moon pool, it is accessed by the **Hall of Celestial Kings**, where statues of the four kings of heaven stand guard to repel evil, symbolized by the demons under their feet. The kings flank Maitreya Bodhisattva, the **laughing Buddha**, believed to grant good luck if you rub his stomach. Beyond, a courtyard dotted with bonsai plants and lilies in dragon jars leads to the main Mahavira Hall, where a sakyamuni Buddha in lotus position takes centre stage. To his right is the medicine Buddha, the great healing teacher, and to his left, the Amitabha. Elsewhere in the compound is a grand hall with a 100-armed Kuan Yin, goddess of mercy, flanked by chandeliers; and the seven-tiered **Dragon Light Pagoda**. To **get here**, take the MRT to Toa Payoh station, from where the temple is a ten-minute walk.

Phor Kark See Temple

The largest temple complex in Singapore – and one of the largest in Southeast Asia – lies north of MacRitchie Reservoir, right in the middle of the island. **Phor Kark See Temple** (known in full as the Kong Meng San Phor Kark See Temple Complex; daily 7am–5pm), at 88 Bright Hill Drive, spreads over nineteen acres and combines temples, pagodas, pavilions, a Buddhist library and a vast crematorium to such impressive effect that it has been used several times as a backdrop to Chinese kung fu movies. More modern than Lian Shan Shuang Lin, Phor Kark See boasts none of the faded charm of Singapore's older temples, but relies instead on its sheer magnitude and exuberant decor for effect. Multi-tiered roofs bristle with ceramic dragons, phoenixes, birds and human figures, while around the complex are statues of various constructions and deities, including a nine-metre-high marble statue of Kuan Yin, goddess of mercy, and a soaring pagoda capped by a golden *chedi* (a reliquary tower). The inauguration, in early 2006, of a prayer hall housing a vast seated Buddha reputed to be the biggest in Southeast Asia rendered the complex even more striking. Even the **crematorium**, conveniently placed for the nearby Bright Hill Evergreen Home for the elderly – doesn't do things by halves. Housed below a Thai-style facade of elaborately carved, gilt wood, it can cope with five ceremonies at a time. Below the crematorium is a pair of ponds, where thousands of turtles sunbathe precariously on wooden planks that slant into the water. Letting new turtles into the ponds is supposed to bring good luck. Beside the viewing gallery, old ladies sell bunches of vegetables, which purchasers then throw to the lucky turtles.

Take bus #130 up Victoria Street to reach the complex, alighting at the far end of Sin Ming Drive.

Eastern Singapore

Thirty years ago, **eastern Singapore** was largely rural, dotted with Malay kampungs that perched on stilts over the shoreline and harbouring the odd weekend retreat owned by Europeans or moneyed locals. Massive **land reclamation** and development programmes have altered the region beyond recognition, wiping out all traces of the kampungs and throwing up huge housing projects in their place. Today, former seafront suburbs like Bedok are separated from the Straits of Singapore by a broad crescent of man-made land, much of which constitutes the **East Coast Park**, whose five kilometres incorporate leisure and watersports facilities, imported sand beaches and seafood restaurants. Despite the massive upheavals that have ruptured the communities of the east coast, parts of it, including the suburbs of **Geylang** and **Katong**, have managed to retain a strong Malay identity.

Dominating the eastern tip of the island is Changi airport and, beyond that, **Changi Village**, in whose prison the Japanese interned Allied troops and civilians during World War II. From Changi Point, it's possible to take a boat to **Pulau Ubin**, a small island with echoes of pre-development Singapore.

Geylang and Katong

Malay culture has held sway in and around the adjoining suburbs of **GEYLANG** and **KATONG** since the mid-nineteenth century, when Malays and Indonesians first arrived to work in the local *copra* (dried coconut kernel) processing factory and later on its *serai* (lemon grass) farms. Many of the shophouses, restaurants and food centres in the area are Malay-influenced, less so the thriving trade in prostitution that carries on here, unchecked by the local authorities.

The continuation of Victoria Street and Kallang Road, **Geylang Road** – the main thoroughfare of Geylang – runs east from the Kallang River. Off Geylang Road's main stem shoot 42 *lorongs* (lanes), down which are clusters of brothels, recognizable by their exterior fairy lights. At its far end, 2km east and near Paya Lebar MRT station, Geylang Road meets **Joo Chiat Road**, which runs south and has a refreshingly laid-back and shambolic air after the restrictions of downtown Singapore. In the **Joo Chiat Complex**, at the northern end of Joo Chiat Road, textile merchants drape their wares on any available floor and wall space, transforming the drab interior. More market than shopping centre, it's a prime destination for anyone interested in buying cheap silk, batik, rugs or muslin worn by Malay women. Stalls around the perimeter of the complex sell dates, honey, Malay CDs and *jamu* (Malay medicine).

Before striking off down Joo Chiat Road, cross Changi Road, to the north, where, east of a side street called Geylang Serai, a hawker centre and wet market of the same name provide more Malay atmosphere, from the clove cigarettes to the line of sarong sellers beyond the food stalls. Geylang Serai market is due to be demolished and then rebuilt on the same site in mid-2006. The chances are that when it is complete, the new market will still be a more authentic slice of life than the **Malay Village** (daily 10am–10pm; S$5/3 for attractions, otherwise free) on the other side of Geylang Serai, and a short walk from Paya Lebar MRT. Opened in 1990, and conceived as a celebration of the cuisine, music, dance, arts and crafts of the Malay people, the village conspicuously failed either to woo tourists or to rent out its replica wooden-kampung-style shops to locals, and seems to be dying a slow but certain death. Its tourist lures pack little punch: the **Kampung Museum** features a humdrum array of household instruments, textiles, kites and *kris*, and a mock-up of a Malay wedding scene; the dismal **Kampung Days** exhibition reproduces a traditional Malay kampung homestead, complete with fishing and rice-pounding scenes, a *wayang kulit* stage, an open-air cinema, and another (seemingly obligatory) wedding scene; and the Cultural Demonstration Corner hosts half-hearted exhibitions of Malay games and crafts. If you give these attractions a miss, you're left with the village's numerous **shops**, selling batik, kites, spinning tops, bird cages and textiles, and the evening **food court** with free cultural performances on Saturday and Sunday nights.

As you walk south down Joo Chiat Road you'll have to negotiate piles of merchandise that spill out of shophouses and onto the pavement. With its ochre tiled roof and green walls, low-key **Khalid Mosque**, a stone's throw from the Joo Chiat Complex, belies the eye-catching architecture on view elsewhere on or around Joo Chiat Road. Joo Chiat itself has some beautifully restored shophouses (like Chiang Pow Joss Paper Trading at no. 252, where funerary paraphernalia is made beneath elaborate facades of flowers and dragons) but none as magnificent as the immaculate **Peranakan shophouses** on Koon Seng Road (on the left halfway down Joo Chiat Road), where painstaking work has restored multicoloured facades, French windows, eaves and mouldings.

Back on Joo Chiat, several shops are worthy of a detour: Kway Guan Huat at no. 95 makes *popiah* skin; mackerel *otah* is produced at no. 267; there are non-alcoholic perfumes and Arab CDs at Haruman Makkah at no. 142; and Malay medicines next door at Fatimah Trading.

Hang a right when Joo Chiat hits East Coast Road and at no. 113 you'll find **Rumah Bebe**, a delightful Peranakan shop that sells beaded shoes and handbags, costume jewellery, porcelain tiffin carriers and the traditional garb – *kebaya* and *sarong* – of Nonya women. From Rumah Bebe, it's just a couple of minutes' walk east to the **Katong Antiques House** at 208 East Coast Road where owner Peter Wee has amassed a treasure trove of Peranakan artefacts, from wedding costumes to furniture. You'll need to call ahead (T63458544) to book an appointment. Head west from Rumah Bebe, to the junction with Ceylon Road, and you'll find a clutch of venerable food stalls selling peerless Katong *laksa*.

To get to the western end of Geylang Road, take the MRT to the Kallang stop, from where Geylang Road is a short walk south. Two stops east is Paya Lebar station, from where a short walk left out of the station, across Sims Avenue and left again onto Geylang Road, brings you to the Joo Chiat Complex. Alternatively, bus #16 from Orchard and Bras Basah roads deposits you right in the middle of Joo Chiat Road.

Changi Museum

Infamous Changi Prison was the site of a World War II POW camp in which Japanese jailers subjected Allied prisoners to the harshest of treatment. The prison itself is still in use (drug offenders are periodically executed here), and its terrible past is marked in the hugely moving **Changi Museum** (daily 9.30am–4pm; free; T62142451, W www.changimuseum.com), just up the road.

Following a recent relocation of the museum, an appeal for artefacts by the Singapore Tourism Board to Australian veterans' associations mustered a Samurai sword, a prisoner's chipped enamel mug, ration cards, a Nippon-Go primer and assorted other relics. In truth, though, the museum's power lies more in the many cruelties it portrays, than in the miscellanies it has amassed. Sketches, photographs and information boards plot the Japanese occupation of Singapore and the fate of the soldiers and civilians subsequently incarcerated in camps around the Changi area. Most movingly of all, though, is the board of remembrance, where children, wives and compatriots have pinned messages to the dead.

Novelist **James Clavell** was a young British artillery officer in Singapore at the time of the Japanese invasion; later he drew on his own experience of the "obscene forbidding prison" at Changi in writing *King Rat*, never forgetting that in the cells of the prison camp, "the stench was nauseating. Stench from rotten bodies. Stench from a generation of confined human bodies." You can get the merest sense of what Clavell means by entering the **Changi Cell**, a dark, stuffy alleyway that approximates the cramped confinement suffered by POWs, and in which the voices of former POWs recall enduring the "howling, crying, shouting" of fellow inmates being tortured in the middle of the night.

Clavell's recollections are borne out by the selection of photos by **George Aspinall**, in a cabinet at the entrance to the museum. Aspinall, then a young Australian trooper, recorded the appalling living conditions and illnesses suffered by POWs in Malaya and Thailand during the occupation using a folding Kodak 2 camera, later developing his shots with a stock of processing materials which he found while working in a labour gang in Singapore's docks.

The museum's **gallery** section showcases the work of various prison artists, among them W.R.M. Haxworth, who produced over four hundred paintings and sketches during his internment. Haxworth's tongue-in-cheek sketches of daily Changi life reveal the dry sense of humour and stiff upper lips that sustained internees in the face of adversity. One, entitled *Changi Comforts*, depicts a variety of rickety stools, some fruit and a battered biscuit tin. Another sketch, in which a character holds up two shirts, one white and one black, is entitled *White and Changi white*. Elsewhere, there are full-scale reproductions of the murals of Stanley Warren, who used camouflage paint, crushed snooker chalk and aircraft paints smuggled in by fellow POWs to paint Bible scenes on a Changi chapel wall.

Outside in a courtyard is a replica of a simple wooden **chapel**, typical of those erected in Singapore's wartime camps; the brass cross on its altar was crafted from spent ammunition casings, while its walls carry more poignant messages of remembrance penned by visiting former POWs and relatives.

Journey's end is at the museum **shop**, where a video screen plays footage of the Japanese attack and the living conditions in Changi. On a lighter note, among the war-related books stocked in the shop is *The Happiness Box*, the first copy of which was written, illustrated and bound by POWs in Changi in 1942 as a Christmas present for children in the prison. The Japanese became suspicious of the POWs' motives when they noticed one of the book's central characters was called Winston, but it was buried in the prison grounds before it could be confiscated, and only recovered after the war had ended.

From Chinatown and Victoria Street, bus #2 travels east and past the museum; alternatively, you could take the MRT to Tanah Merah station, and pick up the #2 there.

Changi Village

Journey's end for bus #2 is at the terminal at **CHANGI VILLAGE**, ten minutes further on from the prison. Apart from a moment's respite from the thrum of downtown life, there's little to bring you out to sleepy Changi Village, save to catch a boat from **Changi Point**, behind the bus terminal, for Pulau

Ubin, or for the coast of Johor in Malaysia (see p.629). The left-hand jetty is for Ubin, the right-hand one for bumboats to Johor.

A stroll over the footbridge to the right of the two jetties takes you to **Changi Beach**, the execution site of many thousands of Singaporean civilians by Japanese soldiers in World War II. As a beach it wins few prizes – apart from its *casuarinas* and palms, its most pleasant aspect is its view. To your left as you look out to sea is Pulau Ubin; slightly to the right is the island of Tekong (a military zone), behind which you can see a hill on mainland Malaysia. In the water you'll see *kelongs*, and boats galore, from bumboats to supertankers. Changi Village Road, the village's main drag, has a growing number of decent restaurants and a few bars, or try the hawker centre near the bus terminal.

Pulau Ubin

Pulau Ubin, 2km offshore, gives visitors a pretty good idea of what Singapore would have been like fifty years ago. A lazy backwater tucked into the Straits of Johor, it's a great place to come if you're tired of shops, high-rises and traffic. It's almost worth coming for the ten-minute boat trip alone, made in an old oil-stained bumboat (S$2 each way) that chugs noisily across Serangoon Harbour, belching fumes all the way. Boats depart from Changi Point throughout the day from 6am onwards, leaving whenever they are full. The last boat back to Changi leaves as late as 10pm, if there's a demand, but plan to be at the jetty by 8.30pm at the latest, just in case.

Boats dock at the pier in **Ubin Village**, where palm trees slope and Malay stilt houses teeter over a sludgy mangrove beach that's stippled with the remains of collapsed, rotting jetties. Bear left from the jetty, and you'll soon hit the village square – but before that, swing by the **information kiosk** (daily 8.30am–5pm; ☎65424108, ⓦwww.nparks.gov.sg) to the right of the jetty for an island map. A short, circular **sensory trail** created by the Singapore Society for the Visually Handicapped, starts and finishes at the kiosk, taking in herbs, spices and orchids en route.

The main road into the village is lined with scores of battered old mopeds, locals sit around, watching the day take its course, roosters run free in the dirt and dogs bask under the hot sun. The best, and most enjoyable, way to explore the dirt tracks of Ubin is by **mountain bike**. A cluster of bike rental shops operates along the jetty road, charging S$2–15 for a day's rental, depending upon the bike and the season (it's most expensive during school holidays). A labyrinthine network of tracks veins Ubin, but it's only a small island (just 7km by 2km) and all roads are well signposted, so you won't get lost. As you go, look out for the monitor lizards, long-tailed macaques, lizards, butterflies, kites and eagles that inhabit Ubin, and listen for the distinctive rattle-buzz of cicadas.

The hall on the left flank of the **square** is used periodically for Chinese opera, ceremonial occasions and other Ubin functions. Opposite it is a tiny, fiery red Chinese temple. Bear left past the hall until you come to a basketball court, where a left turn takes you to the west of the island, and a right turn takes you to the east.

Turn left towards the west of the island and, after about five minutes, you'll come to an impressively deep **quarry**, from which granite was taken to build the causeway linking Singapore to Johor Bahru – Ubin is the Malay word for granite. Don't swim in this or any other Ubin quarry, however tempting it might be: the government has erected signs warning of hefty fines for doing so. A right turn after the first bridge you cross takes you to a peaceful lean-to **Chinese Temple** fronted by wind chimes, a shrine holding three colourful figurines of tigers and a pool of carp, and shielded from the surrounding mangrove by a pretty lily-pad pond.

Further north along the track, over a second bridge and down a right-turn marked Jalan Wat Siam, is a rather incongruous **Thai Buddhist Temple** fronted by two big, polished wooden elephants, complete with portraits of the king and queen of Thailand, and a bookcase full of Thai books. Pictures telling the story of the life of Buddha ring the inner walls of the temple, along with images of various Buddhist hells – the most disturbing of which depicts demons pouring boiling liquid down the mouths of "those who always drink liquor". Boonrai, the temple's head monk, holds free **meditation classes** every Saturday and Sunday; call ☏65423468 to book yourself on a class.

En route to the Thai Temple you'll pass the *Ubin Lagoon Resort*, whose myriad outward-bound facilities can be used by non-guests, upon payment of a day rate. The Outward Bound Singapore centre beyond the Thai Temple is, however, out of bounds.

Biking eastwards of the basketball court takes you past the prawn and fish farms, rubber trees and raised kampung houses of the centre and eastern side of Ubin. **Noordin Beach**, at the top of the island, offers an unprepossessing but smart enough patch of sand, though its views across the Johor Straits to southern Malaysia have been spoilt by the ugly metal fence recently erected in the water to keep out illegal immigrants. Further east, towards **Kampong Melayu**, are some beautifully maintained and brightly painted examples of kampung-style stilt houses. Beyond the village, Tanjong **Chek Jawa**, the far eastern tip of the island, constitutes Ubin's most pristine patch of mangrove; call the information kiosk on ☏65024108 to pre-arrange a free, guided tour of the mudskippers, crabs, seabirds and other wildlife here.

You'll happen upon the odd drinks stop as you bike around Ubin. For **food**, there's a restaurant (daily 8am–10pm) at the resort. Otherwise, of the several eating options in the village, the best bets are the *Sin Lam Huat*, in the village, for its chilli crab and kampung chicken dishes, or the Malay coffee shop beside the jetty, which knocks out curries, noodles and *rendangs*.

Escape Theme Park

With kids in tow, you'll be glad of the **Escape Theme Park** (Mon & Wed–Fri 4–10pm, Sat & Sun 10am–10pm, adults S$16, children S$8 – includes all rides and one go-kart ride; ☏65819112, ⓦwww.escapethemepark.com.sg), at 1 Pasir Ris Close. Singapore's largest theme park, it boasts fifteen rides, among them the Cadbury Inverter, the Daytona Multi-tier Go Kart and Asia's highest flume ride, Wet & Wild. Clowns wander the park's byways, offering light relief while you queue for rides; and in the central pavilion there are oodles of games, galleries and food outlets. From Pasir Ris MRT, you'll need to hop on bus #354.

Western Singapore

Since the government's industrialization programme began in the late 1960s, far **western Singapore** has developed into the manufacturing heart of the state, and today thousands of companies occupy units within the towns of Jurong and Tuas. Manufacturing has proven the backbone of Singapore's economic success – the state presently produces a sizeable proportion of the world's hard-disk drives, for example. Despite this saturation, much of the western region – crafted from former swampland and wasteland – remains remarkably verdant, and perhaps surprisingly, given the industrial surroundings, several major tourist attractions are located here, including **Haw Par Villa**, as garish a theme park as you'll ever set eyes on, though the pick of the bunch is fascinating **Jurong Bird Park**. Slightly further east, the **Singapore Science Centre** is packed with imaginative and informative exhibitions, and is not to be missed if you've got kids to entertain. Just west of Chinatown is the district of **Telok Blangah**, once the seat of Singapore's *temenggong* or chieftain, and dominated by Mount Faber, as well as the **HarbourFront** complex, from where cable cars, boats and buses make for Sentosa Island. It's just a short hop west of Mount Faber to two reminders of World War II at **Labrador Secret Tunnels** and **Reflections at Bukit Chandu**. All of these places are easily reached from the city centre, using either buses or the MRT.

Telok Blangah, HarbourFront and Mount Faber

A twenty-minute walk west of Chinatown is the district known as **Telok Blangah**, home to **HarbourFront**, a shopping-centre-cum-marine terminal from where boats depart for Indonesia's Riau Archipelago, and from which cable cars rock across the skyline, on their way to and from Mount Faber and across to Sentosa Island (see p.699).

Mount Faber, 600m north of HarbourFront, was named in 1845 after government engineer Captain Charles Edward Faber. The top of the "mount" ("hillock" would be a better word) commands fine views of Keppel Harbour and, to the northeast, central Singapore – views which are even more impressive at night, when the city is lit up. It's a long, steep walk from Telok Blangah Road up to the top of Mount Faber – it's better to take the **cable car** from HarbourFront (daily 8.30am–9pm; S$10.90 return, children S$5.50 for up to four stations; S$15, children S$8 for glass cabin). An accident in 1983, when a ship's mast clipped the cables on which the cars are suspended, cost seven passengers their lives, but today laser eyes ensure history won't repeat itself. As you'd expect, there's a correspondingly strong souvenir shop presence up here, though you can escape this by moving away from the area immediately around the cable-car station and up into the palms, bougainvilleas and rhododendrons of **Mount Faber Park**. In the **Jewel Box**, the park also boasts a sophisticated bar and restaurant complex with thrilling views out to sea – though undoubtedly the area's most thrilling culinary experience is to **dine in a cable car** (daily 6.30–8.30pm; ☎63779633; set meals for two from S$88).

In the early days of colonial rule, Temenggong Abdul Rahman played prime minister to Sultan Hussein Shah's president, and his signature graced the treaty authorizing the East India Company to operate out of Singapore. All that's left of his settlement on the southern slopes of Mount Faber is its pillared mosque – the **State of Johor Mosque** – and, behind that, a small Malay cemetery and a portion of the brickwork that once housed the *temenggong*'s baths. The mosque lies five minutes' walk east of the HarbourFront Centre, and can be reached on any HarbourFront-bound bus.

From HarbourFront, it's 1500m as the crow flies to **Labrador Park**, where the **Labrador Secret Tunnels** (hourly guided tours daily 10am–6pm; S$8/5) recall the days when Fort Pasir Panjang stood on this spot. It's hard to see where the S$5m development cost was spent: the two dark tunnels feature old copies of the *Straits Times*, dummies in wartime costume and the detritus – shell fragments, kerosene lamps, mess tins – of army life. Realistically, if you are going to visit just one set of wartime tunnels, you'd do better to go to **Fort Siloso** (see p.701) or **Battle Box** (see p.656). Elsewhere in the park, there are gun emplacements, 6-inch guns and bronze statues of soldiers; you'll also get some fine views of Sentosa and the surrounding bay.

Reflections at Bukit Chandu

The 1st and 2nd Battalion of the Malay Regiment's defence of Pasir Panjang against the Japanese, in 1942, is remembered at **Reflections at Bukit Chandu** (Tues–Sun 9am–5pm; S$2/1; ☎63327978, ⓦwww.1942.org.sg), a low-key attraction 3km west of Telok Blangah, at 31K Pepys Rd. Facing some 13,000 advancing Japanese soldiers, the battalions chose to fight to the death rather than retreat. Wordily billed as a "World War II interpretive centre", Reflections uses exhibits and photographs to tell their story, and to track the unsuccessful defence of Malaya. Visitors experience the sounds of battle, the cold weight of a cast-iron helmet and a rifle, and the fear and claustrophobia of watch duty in a pillbox. However, this is no celebration of war. Rather, the emphasis is upon sombre meditation, with elements such as the Well of Reflection and the Windows of Memories encouraging visitors to ponder the purpose of war and to muse over the terrible loss of life that occurred in this part of Singapore.

Haw Par Villa

As an entertaining exercise in bad taste, **Haw Par Villa** (daily 9am–7pm; free) has few equals. Located 7km from the downtown area at 262 Pasir Panjang Road, it describes itself as a "historical theme park founded on Chinese legends and values", for which read a gaudy, gory parade of over a thousand grotesque statues. Previously known as Tiger Balm Gardens, the park now takes its name from its original owners, the Aw brothers, Boon Haw and Boon Par, who made a fortune early last century selling Tiger Balm – a cure-all unction created by their father. When the British government introduced licensing requirements for the possession of large animals, the private zoo that the brothers maintained on their estate here was closed down and replaced by statues.

The rides, theatre shows and multimedia attractions that were added a few years back to broaden the appeal of the place actually did no such thing. All have now been closed, leaving only the statues for which the park is famous. These statues feature characters and creatures from Chinese legend and religion, Fu Lu Shou, Confucius and the Laughing Buddha among them, as well as a fantastical menagerie of snakes, dragons, elephants, kissing locusts, monkeys and crabs with women's heads.

△ Haw Par Villa

The best – and most gruesome – series of statues lies in the **Ten Courts of Hell** exhibit (daily 9am–5pm, S$2), whose explanation of the Buddhist belief in punishment for sins and reincarnation is not for the faint-hearted. Accessed through the open mouth of a huge "walk-in" dragon, the statues depict sinners undergoing a ghastly range of tortures meted out by hideous, leering demons, before being wiped of all memory in the Pavilion of Forgetfulness and sent back to earth to have another stab at godliness. Prostitutes are shown drowned in pools of blood, drug addicts tied to a red-hot copper pillar, thieves and gamblers frozen into blocks of ice and moneylenders who charge exorbitant interest rates thrown onto a hill of knives. If you are thinking of cracking the spine on this guidebook, bear in mind that being sawn in two is the penalty for the misuse of books. Before you enter the courts of hell, check out the replica of Aw Boon Haw's **tiger car** at the ticket desk, which had a huge tiger's head across the radiator to advertise the family wares.

Elsewhere, another series of statues retells the classic Chinese legend of the monk Xuanzang's **Journey to the West** in search of Buddhist scriptures. The trials and tribulations that beset the monk and his disciples, featuring such characters as the spider women, the monkey god and the scarlet child, are all colourfully depicted.

A new attraction, the **Hua Song Museum** (Tues–Sun noon–7pm; S$8.40/5.25), has taken up residence on the western flank of the compound. Roughly translated, its name means "in praise of the Chinese", making it an appropriate addition to a park so dedicated to Oriental faith and legend. The museum traces the struggles of early Chinese immigrants as they settled, assimilated and flourished around the world, also focusing on the global impact upon the world of the Chinese diaspora.

"Robust like bamboo, able to thrive in rich soil and stay alive in poor soil", reads one sign in the museum, "the early Chinese immigrant had to bend and blend in to survive." Successive **galleries** describe how this survival was effected. Visitors follow the Chinese migrants' long road from village to dockside and from dockside to far-flung corners of the world. In the Floating Hell gallery, displays and exhibits convey the hardships they endured on board the junks that transported them to their new lives and the struggles they had to stay alive when they came ashore. From there, the museum tells of how they assimilated into their adopted lands while still, with the support of their clan associations, preserving ancestral identities. The lion's share of the museum's focus falls on China's male migrants but one gallery highlights the peculiar challenges that confronted female migrants – examples are the young girl sold into slavery at auction and the Samsui woman working on Singapore building sites. Food, one of the cornerstones of Chinese culture, merits its own gallery, where visitors become acquainted with the **cooking** implements and ingredients of the cuisine.

To **get to** Haw Par Villa, take bus #200 from Buona Vista MRT, bus #143 from HarbourFront or #51 from Chinatown.

Holland Village

A couple of kilometres north of Haw Par Villa and west of the Botanic Gardens, **Holland Village**, previously home to some of the British soldiers based in Singapore, continues to be an expat stronghold, with a plethora of Western restaurants and shops. The **Holland Road Shopping Centre** at 211 Holland Ave is the place to head for if you want to buy Asian art, crafts or textiles: there are shops on two levels where you can buy anything from an Indian pram to a Chinese opium pipe, while outside, cobblers, key-cutters and newsagents set up stall. Off Lorong Liput, the small road alongside the shopping centre, shoots Lorong Mambong, home to a thriving restaurant scene and to **craft shops** that specialize in ceramic elephants, dragon pots, porcelain, rattan and bamboo products. **Pasar Holland**, opposite the shops on Lorong Mambong, is a small, tumbledown market selling fruit, flowers, fish and meat, as well as housing a handful of hawker stalls.

Holland Village is a short walk from Buona Vista station, or take bus #7 from Orchard Boulevard.

Around Jurong Lake and beyond

Several tourist destinations are dotted around the environs of tranquil **Jurong Lake**, about 4km northwest of the new town of Clementi. You're far more likely to want to come out this way if you've got children in tow.

Singapore Science Centre

At the **Singapore Science Centre** (Tues–Sun 10am–6pm; S$6; ☏ 64252500, ⓦ www.science.edu.sg), situated southwest of Jurong Lake, a broad range of exhibition galleries hold over 850 hands-on exhibits designed to inject interest into even the most impenetrable scientific principles. The majority of the centre's visitors are local schoolchildren, who sweep around the galleries in vast, deafening waves, frantically trying out each interactive display. Exhibitions focusing on aviation, genetics, space science, marine ecology, IT, biotechnology and other disciplines allow you to experience sight through an insect's eyes, write in Braille, make smoke rings, speak with a frog's voice and see a thermal heat reflection of yourself. The **Omni-Theatre** (various times; S$10/5; call ☏ 64252500 for details of current movie), within the centre's grounds, features heart-stopping movies about science, space, history and adventure sports, shown planetarium-style on a huge dome screen. Recently it has also started showing blockbusters like Harry Potter and Lord of the Rings; check the local press for details of current showings. It takes ten minutes at most to reach the Science Centre on foot from Jurong East MRT – or hop onto bus #335.

Snow City

Hi-tech machines at **Snow City** (Tues–Sun 9am–8.30pm; S$12 including loan of jackets and boots; ☏ 63371511, ⓦ www.snowcity.com.sg), let it snow twelve months a year in one corner of equatorial Singapore. Don't come expecting an Alpine piste: the slope at this indoor centre, one stop north of the Science Centre on bus #335, at 21 Jurong Town Hall Road, is just 60m long and less than three storeys high, meaning that there's no scope for meaningful skiing or snowboarding, only for tobogganing on rubber rings. Nevertheless, the complex offers an invigorating alternative to the hot sun, its constant temperature of -5°C setting it on a par with most Singaporean cinemas. Snow City is an offshoot of the Singapore Science Centre, meaning that there is an educational, as well as a recreational slant, in the shape of a very worthy cold temperature science exhibition. Faced with the chance to explore an igloo, make snowmen, engage in snow-gun combat and even come face to face with the Abominable Snowman, kids are likely to eschew extracurricular studies.

Chinese and Japanese Gardens

The **Chinese and Japanese Gardens** (daily 6am–11pm; free), situated just south of Jurong Lake, defy categorization, being too expensive and too far out to visit for just a sit-down in the park and too dull to be a fully fledged tourist attraction.

In the **Chinese Garden** (or Yu Hwa Yuan), pagodas, pavilions, bridges, arches and weeping willows attempt to capture the style of Beijing's Summer Palace – and fail. That said, if you are out this way, the **Bonsai Garden** (daily 9am–5pm, free), with its hundreds of miniature trees on raised plinths, is worth a look. The same cannot be said for the **Live Turtle and Tortoise Museum** (daily 9am–6pm; S$5), a faintly depressing collection of creatures, whose prize exhibit, a two-headed turtle, is straight out of a freakshow.

If you visit at the weekend, be prepared to be confronted by hordes of newlyweds scouring the garden for a decent photo opportunity. The Chinese Garden is best explored on the day of the annual Moon Cake Festival (see p.74), when children parade with their lanterns after dark. Across from the Chinese Garden, over the impressive, 65-metre "Bridge of Double Beauty", is the **Japanese Garden** (or Seiwaen, "Garden of Tranquillity"), whose wooden bridges, carp ponds, pebble footpaths and stone lanterns are currently under renovation.

Alighting at Chinese Gardens MRT leaves you a hop and a skip from the gardens.

Jurong Bird Park

The **Jurong Bird Park** (daily 9am–6pm; S$14/7; ☎62650022, ⓦwww .birdpark.com.sg) on Jalan Ahmad Ibrahim has one of the world's largest bird collections, with nine thousand birds representing over six hundred species, ranging from Antarctic penguins to New Zealand kiwis. A ride on the **Panorail** (9am–5pm; S$4/2) is a good way to get your bearings; the bullet-shaped monorail skims over, past or through all the main exhibits, with its running commentary pointing out the attractions.

Be sure at least to catch the **Waterfall Aviary**, which allows visitors to walk amongst 1500 free-flying birds in a specially created tropical rainforest, dominated by a thirty-metre-high waterfall. Other exhibits to seek out are the Australian **Lory Loft**, the colourful **Southeast Asian Birds**, where a tropical thunderstorm is simulated daily at noon; the **Penguin Parade** (feeding times 10.30am & 3.30pm); and the **World of Darkness**, a fascinating exhibit which swaps day for night with the aid of a system of reversed lighting, in order that its cute collection of nocturnal residents doesn't snooze throughout the park's opening hours. There are **bird shows** throughout the day. The best is undoubtedly the "Kings of the Skies" show (4pm) – a *tour de force* of speed-flying by trained eagles, hawks and falcons. Entrance to this, and to the similar "World of Hawks" show (10am) and "All Star Bird Show" (11am & 3pm), is free.

To get to the bird park, take either bus #194 or #251 from the bus interchange outside Boon Lay MRT station, a ten-minute ride.

The Singapore Discovery Centre and Tiger Brewery

The hands-on **Singapore Discovery Centre** (Tues–Fri 9am–7pm; S$9/5; ☎67926188, ⓦwww.sdc.com.sg) at 510 Upper Jurong Road is mainly geared towards local school parties. The emphasis is on Singapore's history, technological achievements and national defences, but there are exhibits with broader appeal, such as **motion simulator** rides that let you experience flying a jet or driving a tank, and a clutch of **virtual reality** games. In the grounds outside the centre are a cluster of military vehicles of varying vintages, and an imaginative playground complete with its own maze. To reach the Singapore Discovery

Centre, travel to Boon Lay MRT and transfer to bus #193. It was closed for renovation at the time of writing, though a new paintball park is promised to be included in the complex.

Tiger Beer, now the flagship brew of Asia Pacific Breweries Limited, has been brewed in Singapore since 1931, though back then its home was the Malayan Breweries on Alexandra Road, where it was developed with help from Heineken. A few years later, the establishment of Archipelago Brewery by German giants Beck's seemed to set the scene for a Singaporean beer war, especially when Tiger's newer rival, Anchor beer was priced slightly lower, But in 1941, Archipelago was bought out by Malayan Breweries, since when the organization has gone from strength to strength, moving in 1990 into new holdings in Tuas, and changing its name to reflect the "new international role the company has assumed", although it's still commonly known as the Tiger Brewery.

Today, the tiger beneath a palm tree that adorns the label on every bottle of Tiger beer can be seen in ads across the state. The original slogan for the beer, was used by **Anthony Burgess** as the title of his debut novel, *Time for a Tiger*. As the embattled, debt-ridden policeman, Nabby Adams, gulps down another beer, Burgess wrote, "fresh blood flowed through his arteries, the electric light seemed brighter, what were a few bills anyway?"

A **tour** of the brewery (Mon–Fri 9.30am, 11am, 2.30pm & 5.30pm, free; ☎68603007) is made up of three component parts, arranged in rising order of appeal: first comes a film show which fills visitors in on the history of the set-up; next a walk through the space-age brewing, canning and bottling halls; and finally an hour or two's free drinking in the company's own bar – Nabby would have approved. You need at least ten people in the party, though all is not lost if you are travelling alone – phone up, and if there is a tour already arranged, ask to tag along.

To reach the brewery, take bus #192 from Boon Lay MRT.

Sentosa and the southern isles

Of the many little **islands** that stud the waters immediately south of Singapore, some, like Pulau Bukom, are owned by petrochemical companies and are off limits to tourists. Others, like **Sentosa**, **St John's** and **Kusu** – are served by ferries and can be visited without difficulty, though their accessibility has geared them very much to tourism. If you crave a more secluded spot, you'll have to charter a bumboat to one of the **more remote islands** from the Sentosa Ferry Terminal or Clifford Pier (see p.670) or head for Pulau Ubin, off Singapore's east coast (p.692).

Sentosa

Given the rampant development that has transformed **SENTOSA** (☎1800-7368672, ⓦwww.sentosa.com.sg) into the most developed of Singapore's southern islands over the past 25 years, it's ironic that its name means "tranquil" in Malay. The island has come a long way since World War II, when it was a British military base known as Pulau Blakang Mati, or the "Island of Death Behind". Promoted for its beaches, sports facilities, hotels (see p.643) and attractions, and ringed by a speeding monorail, Sentosa is a contrived but enjoyable place. The island is linked to the mainland by a 500-metre causeway and a necklace of cable cars. Big changes are afoot for Sentosa. An S$8bn revamping programme is underway which will spawn a casino, several new hotels and attractions and the Sentosa Express – a light railway linking the island to HarbourFront. Another development, an oceanfront residential project with marina facilities called **Sentosa Cove**, is at an advanced stage of development at the far eastern end of the island. Even before all these initiatives reach fruition, Sentosa is big business: five million visitors descend on this tiny island, which measures just 3km by 1km, every year. Nevertheless, you'll hear mixed reports of the place. Ultimately, it's as enjoyable as you make it; there's certainly plenty to do (though few of the attractions would make the grade at Disneyland), so much so that it's a good idea to arrive early, with a clear plan of action. It's wise to avoid coming at the weekend and the island should be avoided at all costs on public holidays.

Travel practicalities

Admission to Sentosa costs S$2 if you walk across from the mainland, and S$3 if you take the bus from HarbourFront MRT station (Exit A signposted Telok Blangah Road then follow the signs to the island shuttle bus). This route will cease when the light railway currently under construction is completed. However, the most spectacular route is by the **cable cars** (daily 8.30am–9pm) that travel on a loop between mainland Mount Faber (see p.694) and Sentosa. For the round trip from HarbourFront up to Mount Faber, across to Sentosa and back to HarbourFront you'll pay S$10.90 (kids S$5.50), including admission fee.

Sentosa's basic admission fee gives unlimited rides on the island's four **bus routes**. But the best way to get about is to **rent a bike** for the day (S$5–10 an hour depending on the machine) from the kiosk beside the ferry terminal; tandems are also available. You can pick up a **map** of the island, showing the sights and transport routes, at the HarbourFront Centre or upon arrival on Sentosa.

Admission to several attractions is included in the Sentosa entry ticket, though for the more popular attractions a further charge is levied.

The attractions

Three attractions outshine all others on Sentosa. At the **Underwater World** (daily 9am–9pm; S$19.50/12.50) a moving walkway carries you the length of a hundred-metre acrylic tunnel that snakes through two large tanks: sharks lurk menacingly on all sides, huge stingrays drape themselves languidly above you, and immense shoals of gaily coloured fish dart to and fro. This may not sound all that exciting, but the sensation of being engulfed by sea life – there are more than 2500 fishes here – is a really breathtaking one, and the nearest you'll get to the ocean floor without a wet suit. Of particular interest is the **Deadly Corridor**, which is home to electric eels, piranha and stonefish. If that isn't enough to get the adrenaline pumping, there's even the chance to dive with the sharks by pre-arrangement; call ☎62750030 for details. A **touchpool** beside the entrance allows you to pick up starfish and sea cucumbers – the latter rather like socks filled with wet sand – while beyond that is the **Marine Theatre**, screening educational films throughout the day. The **Dolphin Lagoon** (daily 10.30am–6pm, free with Underwater World ticket), though a part of the Underwater World portfolio, is located away on Palawan Beach; the marine acrobatics of its resident school of Indo-Pacific humpback dolphins are best viewed during one of the daily "Meet the Dolphins" sessions (Mon–Fri 11am, 1.30pm, 3.30pm & 5.30pm).

The other major-league attraction is **Images of Singapore** (daily 9am–9pm; S$10/7). Here, life-sized dioramas present the history and heritage of Singapore from the fourteenth century through to the surrender of the Japanese in 1945. Though the scene-setting AV presentation is contrived and flaky, and some of the wax dummies look like they've been pinched from clothes-shop windows, the effect is fascinating. There are more wax dummies on parade in the Festivals of Singapore gallery, this time dolled up in all manner of festive costumes to represent Singapore's various ethnic celebrations. Iconic images from Singapore's past – Raffles forging a treaty with the island's Malay rulers, rubber tappers at the Botanical Gardens, coolies working the Singapore River, the street barber, satay man and *dhoby* washer at work – spring to life, and there are actors dressed as coolies and kampung dwellers on hand to provide further insight. There are more wax dummies in the Singapore Celebrates gallery, this time dolled up in festive costumes to represent Singapore's various ethnic celebrations.

A trip up to **Fort Siloso** (daily 10am–6pm, S$8/5), on the far western tip of the island, forms Sentosa's third real highlight. The fort – actually a cluster of buildings and gun emplacements above a series of tunnels bored into the island – guarded Singapore's western approaches from the 1880s until 1956, but its obsolescence was revealed in 1942, when the Japanese moved down into Singapore from Malaysia. Today, the recorded voice of Battery Sergeant Major Cooper talks you through a mock-up of a nineteenth-century barracks, complete with living quarters, a laundry and an assault course. Be sure to check out the Surrender Chambers, recently moved from Images of Singapore, where life-sized figures re-enact the British and Japanese surrenders of 1942 and 1945, respectively. After that, you can explore the complex's hefty gun emplacements and tunnels, and sit in on the battle for Singapore, when British soldiers were forced to surrender to the Japanese.

The rest of Sentosa has lots of less interesting options. You might consider one of Sentosa's newer attractions: **Sentosa Luge** (Mon–Thurs 10am–6pm, Fri–Sun 10am–7pm; one ride S$S8), an enjoyable go-Carting track; **Sentosa 4D Magix** (daily 10am–9pm; S$16/9.50), where state-of-the-art audiovisual systems, environmental effects and synchronized motion seats combine to breathtaking effect to bring movies to life; or the **Flying Trapeze** (Mon–Fri 4–6pm, Sat & Sun 4–7pm; S$12 for three swings), where safety harnesses allow you to discover your inner Cirque du Soleil.

Scale the 110m-high **Carlsberg Sky Tower** (daily 9am–9pm; S$10/6), and you'll enjoy panoramic views across Singapore to Malaysia and Indonesia; while back at ground level, **Sijori WonderGolf** (daily 9am–7pm; S$8, children S$4) beckons, with 54 crazy holes.

Otherwise you could do worse than strolling in the elegant, scented grounds of the **Sentosa Orchid Gardens** (Mon–Fri 11am–7.30pm, Sat & Sun 11am–10pm; free). For something slightly more exciting head for the **Butterfly Park and Insect Kingdom Museum** (daily 9am–6.30pm; S$10, kids S$6), which is stuffed with all sorts of creepy-crawlies.

Probably the best option, though, after a trip on the monorail and a visit to one or two attractions, is to head for the three **beaches**, named Siloso, Palawan and Tanjong, on Sentosa's southwestern coast. Created with thousands of cubic metres of imported white sand and scores of coconut palms, they offer canoes, surfboards and aqua bikes for rent, as well as plain old deckchairs. The water here is great for swimming and Singapore does not demand the same modesty on its beaches as Malaysia, although topless and nude bathing are out. From Palawan Beach, a suspended rope bridge connects Sentosa with a tiny islet that's the southernmost part of continental Asia. In recent years, Singapore's annual Dragonboat Racing Festival (see p.74) has been held off Siloso Beach. Sentosa holds Singapore-style beach **raves** from time to time, which are advertised in the local press way in advance.

By early evening, many of Sentosa's attractions are closed, but not so the **Musical Fountain** (shows at 5pm, 5.30pm, 7.40pm & 8.40pm), which is either cute or appalling, depending on your point of view. The fountain dances along to a throbbing soundtrack, with lights, lasers, CGI cartoon characters and pyrotechnics adding to the effect. Overlooking the display is the **Merlion**, a 37-metre-high replica of Singapore's tourism totem that takes centre-stage in the shows. It's possible to walk up to the viewing decks at the top of the Merlion (daily 10am–8pm; S$8/5), from where there are great views of Singapore's harbour, skyline and surrounding islands.

Eating and drinking

The *Asian Food Lover's Place*, beside the ferry terminal, is one of the cheapest of Sentosa's many **eating** options; otherwise, try the nearby *Steword's Riverboat* for Tex-Mex and Cajun dishes, or the *SEA Village Restaurant*, near the visitor arrival centre, where there are reasonably priced Asian buffet lunches and dinners.

Kusu and St John's islands

Well kept and clean as they are, Sentosa's beaches do tend to get overcrowded, and so you may do better to head for the decent sand beaches of either **St John's** or **Kusu** islands, which are 6km south of Singapore and connected to the mainland by a ferry from Sentosa Ferry Terminal. Great things are planned for these islands: under S$1bn redevelopment plans that will create restaurants, spas and resorts. Already, St John's has been linked by causeways to adjacent **Lazarus** and **Seringat** islands in preparation for these plans.

Both St John's and Kusu have decent sand beaches, though for the moment the more interesting of the two is Kusu, also known as **Turtle Island**. Singaporean legend tells of a Chinese and a Malay sailor who were saved from drowning by a turtle that transformed itself into an island; a pool of turtles is still kept on Kusu. Another legend describes how an epidemic afflicting a ship moored off Kusu was banished by the god Tua Pek Kong. Whatever the truth in these tales, once a year during the ninth lunar month (usually in October or November), tens of thousands of Singaporean pilgrims descend upon the **Chinese temple** and **Malay shrine** a few minutes' walk from the jetty on Kusu, to pray for prosperity. The island is impossibly crowded during this time, but the rest of the year it offers a tranquil escape from the mainland. There is a modest **cafeteria** on St John's, but if you're going to Kusu it's wise to take a **picnic**.

Ferries (Mon–Sat 10am & 1.30pm, Sun 9am, 11am, 1, 3 & 5pm; S$11, children S$8) for Kusu and St John's depart from the ferry terminal on the north side of Sentosa Island. Check the return times with the boatmen.

Other southern islands

Since no regular ferries run to any of Singapore's other southern islands, you'll have to **charter a bumboat** from Clifford Pier. Boats take up to twelve passengers, and cost at least S$40 an hour. Unless you rent a boat for the whole day, don't forget to arrange to be picked up again.

The attractive **Sister's Island**, which lies in the same cluster of isles as St John's and Kusu, is a popular snorkelling and fishing haunt, as is **Pulau Hantu** ("Ghost Island" in Malay), 12km further west and under the shadow of Shell-owned Pulau Bukum. Most interesting of all, though, is **Pulau Seking**, 3 or

9

4km east of Hantu; here a handful of Malays continue to live in traditional stilt houses that teeter over the sea, their lifestyle almost untouched by the progress that has transformed the mainland. These islands are all very basic, so take a **picnic** and a day's supply of bottled water with you.

Eating

Along with shopping, **eating** ranks as the Singaporean national pastime – the country offers the chance to sample the whole spectrum of Asia's dishes – and an enormous number of food outlets cater for this obsession. However, in Singapore it's the fare, and not the surroundings, that's important and fabulous food can be served in basic set-ups. You may want to choreograph your visit to coincide with July's **Singapore Food Festival**, a celebration of regional cuisines during which food outlets across the island whip up especially interesting local specialities.

The mass of establishments serving **Chinese** food throughout the island reflects the fact that Chinese residents account for around three-quarters of the population. You're most likely to come across Cantonese, Beijing and Szechuan restaurants, though there's not a region of China whose specialities you can't sample. **North and South Indian** cuisines give a good account of themselves too, as do restaurants serving **Malay, Indonesian, Korean, Japanese** and **Vietnamese** food. One thing you won't find, however, is a Singaporean restaurant: the closest Singapore comes to an indigenous cuisine is **Nonya**, a hybrid of Chinese and Malay food that developed following the intermarrying of nineteenth-century Chinese immigrants with Malay women (see p.753).

Naturally, it's possible to eat **Western food** in Singapore – venture beyond the ubiquitous burger chains and pizza parlours, and you'll find a host of excellent restaurants serving anything from haggis to jambalaya. These and other dishes may be enjoyed at establishments geared to the dishes of a particular nation, or at **international restaurants**, whose menus are a patchwork of Western cuisines. A more informal alternative is to opt for a plate of **British** food – fish and chips, say – at a pub or bar.

Several specialist Chinese restaurants and a number of Indian restaurants serve **vegetarian food**, but otherwise vegetarians need to tread very carefully: chicken and seafood will appear in a whole host of dishes unless you make it perfectly clear that you don't want them. **Halal food** is predictably easy to find, given the number of Muslims in Singapore; the Arab Street end of North Bridge Road and Serangoon Road's Zhu Jiao Centre both have proliferations of restaurants and stalls. There are no **kosher** restaurants, but you could try the food store at the Maghain Aboth Synagogue opposite the Church of St Peter and Paul, on Waterloo Street.

By far the cheapest and most fun place to dine in Singapore is in a **hawker centre** or **food court**, where scores of stalls let you mix and match dishes at really low prices. For a few extra dollars you graduate into the realm of proper **restaurants**, ranging from no-frills, open-fronted eating houses and coffee shops to sumptuously decorated establishments – often located in swanky hotels. Restaurant **opening hours**, on average, are 11.30am–2.30pm and 6–10.30pm daily; hawker stall owners tend to operate to their own schedules, but are invariably open at peak eating times. All cafés and restaurants are marked on the **maps** throughout the chapter.

Markets and supermarkets

Some guesthouses do have cooking facilities, and if you want to buy your own food or fancy a bag of fresh fruit, you're most likely to go to a **wet market** – so called due to the pools of water perpetually covering the floor. Vendors are usually very helpful even if you don't know a mango from a mangosteen. Singapore also has plenty of **supermarkets**, most of which have a delicatessen counter and bakery – some offer familiar beers from back home, too.

Markets
Little India is served by the large wet market in the Zhu Jiao Centre, at the southern end of Serangoon Road; the Chinatown Complex market in **Chinatown** rewards a visit as well. All of Singapore's new towns have their own wet markets too.

Supermarkets
Carrefour #01-43 Suntec City, 3 Temasek Blvd. Part of a French chain, and Singapore's first hypermarket.

Cold Storage Branches at Centrepoint, Orchard Rd (Somerset MRT); 293 Holland Rd (Buona Vista MRT or bus #7); 31 Amber Rd, Katong (Paya Lebar MRT, then bus #135). Local chain that stocks a wide range of Western products.

Good Gifts Emporium Golden Mile Complex, 5001 Beach Rd. A smallish supermarket with a leaning towards Thai produce.

Isetan Wisma Atria, 435 Orchard Rd. Japanese department store and supermarket.

NTUC Fairprice Nearly thirty branches, including a branch in Terminal 1 of the airport, make this one of Singapore's most convenient supermarket chains.

Takashimaya Ngee Ann City, 391 Orchard Rd. One of the largest department stores in Singapore; its supermarket has a Fortnum & Mason franchise.

Breakfast, brunch and snacks

Guesthouses sometimes include coffee or tea and toast in the price of the room but the chances are you'll want to head off elsewhere for breakfast. **Western breakfasts** are available, at a price, at all bigger hotels, most famously at *Raffles*. Otherwise, there are a number of cafés and fast food joints serving continental breakfasts. For a really cheap fry-up, though, you can't beat a Western food stall in a hawker centre. Here, S$8 will buy enough steak, chops and sausage for even the most starving carnivore.

Many visitors to Singapore find the local breakfasts a little hard to stomach, but there are some tasty possibilities. The classic Chinese breakfast is *congee*, a watery rice porridge augmented with chopped spring onion, crispy fried onion and strips of meat, though the tidbits that comprise dim sum tend to be more palatable to Western tastes. Among the Malays, an abiding favourite is *nasi lemak*, while curry and bread breakfasts are served up by scores of Indian establishments.

Ann Siang 5 5 Ann Siang Rd, Chinatown ☏ 63230061. Civilized, cheery and airy café, just off trendy Club Street, serving scrambled eggs, Spanish omelettes and tasty homemade cakes. Mon–Sat 9am–11.30pm.

Breakfast With An Orang-utan Singapore Zoo, 80 Mandai Lake Rd ☏ 62693411. A bumper buffet-style spread with seasonal tropical fruits, shared with whichever orang-utan is on duty; S$15.50. Daily 9–10am.

Coffee Bean & Tea Leaf 82 Boat Quay ☏ 65364355. This is the most atmospheric branch of Singapore's most reliable coffee and tea chain. Open Sun–Thurs 10am–11pm, Fri & Sat 10am–2am.

Dôme Ground floor UOB Plaza, Boat Quay ☏ 65333266. Slick café, part of a global chain,

Many of Singapore's swisher hotels advertise that most colonial of traditions, **high tea**, in the local press; below are a few of the more permanent choices. Typically, a Singapore high tea comprises local and Western snacks, both sweet and savoury. If you really want to play the part of a Victorian settler, Singapore's most splendid food outlet at the *Raffles* still serves **tiffin** – the colonial term for a light curry meal (derived from the Hindi word for luncheon).

Café l'Espresso *Goodwood Park Hotel*, 22 Scotts Rd ℡67301743. A legendary array of English cakes, pastries and speciality coffees. Daily 2–5pm.

Halia Singapore Botanical Gardens 1 Cluny Rd ℡64766711. High tea (daily 3–5.30pm) offers cake and coffee or tea for S$7.50.

Rose Verandah *Shangri-La Hotel*, 22 Orange Grove Rd ℡67373644. Rated the best high tea in Singapore by the American Women's Association of Singapore, no less.

Tiffin Room *Raffles Hotel*, 1 Beach Rd ℡63371886. Tiffin lunch (noon–2pm) and dinner (7–10pm) both cost over S$40 per person, though the spread of edibles, and the charming colonial surroundings make them worth considering. Between tiffin sittings, high tea (S$37) is served (3.30–5.30pm).

boasting an impressive list of coffees and teas and a superb view over the Singapore River. Muffins, toast and croissants are reasonable, and a selection of international papers is on hand. Daily 9am–8pm.

Halia Singapore Botanic Gardens, 1 Cluny Rd ℡64766711. The weekend buffet breakfast (S$18) in this peaceful and enchanting restaurant, serenaded by the sound of insects, birds and whispering trees, has to be one of Singapore's most relaxing experiences. Sat & Sun 8–10.45am.

Noorul Ameen 127 Bencoolen St. Does a roaring trade in *roti prata* with curry sauce each morning. Open 24hr.

Pacific Coffee Company B1-26 CityLink Mall, One Raffles Link, opposite Raffles City. Free Net access is laid on for patrons of the fine coffee in this pleasing coffee shop, whose sassy red sofas provide an ideal vantage point for people-watching. Mon–Fri 8am–11pm, Sat & Sun 9am–11pm.

Steeple's Deli #02-25 Tanglin Shopping Centre, 19 Tanglin Rd, off Orchard Rd. Singapore's original deli, *Steeple's* has been knocking out high-quality homemade sandwiches, soups, cakes and savouries for over two decades now. Mon–Sat 9am–9pm.

Tan Hock Seng Cake Shop 88 Telok Ayer St. They've been baking cakes and biscuits on site for more than fifty years at this famous Hokkien shop, just next door to the Fuk Tai Chi Street Museum. Daily 10am–8pm.

Ya Kun Kaya Toast #01-01 Far East Sq, 18 China St, Chinatown ℡64383638. This Hainanese joint started out as a Chinatown stall in 1944, and still offers a stirring start to the day: piping hot, strong coffee with *kaya* toast – a slab of butter and a splodge of egg and coconut spread oozing from folded toast. Mon–Fri 7.30am–7pm, Sat & Sun 9am–5pm.

Hawker centres and food courts

Although **hawker centres** are kept scrupulously clean, they are often housed in functional buildings, which tend to get extremely hot and, if you are seated next to a stall cooking fried rice or noodles, extremely smoky. As a consequence, an increasing number of smaller, air-conditioned **food courts** are popping up, where eating is a slightly more civilized, if less atmospheric affair. Hawker centres and food courts are open from lunchtime through to dinnertime and sometimes beyond, though individual stalls open and shut as they please. Avoid the peak lunching (12.30–1.30pm) and dining (6–7pm) periods, when hungry Singaporeans go to their nearest hawker centre, and you should have no problems finding a seat.

China Square Food Centre Chinatown. Three floors of spick-and-span stalls – mainly Chinese but with Japanese, Korean and Western representation.

Chinatown Complex Smith Street end of New Bridge Road, Chinatown. A huge range of dishes with a predictably Chinese bias.

Food Junction Basement of Seiyu Department Store, Bugis Junction, 200 Victoria St. Happening food court whose trendy piped music provides a stirring soundtrack to your dinner. Culinary themes as diverse as Thai, Japanese, *nasi padang* and claypot are represented, and there's a choice of local desserts or Häagen-Dazs ice creams.

Funan Digitalife Mall 109 North Bridge Rd. Check out the smart basement food court whose stalls serve herbal soup, claypots, Hainanese chicken and local desserts.

Geylang Serai Food Centre Geylang Serai. Turn left out of Paya Lebar MRT and left again onto Sims Avenue; the centre is five minutes' walk along, on your right. In the heart of Singapore's Malay quarter, this place has a corresponding range of stalls offering Malay staples like *nasi lemak* and *nasi campur*.

Kopitiam Plaza by the Park, 51 Bras Basah Rd. Bright and brash 24hr food court, popular among late-night revellers with the munchies.

Lau Pa Sat Festival Market 18 Raffles Quay, Financial District. The smartest hawker stalls in Singapore, and now open round the clock. At lunchtime the place is full to bursting with suits from the city; at night the clubbers take over.

Maxwell Food Centre Junction of South Bridge Road & Maxwell Road. Old-style hawker centre, a stone's throw from the centre of Chinatown.

New Bugis Street A handful of evening hawkers dish up Asian specialities like satay, *laksa*, *kueh* and sushi. This place is very popular with tourists and hence many of the stalls use photograph-driven menus that provide a crash course on hawker cuisine.

Newton Circus Hawker Centre Corner of Clemenceau Ave North and Bukit Timah Rd, very near Scotts MRT station. Prices are a little higher here as it is on the tourist trail, but it has the advantage of staying open until late. Noted for its seafood stalls.

Orchard Emerald Food Court Basement of Orchard Emerald, 218 Orchard Rd. Smart food court, bang in the centre of Orchard Road, where the Indonesian buffet is great value.

Picnic Food Court Scotts Shopping Centre, 6 Scotts Rd. Slap-bang in the middle of Orchard Road, squeaky clean, and with lots of choice.

Sim Lim Square Food Court (Tenco Food Court) 1 Rochor Canal Rd. Convenient if you are staying on Bencoolen Street; it is under the Sim Lim Square Building.

Smith Street At night this narrow Chinatown street is made still narrower by the two rows of food stalls that open up along it.

Tekka Centre Corner of Bukit Timah Road & Serangoon Road, Little India. The bulk of the stalls here, naturally enough, serve Indian food.

Telok Blangah Telok Blangah Rd. Opposite the HarbourFront Centre, and good for a snack before or after a trip to Sentosa.

Restaurants

Below is a representative selection of the thousands of **restaurants** that span Singapore, with the **cuisines** listed alphabetically. **Meal prices**, where quoted, are fairly arbitrary – even in the most extravagant restaurant in Singapore it's possible to snack on fried rice and a soft drink. Equally, a delicacy such as roast suckling pig will send a bill soaring, no matter how unpretentious the restaurant. Individual **opening hours** are given below. If possible, try to book ahead at more upmarket restaurants, particularly on Saturday nights and Sunday lunchtimes, when they are at their busiest. Moreover, bear in mind that many restaurants close over Chinese New Year, and those that don't are often bursting at the seams. There aren't too many establishments that enforce a dress code, though it's always best to dress up a little if you're heading for a hotel restaurant.

Chinese

The majority of the **Chinese** restaurants in Singapore are Cantonese, that is, from the province of Canton (Guangdong) in southern China, though you'll also come across northern Peking (Beijing) and western Szechuan (Sichuan) cuisines, as well as the Hokkien specialities of the southeastern province of

Fukien (Fujian); and Teochew dishes from the area east of Canton. Whatever the region, it's undoubtedly the real thing – Chinese food as eaten by the Chinese. Fish and seafood is nearly always outstanding in Chinese cuisine, with prawns, crab, squid and a variety of fish on offer. Noodles, too, are ubiquitous, and come in wonderful variations. For something a little more unusual, try a steamboat or a claypot. The other thing to note is that at many Cantonese restaurants (and in other regional restaurants, too), lunch consists of **dim sum** – steamed and fried dumplings served in little bamboo baskets.

Cantonese

Capital 44 Bukit Pasoh Rd, Chinatown ☏62223938. The friendly staff in this spotless restaurant recommend fried deer meat with ginger; also worth a try are the fried prawns rolled in bean-curd skin. A feast for two costs less than S$35. Daily noon–2.30pm & 6–10.30pm.

Fatty's Wing Seong Restaurant #01-31 Burlington Complex, 175 Bencoolen St ☏63381087. A Singapore institution where every dish on the wide Cantonese menu is well cooked and speedily delivered. Around S$20 a head. Daily noon–11pm.

Grand City #02-18/19 Raffles City Shopping Centre, 252 North Bridge Rd ☏03003022. Sizeable, enduringly popular restaurant serving oddities like emu with black pepper and Teochew-style goose alongside better-known dishes on the menu. Open Mon–Sat 11.20am–2.30pm & 6.30–10.30pm, Sun 10am–2.30pm & 6.30–10.30pm.

Hai Tien Lo 37th floor *Pan Pacific Hotel*, 7 Raffles Blvd, Marina Sq ☏68268338. If you have money enough for just one blowout, come here for exquisitely presented food and stunning views of downtown Singapore. Extravagant set meals are available, while Sunday lunchtimes are set aside for dim sum (11.30am–2.30pm). Daily noon–2.30pm & 6.30–10.30pm.

Lei Gardens #01-24 CHIJMES, 30 Victoria St ☏63393822. Refreshingly understated, *Lei Garden* lets its classy Cantonese dishes do the talking. Stunning seafood, most of which starts the day swimming in the tanks in the dining room. Four can gorge for S$140, with a special promotion meal (Sat & Sun only). Daily 11.30am–2.30pm & 6–10pm.

Soup Restaurant 25 Smith St, Chinatown ☏62229923. Traditional Cantonese double-boiled

△ A hawker-style fry-up

and simmered soups are the speciality in this steam-heat-dependent soup shop whose elegant tables and low-hung lights recall old Chinatown. The *samsui* ginger chicken comes recommended. Daily 11.30am–10.30pm.

Swee Kee *Damenlou Hotel*, 12 Ann Siang Rd ☏62211900. A Cantonese restaurant with real pedigree: Tang Swee Kee hawked the first bowl of his trademark *ka shou* fish-head noodles more than sixty years ago, and now his son sells this and other well-cooked dishes from the attractive coffee shop on the ground floor of his Chinatown hotel. Daily 11am–2.30pm & 5.30–11pm.

Tekong Seafood #01-2100 Block 6 Changi Village Rd ☏65428923. This Cantonese/Teochew restaurant moved over to the mainland when Pulau Tekong was earmarked as an army shooting range; but the food is as good as ever – the Teochew steamed fish with sour prunes is particularly fab. Daily 11am–2.30pm & 5.30–11pm.

Wang Jiang Lou Block A Clarke Quay ☏3383001. Slick Cantonese–Teochew restaurant where the ingredients of a full seafood menu eye you suspiciously from tanks on the walls. The set menu (S$68 for two) yields five dishes, plus fruit. Daily 11.30am–3pm & 6–11pm.

Yum Cha #02-01 20 Trengganu St (entry via Temple St), Chinatown ☏63721717. Big, buzzing dim sum joint, above the buzz of Trengganu Street. Great fun. Daily 8am–11pm.

Hainanese

Mooi Chin Palace #B1-03 Funan Digitalife Mall, 109 North Bridge Rd ☎63397766. Hainanese immigrants often worked as domestics to colonial families, resulting in crossover dishes like Hainanese mutton soup and Hainanese pork chop – both cooked to perfection in this sixty-year-old place, where whole *pomfret sambal* (S$25) is a speciality, and set menus start at around S$30 for two. Daily 11.30am–3pm & 6–10pm. Open for dim sum daily 7.30–9am.

Yet Con Chicken Rice Restaurant 25 Purvis St, off Beach Rd ☎63376819. Cheap and cheerful, old-time restaurant: try "crunchy, crispy" roast pork with pickled cabbage and radish, or chicken rice, washed down with barley water; S$15 for two people. Daily 10.30am–9.30pm.

Hokkien

Beng Hiang 115 Amoy St, Chinatown ☎62216695. The Hokkien chef relies heavily upon robust soups and sauces, though his most popular dish is a superbly cooked fried *mee*; the lack of a menu makes ordering distinctly tricky, but persistence is rewarded by well-cooked food and you can eat well for under S$15. Daily 11.30am–2.30pm & 6–9.30pm.

Beng Thin Hoon Kee #05-02 OCBC Centre, 65 Chulia St, CBD ☎65332818. Hidden inside the OCBC car park, this minty green restaurant is very popular at lunchtime with city slickers from the nearby business district. Big portions make it a good and filling introduction to Hokkien cuisine. Daily 11.30am–3pm & 6–10pm.

Szechuan & Hunanese

Cherry Garden *The Oriental*, 5 Raffles Ave, Marina Sq ☎68853538. Elegant restaurant, designed to resemble a Chinese courtyard, and serving tasty Szechuan and Hunanese dishes. The Hunanese honey-glazed ham is delectable, as is the Szechuan house speciality, camphor-smoked duck and bean-curd crust (both under S$30); the set lunch costs S$40–60 a head. Daily noon–3pm & 6–11pm.

Magic of Chongqing Hotpot Fourth floor, Tanglin Shopping Centre, 19 Tanglin Rd, off Orchard Rd ☎67348135. Established in 1995, this homely DIY place has got local pundits raving over its zesty Szechuan hotpots: choose a stock, drop in ingredients and fish them out when cooked. Two can dine well for S$70. Daily noon–3pm & 6–11pm.

Teochew

Ban Seng #B1-44 The Riverwalk, 20 Upper Circular Rd ☎65331471. Road-widening caused this venerable, mid-price restaurant to move to this spot on the Singapore River, and the traditional charcoal ovens didn't survive the move. The food

is still top-notch, however: try the steamed crayfish, braised goose or stuffed sea cucumber. Daily noon–2pm & 6–10pm.

Vegetarian

Happy Realm Vegetarian Food Centre #03-16 Pearls Centre, 100 Eu Tong Sen St ☎62226141. "The way to good health and a sound mind", boasts the restaurant's card; tasty and reasonably priced vegetarian dishes. Daily 11am–8.30pm.

Kwan Im Vegetarian Restaurant 190 Waterloo St ☎63382394. A huge display of sweet and savoury *pau* (Chinese-style buns) is the highlight of this unfussy establishment, in the *East Asia Hotel* close to Bencoolen Street. Daily 8am–8.30pm.

Lingzhi #B1-17/18 Orchard Towers, 400 Orchard Rd ☎67343788. A real treat, where skewers of vegetables served with satay sauce are the highlight of an imaginative menu; there's also a takeaway counter. Daily 11am–10pm.

Other speciality restaurants

Chinese Opera Teahouse 5 Smith St, Chinatown ☎63234862. The Sights and Sounds of Chinese Opera Show ($35), a set dinner serenaded by Chinese musicians, and followed by excerpts from Chinese operas, is a memorable cultural treat. The dinner begins at 7pm. If you don't want a dinner but want to catch the show while drinking tea and munching on Chinese snacks, the cost is S$25 and you'll be admitted at 7.50pm. Open Fri & Sat.

Crystal Jade La Mian Xiao Long Bao Ngee An City #04-27 ☎6238 1661; Scotts Shopping Centre #B1-05 ☎6734 0200; Suntec City Mall #B1-028 ☎6337 6678; and other locations. Very popular chain specializing in Shanghai and Beijing cuisine. The name is a bit of a mouthful, but encapsulates their signature dishes – *xiao long bao*, incredibly succulent pork dumplings, and *la mian*, literally "pulled noodles", the strands of dough being stretched and worked by hand (the version cooked with wood-ear fungus is particularly good). Not great for vegetarians, though veggie versions of a few dishes can be made to order.

Doc Cheng's *Raffles Hotel*, 328 North Bridge Rd ☎63311612. East meets West in this ice-cool Raffles joint themed around the global travels of imagined local bon viveur, Doc Cheng. Though the menu betrays Thai, Indian, Japanese and Pacific Rim influences, Chinese culinary ideology provides the backbone of much of the food; the decor presents a similarly eclectic blend of Oriental, Art Deco and modernist influences. Two pay around S$60. Mon–Fri noon–2pm, daily 7–10pm.

Imperial Herbal Restaurant Third floor, *Metropole Hotel*, 41 Seah St, off Beach Rd ☏ 63370491. The place to go if you are concerned about your Yin and Yang balance: after checking your pulse and tongue, a resident Chinese physician recommends either a cooling or a heating dish from the menu. For migraine sufferers, scorpions pickled in foul liquor are, by all accounts, a must; rheumatics should opt for crispy black ants. It's a good old-fashioned gross-out of the type that used to be what travel to the Orient was all about. The downside is the cost – be prepared to pay through the nose. Daily 11.30am–2.30pm & 6.30–10.30pm.
Lao Beijing #03-01 Plaza Singapura, 68 Orchard Rd ☏ 67387207. Charming teahouse-style restaurant. If the braised pork trotters don't appeal, try the more mainstream dishes like sweet and sour fish and *popiah*; the steamboat with lamb slices is exceptional. Daily 11.30am–3pm & 6–10pm.
Singapura Seafood Restaurant #01-31 Selegie House, Block 9, Selegie Rd, south of Little India ☏ 63363255. Sure the seafood is great, but it's hard to see beyond such Foochow classics as steamed white cabbage, fishball soup and Foochow fried noodles. Daily 11am–2.30pm & 6–10.30pm.
Snackworld #01-12/13 Cuppage Plaza, 5 Koek Rd, off Orchard Rd. Hectic terrace restaurant where the Chinese menu is enlivened by hot-plate crocodile meat and emu. Daily 10am–midnight.
Superbowl 80 Boat Quay ☏ 65386066. An affordable range of 47 *congees*, served at marble-topped tables recalling a 1950s coffee shop. Daily 11am–11pm.

Arabic

Café Le Caire 39 Arab St ☏ 6292 0979. This informal diner spearheaded the revival of Arab cuisine in the Arab quarter and remains a good inexpensive bet for Lebanese and Egyptian specialities, plus more obscure Saudi and Yemeni dishes. If you're into hubble-bubbles, take advantage of the huge range of tobaccos – they do over a dozen. Daily 10am til late.

🏃 El Sheikh 18 Pahang St ☏ 6296 9116. Excellent Lebanese restaurant, suitably located in the Arab Quarter. The menu runs the usual gamut, from meze (with plenty for vegetarians) to main courses such as *shish taouk*, filleted chicken done on a skewer. Combination platters ($12) and mains (from S$10) are both good value, and there's a great selection of juices and desserts too.

European & international

🏃 Blu *Shangri-La Hotel*, Orange Grove Rd, off Orchard Rd ☏ 67302598. One of Singapore's most exquisite dining experiences: California fusion cuisine of the highest quality, overlooking downtown Singapore from the *Shangri-La*'s 24th floor. Daily 7–11pm.
Blu Jaz Café 11 Bali Lane, Arab Quarter ☏ 6292 3800. Chilled-out café-restaurant, tucked away on the edge of the Arab quarter. They do reliable Japanese and Western food – everything from beef teriyaki to fish and chips – and a range of local fare too, including satay and *mee goreng*. Not expensive either; a steak will set you back around S$13. Live jazz Fri & Sat eves. Mon–Fri 11am–midnight; Sat til 1am.
🏃 Broth 21 Duxton Hill ☏ 63233353. Superb fusion cuisine in an old shophouse on a delightfully quiet, tree-shaded Chinatown back street. A charming oasis, and recommended. Mon–Fri noon–2.30pm & 6–10.30pm, Sat 6–10.30pm.
Colours by the Bay Esplanade Mall, 8 Raffles Ave. Restaurant collective, offering a full palate of global cuisines, overlooking the bay beside Singapore's new theatre. With luck, your meal will coincide with an alfresco cultural performance.

🏃 Halia Singapore Botanic Gardens, 1 Cluny Rd ☏ 64766711. Moonlit and candlelit after dusk, Halia's magical garden-veranda setting whisks you a world away from downtown Singapore. The East-meets-West lunch menu spans sandwiches, pasta and *laksa*, plus set lunches. At night, there are more substantial dishes like rack of lamb and seafood stew (both S$36). Daily 11am–11pm, also Sat & Sun 8–10.30am for breakfast.
Hot Stones 53 Boat Quay ☏ 65345188. A healthy and novel twist on dining: steaks, chicken and seafood grilled at your table on non-porous alpine rock heated to 200° – no oil, but bags of flavour. Similar to a Korean BBQ, this DIY cookfest is not for the lazy. Daily noon–2.30pm & 6–10.30pm.
Louis' Oyster Bar 36 Boat Quay. The Louis in question is Louis Armstrong, who beams down from all the walls. Oysters cost around S$18 per half-dozen, but the High Society Platter (crayfish, crab, mussels, oysters and prawns on ice; S$60 for two) is hard to resist. Mon–Fri 11am–1am, Sat & Sun 5pm–3am.
Ocho Tapas #01-12 CHIJMES, 30 Victoria St ☏ 68831508. Top tapas: sit inside, amid the rugs,

terracotta tiles and Moorish panels, or venture out onto the terrace, where musicians play Eagles hits, Gypsy Kings-style. The wine list impresses. Sun–Thurs 11am–1am, Fri & Sat 11am–3am.
Original Sin #01-62 Block 43, Jalan Merah Saga, Holland Village ☎64755605. Quality vegetarian Mediterranean food: the mezze plate makes a good appetizer; after that try a pizza Ibiza, topped

with roasted pumpkin, avocado, Spanish onion, asparagus and cheese. Tues–Sun 6–10.30pm, Sat & Sun noon–3pm.
Spizza 29 Club St, Chinatown ☎62242525. Homely, rustic and affordable pizzeria, whose menu boasts a tempting A-Z of thin-crust pizzas, cooked in a traditional wood oven. Daily noon–3pm & 6.30–11pm.

Indian and Nepali

Annalakshmi 104 Amoy St, Chinatown ☎62230809, ⓦwww.annalakshmi.com .sg. Terrific Indian vegetarian buffets served up by volunteers from the Hindu community. They ask you to pay what you feel the meal was worth; be generous (profits go to Kala Mandhir, an Indian cultural association) and don't help yourself to more than you can finish. Mon–Sat 11am–7pm at Amoy St; contact them for details of their new main outlet, which should be open by the time you read this.

Banana Leaf Apolo 56–58 Race Course Rd, Little India ☎62938682. Pioneering fish-head curry (S$30 for two people) restaurant where a wide selection of South Indian dishes are all served on banana leaves. Eating is done with the hands, and make sure to fold over your banana leaf to show that you are full and finished eating, or you'll be given another dollop of rice and curry from the roving waiters. All you can eat. Daily 10am–10pm.

Gandhi Eating House 29 Chandler Rd, Little India. Many locals reckon this open-fronted place off Race Course Road knocks out the best chicken curries in Little India; meals come on banana leaves, water in metal jugs. Daily 11am–11pm.

Gorkha Grill 21 Smith St, Chinatown ☎62270806. There are fish, mutton and chicken dishes galore at this enchanting Nepali place, but be sure to start with *momo* (minced chicken dumplings) and end with *kheer* (rice pudding), a tasty blend of cream, rice and cardamom. Daily 11.30am–11.30pm.

Islamic Restaurant 791–797 North Bridge Rd, Arab Quarter ☎62987563. Aged Muslim restaurant manned by a gang of old men who plod solemnly up and down between the tables. It boasts the best chicken biriyani in Singapore, cooked in the traditional way – heated from above and below with charcoal. S$15 for two. Daily except Fri 9.30am–9.30pm.

Kinara 57 Boat Quay ☎65330412. Exquisite restaurant boasting antique fittings imported from the subcontinent and a marvellous view of the

river from upstairs; the food comprises elegantly presented Punjabi dishes. Around S$60 for two. Daily noon–2.30pm & 6.30–10.30pm.

Komala Villas 76–78 Serangoon Rd ☎62936980. A cramped, popular vegetarian establishment specializing in fifteen varieties of *dosai*. The "South Indian Meal", served upstairs on a banana leaf, is good value at S$12. Daily 7am–10pm.

Madras New Woodlands 12–14 Upper Dickson Rd, Little India ☎62971594. Canteen-style place serving up decent vegetarian food at bargain prices. House specialities are the Thali set meal (S$5.50) and the VIP Thali (S$6.50); samosas, bhajis and other snacks are available after 3pm, and there's a big selection of sweets, too. Recommended. Daily 7.30am–11.30pm.

Moti Mahal 18 Murray St, Chinatown ☎62214338. Not cheap, but one of Singapore's very best, serving tasty tandoori dishes in pleasant surroundings. The special is *murg massalam*, a whole chicken stuffed with rice (S$50 – must be ordered in advance). Daily 11am–3pm & 6–10.30pm.

Orchard Maharajah 25 Cuppage Terrace, Cuppage Rd ☎67326331. Set in a wonderful old Peranakan house off Orchard Rd, this splendid North Indian restaurant has a large terrace and a tempting menu that includes the sublime fish *mumtaz* – fillet of fish stuffed with minced mutton, almonds, eggs, cashews and raisins. The set lunch is good value at S$16. Daily 11am–3pm & 6–11pm.

Our Village Fifth floor, 46 Boat Quay ☎65383092. A hidden gem, with fine North Indian and Sri Lankan food, and peachy views of the river, city and Colonial District from its charming, lamplit roof terrace. Open Mon–Fri 11.30am–1.45pm & 6–10.30pm, Sat & Sun dinner only.

Sri Vijayah 229 Selegie Rd ☎63361748. Hole-in-the-wall vegetarian banana-leaf joint offering unbeatable value for money: S$4 buys a replenishable mountain of rice and vegetable curries, and there's a mouthwatering display of sweetmeats at the front door. Daily 6am–10pm.

Indonesian

Bumbu 44 Kandahar St, Arab Quarter ℡63928628. Crammed with Singaporean antiques amassed by owner, Robert Tan, *Bumbu* is as much a social history document as a restaurant. Happily, the furnishings don't outshine the fine Indonesian/ Thai cuisine on offer. Daily 11am–2pm & 6–10pm.

Cumi Bali 20 Duxton Rd, Chinatown ℡62206619. Slender and jolly *nasi padang* joint whose walls are strung with Indonesian puppets, fishing nets, instruments and batiks. The beef *rendang* and *ikan bakar* (BBQ fish) both hit the spot; or try one of the generous set lunches (S$7). Daily noon–9pm.

House of Sundanese Food 55 Boat Quay ℡65343775. Spicy salads and barbecued seafood characterize the cuisine of Sunda (West Java), served here in simple yet tasteful surroundings. Try the tasty *ikan sunda* (grilled Javanese fish) – an S$18 fish serves two to three people. Mon–Fri 11am–2.30pm & 5–10pm, Sat & Sun 5–10pm.

Rendezvous #02-02 *Hotel Rendezvous*, 9 Bras Basah Rd ℡63397508. Revered *nasi padang* – highly spiced Sumatran cuisine – joint that still turns in lip-smacking curries, *rendangs* and *sambals*; the weighing machine in the corner is an unusual touch. Daily 11am–9pm.

Rumah Makan Minang, 18a Kandahar St. Fiery *nasi padang* in the heart of the Arab Quarter; S$4 ensures a good feed, and buys the popular barbecued fish. Daily noon–2.30pm & 6–10.30pm.

Sanur #04-17/18 Centrepoint, 176 Orchard Rd ℡67342192. Hearty, reasonably priced food served by waitresses in traditional batik dress; the beef *rendang* is terrific. It's best to book ahead. Daily 11.30am–2.45pm & 5.45–10pm.

Warung M Nasir #01-05 1 Liang Seah St, off Beach Rd ℡63395935. Charming, open-fronted *nasi padang* café that's a welcome addition to Liang Seah's burgeoning dining scene. *Rendangs* and curries are taken either at streetside tables or in the *kopitiam*-style dining room. Mon–Sat 10am–10pm.

Japanese

Akashi Japanese Restaurant B1-09 Tanglin Shopping Centre, 19 Tanglin Rd ℡67324438; branch at B1-23 CityLink Mall, 1 Raffles Link ℡62387767. Chain of understated, classical Japanese restaurants, where the *sake teriyaki* and the *tempura* are both good and there's a good range of sakes. Daily noon–3pm & 6.30–10pm.

Shima Yakiniku 2 Murray Terrace, Murray St, Chinatown ℡62235159. A DIY delight: all the meat, salmon, prawns and frogs' legs you can eat, cooked on a hot stone at your table, for just S$18 a head. Daily noon–2.30pm & 6.30–9.30pm.

Tatsu Sushi #01-16 CHIJMES, 30 Victoria St ℡63325868. *Tatsu* is a veteran relative to the notoriously fluid CHIJMES restaurant scene. Owner Ronny Chia's expertise, and the high quality of ingredients used (all fish is flown in from Japan) draw a clientele that's around seventy-five percent Japanese. Mon–Sat noon–3pm & 6.30–10.30pm.

Korean

Korean Restaurant Pte Ltd #05-35 Specialists' Centre 277 Orchard Rd ℡62350018. Singapore's first Korean restaurant, beautifully furnished and serving up a wide range of dependably good dishes at around S$20 per dish. Daily noon–11pm.

Seoul Garden Korean Restaurant #03-119 Marina Sq, 6 Raffles Blvd ℡63391339. Entertaining, busy restaurant where the best value is the "all you can eat" Korean barbecue – a buffet of twenty seasoned meats, seafoods and vegetables which you cook at your table (S$25 per person). Mon–Fri 11am–3pm & 5.30–10.30pm, Sat & Sun 11am–10.30pm.

Malay and Nonya

Belachan 10 Smith St, Chinatown ℡62219810. Friendly, refined *Belachan* (the name is Malay for shrimp paste) offers sanctuary from Smith Street's throng. The *itek manis*, duck stewed in ginger and black beans (S$8), is sensational, though the set lunch (main course, veg, rice and *achar*, S$5) offers best value. Tues–Sun 11.30am–3pm & 6.30–10.30pm, Mon lunch only.

Blue Ginger 97 Tanjong Pagar Rd ℡62223928. Housed in a renovated shophouse, this trendy Peranakan restaurant is proving a yuppie favourite, thanks to such dishes as *ikan masal asam gulai* (mackerel simmered in a tamarind and lemon-grass gravy), and that benchmark of Nonya cuisine, *ayam buah keluak* – braised chicken with Indonesian black nuts. Daily 11.30am–3pm & 6.30–11pm.

🏃 **Guan Hoe Soon** 214 Joo Chiat Rd, Katong ☎63442761. Over fifty years old, this place still turns out fine Nonya cuisine; try the *chendol* (coconut milk, red beans, sugar, green jelly and ice), a refreshing end to a meal. Around S$40 for two, with beer. Daily except Tues 11am–3pm & 6–9.30pm.

🏃 **Peranakan Inn** 210 East Coast Rd ☎64406195. As much effort goes into the food as went into the renovation of this immaculate, bright-green shophouse restaurant, which offers authentic Nonya favourites at reasonable prices; around S$8 a dish. Daily 11am–3pm & 6–10.30pm.

Thai and Vietnamese

Cuppage Thai Food Restaurant 49 Cuppage Terrace ☎67341116. Nondescript inside, but boasting a great outdoor terrace, this cheap and cheerful restaurant offers quality Thai dishes at around S$8. Daily 11am–3pm & 6–11pm.

Golden Mile Complex 5001 Beach Rd. Known locally as "Thai Village", the Golden Mile is always full of Thais waiting to catch buses home. Drop by any one of its countless Thai cafés and you're guaranteed authentic, affordable Thai cuisine and an atmosphere that's pure Bangkok.

🏃 **Indochine** 49B Club St, Chinatown ☎63230503. One of Singapore's most elegant restaurants, with beautiful fixtures complemented by a truly great menu embracing Vietnamese, Laotian and Cambodian cuisine. Try the Laotian *larb kai* (spicy chicken salad) or the Vietnamese *nha trang* (roast duck and mango salad). The Vietnamese *chao tom* (minced prawn wrapped round sugarcane) is also mouthwatering. Mon–Sat noon–2.30pm & 6–10pm.

Viet Café #01-76 UE Sq Unity St, off River Valley Rd ☎63336453. The heady aromas of Vietnamese *pho* (soup) – mint, basil and citrus – hang heavy in the air at this sleek establishment. Follow the pebble path that leads up to the balcony or, better still, sit out on the forecourt and enjoy the night air. Handy for a late-night snack after a beer along Mohamed Sultan Road. Daily noon–3am.

Viet Lang #01-26 Block A CHIJMES, 30 Victoria St ☎63373379. The main dining room is dominated by a vast painting of Vietnamese women borne on a sea of flowers; there's a similar textured lushness to the food. Start with a zingy pomelo salad, then move on to the grilled pork chop with lemon grass, washed down with a 333 beer. Daily 11am–10pm.

US

Bobby Rubino's #B1-03 Fountain Court, CHIJMES, 30 Victoria St ☎63375477. Ribs are their speciality, but steaks, burgers and other big-boy platters are available; eschew the "wine-rack" partitions and rough-hewn red-brick interior and make for the terrace, superbly located below CHIJMES' looming convent. Daily 11am–midnight.

Café Iguana #01-03 Riverside Point, 30 Merchant Rd, near Clarke Quay ☎62361275. Riverfront Mexican tucker, in colourful surrounds. Tortillas, chili, *quesadillas* and all the other favourites feature on the menu, plus a huge selection of tequilas. Daily 6pm–3am.

Cha Cha Cha 32 Lorong Mambong, Holland Village ☎64621650. Classic Mexican dishes in this vibrantly coloured restaurant range from S$10 to S$22; outside are a few open-air patio tables, ideal for posing with a bottle of Dos Equis beer, but book ahead for these. Daily 11am–11pm.

Dan Ryan's Chicago Grill #B1-01 Tanglin Mall, Tanglin Rd ☎67383800. Chug back a Budweiser and get stuck into "American portions" of ribs, burgers and chicken in a dining room that's crammed with Americana; main courses cost around S$15. Daily 11.30am–midnight.

🏃 **Ponderosa** #02-20 Raffles City Shopping Centre, 252 North Bridge Rd ☎63344926. The perfect cure for vitamin deficiency – chicken, steak and fish set meals come with baked potato, sundae and as much salad as you can eat, all for S$32. Daily noon–10.30pm.

Seah Street Deli *Raffles Hotel*, 1 Beach Rd ☎3371886. New York-style deli boasting mountainous sandwiches at around S$10 each. The soda and root beer signs and outsized Americana on the walls make this the most uncolonial establishment in *Raffles Hotel*. Sun–Thurs 11am–10pm, Fri & Sat 11am–11pm.

Drinking and nightlife

Singapore's **nightlife** has gone from strength to strength over the past decade. The island's well-developed **bar and pub** scene means there is now a vast range of drinking holes to choose from, with the Colonial District, Riverside and Orchard Road areas offering particularly good pub-crawl potential. With competition so hot, more and more bars are turning to **live music** to woo punters, though this is usually no more than cover versions performed by local bands. That said, big-name groups do occasionally make forays here. **Clubs** also do brisk business; glitzy and vibrant, they feature the latest imported pop, rock and **dance music**, and attract the world's best DJs.

Bars and pubs

With the **bars and pubs** of Singapore ranging from slick cocktail joints through elegant colonial chambers to boozy dives, you're bound to find a place that suits you. Establishments open either in the late morning (to catch the lunchtime dining trade) or in the early evening, closing anywhere between midnight and 3am. On Friday and Saturday, **opening hours** almost invariably extend by an hour or two. Many serve snacks throughout the day, and a few offer more substantial dishes. It's possible to buy a small glass of beer in most places for around S$8, but **prices** can be double or treble that amount, especially in the Orchard Road district. A glass of wine usually costs much the same as a beer, and spirits a dollar or two more. One way of cutting costs is to arrive in time for **happy hour** in the early evening, when bars offer local beers and house wine either at half price, or "one for one" – you get two of whatever you order, but one is held back for later.

Singaporeans adore **rock** and jazz, and a plethora of bars panders to this, presenting nightly performances by local or Filipino covers bands. Also hugely popular is **karaoke**, which almost reaches an art form in some Singapore bars.

The Quays

BQ Bar 39 Boat Quay ☎65369722. Arguably Boat Quay's coolest venue, thanks to its chilled dance music, comfy sofas and friendly staff. The second level affords memorable views of the river. Tues–Sat 11am–1am, Sun & Mon 11am–midnight.

Crazy Elephant #01-07 Trader's Market, Clarke Quay. The only bar with any real clout along Clarke Quay, playing decent rock music on the turntable between live sessions by the house band; outside, there are tables by the water's edge. Mon–Thurs & Sun 5pm–1am, Fri & Sat 5pm–2am. Happy hour is daily 5–9pm.

Harry's Quayside 28 Boat Quay. There's live jazz and R&B Tuesday to Saturday in this upmarket place, and a blues jam every Sunday evening. Light lunches are served too. Daily 11am–1am.

Home Beach Bar 15 Merbau Rd. Deckchairs, lanterns, reggae sounds – close your eyes and you'll swear there's sand, not concrete, underfoot at this mellow riverfront venue, where happy hour lasts from 5–8pm. Avoid the bar food, which will only disappoint. Daily 3pm–1am.

Jazz @ Southbridge 82b Boat Quay ☎63274671. The crowd here can be rather self-consciously jazzy, but there's no faulting the quality of the nightly live music sessions. Sun–Thurs 11am–1am, Fri & Sat 11am–2am.

Milk Bar #01-09 *The Gallery Hotel*, Robertson Quay. Singapore's hippest hotel is also home to one of its coolest bars. *Milk's* split levels allow punters to chill out downstairs, and get down, upstairs. Sun–Thurs 5pm–1am, Sat & Sun 5pm–2am.

The Colonial District

Balaclava #01-01b Suntec City Convention Ctr, 1 Raffles Blvd ☎63391600. Homage to G-Plan or nod to 1960s James Bond movies? Both could be said of this retro jazz bar, whose leather chairs, sassy red lamps and dark wood veneers may make the ambience too oppressive for some tastes. There's live jazz from 8.30pm, and happy hour is 3–9pm. Mon–Thurs 3pm–1am, Fri & Sat 3pm–2am.

Bar and Billiards Room *Raffles Hotel*, 1 Beach Rd ☏ 63371886. A Singapore Sling in the colonial elegance of the hotel where Ngiam Tong Boon invented it in 1915, is required drinking on a visit to Singapore. Snacks are available through the afternoon, and billiards costs by the hour. Daily 11.30am–midnight.

Bar Opiume Asian Civilizations Museum, 1 Empress Place ☏ 63392876. Cool-as-ice cocktail bar, where the barmen mix a mean Singapore Sling. Outside, are drop-dead gorgeous views of the waterfront; inside is a bar of mature sophistication, graced by huge crystal chandeliers, modish, square-cut leather furniture and a lordly standing Buddha statue. Recommended. Mon–Thurs 5pm–2am, Fri & Sat 5pm–3am.

City Space 70th floor, *Swissôtel the Stamford*, 2 Stamford Rd. Exquisitely appointed lounge bar – but decor be hanged: you come to *City Space* to drink in the peerless, 70-storey views across Singapore to southern Malaysia. The cocktails aren't cheap, but the warmed chili cashews that come with them are to die for. Sun–Thurs 5pm–1am, Fri & Sat 5pm–2am.

Divine Society Parkview Sq, 600 North Bridge Rd ☏ 63964466. All the decadence and excess of 1920s café society comes outrageously to life at *Divine*, a big, bonkers bar whose adoption of a wine angel (a waitress, kitted out in wings and harness, who is winched up and down the 12m wine rack) might just be the most politically incorrect thing you'll ever see. Elsewhere, Art Deco murals of prancing deer line the walls, vast brass lamps hang from the lofty ceiling, and there are life-sized mannequins of Duke Ellington, Billie Holliday and Louis Armstrong. This is supposed to be a members' only establishment, but dress sharp and you'll have no trouble getting in. Mon–Sat noon–midnight.

Fat Frog Café The Substation, 45 Armenian St ☏ 63386201. Relaxed courtyard café, sited within the Substation arts centre, where Singapore's culture vultures come to sip coffees and cold drinks and deconstruct the latest arts sensation under the shade of the whispering trees. Sun–Thurs 11.20am–11.30pm, Fri & Sat 11.30am–2am.

Liberté #01-19/20 CHIJMES, 30 Victoria St. *Liberté* holds centre stage on CHIJMES' main square – and rightly so. Its artsy wall hangings, flickering tea lights, mellow, middle-eastern influenced sounds and excellent cocktails make it one of the few CHIJMES addresses where you actually want to stay inside, rather than head out onto the terrace. Better still, there are free drinks for women from 9pm to midnight on Thurs. Mon–Wed 5pm–2am, Thurs–Sat 5pm–3am, Sun 4pm–1am.

Lot, Stock and Barrel Pub 29 Seah St, north of Bras Basah Road. Frequented by a daytime office crowd and later a backpacker crowd (the guest-houses of Beach and North Bridge roads are just around the corner), who come for the rock classics on the jukebox. Daily 4pm–midnight; Happy hour daily 4–8pm.

Little India and around

Leisure Pub #B1-01 Selegie Centre, 189 Selegie Rd. Tame but endearing, darts-orientated establishment that's ideal for a quiet chat. Daily 5pm–midnight; Happy hour daily 4–9pm.

Roshni #02-01 Little India Arcade, 48 Serangoon Rd. Once the dinner plates and cutlery have been cleared away, there's swinging Hindi and Tamil dance music into the night. Daily 11.30am–midnight.

Orchard Road

Alley Bar 2 Emerald Hill Rd ☏ 67388818. Stand up at the bar counter and you'll swear you are imbibing under the stars, such is the ingenuity of the decor in this slightly pricey joint, off Orchard Road. The candlelit, seated area behind the bar is cosier. Sun–Thurs 5pm–2am, Fri & Sat 5pm–3am.

Anywhere #04-08/09 Tanglin Shopping Centre, 19 Tanglin Rd. Tania, Singapore's most famous cover band, plays nightly to a boozy roomful of expats that's at its rowdiest on Friday nights. Mon–Sat 6pm–2am; Happy hour Mon–Fri 6–8pm.

Dubliner Windsland House, 165 Penang Rd. Set up in a colonial-era mansion, this is not your typical prefab Irish pub. The grub is a notch above as well, and there are sometimes live bands on offer. However, enjoying a beer while parked out on the veranda may be the best seat in the house. Sun–Thurs 11.30am–1am, Fri & Sat 11.30am–2am.

Ice Cold Beer 9 Emerald Hill Rd. Noisy, hectic and happening place where the beers are kept on ice under the glass-topped bar. Sun–Thurs 5pm–2am, Fri & Sat 5pm–3am; Happy hour daily 5–9pm.

No 5 Emerald Hill 5 Emerald Hill Rd. Quite a pleasant Peranakan-style bar/restaurant, if you can stomach the constant crunch of peanut shells underfoot. There's nightly live jazz in the upstairs bar. Daily noon–2am; Happy hours noon–9pm & 1–2am.

Observation Lounge 38th floor, *Mandarin Hotel*, 333 Orchard Rd. Swanky cocktail bar offering awesome views over downtown Singapore. Mon–Thurs & Sun 11am–1am, Fri & Sat 11am–2am.

Snackworld Cuppage Terrace, Cuppage Rd. Buy a bottle of Tiger from *Snackworld* and watch the world drifting by – a great place to hang out. Daily 11am–midnight.

Vintage Rock Café #01-23 Orchard Plaza, 150 Orchard Rd. Friendly staff and locals, great R&B music on the speakers and cheapish beer. Daily 4–11pm; Happy hour 4–8pm.

River Valley Road and around

Next Page Pub 17–18 Mohamed Sultan Rd. Cool, popular pub, with a pool table out back. The decor is a mixture of Chinese wooden screens, lanterns and rough brick wall. The adjacent *Front Page* annexe, with its deep leather armchairs, is quieter and more relaxed. Daily 3pm–1am.

Siam Supper Club #01-53/55 UE Sq, River Valley Rd. Semi-circular red leather booths, a circular bar and lustrous red oval lamps lend the *Supper Club* a soothing fluidity. Buddha effigies in wall niches add an Asian twist. Cocktails are S$12 and bar snacks range from chicken wings to sashimi. Mon–Sat 3pm–3am; Happy hour 5–9pm.

The Yard 294 River Valley Rd. River Valley's elder statesman is a busy English pub with bar snacks available. Mon–Thurs 3pm–1am, Fri & Sat 3pm–2am, Sun 5pm–1am; Happy hour daily 3–8pm.

Chinatown and around

Bar Savanh 49 Club St. Candlelit, and crammed with Buddha effigies, scatter cushions and plants, the *Savanh* (the name means "Heaven" in Lao) is a mellow bar if ever there was one. The cool acid-jazz sounds round things off nicely. Mon–Thurs 5pm–2am, Fri & Sat 5pm–3am, Sun 5pm–1am; Happy hour 5–8pm.

Carnegie's #01-01 Far East Sq, 44-45 Pekin St. Good-time pub-disco, where Dutch courage sees to it that there's always a clutch of revellers dancing on the bar. All standard drinks are S$6 during Crazy Hour (6–7pm). Sun & Mon 11am–midnight, Tues–Thurs 11am–2am, Fri & Sat 11am–3am.

Embargo #01-06 One Fullerton, 1 Fullerton Rd. Pre-clubbing cocktails with views out over the bay are the order of the day at *Embargo*, so don't come along in jeans and pumps and expect to blend in with the beautiful people that frequent the place. Daily 5pm–3am.

Around Singapore

Full Moon Beach Bar & Grill #01-01 Costa Sands Resort, 1110 East Coast Parkway. The South China Sea is just a stone's throw away from this breezy, open-fronted beachfront bar. Sun–Thurs noon–2am, Fri & Sat noon–3am.

Wala Wala Café & Bar 31 Lorong Mambong, Holland Village. Rocking Holland Village joint, now into its second decade, serving Boddington's, Stella and Hoegaarden and featuring a generous happy hour (4–9pm). A live band plays in the bar upstairs. Sun–Thurs 4pm–1am, Fri & Sat 4pm–2am.

Clubs

The Singaporean **nightclub** scene has transformed itself over the last few years. Clubs are far more self-aware, and the dance music on the decks is far more cutting-edge, than previously. The cult of the celebrity DJ has taken a firm hold. Happily, Singaporean clubbers themselves remain, on the whole, more intent on enjoying themselves than on posing. European and American dance music dominates (though some play Cantonese pop songs, too), and many feature live bands playing cover versions of current hits and pop classics.

Clubs tend to open around 9pm, though some start earlier in the evening with a happy hour. Indeed, the difference between bars and discos has recently begun to blur, and some now include bars or restaurants that kick off at lunchtime. Most have a **cover charge**, at least on busy Friday and Saturday nights, which fluctuates between S$15 and S$30, depending on what day it is and what sex you are, and almost invariably entitles you to a drink or two. It's worth checking the local press to see which venues are currently in favour; a scan through *8 Days*, *I-S* or *Juice* magazines will bring you up to date.

Singapore's **gay scene** has done a couple of odd reversals in the past half decade. First official attitudes seemed to become more tolerant, but then a few years later a change seemed to come about with denial for permission to organize a local gay pride festival that had been held annually since 2001. Surely Singapore has not completely reverted to its prudish past, but discretion is still advisable in this country where homosexual acts are still illegal. The gay nightlife scene centres on a number of clubs in Chinatown and Tanjong Pagar. Ⓦwww.sgboy.com has a listings sections of gay-oriented clubs and restaurants.

Singapore also has a plethora of seedy **hostess clubs**, in which aged Chinese hostesses working on commission try to hassle you into buying them a drink. Extortionately expensive, these joints are to be avoided, not least because they attract a decidedly unsavoury clientele. Fortunately, they are easy to spot: even if you get beyond the heavy wooden front door flanked by brandy adverts, the pitch darkness inside gives the game away.

Bar None *Marriott Hotel,* 320 Orchard Rd. Popular *Bar None's* house band Energy are a Singapore institution; when they aren't playing their polished rock covers sets, the DJs veer from Latino to alternative, and from R&B to top 40 hits. Daily 6pm–3am; Happy hour 7–9pm.

Brix 10–12 Scotts Rd. Formally known as *Brannigan's,* this large basement bar has shed its pick-up joint reputation, roughed up its decor a bit, and moved up into the premier league of Singapore clubs. There are salsa lessons on Monday nights, and a S$20 cover charge applies Thurs–Sun. Tues–Sun 7pm–2am, Wed–Sat 7pm–3am.

Centro #02-02 One Fullerton, 1 Fullerton Rd. Should you tire of ogling the glamorous clubbers, there are great views out to the Singapore harbour from sophisticated *Centro.* The intimate dance floor moves to house and garage sounds, celebrity guest DJs have included Judge Jules and Roger Sanchez. A S$30 cover charge applies except on Wed, when women get free entry, champagne and house spirits. Wed–Sun 9pm–3am.

China Black 12th floor Pacific Plaza, 9 Scotts Rd ☏67347677. *China Black's* emphasis on chart hits and R&B makes it a safe haven for occasional clubbers who don't know their trance from their handbag house. Fri 5pm–3am, Sat 7pm–3am, Sun 9pm–3am.

DBL-O #01-24 Robertson Walk, 11 Unity St. With its massive dance floor, sassy *DBL-O* really can pack in the punters. House, garage and R&B are the favoured musical styles. Wednesday night is free for women; on other nights, cover charges range from S$15–25. Wed–Sat 8pm–3am.

Gold Dust 400 Orchard Rd ☏62357170. Drag queen Kumar, formerly of the infamous Bugis Street *Boom Boom Room,* hosts a nightly show of cabaret and gay-oriented stand-up comedy.

Home Club #B01-06 The Riverwalk, 20 Upper Circular Road Ⓦwww.homeclub.com.sg. The fringes of a shopping mall might seem a strange place for a happening club, but this cosy venue makes the best of the riverside location with a chilled-out patio area outside; inside DJs spin a range of sounds, from R&B to 1980s synth-pop depending on the evening. Friday nights see a switch to indie, however, as a bunch of local bands play original material that wouldn't sound out of place on US college radio. Cover charge of around S$20 most nights. Closed Mon.

Liquid Room #01-05 *The Gallery Hotel,* 76 Robertson Quay. Bring your dancing shoes – *Liquid Room* is a dark, cramped, pumping place majoring on trance and techno, and the dance floor is a sea of bodies. Daily 7pm–3am.

Madam Wong's 28/29 Jalan Mohamed Sultan. Vast warren of a pub-cum-disco in a former rice warehouse, where scruffy red walls, weathered Chinese signage, opium beds and scatter cushions evoke an entrancing retro-Asian chic. Early-evening acid jazz gives way to higher-octane dance music later on. Cover charge of S$15 applies after 9pm, Fri & Sat. Daily 5pm–3am; Happy hour 5–10pm.

Ministry of Sound The Cannery, River Valley Rd Ⓦwww.ministryofsound.com.sg. Claiming to be the largest *MoS* franchise in the world, spilling over into various annexes, this heavyweight club boasts regular appearances by big-name DJs, a water feature doubling as a screen for visuals, and sounds ranging from funky house to R&B and soul. Cover charge of around S$20 most nights, though women get in free Wednesdays. Wed–Sun 9pm–4am.

Phuture 17 Jiak Kim St. Dark, smoky joint, with harder hip-hop, break beat and drum and bass sounds than the other *Zouk* venues, and therefore a more youthful crowd. Cover charge is S$15 before 9pm, then S$25. Wed–Sat 7pm–3am.

Velvet Underground 17 Jiak Kim St. Less thumping than *Phuture* and *Zouk*, and with a correspondingly older, less frenetic crowd. Lava lamps create a suitably dreamy ambience. The cover charge (S$25 for women, S$35 for men)

affords access to *Zouk* and *Phuture*. Tues–Sat 9pm–3am.

Zouk 17–21 Jiak Kim St. Singapore's trendiest club, fitted out with palm trees and Moorish tiles to create a Mediterranean feel. As well as *Zouk* itself, the warehouse it occupies hosts *Phuture* and *Velvet Underground* (above). Renowned DJs like Paul Oakenfold guest occasionally. Cover charge is S$15 before 9pm, then S$25. Wed–Sat 7pm–3am.

Live music

Singapore has a thriving live music scene and has recently attracted big names like Oasis, Mogwai, and Damien Rice. Have a look at *8 Days* or *I-S* magazine to see if any concerts are scheduled. Rivalling Western music in terms of popularity in Singapore is **Canto-pop**, a bland hybrid of Cantonese lyrics and Western disco beats; Hong Kong Canto-pop superstars visit periodically, and the rapturous welcomes they receive make their shows quite an experience. No matter who else is in town, you can always catch a set of cover versions at one of Singapore's bars and clubs.

Anywhere See p.714. Good-time rock music by local favourites Tania.
Balaclava See p.713. Live torch song and jazz sets nightly.
Crazy Elephant See p.713. Live blues and rock throughout the week.
Harry's Quayside See p.713. Live jazz Wednesday to Saturday, and a blues jam on Sunday evening.
Jazz @ Southbridge See p.713. Mellow jazz played live.

No 5 Emerald Hill See p.714. Live jazz upstairs nightly.
Singapore Indoor Stadium The usual venue for big-name bands in town.
Theatres on the Bay See p.649. Western and Asian stars take the stage, between musicals.
HarbourFront Centre See p.694. Hosts international acts from time to time, as well as presenting free local gigs in its amphitheatre.

The arts and culture

The opening of the Esplanade – Theatres on the Bay centre has transformed Singapore's **performing arts** scene, and given the island a cultural focal point. But there is a plethora of venues away from Esplanade that also serve up notable performances. Of all the performing arts, **drama** gets the best showing in Singapore, the island's theatres staging productions that range from English farces to contemporary productions by local writers. **Classical music** also gets a good showing, thanks to the busy schedule of the Singapore Symphony Orchestra. Western and Asian **dance** performances crop up periodically; you are sure to see some, if you time your trip to coincide with the annual **Singapore Festival of Arts** in June. **Asian culture** is showcased in Singapore's major venues from time to time, but tends to appear more often on the street than in the auditorium, particularly around the time of the bigger festivals. Cinema is big business in Singapore, with up-to-the-minute Asian and Western movies all drawing big crowds, and the annual **Singapore International Film Festival** in April.

For **information** on cultural events and performances, pick up a copy of either the *Singapore Straits Times* (whose daily "Life!" supplement has a good "what's on" section), *8 Days* magazine, or the free magazines *I-S* (fortnightly) and *Where Singapore* (monthly), available at most hotel lobbies. **Tickets** for music shows, theatre and dance are sold either at the venue itself, or through two ticketing agencies, Sistic (℡63485555, ⓦwww.sistic.com.sg) and CalendarONE TicketCharge (℡62962929, ⓦwww.ticketcharge.com.sg). You can expect to pay at least S$10 to attend a performance, though international acts command substantially higher prices.

Classical music

At the heart of the **Western** classical music scene in Singapore is the **Singapore Symphony Orchestra**. Performances by the national orchestra take place at Esplanade – Theatres on the Bay and often feature guest soloists, conductors and choirs from around the world; occasional **Chinese** classical music shows are included in the programme. From time to time, ensembles from the orchestra also give **lunchtime concerts** at various spots around the island. In addition, the Singapore Symphony Orchestra gives occasional free performances in Singapore's parks while Sentosa Island also hosts regular Sunday concerts – the shows themselves are free, but the usual Sentosa entry fee applies (see p.700).

Chinese Opera Teahouse 5 Smith St ℡63234862. S$35 buys you Chinese dinner and an opera performance. See p.666 for details.
Nanyang Academy of Fine Arts Chinese Orchestra 111 Middle Rd ℡63377636. Chinese classical and folk music.
Singapore Chinese Orchestra Singapore Conference Hall, 7 Shenton Way ℡64403839, ⓦwww.sco.com.sg. Performances of traditional Chinese music through the year, plus occasional free concerts.
Singapore Symphony Orchestra Esplanade – Theatres on the Bay ℡63381230, ⓦwww.sso .org.sg. Performances throughout the year.

Cultural performances

If you walk around Singapore's streets for long enough, you're likely to come across some sort of streetside **cultural event**, most usually a *wayang*, or Chinese opera, played out on tumbledown outdoor stages that spring up overnight next to temples and markets, or just at the side of the road. *Wayang*s are highly dramatic and stylized affairs, in which garishly made-up and costumed characters enact popular Chinese legends to the accompaniment of the crashes of cymbals and gongs. They're staged throughout the year, but the best time to catch one is during the Festival of the Hungry Ghosts, when they are held to entertain passing spooks, or during the Festival of the Nine Emperor Gods (see p.74). The Singapore Tourism Board may also be able to help you track down a *wayang*, and as usual the local press is worth checking. Another fascinating traditional performance, **lion dancing**, takes to the streets during Chinese New Year, and **puppet theatres** appear around then, as well.

Film

With over fifty **cinemas** on the island, you should have no trouble finding a movie that appeals to you, and at a price (S$5–8) that compares favourably with cinemas in Europe and America. As well as the latest Hollywood blockbusters, a wide range of Chinese, Malay and Indian movies, all with English subtitles, are screened. **Chinese** productions tend to be a raucous blend of slapstick and martial arts, while **Malay** and **Indian** movies are characterized by exuberant song and dance routines. **Western** movies in languages other than English also pop up occasionally. The Alliance Française at 1 Sarkies Road (℡67378422) screens free French movies (Tues 9pm) and holds an annual film festival in

November. There are also regular presentations at the British Council, 30 Napier Road (☎64731111) and the Goethe Institute, #05-01, 163 Penang Rd (☎67354555). The annual **Singapore International Film Festival** (🌐www .filmfest.org.sg) takes pace in April and screens over 150 films and shorts – mostly by Asian directors – over two weeks; smaller festivals are occasionally mounted by the Singapore Film Society (🌐www.sfs.org.sg).

Cinema-going is a popular pastime here, so if you plan to catch a newly released film, turn up early to secure your tickets – and take along a sweater, as the a/c units are perpetually on full blast. Be prepared, also, for a lot of noise during shows: Singaporeans are great ones for talking all the way through the movie, and the sound of a bag of popcorn being rustled pales next to the sound of melon seeds being cracked and crunched. The most central cinemas are listed below, but check the local press for a full rundown of any special events or one-offs that might be taking place.

Golden Village GV Grand #03-29 Great World City, 1 Kim Seng Promenade ☎67358484. Singapore's poshest cinema, with state-of-the-art digital sound and fully reclinable seats. Pricey at S$25 a ticket.

Lido Level 5, Shaw House, 1 Scotts Rd ☎67380555. Five screens, including the luxurious Lido Classic.

Omni-Theatre Singapore Science Centre, 15 Science Centre Rd ☎64252500. Hair-raising 3D movies; see p.697 for more details.

Orchard Cineplex 8 Grange Rd ☎62351155. Central and recently renovated cinema, with a swish new shopping centre constructed around it.

Suntec Cineplex #03-51 Suntec City Mall, 3 Temasek Blvd ☎68369074. Latest releases and Asian blockbusters.

United Artists Beach Rd, Level 4, Shaw Leisure Gallery, 100 Beach Rd ☎63912550. This cinema has a reputation for screening slightly more cerebral movies than most.

United Artists Bugis Junction, 200 Victoria St ☎63912550. Posh and central cinema, showing Western and Chinese blockbusters.

Yangtse Pearl Centre, 100 Eu Tong Sen St ☎62237529. In the heart of Chinatown, this place shows Western and Asian films.

Theatre and the performing arts

Singapore now boasts a thriving **drama** scene encompassing lavish musicals like *Singin' in the Rain* and the tiniest of repertory companies. Ticket prices range from about S$15 upwards. Foreign companies visit regularly and usually perform at Esplanade – Theatres on the Bay or the Victoria or Kallang theatres. Performances of **dance** are also common – most notably by the Singapore Dance Theatre (☎63380611, 🌐www.singaporedancetheatre.com), which performs contemporary and classical works at various venues, and sometimes by moonlight, at Fort Canning Park.

Singapore's annual **Festival of the Arts** attracts class acts from all over the world. A schedule of events is published in May, a month before the festival begins so, unless you are in Singapore for quite a while, you'll probably have trouble getting tickets for more popular events. Still, an accompanying **fringe festival** takes place concurrently, and its programme always includes free street and park performances. Singapore also hosts a biennial **Festival of Asian Performing Arts**, showcasing the cultures of neighbouring nations.

Action Theatre 42 Waterloo St ☎68370842. Showcases contemporary works by Singaporean playwrights.

Drama Centre Canning Rise Fort, Canning Park ☎63360005. Proficient drama performed by local companies.

Esplanade – Theatres on the Bay 1 Esplanade Drive ☎68288222. Sucks up all the biggest events to hit Singapore's shores.

Jubilee Hall *Raffles Hotel,* 1 Beach Rd ☎63371886. Occasionally stages plays.

Kala Mandhir Cultural Association *Peninsula Excelsior Hotel,* 5 Coleman St ☎63390492, www.templeoffinearts.org. Dedicated to perpetuating traditional Indian art, music and dance. **Kallang Theatre** 1 Stadium Walk ☎ 63454888. Hosts visiting companies such as the Bolshoi Ballet and touring musical productions like *Chicago*. **Singapore Repertory Theatre** DBS Drama Centre, 20 Merbau Rd, Robertson Quay ☎ 67338166. English-language theatre, showcasing Western plays with Asian actors.

Substation 45 Armenian St ☎ 63377800. Self-styled "home for the arts" with a multipurpose hall that presents drama and dance, as well as art, sculpture and photography exhibitions in its gallery. **Victoria Concert Hall and Theatre** 11 Empress Place ☎ 63396120. Visiting performers and successful local performances that graduate here from lesser venues.

Shopping

For many stopover visitors, Singapore is synonymous with **shopping**, though, contrary to popular belief, prices aren't necessarily much cheaper than in Western cities, due to the consistently strong Singaporean dollar and a rising cost of living. Good deals can, however, be found on watches, cameras, electrical and computer equipment, fabrics and antiques, and cut-price imitations – Rolexes, Lacoste polo shirts and so on – are rife. What's more, come during the **Great Singapore Sale** (from late May to late July; www.greatsingaporesale.com .sg), and you'll find seriously marked-down prices in many outlets across the island. Choice and convenience make the Singapore shopping experience a

Orchard Road shopping centres

The main Orchard Road shopping centres are detailed below; see map on pp.680–681.

Centrepoint Dependable all-round complex, whose seven floors of shops include the second incarnation of Robinsons, Singapore's oldest department store.

C.K. Tang's Singapore's most famous department store, whose pagoda-style construction provides Orchard Road with one of its most recognizable landmarks.

Delfi Orchard Good for crystalware, glassware and art galleries.

Forum the Shopping Mall Kids' clothes, toyshops, modelling specialists and clothes stores.

Lucky Plaza Crammed with tailors and electronics, this is Orchard Road's classic venue for haggling.

Ngee Ann City A brooding twin-towered complex – Singapore meets Gotham City – with a wealth of good clothes shops and Kinokuniya, the biggest bookstore on the island.

Orchard Plaza Tailors, leather jackets and silks galore, as well as a glut of audio, video and camera stores where haggling is par for the course.

Palais Renaissance One of Singapore's classiest complexes, featuring Prada, Versace, Ralph Lauren, Gucci, Christian Dior and other heavyweights.

Plaza Singapura Sportswear and sports equipment, musical instruments, audio, video and general electrical equipment.

Tanglin Shopping Centre Unsurpassed for art, antiques and curios.

Wheelock Place One of the newer shopping centres on the block, this impressive pyramid of a building boasts a well-stocked Border's bookshop and a Marks & Spencer.

Wisma Atria Hosts a good range of local and international fashion designers over five floors.

rewarding one, with scores of shopping centres and department stores meaning that you're rarely more than an air-con escalator ride away from what you want to buy. Usual **shopping hours** are daily 10am–9pm, though some shopping centres, especially those along Orchard Road, stay open until 10pm. The **Mustafa Centre**, on the northern edge of Little India, is known all over the island for being open 24/7.

Singapore's goods and services **tax** (GST) adds a five percent sales tax to all goods and services, but tourists can claim a refund on purchases over a certain amount at retailers displaying a **Tax Refund** or **Tax Free Shopping** sticker. It's fairly complicated and only really worth the trouble if you are going to spend a large amount of money on electronics or something similar. For detailed information have a look at ⓦ www.customs.gov.sg/travel2.html.

Should you have a complaint that you can't resolve with a particular store, contact the Retail Promotions Centre at ⓣ 64502114. Or you can go to Singapore's Small Claims Tribunal, Subordinate Courts, 5th floor, Apollo Centre, 2 Havelock Rd ⓣ 65356922, ⓦ www.smallclaims.gov.sg, which has a fast-track system for tourists; it costs S$10 to have your case heard.

For clothes (either by Western or local designers – the latter are far more reasonably priced), tailor-made suits, sports equipment, electronic goods or antiques, the shopping malls of **Orchard Road** have all you could possibly want. At **Arab Street** (p.660), you find exquisite textiles and batiks, robust basketware and some good deals on jewellery, as well as more unusual Muslim items. From here, make a beeline for **Little India** (p.671), where the silk stores and goldsmiths spoil you for choice; en route you pass the intersection of **Bencoolen Street and Rochor Road**, where a gaggle of shopping centres stock electrical goods galore. As well as its souvenir shops, **Chinatown** boasts some more traditional outlets stocking Chinese foodstuffs, medicines, instruments and porcelain – Chinatown's shopping highlights are listed on p.668. For souvenirs, head for the Singapore Handicraft Centre in Chinatown Point (see p.668) or for the cluster of Asian antique and curio shops that have sprung up along South Bridge Road. Pick up any tourism leaflet in Singapore, and you are sure to find plenty of suggestions as to where to spend your hard-earned cash. The free monthly, *Where Singapore*, has a decent shopping section, and the STB publishes a free monthly *Singapore Shopping Guide*. As well as the various shops and outlets picked out in the text, check out any of the following as you travel around Singapore.

Antiques Antiques of the Orient, #02-40 Tanglin Shopping Centre, 19 Tanglin Rd, specializes in antiquarian books, maps and prints; Cho Lon Galerie, 43 Jalan Merah Saga, Holland Village, specializes in Chinese and Vietnamese furniture and crafts; Far East Inspiration, 33 Pagoda St, Chinatown, is the classiest of several antique shops along this street, stocking Asian furniture, porcelain-based lamps, prints and watercolours; Katong Antiques House, 208 East Coast Rd, Katong, is an Aladdin's cave of tiffin carriers, Peranakan slippers and textiles, and Chinese porcelain.

Artworks Jasmine Fine Arts, #04-14 Orchard Point, 160 Orchard Rd, stocks appealing artwork from all over the world; Kwok Gallery, #03-01 Far East Shopping Centre, 545 Orchard Rd, has a broad and impressive inventory of antique Chinese artworks; MITA Building, 140 Hill St, houses as good a selection of art galleries as you'll find in Singapore.

Buddhist goods Nanyang Buddhist Culture Service, #01-13 Block 333, Kreta Ayer Rd, Chinatown, sells effigies, trinkets, necklaces and books. Otherwise, head for the stretch of Waterloo Street beside Kuan Yim Temple, where there is a proliferation of stores selling Buddhist goods.

Computers and software Funan Digitalife Mall, 109 North Bridge Rd, at the junction with High St.

Electronic equipment Sim Lim Tower, 10 Jalan Besar; Lucky Plaza, 304 Orchard Rd.

Fabrics and silk Dakshaini Silks, 164 Serangoon Rd, Little India, sells premier Indian embroidered silks; Goodwill Trading Co, 56 Arab St, has Indonesian batik sarongs heaped on varnished wood shelves.

Jewellery The entire first floor of the Pidemco Centre, 95 South Bridge Rd, is a jewellery market; CT Hoo, #01-22 Tanglin Shopping Centre, 19 Tanglin Rd, specializes in pearls; Richard Hung Jewellers, #01-24 Lucky Plaza, 304 Orchard Rd are well regarded, and all of their staff are qualified gemologists; Risis, Botanic Gardens, Cluny Rd, sells jewellery made by gold-plating flora of all kinds – from ferns to orchids.

Music HMV Singapore, #01-11 The Heeren Shops, 260 Orchard Rd; Jothi Music Corner, #01-77 Little India Arcade, 48 Serangoon Rd, for Indian music on tape; Flux Us, #04-34 Peninsula Shopping Centre, 3 Coleman St, with music, books and DVDs of a more indie nature; Roxy Records, #03-36 Funan Digitalife Mall, 109 North Bridge Rd, for indie and dance records, plus Singaporean artists; Supreme Record Centre, #03-28 Centrepoint, 175 Orchard Rd; That CD Shop, #01-17 Tanglin Mall, 163 Tanglin Rd, for new age, acid jazz and classical CDs; Tower Records, second floor, Suntec City Mall, 3 Temasek Blvd.

Porcelain Ming Village, 32 Pandan Rd ℡ 62657711 (Clementi MRT and then bus #78), where all the work on Ming and Qing Dynasty reproductions is done by hand, according to traditional methods – most fascinating is the painstaking work of the painters.

Souvenirs China Mec, #03-31/32 Raffles City Shopping Centre, 250 North Bridge Rd, for Beijing *cloisonné* goods; Eng Tiang Huat, 284 River Valley Rd, for oriental musical instruments, *wayang* costumes and props; Funan Stamp and Coin Agency, #03-03 Funan the IT Mall, 109 North Bridge Rd; Lim's Arts & Living, #02-01 Holland Rd Shopping Centre, 221 Holland Ave, is a sort of Asian Conran Shop, packed with bamboo pipes, dainty tea pots, cherrywood furniture and lamps crafted from old tea jars; One Price Store, 3 Emerald Hill Rd, off Orchard Road, carries everything from carved camphorwood chests to Chinese snuff bottles; Red Peach Gallery, 68 Pagoda St, for Asian arts, incense sticks, tea sets, fabrics and chopsticks; Royal Selangor Pewter, 32 Pandan Rd ℡ 62657711, for pewterwork demonstrations and products; Singapore Handicraft Centre, Chinatown Point, 133 New Bridge Rd, gathers around fifty souvenir shops under one roof; Tatami Shop, #02-10 Esplanade Mall, 8 Raffles Ave, specializes in Japanese tatami mats, rugs and miscellanea; TeaJoy #01-05 North Bridge Rd, sells Chinese tea sets with special attention paid to oolong accoutrements; Zhen Lacquer Gallery, 1a/b Trengganu St, specializing in boxes, bowls and paintings whose polished finish is crafted from the resin of the lacquer tree.

Listings

Airlines Aeroflot #01-02/#02-00 Tan Chong Tower, 15 Queen St ℡ 63361757; Air Canada #02-43/46 Meridien Shopping Centre, 100 Orchard Rd ℡ 62561198; Air India #17-01 UIC Building, 5 Shenton Way ℡ 62259411; Air New Zealand #24-08 Ocean Bldg, 10 Collyer Quay ℡ 65358266; American Airlines #06-05 Cairnhill Place, 15 Cairnhill Rd ℡ 67370900; Berjaya Air 67 Tanjong Pagar Rd ℡ 62273688; British Airways #06-05 Cairnhill Place 15 Cairnhill Rd ℡ 65897000; Cathay Pacific #16-01 Ocean Bldg, 10 Collyer Quay ℡ 65331333; Garuda #12-03 United Sq, 101 Thompson Rd ℡ 62505666; KLM #12-06 Ngee Ann City Tower A, 391a Orchard Rd ℡ 67377622; Lufthansa #05-07 Palais Renaissance, 390 Orchard Rd ℡ 68355912; MAS #02-09 Singapore Shopping Centre 190 Clemenceau Ave ℡ 63366777; Philippine Airlines #01-10 Parklane Shopping Mall, 35 Selegie Rd ℡ 63361611; Qantas #06-05/08 The Promenade, 300 Orchard Rd ℡ 65687000; Royal Brunei #03-11 UE Shopping Mall, 81 Clemenceau Ave ℡ 62354672; Royal Nepal Airlines #03-09 Peninsula Shopping Centre, 3 Coleman St ℡ 63395535;

Silkair #08-01 Temasek Tower, 8 Shenton Way ℡ 62238888; Singapore Airlines #02-26 The Paragon, 290 Orchard Rd ℡ 62236666; SriLankan Airlines #13-02 Keck Seng Tower, 133 Cecil St ℡ 62257233; Thai Airways #02-00 The Globe, 100 Cecil St ℡ 62249977; United Airlines #44-02 Hong Leong Bldg, 16 Raffles Quay ℡ 68733533.

Airport For Changi airport flight information, call ℡ 1-800/5424422 (toll-free).

Banks and exchange All Singapore's banks change traveller's cheques; normal banking hours are Mon–Fri 9.30am–3pm & Sat 9.30am–12.30pm. Licensed moneychangers, offering slightly more favourable rates also abound – particularly in Arab Street, Serangoon Road's Mustafa Centre, and the Orchard Road shopping centres. Credit cards can be used either in ATM machines or over the counter.

Bookshops One of Singapore's biggest bookshops is Books Kinokuniya, #03-10 Ngee Ann City, 391 Orchard Rd. Times bookshops stock a wide choice of titles, and crop up all over town: one of its most central branches is at #04-08/15 Centrepoint, 175 Orchard Rd. MPH shops are also well stocked, with branches at B1-26a CityLink Mall, 1 Raffles Link and #02-24 Raffles City Shopping Centre, 252 North Bridge Rd. Borders has a Singapore branch at Wheelock Place, 501 Orchard Rd, which also carries an excellent range of newspapers and magazines. One of the best small bookshops in town is Select Books, #03-15 Tanglin Shopping Centre, 19 Tanglin Rd @ www.selectbooks.com .sg, which offers a huge array of books on the history, culture, society and attractions of Malaysia and Singapore, plus a variety of more specialized literature on Southeast Asia in general.

Car rental Avis, 01-0 Waterfront Plaza, 392 Havelock Rd ☏ 67371668 and Terminal 1 and 2, Changi airport ☏ 65450800, ☏ 65428855; Hertz, 01-01 Thong Teck Building, 15 Scotts Rd ☏ 1800-734 4646 and Terminal 2 Changi airport, ☏ 65425300; Sintat, 8 Kim Keat Lane ☏ 62952211 and Terminal 1, Changi airport ☏ 65427288.

Cookery schools Coriander Leaf Cookery School #02-01 *The Gallery Hotel*, 76 Robertson Quay ☏ 67323354; Raffles Culinary Academy #02-17 *Raffles Hotel* Arcade, 328 North Bridge Rd ☏ 64121256.

Credit-card helplines American Express ☏ 1800-299 1997; Diners Club ☏ 62944222; MasterCard ☏ 65332888; Visa ☏ 64375800.

Dentists Listed in the *Singapore Buying Guide* (equivalent to the *Yellow Pages*) under "Dental Surgeons", and "Dentist Emergency Service".

Disabled travellers The best resource for pre-trip advice is the Disabled People's Association of Singapore, #02-00 Day Care Centre, 150a Pandan Gardens ☏ 68891220, @ www.dpa.org.sg. Their informative website links to *Access Singapore*, a Singapore Council of Social Service publication which, while in need of updating, is still an informative booklet detailing amenities for the disabled in Singapore's hotels, hospitals, shopping centres, banks and cinemas.

Embassies and consulates Australia ☏ 68384100; Brunei ☏ 67339055; Canada ☏ 62253240; France ☏ 68807800; Germany ☏ 67371355; India ☏ 67376777; Indonesia ☏ 67377422; Ireland ☏ 62387616; Malaysia ☏ 62350111; New Zealand ☏ 62359966; Philippines ☏ 67373977; Sri Lanka ☏ 62544595; Thailand ☏ 67372644; UK ☏ 64739333; US ☏ 64769100; Vietnam ☏ 64625938.

Emergencies Police ☏ 999; Ambulance and Fire Brigade ☏ 995 (all toll-free); larger hotels have doctors on call at all times.

Hospitals Singapore General, Outram Road ☏ 62223322; Alexandra Hospital, Alexandra Road ☏ 64722000; and National University Hospital, Kent Ridge ☏ 67795555. All are state hospitals and all

have casualty departments. Raffles Hospital, 585 North Bridge Rd ☏ 63111555 is private but very central.

Internet access There are numerous Internet cafés in Singapore, including at most places of accommodation. Typical charges are S$3 per half-hour or S$5 per hour.

Laundry DryClean Express offer a pick-up and delivery service ☏ 68615933 or 62860811; Washy Washy, #01-18 Cuppage Plaza, 5 Koek Rd (Mon–Sat 10am–7pm).

Pharmacies Guardian Pharmacy has over forty outlets, including ones at Centrepoint, 176 Orchard Rd; Raffles City Shopping Centre, 252 North Bridge Rd; and Clifford Centre, 24 Raffles Place. Usual hours are 9am–6pm, but some stay open until 10pm. There are also around fifty outlets of Watson's pharmacy across Singapore.

Police In an emergency, dial ☏ 999; otherwise call the freephone police hotline, ☏ 1800-255 0000.

Post offices The GPO (Mon–Fri 8am–6pm, Sat 8am–2pm) is at 10 Eunos Road beside Paya Lebar MRT; poste restante/general delivery is here (take your passport). There are more than sixty other post offices across the state, with usual opening hours of Monday to Friday 8.30am–5pm and Saturday 8.30am–1pm, though some central postal offices keep extended hours, notably at 1 Killiney Road (until 9pm Mon–Fri, until 4pm Sat, plus Sun 10am–4pm). Branches also at Changi airport. Singpost (☏ 1605, @ www.singpost.com.sg) does an efficient job of running mail services in Singapore. Aerogrammes here cost 000.50 each, while airmail starts at S$0.70 to Australasia.

Swimming Katong Swimming Complex, Wilkinson Road, and Buona Vista Swimming Complex, Holland Drive.

Telephones Local calls from private phones cost next to nothing; calls from public phones cost 10¢ for three minutes, though Changi airport's courtesy phones are free. Singapore has no area codes – the only time you'll punch more than eight digits for a local number is if you're dialling a toll-free (☏ 1-800) number or a pager. Cardphones have taken over from payphones: cards are available from the Comcentre on Killiney Road, post offices, 7-Elevens, stationers and bookshops and come in S$3–50 denominations. International calls can be made from all public cardphones and credit-card phones. International cards come in S$10–50 denominations. IDD calls from hotel rooms in Singapore carry no surcharge. For directory enquiries, call ☏ 100 and for IDD information, call ☏ 100 or 1607, or ☏ 104 for international enquiries. Internet cafés are increasingly offering the services of Skype or other Voice over Internet

Protocol (VoIP) technology to let customers make long-distance calls for a fraction of what a normal long-distance call would cost.

Tour operators Holiday Tours ☎67382622, RMG Tours ☎62201661 and SH Tours ☎67349923 can all arrange sightseeing tours of Singapore. For the kids (and fun-loving adults), Singapore Ducktour (hourly 9.30am–7.30pm; S$33, children S$17; ☎63333825, ⓦwww.ducktours.com.sg) provides an hour-long land and sea tour on an amphibious craft dating from the Vietnam War.

Travel agents The following organizations are good for discounted airfares and buying bus tickets to Malaysia and Thailand: Airpower Travel, 131a Bencoolen St ☎63346571; Harharah Travel, first floor, 171a Bencoolen St ☎63372633; STA Travel, 33a Cuppage Terrace ☎67377188, ⓦwww .statravel.com.sg; Sunny Holidays, #01-70 Parco Bugis Junction, 200 Victoria St ☎63345545.

Vaccinations Travellers' Health & Vaccination Clinic, Tan Tock Seng Hospital Medical Centre, 11 Jalan Tan Tock Seng ☎63572222.

Watersports Cowabunga Ski Centre, Kallang Stadium Lane ☎63448813; Pasta Fresca Sea Sports Centre, 1210 East Coast Parkway ☎64495118; Ponngol Sea-Sports, Ponngol Marina, 600 Ponngol 17th Ave ☎63864736; William Water Sports Centre 35 Ponngol 24th Ave, Ponngol Point ☎62575859.

Women's helpline AWARE is a women's helpline ☎1-800/7745935, ⓦwww.aware.org.sg.

Travel details

Trains

Singapore Railway Station to: Kuala Lumpur (4 daily; 6hr 30min); Gemas (4 daily; 4hr); Seremban (3 daily; 5hr).

Buses

Ban San Terminal to: Kuala Lumpur (4 daily; 6hr); Johor Bahru (every 10min; 40min);.

Golden Mile Complex to: Hat Yai (several daily; 12hr); Kuala Lumpur (Transtar luxury buses; 5 daily; 6hr).

Lavender MRT Station (Transtar luxury buses only) to: Kuala Lumpur (5 daily; 6hr); Melaka (daily; 3hr 30min); Penang (daily; 10hr).

Lavender Street Terminal to: Butterworth (at least 2 daily; 8hr 30min); Ipoh (2 daily; 7hr 30min); Kota Bharu (1 daily; 12hr 30min); Kuala Lumpur (8 daily; 5hr 30min); Kuantan (5 daily; 6hr 30min); Melaka (6 daily; 3hr 30min); Mersing (at least 2 daily; 3hr).

Ferries

Changi Ferry Terminal to: Tanjung Belungkor (Johor; 3 daily; 45min).

Changi Point to: Kampung Pengerang (for Desaru; hourly; 45min); Pulau Ubin (every 45min; 25min).

HarbourFront Centre to: Batam (Indonesia; every 30min; 40min).

Tanah Merah Ferry Terminal to: Tanjung Pinang (Indonesia; 4 daily; 1hr); Tioman (March–Oct 1 daily; 4hr 30min).

Flights

Changi Airport to:

Bandar Seri Begawan (2–3 daily; 2hr); Kota Kinabalu (2 daily; 2hr 30min); Kuala Lumpur (11 daily; 55min); Kuching (2 daily; 1hr 20min); Langkawi (8 weekly; 1hr 30min); Penang (8 daily; 1hr 15min).

Seletar Airport to: Pulau Redang (March–Oct 4 weekly; 1hr 30min); Pulau Tioman (daily; 35min).

Contexts

Contexts

History

The modern-day nations of **Malaysia**, **Singapore** and **Brunei** only acquired independent status in 1963, 1965 and 1984 respectively. Before that, the history of these countries was inextricably linked with events in the larger Malay archipelago, from Sumatra, across Borneo to the Philippines.

The problem for any historian is the lack of reliable source material for the region: there's little hard archeological evidence pertaining to the prehistoric period, while the events prior to the foundation of Melaka are known only from unreliable written accounts by Chinese and Arab traders. However, there are two vital sources for an understanding of events in the formative fourteenth and fifteenth centuries: the **Suma Oriental** (Treatise of the Orient), by Tomé Pires, a Portuguese emissary who came to Melaka in 1512 and wrote a history of the Orient based upon his own observations, and the **Sejarah Melayu**, the seventeenth-century "Malay Annals", which recorded oral historical tales recounted in a poetic, rather than strictly chronological, style. Although differing in many respects, not least in timescale, both volumes describe similar events.

Portuguese and Dutch **colonists** who arrived in the sixteenth and seventeenth centuries provided **written records**, though these tended to concern commercial rather than political or social matters. The wealth of information from **British colonial** times (from the early nineteenth century onwards), though giving detailed insights into Malay affairs, is imprinted with an imperialistic bias. It is only in the twentieth century, when Malay sources come into play, that a complete picture can be presented.

Beginnings

The oldest remains of *Homo sapiens* in the region were discovered in the Niah Caves in Sarawak in 1958, and are thought to be those of hunter-gatherers, between 35,000 and 40,000 years old; other finds in the Peninsular state of Kedah are only 10,000 years old. The variety of **ethnic groups** found in both East and West Malaysia – from small, dark-skinned Negritos through to paler Austronesian Malays – has led to the theory of a slow filtration of peoples through the Malay archipelago from southern Indochina – a theory backed by an almost universal belief in animism, celebration of fertility and ancestor worship among the various peoples.

The Malay archipelago acquired a strategic significance thanks largely to the **shipping trade**, which flourished as early as the first century AD. This was engendered by the two major markets of the early world – India and China – and by the richness of its own resources. From the dense jungle of the Peninsula and from northern Borneo came aromatic woods, timber and *nipah* palm thatch, traded by the forest-dwelling Orang Asli with the coastal Malays, who then bartered or sold it on to Arab and Chinese merchants. The region was also rumoured to be rich in **gold**, leading to its description by Greek explorers as "The Golden Chersonese" (*chersonese* meaning "peninsula"). Although gold was never found in the quantities supposed to exist, ornaments made of the precious metal helped to develop decorative traditions among craftsmen, and still survive today. More significant, however, were the **tin fields** of the Malay

Peninsula, mined in early times to provide an alloy used for temple sculptures. Chinese traders were also attracted by the medicinal properties of various sea products, such as sea slugs, collected by the Orang Laut (sea people), as well as the aesthetic value of pearls and tortoise shells.

In return, the indigenous peoples acquired cloth, pottery, glass and new beliefs from foreign traders. From as early as 200 AD, **Indian traders** brought with them their Hindu and Buddhist practices, and archeological evidence from later periods, such as the tenth-century temples at Lembah Bujang (p.220), suggests that the local population not only tolerated these new belief systems, but adapted them to suit their own experiences. Perhaps the most striking contemporary example of such cultural interchange is the traditional entertainment of *wayang kulit* (shadow plays), whose stories are drawn from the Hindu Ramayana.

Contact with **China**, the other significant trading source, was initially less pronounced due to the pre-eminence of the Silk Road, further to the north. It wasn't until much later, in the eighth and ninth centuries, that Chinese ships ventured into the archipelago.

There's little evidence to reveal the structure of society in these early times. All that is certain is that by the time Srivijaya (see below) appeared on the scene, there were already a number of states – particularly in the Kelantan and Terengganu areas of the Peninsula – that were sending envoys to China.

Srivijaya

The calm Melaka Straits provided a refuge for ships which were forced to wait several months for a change in the monsoon winds. The inhabitants of the western Peninsula and eastern Sumatra were quick to realize their geographical advantage, and from the fifth century onwards a succession of **entrepôts** (storage ports) were created to cater for the needs of passing vessels.

One entrepôt eventually became the mighty empire of **Srivijaya**, eminent from the beginning of the seventh century until the end of the thirteenth, and encompassing all the shores and islands surrounding the Straits of Melaka. The exact location of Srivijaya is still a matter for debate, although most sources point to **Palembang** in southern Sumatra. The empire's early success was owed primarily to its favourable relationship with China, which it plied with tributes to ensure profitable trade. The entrepôt's stable administration attracted commerce when insurrection elsewhere frightened traders away, while its wealth was boosted by extracting tolls and taxes from passing ships. **Piracy** in the surrounding oceans was rife, but was kept in check in Srivijayan waters by the fearsome Orang Laut who formed the linchpin of the navy. Indeed, they might otherwise have turned to piracy themselves had not the prestige of association with the empire been so great.

Significant political concepts developed during the period of Srivijayan rule were to form the basis of Malay government in future centuries. Unquestioning **loyalty** among subjects was underpinned by the notion of *daulat*, the divine force of the ruler (who was called the Maharaja, further evidence of Indian influence), which would strike down anyone guilty of *derhaka* (treason) – a powerful means of control over a deeply superstitious people. Srivijaya also became known as an important centre for **Mahayana Buddhism** and learning. Supported by a buoyant economy, centres for study sprang up all over the empire, and monks and scholars were attracted from afar by Srivijaya's academic reputation. When the respected Chinese monk, I Ching, arrived in 671 AD, he found more than a thousand monks studying the Buddhist scriptures.

The decision made between 1079 and 1082 to shift the capital (for reasons unknown) from Palembang to **Melayu**, in the Sungai Jambi area to the north, seems to have marked the start of Srivijaya's decline. Piracy became almost uncontrollable, with even the loyal Orang Laut turning against their rulers, and soon both local and foreign traders began to seek safer ports, with the area that is now Kedah becoming one of the main beneficiaries. Other regions were soon able to replicate the peaceable conditions and efficient administration conducive to commercial success. One such was **Puni** in northwest Borneo, thought to be the predecessor of Brunei, which had been trading with China since the ninth century and which continued to prosper over the next three hundred years.

Srivijaya's fate was sealed when it attracted the eye of envious foreign rivals, among them the Majapahit Empire of Java, the Cholas of India and, latterly, the Thai kingdom of Ligor. In 1275, the Majapahits invaded Melayu and made inroads into many of Srivijaya's peninsula territories. The Cholas raided Sumatra and Kedah, while Ligor enforced its territorial claims by the instigation of a **tribute system**, whereby local Malay chiefs sent gifts of gold to their Thai overlords as recognition of their vassal status, a practice which continued until the nineteenth century. Moreover, trading restrictions in China were relaxed from the late twelfth century onwards, which made it more lucrative for traders to go directly to the source of their desired products, bypassing the once mighty entrepôt. Around the early fourteenth century Srivijaya's name disappears from the record books.

The Melaka Sultanate

With the collapse of Srivijaya came the beginning of the Malay Peninsula's most significant historical period, the establishment of the **Melaka Sultanate**. Both the *Sejarah Melayu* and the *Suma Oriental* document the story of a Sumatran prince from Palembang named **Paramesvara**, who fled the collapsing empire of Srivijaya to set up his own kingdom, finally settling on the site of present-day Melaka.

As well placed as its Sumatran predecessor, with a deep, sheltered harbour and good riverine access to its own lucrative jungle produce, Melaka set about establishing itself as an international marketplace. The securing of a special agreement in 1405 with the new Chinese emperor, Yung-lo, guaranteed trade to Melaka and protected it from its main rivals. To further ensure its prosperity, Melaka's second ruler, Paramesvara's son **Iskandar Shah** (1414–24), took the precaution of acknowledging the neighbouring kingdoms of Ayuthaya and Majapahit as overlords. In return Melaka received vital supplies and much-needed immigrants, which bolstered the expansion of the settlement.

To meet the needs of passing traders, port taxes and market regulations were managed by four **shahbandars** (harbour masters). Each was in charge of a group of nations: one for the northwest Indian state of Gujarat alone; another for southern India, Bengal, Samudra-Pasai and Burma; the third for local neighbours such as Java, Palembang and Borneo; and the fourth for the eastern nations, including China and Japan.

Hand in hand with the trade in commodities went the exchange of ideas. By the thirteenth century, Arab merchants had begun to frequent Melaka's shores, bringing with them their religion, **Islam**, which their Muslim Indian counterparts helped to propagate among the Malays. The sultanate's **conversion** helped to increase its prestige by placing it within a worldwide community which worked to maintain profitable trade links. Melaka also amplified its reputation by territorial expansion which, by the reign of its last ruler **Sultan Mahmud Shah** (1488–1528), included the west coast of the Peninsula as far as Perak, Pahang, Singapore, and most of east-coast Sumatra.

The legacy of **Melaka's golden age** reaches far beyond memories of its material wealth. One of the most significant developments was the establishment of a **court structure** (see p.362), which was to lay the foundations for a system of government lasting until the nineteenth century. According to Malay royal tradition, the **sultan**, as head of state, traced his ancestry back through Paramesvara to the maharajas of ancient Srivijaya; in turn Paramesvara was believed to be descended from Alexander the Great (Iskandar Zulkarnain). The sultan also claimed divinity, a claim strengthened by the sultanate's conversion to Islam, which held Muslim rulers to be Allah's representatives on earth. To secure further his power, which was always under threat from the overzealous nobility, the sultan embarked on a series of measures to emphasize his "otherness": no one but he could wear gold unless it was a royal gift, and yellow garments were forbidden among the general population.

The Melaka Sultanate also allowed the **arts** to flourish; the principal features of the courtly dances and music of this period can still be distinguished in traditional entertainments today. Much more significant, however, was the refinement of **language**, adapting the primitive Malay that had been used in the kingdom of Srivijaya into a language of the elite. Such was Melaka's prestige that all who passed through the entrepôt sought to imitate it, and by the sixteenth century, Malay was the most widely used language in the archipelago. Tellingly, the word *bahasa*, although literally meaning "language", came to signify Malay culture in general.

The Portuguese conquest of Melaka

With a fortune as tempting as Melaka's, it wasn't long before Europe set its sights on the acquisition of the empire. At the beginning of the sixteenth century, the **Portuguese** began to take issue with Venetian control of the Eastern market. They planned instead to establish direct contacts with the commodity brokers of the East by gaining control of crucial regional ports.

The key player in the subsequent **conquest** of Melaka was Portuguese viceroy **Alfonso de Albuquerque**, who led the assault on the entrepôt in 1511, forcing its surrender after less than a month's siege. There are few physical reminders of the Portuguese in Melaka, apart from the gateway to their fort, A Famosa (see p.367), and the small **Eurasian** community, descendants of intermarriage between the Portuguese and local Malay women. The colonizers had more success with religion, however, converting large numbers of locals to **Catholicism**; their churches still dominate the city. Aloof and somewhat effete in their high-necked ruffs and stockings, the Portuguese were not well liked, but despite the almost constant attacks from upriver Malays, the Portuguese controlled Melaka for the next 130 years.

Brunei

During the period of Melaka's meteoric rise, **Brunei** had been busily establishing itself as a trading port of some renown. The Brunei Sultanate's conversion to **Islam**, no doubt precipitated by the arrival of wealthy Muslim merchants fleeing from the Portuguese in Melaka, also helped to increase its international prestige. When geographer **Antonio Pigafetta**, travelling with **Ferdinand Magellan**'s expedition of 1521, visited Brunei, he found the court brimming with visitors from all over the world. This, indeed, was Brunei's "golden age", with its borders embracing land as far south as present-day Kuching in Sarawak, and as far north as the lower islands of the modern-day Philippines. Brunei's efforts, however, were soon curtailed by Spanish colonization in 1578, which, although lasting only a matter of weeks, enabled the Philippine kingdom of Sulu to gain a hold in the area – a fact which put paid to Brunei's early expansionist aims.

The kingdom of Johor

Fleeing Melaka, after its fall to the Portuguese, the deposed sultan, Sultan Mahmud Shah made for Pulau Bentan in the Riau archipelago, just south of Singapore, where he established the first **court of Johor**. When, in 1526, the Portuguese attacked and razed the settlement, Mahmud fled once again, this time to Sumatra, where he died in 1528. It was left to his son, Alauddin Riayat Shah, to found a new court on the upper reaches of the Johor River, though the capital of the kingdom then shifted repeatedly, during a century of assaults on Johor territory by Portugal and the Sumatran Sultanate of Aceh.

The **arrival of the Dutch** in Southeast Asia towards the end of the sixteenth century marked a distinct upturn in Johor's fortunes. Hoping for protection from its local enemies, the court aligned itself firmly with the new European arrivals, and was instrumental in the successful siege of Portuguese Melaka by the Dutch in 1641. Such loyalty was rewarded by trading privileges and by assistance in securing a treaty with Aceh which at last gave Johor the breathing space to develop. Soon it had grown into a thriving kingdom, its sway extending some way throughout the Peninsula.

Johor was the supreme Malay kingdom for much of the seventeenth century, but by the 1690s its empire was fraying under the despotic rule of another Sultan Mahmud. Lacking strong leadership, Johor's Orang Laut turned to piracy, scaring off trade, while wars with the Sumatran kingdom of Jambi, one of which resulted in the total destruction of Johor's capital, weakened it still further. No longer able to tolerate his cruel regime, Mahmud's nobles stabbed him to death in 1699. Not only did this change the nature of power in Malay government – previously, law deemed that the sultan could only be punished by Allah – but it marked the end of the Melaka Dynasty.

The Dutch in Melaka

Already the masters of Indonesia's valuable spice trade, the Vereenigde Oost-indische Compagnie (VOC), or **Dutch East India Company**, began a bid to gain control of its most potent rival, Melaka. After a five-month siege, the Dutch flag was hoisted over Melaka in 1641. Instead of ruling from above as the Portuguese had tried to do, the Dutch cleverly wove their subjects into the fabric of government: each racial group was represented by a kapitan, a respected figure from the community who mediated between his own people and the new administrators – often becoming a very wealthy and powerful person in his own right. The Dutch were also responsible for the rebuilding of Melaka, much of which had been turned to rubble during the protracted takeover of the city; many of these structures, in their distinctive Northern European style, still survive today.

By the mid-eighteenth century, the conditions for trade with China were at their peak: the relaxation of maritime restrictions in **China** itself had opened up the Straits for their merchants, while Europeans were eager to satisfy the growing demand for tea. The Chinese came to Melaka in droves and soon established themselves as the city's foremost entrepreneurs. Chinese intermarriage with local Malay women created a new cultural blend, known as **Peranakan** (literally, "Straits-born") or Baba-Nonya – the legacies of which are the opulent mansions and unique cuisine of Melaka (see box, p.374).

But a number of factors prevented Dutch Melaka from fulfilling its potential. Since their VOC salary was hardly bountiful, Dutch administrators found it more lucrative to trade on the black market, taking backhanders from grateful merchants, a situation which severely damaged Melaka's commercial standing. High taxes forced traders to more economical locations such as the newly established British port of **Penang**, whose foundation in 1786 heralded the awakening of British interest in the Straits. In the end, given the VOC's overall strategy in the archipelago, Melaka never stood a chance: Batavia (modern-day Jakarta) was the VOC capital, and Johor's penchant for commerce suited Dutch purposes too much for it to put serious effort into maintaining Melaka's fortunes.

The Bugis and the Minangkabaus

Through the second half of the seventeenth century, a new ethnic group, the **Bugis** – renowned for their martial and commercial skills – had been trickling into the Peninsula, seeking refuge from the civil wars which wracked their homeland of Sulawesi (in the mid-eastern Indonesian archipelago). By the beginning of the eighteenth century, there were enough of them to constitute a powerful court lobby, and in 1721 they took advantage of factional struggles to capture the kingdom of Johor – now based in Riau. Installing a Malay puppet sultan, Sulaiman, the Bugis ruled for over sixty years, making Riau an essential port of call on the eastern trade route; they even almost succeeded in capturing Melaka in 1756. But when Riau-Johor made another bid for Melaka in 1784, the Dutch held on with renewed vigour and finally forced a treaty placing all Bugis territory in Dutch hands.

In spiritual terms, the **Minangkabaus** (see p.356), hailing from western Sumatra, had what the Bugis lacked, being able to claim cultural affinity with the ancient kingdom of Srivijaya. Although this migrant group had been present in the Negeri Sembilan region since the fifteenth century, the second half of the seventeenth century brought them to the Malay Peninsula in larger numbers. Despite professing allegiance to their Sumatran ruler, the Minangkabaus were prepared to accept Malay overlordship, which in practice gave them a great deal of autonomy. Accredited with supernatural powers, the warrior Minangkabaus were not natural allies of the Bugis or the Malays, although they did occasionally join forces in order to defeat a common enemy. In fact, over time the distinction between various migrant groups became less obvious, as intermarriage blurred clan demarcations, and Malay influence, such as the adoption of Malay titles, became more pronounced.

The arrival of the British

At the end of the eighteenth century, Dutch control in Southeast Asia was more widespread than ever, and the VOC empire should have been at its height. Instead, its coffers were bare and it faced the superior trading and maritime skills of the British. The disastrous defeat of the Dutch in the Fourth Anglo-Dutch War (1781–83) lowered their morale still further, and when the British, in the form of the **East India Company** (EIC), moved in on Melaka and the rest of the Dutch Asian domain in 1795, the VOC barely demurred.

Initially, the British agreed to a caretaker administration, whereby they would assume sovereignty over the entrepôt to prevent it falling under French control, now that Napoleon had conquered Holland. The end of the Napoleonic wars in Europe put the Dutch in a position to retake Melaka between 1818 and 1825, but in the meantime, the EIC had established the stable port of **Penang** and – under the supervision of **Sir Thomas Stamford Raffles** – founded the new settlement of **Singapore**.

The strategic position and free-trade policy of Singapore – backed by the impressive industrial developments of the British at home – threatened the viability of both Melaka and Penang, forcing the Dutch finally to relinquish their hold on the former to the British, and leaving the latter to dwindle to a backwater. In the face of such stiff competition, smaller Malay rivals inevitably linked their fortunes to the British.

The consolidation of British power in the Peninsula

To a degree, the British presence in Malay lands was only the most recent episode in a history of foreign interference that stretched back centuries. What differed this time, however, was the rapidity and extent of the takeover – aided by technological developments in the West that improved communications.

The British assumption of power was sealed by the **Anglo–Dutch Treaty of 1824**, which divided territories between the two countries using the Straits of Melaka and the equator as the dividing lines, thereby splitting the Riau-Johor kingdom as well as ending centuries of cultural interchange with Sumatra. This was followed in 1826 by the unification of Melaka, Penang and Singapore into one administration, known as the **Straits Settlements**, with Singapore replacing Penang as its capital in 1832.

Raffles had at first hoped that **Singapore** would act as a market to sell British goods to traders from all over Southeast Asia, but it soon became clear that **Chinese** merchants, the linchpin of Singapore's trade, were interested only in Malay products such as birds' nests, seaweed and camphor. But passing traders were not the only Chinese to come to the Straits. Although settlers had trickled into the Peninsula since the early days of Melaka, new pepper and gambier (an astringent product used in tanning and dyeing) **plantations**, and the rapidly expanding **tin mines**, attracted floods of willing workers eager to escape a life of poverty in China. By 1845, the Chinese formed over half of Singapore's population, while principal towns along the Peninsula's west coast (site of the world's largest tin field) and, for that matter, Kuching, became predominantly Chinese.

Civil conflict

Allowed a large degree of commercial independence by both the British and the Malay chiefs, the Chinese carried their traditions into the social and political arena with the formation of **kongsis**, or clan houses, and secret societies (triads). Struggles between clan groups were rife, sometimes resulting in large-scale riots, such as those in Penang in 1867 where the triads allied themselves with Malay groups in a bloody street battle lasting several days.

Malays, too, were hardly immune from factional conflicts, which frequently became intertwined with Chinese squabbles, causing a string of **civil wars**. **Pahang**'s skirmishes (1858–63) involved rival political claims by two brothers, Mutahir and Ahmad, although this time the British were much more directly involved: on hearing that the Thais had backed Ahmad, the Straits Governor Cavenagh hastily aligned himself with Mutahir by attacking Kuala Terengganu – then a Thai vassal town – in order to ward off further foreign involvement in the Peninsula. But the British government was outraged by this decision and forbade any other action to prevent Ahmad's succession.

Lawlessness like this was detrimental to commerce, giving the British an excuse to increase their involvement in local affairs. A meeting involving the chiefs of the Perak Malays was arranged by the new Straits Governor, Andrew Clarke, on Pulau Pangkor, just off the west coast of the Peninsula. In the meantime, Raja Abdullah, the man most likely to succeed to the Perak throne, had written to Clarke asking for his own position as sultan to be guaranteed; in return, he offered the British the chance to appoint a **Resident**, a senior British civil servant whose main function would be to act as advisor to the local sultan, but who would also oversee the collecting of local taxes. On January 20, 1874, the **Pangkor Treaty** (p.188) was signed between the British and Abdullah, formalizing British intervention in the political affairs of the Malay people.

Perak's first Resident, J.W.W. Birch, was not sympathetic to the ways of the Malays. Upon becoming sultan, Abdullah opposed Birch's centralizing tendencies, and senior British officials, fearful of a Malay rebellion, announced that judicial decisions would from now on be in the hands of the British, which was against the letter of the Pangkor Treaty. Furious Malays soon found a vent for their frustration: on November 2, 1875, Birch was killed on an upriver visit, although the attack was not followed by further assaults on colonial staff. It wasn't until the appointment of the third Resident of Perak, the respected Hugh Low, that the system began working far more smoothly.

British Malaya

By 1888 the name **British Malaya** had been brought into use – a term which reflected the intention to extend British control over the whole Peninsula. Over subsequent decades, the Malay sultans' economic and administrative powers were gradually eroded, while the introduction of rubber estates during the first half of the twentieth century made British Malaya one of the most productive colonies in the world.

Each state soon saw the arrival of a **Resident** and agreements along the lines of the Pangkor Treaty were drawn up with Selangor, Negeri Sembilan and Pahang in the 1880s, and in 1896 these three became bracketed together under the title of the **Federated Malay States**, with the increasingly important town of Kuala Lumpur made the regional capital.

The gradual extension of British power brought further unrest, particularly in the east-coast states, where the Malays proved just as resentful of British control as in Perak. In Pahang a set of skirmishes took place in the early 1890s, when Malay chiefs protested about the reduction of their former privileges. One powerful chief, Dato' Bahaman, was stripped of his title by Pahang's Resident, Hugh Clifford, as a result of which the Dato' led a small rebellion which – though never a serious military threat to the British – soon became the stuff of legends. One fighter, **Mat Kilau**, gained a place in folklore as a heroic figure who stood up to the British in the name of Malay nationalism. From this time onwards, Malays would interpret the uprisings as a valiant attempt to safeguard Malay traditions and preserve Malay autonomy.

By 1909, the northern Malay states of Kedah and Perlis were brought into the colonial fold. In 1910, Johor accepted a British general-adviser; a 1914 treaty between Britain and Johor made his powers equal to those of Residents elsewhere. Terengganu, which was under Thai control, was the last state to accept a British adviser, in 1919. These four states, together with Kelantan, were sometimes referred to as the Unfederated Malay States, though they shared no common administration.

By the outbreak of World War I, British political control was more or less complete. The Peninsula was subdivided into groups of states and regions with the seat of power split between Singapore and Kuala Lumpur.

The expansion of British interests in Borneo

The Anglo-Dutch Treaty did not include **Borneo**, where official expansion was discouraged by the EIC, who preferred to concentrate on expanding their trading contacts rather than geographical control. The benefits of Borneo did not, however, elude the sights of one British explorer, **James Brooke** (1803–68). Finding lawlessness throughout the island, Brooke persuaded the sultan of Brunei to award him his own area – **Sarawak** – in 1841, becoming the first of a line of "**White Rajahs**" that ruled the state until the start of World War II. By involving formerly rebellious Malay chiefs in government, he quickly managed to assert his authority, although the less congenial Iban tribes in the interior proved more of a problem. Despite the informal association of the British with Rajah Brooke (Sarawak was not granted the status of a protectorate, and Brooke was careful not to encourage European contacts that might challenge his hold on the state), trade between Singapore and Sarawak flourished. By the mid-nineteenth century, however, the British attitude had mellowed considerably; they chose Brooke as their agent in Brunei, and found him a useful deterrent against French and Dutch aspirations towards the valuable trade routes. As well, Brooke and his successors were adept at siphoning more land into the familial fiefdom.

In 1888, the three states of Sarawak, Sabah and Brunei were transformed into **protectorates**, a status which handed over the responsibility for their foreign policy to the British in exchange for military protection. The legacy of James Brooke was furthered by his nephew Charles in the closing years of the nineteenth century. Like his uncle before him, **Charles Brooke** ruled Sarawak in a paternalistic fashion, recruiting soldiers, lowly officials and boatmen from the ranks of the ethnic groups and leaving the Chinese to get on with running commercial enterprises and opening out the interior.

The rule of the last white rajah, **Vyner Brooke**, Charles' eldest son (1916–41), saw no new territorial acquisitions, but there was a steady development in rubber, pepper and palm-oil production. The ethnic peoples mostly continued living a traditional lifestyle in longhouses along the river systems and, with the end of groups' practice of head-hunting, there was some degree of integration among the country's varied racial groups.

By way of contrast, the **British North Borneo Chartered Company**'s writ in what became Sabah encountered some early obstacles. Its plans for economic expansion involved clearing the rainforest and planting **rubber** and **tobacco** over large areas, and levying taxes on the ethnic groups. Resistance followed, with the most vigorous action, in 1897, led by a Bajau chief, **Mat Salleh**, whose men rampaged through the company's outstation on Pulau Gaya. Another rebellion by the Murut tribespeople in 1915 resulted in a heavy-handed response from British forces, who killed hundreds.

By the start of the twentieth century, the majority of the lands of the erstwhile powerful **Sultanate of Brunei** had been dismembered – the sultanate was now surrounded by Sarawak. But the sultan's fortunes had not completely disappeared and with the discovery of oil in 1929, the British thought it prudent to appoint a Resident. Exploitation of the small state's oil beds picked up pace in the 1930s following investment from British companies.

Economic development and ethnic rivalries

In the first quarter of the twentieth century hundreds of thousands of **immigrants** from China and India were encouraged by the British to emigrate to sites across Peninsular Malaysia, Sarawak, North Borneo and Singapore. They came to work as tin miners or plantation labourers, and Malaya's population in this period doubled to four million. The main impact was an increase in resentment among the Malays, who believed that they were being denied the economic opportunities advanced to others. The British barely noticed the deepening differences between the ethnic groups – a factor which contributed to racial violence in later years.

A further deterioration in Malay–Chinese relations followed the success of the mainland Chinese revolutionary groups in Malaya. Chinese-educated Chinese, who joined the **Malayan Communist Party** (MCP) from 1930 onwards, formed the backbone of the politicized Chinese movements after World War II, which demanded an end to British rule and to what they perceived as special privileges extended to the Malays. For their part, the Malays – specifically those influenced by radical Islamic movements – saw better education as the key to their future. The **Singapore Malay Union**, established in 1926, gradually gained support in Straits Settlement areas where Malays were outnumbered by Chinese. It held its first conference in 1939 and advocated a Malay supremacist line. A year earlier, the first All-Malaya Malays Conference, organized by the Selangor Malays Association, had been held in Kuala Lumpur.

Despite the argument put forward by the British in the 1930s that a Union for Malaya (incorporating the Unfederated Malay States) would decentralize power and integrate the regional state groupings, little progress had been made on the burning issue of independence by the time Malaya was invaded by the Japanese in late 1941.

The Japanese Occupation

The **surrender** of the British forces in Singapore in February, 1942 ushered in a Japanese regime which proceeded to brutalize the Chinese, largely because of Japan's history of conflict with China; up to fifty thousand people were tortured and killed in the two weeks immediately after the surrender of the island by the British military command. Allied POWs were rounded up into prison camps; many of the troops were subsequently sent to build the infamous "Death Railway" in Burma.

In **Malaya**, towns and buildings were destroyed as the Allies attempted to bomb strategic targets. But with the Japanese firmly in control, the occupiers ingratiated themselves with some of the Malay elite by suggesting that after the war the country would be given independence. Predictably, it was the Chinese activists in the MCP, more so than the Malays, who organized resistance during wartime; in the chaotic period directly after the war it was the MCP's armed wing, the **Malayan People's Anti-Japanese Army** (MPAJA), who maintained order in many areas.

The Japanese invasion of **Sarawak** in late 1941 began with the capture of the Miri oil field and spread south, encountering little resistance. Although the Japanese invaders never penetrated the interior, they quickly established complete control over the populated towns along the coast. The Chinese in Miri, Sibu and Kuching were the main targets: the Japanese put down rebellions against their rule brutally, and there was no organized guerrilla activity until late in the occupation. What resistance there was arose from the presence of Major **Tom Harrisson** and his team of British and Australian commandos, who parachuted into the remote Kelabit Highlands to build a resistance movement.

In **North Borneo**, the Japanese invaded Pulau Labuan on New Year's Day, 1942. Over the next three years the main suburban areas were bombed by the Allies, and by the time of the Japanese surrender in September 1945, most of Jesselton (modern-day KK) and Sandakan had been destroyed. Captured troops and civilians suffered enormously – the worst single outrage being the "Death March" in September 1944 when 2400 POWs were forced to walk from Sandakan to Ranau (see p.572).

The Allies had been preparing to retake Singapore, but just prior to the planned invasion the **Japanese surrendered** on September 9, 1945, on Pulau

Labuan, following the dropping of atom bombs on Nagasaki and Hiroshima. The surrender led to a power vacuum in the region, with the British initially left with no choice but to work with the MPAJA to exert political control. Violence occurred between the MPAJA and Malays, particularly against those accused of collaborating with the Japanese.

Postwar developments

Immediately after the war, the British introduced the **Malayan Union**, in effect turning the Malay States from a protectorate into a colony, as part of which the Malay rulers had their sovereignty removed. One impact of these new arrangements was to make the Chinese and Indian inhabitants full citizens and give them equal rights with the Malays. This erosion of their superior position quickly aroused opposition among the Malays, with Malayan nationalists forming the **United Malays National Organization** (UMNO) in 1946. Its main tenet was that Malays should retain their special privileges, largely because they were the region's first inhabitants and that the uniquely powerful position of the sultans should not be tampered with.

UMNO supporters displayed widespread resistance to the British plan, and the idea of union was subsequently replaced by the **Federation of Malaya** which restored the sovereign position of the rulers. Established in 1948, this upheld the sultans' power and privileges and brought all the regional groupings together under one government, with the exception of Chinese-dominated Singapore, whose inclusion would have led to the Malays being in a minority overall. Protests erupted in Singapore at its exclusion, with the **Malayan Democratic Union** (MDU), a multiracial party, calling for integration with Malaya – a position that commanded little support among the Chinese population. After the communists took control of China in 1949, most of the Malayan Chinese ceased to look to China and the most political among them founded a new political party, the **Malayan Chinese Association**, in Kuala Lumpur.

In **Borneo**, after the Japanese surrender, the Colonial Office in London stepped into the breach and made Sarawak and North Borneo **Crown Colonies**, with Vyner Brooke offering no objection. Britain also signed a Treaty of Protection with the sultan of Brunei, making Sarawak's high commissioner the governor of Brunei – a purely decorative position, as the sultan remained the chief power in the state.

Although Sarawak's ruling body, the Council Negeri (composed of Malays, Chinese, Iban and British) had voted to transfer power to Britain, some Malays and prominent Iban in Kuching opposed their country's new status. Protests reached a peak with the assassination in Sibu in 1949 of the senior official in the new administration, Governor Duncan Stewart. But on the whole, resentment at the passing of the Brooke era was short-lived as the economy expanded and infrastructure improved.

The Emergency

In the Peninsula, many Chinese were angered by the change of the status of the country from a colony to a federation, in which they effectively became second-class citizens. According to the new laws, non-Malays could only qualify as citizens if they had lived in the country for fifteen out of the last twenty-five years, and they also had to prove they spoke Malay or English.

The impact of the Emergency on the **Orang Asli** of the interior was dramatic. All but the most remote tribes were subject to intimidation and brutality, from guerrillas on one side and government forces on the other. In effect, the Orang Asli's centuries-old invisibility had ended; the population of Malaysia was now aware of their presence, and the government of their strategic importance.

The Orang Asli had no choice but to grow food and act as porters for the guerrillas, as well as – most important of all – provide intelligence, warning them of the approach of the enemy. Meanwhile, government forces built eleven jungle forts, some near the towns of Raub and Tanjung Malim. In near desperation they implemented a disastrous policy of removing Orang Asli from the jungle and relocating them in new model villages near Raub and Gua Musang, which were no more than dressed-up prison camps. Thousands were placed behind barbed wire and hundreds died in captivity before the government dismantled the camps. By then, not surprisingly, active support for the insurgents among the Orang Asli had risen – though allegiances were switched to the security forces when the guerrillas' fortunes waned and their defeat became inevitable. Government attempts to control the Orang Asli during the Emergency turned out to be the precursor to initiatives that persist to the present day, drawing the Orang Asli away from their traditional lifestyle and into the framework of the Malaysian nation-state.

C

CONTEXTS | History

More Chinese began to identify with the MCP, which, under its new leader, **Chin Peng**, declared its intention of setting up a Malayan republic. Peng fused the MCP with the remains of the wartime resistance movement, the MPAJA, and using the arms supplies which the latter had dumped in the forests, from June 1948 he launched sporadic attacks on rubber estates, killing planters and employees as well as spreading fear among rural communities. At the peak of the conflict, around ten thousand of his guerrillas were hiding out in dozens of camouflaged jungle camps. For a long time they milked a support network of Chinese-dominated towns and villages in the interior, in many cases cowing the inhabitants into submission by means of public executions – although in some areas many of the poor rural workers identified with the insurgents' struggle. It was only when the government successfully planted informers that the security services started to get wind of guerrilla operations.

The period of unrest (1948–60) was referred to as **the Emergency**, rather than the civil war it undoubtedly was. This was mainly for insurance purposes – planters would have had their premiums cancelled if war had been officially declared. Although the Emergency was never fully felt in the main urban areas, the British rubber estate owners would arrive at the *Coliseum Hotel* in KL with harrowing stories of how the "Communist Terrorists" had hacked off the arms of rural Chinese workers who had refused to support the cause, and of armed attacks on plantations.

The British were slow to respond to the threat, but once Lieutenant-General Sir Harold Briggs was put in command of police and army forces, Malaya was on a war footing. The most controversial policy Briggs enacted was the **resettlement** of 400,000 rural Chinese – mostly squatters who had moved to the jungle fringes to avoid the Japanese during the war – as well as thousands of Orang Asli (see box above). Although these forced migrations were successful in breaking down many of the guerrillas' supply networks, they had the effect of making both Chinese and Orang Asli more sympathetic to the idea of a Communist republic.

The violence peaked in 1950 with ambushes and attacks on plantations near Ipoh, Kuala Kangsar, Kuala Lipis and Raub. The most notorious incident occurred in 1951 on the road to Fraser's Hill, when the British high commissioner to Malaya, **Sir Henry Gurney**, was assassinated. Under his replacement, Sir Gerald Templer, a new policy was introduced to win hearts and minds. "White Areas", regions perceived as free of guerrilla activity, were established; communities in these areas had food restrictions and curfews lifted, a policy which began to dissipate guerrilla activity over the next three years. The leaders were offered an amnesty in 1956, which was refused, and Chin Peng and most of the remaining cell members fled over the border to Thailand where they received sanctuary.

Towards independence

The Emergency had the effect of speeding up the political processes prior to independence. Although UMNO stuck to its "Malays first" policy, **Tunku Abdul Rahman** (the chief minister of Malaya and brother of the sultan of Kedah), won the 1955 election by co-operating with the Malayan Chinese Association (MCA) and the Malayan Indian Association. The result was called the **UMNO Alliance**, and it swept into power under the rallying cry of **Merdeka** (Freedom). The hope was that ethnic divisions would no longer be a major factor if **Malayan independence** was granted, though the deep-seated differences between the various ethnic groups' positions still hadn't been eradicated.

With British backing, *Merdeka* was promulgated on August 31, 1957 in a ceremony in Kuala Lumpur's padang – promptly renamed Merdeka Square. The British high commissioner signed a treaty which decreed that the Federation of Malaya was now independent of the Crown, with Tunku Abdul Rahman as the first prime minister. The new **constitution** allowed for the nine Malay sultans to alternate as king, and established a two-tier **parliament**, comprising a house of elected representatives and a senate with delegates from each of the states. Although the system was, in theory, a democracy, the Malay-dominated UMNO remained by far the most influential element in the political equation.

Under Rahman, the country was fully committed to economic expansion, with foreign investment actively encouraged. These policies remain the basis for economic management today.

Similarly, in **Singapore** the process of gaining independence gained momentum throughout the 1950s. In 1957 the British gave the go-ahead for the setting up of an elected 51-member assembly, and full **self-government** was attained in 1959, when the People's Action Party (PAP) under **Lee Kuan Yew** won most of the seats. Lee immediately entered into talks with Tunku Abdul Rahman over the notion that Singapore and Malaya should be joined administratively – Rahman initially agreed, although he feared the influence of pro-Communist extremists in the PAP.

In 1961 Tunku Abdul Rahman announced that the two Crown Colonies of Sarawak and North Borneo should join Malaya and Singapore in a revised federation. Many in Borneo would have preferred the idea of a separate Borneo Federation, but the advent of the **Konfrontasi** (see opposite) played into Rahman's hands – those against his proposals could see how vulnerable the states were to attack from Indonesia.

Behind Rahman's proposal was the concern that demographic trends would in time lead to Malaya having a greater Chinese population than Malay.

Consequently he campaigned hard for the inclusion of the two Borneo colonies into the proposed federation, to act as a demographic balance to the Chinese in Singapore.

Federation and the Konfrontasi

In September 1963 North Borneo (quickly renamed Sabah), Sarawak and Singapore joined Malaya in the **Federation of Malaysia** – "Malaysia" being a term first coined by the British in the 1950s when the notion of a Greater Malaya had been propounded. Both Indonesia, which laid claim to Sarawak, and the Philippines, which argued it had jurisdiction over Sabah as it had originally been part of the Sulu Sultanate, reacted angrily to the new federation and border skirmishes known as the **Konfrontasi** ensued. The conflict intensified as Indonesian soldiers crossed the border, and a wider war was only just averted when Indonesian President Sukarno backed away from costly confrontations with British and Gurkha troops brought in to boost Sarawak's small armed forces.

Within the federation, further differences surfaced in Singapore in this period between Lee Kuan Yew and the Malay-dominated Alliance Party over the lack of egalitarian policies – although the PAP had dominated recent elections in Singapore, many Chinese were concerned that UMNO's overall influence in the federation was too great. Tensions rose on the island and ugly racial incidents developed into full-scale **riots** in 1964, in which several people were killed.

These developments were viewed with great concern by Tunku Abdul Rahman in Kuala Lumpur, and when the PAP subsequently attempted to enter Peninsular politics, he decided it would be best if Singapore left the federation. This was emphatically not in Singapore's best interests, since it was an island without any obvious natural resources; Lee cried on TV when the expulsion was announced and Singapore acquired full **independence** soon after on August 9, 1965. The severing of the bond between Malaysia and Singapore has led to a kind of sibling rivalry between the two nations ever since.

Although Abdul Rahman had wanted **Brunei** to join the Malaysian Federation, too, along with neighbouring Sarawak and Sabah, Sultan Omar refused when he realized Rahman's price – a substantial proportion of Brunei's oil and gas revenues. Brunei remained under nominal British jurisdiction until **independence** was declared on December 31, 1983. For more on Brunei's history, in particular recent developments, see p.595.

Racial issues and riots

The exclusion of Singapore from the Malaysian Federation was not enough to quell ethnic tensions. Resentment built among the Malaysian Chinese over the principle that Malay be the main language taught in schools and over the privileged employment opportunities offered to Malays. In 1969 the Malay-dominated UMNO Alliance lost regional power in parliamentary elections, and Malays in major cities reacted angrily to a perceived increase in power of the Chinese, who had commemorated their breakthrough with festivities in the streets, triggering counter-demonstrations by Malays. Hundreds of people, mostly Chinese, were killed and injured in the **riots** which followed, with Kuala Lumpur in particular becoming a war zone where large crowds of youths went on the rampage. Rahman kept the country under a state of emergency for nearly two years, during which the draconian **Internal Security Act** (ISA) was used to arrest and imprison activists, as well as many writers and artists, setting a sombre precedent for authoritarian practices still followed today.

The New Economic Policy

Rahman never recovered full political command after the riots and resigned in 1970. In September that year, the new prime minister, **Tun Abdul Razak**, took up the reins with a less authoritarian stance – though still implementing the ISA. He brought the parties in Sarawak and Sabah into the political process and initiated a a form of state-orchestrated positive discrimination called the **New Economic Policy** (NEP; see p.752), which to this day gives ethnic Malays and members of Borneo's tribes favoured positions in business and other professions.

Malaysia under Mahathir

For all but the last few years since his retirement in October 2003, Malaysian politics has been totally dominated by prime minister, **Dr Mahathir Moha-mad**, victor at every election since winning the leadership of UMNO in 1981. UMNO is the dominant party in a coalition, the **Barisan Nasional** (BN),

---

The Anwar affair

The chief fallout of the Asian economic crisis of the late 1990s was to heighten the growing rift between Mahathir and his deputy **Anwar Ibrahim**, a former student leader who'd developed into an espouser of progressive Islamic policies, and had for some years been groomed to succeed Mahathir. In September 1998, Mahathir sacked Anwar, who was also finance minister, from the government; within a week, Anwar was arrested on corruption and sexual misconduct charges which stunned the nation. A succession of demonstrations in support of Anwar ensued. When Anwar appeared in court on the corruption charge he had a black eye, prompting concern to be expressed over his treatment in detention. Anwar was subsequently found guilty – leading many observers to question the independence of the judiciary – and sentenced to six years in prison. In August 2000 he was found guilty of sodomy and sentenced to nine years in prison on top of his jail term for corruption.

Throughout 1999, Anwar's wife **Wan Azizah Wan Ismail** became the focus of opposition to Mahathir for many. Azizah formed a new party, **Keadilan** ("Justice"), which contested the November 1999 elections in alliance with other opposition parties including the ethnic Chinese dominated Democratic Action Party (DAP) and the Islamist PAS. In the event, PAS made significant gains at UMNO's expense, while Keadilan achieved a very creditable six seats in parliament, though ultimately the BN retained a comfortable majority.

In mid-2003 Anwar lost an appeal against the sodomy conviction and returned to prison, only to be released in September 2004 following Mahathir's retirement. The prospects for Anwar and his wife's Keadilan party are uncertain. Anwar himself remains banned from politics until 2008 as his convictions have not been overturned, while Keadilan has yet to make a major breakthrough, as issues of human rights and transparency don't resonate massively among the electorate. Nonetheless he and the party remain a potential threat to UMNO, and are well placed to capitalize on any economic failings or loss of direction on the part of the government.

which was formed in 1974 under Razak and includes representatives from the other mainstream Chinese and Indian parties and – since the 1990s – members of the indigenous parties in Sabah and Sarawak.

During Mahathir's first ten years in power, UMNO's prime concern had been to extend the concept of the NEP as well as maintaining overall Malay political dominance. Initially, the NEP had been underwritten by oil and timber revenues, while Malaysia looked away from the West, preferring to rely on other Southeast Asian countries, especially Singapore, as economic partners. But as the costs of the NEP started to bite, Mahathir galvanized Western investment, offering juicy financial incentives like low tax rates and cheap labour; the UK soon became the main foreign investor in Malaysia.

Although the NEP was understandably popular with Malays, many of whom got richer through its tax, educational and financial breaks, it was deeply resented by Chinese and Indian citizens, although outspoken critics of the government were few. In 1991, the NEP was succeeded by the **National Development Policy (NDP)**. Critics say the favoured position of the Malays was just being continued under a new name, but Mahathir has been careful to remove some of the most ill-regarded elements, such as the use of quotas to push Malays into powerful positions.

The structure of Malaysia's expanding **economy** has changed over the last twenty years. Manufacturing output overtook agriculture as the biggest earner in the late 1980s, while the shift to export-dominated areas, notably hi-tech industries and the service sector, has changed the landscape of regions like the Klang Valley, Petaling Jaya and Johor, where industrial zones have mushroomed. However, in 1997, the economy suffered a major setback when the **Asian economic crisis**, which had begun in Thailand and Korea, sucked Malaysia in. Mahathir took personal charge of the effort to get the economy back on track, sacking his deputy (see box opposite) and ignoring recommendations from the International Monetary Fund on how best to bring the situation under control. To Mahathir's credit, the economy soon achieved a measure of stability, but at the expense of a major devaluation of the ringgit, a drop in living standards for many of the population and the cancelling of a number of high-profile projects.

The impact of September 11, 2001

Mahathir, ever a leader with a golden glove, was to benefit significantly from the global changes brought about by the terrorist attacks of **September 11, 2001**. Scores of people were detained in Malaysia in the aftermath, mainly said to be members of **Jemaah Islamiyah** (JI), a pan-ASEAN militant group committed to creating an orthodox Islamic state based on Sharia law by any means necessary. Mahathir, predictably, used the repressive ISA which was extended to allow suspects to be detained for up to two years without charge or trial; subsequently very few, if any, of those arrested have received sentences.

The Singaporean government for its part in early 2002 also detained more than a dozen members of JI suspected of involvement in a plot to blow up the US Embassy on the island state.

The aftermath of the 9/11 attacks pushed many Muslims across the region, and particularly in Malaysia, towards a more moderate version of Islam, countering the region's unwanted reputation as a hotbed of extremists. Mahathir adroitly exploited Malaysian's fear of a militant Islamic opposition, winning back some of the burgeoning middle class – Chinese as well as Malay – who had flirted with PAS or Keadilan.

Malaysia today: the Badawi era

Momentously, in 2003 Mahathir Mohamad, after 22 years as prime minister, resigned and handed the reins of power to foreign minister **Abdullah Badawi**. From Penang, Badawi (often referred to as Pak Lah) is a genial man, cutting a very different figure to his abrasive predecessor, but asserted himself quickly and effectively, winning a landslide 2004 general election victory for an UMNO seemingly untarnished by accusations of authoritarianism and corruption. Badawi, however, faced a personal crisis in 2005 when his wife, Endon Mahmood, died of cancer.

Looking to the future, it would seem that prospects for Malaysia and Badawi's government are promising. Despite its relatively small population, Malaysia has become the world's seventeenth-largest trading nation, and has successfully diversified away from its traditional reliance on rubber, palm oil and tin, into service industries, manufacturing and IT. However, there are plenty of issues for Badawi to tackle, notably the **lack of transparency** and efficiency in government, a sizeable **wealth gap** between rich and poor, and the question of whether the **NEP/NDP** policy of economic discrimination in favour of Malays and tribal people should be amended. The latter is the hottest of political hot potatoes: the policy rightly attempts to redistribute wealth to some of the poorest sectors of society, but remains deeply resented by Malaysia's Chinese and Indian citizens, and in a few cases has perpetuated inefficiency and a lack of

Neighbourly spats: the case of Malaysia and Singapore

Ever since the 1960s, when Singapore left the Federation of Malaysia after just two bitter years of membership, relations between the governments of the two countries have been characterized by constant **bickering**. Early on, tiny Singapore attempted to bolster its security by establishing close ties with Indonesia and military links with Israel, moves which could only annoy Malaysia. Subsequent decades have seen a series of issues souring relations, ranging from arguments over how to administer the main **rail line** in Singapore – the line itself, plus Singapore's station, which sits on prime land in Tanjong Pagar, remain in Malaysian ownership – to recriminations over unguarded remarks made by various leaders, including an episode several years ago when Singapore's ex-prime minister, Lee Kuan Yew, appeared to intimate that Johor Bahru was some kind of hotbed of crime. The terms under which Singapore receives mains **water** from Malaysia have long been a bone of contention, to the point that the crowded island has committed itself to building an ambitious freshwater lagoon to wean itself off reliance on Malaysian supplies. Of late, there have also been tensions over Malaysia's creation of a port at **Tanjung Pelepas** in southern Johor, which Singapore sees as a threat to its historic raison d'etre in shipping. Furthermore, Malaysia for a time threatened to build a bizarre **"crooked bridge"** replacing the half of the causeway within its waters, in order, so it argued, to improve access to ports on its side.

Ironically, all this belies the fact that the two countries are like a pair of squabbling Siamese twins, unable to get along despite having a vast amount in common and many **shared interests**. Each has significant investments on the opposite side of the causeway; many Malaysians seek better-paid jobs in Singapore, as queues of workers crossing from Johor to Singapore each morning attest; and – perhaps the ultimate test – whenever a bunch of Malaysians and Singaporeans get together, it's often impossible to distinguish between the two in terms of their speech, food or behaviour. At least there has been a recent thaw in relations, with the two countries' new prime ministers, Abdullah Badawi and Lee Hsien Loong, starting off on a fresh footing.

professionalism by cosseting the communities it's meant to assist. Should Badawi choose to weaken the policy, he risks not only a backlash from within his party but also the support of UMNO's own Malay constituency, with PAS still potentially posing an electoral threat in the important northern and east-coast states. Meanwhile, the government continues to invest huge sums to meet Mahathir's target of Malaysia becoming a developed country by 2020, though the impact on the nation's architectural and natural heritage sometimes seems barely to be recognized. Still, there is much to commend: economic growth moves steadily on, Islamic fundamentalism is held in check, corruption is far less than in many Asian states, and race relations are generally harmonious.

Religion

I n Malaysia, **Islam** is a significant force, given that virtually all Malays, who comprise just over half the population, are Muslim; in Singapore, where three-quarters of the population are Chinese, **Buddhism** is the main religion. There's a smaller, but no less significant, **Hindu** Indian presence in both countries, while the other chief belief system is **animism**, adhered to by many of the indigenous ethnic peoples of Malaysia – including the Orang Asli in the Peninsula and the various Dayak groups in Sarawak. The colonial period inevitably drew **Christian missionaries** to the region, but the British, in a bid to avoid unrest among the Malays, were restrained in their evangelical efforts. Christian missionaries had more success in Borneo than on the Peninsula; indeed, the main tribal group in Sabah, the Kadazan, is Christian, as are the Kelabit in Sarawak. That said, Christianity is a significant minority religion in Peninsular Malaysia and Singapore, with a notable following among middle-class Chinese and Indians. The brief survey below is not intended to explain the tenets of each belief, but rather outlines the historical role of these faiths in the region, and considers the ways in which they continue to permeate local life today – both tangibly, through the **places of worship** which decorate cities and towns, and less obviously in the way religion influences society and customs.

One striking feature of religion in the region is that it is sometimes **syncretic** – featuring a blend of beliefs and influences. In part, this is due to elements which have been integrated from indigenous beliefs over the centuries. On another level, in a region where fusion is noticeable in everything from food to language, it's not hard to come across individuals who profess one faith, yet pray or make offerings to deities of another, in the warm-hearted and woolly belief that all religions contain some truth, and that it therefore makes sense not to put all your spiritual eggs in one devotional basket.

Animism

Although many of Malaysia's indigenous groups are now nominally Christian or Muslim, many of their old animist beliefs and rites still survive. In the animist world-view, everything in nature – mountains, trees, rocks and lakes – has a controlling soul or spirit (**semangat** in Malay) which has to be mollified. For the Orang Asli groups in the interior of the Peninsula, their remaining animist beliefs often centre on healing and funereal ceremonies. A sick person, particularly a child, is believed to be invaded by a bad spirit, and drums are played and incantations performed to persuade the spirit to depart. The death of a member of the family is followed by a complex process of burial and reburial – a procedure which, hopefully, ensures an easy passage for the person's spirit.

In Sarawak, birds, especially the hornbill, are of particular significance to the Iban and the Kelabit peoples. Many Kelabit depend upon the arrival of migrating flocks to decide when to plant their rice crop, while Iban hunters still interpret sightings of the hornbill and other birds as good or bad omens. In the Iban male rite-of-passage ceremony, a headdress made of hornbill feathers adorns the young man's head.

Hinduism

Hinduism arrived in Malaysia long before Islam, brought by Indian traders more than a thousand years ago. Its central tenet is the belief that life is a series of rebirths and reincarnations that eventually leads to spiritual release. A whole variety of deities are worshipped, which on the surface makes Hinduism appear complex; however, a loose understanding of the Vedas – the religion's holy books – is enough for the characters and roles of the main gods to become apparent. The deities you'll come across most often are the three manifestations of the faith's supreme divine being: **Brahma** the creator, **Vishnu** the preserver and **Shiva** the destroyer.

The earliest Hindu archeological remains in Malaysia are in Kedah (see p.220) and date from the tenth century, although the temples found here indicate a synthesis of Hindu and Buddhist imagery. Although almost all of the region's Hindu past has been obliterated, elements live on in the popular arts like *wayang kulit* (shadow plays), for which sacred texts like the Ramayana form the basis of the plots.

Hinduism returned to the region in the late nineteenth century when immigrants from southern India, having arrived to work on the Malayan rubber and oil-palm plantations, built temples to house images of popular deities. The Hindu celebration of Rama's victory – the central theme of the Ramayana – in time became the national holiday of **Deepavali** (the festival of lights), while another Hindu festival, **Thaipusam**, when Lord Subramaniam and elephant-headed Ganesh, the sons of Shiva, are worshipped, is the occasion for some of the most prominent religious gatherings in the region.

Step over the threshold of a **Hindu temple** and you enter a kaleidoscope world of colourful gods and fanciful creatures. The style is typically Dravidian (South Indian), as befits the largely Tamil population, with a soaring **gopuram**, or entrance tower, teeming with sculptures and a central courtyard leading to an inner sanctum to the presiding deity. In the temple precinct, there are always busy scenes – incense burning, the application of sandalwood paste to the forehead, and the *puja* (ritualistic act of worship).

Islam

The first firm foothold Islam made in the Malay Peninsula was the conversion of Paramesvara, the ruler of **Melaka**, in the early fifteenth century. The commercial success of Melaka accelerated the spread of Islam and, one after another, the powerful Malay court rulers took to the religion, adopting the Arabic title sultan ("ruler"), either because of sincere doctrinal conversion or because they took a shrewd view of the practical advantages to be gained by embracing the new faith. On a wider cultural level, too, Islam had great attractions – its revolutionary concepts of equality in subordination to Allah freed people from the feudal Hindu caste system which had previously dominated parts of the region. Though the Melaka Sultanate fell in 1511, the hold of Islam in the region was strengthened by the subsequent migration of Muslim merchants to Brunei.

The first wave of Islamic missionaries were mostly **Sufis**, representing the mystical and generally more liberal wing of Islam. Sufi Islam integrated some animist elements and Hindu beliefs: the tradition of pluralist deity worship which is central to Hinduism continued. However, in the early nineteenth century the influence of Sufism declined when a more puritanical sect within mainstream **Sunni** Islam, the Wahhabis, captured Mecca. The return to the Koran's basic teachings became identified with a more militant approach, leading to several jihads (holy wars) in Kedah, Kelantan and Terengganu against the Malay rulers' Siamese overlords and, subsequently, the British. Islam in Malaysia and Singapore today is a mixture of Sunni and Sufi elements, and its adherents are still largely comprised of Malays, though a small minority of the Indian community is Muslim, too. Notably, with virtually all Malays being Muslim, the Malaysian **constitution** practically regards being Malay as equivalent to being Muslim.

While Islam as practised locally is relatively liberal, the trend that has swept the Muslim world in the last two or three decades, away from tacit secularism towards a more devout approach, has not left the two countries untouched. There's now a better understanding of Islam's tenets – and thus better compliance with those principles – among Muslims in both countries, thanks partly to increasing educational sophistication, but the drift is not purely about the spiritual realm, as there are social and political dimensions too. Against the backdrop of Malaysia's complex ethnic milieu, Islam is something of a badge of identity for the Malays; thus Malaysia has seen an increase in religious programming on TV and in state spending on often ostentatious new mosques, while even in consumerist Singapore, the Malay minority has shown signs of becoming much more actively engaged in religion. All of this said, it's important not to jump to conclusions of profound change: for most young Muslims in Malaysia and Singapore, Islam is not a matter of dogma but about blending a personal interpretation of the religion with living in a multifaith community and a fast-growing economy, with all the opportunities for technological, artistic and personal development that implies.

Islam and Malay law

One striking way in which Islam influences day-to-day affairs is the fact that in certain areas, Muslim and non-Muslim citizens are subject to different **laws**. In Malaysia, for example, a Muslim man may avail himself of the Islamic provision for a man to take up to four wives, if certain stringent criteria are met, but non-Muslim men are subject to the usual injunctions against bigamy and polygamy. Likewise, while it would be acceptable for an unmarried couple to share a hotel room if neither person is Muslim, it would be illegal (an act known as **khalwat**) if both were Muslim (and if only one of them were Muslim, only that person would be committing an illegal act). This legal divide is reflected in the judicial systems of both Malaysia and Singapore, in which **syariah** (sharia) courts interpreting Islamic law exist alongside courts and laws derived from the British legal system. However, both Malaysia and Singapore limit Islamic jurisprudence to matters concerning the family and certain types of behaviour deemed transgressions against Islam, such as *khalwat*, or for a Muslim to drink in public. In this regard, the *syariah* courts are in many ways subservient to the secular legal framework. This also means the harsher aspects of Islamic justice do not, in practice, apply. For example, punishments such as stoning or the cutting off of a thief's hand are not deemed permissible, and an attempt in the 1990s by the state government of Kelantan, run by the Islamist opposition PAS party, to introduce them within the state was thwarted by the federal government. The Islamic standard of proof in a case concerning rape – requiring the victim to be able to produce four witnesses – also does not apply, since rape cases are tried within the secular system.

Bomoh

An important link between animism and the Islam of today is provided by the Malay **bomoh** (shaman or medicine man). While *bomohs* keep a low profile in these times of greater Islamic orthodoxy – no *bomoh* operates out of an office, and there are no college courses to train *bomohs* or listings of practitioners in the telephone directory – the fact is that every Malay community can still summon a *bomoh* when it's felt one is needed, to cure disease, bring rain during droughts, exorcize spirits from a newly cleared plot before building work starts, or rein in the behaviour of a wayward spouse. A central part of the *bomoh's* trade is recitation, often of sections of the Koran, while – like his Orang Asli counterparts – he uses techniques such as burning herbs to cure or ease pain and disease.

Mosques

In Malaysia, every town, village and hamlet has its mosque, while the capital city of each state hosts the **Masjid Negeri** or state mosque, always more grandiose than its humble regional counterparts. Designs reflect tradition, and you'll rarely see contemporary mosques varying from the standard square building topped by onion domes and minarets. (In Melaka state, where some of Malaysia's oldest mosques are located, the architecture becomes more interesting, revealing unusual Sumatran influences.) Two additional standard features can be found inside the prayer hall, namely the **mihrab**, a niche indicating the direction of Mecca, towards which believers face during prayers (the green *kiblat* arrow on the ceiling of most Malaysian hotel rooms fulfils the same function), and the **mimbar** (pulpit), used by the imam.

One of the five **pillars of Islam** is that the faithful should pray five times a day – at dawn (called the *subuh* prayer in Malay), midday (*zuhur*, or *jumaat* on a Friday), mid-afternoon (*asar*), dusk (*maghrib*) and mid-evening (*isyak*). Travellers soon become familiar with the sound – sometimes recorded – of the **muezzin** calling the faithful to prayer at these times; loudspeakers strapped to the minaret amplify his summons, though a few mosques have their own distinctive methods for summoning the faithful, such as at the Masjid Langgar in Kota Bharu, where traditionally a giant **drum** is banged before prayer time. Once at the mosque, Muslims ritually wash their hands, feet and faces three times in the outer chambers. The men enter the main prayer hall, while women congregate in a chamber beside or above. On **Friday** – the day of communal prayer – Muslims converge on their nearest mosque around noon, to hear the imam lead prayers and deliver a sermon applying the teachings of Allah to the contemporary context. All employers allow Muslim staff a three-hour break for *jumaat* prayers, plus lunch and the attendant socializing.

Chinese religions

The three different strands in Chinese religion ostensibly lean in very different directions: **Confucianism** began as a philosophy based on piety, loyalty, humanitarianism and familial devotion, and has transmuted into a set of principles that permeate every aspect of Chinese life; **Buddhism** is primarily concerned with the attainment of a state of personal enlightenment, nirvana; and **Taoism** propounds unity with nature as its chief tenet. When Chinese pioneers opened up the rivers of Sarawak to trade, it was thanks to the Taoist emphasis on harmony with nature that they identified with many of the animist practices of the Iban and Melanau tribesmen they dealt with.

Malaysian and Singaporean Chinese usually consider themselves Buddhist, Taoist or Confucianist, although in practice they are often a mixture of all three. The combination comprises a system of belief which is first and foremost pragmatic. The Chinese use their religion to ease their passage through life, whether in the spheres of work or family, while temples double as social centres, where people meet and exchange views.

Most visitors are more aware of the region's Chinese religious celebrations than of the Muslim or Hindu ones, largely because the festivals themselves are particularly welcoming of tourists and are often exciting. Most are organized by *kongsis*, or clan houses, which are the cornerstone of all immigrant Chinese communities in Malaysia and Singapore and traditionally provided housing, employment and a social structure for the newly arrived.

Chinese temples

The rules of **feng shui** are rigorously applied to the construction of Chinese temples, so that each building has a layout and orientation rendering it free from evil influences. Visitors wishing to cross the threshold of a temple have to step over a kerb that's intended to trip up evil spirits, and walk through doors painted with fearsome door gods; fronting the doors are two stone lions, whose roars provide yet another defence.

Temples are normally constructed around a framework of huge, lacquered timber beams, adorned with intricately carved warriors, animals and flowers. More figures are moulded onto outer walls, which are dotted with octagonal, hexagonal or round grille-worked windows. Larger temples typically consist of a front entrance hall opening onto a walled-in courtyard, beyond which is the hall of worship, where joss sticks are burned below images of the deities.

The most important and striking element of a Chinese temple is its **roof** – a grand, multitiered affair with low, overhanging eaves, the ridges alive with auspicious creatures such as dragons and phoenixes and, less often, with miniature scenes from traditional Chinese life and legend. *Feng shui* comes into play again inside the temple, with auspicious room numbers and sizes, colour and sequence of construction. Elsewhere in the temple grounds, you'll see sizeable ovens, stuffed constantly with paper money, prayer books and other offerings; or a **pagoda** – a tall, thin tower thought to keep out evil spirits.

Peop[e]s

L argely because of their pivotal position on the maritime trade routes between the Middle East, India and China, the present-day countries of Malaysia, Singapore and Brunei have always been a cultural melting-pot. During the first millennium, Malays arrived from Sumatra and Indians from India and Sri Lanka, while later the Chinese migrated from mainland China and Hainan Island. But all these traders and settlers arrived to find that the region already contained a gamut of indigenous tribes, thought to have migrated here around 50,000 years ago from the Philippines, which was then connected by a land bridge to Borneo and Southeast Asia. The indigenous tribes still existing on the Peninsula are known there as the Orang Asli, Malay for "the original people". Some of these are more commonly known in English by the term "Negritos", given to them by Spaniards who colonized the Philippines.

Original people they may have been, but the descendants of the various indigenous groups now form a small minority of the overall populations of the three countries. Over the last 150 years a massive influx of Chinese and Indian immigrants, escaping poverty, war and revolution, has swelled the population of **Malaysia**, which now stands at over 25 million. Just under half are Malays, while the Chinese make up a quarter of the population, the Indians seven percent, and the various indigenous groups just over a tenth.

Brunei's population of around 370,000 is heavily dominated by Malays, with minorities of Chinese, Indians and indigenous peoples. In **Singapore**, there were only tiny numbers of indigenes left on the island by the time of the arrival of Raffles. They have no modern-day presence in the state and more than three-quarters of the 4.4-million strong population are of Chinese extraction, while around fourteen percent are Malay and seven percent Indian.

The Malays

The **Malays**, a Mongoloid people believed to have originated from the meeting of Central Asians with Pacific islanders, first moved to the west coast of the Malay Peninsula from Sumatra in early times. Known as Orang Laut (sea people), they sustained an economy built around fishing, boat-building and, in some communities, piracy. It was the growth in power of the Malay sultanates from the fifteenth century onwards – coinciding with the arrival of Islam – that established Malays as a force to be reckoned within the Malay Peninsula and in Borneo. They developed an aristocratic tradition, courtly rituals and a social hierarchy (for more on which, see p.362) which have an influence even today. The rulers of the Malaysian states still wield immense social and economic power, reflected in the sharing of the appointment of the Yang Dipertuan Agong, a pre-eminent sultan nominated on a five-year cycle. Although it's a purely ceremonial position, the *agong* is seen as the ultimate guardian of Malay Muslim culture and, despite recent legislation to reduce his powers, is still considered to be above the law. The situation is even more pronounced in **Brunei**, to which many Muslim Malay traders fled after the fall of Melaka to the Portuguese in 1511. There, the sultan is still the supreme ruler (as his descendants have been, on and off, for over five hundred years).

Even though Malays have been Muslims since the fifteenth century, the region as a whole is not fundamentalist in character. Only in Brunei is alcohol banned, for instance, and while fundamentalist groups do hold some sway in the eastern states of Kelantan and Terengganu, their influence is rarely oppressive.

The main contemporary change for Malays in Malaysia was the introduction of the **bumiputra** policy – a Malay word meaning "sons of the soil." It was brought in as part of the New Economic Policy (NEP) that followed the race riots of May 1969 which pitted the wealthier Chinese against the poorer Malays. The policy was intended to provide a more level economic playing field for those ethnic groups (Malays, Orang Asli and the indigenous peoples of East Malaysia, though it's the Malays and not the Orang Asli who have benefited) who had fallen behind the more successful Chinese and Indian immigrant minorities. Business in Malaysia by the late 1960s was heavily Chinese dominated, both the result of a natural Chinese affinity for business (and a culture strongly orientated around notions of achieving prosperity) and the British colonial policy of keeping the races largely separate; the Malays as farmers in the countryside, the Chinese as businesspeople in the towns and the Indians as workers on the railways and on the plantations. The policy gave privileges to Malays such as subsidized housing, easier access to higher education (with generous grants being paid to help Malays study abroad) and forced companies to appoint Malay directors. Since the early 1990s, when the NEP had officially run its course, the rules have been relaxed. However non-bumiputra groups continue to complain that they are discriminated against, particularly in education. The policy has resulted in an easing of the ethnic tensions as it has created a Malay super-rich class who have much to lose from unrest, however, it still causes resentment. Despite his role in its formation, former prime minister, Dr Mahathir Mohamad came to lament the response of Malays to the policy. He accused them of laziness, (not an uncommon accusation from others in private) while the Malay-dominated public sector appears ripe for the chill wind of free-market competition to remind salary-men and women that a job for life does at times involve work and not simply sitting behind a *tutup* (closed) sign and chatting with co-workers.

The situation is different in **Singapore**, where the policy doesn't hold sway: despite being greatly outnumbered by their Chinese compatriots, Singapore's Malay community appears content to stay south of the causeway and enjoy the state's higher standard of living.

The Chinese and Straits Chinese

Chinese traders began visiting the region in the seventh century, but it was in Melaka in the fifteenth century that the first significant community established itself. However, the ancestors of the majority of Chinese now living in Peninsular Malaysia emigrated from southern China in the nineteenth century to work in the burgeoning tin-mining industry. In Sarawak, Foochow, Teochew and Hokkien Chinese from southeastern China played an important part in opening up the interior, establishing pepper and rubber plantations along Batang Rajang; while in Sabah, Hakka Chinese labourers were recruited by the British North Borneo Chartered Company to plant rubber, and many stayed on, forming the core of the Chinese business community there.

Although many Chinese in the Peninsula came as labourers, they graduated quickly to shopkeeping and business ventures, both in established towns like

Melaka and fast-expanding centres like KL, Penang and Kuching. Chinatowns developed throughout the region, even in Malay strongholds like Kota Bharu and Kuala Terengganu, while **Chinese traditions**, religious festivities, theatre and music became an integral part of a wider Malayan, and later Malaysian, multiracial culture. On the political level, the Malaysian Chinese are well represented in parliament and occupy around a quarter of the current ministerial positions. By way of contrast, **Chinese Bruneians** are not automatically classed as citizens and suffer a fair amount of discrimination at the hands of the majority Malay population.

Singapore's nineteenth-century trade boom drew large numbers of Cantonese, Teochew, Hokkein and Hakka Chinese traders and labourers, who quickly established a Chinatown on the south bank of the Singapore River. Today, the Chinese account for 77 percent of the state's population and are the most economically successful racial group in Singapore. As the proportion of Singaporean Chinese born on the island increases, the government's efforts to cultivate a feeling of Singaporean national identity are beginning to show signs of working, especially among the younger generation. Consequently, the main difference between the Chinese in Singapore and those in Malaysia is that Singapore's Chinese majority prefers to think of itself simply as Singaporean. Nevertheless, as in Malaysia, they still display their traditional work ethic and spurn none of their cultural heritage.

One of the few examples of regional intermarrying is displayed in the **Peranakan** or "Straits-born Chinese" heritage of Melaka, Singapore and, to a lesser extent, Penang. When male Chinese immigrants settled in these places from the sixteenth century onwards to work as miners or commercial entrepreneurs, they often married local Malay women, whose male offspring were termed "Baba" and the females "Nonya". **Baba–Nonya** society, as it became known, adapted elements from both cultures to create its own traditions: the descendants of these sixteenth-century liaisons have a unique culinary and architectural style (for more on which see p.374). Although Baba-Nonyas dress as Malays (the men in stiff-collared tunics and *songkets* and the women in sarongs and fitted, long-sleeved blouses), their Malay is a distinct dialect, and most follow Chinese Confucianism as their religion. Nowadays though, the cultural idiosyncrasies of the Straits Chinese have largely been assimilated into the ways of Singapore and Malaysia as a whole, meaning that you'll need to visit museums to see evidence of them.

The Indians

The second-largest non-*bumiputra* group in Malaysia, the **Indians**, first arrived as traders more than two thousand years ago, although few settled and it wasn't until the early fifteenth century that a small community of Indians (from present-day Tamil Nadu and Sri Lanka) was based in Melaka. But, like the majority of Chinese, the first large wave of Indians – Tamil labourers – arrived in the nineteenth century as indentured workers, to build the roads and railways and to work on the European-run rubber estates. But an embryonic entrepreneurial class from North India soon followed and set up businesses in Penang and Singapore; these merchants and traders, most most of whom were Muslim, found it easier to assimilate themselves within the existing Malay community than the Hindu Tamils did.

Although Indians comprise only ten percent of Malaysia's population (seven percent in Singapore) their impact is felt everywhere. The Hindu festival of *Thaipusam* is celebrated annually at KL's Batu Caves by upwards of a million people (with a smaller, but still significant celebration in Singapore); the festival of *Deepavali* is a national holiday; and Indians are increasingly competing with Malays in the arts, and dominate certain professional areas like medicine and law. And then, of course, there is the area of food – very few Malaysians these days could do without a daily dose of *roti canai*, so much so that this North Indian snack has been virtually appropriated by Malay and Chinese cafés and hawkers.

Even today in Malaysia, many Tamils work on private plantations and are unable to reap many of the benefits of the country's economic success. The Indians' political voice has also traditionally been weak, although there are signs that a younger generation of political leaders from the two Indian-dominated political parties, the Malaysian Indian Congress and the Indian Progressive Front, are asserting the community's needs more effectively.

Indigenous peoples

The **Orang Asli** – the indigenous peoples of Peninsular Malaysia – mostly belong to three distinct groups, within which various tribes are related by geography, language or physiological features.

The largest of the groups is the **Senoi** (the Asli word for "person"), who number about 40,000. They live in the large, still predominantly forested interior, within the states of Perak, Pahang and Kelantan, and divide into two main tribes, the Semiar and the Temiar, which still live a traditional lifestyle, following animist customs in their marriage ceremonies and burial rites. On the whole they follow the practice of shifting cultivation (a regular rotation of jungle-clearance and crop-planting), although government resettlement drives have successfully persuaded many to settle and farm just one area.

The **Semang** (or Negritos), of whom there are around 2000, live in the northern areas of the Peninsula. They comprise six distinct, if small, tribes, related to each other in appearance – they are mostly dark-skinned and curly haired – and share a traditional nomadic, hunter-gatherer lifestyle. However, most Semang nowadays live in settled communities and work within the cash economy, either as labourers or selling jungle produce in markets. Perhaps the most frequently seen Semang tribe are the Batek, who live in and around Taman Negara.

The third group, the so-called **Aboriginal Malays**, live in an area roughly south of the Kuala Lumpur–Kuantan road. Some of the tribes in this category, like the Jakun who live around Tasek Chini and the Semelais of Tasek Bera, have vigorously retained their animist religion and artistic traditions despite living in permanent villages near Malay communities and working within the regular economy. These are among the easiest of the Orang Asli to approach, since some have obtained employment in the two lakes' tourist industries; others are craftspeople selling their wares from stalls beside the water.

These three main groupings do not represent all the Orang Asli tribes in Malaysia. One, the Lanoh in Perak, are sometimes regarded as Negritos, but their language is closer to that of the Temiar. Another group, the semi-nomadic Che Wong, of whom just a few hundred still survive on the slopes of Gunung Benom in central Pahang, are still dependent on foraging to survive and live in temporary huts made from bamboo and rattan. Two more groups, the Jah Hut of Pahang and the Mah Meri of Selangor, are particularly fine carvers, and it's possible to buy their sculptures at regional craft shops.

The tribes of Tasek Chini and Tasek Bera apart, it's difficult to visit most Orang Asli communities. Many live way off the beaten track and can only be reached if you go on a tour (some operators do visit Orang Asli settlements in Tasek Bera or Endau Rompin National Park). It's most unlikely that visitors would ever chance upon a remote Orang Asli village, though you will sometimes pass tribe members in the national parks or on inaccessible roads in eastern Perak, Pahang and Kelantan. To learn more about the disappearing Asli culture, the best stop is KL's Orang Asli Museum (see p.150).

Sarawak

In direct contrast to the Peninsula, indigenous groups make up a substantial chunk of the population in **Sarawak**, which is what attracts many visitors there in the first place (see the "Sarawak" chapter for all the details). Although the Chinese comprise 29 percent of the state's population and the Malays and Indians around 24 percent together, the remaining 47 percent are made up of various indigenous **Dyak** groups – a word derived from the Malay for "upcountry".

The largest Dyak groups are the Iban, Bidayuh, Melanau, Kayan, Kenyah, Kelabit and Penan tribes, all of which have distinct cultures, although most have certain things in common, including a lifestyle predominantly based outside towns. Many live in **longhouses** along the rivers or on the sides of hills in the mountainous interior, and maintain a proud cultural legacy which draws on animist religion (see the *Longhouse culture* colour section for more on this), arts and crafts production, jungle skills and a rich tradition of **festivals**. The *ngajat*, a dance traditionally performed by warriors on their return from battle, is now more commonly performed in the longhouses, albeit in a milder, truncated form, often for tourists. Spectacular costumes featuring large feathers are worn by the dancers who, arranged in a circle, perform athletic leaps to indicate their virility.

The **Iban** make up nearly one-third of Sarawak's population. Originating hundreds of miles south of present-day Sarawak, in the Kapuas Valley in Kalimantan, the Iban migrated north in the sixteenth century, coming into conflict over the next two hundred years with the Kayan and Kenyah tribes and, later, the British. Nowadays, Iban longhouse communities are found in the Batang Ai river system in the southwest. These communities are quite accessible, their inhabitants always hospitable and keen to illustrate aspects of their culture like traditional dance, music, textile-weaving, blowpiping, fishing and games. In their time, the Iban were infamous head-hunters – some longhouses are still decorated with authentic shrunken heads. (For more details about the Iban, see p.458).

The most southern of Sarawak's indigenous groups are the **Bidayuh**, who – unlike most Dyak groups – traditionally lived away from the rivers, building their longhouse on the sides of hills. Culturally, they are similar to the Iban, although in temperament they are much milder and less gregarious, keeping themselves to themselves in their inaccessible homes on Sarawak's mountainous southern border with Kalimantan.

The **Melanau** are a coastal people, living north of Kuching in a region dominated by mangrove swamps. Many Melanau, however, now live in towns, preferring the kampung-style houses of the Malays to the elegant longhouses of the past. They are expert fishermen and cultivate sago as an alternative to rice. Many Melanau died in the battles that ensued when the Iban first migrated northwards, and the survival of their communities owes much to the first white rajah, James Brooke, who protected them in the nineteenth century. He had a soft spot for the Melanau, thinking them the most attractive of the state's ethnic peoples and employing many as boat-builders, labourers and domestic servants.

The **Kelabit** people live on the highland plateau which separates north Sarawak from Kalimantan. Like the Iban, they live in longhouses and maintain a traditional lifestyle, but differ from some of the other groups in that they are Christian. The highlands were totally inaccessible before the airstrip at Bario was built; now the area has become popular for hikers, since many longhouses which welcome visitors lie within a few days' walk of Bario (see p.510 for more).

The last main group is the semi-nomadic **Penan**, who live in the upper Rajang and Limbang areas of Sarawak in temporary lean-tos or small huts. They rely, like some of the Orang Asli groups in the Peninsula, on hunting and gathering and collecting jungle produce for sale in local markets. They also have the lightest skin of all the ethnic groups of Sarawak, largely because they live within the shade of the forest, rather than on the rivers and in clearings. In recent years the state government has tried to resettle the Penan in small villages, a controversial policy not entirely unconnected with the advance of logging in traditional Penan land, which has caused opposition from the Penan themselves and criticism from international groups. Some tour operators now have itineraries which include visiting Penan communities in the Baram river basin and in the primary jungle that slopes away from the Kelabit Highlands.

Most of the other groups in Sarawak fall into the catch-all ethnic classification of **Orang Ulu** (people of the interior), who inhabit the more remote inland parts of the state, further north than the Iban, along the upper Rajang, Balui and Linau rivers. The most numerous, the **Kayan** and the **Kenyah**, are closely related and in the past often teamed up to defend their lands from the invading Iban. But they also have much in common with their traditional enemy, since they are longhouse-dwellers, animists and shifting cultivators. The main difference is the more hierarchical social structure of their communities, each of which has one leader, a *penghulu*, who has immense influence over the other inhabitants of the longhouse. Nowadays, many Kayan and Kenyah are Christians – converted after contact with missionaries following World War II – and their longhouses are among the most prosperous in Sarawak. Like the Iban, they maintain a tradition of *bejelai*, and the return of the youths from their wanderings is always an excuse for a big party, at which visitors from abroad or from other longhouses are always welcome. (There's more information on both the Kenyah and Kayan on p.475).

Sabah

Sabah has a population of around 1.6 million, made up of more than thirty distinct racial groups, between them speaking over eighty different dialects. Most populous of these groups are the **Dusun**, who account for around a third of Sabah's population. Traditionally agriculturists (the word Dusun means "orchard"), the *Dusun* are divided into subgroups which inhabit the western coastal plains and the interior of the state. These days they are known generically as **Kadazan/Dusun**, although strictly speaking "Kadazan" refers only to the Dusun of Penampang. Other branches of the Dusun include the **Lotud** of Tuaran and the **Rungus** of the Kudat Peninsula, whose convex longhouses are all that remain of the Dusun's longhouse tradition. Although most Dusun are now Christians, remnants of their animist past are still evident in their culture, most obviously in the harvest festival, or *pesta kaamatan*, when their *bobohizans*, or priestesses, perform rituals to honour the *bambaazon*, or rice spirit. In the *samazau* dance – almost the national dance of East Malaysia – the costumes worn are authentically Kadazan. Two rows of men and women dance facing each other in a slow, rhythmic movement, flapping their arms to the pulse of the drum, their hand gestures mimicking the flight of birds. Not to be outdone, the women of the Kwijau community have their own dance, the *buloh*, which features high jumping steps to the percussive sounds of the gong and bamboo.

The mainly Muslim **Bajau** tribe drifted over from the southern Philippines some two hundred years ago, and now constitute Sabah's second largest ethnic group, accounting for around ten percent of the population. Their penchant for piracy quickly earned them the sobriquet "Sea Gypsies", though nowadays they are agriculturalists and fishermen, noted for their horsemanship and their rearing of buffalo. The Bajau live in the northwest of Sabah and annually appear on horseback at Kota Belud's market (see p.553).

Sabah's third sizeable tribe is the **Murut**, which inhabits the area between Keningau and the Sarawak border, in the southwest. Their name means "hill people", though they prefer to be known by their individual tribal names, such as Timugon, Tagal and Nabai. The Murut farm rice and cassava by a system of shifting cultivation and, at times, still hunt using blowpipes and poison darts. Though their head-hunting days are over, they retain other cultural traditions, such as the construction of brightly adorned grave huts to house the graves and belongings of the dead. Another tradition that continues is the consumption at ceremonies of *tapai* or rice wine, drawn from a ceremonial jar using bamboo straws. Although the Murut now eschew longhouse life, many villages retain a ceremonial hall, complete with a *lansaran*, or bamboo trampoline, for festive dances and games.

Development and the environment

Malaysia is gradually becoming more environmentally friendly, largely as a result of well-organized and scientifically persuasive organizations within the country, rather than pressures from outside, but the pace of change remains slow and huge problems still remain. Logging and large-scale development projects have for decades hogged the spotlight, and are still a prime focus for NGOs, but just as pressing are concerns over oil-palm cultivation and wetlands erosion, as well as the impact of environmental degradation on the lifestyles of indigenous groups. For the majority of Malaysians, these are distant matters relating to faraway Sarawak and Sabah – they are more concerned over fears that the haze, caused by forest fires in neighboring Indonesian territories, will flare up again and blanket the region.

Far less controversy surrounds environmental issues in **Singapore**. Of course as a small island there are not many wild places left to spoil; nevertheless the nation appears to value protection policies opening new bird sanctuaries and small parklands. More so than in Malaysia, ordinary people appear to be increasingly sensitive to environmental concerns, and support laws controlling littering and waste emissions which have been tightened in recent years.

The tiny kingdom of **Brunei** is perhaps the most enlightened of all. With a small, wealthy population there is no rampant commercial exploitation of natural resources as in Malaysia. Forest protection is successfully applied and the state's small percentage of indigenous peoples treated respectfully.

Logging and deforestation

The **sustainable exploitation** of forest products by the indigenous population has always played a vital part in the domestic and export economy of the region – for almost two thousand years, the ethnic tribes have bartered products like rattan, wild rubber and forest plants with foreign traders.

Although blamed for much of the deforestation in Sarawak and Sabah, the bulk of indigenous agricultural activity occurs in secondary rather than primary (untouched) forest. Indeed, environmental groups believe that only around one hundred square kilometres of primary forest – a tiny proportion compared to the haul by commercial timber companies – is cleared by the indigenous groups annually. Logging, despite having slowed is still a cause of huge grievances among the indigenous peoples of East Malaysia.

The Peninsula

Peninsular Malaysia's pre-independence economy was not as reliant on timber revenues as those of Sabah and Sarawak. Although one-sixth of the region's 120,000 square kilometres of forest, predominantly in Johor, Perak and Negeri Sembilan states, had been cut down by 1957, most of the logging had been done gradually and on a small, localized scale. As in Sabah, it was the demand for rail sleepers – for the expansion of the Malayan train network in the 1920s – which had first attracted the commercial logging companies, but wide-scale clearing and conversion to rubber and oil-palm plantations in the more remote areas of Pahang, Perlis, Kedah and Terengganu didn't intensify until the 1960s. By the end of the 1970s, more efficient extraction methods, coupled with a massive increase in foreign investment in the logging industry, had led to over forty percent of the Peninsula's remaining forests being either cleared for plantation purposes or partially logged.

Only in the last fifteen years has logging in West Malaysia slowed significantly, with more stringent assessments of the environmental impact being carried out before logging is allowed to proceed. Legislation enacted by the government has provided more protection for the environment. One particularly positive piece of legislation is the creation of Permanent Forest Reserves, which in time will ensure that more land will be preserved in permanent reserves under the various Malaysia Plans. But unfortunately while this sounds good, it doesn't represent a watertight system: even if a parcel of land is labelled a reserve, it can still be partially logged. But at least now the work must be carried out in a sustainable manner integrating checks and impact assessments.

Sabah

Commercial logging started in **Sabah** (then North Borneo) in the late nineteenth century, when the British Borneo Trading and Planting Company began to extract large trees from the area around Sandakan to satisfy the demand for timber sleepers for the expanding railway system in China. By 1930 the larger **British Borneo Timber Company** (BBTC) was primarily responsible for the extraction of 178,000 cubic metres of timber, rising to nearly five million cubic metres by the outbreak of World War II, and Sandakan became one of the world's main timber ports. Most areas were logged indiscriminately, and the indigenous tribal groups who lived there were brought into the economic system to work on North Borneo's rubber, tobacco and, later, oil-palm plantations. The process intensified as the main players in Sabah tapped the lucrative Japanese market, where postwar reconstruction costing billions of dollars was underway.

By the early 1960s, timber had accelerated past rubber as the region's chief export and by 1970 nearly thirty percent of Sabah had been extensively logged, with oil palm and other plantation crops replacing around a quarter of the degraded forest. Timber exports had accounted for less than ten percent of all exports from Sabah in 1950; by the 1970s, this had rocketed to over seventy percent. Nowadays much of the logged land is used for oil-palm cultivation with powerful companies continuing to pressure the state government for access to more of the remaining forests to expand further this lucrative, and ecologically suffocating mono-culture.

Sarawak

A much larger share of contemporary logging takes place in **Sarawak** – around eighty percent of the total Malaysian output. The development of large foreign-run plantations in the state was hindered initially by the white rajahs, James and Charles Brooke, who largely kept foreign investment out of their paternalistically run fiefdom. But once the BBTC was given rights to start logging in northern Sarawak in the 1930s, timber extraction grew rapidly, especially since the third white rajah, Vyner Brooke, was less stringent in his opposition. Timber was viewed as a vital commercial resource to be utilized in the massive reconstruction of the state, following the devastating Japanese occupation. During its short postwar period as a Crown Colony and, after 1963, as a Malaysian state, logging in Sarawak grew to become one of its chief revenue earners, alongside oil extraction. The state government encouraged foreign investment and issued timber concessions to rich individuals, who were encouraged to carve up ever more remote areas. Today, most of the Baram basin in the north of the state has been logged – the river is now a soupy brown sludge due to the run-off of earth and silt caused by the extraction process – and attention has switched to the remote Balui River and its tributaries in the east of the state, where the Bakun Dam project (see p.476), nearly shelved due to financial constraints, is now back on course.

Accurate figures as to the current state of Sarawak's forests are, however, notoriously hard to come by. Suaram, a coalition of East Malaysian environmental NGOs, says that less than half of Sarawak's 124,000 square kilometres remains as forest; the state claims the figure is more like three-quarters – though it includes oil palm and other plantation zones in its calculations.

Government initiatives

Since the mid 1990s logging has slowed down as a result of the **National Forestry Policy** (NFP). This has led to deforestation being reduced to 900 square kilometres a year, almost a third slower than the previous rate, with a further target of reducing timber harvesting by ten percent each year, although critics say this isn't enough to save the forests, which within twenty years will cover less than twenty percent of the surface of the country instead of the current 55 percent.

The Malaysian government is naturally keen to deflect attention away from the accusation that the timber concessions it grants are solely responsible for unsustainable timber production. Re-forestation schemes within the **Permanent Forest Estates** – government-run tracts of land given over to tree cultivation – are on the increase. And organizations like the Forest Resource Institute of Malaysia (FRIM), which sustains an area of secondary forest on the edge of Kuala Lumpur, prove how rainforest habitats can be renewed. FRIMS' ecological management plan ensures that a comprehensive range of flora, including tree species and a wide spectrum of plants, are planted and monitored over a long period. It must be stressed, however, that FRIM is the exception rather than the rule, and most environmentalists within Malaysia don't believe that renewable forestry can offset the damage caused by current timber extraction techniques which seldom aid re-growth.

In East Malaysia various initiatives aim to protect the remaining forests. In early 2006 WWF Malaysia announced The Heart of Borneo project, an international agreement between the governments of Malaysia, Indonesia and Brunei to protect 220,000 square kilometres of forest straddling the Bornean foothills and highlands where the three nations' borders meet.

Dam construction

Massive **dam construction** is another issue often on the environmental agenda. The current prime example is the **Bakun** Dam project in Sarawak in Belaga district. In preparation for construction – due for completion in 2007 – over ten thousand ethnic peoples were moved from their longhouses along the Balui River to a dry location, Asap. Environmentalists opposed to the scheme say it ignored scientific evidence indicating the adverse effects of flooding of an area the size of Singapore. It isn't simply the uprooting of ethnic peoples, but also the eradication of the region's unique biodiversity, that has caused such controversy.

The international funding of such projects was highlighted in 1994 when it became clear that £1.3 billion's worth of defence contracts awarded to British companies had been linked to £234 million of British aid money for the building of a hydroelectric dam at **Pergau** in northern Kelantan. British civil servants declared the dam "a bad buy", but the British government went ahead, it was suggested, because the Malaysians had made the arms purchases conditional on the aid money to underwrite the dam. A parliamentary committee in Britain launched an inquiry, but the issue was firmly swept under the carpet in Malaysia where the press stood right behind former prime minister, Mahathir Mohamad.

Air pollution

For the inhabitants of Peninsular Malaysia and Singapore, the environmental issue which has affected them most has not been forest depletion or land rights, but **air pollution**, particularly dust and smoke caused by forest fires – dubbed "the haze" by the local media. Although such events had occurred sporadically during the 1990s, in 1997/8 the region suffered a severe, prolonged episode, when the haze was so bad that motorists were warned to keep their distance from one another and there was an alarming rise in respiratory illnesses. Visibility in the Straits of Melaka – one of the world's busiest shipping routes – also dropped dramatically.

The Malaysian government originally suggested that the agricultural methods of the indigenous peoples – which involve the burning of excess vegetation at the end of growing cycles – were to blame. However, further research indicated that small longhouse communities could not have caused such extensive fires. It's now thought that the haze is caused by Indonesian plantation companies using fire to clear large areas of forest to facilitate the planting of crops such as oil palm and acacia. The Indonesian government does not appear to have been able to change the habits of its forest developers given that the 1997 catastrophe was repeated, albeit to a lesser extent, in 2000, 2002 and 2005. The 2005 event – cause by forest fires in Sumatra – prompted a state of emergency to be declared and crisis talks with Indonesia.

The threat to traditional lifestyles

Although large-scale projects such as the Bakun Dam are the most prevalent threat to indigenous tribes' way of life, illegal logging still threatens to underscore the gains made over the last ten years. In the case of Sarawak, customary land tenure or *adat*, which was enshrined in law throughout the white rajah period and forms the basis of the 1958 Sarawak Land Code, should protect the land claimed by the state's tribal groups. In practice, much commercial logging has ignored this. The forest-dependent people of northern Sarawak have responded to logging encroachment with spontaneous actions (such as destruction of machinery) through the 1960s and 1970s and developing collective actions (blockades) in the late 1980s and 1990s. Protests still sporadically take place today, achieving small mentions in the local press even though logging has been substantially scaled back. The failure to respect *adat* has led to the desecration of locations of special importance – burial places, access routes and sections of rivers used for fishing – as it is hard for indigenous people to prove conclusively that they have lived and farmed here for generations.

The forests around Bintulu, Belaga and Limbang have suffered in this way, although the Iban in southwest Sarawak have had more success. A historic court case in 2001, Rumah Nor v. Borneo Pulp and Paper, should have proved a milestone in shifting the goal posts more the indigenes way. Here the court ruled in favour of the longhouse community, after the community's map was accepted as court evidence for ownership of land. Emboldened by this ruling, a growing number of communities filed complaints but in many cases the courts have not been able to stand up to the powerful timber companies.

Counter-mapping

The authorities had long been able to reject *adat* claims as the indigenes had not been able to prove conclusively, within Malaysian law, that the land had been in their ownership for generations. In response to this, **counter-mapping**, introduced in the 1990s, has been employed as an empowerment tool for reassertion of Native Customary Right (NCR). Essentially the process involves utilizing technology to draw up detailed maps of a community's boundaries. Members of local NGOs have been trained in mapping, using GPS (global positioning system) and even the more sophisticated GIS (geo-information system).

Land conflicts

Another hot issue in Sarawak and Sabah in recent years has been **oil-palm cultivation**, the state governments launching joint ventures with private companies to open up new plantations in the states. There have been many examples of plantations taking over sizeable areas previously designed as customary land, with the authorities compelling longhouse communities to resettle in model villages nearby. The communities are then offered work at low rates in the emerging oil-palm cash economy.

The authorities are quick to defend themselves, insisting that mono-agricultural enterprises, like oil palm, and massive energy projects like Bakun generate substantial profits which in turn fund initiatives like new housing and education for the poorer sections of society. Indigenous groups argue that most profits from these businesses are in fact not ploughed back into social policies but return to private company accounts, often in Peninsular Malaysia or, increasingly, to China and Korea.

In 2005, research by campaigning group, Friends of the Earth showed that oil-palm expansion directly threatens the survival of animals. **Protected species**, including the orang-utan and pygmy elephant, were being prevented from migrating as wildlife corridors were fragmented by estate developers.

The Penan

The **Penan**, hunter-gatherers from northern Sarawak, have arguably been the worst hit from industrial logging. Unlike many of the ethnic groups close by – the Ukit, Kenyah and Kayan – who can base their customary land claims on a settled history of farming, the nomadic lifestyle of the Penan, and the particular ways in which they utilize the land, makes it harder for their land rights to be defined and recognized. An additional factor in the case of the Penan has been that since the mid-1980s the Sarawak state government's avowed policy has been to bring them into what it views as the development process (as has been applied to the more settled Dayak and Orang Ulu groups for many decades), urging them to move to permanent longhouses, work in the cash economy and send their children to school.

The Penan have proved resilient to these attempts to assimilate them into the wider Malaysian social system, largely because the government diktats seem to go suspiciously hand in hand with an expansion of logging in their customary land areas. Very often, there's been no warning that Penan land has been earmarked for logging until the extraction actually begins – examples in remote areas of the Belaga district have been well documented by the environmental group **Sahabat Alam Malaysia** (Ⓦ www.surforever.com/sam). In retaliation, some Penan tribes-people have applied for **communal forest areas** (so-called "Penan zones") to be designated, so that some of their land would receive protection, but until now, all such applications have been refused. Up to the mid 1990s the Penan had became a well-organized passive resistance force with the help of Swiss environmentalist Bruno Manser, who for a time topped Malaysia's most-wanted persons list. (Manser went missing in 2000 under suspicious circumstances.) However, over the last few years Penan resistance has sadly withered; the vast majority now live in squalid resettlement camps and hold on as best they can to their traditional culture.

Wildlife

There's an extraordinary tropical biodiversity in the Malay Peninsula and in Borneo, with over six hundred species of birds; more than two hundred kinds of mammals, including the tiger, Asian elephant, orang-utan and tapir; many thousands of flowering plant species, among them the insectivorous pitcher plant and scores of others of known medicinal value; and over one thousand species of brightly coloured butterflies. This enormous variety of bird, plant and animal life makes any trip to a tropical rainforest a memorable experience. Wherever you visit, it's important to remember that observing wildlife in tropical forests requires much patience, and on any one visit it is unlikely that you will encounter more than a fraction of the wildlife living in the forest; many of the mammals are shy and nocturnal.

Despite being separated by the South China Sea, the wildlife and plant communities of Peninsular and East Malaysia are very similar, since the island of Borneo was joined to the Asian mainland by a land bridge until after the last ice age. Nonetheless, there are some specific differences. The forests of the Peninsula support populations of several large mammal species, such as tiger, tapir and gaur (forest-dwelling wild cattle), which are absent from Borneo. Other large mammals, for example the Asian elephant, and birds such as the hornbill, occur both on Borneo and on the Peninsula; while Borneo features the orang-utan (the "man of the forest") and the proboscis monkey. Indeed, this latter species is endemic to the island of Borneo.

Below we feature two of the most exciting – and accessible – areas in Peninsular Malaysia in which to view wildlife, namely **Taman Negara** and **Fraser's Hill**; the round-ups of bird, plant and animal life at these two sites should be read in conjunction with the general accounts of both places in the Guide. East Malaysia and Brunei also offer many opportunities for observing wildlife. It's easy to spot proboscis monkeys along **Sungai Kinabatangan** in Sabah and at **Bako National Park** in Sarawak, the former also a good place to watch orang-utans. Those with an interest in birdlife should head for Sarawak's **Loagan Bunut National Park**, whose shallow lake is home to many different bird species, or to Brunei's **Ulu Temburong National Park**.

Singapore, on the other hand, is not the sort of place you would expect to find much plant or animal life. The rapid urbanization of the island has eradicated many of its original forest plant species, all its large mammals and many of its ecologically sensitive bird species. However, several remnants of its more verdant tropical past still survive. The most noteworthy of these are the pocket of primary rainforest at **Bukit Timah Nature Reserve**, the splendidly manicured Botanic Gardens, and the **Sungei Buloh Nature Wetland Reserve** in the far north of the island. Day-trippers to Pulau Ubin, just off the island of Singapore, can also visit the mangrove flats of **Chek Jawa**.

Poaching and habitation loss due to deforestation means that the future of the region's wildlife is far from assured. Fortunately, many **not-for-profit organizations** are campaigning to preserve the species and terrains most under threat. A visit to the website of the World Wildlife Foundation (ⓦwww.wwfmalaysia .org) unearths a mine of information about Malaysia's natural riches and the regional projects the WWF is currently pursuing there. SOS Rhino's more specific goal is to preserve the world's various rhino species; among the group's various projects, is one to protect the handful of the Bornean sub-species of the Sumatran rhino known to live within Sabah's Tabin Wildlife Reserve. For

more information, go to ⊛www.sosrhino.org. Finally, the EIA (⊛www.eia
-international.org) is another group conducting activist work on behalf of
orang-utans and the forest.

For **books** on the wildlife of Malaysia, Singapore and Brunei, see p.781.

Taman Negara

The vast expanse (4343 square kilometres) of **Taman Negara** contains one of
the world's oldest tropical rainforests, and is generally regarded as one of Asia's
finest national parks. It has an **equatorial climate**, with rainfall throughout
the year and no distinct dry season. Temperatures can reach 35°C during the
day, with the air often feeling very muggy. Most rain falls as heavy convectional
showers in the afternoon, following a hot and sunny morning – from November to February, heavy rains may cause flooding in low-lying areas.

Forest trees

The natural richness of the habitat is reflected in the range of forest types found
within the park. Only a small proportion of Taman Negara is true **lowland
forest**, though it's here that most of the trails and hides are located. The
lowlands support **dipterocarp** (meaning "two-winged fruit") evergreen forest,
featuring tall tropical hardwood species and thick-stemmed lianas. There are
more than four hundred dipterocarp species in Malaysia, and it's not uncommon to find up to forty in just one small area of forest. Among other trees
present at Taman Negara are the majestic fifty-metre tall *tualang*, Southeast
Asia's tallest tree; many others have broad, snaking buttress roots and leaves the
size of dinner plates. Several species of **fruit trees**, such as durian, mango, guava
and rambutan also grow wild here.

Montane forest predominates above 1000m, mainly oak and native conifers
with a shrub layer of rattan and dwarf palm. Above 1500m on Gunung Tahan
is **cloudforest**, where trees are often cloaked by swirling mist, and the damp
boughs bear thick growths of mosses and ferns; at elevations of over 1700m,
miniature montane forest of rhododendron and fan palms is found.

Mammals

The best method of trying to see some of the larger herbivorous (grazing)
mammals is to spend the night in a **hide** overlooking a salt lick. There are six
hides in the park, and to maximize your chances of spotting mammals you need
to stay overnight at one. Animals commonly encountered include the Malayan
tapir, a species related to horses and rhinos, though pig-like in appearance with
a short, fat body, a long snout and black-and-white colouring. The **gaur** (wild
cattle) is dark in colour apart from its white leg patches, which look like ankle
socks. There are also several species of **deer**: the larger *sambar*; the *kijang* or
barking deer, the size of a roe deer; and the lesser and greater mouse deer, these
last two largely nocturnal, and not much bigger than rabbits.

Primates (monkeys and gibbons) are found throughout the park, although
they are quite shy since they have traditionally been hunted for food by the
park's indigenous groups. The dawn chorus of a white-handed **gibbon** troupe
– making a plaintive whooping noise – is not a sound which will be quickly
forgotten. Other primates include the long-tailed and pig-tailed **macaques**,

which come to the ground to feed, the latter identified by its shorter tail, brown fur and pinkish-brown face. There are dusky (or spectacled – with white patches around the eyes) and banded **leaf monkeys**, too, which can be recognized by their long, drooping tails (gibbons are tailless) and their habit of keeping their bodies hidden among the foliage. Whereas macaques sometimes feed on the ground, both leaf monkeys and gibbons keep to the trees.

Several **squirrel** species, including the black and common giant squirrels, are present in the park, and towards dusk there's a chance of seeing the nocturnal red flying squirrel shuffling along the highest branches of a tree before launching itself to glide across the forest canopy to an adjacent tree. This squirrel can make continuous glides of up to 100m at a time.

Other mammals you might encounter by – admittedly fairly remote – chance are the Asian **elephant**, with smaller ears and a more humped back than the African; **tigers**, of which a reasonably healthy population exists due to an abundance of prey and the relatively large size of the protected area; and **sun bears**. The bears are an interesting species: standing about 70cm high on all fours, and around 1.5m in length, they are dark brown or black, with muzzle and breast marked dirty white to dull orange, and live on fruit, honey and termites. Their behaviour towards humans can be unpredictable, particularly if there are cubs nearby.

Also present are **clouded leopards**, a beautifully marked cat species with a pattern of cloud-like markings on the sides of the body. They live mostly in the trees, crossing from bough to bough in their search for food, eating monkeys, squirrels and birds, which they swat with their claws; they're most active at twilight. Smaller predators include the **leopard cat** (around the size of a large domestic cat) and several species of nocturnal **civet**, some of which have been known to enter the hides at night in search of tourists' food. Smooth **otters** may also sometimes be seen, in small family groups along Sungai Tembeling.

Birds

Over 250 species of birds – including some of the most spectacular forest-dwelling birds in the world – have been recorded in Taman Negara, though many species are shy or only present in small numbers. Birds are at their most active from early to mid-morning, and again in the late afternoon and evening periods; the areas around Kuala Keniam, and the Kumbang and Tabing hides are particularly worth visiting.

Resident forest birds include several species of **green pigeon**, which feed on the fruiting trees; **bulbuls**, vocal, fruit-eating birds which often flock to feed; **minivets**, slender, colourful birds with long, graduated tails, white, yellow or red bands in the wings and outer tail feathers of the same colour; and **babblers**, various short-tailed, round-winged, often ground-dwelling species. The period from September to March is when the visitor can hope to encounter the greatest diversity of birds, with resident species joined by **wintering birds** from elsewhere in Asia, such as warblers and thrushes. At this time of year, up to seventy species altogether can be seen near the park headquarters, particularly if the trees are in fruit.

Pittas, brilliantly coloured in hues of red, yellow, blue and black, are ground-dwelling birds generally occurring singly or in pairs, though they are notoriously shy and difficult to approach. The resident species are the giant, garnet and banded pittas, with blue-winged and hooded pittas being winter visitors.

In addition, several species of pheasant may be seen along the trails, including the **Malaysian peacock pheasant**, a shy bird with a blue-green crest and a patch of bare, orange facial skin; the feathers of the back and tail have green *ocelli* (eye-spots). The crested and crestless **fireback** are similar species of pheasant, differing in the crested fireback's black crest, white tail-plumes, blue-sheen upper parts and white-streaked (rather than plain black) belly. The **great argus** is the largest pheasant species present in the area, with the male birds reaching a maximum of 1.7m in length including their long tail feathers; its penetrating "kwow wow" series of call notes is audible most days in the park. Finally, the mountain **peacock pheasant** – very similar in plumage to the Malaysian peacock pheasant and endemic to Malaysia – is found high on Gunung Tahan.

You may also see birds of prey, with two of the most common species, the **crested serpent eagle** and the **changeable hawk eagle**, often spotted soaring over gaps in the forest canopy. The crested serpent eagle (with a 75cm wingspan; about the size of a buzzard) can be identified by the black and white bands on the trailing edge of the wings and on the tail.

Other species confined to tropical forests are **trogons** (brightly coloured, mid-storey birds), of which five species are present at Taman Negara; and several species of **hornbill** – large, broad-winged, long-tailed forest birds with huge, almost outlandish bills.

Reptiles and amphibians

Reptiles and amphibians are well represented in the area. **Monitor lizards** (which can grow to be over 2m long) can be found close to the park headquarters, as can **skinks** (rather short-legged types of lizard which wriggle as much as run among the leaf litter).

Several species of snakes are present, too, including the reticulated **python** (which feeds on small mammals and birds and can grow to a staggering 9m in length), and the king and common **cobras**; king cobras, the largest venomous snake in the world, grow up to five metres long. These are all pretty rare in Taman Negara, though, and you're more likely to come across **whip snakes** (which eat insects and lizards) and – most common of all – harmless green **tree snakes** (which, not surprisingly, live in the trees, and eat small lizards).

Fraser's Hill

At **Fraser's Hill**, visitors can escape the stultifying tropical heat of the lowlands and venture into the cool breezes and fogs of the mountain forests, where ferns and pitcher plants cling to damp, moss-covered branches. It's a noted area for birdwatching, with the hill itself harbouring several montane species of birds, while mammals represented in the area include those normally restricted to more mountainous regions, in addition to some lowland species.

Much of the **forest** at Fraser's Hill is in pristine condition and the route there takes you from lowland forest through sub-montane to montane forest. Higher up on the hill, there are more evergreen tree species present, while the very nature of the vegetation changes: the trees are more gnarled and stunted, and the boughs heavily laden with dripping mosses and colourful epiphytic orchids (ie, orchids which grow on other plants and trees).

Mammals

The more strictly montane mammal species at Fraser's Hill include the **siamang gibbon**, a large, all-black gibbon that spends its time exclusively in

CONTEXTS | Wildlife

trees. There are also several species of **bat**, including the montane form of the Malayan fruit bat and the grey fruit bat; and several **squirrel** species such as the mountain red-bellied squirrel and the tiny Himalayan striped squirrel, the latter species having a pattern of black-and-yellow stripes running along the length of its back. Lowland mammal species which may be encountered are the tiger, clouded leopard, sun bear and leaf monkeys (see the "Taman Negara" section of this piece). However, most of these are scarce here, and you can realistically expect to encounter only monkeys, squirrels and, possibly, siamangs.

Birds

A feature of montane forest bird flocks is the **mixed feeding flock**, which may contain many different species. These pass rapidly through an area of forest searching for insects as they go, and it's quite likely that different observers will see entirely different species in one flock. Species which commonly occur within these flocks are the **lesser racket-tailed drongo**, a black crow-like bird with long tail streamers; the **speckled piculet**, a small spotted woodpecker; and the **blue nuthatch**, a small species – blue-black in colour with a white throat and pale eye ring – which runs up and down tree trunks. Several species of brightly coloured **laughing thrushes**, small thrush-sized birds which spend time foraging on the ground or in the understorey, also occur in these flocks. One sound to listen out for is the distinctive cackling "took" call of the **helmeted hornbill** echoing up from the lowlands.

Fraser's Hill itself peaks at 1310m at the High Pines, where a ridge trail begins. Here, there's the possibility of encountering rare species unlikely to be seen at lower altitudes, including the brown bullfinch and the **cutia** – a striking bird, with blue cap, black eyeline and tail, white underparts barred black and a chestnut-coloured back.

Tony Stones, with additional contributions by Charles de Ledesma.

Music

At its best, Malaysian music boasts some of the finest sounds never to burst onto the radar of the West's Africa-centric world-music scene. Malaysia's contemporary sounds encompass everything from Malay rock to English-language indie (also a notable feature of Singapore's scene), Chinese grunge and Tamil hip-hop. And despite Malaysia's rapid modernization, traditional sounds are clinging on, including music to accompany folk dances, as well as the largely hidden delights of the indigenous music of Sarawak and Sabah.

A brief survey can't hope to cover this diversity, and thus here the focus is on Malay sounds, both traditional and modern, plus the tribal music of East Malaysia. For a broader exploration of Malaysian music, consult the *Encyclopedia of Malaysia* series (published by Editions Didier Millet in Kuala Lumpur and Singapore; Volume 8 covers the performing arts in general, and has some useful sections on music) or the excellent musicological monograph *The Music of Malaysia*, by Patricia Matursky and Tan Sooi Beng (Ashgate Publishing). Websites such as Malaysia's ⓦricecooker.kerbau.com and Singapore's ⓦwww.audioreload.com offer a glimpse of the alternative scene.

Influences

Malaysia's music betrays a wide range of influences. The peoples of Malaysia share in the wider heritage of Indonesia and the Philippines, the cultures of the three nations having borrowed and adapted elements from one another from pre-Islamic times down to the present day. Furthermore, Malaysia lies at the hub of global trade routes which have brought a rich mixture of influences, most significantly Islam from the Middle East. Much of this can be seen in the instruments used in Malay music: the bronze gong is thought to be part of the Chinese influence, the Indonesian gamelan ensemble being one of its most refined derivatives; the skin drum in its many forms was first brought in by seafaring Arabs, who also introduced the three-string spiked fiddle (*rebab*), lute (*gambus*) and the choral tradition of *hadrah* (religious songs accompanied by tambourines); a species of oboe (*serunai*) is thought to be of Indian origin. To this mix, the aboriginal inhabitants of the Peninsula and Borneo contributed strong rhythms, reed flutes, and a wooden xylophone to the modern-day "national music". The policy of borrowing and adapting has continued, and today, traditional styles are still played on violins, accordions and hand drums, though electric guitars and electronic keyboards may also feature.

Traditional styles

Authentic traditional Malaysian music still exists these days but has only a small presence on the CD racks in Malaysian music stores. You're more likely to come across live performances, particularly **asli** (literally "original"), a slow traditional music played by small ensembles. These also play the faster **joget** and **zapin** dances, the former with Portuguese roots, the latter considered typically Malay (and popular throughout the Peninsula), though actually of Arabic origin. In their traditional form, both *asli* and *zapin* dances or songs are accompanied by the *gambus* and a couple of two-headed frame drums beating out an interlocking rhythm. These are often supplemented by violin and harmonium (or accordion), flute, keyboards and guitars. The traditional *joget* ensemble is not dissimilar to those for *asli*, but in Terengganu there's also *joget-gamelan*, featuring an assembly of ten gongs and metallophones, which originally came from the Riau islands of Indonesia.

Ghazal, associated particularly with Kuala Lumpur and Johor, is a sentimental form of folk pop derived from the poetic love songs of Indian light classical music. The great star of the genre remains the late Kamariah Noor, whose recordings are still available. Her voice, both intense and languid, enabled her to bend and hold notes, milking them for every last drop of emotion. Kamariah often sang with her husband Hamzah Dolmat, Malaysia's greatest **rebab** player, famous for his slow rather mournful style combined with a wonderful melodic creativity.

The six-stringed Arabic lute, known as *gambus* in Malay, is used as an accompanying instrument for singers of *ghazal* and *asli* music as well as in ensembles for dance music. Malaysia's recognized master of the *gambus* was the late Fadzil Ahmad, who started performing in the 1950s and later assisted in the formation of several cultural groups dedicated to preserving traditional Malay-Arabic music.

Melaka

Like its buildings, a strange mix of Portuguese, Dutch and Chinese architecture, **Melaka**'s music is a confluence and compromise between styles. Modern Malaysia accepts the Malaccan *ronggeng* as its own "folk music" – a music played on the violin and the button accordion, accompanied by frame drums, hand drums and sometimes a brass gong. The melodies speak of their Portuguese origin, with faint echoes of Moorish intervals and motifs. The fiddle holds the floor until the singers join in, when it recedes to a plaintive accompaniment.

Another musical genre associated with Melaka is **dondang sayang**, a slow, intense, majestic form led by sharp percussive drum rolls which trigger a shift in melody or a change in the pace of rhythm. This is a typically Malaysian style, in fact an amalgam of Hindu, Arabic, Chinese and Portuguese instruments and musical styles. *Tabla* and harmonium, double-headed *gendang* drum and tambourine create the rhythm, while the violin (and sometimes the accordion) carries the melody.

The east coast

Kelantan, **Terengganu** and southeastern Thailand share a distinctive Malay culture, seaborne traffic having linked this region more to the cultures of the South China Sea and less to Western influence than is the case with the west coast of the Peninsula.

A Kelantan performance of *silat*, the Malay martial art, is accompanied by a small ensemble of long drums, Indian oboes and gongs, which generate a loose set of cross rhythms. The music rises to a crescendo as the *silat* intensifies, the *serunai* screeching atonally while the drums and gongs quicken their loose rhythm. **Kertok**, a form of music which originated with the Orang Asli, is played by a very different sort of ensemble, in which six to twelve men play pentatonically tuned wooden xylophones. The rhythmic melody they hammer out in unison is fast and jolly and all the players end each piece at precisely the same time, raising their beaters overhead as they do so.

Wayang kulit (shadow puppetry), an ancient artistic tradition of Southeast Asia, serves as a good example of the meeting and intermingling of cultures in the Malay Peninsula: the *wayang*'s roots are in the Hindu epic, the *Ramayana*; the craftsmanship of the puppets is Indonesian/Malay; while the music is produced by something similar to a *silat* ensemble, enhanced by the wooden xylophone and sometimes small hand drums. Another form of Malaysian drama, **mak yong**, traditionally performed as entertainment for the court ladies of Kelantan, is accompanied by the music of *rebab* or violin, oboes and percussion. A pre-Islamic art form, *mak yong* is disapproved of by some, and is currently banned in religiously conservative Kelantan.

The popular traditional music of the east coast is **dikir barat**, probably based on *zikir*, an Islamic (particularly Sufi) style of singing, featuring verses in praise of Allah sung to the beat of a single tambourine, sometimes accompanied by hand-clapping. *Dikir barat*, practised at evening markets or neighbourhood parties, features teams of men singing impromptu verses on local politics, village gossip or any subject of general interest.

East Malaysia

The music of the various tribal groups of **Borneo** has been preserved in a relatively pure form, without the admixtures of European and other Asian styles that have entered into Malay music. That said, the music now fights for survival against social change and against the radios, televisions and CDs that have made their way into the remotest river tributary or mountain valley. However, a recent increase in interest in Borneo's culture – both from tourists and the "root searching" urban middle classes of East Malaysia – may yet help to reverse the decline in interest in traditional music.

In a longhouses, everybody and their grandmother can play the **gongs**, on which traditional **Iban** music accompanying dances is played. The lead instruments – the "melody gongs" – are heirloom pieces in sets of six or eight, laid in a wooden frame over a bed of string and played with two beaters. Rhythm is kept by the larger gongs, which are suspended singly.

The principal Orang Ulu instrument, the lute-like **sape**, has seen a conscious attempt at a revival, and is one of the real joys of Sarawak music when played by a master. Visually striking, the *sapé* has a body hollowed out from a single block of wood, and often painted with traditional geometric designs. There are three or four strings, of which the lowest is the melody string and the others drones. *Sapés* are commonly played in pairs, or even larger groups, possibly because they are rather soft despite their large size – though these days some players, notably **Jerry Kamit**, have fitted their instruments with electric-guitar pickups. In an ensemble, *sapés* may be joined by a wooden xylophone, whose top end can be fastened to an upright support (in a longhouse, one of the house pillars) while the lower end is tied to the performer's waist. In the Orang Ulu longhouses you often see old "mouth-organs", called *keluré* or *kediri*, made from a gourd into which are fixed bamboo pipes; these instruments were once used to accompany dances or processions, though nowadays you really have to hunt to find anyone who can play one.

There are, however, many types of **mouth and nose flute** all over Borneo. The **Lun Bawang** people are particularly active players and have formed "bamboo bands" incorporating every flute known to man, including a "bass flute" that looks more like a bamboo tuba than anything else. Schools and villages of east Sarawak and west Sabah have resounding bamboo bands, playing anything from *Onward Christian Soldiers* to the patriotic march *Malaysia Berjaya*.

The ethnic music of Sarawak and Sabah may be heard during harvest festivals (in June; see the chapters on these two states for more details) and at the Rainforest World Music Festival in Kuching (see p.447).

Contemporary music

Modern music in Malay was almost entirely Indonesian, of the sentimental **kroncong** variety, until **P. Ramlee**'s mellifluous baritone sang its way into Malaya's heart in the 1950s. Penang-born, Ramlee (1929–73) started crooning and writing songs during his teens, landing himself an invitation to become involved in the Malay film industry, then centred in Singapore. He soon became one of the biggest Malay stars of the era, appearing in (and later also directing) dozens of films, for which he composed and performed some gorgeous melodies. Musically, he steered Malay singing along a new course, abbreviating the songs, adapting the folk instrument repertoire and also often recording with a dance hall orchestra, reflecting the popularity of Latin ballroom music in the postwar period. Ramlee's great duets with his wife, Saloma, are regarded as Malaysian pop's glorious dawn.

Prominent among performers of "modern classical" Malay songs is **Sharifah Aini**, whose strong, sweet voice seems to improve with the years. In the popularity stakes, however, it's **Siti Nurhaliza** who is right at the front of the pack. Equally at home with both contemporary and traditional styles, she is regarded by her many fans as having genuine international appeal, but has yet to make a breakthrough abroad. **Sheila Majid** is also among Malaysia's best-known pop stars and was the first Malaysian to penetrate the Asian market, particularly in Indonesia. Her foundation in classical music has stood her in good stead as she sings her way from soft rock towards jazz – mostly in the Malay *balada* genre, though she is equally at home in English.

For one reason or another, Malay audiences have a particular affinity with rock, often 1970s-style pop-rock or straightforward heavy metal, though grunge has also had a big impact. Long-established rockers M. Nasir and Ramli Sarip, both Singapore-born though based in KL, retain a major following. Arguably the greatest pop musician Singapore has ever produced, singer-artist-actor **M. Nasir** remains, sadly, relatively unknown in the country of his birth except among the Malay community, but has over his 25-year career written more hits (many for other performers) and won more industry awards than anyone else, and not without good reason; at his best, he's a genuinely distinctive, articulate songsmith with an ear for a great tune, yet not given to the formulaic crassness that the Malaysian music industry tends to be afflicted by – and he really can sing. **Ramli Sarip** is nearly as iconic, a kind of Malaysian Neil Young, with a voice that makes Rod Stewart's sound positively velvety.

Among a number of disparate trends in recent years has been the advent of Malay rap and hip-hop, spearheaded by groups such as **KRU**, **Too Phat** and the more politically conscious **Ahlifiqir**. These groups have been no strangers to controversy in their lyrics, something that could not be less true of groups allied to the other major vogue of recent years, the style known as **nasyid** – the Muslim equivalent of gospel pop. Reflecting the more conservative bent of the last couple of decades, *nasyid* is performed by all-male or all-female groups to the accompaniment of drums and tambourines. Foremost in this vein is the group **Raihan**, whose debut album *Puji-Pujian* sold an unprecedented 600,000 copies in the late 1990s. Having sustained a successful recording career ever since, they are among very few Malaysian groups to perform outside Asia regularly.

Not a *nasyid* singer as such, but certainly the poster boy for the more pious side of current pop, is **Mawi**. A sometime religious education teacher from Johor, he was propelled into the limelight – amid frenzied press interest – after he won a nationally televised talent contest in 2005. The Malaysian media's obsession with Mawi has barely died down at the time of writing, a year on from his arrival on the scene, but it remains to be seen whether, despite a reasonable debut album, he will prove to be anything other than a flash in the pan.

Discography

Very few recordings of Malaysian music see the light of day abroad, so shop around at Tower Records in KL for mainstream releases, or try the various outlets in the Campbell Shopping Centre in KL (on Jalan Dang Wangi, not far from Little India) or the Queensway Shopping Centre in Singapore (at the junction of Queensway and Alexandra Road).

Traditional

Fadzil Ahmad *Raja Gambus Malaysia* (Ahas Productions). Featuring instrumentals as well as songs, this is a great illustration of the art of Fadzil Ahmad, "Malaysia's king of the *gambus*", as the album's title has it.

Siti Nurhaliza *Cindai* (SRC, Malaysia). In a rootsy style, the band featuring *rebana* (drums), *tabla* and bamboo flutes, *Cindai* achieved sales of 200,000 copies, all the more staggering considering its release during the economic woes of the late 1990s.

Tusau Padan *Masters of the Sarawakian Sapé, featuring Tusau Padan* (Pan, Netherlands). Tusau Padan, who died

in 1996, was an acknowledged exponent of the *sapé*, but no recordings of his survive other than these, featuring traditional dances plus a couple of duets with younger players.

Various *Muzik Tarian Malaysia* (Life Records). Two-CD set of *joget, zapin* and other traditional dances played by a small instrumental ensemble. Classical and refined.

Various *The Rough Guide to the Music of Malaysia* (World Music Network). A largely traditional compilation with a couple of excellent tracks, notably the S.M. Salim/ Rosiah Chik duet *Berdendang Sayang*, plus Siti Nurhaliza's *Cindai*.

Contemporary

Ahlifiqir *Hari Ini Dalam Sejarah* (Powder/Warner Music, Malaysia). An audacious and uncompromising debut, in which Ahlifiqir stick their necks out by railing against the Malay establishment – a fact which appears all the more daring when you consider

that three of the four members come from Singapore, not a place noted for encouraging outspokeness among its citizens. As a blend of hip-hop and Malay melodic influences, it's totally listenable even if you don't understand the language.

Farid Ali *Turning Point: Gambus Goes Jazz* (Lite Ears). Like quite a few of his fellow alumni from Boston's prestigious Berklee College of Music, Farid started out as a jazz guitarist, influenced by the likes of George Benson and Earl Klugh. Later, however, he returned to his Malay roots by taking up the *gambus*, as showcased on this fine debut.

Alleycats *No. 1s* (Universal). Since the 1970s Penang's Alleycats, led by two Tamil brothers, David and Loga Arumugam, have been seen as Malaysia's answer to the Bee Gees, having chalked up a string of easy-listening hits, both uptempo tunes and ballads. If you ever get to sample a Malay karaoke bar, expect some tune or other from this twenty-song compilation (half of which was written by M. Nasir) to crop up at some point.

Butterfingers *Selamat Tinggal Dunia* (Butterworld/EMI). After releasing a slew of albums in English, grungers Butterfingers hit their creative peak with this, their first Malay-language CD, using northern slang (from Kedahan to Kelantanese) to convey their disenchantment with the new Malay middle class and the Malay mass media. A terrific slice of angst-ridden Malay rock.

Gerhana Skacinta *The New Authentic* (Clockwork/EMI). It's not every day a bunch of erstwhile punk rockers based in KL decides to take a swerve into Jamaican sounds. Somehow, the resulting Malay ska by Gerhana Skacinta makes total sense, best sampled on this, the group's second album, which features some stonking original tunes, plus their cover of the Jamaican evergreen *My Boy Lollipop*, which made the local charts.

Kembara *No. 1s* (Universal). A collection of Kembara's work from the early 1980s, when the group's

singer-songwriters – A. Ali, S. Amin Shahab and M. Nasir – created something of a folk rock sensibility, building up barbed tunes from acoustic settings and tackling in their lyrics issues such as youth unrest, urban migration and the plight of rice farmers.

Sheila Majid *Ratu* (Warner Music, Malaysia). Easy-listening Malaysian-style, and superbly produced, justifying her claim to being one of Malaysia's few jazz singers.

M. Nasir *No. 1 "Dulu Dan Kini"* (Sony BMG). A whole bunch of Malay pop-rock standards on one album, including *Ekspres Rakyat, Mentera Semerah Padi* and *Keroncong Untuk Ana*. Indispensable.

M. Nasir *Phoenix Bangkit* (Warner Music, Malaysia). The rootsiest, most ambitious record by this veteran musician, bringing together his top-drawer songwriting and a lush production that makes traditional and modern instruments sound completely at home with each other. The last three tracks, in particular, are absolute killers. Sadly the album proved too sophisticated for most of the domestic audience and was not released abroad until several years on, when it became one of very few Malaysian albums on iTunes.

Raihan *Puji-pujian* (Warner Music, Malaysia). Fresh young voices and sophisticated percussion character-ize Raihan's huge-selling debut, still worth picking up even though *nasyid* itself has come off the boil a bit of late.

P. Ramlee *Sri Kenangan Abadi Vols I–III* (EMI, Malaysia). Any of these three CDs are recommended as an introduction to P. Ramlee's most popular tunes.

S.M. Salim *Raja Irama Malaysia* (Warner Music, Malaysia). With a career stretching back to the days of Merdeka, S.M. Salim is one of the Malay music scene's great icons. This 26-track compilation ranges from much-loved *asli* and *joget* songs to hit-or-miss collaborations with the likes of M. Nasir, Siti Nurhaliza, Ramli Sarip, Raihan and the Malaysian Philharmonic Orchestra. File under "National Treasure".

Ramli Sarip *Kalam Kesturi* (Warner Music, Malaysia). A return-to-roots album, stylistically messy but still full of rousing melodies, including the superb *Nyanyian Serambi*.

Search *Terunggul* (Sony BMG). The story of Johor hard-rock outfit Search is one of good old rock 'n' roll excess, with a Malaysian spin. Back in the 1980s they were busted for drugs and – once a big issue given domestic sensibilities – long hair, but they've survived to become one of the most respected local bands. This 28-track retrospective, focusing on the band's chart-busting back catalogue, is of variable quality, but there are enough decent faux glam-rock numbers and ballads here to make it worth investigating.

Abridged from the article by Heidi Munan in *The Rough Guide to World Music*, second edition, with additional contributions from Richard Lim

Books and maps

There's no shortage of **books** about Malaysia, Singapore and Brunei. In the past, the majority tended to be penned by Western visitors to the region, but in the last couple of decades local writing and publishing in English has really gathered momentum. Among the more interesting independent **publishers** are Select Books (Ⓦ www.selectbooks.com.sg), Editions Didier Millet (Ⓦ www.edmbooks.com), Pelanduk (Ⓦ www.pelanduk .com), Media Masters (Ⓦ www.mediamasters.com.sg), Silverfish Books (Ⓦ www .silverfishbooks.com) and Natural History Publications, Borneo (Ⓦ www .nhpborneo.com). It's obviously easiest to buy locally published material while you're travelling around the countries concerned, though a few titles are available internationally, while Select Books and MPH (Ⓦ www.mph.com.my) have online mail-order services.

As for **maps**, it's unfortunately the case that many aren't up to speed with the frenzied highway construction taking place in the Peninsula. The *Rough Guide Map: Malaysia*, printed on tearproof plastic, does show all the key expressways, and is among the best of the general maps available. Otherwise, your best bet is to investigate the extensive range of Malaysia maps published by the Johor Bahru-based World Express Mapping. They produce maps of most of the individual states plus, usefully, KL and Penang, which are available in the larger Malaysian bookshops.

In the reviews that follow, books published outside the UK and US have the publisher listed. Books marked 🎿 are especially recommended, while o/p signifies that a book is out of print. Note that, as per Chinese custom, surnames are given first for those Chinese authors who don't have Christian names.

Travel and general interest

🎿 *Encyclopedia of Malaysia* (Editions Didier Millet). A brilliantly produced series of tomes on different aspects of Malaysia, all beautifully illustrated and – not always the case with locally published material – competently edited. The volumes on the performing arts and architecture are particularly recommended, but really, they're all good. Available to buy as individual volumes (11 out of 16 had been published at the time of writing) or as a set.

James Barclay *A Stroll Through Borneo* (o/p). A seminal tour of Sarawak and Indonesian Kalimantan by the doyen of travel writers; particularly perceptive on the Kayan ethnic group.

🎿 **John Bastin** (ed) *Travellers' Singapore*. Singapore-related vignettes from as early as 1819 and as late as the Japanese conquest of 1942.

Isabella Bird *The Golden Chersonese*. Delightful epistolary romp through old Southeast Asia, penned by the intrepid Bird, whose adventures in the Malay states in 1879 ranged from strolls through Singapore's streets to elephant-back rides and encounters with alligators. Available as a free download from various online libraries.

Margaret Brooke *My Life in Sarawak*. Engaging account by White Rajah Charles Brooke's wife of nineteenth-century Sarawak, which reveals a sympathetic attitude to her subjects (which extended to rubbing eau de cologne into a Dyak warrior's forehead). Her eye for detail conveys the wonder of an unprejudiced colonial embracing an alien culture.

Anthony Burgess *Little Wilson and Big God.* An application for a teaching post in Malaya while drunk on cider took Burgess ("novelist, composer, traveller, teacher, raconteur, linguist, soldier, husband, boozer, and amorous adventurer") to Kuala Kangsar's Malay College in 1954. His unerring eye for extraordinary characters and customary relish for cultural and semantic detail make the Asian segment of this autobiography an entertaining time capsule of 1950s Malaysia.

Harry Foster *A Beachcomber in the Orient.* Recently reissued in the US, this is a hilarious first-person account of a proto-backpacker who travelled through Malaya and other parts of Southeast Asia in the 1920s.

G.M. Gullick *They Came To Malaya.* A cornucopia of accounts and of people, places and events, written by the governors, planters and explorers who tamed Malaya.

Eric Hansen *Orchid Fever.* Hansen's epic search for the world's most elusive strain of orchid took him from the Bornean jungle to Kew Gardens and from the Orinoco River to the peat bogs of Minnesota. The resulting account is a funny and compelling tale of orchids and obsession.

Eric Hansen *Stranger in the Forest.* A gripping book, the result of a seven-month tramp through the forests of Sarawak and Kalimantan in 1982, that almost saw the author killed by a poison dart.

Judith M. Heimann *The Most Offending Soul Alive: Tom Harrisson and His Remarkable Life.* From his first expedition there in 1932 onwards,

Tom Harrisson's life was inextricably linked with Sarawak. Heimann's biography tracks Harrisson's many dealings with Borneo, from his wartime exploits raising a headhunter army against the Japanese, to his subsequent work as curator of the Sarawak Museum.

Agnes Keith *Land Below the Wind.* Bornean memories galore, in this charming account of expat life in prewar Sabah; Keith's true eye and assured voice produce a heart-warming picture of a way of life now long gone. Her naïve sketches complement perfectly the childlike wonder of the prose.

Victor T. King *The Best of Borneo Travel.* Compendium of extracts from Bornean travel writing since the sixteenth century; an interesting travelling companion.

Redmond O'Hanlon *Into The Heart of Borneo.* A hugely entertaining yarn recounting O'Hanlon's refreshingly amateurish romp through the jungle to a remote summit on the Sarawak/Kalimantan border, partnered by the English poet James Fenton.

Spenser St John *Life in the Forests of the Far East* (o/p). A description of an early ascent of Mount Kinabalu is a highlight of this animated nineteenth-century adventure, written by the personal secretary to Rajah Brooke.

Robert Twigger *Big Snake* (o/p). His hunt for the world's longest python takes Twigger on an entertaining and eventful jaunt from the sewers of KL to the forests of Sabah.

Michael Wise (ed) *Travellers' Tales of Old Singapore.* Identical in theme to Bastin's *Travellers' Singapore*, though Wise's selection of tales is the more catholic and more engrossing of the two.

History and politics

Munshi Abdullah *The Hikayat Abdullah*. Raffles' one-time clerk, Melaka-born Abdullah became diarist of some of the most formative years of Southeast Asian history; his first-hand account is crammed with illuminating vignettes and character portraits.

Syed Husin Ali *Two Faces (Detention without Trial)* (Insan, Malaysia). In 1974, Syed, a sociology professor at Universiti Malaya, was taken from his home and detained under the Internal Security Act. He was held for six years in Kamunting, Malaysia's own gulag; this is his harrowing, eye-opening story.

Barbara Watson Andaya and Leonard Andaya *The History of Malaysia*. Unlike more paternalistic histories penned by former colonists, this standard text on the region takes a more even-handed view of Malaysia, and finds time for cultural coverage, too.

Noel Barber *War of the Running Dogs*. Illuminates the Malayan Emergency with a novelist's eye for mood.

Nigel Barley *White Rajah*. A highly readable biography of Sir James Brooke, focusing particularly on letters and other primary sources.

James Bartholomew *The Richest Man in the World*. Despite an obvious (and admitted) lack of sources, Bartholomew's study of the Sultan of Brunei makes fairly engaging reading – particularly the astounding facts and figures used to illustrate the sultan's wealth.

David Brazil *Insider's Singapore*. An Aladdin's cave of Singaporean history and trivia that remains fascinating throughout.

Maurice Collis *Raffles* (Graham Brash). The most accessible and enjoyable biography of Sir Stamford Raffles.

Roy Follows *The Jungle Beat*. The Malaysian jungle proved as unforgiving an enemy as the Malayan Communist insurgents when Follows joined the Malay police in the 1950s. His story engages from beginning to end.

Mary Somers Heidhues *Southeast Asia: A Concise History*. A Thames & Hudson text packed with photographs and sketches reflecting the history of the region described within its readable prose.

John Hilley *Malaysia: Mahathirism, Hegemony and the New Opposition*. At last, the critical book on Malaysia's long-standing prime minister with much attention given to Mahathir's vilification of his deputy Anwar and the galvanization of the opposition movement that resulted.

Images of Asia series Maya Jayapal's *Old Singapore* and Sarnia Hayes Hoyt's *Old Malacca* and *Old Penang* chart the growth of three of the region's most important outposts, drawing on contemporary maps, sketches and photographs to engrossing effect.

Patrick Keith *Ousted* (Media Masters). Most of the largely young population of Malaysia and Singapore know little of the events which saw Singapore leaving the federation in 1965. And yet, as this excellent memoir by a former Malaysian government advisor demonstrates, many of the issues which led to the rift continue to shape both countries and their mutual ties today – Malaysia is still laden with ethnically based politics, while Singapore remains the fiefdom of the PAP.

Wendy Khadijah-Moore *Malaysia: A Pictorial History 1400–2003*

(Editions Didier Millet). If you're going to do coffee-table books on Malaysia's history, you could come up with a lot worse than this well-illustrated portable museum. Don't come to it expecting trenchant commentary, though: the Anwar affair, for instance, gets a mere couple of lines.

Lee Kuan Yew *The Singapore Story* (Times Editions). Spanning the first 42 years of Lee Kuan Yew's life, up to Singapore's separation from Malaysia in 1965, this first volume of memoirs by the granddaddy of contemporary Singapore is essential reading for anyone wanting the inside story on the island's huge economic expansion over the past fifty years.

Eric Lomax *The Railway Man*. Such is the power of Lomax's artless, redemptive and moving story of capture during the fall of Singapore, torture by the Japanese and reconciliation with his tormentor after fifty years, that many reviewers were moved to tears.

James Minchin *No Man Is An Island* (o/p). A well-researched, and at times critical study of Lee Kuan Yew, which refuses to kowtow to Singapore's ex-prime minister and is hence unavailable in Singapore itself.

Bob Reece *The White Rajahs of Sarawak* (Editions Didier Millet). A handsome coffee-table book about the extraordinary Brooke dynasty.

World War II and the Japanese occupation

Noel Barber *Sinister Twilight*. Documents the fall of Singapore to the Japanese, by re-imagining the crucial events of the period.

Russell Braddon *The Naked Island*. Southeast Asia under the Japanese: Braddon's disturbing yet moving first-hand account of the POW camps of Malaya, Singapore and Siam displays courage in the face of appalling conditions and treatment; worth scouring secondhand stores for.

Spencer Chapman *The Jungle is Neutral*. This riveting first-hand account of being lost, and surviving, in the Malay jungle during World War II reads like a breathless novel.

Peter Elphick *Singapore: The Pregnable Fortress*. Drawing on documents only made available in 1993, Elphick has produced the definitive history of the fall of Singapore, showing the gaffes, low morale and desertion that led to it; a scholarly tour de force.

Agnes Keith *Three Came Home*. Pieced together from scraps of paper secreted in latrines and teddy bears, this is a remarkable story of survival in the face of Japanese attempts to eradicate the "proudery and arrogance" of the West in the World War II prison camps of Borneo.

Colin Smith *Singapore Burning: Heroism and Surrender in World War II*. Highly detailed, definitive account of the fall of Singapore, written with a journalist's instinct for excitement.

Culture and society

Salleh Ben Joned *As I Please* (Skoob; Atrium). Named after his occasional column in the *New Straits Times*, Salleh's articles are candid observations on Malaysian society with titles such as "The Art of

Pissing" and "Kiss My Arse – In the Name of Common Humanity". Don't let this mislead you. Although he's outspoken, Salleh is thoughtful and intensely proud of his Malay roots.

James Harding and Ahmad Sarji *P. Ramlee: The Bright Star* (Pelanduk). An uncritical but enjoyable biography of the Malay singer, actor and director sometimes likened to Malaysia's Harry Belafonte, this book gives a blow-by-blow account of most of P. Ramlee's films. More importantly, it's a lovely window onto what seems like a different era – though only half a century ago – when Singapore was the centre of the Malay entertainment universe, and when things felt, frankly, a little more carefree and less pious than today.

Tom Harrisson *A World Within* (o/p). The only in-depth description of the Kelabit peoples of Sarawak, and a cracking good World War II tale courtesy of Harrisson, who parachuted into the Kelabit Highlands to organize resistance against the Japanese.

Leslie Layton *Songbirds in Singapore*. A delightful examination of songbird-keeping in Singapore, detailing all facets of the pastime, from its growth in the nineteenth century.

Gerrie Lim *Invisible Trade: High-Class Sex for Sale in Singapore* (Monsoon Books). This exposé of the escort industry in Singapore makes for an entertaining but somewhat unsatisfying read, its basic flaw being the assumption that showing Singapore to be much less squeaky clean than it appears is somehow revelatory.

Andro Linklater *Wild People*. As telling and as entertaining a glimpse into the lifestyle of the Iban

as you could find, depicting their age-old traditions surviving amid the T-shirts, baseball caps and rock posters of Western influence.

Heidi Munan *Culture Shock! Malaysia*. Cultural do's and don'ts for the leisure and business traveller to the region, spanning subjects as diverse as handing over business cards and belching after a fine meal.

Colin Nicholas *The Orang Asli and the Contest for Resources* (International Workgroup for Indigenous Affairs). An invaluable read if you intend to spend time among Orang Asli communities in the interior, this puts into context the way in which the Orang Asli have been both drawn into mainstream society and yet marginalized over the years.

Karim Raslan *Ceritalah: Malaysia in Transition* (Times Editions). Collection of the young lawyer-turned-journalist's articles from local newspapers and magazines, providing an insight into modern Malaysia. Raslan may at times be sentimental and an apologist for the excesses of Malaysia's political and social set-up, but he is always entertaining. The essay "Roots", about his family, is excellent.

James Ritchie *Who Gives A DAM! The Bakun Odyssey* (Wisma Printing). Engaging, balanced account of the social and political consequences of the controversial Bakun Dam in Sarawak where over 10,000 indigenous peoples wer moved from their lands to make way for a massive development project.

Tan Kok Seng *Son Of Singapore*. Tan Kok Seng's candid and sobering autobiography on the underside of the Singaporean success story, telling of hard times spent as a coolie.

Cookbooks

Aziza Ali *Aziza's Creative Malay Cuisine* (PEN). A very posh take on Malay food, by the woman who, for years, ran one of the best Malay restaurants in Singapore. Naturally, it's quite southern in approach, so you won't find *nasi kerabu* or *laksam* in here, but then many of the recipes are intended more to impress at dinner parties than to reflect what's served on the street.

Betty Saw *Rasa Malaysia* (Marshall Cavendish). A nicely illustrated cookbook that covers dozens of the standard dishes you'll find served at food courts and in homes around the country, including various Chinese and Nonya recipes, though very little South Indian fare. It's all organized by state, which helps give a feel for regional cuisine, but annoyingly there's no index.

Natural history and ecology

Odoardo Beccari *Wanderings in the Great Forests of Borneo* (o/p). Vivid c.1900 account, reissued in the 1990s though now hard to find, of the natural and human environment of Sarawak.

Chua Ee Kiam *Chek Jawa: Discovering Singapore's Biodiversity* (Select Books). The shallow tidal flats of Chek Jawa, on Pulau Ubin's east coast were saved from the redevelopers in 2001. This beautiful book traces its salvation, and features stunning photography of its rich wildlife.

Fadzilah Majid Cooke *The Challenge of Sustainable Forests*. A thought provoking work, which presents the argument that destruction or conservation of forests is, above all, a social question.

G.W.H. Davison and Chew Yen Fook *A Photographic Guide to Birds of Borneo*; **M. Strange and A. Jeyarajasingam** *A Photographic Guide to Birds of Peninsular Malaysia and Singapore*; **Charles M. Francis** *A Photographic Guide to the Mammals of Southeast Asia*. Well-keyed and user-friendly, these slender volumes carry oodles of glossy plates that make positive identifying a breeze.

Robin Hanbury-Tenison *Mulu: The Rain Forest*. Hanbury-Tenison's overview of the flora, fauna and ecology of the rainforest, the result of a 1977 Royal Geographical Society field trip into Sarawak's Gunung Mulu National Park; makes enlightening reading.

Jeffrey McNeely *Soul of the Tiger*. Offers insights into the wide-ranging importance of wildlife for Southeast Asia's indigenous peoples. Particularly fascinating is the chapter on Borneo, which suggests that birds are viewed as "messengers from the gods" in local culture.

Ivan Polunin *Plants and Flowers of Malaysia* (Times Editions). A single volume simply can't do justice to the vast quantity of flora packed into tropical rainforest, and this doesn't attempt to try, instead providing a handy illustrated survey of plants in a variety of environments, from sandy beach to upland forest.

Alfred Russel Wallace *The Malay Archipelago*. Wallace's peerless account of the flora and fauna of Borneo, based on travels made between 1854 and 1862 – during which time he collected over one hundred thousand specimens. Still required reading for nature lovers.

Art and architecture

Jacques Dumarcay *The House in Southeast Asia*. An overview of regional domestic architecture, covering the rituals and techniques of house construction.

Norman Edwards *Singapore House and Residential Life*. The development of the Singapore detached house, traced from early plantation villas, through colonial bungalows to Chinese landowners' mansions; beguiling photographs.

M. Heppell *Iban Art: Sexual Selection and Severed Heads* (KIT Publishers). Impressive illustrated volume exploring how Iban betrothals were crucially influenced by the prowess of the prospective partners at producing artwork and artefacts, as well as head-hunting.

Khoo Su Nin *Streets of George Town Penang* (Janus Print). This photograph-driven guide to Penang's traditional architecture is the perfect companion while strolling the lanes of Georgetown. Try the Cheong Fatt Tze Mansion in Georgetown or Select Books in Singapore for a copy.

Lim Huck Chin and Fernando Jorge *Malacca: Voices From the Street* (self-published; www.malaccavoices.com). By the architects responsible for the restoration of 8 Heeren Street (see p.373), this labour of love chronicles the evolution of Melaka over the generations, street by street. The book also documents the decline of traditional trades and pastimes, and the degeneration of some areas into a crass modernity – sadly, a fate mirroring what has happened to parts of Penang, KL and Singapore. Printed on heavy-duty paper and illustrated with the author's own colour photographs.

Farish A. Noor and Eddin Khoo *The Spirit of Wood: The Art of Malay Woodcarving* (Periplus). Much weightier in tone than your average coffee-table book, this deals not only with the superb woodcarving produced on the east coast of the Peninsula and in southern Thailand, but also with the whole pre-Islamic consciousness that subtly imbues the woodcarver's art. Packed with great photos, too, of gorgeous timber mosques, incredibly detailed *kris* hilts and the like.

Roxana Waterson *The Living House*. More authoritative than Dumarcay's slender introduction to Southeast Asian dwellings, and required reading for anyone with an interest in the subject.

Robert Winzeler *The Architecture of Life and Death in Borneo*. Highly readable, illustrated study of the traditional architecture of Borneo, looking at the evolution of longhouses over the years and symbolism in building design.

Fiction

Charles Allen *Tales from the South China Seas*. Memoirs of the last generation of British colonists, in which predictable Raj attitudes prevail, though some of the drama of everyday lives, often in inhospitable conditions, is evinced with considerable pathos.

Gopal Baratham *Moonrise, Sunset*. When How Kum Menon's fiancée is murdered while sleeping by his side in Singapore's East Coast Park, it seems everyone he knows has a motive. How Kum turns detective, and an engaging whodunnit emerges. In the earlier *A Candle or the Sun*, Baratham swallows hard and tackles the thorny issue of political corruption.

Anthony Burgess *The Long Day Wanes*. Burgess's Malayan trilogy – *Time for a Tiger*, *The Enemy in the Blanket* and *Beds in the East* – published in one volume, provides a witty and acutely observed vision of 1950s Malaya, underscoring the racial prejudices of the period. *Time for a Tiger*, the first novel, is worth reading for the Falstaffian Nabby Adams alone.

James Clavell *King Rat*. Set in Japanese-occupied Singapore, a gripping tale of survival in the notorious Changi Prison.

Joseph Conrad *Lord Jim*. Southeast Asia provides the backdrop to the story of Jim's desertion of an apparently sinking ship and subsequent efforts to redeem himself; modelled upon the sailor, A.P. Williams, Jim's character also yields echoes of Rajah Brooke of Sarawak.

Alastair Dingwall (ed) *South-east Asia Traveller's Literary Companion*. Among the bite-sized essays in this gem of a book are enlightening segments on Malaysia and Singapore, into which are crammed biopics, a reading list and historical, linguistic and literary background. Excerpts range from classical Malayan literature to work by the nations' leading contemporary lights.

J.G. Farrell *The Singapore Grip*. Lengthy novel – Farrell's last – of World War II Singapore in which real and fictitious characters flit from tennis to dinner party as the countdown to the Japanese occupation begins.

Henri Fauconnier *The Soul of Malaya*. Fauconnier's semi-autobiographical novel is a lyrical, sensory tour of the plantations, jungle and beaches of early-twentieth-century Malaya, and pierces deeply into the underside of the country.

Lloyd Fernando *Scorpion Orchid*; *Green is the Colour* (Landmark Books, Singapore). Social politics form the basis of Fernando's works. In *Scorpion Orchid*, he concerns himself with the difficulties of adjusting to the move towards Merdeka and new nationhood; *Green is the Colour* is a remarkable novel, exploring the deep-seated racial tensions brought to light by the Kuala Lumpur demonstrations of May 1969.

K.S. Maniam *The Return; In A Far Country; Haunting the Tiger*. The purgative writings of this Tamil-descended Malaysian author are strong, highly descriptive and humorous – essential reading.

Wong Phui Nam *Ways of Exile*. Chinese-Malaysian poet's first collection published outside Malaysia; evocative works rooted in the interaction of cultures and ethnicity.

Rex Shelley *The Shrimp People* (Times). Eurasian family saga, critically acclaimed in Singapore, that's played out against the backdrop of the years of race riots and confrontation in Singapore, Malaysia and Indonesia.

I.K. Ong and C.Y. Loh (eds) *Skoob Pacifica Anthology No. 2*. A compendium of writings from the Pacific Rim, including K.S. Maniam and Salleh Ben Joned, rubbing shoulders with the likes of Toni Morrison.

W. Somerset Maugham *Short Stories Volume 4*. Peopled by hoary sailors, bored plantation-dwellers and colonials wearing mutton-chop whiskers and *topees*, Maugham's short stories resuscitate Malaya c.1900; quintessential colonial literature graced by an easy style and a steady eye for a story.

Paul Theroux *Saint Jack; The Consul's File*. *Saint Jack* tells the compulsively bawdy tale of Jack Flowers, an ageing American who supplements his earnings at a Singapore ship's chandlers by pimping for Westerners; Jack's jaundiced eye and Theroux's rich prose open windows on Singapore's past. In *The Consul's File*, the fictitious American consul to interior Malaya recounts a series of short stories.

Leslie Thomas *The Virgin Soldiers*. The bawdy exploits of teenage British Army conscripts snatching all the enjoyment they can, before being sent to fight in troubled 1950s Malaya.

Beth Yahp *The Crocodile Fury* (Strategic Information Research). Described by one reviewer as a "spicy Malaysian curry" to Amy Tan's "lightly seasoned Chinese soup", Yahp has produced a garlicky, rambunctious storytelling treat that shadows the lives of three women – grandmother, mother and daughter – in colonial and post-colonial Malaysia.

C

CONTEXTS | Books and maps

Language

Language

Language

M alay, officially referred to as Bahasa Melayu (literally "Malay language"), is the national language of Malaysia, Singapore and Brunei. Part of the Austronesian language family, it's an old tongue, which was refined by its use in the ancient kingdom of Srivijaya and during the fifteenth-century Melaka Sultanate into a language of prestige, becoming something of a regional lingua franca. Native speakers of Malay are found not just in Peninsular Malaysia and northern Borneo but also in pockets of hugely populous Indonesia, where a version of Malay has been adopted as the official language, designated Bahasa Indonesia.

Of course, Malay is only one of many languages used in the three countries covered in this book. In Singapore, English, Mandarin and Tamil are also official tongues, with English pre-eminent as the language of government and business, while Hokkien is the most used regional Chinese dialect. In Malaysia itself, English retains an important position in business and intellectual discourse, Tamil is widely spoken among the Indian community, while Mandarin is much used by the Chinese, as are Chinese dialects such as Cantonese (especially in KL and Ipoh) and Hokkien (in Penang, Johor and on the east coast).

In practice, you'll be able to get by with **English** except in remote areas and in the more Malay-dominated parts of the country, such as the east coast and the north of the Peninsula, where it really does pay to pick up a few words of Malay, especially since the basics are simple enough to learn. Besides, it's entertaining to get to grips with a tongue which, like English, is clearly a ready absorber of loan words. The influence of English on modern Malay is readily apparent to most travellers, and with an awareness of Asian languages, it's not hard to discern the huge infusion of words from Sanskrit (thanks to the ancient impact of Hinduism on Southeast Asia), such as *jaya* ("success") and *negara* ("country"), as well as from Arabic, which has contributed words like *maaf* ("sorry") and many terms to do with Islam.

To pick up the language, it's best to buy a coursebook that focuses on **vernacular** Malay, as our vocabulary section does, rather than the formal language used in print and in broadcasting. The most recommendable book by some way is *A Course in Conversational Malay* by Malcolm W. Mintz (SNP Publishing Singapore).

Pronunciation

Malay was once written in Arabic script, but over the years this has been almost completely supplanted by a Romanized form. However, the Romanized **spellings** are prone to inconsistencies, as reforms meant to achieve uniformity with Bahasa Indonesia aren't strictly adhered to. Thus it is, for example, that *baru*, "new", crops up in variant forms in place names like Johor Bahru and Kota Bharu, while new and old spellings of certain very common words still coexist, for example *sungai/sungei, kampung/kampong, kucing/kuching,* and so forth.

Spelling quirks aside, Bahasa Malaysia is one of the more straightforward languages to pronounce, once you get your head round a few rules. One basic

Manglish and Singlish

As diverting and as incomprehensible as Jamaican patois, Manglish and Singlish are aberrant forms of English widely spoken in Malaysia and Singapore respectively. They're really two sides of the same coin: in both, conventional English syntax gives way to a word order that's more akin to that of Malay or Chinese, and tenses and pronouns are discarded. Ask someone if they've ever been abroad, and you might be answered "I ever", while enquiring whether they've just been shopping might yield "Go, come back already". Pronunciation is so staccato that many words are rendered almost unrecognizable – "traffic light", for example, might be rendered "traffylie". Responses are almost invariably distilled down to single-word replies, often repeated for stress. Request something in a shop and you'll hear "have, have", or "got, got". Other stock manglings of English include:

ackchwurly	"Actually", used as a sentence starter
aidontch-main	"I don't mind"
baiwanfriwan	"Buy one and you'll get one free", a sales ploy
betayudon(lah)	"You'd better not do that!"
debladigarmen	A contraction of "the bloody government"
is it?	(pronounced *eezeet*?) "Really?"
tingwat	"What do you think?"
watudu	"What can we do?", a rhetorical question
yusobadwan	"You're such a bad one!" meaning "that's not very nice!"

Suffixes and **exclamations** drawn from Malay and Hokkien complete this patois, the most ubiquitous being the Malay intensifier "lah", which seems to finish off just about every other utterance. In Malaysia you may hear the Malay question marker "kah" at the ends of queries, while Chinese on both sides of the Causeway might apply the suffix "ah", as in "so cheap one ah", which translates as "is it really that cheap?" or "wow, that's cheap" depending on the intonation; "ah" can also mean "yes" if on its own, especially if accompanied by a nod of the head. If Manglish and Singlish have you totally baffled, you might try raising your eyes to the heavens and crying either "ayoh" (with a drop of tone on the second syllable) or "alamak", both expressions denoting exasperation or even regret at the situation.

Amusing though all this linguistic deviation is, the governments of both countries are concerned at how **standards of English** appear to be slipping. During the colonial period, the minority who could speak English tended to have a fair facility for the language. Today virtually everyone learns some English in school (in Singapore, English-language schools dominate) but too often students emerge with a weak grasp of the language, and sometimes with only a mediocre appreciation of their mother tongue to boot. In Malaysia, former prime minister Mahathir Mohammed recognized the problem when, at the end of his career, he reintroduced the use of English in mathematics and science lessons, thus back-pedalling on his own longstanding policy of emphasizing Malay in state education. For its part, Singapore, a country with a history of preachy state campaigns, has seen the creation of the government-run Speak Good English movement (@www.speakgoodenglish.org.sg), rejoicing in the faintly awkward slogan "Speak up, speak out, speak well".

point to remember is that the consonants **k, p, t** have slightly less force in Malay than in English (to be precise, they aren't aspirated in Malay); if you emulate the sounds at the start of the Spanish words *cuatro*, *pero* and *toro*, you'd be in the right ball park. Other points of difference are listed below.

Syllable stress isn't that complicated in Malay. As a general rule, the stress lands on the **penultimate syllable** of a word (or, with words of two syllables, on the first syllable), a pattern which can lead to a few counterintuitive stress placements (eg SaRAwak, TerengGAnu). The chief exception to this rule concerns two-syllable words whose first syllable contains a short vowel (usually denoted by an "e"); in such cases, the stress sometimes falls on the second syllable – as in beSAR (big), leKAS (fast), and so forth, though unfortunately this isn't predictable.

Vowels and diphthongs

a somewhere in between the vowels of carp and cup, but changes to a short indeterminate vowel if at the end of a word, as in banana

aa like two "a" vowels separated by the merest pause; thus *maaf* (forgiveness) is rendered *ma + af*

ai as in fine (written "ei" in some older spellings)

au as in how

e as in her, though in many instances (not easy to predict) it is like the French é of

sauté, as in *kereta* (car), pronounced *keréta*; in yet others it denotes a short indeterminate vowel (schwa)

i somewhere between the i of tin and the ee of teen

o as in stone, though shorter and not as rounded as in English

u sometimes short as in pull, sometimes long (eg, if at the end of a word) as in pool

ua as in doer

Consonants

c as in chip (and written "ch" in older spellings), though slightly gentler than in English

d becomes t when at the end of a word

g hard, as in girl

h can drop out when flanked by vowels; thus *tahu*, "know", is usually pronounced as though spelt *tau*

k drops out if at the end of the word or if followed by another consonant, becoming a glottal stop (a brief pause); thus *rakyat* (people) is pronounced *ra + yat*

kh as in the Scottish loch; found in loan words from Arabic

l unlike in English, l is not swallowed if it occurs at the end of a word

ng as in tang (the "g" is never hard – thus *telinga*, "ear", is te-ling-a and not te-lin-ga); can occur at the start of a word

ngg as in tango

ny as in mañana; can occur at the start of a word

r is lightly trilled (though in some accents it can be rendered like the French r of Paris); drops out at the ends of words when preceded by a vowel

sy as in shut

Grammar

Word order in Malay is similar to that in English, though note that adjectives usually follow nouns. **Nouns** have no genders and don't require an article, while the **plural** form is constructed either by saying the word twice, if the number of objects is unspecified (thus "book" is *buku*, "books" *buku-buku*, sometimes written *buku2*), or by specifying the number of objects before the singular noun ("three books" is thus *tiga buku*). **Verbs** have no tenses either, the time of the action being indicated either by the context, or by the use of words such as *akan* (functioning like "will") and *sudah* ("already") for the future and past. The verb "to be" seldom appears explicitly, so, for example, *saya lapar* literally means "I [am] hungry". There are two words for **negation**: *bukan*, used before nouns (for example *saya bukan doktor*, "I'm not a doctor"), and *tak* (formally *tidak*), used before verbs and adjectives (as in *saya tak lapar*, "I'm not hungry"; *saya tak makan*, "I've not eaten"). Possessive constructions are achieved simply by putting the "owner" after the thing that's "owned"; thus *kampung saya*, literally "village [of] I", is "my village".

Malay words and phrases

One point to note regarding **pronouns** is that Malay lacks a convenient word for "you", all the options being either too formal or informal. In fact, the normal way to address someone is to use their name to their face, which can seem strange to English-speakers. If, as in most cases, you don't know someone's name, then you can use *abang* (brother) or *kak* (sister) to address a person of roughly the same age as you, or *adik* to a child, or *pak cik* or *mak cik* to a much older man or woman respectively.

You'll often see the word Dato' (or Datuk) or Tun placed before the name of a government official or some other worthy. Both are honorific titles of distinction roughly equivalent to the British "Sir". Royalty are always addressed as Tuanku.

Personal pronouns

Saya	I/my	Dia	He/she
Kami	We (excludes the person person being spoken to) or kita (includes the person being spoken to)	Mereka	They
		Encik or Tuan	Mr
		Puan	Mrs
		Cik	Miss
Anda	You (formal) or awak (informal)		

Greetings and other basics

"Selamat" is the all-purpose greeting derived from Arabic, which communicates a general goodwill.

Selamat pagi	Good morning	Baik or bagus	Fine
Selamat petang	Good afternoon	Jumpa lagi	See you again
Selamat tengah hari	Good midday (used around noon)	Tolong	Please
		Terima kasih	Thank you
Selamat malam	Good evening	Sama-sama	You're welcome
Selamat tidur	Good night (literally "peaceful sleep")	Maaf	Sorry/excuse me
		Tak apalah	Never mind, no matter
Selamat tinggal	Goodbye (literally "peaceful stay"; used by someone leaving)	Ya	Yes (sometimes pronounced a bit like "year")
		Tidak	No
Selamat jalan	Safe journey	Ini/Itu	This/that
Selamat datang	Welcome	Sini	Here
Selamat makan	Bon appetit	Situ	There (very nearby), sana (further away)
Apa khabar?	How are you?		

Siapa nama awak?	What is your name?	Boleh cakap bahasa Inggeris?	Do you speak English?
Nama saya...	My name is...	Saya (tak) faham	I don't understand
Dari mana?	Where are you from?	Boleh	That's fine/allowed
Saya dari...	I come from...	Boleh tolong saya?	Can you help me?
...England	...England	Boleh saya ...?	Can I ...?
...Amerika	...America	Ada	To have, there is/are
...Australia	...Australia	Apa?	What?
...Kanada	...Canada	Apa ini/itu?	What is this/that?
...Zealandia Baru	...New Zealand or just "New Zeelan"	Bila?	When?
...Irlandia	...Ireland	Di mana?	Where?
...Skotlandia	...Scotland	Siapa?	Who?
Suami	Husband	Mengapa? or Kenapa?	Why?
Isteri	Wife	Bagaimana?	How?
Kawan	Friend	Berapa?	How much/many?
Orang	Person		

Useful adjectives

Bagus	Good	Cukup	Enough
Banyak	A lot	Buka/tutup	Open/closed
Sikit or sedikit	A little	Lapar	Hungry
Murah/mahal	Cheap/expensive	Haus	Thirsty
Panas/sejuk	Hot/cold	Letih	Tired
Besar/kecil	Big/small	Sakit	Ill

Useful verbs

Datang/pergi	Come/go	Kenal	Know (someone)
Buat	Do	Suka	Like
Makan/minum	Eat/drink	Tolak/tarik	Push/pull
Masuk	Enter, go in	Tengok	See
Beri/ambil	Give/take	Duduk	Sit
Punya or ada	Have, possess	Tidur	Sleep
Dengar	Hear	Mahu	Want
Tolong	Help	Nak	Wish to, intend to
Tahu	Know (something)		

Getting around and directions

Di mana...?	Where is ...?	Jam berapa keretapi sampai?	What time does the train arrive?
Saya mahu pergi ke...	I want to go to...	Naik	Go up, ride
Bagaimanakah saya boleh ke sana?	How do I get there?	Turun	Get down, disembark
Berapa jauh?	How far?	Dekat/jauh	Nearby/far away
Berapa lama?	How long will it take?	Berhenti	Stop
Bila bas berangkat?	When will the bus leave?	Tunggu	Wait
		Belok	Turn

Kiri	Left	Kereta	Car
Kanan	Right	Motosikal	Motorcycle
Terus	Straight on	Kapal terbang	Plane
Di depan or di hadapan	In front	Teksi	Taxi
Di belakang	Behind	Beca	Trishaw
Utara	North	Tiket	Ticket
Selatan	South	Tambang (dewasa/ kanak-kanak)	Fare (adults/ children)
Timur	East	Rumah	House
Barat	West	Pejabat pos	Post office
Jalan	Street	Restoran	Restaurant
Lapangan terbang	Airport	Gereja	Church
Stesen bas or sometimes hentian bas	Bus station	Masjid	Mosque
Stesen keretapi	Train station	Tokong	Chinese temple
Jeti or pangkalan	Jetty	Muzium	Museum
Baisikal	Bicycle	Taman	Park, reserve
Bot or bot penambang	Boat (the latter is used of small passenger-carrying craft)	Tandas (lelaki/ perempuan)	Toilet (men/women)
		Masuk	Entrance
		Keluar	Exit

Accommodation

Hotel	Hotel	Saya perlu satu bilik	I need a room
Rumah tumpangan or rumah rehat	Guesthouse	Saya mahu tinggal ... malam	I'm staying for ... nights
Asrama	Dorm	Tolong bersih-kan bilik saya	Please clean my room
Bilik (untuk dua/satu)	Room (double/single)		
Katil (kelamin/bujang)	Bed (double/single)	Boleh titip barang?	Can I store my luggage here?
Kipas	Fan		
Berhawa dingin	Air-conditioned	Saya nak bayar	I want to pay
Mandi	Bath, shower		

Banking and shopping

Berapa harga ...?	How much is...?	Kedai	Shop
Saya mahu beli...	I want to buy...	Pasar	Market
Boleh kurang?	Can you reduce the price?	Pasar malam	Night market
		Pasaraya	Supermarket
Saya bayar tidak lebih dari...	I'll give you no more than ...	Bank	Bank
		Wang or duit	Money
Saya hanya lihat-lihat	I'm just looking	Pengurup wang	Moneychanger

Numbers

Kosong	0	Sepuluh	10
Satu (sometimes shortened to the prefix "se-" when used with a noun)	1	Sebelas	11
		Duabelas	12
		Duapuluh	20
		Duapuluh satu	21
Dua	2	Seratus	100
Tiga	3	Seratus duapuluh satu	121
Empat	4	Duaratus	200
Lima	5	Seribu	1000
Enam	6	Duaribu	2000
Tujuh	7	Sejuta	1 million
Lapan	8	Setengah	A half
Sembilan	9		

Time and days of the week

Pukul jam berapa?	What time is it?	Hari ini	Today
Pukul ...	Time is ...	Esok or besok	Tomorrow
Tiga	Three o'clock	Semalam or on the east coast kelmarin	Yesterday
Empat sepuluh	Ten past four		
Lima suku	Quarter past five	Sekarang	Now
Lima tiga suku ("five three-quarters")	Quarter to six	Nanti	Later
		... depan	Next ...
Enam setengah ("six half")	Six-thirty	.... yang lalu, ... lepas	Last ...
		Belum lagi	Not yet
Tujuh pagi	7am	Tak pernah	Never
Lapan malam	8pm	Hari Isnin	Monday
Jam	Hour	Hari Selasa	Tuesday
Minit	Minute	Hari Rabu	Wednesday
Detik	Second	Hari Kamis	Thursday
Hari	Day	Hari Jumaat	Friday
Minggu	Week	Hari Sabtu	Saturday
Bulan	Month	Hari Ahad or Minggu	Sunday
Tahun	Year		

Food and drink glossary

The list below concentrates on Malay terminology, though a few Chinese and Indian terms appear (unfortunately, transliteration of these varies widely), as well as definitions of some culinary words used in local English.

Basics, including cooking methods

Deciphering menus and ordering is sometimes a matter of matching ingredients and cooking methods – for example, to get an approximation of chips or French fries, you'd ask for *kentang goreng*, literally "fried potatoes". If you don't want your food spicy, say *jangan taruh cili* ("don't add chilli") or *saya tak suka pedas* ("I don't like spicy [food]").

Bakar Baked
Bubur Porridge
Garpu Fork
Goreng Fried
Istimewa Special (as in "today's special")
Kari Curry
Kedai kek Bakery ("cake shop")
Kedai kopi A diner ("coffee shop") concentrating on inexpensive rice spreads, noodles and other dishes, while serving some beverages
Kering Dried
Kopitiam Hokkien Chinese term for a *kedai kopi*; commonly used in Singapore
Kuah Gravy
Kukus Steamed
Lemak "fatty"; often denotes use of coconut milk

Makanan/minuman Food/drink
Mangkuk Bowl
Manis Sweet
Masam Sour
Masin Salty
Medan selera Food court
Panggang Grilled
Pedas Spicy
Pinggan Plate
Pisau Knife
Rebus Boiled
Restoran Restaurant
Sedap Tasty
Sudu Spoon
Sup/sop Soup
Tumis Stir-fried, sautéed
Warung Stall

Meat (*daging*) and poultry

Ayam Chicken
Babi Pork
Burong puyuh Quail
Char siew Cantonese honey roast pork
Daging lembu Beef

Itek Duck
Kambing Mutton
Lap cheong Sweetish, fatty pork sausage; Cantonese

Fish (*ikan*) and other seafood

Ambal Bamboo clams, a Sarawak delicacy
Fishball Spherical fish dumpling, rubbery in texture, often added to noodles and soups
Fishcake Fish dumpling in slices, often added to noodles
Ikan bawal Pomfret
Ikan bilis Anchovy
Ikan keli Catfish
Ikan kembong Mackerel
Ikan kerapu Grouper
Ikan kurau Threadfin
Ikan merah Red snapper

Ikan pari Skate
Ikan siakap Sea bass
Ikan tongkol Tuna
Ikan yu or **jerung** Shark
Kepiting or **ketam** Crab
Kerang Cockles
Keropok lekor Tubular fish dumplings (an east-coast speciality)
Sotong Squid, cuttlefish
Udang Prawn
Udang galah Lobster

Vegetables (*sayur*)

Bangkwang A radish-like root (also called *jicama*), used in Chinese *rojak* and in *popiah* fillings

Bawang Onion

Bawang putih Garlic

Bayam Spinach or spinach-like greens

Bendi Okra, ladies' fingers

Bunga kobis Cauliflower

Cendawan Mushroom

Chye sim or choy sum Brassica greens, similar to *pak choy*

Cili Chilli

Halia Ginger

Jagung Corn

Kacang Beans, pulses or nuts

Kangkung Convolvulus greens with narrow leaves and hollow stems; aka water spinach or morning glory

Keladi Yam

Keledek Sweet potato

Kentang Potatoes

Kobis Cabbage

Lada Chilli

Lobak Radish

Lobak merah Carrot

Midin Jungle fern, native to Sarawak

Pak choy or pek chye Soft-leaved brassica greens with broad stalks

Petai Beans in large pods from a tree, often sold in bunches

Pucuk paku Fern shoots, eaten as greens

Rebung Bamboo shoots

Tauge Beansprouts

Terung Aubergine

Timun Cucumber

Ubi kayu Tapioca

Other ingredients

Asam Tamarind; also used to indicate a dish flavoured with tamarind

Belacan Pungent fermented shrimp paste

Budu Sauce made from fermented anchovies; found on the east coast

Daun pandan Pandanus (screwpine) leaf, imparting a sweet bouquet to foods with which it's cooked; used not only in desserts but also in some rice dishes

Garam Salt

Gula Sugar

Gula Melaka Palm-sugar molasses, used to sweeten *cendol* and other desserts

Kaya Orange or green curd jam made with egg and coconut; delicious on toast

Kicap Soy sauce

Kicap manis Sweet dark soy sauce

Mentega Butter

Minyak Oil

Tahu Tofu (beancurd)

Telur Egg

Tempeh Fermented soybean cakes, nutty and slightly sour

Noodles and noodle dishes

The three most common types of noodle are *mee* (or *mi*), yellow egg noodles made from wheat flour; *bee hoon* (or *bihun* or *mee hoon*), like vermicelli; and *kuay teow* (or *hor fun*), like tagliatelle.

Char kuay teow Chinese fried *kuay teow*, often seasoned with *kicap manis*, and featuring any combination of prawns, Chinese sausage, fishcake, egg, vegetables and chilli.

Foochow noodles Steamed and served in soy and oyster sauce with spring onions and dried fish.

Hokkien fried mee *Mee* and *bee hoon* fried with pieces of pork, prawn and vegetables; a variant in KL has the noodles cooked in soy sauce with *tempeh*.

Kang puan (or kampua) mee A rich Sibu speciality – noodles cooked in lard.

Kolok mee *Mee* served dryish, accompanied by *char siew* slices.

Laksa Basically noodles in a curried soup featuring some seafood and flavoured with the *laksa*-leaf herb (*daun kesom*); variations include Nonya *laksa* (featuring coconut milk), *asam* laksa (Penang-style, with tamarind) and *laksa* Johor (made with spaghetti).

Laksam *Kuay teow* rice noodles in a fish sauce made with coconut milk and served with *ulam* (salad); an east-coast speciality.

Mee bandung *Mee* served in thickish gravy flavoured with beef and prawn (both of which garnish the dish).

Mee goreng Indian or Malay fried noodles; Indian versions are particularly spicy.

Mee hailam *Mee* in an oyster-sauce-based gravy.

Mee kari Noodles in a curried soup.

Mee pok Teochew dish using ribbon-like yellow noodles, served with fishballs and a chilli dressing.

Mee rebus Boiled *mee*; varies regionally, but one of the best is that sold in Singapore, featuring *mee* in a sweetish sauce made with yellow bean paste, and garnished with boiled egg and tofu.

Mee siam Not really Thai as its name might suggest, *mee siam* is *bee hoon* cooked in tangy-sweet soup flavoured with tamarind, and garnished with slices of hard-boiled egg and beancurd.

Mee suah Like *bee hoon* but even more threadlike and soft; can be made crispy if fried.

Sar hor fun Flat rice noodles served in a chicken-stock soup, to which prawns, fried shallots and beansprouts are added; a speciality in Ipoh.

Wan ton mee Roast pork, noodles and vegetables, accompanied by pork dumplings.

Rice (*nasi*) dishes and spreads

Char siew fan Common one-plate meal, featuring *char siew* and gravy on a bed of steamed rice.

Claypot rice Chinese dish of rice topped with meat (such as *lap cheong*), cooked in an earthenware pot over a fire to create a smoky taste.

Daun pisang Malay term for banana-leaf curry, a Southern Indian meal with chutneys and curries, served on a mound of rice, and presented on a banana leaf with poppadums.

Hainanese chicken rice Singapore's unofficial national rice dish; steamed or boiled chicken slices served on rice cooked in chicken stock, and accompanied by chicken broth, and a chilli and ginger dip.

Lemang Glutinous rice stuffed into lengths of bamboo.

Nasi ayam Malay version of Hainanese chicken rice.

Nasi berlauk Just means "rice with dishes".

Nasi biryani Saffron-flavoured rice cooked with chicken, beef or fish; a North Indian speciality.

Nasi campur Standard term for a rice spread, served with an array of meat, fish and vegetable dishes to choose from.

Nasi dagang East-coast speciality; a slightly glutinous rice steamed with coconut milk, and often brownish in appearance, usually served with fish curry.

Nasi goreng Rice fried with diced meat and vegetables and sometimes a little spice.

Nasi kandar A spread of rice and curries originating with Indian Muslim caterers in Penang; the rice is often stored in a container made of wood, which is said to give it a distinctive flavour.

Nasi kerabu Blue or green rice traditionally coloured with flower pigments, though these days food colourings may be used; found particularly in Kelantan, it's usually served with a fish curry.

Nasi kunyit Rice given a bright yellow colour by turmeric.

Nasi lemak A Malay classic, rice cooked with a little coconut milk and served with *ikan bilis*, cucumber, fried peanuts, fried or hard-boiled egg slices and *sambal*.

Nasi Minang Rice spread featuring dishes cooked in the style of the Minang Highlands of western Sumatra; similar to *Nasi Padang*.

Nasi minyak Rice cooked with *ghee*.

Nasi Padang Rice spread with the dishes cooked in the style of Padang, Sumatra.

Nasi putih Plain boiled rice.

Nasi ulam Rice containing blanched herbs and greens.

Pulut Glutinous rice.

Roti *(bread)* dishes

The word *roti* refers both to griddle breads and to Western bread, depending on the context.

Murtabak Thick griddle bread, usually savoury stuffed with onion, egg and chicken or mutton.

Murtabak pisang A sweet version of *murtabak*, stuffed with banana.

Roti bakar Toast, usually served with butter and *kaya*.

Roti bom An especially greasy *roti canai*, containing a cheesy-tasting margarine.

Roti canai Light, layered griddle bread served with a thin curry sauce.

Roti John Simple Indian dish, a French loaf split and stuffed with an egg, onion and sweet chilli sauce mixture; versions containing meat are occasionally seen.

Roti kahwin Toast with butter and *kaya*.

Roti prata Singapore name for *roti canai*.

Roti telur *Roti canai* with an egg mixed into the dough.

Roti telur bawang *Roti canai* with an egg and chopped onion mixed into the dough.

Other specialities

Ayam goreng Malay-style fried chicken.

Ayam percik Barbecued chicken with a creamy coconut sauce; a Kota Bharu speciality.

Bak kut teh Literally "meat bone tea", a Chinese soup made by boiling up pork ribs with soy sauce, ginger, herbs and spices.

Chap chye A Nonya stew of mixed vegetables, fungi and sometimes also glass noodles (aka *tang hoon*, a rather elastic vermicelli).

Chee cheong fun Cantonese specality, vaguely like ravioli, featuring minced shrimp rolled up in rice-flour sheets, steamed and dredged in a sweet-salty red sauce.

Chye tow kuay Also known as "carrot cake", comprising a rice flour/white radish mixture formed into cubes and fried with egg and garlic; a savoury-sweet version with added *kicap manis* is also worth trying.

Congee Watery rice gruel eaten with slices of meat or fish or omelette; sometimes listed on menus as "porridge".

Dim sum Chinese meal of titbits – dumplings, pork ribs, etc – steamed or fried and served in bamboo baskets.

Dosa/dosai/thosai Southern Indian pancake, made from ground rice and lentils, and served with dal (lentils); *masala dosa* features a potato stuffing, while *rava dosa* has grated carrot in the batter.

Fish-head curry The head of a red snapper (usually), cooked in a spicy curry sauce with tomatoes and okra.

Gado-gado Malay/Indonesian salad of lightly cooked vegetables, boiled egg, slices of rice cake and a crunchy peanut sauce.

Idli South Indian rice-and-lentil cakes, steamed.

Kari kepala ikan See fish-head curry.

Kongbian Chinese-style bagels, found only in Sibu.

Kuih pai tee Nonya dish vaguely resembling fried spring rolls, except that the *pai tee* are shaped like cup cakes; filling is like that for *popiah*.

Lontong A pairing of a *sayur lodeh*-like curry with rice cakes similar to *ketupat*.

Oothapam Rice-and-lentil pancakes; South Indian.

Otak-otak Mashed fish mixed with coconut milk and chilli paste, then steamed in strips wrapped in banana leaf; a Nonya dish.

Popiah Spring rolls, consisting of a steamed dough wrapper filled with peanuts, egg, bean shoots, vegetables and a sweet sauce; sometimes known as *lumpia*.

Rendang Dry, highly spiced coconut curry with beef, chicken or mutton.

Rojak The Chinese version is a salad of greens, beansprouts, pineapple and cucumber in a peanut and prawn-paste sauce; quite different is Indian *rojak*, a variety of fritters with sweet chilli dips.

Satar Similar to *otak-otak* but made in triangular shapes; found on the east coast.

Satay Marinated pieces of meat, skewered on small sticks and cooked over charcoal; served with peanut sauce, cucumber, raw onion and *ketupat* (rice cake).

Sayur lodeh Mixed vegetables stewed in a curry sauce containing coconut milk.

Sop ekor Malay oxtail soup.

Sop kambing Spicy Malay mutton soup.

Sop tulang Malay beef-bone soup.

Steamboat Chinese fondue; raw meat, fish, veggies and other titbits dunked into a steaming broth until cooked.

Umai Raw fish salad, mixed with shallots and lime, found in East Malaysia and Brunei.

Umbut kelapa masak lemak Young coconut shoots, cooked in coconut milk.

Vadai South Indian fried lentil patty.

Yam basket Sarawak speciality: meat, vegetables and soya bean curd in a fried yam crust.

Yong tau foo Bean curd, fishballs and assorted vegetables, poached and served with broth and sweet dipping sauces.

Snacks and accompaniments

Acar Pickle, often sweet and spicy.

Bak kwa Chinese-style sweet barbecued pork slices, eaten as a snack.

Cempedak goreng *Cempedak* (see opposite) fried in batter, allowing not just the flesh but also the floury stones to be eaten.

Curry puff Also called *karipap* in Malay; a semicircular pastry parcel stuffed with curried meat and vegetables.

Kerabu Not to be confused with *nasi kerabu*, this is a salad of grated unripe fruit, mixed with chilli, grated coconut, cucumber and other ingredients.

Keropok (goreng) Deep-fried prawn or fish crackers, derived from a dough like that used to make *keropok lekor* (see p.794).

Ketupat Unseasoned rice cubes boiled in packets of woven coconut-leaf strips, served as an accompaniment to satay.

Pau or pow Chinese stuffed bun made with a sweetish dough and steamed; *char siew pau* contains Cantonese honey-roast pork, *kai pau* chicken and egg, while there are also *pau* with sweet fillings include bean paste, dried coconut or *kaya*.

Rasam Sour-spicy southern Indian soup flavoured with tamarind and tomato.

Sambal Dip made with pounded or ground chilli; *sambal belacan* is augmented with a little *belacan* for extra depth of flavour.

Sambar Watery South Indian curry served with *dosa*.

Ulam Malay salad of raw vegetables and herbs.

Yew char kuay Chinese fried dough sticks, good dunked in coffee; not unlike Spanish *churros* in flavour and texture.

Drinks

When ordering beverages in a *kedai kopi*, there are standard terms to bear in mind. *Kosong* ("zero") after the name of the drink means you want it black and unsugared; the suffix -o (pronounced "oh") means black with sugar, *susu* means with milk (invariably of the sweetened condensed variety), *ais* or *peng* means iced, *tarik* ("pulled") denotes the popular practice of frothing a drink by pouring it repeatedly from one mug to another and back, and finally *kurang manis* ("lacking sweetness") means to go easy on the sugar or condensed milk. It's quite possible to combine these terms, so in theory, you could order *kopi susu tarik kurang manis peng*, which would be a frothy milky coffee, iced and not too sweet. Note that condensed milk is often assumed to be wanted even if you don't say *susu*.

Air botol A bottled drink (usually refers to soft drinks).

Air kelapa Coconut water.

Air laici Tinned lychee juice, very sweet, usually with a couple of lychees in the glass.

Air minum Drinking water.

Air tebu Sugar-cane juice.

Bandung or air sirap bandung A sweet drink, bright pink in colour, made with rose essence and a little milk.

Bir Beer.

Chrysanthemum tea Delicately fragrant tea made from chrysanthemum blossom, and served slightly sweet, either hot or cold.

Cincau or chinchow Sweet drink, the colour of cola or stout, made with strips of jelly-like seaweed.

Jus Juice (the word *jus* is usually followed by the name of the fruit in question).

Kopi Coffee; some *kedai kopis* offer it freshly brewed, others serve instant.

Kopi jantan Coffee that's claimed to be a male tonic, often advertised with posters showing avuncular Malay men apparently endorsing the drink.

Kopi tongkat Ali Similar to *kopi jantan* (*tongkat Ali* is a herb that Malays believe has aphrodisiac qualities for men).

Lassi Indian sweet or salty yoghurt drink.

Susu Milk.

Teh Tea.

Teh bunga kekwa Chrysanthemum.

Teh limau ais Iced lemon tea.

Tuak Rice wine (Borneo).

Fruit (*buah*)

Belimbing Starfruit

Betik Papaya

Cempedak Similar to jackfruit

Duku, duku langsat Small round fruits containing bittersweet segments

Durian Famously stinky large fruit containing rows of seeds coated in sweet creamy flesh

Durian belanda Soursop

Epal Apple

Jambu batu Guava

Kelapa Coconut

Laici Lychee

Limau Lime or lemon

Limau bali Pomelo

Mangga Mango

Manggis Mangosteen

Nanas Pineapple

Nangka Jackfruit

Nyiur Alternative term for coconut

Oren Orange

Pisang Banana

Rambutan Hairy-skinned stone fruit with sweet white flesh

Salak Teardrop-shaped fruit with scaly brown skin and bitter flesh

Tembikai Watermelon

Desserts

Agar-agar Seaweed-derived jelly served in squares or diamonds, and often with coconut milk for richness.

Air batu campur ("ABC") Another name for *ais kacang*.

Ais kacang Ice flakes with red beans, cubes of jelly, sweetcorn, rose syrup and evaporated milk.

Bubur cha cha Sweetened coconut milk with pieces of sweet potato, yam and tapioca.

Cendol Coconut milk, palm sugar syrup and pea-flour noodles poured over shaved ice.

Cheng tng Clear, sweet Chinese broth containing fungi and dried fruit.

Kuih or kuih-muih Malay/Nonya sweetmeats, ranging from something like a Western cake to fudge-like morsels made of mung bean or rice flour.

Kuih lapis Layer cake; either a simple rice-flour confection, or an elaborate wheat-flour sponge comprising numerous very thin layers and unusually rich in egg.

Pisang goreng Bananas or plantains coated in a thin batter and fried.

Glossary

Adat Customary or traditional law.

Air Water.

Air panas Hot springs.

Air terjun Waterfall.

Atap/attap Palm thatch.

Baba Straits-born Chinese (male).

Bandar Town.

Bandaraya City.

Bangunan Building.

Banjaran Mountain range.

Batang River system.

Batik Wax and dye technique of cloth decoration.

Batu Rock/stone.

Bejalai Period in an Iban youth's life when he ventures out from the longhouse to experience life in the towns.

Belian A hardwood traditionally used to construct Sarawak longhouses.

Belukar Secondary rainforest, essentially woodland that regrows in areas where primary forest has been disturbed or cut down.

Bomoh Traditional spiritualist healer.

Bukit Hill.

Bumbun Hide.

Bumiputra Person deemed indigenous to Malaysia ("son of the soil").

Bungalow In local English, any detached house.

Candi Temple.

Cantonese Pertaining to the Guangdong province of southeast China.

Daerah An administrative district.

Daulat Divine force possessed by a ruler that commands unquestioning loyalty.

Dipterocarp The predominant family of tree in the rainforest, comprising many types of exceptionally tall tree reaching up to the top of the forest canopy.

Ekspres Express (used of boats and buses).

Empangan Dam.

Foochow Pertaining to Fuzhou, a city in Fujian province, southeast China.

Gasing Spinning top.

Gawai Annual festivals celebrated by indigenous groups in Sarawak.

Gelanggang seni Cultural centre.

Gereja Church.

Godown Warehouse.

Gongsi Chinese clan-house.

Gopuram Sculpted deities over the entrance to a Hindu temple.

Gua Cave.

Gunung Mountain.

Hainanese Pertaining to Hainan Island, southeast China.

Halal Something permissible in Islam.

Hill station A settlement or resort at relatively high altitude usually founded in colonial times as an escape from the heat of the lowlands.

Hokkien Pertaining to the Fujian province of southeast China, the dialect of which is more formally called *minnan*.

Hutan Forest.

Ikat Woven fabric.

Istana Palace.

Jalan Road, street.

Jambatan Bridge.

Kampung Village.

Kelong A kind of fishing platform that can be seen extending out to sea from some beaches; it comprises two rows of vertical poles in the sea bed with a net at the far end, to which the fish are lured by a light hung over the water.

Kerangas Sparse forest ("poor soil").

Khalwat An offence under Islamic law, typically involving an unmarried Muslim couple being together in private.

Kongsi Chinese clan-house/temple; has entered Malay as a word meaning "share".

Kota Fort.

Kris Wavy-bladed dagger.

Kuala River confluence or estuary.

Labu Gourd; also used of the gourd-like ceramic bottles made as souvenirs in some parts of the Peninsula.

Lata Waterfall.

Laut Sea.

Lebuh Avenue.

Lebuhraya Highway/expressway.

Lorong Lane.

Mak yong Courtly dance-drama.

Makam Grave or tomb.

Malaya Old name for the area now called Peninsular Malaysia.

Mamak Indian Muslim; used particularly of restaurants run by Indian Muslims.

Mandi Asian method of showering by dousing with water from a tank using a small bucket or dipper.

Masjid Mosque.

Mat Salleh Malaysian colloquial term for a foreigner, usually a white person.

Melayu Malay.

Menara Minaret or tower.

Merdeka Freedom, in general; can specifically refer to Malaysian independence.

Minangkabau Matriarchal people from Sumatra.

Negara National.

Nipah A type of palm tree.

Nonya Straits-born Chinese (female); sometimes Nonya.

Orang Asli Peninsular Malaysia aborigines ("original people"); also Orang Ulu (upriver people) and Orang Laut (sea people).

Padang Field/square; usually the main town square.

Pangkalan Jetty or port (literally "base").

Pantai Beach.

Parang Machete.

Pasar Market.

Pasar malam Night market.

Pasir Sand.

Pejabat Daerah District office.

Pejabat Pos Post office.

Pekan Town.

Pelabuhan Port/harbour.

Penghulu Chieftain, leader.

Peranakan Straits-born Chinese.

Perigi Well.

Persekutuan Federal.

Pintu Arch/gate/door.

Pondok Hut or shelter.

Pulau Island.

Raja Prince.

Ramadan Muslim fasting month.

Rebana Drum.

Rotan Rattan cane; used in the infliction of corporal punishment.

Rumah persinggahan Lodging house.

Rumah rehat Older guesthouse (literally "rest house"), now mainly privately run, though once state-owned.

Rumah tumpangan Boarding house.

Samping *Songket* worn by a man as a short sarong over loose trousers.

Saree Traditional Indian woman's garment, worn in conjunction with a *choli* (short-sleeved blouse).

Sarung/sarong Cloth worn as a wrap around the lower body.

Sekolah School.

Semenanjung Peninsula.

Seni Art or skill.

Shophouse A two-storey terraced building found mainly in town centres, and often featuring a facade that is recessed at street level, providing a shaded walkway that serves as a pavement.

Silat Malay art of self-defence.

Songket Brocade.

Songkok Malay male headgear, a little like a flattish fez, made of black velvet over cardboard.

Storm corridor An exterior pathway with an overhead shelter throughout its length.

Sultan Ruler.

Sungai/sungei River.

Tai chi Chinese martial art; commonly performed as an early-morning exercise.

Taman Park.

Tamu Market/fair.

Tanjung/tanjong Cape, headland.

Tasik/tasek Lake.

Telaga Freshwater spring or well.

Teluk/telok Bay or inlet.

Teochew Pertaining to Chaozhou, a city in Fujian province, southeast China.

Tokong Chinese temple.

Towkay Chinese merchant.

Tuai Tribal headman (Sarawak).

Wau Kite.

Wayang Show, ranging from a film screening to Chinese opera.

Wayang kulit Shadow-puppet play (literally "skin show", after the fact that the puppets are made of hide).

Wisma House (used of commercial buildings rather than residences).

Acronyms

ASEAN Association of Southeast Asian Nations, an economic and political grouping of ten regional states, including Malaysia, Singapore and Brunei.

BN Barisan Nasional or National Front – the coalition, dominated by UMNO, that has governed Malaysia since 1974.

KTM Keretapi Tanah Melayu, the Malaysian national railway company.

MAS Malaysia Airlines.

MCA Malaysian Chinese Association, the Chinese wing of the governing BN.

MCP Malayan Communist Party.

MRT Singapore's Mass Rapid Transit system.

PAP Singaporean People's Action Party.

PAS Parti Islam SeMalaysia, the Pan-Malaysian Islamic Party.

SIA Singapore Airlines.

UMNO United Malays National Organization.

Small print and
Index

A Rough Guide to Rough Guides

Published in 1982, the first Rough Guide – to Greece – was a student scheme that became a publishing phenomenon. Mark Ellingham, a recent graduate in English from Bristol University, had been travelling in Greece the previous summer and couldn't find the right guidebook. With a small group of friends he wrote his own guide, combining a highly contemporary, journalistic style with a thoroughly practical approach to travellers' needs.

The immediate success of the book spawned a series that rapidly covered dozens of destinations. And, in addition to impecunious backpackers, Rough Guides soon acquired a much broader and older readership that relished the guides' wit and inquisitiveness as much as their enthusiastic, critical approach and value-for-money ethos.

These days, Rough Guides include recommendations from shoestring to luxury and cover more than 200 destinations around the globe, including almost every country in the Americas and Europe, more than half of Africa and most of Asia and Australasia. Our ever-growing team of authors and photographers is spread all over the world, particularly in Europe, the USA and Australia.

In the early 1990s, Rough Guides branched out of travel, with the publication of Rough Guides to World Music, Classical Music and the Internet. All three have become benchmark titles in their fields, spearheading the publication of a wide range of books under the Rough Guide name.

Including the travel series, Rough Guides now number more than 350 titles, covering: phrasebooks, waterproof maps, music guides from Opera to Heavy Metal, reference works as diverse as Conspiracy Theories and Shakespeare, and popular culture books from iPods to Poker. Rough Guides also produce a series of more than 120 World Music CDs in partnership with World Music Network.

Visit www.roughguides.com to see our latest publications.

Rough Guide travel images are available for commercial licencing at www.roughguidespictures.com.

Rough Guide credits

Text editors: Edward Aves, Sarah Eno, Helen Marsden and Andy Turner
Layout: Jessica Subramanian
Cartography: Rajesh Chhibber
Picture editors: Simon Bracken, Andrea Sadler and Jj Luck
Production: Aimee Hampson
Proofreader: Anna Leggett
Cover design: Chloë Roberts
Editorial: London Kate Berens, Claire Saunders, Geoff Howard, Ruth Blackmore, Polly Thomas, Richard Lim, Alison Murchie, Karoline Densley, Keith Drew, Nikki Birrell, Alice Park, Joe Staines, Duncan Clark, Peter Buckley, Matthew Milton, Tracy Hopkins, David Paul, Lucy White, Ruth Tidball; **New York** Andrew Rosenberg, Steven Horak, April Isaacs, AnneLise Sorensen, Amy Hegarty, Sean Mahoney, Ella Steim
Design & Pictures: London Dan May, Diana Jarvis, Mark Thomas, Harriet Mills; **Delhi** Madhulita Mohapatra, Umesh Aggarwal, Ajay Verma, Ankur Guha, Pradeep Thapliyal, Sachin Tanwar, Anita Singh

Production: Sophie Hewat, Katherine Owers
Cartography: London Maxine Repath, Ed Wright, Katie Lloyd-Jones; **Delhi** Jai Prakash Mishra, Ashutosh Bharti, Rajesh Mishra, Animesh Pathak, Jasbir Sandhu, Karobi Gogoi, Amod Singh, Alakananda Bhattacharya
Online: New York Jennifer Gold, Suzanne Welles, Kristin Mingrone; **Delhi** Manik Chauhan, Narender Kumar, Rakesh Kumar, Amit Verma, Amit Kumar, Rahul Kumar
Marketing & Publicity: London Richard Trillo, Niki Hanmer, Louise Maher, Jess Carter; **New York** Geoff Colquitt, Megan Kennedy, Katy Ball; **Delhi** Reem Khokhar
Custom publishing and foreign rights: Philippa Hopkins
Manager India: Punita Singh
Series editor: Mark Ellingham
Reference Director: Andrew Lockett
PA to Managing and Publishing Directors: Megan McIntyre
Publishing Director: Martin Dunford

SMALL PRINT

Publishing information

This fifth edition published October 2006 by **Rough Guides Ltd**,
80 Strand, London WC2R 0RL, UK
345 Hudson St, 4th Floor,
New York, NY 10014, USA
14 Local Shopping Centre, Panchsheel Park,
New Delhi 110017, India
Distributed by the Penguin Group
Penguin Books Ltd,
80 Strand, London WC2R 0RL, UK
Penguin Putnam, Inc.
375 Hudson Street, NY 10014, USA
Penguin Group (Australia)
250 Camberwell Road, Camberwell,
Victoria 3124, Australia
Penguin Books Canada Ltd,
10 Alcorn Avenue, Toronto, Ontario,
M4V 1E4, Canada
Penguin Group (New Zealand)
Cnr Rosedale and Airborne Roads,
Albany, Auckland, New Zealand
Original cover design by Peter Dyer.

Typeset in Bembo and Helvetica to an original design by Henry Iles.

Printed and bound in Italy by Legoprint S.p.A

824pp includes index
A catalogue record for this book is available from the British Library
ISBN 13: 978-1-84353-687-1
ISBN 10: 1-84353-687-0

Help us update

We've gone to a lot of effort to ensure that the fifth edition of **The Rough Guide to Malaysia, Singapore and Brunei** is accurate and up to date. However, things change – places get "discovered", opening hours are notoriously fickle, restaurants and rooms raise prices or lower standards. If you feel we've got it wrong or left something out, we'd like to know, and if you can remember the address, the price, the time, the phone number, so much the better.

We'll credit all contributions, and send a copy of the next edition (or any other Rough Guide if you prefer) for the best letters. Everyone who writes to us and isn't already a subscriber will receive a copy of our full-colour thrice-yearly newsletter.

Please mark letters: "**Rough Guide Malaysia, Singapore and Brunei Update**" and send to: Rough Guides, 80 Strand, London WC2R 0RL, or Rough Guides, 4th Floor, 345 Hudson St, New York, NY 10014. Or send an email to **mail@roughguides.com**

Have your questions answered and tell others about your trip at
www.roughguides.atinfopop.com

Acknowledgements

Charles de Ledesma In Brunei, Charles would like to thank: Jungle Dave from *MonaFlora*; dental supremo Colonel Ian Hamilton and his partner Jean, who showed him the *Empire and Country Club*; and the great staff at the wonderful *Terrace Hotel*. In Kota Kinabalu: Robin Chin from Sabah Tourism helped whenever he could; and the *Kinabalu Daya Hotel* proved to be the most user-friendly in town. Also in Sabah, the *Mesilau Nature Resort* was a restful – and cool – sanctuary and the *Borneo Hotel* in Sandakan's staff kind. In Kuching, thanks as usual to: Wayne Tarman and Mike Reed for toiling round town; and to Audrey Wan-Ullock at the always comfortable *Telang Usan Hotel*. And Charles could never forget his partner Karen for all her support.

Richard Lim thanks everyone who provided assistance in his research for this book, including: Abang Din; Abdul Wahab Abdullah; Amma Addai; Zawawi Ahmad; Sabrina Ali; Meor Amran; Appu; Ardiana; Mr Aziz; Firdaus Cathyaoki; Cheong Chai Yen; Sanadure Durei; Esa; Art Fazil; Colin Goh; Hani; Ishak Ibrahim; Rajan Jones; Ju; Ibrahim Kamaruddin; Diana Lee; Lokman; Mervyn and Khalid; Masjaliza Hamzah; Nazir Zaman; Rahayu; Rugayah Muhamad; Rosmawati Abdul Hamid; Mr Saiful; Sakthiswaran; Shariana Shaharudin; Mr Tawfik and other Jabatan Perhilitan staff; Trish and Junaidi; and Brian Y. Special thanks to: Amie and Amelia; J. Anu; Arnold Barkhordarian; "Jascion" C.; John Gee; Roselan Hanafiah and Azahari; Alex Kang; Professor Khoo Kay Kim; Professor Ulrich Kratz; Alex Lee, Maznah, Johari, Shukri and all at Ping Anchorage; David Leffman; Lim Ee Lin and Elizabeth Cardosa; Lim Huck Chin; Ian M.; Pete Mancuso; Martin T.J.; Mohd Fazil Ismail at KTM; Dr Mushrifah; the elusive Joe Ng; Moses Ng; Colin Nicholas; Andrew Sebastian; Karol Szlichcinski; Kamal Yasin; and Professor Wan Zawawi. Above all, thanks to my family in Singapore and to the incomparably gingery Son of Colin.

Steven Martin Special thanks to: Benjamin Sirirat; Jack Barton; Karishma Vyas; Michael Newbill; Angeline Thangaperakasam; Dr Zheng Yangwen; Ronni Pinsler; Yishane Lee; Eric & Jennifer Ho; Besti & Wiwik Gula; Wellington Wang; and the lovely Loog sisters.

Readers' letters

Thanks to all the following who wrote in to us with corrections and updates to the fourth edition of this book (with apologies to anyone we've inadvertently forgotten to name):

Ilene Africk; Amanda Armitage; Janine Baggs; Rob Beaty; S.K. Bird; Johan G. Borchert; David Clark; Maggie Coaton; Marjan Crabtree-Nieuwland; Jamie Crisp and Angelika Klemm; Hannah Dixey-Williams; Rodney Eckart; Charles Elder and Nicky Harmer; Donna Ellis; Tim Frier; Karen Goode; Heather Hapeta; Jacqueline Harvey; Ian Hawker; Peter Heller; Alan Hickey; Tine Hjetting; Rosalind Hoffler; Quentin and Ann Hunter; David Ince; Kong Ling Teck; Andrea Leman; Melissa K. Ma; Mon Mackaness; Jonny Mackrill; Dave Morgan; Steve O'Leary; Maya Patel; Emma Perry; Darren and Ann Petersen; Poul Petersen; Suzanne Phillips; John Pinnells; Phua Kai Lit; Christopher Portway; Richard Price; Ivan Purdy; Charles Smith; David Stevens; Derek Stokes; Josua Tascali; Cyrus Tiz; Ivan Valencic; Hans van Leeuwen; Rachel Wingate; Tony Wright; and Randy Yuen.

Photo credits

All photos © Rough Guides except the following:

Title page
Rinoceros hornbill in flight © Timothy Laman/
Getty

Full page
Fishing village, Pulau Mabul © Sergio Pitamitz/
Corbis

Introduction
Kenyah "tree of life" painting, Sarawak © Charles
& Josette Lenars/Corbis
Elephants at Kinabatangan Wildlife Sanctuary,
Sabah © Timothy Laman/Getty
Iban tattooed legs, Rumah Lasong longhouse,
Sarawak © Robert Holmes/Corbis
Petronas Towers and Asy-Syakirin Mosque, Kuala
Lumpur © Tibor Bognar/Corbis
Orang Asli settlement, Cameron Highlands © Neil
Rabinowitz/Corbis
Singapore waterfront © Kevin Christopher Ou
Photography/Corbis
Pulau Lang Tengah © Malaysian Tourist Board

Things not to miss
01 Orang Ulu longhouse, Sarawak Cultural Village
© Neil McAllister/Alamy
02 Ulu Temburong Park © Graham Tim/Corbis
Sygma
03 Chinese mansion doorway, Georgetown
© Anthony Brown/Alamy
04 Female orang-utan with young © Daniel J
Cox/Getty
06 Barbecued chicken satay, Chinatown, Kuala
Lumpur © David Noton/Alamy
07 Diving at Pulau Sipadan © Malaysian Tourist
Board
08 Omar Ali Saifuddien Mosque, Brunei
© J Marshall – Tribaleye Images/Alamy
09 Workers on tea plantation, Cameron Highlands
© Dave Jacobs/Getty
10 Perhentian Islands © Robert Harding Picture
Library Ltd/Alamy
11 Datai Bay, Langkawi © Malaysian Tourist Board
12 Jerry Kamit at the Rainforest Music Festival
© Sarawak Tourism Board
13 KLCC shopping mall, Kuala Lumpur
© Malaysian Tourist Board
14 Proboscis monkey, Bako National Park © Nick
Garbutt/NHPA
16 Theatre performance, Singapore © Peter
Bowater/Alamy
17 Kampung Ayer, Bandar Seri Begawan
© Michael S. Yamashita/Corbis
18 Mount Kinabalu © Sabah Tourism
19 Petronas Towers © Malaysian Tourist Board
20 Traditional crafts © Malaysian Tourist Board
21 Shadow puppet play (*wayang kulit*), Kota
Bharu © Pat Behnke/Alamy

22 Kuching riverside promenade © Neil
McAllister/Alamy
23 Mulu Caves © Robert Harding Picture Library
Ltd
24 East Malaysian rainforest © Roine
Magnusson/Getty
25 Christ Church, Melaka © Norman Price/Alamy
26 The Pinnacles, Mulu National Park © Robert
Holmes/Corbis
27 White-water rafting, Kinabalu National Park
© Malaysian Tourist Board

Malay life colour insert
Master kite maker © Hugh Sitton/Getty
Muslim girls in headscarves, Malaysia
© Angel Terry/Alamy
Spinning tops, Kota Bharu © Hugh Sitton
Photography/Alamy
Kampung house, Pulau Pangkor © Andrew
Woodley/Alamy
Silat competition © Pat Behnke/Alamy
Dancer at the Colours of Malaysia Festival, Kuala
Lumpur © Lightworks Media/Alamy
Wayang kulit © Reuters/Corbis

Longhouse culture colour insert
Iban warrior wearing a headdress of feathers
© Peter Guttman/Corbis
Rice-drying at an Iban longhouse, Sungai
Engkari, Batang Ai © Thomas Hoepker/
Magnum Photos
Melanau longhouse, Sarawak Cultural Village
© Neil McAllister/Alamy
Dusun harvest dancer, Sabah © Nik Wheeler/
Corbis
Shrunken heads © Thomas Hoepker/Magnum
Photos
Basket making, Sarawak Cultural Village © Neil
McAllister/Alamy

Black and white photos
p.90 Kuala Lumpur skyline © Josef Beck/Getty
p.112 Sultan Abdul Samad Building, Kuala
Lumpur © Jon Hicks/Corbis
p.115 Jalan Petaling Market, Kuala Lumpur
© Richard Lim
p.124 Aquarium, Kuala Lumpur © Darby
Sawchuck/Alamy
p.130 Outdoor food stalls, Chinatown, Kuala
Lumpur © Oriental Touch
p.150 Hindu devotees dragging *kavadi* during
Thaipusam, Batu Caves © Zainal Abd Halim/
Reuters/Corbis
p.158 Khoo Kongsi, Georgetown © AA World
Travel Library
p.164 British phone box, Cameron Highlands
© Andrew Woodley
p.175 Kellie's Castle © Ted Adnan Photography

Index

Map entries are indicated in colour. For a list of map symbols used in this book, see p.823. Islands are indexed under "Pulau", rivers under "Sungai", lakes under "Tasik" and mountains under "Gunung".

INDEX

N

O

INDEX

Map symbols

maps are listed in the full index using coloured text

▬·▬·	International borders		👁	Lighthouse
▬ ··	Malaysian state boundary		🕱	Waterfall
▬ ▬ ▬	Chapter division boundary		⋮⋮	Marshland
▬▬▬	Highway		✈	Airport
══	Road		✈	Airfield
-----	Path		★	Bus stop
▬▬•▬	Railway		⊖	MRT station (Singapore)
⊪⊪⊪⊪	Funicular		🅿	Parking
– –	Ferry route		Å	Campsite
▬▬	Waterway		🏠	Refuge
♦	Point of interest		◉	Accommodation
✝	Church (regional maps)		■	Restaurant/café
🕌	Mosque		⊠	Gate
✝	Buddhist temple		@	Internet access
▲	Hindu temple		⊞	Hospital
✡	Synagogue		ⓘ	Tourist office
🏯	Chinese temple		✉	Post office
∴	Ruins		ℰ	Telephone
♛	Castle/fort		♟	Golf course
♦	Museum		▬▬	Building
🏛	Monument		⊞	Church (town maps)
☨	Public gardens		⟊	Christian cemetery
◖	Cave		⟊	Muslim cemetery
🪨	Rocks		▦	Park
▲	Peak		▨	Pedestrianized area
⋚	Viewpoint			

WHEREVER YOU ARE,

WHEREVER YOU'RE GOIN

WE'VE GOT YOU COVERED!

Simms Library
Albuquerque Academy
6400 Wyoming Blvd NE
Albuquerque, NM 87109